Albion's See

MW00753860

A M E R I C A
A CULTURAL HISTORY

VOLUME I: ALBION'S SEED
VOLUME II: AMERICAN PLANTATIONS

ALBION'S SEED

FOUR BRITISH FOLKWAYS IN AMERICA

BY

DAVID HACKETT FISCHER

OXFORD UNIVERSITY PRESS
New York   Oxford

Oxford University Press

Oxford   New York
Athens   Auckland   Bangkok   Bombay
Calcutta   Cape Town   Dar es Salaam   Delhi
Florence   Hong Kong   Istanbul   Karachi
Kuala Lumpur   Madras   Madrid   Melbourne
Mexico City   Nairobi   Paris   Singapore
Taipei   Tokyo   Toronto

and associated companies in
Berlin   Ibadan

Copyright © 1989   by David Hackett Fischer

First published in 1989 by Oxford University Press, Inc.,
198 Madison Avenue, New York, New York 10016

First issued as an Oxford University Press paperback, 1991

Oxford is a registered trademark of Oxford University Press

Library of Congress Cataloging-in-Publication Data
Fischer, David Hackett, 1935–
Albion's seed : four British folkways in America /
David Hackett Fischer.
p.   cm.   (America, a cultural history ; v. 1)
Bibliography: p.   Includes index.
ISBN 0-19-503794-4
ISBN 0-19-506905-6 (Pbk.)
1. United States—Civilization—To 1783.
2. United States—Civilization—English influences.
I. Title.   II. Series: Fischer, David Hackett, 1935–
America, a cultural history; v. 1.
E169.1.F539   vol. 1   [E162]   973 s–dc20   [973]   89-16069   CIP

19 20

Printed in the United States of America
on acid-free paper

For Robert and Patricia Blake

PREFACE

❧ An Idea of Cultural History

> History is culturally ordered, differently so in differ-
> ent societies . . . The converse is also true: cultural
> schemes are historically ordered.
> —Marshall Sahlins, 1985

THIS BOOK is the first in a series, which will hopefully comprise a cultural history of the United States. It is cultural in
an anthropological rather than an aesthetic sense—a history of American folkways as they have changed through time.

Each volume (five are now in draft) centers on a major problem
in American historiography. The first volume, *Albion's Seed,* is
about the problem of cultural origins. The second volume, *American Plantations,* studies the problem of culture and environment
in the colonial era. The third volume examines the coming of
independence as a cultural movement. Volume four takes up the
problem of cultural change in the early republic, and volume five
is about the Civil War as a cultural conflict. Other volumes will
follow if the author is allowed to complete them.

This project has grown from an intellectual event that happened in the 1960s—a revolution in the writing of history, very
much like the thought-revolutions described in Thomas Kuhn's
essays on the history of science, and Michael Foucault's studies
of social thought. Three generations ago, there was an established
"paradigm" or "episteme" of historical knowledge. A writer had
only to call his book a history in order to announce what sort of
work it was, for history books were very much the same. History
was about the past. It was a narrative discipline—a story-telling
art. The stories that it told were about the organization of power
and authority. Not all historians wrote political history, but most

were interested in the politics of the subjects they studied. Labor historians wrote about labor leaders; historians of eduction studied school systems and the men who ran them; historians of women wrote about suffrage leaders and reform elites. Large masses of less eminent people also passed through the history books, or loitered in the wings like armies of anonymous extras on a Hippodrome stage. But the leading actors were small and highly individuated power-elites.

Historians studied these people through documentary sources. The results were organized as narratives and presented in the form of testimony—sometimes with specific citations, but for the most part historians testified to their readers, "I have steeped myself in the sources, and here is what I believe to have happened," and they were believed, for this was a time when scholars were gentlemen, and a gentleman was as good as his word.

All of this activity created a coherent and plausible idea of history, which was at once a body of knowledge about the past and also a way of knowing it. Its masters were the great "narrative" historians such as Macaulay, Michelet, Ranke and Parkman. The last of this breed in America were Allan Nevins and Samuel Eliot Morison, who are both in their graves.

Early in the twentieth century, this paradigm of history began to come apart. Its ethical framework disintegrated. Suddenly, there were many new interests and problems that no longer seemed to fit. Anomalies were found; young scholars were promoted primarily for finding them. For two generations, historians became hunters after the anomalous fact. Each of their successes was a blow against the old synthesis, which was soon reduced to something like a ruin.

Some scholars struggled to repair it. Others attempted to replace it with a new synthesis. In the United States, the work of Turner, Beard, Parrington, Hofstadter, Boorstin and Hartz might be understood as a series of highly tentative paradigm sketches. But nobody could put the pieces together again. This was the period (1935–60) when historical relativism came into fashion, and every convention of the American Historical Association became an organized expression of professional *Angst*.

Then, in the decade of the 1960s, something new began to happen. Young scholars in Europe and America were inspired by the French school of the *Annales* to invent a new kind of history which differed from the old paradigm in all of the characteristics mentioned above. This new history was not really about the past at all, but about change—with past and present in a mutual per-spective. It was not a story-telling but a problem-solving disci-pline. Its *problematiques* were about change and continuity in the acts and thoughts of ordinary people—people in the midst of others; people in society. The goal of this new social history was nothing less than an *histoire totale* of the human experience. To that end, the new historians drew upon many types of evidence: documents, statistics, physical artifacts, iconographic materials and much more. They also presented their findings in a new way—not as testimony but as argument. An historian was required not only to make true statements but also to demon-strate their truthfulness by rigorous methods of logic and empi-ricism. This epistemic revolution was the most radical innovation of the new history. It was also the most difficult for older scholars to understand.

In its early years, the new social history claimed to be not merely a new subdiscipline of history but the discipline itself in a new form. It promised to become a major synthesizing discipline in the human sciences—even *the* synthesizing discipline. Unhap-pily, these high goals were not reached. The new social history succeeded in building an institutional base, and also in exploring many new fields of knowledge. But in Fernand Braudel's words, it was overwhelmed by its own success. Instead of becoming a syn-thesizing discipline, it disintegrated into many special fields—women's history, labor history, environmental history, the history of aging, the history of child abuse, and even gay history—in which the work became increasingly shrill and polemical. More-over, too many important subjects were excluded from the new history—politics, events, individuals, even ideas—and too many problems were diminished by materialist explanations and "mod-ernization models." By the 1980s the new social history had lost much of its intellectual momentum, and most of its conceptual range. It had also lost touch with the larger purposes that had called it into being.

From this mixed record of success and failure, a question inev-itably arises. What comes after the new history? How can we con-tinue to move forward? How might we strengthen the weakened hand of synthesis in an analytic discipline? What larger intellec-tual and cultural purposes might an historian seek to serve?

To those questions, this series offers an answer in its organizing idea of cultural history. Briefly, it seeks to find a way forward by combining several elements which the old and new histories have tended to keep apart. In terms of substance, it is about both elites and ordinary people, about individual choices and collective experiences, about exceptional events and normative patterns, about vernacular culture and high culture, about the problem of society and the problem of the state. To those ends, it tries to keep alive the idea of *histoire totale* by employing a concept of culture as a coherent and comprehensive whole.

In causal terms, this inquiry searches for a way beyond reductive materialist models (of both the left and the right) which are presently in fashion among historians in the United States and Britain, where materialism became a cultural mania during the Reagan and Thatcher years. Without denying the importance of material factors in history, one might assert that they are only a part of a larger whole, and that claims for their priority are rarely grounded in empirical fact. This inquiry seeks to place them in their proper context.

In terms of epistemology, this work tries to find a way forward in yet another way. The old history was idealist in its epistemic assumptions. Its major findings were offered as "interpretations" which tended to be discovered by intuition and supported by testimony. The new social history aspired to empiricism, but the epistemic revolution was incomplete—and something of the old interpretative sweep was lost in the process. This work tries to combine the interpretative thrust of the old history with the empiricism of the new—interpretative sails and empirical anchors, so to speak.

In its temporal aspect, this inquiry seeks a new answer to an old problem about the relationship between the past and the present. Many working historians think of the past as fundamentally separate from the present—the antiquarian solution. Others study the past as prologue to the present—the presentist solution. This work is organized around a third idea—that every period of the past, when understood in its own terms, is immediate to the present. This "immediatist" solution cannot be discussed at length here; it must be defined ostensively by the work itself, and especially by the conclusion. Suffice to say that the temporal problem in this volume is to explore the immediacy of the earliest period of American history without presentism, and at the same time to understand the cultures of early America in their own terms without antiquarianism.

An immediatist idea of a relationship between the past and present might also support a more spacious relationship between history and other fields of knowledge. The old history was conceived as an autonomous discipline. The new history was more interdisciplinary—but its efforts consisted mainly of borrowings from other fields. This work is meant to suggest that major problems in many disciplines are insoluble without the application of historical knowledge. A case in point is the problem of wealth distribution; this work will argue, for example, that the distribution of wealth is determined not merely by timeless economic laws but by the interplay of cultural values and individual purposes which are rooted in the past.

Such an approach to the relationship between past and present might also help to enlarge historical inquiry in its ethical dimension. This work, for example, tries to apply new empirical methods and findings to old problems about the history of freedom in the world. It suggests that the problem of liberty cannot be discussed intelligently without a discrimination of libertarianisms which must be made in historical terms. Empirical knowledge of the past is not merely useful but necessary to an understanding of our moral choices in the present.

Finally, in terms of rhetoric, a problem has arisen from the empirical requirements of the new history, which have destroyed the possibility of simple story-telling in original scholarship without changing the narrative nature of the writing that historians do. This series seeks to combine story-telling and problem-solving in a "braided narrative" of more complex construction.

In all of those many ways, this idea of cultural history rests upon an assumption that the old and the new history are not two disciplines but one. The progress of historical knowledge is best served by their creative integration.

Old Headington, Oxford   D.H.F.
Wayland, Massachusetts

CONTENTS

ILLUSTRATIONS

Drawings
by Jennifer Brody

Maps
by Andrew Mudryk

Tables

Albion's Seed

INTRODUCTION

❧ The Determinants of a Voluntary Society

> Where do we come from? Who are we?
> Where are we going?
> —Paul Gauguin, 1897

IN BOSTON'S MUSEUM OF FINE ARTS, not far from the place where English Puritans splashed ashore in 1630, there is a decidedly unpuritanical painting of bare-breasted Polynesian women by Paul Gauguin. The painting is set on a wooded riverbank. In the background is the ocean, and the shadowy outline of a distant land. The canvas is crowded with brooding figures in every condition of life—old and young, dark and fair. They are seen in a forest of symbols, as if part of a dream. In the corner, the artist has added an inscription: "D'ou venons nous? Qui sommes nous? Ou allons nous?"

That painting haunts the mind of this historian. He wonders how a Polynesian allegory found its way to a Puritan town which itself was set on a wooded riverbank, with the ocean in the background and the shadow of another land in the far distance. He observes the crowd of museumgoers who gather before the painting. They are Americans in every condition of life, young and old, dark and fair. Suddenly the great questions leap to life. Where do *we* come from? Who are we? Where are we going?

The answers to these questions grow more puzzling the more one thinks about them. We Americans are a bundle of paradoxes. We are mixed in our origins, and yet we are one people. Nearly all of us support our republican system, but we argue passionately

3

(sometimes violently) among ourselves about its meaning. Most of us subscribe to what Gunnar Myrdal called the American Creed, but that idea is a paradox in political theory. As Myrdal observed in 1942, America is "conservative in fundamental principles . . . but the principles conserved are liberal and some, indeed, are radical."[1]

We live in an open society which is organized on the principle of voluntary action, but the determinants of that system are exceptionally constraining. Our society is dynamic, changing profoundly in every period of American history; but it is also remarkably stable. The search for the origins of this system is the central problem in American history. It is also the subject of this book.

❧ The Question Framed

The organizing question here is about what might be called the determinants of a voluntary society. The problem is to explain the origins and stability of a social system which for two centuries has remained stubbornly democratic in its politics, capitalist in its economy, libertarian in its laws, individualist in its society and pluralistic in its culture.

Much has been written on this subject—more than anyone can possibly read. But a very large outpouring of books and articles contains a remarkably small number of seminal ideas. Most historians have tried to explain the determinants of a voluntary society in one of three ways: by reference to the European culture that was transmitted to America, or to the American environment itself, or to something in the process of transmission.

During the nineteenth century the first of these explanations was very much in fashion. Historians believed that the American system had evolved from what one scholar called "Teutonic germs" of free institutions, which were supposedly carried from the forests of Germany to Britain and then to America. This idea was taken up by a generation of historians who tended to be Anglo-Saxon in their origins, Atlantic in their attitudes and Whiggish in their politics. Most had been trained in the idealist and institutional traditions of the German historical school.[2]

---

[1] Gunnar Myrdal, *An American Dilemma* (1944, rpt. New York, 1962), 7.

[2] The exponents of the germ theory were especially interested in continuities of land tenure such as *socage,* and political institutions such as the *tun* and *folk-moot.* Many early dissertations

For a time this Teutonic thesis became very popular—in Boston and Baltimore. But in Kansas and Wisconsin it was unkindly called the "germ theory" of American history and laughed into oblivion. In the early twentieth century it yielded to the Turner thesis, which looked to the American environment and especially to the western frontier as a way of explaining the growth of free institutions in America. This idea appealed to scholars who were middle western in their origins, progressive in their politics, and materialist in their philosophy.[3]

In the mid-twentieth century the Turner thesis also passed out of fashion. Yet another generation of American historians became deeply interested in processes of immigration and ethnic pluralism as determinants of a voluntary society. This third approach was specially attractive to scholars who were not themselves of Anglo-Saxon stock. Many were central European in their origin, urban in their residence, and Jewish in their religion. This pluralistic "migration model" is presently the conventional interpretation.[4]

Other explanations have also been put forward from time to time, but three ideas have held the field: the germ theory, the frontier thesis, and the migration model.

This book returns to the first of those explanations, within the framework of the second and third. It argues a modified "germ thesis" about the importance for the United States of having been British in its cultural origins. The argument is complex, and for the sake of clarity might be summarized in advance. It runs more or less as follows.

---

at Johns Hopkins attempted to establish these linkages, with limited success. No historian in the late 19th century had a sufficient command of archives on both sides of the Atlantic to settle the question. The germ theory lay beyond the empirical reach of American historical scholarship for three generations. For a survey of this literature see J. M. Vincent et al., *Herbert B. Adams* (Baltimore, 1902), with a bibliography of his students' works from 1876 to 1902.

[3]The Turner thesis is older than Frederick Jackson Turner himself. Similar arguments were made by Cotton Mather and Benjamin Franklin, but Turner gave this idea its classical statement. He preserved the structure of the Teutonic "germ theory," but argued that the European "germs" were less important than the American environment in which they grew, and specifically that "free land" encouraged the growth of democracy, capitalism and individualism. See generally Ray Billington, *Westward Expansion* (4th ed., New York, 1974), with a full bibliography; Lee Benson, *Turner and Beard* (Glencoe, Ill., 1960); Ray Billington, *Frederick Jackson Turner* (New York, 1963); Richard Hofstadter, *The Progressive Historians* (New York, 1969).

[4]Leading examples of the migration model are to be found in the work of Arthur Schlesinger Sr., Marcus Hansen, Oscar Handlin, and most recently Bernard Bailyn, *The Peopling of British North America* (New York, 1986), and *Voyagers to the West: A Passage in the Peopling of America on the Eve of the Revolution* (New York, 1986).

❧ The Argument Stated

During the very long period from 1629 to 1775, the present area of the United States was settled by at least four large waves of English-speaking immigrants. The first was an exodus of Puritans from the east of England to Massachusetts during a period of eleven years from 1629 to 1640. The second was the migration of a small Royalist elite and large numbers of indentured servants from the south of England to Virginia (ca. 1642–75). The third was a movement from the North Midlands of England and Wales to the Delaware Valley (ca. 1675–1725). The fourth was a flow of English-speaking people from the borders of North Britain and northern Ireland to the Appalachian backcountry mostly during the half-century from 1718 to 1775.

These four groups shared many qualities in common. All of them spoke the English language. Nearly all were British Protestants. Most lived under British laws and took pride in possessing British liberties. At the same time, they also differed from one another in many other ways: in their religious denominations, social ranks, historical generations, and also in the British regions from whence they came. They carried across the Atlantic four different sets of British folkways which became the basis of regional cultures in the New World.

By the year 1775 these four cultures were fully established in British America. They spoke distinctive dialects of English, built their houses in diverse ways, and had different methods of doing much of the ordinary business of life. Most important for the political history of the United States, they also had four different conceptions of order, power and freedom which became the cornerstones of a voluntary society in British America.

Today less than 20 percent of the American population have any British ancestors at all. But in a cultural sense most Americans are Albion's seed, no matter who their own forebears may have been.[5] Strong echoes of four British folkways may still be

---

[5]Albion was the first recorded name for the island of Britain, which was known to the Greeks in the 6th century B.C. as the "island of the Albiones." This usage persisted for a thousand years. The venerable Bede began his *History of the English Church and People* thus: "Britannia, oceani insula, cui quondam Albion nomen fuit . . ." (*Historical Works*, ed. J. E. King (2 vols., London, 1929), I, 1011). The connotation of *Albion* changed through time; the Romans made "Albion" into a Latin pun on *albus*, "white," for the cliffs of Dover. In German, it is still erroneously translated *Weissland*, "white land." In French, "Albion" has become a pejorative for a

heard in the major dialects of American speech, in the regional patterns of American life, in the complex dynamics of American politics, and in the continuing conflict between four different ideas of freedom in the United States. The interplay of four "freedom ways" has created an expansive pluralism which is more libertarian than any unitary culture alone could be. That is the central thesis of this book: the legacy of four British folkways in early America remains the most powerful determinant of a voluntary society in the United States today.

✎ The Problem of Folkways

Before we study this subject in detail, several conceptual problems require attention. All are embedded in the word "folkways." This term was coined by American sociologist William Graham Sumner to describe habitual "usages, manners, customs, mores and morals" which he believed to be practiced more or less unconsciously in every culture. Sumner thought that folkways arose from biological instincts. "Men begin with acts," he wrote, "not with thoughts."[6]

In this work "folkway" will have a different meaning. It is defined here as the normative structure of values, customs and meanings that exist in any culture. This complex is not many things but one thing, with many interlocking parts. It is not primarily biological or instinctual in its origins, as Sumner believed, but social and intellectual. Folkways do not rise from the unconscious in even a symbolic sense—though most people do many social things without reflecting very much about them. In the modern world a folkway is apt to be a cultural *artifact*—the conscious instrument of human will and purpose. Often (and increasingly today) it is also the deliberate contrivance of a cultural elite.

A folkway should not be thought of in Sumner's sense as something ancient and primitive which has been inherited from the distant past. Folkways are often highly persistent, but they are

---

nation which is thought to preach high ideals but not to practice them; an example was Napoleon's sneer against "Albion perfide." In the 19th century, romantic poets made Albion into an ornate alias for England rather than Britain, which was its original meaning.

[6]William Graham Sumner, *Folkways: A Study of the Sociological Importance of Manners, Customs, Mores and Morals* (Boston, 1907), 2.

never static. Even where they have acquired the status of a tradition they are not necessarily very old. Folkways are constantly in process of creation, even in our own time.[7]

Folkways in this normative sense exist in advanced civilizations as well as in primitive societies. They are functioning systems of high complexity which have actually grown stronger rather than weaker in the modern world. In any given culture, they always include the following things:

—*Speech ways,* conventional patterns of written and spoken language: pronunciation, vocabulary, syntax and grammar.

—*Building ways,* prevailing forms of vernacular architecture and high architecture, which tend to be related to one another.

—*Family ways,* the structure and function of the household and family, both in ideal and actuality.

—*Marriage ways,* ideas of the marriage-bond, and cultural processes of courtship, marriage and divorce.

—*Gender ways,* customs that regulate social relations between men and women.

—*Sex ways,* conventional sexual attitudes and acts, and the treatment of sexual deviance.

—*Child-rearing ways,* ideas of child nature and customs of child nurture.

—*Naming ways,* onomastic customs including favored forenames and the descent of names within the family.

—*Age ways,* attitudes toward age, experiences of aging, and age relationships.

—*Death ways,* attitudes toward death, mortality rituals, mortuary customs and mourning practices.

—*Religious ways,* patterns of religious worship, theology, ecclesiology and church architecture.

[7]Eric Hobsbawm and Terence Ranger, *The Invention of Tradition* (Cambridge, 1983). This idea of folkways differs from folklore. The word "folklore" was coined by a British scholar William Thoms in 1846 as "the generic term under which are included traditional institutions, beliefs, arts, customs, stories, songs, sayings and the like current among backward peoples or retained by the less cultured classes of more advanced peoples."

This idea of folklore was modified by scholars in the 20th century, but some of its biases still survive. Architectural historian Dell Upton observes that "in many treatments of folk culture, change is viewed as decay; folk culture is thought to be constantly threatened. It is a 'dying' thing which somehow never manages to expire." This problem has led scholars such as Upton, James Deetz and Henry Glassie to shift their thinking from "folk" to "vernacular" culture. Cf. Dell Thayer Upton, "Early Vernacular Architecture in Southeastern Virginia" (thesis, Brown, 1980); Richard M. Dorson, *Handbook of American Folklore* (Bloomington, 1983), xi–xii, xiv, 115, 323–40.

—*Magic ways,* normative beliefs and practices concerning the supernatural.

—*Learning ways,* attitudes toward literacy and learning, and conventional patterns of education.

—*Food ways,* patterns of diet, nutrition, cooking, eating, feasting and fasting.

—*Dress ways,* customs of dress, demeanor, and personal adornment.

—*Sport ways,* attitudes toward recreation and leisure; folk games and forms of organized sport.

—*Work ways,* work ethics and work experiences; attitudes toward work and the nature of work.

—*Time ways,* attitudes toward the use of time, customary methods of time keeping, and the conventional rhythms of life.

—*Wealth ways,* attitudes toward wealth and patterns of its distribution.

—*Rank ways,* the rules by which rank is assigned, the roles which rank entails, and relations between different ranks.

—*Social ways,* conventional patterns of migration, settlement, association and affiliation.

—*Order ways,* ideas of order, ordering institutions, forms of disorder, and treatment of the disorderly.

—*Power ways,* attitudes toward authority and power; patterns of political participation.

—*Freedom ways,* prevailing ideas of liberty and restraint, and libertarian customs and institutions.

Every major culture in the modern world has its own distinctive customs in these many areas. Their persistent power might be illustrated by an example. Consider the case of wealth distribution. Most social scientists believe that the distribution of wealth is determined primarily by material conditions. For Marxists the prime mover is thought to be the means of production; for Keynesians it is the process of economic growth; for disciples of Adam Smith it is the market mechanism. But to study this subject in a comparative way is to discover that the distribution of wealth has varied from one culture to another in ways that cannot possibly be explained by material processes alone. Another powerful determinant is the inherited structure of values and customs which might be called the "wealth ways" of a culture.

These wealth ways are communicated from one generation to the next by many interlocking mechanisms—child-rearing pro-

cesses, institutional structures, cultural ethics, and codes of law—
which create ethical imperatives of great power in advanced societies as well as primitive cultures. Indeed, the more advanced a
society becomes in material terms, the stronger is the determinant power of its folkways, for modern technologies act as ampli-
fiers, and modern institutions as stabilizers, and modern elites as
organizers of these complex cultural processes.[8]

The purpose of this book is to examine those processes at work
in what is now the United States, where at least four British folk
cultures were introduced at an early date. Their variety makes
them unusually accessible for study, as William Graham Sumner
himself was one of the first to observe. He found his leading
example of folkways not in primitive tribes but in the regional
culture of New England. Sumner wrote:

> The mores of New England, however, still show deep traces of the
> Puritan temper and world philosophy. Perhaps nowhere else in
> the world can so strong an illustration be seen, both of the persis-
> tency of the spirit of mores, and their variability and adaptability.
> The mores of New England have extended to a large immigrant
> population, and have won control over them. They have also been
> carried to the new states by emigrants, and their perpetuation
> there is an often-noticed phenomenon.[9]

The same historical pattern appears in the American south.
However different that region may be from New England, it also
has preserved its own distinctive folkways through many generations. Something similar also happened in the American midlands, and in the American west. Throughout all four of these
broad areas we find the same processes of cultural persistence,
variability and adaptability that William Graham Sumner
observed in New England. Even as the ethnic composition of
these various regions of the United States has changed profoundly, regional cultures themselves have persisted, and are still

---

[8]Scholars regularly rediscover the persistent power of ethnicity and regional culture in modern societies without being able to explain it except in material terms. See, for example, Michael
Hechter, *Internal Colonialism: The Celtic Fringe in British National Development, 1536–1966* (London, 1975), which argues that the survival of "ethnic solidarity" in Britain was caused by a
division of labor in which some ethnic groups were kept in inferior positions by a process of
"internal colonialism." The argument of the present work is different—that cultural systems
have their own imperatives, and are not mere reflexes of material relationships. This is not to
argue against the power of material forces, but for a more balanced conception of the
problem in which material structures are seen as part of a cultural whole.

[9]Sumner, *Folkways*, 86.

very powerful even in our own time. All of them derive from folkways that were planted in the American colonies more than two centuries ago.

If these folkways are to be understood truly, they must be described empirically—that is, by reference to evidence which can be verified or falsified. In this work, descriptive examples are presented in the text for illustrative purposes, and empirical indicators are summarized in the notes.[10] Not all of these folkways can be treated empirically, but the work of many scholars has produced a broad range of historical evidence for each of the four major cultures in British America. Let us begin with Puritan New England, which was founded by the first great migration, and take up the others in chronological order.

[10]The following empirical indicators are employed here:

Folkway	Qualitative Indicators	Quantitative Indicators
Speech	pronunciation, vocabulary, grammar	speech frequencies
Building	styles, plans, methods, materials	modal building types
Family	family ideas, language and law	completed size, household composition
Marriage	courtship and marriage customs	age at marriage, proportion married
Gender	ideas and language	
Sex	ideas and language	prenuptial pregnancy; bastardy; fertility
Naming	qualities of namesakes	forename frequencies, descent ratios, etc.
Child-rearing	ideas of child nature and nurture	sending-out frequencies
Age	ideas of age relations	age-heaping patterns
Death	ideas of fatalism	
Religion	worship rituals; church architecture	church membership
Magic	magic customs	frequency of witchcraft proceedings
Learning	institutions and rituals	total education rate
Literacy	attitudes toward literacy and orality	signature-mark frequencies
Food	foods, cooking and eating methods	foodstuff frequencies
Dress	sumptuary laws, dress norms	
Sport	common games, ideology of sport	
Work	work ethics	work force composition
Time	ideas of time; calendars; holidays	seasonality indicators
Wealth	ideas of wealth	grants, Gini ratios, SSTT, zero-holdings
Inheritance	intestacy rules	sibling shares
Rank	criteria, language, rituals of rank	rank distribution
Association	ideals of settlement	settlement patterns, persistence
Order	ideas of order and ordering institutions	crime rates; indictments; penalties
Power	institutions of local government	voting, officeholding, taxing and spending
Freedom	libertarian ideas and customs	

EAST ANGLIA TO MASSACHUSETTS

❧ The Exodus of the English Puritans, 1629–1641

> You talk of New England; I truly believe
> Old England's grown new and doth us deceive.
> I'll ask you a question or two, by your leave:
>   And is not old England grown new?
>
> New fashions in houses, new fashions at table,
> The old servants discharged, the new are more able;
> And every old custome is but an old fable!
>   And is not old England grown new? . . .
>
> Then talk you no more of New England!
> New England is where old England did stand,
> New furnished, new fashioned, new womaned, new manned
>   And is not old England grown new?
>   —Anonymous verse, c. 1630[1]

ON A BLUSTERY MARCH MORNING in the year 1630, a great ship was riding restlessly at anchor in the Solent, near the Isle of Wight. As the tide began to ebb, running outward past the Needles toward the open sea, a landsman watching idly from the shore might have seen a cloud of white smoke billow from the ship's side. A few seconds later, he would have heard the sharp report of a cannon, echoing across the anchorage. Another cannon answered from the shore, and on board the ship the flag of England fluttered up its halyard—the scarlet cross of Saint George showing bravely on its field of white. Gray sails blossomed below the great ship's yards, and slowly she began to move toward the sea. The landsman might have observed that she lay deep in the water, and that her decks were crowded with passengers. He would have noticed her distinctive figurehead—a great prophetic eagle projecting from her bow. And he might have made out her name, gleaming in newly painted letters on her hull.

13

She was the ship *Arbella,* outward bound with families and freight for the new colony of Massachusetts Bay.[2]

Arbella was no ordinary emigrant vessel. She carried twenty-eight great guns and was the "admiral" or flagship of an entire fleet of English ships that sailed for Massachusetts in the same year. The men and women who embarked in her were also far from being ordinary passengers. Traveling in the comfort of a cabin was Lady Arbella Fiennes, sister of the Earl of Lincoln, in whose honor the ship had received her name. Also on board was her husband, Isaac Johnson, a rich landowner in the county of Rutland; her brother Charles Fiennes; and her friend the future poet Anne Dudley Bradstreet, who had grown up in the household of the Earl of Lincoln. Other berths were occupied by the Earl's high stewards Simon Bradstreet and Thomas Dudley; by an English gentleman called Sir Richard Saltonstall; and by a Suffolk lawyer named John Winthrop who was destined to become the leader of the colony.[3]

Most of *Arbella*'s passengers were families of lesser rank, but very few of them came from the bottom of English society. Their dress and demeanor marked them as yeomen and artisans of middling status. Their gravity of manner and austerity of appearance also said much about their religion and moral character.

Below decks, the great ship was a veritable ark. Its main hold teemed with horses, cattle, sheep, goats, pigs, dogs, cats and dunghill fowl. Every nautical nook and cranny was crowded with provisions. In the cabin were chests of treasure which would have made a rich haul for the Dunkirkers who preyed upon Protestant shipping in the English Channel.[4]

The ship *Arbella* was one of seventeen vessels that sailed to Massachusetts in the year 1630. She led a great migration which for size and wealth and organization was without precedent in

[1]Ashmole Ms. 36.37 folio 100v, Bodleian Library, Oxford.

[2]This, the departure from Cowes on the morning of March 29, 1630, proved to be a false start. But John Winthrop took it in his journal to be the true beginning of his voyage. In fact the ship did not pass through the Needles until 8 April 1630. *Winthrop's Journal,* ed. James K. Hosmer (2 vols., New York, 1908), I, 23, 29 March 1630.

The spelling of the ship's name is disputed by New England historians. Winthrop wrote it as *Arbella,* others as *Arabella;* see Edward Channing, *History of the United States* (6 vols., New York, 1905–25), I, 330n; and *Winthrop Papers,* Stewart Mitchell, ed. (5 vols., 1929, rpt. New York, 1968), II, 239n.

[3]A passenger list compiled by C. K. Bolton appears in Albert K. Rogers, *Voyage of the Arbella, 1630* (Boston, 1930); another list is in the *Winthrop Papers,* II, 276.

[4]*Winthrop's Journal,* I, 23–49.

These Puritan leaders personified the spiritual striving that brought the Bay colonists to America. John Winthrop (center front) was a pious East Anglian lawyer who became governor of Massachusetts. His son John Winthrop, Jr. (center rear) was governor of Connecticut, entrepreneur, and scientist, much respected for what Cotton Mather called his "Christian qualities . . . studious, humble, patient, reserved and mortified." Sir Harry Vane (right rear) was briefly governor of Massachusetts at the age of 24. He was reprimanded for long hair and elegant dress, but was so rigorous in his Puritanism that he believed only the thrice-born to be truly saved. Sir Richard Saltonstall (right front) founded Watertown and colonized Connecticut, but dissented on tolera-tion and returned to England. William Pynchon (left front) founded Spring-field and wrote a book on atonement that was ordered burned in Boston. Hugh Peter (left rear) was minister in Salem, a founder of Harvard and an English Parliamentary leader who was executed in 1660. The original portraits are in the Am. Antiq. Soc., Essex Institute, Mass. Hist. Soc., Queens College (Cam-bridge) and the Victoria and Albert Museum.

England's colonization of North America. Within a period of eleven years, some 80,000 English men, women and children swarmed outward from their island home. This exodus was not a movement of attraction. The great migration was a great flight from conditions which had grown intolerable at home. It continued from 1629 to 1640, precisely the period that Whig historians called the "eleven years' tyranny," when Charles I tried to rule England without a Parliament, and Archbishop William Laud purged the Anglican church of its Puritan members. These eleven years were also an era of economic depression, epidemic disease, and so many sufferings that to John Winthrop it seemed as if the land itself had grown "weary of her Inhabitants, so as man which is most precious of all the Creatures, is here more vile and base than the earth they tread upon."[5]

In this time of troubles there were many reasons for leaving England, and many places to go. Perhaps 20,000 English people moved to Ireland. Others in equal number left for the Netherlands and the Rhineland. Another 20,000 sailed to the West Indian islands of Barbados, Nevis, St. Kitts, and the forgotten Puritan colony of Old Providence Island (now a haven for drug-smugglers off the Mosquito Coast of Nicaragua). A fourth contingent chose to settle in Massachusetts, and contributed far beyond its numbers to the culture of North America.[6]

The seventeen vessels that sailed to Massachusetts in 1630 were the vanguard of nearly 200 ships altogether, each carrying about a hundred English souls. A leader of the colony reckoned that there were about 21,000 emigrants in all. This exodus continued from 1630 to the year 1641. While it went on, the North Atlantic Ocean was a busy place. In the year 1638, one immigrant sighted

---

[5]John Winthrop, "General Observations for the Plantation of New England," May 1629, *Winthrop Papers,* II, 114.

[6]For general discussions of the great migration, see C. M. Andrews, *The Colonial Period of American History* (4 vols., New Haven, 1934–38), I, chap. 18; and Carl Bridenbaugh, *Vexed and Troubled Englishmen* (New York, 1967), chaps. 11, 12; Puritan movement to the Caribbean is the subject of A. P. Newton, *The Colonising Activities of the English Puritans* (New Haven, 1914), and Susanna Fischer, "The Providence Adventure" (thesis, Princeton, 1983); for emigration to Ireland see Philip S. Robinson, *The Plantation of Ulster; British Settlement in an Irish Landscape, 1600–1670* (Dublin, 1984).

On the history of the great migration, the Essex County Record Office in Chelmsford, Essex, contains in its reading room many unpublished dissertations, both British and American, touching various aspects of this subject. Of particular value is Norman C. P. Tyack, "Migration from East Anglia to New England before 1660" (thesis, Univ. of London, 1951); David Cressy, *Coming Over: Migration and Communication between England and New England in the Seventeenth Century* (Cambridge, 1987).

no fewer than thirteen other vessels in midpassage between England and Massachusetts.[7]

After the year 1640, New England's great migration ended as abruptly as it began. The westward flow of population across the Atlantic suddenly stopped and ran in reverse, as many Massachusetts Puritans sailed home to serve in the Civil War. Migration to New England did not resume on a large scale for many years—not until Irish Catholics began to arrive nearly two centuries later.[8]

The emigrants who came to Massachusetts in the great migration became the breeding stock for America's Yankee population. They multiplied at a rapid rate, doubling every generation for two centuries. Their numbers increased to 100,000 by 1700, to at least one million by 1800, six million by 1900, and more than sixteen million by 1988—all descended from 21,000 English emigrants who came to Massachusetts in the period from 1629 to 1640.

The children of the great migration moved rapidly beyond the borders of Massachusetts. They occupied much of southern New England, eastern New Jersey and northern New York. In the nineteenth century, their descendants migrated east to Maine and Nova Scotia, north to Canada, and west to the Pacific. Along the way, they founded the future cities of Buffalo, Cleveland, Chicago, St. Paul, Denver, Seattle, San Francisco and Salt Lake City. Today, throughout this vast area, most families of Yankee descent trace their American beginnings to an English ancestor who came ashore in Massachusetts Bay within five years of the year 1635.

---

[7]This standard estimate, contemporary with the event, was made by Edward Johnson of Woburn, who migrated to the New World in 1630, probably in the ship *Arbella* with Governor Winthrop. Johnson reckoned that between 1630 and 1640 the number of "Men, Women and Children passing over this wide Ocean, is near as at present can be gathered, is also supposed to be 21,200 or thereabout." His estimate of the number of emigrant ships is clouded by a typographical error. One passage reported 298 vessels; another, 198. Winthrop's journal mentioned more than 100 vessels (many by name), and in approximately sixty instances supplied the number of passengers, at a little above 100 per ship. This suggests that the correct number of shiploads is 198. For text and learned commentary see Edward Johnson, *Johnson's Wonder-working Providence 1628–1651*, ed. J. F. Jameson (New York, 1910), 58–61.

A radically different estimate has recently been offered by an American economist who argues that the true size of the great migration to New England was only a little above 10,000. He obtains this result as a residual from estimates of fertility, mortality, emigration and total population—some of which may be mistaken; cf. Henry A. Gemery, "Emigration from the British Isles to the New World, 1630–1700; Inferences from Colonial Populations," *Research in Economic History* V (1980), 179–233; this difficult question will be discussed in more detail in a forthcoming work.

[8]Only one of the 198 vessels in the great migration was lost—the ship *Gabriel*, on the coast of Maine near Pemaquid in 1635; Johnson, *Wonder-working Providence*, 61.

❧ Religious Origins of the Great Migration

For these English Puritans, the new colony of Massachusetts had a meaning that is not easily translated into the secular terms of our materialist world. "A letter from New England," wrote Joshua Scottow, ". . . was venerated as a Sacred Script, or as the writing of some Holy Prophet. 'Twas carried many miles, where divers came to hear it."[1]

The great migration developed in this spirit—above all as a religious movement of English Christians who meant to build a new Zion in America. When most of these emigrants explained their motives for coming to the New World, religion was mentioned not merely as their leading purpose. It was their only purpose.[2]

This religious impulse took many different forms—evangelical, communal, familial and personal. The Massachusetts Bay Company officially proclaimed the purpose of converting the natives. Its great seal featured an Indian with arms beckoning, and five English words flowing from his mouth: "Come over and help us." However bizarre this image may seem to us, it had genuine meaning for the builders of the Bay Colony.[3]

A very different religious motive was expressed by many leaders of the Colony, who often declared their collective intention to build a "Bible Commonwealth" which might serve as a model for mankind. The classical example was John Winthrop's exhortation which many generations of New England schoolchildren have been made to memorize: "We shall be as a City upon a Hill, the

---

[1]MAHSC, 4th series, IV, 293.

[2]Most American historians agree on the centrality of religion in the Puritan great migration, but some English historians take a more secular view, and one wishes to abolish the word "Puritan" from historical usage altogether; see Tyack, "Migration from East Anglia"; Cressy, *Coming Over*, 74–106; Patrick Collinson, "Concerning the Name Puritan," *JECH* 31 (1980), 483–88.

Empirical evidence for the primacy of religion appears in repeated statements not only by leaders such as Richard Mather, John Winthrop, Thomas Dudley, John Cotton, Thomas Shepard and Thomas Hooker, but also by ordinary emigrants such as indentured servant Roger Clap, tailor John Dane, housewife Lucy Downing and many others. Evidence to the contrary consists of occasional complaints by Puritan leaders that some migrants were not religious enough; and of criminal proceedings against men such as bigamist Christopher Gardiner (banished from the Bay Colony) and fugitive William Schooler (hanged for rape and murder). Altogether, most American historians agree with John White, who observed the great migration at first hand and wrote as early as 1630, "necessity may press some, novelty draw on others, hopes of gain in time to come may prevail with a third sort; but that the most and most sincere and godly part have the advancement of the Gospel for their main scope I am confident" (*The Planter's Plea* (London, 1630)).

[3]*Records of the Governor and Company of the Massachusetts Bay in New England,* ed. Nathaniel B. Shurtleff (5 vols., Boston, 1853–54), I, 1.

Ninety Puritan ministers came to New England in the Great Migration. They were a close-knit cultural elite, strong in their spiritual purposes, and highly respected for intellect and character. John Cotton (front center) was a leading theologian of the Congregational middle way and minister in Boston, a leader much loved for his piety and wisdom. Richard Mather (front left) became minister in Dorchester, and architect of the Cambridge Platform (New England's system of church discipline). John Eliot (left rear) served as minister in Roxbury and Indian missionary who founded the "praying town" of Natick and translated the Bible into Algonkian. Peter Bulkeley (right rear) was minister in Concord, and a gentleman of old family and large fortune which he devoted to God's work in America. John Davenport (front right) was a Londoner who founded New Haven, the most conservative and purse-proud colony in New England. Their portraits are owned by the American Antiquarian Society, Peter Bulkeley Brainerd, the Connecticut Historical Society, Harvard University and the Huntington Library.

eyes of all people are upon us. . . . we shall be made a story and a byword throughout the world."[4]

But most emigrants did not think in these terms. They were not much interested in converting heathen America, and had little hope of reforming Christian Europe. Mainly they were concerned about the spiritual condition of their own families and especially their children. Lucy Downing, the Puritan wife of a London lawyer, wrote to her brother in New England on the eve of her own sailing:

> If we see God withdrawing His ordinances from us here, and enlarging His presence to you there, I should then hope for comfort in the hazards of the sea with our little ones shrieking about us . . . in such a case I should [more] willingly venture my children's bodies and my own for them, than their souls.[5]

Many others embarked upon entirely personal errands. A tailor named John Dane explained that he "bent myself to come to New England, thinking that I should be more free here than there from temptations." His parents did not approve, but agreed to settle the question by consulting the Bible. Dane wrote afterwards:

> To return to the way and manner of my coming: . . . My father and mother showed themselves unwilling. I sat close by a table where there lay a Bible. I hastily took up the Bible, and told my father if, where I opened the Bible, there I met with anything either to encourage or discourage, that should settle me. I, opening of it, not knowing no more than the child in the womb, the first I cast my eyes on was: "Come out from among them, touch no unclean thing, and I will be your God and you shall be my people." My father and mother never more opposed me, but furthered me in the thing, and hastened after me as soon as they could.

John Dane and his family did not emigrate to escape persecution. Even that motive, which we call "religious" in our secular age, was more worldly than his own thinking. He never wrote in grand phrases about a "city on a hill," and showed no interest in saving any soul except his own. John Dane's purpose in coming to New England was to find a place where he could serve God's will and

---

[4]John Winthrop, "A Modell of Christian Charity Written on Board the Arrabella on the Atlantick Ocean," *Winthrop Papers*, II, 282–95.

[5]Frederick J. Simmons, *Emmanuel Downing* (n.p., 1958), 43.

be free of temptation. The New World promised to be a place where he would "touch no unclean thing." In that respect, he was typical of the Puritan migration.[6]

Most immigrants to Massachusetts shared this highly personal sense of spiritual striving. Their Puritanism was not primarily a formal creed or reasoned doctrine. In Alan Simpson's phrase it was the "stretched passion" of a people who "suffered and yearned and strived with an unbelievable intensity."[7]

That "stretched passion" was shared by the great majority of immigrant families to Massachusetts. This truth has been challenged by materialist historians in the twentieth century, but strong evidence appears in the fact that most adult settlers, in most Massachusetts towns, joined a Congregational church during the first generation. This was not easy to do. After 1635, a candidate had to stand before a highly skeptical group of elders, and satisfy them in three respects: adherence to Calvinist doctrines, achievement of a godly life, and demonstrable experience of spiritual conversion.[8]

These requirements were very rigorous—more so than in the Calvinist churches of Europe. Even so, a majority of adults in most Massachusetts towns were willing and able to meet them. In the town of Dedham, for example, 48 people joined the church by 1640—25 women and 23 men, out of 35 families in the town. Most families included at least one church member; many had two. By 1648, Dedham's church members included about 70 percent of male taxpayers and an even larger proportion of women.[9] That pattern was typical of country towns in Massachusetts. In Sudbury, 80 were admitted out of 50 or 60 families. In Watertown, 250 were in "church fellowship" out of 160 families. In Rowley, we are told that "a high percentage of men" joined the church—and probably a higher percentage of women—despite

[6]John Dane, "A Declaration of Remarkabell Prouidenses in the Corse of My Lyfe," *NEHGR* 8 (1854), 154; for many testimonies to the importance of personal religion as the primary motive for migration see George Selement and Bruce C. Woolley, eds., *Thomas Shepard's Confessions*, CSM *Pubs.* 58 (1981), 108, 113, 131; Alexander Young, *Chronicles of the First Planters of the Colony of Massachusetts Bay* (1846, rpt. Williamstown, 1978); and Cotton Mather, *Magnalia Christi Americana* (1702, rpt. 1852, New York, 1967), which publishes excerpts from journals since lost.

[7]Alan Simpson, *Puritanism in Old and New England* (Chicago, 1955), 21.

[8]Edmund S. Morgan, *Visible Saints; The History of a Puritan Idea* (New York, 1963), chaps. 1–3.

[9]Kenneth A. Lockridge, "The History of a Puritan Church, 1637–1736," *NEQ* 40 (1967), 397–424.

local requirements that were even more stringent than in the Colony as whole.[10]

Church membership was not as widespread in seaport towns such as Salem or Marblehead. But even in Salem more than 50 percent of taxable men joined the church in the mid-seventeenth century. Those who did not belong were mostly young men without property.[11]

This pattern of church membership reveals a vital truth about New England's great migration. It tells us that the religious purposes of the colony were not confined to a small "Puritan oligarchy," as some historians still believe, and that the builders of the Bay Colony did not come over to "catch fish," as materialists continue to insist. The spiritual purposes of the colony were fully shared by most men and women in Massachusetts. Here was a fact of high importance for the history of their region.[12]

The religious beliefs of these Puritans were highly developed before they came to America. Revisionist historians notwithstanding, these people were staunch Calvinists. Their spiritual leader John Cotton declared, "I have read the fathers and the schoolmen, and Calvin too; but I find that he that has Calvin, has them all." Many other ministers agreed.[13]

Without attempting to describe their complex Calvinist beliefs in a rounded way, a few major doctrines might be mentioned briefly, for they became vitally important to the culture of New

---

[10]In Rowley the local minister, Ezekiel Rogers, added as a test for membership his own creed, "I professe myselfe to have lived and to dye an unfeigned Hater of all the Base opinnions of the Anabaptists and antinomians, and all other phrentiche dotages of the times that spring from them which God will ere longe cause to be as dung upon the earth." Quoted in Patricia O'Malley, "Rowley, Massachusetts" (thesis, Boston College, 1975), 23; statistics of church membership in Sudbury and Watertown are from Johnson, *Wonder-working Providence,* 74, 197.

[11]Richard Gildrie found the following pattern in church membership of Salem men, by wealth:

Land Holdings (acres)	Church Members (%)	N
100+	83.3	30
60–99	81.3	16
30–59	75.1	42
10–29	41.7	67
.1–10	35.4	79
None	25.0	4
Total	53.4	238

Source: Richard P. Gildrie, "Salem, 1626–1668: History of a Covenanted Community" (thesis, Univ. of Va., 1971), 153.

[12]Thomas J. Wertenbaker, *The Puritan Oligarchy* (New York, 1947).

[13]Mather, *Magnalia Christi Americana,* I, 274.

England. These Puritan ideas might be summarized in five words: depravity, covenant, election, grace, and love.[14]

First was the idea of *depravity* which to Calvinists meant the total corruption of "natural man" as a consequence of Adam's original sin. The Puritans believed that evil was a palpable presence in the world, and that the universe was a scene of cosmic struggle between darkness and light. They lived in an age of atrocities without equal until the twentieth century. But no evil ever surprised them or threatened to undermine their faith. One historian remarks that "it is impossible to conceive of a disillusioned Puritan." They believed as an article of faith that there was no horror which mortal man was incapable of committing. The dark thread of this doctrine ran through the fabric of New England's culture for many generations.[15]

The second idea was that of the *covenant*. The Puritans founded this belief on the book of Genesis, where God made an agreement with Abraham, offering salvation with no preconditions but many obligations. This idea of a covenant had been not prominent in the thinking of Luther or Calvin, but it became a principle of high importance to English Puritans. They thought of their relationship with God (and one another) as a web of contracts. As we shall see, the covenant became a metaphor of profound importance in their thought.[16]

A third idea was the Calvinist doctrine of *election*—which held that only a chosen few were admitted to the covenant. One of Calvinism's Five Points was the doctrine of limited atonement, which taught that Christ died only for the elect—not for all humanity. The iron of this Calvinistic creed entered deep into the soul of New England.

[14]For annotated texts of the creeds and covenants of Salem Church (1629, 1636), Boston Church (1630), Windsor Church (1647), and the two Cambridge Platforms (1646, 1648) see Williston Walker, ed., *The Creeds and Platforms of Congregationalism* (1893, rpt. Boston, 1960).

[15]The Synod of Dort (1618–19) of the Dutch Reformed Church, with German Calvinists and English Puritans sitting in, produced the "Five Points" of Calvinism which included: (1) total depravity, (2) limited atonement, (3) unconditional election, (4) irresistible grace and (5) the final perseverance of the saints (that is, no backsliding). These doctrines emerged in the process of declaring the teachings of Jacobus Arminius to be a Calvinist heresy. The Five Points were generally accepted by Congregationalists in New England; the texts appear with an English translation in Philip Schaff, *The Creeds of Christendom* (4th ed., New York, 1905), III, 540–97. See also A. W. Harrison, *The Beginnings of Arminianism to the Synod of Dort* (London, 1926).

[16]A major statement was John Cotton, *Covenant of God's Free Grace* (London, 1645). The importance of the idea of the covenant to the Puritans was developed by Champlin Burrage, *The Church Covenant Idea* (Philadelphia, 1904), and enlarged by Perry Miller in "The Marrow of Puritan Divinity," *Errand into the Wilderness* (Cambridge, 1956), 48–98; and *The New England Mind: the Seventeenth Century* (1939, rpt. Cambridge, 1954).

A fourth idea was *grace,* a "motion of the heart" which was God's gift to the elect, and the instrument of their salvation. Much Puritan theology, and most of the Five Points of Calvinism, were an attempt to define the properties of grace, which was held to be unconditional, irresistible and inexorable. They thought that it came to each of them directly, and once given would never be taken away. Grace was not merely an idea but an emotion, which has been defined as a feeling of "ecstatic intimacy with the divine." It gave the Puritans a soaring sense of spiritual freedom which they called "soul liberty."[17]

A fifth idea, often lost in our image of Puritanism, was *love.* Their theology made no sense without divine love, for they believed that natural man was so unworthy that salvation came only from God's infinite love and mercy. Further, the Puritans believed that they were bound to love one another in a Godly way. One leader told them that they should "look upon themselves, as being bound up in one *Bundle of Love;* and count themselves obliged, in very close and Strong Bonds, to be serviceable to one another." This Puritan love was a version of the Christian *caritas* in which people were asked to "lovingly give, as well as lovingly take, admonitions." It was a vital principle in their thought.[18]

These ideas created many tensions in Puritan minds. The idea of the covenant bound Puritans to their worldly obligations; the gift of grace released them from every bond but one. The doctrine of depravity filled their world with darkness; the principle of election brought a gleam of light. Puritan theology became a set of insoluble logic problems about how to reconcile human responsibility with God's omnipotence, how to find enlightenment in a universe of darkness, how to live virtuously in a world of evil, and how to reconcile the liberty of a believing Christian with the absolute authority of the word.

For many generations these problems were compressed like coiled springs into the culture of New England. Long after Puritans had become Yankees, and Yankee Trinitarians had become New England Unitarians (whom Whitehead defined as believers in one God at most) the long shadow of Puritan belief still lingered over the folkways of an American region.

---

[17]Norman Pettit, *The Heart Prepared; Grace and Conversion in Puritan Spiritual Life* (New Haven, 1966); Philip F. Gura, *A Glimpse of Sion's Glory; Puritan Radicalism in New England, 1620–1640* (Middletown, Conn., 1984), 50.

[18]Cotton Mather, *Bonifacius,* ed. David Levin (1710, rpt. Cambridge, 1966), 64–65. An excellent discussion of the Puritan idea of love appears in Stephen Foster, *Their Solitary Way* (New Haven, 1971), 41–64.

❧ Social Origins of the Puritan Migration

The builders of the Bay Colony thought of themselves as a twice-chosen people: once by God, and again by the General Court of Massachusetts. Other English plantations eagerly welcomed any two-legged animal who could be dragged on board an emigrant ship. But Massachusetts chose its colonists with care. Not everyone was allowed to settle there. In doubtful cases, the founders of the colony actually demanded written proof of good character. This may have been the only English colony that required some of its immigrants to submit letters of recommendation.[1]

Further, after these immigrants arrived, the social chaff was speedily separated from Abraham's seed. Those who did not fit in were banished to other colonies or sent back to England. This complex process of cultural winnowing created a very special population.[2]

To a remarkable degree, the founders of Massachusetts traveled in families—more so than any major ethnic group in American history. In one contingent of 700 who sailed from Great Yarmouth (Norfolk) and Sandwich (Kent), 94 percent consisted of family groups. Among another group of 680 emigrants, at least 88 percent traveled with relatives, and 73 percent arrived as members of complete nuclear families. These proportions were the highest in the history of American immigration.[3]

The nuclear families that moved to Massachusetts were in many instances related to one another before they left England. A ballad of the great migration commemorated these ties:

> Stay not among the Wicked,
> Lest that with them you perish,
> But let us to New-England go,
> And the Pagan people cherish . . .

[1]Some of these recommendations appear in Young, *Chronicles of the First Planters*, 165ff., and in the *Winthrop Papers*.

[2]The first and in many ways the most detailed analysis was Tyack, "Migration from East Anglia." Tyack has also published "The Humble Puritans of East Anglia and the New England Movement: Evidence from the Court Records of the 1630's," *NEHGR* 138 (1984), 79–106. Other studies include T. H. Breen and Stephen Foster, "Moving to the New World: The Character of Early Massachusetts Immigration," *WMQ3* 30 (1973), 189–222; and Virginia DeJohn Anderson, "Migrants and Motives: Religion and the Settlement of New England, 1630–1640," *NEQ* 58 (1985), 339–83.

[3]Breen and Foster, "Moving to the New World," 189–222. Anderson, "Migrants and Motives," 339–83. Of major ethnic stocks, in American history, only the Germans approached this proportion of migration in family groups.

> For Company I fear not,
> There goes my cousin Hannah,
> And Reuben so persuades to go
> My Cousin Joyce, Susanna.
>
> With Abigail and Faith,
> And Ruth, no doubt, comes after;
> And Sarah kind, will not stay behind;
> My cousin Constance daughter.[4]

From the start, this exceptionally high level of family integration set Massachusetts apart from other American colonies.

Equally extraordinary was the pattern of age distribution. America's immigrants have typically been young people in their teens and twenties. A distribution which is "age-normal" in demographic terms is decidedly exceptional among immigrant populations. But more than 40 percent of immigrants to the Massachusetts Bay Colony were mature men and women over twenty-five, and nearly half were children under sixteen. Only a few migrants were past the age of sixty, but in every other way the distribution of ages was remarkably similar to England's population in general.[5]

Also unusual was the distribution of sexes, which differed very much from most colonial populations. The gender ratio of European migrants to Virginia was four men for every woman. In New Spain it was ten men for every woman; in Brazil, one hundred

---

[4]"The Zealous Puritan," 1639, in C. H. Firth, *The American Garland; Being a Collection of Ballads Relating to America, 1563–1759* (Oxford, 1915), 25–26.

[5]Anderson shows that this distribution of ages was remarkably similar to the population of England in 1636:

New England's Immigrants (Anderson)		England's Population (1636) (Wrigley and Schofield)	
0–14	11.6%	0–14	12.4%
5–14	19.6%	5–14	19.7%
15–24	26.15%	15–24	17.7%
25–59	41.65%	25–59	42.03%
60+	00.97%	60+	8.12%

The only exception was the proportion of immigrants over sixty. The Massachusetts Puritans, because of the intensity of their respect for age, gave much attention to the presence of elderly emigrants among them. Thomas Welde in 1632 reported "many aged passengers" in his ship, "twelve persons being in all able to make well nigh one thousand years." But every quantitative test shows that the proportion of emigrants over sixty was in fact very small—less than 1%, compared with 8–10% in England at that time. Cf. Everett Emerson, ed., *Letters from New England: The Massachusetts Bay Colony, 1629–1638* (Amherst, 1676); Anderson, "Migrants and Motives," 195, 339–83; E. A. Wrigley and R. S. Schofield, *The Population History of England, 1541–1871* (Cambridge, 1981), table A3.1.

men for every Portuguese woman. Only a small minority of immigrants in those colonies could hope to live in households such as they had left behind in Europe. But in the Puritan migration to Massachusetts, the gender ratio was approximately 150 males for every 100 females. From an early date, normal family life was not the exception but the rule. As early as 1635, the Congregational churches of New England had more female than male members. Our stereotypical image of the Puritan is a man; but the test of church membership tells us that most Puritans were women. One historian infers from the gender ratio that "many Puritans brought their wives along"; it would be statistically more correct to say that many Puritans led their husbands to America.[6]

In terms of social rank, most emigrants to Massachusetts came from the middling strata of English society. Only a few were of the aristocracy. Two sisters and a brother of the Earl of Lincoln settled in Massachusetts, but all were gone within a few years. The gentry were rather more numerous; as many as 11 percent of male heads of households in the Winthrop fleet were identified as gentlemen.[7] Many New England towns attracted a few "armigerous" families whose coats of arms were on record at the College of Heralds in London. This elite, as we shall see, contributed much to the culture of Massachusetts, but comparatively little to its population.[8]

The great majority were yeomen, husbandmen, artisans, craftsmen, merchants and traders—the sturdy middle class of England. They were not poor. A case in point was Benjamin Cooper, an emigrant who died on the way to America in the Ship *Mary Anne* (1637). He had modestly described himself as "husbandman" in the passenger list. But when his estate was settled he was found

---

[6]Computed from shipping lists in John C. Hotten, *The Original Lists of Persons of Quality; Emigrants and Religious Exiles . . . Who Went from Great Britain to the American Plantations,* (rpt. Baltimore, 1962); slightly different estimates appear in Herbert Moller, "Sex Composition and Correlated Culture Patterns of Colonial America," *WMQ3* 2 (1945), 113–53; Breen and Foster, "Moving to the New World"; Tyack, "Migration from East Anglia"; and Anderson, "Migrants and Motives."

[7]They included the Hon. Charles Fiennes; Sir Richard Saltonstall and his son; Isaac Johnson, Esq.; John Winthrop, Esq.; and Messrs. Benjamin Brand, Robert Feake, Josiah Plaistow, William Pynchon, George Alcock, Simon Bradstreet, Richard Browne, William Coddington, Robert Cole, John Dillingham, Thomas Dudley, Samuel Freeman, Ralph Glover, Edward Jones, John Masters, Thomas Mayhew, William Pelham, Israel Stoughton and Thomas Stoughton, Nathaniel Turner, Arthur Tyndale and William Vassall. Altogether these gentlemen were 27 out of 247 heads of families in the Winthrop fleet. Others also arrived in the great migration. See Charles E. Banks, *The Winthrop Fleet of 1630* (Boston, 1930), 52–54.

[8]Tyack, Anderson, and Breen and Foster all generally agree on this question, with minor differences of emphasis.

to be worth £1,278. This was a large fortune in that era, much above the usual idea of a "husbandman's" condition.[9]

Remarkably few of these migrants came from the bottom of English society, to the surprise of some immigrants themselves. "It is strange the meaner people should be so backward [in emigrating]," wrote Richard Saltonstall in 1632. But so they were. On three occupational lists, less than 5 percent were identified as laborers—a smaller proportion than in other colonies.[10] Only a small minority came as servants—less than 25 percent, compared with 75 percent in Virginia. Most New England servants arrived as members of household, rather than as part of a labor draft as in the Chesapeake.[11]

The leaders of the great migration actively discouraged servants and emigrants of humble means. Thomas Dudley, for example, urged the Countess of Lincoln to recruit "honest men" and "godly men" who were "endowed with grace and furnished with means." But he insisted that "they must not be of the poorer sort." When John Winthrop's son asked permission to send a servant named Pease, the governor replied: "people must come well provided, and not too many at once. Pease may come if he will, and such other as you shall think fit, but not many and let those be good, and but few servants and those useful ones."[12]

As a result of this policy, nearly three-quarters of adult Massachusetts immigrants paid their own passage—no small sum in 1630. The cost of outfitting and moving a family of six across the ocean was reckoned at £50 for the poorest accommodation, or £60 to £80 for those who wished a few minimal comforts. A typical English yeoman had an annual income of perhaps £40 to £60. A husbandman counted himself lucky to earn a gross income of £20 a year, of which only about £3 or £4 cleared his expenses. Most ordinary families in England could not afford to come to Massachusetts.[13]

The social status of these people also appeared in their high levels of literacy. Two-thirds of New England's adult male immi-

---

[9]Anderson, "Migrants and Motives," 366.

[10]Emerson, *Letters from New England*, 92; Anthony C. Salerno, "The Character of Emigration from Wiltshire to the American Colonies" (thesis, Univ. of Va., 1977), table IV.

[11]Cressy, *Coming Over*, 52–63, is a valuable discussion of this neglected subject but Cressy counts as servants everyone in a household of a different name—an upper-bound estimate.

[12]Thomas Dudley to the Countess of Lincoln, 12 March 1630/31, *NHHSC* 4 (1834), 224–49; John Winthrop to John Winthrop, Jr., 23 July 1630, *Winthrop Papers*, II, 306.

[13]The Puritans themselves reckoned the cost at £54 for a family of six; a modern computation yields the same result; see Cressy, *Coming Over*, 108.

Dr. John Clark was a Puritan physician in the Great Migration. Trained in England as a specialist in "cutting for the stone," he sailed to Massachusetts in 1638 and became more generally employed as a physician, surgeon, apothecary, merchant, landowner, distiller, inventor, magistrate in Essex County, and representative in the General Court. His left hand holds a crown saw which was used to trepan skulls, an operation he may have been the first to perform in New England. Behind the skull is a Hey's saw, another tool of his trade. Clark's wealth was subtly displayed by a small finger ring which was painted with actual gold dust. His Puritan faith appears in his physiognomy, dress and demeanor. This drawing follows a portrait (1664), the earliest dated in New England, which hangs in the Countway Library of the Harvard Medical School.

grants were able to sign their own names. In old England before
1640, only about one-third could do so. By this very rough "signature-mark test," literacy was nearly twice as common in Massachusetts as in the mother country.[14]

These colonists were also extraordinary in their occupations. A
solid majority (between 50 and 60%) had been engaged in some
skilled craft or trade before leaving England. Less than one-third
had been employed primarily in agriculture—a small proportion
for a seventeenth-century population. The ballads of the great
migration remarked upon this fact:

> Tom Taylor is prepared,
> And th' Smith as black as a coal;
> Ralph Cobler too with us will go.
> For he regards his soul;
> The Weaver, honest Simon . . .
> Professeth to come after.

That lyrical impression was solidly founded in statistical fact.[15]

This was mainly an urban migration. Approximately one-third
of the founders of Massachusetts came from small market towns
in England. Another third came from large towns—a much
greater proportion than in the English population as a whole.
Less than 30 percent had lived in manorial villages, and a very
small proportion had dwelled on separate farms.[16]

---

[14]Kenneth Lockridge, *Literacy in Colonial New England* (New York, 1974); David Cressy, *Literacy and the Social Order: Reading and Writing in Tudor and Stuart England* (Cambridge, 1980). These two works are not precisely comparable. Lockridge's estimates should be treated as an upper-bound estimate of illiteracy in Massachusetts; Cressy's as a lower-bound of illiteracy in England. The difference was probably even greater; see below, "Massachusetts Learning Ways."

[15]Five tabulations of occupations among emigrants to New England yield the following result:

Occupations	Anderson (n = 139)	Tyack (n = 147)	Salerno (n = 124)	Breen–Foster (n = 42)	Cressy (n = 242)
Professional	3.6%	27.2%	2.4%	4.8%	2.1%
Agriculture	33.8%	16.3%	28.2%	26.2%	22.3%
Cloth trades	25.2%	23.1%	24.2%	23.8%	20.7%
Other crafts and trades	35.3%	29.9%	45.2%	40.5%	28.9%
Maritime	2.2%	3.4%	0.0%	4.8%	1.2%
Laborers	n.a.	n.a.	n.a.	n.a.	4.1%
Servants	n.a.	n.a.	n.a.	n.a.	20.7%
Total	100.1%	99.9%	100.0%	100.1%	100.0%

[16]Anderson, "Migrants and Motives," 358. Of 590 immigrants, more than 200 came from the city of London and the six large towns of Canterbury, Dover, Maidstone, Great Yarmouth, Norwich and Salisbury. This pattern is partly the result of bias in the ship lists available to Anderson, as she herself points out. But other inquiries yield much the same result.

In summary, by comparison with other emigrant groups in American history, the great migration to Massachusetts was a remarkably homogeneous movement of English Puritans who came from the middle ranks of their society, and traveled in family groups. The heads of these families tended to be exceptionally literate, highly skilled, and heavily urban in their English origins. They were a people of substance, character, and deep personal piety. The special quality of New England's regional culture would owe much to these facts.

∾ Regional Origins of the Puritan Migration

Another important fact about the founders of Massachusetts was their region of origin in the mother country. When one examines the ship lists in these terms, the first impression is one of extreme diversity. One "sample" of 2,885 emigrants to New England came from no fewer than 1,194 English parishes. Every county was represented except Westmorland in the far north and Monmouth on the border of Wales.[1]

But closer study shows that some counties contributed more than others, and that one region in particular accounted for a majority of the founders of Massachusetts. It lay in the east of England. We may take its geographic center to be the market town of Haverhill, very near the point where the three counties of Suffolk, Essex and Cambridge come together. A circle drawn around the town of Haverhill with a radius of sixty miles will circumscribe the area from which most New England families came.[2] That great circle (or semicircle, for much of it crosses the North Sea) reached east to Great Yarmouth on the coast of Norfolk, north to Boston in eastern Lincolnshire, west to Bedford and Hertfordshire, and south to the coast of East Kent. This area of approximately 7,000 square miles (about 8% of the land area of Britain today) roughly included the region that was defined in 1643 as the Eastern Association—Norfolk, Suffolk, Essex, Hertfordshire, Cambridgeshire, Huntingdonshire and Lincolnshire—plus parts of Bedfordshire and Kent.

[1]Charles E. Banks, *Topographical Dictionary of 2885 English Emigrants to New England, 1620–1650* (Philadelphia, 1937).

[2]G. Andrews Moriarity, "Social and Geographic Origins of the Founders of Massachusetts," in A. B. Hart, ed., *Commonwealth History of Massachusetts* (5 vols., rpt. New York, 1966), I, 49–65.

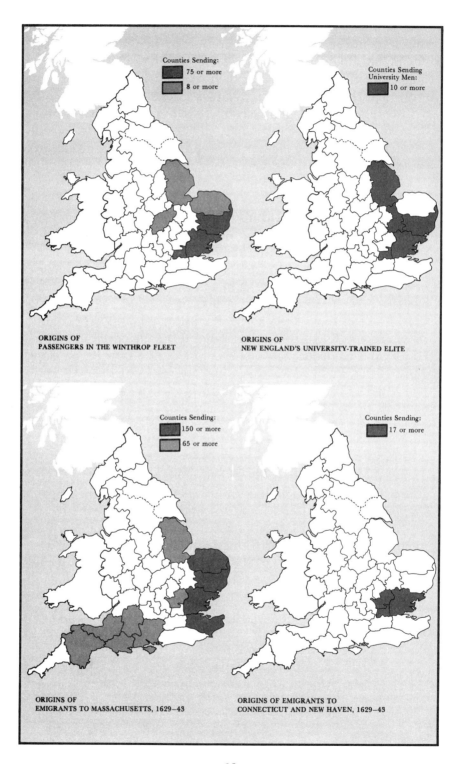

Counties Sending:
75 or more
8 or more

Counties Sending
University Men:
10 or more

ORIGINS OF
PASSENGERS IN THE WINTHROP FLEET

ORIGINS OF
NEW ENGLAND'S UNIVERSITY-TRAINED ELITE

Counties Sending:
150 or more
65 or more

Counties Sending:
17 or more

ORIGINS OF
EMIGRANTS TO MASSACHUSETTS, 1629–43

ORIGINS OF EMIGRANTS TO
CONNECTICUT AND NEW HAVEN, 1629–43

Approximately 60 percent of immigrants to Massachusetts came from these nine eastern counties. Three of the largest contingents were from Suffolk, Essex and Norfolk. Also important was part of east Lincolnshire which lay near the English town of Boston, and a triangle of Kentish territory bounded by the towns of Dover, Sandwich and Canterbury. These areas were the core of the Puritan migration.[3]

On the periphery of New England's primary recruiting ground lay the great city of London. Less than 10 percent of emigrants to Massachusetts came from the metropolis. London was an important meeting place and shipping point for the builders of the Bay Colony, but it was not their English home. Those who had lived in the capital tended not to be native Londoners, but transplanted East Anglians to whom London seemed a foreign place, more alien even than the American wilderness. An example was Lucy Winthrop Downing, a Puritan lady who had moved from East Anglia to London because of her husband's business. In 1637, Lucy Downing was expecting the birth of a child. She wrote her brother in New England that she wanted to have her baby in Massachusetts rather than in London. "I confess could a

---

[3]Eight studies have obtained similar results. The largest and most detailed is still Charles E. Banks, *The Planters of the Commonwealth; A Study of the Emigrants and Emigration in Colonial Times* . . . (Boston, 1930), and *Topographical Dictionary*. His tabulations show that 51.3% of 2,885 emigrants came from the nine eastern counties. Banks was a careful historian, but the *Topographical Dictionary* was a posthumous work, and other scholars have found many inaccuracies. Its statistical results also understate the East Anglian connection with Massachusetts Bay, for they include emigrants to Plymouth (a different group), to New Haven (which drew heavily from London), and to New Hampshire and Maine (which attracted disproportionate numbers from the West Country).

Moriarity independently reached the same results in his "Social and Geographical Origins of the Founders of Massachusetts," 49–65. Anderson found a similar concentration in her study of seven ship lists in the period 1635–38. Of 592 passengers whose origins she could identify, 188 (32%) came from Norfolk and Suffolk; 182 (31%) were from Kent; and another third were scattered widely through the other counties of England. This pattern was partly produced by her sample, but is broadly consistent with other results ("Migrants and Motives," 339–83). Anders Orbeck, in a study for his thesis on New England speech, concluded that "67.73 percent of New England immigrants came from the coast counties from (and including) London to the Wash." That area comprises Essex, Suffolk, Norfolk and Lincoln; see Orbeck, *Pronunciation in Early New England* (Ann Arbor, 1927).

Similar conclusions were reached by Tyack, and also by Breen and Foster. David Grayson Allen does not directly address this question in *In English Ways: The Movement of Societies and the Transferal of English Local Law and Custom to Massachusetts Bay in the Seventeenth Century* (Chapel Hill, 1981), but in his unpublished dissertation he included a survey of geographical origins to all New England towns before 1650. The results, once again, appear to be broadly similar. Cf. "In English Ways" (thesis, Univ. of Wisconsin, 1974), appendix I, 415–26.

Breen and Foster have raised the important question of bias in ship lists, but precisely the same patterns also appear in independent evidence of elite origins and New England place names, reported below.

wish transport me to you," she declared, "I think, as big as I am, I should rather bring an Indian than a Cockney into the world."[4]

The Puritan migration also drew from other parts of England, but often it did so through East Anglian connections. Throughout England, there were scattered parishes where charismatic ministers led their congregations to Massachusetts. But these leaders were themselves often East Anglians. A case in point was the parish of Rowley in Yorkshire, whence the Reverend Ezekiel Rogers brought a large part of his congregation to Massachusetts, where they founded another community called Rowley in the New World. Rogers was himself an East Anglian, born at Wethersfield in Essex, educated at Christ's College, Cambridge, and for twelve years a chaplain at Hatfield Broad Oak. He had moved to Yorkshire as a Puritan missionary, "in the hope that his more lively ministry might be particularly successful in awakening those drowsy corners of the north."[5]

It would be a mistake to exaggerate the role of the eastern counties in the peopling of New England. A large minority (40%) came from the remaining thirty-four counties of England. An important secondary center of migration existed in the west country, very near the area where the counties of Dorset, Somerset and Wiltshire came together.[6] But many of these West Country Puritans did not long remain in the Bay Colony. They tended to move west to Connecticut, or south to Nantucket, or north to Maine. Diversity of regional origins became a major factor in the founding of other New England colonies.[7]

---

[4]Lucy Winthrop Downing to John Winthrop, 4 March 1636/37; Simmons, *Emmanuel Downing*, 44.

[5]Mather, *Magnalia Christi Americana*, I, 409; Allen, *In English Ways*, 166.

[6]A detailed study has been made of one shipload of West Country Puritans who sailed in the *Mary and John*. They were recruited by the Rev. John White from Dorset, Devon and Somerset, and founded the town of Dorchester in Massachusetts. But many left the Bay Colony within a few years, and settled in Connecticut. The descendants of this one shipload included many leading Connecticut families: Wolcott, Griswold, Ellsworth, Gibbs, Dewey, Burr and Gallup. John Winthrop called these settlers "the west country people." Dudley referred to them as "the western men." See Winthrop, *Journal*, I, 50; Dudley to Countess of Lincoln, 12 March 1631, Young, *Chronicles of the First Planters*, 314; and for a genealogy, Maude P. Kuhns, The *"Mary and John"* (Rutland, Vt., 1943).

[7]Origins of New England's immigrants, the Banks sample (corrected for errors of computation), were as follows:

County	Mass.	Conn.	N.H.	R.I.	Maine	L.I.	Unknown	Total
Suffolk	270	9	3	7	3	1	5	298
Essex	215	27	0	9	3	0	5	259
London	168	14	5	5	7	0	4	203
Kent	163	11	0	3	5	2	12	195

The concentration of Puritans from East Anglia, and from the county of Suffolk, was especially great in the Winthrop Fleet of 1630.[8] In the New World, their hegemony became very strong in the present boundaries of Suffolk, Norfolk, Essex and Middlesex counties in Massachusetts. This area became the heartland of its region; its communities are called "seed towns" in New England because so many other communities were founded from them. Most families in these seed towns came from the east of England. The majority was highly concentrated in its regional origin while

County	Mass.	Conn.	N.H.	R.I.	Maine	L.I.	Unknown	Total
Norfolk	157	0	9	1	0	1	0	168
Somerset	124	12	3	5	3	0	5	152
Dorset	112	2	0	3	2	3	5	127
Wiltshire	95	3	0	1	2	0	9	107
Devonshire	82	0	17	5	50	2	5	161
Hertfordshire	81	19	0	6	1	2	0	109
Hampshire	65	1	2	3	0	2	0	73
Lincolnshire	65	1	9	0	0	0	0	75
Yorkshire	62	12	0	0	1	2	3	80
Middlesex	62	3	1	4	2	1	5	78
Northamptonshire	62	3	0	2	0	1	2	70
Buckinghamshire	59	10	0	5	1	1	1	77
Surrey	43	7	1	1	0	1	2	55
Gloucestershire	52	3	4	1	10	0	2	72
Bedfordshire	45	3	0	2	2	1	0	53
Warwickshire	39	10	5	2	3	0	2	61
Lancashire	37	2	0	1	3	0	0	43
Leicestershire	33	5	4	0	0	0	0	42
Berkshire	31	0	0	1	0	0	0	32
Oxfordshire	24	1	0	1	0	1	0	27
Nottinghamshire	24	0	1	0	1	0	3	29
Sussex	22	2	0	3	3	0	1	31
Cambridgeshire	21	6	0	1	1	0	0	29
Northumberland	18	1	0	0	0	0	0	19
Derbyshire	13	4	2	0	1	4	0	24
Staffordshire	13	0	0	0	0	1	0	14
Shropshire	9	2	0	0	3	0	0	14
Cheshire	7	5	1	0	0	0	0	13
Huntingdonshire	5	2	0	0	0	1	0	8
Rutland	5	4	0	0	0	0	0	9
Durham	1	0	0	0	1	1	0	3
Cumberland	0	0	0	1	0	0	0	1

Compiled by Jonathan Schwartz from data in Banks, *Topographical Dictionary*, whose totals differ in several details.

[8]Regional origins of emigrants in the Winthrop fleet (1630) were as follows: Suffolk, 159; Essex, 92; London, 78; Lincolnshire, 17; Norfolk, 8; Northamptonshire, 22; Yorkshire, 8; Leicestershire, 7; Kent, 7; Nottinghamshire, 5; Lancashire, 6; Surrey, 5; Wiltshire, 1; Oxfordshire, 3; Warwickshire, 2; Middlesex, 3; Buckinghamshire, 2; Hertfordshire, 2; Hampshire, 5; Rutland, 2; Berkshire, 1; Cambridgeshire, 1; Cheshire, 1; Netherlands 5. Compiled by Hadley Lewis from Banks, *The Winthrop Fleet.*

the minority was widely scattered. As a consequence, the East Anglian core of New England's population had a cultural importance greater even than its numbers would suggest.[9]

❧ Regional Origins: Names on the New Land

The same pattern of regional origins also appeared in English place names that were given to the new settlements of Massachusetts. The first counties in the Bay Colony were called Suffolk, Essex, Norfolk and Middlesex. Three out of four received East Anglian names.

Town names showed a similar tendency. A few Massachusetts communities were named after natural features (Marblehead, Watertown). Others expressed the social ideals of their founders. Salem took its name from the Hebrew word for peace—Shalom. The first town in the interior was named Concord. The town of Dedham wanted to call itself Contentment, but that idea caused such rancor in the General Court that it had to be given up. Only one town in Massachusetts (Charlestown) was named for any member of the royal family during the first generation—a striking exception to the monarchical rule in most British colonies

---

[9]Another way of approaching this problem is to study the English origins of householders in individual towns. Studies of seven towns yield the following results: Boston (n = 141): Suffolk and Essex, 59%; London 10%; scattering, 31%; Sudbury (n = 52): Suffolk, Essex and Hertford, 36%; Wiltshire, Dorset and Hampshire, 36%; London, 9%, scattering, 19%; Ipswich (n = 121): Suffolk, 20%; Essex, 20%; Herts., Norf., Lincs., and Kent, 23%; Middlesex, 9%; scattering, 28%; Hingham (n = 114): Norfolk, 59%; other Eastern counties, 16%; scattering 25%; Watertown (n = 82): Suffolk, 51%; Essex 17%; London and Middlesex, 12%; scattering, 20%; Rowley (n = 32): Yorkshire, 91%; East Anglia, 9%; Newbury (n = 74): Wiltshire and Hampshire, 61%; East Anglia, 10%; scattering, 29%. By and large, towns in what are now Essex, Suffolk, Norfolk and Middlesex counties of Massachusetts drew most heavily from East Anglia. The area around Scituate harbor on the South Shore was settled from Kent. Exceptions included the towns of Dorchester (Dorset and Lancashire), Lancaster (Lancashire and Yorkshire) and Weymouth (Dorset and Somerset). Other colonies in New England, beyond the borders of Massachusetts, drew from different sources: Plymouth (n = 40): London, 55%; Yorkshire, 13%; Essex and Norfolk, 10%; scattering, 22%; New Haven (n = 110): London, 52%; East Anglia, 22%; Kent, 9%; Yorkshire, 9%; scattering, 8%. Sources include Darrett B. Rutman, *Winthrop's Boston: Portrait of a Puritan Town, 1630–1649* (Chapel Hill, 1965), 138; Edward S. Perzel, "The First Generation of Settlers in Colonial Ipswich, Massachusetts 1633–1660" (thesis, Rutgers, 1967), appendix II; and Allen, *In English Ways*, appendix; William Bradford, *Of Plymouth Plantation, 1620–1647,* ed. S. E. Morison (New York, 1952), appendix; and Floyd Shumway, "Early New Haven and Its Leadership" (thesis, Columbia, 1971), 22; impressionistic but generally accurate generalizations about many other towns appear in Moriarity, "Social and Geographic Origins of the Founders of Massachusetts," 49–65; also helpful is Anne R. Yentsch, "Expressions of Cultural Diversity and Social Reality in Seventeenth Century New England," (thesis, Brown, 1980).

ENGLISH ORIGINS OF
MASSACHUSETTS PLACE NAMES
BEFORE 1660

throughout the world, from the sixteenth to the twentieth century.[1]

Every other Massachusetts town founded before 1660 was named after an English community. Of thirty-five such names, at least eighteen (57%) were drawn from East Anglia and twenty-two (63%) from seven eastern counties. Most were named after English towns within sixty miles of the village of Haverhill.[2]

As the Puritans moved beyond the borders of New England to other colonies, their place names continued to come from the east of England. When they settled Long Island, they named their county Suffolk. In the Connecticut Valley, their first county was called Hartford. When they founded a colony in New Jersey, the most important town was called the New Ark of the Covenant (now the modern city of Newark) and the county was named Essex. In general, the proportion of eastern and East Anglian place names in Massachusetts and its affiliated colonies was 60 percent—exactly the same as in genealogies and ship lists.[3]

[1]Charlestown (pronounced Charlton) was not named directly for Charles I, but after the Charles River, which Captain John Smith had named long before the Puritans arrived.

[2]The following towns in the Massachusetts Bay Colony were named after English communities through 1660:

Haverhill (Suffolk)	Newbury (Berkshire)	Rowley (Yorkshire)
Ipswich (Suffolk)	Salisbury (Wiltshire)	Weymouth (Dorset)
Lynn (Norfolk)	Medford (Kent)	Sudbury (Suffolk)
Cambridge (Cambridge)	Boston (Lincoln)	Dorchester (Dorset)
Dedham (Essex)	Braintree (Essex)	Hingham (Norfolk)
Woburn (Bedfordshire)	Andover (Hampshire)	Chelmsford (Essex)
Groton (Suffolk)	Lancaster (Lancashire)	Hadley (Suffolk)
Newton (Norfolk)	Reading (Berkshire)	Wrentham (Suffolk)
Boxford (Suffolk)	Marlborough (Wiltshire)	Framingham (Suffolk)
Springfield (Essex)	Hull (Yorkshire)	Malden (Essex)
Topsfield (Essex)	Billerica (Essex)	Gloucester (Gloucs.)
Manchester (Lancashire)	Northampton (Northamptonshire)	

Of these 35 names, 22 came from the counties of Essex, Suffolk, Norfolk, Kent, Lincolnshire, Cambridgeshire, and Bedfordshire). The rest were scattered broadly throughout England. Two town names (Roxbury and Medfield) were of unknown origin. See William H. Whetmore, "On the Origins of the Names of Towns in Massachusetts," *MAHSP* 12 (1871–73), 391–413. On the naming of Boston by Puritans from Lincoln (not by Capt. John Smith) see evidence cited in G. A. Taylor, "Lincolnshire and Massachusetts," *LNQ* 21 (1930), 4–6.

[3]This finding is important because it confirms the evidence of ship lists. Breen and Foster wondered whether the predominance of East Anglian emigrants in those documents might have been merely a source-bias. The answer is clearly negative. The same pattern appears in place names, and also in the origins of Massachusetts elites. We have three independent sources for English regional origins in the great migration. All yield similar results.

❧ Origins of the Massachusetts Elite

This predominance of England's eastern counties was even stronger among the Puritan elite. Of 129 university-trained ministers and magistrates in the great migration, 56 percent had lived in the seven eastern counties of Suffolk, Essex, Norfolk, Lincolnshire, Cambridgeshire, Hertfordshire and Kent before sailing to America. Only 9 percent were Londoners. The rest had been widely scattered through many parts of England.[1]

This statistic refers only to their last known addresses in England. Many more had some other connection with the eastern counties, and with East Anglia in particular. Altogether, 78 percent of New England's college-trained ministers and magistrates had been born, bred, schooled, married, or employed for long periods in seven eastern counties.[2]

This little elite was destined to play a large role in the history of New England. Its strength developed in no small degree from its solidarity. Many of its members had known one another before coming to America. They had gone to the same schools. Nearly half had studied in three Cambridge Colleges—Emmanuel, Magdalen and Trinity. Approximately 30 percent had attended Emmanuel alone. They intermarried with such frequency that one historian describes the leading Puritan families of East Anglia as a "prosopographer's dream."[3]

Several of these genealogical connections were especially important in the history of New England. One centered on the county of Suffolk and included the families of Winthrop, Downing, Rainborough, Tyndal and Fones. A second connection had its base in Emmanuel College and united a large number of eminent Puritan divines, including Samuel Stone, Thomas Hooker,

---

[1] Of 129 university-trained ministers and magistrates known to have settled in New England, last known addresses were as follows: Suffolk, 18; Essex, 15; Lincolnshire, 13; Cambridge, 12; London, 11; Kent, 7; Yorkshire, 7; Hertfordshire, 5; Wiltshire, 5; Devon, 4; Norfolk, 3; Somerset, 3; Lancashire, 3; Buckinghamshire, 2; Cheshire, 2; Hampshire, 2; Lancashire, 2; Northamptonshire, 2; Surrey, 2; Leicestershire, 2; Bedfordshire, Cornwall, Dorsetshire, Gloustershire, Huntingdonshire, Middlesex, Northumberland, Oxfordshire, Rutland, Shropshire, Staffordshire, Wales, Warwickshire and Worcester, 1 each; unknown, 1. Compiled mainly from biographical data in S. E. Morison, *The Founding of Harvard College* (Cambridge, 1935), 359–410; see also Harry S. Stout, "University Men in New England, 1620–1660: A Demographic Profile," *JIH* 4 (1974), 357–400; *idem,* "The Morphology of Remigration: New England University Men and Their Return to England, 1640–60," *JAS* 10 (1976), 151–172.

[2] Computed from the same sources.

[3] At least 35 are known to have studied at Emmanuel, 13 at Trinity and 7 at Magdalen College, Cambridge. These are lower-bound estimates.

Thomas Shepard, John Wilson and Roger Newton, all of whom came to New England. These men had known each other at Cambridge. Most had held livings in East Anglia and had been removed for their Puritan beliefs. They were often related by marriage or other ties of kinship.[4]

A third group had its seat in the household of the Earl of Lincoln. It included two of the Earl's sisters and a younger brother, all of whom came to Massachusetts. Also in this connection were Thomas Dudley and Simon Bradstreet, stewards of the Earl of Lincoln; and Thomas Leverett and Richard Bellingham, alderman and recorder of the town of Boston in Lincolnshire.

A fourth connection had its home in the parish of Alford, Lincolnshire. This was a small settlement six miles from the sea, in the "fat marsh" country that ran many miles across east Lincolnshire from the Humber to the Wash. Alford sent three families who loomed large in the history of Massachusetts: the Hutchinsons (an armigerous family of county gentry), the Storres or Storys (prosperous yeomen), and the Marburys (a clerical family). These three groups were linked to many other families in the surrounding countryside, including the Coddingtons, Wentworths, Quincys and Rishworths, who would also play prominent parts in New England and Old Providence Island.

The spiritual leader of this flock was the Reverend John Cotton, vicar of Boston's St. Botolph's church—the largest parish church in England. Its tremendous tower called Boston Stump, 272 feet high, served mariners as a seamark, and the Puritans as a spiritual beacon. On Sundays the Marburys and Hutchinsons traveled twenty miles through the Lincoln fens toward Boston Stump where they heard John Cotton preach from the beautiful pulpit that still stands in the church.[5]

In Massachusetts, these various Puritan connections were soon united in a single cousinage. Genealogists have remarked upon "the vast number of unions between the members of the families of Puritan ministers." One commented that "it seemed to be a law of social ethics that the sons of ministers should marry the daughters of ministers." Mathers, Cottons, Stoddards, Eliots,

---

[4]Rebecca Seward Ralph, "Emmanuel College, Cambridge, and the Puritan Movements of Old and New England" (thesis, Univ. of Southern California, 1979); Morison, *Founding of Harvard College*, 92–107.

[5]Reginald C. Dudding, "Alford and America," in *History of the Parish and Manors of Alford . . .* (Horncastle, 1930), 145–81; the family linkages appear in *The Parish Register of Alford . . . ; LRS* V (1917), 6.

The East-Anglian Puritan Elite of Massachusetts
The Winthrop-Downing-Dudley-Endecott-Bradstreet-Cotton-Mather Connection

I. Descendants of Adam Winthrop
(1548–1623)

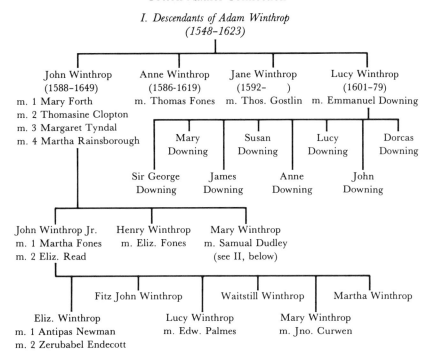

John Winthrop
(1588–1649)
m. 1 Mary Forth
m. 2 Thomasine Clopton
m. 3 Margaret Tyndal
m. 4 Martha Rainsborough

Anne Winthrop
(1586-1619)
m. Thomas Fones

Jane Winthrop
(1592–   )
m. Thos. Gostlin

Lucy Winthrop
(1601–79)
m. Emmanuel Downing

Mary Downing

Susan Downing

Lucy Downing

Dorcas Downing

Sir George Downing

James Downing

Anne Downing

John Downing

John Winthrop Jr.
m. 1 Martha Fones
m. 2 Eliz. Read

Henry Winthrop
m. Eliz. Fones

Mary Winthrop
m. Samual Dudley
(see II, below)

Fitz John Winthrop

Waitstill Winthrop

Martha Winthrop

Eliz. Winthrop
m. 1 Antipas Newman
m. 2 Zerubabel Endecott

Lucy Winthrop
m. Edw. Palmes

Mary Winthrop
m. Jno. Curwen

II. Descendants of Thomas Dudley
(1576–1653)

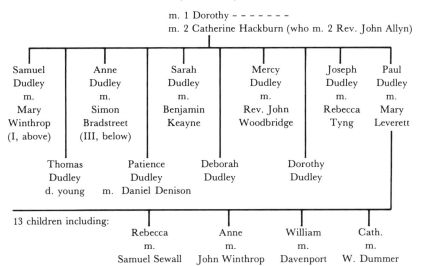

m. 1 Dorothy - - - - - - -
m. 2 Catherine Hackburn (who m. 2 Rev. John Allyn)

Samuel Dudley
m.
Mary Winthrop
(I, above)

Anne Dudley
m.
Simon Bradstreet
(III, below)

Sarah Dudley
m.
Benjamin Keayne

Mercy Dudley
m.
Rev. John Woodbridge

Joseph Dudley
m.
Rebecca Tyng

Paul Dudley
m.
Mary Leverett

Thomas Dudley
d. young

Patience Dudley
m. Daniel Denison

Deborah Dudley

Dorothy Dudley

13 children including:

Rebecca
m.
Samuel Sewall

Anne
m.
John Winthrop

William
m.
Davenport

Cath.
m.
W. Dummer

III. Descendants of Simon Bradstreet

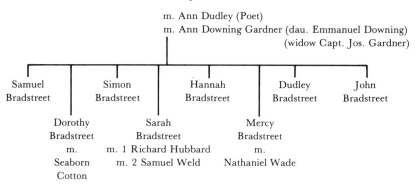

m. Ann Dudley (Poet)
m. Ann Downing Gardner (dau. Emmanuel Downing)
(widow Capt. Jos. Gardner)

Samuel Bradstreet	Simon Bradstreet	Hannah Bradstreet	Dudley Bradstreet	John Bradstreet

Dorothy Bradstreet m. Seaborn Cotton

Sarah Bradstreet m. 1 Richard Hubbard m. 2 Samuel Weld

Mercy Bradstreet m. Nathaniel Wade

IV. Descendants of Sarah Story

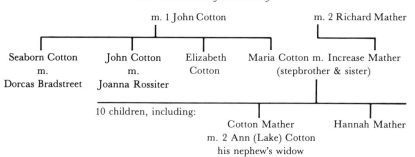

m. 1 John Cotton

m. 2 Richard Mather

Seaborn Cotton m. Dorcas Bradstreet

John Cotton m. Joanna Rossiter

Elizabeth Cotton

Maria Cotton m. Increase Mather (stepbrother & sister)

10 children, including:

Cotton Mather m. 2 Ann (Lake) Cotton his nephew's widow

Hannah Mather

Note: In these and subsequent charts not all children are included.

Williamses, Edwardses, Chaunceys, Bulkeleys and Wigglesworths all came to be related to one another within a generation.[6]

A case in point was the web that formed between the Mather and Cotton families. The founders of these two houses in America, John Cotton and Richard Mather, both married the same woman, Sarah Story. John Cotton's daughter Maria Cotton became the wife of Richard Mather's son Increase Mather. A child of that union was the eminent minister Cotton Mather. By these various connections, John Cotton was simultaneously Cotton Mather's natural grandfather on the mother's side, and his step-grandfather on his father's side. At the same time, Richard Mather was both Cotton Mather's paternal grandfather, and his maternal step-grandfather. To compound the confusion, Cotton Mather married Ann Lake Cotton Mather, who was both his cousin and also his nephew's widow.

The matriarch of this family, Sarah Story Cotton Mather, might be taken as the genealogical center of New England's elite. By the mid-eighteenth century many leading families in eastern Massachusetts were related to her by linear or collateral descent.[7] Important marriages joined the Mather-Cotton dynasty to the Dudleys, Bradstreets, Winthrops, Sewalls and other leading families in Massachusetts. So dense was this web that Samuel Sewall, in his diary and letterbook, addressed as cousin at least forty-eight people with thirty-eight family names. This was the cousinage that governed Massachusetts. It went to the same schools, visited constantly with one another, joined in the same working associations, and dominated the public life of the Bay Colony for many generations.[8]

The ministers who belonged to this cousinage were forbidden to hold political office. But in every other way their power was very great. When a stranger made the mistake of asking the Reverend Phillips of Andover if he were "the parson who serves here," he was abruptly told, "I am, sir, the parson who rules here."[9]

This elite maintained its regional hegemony well into the nineteenth century. Harriet Beecher Stowe testified from the experi-

[6]Alice Morse Earle, *Customs and Fashions in Old New England* (New York, 1893, rpt. Rutland, Vt., 1973), 71.

[7]Sarah Story's name was variously spelled Storey or Storre.

[8]Edmund Morgan, *The Puritan Family: Religion & Domestic Relations in the Seventeenth Century* (1944, rev. ed., New York, 1956), 150.

[9]Charles M. Andrews, *Pilgrims and Puritans* (New Haven, 1926), 166.

ence of her own generation that "In those days of New England, the minister and his wife were considered the temporal and spiritual superiors of everybody in the parish."[10] The moral ascendancy of this elite was very great. Its role in forming the folkways of New England was even greater.

❧ The East of England before the Great Migration

The parts of eastern England from which these Puritans came— East Anglia, eastern Lincolnshire, eastern Cambridge and the northeastern fringe of Kent—are not recognized as a single region today. But in the seventeenth century they shared many qualities in common. In physical terms, all of these territories tended to be flat, open country, with long vistas and unbroken views of the sky. Some parts of this land were highly fertile. Other parts were so very poor that Charles I once suggested that the soil of Norfolk should be divided to make highways in the other counties of England.[1]

Despite its poor resources, methods of farming were more advanced in the eastern counties than elsewhere in England. The agricultural revolution came early to East Anglia, as also it did to the Netherlands; "replenishing crops" were used as early as the mid-seventeenth century.[2] The great reformer Arthur Young observed as he traveled through the eastern counties that England's best farmers lived on its worst soil. Agriculture in this region was mostly a regime of mixed farming, which supplied food for urban markets and wool for a local textile industry.[3]

---

[10]Harriet Beecher Stowe, *Oldtown Folks* (1869), in Kathryn Kish Sklar, ed., *Harriet Beecher Stowe* (New York, 1982), 891.

[1]This apocryphal remark is attributed both to Charles I and to Charles II. East Anglians quote it as a comment on the excellence of their roads; others remember it as a complaint against the poverty of their soil; cf. N. Kent, *General View of the Agriculture of Norfolk* (London, 1796), 16.

[2]For the use of "turnips and pease [to] manure the land," see Sir Thomas Sclater Manor Book, CAMBRO.

[3]B. A. Holderness, "East Anglia . . . ," in Joan Thirsk, ed., *The Agrarian History of England and Wales, 1640–1750*, vol. 5.1, *Regional Farming Systems* (Cambridge, 1984), 197–238; M. R. Postgate, "Field Systems of East Anglia," in Alan R. H. Baker and Robin A. Butlin, eds., *Studies of the Field Systems in the British Isles* (Cambridge, 1973), 281–324; N. Riches, *The Agricultural Revolution in Norfolk* (Chapel Hill, 1937); Eric Kerridge, *The Agricultural Revolution* (London, 1967); R. A. C. Parker, *Coke of Norfolk* (Oxford, 1975); Arthur Young, *A Farmer's Tour in the East of England* (4 vols., London, 1771).

Cambridge: The Emmanuel Connection

Rev. Thomas Hooker m. Susanna Garbrand
(1586–1647)

John Hooker	Rev. Samuel Hooker

Sarah Hooker	Joanna Hooker	Mary Hooker
m. Rev. John Wilson	m. Rev. Thomas Shepard	m. Rev. Roger Newton

Note: Other Emmanuel men who came to New England (with dates of matriculation in the college) included Nathaniel Ward (1596); Thomas Hooker (1604); Samuel Stone; John Harvard (1627); Samuel Dudley (1626); George Alcock who married the sister of Thomas Hooker; Thomas Allen who married the widow of John Harvard; Wm. Blackstone (1614); Simon Bradstreet (1618); Edmund Browne (1624); Ezekiel Cheever (1633); John Cotton (1606); Giles Firmin (1629) who married a daughter of Nathaniel Ward; Isaac Johnson (1616); William Mildmay (1640); William Pelham (1615); William Perkins (1624); John Phillips (1600) who married a sister of William Ames; Peter Prudden (1620); Nathaniel Rogers (1614); Richard Sadler (1636); Richard Saltonstall Jr.; Nicholas Street (MA 1636); Zechariah Symmes (1617); William Walton (1621); John Ward son of Nathaniel Ward (1622); Samuel Whiting (1613) whose second wife was sister to Oliver St. John and cousin to Peter Bulkeley and John Wilson.

Lincolnshire: The Fiennes–Clinton Connection

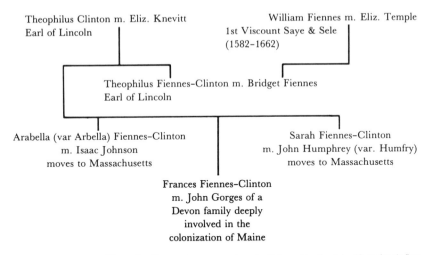

Theophilus Clinton m. Eliz. Knevitt
Earl of Lincoln

William Fiennes m. Eliz. Temple
1st Viscount Saye & Sele
(1582–1662)

Theophilus Fiennes–Clinton m. Bridget Fiennes
Earl of Lincoln

Arabella (var Arbella) Fiennes–Clinton
m. Isaac Johnson
moves to Massachusetts

Sarah Fiennes–Clinton
m. John Humphrey (var. Humfry)
moves to Massachusetts

Frances Fiennes–Clinton
m. John Gorges of a
Devon family deeply
involved in the
colonization of Maine

Note: The Fiennes–Clinton Family was also connected to the Pelham Family. John Humphrey's first wife was a Pelham; William Pelham sailed in *Arbella*. Penelope Pelham aged 16 also sailed to Massachusetts in 1635. Also connected to this family was Thomas Dudley, a close friend and steward to the Earl of Lincoln, and Simon Bradstreet, also steward to the Earl of Lincoln and Dudley's son-in-law.

Sources: A. M. Cook, *Boston* (Boston, Lincolnshire, 1948); H. A. Doubleday et al., *The Complete Peerage* (London, 1929); and genealogical materials in LINCRO.

Alford, Lincolnshire: The Wentworth–Marbury–Storre–Hutchinson–Oliver Connection

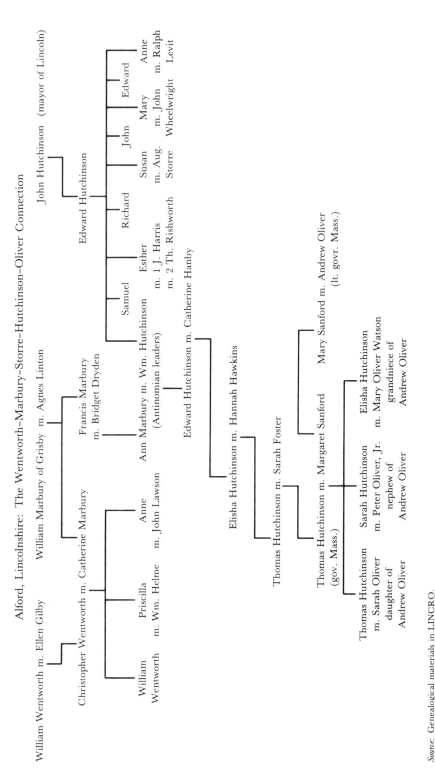

Source: Genealogical materials in LINCRO.

Today, East Anglia seems very rural by comparison with other English regions. But in the early seventeenth century, it was the most densely settled and highly urbanized part of England, and had been so for many centuries. Norwich was England's second largest city in 1630—a dynamic center whose population had trebled in the preceding fifty years. There were also many small seaports and market towns. In 1600, no fewer than 130 little ports of entry existed on the coast of Essex alone.[4]

Many inhabitants of East Anglia were artisans and skilled craftsmen. In 1630, half the adult population of Essex was employed in the cloth trade. Suffolk, Norfolk, Cambridge and Kent were also major textile centers, specializing in the manufacture of light woolens favored in southern Europe, and also in luxurious "Suffolk shortcloths," which were worn by the rulers of the Western world. This trade had been deeply depressed by wars with Spain (1625–30) and France (1627–29) and by a general depression of commerce in this period. As a result, unemployment and poverty were major problems in East Anglia on the eve of the great migration. In 1629, unemployed weavers besieged the courts at Braintree and Sudbury in search of work. Their suffering was deepened by a severe "scarcity and dearth of corn" in that year.[5]

Local scarcities were made worse by the wretched state of overland communications. Even short trips were so dangerous that the D'Ewes family left an infant with a wet nurse rather than expose it to the danger of even a single day's journey.[6] Travel by land was slow and painful; but travel by water was cheap and easy. The sea linked East Anglia, Kent and Lincolnshire with each other, and also with the Netherlands, in a cultural nexus of great importance in the seventeenth century.[7] East Anglia was invigorated by Dutch trade, Dutch immigrants, Dutch architecture, Dutch religion and Dutch culture. The culture of New England,

[4]John Patten, "Towns in the National Urban System—East Anglia," *English Towns, 1500–1700* (Folkestone, Kent, 1978), 244–96; Felix Hull, "Agriculture and Rural Society in Essex, 1560–1640" (thesis, Univ. of London, 1950), 3; two very rich sources for this region are Thomas William Bramston, ed., *The Autobiography of Sir John Bramston, K.B.* (London, 1845); and John Bruce, ed., *Diary of John Manningham* (Westminster, 1868).

[5]B. E. Supple, *Commercial Crisis and Change in England, 1600–1642: A Study in the Instability of a Mercantile Economy* (Cambridge, 1959), 102–12.

[6]J. O. Halliwell ed., *The Autobiography and Correspondence of Sir Simonds D'Ewes, Bart., during the Reigns of James I and Charles I* (2 vols., London 1845), ca. 1603.

[7]Arne Bang-Andersen, Basil Greenhill and Egil Harald Grude, *The North Sea: A Highway of Economic and Cultural Exchange; Character—History* (Stavanger, Norway, 1985), 9–26, 151–66.

as we shall see, owed much to this Dutch connection, as did the folkways of East Anglia itself.[8]

At the same time, the sea also exposed East Anglia to many hazards. For more than a thousand years, sea raiders had fallen upon the English coast, and the memory of their depredations was very much alive in 1630. In that year, at least two towns in Essex and the village of Linton in Cambridge still had nailed to their church doors the human skins of marauding Danes who had been flayed alive by their intended victims.[9] Raiders from the sea had attacked East Anglia as recently as 1626 and 1627 when the dreaded "Dunkirkers" came ashore—killing, looting and raping as so many other sea people had done before.[10]

Through the centuries, some of these many waves of raiders had remained to settle there, particularly the people known as Angles, and later those called Danes in East Anglia and Jutes (from Jutland) in Kent. It was in part the culture of these people that gave East Anglia and Kent their special character. As early as the sixth century, both East Kent and East Anglia were very different from Wessex, Mercia and the north of England in their comparatively large numbers of freemen, and small numbers of *servi* and *villani*. Also, in the words of historian K. P. Witney, they were special in "the greatly superior status enjoyed by the ordinary freemen."[11]

The eastern counties were also distinctive in their political character. Many rebellions against arbitrary power had occurred there—Jack Straw's Rising in Suffolk, Wat Tyler's Rebellion, John Ball's Insurrection in Kent, and Robert Kett's Rebellion in Norfolk, where the leader sat under an oak called the "tree of reformation" while the terrified gentry were tried before a makeshift jury of their former victims. The Peasants' Rebellion of 1381

[8]For graphic details of the Dutch presence in East Anglia, see Thomas William Bramston, *Autobiography* (London, 1845), 108; for East Anglian Puritans in the Netherlands, see Raymond P. Stearns, *Congregationalism in the Dutch Netherlands: The Rise and Fall of the English Congregational Classis, 1621–1635* (Chicago, 1940).

[9]Arthur Gray, "Massacre at the Bra Ditch," *Cambridge Antiq. Comm.* 31 (1931), 77–87; W. M. Palmer, "Notes on Linton" (1937), ms. B20, Cambridge Univ. Library, 39.

[10]Francis Hervey, ed., *Suffolk in the Seventeenth Century; The Breviary of Suffolk by Robert Reyce, 1618* (London, 1902), 13; for the raids of 1626–27 and the panic they caused, see Ruth Hughey, ed., *The Correspondence of Lady Katherine Paston, 1603–1627* (Norwich, 1941), 91; and Mary Anne Everett Green, *Diary of John Rous, Incumbent of Santon Downham, Suffolk, from 1625 to 1642, CS* 66 (1856), 9 (15 March 1627).

[11]K. P. Witney, *The Jutish Forest* (London, 1976).

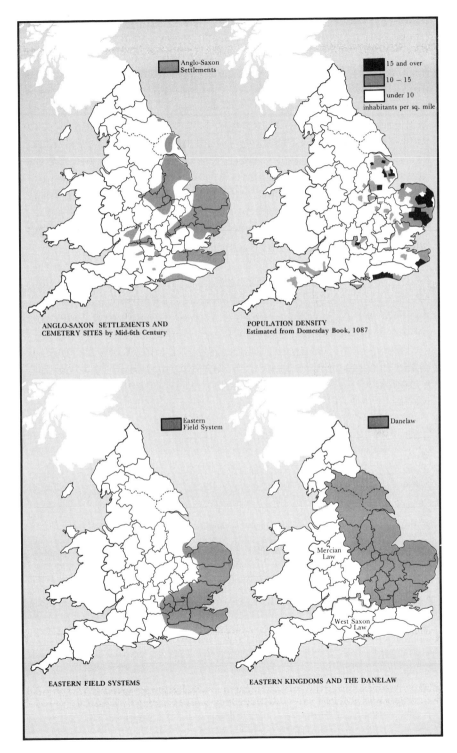

ANGLO-SAXON SETTLEMENTS AND
CEMETERY SITES by Mid-6th Century

Anglo-Saxon
Settlements

POPULATION DENSITY
Estimated from Domesday Book, 1087

15 and over

10 – 15

under 10

inhabitants per sq. mile

EASTERN FIELD SYSTEMS

Eastern
Field System

EASTERN KINGDOMS AND THE DANELAW

Danelaw

Mercian
Law

West Saxon
Law

was heavily concentrated in nine eastern counties. So also was Clarence's Rising in 1477 and Buckingham's Revolt in 1483.[12]

This region also became a major center of resistance to Charles I after 1625. When the Civil War began in 1642, Parliamentary forces found their greatest strength in the counties called the Eastern Association—the same area from which Massachusetts was settled.[13]

The religious life of this region also differed from other parts of England. It had been marked by dissent for centuries before Martin Luther. During the early fifteenth century, the movement called Lollardy found many of its followers in East Anglia. After its suppression, the underground cells of Lollards who met to study the scriptures were exceptionally numerous in eastern counties from Lincoln and Norfolk to Kent.[14]

The Protestant Reformation of the sixteenth century also flourished in East Anglia, more than elsewhere in England. The Marian martyrs—men and women executed for their Protestant faith in the reign of the Queen Mary—came mostly from this region. Of 273 Protestants who were burned at the stake for heresy during the counter reformation of the Catholic Queen (1553–58), no fewer than 225 (82%) came from nine eastern counties.[15] In the era of Elizabeth I, nearly half of Puritan ministers came from the East Anglian counties of Essex, Suffolk and

---

[12]The Peasants' Rebellion occurred mainly in Kent, Essex, Suffolk, Norfolk, Cambridge, Huntingdon, Hertford, Middlesex and Surrey. See Edgar Powell, *The East Anglian Rising in 1381* (Cambridge, 1896); for the ethnic character of this movement see Witney, *The Jutish Forest*, 186 (Walsingham: "totem illud Kentensium et Juttorum"). For Clarence's Rising and Buckingham's Revolt see E. F. Jacob, *The Fifteenth Century, 1399–1485* (Oxford, 1961), 580, 625–26.

[13]Clive Holmes, *The Eastern Association in the English Civil War* (Cambridge, 1974).

[14]Lollardy was a movement that arose in the 14th century, and generally espoused doctrines of predestination, limited atonement, and consubstantiation. The social and theological attitudes of the Lollards were similar in some ways to those of the Puritans three centuries later. Lollardy was by no means confined to the eastern counties. But after its suppression it proved most persistent in East Anglia, Kent and the Thames Valley. For the distribution of leading centers of Lollardy before and after Oldcastle's Rising in 1414 see Malcolm Falkus and John Gillingham, *Historical Atlas of Britain* (New York, 1981), 80; see also Claire Cross, *Church and People, 1450–1660* (Glasgow, 1978); Kenneth W. Skipps, "Lay Patronage of East Anglian Puritan Clerics in Pre Revolutionary England" (thesis, Yale, 1971); J. D. Fines, "Studies in the Lollard Heresy; Being an Examination from the Dioceses of Norwich, Lincoln, Coventy, Lichfield, and Ely" (thesis, Sheffield, 1964).

[15]The distribution of Marian martyrs was as follows: Kent, 59; Essex, 52; London, 47; Sussex, 27; Suffolk, 25; Middlesex, 13; Hertfordshire, 13; Norfolk, 10; Cambridgeshire, 3; the rest of England and Wales, 35. See John D. Gay, *The Geography of Religion in England* (London, 1971); P. Hughes, *The Reformation in England* (London, 1953), II, 260–64.

Norfolk. If other eastern counties were included, the proportion rose to 75 percent.[16]

People of every religious party agreed that Puritanism was specially strong in the eastern counties. The Puritan leader John Hampden said of Essex that it was "the place of the most life of religion in the land." The Puritans' great enemy, Archbishop William Laud, complained that East Anglia was the throbbing heart of heresy in England.[17]

Within East Anglia, the Puritan movement was strongest in the small towns whence so many migrants left for Massachusetts. Of Colchester (Essex) one Puritan leader said that "the town, for the earnest profession of the gospel, became like unto a city upon a hill, and as a candle upon a candle stick." That passage from St. Matthew, however inappropriate it may have been to the topography of East Anglia, was often used by Puritans to describe the spiritual condition of this region. When John Winthrop described his intended settlement in Massachusetts as "a city upon a hill," he employed a gospel phrase that had become a cliché in the communities of eastern England.[18]

The Puritanism of eastern England was not all of a piece. Several distinct varieties of religious dissent developed there, each with its own base. A special strain of religious radicalism which

---

[16]During the 1580s, the distribution of Puritan ministers has been estimated as follows:

	Ministers	Locations
Essex	88	78
Suffolk	77	58
Norfolk	51	47
Rutland and Northamptonshire	49	42
Lincoln	33	33
Kent	30	27
Sussex	27	24
Cambridgeshire	13	14
Hertfordshire	20	12
Bedfordshire and Huntingdonshire	11	9
Other counties	103	97
Total	502	441

Source: Allen, *In English Ways,* 10, tabulating data from Patrick Collinson, "The Puritan Classical Movement in the Reign of Elizabeth I" (thesis, Univ. of London, 1957), II, 1252–81. A few counties are missing, but would not alter the result in a material way. An independent study which obtained the same result was Ronald G. Usher, *The Reconstruction of the English Church* (2 vols., New York, 1910), I, 248.

[17]William Hunt, *The Puritan Movement: The Coming of the Revolution in an English County,* (Cambridge, 1983), x.

[18]Quoted in John Strype, *Analysis of the Reformation* (Oxford, 1824), II, pt. 2, p. 282.

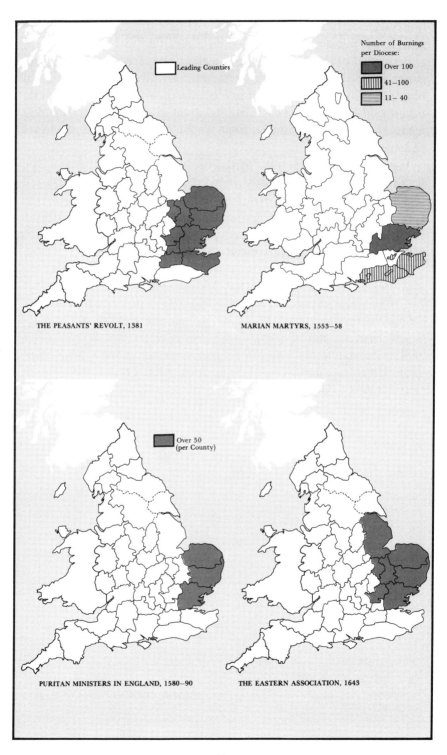

Number of Burnings per Diocese:

■ Over 100

▦ 41–100

▨ 11– 40

☐ Leading Counties

THE PEASANTS' REVOLT, 1381

MARIAN MARTYRS, 1553–58

■ Over 50 (per County)

PURITAN MINISTERS IN ENGLAND, 1580–90

THE EASTERN ASSOCIATION, 1643

put heavy stress upon the spirit (Antinomianism) flourished among Puritans in eastern Lincolnshire. The more conservative and highly rationalist variant of Calvinism (Arminianism) found many adherents in London, Middlesex and Hertfordshire. In between were men and women from the counties of Suffolk, Essex and Norfolk who adopted a Puritan "middle way." Their faith became the official religion of Massachusetts for two centuries.[19]

East Anglia was also exceptional in its educational and cultural attainments. In the seventeenth century, rates of literacy were higher there than in other English regions. When Havelock Ellis undertook to measure the geography of intellectual distinction in English history, he found that a larger proportion of scholars, scientists and artists came from East Anglia than from any other part of England.[20]

Many cultural stereotypes attached to the people of eastern England. East Anglian historian R. W. Ketton-Cremer writes, "The Norfolk man, gentle or simple, tended to be dour, stubborn, fond of argument and litigation, strongly Puritan in his religious views. The type was far from universal . . . but it was a type to which the majority of all classes to some degree conformed."[21] These images added yet another dimension to regional identity in the seventeenth century.

[19]On the connection between Arminianism and Lincolnshire, see Emory Battis, *Saints and Sectaries: Anne Hutchinson and the Antinomian Controversy in the Massachusetts Bay Colony* (Chapel Hill, 1962), 249–85; for the linkage between London, Middlesex and Arminianism, see Shumway, "Early New Haven," and Isabel Calder, *New Haven Colony* (New Haven, 1934); on the Puritan "middle way," the classical work is still Cotton Mather, *Magnalia Christi Americana*. The argument of this work was developed in scholarly detail by Congregational historians in the 19th century, in particular Henry Martin Dexter and Williston Walker. Their work in turn was generalized by Perry Miller. These historians showed little interest in the social or regional origins of the Puritan middle way. But if one compares the small number of religious writers whom Perry Miller drew together as *The New England Mind*, most came from Suffolk, Essex and Norfolk, and were educated at Cambridge.

[20]Cressy, *Literacy and the Social Order;* Havelock Ellis, *A Study of British Genius*, new ed. (Boston, 1926), 25–36.

[21]R. W. Ketton-Cremer, *Norfolk in the Civil War* (1969, Norwich, 1985), 20.

❧ A "New Paradise" for Puritans: Massachusetts Bay

As these Puritans from the east of England sailed slowly across the western sea, every family among them was ordered by the Massachusetts Bay Company to keep a journal, which became a running record of their hopes and apprehensions for the New World. Francis Higginson's advance party sailed in the ships *Talbot* and *Lion's Whelp.* Their first sight of America was not encouraging. In the month of June 1629, when England was all in bloom, these weary travelers reached the Grand Bank of Newfoundland. Suddenly the wind turned bitter cold, and they passed an enormous iceberg hard aground in forty fathoms of frigid water, with the green Atlantic surf roaring against it. It seemed to be "a mountain of ice, shining as white as snow, like to a great rock or cliff," towering above their little ships. In great fear they sailed onward through a foggy night, while drift ice scraped dangerously against fragile hulls, and the ships' drums beat mournfully in the darkness.

A few days later the weather moderated and spirits revived. As these weary travelers approached New England, the ocean teemed with "infinite multitudes" of mackerel and "great whales puffing up water." The surface of the sea was covered with what Francis Higginson took to be brilliant yellow flowers. Rounding Cape Ann into Massachusetts Bay, they saw "every island full of gay woods and high trees," and the Higginsons suddenly felt very good about their new home:

> What with fine woods and green trees by land, and these yellow flowers painting the sea, made us all desirous to see our new paradise of New England, whence we saw such forerunning signals of fertility.[1]

Not many people would have seen that stormy, cold and rockbound coast as a "new paradise." But the Puritans looked upon the world through very special lenses. "*Geography,*" wrote Cotton Mather, "must now find work for a *Christianography.*"[2]

The New England location of this Bible Commonwealth was not an accident; its site was carefully chosen by the Puritans with an eye to their special requirements. It proved to be a perfect

---

[1] Francis Higginson, "Journal," in Young, *Chronicles of the First Planters*, 228–33.
[2] Mather, *Magnalia Christi Americana*, I, 42.

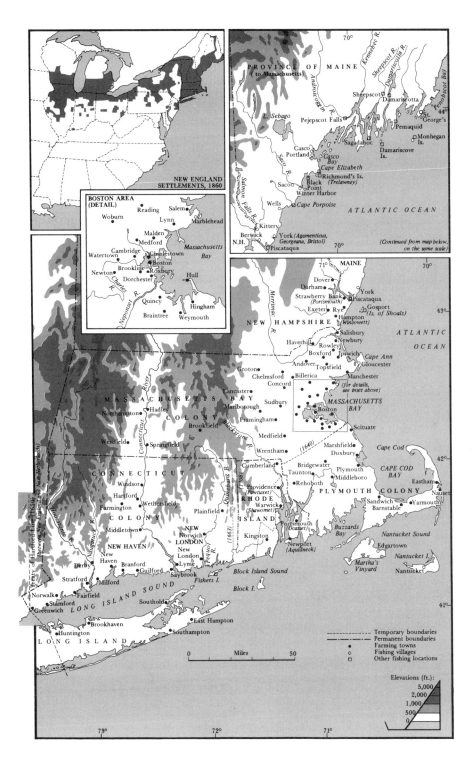

NEW ENGLAND
SETTLEMENTS, 1860

BOSTON AREA
(DETAIL)

Reading   Salem
Woburn   Lynn
              Marblehead
        Malden
        Medford
Watertown Cambridge   Massachusetts
      Brookline Charlestown   Bay
Newton   Boston
        Dorchester Roxbury
                  Hull
      Quincy
              Hingham
    Braintree   Weymouth

PROVINCE OF MAINE
(to Massachusetts)

Kennebec R.
Sheepscot R.
Damariscotta R.
Penobscot Bay

Androscoggin R.
L. Sebago
Sheepscot Damariscotta
Pejepscot Falls
                      St.
                  Pemaquid George's
Saco R.   Sagadahoc   Monhegan
Casco   Damariscove   Is.
Portland Casco   Is.
        Bay
    Cape Elizabeth
Salmon Falls R.   Richmond's Is.
        Black   (Trelawney)
Saco   Point
    Winter Harbor
Wells   Cape Porpoise   ATLANTIC OCEAN

Kittery
Berwick   York (Agamenticus,
N.H.   Georgeana, Bristol)   (Continued from map below,
      Piscataqua   70°   on the same scale)

MAINE
Dover
Durham
Strawberry Bank   York
(Portsmouth) Piscataqua
Exeter Rye   Gosport
          (Is. of Shoals)   ATLANTIC
Hampton
(Wincowett)   OCEAN
NEW HAMPSHIRE   Salisbury
        Newbury
Haverhill Rowley
        Boxford Ipswich
        Andover Topsfield Cape Ann
Groton   Manchester Gloucester
Chelmsford Billerica
Lancaster   Concord   Manchester
              (for details,
Sudbury   see inset above)
Marlborough   MASSACHUSETTS
Hadley   BAY
Northampton   Framingham Boston
        Brookfield
                      Scituate
        Medfield
Westfield   Cape Cod
    Springfield
        Wrentham (1640)   Marshfield
                  Duxbury
Cumberland   Bridgewater Plymouth   CAPE COD
        Taunton Middleboro BAY
        Rehoboth
Windsor Providence   Eastham
    (Pawtucket)   PLYMOUTH COLONY   Nauset
Hartford RHODE
Farmington Warwick Sandwich Yarmouth
Plainfield (Shawomet) Barnstable
Middletown ISLAND Portsmouth Buzzards
        (Ocasset)   Bay   Nantucket Sound
    NEW   Kingston
Norwich LONDON   Newport Edgartown
New London (Aquidneck)   Nantucket I.
Derby New   Martha's Nantucket
    Haven Branford Vinyard
Stratford Guilford
    Milford Saybrook Block Island Sound
Norwalk Fairfield Fishers I. Block I.
Stamford Southold
Greenwich Brookhaven East Hampton
Huntington   Southampton
LONG ISLAND

CONNECTICUT
COLONY
NEW HAVEN

MASSACHUSETTS BAY COLONY
Connecticut River
Blackstone R.
Quinebaug R.
Thames R.
Merrimac R.
Connecticut R.
Naugatuck R.
Housatonic R.
Charles R.
Neponset R.

LONG ISLAND SOUND

Temporary boundaries
Permanent boundaries
• Farming towns
○ Fishing villages
□ Other fishing locations

Elevations (ft.):
5,000
2,000
1,000
500
0

0   Miles   50

choice for a Calvinist utopia. Even the defects of the place were blessings in disguise for the builders of the Bay colony.

The first and most important environmental fact about New England is that it was cold—much colder in the seventeenth and eighteenth centuries than today. The Puritans arrived in a period of the earth's history which climatologists call the "little ice age." Ocean temperatures off the coast of New England were three degrees centigrade colder in the eighteenth century than the mid-twentieth. In the coldest years of the seventeenth century, the water temperature off New England approached that near southern Labrador today.[3] The Puritans complained of "piercing cold," and salt rivers frozen solid through the winter. One wrote that many lost the use of fingers and feet, and "some have had their overgrown beards so frozen together that they could not get their strong-water bottles into their mouths."[4]

But after the first few years, this cold climate proved to be a blessing. It created an exceptionally healthy environment for settlers from northern Europe. Insect-born diseases such as malaria and yellow fever were less dangerous than in southern settlements. Water-borne infections including typhoid fever and dysentery were much diminished by the cold temperatures of Massachusetts Bay. Summer diseases such as enteritis, which were the great killers of children in the seventeenth century, tended to be comparatively mild in the Puritan colonies. These New England advantages were only relative; terrible epidemics would develop throughout this region. But average rates of mortality in Massachusetts fell far below most other places in the Western world.[5]

At the same time, the cold climate also had other cultural consequences. It proved to be exceptionally dangerous to immigrants from tropical Africa, who suffered severely from pulmonary infections in New England winters. Black death rates in colonial Massachusetts were twice as high as whites'—a pattern very different from Virginia where mortality rates for the two races were not so far apart, and still more different from South Carolina where white death rates were higher than those of blacks. So high was mortality among African immigrants in New England that race slavery was not viable on a large scale, despite

[3]Hubert H. Lamb, *The Changing Climate: Selected Papers* (London, 1966), 16.

[4]William Wood, *New England's Prospect*, ed. Alden Vaughan (1634, rpt. Amherst, Mass., 1977), 29.

[5]These generalizations summarize demographic patterns of high complexity, which will be discussed in forthcoming monograph on death in New England.

many attempts to introduce it. Slavery was not impossible in this region, but the human and material costs were higher than many wished to pay. A labor system which was fundamentally hostile to the Puritan ethos of New England was kept at bay partly by the climate.[6]

The climate also had its impact on the growing season, which was shorter in the seventeenth century than today. There were only about five months between killing frosts. This period, from late May to early October, was two months shorter than in tidewater Virginia. Family farms flourished in New England, but large-scale staple agriculture was not as profitable as in warmer climes.

Another environmental factor was the land. New England's terrain was immensely varied, with pockets of highly fertile soil. "At Charles River," wrote Francis Higginson, "is as fat black earth as can be seen anywhere." Concord, Sudbury and Dedham also had excellent soil, as did many other towns in Essex and Middlesex County. But most of the land was very poor—thin sandy scrub on the south shore of Massachusetts, and stony loams to the north. Much of the coast consisted of rocky shoals or marshes, and the rivers were not navigable for more than a few miles into the interior. By comparison with the Chesapeake estuary, there were comparatively few points of access for ocean shipping. Both of these factors—the distribution of pockets of good soil and the configuration of the coastline—encouraged settlement in nucleated towns.[7]

The climate of New England was wet and stormy—with forty inches of precipitation a year, compared with twenty-five inches in East Anglia. The weather in the seventeenth century was even more variable than in the twentieth. It was kept in constant turmoil by the continuing collision of warm dry air from the west, cold dry air from the north, cold wet air from the east, and warm wet air from the south. When these air masses met above New England, the meteorological effects were apt to be spectacular. The countryside was lashed by violent blizzards, drenched by thunderstorms, raked by tornadoes, and attacked by dangerous

[6]An exception was the Narragansett or "South Country" of Rhode Island and southeastern Connecticut, where the climate was similar to southern New Jersey or northern Maryland. This subject will be discussed in volume II; for attempts to introduce slavery to Massachusetts see Lorenzo Johnston Greene, *The Negro in Colonial New England* (New York, 1924).

[7]These places are identified in Bernard and Lotte Bailyn, *Massachusetts Shipping, 1697–1714* (Cambridge, 1959).

three-day nor'easters which churned the coastal waters of New England into a seaman's hell.[8]

But there were no dry and rainy seasons in New England. The average distribution of precipitation through the year was remarkably even; no month averaged more than four inches of moisture or less than three. As a consequence, the water supply in New England was abundant and stable, with little need for hydraulic projects or public regulation.[9]

Cool temperatures and a variable climate created an immensely stimulating environment for an active population. European travelers repeatedly observed with astonishment the energy of the inhabitants. One visitor noted that New England children seem normally to move at a full run. Another remarked that their elders invented the rocking chair so they could keep moving even while sitting still. These impressions have been empirically confirmed by the new science of biometeorology which measures the animating effect of variability in atmospheric pressure and ozone levels. It finds that the New England climate was in fact immensely stimulating to human enterprise.[10]

Altogether, the environment of Massachusetts proved to be perfectly suited for a Puritan experiment. The climate was rigorous but healthy and invigorating. The land was challenging but rewarding. For historian Arnold Toynbee, New England was the classical example of a "hard country" which stimulated its inhabitants to high achievements through a process of "challenge and response." The vitality of this regional culture owed much to its physical setting.[11]

[8]W. R. Baron, "Eighteenth Century New England Climate Variation and Its Suggested Impact on Society," *MEHSQ* 21 (1981–82), 201–14; David C. Smith, "Climate Fluctuations and Agriculture in Southern and Central New England," *ibid.,* 179–200.

[9]In the environmental history of New England, one might stand the Wittfogel thesis on its head. The absence of hydraulic problems allowed an open society to develop; cf. Karl Wittfogel, *Oriental Despotism: A Comparative Study of Total Power* (New Haven, 1957).

[10]S. W. Tromp, *Medical Biometeorology: Weather, Climate and the Living Organism* (Amsterdam, 1963).

[11]Arnold Toynbee, *A Study of History* (12 vols., 1934–61, rpt. New York, 1962), II, 65.

❧ The Colonial Mood:
Anxiety and Nostalgia in Massachusetts Bay

The main body of the Winthrop fleet reached New England in the month of June 1630. After the euphoria of arrival wore off, moods rapidly began to change. "Salem, where we landed, pleased us not," Dudley wrote. Most of the new settlers moved south to Charlestown, where they made a camp of "cloth tents" and small huts near the water's edge. Many were weak with scurvy after their long sea voyage. Fevers spread swiftly through the unhealthy camp, and people began to die. The Bay Colony knew nothing like the "starving time" of Jamestown or Plymouth, but every day there were several dead colonists to bury.

"The first beginning of this work seemed very dolorous," Isaac Johnson remembered, ". . . almost in every family, lamentation, mourning and woe was heard." When the immigrant ships left for home, nearly one hundred settlers decided to return with them, and the remainder watched with sinking hearts as the topsails disappeared beyond the horizon. A melancholy spirit settled over the colony, as it did in every new settlement. Many colonists felt desperately homesick, and regretted what Isaac Johnson called their "voluntary banishment" from the "mother country." Something of this colonial mood persisted for many years.[1]

This aching sense of physical separation from the European homeland became a cultural factor of high importance in colonial settlements.[2] The effect of distance created feelings of nostalgia, anxiety and loss. The prevailing cultural mood became profoundly conservative—a spirit reinforced by emigration from England, by the rigors of the Atlantic passage, and by the sense of distance from the Old World. "For my own part," wrote Lucy Winthrop Downing, "changes were ever irksome to me, and the sea much more."[3]

In the early records of the Bay Colony, the adjectives "new" and "novel" were pejorative terms. In 1639, for example, a special "day of humiliation" was called in Massachusetts on account

[1]Thomas Dudley to Countess of Lincoln, 12 March 1631, in Young, *Chronicles of the First Planters,* 312; Johnson, *Wonder-working Providence,* 66.

[2]American historians have much to learn from Geoffrey Blainey, *The Tyranny of Distance; How Distance Shaped Australia's History* (Melbourne, 1966, 1974).

[3]Lucy Winthrop Downing to John Winthrop, n.d., Winthrop Papers, MAHS; Simmons, *Emmanuel Downing,* 43.

of "novelties, oppression, atheism, excesse, superfluity, idleness, contempt of authority, and trouble in other parts to be remembered." In this catalogue of depravity, it is interesting to observe that "novelty" led the list.[4] Dissenters were severely punished for "innovation." Roger Williams was banished for opinions that were condemned not merely as dangerous, but "new and dangerous." Thomas Makepeace was warned by the General Court that "because of his novile disposition . . . we were weary of him unless he reform."[5]

As that statement implies, reform was regarded in Massachusetts mainly as a process of recovery and preservation. Reformation meant going backward rather than forward, on the assumption that error was novel and truth was ancient in the world. The Protestant Reformation meant a reversion to primitive Christianity. In politics, reform was a return to the ancient constitution. In society, it meant a revival of ancestral ways.

These ideas were deepened by feelings of nostalgia for the "mother country," as the Puritans called England. The passengers who sailed in the *Arbella* wrote from shipboard "we . . . cannot part from our native country . . . without much sadness of heart, and many tears in our eyes, ever acknowledging that such hope and part as we have obtained in the common salvation, we have received in her bosom, and sucked it from her breasts."[6] For many years, the people of Massachusetts called themselves "the English." Nearly two centuries would pass before they could think of themselves as American.[7]

These attitudes grew even stronger among the children and grandchildren of these migrants—reinforced by a mood of cultural anxiety which developed in most colonies, no matter whether English, French, Spanish, Dutch or Portuguese. In all of these settlements there was an abiding fear of what Cotton Mather called "Criolian degeneracy." Change of any sort seemed to be cultural disintegration. In consequence, the founders of Massachusetts and their descendants for many generations

[4]Nathaniel B. Shurtleff, *Records of the Governor and Company of the Massachusetts Bay in New England* (5 vols. in 6, Boston, 1853–54), I, 252–53; 13 Mar. 1639.

[5]*Ibid.*, I, 104, 152, 1 Apr. 1633; 7 July 1635.

[6]John Winthrop, Charles Fiennes, Richard Saltonstall, Isaac Johnson, George Philips, Thomas Dudley, William Coddington and others, *The Humble Request of His Majesties Loyal Subjects, the Governour and the Company Late Gone for New England; to the Rest of Their Brethren in and of the Church of England* (London, 1630). Contemporary comment on this work appears in John Rous, *Diary*, 54, 7 June 1630.

[7]*Mass. Bay Records*, II, 228 (1648).

tended to cling to the cultural baggage which they had carried out of England.[8]

This mood of cultural conservatism created a curious paradox in colonial history. New settlements tended to remain remarkably old-fashioned in their folkways. They missed the new fads and customs that appeared in the mother country after they were planted. They tended also to preserve cultural dynamics that existed in the hour of their birth. It was as if they were caught in a twist of time, and held in its coils while the rest of the world moved beyond them.

A case in point was the history of language in new colonies. Much recent scholarship has repeatedly rediscovered the same pattern of linguistic conservatism in colonial cultures. The language of Iceland is an archaic form of Norwegian. The *patois* of Quebec preserves much of old French. The speech called Afrikaans is in many ways an antique Dutch dialect. The Spanish of Mexico and Peru retain many old-fashioned Castilian expressions. None of these colonial languages have been static or frozen. All of them diverged from the homeland by complex processes of change in their new environments. But the continuities were also very strong. A classical example was the language of Massachusetts.[9]

❧ Massachusetts Speech Ways: Yankee Twang and Norfolk Whine

In remote corners of East Anglia today, country folk still speak in a harsh, high-pitched, nasal accent unkindly called the "Norfolk whine." This dialect is the survivor of a family of accents that were heard throughout the east of England in the seventeenth century, from the fens of east Lincolnshire to the coast of Kent.[1]

---

[8]Cotton Mather, *The Way to Prosperity* (Boston, 1690), 33; Samuel Eliot Morison, *The Intellectual Life of Colonial New England* (1936, rpt. Ithaca, 1956), 75.

[9]Albert H. Marckwardt, *American English* (2d ed., rev., New York, 1980), chap. IV, "Colonial Lag and Leveling," 69–90.

[1]The Norfolk whine was one of a family of closely related eastern dialects. A leading authority defines this "southeastern speech region" as having extended from "Norfolk to Kent inclusive" in the period from 1500 to 1700; see E. J. Dobson, *English Pronunciation, 1500–1700* (2 vols., Oxford, 1968), I, xxv.

H. T. Armfield argues that "the speech of the New Englanders is largely indebted to the county of Essex, and especially to the valley of the Colne" in "The Essex Dialect and Its Influ-

In the Puritan great migration, these English speech ways were carried to Massachusetts, where they mixed with one another and merged with other elements. During the seventeenth century, they spread rapidly throughout New England, and became the basis of a new regional accent called the Yankee twang.[2]

This developing New England dialect was distinctive in its vocabulary, idiom and grammar.[3] But mainly it was known for the way that it sounded its words. The people of Massachusetts, like the fictional Yankee whom James Fenimore Cooper named

---

ence in the New World," *EAST* 4 (1893), 245–53; see also S. F. Hoar, "The Obligations of New England to the County of Kent," *AAS Proceedings*, n.s. 3 (1885), 344–71; see also Augustus M. Kelley, *Suffolk Words and Phrases* (1823, rpt. New York, 1970); Edward Gepp, *An Essex Dialect Dictionary* (London, 1923); Helge Kokeritz, "The Juto-Kentish Dialect Boundary," *AS* 16 (1941), 270–77.

On the Norfolk whine, see R. Forby, *The Vocabulary of East Anglia* (2 vols., 1830); G. J. Chester, "Norfolk Words Not in Forby's Vocabulary," *NA* 5 (1859), 188–93; W. G. Waters, "Norfolk Words Not Found in Forby's Vocabulary," *NA* 8 (1879), 167–74; H. Orton and P. M. Tilling, *Survey of English Dialects:* III, *The East Midland Counties and East Anglia* (Leeds, 1969–71).

Also related was the dialect of east Lincolnshire. In the northern and western parts of that county, people spoke a broad midland accent, similar to that of Nottinghamshire, Derbyshire and south Yorkshire. But the fen dwellers of Lincoln and Norfolk had similar speech ways in the 17th century. This east Lincoln accent included words such as argify, ax, arsy-varsy, begum, bile (for boil), blab (for talk), bust, caant (for cannot), codger, consarn, dowter (for daughter), edicated, forrard, hessle (to chasten), jabber, kid (for child), mawkin, quality (for gentry), rumpus, shaant, talk (conversation), teeny (small), uppish (proud), varmint (for vermin). See Jabez Good, *A Glossary or Collection of Words, Phrases, Place Names, Superstitions, etc., Current in East Lincolnshire* (n.p., n.d., copy in LINCRO); see also R.E.G. Cole, *Glossary of the Words in Use in South-West Lincolnshire (Wapentake of Graffoe)* (London, 1886); and J. Ellet Brogden, *Provincial Words and Expressions Current in Lincolnshire* (London, 1866); Edward Peacock, *A Glossary of Words Used in the Wapentakes of Manley and Corringham, Lincs.* (London, 1889).

[2]Most scholars agree. Anders Orbeck writes, "We are to look for the roots of Eastern Massachusetts speech in the eastern dialects of England" (*Early New England Pronunciation as Reflected in Some Seventeenth Century Town Records of Eastern Massachusetts* [thesis, Columbia, 1925, rev. ed., Ann Arbor, 1927]). M. Schele de Vere observes of the first generation in Massachusetts that "they brought not only their words which the Yankee still uses, but also a sound of voice and a mode of utterance which have been faithfully preserved, and are now spoken of as the 'New England drawl,' and the high metallic ring of the New England voice . . . is nothing but the well-known 'Norfolk Whine.'" *Americanisms; The English of the New World* (New York, 1872); see also Herbert J. Tjossem, "New England Pronunciation before 1700" (thesis, Yale, 1955).

One of the best general discussions is still George Philip Krapp, *The English Language in America* (2 vols., New York, 1925), II, 124; see also G. H. Grandgent, "From Franklin to Lowell: A Century of New England Pronunciation," *PMLA* 14 (1899), 207–39; Henry Alexander, "The Language of the Salem Witch Trials," *AS*, 3 (1927–28), 390–400; C. H. Grandgent, *Fashion and the Broad A in Old and New England* (Cambridge, 1920).

[3]Through many centuries it preserved archaic constructions such as *housen* for houses, and *blowth* for blossoms which were rarely recorded in other parts of British America, and had been commonly used in East Anglia. S. A. Green, *Natural History and Topography of Groton, Massachusetts* (Groton, 1912), 74; James Russell Lowell, *The Biglow Papers*, series II (Boston, 1867), introduction.

Remarkable Pettibone, became "provarbal for pronounsation" throughout the English-speaking world.[4]

This Yankee accent also tended to be exceptionally harsh and high-pitched. The early American orthographer John Pickering described it as "a sort of nasal twang." The English traveler John Lambert agreed that it was "a nasal twang." It had, as James Russell Lowell observed, a "partiality for nasals."

New Englanders omitted *h* after *w*, so that *whale* became *wale*, and added an extra *e* before *ou*, so that *now* became a nasal *neow*. Soft vowels became hard and metallic, as *insine* for *ensign*. The rhyme-schemes of New England poets in the seventeenth and eighteenth centuries tell us that *glare* was pronounced *glar; hair* was *har; air* was *ar;* and *war* rhymed with *star*. Other common pronunciations were *hev* for *have, yistidy* for *yesterday, ginral* for *general, dafter* or *darter* for *daughter, drownd* for *drown, gownd* for *gown, Americur* for *America* and *kiver* for *cover*. Peace officers were addressed as *cunstibles*. The town of Charlestown was *Charlton*. Governor Winthrop's name was sometimes spelled as it was sounded—*Wyntropp*. The minister John Eliot was known as *Eli't*.[5]

---

[4]Speech ways in Massachusetts and East Anglia were dynamic in their nature. Patterns of pronunciation recorded in the 20th century are only an echo of earlier practices. The best guides to the Yankee twang in its classical form are not the speech maps of scholars in the 20th century, but more casual descriptions, rhyming patterns and orthography in the 17th, 18th and 19th centuries. See John Pickering, *A Vocabulary or Collection of Words and Phrases . . . Peculiar to the United States* (Boson, 1816), 42; John Lambert, *Travels through Canada and the United States* (3 vols., London, 1814), II, 505; see also Noah Webster, *A Grammatical Institute of the English Language* (Hartford, 1783), I, 6; *Groton Records*, 130; *New Haven Records*, 97; *Mass Bay Records*, I, 238, 241; J. F. Cooper, *Pioneers*, ed. J. F. Beard (Albany, 1980), chap. xv.

In East Anglia similar pronunciations in "the eastern dialect" were recorded by Alexander Gil in his *Logonomia Anglica* in 1916; for a general discussion see Dobson, *English Pronunciation, 1500–1700* I, 147–52.

[5]A New England word list compiled in the 19th century by J. B. Moore may be taken as representative of many such lists. He compared the speech of the "typical Yankee" or "country Jonathan" with standard English, as follows:

"*Airnest* for earnest; *Actilly,* actually; *Ax,* ask; *Arter,* after; *Airly,* early; *Ain't,* is not; *Bellowses,* bellows; *Beller,* bellow; *Bin,* been; *Bile,* boil; *Bimeby,* by and by; *Blurt out,* to speak bluntly; *Bust,* burst; *Caird,* carried; *Chunk,* a piece; *Cuss,* curse, [also] a mean fellow; *Close,* clothes, *Darsn't,* dare not; *Darned,* a polite way of saying damned; *Desput,* desperate; *Du,* do; *Dunno,* don't know; *Dror,* draw; *Eend,* end; *Tarnal,* eternal; *Etarnity,* eternity; *Ef,* if; *Emptins,* yeast; *Es,* as; *Fur,* far; *Forrard,* forehead, or forward; *Ferfle,* fearful; *Ferrel,* ferrule; *Feller,* fellow; *Fust,* first; *Foller,* follow; *Furrer,* furrow; *Git,* get; *Gret,* great; *Gal,* girl; *Grouty,* sulky; *Gut,* got; *Gump,* a foolish or full fellow; *Gum,* to impose upon; *Hed,* had; *Housen,* houses; *Het,* heated; *Hull,* whole; *Hum,* home; *Hev,* have; *Ideno,* I don't know; *Inimy,* enemy; *Idees,* ideas; *Insine,* ensign; *Inter,* into; *Jedge,* judge; *Jest,* just; *Jine,* join; *Jint,* joint; *Keer,* care; *Ketch,* catch; *Kinder,* similar; *Kittle,* kettle; *Let daylight into him,* to shoot or destroy him; *Lick,* to beat or whip; *Lights,* lungs; *Mash,* marsh; *Mean,* stingy; *Offen,* often; *Ole,* old; *Peek,* peep; *Pint,* a point; *Popler,* popular; *Popple,* poplar; *Put out,* troubled, or vexed; *Riled,* angry; *Riz,* rose or risen; *Sass,* sauce; *Sassy,* impertinent; *Sartin,* certain; *Set by* or sot by, admired; *Sich,* such; *Slarter,* slaughter; *No great shakes,* not much

Yankee speech owed much of its distinctive character to its pronunciation of the letter *r*. Postvocalic *r*'s tended to disappear altogether, so that *Harvard* became *Haa-v'd* (with the *a* pronounced
as in *happen*). This speech-habit came from East Anglia and may
still be heard in the English counties of Suffolk, Norfolk and
Kent. At the same time, other *r*'s were added. *Follow* was pronounced *foller*, and *asked* became *arst*—a spelling which often
appeared in town meeting records during the seventeenth century. Precisely the same sounds still exist today in remote parts of
East Anglia.[6]

The Yankee twang did not develop in a perfectly uniform way
throughout New England. In Boston it was spoken at a speed
which made it incomprehensible even to others of the same
region. Yale President Timothy Dwight complained of Bostonians
that "the rapidity of their pronunciation contracts frequently two
short syllables into one, and thus renders the language, in itself
too rough, still rougher by a violent junction of consonants. . . .

---

account; *Meetin' heouse*, meeting house; *Nower's*, nowhere; *Pooty*, pretty; *Pizen*, poison; *Scaly*,
mean; *Scrouging*, hard labor; *Sot*, sat; *Picter*, picture; *Snaked out*, pulled out; *Streaked*, mean; *Scoot*,
to run away; *Sogerin*, shirking; *'Somers*, somewhere, *Suthin*, something; *Take on*, to mourn; *Taters*,
potatoes; *Tetch*, touch; *Sost*, so as to; *Darter*, daughter; *Wal*, well; *Wuz*, was; *Puddn*, Pudding;
Winder, window; *Hins*, hens; *Ter rites*, presently; *Harrer*, harrow; *Harrer* up yer feelins, to excite
your feelings; *Put out*, offended; *Straddle over*, step over; *Grouty*, cross or angry; *Terbarker* or
Barker, tobacco; *Pester*, annoy; *Sharder*, shadow; *Pesky*, offensive; *Larnin*, learning; *Turkle*, turtle;
Tootin, blowing on an instrument; *Sho*, an exclamation of surprise; *Duds*, clothes; *Nuther*, neither; *Natur*, nature; *Yaller*, yellow; *I swow*, or *I swan*, another way of saying I swear; *Edicated*,
educated; *This ere*, this here; *That are*, that there; *Seed*, saw; *Hist*, hoist; *T'other*, the other. Words
ending with the syllable ing were pronounced as though the final consonant, g, was silent."

Moore commented that "for many years after the settlement of New England, the majority
of the people who were not well educated were in the habit of pronouncing many of the common words in use in a very peculiar manner. . . . The typical Yankee or country Jonathan always
talked in this dialect." *History of the Town of Candia* (Manchester, N.H., 1893), 324; other early
New England word lists and records of pronunciation appear in Timothy Dwight, *Travels in
New England and New York*, ed. Barbara Miller Solomon (3 vols., Cambridge, Mass., 1969); John
Drayton, *Letters Written during a Tour through the Northern and Eastern States of America* (Charleston, S.C., 1794), 58; and Andrew Beers, *Beers' Almanack for the Year 1808* (New Haven, 1807),
23.

The pattern of orthography in town and colony records also contains many clues which have
been studied systematically by Anders Orbeck, with results summarized in *Early New England
Pronunciation*.

[6]Bernard Bloch, "The Treatment of Middle English Final and Preconsonantal R in the Pres-
ent-Day Speech of New England" (thesis, Brown, 1935); and "The Post Vocalic R in New
England Speech," *Actes du IVe Congrès Internationale de Linguistes* (Copenhagen, 1938), 195–97;
Gordon E. Bigelow, "More Evidence of Early Loss of [r] in Eastern American Speech," *AS* 30
(1955) 154–56; Vivian S. Lawrence, "Dialect Mixture in Three New England Pronunciation
Patterns: Vowels and Consonants" (thesis, Columbia, 1960); Robert L. Parslow, "The Pronunciation of English in Boston, Massachusetts: Vowels and Consonants" (thesis, Univ. of Michigan,
1967); Peter and Jane Benes, *American Speech: 1600 to the Present, DSNEF, 1983* (Boston, 1985).

Thus Sweden, Britain, garden and vessel are extensively pronounced *Swed'n, Brit'n, gard'n, vess'l.* By this contraction, also, the harshness of the language is increased."[7]

Many country towns in New England also developed individual speech ways. Even neighboring communities differed in their pronunciation—a fact which tells us much about the intensity of life within them. A case in point were two little villages founded by New Englanders on eastern Long Island. In 1798 a local gentleman noted that the speech of an Easthampton man might be distinguished from that of a Southampton man, "as well as a native of Kent might be distinguished from a Yorkshireman."[8] But these local customs were variations on a regional pattern which existed throughout New England.

The character of this pattern derived in large measure from the influence of an East Anglian elite who became ministers and magistrates in the Puritan colonies. One bizarre indicator of their influence was a layer of Latinate complexity that came to be grafted upon the language of New England. An early example (1647) appeared in the prose of Puritan minister Nathaniel Ward: "If the whole conclave of Hell," he wrote, "can so compromise, exadverse, and diametricall contradictions, as to compolitize such a multimonstrous maufrey of heteroclytes and quicquidlibets quietly; I trust I may say with all humble reverence, they can do more than the Senate of Heaven."[9]

The people of Massachusetts were constantly bombarded with this pedantry. Every Sunday they sat with bowed heads while showers of polysyllables rained down upon them from the pulpit. Inspired by this show of Cambridge learning, the country people of New England studded their speech with quasi-classical folk-

---

[7]Dwight, *Travels,* I, 368–69.

[8]Edmund B. O'Callaghan, ed., *Documentary History of the State of New York* (4 vols., Albany, 1849–51), I, 678; see also Martha Jane Gibson, "Early Connecticut Pronunciation: Guilford, 1639–1800; Branford, 1644–1800" (thesis, Yale, 1933); Claude Mitchell Simpson, "The English Speech of Early Rhode Island, 1636–1700" (thesis, Harvard, 1936); and Tjossem, "New England Pronunciation before 1700."

There were also individual variations. New England's Puritan poet Edward Taylor constructed his rhyme schemes with a distinct Leicester accent. Taylor was a comparative latecomer to New England, having been born in Sketchley, Leicestershire, probably in the year 1642; he emigrated in 1668. See Bernie Eugene Russell, "Dialectical and Phonetic Features of Edward Taylor's Rhymes: A Brief Study Based upon a Computer Concordance of his Poems (6 vols., thesis, Univ. of Wisconsin, 1973); also Karl Keller, *A Concordance to the Poems of Edward Taylor* (Washington, 1973), and Donald E. Stanford, ed., *The Poems of Edward Taylor* (New Haven, 1960.

[9]Nathaniel Ward, *The Simple Cobler of Aggawam* (London, 1647).

coinages of their own invention such as *rambunctious, absquatulate, splendiferous,* and many other words ending in *ize, ous, ulate, ical, iction, acious, iferous,* and *ticate.* Language of this sort became a distinguishing mark of New England speech, especially in the neighborhood of Boston. Late in the eighteenth century, Timothy Dwight wrote that "The Boston style is a phrase proverbially used throughout a considerable part of this country to denote a florid, pompous manner of writing, and has been thought by persons at a distance to be the predominant style of this region."[10]

Today, these regional speech ways are growing fainter on both sides of the Atlantic. The Norfolk whine has retreated to the remote northern coast of East Anglia. The old Yankee twang survives mainly in the hill towns of interior New England. But throughout these larger regions, a trained ear can still detect the old accents in more muted forms. The postvocalic *r* still tends to disappear in rural East Anglia, and traces of Yankee speech may yet be heard in every part of America where the children of the Puritan great migration pitched their homes.

❧ Massachusetts Building Ways: East Anglian and Kentish Origins of New England Houses

The same pattern of persistence and change also appeared in the vernacular architecture of New England. By an early date in the seventeenth century, a distinctive building style developed in Massachusetts Bay. It was not invented in the New World, but adapted from customs and fashions that had prevailed in eastern England during the period of the great migration.[1]

---

[10]Dwight, *Travels,* I, 368.

[1]The best introduction to English vernacular architecture is Eric Mercer, *English Vernacular Houses* (London, 1975); see also R. W. Brunskill, *Timber Building in Britain* (London, 1985); and John and Jane Penoyre, *Houses in the Landscape: A Regional Study of Vernacular Building Styles in England and Wales* (London, 1978); more specialized works include C. A. Hewett, "Timber-Building in Essex," *AMST,* n.s. 9 (1961), 32–56; O. Rackham, "Grundle House: On the Quantities of Timber in Certain East Anglian Buildings in Relation to Local Supplies," *VA* 13 (1982), 39–47; H. C. Hughes, "Some Notes on the Character and Dating of Domestic Architecture in the Cambridge District," *CASP* 37 (1935–36), 1–23; F. W. Steer, *Farm and Cottage Inventories of Mid-Essex, 1635–1749* (Colchester, 1950); F. A. Gurling, "Suffolk Chimneys of the Sixteenth Century," *SIAP* 22 (1934–36), 104–7.

Specially helpful are careful modern studies of demolished buildings in the east of England; D. G. Macleod, "Cottages on the East Side of Rochford Market Square," *EJ* I (1966), 25–37;

This architecture could be recognized in part by its choice of building materials. Through nearly four centuries, New England houses have been made of wood. In the seventeenth and eighteenth centuries when hardwoods were abundant, they were given frames of oak, sills of hackmatack, floor of white pine and outer skins of cedar. As these species slowly disappeared, cheaper softwoods became more common. But wood itself remained the dominant building material in Massachusetts from the seventeenth century to our own time—more so than in any other American region.

This preference for wood was not merely a reflexive response to the North American forest. It was an old folk custom that had been carried from the east of England, where even today timber-framed houses are more common than elsewhere in the British Isles. Historian R. J. Brown, in a survey of English domestic architecture, finds that the county of Essex "probably contains more timber-framed buildings than any other."[2] Wood-sheathing and particularly wooden clapboards are also found more frequently in East Anglia, Kent and East Sussex than elsewhere in England, just as they are more common in New England than in other parts of the United States.[3]

Techniques of building also showed similar patterns. House carpentry in Massachusetts was much like that of eastern England in the many complex details of post-and-beam construction—such as the design of windbraces, the placing of pegs, the shape of mortise and tenon joints, and the design of crownposts, rafters, purlins and scantling.[4]

---

and Ian G. Robertson, "The Archaeology of the M1 Motorway in Essex, 1970–1975," *EJ* 10 (1975), 68.

On New England architecture see Abbott L. Cummings, *The Framed Houses of Massachusetts Bay, 1625–1675* (Cambridge, 1979); R. G. St. George, "Set Thine House in Order . . . ," in *New England Begins: The Seventeenth Century* (3 vols., Boston, 1982), II, 159–351; and Anthony Garvan, "The New England Plain Style," *CSSH* 3 (1960), 106–22.

[2] R. J. Brown, *The English Country Cottage* (London, 1979), 105.

[3] This form of sheathing is called weatherboarding or woodcladding in England today. But in the 17th century it was called clapboarding—a term which survives in the United States. On wooden clapboards as "indigenous to the South-east," see R. J. Brown, *English Farmhouses* (London, 1982), 172. They were particularly common in Kent, Essex and eastern Hertfordshire near the Essex border.

[4] These patterns are highly complex. To summarize briefly, framing techniques in East Anglia and New England were similar in the following respects:

1. Crownposts and clasped purlins were common in the east; roof construction in other English regions (especially the north) ran more to king-posts (if box-built).
2. Internal chimney-stacks were preferred to chimneys on gable ends.

The interior plans of buildings in Massachusetts also resembled those of eastern England. One common design for a farmhouse in southern New England was a simple rectangle of two stories, with a central chimney stack and a steep "twelve pitch" roof. A one-story lean-to was often added to the back for the kitchen, and by 1680 was built as an integral part of the house. To cover it the back roof was carried down in a straight line, creating the classic "salt-box" silhouette that gave this house its name.[5]

The salt-box house was not a New England invention. It had been common throughout Kent and East Anglia before the great migration. A case in point was a seventeenth-century wood-framed house at Parsonage Lane, Darenth, Kent, which was exactly like a New England salt-box in every respect—two stories in front and one in back, a central chimney stack, a kitchen lean-to behind, creating the classical salt-box silhouette. The interior was divided in two large chambers on the ground floor, and smaller rooms upstairs. It was not a large structure—only twenty-six feet square. But it made a comfortable home for an artisan or husbandman. Not many of these wooden salt-box houses survive in old England today. Most have fallen victim to damp, decay, and changing fashion. But in the late sixteenth and early seventeenth century they were common in the eastern counties, and were carried to New England with comparatively very little change.[6]

Another New England style was the Cape Cod box—a small structure of one and one-half stories. This house also had developed in eastern England during the late sixteenth and early seventeenth century, as cottagers "chambered over" their wood-framed houses by adding separate sleeping quarters above. It was

---

3. Tenons were secured by one or two pins at most, even on chimney girts.
4. Roof-frames consisted of close-built principal and common rafters; rather than principal rafters, ridge pieces, and common purlins.
5. Roof scantling (and other timbers) tended to be more slender than in the west and north of England.
6. Bays were functionally spaced on the lower floor but regularly spaced on the upper floor.
7. Windbraces in the roof sometimes rose above the purlins rather than falling below them.

The leading authorities are C. A. Hewett, *The Development of English Carpentry, 1200–1700: An Essex Study* (London, 1969); and "Some East Anglian Prototypes for Early Timber Houses in America," *PMA* 3 (1969), 100–121; "Seventeenth Century Carpentry in Essex," *PMA* 5 (1971), 77–087; and Cummings, *Framed Houses of Massachusetts Bay*, 95–117.

[5]A "twelve pitch" roof in the lexicon of New England house carpenters is a roof that rises 12 inches in height for every 12 inches in depth.

[6]When this house was demolished in 1961, it was studied in close detail; see *AC* 77 (1961), 92–93; C. W. Chalkin, *Seventeenth-Century Kent* (London, 1965), 237.

Whitman House, Farmington, Connecticut, 1664

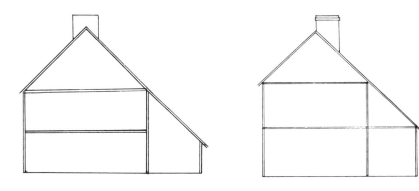

Parsonage Lane Cottage   *Moulthorp House*
Darenth, Kent   *East Haven, Connecticut*

The Salt Box House was not invented in New England. In the early seventeenth century, it was an established form of vernacular architecture in East Anglia and Kent. An example was this cottage (now pulled down) which stood in Parsonage Lane, Darenth, Kent. Its plan and elevation were similar in every important way to a New England Salt Box House. Timber framing and wood sheathing were commonplace in southeastern England, and rare in other British regions. Sources for these sketches include Morrison, Early American Architecture, *57; AC LXXVII, 92–93; Chalkin,* Kent, *237; drawing by J. Frederick Kelley in Dow,* Everyday Life in Massachusetts, *24f.*

in common use throughout New England during the seventeenth and eighteenth centuries, and was revived in the twentieth. The "cape" as it is called today remains very popular, long after it was abandoned in England.[7]

A more pretentious New England plan was the stretched box, a wooden rectangle much like the salt box, with additions to the sides instead of the rear. The result was an imposing facade of exceptional breadth, and more room for the complex households of the rich. In eastern England and Massachusetts the stretched box became the house of prosperous yeomen and lesser gentry.[8]

Yet a fourth design was the gabled box. An example was the Downing-Bradstreet house in Salem, with three front gables, and double windows and two massive chimney stacks. These were the most opulent private houses in seventeenth-century Massachusetts, and resembled the homes of lesser gentry in East Anglia.[9] They were often enlarged by the addition of gables and wings without regard to symmetry—a custom which was also common in East Anglia, where we find that "complex roof-gable shapes" were more common than in other parts of England.[10]

A distinctive characteristic of these larger houses was a projecting second story (which in England is called the first story). The front of this second floor extended a foot or two beyond the first floor in a design called a "jetty" in the seventeenth century. This fashion had been specially popular in the villages and towns of East Anglia. It was much used in New England for a century after settlement.[11]

Site plans in Massachusetts also showed an architectural kinship to East Anglia. Houses in the Bay Colony were customarily

---

[7]Basil Oliver, *Old Houses and Village Buildings in East Anglia, Norfolk, Suffolk and Essex* (London, 1912); Arthur Oswald, *Country Houses of Kent* (London, 1933); Abbott Cummings observes of the "hall and parlor" plan of the Mayflower Cottage of Colne Engaine, Essex, that "this well established plan type set a pattern which has persisted through three and a half centuries and survives today in modified form in the modern American builder's vocabulary of styles as Garrison, Colonial and Cape Cod house." (*Framed Houses of Massachusetts Bay*, 6.)

See also Allen G. Noble, *Wood, Brick and Stone, The North American Settlement Landscape;* vol I, *Houses* (Amherst, 1984), 23–25; Alfred E. Poor, *Colonial Architecture of Cape Cod, Nantucket and Martha's Vineyard* (New York, 1932); Ernest A. Connally, "The Cape Cod House," *SAHJ*, 19 (1960), 47–56; Henry Glassie, *Pattern in the Material Folk Culture of the Eastern United States* (Philadelphia, 1968), 128–30, discusses the spread of the Cape Cod house through upstate New York and the Old Northwest (the states of Ohio, Indiana, Illinois, Michigan and Wisconsin).

[8]For an example from central Kent, see Chalkin, *Kent,* 237.

[9]This structure was destroyed in the 18th century; it is known through a drawing of doubtful authenticity, reproduced in Cummings, *Framed Houses of Massachusetts Bay,* 144.

[10]Penoyre and Penoyre, *Houses in the Landscape,* 78.

[11]*Ibid.*

The Corwin House, Salem, Essex County

Church Hall, Boxted, Essex, circa 1600

The Gabled Box was the most opulent of New England's early house-types. These complex framed structures had multiple bays and wings, and often a rambling ell in the rear. One example was the Corwin House in Salem, here reproduced from an old drawing. Its central porch was two stories high, flanked by large gables projecting to the front and sides. A massive central chimney stack heated many rooms, and the roof-peaks bore large ornaments at each gable end. Many of these houses were built in Boston, Salem, Ipswich and Saugus. They closely resembled large houses in the east of England. Sources for these sketches include a drawing by Samuel Bartol in the Essex Institute, and a photograph in Cummings, Framed Houses of Massachusetts, *13.*

built facing south. They stood so close to the road that carts rumbled by only a few feet from the door. This tendency in New England has sometimes been explained as a response to the environment—a way of reducing the labor of "breaking out" in snowy winters. But precisely the same pattern may still be seen on the old roads and byways of East Anglia.[12]

The building ways of Massachusetts were never static. In the eighteenth century major changes would be made in fenestration, as casement windows yielded to small guillotine sash windows and later to large double-hung windows. During the nineteenth century, the framing of houses was revolutionized by a shift from hardwood posts and beams to a "balloon frame" of light softwood studs and joists. The proportions of the house were enlarged, and other changes were introduced in the interior, by a subdivision of rooms for greater privacy. Aesthetic tastes in New England houses were also transformed by Palladian forms in the eighteenth century, and by the Greek Revival in the nineteenth. But behind these changes in taste, there was an underlying continuity in building materials, methods, plans, styles and sites. For three centuries, domestic architecture in Massachusetts preserved a special character that derived from the culture of eastern England.

❧ Massachusetts Family Ways:
The Puritan Idea of the Covenanted Family

The builders of the Bay Colony also created special forms of family life which were as distinctive as their speech and architecture. The Puritans were deeply self-conscious in their familial acts. They wrote at length about the family, in a literature of prescription which was remarkably consistent with actual conditions in their households.[1]

The people of Massachusetts thought of the family not as an end in itself, but as an instrument of their highest religious pur-

---

[12]Elizabeth G. Farrell, "Essex Rural Settlement" (thesis, Wales, 1969).

[1]On this subject we have two classics of American historiography: Edmund Morgan, *The Puritan Family,* and John Demos, *A Little Commonwealth: Family Life in Plymouth Colony* (New York, 1970). Morgan's work is strong on ideas of the family; Demos gives more attention to actual conditions as revealed in probate and court records. I am much indebted to both historians.

poses. The Puritan writer Jonathan Mitchell declared, "a Christian may and ought to desire many things as means, but God alone as his end."[2] This was their way of thinking about the family in particular, which was also described as "the root whence church and commonwealth cometh."[3]

Concern for the family in this culture was also given a special intensity by an attitude which historian Edmund Morgan calls "Puritan tribalism," that is, the Hebraic idea that the founders of New England were God's chosen people. The Puritans were encouraged by their ministers to think of themselves as "the saints," and to believe that grace descended to their children. John Cotton explained this process in explicitly genealogical terms: "The Covenant of God is, *I will be thy God, and the God of thy seed after thee*," he wrote.[4] The Puritan minister William Stoughton went even farther. He prophesied, ". . .the books that shall be opened at the last day will contain *Genealogies* among them. There shall be brought forth a *Register of the Genealogies of New-England's sons and daughters*."[5]

This obsession with family and genealogy became an enduring part of New England's culture. Two centuries after the great migration, Harriet Beecher Stowe observed:

> among the peculiarly English ideas which the Colonists brought to Massachusetts, which all the wear and tear of democracy have not been able to obliterate, was that of *family*. Family feeling, family pride, family hope and fear and desire, were, in my early day, strongly-marked traits. Genealogy was a thing at the tip of every person's tongue, and in every person's mind. . . . "Of a very respectable family," was a sentence so often repeated at the old fireside that its influence went in part to make up my character.[6]

New England's interest in genealogy was not the same as that of high-born families in England or Virginia. It was not a pride in rank and quarterings, but a moral and religious idea that developed directly from the Puritan principles of the founders.

Puritan ideas also had an impact on New England's family ways in yet another way. The builders of the Bay Colony cast their idea

---

[2]Jonathan Mitchell, "Sermons from Psalms," n.d., MAHS; quoted in Morgan, *Puritan Family*, 15.

[3]Boston Sermons, 14 Jan. 1672, MAHS, as quoted in Morgan, *Puritan Family*, 143.

[4]John Cotton, *The Covenant of God's Free Grace* (London, 1645), 19–20.

[5]William Stoughton, *New Englands True Interest, Not to Lie* (Cambridge, 1670), 33.

[6]Stowe, *Oldtown Folks*, 1102.

of the family in terms of the covenant theology which was so central to their faith. They believed that God's covenant with each individual Christian was enlarged into another sort of contract which they called the family covenant. John Cotton explained, "God hath made a covenant with parents and householders," which bound them not only on their own account, but also in regard to "wives, and children, and servants, and kindred, and acquaintances, and all that are under our reach, either by way of subordination, or coordination."[7]

Thus, the covenanted family became a complex web of mutual obligations between husbands and wives, parents and children, masters and servants. The clarity of this contractual idea, the rigor of its enforcement and especially the urgency of its spiritual purpose, set New England Puritans apart from other people— even from other Calvinists—in the Western world.[8]

Like most of their contemporaries, the Puritans thought of the family as a concentric set of nuclear and extended rings. But within that conventional idea, they gave special importance to the innermost nuclear ring. Strong quantitative evidence of this attitude appeared in their uniquely nuclear naming customs. As we shall see below, the Puritans of Massachusetts gave high priority to the descent of names from parents to children within the nuclear family. This naming strategy was unique to the Puritans, and very different from other cultures in British America.[9]

Similar tendencies also appeared in customs of inheritance, which were more nuclear in New England than in other American colonies during the seventeenth century. One study of 168 wills in Newbury, Massachusetts, for example, found that only 6.5 percent left bequests to a niece or nephew, and 3.0 percent to other kin. None whatever bequeathed property to a cousin—a pattern different from the Chesapeake colonies.[10]

The same nuclear pattern also appeared in the composition of

[7]Cotton, *God's Free Grace,* 19.

[8]John Cotton, *Christ the Fountaine of Life* (London, 1651), 33; quoted in Morgan, *Puritan Family,* 6–7; the Puritan idea of the family covenant is discussed in *ibid.,* 6–9, 181; see also Champlin Burrage, *The Church Covenant Idea* (Philadelphia, 1904); Leonard J. Trinterud, "The Origins of Puritanism," *Church History* 20 (1951), 55; Miller, *Errand into the Wilderness* and *The New England Mind,* 366–97.

[9]The magnitudes of difference were very great, and have been replicated in many studies. See below, "Massachusetts Naming Ways."

[10]Robert L. Goodman, "Newbury, Massachusetts, 1635–1685: The Social Foundations of Harmony and Conflict" (thesis, Michigan State Univ., 1974), 65; the magnitudes of difference between Puritan and non-Puritan colonies cannot be accounted for by mortality rates.

households. By comparison with other colonies, households throughout Massachusetts and Connecticut included large numbers of children, small numbers of servants and high proportions of intact marital unions. In Waltham, Massachusetts, for example, completed marriages formed in the 1730s produced 9.7 children on the average. These Waltham families were the largest that demographic historians have found anywhere in the Western world, except for a few Christian communes which regarded reproduction as a form of worship. But they were not unique. In many other New England towns fertility rates rose nearly as high, and the number of children was larger than French demographer Louis Henry defined as the biological maximum in a normal population.[11]

[11]Total numbers of children known to have been born to completed families and all families in New England were as follows:

Town	Marriage Cohort	Comp.	All	Town	Marriage Cohort	Comp.	All
Plymouth	1st gen.	8.3	n.a.		1710–40	7.4	n.a.
	2nd gen.	8.7	n.a.		1740–50	7.4	n.a.
	3rd gen.	9.3	n.a.		1750–60	7.8	n.a.
Andover Mass.	1st gen.	8.3	8.3		1760–70	8.3	n.a.
	2nd gen.	8.7	8.1	Concord Mass.	1750–70	7.1	5.4
	3rd gen.	7.6	7.2	Sturbridge Mass.	1730–59	8.8	n.a.
Waltham Mass.	1671–80	9.0	n.a.	Brookline Mass.	1710–1810	7.2	6.5
	1691–1700	8.3	n.a.	Windsor Conn.	1640–59	7.7	n.a.
	1701–10	8.4	n.a.		1660–79	8.0	n.a.
	1711–20	8.5	n.a.		1680–99	7.2	n.a.
	1721–30	9.0	n.a.		1700–19	6.2	n.a.
	1731–40	9.7	n.a.		1720–39	7.6	n.a.
Hingham Mass.	pre-1660	7.5	6.4		1740–59	6.6	n.a.
	1661–80	7.9	7.7		1760–79	7.1	n.a.
	1681–1700	6.0	5.5	Hampton N.H.	1638–74	8.6	7.5
	1701–20	5.6	4.8		1675–99	7.3	6.7
	1721–40	6.8	5.7		1700–24	7.7	6.4
	1741–60	7.2	6.3		1725–49	7.2	6.9
Milford Mass.	1660–1710	8.4	n.a.	Nantucket	1680–1739	7.2	n.a.

Compiled from Demos, *A Little Commonwealth,* 192; Philip J. Greven, Jr., *Four Generations: Population, Land, and Family in Colonial Andover, Massachusetts* (Ithaca, 1970); D. S. Smith, "Population, Family, and Society in Hingham, Massachusetts, 1635–1880" (unpubl. thesis, Berkeley, 1975); unpublished family reconstitution projects conducted under the direction of the author at Brandeis on Milford, Mass., by Sally Barrett; on Hampton, N.H., by Lawrence Kilbourne; on Nantucket by Carol Shuchman and Edward Byers; on Waltham by Susan Simmons; on Concord by Marc Harris, Susan Kurland, James Kimenker, Richard Weintraub and Joanne Early Levin; and on Brookline by Beth Linzner, Kenneth A. Dreyfuss, Alisa Belinkoff Katz and Bethamy Dubitzky Weintraub, and on Windsor, Conn., by Linda Auwers. Results have been partly published by Marc Harris, "The People of Concord: A Demographic History, 1750–1850," in D. H. Fischer, ed., *Concord, The Social History of a New England Town, 1750–1850* (Waltham, 1983); Beth Linzner, "Population and Society: A Demographic History of Brookline," in D. H. Fischer, ed., *Brookline the Social History of a Suburban Town* (Waltham, 1986), 7–48; Lawrence J.

The number of servants in New England, however, was very small—less than one per family. At any given time, most households in this region had no servants at all—a pattern very different from the Chesapeake and Delaware colonies. In short, the New England household more closely coincided with the nuclear unit, and the nuclear family was larger and stronger than elsewhere in the Western world.

The strength of the nuclear unit was merely one of many special features of New England families. Another was a strong sense of collective responsibility for maintaining its individual integrity. The people of the Bay Colony worked through many institutions to preserve what they called "family order" and "family government" within each nuclear unit. Other cultures also shared these concerns, but once again Puritan New England did things in its own way, with a special intensity of purpose. The selectmen and constables of each town were required by law to inspect families on a regular basis. Where "good order" broke down within a household, their task was to restore it. In nuclear families that were persistently "disorderly"—a word that covered a multitude of misdeeds—the selectmen were required to remove the children and servants and place them in other homes. Thus, in 1675, Robert Styles of Dorchester was presented for many sins, and ordered to "put forth his children, or otherwise the selectmen are hereby empowered to do it, according to law."[12]

In the second generation, responsibility for inspecting families passed from selectmen to special town officers called tithingmen. A statute in 1675 ordered that each tithingman "shall take charge of ten or Twelve families of his Neighborhood, and shall diligently inspect them." This office did not exist in Anglican Virginia or Quaker Pennsylvania. But it was not a New England innovation. Tithingmen had long existed as parish functionaries in East Anglia and other parts of England. Here again an old English custom was taken over by the Puritans and given a new intensity of purpose.[13]

Kilbourne, "The Fertility Transition in New England: The Case of Hampton, New Hampshire, 1655–1840," in Robert M. Taylor, Jr., and Ralph J. Crandall, eds., *Generations and Change: Genealogical Perspectives on Social History* (Mercer, Ga., 1986).

[12]Samuel E. Morison, ed., *Records of the Suffolk County Court, CSM Collections* 29–30 (1933), 646, 23 Nov. 1675.

[13]Morgan, *Puritan Family,* 148–149; still useful is Herbert Baxter Adams, *Saxon Tithingmen in America* (Baltimore, 1883).

So important was the idea of a covenanted family in Massachusetts that everyone was compelled by law to live in family groups. As early as 1629 the Governor and Deputies of the colony ordered that:

> For the better accommodation of businesses, we have divided the servants belonging to the Company into several families, as we desire and intend they should live together. . . . Our earnest desire is, that you take special care, in settling these families, that the chief in the family (at least some of them) be grounded in religion; whereby morning and evening family duties may be duly performed, and a watchful eye held over all in each family . . . that so disorders may be prevented, and ill weeds nipped before they take too great a head.

The provinces of Connecticut and Plymouth also forbade any single person to "live of himself."[14]

These laws were enforced. In 1668 the court of Middlesex County, Massachusetts, systematically searched its towns for single persons and placed them in families.[15] In 1672 the Essex County Court noted:

> Being informed that John Littleale of Haverhill lay in a house by himself contrary to the law of the country, whereby he is subject to much sin and iniquity, which ordinarily are the companions and consequences of a solitary life, it was ordered . . . he remove and settle himself in some orderly family in the town, and be subject to the orderly rules of family government.

One stubborn loner, John Littleale, was given six weeks to comply, on pain of being sent to "settle himself" in the House of Correction.[16]

This custom was not invented in New England. It had long been practiced in East Anglia. From as early as 1562 to the mid-seventeenth century, The High Constables' Sessions and Quarter Courts of Essex County in England had taken similar action against "single men," "bachelors," and "masterless men." The Puritans took over this custom and endowed it with the spiritual intensity of their faith.[17]

---

[14]*Mass. Bay Records*, 21 April 1629, I, 397.

[15]Morgan, *Puritan Family*, 146.

[16]*Essex County Court Records*, V, 104.

[17]F. G. Emmison, *Elizabethan Life: Home, Work and Land; From Essex Wills and Sessions and Manorial Records* (Chelmsford, 1976), I, 148–49; also *idem, Elizabethan Life: Disorder; Mainly from Essex Sessions and Assize Records* (Chelmsford, 1970), 31, 33, 46, 210, 222–24.

Family order was an hierarchical idea to the people of the Bay Colony. In that belief they were typical of their age. But the structure of that hierarchy had a special cast in their thinking. In Puritan New England, the family hierarchy had more to do with age, and less with gender and rank, than in other English-speaking cultures. The evidence appears not only in prescriptive literature, but also in the ordering of daily functions such as eating and sleeping. Families in Massachusetts did not dine together. Laurel Thatcher Ulrich discovered that in New England "servants and children . . . sat down to eat after their master and mistress." This, as we shall discover, differed from table customs in other Anglo-American cultures.[18]

The same hierarchy of ages also appeared in sleeping arrangements. Adults and heads of families slept on the ground floor in rooms called the parlor or principal chamber. Children commonly slept in upstairs, in lofts or low rooms. Architectural historians find that this arrangement was typical of East Anglia, but not of other regions in England. "In East Anglia," writes Abbott Cummings, "the sleeping arrangements for adults were confined almost entirely to the ground floor." Cummings discovered that in the west of England, adults and children slept in upstairs chambers, but "by the early seventeenth century, in southeastern England at least, the parlor had become the principal ground floor sleeping room and this continues to be its chief function in Massachusetts as reflected in inventories for houses with a plan of two or more rooms . . . the ground floor parlor remained the master bedroom for the head of the family into the eighteenth and even in some cases into the nineteenth century in some rural areas."[19]

This hierarchy of age within the family was written into the laws of Massachusetts, which in 1648 required the death penalty as a punishment for stubborn or rebellious sons over the age of sixteen who refused to obey either their father or mother. The same punishment was also provided for children who struck or cursed

---

[18]Laurel Thatcher Ulrich, "'It Went Away She Knew Not How': Food Theft and Domestic Conflict in Seventeenth Century Essex County," *Foodways in the Northeast, DSNEF for 1982*, 97.

[19]Cummings, *Framed Houses of Massachusetts Bay*, 5, 28. William Bentley in Salem recalled that "no . . . heads of families lodged on the second stories" during the 17th century. See *The Diary of William Bentley* (4 vols., rpt. Gloucester, 1962), IV, 127. In Virginia, as we shall see, everyone normally slept on the same floor; in the backcountry, the entire family often slept in the same room.

their parents. No child was ever executed under this law, but several were fined or whipped by the courts for being rude or abusive to their parents. Some of these errant "children" were in their forties, and their parents were of advanced age.[20]

At the same time, other laws ordered that younger children who were "rude, stubborn and unruly" and could not be kept in subjection by their parents, should be removed and placed under a master who would "force them to submit to government."[21]

The intensity of these Puritan beliefs in the covenanted family as an instrument of larger purposes, and in the instrumental family as primarily a nuclear unit, and also in the nuclear family as a hierarchy of age all distinguished the family customs of New England from other cultures in British America. The Puritans also developed these ideas in elaborate detail, with regard to relations between husband and wife, children and elders, marriage and divorce, sex and death.

❧ Massachusetts Marriage Ways: The Puritan Idea of Marriage as a Contract

Marriage customs in Massachusetts were not what one might expect to find in a new country. Despite the vast abundance of land, young people did not rush to tie the knot. By comparison with other colonies, age at first marriage was remarkably advanced. After the first few years of settlement, men tended to marry at the age of 26, and women at about 23. These patterns persisted in the Puritan colonies for nearly a century.[1]

---

[20]"If a man have a stubborn or rebellious son, of sufficient years and understanding (viz) sixteen years of age, which will not obey the voice of his father or the voice of his mother, and that when they have chastened him will not harken unto them . . . such a son shall be put to death." This law followed the text of Deuteronomy 21:18–21 (King James version). Massachusetts Laws of 1648, 6; *Connecticut Laws of 1673,* 78; *The Compact with the Charter and Laws of the Colony of New Plymouth,* 100. Instances of actual punishment appear in the *Plymouth Colony Records,* III, 201; VI, 20; *Mass. Bay Records,* I, 155; *Essex Records,* I, 19; *Assistants Records,* III, 138–39, 144–45.

[21]For a summary of laws and court cases, see Morgan, *Puritan Family,* 78.

[1]Twenty town studies of mean age at marriage yield a normal New England pattern and three regional variations. The norm appeared in the seed towns of Congregational Massachusetts, New Hampshire and Connecticut by the second generation. Variation I in new interior towns combined a near-normal age for men and an early age for women, converging on the regional standard by the 2d or 3d generation. Variation II among Plymouth Separatists, Rhode Island Baptists and Nantucket families was marriage at a slightly earlier age for both sexes. Variation

Another anomaly appeared in the proportion of young people who never married at all. In most societies where age at marriage is advanced, the proportion never marrying tends to be high. This pattern did not appear in New England. Marriage was delayed ten

III among Boston elites and Massachusetts ministers was marriage at an advanced age for males and a near-normal age for females. Mean age at marriage was as follows:

Town	Marriage Cohort	Men	Women	Town	Marriage Cohort	Men	Women
Dedham	1640–90	25.5	22.5	Ipswich	1652–1700	27.2	21.1
(Lockridge)				(Norton)	1701–25	26.5	23.6
Andover	1st gen.	26.8	19.0		1726–50	24.0	23.3
(Greven)	2nd gen.	26.7	22.3				
	3rd gen.	27.1	24.5	Topsfield	1701–25	28.3	23.3
	4th gen.	25.3	23.2	(Norton)	1726–50	27.8	25.3
					1751–75	16.1	24.3
Rowley	1st gen.	26.6	22.0				
(O'Malley)	2nd gen.	26.5	24.1	Boxford	1701–25	26.9	22.8
	3rd gen.	24.5	23.5	(Norton)	1726–50	26.6	23.7
					1751–75	25.5	22.8
Hingham	1641–1700	26.8	22.6				
(Smith)	1701–20	27.8	24.3	Wenham	1701–25	24.8	22.2
	1721–40	26.3	23.3	(Norton)	1726–50	24.0	23.6
	1741–60	25.7	22.5		1751–75	24.7	23.7
Concord	1750–70	25.1	21.1	Sturbridge	1730–59	24.8	19.5
(Harris)	1770–90	26.2	23.9	(Osterud and	1760–79	25.4	21.6
				Fuller)			
Brookline	1710–30	26.6	23.0	Deerfield	1741–79	n.a.	21.1
(Linzner)	1731–50	26.4	23.0	(Temkin-Greene			
				and Swedlund)			
Hampton, N.H.	1655–99	25.7	21.5	Greenfield	1741–79	n.a.	18.5
(Kilbourne)	1700–1719	26.7	23.3	*(Idem)*			
Windsor, Conn.	1640–59	26.7	n.a.	Shelburne	1741–79	n.a.	23.7
(Auwers)	ca.1660–75	25.1	19.8	*(Idem)*			
	ca.1670–85	25.4	20.6				
	ca.1680–95	26.4	21.8	Nantucket	1710–19	23.3	21.6
	ca.1690–1705	26.3	23.0	(Byers)	1720–29	24.0	20.0
					1730–39	24.6	19.3
Plymouth	1st gen.	27.0	20.6		1740–49	22.6	20.0
(Demos)	2nd gen.	26.0	20.2		1750–59	22.7	20.6
	3rd gen.	25.4	21.3		1760–69	23.0	21.7
	4th gen.	24.6	22.3		1770–79	23.6	20.7
Boston elites	1710–20	27.7	22.2	Bristol, R.I.	before 1750	23.9	20.5
(Simmons)				(Demos)	after 1750	24.3	21.1

Sources include Kenneth Lockridge, "The Population of Dedham, Massachusetts, 1636–1676," *ECHR* 19 (1966), 331; Greven, *Four Generations,* 34; Smith, "Population, Family and Society in Hingham," 55; Harris, "Concord," 89; Linzner, "Brookline," 24; Nancy Osterud and John Fulton, "Family Limitation and Age at Marriage: Fertility Decline in Sturbridge, Massachusetts, 1730–1850," *PS* 30 (1976), 481–94; Susan Norton, "Population Growth in Colonial America: A Study of Ipswich, Mass.," *PS* 25 (1971), 445; Patricia O'Malley, "'Beloved Wife' and 'Invei-gled Affections': Marriage Patterns in Early Rowley, Massachusetts," in Robert M. Taylor and Ralph J. Crandall, eds., *Generations and Change* (Macon, Ga., 1986), 181–202; Demos, *A Little Commonwealth,* 193; *idem,* "Families in Colonial Bristol, Rhode Island," *WMQ3* 25 (1968), 55; unpublished data by Lawrence Kilbourne on Hampton, Susan Simmons on Boston elites, Edward Byers and Carol Shuchman on Nantucket.

years beyond puberty but nearly everyone married—94 percent of women, and 98 percent of New England men.[2]

This pattern which seems natural to us today was very different from western Europe in the mid-seventeenth century. In that rigid and rank-bound society, many young men and women were never able to marry at any age. As many as 27 percent of England's adult population reached maturity without marrying.[3]

From the start, things were different in the Puritan colonies. In the town of Rowley, Massachusetts, historian Patricia O'Malley concludes from close research that "almost every child who reached adulthood" in the seventeenth century found a marriage partner. In the first generation, there was only one old bachelor in the town.[4] The marriage imperative was strong in this culture. Women who did not find a partner by the age of thirty were called "thornbacks" in Massachusetts—as they had been in England. Worse, Puritans suspected that failure to marry was a sign of God's ill favor. There was a New England proverb that "women dying maids lead apes in hell."[5]

Behind these demographic patterns was a cultural idea of marriage that was unique to the Puritan colonies. The Church of England had taught that matrimony was a sacred union that must be solemnized by a priest. Anglicans also insisted that after the sacred knot was firmly tied, it could never be "put asunder" by mortal hands. Exceptions were allowed for monarchs and great lords, but for ordinary English men and women there was virtually no possibility of divorce in the seventeenth century.[6]

The Puritans of New England rejected all of these Anglican ideas. They believed that marriage was not a religious ceremony but a civil contract. They required that this covenant must be

---

[2] The proportion of women who remained single among Andover's third generation was 7.4%; among Hingham women before 1700 it was 5.3%. Bachelorhood was less common— below 2.6% in Hingham; Greven, *Four Generations,* 121; Smith, "Population, Family and Society in Hingham," 12.

[3] J. Hajnal, "European Marriage Patterns in Perspective," in D. V. Glass and D. E. C. Eversley, eds., *Population in History* (London, 1965), 101–46; subsequent research has confirmed the Hajnal thesis for Britain; see E. A. Wrigley and R. S. Schofield, *The Population History of England, 1541–1871* (Cambridge, 1981), 160.

[4] O'Malley, "Beloved Wife," 181–201.

[5] Alice Morse Earle, *Customs and Fashions in Old New England* (1893, Rutland, Vt., 1973), 38; *OED,* s.v., "thornback."

[6] George Elliott Howard, *A History of Matrimonial Institutions* (2 vols., Chicago, 1964), I, 364–402. The Anglican position on matrimony was a compromise—complex, inconsistent and unstable; a typical product of the halfway reformation which created the Church of England. Church law declared that marriage was not a true sacrament. But the customs of the church required that it should be solemnized in a sacramental ceremony.

"agreed" or "executed" (not "performed" or "solemnized") before a magistrate, and not a minister. They also insisted that if the terms of the marriage covenant were broken, then the union could be ended by divorce. These attitudes became the basis of regional marriage customs throughout New England. But they were not invented in America, or even in England. William Bradford noted that they were established "according to the laudable custom of the low countries," with which East Anglian Congregationalists were in close communication.[7] They were also briefly introduced in England by Oliver Cromwell's Civil Marriage Act of 1653.[8]

The Puritans required in most cases that both parents and children must give their free consent to marriage. Massachusetts courts fined children for an offense called "self-marriage," which meant marrying without the consent of parents or magistrates. But parents were forbidden to withhold their approval arbitrarily; in some cases, children successfully sued fathers and mothers for refusing permission to marry.[9]

The process of a covenanted marriage began with complex rituals of courtship that were strictly regulated by law and custom. Diaries kept by Samuel Sewall in Massachusetts and Ralph Josselin in East Anglia described these rituals in very much the same way. By and large, Puritan parents did not arrange the marriages of their children. Suitors carefully sought the consent of parents before beginning a courtship, and sent small presents to ease the way. A suitor of Samuel Sewall's daughter Judith sent the mother "a present of oranges and a shattuck [a grapefruit, a rare treat in Boston], and to my daughter Judith a Stone-Ring and a Fan."[10]

---

[7]Bradford, *Of Plymouth Plantation,* 86; Howard, *Matrimonial Institutions,* II, 129.

[8]Alan Macfarlane, *The Family Life of Ralph Josselin* (Cambridge, 1970), 31.

[9]An example was Col. William Dudley's unsuccessful courtship of Samuel Sewall's daughter Judith: "September 26, 1719, Col. Wm. Dudley calls, and after other discourse, asked me [permission] to wait on my daughter Judith home, when 'twas fit for her to come. I answered, It was reported he had applied to her and he said nothing to me . . . his waiting on her might give some Umbrage: I would speak with her first . . . October 13, 1719, Governor Dudley visits me in his Chariot; speaks to me in behalf of Colonel William Dudley, that I would give him leave he might visit my daughter Judith. I said 'twas a weighty matter. I would consider of it &c." On 12 May 1720, Judith married the Reverend William Cooper (*The Diary of Samuel Sewall,* ed. Milton Halsey Thomas (2 vols. New York, 1973), II, 929, 931, 948).

Precisely the same rituals were kept by Puritan families in East Anglia. "Jonathan Woodthorp of our town, a Tanner, asked my consent to come to my daughter Jane and had it, on this ground especially that he was a sober, hopeful man his estate about 500 pounds" (*The Diary of Ralph Josselin, 1616–1683,* ed. Alan Macfarlane (London, 1976), 551; 21 Jan. 1669–70; see also Howard, *Matrimonial Institutions,* II, 202).

[10]Sewall, *Diary,* II, 937, 1 Jan. 1719/20.

Puritan males made awkward suitors. When Samuel Sewall was courting Katherine Brattle Winthrop, she asked him to help her "draw off" her glove. He bluntly refused, and made a clumsy joke that "twas great odds between handling a dead goat and a living lady." This specimen of Puritan *savoir faire* suggests something of the hostility in this culture to the arts of courtship that flourished in cavalier circles.[11]

But in their bluff and awkward way, the Puritans cherished true love, and insisted that it was a prerequisite of a happy marriage.[12] The Puritans used the expression "falling in love." They believed that love should normally precede marriage. Their courtship rituals were designed to promote this order of events. East Anglian Puritan Mary Josselin refused a suitor partly on the ground that he was "not loving," and her father acquiesced, even though he strongly favored the match:

> Mary quitted Mr. Rhea [Rev. Ambrose Rhea, rector of Wakes Colne, Essex]. Her exceptions were his age, being 14 years older, she might be left a widow with children. She checked at his estate being not suitable to her portion . . . [and] he seemed to her not loving. It was no small grief to me, but I could not desire it, when she said it would make both their lives miserable.[13]

Customs of courtship in New England were carefully designed to allow young people privacy enough to discover if they loved one another, at the same time that parents maintained close supervision. This was the purpose of "bundling," a European custom which became widespread in New England. The courting couple were put to bed together, "tarrying" all night with a "bundling board" between them. Sometimes the young woman's legs were bound together in a "bundling stocking" which fitted her body like a glove.[14]

Another regional custom was the "courting stick," a hollow pole six or eight feet long, with an earpiece at one end and a mouthpiece at the other. The courting couple whispered quietly

[11]Sewall, *Diary*, 960 (12 Aug. 1720).

[12]Many historians have followed Edmund Morgan in an uncharacteristic error on this point. Morgan concluded that Puritans believed that love should follow marriage, but not necessarily precede it. This is not correct.

[13]Josselin, *Diary*, 632 (4 June 1681).

[14]Henry R. Stiles, *Bundling: Its Origins, Progress and Decline* (1869, rpt. Mt. Vernon, N.Y., n.d.); Laurel Thatcher Ulrich, *Good Wives: Image and Reality in the Lives of Women in Northern New England, 1650–1750* (New York, 1982), 122–23.

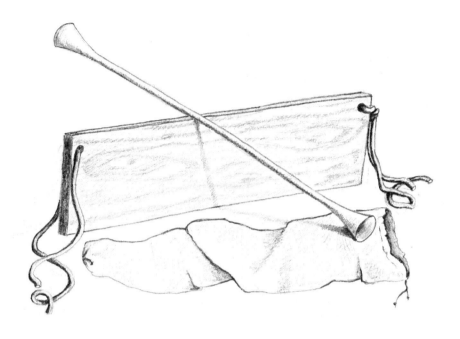

The apparatus of courtship in New England had a double purpose—to combine close supervision by elders with free choice by the young. To that end, New Englanders invented the courting stick, a tube six or eight feet long with an open bell at each end. A New England antiquarian wrote more than a century ago, "in the presence of the entire family, lovers seated formally on either side of the great fireplace carried on this chilly telephonic love-making. One of these batons of propriety still is preserved in Long Meadow, Massachusetts."

Other folk inventions were the bed board, bundling stocking and bundling apron. A courting couple were securely "bundled" together in a bed with a wooden board between them. Sometimes the young woman's legs were securely fastened together in a bundling stocking, or wrapped in a bundling apron which left the upper body exposed. An old New England ballad tells us:

> *But she is modest, also chaste*
> *While only bare from neck to waist,*
> *And he of boasted freedom sings,*
> *Of all above her apron strings.*

to one another through this tube, while members of the family remained in the room nearby.[15]

Bundling boards and courting sticks were not merely pieces of amusing social trivia. These two ingenious folk-inventions were instruments of an important cultural purpose. They were designed to reconcile two requirements of New England courtship—the free consent of the young, and strict supervision by their elders. Both of these elements were thought necessary to a covenanted marriage.

After the courtship was complete, the ritual of the wedding in Massachusetts began with a betrothal ceremony which was called the "precontract" in Plymouth and the "contraction" in the Massachusetts Bay Colony. Cotton Mather explained: "There was maintained a solemnity called a Contraction a little before the consummation of a marriage was allowed of. A Pastor was usually employed and a sermon was preached on this occasion."[16] This custom was also called the "walking out," or the "coming out." It was a great event in a small New England town. The intended bride was commonly invited to choose the text for the minister's sermon with all the care and attention that a young woman in the twentieth century would select her bridesmaids' matching dresses and shoes.

Betrothed couples were also required to post their "banns" (a public announcement) at the meeting house on at least three lecture days. Those who failed to do so risked punishment for "disorderly marriage." If no impediment was found, the wedding was arranged, commonly for a date in November which was the favorite season in Puritan New England.[17]

The wedding was performed at home by a magistrate in a simple civil ceremony. There were no holy vows or wedding rings—which the Puritans disapproved. A single question was addressed to the bride and groom; when they freely answered in the affirmative, the event was over.[18] The couple were required to register their marriage in a civil book kept by the town clerk. Then a small celebration followed—not a great feast, but a modest wedding dinner with bridal cakes and a cup of sack posset. The sober settlers of Massachusetts did not approve of wild wedding parties.

[15]Earle, *Customs and Fashions in Old New England,* 64.

[16]*Ibid.,* 68.

[17]*Mass. Bay Records,* I, 275.

[18]Only after 1686 were ministers allowed to conduct marriages in Massachusetts by order of the Crown; before that date they were forbidden to do so.

The clergy condemned extravagant display as "vain marriage." The most important part of the dinner was the singing of a psalm. Dancing was sternly forbidden; so also were excessive dining and drinking.

On the wedding night, the bride dressed in a special gown, and was put to bed by friends who accompanied the couple into the chamber, and then gave them a joyous charivari with much banging and bell-ringing outside the chamber. This custom was commonly kept throughout Christian Europe—both the "chambering" and the charivari. But the marriage ways of Massachusetts in their totality were a unique amalgam of Puritan ideas and East Anglian practices. As we shall see, they differed in many important ways from other regional folkways in British America.

Divorce customs also differed from other English-speaking cultures. The Puritans recognized many grounds for divorce that were consistent with their conception of marriage. The statutes of Connecticut allowed divorce for adultery, fraudulent contract, wilful desertion and total neglect for three years, and "providential absence" for seven years. Massachusetts granted divorces in the seventeenth century for adultery, desertion, cruelty, and "failure to provide."[19] Physical violence was also recognized as a ground for divorce. Husbands and wives were forbidden to strike one another in Massachusetts; there was no such thing as "moderate correction" in the laws of this colony. The courts often intervened in cases of wife-beating, and sometimes of husband-beating too.[20]

These various grounds for divorce also defined the idea of marriage in Massachusetts. It was to be a close and companionate relationship, a union of love and harmony, an act of sexual fulfillment, and an institution with a firm economic base. All of these requirements were part of the Puritan idea of the marriage convenant, which could be dissolved if any of its major terms were not kept. These Puritan marriage ways were unique to New England in the seventeenth century.

---

[19]Howard, *Matrimonial Institutions*, II, 333.
[20]Nancy F. Cott, "Divorce and the Changing Status of Women in Eighteenth-Century Massachusetts," *WMQ3*, 33 (1976), 586–614.

❧ Massachusetts Gender Ways:
The Puritan Idea of a Covenant Between Unequals

Within Massachusetts marriages, conjugal relations rested upon an assumption of inequality between the sexes. This conventional idea was routinely asserted by men and acknowledged by women—even women of high estate. The New England gentle-woman Anne Bradstreet eloquently expressed this idea in her poetry:

> Let Greeks be Greeks, and women what they are,
> Men have precedency and still excel,
> It is but vain, unjustly to wage war;
> Men can do best, and women know it well;
> Preheminence in each and all is yours,
> Yet grant some small acknowledgement of ours.[1]

A similar attitude was expressed by that spirited Puritan lady Lucy Winthrop Downing, who wrote to her brother John Winthrop, "I am but a wife and therefore it is sufficient for me to follow my husband."[2]

This idea of gender inequality, however, was modified in important ways by the religious faith of the founders. The Puritans deeply believed that women and men were equally capable of joining the church, receiving grace and entering the kingdom of heaven. Further, many women took an active role in the Congregational churches of Massachusetts. Ordination was denied to them; women were not allowed to become ministers in a formal sense, and were explicitly forbidden to preach to men. But Puritan women ministered to others of their sex, and were admitted to church membership more often than their husbands. The Christian ideal of spiritual equality between the sexes was specially powerful in the seventeenth century, when the fires of faith burned so brightly in the Calvinist colonies.[3]

---

[1]Anne Bradstreet, *The Tenth Muse, Lately Sprung Up in America* (London, 1650, rpt. Gainesville, 1965), 4.

[2]Simmons, *Emmanuel Downing*, 43.

[3]On the English side, consult Claire Cross, "He-Goats before She-Flocks: A Note on the Part Played by Women in the Founding of Some Civil War Churches." *Studies in Church History* 8 (1972), 195–202; Keith Thomas, "Women and the Civil War Sects," *PP* 13 (1958), 42–62; E. M. Williams, "Women Preachers in the Civil War," *JMH* 1 (1929), 561–69; R. L. Greaves, "The Ordination Controversy and the Spirit of Reform and Puritan England," *JEH* 21 (1970), 225–

In the culture of New England, these two contrary ideas of equality in "the soul's vocation" and inequality in other spheres were combined in structures of delicate complexity. Puritan minister Samuel Willard wrote on the subject of relations between husbands and wives, ". . . of all the orders which are unequals, these do come nearest to an Equality, and in several respects they stand upon an even ground. These two do make a pair, which infers so far a parity."[4]

The Puritans often quoted the Pauline expression that the husband was "the head of the wife." Sermons and advice-books (all written by men) uniformly urged that a woman was duty-bound to submit to her husband, and counseled obedience and resignation in that respect. Ministers also preached that the husband ruled with God-given authority, and even represented divine sovereignty in the family. This idea was summarized in one of Milton's mighty lines: "He for God only; She for God in Him."[5]

On the other hand, the laws of Massachusetts gave women many protections. Every woman without exception was equally entitled to the physical protection of the law. Her husband could not beat her, or even verbally abuse her—a rule that was sternly enforced. There was also an elastic clause that forbade husbands to command their wives to do anything contrary to the law of God. Further, the common law of New England recognized that women both single and married could own property, and execute contracts.[6]

41; Patricia Higgins, "Women in the Civil War" (thesis, Manchester Univ., 1965); Roger Thompson, *Women in Stuart England and America; A Comparative Study* (London, 1974).

Some American historians have been misled by the exceptional events of the Antinomian Controversy; cf. Lyle Koehler, *A Search for Power: The Weaker Sex in Seventeenth Century New England* (Urbana, Ill., 1980); and the same author's "The Case of the American Jezebels: Anne Hutchinson and Female Agitation during the Years of Antinomian Turmoil, 1636–1640," *WMQ3* 31 (1974), 55–78.

More balanced interpretations appear in Laurel Ulrich, "Vertuous Women Found: New England Ministerial Literature, 1668–1735," *AQ* 28 (1976), 20–40; Margaret Masson, "The Typology of the Female as a Model for the Regenerate . . . ," *Signs* 2 (1976), 304–15; and Lonna Malmsheimer, "Daughters of Zion: New England Roots of American Feminism," *NEQ* 50 (1977), 484–504.

[4]Samuel Willard, *A Complete Body of Divinity* (Boston, 1726), 609–612; quoted in Ulrich, "Vertuous Women Found," 28–30.

[5]Milton, *Paradise Lost*, book IV, line 297.

[6]The courts in all New England colonies frequently recognized the right of married women to hold property independently of their husbands. In 1660, for example, a court in Connecticut recorded an agreement that "Jeremiah Adams did resign all power of disposing the estate (left by Thomas Greenhill to Goodwife Adams) unto his wife's hands to be wholly at her dispose."

Normally, Puritan moralists preached that husbands and wives should not have separate property. They were expected to work together for the common welfare of the family. There was no clear idea of "separate spheres" in this culture. Depositions filed in the court of Essex County, Massachusetts, during the late seventeenth century describe women routinely doing heavy field labor, carrying sacks of grain to the mill, cutting firewood, tending swine, and castrating steers. One minister wrote that a woman "in her husband's absence, is wife and deputy-husband."[7]

A Puritan writer also argued that "tho the Husband be the head of the wife, yet she is the head of the family."[8] Custom as well as law in the Bay Colony required husbands to treat their wives not only with decency, but respect. When a man in Essex County told his spouse that "she was none of his wife, she was but a servant," the neighbors brought a criminal complaint against him, and though the wife herself refused to support the prosecution, he was heavily fined by the court.[9]

Puritan moralists on the family universally routinely agreed that husbands and wives should love one another and live in harmony together. In these beliefs, they were no different from most people in the Western world. But Puritanism was a form of social striving which labored obsessively to close the gap between ideals and actuality. Surviving letters between husbands and wives in Massachusetts commonly described a world in which both partners worked very hard at perfecting their relationship, in a mutual effort to achieve love and harmony within the household.

There was also a darker side of family life. The court records of Massachusetts contained cases of unhappy families in the Bay Colony. But this evidence points two ways. When outward signs of trouble appeared, the entire neighborhood was apt to swing into action; then the churches intervened; and finally the courts.

See J. Hammond Trumbull, ed., *The Public Records of the Colony of Connecticut* (Hartford, 1850), I, 360, 14 March 1660. Of Plymouth Colony, a leading authority writes, "... one finds the Court sustaining certain kinds of contracts involving women on a fairly regular basis." Both prenuptial and postnuptial contracts were enforced for women living with their husbands. See Demos, *A Little Commonwealth,* 85–86; cf. Marylynn Salmon, *Women and the Law of Property in Early America* (Chapel Hill, 1986).

[7] C. Dallett Hemphill, "Women in Court: Sex Role Differentiation in Salem, Massachusetts, 1636–1683," *WMQ3* 39 (1982), 164–75; Thomas Fuller, *The Holy State and Prophane State* (1642), quoted in Ulrich, *Good Wives,* 36.

[8] Morgan, *Puritan Family,* 46–47.

[9] *Ibid.,* 45.

It did not take much of a domestic disturbance to set this social machinery in motion. A sudden quarrel between husband and wife could end in a criminal indictment. The object of these proceedings was not punishment or retribution, but the restoration of good relations within the family. The Puritans had a very low tolerance of domestic discord, and high expectations for peace and harmony.[10]

It is also important to note that these disciplinary proceedings tended to be remarkably even-handed as to the treatment of husbands and wives. A comparative study of adultery in New England and the Chesapeake finds that men and women convicted of this offense commonly received similar punishments in Massachusetts. But in Maryland courts, women were punished much more severely than men.[11]

The Puritans also expected that important family decisions would be taken by the husband and wife together. Agreements for the sending out of children referred to both the husband's and the wife's consent. Business ventures were often undertaken jointly. Men and women were not equals in these relationships, but they were partners in the conduct of their affairs.[12]

Between husbands and wives, the culture of New England sought to create a covenant of unequals which was cemented by a spiritual communion of love, harmony, caring, forbearance and mutual respect. The ideal was captured in an immortal verse of Anne Bradstreet, addressed to her "dear and loving husband." The first lines of her poem are most often quoted, but the last lines are the key to this covenanted relationship:

> If ever two were one, then surely we.
> If ever man were lov'd by wife, then thee;

---

[10]One must be very careful in the use of court records as a source for family history. In Massachusetts, judicial materials have survived in more abundance than other types of evidence, and they also tend to be exceptionally graphic. But to build an interpretation of Puritan families upon that base would be comparable to writing a history of the American family today from record of intervention by the police in family quarrels. Many scholars (including the author) have also used the testimony of court depositions, which are rich sources of information on problems far removed from their nominal subject or theme. But these inferences must also be drawn with caution, for court depositions do not derive from a cross-section of New England's population. Opposite biases exist in prescriptive sources. Accuracy requires a balance between these forms of evidence.

[11]Miriam Hibel, "Adultery in Maryland and Massachusetts" (unpublished paper, Brandeis, 1978.)

[12]Demos, *A Little Commonwealth*, 88.

If ever wife was happy in a man,
Compare with me ye women if you can. . . .

Thy love is such I can no way repay,
The heavens reward thee manifold I pray.
Then while we live, in love let's persever,
That when we live no more, we may live ever.[13]

❧ Massachusetts Sex Ways: Puritan Ideas of Flesh and the Spirit

Sex among the Puritans was very far from being puritanical in the popular sense. Copulation was not a taboo subject in seventeenth-century Massachusetts, as it later became in the nineteenth. It was discussed so openly that the writings of the Puritans required heavy editing before they were thought fit to print even in the mid-twentieth century.[1] But sex in Massachusetts was distinctly puritanical in another meaning. The sexual attitudes and acts of the Bay colonists were closely linked to religious beliefs. Where controlled regional comparisons can be made by a quantitative method, we find that their sexual behavior was distinctly different from the non-Puritan colonies. At the same time, Massachusetts sex ways were remarkably similar to prevailing customs in East Anglia, as distinct from other parts of England.

The Puritans never encouraged sexual asceticism. They did not value chastity in the Roman Catholic sense as highly as other Christians did. The Boston minister Samuel Willard explicitly condemned "the Popist conceit of the excellency of virginity." John Cotton wrote that "women are creatures without which there is no comfortable living for man: it is true of them what to be said of governments, that bad ones are better than none."[2]

Puritans also commonly believed that an intimate sexual bond

[13]Anne Bradstreet, "To My Dear and Loving Husband," in *Seventeenth Century American Poetry*, ed. Harrison T. Meserole (1968, rpt. New York, 1972), 32.

[1]Edmund Morgan, "The Puritans and Sex," *NEQ* 15 (1942), 591–607; counter-arguments appear in M. Zuckerman, "Pilgrims in the Wilderness: Community, Modernity and the Maypole at Merry Mount," *NEQ* 50 (1977), 265; Philip J. Greven, *The Protestant Temperament* (New York, 1977).

[2]Morgan, "Puritans and Sex," 591; Samuel Willard, *A Compleat Body of Divinity* (Boston, 1726), 125, 608–13; John Cotton, *A Meet Help* (Boston, 1699), 14–15.

between husbands and wives was an important and even a necessary part of marriage. Correspondence between Puritan husbands and wives often expressed their love for one another in
strong sensual terms. John Winthrop and his wife Margaret wrote
often in this way: "My dearly beloved wife," he began, ". . . my
heart is at home, and specially with thee my best beloved . . . with
the sweetest kisses and pure embracings of my kindest affection I
rest thine. . . ."[3]

Sexual relations within marriage were protected by the Puritans from the prying eyes of others, and surrounded with as much
privacy as was possible in that culture. A court in New England
indicted a man because "he could not keep from boys and servants, secret passages betwixt him and his wife about the marriage
bed."[4]

Sex outside of marriage, however, was regarded very differently. The Puritans followed the teachings of the Old Testament
in believing that adultery was a sin of the deepest dye. They
defined an adulterous act in the conventional way as extramarital
sex involving a married woman (not necessarily a married man),
but punished both partners with high severity. Their criminal
codes made adultery a capital crime, and at least three people
were actually hanged for it in the Puritan colonies.

When cases of adultery occurred, it was not uncommon for
entire communities to band together and punish the transgressors.[5] In the town of Ipswich, Massachusetts, for example, a married woman named Sarah Roe had an affair with a neighbor
named Joseph Leigh while her mariner-husband was away at sea.
Several townsmen warned them to stop. When they persisted, no
fewer than thirty-five Ipswich neighbors went to court against
them and gave testimony that communicated a deep sense of
moral outrage. In this case, adultery could not be proved according to New England's stringent rules for capital crime, which
required two eye-witnesses to the actual offense. But the erring
couple were found guilty of "unlawful familiarity" and severely
punished. Joseph Leigh was ordered to be heavily whipped and
fined five pounds, and Sarah Roe was sent to the House of Correction for a month, with orders that she was to appear in Ipswich
meetinghouse on lecture day bearing a sign, "For My baudish

---

[3]John Winthrop to Margaret Winthrop, 9 May 1621, *Winthrop Papers,* I, 261–62.
[4]David H. Flaherty, *Privacy in Colonial New England* (Charlottesville, 1972), 80.
[5]For one such case in the town of Newbury, Massachusetts, see Ulrich, *Good Wives,* 89.

Carriage," written in "fair capital letters." In this case as in so many others, the moral code of Puritan Massachusetts was not imposed by a small elite upon an unwilling people; it rose from customs and beliefs that were broadly shared throughout the Puritan colonies.[6]

In cases of fornication the rules were also very strict. For an act of coitus with an unwed woman, the criminal laws of Puritan Massachusetts decreed that a man could be jailed, whipped, fined, disfranchised and forced to marry his partner. Even in betrothed couples, sexual intercourse before marriage was regarded as a pollution which had to be purged before they could take its place in society and—most important—before their children could be baptized. In both courts and churches, the Puritans created an elaborate public ritual by which fornicators were cleansed of their sin, so that they could be speedily admitted to full moral fellowship.

In New England, unlike other parts of British America, men and women were punished in an exceptionally even-handed way for sexual transgressions. Where differences appeared in penalties for fornication, males suffered more severely than females in New England. The custom of the Chesapeake colonies was the reverse.[7]

These rules were obeyed. In Massachusetts during the seventeenth century, rates of prenuptial pregnancy were among the lowest in the Western world. In the towns of Hingham, Sudbury and Concord, the proportion of brides who were pregnant on their wedding day approached zero in the period from 1650 to 1680. This pattern was not universal in New England. Premarital pregnancy was more common in seaports on the social periphery

[6]Amy Buchbinder, "Unlawful Familiarity in Ipswich," (paper, Brandeis, 26 Nov. 1986); the case appears in *Records and Files of the Quarterly Courts of Essex County,* V, 143–46 (1672). There was, however, strong reluctance to impose capital punishment for adultery. In Connecticut, Governor John Winthrop, Jr., refused to approve a death sentence imposed on Hannah Hackleton after she had freely confessed to adultery. The magistrates refused to approve his decision for a year, while Hannah languished in a Connecticut jail. Finally her sentence was commuted to a whipping, and the law was changed so that adultery ceased to be a capital crime in Connecticut. In Massachusetts, nobody was sentenced to death for this offense after 1644, but many were punished by banishment, imprisonment, whippings and fines. See John Murrin, "Trial by Jury in Seventeenth-Century New England," in David D. Hall, John Murrin and Thad Tate, eds., *Saints and Revolutionaries* (New York, 1984), 190–93.

[7]Sheri Keller, "Adultery and Fornication in Massachusetts and Maryland" (paper, Brandeis, 1987); the gender ratio of punishments for fornication changed through time. In the first generation most proceedings were against men. By the end of the 17th century the proportion was nearly even.

of the region and in the pluralist settlements of Rhode Island. Everywhere it tended to increase during the late seventeenth century. But by comparison with other colonies it remained exceptionally low in most parts of New England during the first fifty years of settlement.[8]

Bastardy was also very rare in the Puritan colonies. Few cases occurred in the first generation, and were punished with great rigor. As time passed, rates of illegitimacy tended to rise throughout New England, but always remained lower than in other parts of British America.[9]

This New England pattern, which differed very much from other colonies, was similar to East Anglia in the sixteenth and seventeenth centuries. Historian Peter Laslett and his colleagues find that the eastern counties in general, and the counties of Suf-

---

[8]Rates of prenuptial pregnancy in 9 Massachusetts towns were as follows:

Town	Marriage Cohort	Proportion of First Births Within			
		7 mos.	8 mos.	8.5 mos.	9 mos.
Hingham	pre-1660	0.0	0.0	0.0	0.0
	1661–80	5.0		11.2	11.2
Watertown	pre-1660		11.1		
	1661–80		8.6		
Nantucket	pre-1699		11.1		
	1700–1709		0.0		
Dedham	1661–69	4.8		4.8	4.8
	1671–80	2.8		8.5	11.1
Andover	1655–74				0.0
	1675–99				12.5
Topsfield	1660–79	7.7		7.7	7.7
	1680–99	2.3		4.5	6.8
Salem	1651–70				5.3
	1671–1700				8.2
Boston	1651–55	3.6		6.0	14.3
Ipswich	1651–87	3.8		6.0	8.2

Daniel Scott Smith and M. S. Hindus, "Premarital Pregnancy in America, 1640–1971," *JIH* 5 (1975), 537–70; Daniel Scott Smith, "The Long Cycle in American Illegitimacy and Prenuptial Pregnancy," in Peter Laslett et al., *Bastardy and Its Comparative History* (Cambridge, Mass., 1980), 362–78; Robert V. Wells, "Illegitimacy and Bridal Pregnancy in Colonial America," *ibid.*, 349–61. Rates of prenuptial pregnancy in most parts of England and the Chesapeake colonies were generally much higher in the same period. For another study which also concludes that the ratio of bridal pregnancy in the county of Middlesex, Massachusetts, was "minuscule in comparison with England or the Southern colonies" see Roger Thompson, *Sex in Middlesex: Popular Mores in a Massachusetts County, 1649–1699* (Amherst, 1986), 70.

[9]As late as 1764, the rate of illegitimacy in Middlesex County, Massachusetts, was 7.7 per 1000 live births. This as we shall see was lower even than among Quaker families, and very far below bastardy rates in the Chesapeake colonies, which were ten to twenty times higher. See Robert V. Wells, "Illegitimacy and Bridal Pregnancy in Early America," and Daniel Scott Smith, "The Long Cycle," in Laslett, *Bastardy and Its Comparative History*, 349–61, 362–78.

folk and Norfolk in particular, had the lowest rates of illegitimacy in England.[10]

The sexual discipline of the Puritan colonies was not achieved by Christian asceticism. Relationships between men and women were highly charged with sexual tension in this culture. It was assumed by the courts that if healthy adult men and women were alone together, they would probably be engaged in a sexual relationship. Married men and women were generally forbidden to meet privately with others of the opposite sex, unless related. Unmarried people were carefully watched by the community, and offenders were publicly denounced. When one wayward Puritan attempted to seduce a woman in 1650, she told him, "I will make you a shame to all New England." Undeterred, he forced himself upon her, even though her child lay beside her in the bed. Afterwards, she told him, "Put your finger but a little in the fire [and] you will not be able to endure it, but I must suffer eternally."[11]

Puritan attitudes were almost maniacally hostile to what they regarded as unnatural sex. More than other religious groups, they had a genuine horror of sexual perversion. Masturbation was made a capital crime in the colony of New Haven. Bestiality was punished by death, and that sentence was sometimes executed in circumstances so bizarre as to tell us much about the sex ways of New England. One such case in New Haven involved a one-eyed servant named George Spencer, who had often been on the wrong side of the law, and was suspected of many depravities by his neighbors. When a sow gave birth to a deformed pig which also had one eye, the unfortunate man was accused of bestiality. Under great pressure, he confessed, recanted, confessed again, and recanted once more. The laws of New England made conviction difficult: bestiality was a capital crime and required two wit-

---

[10]Laslett reports the following illegitimacy ratios (that is, bastards as a percent of baptisms) by English region in the period of American colonization:

Region	1581–1640	1661–1720
Eastern Counties	1.2	1.0
Southern Counties	2.1	1.4
Midland Counties	1.6	1.3
West and Northwest	3.6	1.4
Northern Counties	2.9	1.3

Source: Peter Laslett, "Long-term Trends in Bastardy in Britain," in *Family Life and Illicit Love in Earlier Generations* (Cambridge, 1977), 137–42.

[11]Ulrich, *Good Wives*, 99.

nesses for conviction. But so relentless were the magistrates that the deformed piglet was admitted as one witness, and the recanted confession was accepted as another. George Spencer was hanged for bestiality.

That case was not unique in the sexual history of New Haven. When a second deformed pig was born in that troubled town, another unfortunate eccentric was also accused of bestiality by his neighbors. Even though he could not be convicted under the two-witness rule, he was imprisoned longer than anybody else in the history of the colony. When yet a third defective piglet was born with one red eye and what appeared to be a penis growing out of its head, the magistrates compelled everyone in town to view it in hopes of catching the malefactor. The people of New Haven seem to have been perfectly obsessed by fear of unnatural sex. When a dog belonging to Nicholas Bayly was observed trying to copulate with a sow, neighbors urged that it be killed. Mrs. Bayly refused and incautiously made a joke of it, saying of her dog, "if he had not a bitch, he must have something." The magistrates of New Haven were not amused. Merely for making light of bestiality, the Baylys were banished from the town.[12]

Two people were also hanged for bestiality in Massachusetts, and even jests on that subject were punished ferociously in the Bay Colony. Bestiality was also a capital crime in other English jurisdictions, but New England's intensity of concern was something special.[13]

This hostility to unnatural sex had a demographic consequence of high importance. Puritan moralists condemned as unnatural any attempt to prevent conception within marriage. This was not a common attitude in world history. Most primitive cultures have practiced some form of contraception, often with high success. Iroquois squaws made diaphragms of birchbark; African slaves used pessaries of elephant dung to prevent pregnancy. European women employed beeswax disks, cabbage leaves, spermicides of lead, whitewash and tar. During the seventeenth and early eighteenth century, coitus interruptus and the use of sheepgut condoms became widespread in Europe.[14]

But the Puritans would have none of these unnatural practices.

[12]John M. Murrin, "Trial by Jury in Seventeenth-Century New England," in John M. Murrin et al., *Saints and Revolutionaries* (New York, 1983), 177.

[13]Roger Thompson, *Sex in Middlesex: Popular Mores in a Massachusetts County, 1649–1699* (Amherst, 1986), 74.

[14]Norman Himes, *Medical History of Contraception* (Baltimore, 1936).

They found a clear rule in Genesis 38, where Onan "spilled his seed upon the ground" in an effort to prevent conception and the Lord slew him. In Massachusetts, seed-spilling in general was known as the "hideous sin of Onanism." A Puritan could not practice coitus interruptus and keep his faith. Every demographic test of contraception within marriage yields negative results in Puritan Massachusetts.[15] The burden of this taboo rested heavily upon families throughout New England. One minister wrote wearily in his diary, ". . . uxor praegnans est; sic semper uxoribus."[16] Samuel Sewall, at the age of 49, recorded the birth of his fourteenth child, and added a prayer, "It may be my dear wife may now leave off bearing." So she did, but only by reaching the age of menopause.[17]

This general pattern of sexual attitudes—strong encouragement of sexual love and sensual bonds within marriage, strict punishment of fornication and adultery, a maniacal horror of unnatural sex, and rigid taboos against contraception within marriage—was in its totality unique to New England. By and large, this culture was not a system of sexual tyranny and repression. The sex ways of Massachusetts rested upon an intensity of moral and religious purpose which marked so many aspects of this culture.

ᴥ Massachusetts Child-naming Ways: Puritan Onomastics

"The naming of children," writes historian Daniel Scott Smith, "is culturally never a trivial act." This was specially so among the Puritans. One of their ministers declared, ". . . a good name is as a thread tyed about the finger, to make us mindful of the errand we came into the world to do for our master."[1]

---

[15]These tests for contraception within marriage include age-specific intramarital fertility, total marital fertility, the wife's age at last birth, intergenesic intervals, completed family size, and fertility by age at marriage. Family reconstitution studies have been completed by the author and his students and research assistants for the New England towns of Concord, Brookline, Nantucket, Hampton, Windsor, Milford, Waltham and Boston. Other studies have been done elsewhere for Salem, Ipswich, Sturbridge, Dedham, Andover, Rowley, Deerfield and Hingham. All yield firmly negative results for contraception within marriage before 1790, except Nantucket with its large Quaker population, and one cohort in Hingham. The data will appear in volume four, *Deep Change: America's Age of Cultural Revolution.*

[16]J. Potter, "Growth of Population in America, 1700–1860," in Glass and Eversley, eds., *Population in History*, 647.

[17]Sewall, *Diary*, I, 458; 6 Jan. 1701/02.

[1]Many studies of naming in New England have been completed, by different methods but

The Puritan families of Massachusetts named their newborn infants in ways that differed very much from other English-speaking people. The most striking feature of their onomastic customs was their strong taste for biblical names. In seventeenth-century Boston, 90 percent of all first names were taken from the Bible; in Concord, 91 percent; in Hingham, 95 percent. That proportion was nearly twice as great as in non-Puritan colonies.[2]

Few biblical names failed to be bestowed upon one New England baby or another. Some parents cultivated a spirit of scriptural uniqueness. One unfortunate child was named *Mahershalalhasbaz,* the longest name in the bible. Another, the son of Bostonian Samuel Pond, was baptized *Mene Mene Tekel Upharsin* Pond. There is evidence that parents sometimes shut their eyes, opened the good book and pointed to a word at random, with results such as *Notwithstanding* Griswold and *Maybe* Barnes.[3]

But onomastic eccentricities of that sort were rare in New England. A remarkably small number of biblical names accounted for a very large proportion of choices. In the Massachusetts Bay Colony as a whole during the seventeenth century, more than 50 percent of all girls were named *Mary, Elizabeth* or *Sarah.*[4] These biblical namesakes were carefully selected for the moral qualities which they personified. *Mary,* the mother of Jesus, appeared to the Puritans as humble, devoted, thoughtful, sensitive and serious. *Elizabeth* was the faithful wife of Zecharias and mother of John the Baptist. *Sarah* was the wife of Abraham, mother of Isaac and "mother of nations." Also very popular was *Rebecca,* wife of Isaac and mother of two nations, who appears in the Bible with a pitcher perched upon her shoulder. The few female prophets—

with broadly similar results; see George Stewart, "Men's Names in Plymouth and Massachusetts in the Seventeenth Century," *University of California Publications in English* (Berkeley and Los Angeles, 1948); Daniel Scott Smith, "Child-naming Practices, Kinship Ties, and Change in Family Attitudes in Hingham, Massachusetts, 1641 to 1880," *JSH* 19 (1985), 541–66; D. H. Fischer, "Forenames and the Family in New England: An Exercise in Historical Onomastics," *Chronos* I (1981), 76–111, also published in *Generations and Change,* eds. Robert M. Taylor, Jr., and Ralph S. Crandall (Macon, 1986), 215–42; David W. Dumas, "The Naming of Children in New England, 1780–1850," *NEHGR* 132 (1978), 196–210; Donald Lines Jacobus, "Early New England Nomenclature," *NEHGR* 77 (1923), 10–20; John J. Waters, "Naming and Kinship in New England: Guilford Patterns and Usage, 1693–1759," *NEHGR* 138 (1984), 196–210.

    [2]Many published studies yield similar results; see Stewart, "Men's Names in Plymouth and Massachusetts," 118; Smith, "Child-naming Practices," 541–66; Fischer, "Forenames and the Family," 76–111.

    [3]Donald Lines Jacobus, "Early New England Nomenclature," *NEHGR* 77 (1923), 11–12; N. I. Bowditch, *Suffolk Surnames* (London, 1861), 5–27, 473–79.

    [4]George R. Stewart, *American Given Names* (New York, 1979), 15; Fischer, "Forenames and the Family," 82.

Anne, Hannah, Deborah and *Huldah*—were often honored in New England. So was *Abigail,* who bravely defended her husband against a monarch's wrath, and *Rachel* who stood up for her husband even against her own father. Many a daughter of New England was named for *Ruth,* industrious and obedient, who gleaned the field and beat out her gleanings and lay down her head at the foot of her husband Boaz.[5] Most feminine namesakes were firmly anchored in a domestic role. At the same time they were also notable for intellect, courage, integrity and strength of character. The feminist movement has trained us to think disjunctively of these qualities; but in early New England they were one.

For boys, the leading namesake was *John,* the most Christlike of the apostles, the disciple whom Jesus loved for his goodness of spirit. Another favored namesake was *Joseph,* not the father of Jesus but the first Joseph, whom the Puritans specially respected for strength of character. Other favorites were *Samuel* the upright judge, and *Josiah* the just ruler. The names of many great patriarchs and lawgivers were rarely used. Among 1,000 families in Concord, the name *Moses* was uncommon and *Adam* was virtually unknown. Few children were named *Abraham* or *Solomon.* A surprising omission was *Paul,* despite the fact that New England Puritanism lay squarely within the Pauline tradition of Christianity.[6]

Other common Christian names did not appear in Massachusetts. Puritan children were not named *Jesus,* or *Angel* or *Emmanuel* or *Christopher,* all of which were taboo among English Calvinists. A minister explained the reason: "*Emmanuel* is too bold," wrote Thomas Adams. "The name is properly to Christ, and therefore not to be communicated to any creature." Adams also thought it "not fit for Christian humility to call a man *Gabriel* or *Michael,* giving the names of angels to the sons of mortality." The archangels were common namesakes in Anglican families of Virginia, but Puritan parents carefully matched biblical names to their mortal condition in the great chain of being.[7]

With equal care, Puritan parents also chose scriptural names which seemed suitable to their social rank. On New England muster rolls, the name of *Hezekiah* the king of Judah appeared ten

---

[5]The quantitative evidence appears in Fischer, "Forenames and the Family."
[6]*Ibid.*
[7]Thomas Adams, *Meditations upon the Creed* (1629; rpt. London, 1872), III, 213.

times as often for officers as for enlisted men. *Amos,* the name of a simple herdsman, was generally more common among the rank and file.[8]

Onomastic customs of Massachusetts were also unique in another way—the descent of names within the family. Children in Calvinist families were not named after godparents; this was a "Popish" practice which Puritans detested. In Massachusetts, two-thirds of first-born sons and daughters were given the forenames of their parents. This nuclear naming strategy persisted through many generations in Massachusetts. As we shall see, it was very different from other cultures in British America.[9]

Still another onomastic custom in Massachusetts was the use of necronyms. When a child died, its name was usually given to the next-born baby of the same sex. A case in point was the Concord family of Ephraim and Elizabeth Hartwell who married in 1732 and had five children named *Ephraim, Samuel, John, Elizabeth* and *Isaac.* In 1740, the "throat Distemper" came to Concord, and the Hartwells watched helplessly as all their children died within a single month. But the parents survived and nine more children were born; their names were *Elizabeth, Samuel, Abigail, Ephraim, John, Mary, Sarah, Isaac* and *Jonas.* The name of every dead child was used again. The Hartwells were exceptional only in the scale of their suffering. When New England families lost a child, its name was used again in 80 percent of all cases where another baby of the same sex was born. Necronyms were a normal part of New England's naming system and of other cultures in the seventeenth century.[10]

Massachusetts onomastics were the product of what has been called a "Puritan naming revolution," in England during the late sixteenth and early seventeenth century. It is interesting that this revolution took different forms in various parts of England, and that once again it was the East Anglian pattern that came to Massachusetts, rather than naming customs from the south or west or north of England.[11]

---

[8]Stewart, *American Given Names,* 26.

[9]In Hingham, more than two-thirds of first-born male and female children received the same forenames as their parents. The pattern was much the same in Concord. See Smith, "Child-naming Practices," 548; Fischer, "Forenames and the Family," 85–89.

[10]Fischer, "Forenames and the Family," 91.

[11]An Anglican student of Puritan onomastics dates the "Hebrew invasion of font names" from the year 1560, when the Geneva Bible was published in a compact English quarto edition. See Charles W. Bardsley, *Curiosities of Puritan Nomenclature* (London, 1897), 38–108.

A great many English Puritans lived in Sussex, for example, but only about 1 percent of New England's immigrants came from that county. Sussex Puritans made heavy use of hortatory names such as Be-courteous Cole (in the Parish of Pevensey), Safely-on-high Snat (Uckfield), Fight-the-good-fight-of-faith White (Ewhurst), Small-hope Biggs (Rye), Humiliation Scratcher (Westham), Kill-sin Pemble (also Westham), and Mortifie Hicks (Hailsham). A classic example was an unfortunate young woman named ffly fornication Bull, of Hailsham, Sussex, who was made pregnant in the shop of a yeoman improbably called Goodman Woodman. So popular were these hortatory names among Sussex Puritans that in the parish of Warbleton, for example, more than 43 percent of children received them in the period between 1570 and 1600.[12]

In East Anglia, on the other hand, hortatory names were uncommon among Puritan families—less than 4 percent of children were given them. Massachusetts followed the East Anglian rather than the Sussex pattern; its onomastic customs were both religious and regional in their origins.[13]

❧ Massachusetts Child-rearing Ways: Breaking of Will

Puritan conventions of child-naming were closely related to customs of child rearing in New England—a business of high importance in this culture. "Remember . . . the children," Puritan minister John Wilson told his New England congregation, "you came hither for your children." In their concern for the young, the builders of the Bay Colony brought to America a special set of

---

[12]"Examination of ffly fornication Bull of Hailsham Single Woman taken ye 21 of september 1646 who sayeth shee is with childe by Nathaniel Hugget of Hailsham, husbandman—that the said Hugget lay with her a littell before the harvest last in Goodman Woodman's shop of Hailsham, & that he never lay with her but once & that no other person ever lay with her but ye sd Hugget." Sussex Quarter Sessions Records, QR/E/73-91, ESUSRO, Lewes.

[13]The popularity of hortatory names in Sussex was promoted by a minister named Thomas Hely; see Jeremy Goring, *Church and Dissent in Warbleton, c. 1500–1900* (Warbleton and District History group, 1980), ESUSRO; for their vogue among Sussex Puritans see Brian Phillips, "Analyzing Christian Names," *SFH* 6 (1985), 212–16; also Hylda Rawlings, "Note," *Danehill Parish Historical Society Magazine* 2 (1982), 25; L. F. Salzmann, *The History of the Parish of Hailsham* (Lewes, 1901), 49–50; Charles Thomas-Stanford, *Sussex in the Great Civil War*, 24; for their unpopularity in East Anglia and Massachusetts see Smith, "Child-naming Practices," 544; and Fischer, "Forenames and the Family," 81.

child-rearing customs which were shaped by Puritan ideas and East Anglian experiences.[1]

Behind these practices lay an explicit assumption, deeply rooted in Calvinist theology, about the natural depravity of the newborn child. The Puritans believed that in consequence of Adam's sin, all infants were born ignorant and empty of all good things, and that small children were naturally disposed to do evil in the world. This Calvinist dogma appeared in Puritan sermons and child-rearing books, and also in New England autobiographies, which commonly remembered childhood not with the nostalgia of modern memoirs but with persistent feelings of pain and guilt. The same attitude suffused the high literature of New England, as in Anne Bradstreet's poem, "The Four Ages of Man," which makes Childhood speak these words:

> Ah me! conceiv'd in sin, and born in sorrow,
> A nothing, here to day, but gone tomorrow.
> Whose mean beginning, blushing cann't reveal,
> But night and darkness, must with shame conceal. . . .

> With tears into this world I did arrive;
> My mother still did waste, as I did thrive:
> Who yet with love, and all alacrity,
> Spending was willing, to be spent for me.

> With wayward cries, I did disturb her rest;
> Who sought still to appease me, with her breast.
> With weary armes, she danced, and Bye, Bye, sung,
> When wretched I (ungrate) had done the wrong.

> When infancy was passed, my childishness,
> Did act all folly, that it could expresse . . .
> From birth stained, with Adam's sinful fact
> Fron thence I 'gan to sin as soon as act.

> A perverse will, a love to what's forbid:
> A serpent's sting in pleasing face lay hid.
> A lying tongue as soon as it could speak,
> And fifth commandment do daily break.[2]

This dual idea of the depravity of infants and the perversity of their natural will led Puritans to the conclusion that the first and most urgent purpose of child rearing was what they called the

---

[1] John Wilson, *A Seasonable Watchword* (Cambridge, 1677), 8.
[2] Bradstreet, *The Tenth Muse,* 43–45.

"breaking of the will." This was a determined effort to destroy a spirit of autonomy in a small child—a purpose which lay near the center of child rearing in Massachusetts.[3]

The idea of "will-breaking" was not invented in New England. It also appeared among Puritan clergy in the east of England, and among Calvinist writers from the Netherlands to Hungary. One of the classical texts was written by English Puritan John Robinson, a Cambridge scholar who had preached in the East Anglian metropolis of Norwich before moving to the Netherlands where he became minister to the Pilgrims. On the subject of child rearing, he declared:

> Children . . . are a blessing great but dangerous. . . . how great and many are their spiritual dangers, both for nourishing and increasing the corruption which they bring into the world with them. . . . parents must provide carefully . . . that children's wills and willfulness be restrained and repressed. . . . Children should not know, if it could be kept from them, that they have a will of their own, but in their parents' keeping. Neither should these words be heard from them, save by way of consent, "I will," or "I will not." And, [if] will be suffered at first to sway in them in small and lawful things, they will hardly after be restrained in great and ill matters.[4]

This process of will-breaking was achieved in Puritan households by strict and rigorous supervision. Fathers took an active and even a leading part. The Puritan diaries of Samuel Sewall in New England and Ralph Josselin in East Anglia, both described their busy child-rearing roles. The care of infants was mainly in the hands of the mother, but Sewall and Josselin both taught their youngsters to read and write, instructed them in religion, and took sons and daughters on day-trips. They made the major decisions about naming their children, schooling, discipline and the decision to send their children into other homes. Sewall and Josselin helped their children to make the major decisions about work and marriage. A close relationship continued to the end of life.

The Sewall and Josselin diaries suggest that the tone of these relationships was normally warm and affectionate. Both fathers expressed deep concern about the welfare and happiness of their

---

[3]For good general discussions, see Morgan, *Puritan Family*, chaps. 3, 4; Demos, *A Little Commonwealth*, chaps. 6, 9; Greven, *The Protestant Temperament*, chaps. 2, 3.

[4]John Robinson, *New Essays; Or, Observations Divine and Moral* (1628), in *Works*, ed. Robert Ashton (Boston, 1851), I, 246; on Robinson's preaching in Norwich, see Timothy George, *John Robinson and the English Separatist Tradition* (Macon, Ga., 1982), 69–80.

Will-breaking was mainly a form of mental discipline, but when all else failed New England parents did not hesitate to use physical constraints. Restless children were rolled into small squirming human balls with their knees tied firmly beneath their chins, and booted back and forth across the floor by their elders. Other youngsters were dangled by their heels out of windows, or forced to kneel on sharp sticks, or made to sit precariously for long periods on a one-legged stool called the unipod, or compelled to wear a painful cleft stick on the tip of the nose. Partners in juvenile crime were yoked together in miniature versions of an oxbow. Small malefactors were made to wear shame-signs that proclaimed their offenses: "Lying Ananias," or "Bite-Finger-Baby." Large children were caned or whipped; little ones were slapped with ferules, and tiny infants were tapped sharply on the skull with hard ceramic thimbles. Another common punishment was a wooden bit called the whispering stick, firmly set between the teeth and fastened by a cord behind the neck. To the front was added a shame-paper that read, "he whispers." Several of these devices have survived, and are sketched here from old photographs.

children, and wrote of them with love and tenderness. Both subscribed to the Puritan epigram, "better whipped than damned,"
but they disliked corporal punishment and used it only in extreme
circumstances (commonly when a child threatened danger to
itself or others), and much preferred to lead their children by
precept, example, reward and exhortation.[5]

Both of these Puritan fathers, New Englander Samuel Sewall
and East Anglian Ralph Josselin, trained their children to regard
elders with what one English Puritan called "filial awe and reverence," in which love and fear were mixed. Children were
required to stand and bow when their parents approached. They
were forbidden to show that "fondness and familiarity [which]
breeds and causeth contempt and irreverence." This ritual display of deference was another method of curbing the will.[6]

An important part of child-rearing in Massachusetts was the
custom called "sending out." Parents routinely sent away their
youngsters to be raised in other homes, sometimes at the same
time that they took in children of the same age from other families.[7] This folkway often had a practical purpose—to place a child
close to a school, to prepare it for a calling, to remove it from a
pestered place, or to put it in an intact family after the loss of a
parent. At the same time, sending out also had another purpose—a child was thought to learn better manners and behavior
in another home.[8]

Sending out was customary in Puritan families of all ranks—
high and low, rich and poor, urban and rural. The diary of Samuel Sewall recorded the sending out of all his children in much
detail. Sewall's purposes varied. One sickly youngster was put into
the home of a famous healer. Another studious child was sent
away to school. Two girls were dispatched to housewives to learn
sewing and knitting. The eldest son was apprenticed to several
tradesmen in Boston until he found his calling. The children were
consulted in the choice of a home, but they were compelled to
go, often much against their will. Sewall recorded the unhappiness of his daughter Hannah when she was sent away to Salem.

[5]On this subject I have been taught by my students Gail Goldberg, "Puritan Fathers," and
Naomi Levitsky, "Ralph Josselin and Samuel Sewall: Two Puritan Fathers" (unpublished papers,
Brandeis, 26 Nov. 1986).

[6]Thomas Cobbett, *A Fruitfull and Usefull Discourse Touching the Honour Due from Children to
Parents and the Duty of Parents toward Their Children* (London, 1656).

[7]In 1633, Samuel Fuller sent his daughter Mercy into another household at the same time
that he took three other children into his own home. "Abstract of the First Wills in the Probate
Office, Plymouth," *NEHGR* 4 (1850), 33.

[8]Morgan, *Puritan Family*, 77.

When her father carried her away to new home, the thirteen-year-old child wept bitterly, begging not be be abandoned. "Much adoe to pacify my dear my dear daughter, she weeping and pleading to go with me," the father wrote. A similar scene occurred when Samuel Sewall junior was sent to learn a trade in Boston. His father recorded that "Sam was weeping and much discomposed and loth to go." But Sam went.[9]

The age at which Sewall's children were sent away from home varied with the cause. Those who were "put out" for their health tended to go at an exceptionally early age. But most departures occurred near the age of puberty. A twentieth-century scholar observes that "It is surely more than a coincidence that it was exactly at this age that they all left home to be subjected to outside discipline and freed from the incestuous dangers of crowded living." Whether or not this modern reading is correct, there were undoubtedly deeper motives than the rationale itself.

These were not casual arrangements. The terms were settled with great care between households.[10] The custom of sending out was much the same among Puritans in East Anglia and Massachusetts, and very different from child-rearing ways in other regions of British America.[11]

---

[9]Sewall, *Diary*, 12–13 Oct. 1693, 10 Feb. 1696.

[10]Another example appears in the diary of Ebenezer Parkman of Westborough, Mass., 30 miles west of Boston. "Captain [Rowland?] Storey [of Boston] conversed with me about his Sons living with me. His words were these about the Conditions of our Discourse. 'Take the Lad, Sir, till about May, when I expect to return from Sea, but if it please God to prevent me, if you like the boy keep him till he is 15 or 16 years old, when I would have him put to apprentice. All I desire is that you keep him warm, and feed him Suitably. Instruct him [in] Christianity. My main expectation and hope is that you'll give him Education proper to such an one. Let him serve you as he is able, impose not on him those heavy burthens that will either Cripple him or Spoil his Growth. But in all regards I am willing he should Serve you to his Utmost. Upon my Consenting to this he said he has no Hatt. Let him have one of yours, and if it should so happen that he doth not remain with you I'll pay for it.' Upon all I got him a Hatt at my Brothers and took him with Me at the Entrance of the Evening. It was very Cold and for the Sake of the Boy I was forc'd to call in twice by the way to Cambridge." Young John Storey duly entered the Parkman household. Parkman, *Diary*, I, 8, 13 (20 Jan., 6 June 1726).

[11]A comparison of "sending out" in two Puritan households in East Anglia and Massachusetts yields the following result:

The Children of Samuel Sewall, Boston, Mass.

Name	Date Sent Out	Age (yr.month)	Place and Purpose
Samuel Jr.	11.10.1694	16.4	Boston, bound apprentice
Hannah	11.10.1693	13.8	Rowley, learning housewifery
Elizabeth	24.08.1696	14.8	Salem, learning needlework
Joseph	16.08.1703	15.0	Cambridge, attends college
Mary	02.11.1696	5.0	Boston, learning to read and knit
Judith	27.04.1704	2.7	Dedham, "to be healed of her rupture"

❧ Massachusetts Age Ways:
The Puritan Idea of the Elder-Saint

From childhood to the grave, the Puritans of Massachusetts had strong views on every stage of life. This was specially the case in regard to old age, and age-relations in general. On these subjects, the customs of New England were shaped by Puritan beliefs.

In the twentieth century, Americans share an exceptionally strong bias toward youth. We fear the process of aging, and despise old age. Further, our system of social rank is so centered on wealth that other criteria of status such as age operate only when they can be translated into materialist terms. So dominant is our materialistic ranking system today that other customs are not merely unfamiliar; they are inconceivable.[1]

The people of seventeenth-century New England lived in another world. They carefully cultivated an attitude of respect for the old, and ranked people in proportion to their age. "These two qualities go together, the ancient and the honorable," wrote Cotton Mather. "If any man is favored with long life," wrote Increase Mather, "it is God who has lengthened his days."[2]

The moral posture which young people were taught to assume before their elders was unlike that of any other social relation-

---

The Children of Ralph Josselin, Earls Colne, Essex

Name	Date Left	Age (yr.month)	Place and Purpose
Thomas	25.05.1659	15.5	London, bound apprentice
Jane	21.04.1656	10.6	Colchester, education
John	09.01.1667	15.4	London, bound apprentice
Anne	24.06.1668	14.0	London, bound as servant
Mary	02.02.1668	10.0	White Colne, education
Elizabeth	23.04.1674	13.9	Bury St. Edmunds, education
Rebecka	17.05.1677	13.5	London, bound as servant

Sources: Sewall, *Diary;* Alan Macfarlane, *The Family Life of Ralph Josselin, A Seventeenth-Century Clergyman: An Essay in Historical Anthropology* (Cambridge, 1970), 93.

[1] This section combines new materials with those presented in *Growing Old in America* (exp. ed., New York, 1978), 26–77. For subsequent scholarship which has replicated results as to age heaping, life expectancy, the language of age relations, church seating, office holding, retirement, and property holding, see Heather Green Campbell, "A Study of Old Age in Early America, 1607–1820" (thesis, Univ. of Houston, 1986).

[2] Cotton Mather, *A Good Old Age* (Boston, 1726), 4; Increase Mather, *Two Discourses Shewing, I, That the Lord's Ears Are Open to the Prayers of the Righteous, and II, The Dignity and Duty of Aged Servants of the Lord* (Boston, 1716), 52.

ship. It was summarized in a word now lost from common usage: *veneration,* which came from the Latin deponent verb *veneror, venerari,* "to regard with religious awe and reverence." Veneration took on a special meaning among the Puritans, who more than others made a cult of age. The Calvinist doctrine of limited atonement—that Jesus died only for the elect—created a difficult problem. How could election be known?

Old age, in short, was a sign. The Puritans had need of signs. They argued that elderly people had "a peculiar acquaintance with the Lord Jesus." Further, their cosmology taught that everything in the world happened according to God's purpose. They believed that the small numbers of godly men and women who lived to old age were the saving remnant of the race.[3]

Every Puritan moralist who wrote upon this subject agreed that old age was a sign of grace. This belief was powerfully joined to a demographic reality. In Massachusetts, there were not very many older people. The proportion of men and women over sixty-five in that population was not more than 2 percent, compared with more than 12 percent in 1988. This was mainly because rates of fertility were high, and the number of children was relatively large. But mortality also made a difference in another way: the chances of living a biblical span of seventy years were approximately 20 percent at birth, compared with 80 percent today. The odds of reaching the age of seventy were highly unfavorable—in fact, four to one against. This demographic fact deepened a theological perception.[4]

Respect for age was not merely an ideal. It became a living reality in New England. Evidence appears in the assumptions that writers tacitly made about the ways in which people normally behaved in this culture. A case in point was the following passage by New England clergyman Job Orton:

> One is sometimes ready to wish that the aged who have the most wisdom and experience, had most strength; but while we have old heads to contrive and advise, and young hands to work, it comes to much the same. Besides, had the aged the strength of youth, they would be more ready to despise the young than they now are.[5]

[3]Mather, *Two Discourses,* 52.
[4]Fischer, *Growing Old in America,* 275–77.
[5]Job Orton, *Discourses to the Aged* (Salem, Mass., 1801).

Orton assumed in this extraordinary passage that "old heads" *did* effectively control "young hands." Further, he also assumed that the major problem was not that young people would despise their elders, but that elders would despise the young. This evidence is most interesting for the truth that it betrays about Puritan assumptions which were so different from our own.

Evidence of these attitudes also appeared in census tracts and depositions. When people report their ages today they are apt to bend the truth, and make themselves a little younger than they actually are. The result is a tendency called "age-heaping," by people who prefer to be 39 rather than 40; similar distortions are caused by others who claim to be 49, 59, 69 and even 79. In early New England the pattern of age-bias was very different. On balance, people of advanced age tended to make themselves older rather than younger than they actually were—the opposite of the modern bias.[6]

[6]The early New England pattern in age-heaping showed a bias toward youth in early adulthood, and bias toward old age in the later years of life. The transition occurred in the fifties. This differed from age heaping in the 19th and 20th centuries (youth bias throughout), and as we shall see, from other colonial cultures. Three New England samples show the following trends:

Age	Essex County, Mass. Depositions 1636–72 (n = 4106)	Middlesex County, Mass. Depositions 1661–75 (n = 251)	New Haven, Conn. Census 1787 (n = 5085)
29	.793	.617	.798
30	2.716	1.944	1.575
31	.498	.597	.949
39	.503	.166	1.014
40	3.939	2.449	1.557
41	.363	.392	.879
49	.669	.222	.585
50	4.161	4.286	1.934
51	.254	.541	.923
59	.327	.416	.522
60	4.139	6.875	2.456
61	.365	.385	.902
69	.345	n.a.	n.a.
70	3.354	n.a.	n.a.
71	.384	n.a.	n.a.

For any given age cohort these data can be converted into a single age-heaping ratio which measures the relative strength and direction of bias in age-reporting. Where no net bias exists, the ratio is 1.0; that is, the same proportion of people are distorting their ages up and down, toward age and youth. Where a youth bias exists, the age-heaping ratio falls below 1.0; a bias toward old causes the ratio to rise above 1.0.

This attitude of respect for age was also woven into the fabric of New England's institutions. It appeared in the custom of "seating the meeting." Throughout rural Massachusetts, older men and women were given the places of highest "dignity" and the entire population was distributed according to its age. Women of advanced age shared this honor equally with men.[7] Elderly women in general were respectfully addressed as "Gran'mam," and older men were greeted as "Grandsire" throughout this region.[8]

The same attitudes also appeared in patterns of officeholding. The higher the office, the older the incumbent was likely to be. In Plymouth Colony, for example, five out of six governors served into old age: four died in office at advanced ages; the last was seventy-three when Plymouth was annexed by Massachusetts. The same was true of assistants who "rarely left their posts of

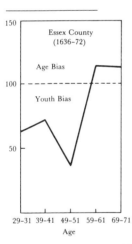

Age	Essex Co. (1636–72)	Middlesex Co. (1661–75)	New Haven (1787)	New England (Mean)	U.S. (1950)
29–31	.63	.97	1.18	.93	.94
39–41	.72	2.36	.87	1.31	.93
49–51	.38	2.43	1.58	1.46	.93
59–61	1.12	.93	1.72	1.26	.92
69–71	1.11	n.a.	n.a.	n.a.	.91

Sources: Carol Shuchman, "Examining Life Expectancies in Seventeenth Century Massachusetts" (Unpub. paper, Brandeis, 1976); unpub. data furnished by John Demos; Fischer, *Growing Old in America*, 85; Ansley J. Coale and Melvin Zelnick, *New Estimates of Fertility and Population in the United States* (Princeton, 1963), 127–28.

When this test was invented by the author as an empirical indicator of age-bias, American historians and social scientists responded with expressions of incomprehension and disbelief; but European historians replicated the test and obtained similar results; see David Herlihy and Christiane Klapisch-Zuber, *Tuscans and Their Families* (New Haven, 1985), 169–81; for sources, methods and equations see Fischer, *Growing Old in America*, 85ff; data for the United States in 1950 are from Ansley J. Coale and Melvin Zelnik, *New Estimates of Fertility and Population in the United States* (Princeton, 1963), 90–138.

[7] Seating committees usually employed three criteria—age, wealth and something else variously called rank or usefulness or office. A study by Robert Gross of Concord's 1774 list found that people were seated first by age, then within age groups by wealth, and finally within wealth groups by status. Procedures varied in detail from one community to another. Some purse-proud trading towns such as New Haven gave wealth priority over age. But in most places, age came first. See Fischer, *Growing Old in America*, 39.

[8] Sarah Knight, "Journal," in Newton D. Mereness, ed., *Travels in the American Colonies* (New York, 1961), 14.

The iconography of old age in New England appears in this portrait of Mistress Anne Pollard of Boston (1621–1725), "Aetatis Suae 100 & 3 Months." This much-venerated lady was born at Saffron Walden (Essex) and emigrated at the age of nine. Long afterward she claimed to be the first female in the Great Migration to land on Boston's shore. Later she married Boston innkeeper William Pollard (ca. 1643), bore him 12 children, and survived to a great age, much revered in New England. When she died in 1725 at the age of 104 she was buried with the body of a great-grandchild cradled in her arms. The two corpses were carried to the grave by six of Boston's elders including diarist Samuel Sewall, who noted that the ages of the bearers "join'd together, made 445."

This icon of Anne Pollard was painted in April 1721. She wears a sad brown dress, white cap and bonnet, a graceful bib and lace cuffs, and holds a small book in her right hand. The artist has elongated her features and made heavy use of light and shadow to bring out the arched brow, long nose and firm chin. There is nothing frail or weak about this old woman. Her image combines the strength, resolve, seriousness, dignity, virtue and gravitas that Puritans expected from elders. This sketch follows a painting in the Massachusetts Historical Society.

their own accord, nor were they often voted out of office by their constituents. Usually their tenure was ended by death, which in some instances was very long delayed."[9]

Yet another sign was the tendency of New England to turn to older people in time of crisis. A classical example was William Goffe (c. 1607–79), a Puritan soldier and "Regicide" who sentenced Charles I to death. After the Restoration, Goffe fled to New England, and found refuge first in New Haven and later in Hadley, Massachusetts, where he lived in hiding, unknown to most people of that frontier town. In 1675, an Indian war began, and the townspeople repaired to their meetinghouse—all but Goffe himself who remained in hiding. As he watched from a window, he saw an Indian war party stealing upon the town. Goffe left his place of concealment and ran to the meetinghouse, where his sudden appearance caused panic among the people:

"I will lead," the old man said. "Follow me!" The people instantly obeyed him. They had an old cannon, but knew not how to use it. Goffe trained it upon the Indians and his first shot crashed against a chimney above their heads, and sent them fleeing through a shower of brick and mortar. He rallied the townsmen, and ordered them in pursuit. When they returned he had vanished as miraculously as he had arrived. Later, it was written that "His venerable form, silvery locks, mysterious appearance and sudden disappearance, with the disposition of the pious in those days to recognize in any strange event a special providence, led the inhabitants to regard their deliverer as an angel, who after fulfilling the purpose of his missions, had rescended to heaven. They very likely never knew who he was."[10]

This episode became a folk legend in New England. It was the basis for Nathaniel Hawthorne's story, "The Grey Champion," in which another old man with venerable appearance and silvery locks appeared as if by miracle to lead New England against Sir Edmund Andros in the Glorious Revolution. There were many "grey champions" in New England's history and more in its collective imagination—Captain Samuel Whittemore who fought at Lexington at the age of 78; Deacon Josiah Haynes led his townsmen to Concord at the age of 80 and Congressman John Quincy Adams who stood as firm as New England granite against the

---

[9]Demos, *A Little Commonwealth,* 174; Fischer, *Growing Old in America,* 46.

[10]John L. Sibley, *Biographical Sketches of Graduates of Harvard College* (Cambridge, 1873), I, 114.

"slave power" at the age of 81. The idea of the "grey champion" became a cliché in New England culture.[11]

John Adams used another New England cliché when he wrote that "none were fit for Legislators and magistrates but 'sad men,' . . . aged men who had been tossed and buffeted by the vicissitudes of Life, forced upon profound reflection by grief and disappointments, and taught to command their passions."[12] In this context, "sad" preserved its old English meaning of "grave, serious, wise, discreet, settled, steadfast and firm"—qualities which the people of New England associated with old age.[13]

When Harvard sought a president in 1672, Richard Saltonstall insisted that old age was a requirement for that office, and youth or even middle age a disqualification. He argued:

> First, Paul the aged, or Paul at the age of 60, or 70 years, is not only as good, but in some respects much better, than Paul not so old by ten or twenty years. Aged persons eminently righteous, by virtue of the promise [in] Psalm the 92:14, shall certainly yield more, better, sweeter and fairer fruit, than they did, or could have done, when they were not so old. . . .
>
> Secondly, the scripture giveth great and weighty caution concerning youth or younger men.[14]

These principles were also incorporated in the institution of Christian eldership, which became a formal part of the New England Way. "Reverend Elders" were the official guardians of religion and morality in the Bay Colony. Difficult questions were specifically referred to them by the General Court. In 1641, for example, the legislature resolved that "it is desired that the elders would make a catechism for the instruction of youth in the grounds of religion."[15]

Respect for age rested upon a solid material base. The system of land-holding in New England was purposely used to maintain a proper attitude of subordination in the young. Puritan elders

[11]Nathaniel Hawthorne, *Twice Told Tales* (Boston, 1851).

[12]John Adams to Jefferson, in *The Adams-Jefferson Letters*, ed. Lester J. Cappon (2 vols., Chapel Hill, 1959), II, 582.

[13]*OED*, s.v. "sad," A2,3,4.

[14]The 92nd Psalm taught that "the righteous shall flourish like the palm tree: he shall grow like a cedar in Lebanon. Those that be planted in the house of the Lord shall flourish in the courts of our God. They shall still bring forth fruit in old age: they shall be fat and flourishing; to shew that the Lord is upright." Richard Saltonstall to the Governor and Council of Massachusetts and to the Overseers of Harvard College, 5 March 1671/2, *Saltonstall Papers*, I, 159.

[15]*Mass. Bay Records*, I, 328.

tended to retain land for an unusually prolonged period. Sons who married at twenty-five or twenty-six sometimes did not receive land of their own until well into their thirties, and continued in a state of dependency upon their aged parents.[16]

This system of age relations also had its underside. Exceptions to the principle of veneration were made for older people who violated the moral precepts of this culture. Many of those who did so were not despised but feared; in Essex County, perhaps as many as one out of four women over the age of forty-five was accused of witchcraft in 1692.[17]

Most elderly people were treated with respect in New England, no matter whether rich or poor, male or female, weak or strong. But sometimes they were not much loved. Veneration was a cold emotion, closer to awe than to affection. The control which elders maintained over the young created strong resentments. "Love rather descends than ascends," wrote John Robinson.[18] A case in point was Timothy Cutler (1684–1765), the rector of Yale College. He was said to be "haughty and overbearing in his manner; and to a stranger, in the pulpit, appeared as a man fraught with pride. He never could win the rising generation, because he found it so difficult to be condescending, nor had he intimates of his own age and flock. But people of every denomination looked upon him with a kind of veneration, and his extensive learning excited esteem and respect where there was nothing to move or hold the affections of the heart."[19]

Within the family, there was also an ambivalence of another sort. One pair of Puritan parents instructed their daughter how to regard her "good Grandmother":

> Deny your self very far to please her. Consider [that] her relation, age, [and] goodness all call for honor and respect from you. Her weakness of body and infirmities of old age call for patience and pity from you. Consider if you should live to be old you may stand in need of the same from others. It is certainly your duty next to pleasing God and your husband.[20]

---

[16]Greven, *Four Generations,* 88–92.

[17]Personal communication from John Murrin; Carol F. Karlsen, *The Devil in the Shape of a Woman* (New York, 1987).

[18]John Robinson, *New Essays, Or Observations Divine and Moral* (London, 1628), 246.

[19]John Eliot, *Biographical Dictionary* (Salem, 1809), 44.

[20]Elizabeth and Nathaniel Saltonstall to Elizabeth (Saltonstall) Denison, 6 Dec. 1688, *Saltonstall Papers,* I, 186.

The idea of "honor and respect, patience and pity" for age was not in itself unique to New England. As we shall discover, it also was very strong in other cultures of British America before 1750. But among the people of the Bay Colony, the Puritan idea of veneration and the Calvinist image of the "elder-saint" gave it a special form and meaning.

❧ Massachusetts Death Ways: The Puritan Idea of Instrumental Fatalism

Ideas of old age were closely linked to attitudes toward death in Massachusetts. The same theological problems which caused Puritans to think of old age as a Calvinist sign also led to a way of thinking about death which had an exceptional intensity even by the macabre standards of their age. "Men fear death," wrote Francis Bacon of his contemporaries, "as children fear to go into the dark; and as that natural fear in children is increased by tales, so is the other."[1]

The Puritans had many tales to tell upon the subject of death and dying. In that process, they created death-fears and also death-hopes of extraordinary power. This was so, notwithstanding the fact that New England proved to be unusually healthy for colonists from northern Europe. The first years were difficult, but the Bay Colony suffered nothing like the "starving time" that afflicted Jamestown and Plymouth. Rates of mortality in New England remained moderately low by comparison with other places.[2]

Even so, the mid-seventeenth century was a very grim period in Europe, Asia and America. This was the only era after the

---

[1]Francis Bacon, *Essays* (1625), "Of Death," quoted in David Stannard, *The Puritan Way of Death* (New York, 1977). Two histories of Puritan death ways argue opposite theses. Stannard stresses the death-fears which were highly developed in this culture; Geddes, *Welcome Joy: Death in Puritan New England* (Ann Arbor, 1981), brings out death-hopes, which were equally intense. Both of these interpretations accurately describe one side of a complex culture, in which hopes and fears were closely intertwined.

[2]The seventeen shiploads of immigrants in the Winthrop fleet suffered much in 1630. Thomas Dudley wrote home that "many were interrupted with sickness and many died weekly, yea almost daily." Altogether, he counted about 200 deaths from April to December 1630, with a crude mortality rate of perhaps 125 per thousand, assuming a population of "1600 English." In Plymouth, the crude death rate was 500 per thousand in the first year; in Virginia, it was near 700 per thousand. See Thomas Dudley to Countess of Lincoln, 12 March 1630, *NHHSC*, 4 (1834), 224–49.

Black Death when the population of the Western world actually declined.[3] New England, fortunate as it may have been in a comparative way, was not exempt from the general suffering. The death rate in Massachusetts was approximately 25 per thousand in the seventeenth century: lower than in western Europe, and much below Virginia. But it was three times higher than in our own time. During the late seventeenth and early eighteenth century, mortality rates tended to rise in Massachusetts, reaching levels above 30 per thousand in the 1730s and 1740s, when epidemic disease ravaged the region.[4]

Throughout this period, the death rate in New England was also highly unstable. As the country became more densely settled, epidemics of smallpox, measles and diphtheria struck with increasing frequency and force.[5] Despite the comparative advantages of their environment, the builders of the Bay Colony shared with most other people in the seventeenth century the same dark foreboding of danger and insecurity. Journals and letters in this period were filled with stories of sudden deaths. "Mr. Creswell, was suddenly seized of an illness, which carried him off in a few minutes," wrote a diarist in 1728. Epidemics struck families and even entire communities with the same appalling force.[6]

The Puritans of Massachusetts shared this feeling of insecurity in an exaggerated degree because of their theology. Their Calvinist faith was one of the most harsh and painful creeds that believing Christians have ever inflicted upon themselves. One New Englander described this dark philosophy as a "bitter pill in a chestnut burr." The fabled "Five Points" of New England's Calvinist orthodoxy insisted that the natural condition of humanity was total depravity, that salvation was beyond mortal striving, that grace was predestined only for a few, that most mortals were condemned to suffer eternal damnation, and no earthly effort could save them.

The people of Massachusetts were trained by their ministers never to be entirely confident of their own salvation. From childhood, they were taught to believe that a sense of certainty about

---

[3]Colin McEvedy and Richard Jones, *Atlas of World Population History* (New York, 1978), 69–71 passim.

[4]These estimates are higher than those of other scholars; they are discussed at greater length in "The Dying Time," forthcoming.

[5]Evidence (from mortality registers privately kept in most Massachusetts towns) will appear in "The Dying Time."

[6]Clegg, *Diary*, I, 35, 22 May 1728.

salvation was one of the surest signs that one was not saved. "This was the constant message of Puritan preachers," writes historian Edmund Morgan, "in order to be sure one must be unsure." This attitude of cultivated insecurity, coming on top of the dangers of life itself, created a brooding darkness that hovered over the collective consciousness of New England for two centuries.[7]

Harriet Beecher Stowe, who lived in the twilight of this culture, understood these feelings very well. "The underlying foundation of life . . . in New England," she wrote, "was one of profound, unutterable, and therefore unuttered, melancholy, which regarded human existence itself as a ghastly risk, and, in the case of the vast majority of human beings, an inconceivable misfortune."[8]

This way of thinking led New Englanders to adopt some of more lugubrious deathlore which human ingenuity has invented. One of these customs was an exceptionally brutal method of preparing the young for death. Puritan parents compelled their youngsters to stare death in the face. Children were forced to read some of the most gruesome verses in the Bible until they dissolved in tears of terror and despair. They were lectured at length about the sudden deaths of other children, which happened to young Samuel Sewall until "he burst out in a bitter cry and said he was afraid he should die." They were dragged screaming and twisting to the edge of an open grave and made to stare into the void and to reflect upon their own mortality. They were also taught always to doubt if they had been elected to grace, and never to feel entirely confident of salvation. Young Elizabeth Sewall repeatedly suffered torments of salvation-angst; at the age of fifteen she came to her father early in the morning and told him that she was "afraid to go to hell, was like Spira, not Elected." All of this left a permanent mark upon Puritan personalities, and set them apart from other Christians in their own time.[9]

Another curious death custom in Puritan New England was an adult ritual which Cotton Mather called "daily dying." This was a set of spiritual calisthenics, designed to warm the Calvinist soul. "A prudent man," wrote Cotton Mather, "will die daily; and this is one thing in our doing too: tis to live daily under the power of

[7]Morgan, *Visible Saints*, 69–70; Simpson, *Puritanism in Old and New England*, 3.
[8]Stowe, *Oldtown Folks*, chap. 29, 1238.
[9]Sewall, *Diary*, 10 Jan. 1689/90, 13 Jan., 22 Feb., 3 May, 12 Nov. 1696.

such impressions, as we shall have upon us, when we come to die." The diaries of individual Puritans tell us that "daily dying" became a living reality in ordinary lives.[10]

Yet a third death custom appeared in the responses of Puritans to the deaths of others. When a relative or friend or child died, the Puritans seized upon their grief, and nourished it, and tried to turn it to a constructive spiritual purpose. An English Puritan who lost his daughter when she was barely twelve, wrote in his diary:

> May I never forget the afflicting stroke
> Remember where I was and what I was doing when she was seized.
> Remember the vows and promises then made.
> Remember her patient suffering of grievous pain.
> Remember her dying looks and parting sigh.
> God grant the impressions made may never wear off.

Puritans never insulated themselves from the pain of death. They drove themselves toward the opposite extreme, and even prayed that their grief would "never wear off."[11]

Yet another custom was a cultivated bleakness of burial practices throughout New England. The Puritans had little interest in the physical remains of the dead. They did not approve of embalming, elaborate funerals, or extravagant tombs. "Burials now among the reformed in England," wrote one unsympathetic observer at the time of the great migration, "are in a manner prophane, in many places the dead being thrown into the ground like dogs, and not a word said."[12] In early New England, corpses were hurried into the ground with little ceremony. Burials often occurred late in the day, very near to sunset. The grave was marked by a simple granite rock, or a rough wooden paling.[13] The funeral itself was a separate occasion—a sermon in which the minister made a point of not exaggerating the virtues of the dead. One New Englander attacked the hypocrisy of those "who in preaching Funeral Sermons, by mis-representing the dead, have dangerously misled the living."

As time passed, burial and funeral customs grew more elaborate. The mourners wore small tokens of remembrance—black

---

[10]Stannard, *Puritan Way of Death*, 77.

[11]Clegg, *Diary*, I, 28 Aug. 1723.

[12]Stannard, *Puritan Way of Death*, 105.

[13]One of these marker-rocks still survives in the original Sudbury burying ground, now part of the town of Wayland, Mass.

scarves, ribbons, cloaks and gloves. The coffin became a piece of fine cabinet work, covered with a pall or shroud. But the people of New England were uncomfortable with this display, and a series of laws repeatedly sought "to retrench the extraordinary expence at Funerals."[14]

Outward displays of grief were generally discouraged. Mourners were expected to maintain an outward appearance of disciplined calm which struck others as cold, callous and emotionless. In fact it was not so. But Massachusetts mourning customs made a striking contrast with the paroxysms of weeping and wailing and self-destruction that occurred in other cultures.

After the funeral, food and drink were served. Then suddenly the restraints were removed on one of the few occasions when New Englanders drank to excess. Entire communities became intoxicated. Even little children went reeling and staggering through the bleak burying grounds. There are descriptions of infants so intoxicated that they slipped into the yawning grave.

Altogether, Puritan death ways encouraged a manic combination of hope and fear about the "dying time" that became a central part of life. These attitudes included a sense of fatalism about the coming of death. In the seventeenth century all the world was fatalistic; but it was not all fatalistic in the same way. Every culture taught that vital events were beyond human control. The Puritans shared this cosmic sense of inexorability. But their uncertainty about the outcome of salvation encouraged a spirit of restless striving for assurance which set the fatalism of Puritan New England apart from other cultures.

This special fatalism of the Puritans was carefully recorded in their diaries and autobiographies. A case in point was the New England minister Thomas Shepard. Every day for him was a spiritual trial with a different verdict. On February 16, 1641, for example, he was convinced that he was saved:

> February 15. I was in prayer, and in the beginning of it that promise came in, Seek me, and you shall live . . . my heart made choice of God alone, and he was a sweet portion to me.

The next day, Shepard's mood suddenly changed.

> February 16. I saw my heart was not prepared to die because I had not studied to wean my heart from the world. . . . Oh Lord, help me . . . a perishing thing.

---

[14]Geddes, *Welcome Joy,* chaps. 5, 6; Stannard, *Puritan Way of Death,* chap. 5.

There were no diary entries for a week. Then, Shepard's spirits lifted:

> February 23. On bed I considered how sweetly the Lord was some-
> times with me, and so how I should preserve that spirit and go
> forward . . .

But that same night he was overtaken by despair:

> February 23. At night after lecture I saw my vileness . . . the Lord
> made me see nothing but shame to belong to me.

A similar rhythm appeared in the thoughts of many Puritans on both sides of the Atlantic. Historian Alan Simpson has described the spiritual career of the English Puritan Thomas Goodwin:

> At six, young Thomas was warned by a servant that, if he did not
> repent of his sins, Hell awaited him. At seven, he had learned to
> weep for them and to look for the signs of grace. At twelve he
> thought he had more grace than anyone else in his village. At thir-
> teen, he went up to Christ's College, Cambridge . . . oscillating
> between hope and despair. For the real experience had not yet
> come. . . . It came to him of course through the medium of a ser-
> mon: the normal means employed by God to hammer the hard-
> ened heart. The text was, "Defer not thy repentence. . . ." Always
> before, when he wept for his sins, he had kept some feeling of
> human merit. Now he knows he has none, that the natural man,
> even when seemingly a good man, is only a beautiful abomination,
> for the natural man has had no merit since Adam's disobedience,
> and Hell is his just destination. Then, in the midst of his horror,
> comes the act of mercy: the voice that says to the dead soul "Arise
> and live." Goodwin compares himself to a traitor whom a king has
> pardoned and then raised to the position of friend and favorite.
> But if the favorite has tremendous privileges, he also has tremen-
> dous duties. His life must be an endless war against the sin which
> dishonors his sovereign. . . .[15]

These feelings were widely shared among the Puritans. Simpson writes, ". . . there is almost no famous Puritan who has not left some account of this experience, even though it is only a few haunted lines written to a cousin in the midst of his travail."[16] These wild swings of hope and despair colored Puritan attitudes toward life and death itself. They created the paradox of a Puri-tan fatalism which quickened the pulse of life itself and became an important part of the "New England Way."

---

[15]Simpson, *Puritanism in Old and New England*, 3–5.
[16]*Ibid.*

❧ Massachusetts Religious Ways:
The Puritan Meeting and Lecture Style

When the builders of the Bay Colony spoke of the "New England Way," what they usually meant was their religion. We have already studied this subject in several of its aspects—its origins in East Anglia, its role in the great migration and its tenets of belief. Here we shall examine the ritual of worship as a religious folkway in Congregational New England.

Many different forms of Christian ritual flourished in British America—the liturgical style of Anglican churches; the evangelical style of Presbyterian field meetings; the communal style of Baptist fellowships; the spiritual style of the Society of Friends. The people of New England adopted still another form of worship which might be called the meeting and lecture style. It was fully developed in Massachusetts by the mid-seventeenth century, and persisted throughout the Puritan colonies for many generations.

This New England Way was distinguished by its exceptional austerity. "Everything was stripped bare," wrote Harriet Beecher Stowe, "all poetic forms, all the draperies and accessories of religious ritual, have been rigidly and unsparingly retrenched." It claimed to be a religion without ritual, but in fact it replaced one set of rituals with another.[1]

Like every other form of worship, the New England Way created its own unique physical setting in the architecture of its Congregational meetinghouse. More than 200 of these buildings were constructed in the Puritan colonies before 1700. They were very different from the white neo-classical picture-postcard churches of a later period. Seventeenth-century meetinghouses tended to be compact squarish buildings, with a steep four-sided roof rising to support a central "turret." They were constructed on the model of secular buildings in East Anglia such as courthouses and markets.[2]

The meetinghouses of New England were often set high on a commanding hilltop. Roxbury's aged minister John Eliot was heard to say as he climbed meetinghouse hill on the arm of a townsman, "This is very like the way to heaven; 'tis uphill. The

---

[1] Stowe, *Oldtown Folks*, 909.

[2] Details of 203 17th-century Congregational meetinghouses in British America before 1701 appear in Marian Card Donnelly, *The New England Meeting Houses of the Seventeenth Century* (Middletown, 1968), 121–30.

Lord by his grace fetch us up."[3] Most meetinghouses faced due south; like so many domestic buildings in New England, they were "sun-line structures," carefully planned so as to be "square with the sun at noon."[4]

From the outside, these buildings made a grim appearance. The walls were rough unpainted clapboards. On them were nailed the bounty-heads of wolves with dark crimson bloodstains below. The doors were covered with tattered scraps of faded paper which told of intended marriages, provincial proclamations, sales of property, and sometimes rude insults in which one disgruntled townsman denounced another.

The interiors were very plain. The Puritan meetinghouse was fundamentally a lecture room, intended for the hearing of the word. Its design was the same as Calvinist meetinghouses throughout western Europe. There was never an altar in Congregational New England; only a simple table which usually stood on the north wall rather than the east as in an Anglican church. Beside the table, a steep stairway or ladder rose to a high tub pulpit which dominated the room. Alice Morse Earle remembered that "the pulpit of one old unpainted church retained . . . as its sole decoration, an enormous, carefully painted, staring eye, a terrible and suggestive illustration to youthful wrong-doers."[5]

Above the pulpit a sounding board leaned ominously outward over the minister's head. In front of him was a lectern and a large wooden hourglass. Beneath the pulpit was the elders' seat, facing outward. The congregation sat before the pulpit, on rows of backless benches, later to be replaced by pews. Men were seated on one side of an aisle and women on the other, all carefully arranged in order of age, wealth and reputation. Most meetings had no ornaments except that terrible staring eye—no paint, no curtains, no plaster, no pictures, no lights—nothing to distract the congregation from the spoken word.

There was no heat in these buildings, partly because the earliest meetinghouses also served as powder magazines, and fires threatened to blow the entire congregation to smithereens. They were bitter cold in winter. Many tales were told of frozen communion bread, frostbitten fingers, baptisms performed with chunks of ice and entire congregations with chattering teeth that sounded like

[3]Alice Morse Earle, *The Sabbath in Puritan New England* (New York, 1891), 5.
[4]Ola Elizabeth Winslow, *Meetinghouse Hill* (New York, 1952), 55.
[5]Earle, *The Sabbath in Puritan New England*, 16.

Meetinghouses in seventeenth-century New England were very different from the later white-painted Greek Revival temples that live in the national memory. The only survivor is Hingham's Old Ship Meeting House, its windows and proportions much altered by passing generations. Early meetinghouses were rude square buildings, with unpainted wooden sides, a hipped roof and sometimes a central spire. They closely followed the conventions of secular buildings such as markets and town halls in East Anglia. Their austerity made a striking contrast with liturgical complexities of Anglican church architecture.

a field of crickets. It was a point of honor for the minister never to shorten a service merely because his audience was frozen. But sometimes the entire congregation would begin to stamp its feet to restore circulation until the biblical rebuke came crashing down upon them: "STAND STILL and consider the wonderous work of God." Later generations built "nooning houses" or "sabbaday houses" near the church where the congregation could thaw out after the morning sermon and prepare for the long afternoon sermon to come. But unheated meetings remained a regional folkway for two hundred years.

The ritual of worship in these buildings had nothing to do with the lights and incense of Anglican devotionalism, or with the spontaneous movements of the spirit among Radical Protestant sects. Puritan worship centered on the Bible, the lecture and the relentless hearing of the word.

On Lord's days and lecture days at nine o'clock in the morning the town was summoned by the sound of a bell, or the rasping cry of a conch shell, or often in the seventeenth century the rattle of a drum. The congregation arrived in orderly family groups, husbands and wives walking side by side, followed by children, servants and dogs. By a law of 1640, the men were required to carry arms to meeting, and sentries were posted at the doors. These precautions were repeated whenever danger threatened. As late as 1775, townsmen within twenty miles of the sea were urged to carry arms to church lest godless British raiding parties surprise them while at worship. After the service, the men left the meeting first—a regional folkway that continued long after its military origins had been forgotten.

After the townsfolk entered the meetinghouse and took their seats, the minister and his family made a grand entrance. In the mid-seventeenth century he usually dressed in a black flowing cape and black skullcap. The entire congregation rose respectfully to its feet until he had climbed into the pulpit. "Our fathers were no man worshippers," wrote Harriet Stowe, "but they regarded the minister as an ambassador from the great Sovereign of the universe." Many Calvinist tracts in the seventeenth century described their clergy in precisely these terms, as ambassadors from Christ.[6]

An important part of every service was a ritual of purification. Members of the congregation who had committed various sins

---

[6]Stowe, *Oldtown Folks,* 940.

were compelled to rise and "take shame upon themselves." Often they wore signs that proclaimed their misdeeds, as in Essex County where Elizabeth Julett was ordered to appear on lecture day with "a paper to be pinned upon her forehead with this inscription in capital letters: A SLANDERER OF MR. ZEROB-ABEL ENDECOTT."[7] Sometimes they dressed in rags and smeared streaks of dirt upon their faces to deepen their humiliation. Occasionally, they were compelled literally to crawl before the congregation.

The major part of the service was the sermon. Church-going New Englanders normally heard two sermons every Sunday—one in the morning and another in the afternoon, each two hours long (or longer). Sometimes a third short sermon was added in the nooning house. It was not uncommon for a congregation to sit through five or six hours of instruction every Sunday. These sermons were very austere. In stained-glass words, as well as stained-glass windows, Puritans saw only an impediment to light. The style of preaching was a relentless cultivation of the plain style. John Cotton set the model. At Cambridge in England he startled his listeners by preaching in a "plain and profitable way, by raising of doctrines, with propounding the reasons and uses of the same." His auditors were so shocked that they "sat down in great discontent, pulling their hats over their eyes, to express their dislike of the sermon."[8] But this was the style that caught on in New England—the "text-and-context" sermon. It began with a powerful and usually puzzling scrap of Scripture which was relentlessly analyzed and ramified in a prolonged discussion called "the finding out." The plain style was carefully cultivated throughout. Of Increase Mather it was said that he "concealed every other art, that he might pursue and practice the art of being intelligible."[9]

A modern reader might imagine that these sermons were very dull and dreary. Popular historians in the twentieth century have painted an image of bored and sleepy congregations nodding in their seats. Nothing could be more mistaken. Puritan listeners sat on the edge of their benches through these long sermons. It was said of Thomas Shepard's church that he "scarce ever preached a sermon, but some or other of his congregation . . . cried out in

---

[7]*Records of the Quarterly Court of Essex County*, 1654.
[8]Mather, *Magnalia Christi Americana*, I, 256; Miller, *New England Mind*, 331.
[9]Miller, *New England Mind*, 358.

agony, 'What shall I do to be saved?'" Many Puritan sermons were an answer to this great question.[10]

Another important part of the service was the prayer, which was nothing like the liturgical rites of the Roman and Anglican churches. In Congregational New England, there was no kneeling or genuflection. In the first generation there was not even a bowing of heads or the closing of eyes. A Puritan prayed on his feet, standing upright and looking God in the eye. These prayers were original compositions, usually delivered by the minister at very great length. Cotton Mather recorded that at his ordination service he "prayed about an hour and a quarter, and preached . . . about an hour and three quarters." Samuel Sewall recorded prayers of several hours' duration. These addresses tended to be closely argued statements of great density, in which Puritans reasoned as relentlessly with their maker as they did with one another.[11]

In the first generation, the ritual of Puritan worship sometimes had another part which was called "the prophesying." This was a moment when members of the congregation other than the minister rose to "expound and apply" passages from the Bible, sometimes with much emotion. Prophesying had long occurred in the more radical Protestant sects, and was permitted for a time in some New England churches. It seems to have been practiced with comparative restraint in Massachusetts, but prophesying was regarded with grave suspicion by ministers and magistrates. After the disorders of the Antinomian crisis, it was suppressed.[12]

At the end of a New England service a psalm was sung, if singing is the word to describe the strange cacophony that rose from a Puritan congregation. Here again, the emphasis was on words rather than music. The psalm would be begun with a line by a member of the congregation. Then each individual "took the run of the tune" without common tempo, pitch or scale. One observer wrote in 1720, ". . . everyone sang as best pleased himself." Another described the effect as a "horrid medley of confused and disorderly noises." Strangers were astounded by the noise, which carried miles across the quiet countryside. But New Englanders were deeply moved by this "rote singing" as it was

[10]George Selem and Bruce C. Woolley, eds., *Thomas Shepard's Confession* (Boston 1981), 13.

[11]*The Diary of Cotton Mather*, ed. Worthington Chauncey Ford (2 vols., 1911, rpt. New York, 1957), I, 98 (13 May 1685).

[12]Morgan, *Visible Saints*, 27, 58–59, 82, 99; Gura, *A Glimpse of Sion's Glory*, 37, 61–62, 73, 97, 111, 162, 242, 286–87, 299.

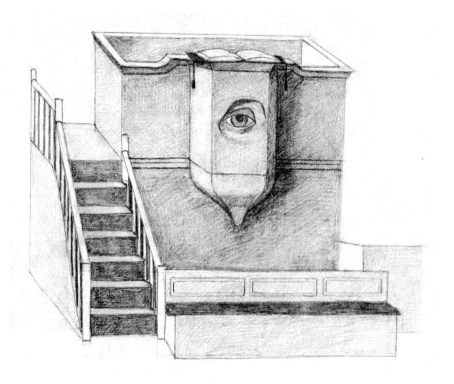

The center of attention in a Calvinist meetinghouse was the pulpit from which the minister preached. New England historian Alice Morse Earle remembered that "the pulpit of one unpainted church retained until the middle of this [nineteenth] century, as its sole decoration, an enormous, carefully painted, staring eye, a terrible and suggestive illustration to youthful wrong-doers of the great all-seeing eye of God." Beneath the pulpit was the elder bench, on which the lay leaders of the church sat facing the congregation, sternly monitoring every move during the long sermons and prayers. Here was a symbol of the Christian watch-care that came to be so highly developed in this culture.

called, and strenuously resisted efforts to improve it. The result was a major controversy in the eighteenth century between what was called "rote singing" and "note singing."[13]

Much later, Harriet Beecher Stowe remembered that "the rude and primitive singing in our old meeting house always excited me powerfully. It brought over me, like a presence, the sense of the infinite and the eternal, the yearning and the fear and the desire of the poor finite being, as if walking on air, with the final words of the psalm floating like an illuminated cloud around me."[14]

Every part of the religious ritual of Congregational New England was thus centered on the word of God—the design of the meetinghouse; the enforcement of Mosaic law; the structure of the sermon; the pattern of Puritan prayer; the form of psalmody. This communal harkening to the word of God was the primary purpose of Puritan worship.

Worship also had another meaning in this culture. Harriet Stowe explained that it was the only moment in the week when the entire town gathered together. "Nobody thought of staying away,—and for that matter, nobody wanted to stay away. . . . our weekly life was simple, monotonous and laborious; and the chance of seeing the whole neighborhood together in their best clothes . . . appealed to the idlest and most unspiritual. . . . the meeting on Sunday united in those days, as nearly as possible, the whole population of a town." She recalled her unhappiness when forced by illness to stay home. "How ghostly and supernatural the stillness of the whole house and village outside the meeting-house used to appear to me, how loudly the clock ticked and the flies buzzed down the window-pane, and how I listened in the breathless stillness to the distant psalm-singing, the solemn tones of the long prayer, and then to the monotone of the sermon, and then again to the closing echoes of the last hymn."[15]

This ritual of worship became a powerful instrument of cultural continuity in New England for two hundred years. Stowe

---

[13]Zoltan Haraszti, *The Enigma of the Bay Psalm Book* (Chicago, 1956), 61–71; Percy A. Scholes, *The Puritans and Music in England and America* (London, 1934); Waldo S. Pratt, *The Music of the Pilgrims* (Boston, 1921); Robert Stevenson, *Protestant Church Music in America* (New York, 1966), 13–31.

[14]Stowe, *Oldtown Folks*, 942; the music of the old New England hymns was very beautiful in a somber way. Most were sung in the minor key. The tune that Puritans called High Dutch was the old Lutheran chorale *Vater unser im Himmelreich* which is a motif in many Bach chorales (BMV 636, 682, 683, 737, 760–62). Westminster was a melody by Orlando Gibbons. York was the Scottish hymn commonly called The Stilt.

[15]*Ibid.*, 927.

remembered that "rude and primitive as our meeting-houses were, this weekly union of all classes in them was a most powerful and efficient mode of civilization. The man and woman cannot utterly sink who on every seventh day is obliged to appear in decent apparel, and to join with all the standing and respectability of the community in a united act of worship."[16]

There was also a deeper sort of union in these rituals, which were an act of cultural communion that joined the past to the present, the living to the dead. Every Sunday, for many generations, the people of Congregational New England returned to the first purposes of their regional culture and reenacted its founding impulse. The persistence of that culture owed much to the power of these religious rituals.

◥ Massachusetts Magic Ways:
The Puritan Obsession with Witchcraft

The Puritan founders of Massachusetts, like most of their Christian contemporaries, lived in a world of wonders. They believed that unicorns lived in the hills beyond the Hudson, that mermaids swam in waters off Cape Ann, and that tritons played in Casco Bay. "There are many stranger things in the world than are to be seen between London and Staines," wrote John Josselyn of supernatural wonders in New England.[1]

In sharing these beliefs, the English Puritans were not very different from others of their generation.[2] But they also carried to New England several forms of magical obsession which, though not unique, were very special in their intensity. One of these beliefs might be called providential magic, for it was closely linked to the Puritans' faith in the all-powerful rule of God's Providence. Even more than most people in their time, they searched constantly for clues to God's purposes in the world. It was this impulse which led so many English Puritans to study nature with

[16]*Ibid.*, 940.

[1]John Josselyn, *An Account of Two Voyages to New-England*, ed. Paul J. Lindholdt (1674, rpt. Hanover, 1988), 20; Edward Eggleston, *The Transit of Civilization from England to America in the Seventeenth Century* (1900, rpt. Boston, 1959), 15; Staines is a suburb of London, now very near to Heathrow Airport.

[2]Writing generally upon the subject of magic in 16th- and 17th-century England, historian Keith Thomas observes that "sometimes they were parasitic upon Christian teaching; sometimes they were in sharp rivalry to it." *Religion and the Decline of Magic* (New York, 1971), ix.

that extraordinary intensity which played a central part in the birth of modern science. It also expressed itself in a continuing obsession with any "wonder" that might possibly be a sign of what they called "God's remarkable Providences in the world," or "remarkables" for short.[3]

Many such wonders presented themselves to the people of New England. Their diaries tell us that heads without bodies would sometimes appear before them. Animals would appear to change their shapes; dishes would suddenly dance upon the table; doors and windows would mysteriously fly open and shut. They heard God and the Devil speak to them through the mouths of children. Dark warnings were detected in the whisper of the wind and the babbling of streams. Heavenly messages of high significance were thought to be written in clouds that scudded across the ever-changing New England sky.[4]

The founders of Massachusetts were not alone in these beliefs. In the seventeenth century, most people searched the world for supernatural signs. But there was a special intensity to Puritan searching. The leaders of the Bay Colony kept meticulous records of signs and portents. The diaries of leading magistrates John Winthrop and Samuel Sewall were much the same in this respect as those of the merchant John Hull, the minister Cotton Mather and the shoemaker John Dane. Elaborate instructions were given for providential record keeping, and hundreds of diaries were compiled in New England, as running records of God's "remark-ables." The great scholars of New England gave close attention to these questions in treatises where history, religion, science and magic all became one.[5]

One example (among many) of this official concern was a church register kept by Roxbury's minister John Eliot. He wrote:

> 1644 A strange providence of God fell out at Boston, where a piece of iron in a dung-cart was smote into the head and brains of the daughter of Jacob Eliot, deacon of the church, and brought

[3]On Puritanism and science see Robert Merton, *Science, Technology and Society in Seventeenth Century England* (New York, 1970); the Merton thesis has stimulated a large controversial literature which is reviewed in *idem, Sociology of Science in Europe* (Carbondale, 1977).

[4]Edward Eggleston, *Transit of Civilization from England to America in the Seventeenth Century*, ed. Arthur M. Schlesinger (1900, Boston, 1959), 1–47; an excellent survey of this subject appears in David D. Hall, "The Mentality of the Supernatural in Seventeenth Century New England," *CSMP* 63 (1964), 239–74.

[5]Increase Mather, *Essay for the Recording of Illustrious Providences* (Boston, 1684), reprinted in *Narratives of the Witchcraft Cases, 1648–1706* (New York, 1914), 9, 12–13. *Idem, Heaven's Alarm to the World* (Boston, 1682); *idem, Kometographia* (Boston, 1684); Johnson, *Wonder-working Providence;* Cotton Mather, *Wonders of the Invisible World* (1692, rpt. London, 1862).

forth some of the brains. And after more of the brains came forth. And yet the Lord cured the child, the brains lying next the skin in that place.

Soon after that one William Curtis of Roxbury was cast off from a cart of logs onto the ground with such violence that his head and one side of his face were bruised, blood gushed out of his ear, his brain was shaken he was senseless diverse days; yet by degrees through God's mercy he recovered his senses, yet his cheek drawn awry and paralytic; but in a quarter of a year he was pretty well recovered to the wonder of all men.

1645 Toward the end of the first month, called March, there happened (by God's providence) a very dreadful fire in Roxbury street. None knoweth how it was kindled, but being a fierce wind it suddenly prevailed . . . in this fire were many strange preservations of God's providence to the neighbors and town; for the wind at first stood to carry the fire to other houses but suddenly turned.[6]

John Eliot had no conception of what we would call an accident. There were no random events in Puritan thinking. Everything was thought to happen for a purpose.

At the same time that the Puritans searched constantly for signs of God's Providence, they also were deeply concerned about other forms of magic that threatened to usurp God's powers. Black magic was sternly suppressed in Massachusetts. Even white magic was regarded as a form of blasphemy. In 1637, for example, Jane Hawkins was punished for selling oil of mandrakes in Boston as a magic potion. Many other magicians and sorcerers were treated in the same fashion.

Most of all, the practice of black magic was regarded with obsessive fear and hatred by Puritans. The biblical injunction weighed more heavily upon them than upon others of their age: "Thou shalt not suffer a witch to live." A great many people were formally accused of witchcraft in New England—at least 344 individuals altogether. Of that number, 35 were actually executed, and another person who refused to testify was pressed to death with heavy stones. These terrible events happened much more frequently in New England than in other colonies. More than 95 percent of all formal accusations and more than 90 percent of executions for witchcraft in British America occurred in the Puritan colonies.[7]

---

[6]John Eliot, "Records of the First Church of Roxbury . . . ," *NEHGR* 33 (1879), 373–74.

[7]In the past twenty years, historians have discovered many more cases of witchcraft than had been previously known. In 1968, Frederick Drake's count of witchcraft cases in the American

In England, every quantitative study has found that recorded cases of witchcraft were most frequent in the eastern counties from which New England was settled. The American historian John Demos concludes, ". . . interestingly, the figures look most nearly equivalent when New England is matched with the [old English] county of Essex alone. Essex was beyond doubt a center of witch-hunting within the mother country; and Essex supplied a disproportionately large complement of settlers for the new colonies across the sea. The linkage is suggestive, to say the least." When weighted by population, the annual frequency of witchcraft indictments in Essex County, England (5.42 indictments per 100,000 population from 1560–1680), was very similar to that in New England (6.69 per 100,000 from 1630 to 1700).[8]

---

colonies from 1647 to 1692 yielded the following result: Connecticut, 42; Massachusetts Bay, 20; New Haven, 6; Maryland, 3; Virginia, 3; New Hampshire, 2; Plymouth, 1; Puritan settlements on Long Island, 1; these 58 accusations ended in 20 executions. Of that total, the Puritan colonies accounted for 90% of accusations and 85% of executions. The executions outside of New England occurred on ships at sea, bound to or sailing from America. Every execution for witchcraft in the colonies themselves from 1647 to 1662 was carried out by the Puritans. From 1663 to 1692, Drake found another 37 accusations and 2 executions, which were also heavily centered in New England. In the great Salem outbreak, there were an additional 141 indictments or formal complaints which further swelled New England's total. See Frederick C. Drake, "Witchcraft in the American Colonies, 1647–1692." *AQ* 20 (1968), 694–726.

Subsequent research by other scholars has uncovered many more cases in the Puritan colonies. John Demos, in a project confined to New England, found 93 complaints filed or indictments for witchcraft from 1620 to 1700, not counting the Salem cases. With the addition of Salem, Demos's count rose to 234 New England indictments or complaints filed, of which 36 ended in execution. An inquiry by Lyle Koehler identified 315 accusations in New England, and yet another other study by Carol Karlsen has identified 344 accusations of witchcraft and 35 executions in New England from 1620 to 1725.

Proceedings for witchcraft were "uncommon in other parts of British America" (John Demos, *Entertaining Satan* (New York, 1982), 12, 401–9). But they were not unknown. For witchcraft in other colonies see Lawrence J. Spagnola, "The Witchcraft Cases of Maryland and Virginia, 1626–1712," (undergraduate thesis, Harvard, 1977); Richard Beale Davis, "The Devil in Virginia in the Seventeenth Century," *VMHB* 65 (1957), 131–49; F. N. Parke, "Witchcraft in Maryland," *MDHM* 31 (1936), 271–98; "Witchcraft in New York," *NYHSC* (1869), 273–76; Tom P. Cross, "Witchcraft in North Carolina," *SP* 16 (1919), 217–87; Lyle Koehler, *A Search for Power: The "Weaker Sex" in Seventeenth Century New England* (Urbana, 1980), 474–91; Carol F. Karlsen, *The Devil in the Shape of a Woman* (New York, 1987), 47.

[8]Demos, *Entertaining Satan,* 12; for other studies which reach a similar result see C. L. Ewen, *Witchcraft and Demonianism* (London, 1933), which tabulated 83 cases, of which the leading areas were: Essex, 7; Suffolk, 6; London, 6; Somerset, 6; Kent, 5, and Yorkshire, 5. The rest were scattered through many counties. The same pattern was found by Wallace Notestein, *A History of Witchcraft in England from 1558 to 1718* (Washington, 1911), appendix C, which tabulated 299 cases of which nearly half came from nine eastern counties. The leading counties were Middlesex, 51; Yorkshire, 32; Norfolk, 21; Northumberland, 19; Kent, 18; Wiltshire, 15; Lancashire, 14; Essex, 14; Somerset, 13; Suffolk, 11. Macfarlane makes a contrary argument, but is contradicted by his own evidence. Keith Thomas, in conversation with the author, urges caution on the ground that judicial records are more abundant for the eastern counties—a problem which also exists in America. But the studies of Ewen and Notestein seem not to be seriously affected by this problem.

Spirit Stones were erected in New England by a people who lived in daily dread of the Devil's work. To keep evil forces at bay, special signs were carved on boundary markers, thresholds and doorposts. Four spirit stones survive today. They were erected on a property later called Witchstone Farm, in Essex County, Massachusetts. The stone shown here is a little more than 50 inches high and bears a crude figure in a posture of defiance, surrounded by various magical signs and charms. These stones have been attributed to Richard Dummer (1598–1679), who led a group of West Country Puritans from Hampshire, Wiltshire and Berkshire to the New England town called Newbury. But the oldest of them bears the date 1636, before he arrived in the colony. The original is now in the Smithsonian Museum.

Here again, we find a striking similarity between East Anglia and Massachusetts. Despite arguments to the contrary by loyal sons of the Puritans in the twentieth century, there is strong and compelling evidence that New England was indeed, in the words of Cotton Mather, "a country . . . extraordinarily alarum'd by the wrath of the Devil." In the mother country, George Gifford described the country of Essex as "one of the worst in England" for witchcraft. Here again, the Puritan colonies resembled the English region from whence they sprang.[9]

❧ Massachusetts Learning Ways:
The Puritan Ethic of Learning

More than most Christians, the founders of Massachusetts were people of the book. Their faith was founded entirely on the Bible. John Cotton wrote that the "scriptures of God do contain a short *upoluposis,* or platform, not only of theology, but also of other sacred sciences . . . ethics, economics, politics, church government, prophesy, academy." In the language of a later age, the Puritans were biblical fundamentalists who believed that every authentic word of Scripture was literal truth, and every command was binding upon them. On even the most mundane social questions, they searched the Scriptures for guidance. In the Massachusetts Bay Colony the standard size of a barrel of beer was set according to a rule in the book of Deuteronomy.[1]

This religious attitude was closely linked to a social fact of some importance. By the standards of the seventeenth century, a very large proportion of adults in the Bay Colony were able to read and write. In 1660, approximately two-thirds of New England men and more than one-third of women were able to sign their wills. By 1760, these rates of "signature-mark" literacy had risen above 84 percent for men and 50 percent for women.[2]

---

[9]Mather, *Wonders of the Invisible World,* 79; George Gifford, *A Dialogue Concerning Witches and Whitchcraftes* (London, 1593).

[1]"Certain Proposals Made by Lord Say, Lord Brooke and Other Persons of Quality . . ." (1636), reprinted in Thomas Hutchinson, *The History of the Colony and Province of Massachusetts Bay* (3 vols. with addenda, Cambridge, 1936), I, 415.

[2]Kenneth Lockridge, *Literacy in Colonial New England: An Inquiry into the Social Context of Literacy in the Early Modern West* (New York, 1974), 13–23. Lockridge, among the first to control for age and wealth, raised the history of literacy to a new level of sophistication. But his raw data are at odds with three other studies by George H. Martin, William Kilpatrick and Clifford

These estimates, it should be understood, refer not to literacy itself, but to the proportion of men and women who were able to sign their names. More people in the seventeenth century could read than write: as many as half of those who could not scrawl their own names may have been able to make out a few words.[3] The signature-mark test was only a rough indicator of literacy. Even so, it shows beyond doubt that literacy was higher in New England than in any other part of British America.[4]

Here we find another similarity between Massachusetts and East Anglia, where rates of literacy were higher than any other part of rural England. This was particularly the case in the county of Suffolk, where during the period of the great migration most people were able to write their own names. Approximately 55 percent could sign their names in that county, compared with 30 percent in England as a whole. The rate of literacy in Suffolk was higher than any rural county in England for which comparable evidence survives (22 counties in all). The next highest literacy rate in rural England was in the neighboring county of Essex.[5]

Within East Anglia, rates of literacy were even higher among that part of the population which moved to Massachusetts. One study in the county of Essex estimated that as many as 85 percent of people with Puritan leanings could sign their names to documents.[6] In economic and social terms, the middling ranks of East

---

Shipton. Kilpatrick found in a study of Suffolk County deeds (1653–56) that 89% of men and 42% of women could sign their names. Clifford Shipton, in another inquiry based on 2,729 names on petitions, addresses and other legal documents, obtained the following result:

Colony	Date	Signing	Marking
Massachusetts	1640–1660	670 (93%)	47 (7%)
Massachusetts	1681–1680	641 (98%)	14 (2%)
Connecticut	1640–1679	442 (94%)	26 (6%)
Connecticut	1680–1700	547 (95%)	28 (5%)

Shipton found remarkably little variance throughout Massachusetts and Connecticut. Signature-mark ratios ranged from a high of 99% in older eastern towns to a low of 90% in new settlements. Significantly lower were signature-mark rates in Plymouth Colony (81% signing). The difference between these estimates and those of Lockridge cannot be accounted for by age, biases of wealth, or name repetition. Lockridge's sample also yields lower raw numbers than another New England sample in W. H. Kilpatrick, *The Dutch Schools of New Netherland* (New York, 1912), 229; see also Samuel E. Morison, *The Puritan Pronaos* (Ithaca, 1936), 83–84.

[3] Lockridge and Morison agree; cf. Morison, *Puritan Pronaos*, 85; and Lockridge, *Literacy in Colonial New England*, 14.

[4] Lockridge, *Literacy in Colonial New England*, chap. 1.

[5] Cressy, *Literacy and the Social Order*, 74–75; see also Lawrence Stone, "Literacy and Education in England," *Past and Present* 42 (1969), 100.

[6] K. E. Wrightson, "The Puritan Reformation of Manners," (thesis, Cambridge Univ., 1973), 121.

Anglian yeomen, tradesmen and skilled artisans who came to
Massachusetts in large numbers were mostly able to write their
names by 1640. So also were most men who lived in the commercial towns of East Anglia.[7]

The zeal for learning and literacy in New England was not
invented in America. The proportion of men and women in the
Bay Colony who could sign their own names was almost exactly
the same as yeomen and their wives in eastern England. This pattern had existed among East Anglian Puritans of middling rank
for at least half a century before the great migration.[8]

The culture of this English region encouraged literacy in many
ways. Its towns, its commercial economy, its connections with the
Netherlands, and especially its predilection for Puritanism, all
created conditions more favorable to literacy than those in other
parts of England.[9]

In New England, this special concern for literacy was expressed
in a unique set of laws and institutions, within a few years of the
great migration. As early as 1642, the Massachusetts Bay Colony
required that all children should be trained to read by their parents or masters. This law was copied by all the Puritan colonies:
Connecticut in 1650, New Haven in 1655 and Plymouth in
1671.[10]

In 1647, this first act was followed by another Massachusetts
statute called the "Old Deluder Law" after its immortal pream-
ble, which began:

> It being one chief project of that old deluder, Satan, to keep men
> from the knowledge of the scriptures, as in former times keeping
> them in an unknown tongue, so in these later times by persuading
> from the use of tongues, that so at least the true sense and mean-
> ing of the Original might be clouded with false glosses of saint-
> seeming deceivers; and that Learning may not be buried in the
> graves of our forefathers in Church and Commonwealth, the Lord
> assisting in our endeavors.[11]

---

[7]Cressy, *Literacy and the Social Order,* 118–41.

[8]David Cressy found that during the period 1580–1640 the proportion of East Anglian men
who were unable to sign their own names was 44% for yeomen. In New England, from 1650 to
1670, a roughly comparable figure for all males was 40%. A much larger proportion of women
were unable to sign their names—90–95% in East Anglia, 70% in New England. Cf. David
Cressy, "Education and Literacy in London and East Anglia, 1580–1700" (thesis, Cambridge
Univ., 1972); Lockridge, *Literacy in Colonial New England,* chaps. 1–3.

[9]Keith Wrightson, *English Society, 1580–1680,* (London, 1982), 186.

[10]The texts of all these statutes appear in Marcus W. Jernegan, *Laboring and Dependent Classes
in Colonial America, 1607–1783* (Chicago, 1931), 87–99.

[11]*The Book of the General Lawes and Libertyes . . .* (Cambridge, Mass., 1660), 47.

The Old Deluder Law compelled every town of fifty families to hire a schoolmaster, and every town of one hundred families to keep a grammar school which offered instruction in Latin and Greek, "the masters thereof being able to instruct youth so far as they may be fitted for the university." This statute did not demand compulsory school attendance. But it did require compulsory maintenance of "public schools," as the Puritans began to call them in the seventeenth century. These laws were enforced. A system of town-supported schools developed rapidly throughout Massachusetts. As a result, children in Massachusetts received more than twice as many years of schooling as did youngsters in Virginia.[12]

The Puritans also actively supported higher learning in New England. Before the War of American Independence they founded four colleges—nearly as many as all other mainland colonies combined. These institutions existed primarily to train ministers and magistrates, but they had a broad base of support. In Massachusetts, every family was asked to contribute a peck of grain each year to the college at Cambridge. A great many did so—twenty-five heads of households in the town of Wenham, twenty-three in Woburn, thirty-three in York, Maine, and forty-two in Concord. Some of these donors were themselves illiterate. Altogether, many hundreds of families throughout New England freely gave this gift of "College Corn," and in the process formed a firm sense of kinship with the institution.[13]

Every cultural region of British America gave some encouragement to formal learning. But New England, as we shall see, was unique in its strong support for both common schools and higher learning. This concern was reinforced by the colonial mood. Historian Samuel Eliot Morison was one of the first to perceive that the Puritans lived in fear of losing their cultural heritage in the New World—a process which one of them called "Criolian degeneracy." In part because of this fear, levels of schooling and school support were consistently higher in New England than in the mother country.[14]

[12]The idea of "public" education appears in Thomas Shepard, *Eye-Salve* (Cambridge, 1673).

[13]Margery Somers Foster, *"Out of Small Beginnings . . ." An Economic History of Harvard College in the Puritan Period* (Cambridge, 1962), 88; Morison, *The Founding of Harvard College;* and *Harvard College in the Seventeenth Century* (2 vols., Cambridge, 1936).

[14]Morison quoted Cotton Mather's complaint against "the too general want of Education in the Rising Generation; which, if not prevented, will gradually dispose us, to a sort of Criolian degeneracy"; Cotton Mather, *The Way to Prosperity* (Boston, 1690), 33–34; quoted in Morison, *Puritan Pronaos,* 75.

One consequence of New England's support of learning was an exceptionally high level of intellectual achievement in this region: by far the highest in British America. During the late nineteenth century, Henry Cabot Lodge did a study of intellectual distinction by region in the United States. Lodge, of course, had an ethnic axe to grind, but the quantitative result of his inquiries had a truth value independent of the motives that inspired them. He found that by most empirical tests of intellectual eminence, New England led all other parts of British America from the seventeenth to the early twentieth century.[15]

At about the same time that Lodge did this research, the English scholar Havelock Ellis made a study of intellectual achievement in his own country, and also found strong differences between regions. The eastern counties of England and East Anglia most of all accounted for a much larger proportion of literary, scientific and intellectual achievement than any other part of England. Here was yet another striking parallel between the two kindred cultures of East Anglia and New England through many generations.[16]

❧ Massachusetts Food Ways:
Origins of New England's "Canonical Dish"

The culture of New England was both a moral and a material order. It defined not only what people thought and felt, but also what they owned and even ate. A case in point was this region's food ways, which emerged as the combined product of Puritan ideals, East Anglian tastes and American conditions.

The founders of Massachusetts introduced a characteristic attitude toward food which combined Puritan ideals and English tastes. The leading historian of this subject finds a strong culinary conservatism in the first generation. "Seventeenth century New

---

[15]Henry Cabot Lodge, "The Distribution of Ability in the United States," in *Historical and Political Essays* (Cambridge, 1892), 138–68; Lodge quantified *Appleton's Cyclopaedia of American Biography*. Half a century later, similar inquiries were made by southern scholars, who quantified the *Dictionary of American Biography* with the same result. Cf. Rupert Vance, "The Geography of Distinction: The Nation and Its Regions, 1790–1927," *SF* 18 (1939), 168–79; Dumas Malone, "The Geography of American Achievement," *AM* 154 (1934), 666–79.

[16]Havelock Ellis, *A Study of British Genius* (rev. ed., Boston, 1926). Ellis quantified the *Dictionary of National Biography*.

England," writes Sarah McMahon, "was intent on maintaining the traditional English fare."[1]

New England's food ways also owed much to the Christian asceticism of its founders, who were among the earliest Americans to associate plain cooking with piety, and vegetables with virtue. "Let no man make a jest at pumpkins," wrote Edward Johnson, "for with this fruit the Lord was pleased to feed his people."[2]

The private diaries of the Puritans commonly expressed a settled hostility to sensual indulgence at table. John Winthrop, after a trip to London, scourged himself for overeating:

> I grew drowsy and dull in every good duty; it made me marvel at myself when I remembered my former alacrity; I prayed and I wept, yet still I grew more discouraged. God being merciful unto me, hereby to revive me, at length I fell to prayer and fasting, whereto the flesh was as unwilling as the bear at the stake, yet it pleased God that hereby I recovered life and comfort, and then I found plainly that not keeping a strict watch over my appetite, but feeding more liberally than was meet . . . the flesh waxed wanton, and would no longer wear the yoke, but began to grow jolly and slothful. . . .
>
> I find by oft and repeated experience, that when I hold under the flesh by temperate diet, and not suffering the mind or outward senses to have everything that they desire, and wean it from the love of the world, I ever then pray without weariness, or ordinary wandering of heart, and am far more fit and cheerful in the duties of my calling.[3]

This passage revealed many things about John Winthrop's attitudes toward food. He thought of eating as "feeding," fasting as a form of "revival," appetite as "a bear at the stake," and the "outward senses" as a source of spiritual danger. These attitudes comprised a gastronomic Puritanism which persisted in New England long after the Five Points had been forgotten.

The Puritans of Massachusetts created one of the more austere food ways in the Western world. For three centuries, New England families gave thanks to their Calvinist God for cold

[1]Sarah McMahon, "A Comfortable Subsistence," *WMQ3* 42 (1985), 26–65, which draws from her thesis, "A Comfortable Subsistence: A History of Diet in New England, 1630–1850" (Brandeis, 1982); see also Jay Allan Andrews, "A Solid Sufficiency; An Ethnohistory of Yeoman Foodways in Stuart England" (thesis, Univ. of Pennsylvania, 1971).

[2]Johnson, *Wonder-working Providence*, 85.

[3]John Winthrop, "Experiencia," 1616, *Winthrop Papers*, I, 197.

baked beans and stale brown bread, while lobsters abounded in the waters of Massachusetts Bay and succulent gamebirds orbited slowly overhead. Rarely does history supply so strong a proof of the power of faith.

An important staple of this diet was "pease porridge," which gradually developed into what Lucy Larcom called "the canonical dish of our Forefathers": New England baked beans. Field peas were among the first crops introduced to Massachusetts. As early as the summer of 1629, one colonist reported that "the governor hath store of green pease growing in his garden as good as ever I eat in England."[4]

Peas were boiled or baked, and eaten hot or cold three times a day. Sarah McMahon found that "the winter vegetable supply in seventeenth-century households consisted almost entirely of dried peas. . . . Pease porridge was traditional cold-weather fare for New Englanders of all classes." In the eighteenth century, "pease" yielded to "pea beans" (a change more of nomenclature than of the crops themselves). But in its fundamentals, New England's canonical dish remained the same for three centuries.[5]

Another staple of New England diet was rough brown bread, which the first generation made from a coarse mix of wheat flour and cornmeal. After a disease called wheat rust became a major problem in the 1660s, this mixture was replaced by rye flour and cornmeal—the immortal "rye n' injun" which nourished New Englanders for many generations. This combination produced a crust so hard that it could be used in place of a spoon to scoop up the beans. Wheat flour alone was reserved for special occasions, and ornamental uses such as the top layer of pies—hence the New-England folk expression, "upper crust."

Another favorite dish was the New England boiled dinner: meat and vegetables submerged in plain water and boiled relentlessly without seasonings of any kind. This was not a common cooking method in other parts of Anglo-America. During the early nineteenth century, a Yankee girl who found herself living among southerners wrote with some astonishment: "They think that a boiled dish as we boil it is not fit to eat; it is true they boil

---

[4]Francis Higginson, *New-Englands Plantation* (London, 1630); Young, *Chronicles of the First Planters,* 246.

[5]Sarah McMahon's findings are drawn from a painstaking analysis of food stocks in 1,215 inventories of estates throughout Middlesex County, Massachusetts, from 1653 to 1835. Some of her many findings appear in "A Comfortable Subsistence," 26–65.

their food, but each separate. It won't do to boil cabbage or turnips or beets, carrots and parsnips with their meat."[6]

The common table beverage in Massachusetts was dark English
beer during the seventeenth century, and fermented apple cider
in the eighteenth. There were also fruits and vegetables in season.
But the staples remained much the same throughout the year.
Sarah McMahon concludes that "old practices were adjusted to
new conditions to produce adequate supplies of the traditional
staples without fundamentally changing the diet through the
whole first century."[7]

Yankee food ways provided a healthy diet which was unusually
rich in protein, strong in fiber, abundant in its carbohydrates,
restrained in its animal fats and balanced in most nutrients except
vitamins C and D in winter. The celebrated longevity of New
England natives owed something to their eating habits, as well as
to the life-giving climate.

But in aesthetic terms, New England's cuisine was extraordinarily impoverished, particularly by contrast with the cornucopia
of culinary riches in the region. The coastal waters of New
England teemed with mussels, oysters, lobsters and clams. The
rivers were choked with salmon and shad. Wild fowl flourished in
abundance. Native delicacies such as glasswort sprouted along
the seashore and fiddleheads carpeted the woodlands.

The Puritans showed little interest in these delights except
when driven by hunger to consume them. Shellfish was regarded
with grave suspicion. Shad roe, a gourmet's delight, was used as
fertilizer. In the first year, John Winthrop complained when he
was compelled to eat oysters and wild duck instead of the staples
of old England. "My dear wife," he wrote, "we are here in a paradise, though we have not beef and mutton."[8]

The sense of sameness in New England food ways was deepened by its dining habits. On Yankee tables, every dish arrived at
the same time "all piled together . . . without regard to French
doctrine of courses." Cooking and eating were all of a piece
among these straight-forward folk.[9]

New England's food ways derived not only from the religion of
its founders, but also from their region of origin in the mother

[6]John Mack Faragher, *Sugar Creek* (New Haven, 1986), 46.
[7]McMahon, "A Comfortable Subsistence," 45.
[8]John Winthrop to his wife, 29 Nov. 1630, *Winthrop Papers,* II, 320.
[9]Stowe, *Oldtown Folks,* 1218.

country. Modern studies have discovered that methods of cooking differ even today from one British region to another. The
most detailed inquiry finds three distant culinary regimes of food
preparation, marked by a special taste for frying in the south and
west, for boiling in the north, and for baking in East Anglia. All
methods of cooking, of course, exist in every region. But the balance is distinctly different from one part of England to another—
so much so that even in the twentieth century British merchants
vary their inventories of kitchen equipment according to region.[10]

The East Anglian taste for baking became an important part of
culinary customs in New England, and leavened the general austerity of its regional diet. Harriet Beecher Stowe remembered
that the "old brick oven was a true Puritan institution, and
backed up the devotional habits of good housewives, by the capital care which he took of whatever was committed to his capa-
cious bosom."[11] These brick ovens were amongst the first structures built in Massachusetts.[12] Housewives too poor to own them
used baking kettles and primitive reflector ovens.

New England baking took many forms. The ritual Thanksgiving
dinner came mainly from the oven—baked Turkey, baked
squash, baked beans, baked bread and baked pies in vast profusion. The pie, in particular, became a Yankee folk art. Harriet
Beecher Stowe in her novel *Oldtown Folks* celebrated the social
history of the New England pie:

> The pie is an English institution, which, planted on American soil,
> forthwith ran rampant and burst forth into an untold variety of
> genera and species. Not merely the old mince pie, but a thousand
> strictly American seedlings from that main stock, evinced the
> power of American housewives to adapt old institutions to new
> uses. Pumpkin pies, cranberry pies, huckleberry pies, cherry pies,
> green-currant pies, peach, pear, and plum pies, custard pies, apple
> pies, Marlborough-pudding pies,—pies with top crusts, and pies
> without,—pies adorned with all sorts of fanciful flutings and
> architectural strips laid across and around, and otherwise varied,
> attested the boundless fertility of the feminine mind, when once
> let loose in a given direction.

The oven became New England's cornucopia. As it poured forth
its profusion of cakes and pies, it became a living presence in a

---

[10]David Ellerton Allen, *British Tastes: An Inquiry into the Likes and Dislikes of the Regional Consumer* (London, 1968).

[11]Stowe, *Oldtown Folks*, 1216.

[12]Johnson, *Wonder-working Providence*, 77.

New England household. Mrs. Stowe waxed romantic about her oven:

> In the corner of the great kitchen, during all these days, the jolly old oven roared and crackled in great volcanic billows of flame, snapping and gurgling as if the old fellow entered with joyful sympathy into the frolic of the hour; and then, his great heart being once warmed up, he brooded over successive generations of pies and cakes, which went in raw and came out cooked, till butteries and dressers and shelves and pantries were literally crowded with jostling abundance.

So vast was the production of Mrs. Stowe's oven that her Natick parsonage had a special "pie-room" where frozen baked goods were kept through cold New England winters. She remembered:

> a great cold northern chamber, where the sun never shone, and where in winter the snow sifted in at the window-cracks, and ice and frost reigned with undisputed sway, was fitted up to be the storehouse of these surplus treasures. There, frozen solid, and thus well preserved in their icy fetters, they formed a great repository for all the winter months; and the pies baked at Thanksgiving often came out fresh and good with the violets of April.[13]

The austerity of New England's food ways was softened by its abundance of baked goods. Even so, this culture made a virtue of sensual restraint. For a very long time it preserved a spirit of self-denial which was appropriate to a region that Samuel Adams described as a "Christian Sparta." Even in the nineteenth century, the austerity of New England food ways appeared in the image of Brother Jonathan who stares out at us from his earliest photographs with gaunt body, sallow skin, hollow cheeks, burning eyes and shrunken mouth. To his distrusting cousins, the stereotypical Yankee had a lean and hungry look.

❧ Massachusetts Dress Ways: The Puritan Taste for Simple Clothes and "Sadd" Colors

The typical New England Jonathan—and Abigail as well—were also known by their habits of dress. The founders of Massachusetts had strong views on this subject. For them, clothing was not a matter of cultural indifference. By and large, they believed that

---

[13]Stowe, *Oldtown Folks*, 1211–12.

costume should not be a form of sensual display. This did not mean that the Puritans wore the black suits and gray dresses of historical legend. With a few exceptions, they avoided black—not because it was too plain for their tastes, but because it was not plain enough. Even this strong color was thought to be pretentious in the general population. It was reserved for ruling elders and the governing elite.[1]

The Bay people cultivated a style of dress which drew its inspiration from the customary folk costume of East Anglia in the seventeenth century. The taste of New England ran not to black or gray, but to "sadd colors" as they were called in the seventeenth century. A list of these "sadd colors" in 1638 included "liver color, de Boys, tawney, russet, purple, French green, ginger lyne, deer colour, orange." Other sad colors were called "gridolin" from the French *gris de lin* ("flax blossom"). Still others were called puce, folding color, Kendall green, Lincoln green, barry, milly and tuly.

Specially favored was russet, and a color called philly mort from the French *feuille morte* ("dead leaf"). One country gentleman from the east of England, Oliver Cromwell, made these "sad colors" into a badge of virtue when he celebrated his "plain russet-coated captain that knows what he fights for and loves what he knows."

Sad colors were brought in Massachusetts in the first years of settlement, and their popularity has persisted even to our own time. In a region where nature adorns herself each year in flaming red and orange and yellow, the plain folk of Massachusetts dressed in shades of *feuille morte*.

New England dress ways were also special in the cut of clothing. The Massachusetts Bay Company specified an outfit for men of ordinary rank which included:

4 pair shoes
2 pair Irish stockings

---

[1]There are two historical myths about Puritan costume. One is the image of the black-coated, steeple-hatted, round-headed killjoy. The second myth, a reaction to the first, was set in motion by Samuel Eliot Morison, who wrote that "on great occasions your Puritan might be gaudy. Governor Bradford left a red waistcoat with silver buttons, a colored hat, a violet cloak and a Turkey-red grogram suit" (S. E. Morison, *Builders of the Bay Colony* (Boston, 1930), 140). Other scholars have discovered bright colors in inventories of estates, and some have incautiously concluded that Puritan austerity was largely a fiction. Both myth and countermyth are very much mistaken, as Morison himself knew very well, but others have forgotten. Morison noted that Puritan costume was distinguished by "comparative plainness." It is necessary to find a mediating position.

1 pair knit stockings
1 pair Norwich garters
4 shirts
2 suits of doublet and hose, of leather, lined with oil skin leather, the hose and doublet with hooks and eyes.
1 suit of Hampshire kerseys; the hose lined with skins, the doublet with linen
3 plain falling bands
1 waistcoat of green cotton bound with red tape
1 leather girdle
1 Monmouth cap
1 black hat lined at the brim with leather
5 red knot caps
2 dozen hooks and eyes
1 pair of leather gloves, calfskin or sheepskin[2]

This outfit included the legendary black felt steeple hat, but was otherwise very different from the stereotypical image of the Puritan. It was a remarkably full wardrobe, much superior in quality and cost to the clothing that most Englishmen wore in 1630. The common costume of English laborers and cottagers ran to cheaper fabrics such as frieze, tow and canvas, rather than to these materials.

Leaders and elders in the Bay Colony dressed differently from ordinary people. For godly men and women of "good age" or high rank, black was thought to be suitable. A surviving portrait (ca. 1629) of John Winthrop shows him in a suit of black velvet with slashed sleeves, a starched neck ruff and delicate lace cuffs. In his hand he carried gossamer gloves so thin as to be transparent. Their fragility was meant to show that their wearer did not have to work with his hands. John Winthrop's costume differed in its restraint from the opulent display of Stuart courtiers and Virginia cavaliers, but it was unmistakably the dress of a gentleman.

To discourage excessive display, the Bay Colony passed strict sumptuary laws. Statutes of this sort existed in most American colonies and European states. But the earliest Massachusetts sumptuary laws were very different—they applied not merely to the common people, but to "ordinary wearing" by everyone. One such statute in 1634 forbade men and women of every rank to wear "new fashions, or long hair, or anything of the like nature."

---

[2]*Mass. Bay Records*, I, 23–24.

Steeple hats and "sadd colors" were typical of Puritan dress ways. Both men and women in New England did actually wear the broad-brimmed steeple hats of legend, historical revisionists notwithstanding. One such hat survives today in Pilgrim Hall, Plymouth. It belonged to Constance Hopkins, who arrived in the Mayflower. *Most steeple hats were made of wool felt. In Britain the best were called "beaver hats" and were handsomely blocked. The Massachusetts General Court in 1634 forbade everyone in the colony (not merely the poor) to wear beaver hats and hatbands as "superfluous and unnecessary," on pain of a fine (two shillings sixpence). But it also urged every male immigrant to bring a black wool felt steeple hat.*

Full-length cloaks were also common in New England for both women and men. This one belonged to Richard Smith in Rhode Island (ca. 1659) and is owned by the Rhode Island Historical Society. The fabric is camlet, an untwilled wool closely interwoven with hair; it is lined with a twilled wool called drugget. Its color was "sad green," one of a range of modest and restrained hues which were much favored in New England.

It ordered that "no person, either man or women," could wear "slashed clothes, other than one slash in each sleeve, and another in the back." Also forbidden were "ordinary wearing" of silver, gold, and silk laces, girdles, hatbands, and "immoderate great sleeves . . . great rayles, long wings, etc." These prohibitions applied to everybody in the colony.[3]

The sumptuary laws of Massachusetts also forbade the manufacture and sale of fancy clothing. A statute in 1636 ordered that "no person, after one month, shall make or sell any bone lace, or other lace. . . . neither shall any tailor set any lace upon any garment."[4] The court decreed that "no garment shall be made with short sleeves, whereby the nakedness of the arm may be discovered."[5]

Later in the seventeenth century, the sumptuary laws of Massachusetts became more conscious of rank. In 1651, the General Court complained that "intolerable excess and bravery hath crept in upon us, and especially amongst people of mean condition, to the dishonor of God, the scandal of our profession, the consumption of estates, and altogether unsuitable to our poverty." The selectmen of every town were ordered to judge whether the dress of men and women exceeded their "ranks and abilities." Costly dress was restricted to those whose estates were worth more than 200 pounds, and also to families of magistrates. But subsequent statutes returned to general prohibitions.[6]

The austerity of New England's dress ways also appeared in other customs. Through the seventeenth century this culture maintained an intense hostility to wigs. When a Puritan clergyman named Josiah Willard cut off his natural hair and put on a wig, he was visited by a magistrate who told him that "God seems to have ordained our hair as a test, to see whether we can bring our minds to be content to be at his finding: or whether we would be our own carvers." Attitudes changed in the eighteenth century, when wigs of white or grey (grizzled as if by age) became acceptable. But long youthful curls were strictly condemned in the seventeenth century.[7]

The women of Puritan New England made less use of cosmetics

---

[3]*Mass. Bay Records*, I, 126 (3 Sep. 1634); for sumptuary laws in England see Francis E. Baldwin, *Sumptuary Legislation and Personal Regulation in England* (Baltimore, 1926).

[4]*Mass Bay Records*, I, 183, 28 Oct. 1636.

[5]*Ibid.*, I, 274, 9 Sep. 1639.

[6]*Ibid.*, II, 60, 14 Oct. 1651.

[7]Sewall, *Diary*, 10 June 1701, I, 449.

than most affluent females in the English-speaking world, except the Quakers. Historian Samuel Eliot Morison observes that his ancestors "loved bright-colored paint on ships and houses—but not on women."[8] Cosmetic aids of every kind were condemned not merely as extravagance but as an act of blasphemy. Even false teeth were uncommon, and Josselyn described New England females in 1684 as "pitifully tooth-shaken," a condition not much improved by the Puritans' favorite toothpaste—a suitably strenuous mix of brimstone, butter and gunpowder.[9]

Washing was uncommon amongst these people. Charles Francis Adams recalled that there were no baths in the town of Quincy for two hundred years. But much use was made of scented powders and leaves. Houses were hung with bouquets of herbs. Perfumed leaves were heated over the fire, to mask the ripe aroma of the inhabitants.

There were many exceptions to these general patterns. The dress ways of New England were tempered by the stubborn individuality of its population. Most wills and inventories included a few articles of private extravagance. The will of Jane Humphrey (Dorchester, 1668) listed "my best red kersey petticoat," which was worn beneath outgarments of "sad grey." There was a taste for aprons with "small lace at the bottom" and pocket handkerchiefs with a "little lace" on the edge.

Puritan women were not nearly as austere as Quakers would later become. They normally wore modest lace caps and bright sleeve-ribbons which made a cheery contrast with the "sadd colors" of their skirts and bodices. But these indulgences were monitored by elders who struggled to enforce a rule of restraint. Even Mary Downing, the niece of Governor Winthrop himself, was reprimanded for wearing a little lace, and "crosse clothes." She wrote to her father:

> I wrote my mother for lace not out of any prodigal or proud mind, but only for some crosse clothes, which is the most allowable and commendable dressings here . . . the elders with others entreated me to leave them off, for they gave great offense.[10]

---

[8]Morison, *Builders of the Bay Colony*, 139.

[9]As late as 1893, Alice Earle wrote that "this colonial remedy is still employed on New England farms" (*Customs and Fashions*, 303).

[10]Simmons, *Emmanuel Downing*, 50.

These small excesses made all the more striking the comparative austerity of New England dress ways from the seventeenth century to the twentieth.[11]

After the great migration, the people of New England fought a two hundred years' war to preserve the values of their culture. Young men and women strained against the sartorial limits that elders imposed upon them. From time to time the magistrates cracked down. At Northampton in 1676, thirty-six young ladies received criminal indictments for "overdress chiefly in hoods." One of them, a spirited young woman named Hannah Lyman, defiantly appeared before the court wearing the silken hood for which she had been indicted. The magistrate was not amused; Hannah Lyman found herself in serious trouble not only for "wearing silk," but for "wearing silk in a flaunting manner, in an offensive way, not only before but when she stood presented."[12] Legal evidence of this sort always points two ways. It shows that some New Englanders rebelled against their culture, while others labored to preserve it. It also tells us that even as challenges and changes occurred in the dress ways of this region, elements of continuity remained very strong.

Fashions of dress were never static in this society, but changed as rapidly in Massachusetts as in other parts of the Western world. Doublet and hose yielded to smallclothes, and smallclothes to pantaloons, and pantaloons to sack suits. But through all these changes, the dress ways of Massachusetts have preserved strong continuities. A female traveler wrote in the eighteenth century:

> They are generally very plain in their dress throughout all the colony, as I saw, and follow one another in their modes, that you may know where they belong, especially the women, meet them where you will.[13]

Even in the twentieth century, the descendants of the Puritans still wear suits of slate-grey and philly-mort. In Boston's Back Bay and Beacon Hill, Brahmin ladies still dress in sad colors, and

---

[11]Larger exceptions appeared in Boston, where purse-proud merchants who were increasingly Arminian and even Anglican tended to adopt more gaudy fashions. Many recent revisionist arguments on Puritan costume have drawn their examples from this urban Arminian elite, who were not typical of the region.

[12]This account follows the version in Alice Morse Earle, *Two Centuries of Costume in America, 1620–1820* (2 vols., 1903, Rutland, Vt., 1971).

[13]Knight, "Journal," Peckham, *Narratives*, 35.

their battered hats appear to have arrived in the hold of the *Arbella.*

Sad colors also survive in the official culture of New England. In the older universities of Massachusetts, Rhode Island and New Hampshire, scholars and athletes do not appear in colors such as Princeton's gaudy orange or Oxford's brilliant blues and reds. The color of Harvard is a dreary off-purple euphemistically called crimson. Brown University's idea of high color is dark brown, trimmed with black. On ceremonial occasions, the president of that institution wears a mud-colored garment which is approximately the color of used coffee grounds. Dartmouth prefers a gloomy forest-green. All of these shades were on the official list of "sadd colours" in 1638; and are still in vogue today.

In the New England dialect, it is interesting to discover that clothes have been called "duds" for three centuries. This was an old English term of contempt for dress. A scarecrow, in his cast-off rags was sometimes called a "dudman." The language of dress in New England was a vocabulary of deprecation. That pejorative attitude still survives in the culture of this region.

&smwspace; Massachusetts Sport Ways:
    The Puritan Idea of "Lawful Recreation"

On the subject of sport, Puritan attitudes were typically complex and carefully reasoned. Many sports were condemned in the Bay Colony, but others were permitted, and a few were actually required. Increase Mather wrote, "For a Christian to use recreation is very lawful, and in some cases a great duty."[1] John Winthrop explained the reason in his diary:

> When I had some time abstained from such worldly delights as my heart most desire . . . I grew into a great dullness and discontent: which being at last perceived, I examined by heart, and finding it needful to recreate my mind with some outward recreation, I yielded unto it, and by a moderate exercise herein was much refreshed.
>
>   But here grew the mischief: I perceiving that God and mine own conscience did allow me so to do in my need, I afterwards took occasion from the benefit of Christian liberty to pretend need of

---

[1]Increase Mather, *A Testimony against Several Profane and Superstitious Customs* (Boston, 1688), 37.

recreation when there was none, and so by degrees I ensnared my heart so far in worldly delights as I cooled the graces of the spirit by them. Whereby I perceive that in all outward comforts, although God allow us the use of the things themselves, yet it must be in sobriety, and our hearts must be kept free, for he is jealous of our love.[2]

For John Winthrop, as for other New England Puritans, "outward recreation" was not merely permissible but "needful" as long as it was done in "sobriety" and good restraint. Moderate exercise was thought to be necessary for the refreshment of the spirit. The Puritans believed that sport was not merely a matter of idle play. For them, even games became a serious business, which they approached with their usual high degree of purpose and organization.[3]

The military units of Massachusetts were not merely encouraged to engage in regular sports, but actually required to do so. As early as 1639 the militia companies of Massachusetts sponsored formal athletic competitions and physical exercises on their training days. This practice persisted through the seventeenth century.[4] The faculty of Harvard College also required students to engage in "lawful recreations," and after 1655, a special period of the day was set aside for games.[5] In 1696, when two undergraduates were drowned in a skating accident on Fresh Pond, President Increase Mather consoled their parents with the thought that "although death found them using recreations (which students need for their health's sake) they were lawful recreations."[6]

In seventeenth-century New England, Puritan ministers and magistrates actively encouraged "lawful recreations," and also sternly suppressed sports which they believed to be "unwarrantable" in one way or another. Sports on Sunday were rigorously punished. The clergyman Thomas Shepard, in a sermon long famous in New England, painted an image of Satan "with a ball

---

[2]Winthrop, "Experiencia," *Writings*, I, 201–2.

[3]Nancy Struna, "Puritans and Sport," *JSPH* 2 (1977), 1–21; this important essay demonstrates the error of the oft-repeated idea that "persons inclined to Puritanism were fundamentally hostile to sportive play." See also *idem*, "Sport and Social Values: Massachusetts," *Quest* 27 (1977), 40; Winton Solberg, *Redeem the Time: The Puritan Sabbath in Early America* (Cambridge, Mass., 1977), 49.

[4]Struna, "Puritans and Sport," 6; Benjamin Wadsworth, *Good Soldiers a Great Blessing* (Boston, 1700).

[5]*CSMP* 3 (1935), 330–33.

[6]Shipton, *Harvard Graduates*, IV, 522.

at his foot," ready "to kick and carry God's precious sabbaths out of the world." This was a complaint not against sport itself, but against sport on Sunday.[7]

The builders of the Bay Colony also specially disliked games that were associated with gambling and drinking. The General Court of Massachusetts often legislated against "unlawful games as cards, dice, etc.," and county courts fined tavernkeepers who permitted these pastimes.[8] Shuffle-board was banned; the Essex County court punished a wayward saint for "his misuse of time shuffle-boarding."[9] Gambling was forbidden even in homes. The General Court decreed in 1631 that "all persons whatsoever that have cards, dice or tables in their houses shall make away with them before the next Court, under pain of punishment."[10]

Horse racing was actively discouraged. In the town of Ipswich it was ordered that anyone "convicted of running races upon horses or jades in the streets of Ipswich, or for abetting and encouraging others of laying wagers on any side should pay 40 shillings," an exceptionally heavy fine. Horses were raced even so; by the eighteenth century, purses were openly advertised in the Boston gazettes. But this was the invasion of an alien spirit.[11]

At the same time that these entertainments were discouraged, other forms of lawful recreation flourished. Within the first few years, a distinctive set of games developed in Massachusetts, from the interaction of Puritan ideals and English customs. Chief among them were two amusements. One of them came to be known as the Boston game; the other was variously called the New England game, the Massachusetts game, town ball or round ball. We know them today as American football and baseball, respectively.

The Boston game or American football was descended from a large family of English folk games which involved the kicking of a ball. In many English neighborhoods, a game of football was an annual event on Christmas, or New Year's Day, or Shrove Tuesday or Easter Monday, often with a handsome leather ball spe-

[7]Thomas Shepard, *Theses Sabbaticae* (London, 1649), IV, 49; Samuel E. Morison, *Harvard College in the Seventeenth Century* (2 vols., Cambridge, Mass., 1936), I, 117.

[8]Scott Wiener, "Three Generations of Sports and Games in the Massachusetts Bay Colony" (paper, Brandeis, 26 Nov. 1986).

[9]*Records and Files of Essex Quarterly Court,* I, 91.

[10]*Mass. Bay Records,* I, 85 (22 March 1631).

[11]*Records and Files of the Essex Quarterly Court,* V, 39; VII, 364; Boston *Gazette,* 19–26 April 1725; Wiener, "Three Generations of Sports and Games."

cially made for the occasion by the village cobbler. At Derby, for example, a football match was played every year between the parishes of All Saints and St. Peters. The ball was ceremoniously put in play at the town hall. In the old settlement of Chester-Le-Street, it was "up-streeters" against "down-streeters," each trying to move the ball to the opposite ends of the town. These great games were played by entire communities—old and young, rich and poor, male and female. For one local contest, the men stripped away their coats and waistcoats, whilst the women took off their dresses and even petticoats. Many a kick and blow were exchanged before the match was done.[12]

These rough village games of old England were brought to Massachusetts, where they tended to be regulated by local officials and played in a more orderly manner. In the town of Rowley, one English visitor witnessed a game of football which surprised him by its restraint: "There was that day a great game of football," he wrote, "to be played with their feet, which I thought was very odd; but it was upon a broad sandy shore, free from stones, which made it more easy. Neither were they so apt to trip up one another's heels and quarrel, as I have seen 'em in England."[13]

Football became a controversial question in New England. Many moralists did not hold it in high repute. William Bentley observed in his diary that "the bruising of shins has rendered it rather disgraceful to [illeg] of better education." But in the eighteenth century, it gradually came to be associated with people of better education. An engraving of Yale College in 1807 showed students in beaver hats and swallow-tailed coats playing football on New Haven Common, while an elder who closely resembled college president Timothy Dwight looked on with an air of disapproval.[14]

Classical American football slowly took shape in New England during the eighteenth century as an elaborately rationalized and rule-bound version of an old English folk sport. Football contests between schools were common by the early nineteenth century in eastern Massachusetts, where teams from academies and town schools played each other on a regular basis. A marble monument

---

[12]Alice Bertha Gomme, *The Traditional Games of England, Scotland and Ireland* (2 vols., New York, 1964), I, 136–37.

[13]A. B. Hart, *Commonwealth History of Massachusetts* (5 vols., New York, 1927), I, 280.

[14]Bentley, *Diary*, I, 254.

on Boston Common quietly commemorates the "first football organization in America," which played there long before the intercollegiate contest between Princeton and Rutgers.

Another rule-bound version of an English folk sport was called town ball, the Massachusetts game or the New England game. It was played with a bat, a ball and four bases on a field sixty feet square, by eight to twenty players, each of whom kept his own individual tally. The New England game was also descended from a family of English traditional games, of which perhaps the nearest equivalent was called bittle-battle. Its rules were remarkably similar to modern baseball. Bittle-battle was played with four bases (each about a foot square) 48 feet apart. The pitcher stood 24 feet from home base, and each batter was out if the ball was caught, or if it touched a base before the batter reached it. The game of bittle-battle was played in southeastern England, particularly in Kent. It was brought to Massachusetts in the early seventeenth century, and became so common that by the eighteenth century it bore the name of the region.[15]

The New England game became very popular in schools and towns throughout Massachusetts. A children's book published in Worcester, Massachusetts, included an illustration of this diversion as early as 1787.[16] It was also widely played in New England colleges during the eighteenth and early nineteenth century. A classical description came from Oliver Wendell Holmes, who played it as a Harvard undergraduate in 1829.[17]

Gradually, the New England game spread beyond the region of its origin into New York and northern New Jersey, and began to be called baseball in the eighteenth and nineteenth century. It was played by soldiers at Valley Forge in 1778, and the diary of a Princeton undergraduate mentioned a sport called "baste ball" in 1786.[18] A variant called the New York game was played by Yankee emigrants in that state during the 1820s. Thurlow Weed

[15]William D. Parish, *A Dictionary of the Sussex Dialect* (Lewes, 1875); Gomme, *The Traditional Games of England, Scotland and Ireland*, I, 34, 217–20. Many other folk games have been identified as ancestors of baseball—stoolball, rounders and cat. Stoolball was a game more like cricket but in which the ball was driven from stool to stool. Cat was generally very different— a game in which a small piece of wood was driven with sticks toward a defended hole. Rounders was, I think, a 19th-century invention; I find no reference before 1856. Gomme's American reference to stoolball is inaccurate; the game was played not in Massachusetts Bay but in Plymouth on the second Christmas, much to William Bradford's displeasure.

[16]Isaiah Thomas, *A Little Pretty Pocket Book* (Worcester, 1787).

[17]Jennie Holliman, *American Sport, 1785–1835* (Durham, N.C., 1931), 65–66.

[18]Harold Seymour, *Baseball, The Early Years* (New York, 1980), 7.

belonged to a baseball club with fifty members at Rochester in 1825.[19] In yet another community of transplanted Yankees, Abner Doubleday appears to have codified one of many sets of rules before 1840.[20]

During the first two centuries of American history, ball games were not common in the southern colonies. What is now the American national game was originally a New England folk sport. It still preserves a combination of order and action, reason and emotion, individuality and collective effort which was characteristic of Puritan culture.[21]

❧ Massachusetts Work Ways: Puritan and East Anglian Economies

As it was with play, so also with work. The economic history of Massachusetts was not the inexorable product of its material environment. The history of neighboring colonies shows that the ecology of this region was consistent with many different types of economic development. The Dutch in New Netherlands and the French in Quebec created extractive economies which dealt heavily in products of the forest and the sea—timber, furs, and fish. The builders of the Massachusetts Bay Colony also engaged in these activities, but mainly they constructed a different sort of economic system which reflected their East Anglian origins and Puritan purposes.

From the start, the economy of Massachusetts was remarkably similar to that of eastern England. Some interior New England towns resembled the wood-pasture villages of Suffolk and Norfolk. Others on the coast were more like the small outports of Essex and Kent. The strength of these continuities appeared most clearly in a regional exception. The town of Rowley in Massachusetts was founded by an untypical group of English Puritans who came from the East Riding of Yorkshire, and had been drawn into the great migration by the charisma of their East Anglian minister. Their home in the north of England had been a center for

---

[19]Thurlow Weed, *Autobiography*, ed. Harriet A. Weed (Boston, 1883).

[20]Abner Doubleday was not the inventor of baseball, as the official histories would have us believe. But neither was his association mythical, as some revisionists have suggested. For a review of the evidence see Seymour, *Baseball, The Early Years*, 12.

[21]"Ball playing was less well known in the southern colonies." Seymour, *Baseball, The Early Years*, 7; Holliman, *American Sport*, 7.

the manufacture of coarse linen and hemp textiles by a work
force that consisted largely of children. The new settlement of
Rowley, Massachusetts, rapidly developed the same sort of industry that had existed in Rowley, Yorkshire. John Winthrop noted
in 1643 that the American community's production of hemp and
flax "exceeded all other towns" in New England. Edward Johnson wrote of the Rowley colonists that they "were the first people
that set upon the making of cloth in this western world, for which
end they built a fulling mill, and caused their little-ones to be very
diligent in spinning cotton wool, many of them having been cloth-
iers in England." About the year 1660, Samuel Maverick
described the inhabitants of Rowley as a "very laborious people . . . making cloth and rugs of cotton wool and also sheep's
wool."[1]

Other exceptions which prove the rule were the fishing ports
of Gloucester and Marblehead, which also differed from most
Massachusetts towns in the English origins of their founders. A
large part of their population came from the Channel Islands,
and particularly from the island of Jersey. Many had been fishermen in the Old World, and they continued their ancestral occupation in the New. When a Puritan minister came to Marblehead,
and gave his congregation the usual East Anglian Puritanism, a
grizzled fisherman rebuked him, "You think you are preaching to
the people of the Bay. Our main end was to catch fish."[2]

Catching fish was not the main purpose of most Bay colonists,
in either a literal or a symbolic sense. Despite the gilded cod that
hangs on the wall of the Massachusetts State House, the fisheries
did not become the foundation of their economy. Eighty percent
of the communities in Massachusetts were farm towns, and a
large majority of adult males were engaged in agriculture.[3]

The pattern of farming was in many ways very similar to the
wood-pasture communities of East Anglia—a regime of mixed

---

[1]Winthrop, *Journal,* II, 122 (1643); Johnson, *Wonder-working Providence,* 183; Samuel Maverick, "A Brief Description of New England and the Severall Townes Therein, Together with
the Present Government Thereof," *MAHSP,* 2d series, I (1884–85), 235; David Grayson Allen,
In English Ways (Chapel Hill, 1981).

[2]Christine Heyrman, *Commerce and Culture: The Maritime Communities of Colonial Massachusetts, 1690–1750* (New York, 1984); Stephen Innes, *Labor in a New Land: Economy and Society in
Seventeenth Century Springfield* (Princeton, 1983).

[3]The quantitative research of James Kimenker, Richard Weintraub and Marc Harris have
established that 80 to 90% of Concord's male polls engaged primarily in agriculture before
1790; this proportion may be taken as typical of most farming towns; in the region as a whole
the proportion was a little lower; see D. H. Fischer, ed., *Concord: The Social History of a New
England Town, 1750–1850* (Waltham, 1983), 65–261.

husbandry which combined field crops and farm animals. Most New England towns kept commons for pasture and meadow. Several towns had open fields for tillage as well. But after a transitional period, crops were raised in enclosed fields cultivated by individual families.

The technology of farming was much the same as in England, despite many environmental differences. "The country is very rocky and hilly and some good champion," one colonist wrote from Watertown in 1631. The Puritans specially prized "champion," which was their word for flat, open land without trees or hills. They found it in Dedham, Watertown, Sudbury and Concord—pockets of rich alluvial soil that are still farmed profitably today.[4] From the start, the Puritans worked their American land with English ploughs—a method unlike the hoe husbandry that prevailed in other parts of British America. As early as 1634, John Winthrop wrote home, ". . . our ploughs go on with good success, we are like to have 20 at work next year."[5]

Within a few years of the first settlement, their family farms were producing a surplus and selling it in the market. The size of these transactions was not great by later standards, but large enough to encourage even small farmers to think of their activity in commercial terms. When they came together on Sunday, they talked first of God and then of prices. By 1645, the Connecticut Valley towns were shipping thousands of bushels of grain to market. Cattle were driven to Boston in such number that the town in 1648 petitioned the General Court for permission to have two fairs a year, one for cattle alone.[6] These markets were closely regulated by rules very similar to those that had prevailed in East Anglian communities. Exports were forbidden in times of scarcity. Unfair market practices such as forestalling and regrating were strictly forbidden. Prices and wages were fixed in difficult periods.

---

[4]The soils of New England are exceptionally complex and varied—more so than other American regions. Some are rich and fertile—especially alluvial soil in the flood plains of the Charles, Merrimack and Connecticut river valleys. Farmers in the Connecticut Valley still raise tobacco with high success on productive fields which have been cultivated continuously for three centuries. There is excellent soil in Concord, Dedham and the original Sudbury (now the town of Wayland).

[5]Winthrop to Sir Nathaniel Rich, 22 May 1634, *Winthrop Papers*, III, 167; on farming in Massachusetts see Darrett B. Rutman, "Governor Winthrop's Garden Crop: The Significance of Agriculture in the Early Commerce of Massachusetts Bay," *WMQ3* 20 (1963), 396–415; *idem, The Husbandmen of Plymouth: Farms and Villages in the Old Colony* (Boston, 1967); Robert R. Walcott, "Husbandry in Colonial New England," *NEQ* 9 (1936), 218–52.

[6]Rutman, "Governor Winthrop's Garden Crop," 405.

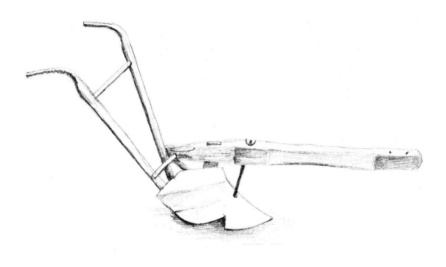

The New England swing plow with its wooden moldboard is a familiar folk artifact, which stands beside the statue of the Minuteman. Folklorist Henry Glassie notes that it was "based on a pattern introduced from Holland into East Anglia probably in the late sixteenth century, and which flourished after 1730 in Scotland and the eastern counties of England. The swing plow was traditional in eighteenth-century New England." This sketch follows a drawing by Henry Glassie.

Massachusetts markets were largely local. Mostly they consisted of one farmer selling to another. But external trade also developed so rapidly that by 1638 more than a hundred vessels engaged in foreign trade from Massachusetts. The West Indies provided a market for grain, meat, fish, butter and many other products. As early as 1647, according to Edward Johnson:

> In a very little space, every thing in the country proved a staple-commodity, wheat, rye, oats, peas, barley, beef, pork, fish, butter, cheese, timber, mast, tar, soap, plankboard, frames of houses, clabboard and pipestaves . . . they have not only fed their Elder Sisters, Virginia, Barbados and many of the Summer Islands that were preferred before her for their fruitfulness, but also the Grandmother of us all, even the fertile isle of Great Britain, beside Portugal hath had many a mouthful of bread and fish from us, in exchange of their Madeira liquor and also Spain, nor could it be imagined, that this wilderness should turn a mart for merchants in so short a space.[7]

At an early date in the seventeenth century, returns from the carrying trade sustained the prosperity of small towns from Portsmouth to Plymouth. An economic historian observes that "New Englanders became the Dutch of England's empire." They did so in more senses than one. The structure of New England's carrying trade was similar in its structure and social function to that which developed on the borders of the North Sea, both in the Netherlands and in the East of England. The combination of mixed agriculture, small villages, and a high level of commercial activity were much the same in East Anglia and Massachusetts. So also was the combination of interior farming villages, and very small seaports that sprang up as thickly in New England as in the Thames estuary and the seacoast of East Anglian coast.[8]

In Massachusetts, this economic system was fully developed by the mid-seventeenth century. Thereafter, for many generations it changed mainly by becoming more elaborately the same. Historian Bernard Bailyn concludes that "the character of the economic system as it emerged in this period remained essentially the same until just before the American Revolution."[9]

Even more persistent than the material structure of New

---

[7]Johnson, *Wonder-working Providence*, 246–47.

[8]John J. McCusker and Russell R. Menard, *The Economy of British America, 1607–1789* (Chapel Hill, 1985), 92; Bernard Bailyn, *New England Merchants in the Seventeenth Century* (Cambridge, Mass., 1955).

[9]Bailyn, *New England Merchants in the Seventeenth Century*, 45.

England's economy was its ethic of work, which the founders of the Bay Colony introduced at an early date. This work ethic was a complex thing. It rested upon an idea that every Christian had two callings—a general calling and a special calling. The first was a Christian's duty to live a godly life in the world. The second was mainly his vocation. The Puritans did not think that success in one's calling was an instrument of salvation, but they believed that it was a way of serving God in the world.

The Puritans did not glorify "capitalist enterprise"—two words which they would not have approved or even understood. They condemned the pursuit of wealth for its own sake, as one rich Puritan merchant named Robert Keayne learned the hard way. Keayne was a Berkshire butcher's boy who became a rich merchant tailor in London, worth "2000 or 3000 pounds in good estate." He brought this capital to Boston, became a member of the Church, married into the ministerial elite and built a flourishing import business. For a time, he may have been Boston's richest merchant, and its fourth largest landowner. But he also gained a reputation for "corrupt practice." John Winthrop noted that "he was wealthy and sold dearer than most other tradesmen." In 1639, when angry customers complained of being overcharged for a bridle and a bag of nails, Keayne was formally charged in General Court with oppression, for having taken "above six-pence in the shilling profit; in some above eight-pence; and in some small things above two for one." The magistrates imposed a fine of £100—one of the heaviest in the history of the colony. But many thought the penalty too light, and the deputies voted a fine of £200. Keayne himself wrote that some wished "corporal punishment was added to it, such as . . . standing openly on a market day with a bridle in his mouth, or at least around his neck."[10]

Boston's Congregational church also made its own investigation of this affair, and found Robert Keayne guilty of "selling his wares at excessive rates." John Cotton denounced him from the pulpit. Keayne was threatened with excommunication until he came weeping before the congregation and "did with tears acknowledge and bewail his covetous and corrupt heart."[11] Thereafter, this once proud Puritan merchant was a shattered man. He gave away large sums in an effort to clear his name,

---

[10] *The Apologia of Robert Keayne: The Self Portrait of a Puritan Merchant* (New York, 1964), 58.
[11] Winthrop, *Journal*, I, 317.

began to drink heavily, lost his public office, and wrote an obsessive defense of his conduct in his last will and testament which became an apologia of 158 pages.[12]

John Cotton was moved by this event to proclaim a code of business ethics for New England. These rules were very strict, and went far beyond medieval ideas of just price. John Winthrop entered them in his *Journal:*

> Some false principles are these: 1. That a man might sell as dear as he can, and buy as cheap as he can. 2. If a man lose by casualty at sea, etc., in some of his commodities, he may raise the price of the rest; 3. That he may sell as he bought, though he paid too dear, etc., and though the commodity be fallen, etc. 4. That, as a man may take advantage of his own skill or ability, so he may take advantage of another's ignorance or necessity. 5. Where one gives time for payment, he is to take like recompense of one as of another.
>
> The rules for trading are these: 1. a man may not sell above the current price. . . . 2. when a man loseth in his commodity for want of skill, etc., he must look at it as his own fault or cross, and therefore must not lay it upon another. 3. Where a man loseth by casualty of sea, or, etc., it is a loss cast upon himself by providence, and he may not ease himself of it by casting it upon another. . . . but where there is a scarcity of the commodity, there men may raise their price; for now it is a hand of God upon the commodity and not the person. 4. A man may not ask any more for his commodity than his selling price, as Ephron to Abraham, the land is worth thus much.[13]

John Cotton forbade merchants to raise prices even to cover their own losses, which they were expected to accept as a judgment upon their sins and not pass on to the consumer. The fact that Boston merchants remained in business tells us that their conduct fell short of John Cotton's ideal. Even so, the Puritan ethic was very far from the spirit of capitalism. For a man such as Robert

---

[12]Bernard Bailyn, "The Apologia of Robert Keayne," *WMQ3* 7 (1950), 568–87; A leading source is Robert Keayne's will which has been republished as *The Apologia of Robert Keayne: The Self Portrait of a Puritan Merchant.* Other important sources are Winthrop's *Journal,* I, 315–18; II, 4, 64–66, 116–20. The judgment of the church appears in *The Records of the First Church in Boston, 1630–1868,* ed. Richard D. Pierce. *CSM Publications,* 39 (1961), 25, 19. Secondary accounts include Rutman, *Winthrop's Boston,* 155, 243–44; Emil Oberholzer, Jr., *Delinquent Saints: Disciplinary Action in the Early Congregational Churches of Massachusetts* (New York, 1956), 188–89; Bernard Bailyn, *The New England Merchants in the Seventeenth Century* (Cambridge, 1955), 41.

[13]Winthrop, *Journal,* I, 318.

Keayne, who tried to be a good Puritan and a good capitalist at the same time, the conflict ended by destroying him.

Altogether, the economy of early New England was neither a system of village communism nor nascent capitalism. It was an old-fashioned system of agricultural production, domestic industry and commercial exchange which bore the impress of East Anglian customs and Calvinist beliefs. At its heart was a Puritan ethic which persisted for many generations.[14]

❧ Massachusetts Time Ways: The Puritan Idea of "Improving the Time"

In most cultures, attitudes toward work are closely connected to conceptions of time. The people of the Bay Colony were no exception. For a Puritan, time was heavily invested with sacred meaning. Fundamentally, it was "God's Time" as Samuel Sewall called it: "God's Time is the best time, God's way the best way."[1]

A central idea in this culture was that of "improving the time," in the seventeenth-century sense of "turning a thing to good account." Time-wasting in the Bay Colony was a criminal offense. As early as 1633 the General Court decreed:

> No person, householder or other, shall spend his time idly or unprofitably, under pain of such punishment as the court shall think meet to inflict; and for this end it is ordered, that the constables of every place shall use special diligence to take knowledge of offenders in this kind, especially of common coasters, unprofitable fowlers and tobacco takers, and to present the same.

A year later, the Court fined two men the heavy sum of twenty shillings each for "misspending their time."[2]

The Puritan magistrate Samuel Sewall was infuriated by the wasting of time, and still more by its profanation. When he observed two men playing "idle tricks" on April Fools' Day he angrily upbraided them:

> In the morning I dehorted Sam. Hirst and Grindal Rawson from playing Idle Tricks because 'twas the first of April. They were the greatest fools that did so. New England men came hither to avoid

---

[14]For the Puritan work ethic see Stephen Foster, *Their Solitary Way: The Puritan Social Ethic in the First Century of Settlement in New England* (New Haven, 1971), 99–126.

[1]Sewall, *Diary,* ed. Thomas, I, 660 (1711).

[2]*Mass. Bay Records,* I, 109, 112 (1 Oct. 1633, 4 March 1633/34).

anniversary days, the keeping of them, such as the 25th of December. How displeasing it must be to God, the giver of our Time, to keep anniversary days to play the fool with ourselves and others.[3]

Puritan writers showed an obsession with time. Their diaries were temporal inventories of high complexity. Birthdays rarely passed in Puritan lives without solemn reflections on the use of time. "I have now lived fifty years much longer than I once expected, blessed be to God," one wrote in 1729, "but oh what abundant cause to be ashamed that I have lived to so little purpose."[4] The turn of each year was marked in the same way. An English Puritan wrote in his diary on one New Year's Eve, "This is the last day of the year and I am sensible a great deal of it hath been lost and misspent."[5]

The daily rhythm of life in the Massachusetts Bay Colony was meant to make the best use of every passing moment. The New England day normally began at the crack of dawn. The country-folk of New England, wrote Mrs. Stowe, "were used to rising at daybreak," to make the best use of every daylight moment.[6] The Puritans also tried to reduce the time for sleep. Increase Mather resolved, "I am not willing to allow myself above seven hours in four and twenty for sleep; but would spend the rest of my time in attending to the duties of my personal or general calling."[7]

For the founders of Massachusetts, "improving the time" was primarily a spiritual idea. Their descendants later turned the same impulse to secular and materialist ends. The classical example was Boston-born Benjamin Franklin. In an essay called *Advice to a Young Tradesman, Written by an Old One* (1748) Franklin wrote:

> Remember that TIME is Money. He that can earn Ten Shillings a Day by his Labour, and goes abroad, or sits idle one half of that Day, tho' he spends but Sixpence during his Diversion or idleness, ought not to reckon That the only Expence; he has really spent or rather thrown away Five Shillings besides.[8]

The sayings of *Poor Richard*, which began to appear in 1733, expressed this idea in many aphorisms:

> Sloth and Silence are a Fool's Virtues.

[3]*Ibid.*, II, 920–21 (1719).
[4]Clegg, *Diary*, I, 68 (20 Oct. 1729).
[5]*Ibid.*, 1727.
[6]Stowe, *Oldtown Folks*, 1424.
[7]Cotton Mather, *Parentator* (Boston, 1724), 38.
[8]*Papers of Benjamin Franklin*, III, 304.

He that wastes idly a Groat's worth of his Time per Day, one Day with another, wastes the Privilege of using £100 each Day.

If you have time, don't wait for time.

Since thou art not sure of a minute, throw not away an hour.

Up, Sluggard, and waste not life; in the grave will be sleeping enough.

Have you somewhat to do to-morrow; do it today.

Who gives promptly, gives twice.

He that riseth late, must trot all day, and shall scarce overtake his business at night.

Idleness is the greatest Prodigality.

Dost thou love Life? Then do not squander Time; for that's the Stuff Life is made of.

Time enough, always proves little enough.

Lost time is never found again.

Procrastination is the thief of time.[9]

Other cultures in Anglo-America showed nothing quite like this obsession with "improving the time," which for more than three centuries became an important part of folkways in New England.

The Puritans in England and America also undertook the improvement of time in another sense—seeking better methods of measuring its passage. This impulse caused the English Puritan Ralph Thoresby to invent an alarm clock. In his diary on 1 November 1680, he made following entry:

> Thinking to have got up by 6 was mistaken, and rose so early that I had read a chapter before it chimed four. Spent most of the time in reading my dear father's diary, and after in writing some things, desiring to redeem my time from sleep I entered into a Resolution that if it might any ways conduce to the glory of God . . . for upon a serious consideration that I usually (now in winter especially) *sleep* away so much precious time which might be redeemed to the ends aforesaid, and then considering the capital *brevity* of our lives, to which a few years will put a period even to the longest, and perhaps a few weeks or days or perhaps minutes to mine in particular, considering these things I resolved in the strength of God to *redeem* more *time,* particularly to retrench my sleeping time, and getting an *Alarm* put to the clock and that set at my *beds-*

---

[9]*Ibid.,* I, 8, 9, 170, 195, 225; II, 296, 333, 334, 337; III, 7; IV, 187.

head to arise every morning by five and first to dedicate the *morning* (as in duty obliged) to the *service of God,* by reading a chapter in an old Bible I have with annotations and then after prayer. . . . [10]

A similar impulse in a more secular form led Benjamin Franklin a century later to invent the idea of daylight saving time. While American minister to France, Franklin was shocked that the people of Paris lost many hours of light by sleeping until midday, and then burned candles far into the night. He tried to enlighten his French friends in an essay called *An Economical Project* which proposed what we call daylight saving time.[11]

Another Puritan idea about time appeared in their notion of "numbering the days." This phrase had many meanings. It meant that time was precious and limited. It also betrayed a quantitative idea of time. Historian Bernard Bailyn observes of the Puritan merchant Robert Keayne:

> the word that expresses best the most basic activity of Keayne's mind is *calculation.* The veil through which he saw the world was not so much colored as calibrated. It was *quantity* that engaged his imagination.[12]

This calculating spirit often appeared in the temporal attitudes of seventeenth-century New England. In diaries and sermons, time usually meant clock time and calendar time. The stages of life were also quantified; old age, for example, was defined as life after sixty. Puritan diaries normally timed events to the nearest hour, or to horological periods such as "between twelve and one," or "one-quarter after one." Minutes were rarely mentioned. New England clocks and watches in the seventeenth century often did not have minute hands. This culture had little need for that degree of temporal refinement. It was a world without our idea of punctuality. In the seventeenth century, "punctual" meant "pertaining to a point." Nevertheless, this world was firmly governed by the discipline of calendars and clocks.[13]

Clocks were costly in the seventeenth century. New Englanders improvised by turning their houses into timepieces. Massachusetts homes were often "sunline houses," which faced due south

---

[10]Ralph Thoresby Diary, 1 Nov. 1680, ms. 21, Yorkshire Archaeological Society, Leeds.

[11]Franklin, "An Economical Project," *Writings,* IX, 183–89.

[12]Bailyn, "The Apologia of Robert Keayne," 577. For a general discussion of these questions see Patricia Cline Cohen, *A Calculating People: The Spread of Numeracy in Early America* (Chicago, 1982).

[13]*OED,* s.v. "punctual."

on a noon sighting. The facade of the house was made into a giant sundial, with hours carved into the facing-boards around the door. By that means, a New England family could tell the hour even in the absence of a mechanical clock on the mantel.

Other forms of time-keeping were also part of this culture. The diurnal rhythm of light and dark was exceptionally important to the Puritans. The coming of darkness, which they called the "candle-lighting," divided each period of twenty-four hours into profoundly different parts. Night was dangerous, threatening and hostile. As the shadows grew longer, New England travelers hurried on the highway, trying desperately to reach their destinations before dark. Samuel Sewall was once overtaken by darkness while on the road to Salem. He kicked his horse into the gallop, racing frantically against the night until the animal stumbled in the dark and "fell upon his nose"; Sewall was lucky to escape with his life. His diary described other moments of danger, fear and even panic when night fell in New England.[14] To the Puritans, the night seemed not only dangerous but evil. The town bells sounded a curfew every night—and still do so in the author's Middlesex village 350 years after its founding. To be abroad after curfew without permission was to risk punishment for a crime called "nightwalking." Altogether, the diurnal rhythms of darkness and light were very pronounced in the time ways of Puritan New England.[15]

Also exceptionally strong in this society was the weekly rhythm defined by the Sabbath. Before coming to America, English Puritans began to observe the Sabbath with extreme rigor—a custom that was kept in Massachusetts from the start. The Puritans followed the Old Testament in reckoning the Sabbath from sundown on Saturday or even earlier. John Winthrop's Sabbath began as early as three o'clock on Saturday afternoon. Historian Winton Solberg observes that "New England was in all likelihood the only region in Christendom where this custom prevailed."[16]

Many activities were forbidden on the Sabbath: work, play, and unnecessary travel. Even minor instances of Sabbath-breaking were punished with much severity. The Essex County Court indicted a man for carrying a burden on the Sabbath, and punished a woman for brewing on the Lord's Day. When Ebenezer Taylor of Yarmouth, Massachusetts, fell into a forty-foot well, his

[14]Sewall, *Diary,* II, 660 (1712).
[15]David H. Flaherty, *Privacy in Colonial New England* (Charlottesville, 1972), 62, 196.
[16]Winton U. Solberg, *Redeem the Time: The Puritan Sabbath in Early America* (Cambridge, 1977), 111.

rescuers stopped digging on Saturday afternoon while they debated whether it was lawful to rescue him on the Sabbath. Other New Englanders were punished for picking strawberries, playing quoits, marking fish, smoking a pipe, and sailing a boat on the Lord's Day. At New London, a courting couple named John Lewis and Sarah Chapman were brought to trial in 1670 merely for "sitting together on the Lord's Day under an apple tree."[17]

Sexual intercourse was taboo on the Lord's Day. The Puritans believed that children were born on the same day of the week as when they had been conceived. Unlucky infants who entered the world on the Sabbath were sometimes denied baptism because of their parents' presumed sin in copulating on a Sunday. For many years Sudbury's minister Israel Loring sternly refused to baptize children born on Sunday, until one terrible Sabbath when his own wife gave birth to twins![18] Altogether, the Puritans created a sabbatical rhythm of unique intensity in the time ways of their culture.[19]

If daily and weekly movements were unusually strong in New England, other common rhythms were exceptionally weak or even absent altogether. The Puritans made a point of abolishing the calendar of Christian feasts and saints' days. The celebration of Christmas was forbidden in Massachusetts on pain of a five-shilling fine. In England, the Puritan Parliament prohibited the observance of Christmas, Easter, Whitsunday, saints' days and holy days.

These Puritan principles made a difference in the rhythm of life. The timing of marriage, for example, differed in New England from other British colonies. In Massachusetts, it was no longer regulated by Anglican prohibitions against matrimony during the period from Ash Wednesday to Easter and also in the

[17]*Ibid.,* 162; Oberholzer, *Delinquent Saints,* 57–77; Ola Elizabeth Winslow, *Meetinghouse Hill, 1630–1783* (New York, 1952), 180; Alice Morse Earle, *The Sabbath in Puritan New England* (New York, 1891), 246. Here again, there are two countervailing myths about New England: the myth of the spurious Connecticut "Blue Laws" which allegedly forbade men to shave and women to kiss their children on the sabbath. These statutes were invented by Samuel Peters, an Anglian clergyman and High Tory who fled New England in the Revolution and wrote a *General History of Connecticut* (London, 1781). Travelers' accounts added other apocrypha. But partisans of the Puritans have created a countermyth in correcting these errors. The sabbath laws of New England were very rigorous, and prosecutions by church and state were sometimes extreme.

[18]Charles Francis Adams, "Some Phases of Sexual Morality and Church Discipline in Puritan New England," *MAHSP,* 2nd series 6 (1891), 495.

[19]Major Puritan works on the Sabbath include Thomas Shepard, *Theses Sabbaticae: Or, The Doctrine of the Sabbath* (London, 1649); William Pynchon, *A Treatise on the Sabbath . . . Whereto Is Annexed a Treatise of Holy Time* (London, 1655).

period before Christmas. New Englanders kept old East Anglian customs without those Episcopal restrictions.[20]

In place of the liturgical calendar, New Englanders created their own annual rhythm of regional festivals, including Election Day, Commencement Day, Thanksgiving, and Training Day. Election Day was a spring event, held on a Wednesday in April, when the charter of Massachusetts required that members of the Bay Company should meet to elect their officers. Gradually this day became a Puritan holiday which was celebrated with sermons and a ritual meal of "election cake" and "election beer."[21] Commencement Day, normally a weekday in July, was an academic ceremony which by 1680 had become a "Puritan midsummer's holiday" when ministers and magistrates assembled at Cambridge to share a dinner, wine and "commencement cake." There was also a great gathering of hucksters and vast crowds of country people on this occasion.[22] Training days happened at various dates from early spring to late summer, when the militia assembled to practice their martial arts. John Winthrop described a training day on 15 September 1641, when 1,200 New England

[20]The definitive study of marriage seasonality in New England is by David Cressy. He reports the following results for six New England towns, including Dedham, which is illustrated in the graph (1638–99).

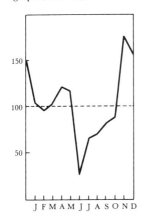

| Month | Marriage Index (m̄ = 100) | |
	Six Towns	Dedham
January	122	103
February	82	97
March	87	103
April	94	121
May	99	117
June	72	25
July	76	64
August	73	69
September	86	81
October	94	88
November	158	177
December	158	156
Total	1200	1200
(N)	(2217)	(256)

(The marriage index is based on the monthly mean; that is, the annual total of marriages is made proportionate to 1200, so that the monthly mean is 100.) Cressy's findings are reproduced here so that they can be compared with other regions, below. Cressy's six-town sample dilutes the distinctive Bay Colony pattern by including Plymouth and Boston. The classic Massachusetts pattern is more clearly visible in the town of Dedham. See David Cressy, "The Seasonality of Marriage in Old and New England," *JIH* 16 (1985), 1–21; for similarities between New England and East Anglia, see Ann Kussmaul, "Time, Space, Hoofs and Grain: The Seasonality of Marriage in England," *JIH* 15 (1985), 755–79.

[21]Winthrop, *Journal*, I, 63 (17 April 1631).

[22]Morison, *Harvard College in the Seventeenth Century*, II, 465–71.

soldiers came together on Boston common. The governor noted with satisfaction that "there was no man drunk, though there was plenty of wine and strong beer in the town, not an oath sworn, no quarrel, nor any hurt done."[23]

A fourth Puritan festival was Thanksgiving, which by 1676 had become an annual event, held on a Thursday in November or December. In earlier years, days of Thanksgiving were appointed *ad hoc* for special occasions by civil authorities. The first Thanksgiving in the Bay Colony happened on 22 February 1630/31, after provision ships arrived just in time to prevent starvation.[24] Approximately twenty-two special days of Thanksgiving were held in the first half-century of the Bay Colony. After New England survived King Philip's War, Thanksgivings began to occur regularly in November. The appointed day was Thursday, which had been lecture day in the churches of Boston and Ipswich. Special days of Thanksgiving continued, but by the late 1670s this event had become an autumn ritual, in which a fast was followed by a family dinner and another fast. The main event was a sermon which reminded New Englanders of their founding purposes. Sabbath rules were enforced on these days; Yankee farmers were prosecuted for ploughing on Thanksgiving.[25]

Gradually Thanksgiving also became a domestic festival when families gathered together and renewed the covenant which was so important to their culture. In the nineteenth century, Harriet Beecher Stowe remembered that Thanksgiving in her family reached its climax after the dinner was done:

> When all was over, my grandfather rose at the head of the table, and a fine venerable picture he made as he stood there, his silver hair flowing in curls down each side of his clear, calm face, while in conformity to the old Puritan custom, he called their attention to a recital of the mercies of God in his dealings with their family.
>
> It was a sort of family history, going over and touching upon the various events which had happened. He spoke of my father's death, and gave a tribute to his memory, and closed all with the application of a time-honored text, expressing the hope that as years passed by we might "so number our days" as to apply our hearts unto wisdom.[26]

---

[23]Winthrop, *Journal*, I, 299–300; II, 42.

[24]*Ibid.*, I, 59

[25]W. DeLoss Love, Jr., *The Fast and Thanksgiving Days of New England* (Boston, 1895); Earle, *Customs and Fashions in Old New England*, 214–33.

[26]Stowe, *Oldtown Folks*, 1218.

The time ways of seventeenth-century New England were distinguished not only by the strength of these regional rituals, but also by weakness of natural rhythms which were very pronounced in other cultures. An example was a fascinating phenomenon which demographic historians call the "conception cycle." Throughout the Western world in the seventeenth century, a large proportion of babies were conceived in the spring. There was a "rutting time" for humans as well as animals—a season of intense sexual activity which was defined by annual cycles of work, nutrition and inherited custom. In Europe twice as many conceptions occurred in the peak month of April as in the summer months during the seventeenth century. This conception cycle also appeared in the baptismal records of New England, but it was fainter than in most parts of the Western world. Conceptions were distributed more evenly throughout the year than was the case in Europe or other American colonies. Sexual behavior in New England was "deseasonalized" in an unusual degree for a seventeenth-century population.[27]

In sum, the time ways of New England embodied Puritan values in many ways. Seasonal rhythms such as the conception cycle were comparatively weak; diurnal and sabbatical rhythms were exceptionally strong. The liturgical calendar of Christian holidays was replaced by festivals which commemorated the founding purposes of New England. Ideas of "improving the time" and "numbering the days" gave a special cast to temporal thinking. Some of these customs appeared elsewhere, but all of them together were unique to New England.

❧ Massachusetts Wealth Ways: Puritan Ideas of the Material Order

As it was with time and work, so also with wealth. The distribution of wealth in Massachusetts was determined not by material processes alone, but mainly by the cultural values and historical experiences of the founders. The builders of the Bay Colony deliberately apportioned the productive assets of their province so as to maintain the social distinctions which they thought proper in a

---

[27]This finding was first reported by Kenneth Lockridge in an unpublished paper presented to a conference on social history at Stony Brook, N.Y., in 1969. Lockridge discovered that New England's spring peak in conceptions was less than half as high as in France, Sweden and Canada during the same era. Marriage rhythms were mixed. Rural towns showed a high peak in November, as in East Anglia; but in Boston there was little variation from month to month.

Bible Commonwealth. Leaders of the community were given larger shares of land; so were those who had held more property in England, and families with many children and servants. Distinctions of social rank were carefully respected, but gross disparities were uncommon. In most cases, town proprietors were men of middling status—yeomen and husbandmen who tended to be neither very rich nor very poor. They distributed the land in such a way as to multiply their own class. There was no small elite of great landlords in most Massachusetts towns during the seventeenth century.

The typical size of land grants in the Bay Colony might be observed in the town of Billerica, where 115 men received land by 1651. The median holding was 60 acres; the mean, 96 acres. Similar patterns appeared in most towns. In the town of Springfield, for example, the largest holding (William Pynchon's) was 237 acres; the smallest, six; the median, near 60. These two towns had very different reputations—Billerica for comparative equality, Springfield for dominance by a single family. But in both communities the distribution of land was much the same. No family was enormously rich; few were entirely landless. Tenancy was uncommon, and in some towns entirely unknown.[1]

When the proprietors of Wallingford, Connecticut, distributed their lands, they divided the population into three parts. Every "high rank man" received 400 acres; every "middle rank man" was given approximately 300 acres, and men of "lower rank" were assigned 200 acres. Other towns distributed their lands on different principles. The town of Dedham, on the other hand, divided its lands by a more complex method which took into account "rank, quality, deserts and usefulness either in the church or commonwealth."

These rules varied in detail from one New England town to another. By and large, the more radical the religious principles of any particular town, the more egalitarian its distribution of lands was apt to be. A case in point was the Separatist settlement which is now the city of Providence, Rhode Island. Its founder,

[1] In Billerica, the number of individual grants were as follows:

10 acres	6	50 acres	11	100 acres	7	220 acres	1
15 acres	6	60 acres	16	140 acres	2	250 acres	1
20 acres	11	70 acres	6	150 acres	5	300 acres	3
30 acres	3	80 acres	18	180 acres	1	400 acres	1
40 acres	5	90 acres	6	200 acres	4	450 acres	1

Source: William Haller, Jr., *The Puritan Frontier; Town-Planting in New England Colonial Development 1630–1660* (New York, 1951), 68. See Stephen Innes, *Labor in a New Land: Economy and Society in Seventeenth-Century Springfield* (Princeton, 1983), 14.

Roger Williams, insisted that he should receive "only unto myself, one single share, equal unto any of the rest of that number. In the intent of Roger Williams, the first division of lands at Providence had a Gini ratio of zero, or perfect equality.[2]

Other towns diverged in the opposite direction. One of the most inegalitarian and materialist communities in the region was New Haven, which was settled by purse-proud London merchants. From the start, its wealth was heavily concentrated in a few hands.

Differences in wealth distribution derived not only from the religious beliefs of the founders, but also from their English regional origins. Historian David Grayson Allen discovered that the size of the average land holdings in the English community of Rowley, Yorkshire, was almost exactly reproduced in the American settlement called Rowley. He also found that the town of Hingham, Massachusetts, replicated the pattern of wealth distribution that had existed in the town of Hingham, East Anglia. Landholdings tended to be larger in New England, but relative sizes remained much the same.[3]

These various English patterns—eastern and northern—were not identical. Landholdings tended to be more egalitarian in East Anglia than in the north or west. Massachusetts towns settled by East Anglians tended to be more equal than those founded by Puritans from other parts of England. Two of the most sharply stratified rural communities in Massachusetts were Rowley, which was founded by a small group of Yorkshire families, and Newbury, which had a large contingent from England's West Country. The builders of the Bay Colony generally followed the model of East Anglian communities, with a few important modifications.[4]

[2]This was the intent. A controversy quickly arose as to whether the first division of land in Providence was only for "use" or for ownership as well. This dispute led to another division which was less egalitarian. See Bartlett, ed., *Records of Rhode Island Colony*, I, 23.

[3]David Grayson Allen found the following patterns in inventoried wealth:

Percent of Total Wealth Held By:	Hingham, Norfolk 1642–88	Hingham, Mass. 1654–92
Top 10%	31.9%	31.0%
Top 25%	66.2%	57.8%
Top 50%	89.3%	81.5%
Bottom 50%	10.7%	18.5%

This refers to personal estate only, as land was not included in English inventories; see Allen, *In English Ways*, 79.

[4]The materialism of New Haven appeared also in the way that it seated its meetinghouse— mainly according to wealth rather than age. Many towns in the Massachusetts Bay Colony reversed this priority.

The overall pattern of wealth distribution in New England was much more equal than in the region of East Anglia as a whole. Outside the towns, there were no great landholders in Massachusetts whose possessions were even remotely comparable to those of the Crown, or the Duke of Norfolk, or other manorial lords who had owned a very large proportion of the manors in the eastern counties of England in the sixteenth century. The large landless proletariat of East Anglia had no counterpart in New England during the seventeenth and early eighteenth century. But the distribution of wealth in Massachusetts towns was similar to patterns among freeholders and leaseholders within East Anglian villages.[5]

These cultural factors were not the only determinants of wealth distribution in Massachusetts. Other factors were also involved. Inland farming towns in New England tended to be more equal than coastal commercial communities. Thus, the Massachusetts village of Newtown (now Cambridge) was more equal than Boston; Watertown was more equal than Newtown; Sudbury was more equal than Watertown; and Marlborough was more equal

[5]Many studies of wealth distribution in 17th-century Massachusetts yield similar results. Gini ratios (the standard measure of concentration which ranges from .00 (perfect equality) to .99 (perfect inequality where the top percentile owns everything)), fell mostly in a narrow middling range of .4 in small farming communities to .6 in seaport towns. One of the most equal patterns appeared in Andover's division lists (.38); least equal were tax assessment lists in Boston and its suburb of Muddy River (now Brookline), which were .64.

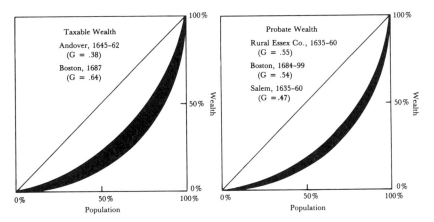

Sources: G. B. Warden, "Inequality and Instability in Boston: A Reappraisal," *JIH* 6 (1976), 505–620; Greven, *Four Generations,* 46; Donald W. Koch, "Income Distribution and Political Structure in Seventeenth Century Salem," *EIHC* 105 (1969), 50–69; Gary Nash, "Urban Wealth and Poverty," *JIH* 61 (1976), 549.

than Sudbury. All of these towns were located on a line that ran due west from Boston.[6]

These material differences, however, existed within a narrow range. Studies of wealth-distribution have been completed for more than twenty-five Massachusetts towns from 1630 to 1750, and also for at least three counties. In most of these places, throughout that period, the top tenth of wealthholders held only 20 to 30 percent of taxable property, and about 30 to 40 percent of estates in probate. This pattern of wealth distribution was egalitarian by comparison with other colonies. With a few urban exceptions such as Salem and Boston, it was typical of New England—and very different from other parts of British America.[7]

[6]William Gately, "Wealth Distribution in Berkhamsted, Weyhill, Sudbury, and Marlboro" (unpublished paper, Brandeis, 1971).

[7]The distribution of wealth in New England has been measured by many different methods. The only statistical indicator common to most inquiries is the size share of the top tenth (SSTT). This appears as follows, in taxable wealth and estate inventories.

| Place | Date | Share Owned by Top Tenth | | List Type |
		Inc. Polls	Exc. Polls	
Boston	1681	42.3		t
	1687		46.9	p
	1650–64		60.0	i
	1665–74		64.0	i
	1685–94		46.0	i
	1684–99		41.2	i
	1705–14		56.0	i
	1700–15		54.5	i
	1715–19		54.0	i
Boxford	1687	25.8	25.7	p, t
	1745	23.9		t
	1746		28.8	p
Andover	1720	21.7		t
	1740	22.6		t
Amherst	1759		24.6	p
	1771	24.6		t
Billerica	1733	22.4		m
	1755	25.0		m
Brookline	1674	36.0		t
	1687	38.0		t
	1688	36.0		t
	1746	30.0		t
	1753	32.0		t
Cambridge	1688	23.9	27.3	t, p
Concord	1717	29.0		l
	1770	30.0		l
Dedham	1710	23.5	27.4	t, p
	1735		29.1	p
Essex Co.	1635–60		36.0	i
	1661–81		49.0	i
Hampshire Co.	1665–64		30.0	i
	1685–94		37.0	i

What is specially interesting in this pattern was its cause. The distribution of wealth in Massachusetts was not determined solely by the organization of the means of production, except in a tautological sense. Neither was it exclusively a function of market relations. It was created largely by a system of value which the founders of Massachusetts drew from their Puritan ideals and East Anglian experiences.

Another major determinant of wealth distribution was the system of inheritance. On this subject, the Bay Colonists had formed strong views while still in England. In 1624, a Puritan list of "grievances groaning for reformation," drafted in the hand of John Winthrop, included an angry indictment of English inheri-

Place	Date	Share Owned by Top Tenth		List Type
		Inc. Polls	Exc. Polls	
	1695–1704		35.0	i
	1705–14		38.0	i
Hadley	1720	28.1		c
	1731	34.4	37.7	c.c
Hingham	1647	22		t
	1680	29		t
	1711	26		t
Leicester	1732	21.3	27.4	m
	1743	22.2	33.7	t, p
Manchester	1696		28.1	m
	1717		30.6	p
Medfield	1697	19.0		c
Newbury	1642		56.4	d
Newbury	1642–1701	33.8		i
Topsfield	1687	26.2	30.4	t, p
	1725	24.3		t
Norton	1711	25.8	33.3	t, p
Rowley	1642	44.5		l
Springfield	1685	34.5		t
Sudbury	1722		25.6	p
Suffolk Co. (rural)	1650–64	37.0		i
	1665–74	37.0		i
	1685–94	34.0		i
	1695–1704	36.0		i
	1705–14	33.0		i
	1715–19	31.0		i
	1750–54	31.0		i
Salem	1683	31.2		t
	1764	38.3	52.2	t, p
Waltham	1740	24.3	29.6	t, p
Watertown	1642	31.0		l
	1642–1700	26.5		i

Note: t = total taxable wealth including polls; p = total taxable wealth excluding polls; m = rates to pay a minister or build a meetinghouse; c = commons division lists; r = real estate valuations or taxes; l = acreage of land owned in the town; i = inventories of estates in probate. Sources include Edward M. Cook, Jr., *The Fathers of the Towns: Leadership and Community Structure in Eighteenth-Century New England* (Baltimore, 1976); unpublished data assembled by the Brandeis Concord, Brookline and Waltham projects; Smith, "Hingham"; Allen, *In English Ways*.

tance practices in general, and an attack upon primogeniture in particular. "It is against all equity that one [son] should be a gentleman to have all, and the rest as beggars to have nothing," he wrote, "it breedeth often times much strife and contention betwixt the elder brother and the rest of the children."[8]

The Bay Colonists found a model that pleased them better in the book of Deuteronomy, which prescribed that a father should honor "the first born [son], by giving him a double portion of all that he hath."[9] This rule had great weight with English Puritans who found in it a "middle way" of the sort which was so congenial to their thinking. The English Puritan William Gouge argued that "houses and families by this means are upheld and continued from age to age," while justice was done to all of the other children.[10]

In Massachusetts this biblical rule was combined with carefully selected East Anglian customs, which had been very mixed.[11] Some communities and individuals in eastern England observed the rule of primogeniture.[12] Others kept a custom called borough English, in which the homestead sometimes went to the youngest son. Many practiced some form of partible descent, which was so common in the eastern counties that small "morcellements" of land became a serious social problem. Some testators even subdivided a single home among their children. In 1585, for example, Margaret Browne of Colchester (Essex) divided one house into five legacies:

> To my son John the hallhouse with the entry coming and going in and from the same; to my son Richard and Joan his wife the chamber over the parlour in which he now dwelleth for the term of their lives; to Anne my daughter now wife of John Glascock of St. Osyth the kitchen and to her heirs for ever; to my son Oliver and his heirs for ever the parlor in which he now dwelleth; to my daughter Katherine now wife of Robert Symon of Colchester weaver the shop with the little buttery in the entry and to his heirs

[8] *Winthrop Papers*, I, 306.

[9] Deuteronomy 21:16; this was also their interpretation of Genesis 48:22 where Israel said unto Joseph, the first born of the true wife, "I have given thee one portion of above thy brethren."

[10] William Gouge, *Of Domesticall Duties* (London, 1622), 575–79; as quoted in Joan Thirsk, "The European Debate on Customs of Inheritance, 1500–1700," in Jack Goody, Joan Thirsk and E. P. Thompson, eds., *Family and Inheritance* (Cambridge, 1976), 189.

[11] Large numbers of these customals survive in county record offices. No scholar, to my knowledge, has studied them systematically.

[12] F. G. Emmison, *Elizabethan Life: Home, Work and Land; From Essex Wills and Sessions and Manorial Records* (Chelmsford, 1976), 107.

forever. . . . My garden and backside to be also equally divided between my said five children. . . .[13]

The founders of Massachusetts drew selectively upon these various English precedents. At an early date, they totally abolished death heriots, reliefs, primer seizins, escheats, licenses, fines and forfeitures which had weighed heavily upon them. They also abandoned primogeniture and entail. In cases of intestacy, Massachusetts courts at first often ordered estates to be divided more or less equally among children of both sexes. Males commonly received land and females were given "moveables" or personal property. In 1648, Massachusetts formally enacted the biblical rule that gave a double portion to the eldest son. This law made no mention of daughters, but in Massachusetts courts children of both sexes shared more equally than in England.[14]

These rules applied only in cases of intestacy. But most property holders in Massachusetts left a will, in which they usually divided their land among their sons, and left a large share of personal property to daughters. In Watertown, for example, one study has found that no two wills were the same in the distribution of property, but every testator with more than one child practiced some form of partible inheritance. One-third gave a double portion to the first-born son. About half left the homestead or house furnishings to the youngest son, a highly practical arrangement which became widely popular in New England. Many testators assigned a life interest in their estates to their widows, with residual rights for the children. These partible customs restrained the growth of inequality in New England.[15]

Material inequalities in Massachusetts existed within a compar-

---

[13]*Ibid.*

[14]*Ibid.*, 275.

[15]A few individual examples from Watertown might illustrate the rule and variations: Deacon Henry Bright, a widower who died in 1686, gave to his oldest son John the homestead and 200 acres of land; his other sons and daughters received 40 or 50 acres each and equal portions of money. Abraham Browne assigned everything to the care of his widow, with the land later to be divided equally among his sons, legacies of livestock for his daughters; but the will could not be proved and the court applied the double-partible rule. John Coolidge in 1691 left everything in the care of his widow, subsequently to be divided equally among five sons, with the homestead to a younger son, and a double portion of money to the eldest. John Whitney of Watertown who died in 1673 left the homestead and "the old mare if she lives" to his youngest son, the furniture to the eldest, a double share of land to the second-born and single shares to his other children. John Warren (d. 1667) left his homestead to his second son Daniel and divided his lands among five children. Roger Wellington (d. 1698) divided his lands equally among three sons and gave his furniture to the youngest. These instances are drawn from Jonathan C. Sorken, "Watertown Inheritance Patterns in the Seventeenth Century" (paper, Brandeis, 26 Nov. 1986). See also Thomas R. Cole, "Family, Settlement and Migration in Southeastern Massachusetts, 1650–1805: The Case for Regional Analysis," *NEHGR* 132 (1978), 171–85.

atively narrow range, but they loomed large in the consciousness of small communities. At the top of this system of wealth distribution were families of lesser gentry. Their houses were commonly at the center of the town, just as small manor houses were in the center of many farming villages in East Anglia.

In the town of Windsor, Connecticut, for example, the Allyns were the leading family. Their two-story wooden house was not very grand by English standards, but it was the largest home in Windsor. It was also painted a vivid red at the time when most New England houses were not painted at all, but slowly weathered to a mottled brown. The Allyn house was the center of society in Windsor and also the seat of justice, where its builder the first Squire Allyn and then his son and grandson after him held court in the great room. So grand did the Allyn house appear that a small child, passing it for the first time, ran home to tell his parents that he had seen "Heaven, the big house where the angels lived."

Even so, by comparison with other cultures, New England was remarkably egalitarian. As late as 1765, a British aristocrat named Lord Adam Gordon traveled widely in New England. He observed with an air of disapproval that "the levelling principle here, everywhere, operates strongly and takes the lead. Everybody has property, and everybody knows it." He was correct both in the fact and the cause. The wealth ways of new England rose in large measure from a "levelling principle" which was embedded in its culture.[16]

❧ Massachusetts Rank Ways:
　A System of Truncated Orders

On board the ship *Arbella,* John Winthrop entertained his fellow passengers with a typical Puritan lay-sermon on the subject of social rank. "God Almighty," Winthrop declared, "in his most holy and wise providence, hath so disposed of the Condition of mankind, as in all times some must be rich some poor, some high and eminent in power and dignity; others mean and in subjection."[1]

---

[16]Lord Adam Gordon, "Journal of an Officer . . . in 1764 and 1765," in Newton D. Mereness, ed., *Travels in the American Colonies* (1916, rpt., New York, 1961), 404–5.

[1]John Winthrop, "A Modell of Christian Charity, Written on Boarde the Arrabella on the Attlantick Ocean," *Winthrop Papers,* II, 282; for the structure of a Puritan lay-sermon, see Perry Miller and Thomas H. Johnson, *The Puritans* (2 vols., New York, 1963), II, 294.

From the beginning, the colony of Massachusetts Bay did indeed make some New Englanders "high and eminent," and others "mean and in subjection." These distinctions derived from East Anglian ranking practices, but were modified in major ways by the builders of the Bay Colony. The system of stratification in eastern England, like that of Europe as a whole during the seventeenth century, was marked by inequality in high degree. At the top was the Crown, the Peerage, and the greater gentry, who held title to much of the farmland in the region, and even to some of its urban centers as well. The county of Norfolk, for example, was divided into approximately 1,500 manors in 1630. Of that number, a majority were owned by a few dozen great landowners.[2] The county of Essex in the year 1640 had approximately 1,100 manors, of which 780 were in private hands. Of that number, 64 were held by the Earl of Warwick alone. Ten families owned 222 Essex manors, and dominated the economic affairs of the county. Entire market towns were owned by single families; the community of Saffron Walden, for example, belonged to the Earl of Suffolk.[3] In Kent the pattern was a little different. Here the Church of England was the largest landowner in the early seventeenth century. But close behind was a temporal peer, the Earl of Thanet, with vast estates that brought him a princely income. After him came twenty or thirty close-knit county families, who owned a very large part of the Kentish countryside.[4]

At the bottom of this social order were large numbers of desperately poor people: small leaseholders and landless laborers. Most adult males held fewer than five acres. A majority possessed no land at all. In the late sixteenth and early seventeenth century, the poor were increasing more rapidly than the population as a whole. In one farming village (Heydon, Essex) during the year 1568, half the householders had struggled to survive on four acres or less. By 1625, that proportion had risen above two-thirds. Similar tendencies appeared in many East Anglian villages. King, peers and gentry all grew richer, while a landless tenantry sank deeper into the slough of poverty and degradation.[5]

---

[2]T. H. Swales, "The Redistribution of the Monastic Lands in Norfolk at the Dissolution," *NA* 34 (1966–69), 14–44; Francis Blomefield, *An Essay towards a Topographical History of Norfolk* (11 vols., 1805).

[3]William Hunt, *The Puritan Moment: The Coming of Revolution in an English County* (Cambridge, 1983), 15.

[4]Chalkin, *Seventeenth Century Kent,* 50; Everitt, *The Community of Kent in the Great Rebellion,* 35.

[5]Of the county of Essex, Felix Hull writes, "The following points stand out. The first is the great proportion represented by the agrarian proletariat holding less than five acres; the second

Even this wretched rural proletariat was not the very lowest stratum of East Anglian society. At the bottom was a large vagrant population of wandering poor who overran the larger towns and much of the countryside as well. On 1 December 1623, for example, the selectmen of the English town of Braintree hired an officer called the Beadle of the Beggars, whose job was "to gather up about dinner and supper time all the beggars at mens' doors."[6] Chronic unemployment was a major problem throughout the region. In the year 1630, many poor men and women, "complaining for want of work," were given make-work jobs by the towns. Women were set to spinning; men, to picking stone. Most towns looked after their own; their records show that elderly residents were often treated with decency, respect and compassion.[7] Many East Anglian towns bought large quantities of coal from Newcastle, butter from local farmers, and bread from bakers to keep the "town-born" poor from perishing of hunger and cold.[8]

But the vagrant poor were treated with great brutality. Pregnant women were expelled so that their newborn babies would not become a charge upon the town. In the English town of Braintree again, the town records recorded that "notice is given to us of a wench entertained at John Beckwith's dwelling that is supposed to have a great belly, which the constables have warning to look after, and to take order to remove."[9] In Essex, some of these vagrants were sent to the county gaol which was kept in the dark dungeons of Colchester castle. Others went to houses of correction and almshouses. The lucky ones found their way to "hospitals," which were hostels for the poor. In the year 1630 when the ship *Arbella* sailed for America, these places were filled to overflowing—so much so in Essex that whenever one person was accepted, someone else had to be removed.[10]

---

is the comparative uniformity in the statistics." Hull reckoned that in the county of Essex generally, holders of five acres or less amounted to 40% of manorial tenants. Similar patterns appeared throughout the eastern counties. In Norfolk and Suffolk, R. H. Tawney calculated that 54% of the copyholders had less than ten acres. See Felix Hull, "Agriculture and Rural Society in Essex, 1560–1640" (thesis, Univ. of London, 1950), I, 75, 477; R. H. Tawney, *The Agrarian Problem in the Sixteenth Century* (London, 1912), 63.

   [6]Braintree Town Records, 1 Dec. 1623; F. G. Emmison, ed., *Early Essex Town Meetings: Braintree, 1619–1636; Finchingfield, 1626–1634* (London, 1970), 23.

   [7]"Old Father Clewes shall receive 3s 4d quarterly for his relief, being aged. . . . the overseers shall provide for old father Paule in the tyme of his sickness." Braintree Records, 2 Aug. 1630. The materialist argument, that old age was treated with respect only when supported by wealth, is certainly mistaken.

   [8]Emmison, *Early Essex Town Meetings,* xi.

   [9]*Ibid.*

   [10]"Robert Eliott being grown aged and poor, shall be put into the Almshouse wherein Baldwin is, and he turned out." Braintree Records, 12 July 1619, ESSRO.

Between these upper and lower ranks of East Anglian society, there were middling strata, from which came the founders of Massachusetts. This broad middle class included lesser gentry, yeomanry, prosperous farmers, artisans and tradesmen, all of whom were more numerous in the eastern counties than in other parts of England. Freeholders were a small minority in most parts of England. But there were many thousands of freeholders in Kent and large numbers in Essex and Suffolk.[11] They held their lands in fee simple. Even so, they were required to pay quitrents and feudal dues which could be very burdensome. These middling families also contributed the great bulk of the king's revenues and the church's tithes, as well as local poor rates. They were thus compelled to support the people who were both above and below them. This double burden lay heavily upon the stratum that sent so many people to New England.

The experience of social oppression in England caused the founders of Massachusetts to modify the ranking system in their society. After much discussion, they deliberately eliminated both the top and bottom strata of the East Anglian social order, and at the same time carefully preserved its middling distinctions. The result was a social revolution which happened not as the result of some "mysterious Atlantic sea change," as one historian has called it, or as a product of the migration process itself, or as a reflexive response to the material environment. This revolution was a conscious act which rose from religious ideals and social purposes of the founders.

One of the critical decisions was made in the year 1636, when a group of Puritan noblemen considered moving to Massachusetts, and sought assurance that their hereditary powers would be protected in the New World. Their letter began with a "demand" that "the commonwealth should consist of two distinct ranks of men, whereof the one should be for them and their heirs, gentlemen of the country, the other for them and their heirs, freeholders." The Puritan peers also asked that honor, power and authority should be made hereditary.

The letter caused consternation in Massachusetts. The magistrates and ministers of the Bay Colony debated the question at length, and commissioned John Cotton, minister of the first church in Boston, to draft a reply. The tone of their answer was conciliatory, and deferential in high degree. But its substance was negative. To "demand one," the leaders of Massachusetts will-

---

[11]Chalkin, *Seventeenth Century Kent,* 46.

ingly granted "hereditary honor," but "hereditary power" was firmly refused. The Bay colonists declared:

> Two distinct ranks we readily acknowledge, from the light of nature and scripture; the one of them called Princes, or Nobles, or Elders (amongst whom Gentlemen have their place). . . . Hereditary honors both nature and scripture doth acknowledge (Eccles xix.17) but hereditary authority and power standeth only by the civil laws of some commonwealths, and yet even amongst them, the authority of the father is nowhere communicated, together with his honors, unto all his posterity.
>
> When God blesseth any branch of any noble or generous family, with the spirit and gifts fit for government, it would be taking God's name in vain to put such a talent under a bushel, and a sin against the honor of the magistracy to neglect such in our public election.
>
> But if God should not delight to furnish some of their posterity with gifts fit for the magistracy, we should expose them rather to reproach and prejudice, and the commonwealth with them, than exalt them to honor, if we should call them forth, when God doth not, to public authority.[12]

The Puritan peers decided to stay home.

Here was an event of no small importance in American history. The founders of Massachusetts, unlike the rulers of other European colonies, deliberately excluded an aristocracy from their ranking system.

At the same time, the leaders of Massachusetts also made a concerted and highly successful effort to discourage immigration from the bottom of English society. They prohibited the entry of convicted felons (many of whom had been punished for crimes of poverty) and placed heavy impediments in the path of the migrant poor. A series of poor laws were enacted in Massachusetts, with rules of settlement and "warning out" that were even more strict than in England.

Poverty persisted in New England, but it had a different meaning from other cultures. An inhabitant of Boston in 1726 defined the poor as those who "always liv'd from hand to mouth, i.e. depended on one day's labor to supply the wants of another."[13]

---

[12]"Certain Proposals Made by Lord Say, Lord Brooke, and Other Persons of Quality, as Conditions of Their Removing to New-England, with the Answers Thereto," in Thomas Hutchinson, *The History of the Province and Colony of Massachusetts Bay,* (ed. Lawrence S. Mayo) (3 vols., Cambridge, Mass., 1936), I, 410–17.

[13]"Letters of John Andrew," *MAHSP,* ser. I, 8 (1864–65), 344; Jackson T. Main, *The Social Structure of Revolutionary America* (Princeton, 1965), 230.

The poor in this sense were remarkably few in New England—a much smaller part of the population than in England or in other parts of British America. Social attitudes were mixed. Most towns made a genuine effort to look after their own poor, as indeed they required to do by law. But for the town poor, provisions went beyond the minimum. In Salem one man was ordered "to be set by the heels in the stocks for being uncharitable to a poor man in distress."[14]

Even as the founders of Massachusetts sought to eliminate extremes of rank from their society, they were very far from being egalitarian. Most Massachusetts towns deliberately preserved inequalities of status and wealth within a narrow range. Practices varied in detail from one town to another. But most communities deliberately attempted to preserve the system of social ranks which had existed within the small villages of East Anglia. The King, peers, great gentry, landless laborers and wandering poor were all outsiders to those little communities. Most actual members belonged to three ranks—the lesser gentry, yeomanry and cottagers. These people lived, worked and worshipped together, in ways that were bound by ancient customs of stratification, which had existed from "tyme out of mind" in East Anglian communities."

Social distinctions between English gentry, yeomen and laborers were reproduced in Massachusetts, and maintained for many generations. John Adams wrote, "Perhaps it may be said in America we have no distinctions of ranks . . . but have we not laborers, yeomen, gentlemen, esquires, honorable gentlemen, and excellent gentlemen?"[15] By "honorable gentlemen" and "excellent gentlemen" John Adams referred to men who were addressed as "Your Honor," and "Your Excellency." These titles of address also continued in Massachusetts. The gentlefolk of the Bay Colony were addressed as "Mister" and "Mistress" just as in England. Yeomen and their wives were called Goodman and "Goodwife," or "Goody" for short. Only landless laborers lacked titles. Legal proceedings of Massachusetts, like those of England, required that every plaintiff and defendant must be identified by social order, as "gentleman," "yeoman," or "laborer," or else the case could be thrown out of court and new papers would have to

---

[14]Quoted in Richard Gildrie, "Salem, 1626–1668: History of a Covenanted Community" (thesis, Univ. of Va., 1971), 203.

[15]C. F. Adams, ed., *Works of John Adams*, IV, 393; Main, *The Social Structure of Revolutionary America*, 233.

be filed. The faculty of Harvard College ranked their students by the social order of their families. Seating committees of New England meetinghouses also used social order as one of several criteria for assigning seats.

By and large, these ranking systems were pluralistic in their definition. The seating committees of most New England towns normally used three criteria in the assignment of benches and pews—age, estate, and a third indicator that was variously called "reputation," "place" or "usefulness." Of these determinants, age was often (but not always) the most powerful. Seaport towns such as New Haven tended to give more weight to wealth. But most New England communities, if their seating lists are an accurate guide, were more respectful of age than estate. In any case, age, estate and reputation tended to be strongly correlated in Puritan New England. Together they defined a ranking system that persisted for many generations.[16]

In short, the ranking system of East Anglia was reproduced in Massachusetts with two decisive differences. First, the top and bottom strata were removed, and inequality persisted within a more narrow range. Second, the importance of material differences was qualified by age and moral standing, for which the Puritans entertained high respect.

There were strict rules of social deference in this society. People of lower rank were expected to bow and curtsy to their superiors, even when passing on a public road. Travelers as late as the early nineteenth century expressed astonishment at the sight of New England children who turned and bowed at the edge of the highway when their "betters" rode by. Most societies in the seventeenth century were deferential systems, but the rules of deference in New England were different from those in other parts of British America. The lines between masters and servants were not so sharply drawn. Servants and even slaves were always called "help," a word that was brought from England in the seventeenth century. Madame Sarah Knight, when traveling in New England wrote that New Englanders were much too "indulgent" to servants and even slaves, "suffering too great familiarity, permitting them to sit at table and eat with them." By comparison with the twentieth century, New England was indeed a deferential society, but in a very special way.[17]

---

[16]Fischer, *Growing Old in America,* chap. 1.
[17]Knight, "Journal," in Mereness, ed., *Travels in the American Colonies,* 30.

∾ The Massachusetts Comity:
Patterns of Migration, Settlement and Association

In the year 1656, the magistrates of Massachusetts heard a charge of fornication against a troubled young woman of humble rank, who was appropriately named Tryal Pore. She pleaded guilty to her indictment and told the court, "By this my sin I have not only done what I can to pull down judgment from the Lord on myself, but also upon the place where I live."[1]

Tryal Pore came from the underclass of the Bay Colony. Her prophetic name hinted at other troubles which her parents had known even before she was born. But for all of her misfortunes, she shared the Puritan purposes of the colony, and showed a strong sense of responsibility for "the place where I live." That sense of belonging became the basis of a comity in Massachusetts which was similar in many respects to that of eastern England.

A modern study has found three types of settlement in East Anglia during the seventeenth century—villages, hamlets and dispersed farmsteads. The leading student of this subject observes that "no single settlement type assumed dominance," but villages and hamlets were common, and isolated homesteads were comparatively rare. Houses were not scattered across the countryside, but grouped in small clusters close to the edges of major roads.

Similar settlement-patterns also appeared in Massachusetts at an early date, and persisted for three centuries—the familiar New England system of nucleated central villages, with small satellite hamlets and isolated farmsteads of "outliers" scattered along the country roads. From the start there were always a few stubborn loners, of whom the General Court complained that they "keep their families at their farms, being remote from any town." But their numbers were comparatively small in Massachusetts. Towns and hamlets became normal units of settlement, as in the east of England.[2]

The builders of the Bay Colony actively encouraged close-built towns. A law in 1635 ordered that "no dwelling house shall be built above half a mile from the meeting house in any new plantation . . . without leave from the Court, except mill houses & farm houses of such as have their dwelling houses in some town."[3]

---

[1]Morgan, *Puritan Family*, 10.
[2]*Ibid.*, I, 190.
[3]*Mass. Bay Records*, I, 157; 3 Sept. 1635.

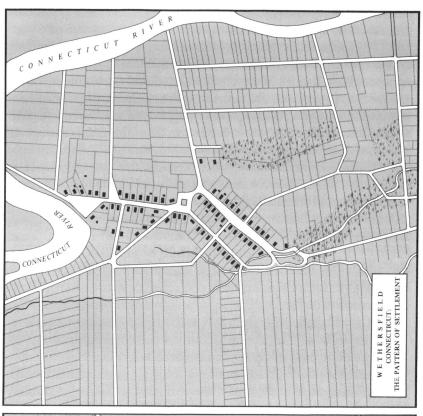

WETHERSFIELD
CONNECTICUT:
THE PATTERN OF SETTLEMENT

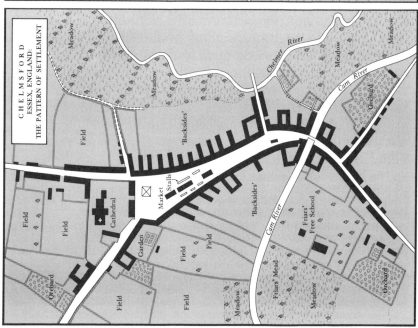

CHELMSFORD
ESSEX, ENGLAND:
THE PATTERN OF SETTLEMENT

Similar laws were also passed in many other colonies, but could not be enforced. In Massachusetts, the policy was made to work because the founders came from the most densely settled region of England, and two-thirds had lived in villages or towns before emigrating. They brought with them an East Anglian habit of settlement which they reproduced in the New World.

In this process of reproduction, changes were inevitably introduced. The New England town became a more formal institution, fixed in its conception, recognized in law, and continuously replicated across the New England countryside. Once again, the major tendency was not the reproduction of an English form but its creative adaptation to the conditions of a new environment.

Within a few years of settlement, the New England town had taken on the character which it retained for three centuries, complete with meetinghouses and schools, stocks and pillories, animal pounds and training fields, town commons and enclosed fields, nucleated centers and rural neighborhoods. Despite many individual differences, the first forty towns in Massachusetts possessed these attributes by 1650, as do most of the 1,600 New England towns that exist today.[4]

In the origin of these settlement patterns, East Anglian folkways played a major role. One may observe their importance in the history of the town of Salem, which was settled by two groups—a party of "old planters" who came from the West Country before 1628, and a contingent of East Anglians who arrived in the great migration during the 1630s. They brought with them two very different ideas of community. Historian Richard Gildrie writes:

> The West Country and East Anglian conceptions of the ideal community tended to differ in material ways. Salem's West Countrymen had originated in an area of dispersed and separate farms. . . . East Anglians tended to envision the ideal community as a compact village. . . . Until 1636 the great difficulty of clearing the wilderness kept the West Countrymen on the peninsula, but as soon as they could, they spread out over the township, building

---

[4]Much, perhaps too much, has been made of differences between towns in 17th-century Massachusetts—between covenanted and uncovenanted towns, seed towns and satellite towns, communal towns and nucleated towns. All of these distinctions existed within a very narrow range, by contrast with other types of local communities in the Western world. Strong similarities sprang from common purposes and common experiences, and also from the laws of the Bay Colony, which strictly regulated many institutions—political, religious, educational, familial and economic.

farms and hamlets in the pattern most familiar to them. East Anglians, however, tended to stay in the original village. . . .[5]

These communities gained a strong hold upon their individual members. One indicator of their social gravity was the rate of internal migration, which was very low in New England before 1780. In the town of Dedham, for example, only 9 percent of taxable inhabitants moved away during the entire decade of the 1690s. Even fewer (7%) moved out of town in the 1670s. In Hingham and Concord the pattern was much the same.[6]

[5]The quantitative data appear in Gildrie, "Salem, 1626–1668," 60. It should be noted that patterns of settlement and field systems were two different but related issues, on which regional customs were very mixed. Open fields in particular were introduced as a matter of expediency in the first generation and rapidly abandoned in most towns. In Salem, East Anglians supported open fields and West Countrymen remained apart from them. In Watertown and Sudbury, the opposite was the case—another indication that the "means of production" were secondary to cultural affiliations.

[6]The following persistence rates have been found in studies of eight New England towns:

Town	Period	Crude Persistence Rate	Refined Persistence Rate I	Refined Persistence Rate II
Rowley, Mass.	1643–53	59%	71%	
Dedham, Mass.	1648–60	51%		63%
	1660–70	78%		88%
	1670–80	76%		93%
	1680–90	73%		91%
	1690–1700	83%		96%
Brookline, Mass.	1674–87	42%	49%	
	1688–93	66%	69%	
	1746–53	63%	69%	
	1753–70	43%	62%	
	1771–83	42%	58%	
	1784–91		71%	
Hingham, Mass.	1670–80	73%	88%	93%
	1754–65	69%	76%	
	1790–1800	62%		82%
Windsor, Conn.	1676–86	57%	71%	
	1686–1702	57%	79%	
Wenham, Mass.	1731–41	68%	76%	83%
	1741–51	58%	67%	73%
	1751–61	53%	70%	74%
	1761–70	59%	70%	76%
Beverly, Mass.	1741–51	50%	66%	
	1751–61	58%	67%	
	1761–71	60%	67%	
Concord, Mass.	1746–57	69%		84%
	1757–70	71%		86%

A crude persistence rate measures the proportion of one population list which reappears upon another list, without regard to mortality. Refined persistence (Type I) removes from the first list all who are known to have died, and assumes that others not persisting have moved. Refined persistence (Type II) assumes that "unknowns" for whom no evidence of death or migration survives tended to share the same persistence rates as others. Computed from data

Those studies refer not to the entire population, but mainly to mature male adults. Young people were more mobile, partly because of the custom of sending out children.[7] Women also moved more often than men because patterns of settlement after marriage tended to be patrilocal.[8] There were many other variations, but in New England as a whole rates of refined persistence were very high—in some older country towns, the highest that have been measured in any adult population throughout the Western world. This pattern continued from the mid-seventeenth century to the late eighteenth.[9]

These patterns of migration and settlement helped to create a special system of association in New England. The vital factors were the comparative immobility of the mature population and the density of town life in this region. A special language of belonging was carried to Massachusetts from the east of England. It appeared in words such as "townsman" and "town-born" which were common in East Anglia during the seventeenth century, and also became part of the social vocabulary of New England. On the night of the Boston massacre, for example, a cry went through the streets of the city, "Town-born, turn out!"

So strong was this sense of belonging that when danger threatened in Massachusetts, people turned instinctively toward their fellow townsmen. A small earthquake in Massachusetts, for example, caused "divers men . . . being at work in the fields, to cast down their working-tools and run with ghastly terrified looks to the next company they could meet withal."[10]

The same feeling also led to strong resentments against outsiders. Rivalries between towns were so intense that they sometimes

---

in Lockridge, "Dedham"; Smith, "Hingham"; Harris, "Concord"; Dreyfuss, "Brookline"; Auwers, "Windsor"; and Douglas Lamar Jones, *Village and Seaport: Migration and Society in Eighteenth-Century Massachusetts* (Hanover, 1981).

[7] High rates of migration in early life explain why so many New Englanders died outside their native towns at the same time that persistence rates on tax lists were very high; cf. John W. Adams and Alice Bee Kasakoff, "Migration and the Family in Colonial New England: The View from Genealogies," *JFH* 9 (1984), 24–43; and "Migration at Marriage in Colonial New England . . . ," in Bennett Dyke and Warren Morrill, eds., *Genealogical Demography* (New York, 1980).

[8] *Mass. Bay Records*, I, 190.

[9] An unanswered question is the similarity of migration in New England and East Anglia. There have been many English studies of internal migration in the east of England, but differences in methods and materials do not permit controlled quantitative comparisons. See John Patten, *English Towns, 1500–1700* (Folkestone, Kent, 1978); and "Patterns of Migration and Movement of Labour to Three Pre-industrial East-Anglian Towns," *JHG* 2 (1976), 111–29; Peter Clark and Paul Slack, *Crisis and Order in English Towns, 1500–1700* (London, 1972); Peter Clark, ed., *The Transformation of English Provincial Towns, 1600–1800* (Oxford, 1982).

[10] Johnson, *Wonder Working Providence*, 185.

led to violence in the seventeenth century. One such clash occurred between the Connecticut towns of Stamford and Greenwich over disputed boundary lines. Another quarrel between New London and nearby towns over a meadow ended in a nasty fight when the farmers of these communities attacked each other with sharpened scythes. A conflict over land between the towns of Windsor and Enfield led to a pitched battle in which 100 men were said to be "fiercely engaged in resolute combat." New England towns were units of passionate identity. Many took on a character and even a personality of their own, and have maintained it through many generations.[11]

The tone and spirit of association within New England towns was very different from other communities. A British traveler observed of New Englanders that "the people are uncommonly stiff and formal." Similar statements were made by many other visitors.[12]

The New England town, for all its solidarity against external threats, was not a unitary structure. The most important unit of daily association in Massachusetts was not the town itself but the neighborhood—a small cluster of houses, inhabited by families who were increasingly related to one another. From an early date in the seventeenth century, these rural neighborhoods appeared on the settlement maps of most New England towns. Urban neighborhoods also appeared at the nucleated centers of these communities. Even the isolated homesteads of "outlyers" tended to be bunched loosely together on a stretch of road, with long unbuilt distances round about.

The existence of neighborhoods was recognized by law in Massachusetts as early as 1633. One statute in that year declared that "no man shall give his swine any corn but such, as being viewed by two or three neighbors, shall be thought unfit for any man's meat."[13] This was a continuation of practices in the east of England, where mundane questions were routinely settled by what was called the "laws of neighbouring men," or the "custom of neighbours."[14]

"Neighboring" was a verb in Massachusetts which described social acts of high complexity. The spirit of a New England neigh-

[11]Andrews, *Pilgrims and Puritans*, 133.

[12]Gordon, "Journal of an Officer," 448.

[13]*Mass. Bay Records*, I, 110.

[14]For examples from Lincolnshire see Joan Thirsk, "Field Systems of the East Midlands," in A. R. H. Baker and R. A. Butlin, eds., *Studies in the Field Systems of the British Isles* (Cambridge, 1979), 279.

"Towne marks" in Puritan Massachusetts were important symbols of belonging and were used for the branding of animals. In the southern colonies every planter had his own individual brand, but in Puritan Massachusetts animals were also marked by town. The General Court of Massachusetts formally agreed on these "towne marks" for horses, "to be set upon one of the near quarters." These marks were (col. 1, left): Charlestown, Cambridge, Concord, Salem, Salisbury, Sudbury, Strawberry Bank (Portsmouth), Dorchester; (col. 2): Dedham, Dover, Boston, Braintree, Roxbury, Rowley, Reading, Watertown; (col. 3): Weymouth, Woburn, Northampton, Lynn, Ipswich, Newbury, Hingham, Hampton; (col. 4): Haverhill, Gloucester, Medford, Manchester, Andover, Hull, Springfield, Exeter. (Mass. Records, II [1647], 225)

borhood was summarized in a proverb by a descendant of the great migration, Benjamin Franklin. "Love your neighbor," said Poor Richard, "but don't pull down your fence." This Yankee proverb was not invented in New England. In England a century earlier, George Herbert had written, "Love your neighbor, yet pull not down your hedges." Even as the granite "fences" of Massachusetts replaced the green hedgerows of England, customs of social "hedging" remained much the same. Here was yet another continuity from the Old World to the New.[15]

One might recognize a ring of modernity in this system, but in other ways, the comity of early New England was far removed from systems of association in our own time. This was specially the case in regard to social reputation, which was urgently important to the Puritans, as to most others of their age. The social cement of their world was a sense of belonging, and an intense fear of "shame," which was the emotion felt when reputation was lost. Punishments were meant to promote a sense of shame. Fornicating couples were sometimes compelled to stand in white sheets before the congregation and confess their sins. Drunkards were forced to wear a great shame-letter D, "made of red cloth and set upon white, and to continue for a year."[16] Serious offenses were punished by excommunication, in which every member of the church was ordered "to forbear to eat and drink with him," and life became an agony of isolation and shame.[17]

The opposite of shame was honor. Puritans had a very strong sense of honor—but one that was very different from what historian Bertram Wyatt-Brown has called the "primal honor" of the cavaliers who came to Virginia. When John Winthrop wrote of honor, which he often did, he meant mainly a condition of Christian sanctification. In 1643, Winthrop instructed his son, ". . . esteem it the greatest honor to lie under the simplicity of Christ crucified." When Cotton Mather celebrated the "honor" of New England's founders, he meant a reputation for being "a studious, humble, patient, reserved and mortified person, and one in whom the love of God was fervent and the love of man sincere."[18] These obsessions with honor and shame were not unique to New England, but the Puritans gave them a special meaning.

[15]Carl Bridenbaugh, *Vexed and Troubled Englishmen* (New York, 1968), 70.
[16]*Mass. Bay Records*, I, 112.
[17]Earle, *The Sabbath in Puritan New England*, 264.
[18]Mather, *Magnalia Christi America*, I, 160–61; references to "honor" and "honorable"

✎ Massachusetts Order Ways:
The Puritan Idea of Order as Unity

Yet another component of this culture was its system of social order. In that regard, New England was characterized by a curious paradox. This was always the most orderly region in British America, but it was also very violent in its ordering acts. This typically Puritan paradox of private order and public violence was specially striking in the seventeenth and eighteenth centuries. For many generations, individual order coexisted with an institutional savagery that appeared in the burning of rebellious servants, the maiming of political dissenters, the hanging of Quakers, the execution of witches and the crushing to death with heavy stones of an old man who refused to plead before the court.

These two tendencies, of individual order and institutional violence, were closely linked. Among the Puritan founders of Massachusetts, order was an obsession. The intensity of their concern—and its distance from our own time—appeared in a startling argument by Puritan minister John Norton, who insisted that it was "better an innocent and a good man should suffer than order; for that preserves the whole."[1]

The prevailing idea of order in Puritan Massachusetts was very different from our own conceptions. It did not primarily mean "a state of peace and serenity" as Webster's Dictionary defines it, but rather a condition where everything was put in its proper place and held there by force if necessary. Order, for the Puritans, meant a condition of organic unity—the order that "preserves the whole" in John Norton's definition—a oneness of the spirit that did not readily admit internal differences. The same idea often appeared in Puritan writings. John Winthrop spoke of order as "the preservation and good of the whole."[2] The Puritan divine Solomon Stoddard explained that "a church is not a confused body of people; but they that are brought into order, and each must observe his proper station: it is compared to a natural body, wherein there are diverse organs appointed to their pecu-

---

qualities appear throughout this work; see, e.g., I, 157, 158, 253, 262, *passim.* See also the discussion of Puritan ideas of honor in Bertram Wyatt-Brown, *Southern Honor; Ethics and Behavior in the Old South* (New York, 1982), 26.

[1]John Norton, *Sion the Outcast Healed of Her Wounds* (Cambridge, Mass., 1664).
[2]John Winthrop, "A Modell of Christian Charity," *Winthrop Papers,* II, 282–83.

liar services."[3] The importance of unity became the leading
theme of Puritan sermons in the seventeenth and early eighteenth century. "Union," declared Jonathan Edwards, "is one of
the most amiable things that pertains to human society; yea, it is
one of the most beautiful and happy things on earth, which
indeed makes earth most like heaven."[4]

This idea of order as organic unity was deeply embedded in the
cosmology of English Calvinism. But the ordering institutions of
New England were drawn from a different source—mainly those
that had existed in the towns of East Anglia. The builders of the
Bay Colony chose very selectively from these English precedents.
In the first generation, for example, they decided not to introduce the office of sheriff. That hated symbol of royal prerogative
and aristocratic power was not welcome in early New England.
Neither, at first, did they have any use for the peace-keeping officers of the Anglican church such as beadles and other parish
policemen who were chosen by vestry and clergy to collect tithes
and keep order. Through the first half of the seventeenth century, The Bay colonists did without these unpopular officials.

Puritan Massachusetts turned instead to the most communitar-
ian of English peacekeepers—the village constable. This was an
ancient office, derived from the borsholders, headboroughs, bor-
oughheads and reeves who were elected by an English township
or tithing, rather than being appointed by higher authority.[5] In
New England, the constable was an officer of the town, chosen by
his neighbors. His duty was to serve processes, execute warrants,
deliver writs, make arrests, and summon town meetings. He could
also be called upon to collect taxes, organize elections, look after
lost goods, recover stray animals, keep a record of newcomers to
the town and arrest "such strange persons as do walk abroad in
the night . . . and sleep in the day; or which do haunt any house,
where is suspicion of bawdie." He was also required to visit and
inspect all the households in the town at least once in every three
months, and each year to read all the laws pertaining to the Sabbath. When serious trouble threatened, the constable was not

---

[3]Solomon Stoddard, *The Way for a People to Live Long in the Land That God Hath Given Them*
(Boston, 1705), 61.

[4]Jonathan Edwards, *A Humble Attempt to Promote Explicit Agreement and Visible Union in God's
People* . . . (Boston, 1747), reprinted in David Austin, *The Millennium* (Elizabethtown, N.J.,
1794), 171; see also David Balch, *A Public Spirit* (Boston, 1749). Kerry A. Trask, "In the Pursuit
of Shadows; A Study of Collective Hope and Despair in Provincial Massachusetts . . ." (thesis,
Univ. of Minn., 1972), 21.

[5]Joan R. Kent, *The English Village Constable, 1580-1642* (Oxford, 1986), 15.

expected to deal with it himself, but to summon all the men of the town, who were required by law to support him. In New England, the community itself was the ultimate peacekeeper.

By and large, the system worked. Violent crime and disorder were comparatively uncommon in Massachusetts. Homicide rates in seventeenth-century New England were less than half those of the Chesapeake colonies.[6] Assaults against persons were also less frequent in New England than in any other part of British America.[7] In the Massachusetts county courts, crimes against property were more common than crimes against persons.[8] But crimes against order were the most common of all. In Massachusetts towns, most adults were prosecuted at least once for criminal offenses against order—commonly small sabbath violations,

[6]In the period from 1657 to 1680, the annual homicide rate in Massachusetts was below 3 per 100,000. In Maryland, it was above 7 per 100,000. Computed from data in William Buttenweiser, "An Examination of Murders, 1630–1692; Frequency, Seasonal Variations, Participants in Maryland and Massachusetts" (unpub. paper, Brandeis, 1978).

[7]The first national crime statistics which allow controlled regional comparisons were for robbery of the U.S. mail. This offense was rare in New England and regional disparities were very great:

State	Number of Offenses, 1790–1827
Maine	0
Massachusetts	5
Rhode Island	1
Vermont	0
New York	1
New Jersey	3
Pennsylvania	10
Maryland	11
Virginia	14
South Carolina	2
Georgia	4
Tennessee	10
Kentucky	6
Ohio	8
Indiana	0

Returns were not given for missing states; *Returns of . . . Offences against the Laws of the United States* (Washington, 1828).

[8]Mark Saloman found the following patterns of criminal prosecution in the county courts of Essex, Suffolk, and Plymouth from 1636 to 1699:

Crimes Against:	Total	Essex Co. 1636–41	Suffolk Co. 1671–80	Plymouth 1651–68	Plymouth 1668–99
Order	503 (51.3%)	40 (60.6%)	251 (44.0%)	162 (66.7%)	50 (51.5%)
Sexual Morality	225 (23.0%)	6 (9.0%)	144 (25.2%)	42 (17.3%)	33 (34.0%)
Property	175 (17.9%)	16 (24.2%)	131 (22.9%)	22 (9.0%)	6 (6.2%)
The Person	74 (7.6%)	4 (6.0%)	45 (7.9%)	17 (7.0%)	8 (8.3%)

Mark Andrew Saloman, "Community and Hierarchy: A Comparative Study of Law, Crime and Punishment in Colonial Massachusetts and Maryland, 1636–1699," (thesis, Brandeis, 1989), 43.

minor cases of disturbing the peace, sexual offenses, idleness, lying, domestic disorder or drunkenness. Criminal proceedings for offenses of this sort were very common, but prosecutions for major crimes of theft and violence were comparatively rare.[9]

Comparatively low rates of violent crime persisted in New England for 300 years and more. Timothy Dwight observed that most people throughout this region never bothered to bar their houses, or to keep their valuables under lock and key, even in seaport towns.[10] A lawyer in Beverly, Massachusetts, wrote in 1840 that "during a practice of nearly forty years, he had never known a native of Beverly convicted of any heinous crime."[11] Harriet Beecher Stowe believed that New England in her generation was a place "where one could go to sleep at all hours of day or night with the house door wide open, without bolt or bar, yet without apprehension of any to molest or make afraid."[12]

Violent crime which invaded the domestic peace of a Puritan household was punished with special rigor in New England. The Massachusetts laws against burglary were exceptionally severe, and court proceedings still more so. The people of this culture had a particular horror of violence which threatened the home.[13]

---

[9]Saloman, "Community and Hierarchy," 37–42. Michael Hindus found that differences between Massachusetts and South Carolina in the relative frequency of crimes persisted into the 18th century.

	Percent of Total Criminal Prosecutions	
	Middlesex Co., Mass. 1760–74	Charleston, S.C. 1769–76
Crimes against persons (murder, assault, rape)	9.5%	53.6%
Crimes against property (larceny, arson)	13.2%	37.8%
Crimes against sexual mores (fornication, bastardy)	57.6%	1.6%
Crimes against order (contempt of authority, riot, vagrancy, church offenses, etc.)	18.4%	1.6%
Slave-related crimes	0.0%	3.1%
Counterfeiting, fraud	1.2%	2.4%
Total	99.9%	100.1%

Similar contrasts continued in the 19th century; see Michael S. Hindus, *Prison and Plantation: Crime, Justice and Authority in Massachusetts and South Carolina, 1767–1878* (Chapel Hill, 1980), 64–65. Another important study is David H. Flaherty, "Crime and Social Control in Provincial Massachusetts," *HJ* 24 (1981), 339–60.

[10]Dwight, *Travels*, I, 141.

[11]Edwin Stone, *History of Beverly* (Boston, 1843), 307.

[12]Stowe, *Oldtown Folks*, 1208.

[13]For evidence of a major difference between Massachusetts and Maryland in prosecutions for burglary, see Saloman, "Community and Hierarchy," 107–31.

Mob violence was also comparatively uncommon in Puritan New England, except in seaport towns such as Salem, Marblehead and Boston. Savage riots sometimes occurred in those troubled communities. The worst happened at Marblehead in 1677. After several fishing crews had been taken by the Indians, a mob of fishermens' wives seized two Indian captives and literally tore them limb from limb. A witness reported:

> The women surrounded them . . . and laid violent hands upon the captives, some stoning us and me in the meantime, because we would protect them. . . . Then, with stones, billets of wood, and what else they might, they made an end of these indians. We were kept at such a distance that we could not see them till they were dead, and then found them with their heads off and gone, and their flesh in a manner pulled from their bones. And such was the tumultation these women made, that . . . they suffered neither constable nor mandrake, nor any other person to come near them, until they had finished their bloody purpose.[14]

Scenes such as this sometimes occurred on the edges of New England society. But in Middlesex County during the mid-seventeenth century only one riot occurred— the pulling down of a maypole. When riots did happen, they were regulated by custom in a curious way. John Adams in 1774 drew a distinction between "public mobs" which defended law and the constitution, and "private mobs" which took to the streets "in resentment of private wrongs." Adams believed that "public mobs" were constitutional, and even a necessary instrument of order. But he added that "private mobs I do and will detest. . . ."[15] By comparison with other colonies, there were very few public mobs and political rebellions in New England.[16]

But when "unconstitutional" disturbances occurred, the people of Massachusetts did not hesitate to suppress them with the utmost rigor. Penalties were arranged in a hierarchy of official

---

[14]James Axtell, ed., "The Vengeful Women of Marblehead," *WMQ3* 31 (1974), 652.

[15]John Adams to Abigail Adams, 7 July 1774, *Adams Family Correspondence,* ed. Butterfield, I, 131; John R. Howe, Jr., *The Changing Political Thought of John Adams* (Princeton, 1966), 13. This was not Adams's view alone, nor merely a rationale for revolution. The same conception of "constitutional mobs" was also held by the Massachusetts tory Thomas Hutchinson, who observed that "mobs, a sort of them at least, are constitutional," even as he fell victim to their violence in Boston. Pauline Maier, "Popular Uprisings and Civil Authority in Eighteenth-Century America," *WMQ3* 27 (1970), 24; see also *idem, From Resistance to Revolution; Colonial Radicals and the Development of American Opposition to Britain, 1765–1776* (New York, 1972), 3–26.

[16]A strong regional pattern appears in the frequency of armed rebellions in the thirteen colonies from 1607 to 1763: New Hampshire, 2; Massachusetts, 1; Rhode Island, 2; Connecticut, 0; New York, 4; New Jersey, 3; Pennsylvania, 3; Delaware, 0; Maryland, 9; Virginia, 9; North Carolina, 7; South Carolina, 3; these data will appear in vol. IV, *Deep Change,* forthcoming.

violence. The most terrible punishment in Massachusetts was burning at the stake—the punishment for cases of petty treason which were defined as the killing of masters by servants. At least two people were burnt alive in Massachusetts. Both were black women: a slave named Maria who was found guilty in 1681 of setting fire to her master's house in the town of Roxbury, and a slave called Phyllis who was burned in Cambridge for having poisoned her master with arsenic.[17]

The next most terrible punishment was death by hanging. The colony of Massachusetts recognized thirteen capital crimes in 1648: witchcraft, idolatry, blasphemy, homicide, rape, adultery, bestiality, sodomy, false witness with intent to take life, and a child of sixteen or older who was a "stubborn" or "rebellious" son, or who "smote" or "cursed" a parent. All of these laws were drawn from the Pentateuch except the punishment for rape.[18]

Next to hanging, in point of violence, were punishments by maiming—the slitting of the nostrils, the amputation of ears, the branding of the face or hands. All of these terrible penalties were administered by the Puritans in Massachusetts. Quakers, for example, were punished with special ferocity. Some were branded in the face and "burned very keep with a red-hot iron with H. for heresie." Others had their ears cut off, faces scarred and nostrils slit open in a saturnalia of sadistic punishment.[19]

For less serious offenses, the penalty was whipping, unless one could pay a fine. These punishments were sometimes very severe. Four Quaker women were ordered to be stripped to the waist, tied to a cart's tail and conveyed "from constable to constable," through twelve New England towns, and to be whipped in every town. The women were flogged so terribly that the blood coursed down their naked backs and breasts, until the horrified townsmen of Salisbury rose against the constables and rescued them.[20] One

---

[17]George Francis Dow, *Every Day Life in the Massachusetts Bay Colony* (Boston, 1935), 210.

[18]Powers estimated in the county courts of Essex and Suffolk, and the Massachusetts Court of Assistants and the Plymouth Court from 1620 to 1692, the death penalty was invoked for the following offenses: witchcraft, 23; murder, 11; piracy, 6; rape, 4; Quakers, 4; bestiality, 2; adultery, 2; arson, 2; treason, 2. Flaherty found that in Massachusetts from 1693 to 1769, 56 people were hanged: murder, 26; infanticide, 15; burglary 8, rape, 3; arson, 3; sodomy, 1. See Flaherty, "Crime and Social Control in Provincial Massachusetts," 339–60; "The Punishment of Crime at the Massachusetts Assizes: An Overview, 1692–1750" (unpub. paper, 1978–79); Edwin Powers, *Crime and Punishment in Early Massachusetts, 1620–1692* (Boston, 1966), 294, 404–8; Kathryn Preyer, "Penal Measures in the American Colonies: An Overview," *AJLH* 26 (1982), 327–53.

[19]Alice Morse Earle, *Curious Punishments of Bygone Days* (1896, Rutland, Vt., 1972), 140; Jones, *Quakers in the American Colonies*, 75.

[20]Earle, *Curious Punishments*, 140.

male Quaker missionary was flogged nearly to death in Massachusetts, and Puritan minister John Norton made a joke of it: "He endeavored to beat the gospel ordinances black and blue, and it was but just to beat *him* black and blue."[21]

Other offenses were punished by various forms of public humiliation—stocks and pillories in particular. Criminals were often required to wear on their clothing a letter of the law, in some contrasting color as a badge of shame—not only the immortal A for adultery, but B for blasphemy or burglary, C for counterfeiting, D for drunkenness, F for forgery, R for roguery, S for sedition, T for Theft—an entire alphabet of humiliation. A man in Deerfield was required to wear "a capital I of two inches long, and proportionable bigness," for the crime of incest.[22]

Calvinist magistrates also invented other ingenious punishments to fit lesser crimes. A woman in Salem had her tongue put in a cleft stick for "reproaching the elders." A dishonest baker was made to stand in the stocks with a lump of dough on his head. Robert Saltonstall, for having "parsimoniously presented a petition on so small and bad a piece of paper," was fined five shillings. Imprisonment was also used as a punishment in New England. Convicts were sometimes confined in holes below ground. In the district of Maine, they were kept through the winter in solitary earth pits that measured nine and a half by four and a half by ten feet deep. Connecticut confined its prisoners in a copper mine.[23]

Justice was swift in New England. The law required four days' interval between sentencing and execution, but this provision was often honored in the breach. For example, two servants (one Scottish, the other French) murdered their master by "knocking him in the head as he was taking tobacco." The crime was committed on 10 February 1675. The two men were hunted down by their neighbors, taken by hue and cry, tried and found guilty, and hanged on 13 February, only three days later.[24]

These applications of official violence were not unique to New England. They also existed in other parts of British America. But the Puritans added their own special intensity of moral purpose to the general rigor of punishment that existed throughout the

---

[21]Jones, *Quakers in the American Colonies*, 71.

[22]Boston *Evening Post*, 7 Oct. 1754.

[23]Richard H. Phelps, *Newgate of Connecticut; Its Origin and Early History, Being a Full Description of the Famous and Wonderful Simsbury Mines and Caverns, and Prison Built over Them* (Hartford, Conn., 1876); Earle, *Curious Punishments*, 92 passim.

[24]Powers, *Crime and Punishment*, 295.

Western world in the seventeenth century. The result was a
regime that combined collective order and institutional violence
in an exceptionally high degree.

❧ Massachusetts Power Ways:
   The Politics of Town Meeting Government

Within a few years of settlement, a unique system of government
by town meetings and selectmen took form in Massachusetts.
Many historians believe that these institutions were invented in
the New World. Leading dictionaries identify the words *town
meeting* and *selectman* as Americanisms.[1] Nothing could be farther
from the case. New England town meetings were transplanted
from East Anglia, where they had existed for many centuries
before the great migration. In the Suffolk County Record Office
at Ipswich, for example, one may find a musty leather-bound
folio volume of great antiquity which contains the records of the
parish of Framlingham—after which the Massachusetts town of
Framingham took its name. On its cover, this volume bears a title
which is written in an old hand: "Town Book." In many East
Anglian communities, the words "town" and "parish" were used
interchangeably. In the great book of Framlingham, the expressions "general parish meeting" and "general town meeting" were
synonyms.[2]

These East Anglian towns governed themselves through officers sometimes called "selectmen." Some East Anglian selectmen
were elected by all the people called "townsmen." Others were
self-perpetuating oligarchies. Always, selectmen were men of substance—prosperous yeomen and artisans for the most part.[3] They
were also men with grey heads, chosen for their maturity, wisdom
and experience in local government. In some East Anglian communities, selectmen were called "ancients."[4]

The selectmen disposed of routine business, but in many parishes of East Anglia, larger questions were dealt with by assemblies explicitly called "town meetings," which brought together

---

[1]Mitford Mathews, *A Dictionary of Americanisms* (Chicago, 1951), *s.v.,* "town meeting,"
"selectman."

[2]Framlingham Town Book; also East Bergholt Town Book, 15 Feb. 1650; both in SUFROIP.

[3]Occupation and rank is given in the town meeting book of East Bergholt, 1650–78,
SUFROIP.

[4]Braintree Town Book, ESSRO.

the "principal inhabitants" of the community. These East Anglian town meetings were diverse in their structure. No two of them were quite the same. But they commonly allowed a large number of townsmen to participate in local government.[5]

Another part of the New England polity was a set of fundamental documents that functioned very much like a written constitution. The East Anglian community of Dedham, for example, had a local constitution called "The Ancient Customs of the Town and Parish of Dedham, County of Essex, which is and hath been, tyme out of minde, of both the lordships there."[6] This document laid down the rules of inheritance, which in Dedham happened to favor the youngest son. It described the processes of law and self-government in that community, and included by-laws for building, farming, and animal keeping such as were commonly covered by manorial customals throughout England during the early decades of the seventeenth century. But the Dedham document was something different from manorial documents. It was a single set of laws that existed for all the manors in the "town." Further, Dedham's "ancient customs" were enforced not by a manorial lord but by all the landholders who lived in the town. "If any man offend in any of these lawes," the document declared, "the tenants may set such fines on their heads as they shall thinke meet and convenient."[7]

Every East Anglian town had its own customs; no two were ever exactly the same and most changed through time. The word *town* itself altered its meaning in this period—slowly beginning to be used in a new sense to describe small urban centers. East Anglia had many towns in this modern sense—more than any other part of England in the early seventeenth century. These places developed systems of self-government that were very different from more rural communities. An example was the market town of Braintree, whose government was mainly in the hands of a local oligarchy called the "Four and Twenty," who functioned much like the ruling elites of many market towns throughout Europe. But when major problems occurred, the "governors of the town" called general town meetings to decide the matter. In September 1625, for example, Braintree's Four and Twenty summoned all the "chiefe inhabitants of the town" to meet in the Church and

---

[5]A selection of these records has been published in Emmison, *Early Essex Town Meetings.*
[6]The Ancient Customs of the Towne and Parishe of Dedham, County of Essex . . . ," ESSRO.
[7]*Ibid.*

to "confer on some course to be taken to set the poor to work at this hard time."[8] In 1630, these institutions were still common throughout the eastern counties of England.

When the Puritans came to America, this ancient system of government by town meetings, selectmen and fundamental laws became the basis of local government in New England. In the year 1636, a statute of the Massachusetts General Court defined town governments in their classical form. Throughout the smaller communities of New England, these institutions have remained remarkably stable for many generations. The institutional building blocks were town meetings, town selectmen, town covenants and town records. Many differences of detail developed from one town to another. The nature of the relationship between selectmen and town meetings, for instance, was very unclear: some Massachusetts towns met more frequently than others; some selectmen were more powerful; some covenants were more formal. In consequence, a variety of town customs developed in New England. But they did so within a narrow range which was fixed by the laws of the colony within a few years of its beginning.

A distinctive pattern of participation in town meetings also developed at an early date in Massachusetts. It was normally characterized by very low levels of turnout—normally in the range of 10 to 30 percent of adult males. But when controversial questions came before the town, participation surged—sometimes approaching 100 percent.[9]

This pattern still exists in New England. The major issues today might be a tax-override or a middle school, rather than the choice

---

[8]Emmison, *Early Essex Town Meetings,* 23.

[9]This pattern in Massachusetts town meetings before 1780 may be seen in the following statistics of voters as a percentage of adult males:

Boston: 1696, 10%; 1698, 25%; 1699, 23%; 1703, 31%; 1703, 16%; 1704, 14%; 1709, 13%; 1711, 10%; 1715, 15%; 1716, 21%; 1717, 16%; 1718, 13%; 1719, 25%; 1721, 13%; 1722, 11%; 1723, 14%; 1724, 10%; 1725, 16%; 1726, 9%; 1727, 9%; 1728, 11%; 1729, 8%; 1730, 22%; 1755, 15%; 1756, 24%; 1757, 24%; 1758, 17%; 1759, 21%; 1760, 45%; 1761, 15%; 1762, 28%; 1763, 49%; 1764, 20%; 1765, 29%; 1766, 34%; 1767, 28%; 1768, 20%; 1769, 23%; 1770, 23%; 1771, 19%; 1772, 33%; 1773, 19%; 1774, 24%. Concord: 1765, 51%; 1765, 62%; 1778, 25%; 1778, 36%. Lynn: 1750, 32%; 1751, 32%; 1752, 37%; 1753, 21%; 1754, 24%; 1756, 28%. Salem: 1735, 24%; 1738, 25%; 1739, 15%; 1740, 21%; 1741, 39%; 1742, 24%. Watertown: 1757, 97%. Weston: 1772, 80%. Dorchester: 1726, 30%; 1750, 37%; 1751, 32%. Stockbridge: 1763, 94% (awm). Cambridge: 1739, 45%. Woburn: 1742, 38%.

Sources: Robert J. Dinkin, *Voting in Provincial America* (Westport, Conn. 1977), 174; Marshall C. Spatz, "Political Power in Colonial Boston, 1679–1721," (thesis, Brandeis, 1966); Susan Kurland, "Democratization in Concord: A Political History, 1750–1850," in D. H. Fischer, ed., *Concord: The Social History of a New England Town, 1750–1850* (Waltham, Mass., 1984), 261–342.

of a new minister or the location of a meetinghouse. But the traditional pattern of very low participation, punctuated by sudden surges of very high turnout, has been characteristic of New England town government for three centuries—and very different as we shall see from voting patterns in other American regions.

New England town governments tended to become very active in the life of their communities. The inhabitants voted to tax themselves heavily by comparison with other parts of British America. On a per capita basis, levels of spending by local government in Massachusetts were two to four times higher than in many other colonies, though much below the cost of government in Europe. These relative patterns have also persisted for three centuries.[10]

Town meeting government in early New England was not really democratic in our majoritarian sense. The object was not rule by majority, but by consensus. The purpose of a town meeting was to achieve that consensual goal by discussion, persuasion and mutual adjustment of differences. The numbers of votes were rarely counted, but merely recorded as the "will of the town." This system was unique to New England, and nearly universal within it. It was the combined product of East Anglian experiences, Puritan ideas, and the American environment.

❧ Massachusetts Freedom Ways: The Puritan Idea of Ordered Liberty

The public life of New England was also shaped by an idea of liberty which was peculiar to the Puritan colonies. To understand its nature, one might begin with the word itself. From the generation of John Winthrop (1558–1649) to that of Samuel Adams (1722–1803), the noun "liberty" was used throughout New England in at least four ways which ring strangely in a modern ear.

First, "liberty" often described something which belonged not to an individual but to an entire community. For two centuries, the founders and leaders of Massachusetts wrote of the "liberty

---

[10]For computations of relative levels of taxation and expenditure see R. R. Palmer, *The Age of Democratic Revolution* (Princeton, 1959), 155; James Henretta et al., *America's History* (Chicago, 1987), 254.

of New England," or the "liberty of Boston" or the "liberty of the Town." This usage continued from the great migration to the War of Independence and even beyond. Samuel Adams, for example, wrote more often about the "liberty of America" than about the liberty of individual Americans.[1]

This idea of collective liberty, or "publick liberty" as it was sometimes called, was thought to be consistent with close restraints upon individuals. In Massachusetts these individual restrictions were numerous, and often very confining. During the first generation, nobody could live in the colony without approval of the General Court. Settlers even of the highest rank were sent prisoners to England for expressing "divers dangerous opinions," or merely because the Court judged them to be "persons unmeet to inhabit here."[2] Others were not allowed to move within the colony except by special permission of the General Court. For a time, the inhabitants of Dedham, Sudbury and Concord were forbidden to move out of their towns, because the General Court believed that those frontier settlements were dangerously under-populated.[3]

This idea of collective liberty also was expressed in many bizarre obligations which New England towns collectively imposed upon their members. Eastham's town meeting, for example, ordered that no single man could marry until he had killed six blackbirds or three crows. Every town book contained many such rules.[4] The General Court also passed sweeping statutes which allowed the magistrates to suppress almost any act, by any means. One such law, for example, threatened that "if any man shall exceed the bounds of moderation, we shall punish him severely." The definition of "exceeding the bounds of moderation" was left to the magistrate.[5]

New Englanders willingly accepted individual restraints, but insisted that they should be consistent with written laws which

---

[1] Samuel Adams to Samuel Cooper, 25 Dec. 1778; Adams to Benjamin Austin, 9 March 1779; Adams to John Scollay, 30 Dec. 1780; Adams to Richard Henry Lee, 15 Jan. 1781, Cushing, ed., *Works of Samuel Adams*, IV, 104, 132, 235–36, 239–40.

[2] *Mass. Bay Records*, I, 83, 159.

[3] "Concord, Sudbury & Dedham . . . being inland towns & not thinly peopled, it is ordered that no man now inhabiting & settling in any of the said town (whether married or single) shall remove to any other town without the allowance of a magistrate or other selectman of that town." *Mass. Bay Records*, II, 122.

[4] "Every unmarried man in the township shall kill six black-birds or three crows while he remains single; as a penalty for not doing it, shall not be married until he obey this order." Eastham Town Records, 1695; Earle, *Customs and Fashions in Old New England*, 37.

[5] *Mass. Bay Records*, I, 110.

they called the "fundamentals of the commonwealth."[6] Further
they demanded the liberty to impose these restraints upon themselves in their own way. This was what they meant by the "publick
liberty" of New England. Interference by outsiders met fierce
and implacable resistance. "Publick liberty" was not merely a
"theoretick idea," as many a brave British soldier learned. New
Englanders were not a warrior people, but many times from 1635
to 1775, they showed themselves willing to defend their "publick
liberty," even to the death.

New Englanders also used the word "liberty" in a second way
which is foreign to our own time. When it referred to individuals,
it often became a plural noun—"liberties" rather than "liberty."
These plural liberties were understood as specific exemptions
from a condition of prior restraint—an idea which had long
existed in East Anglia and in many other parts of the western
world. In the manor of Hengrave (Suffolk), for example, tenants
were granted a specific "liberty" of fishing in the river Lark. Such
a liberty was not universal or absolute; the river was closed to all
other people. There were a great many of these liberties in East
Anglian communities during the early seventeenth century. A
person's status was defined by the number and nature of liberties
to which he was admitted.[7]

The idea of plural liberties as specific exemptions from a condition of prior constraint was carried to Massachusetts. The General Court, for example, enacted laws which extended "liberties
and privileges of fishing and fowling" to certain inhabitants, and
thereby denied them to everyone else. One person's "liberty" in
this sense became another's restraint.[8] In Massachusetts, as in
England, a person's rank was defined by the liberties that he possessed, and vice versa.

The laws of the Bay Colony granted some liberties to all men,
others to all free men, and a few only to gentlemen. For example,
a "true gentleman" and "any man equal to a gentleman," was
granted the liberty not to be punished by whipping "unless his
crime be very shameful, and his course of life vicious and profligate." Other men had a lesser liberty, not to be whipped more
than forty stripes. Other liberties were assigned not to individuals
at all, but to churches and towns and other social groups.[9]

[6]*Ibid.*, I, 174.
[7]John Gage, *The History and Antiquities of Hengrave, in Suffolk* (London, 1822).
[8]*Mass. Bay Records*, 3 April 1632, I, 94.
[9][Nathaniel Ward], "The Massachusetts Body of Liberties (1641), reprinted in *The Colonial Laws of Massachusetts* (Boston, 1889).

This idea of liberty seems very narrow to modern Americans. We do not think of liberty as exemption from prior condition of restraint, but of restraint as an exemption from a prior condition of liberty. But the seventeenth-century idea of plural liberties, however restrictive and limited it may have been, was codified into "laws and liberties" which became what the founders called "the fundamentals of the Commonwealth." The idea of written fundamental laws and liberties existed from the beginning of the Bay Colony.[10] Some of these fundamental "liberties" were specifically extended to everyone. Thus the Massachusetts Body of Liberties in 1641 established that:

> Every man whether inhabitant or foreigner, free or not free shall have liberty to come to any public Court, Council or Town meeting, and either by speech or writing to move any lawful, seasonable, and material question, or to present any necessary motion, complaint, petition, Bill or information, whereof that meeting hath proper cognizance, so it be done in convenient time, due order and respective manner. . . .

> Every man that findeth himself unfit to plead his own cause in any court shall have Liberty to employ any man against whom the court doth not except, to help him. . . . [11]

These plural liberties persisted in Massachusetts for many generations. They appeared in the writings of Samuel Adams and his generation, just as they had done in the world of John Winthrop.[12]

New England Puritans also used the word "liberty" in a third meaning, which became urgently important to the founders of Massachusetts. This was the idea of "soul liberty," or "Christian liberty," an idea of high complexity. Soul liberty was freedom to serve God in the world. It was freedom to order one's own acts in a godly way—but not in any other. It made Christian freedom into a form of obligation.

The founding generation in Massachusetts often wrote of "soul liberty," "Christian liberty" or "liberty of conscience." Many moved to the New World primarily in hopes of attaining it. What they meant was not a world of religious freedom in the modern

---

[10] *Mass. Bay Records,* I, 174.
[11] Ward, "Massachusetts Body of Liberties."
[12] "Candidus," [Samuel Adams], Boston *Gazette,* 27 Jan. 1772; Cushing, ed., *Writings of Samuel Adams,* II, 324.

sense, or even of religious toleration, but rather of freedom for the true faith. In their minds, this idea of religious liberty was thought to be consistent with the persecution of Quakers, Catholics, Baptists, Presbyterians, Anglicans and indeed virtually everyone except those within a very narrow spectrum of Calvinist orthodoxy. Soul liberty also was thought to be consistent with compulsory church attendance and rigorous Sabbath laws. Even the Indians were compelled to keep the Puritan Sabbath in Massachusetts. To the founders of that colony, soul freedom meant that they were free to persecute others in their own way. One New Englander wrote, "Solomon maketh it the joy of a Commonwealth when the righteous are in authority."[13] There was no freedom for "error" in Massachusetts. Even the saints themselves were kept on a short leash. In 1634, for example, Israel Stoughton wrote a book "which occasioned much trouble and offence to the court." Stoughton was himself a deputy, and a staunch Puritan who later returned to England and became an officer in Rainborough's regiment during the Civil War. His book suggested reforms in the government of the colony. The magistrates were so angered by criticism that they decreed not merely that the book should be suppressed, but also ordered that the manuscript should be burned. After heavy pressure from the authorities, the author himself was compelled to confess that he "did desire of the court that the said book might be burnt."[14] To others of different persuasions, the Puritans' paradoxical idea of "soul freedom" became a cruel and bloody contradiction. But to the Puritans themselves "soul liberty" was a genuinely libertarian principle which held that a Christian community should be free to serve God in the world. Here was an idea in which the people of Massachusetts deeply believed, and the reason why their colony was founded in the first place.

The words "liberty" and also "freedom" were used in yet a fourth way by the builders of the Bay Colony. Sometimes, the people of Massachusetts employed the word "freedom" to describe a collective obligation of the "body politicke," to protect individual members from the tyranny of circumstance. This was conceived not in terms of collective welfare or social equality but of individual liberty. It was precisely the same idea that a descen-

---

[13]In 1637 the General Court passed a law "to restrain Indians from profaning the Lord's day"; *Mass. Bay Records,* I, 209.

[14]*Ibid.,* I, 134.

John Winthrop's "Little Speech on Liberty," delivered to the General Court on July 3, 1645, was the classic statement of Puritan ideas of ordered freedom. Winthrop distinguished between natural liberty "to do evil as well as good," and civil or federal liberty, which "may also be termed moral," he wrote, "in reference to the covenant between God and man. . . . It is a liberty to that only which is good, just and honest. This liberty you are to stand for, with the hazard not only of your goods but of your lives if need be. . . . This liberty is maintained and exercised in a way of subjection to authority; it is the same kind of liberty wherewith Christ hath made us free."

To others this argument was a contradiction in terms; but among the Puritans, ordered freedom was a genuine libertarian idea that flourished in this region for many centuries.

dant of the Massachusetts Puritans, Franklin Roosevelt, conceived as the Four Freedoms. That way of thinking was not his invention. It appeared in Massachusetts within a few years of its founding. The Massachusetts poor laws, however limited they may have been, recognized every individual should be guaranteed a freedom from want in the most fundamental sense. The General Court also explicitly recognized even a "freedom from fear." Its language revealed a libertarian conception of social problems (and solutions) that was characteristic of English-speaking people as early as the seventeenth century.[15]

These four libertarian ideas—collective liberty, individual liberties, soul liberty and freedom from the tyranny of circumstance—all had a common denominator. They were aspects of a larger conception which might be called ordered liberty. This principle was deeply embedded in Puritan ideas and also in East Anglian realities. It came to be firmly established in Massachusetts even before the end of the great migration. For many years it continued to distinguish the culture of New England from other parts of British America. Even today, in much modified forms, it is still a living tradition in parts of the United States. But this principle of "ordered liberty" is also opposed by other libertarian ideas, which were planted in different parts of British America.

[15]*Mass. Bay Records*, I, 173.

THE SOUTH OF ENGLAND TO VIRGINIA

❧ Distressed Cavaliers and Indentured Servants,
 1642–75

> Virginia [was] the only city of refuge left in His Majesty's Dominions, in those times, for distressed cavaliers.
> —Ingram's Proceedings, Virginia, 1676

> The gentlemen called Cavaliers are greatly esteemed and respected, and are very courteous and honorable. They hold most of the offices in the country.
> —Durand of Dauphine on Virginia, 1687

> The people of fortune ... are the pattern of all behaviour here.
> —Philip Fithian on Virginia, 1773

IN THE WINTER OF 1641, just as the Puritan migration was coming to an end, a young Englishman boarded an emigrant ship for Virginia. He would have been received with high ceremony by the captain and crew, for he was no ordinary passenger. His appearance was that of a nobleman—short cloak, deep bands, great boots, belted sword, and long hair cascading in ringlets around his patrician face. His manners were those of a courtier, polished by years in the presence of the King. His speech was that of a scholar, full of Oxford learning; and he had the bearing of a soldier, knighted on the field of honor by Charles I. The name of this traveler was Sir William Berkeley. In his baggage, he carried the King's commission as Royal Governor of Virginia.

This proud young cavalier was destined to rule the colony of Virginia for more than thirty years. In that period, he had a profound impact upon its development. At a critical moment, he bent the young sapling of its social system and made it grow in the direction that he wished. The cultural history of an American region is in many ways the long shadow of this extraordinary man.[1]

Sir William Berkeley was born in 1606 to a powerful West Country family which had been seated since the eleventh century at Berkeley Castle in Gloucestershire. The massive battlements of this great building still loom high above the Vale of the Severn, where on a bright fall day one may see the Berkeley Hunt in its distinctive yellow riding coats quartering the countryside, as members of that ancient family have done for more than nine centuries.[2]

The future governor of Virginia belonged to a cadet branch of his family. It kept two houses: one high on a hill above the ancient wool town of Bruton, Somerset; the other in London where the future governor was born. He lived his youth in a broad belt of territory between London and Berkeley Castle—the region which was to become the cradle of Virginia's culture.[3]

---

[1]Sir William Berkeley is known today mainly for the event that ended his long career— Bacon's Rebellion in 1676. By that date he was seventy years old, worn down by ill health, and exhausted by long service. He punished the rebels with a savagery that shocked even the King. "That old fool," Charles II is alleged to have said, "has killed more people in that naked country than I have done for the murder of my father." To this day, liberal historians remember Berkeley as a failed reactionary who was an alien presence in the American past.

A rare revisionary essay argues that Berkeley was a failed progressive whose plans for economic development met defeat. This was true of specific projects such as the silk industry, but in other ways as we shall see the southern colonies developed much as Berkeley intended—in their labor system, class structure, and many of their folkways—and progress had no place in his pantheon; cf. Joan de Lourdes Leonard, "Operation Checkmate: The Birth and Death of a Virginia Blueprint for Progress, 1660–1676," *WMQ3* 24 (1967), 44–74.

Berkeley has been the victim of three strong trends in southern historiography. The first was the work of scholars who heaped ridicule on the so-called "cavalier myth" and argued that "the most significant feature of the Chesapeake aristocracy was its middle class origin" (Carl Bridenbaugh, *Myths and Realities* (Baton Rouge, La., 1952), 12). A second trend appeared in the work of the "Chesapeake group" who were interested in market forces, demographic processes and models of social change which left little latitude for the agency of individuals. A third trend has been a continuing reinterpretation of Bacon's Rebellion in ways unfavorable to Berkeley; e.g., Stephen S. Webb, *1676: The End of American Independence* (New York, 1984). There is no full-length published biography of this neglected man; but see Jane Carson, "Sir William Berkeley" (thesis, Univ. of Va., 1951), and J. R. Pagan, "Notes on Sir William Berkeley," ms., GLOCRO.

[2]H.P.R. Finberg, "Three Centuries in Family History: Berkeley of Berkeley," *Gloucester Studies* (Leicester, 1957), 145–59. The Berkeleys, still securely in possession of their castle, are one of the few landed families in England who can trace their pedigree back before the Norman conquest. They claim descent from Eadnoth the Staller, a Saxon nobleman who joined William the Conqueror and was killed in 1068.

[3]The founder of the Bruton Berkeleys was Sir Maurice Berkeley (ca. 1505–81), a standard bearer of Henry VIII and supporter of Thomas Cromwell. His reward was the land of Bruton Priory, together with Northwood Park near Glastonbury, and other tracts in Berkshire, Buckingham and Surrey. He was also a gentleman of the Privy Chamber before 1539, a member of Parliament for Surrey, and sheriff of Somerset in 1567. The Bruton lands descended to Sir

As a young man, Berkeley showed something of a scholar's bent. He matriculated at The Queen's College in Oxford, earned his degree at St. Edmund Hall and became a fellow of Merton College. After graduating, he took himself to London and became a literary figure of some consequence, publishing a highly polished "tragy comedy" called *The Lost Lady* in 1639. He was also introduced at court by his brother John Lord Berkeley, and made such an impression that the King appointed him Gentleman of the Privy Chamber Extraordinary. In 1639, he was knighted in the field at Berwick, and two years later became Royal Governor of Virginia.[4]

In many ways, Berkeley was not an admirable character. He bullied those beneath him, and fawned on people above. He openly enriched himself from his offices, and set a sad example for peculation that long persisted in Virginia. In 1667, for example, he wrote directly to his superior, Lord Arlington, "Though ambition commonly leaves sober old age, covetousness does not. I shall therefore desire of your lordship to procure of His Majesty the customs of two hundred hogsheads of tobacco."[5]

These were the vices of his age, and Berkeley had them in high degree. But he also had the virtues of candor, courage, fidelity to family and loyalty to a cause. His social values were as highly developed as those of the Puritans—though in a very different

---

Henry Berkeley (d. 1601) and then to Sir Maurice Berkeley (d. 1617), a member of Parliament from various West Country seats (Truro, Minehead) and father of Virginia's future governor. See S. W. Bates-Harbin, *Members of Parliament from the County of Somerset* (Taunton, Eng., 1939); *Visitation of Somerset* (1623), s.v. "Berkeley"; for much unpublished material see ms. 20/i, 137, SOMERO.

Little remains today of the house where Sir William Berkeley lived as a child. It stood near the ruins of the abbey, high on a hill above the stone-built medieval town. St. Mary's Church in Bruton contains many memorials of the Berkeleys. The walls are decorated with their insignia; in the back of the church one may still find the old oil lamps which were used at midnight burials of Berkeleys in the crypt of the church. See *A Walk Round St. Mary's, Bruton* (n.p., ca. 1980); D. A. McCallum, "A Demographic Study of the Parishes of Bruton and Pitcombe," *SANHSP* 121 (1977), 77–87.

[4]According to the records of his various colleges, Sir William Berkeley matriculated at The Queen's College, 14 Feb. 1622–23, took his B.A. in St. Edmund Hall, 10 July 1624, became a Fellow of Merton in 1625, received his M.A. in 1630, and lost his Merton Fellowship to the Puritans in 1649. In 1632, Berkeley was made a gentleman of the Privy Chamber Extraordinary, and was knighted at Berwick on 27 July 1639. He was appointed governor of Virginia in 1641, arrived in 1642, and briefly returned to England in 1644–45. Berkeley's family patronized many writers, including Robert Burton, who dedicated the *Anatomy of Melancholy* to George Berkeley (1613–58). Sir William's play, *The Lost Lady: A Tragy Comedy* (London, 1639), entered the English repertory, and was often reprinted in the 18th and 19th centuries in Dodsley's *Old Plays*. Portraits of Sir William Berkeley hang at Berkeley Castle in Gloucester and Stratford Hall in Virginia.

[5]Berkeley to Lord Arlington, 5 June 1667, *VMHB*, 21 (1913), 43.

direction. And he cared deeply for Virginia. For thirty-five years, Berkeley devoted himself to the welfare of his colony with energy, intelligence, and effect.

When Sir William Berkeley reached Virginia in February 1642, it was a sickly settlement of barely 8,000 souls. The colony had earned an evil reputation "that none but those of the meanest quality and corruptest lives went there." The quality of life in early Virginia was more like a modern military outpost or lumber camp than a permanent society. Its leaders were rough, violent, hard-drinking men. Berkeley's predecessor, Governor John Harvey, had knocked out the teeth of a councilor with a cudgel, before being "thrust out" himself by the colonists in 1635. When Harvey returned with royal warrant to arrest his enemies, he was driven out again in 1639.[6] The colony was in a state of chronic disorder. Its rulers were unable to govern, its social institutions were ill-defined, its economy was undeveloped, its politics were unstable, and its cultural identity was indistinct.[7]

In the thirty-five years of Sir William Berkeley's tenure, Virginia was transformed. Its population increased fivefold from 8,000 to 40,000 inhabitants. It developed a coherent social order, a functioning economic system, and a strong sense of its own special folkways. Most important, it also acquired a governing elite which Berkeley described as "men of as good families as any subjects in England."[8]

This social system did not spring spontaneously from the soil of the new world. No less than New England, the colony of Virginia was the conscious creation of human will and purpose. In that process, Sir William Berkeley played the leading role, laboring through his long years in office to build an ideal society which was the expression of his own values. More than any other individual, he framed Virginia's political system—becoming, in Thomas Ludwell's words, "the sole author of the most substantial

---

[6]Governor Francis Wyatt followed Harvey and also became very unpopular. For various views of these events see Bernard Bailyn, "Politics and Social Structure in Virginia," in James Morton Smith, ed., *Seventeenth Century America: Essays in Colonial History* (Chapel Hill, 1959), 95–96; J. Mills Thornton, "The Thrusting Out of Governor Harvey," *VMHB* 76 (1968), 11–26; Edmund S. Morgan, *American Slavery, American Freedom: The Ordeal of Colonial Virginia* (New York, 1975), 144–45.

[7]The truth of this reputation was conceded even by so fierce a booster as Berkeley himself. "This to our maligners we would easily grant," he wrote, "if they would consent to the omen of it, for was not Rome thus begun?" William Berkeley, *A Discourse and View of Virginia* (London, 1663, rpt. 1914), 3.

[8]*Ibid.*

This portrait of Sir William Berkeley (by Peter Lely, 1661–62) was an image not merely of the man himself but also of the Royalist ideals that guided his actions in Virginia. The governor is dressed for war. He wears an officer's half armor with a baton in hand and a sword hanging at his side. In the background the artist painted a cavalry charge, probably in the Western campaign of 1644, in which Berkeley fought for his King. This painting also reveals an identity with the King in yet another way. Berkeley stands in an unnatural pose with his right hand extended, left hand bent back above the hip, left leg extended forward and head turned sharply to the side. His posture imitated a favorite pose of Charles I which appears in Van Dyck's Roi à la chasse, *now in the Louvre. Even Berkeley's facial expression mimicked that of his royal master. This is a portrait of the governor in middle age. His youth has faded, and his swollen face is ravaged by the chronic illness that afflicted many Virginians. In his cruel eyes we see a hint of the tyranny that lay ahead. But this is a likeness of Sir William Berkeley in the prime of his maturity, secure in his power, and firm in his determination to create in Virginia a Royalist utopia dominated by ideals of honor and hierarchy.*

parts of it, either for laws, or other inferior institutions."[9] When the laws of Virginia were first published, the volume was dedicated to Sir William Berkeley, who was identified as himself "the author of the best of them." Berkeley governed the colony through a pliant "long assembly" which he kept in office for fourteen years, refusing to call an election from 1662 to 1676. Its laws expressed the wishes of the governor; many were drafted by his own hand.[10]

Important as his role as a lawgiver may have been, Berkeley had his greatest impact upon Virginia in another way. More than any other person, he shaped the process of immigration to the colony during a critical period in its history. That process in turn defined its culture, and largely determined the main lines of change for many generations to come.

❧ Sir William Berkeley and Virginia's Elite

Of all Sir William Berkeley's many projects as governor, the most important was his recruitment of a Royalist elite for Virginia. In the words of historian Philip Bruce, he "encouraged the cavaliers to come over in large numbers." When they arrived, he promoted them to high office, granted them large estates and created the ruling oligarchy that ran the colony for many generations.[1]

This cavalier migration continued throughout Berkeley's tenure as governor (1642–76). Much of it occurred during the decade of the 1650s, when a Puritan oligarchy gained the upper hand in England and tried to impose its beliefs by force upon an unwilling people. Virginia's Royalist immigrants were refugees from oppression, just as New England's Puritans themselves had been. Many had fought for Charles I in England's Civil War. Some continued to serve him until his armies were broken by Parliament and the King himself was killed in 1649. Others rallied to the future King Charles II, and in 1651 fought at his side on the field of Worcester, where they were beaten once again.

---

[9]Thomas Ludwell to [Lord Arlington?], 17 Sep. 1666, *VMHB* 21 (1913), 37.

[10]Francis Moryson and Henry Randolph, eds., *The Laws of Virginia Now in Force; Collected out of Assembly Records . . .* (London, 1661).

[1]Philip A. Bruce in *Dictionary of American Biography, s.v.* Berkeley; *idem, Social Life of Virginia in the Seventeenth Century: An Inquiry into the Origin of the Higher Planting Class . . .* (Richmond, 1907).

They suffered severely in this struggle. One Royalist wrote, ". . . in our unnatural wars, most of the ancient gentry were either extinct or undone. The king's side was almost all gentlemen, and of Parliament's few . . . in the quarrel of the Two Roses there were not half as many gentlemen slain."[2] So shattered was the Royalist cause that William Sancroft wrote, ". . . when we meet, it is but to consult to what foreign plantation we shall fly." Indeed, Henry Norwood later remembered that "a very considerable number . . . did fly from their native country, as from a place infected with the plague."[3]

Most of these émigrés took refuge in Europe. But many were recruited by Sir William Berkeley. Some had been his kinsmen and friends before they came to America; others became his relations in the New World. They shared his Royalist politics, his Anglican faith, and his vision for the future of the colony.[4]

These "distressed cavaliers" founded what would later be called the first families of Virginia. But they were not chronologically the first to settle in the colony. Only a few had appeared during the first forty years of its history. Their great migration came later, and was nearly as concentrated in time as the exodus of the English Puritans had been. If most Yankee genealogies commenced within six years of 1635, the American beginnings of Virginia's ruling families occurred within a decade of the year 1655.

The founder of the Carter family, for example, came over in 1649. His forebears had been very rich in England; his children became still richer in Virginia. The first Culpeper also arrived in 1649; as did the first Hammond, Honywood and Moryson. The first Digges migrated in 1650, together with the first Broadhurst, Chicheley, Custis, Page, Harrison, Isham, Skipwith and Landon. The first Northampton Randolph appeared circa 1651, and the first Mason in 1652. The first Madison was granted land in 1653,

[2]Francis Bamford, ed., *A Royalist's Notebook: The Commonplace Book of Sir John Oglander, Kt* [1585–1655] (London, 1931), 109; on economic losses of Royalist families, who mostly suffered *and* survived, see H. J. Habbakuk, "Landowners and the Civil War," *ECHR2* 18 (1965), 130–51; Ann Hughes, *Politics, Society and the Civil War in Warwickshire* (Cambridge, 1987), 267; and many writings by Joan Thirsk, beginning with "The Sales of Delinquent Estates during the Interregnum and the Land Settlement at the Restoration" (thesis, Univ. of London, 1950).

[3]Henry Cary, ed., *Memorials of the Great Civil War* (London, 1842), II, 118; quoted in David Underdown, *Royalist Conspiracy in England, 1649–1660* (New Haven, 1960), 13–14.

[4]"Ingram's Proceedings" [n.d., ca. 1676]; Peter Force, ed. *Tracts and Other Papers Relating Principally to the Origin, Settlement and Progress of the Colonies in North America . . .* (4 vols., 1836–46, New York, 1947), 1.11, 34.

the first Corbin in 1654. The first Washington crossed the ocean in 1657; he was John Washington, the younger son of an Oxford-trained clergyman who had been removed from his living by the Puritans. The family seat was Sulgrave Manor, a few miles north of Oxford. Also in 1657 arrived Colonel William Ball, the ancestor of George Washington's mother, and in 1659 the first Fairfax. Every year of that troubled decade brought a fresh crop of cavaliers to Virginia. Of seventy-two families in Virginia's high elite whose dates of migration are known, two-thirds arrived between 1640 and 1669. A majority appeared between 1647 and 1660.[5]

After the Restoration of Charles II in 1660, Sir William Berkeley continued his recruiting campaign. In 1663 he published a pamphlet addressed to the younger sons of England's great families:

> A small sum of money will enable a younger brother to erect a flourishing family in a new world; and add more strength, wealth and honor to his native country, than thousands did before, that dyed forgotten and unrewarded in an unjust war . . . men of as good families as any subjects in England have resided there, as the Percys, the Barkleys, the Wests, the Gages, the Throgmortons, Wyatts, Digges, Chichelys, Moldsworths, Morrisons, Kemps, and hundred others which I forbear to name, lest I should misherald them in this catalogue.[6]

Sir William Berkeley's recruiting campaign was highly successful. Nearly all of Virginia's ruling families were founded by younger sons of eminent English families during his governorship. Berkeley himself was a younger son with no hope of inheriting an estate in England. This "younger son syndrome," as one historian has called it, became a factor of high importance in the culture of Virginia. The founders of Virginia's first families tried to reconstruct from American materials a cultural system from which they had been excluded at home.[7]

---

[5]Dates of migration for the founders of 72 families in Virginia's high elite as follows: 1607–19, 3; 1620–29, 4; 1630–39, 7; 1640–49, 8; 1650–59, 29; 1660–69, 11; 1670–79, 4; 1680–89, 4; 1690 and after, 2. These data refer to holders of major offices, 1680–1776. Sources include standard genealogical materials indexed in Swem, *Virginia Historical Index,* and English materials in English county record offices; also Bruce, *Social Life of Virginia,* 39–99; Bailyn, "Politics and Social Structure in Virginia," 90–115; Douglas Southall Freeman, *George Washington* (7 vols., New York, 1948–57), I, 15, appendix I-4; Louis Morton, *Robert Carter of Nomini Hall* (Williamsburg, 1945), 3; Nell M. Nugent, *Cavaliers and Pioneers* (Richmond, 1934); William G. and Mary N. Stanard, *The Colonial Virginia Register* (Albany, 1902).

[6]Berkeley, *A Discourse and View of Virginia,* 3.

[7]Joan Thirsk, "Younger Sons in the Seventeenth Century," *H* 54 (1969), 358–77.

Colonel Richard Lee was the younger son of an old Shropshire family. He emigrated to Virginia ca. 1640 and became Attorney General, Secretary of State, and Sir William Berkeley's chief lieutenant. For long and loyal service, he received vast holdings of land and by 1663 owned at least seven plantations and many servants and slaves. Colonel Lee was immensely proud of his lineage. His Saxon family was as ancient as the Berkeley's had been and looked down upon England's Norman nobility as coarse and vulgar upstarts. He lived in high style. In 1655, agents of the Puritan Commonwealth seized Lee's baggage and found "200 ounces of silver plate, all marked with his coat of arms." Above his front door, Lee hung a wood carving of his arms, which still survives with one side broken and faint traces of its original paint. Worked into the design was a crescent, the heraldic mark of a second son which appeared on many escutcheons in Virginia. The Lee family became the archetype of Governor Berkeley's armigerous elite.

File	*Crescent*	*Mullet*	*Martlet*	*Annulet*	*Fleur-de-lis*	*Rose*	*Moline*	*Octofoil*
1st Son	*2d Son*	*3d Son*	*4th son*	*5th son*	*6th son*	*7th son*	*8th son*	*9th son*

The great majority of Virginia's upper elite came from families in the upper ranks of English society. Of 152 Virginians who held top offices in the late seventeenth and early eighteenth century, at least sixteen were connected to aristocratic families, and 101 were the sons of baronets, knights and the rural gentry of England. Seven more came from armigerous urban families, with coats of arms at the college of heralds. Only eighteen were the sons of yeomen, traders, mariners, artisans, or "plebs." None came to Virginia as laborers or indentured servants except possibly the first Adam Thoroughgood who was also the brother of a baronet. Only two were not British, and nine could not be identified.[8]

Some of these families had grown very rich before the Civil War. As early as the sixteenth century, they had made matrimonial alliances with mercantile families and also with others who prospered in the countryside. An example were the Spencers of Althorpe, a family of humble sheep graziers in the fifteenth century who rose so rapidly in the sixteenth century that by 1603 Sir Robert Spencer was reputed to have "the most money of any per-

---

[8]The sixteen with aristocratic connections included Aston, Berkeley, Booth, Culpeper, Digges, Fairfax, Gage, Mason, Mathews, Pawlett, Percy, Spencer, Spotswood, Throckmorton/ Throgmorton, West and Zouch.

Gentry families included Armistead, Ashton, Bacon, Ball, Ballard, Batte, Bathurst, Beckwith, Bedell, Bennett, Bernard, Bland, Booth, Brent, Broadhurst, Brodnax, Burwell, Butt, Cabell, Calthorpe, Carter, Catlett, Chamberlayne, Cheisman, Chicheley, Chilton, Churchill, Claiborne, Clarke, Clayton, Cocke, Cole, Corbin, Croshaw, Custis, Ferrer/Farrar, Fauntleroy, Filmer, Finch, Fleetwood, Fortescue, Fowke/Fowkes, Goldsborough, Goodrich, Grosvenor, Grymes, Hackett, Hammond, Harrison, Honeywell, Horsmanden, Hyde, Isham, Jennings, Kemp, Kingsmill, Landon, Lee, Lear, Leigh, Lightfoot, Littleton, Lovelace, Ludlow, Lunsford, Marshall, Mason, Mayo, Milner, Monroe, Moryson, Norwood, Page, Parke, Peachey/Peachy, Perceval, Peyton, Randolph, Reade, Robinson, Scarborough, Scott, Skipwith, Smith, Spelman, Steward, Tayloe, Thoroughgood, Tucker, Turberville, Warner, Washington, Webb, Welsford, Wentworth, Willoughby, Wingfield, Woodhouse, Wormeley, Wyatt and Yeo.

Armigerous urban families included Bland, Byrd, Cary, Craven, Fitzhugh and Ludwell; all had held the highest offices in their towns, possessed their own arms, and maintained close ties to county gentry.

Lesser ranks included Blair and Donne (professional), Bassett, Beverley and Taylor (yeomen), Bolling, Brooke, Buckner, Chew, Corbin, Hamor, Jones, Munford, Nelson, Perry (merchants, traders and mariners); Allerton, Clopton and Madison (artisans) and Fry ("pleb"). Not of English origin were Taliaferro (Florentine) and Minor (Dutch). Of unknown origins were Duke, Eppes, Hartwell, Jefferson, Lewis, Marable, Porteus, Quary, and Whiting.

Sources include genealogical materials in English county record offices, and works cited in note 6, above. Families of royal governors are included only if other kin settled permanently in Virginia. It should be noted that many men of humble origins became prosperous planters in Virginia but were never admitted to this higher elite. Also many other high-born immigrants came to Virginia, but did not perpetuate themselves in the New World. This list understates aristocratic connections.

Anna Constable Lee, the beautiful wife of Colonel Richard Lee, raised five sons in Virginia. Those children produced a vast progeny of Lees who became the archetypical first gentlemen of Virginia. The carriers of this culture from one generation to the next were women such as Anna Lee. She was a "lady of quality" who came to Virginia in the household of Sir Francis Wyatt, perhaps as his ward. In the handsome features of her portrait, the artist has captured the cultural values that were shared by Virginians of both sexes. Her open expression implies an ideal of candor and an utter contempt for falsehood and deceit. Her erect carriage communicates a pride of rank and reputation that was called honor in a gentleman and virtue in a lady. The firm lines of her mouth and chin suggest independence of mind and strength of character. The costume creates a feeling of simple dignity and grace that requires no ornament for its embellishment. In her eyes one sees a hint of sadness and suffering—which may serve to remind us that the ideals of this culture were continuously tested by its environment, and toughened in the testing. Here was the ideal type of a first lady of Virginia.

son in the kingdom."[9] Some of these Spencers settled in Virginia, as did the children of other great landed families. A few were able to bring capital to Virginia. Others in Oldmixon's phrase were "men of good families and small fortunes," whose pedigrees became their passports to Sir William Berkeley's favor.

These younger sons, by reason of their birth order, were forced to leave the land. Many, perhaps most of them, entered commerce in London and Bristol. There they adopted mercantile and maritime occupations which brought them in contact with Virginia. John Washington followed this path, as did Nicholas Spencer and Thomas Chamberlain and many other progenitors of Virginia's first families. But the roots of all these men were in the English countryside, and Virginia offered a chance to return to the rural life which they preferred. Even the minority of Virginia who had been city-born and city-bred shared this cultural attitude. The first William Byrd found "a private gentleman's life in the country . . . (at this time) most eligible."[10]

With very few exceptions, these immigrants were staunch Royalists. Many had served in the Civil War as military officers of company or field grade. Of those whose opinions are known, 98 percent supported the King in the Civil War. If they had gone to a university, they tended to choose Oxford—especially the colleges of Christ Church, Merton and Queens which had an association with the royal family. They were Anglican in their religion, and their faith was as important to them as it had been to the Puritans.[11]

[9]M. E. Finch, *The Wealth of Five Northamptonshire Families, 1540–1640*, NHANTRS 19 (1954–55, Oxford, 1958), 38; Lawrence and Jeanne C. Fawtier Stone, *An Open Elite? England 1540–1880* (Oxford, 1984), 80–81.

[10]Tinling, ed., *Correspondence of Three Byrds*, I, 122. If the old myths stressed the rural roots of these men, modern historians have made much of their mercantile and maritime careers. Some have argued that the founders of Virginia's first families were really businessmen whose descendants only later acquired the culture and values of a rural gentry. The truth is more complex than either of these interpretations. One must study family backgrounds of these men (mostly younger sons of rural gentry) and their youthful careers (often mercantile and maritime), as well as expressions of value. Statements such as those of William Byrd I, quoted above, should not be explained away. One should also remember the central fact that these men abandoned mercantile and maritime careers for the life of a planter. To understand their values, one must study both their heads and their feet. For three excellent essays with somewhat different emphases, see Martin H. Quitt, "Immigrant Origins of the Virginia Gentry: A Study of Cultural Transmission and Innovation," *WMQ3* 45 (1988), 629–55; Carole Shammas, "English-Born and Creole Elites in Turn-of-the-Century Virginia," in Tate and Ammerman, eds., *The Chesapeake in the Seventeenth Century*, 274–97; Warren M. Billings, "The Growth of Political Institutions in Virginia, 1634 to 1676," *WMQ3* 31 (1974), 225–42.

[11]A few prominent Virginia families were descended from Puritan ancestors; the Harrisons even had a regicide in their family tree. Another unlikely "FFV" was the wayward Pilgrim Isaac

These families came from every part of England. But two-thirds (68%) had lived within a triangle of territory in the south and west of England, stretching from the Weald of Kent to Devon and north to Warwickshire. If emigrants from London are added to this regional group, its proportion rises from two-thirds to nearly three-quarters. Comparatively few came from the north of England (8%), and fewer from East Anglia (7%). There were only a scattering from Cornwall, Wales, Scotland, Ireland, and abroad.[12]

In England, most had lived within a day's journey of London or Bristol. These cities, especially London, had been an important part of their world. One-third of them had lived in London before coming to America.[13]

In 1724 Hugh Jones wrote, "The habits, life, customs, computations, etc., of the Virginians are much the same as about London, which they esteem their home . . . for the most part [they] have contemptible notions of . . . country places in [other parts of] England and Scotland, whose language and manners are strange to them. . . . they live in the same manner, dress after the same fashion, and behave themselves exactly as the gentry in London."[14]

In houses as ancient as the Berkeleys, younger sons and daughters married London merchants. In families as honorable as the Filmers, country cousins did their city business with traders and lawyers who were their kin.[15] At the same time London merchants intermarried with the gentry of Essex and Kent: an example was

---

Allerton, a London tailor's son who emigrated in the *Mayflower* to Plymouth Colony and resettled in Virginia, ca. 1655, where he married into Berkeley's ruling elite. So tightly connected were Virginia's first families that many are qualified for the Society of Mayflower Descendants through kinship with Isaac Allerton.

[12]Counties of origin for 127 families in Virginia's high elite were as follows: Kent, 13; Gloucester, 9, Northampton, 8; Somerset, 8; London, 7; Yorkshire, 6; Surrey, 6; Devon, 5; Berkshire, 4; Hampshire, 4; Shropshire, 4; Bedfordshire, Dorsetshire, Middlesex, Norfolk, Suffolk, Sussex, Warwickshire and Wiltshire, 3 each; Buckinghamshire, Essex, Leicestershire, Lincolnshire, Staffordshire, and Worcestershire, 2 each; Cambridgeshire, Cheshire, Cornwall, Cumberland, Derbyshire, Hertfordshire, Huntingdonshire, Lancashire, Rutland, Westmorland, Channel Islands, West Indies, New England, Italy, the Netherlands, Scotland and Wales, 1 each.

[13]Quitt finds that "altogether, 19 of 59 immigrant leaders whose English locations can be traced are known to have lived in London." Billings reports from another sample that 25 of 75 lived in London. See Quitt, "Origins of Virginia Gentry," 635; Billings, "Political Institutions in Virginia," 237n.

[14]Hugh Jones, *The Present State of Virginia* (1724, rpt. Chapel Hill, 1956), 81, 102; see also Robert Beverley, *The History and Present State of Virginia* (1795, rpt. Chapel Hill, 1947), 287–88.

[15]The record of this business is in Filmer mss, KAO.

the Byrd family, prosperous goldsmiths who were descended from landed gentry and who proudly possessed their own arms.[16]

After 1650 these families continued to intermarry on both sides of the Atlantic, and moved freely back and forth across the ocean. The result was a tightly integrated colonial elite which literally became a single cousinage by the beginning of the eighteenth century. Historian William Cabell Bruce compared the genealogies of these Virginia families to "a tangle of fishhooks, so closely interlocked that it is impossible to pick up one without drawing three or four after it."[17]

One genealogical example was the Filmer-Horsmanden-Byrd-Beverley-Culpeper-Carter connection. The ancient Kentish family of Sir Edward Filmer produced several sons in the early seventeenth century. Among them was Sir Robert Filmer, author of the royalist treatise *Patriarcha* which became a favorite target for Locke and Sydney. This *Patriarcha* Filmer had a son named Samuel Filmer, who married his cousin Mary Horsmanden and moved to Virginia where he died in the dreaded "seasoning." The young widow quickly remarried the prosperous planter William Byrd. She became the mother of William Byrd II, the mother-in-law of Robert Beverley and James Duke, and the grandmother of Thomas Chamberlayne, Charles Carter, Landon Carter and John Page. Within three generations most of Virginia's first families were related to Mary Horsmanden Filmer Byrd, whose genealogy might be titled *Matriarcha*.[18]

That same royalist lady was also related to leading families in other southern colonies. Her first cousin Frances Culpeper married no fewer than three colonial governors in a row: Samuel Stephens, governor of North Carolina; Philip Ludwell, governor of South Carolina; and Sir William Berkeley, governor of Virginia. Frances Culpeper was also the cousin of William Penn and Nathaniel Bacon who became her husband's mortal foe.[19]

---

[16]For the armigerous status of the Byrd family see Lorraine E. Holland, "Rise and Fall of the Ante-bellum Virginia Aristocracy: A Generational Analysis" (thesis, Univ. of Calif. at Irvine, 1980), 33; Alden Hatch, *The Byrds of Virginia* (New York, 1969), 3–5.

[17]William Cabell Bruce, *John Randolph of Roanoke, 1773–1833* (2 vols., New York, 1922), I, 22.

[18]Another candidate for this title was Lucy Higginson, who had three husbands including Lewis Burwell and Philip Ludwell. So numerous were her descendants that Leonard Labaree writes, ". . . one sixth of all Virginia councilors after 1680 could refer to the good lady as 'Grandmother Lucy.'" Leonard W. Labaree, *Conservatism in Early American History* (New York, 1948), 7–8.

[19]Charles H. Townshend, "The Bacons of Virginia and Their English Ancestry," *NEHGR* 37 (1883), 191.

Virginia's Royalist Elite
The Filmer–Byrd–Beverley–Carter–Culpeper–Berkeley Cousinage

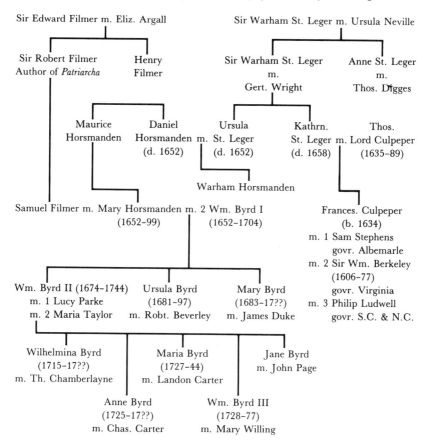

Sir Edward Filmer m. Eliz. Argall

Sir Warham St. Leger m. Ursula Neville

Sir Robert Filmer
Author of *Patriarcha*

Henry
Filmer

Sir Warham St. Leger
m.
Gert. Wright

Anne St. Leger
m.
Thos. Digges

Maurice
Horsmanden

Daniel
Horsmanden
(d. 1652)

Ursula
St. Leger
(d. 1652)

Kathrn.
St. Leger
(d. 1658)

Thos.
m. Lord Culpeper
(1635–89)

Warham Horsmanden

Samuel Filmer m. Mary Horsmanden m. 2 Wm. Byrd I
(1652–99)   (1652–1704)

Frances. Culpeper
(b. 1634)
m. 1 Sam Stephens
govr. Albemarle
m. 2 Sir Wm. Berkeley
(1606–77)
govr. Virginia
m. 3 Philip Ludwell
govr. S.C. & N.C.

Wm. Byrd II (1674–1744)
m. 1 Lucy Parke
m. 2 Maria Taylor

Ursula Byrd
(1681–97)
m. Robt. Beverley

Mary Byrd
(1683–17??)
m. James Duke

Wilhelmina Byrd
(1715–17??)
m. Th. Chamberlayne

Maria Byrd
(1727–44)
m. Landon Carter

Jane Byrd
m. John Page

Anne Byrd
(1725–17??)
m. Chas. Carter

Wm. Byrd III
(1728–77)
m. Mary Willing

Sources: Mildred Campbell Whitaker, *Genealogy of the Campbell, Noble, Gorton, Shelton, Gilmour and Byrd Families* (St. Louis, 1927); Marion Tinling, ed., *The Correspondence of the Three William Byrds of Westover, Virginia, 1684–1776* (2 vols., Charlottesville, 1977), II, 825–36; genealogical materials listed in Swem, *Virginia Historical Index*; William Berry, *County Genealogies: Pedigrees of the Families in the County of Kent* (London, 1830).

The Northampton Connection
The Isham-Washington-Spencer-Randolph-Jefferson-Bland-Beverley-Bolling-Eppes-Hackett Cousinage

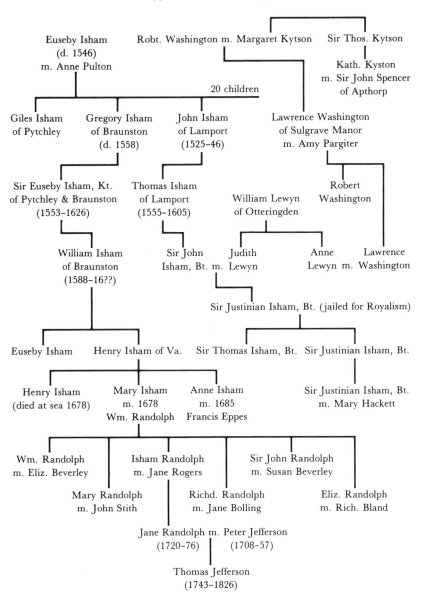

Sources: "The Washington Memorials at Garsden," *WMQ* VI (1910), 482–85; VII (1911), 1–6, 337–43, 452–57, 529–36; Henry Isham Longden, *Visitation of Northamptonshire HARLSP* 87 (1935), 250–63; Henry Isham Longden, *The History of the Washington Family* (Northampton, 1927); Oswald Barron, *Northamptonshire Families* (London, 1906); Finch, *The Wealth of Five Northamptonshire Families*, 141–68.

This Filmer-Byrd-Culpeper-Berkeley connection, centered on the person of Mary Horsmanden Filmer Byrd, was merely one of many alliances among Virginia's ruling families. Another was a Northampton cousinage which formed mainly around the Isham family, and included the Randolphs, Washingtons, and Spencers of Althorp. All of these houses intermarried in Northampton-shire during the sixteenth and seventeenth centuries.[20] They were closely linked to the Filmer connection. For example, the Washingtons of Sulgrave Manor, Northamptonshire (from whom George Washington was descended), had at least three ties to the Filmers. One branch of the Washingtons settled in Kent near Sir Robert Filmer; in the beautiful little church next to the Filmers' seat at East Sutton (now a school for wayward girls) one may still see an old window dedicated to Washingtons who intermarried with Filmers. Another cadet branch resided briefly in Essex when the Reverend Lawrence Washington of Sulgrave (sometime fellow of Brasenose College, Oxford) obtained a place there through the patronage of the Horsmanden family. The sons of this Royalist clergyman migrated to America after his living was taken away by the Puritans. Other Washingtons intermarried with the Fairfax and Culpeper families who lived at Leeds Castle in Kent, only a few miles from the Filmers' estate in East Sutton.[21]

Still a third Virginia connection centered on the family of Sir William Berkeley in Gloucestershire and Somerset. In the old woolen town of Bruton, Somerset, the Berkeleys were related to the Ludwells and Pages, both old and eminent families who had held many high offices. Sir William Berkeley himself was also kin to the Carys who came from the neighboring town of Castle Cary three miles from Bruton, and intermarried with rich merchants in Bristol.

This Berkeley connection was also tied to the Northampton-shire group, and to the Kentish alliance. Sir William Berkeley's family was related to the Washingtons of Northampton and to the Filmers of Kent. Berkeley himself was a cousin of Mary Horsman-

---

[20]The Randolph family in Virginia is commonly traced to William Randolph of Turkey Island, the younger son of Sir Richard Randolph of Morton Hall, Warwickshire, who came to Virginia in 1673. But the true beginning of the family in Virginia was Henry Randolph, the third son of William Randolph of Northamptonshire who emigrated ca. 1650. William Randolph of Turkey Island married Mary Isham, grandaughter of Sir Henry Isham of Braunston, Northamptonshire. Her sister Anne Isham married Francis Eppes in Virginia. The Ishams and Randolphs intermarried in both England and Virginia. See *VCH Northamptonshire Genealogies*, plus ms. genealogies in *NHANTRO*.

[21]Henry Isham Longden, *The History of the Washington Family* (Northampton, 1927), 30; H. Clifford Smith, *Sulgrave Manor and the Washingtons* (London, 1933).

den Filmer Byrd, a kinsman of her father-in-law, *Patriarcha* Filmer, and a second cousin, once removed, of William Byrd. Many of these ties were cemented by cousin marriages, which were carefully planned to create a web of kinship as dense as that of the Roman patriciate. It is difficult to think of any ruling elite that has been more closely interrelated since the Ptolemies.

A case in point was the composition of Virginia's Royal Council. In 1724, there were twelve members of this body; all without exception were related to one another by blood or marriage. Most were kin of Mary Horsmanden Filmer Byrd. They included Robert "King" Carter and his son John Carter, and their cousins William Byrd, Nathaniel Harrison, and Peter Beverley. The other councilors were John Robinson, who had married Katherine Beverley; Philip Ludwell II, who had married Hannah Harrison; James Blair, whose wife was Sarah Harrison; John Lewis, who had married the daughter of Augustine Warner and was tied to all the major connections; Mann Page, who was kin to Judith Wormeley; Edmund Jennings and Cole Digges, who were related by marriage and birth to many of these families.[22]

This elite gained control of the Council during the mid-seventeenth century and retained it until the Revolution. As early as 1660, every seat on the Council was filled by members of five related connections. As late as 1775, every member of that august body was descended from a councilor who had served in 1660.[23]

A seat on the Council was not an empty honor. This small body functioned as the governor's cabinet, the upper house of the legislature and the colony's supreme court. It controlled the distribution of land, and the lion's share went to twenty-five families who held two-thirds of the seats in that body from 1680 to 1775. These same families also controlled other offices of power and profit: secretary, treasurer, auditor general, receiver general, sur-

---

[22]Jones, *The Present State of Virginia,* 103, 235–41.

[23]Labaree found that, of 91 councilors from 1680 to 1775, more than 60% had 23 surnames. David Jordan concludes from this and other evidence that Bacon's Rebellion had less impact on the composition of Virginia's elite than did the 1689 revolt on that of Maryland. See "Political Stability and the Emergence of a Native Elite in Maryland," in Thad W. Tate and David L. Ammerman, eds., *The Chesapeake in the Seventeenth Century* (London, 1975), 245; James L. Anderson, "The Governors' Councils of Colonial America: A Study of Pennsylvania and Virginia, 1660–1776" (thesis, Univ. of Va., 1967); Labaree, *Conservatism in Early American History,* 7; Grace L. Chickering, "Founders of an Oligarchy: The Virginia Council, 1692–1722," in Bruce C. Daniels, ed., *Power and Status: Officeholding in Colonial America* (Middletown, Conn., 1986), 255–77.

Norborne Berkeley, Lord Botetourt, personified the special relationship that long persisted between the Berkeley family and Virginia. Lord Botetourt (1718–70) was "a gracious, amiable and bankrupt nobleman" who became one of Virginia's most popular colonial governors. Appointed to that office in 1768, he conducted himself in the same vice-regal manner as his kinsman had done before him. Just as Sir William Berkeley copied the gestures of Charles I, so Lord Botetourt imitated George III, opening the Assembly much as the King opened Parliament, riding through Williamsburg in a state coach drawn by a matched team of cream-colored Hanoverian horses. When he spoke in public Botetourt mimicked the dress, manners, appearance and even the peculiar speech defects of George III. By 1768, the first gentlemen of Virginia like many old Royalist families in England had become outspoken Whigs. They disagreed with Lord Botetourt on constitutional questions, but they held him in high respect, liked him enormously and accepted him as one of themselves. When Lord Botetourt died suddenly of a tidewater fever in 1770, the Virginians erected a monument that survived the Revolution.

veyor general, collectors and naval officers, and governors of William and Mary College.[24]

In company with a larger group of lesser gentry, they also kept a firm grip on the economic life of the colony. In 1703 an official wrote, ". . . in every river of this province there are men in number from ten to thirty, who by trade and industry have gotten very competent estates. Those gentlemen take care to supply the poorer sort with goods and necessaries, and are sure to keep them always in their debt, and consequently dependent on them. Out of this number are chosen His Majesty's Council, the Assembly, the Justices, and Officers of Government."[25]

This small elite was destined to play a large role in the history of Virginia—not merely in its politics and economics, but also in its society and culture. The formation of southern folkways owed much to their example. An English immigrant who came in 1717 observed, ". . . at the Capitol, at publick times, may be seen a great number of handsome, well-dressed, complete gentlemen." He thought that they made "as fine an appearance . . . as I have seen anywhere."[26] In 1773, a clear-sighted northern visitor to Virginia, Philip Fithian, observed that "the people of fortune . . . are the pattern of all behavior here."[27]

The more hierarchical a society becomes, the stronger is the cultural dominion of its elite. The hegemony of Virginia's first families was exceptionally strong through the first century of that colony's history. One English emigrant named George Fisher remembered being warned about their power:

> John Randolph, in speaking of the disposition of the Virginians, very freely cautioned us against disobliging or offending any person of note in the Colony . . . ; for says he, either by blood or marriage, we are almost all related, and so connected in our interests, that whoever of a stranger presumes to offend any one of us will infallibly find an enemy of the whole. Nor, right or wrong, do we forsake him, till by one means or other his ruin is accomplished.[28]

[24]Fairfax Harrison, *Virginia Land Grants, A Study of Conveyancing in Relation to Colonial Politics* (Richmond, 1925).

[25]Col. Robert Quary to Board of Trade, 16 June 1703, quoted in Chickering, "Founders of an Oligarchy," 262.

[26]Jones, *Present State of Virginia*, 70.

[27]Philip Fithian to Enoch Green, 1 Dec. 1773; in Philip Vickers Fithian, *Journal and Letters 1773–1774: A Plantation Tutor of the Old Dominion* (Williamsburg, 1943), 34–35.

[28]"Narrative of George Fisher . . . ," *WMQ1* 17 (1908–9) 123.

This Virginia elite was firmly established during the governorship of Sir William Berkeley, and remained dominant for more than a century. Throughout this long period, English aristocrats who came to the New World instantly recognized a cultural kinship with the great planters of Virginia. In 1765, for example, Lord Adam Gordon, the first son of the second Duke of Gordon, observed that the "topping families" of Virginia had been founded by "younger brothers of good families of England." He felt perfectly at home among them. "Upon the whole," he wrote, "was it the case to live in America, this province in point of company and climate would be my choice."[29]

The social origins of Virginia's "topping families" were better understood by Lord Adam Gordon than by many middle-class historians in the twentieth century, who have replaced the image of "topping families" and "complete gentlemen" with an idea of upwardly-mobile bourgeois entrepreneurs. But the legend of the Virginia cavalier was no mere romantic myth. In all of its major parts, it rested upon a solid foundation of historical fact.[30]

---

[29]Lord Adam Gordon, "Journal of an Officer . . . in 1764 and 1765," in Newton D. Mereness, ed., *Travels in the American Colonies* (New York, 1916), 404–5.

[30]The historiography of the Virginia cavalier is itself a fascinating subject. In the 19th century, gentlemen-scholars such as Philip Bruce documented the Royalist origins of the Virginia elite, and argued that it came from an integrated group of English gentry and merchants, of whom the latter "traced their pedigrees back, and that not too remotely, to landed proprietors in the different shires" (*Social Life of Virginia*, 83).

Bruce was correct. But another scholar from a very different part of Virginia's society, T. J. Wertenbaker, condemned this interpretation as nostalgic nonsense and made a career of debunking the "cavalier myth." Wertenbaker argued that "few men of good social standing" came to the Chesapeake, and that the "leading settlers in Virginia" were petty tradesmen of "humble extraction" (*Patrician and Plebian in Virginia* (1910, rpt. New York, 1959), 10, 11, 28–30, passim).

Wertenbaker was unable to consult English materials until after he wrote this book, and in the few cases where he made specific attributions of social rank to individual Virginians, he was mistaken in his facts (e.g., Thoroughgood, Cary, Ludwell, even Byrd). By reason of his origins, he also had an axe to grind against the first families of Virginia. But the image of the cavalier was unwelcome in the New South, and his argument was quickly accepted. W. A. Reavis appeared to buttress it with a quantitative test which reported that 82% of Maryland's elite were "not real English gentry at all." But under the heading of "not real" he included younger sons, shrinking fortunes and any sort of commercial connection ("The Maryland Gentry and Social Mobility, 1637–1676," *WMQ3* 14 (1957), 418–28). Similar conclusions appear in Aubrey Land, "Economic Base & Social Structure: The Northern Chesapeake in the Eighteenth Century," *JECH* 25 (1965), 639–54, and "The Planters of Colonial Maryland," *MDHM* 67 (1972), 109–28; but Land had virtually no evidence on English origins, and Maryland was not Virginia. The Wertenbaker thesis has been accepted by social historians of the "Chesapeake group," by cultural historians who write about the "cavalier myth" and by leading historians of the New South.

A few scholars have confirmed parts of the Bruce thesis: as to origins, John E. Manahan, "The Cavalier Remounted: A Study of the Origins of Virginia's Population, 1607–1700" (thesis, Univ. of Va., 1946); as to timing, Bailyn, "Politics and Social Structure in Virginia," 90–118; as

✎ Virginia's Great Migration: Social Origins

The settlement of Virginia had actually begun more than a generation before the arrival of Sir William Berkeley and his elite. Its starting point was the founding of Jamestown (1607) by English colonists in the ship *Susan Constant* and her two small consorts *Godspeed* and *Discovery*. These immigrants succeeded in planting the first permanent English settlement in America. But there is today no Susan Constant Society comparable to that of the Mayflower descendants. Most of Jamestown's founders either died in their new homes or speedily returned to England.[1]

The population of Virginia began to grow rapidly at a later date—after the Puritan migration to New England. Many authorities now agree that English "immigration to the Chesapeake colonies was heavily concentrated in the third quarter of the seventeenth century."[2] From 1645 to 1665, Virginians multiplied more than threefold and Marylanders increased elevenfold, while New Englanders merely doubled. Given the very high mortality rates in the Chesapeake colonies and low birth rates during the first generation, the number of immigrants to the Chesapeake was probably in the range of 40,000 to 50,000 during the period from 1645 to 1670.[3]

---

to beliefs, Bertram Wyatt-Brown in his excellent and useful *Southern Honor: Ethics and Behavior in the Old South* (Oxford, 1982).

[1]Gentry families who survived from the early years of settlement included Archer, Eppes, Forrest, Powell, and Wingfield.

[2]This is the conclusion of Wesley Frank Craven, *White, Red and Black: The Seventeenth Century Virginian* (Charlottesville, 1971); Russell Menard agrees that although this conclusion is "quite accurate . . . one might want to add some qualifications. A more precise timing would probably push its beginning back to the late 1640's and its end up to 1680, and note that it was interrupted several times, severely in the mid-1660's, less so in the mid-50s and early 70s. Two years outside the period, 1635 and 1699, may have witnessed the arrival of more new settlers than any single year between 1650 and 1675. Still, the annual average was almost certainly higher in the third quarter than in any other period of comparable length in the century." These qualifications apply with more force to Maryland than to Virginia; Russell Menard, "Immigration to the Chesapeake Colonies in the Seventeenth Century: A Review Essay," *MDHM* 68 (1973), 323–29.

[3]The pattern appears in the following population estimates:

Colony	1629	1640	1660	1670
Newfoundland	100			
New England	1,000	25,000		50,000
New Netherland	270	2,000	5,000	
Maryland	—	600	4,000	11,000
Virginia	2,500	8,000	30,000	
Bermuda	2,000	3,000	4,000	

Virginia's second great migration differed from the Puritan exodus to Massachusetts in many ways—in its English origins, in its American destination, and especially in its social composition. New England had drawn mostly from the middle of English society. Virginians came in greater numbers from both higher and lower ranks. In quantitative terms, Sir William Berkeley's "distressed cavaliers" were only a small part of the total flow to the Chesapeake colonies. The great mass of Virginia's immigrants were humble people of low rank. More than 75 percent came as indentured servants.[4]

One surviving English register of emigration contains the names of approximately 10,000 servants who sailed from Bristol to America between 1654 and 1678. Roughly half of these emigrants went to Virginia. The rest found their way to the West Indies—mainly the island of Barbados which was much favored

Colony	1629	1640	1660	1670
Barbados	1,400	20,000	42,000	
Jamaica	—	—	3,500	
Leeward Islands	3,150	12,000	10,000	
Providence Island	—	1,000	—	

From 1629 to 1640, English emigrants went mostly to New England and Barbados. The great migration to the Chesapeake occurred from 1640 to 1600, when population grew threefold in Virginia and elevenfold in Maryland, while merely doubling in New England. These estimates are from many sources, mainly those summarized in Carl Bridenbaugh, *Vexed and Troubled Englishmen, 1590–1642* (New York, 1968), 410, 432, 473; Richard S. Dunn, *Sugar and Slaves: The Rise of the Planter Class in the English West Indies, 1624–1713* (Chapel Hill, 1972), 311–13; Russell Menard, "Population, Economy and Society in Seventeenth Century Maryland," *MDHM* 79 (1984), 71–92, and standard works on individual colonies.

For Virginia, a variant estimate appears in Morgan, *American Slavery, American Freedom*, 404, which reckons the population of that colony at 25,600 in 1662, 31,900 in 1674, and 40,600 in 1682, These numbers are too low; Morgan assumed that ratios between tithables and the general population were linear, but in fact the pattern was parabolic with its apogee in 1662. Informed contemporaries believed that Virginia's population had reached 40,000 as early as 1660 (Berkeley, *Discourse and View of Virginia*, 6–7), but this estimate seems too high. A more probable estimate for 1660 was 30,000 (12,000 tithables). The estimates in *HSUS* are far off the mark.

Total immigration has been estimated at 82,000 for Virginia (1607–99), 42,000 for Maryland (1634–99), and 120,000 to 130,000 for the Chesapeake during the 17th century; Berkeley reckoned in 1670 that "yearly, we suppose there comes in, of servants, about 1,500, of which most are English, few Scotch and fewer Irish." This estimate, plus freemen and slaves, is roughly consistent with other evidence. See Craven, *White, Red and Black*, 16; Menard, "Immigration," 323; J.P.P. Horn, "Social and Economic Aspects of Local Society in England and the Chesapeake: A Comparative Study of the Vale of Berkeley, Gloucestershire, with the Lower Western Shore of Maryland, 1660–1700" (thesis, Univ. of Sussex, 1982), 6; William W. Hening, *Hening's Statutes at Large: Being a Collection of All the Laws of Virginia . . .* (13 vols., New York, 1819–1923), II, 515.

[4]Craven found that "the vast majority of the settlers in seventeenth-century Virginia, perhaps 75 per cent or more of them," were indentured servants; *White, Red and Black*, 5.

during the 1650s, and the beautiful little island of Nevis which was preferred in the early 1660s. Scarcely any chose to make New England their home. The main stream flowed from the south and west of England to the Caribbean and the Chesapeake.[5]

Virginia's servants were recruited mainly from the lower strata of English society, but not from the very lowest—"the bottom of the middle ranks," one historian has written, "below their older and wealthier contemporaries, but above the poor laborers, vagrants and the destitute." Unlike most emigrants to New England, their passage was paid by others.[6] They tended to be more rural and agrarian than the founders of Massachusetts. Two-thirds of Virginia's colonists were unskilled laborers, or "farmers" in the English sense—agrarian tenants who worked the land of others. Only about 30 percent were artisans (compared with nearly 60 percent in New England). Most were unable to read or write; rates of literacy in the Chesapeake Bay were much lower than in Massachusetts Bay.[7]

[5]These lists also tell us much about the timing of migration. The number of Bristol emigrants rose steadily through the 1650s, reached a peak in 1659, fell a little in 1660 when Charles II returned to the throne, rose again to high levels in the 1670s, and then dropped sharply and remained at a low ebb through the next 20 years. See Abbot Emerson Smith, *Colonists in Bondage: White Servitude and Convict Labor in America, 1607–1776* (Chapel Hill, 1947), 71, 308–9; David Galenson, *White Servitude in Colonial America: An Economic Analysis* (Cambridge, 1981), 34–39.

Another rough indicator of the rhythm of migration (though not of its rate) in this period is the annual number of headrights in Virginia. This evidence also shows high values in the years from 1635 to 1640, a trough from 1640 to 1649, a great surge from 1650 to 1664, and a decline thereafter. Headrights tended to lag behind migration, and cannot be used to estimate annual immigration. But they are valuable as an indicator of general trends; for a discussion see Craven, *White, Red and Black*, 1–37, which also reports the raw data. See also Edmund Morgan, "Headrights and Head Counts," *VMHB* 80 (1972), 361–71; and Menard, "Immigration."

[6]Horn, "Social and Economic Aspects of Local Society in England and the Chesapeake," 61. On this question a controversy has developed. Marcus Jernegan described Virginia's servants as "dissolute persons of every type," and Abbot Smith took them to be "rabble of all descriptions." But Mildred Campbell argued the contrary proposition that most came from the "middling classes." Mediating positions are taken by David Galenson, who estimated that low to middling occupations predominated, and by Horn, who concluded that they were a "broader cross section."

Horn's thesis includes an interesting comparison between Bristol emigrants and Gloucester militia. He finds that emigrants with listed occupations were more agrarian and less skilled than the militiamen of Gloucester as a whole. Further, no occupations were recorded for 30 to 60% of emigrants; Galenson has argued persuasively that many of these people of unknown origin were in fact unskilled farm laborers.

Servants who sailed from London were more skilled and more urban in their occupations than their Bristol counterparts, but less so than emigrants to New England in the period 1629–40.

[7]Several studies have yielded the following occupational results for Chesapeake immigrants

Patterns of gender were also very different from New England's great migration. Altogether, females were outnumbered by males by more than four to one—in some periods, as much as six to one.[8] Few women freely chose to settle in Virginia. Some were "trapanned" or "snared" and sent against their will, as an old folk ballad called "The Trappan'd Maiden" tells us:

> Give ear unto a Maid, that lately was betray'd,
>   And sent into Virginny, O:
> In brief I shall declare, what I have suffer'd there,
>   When that I was weary, weary, weary, weary, O. . . .
>
> Five years served I, under Master Guy,
>   In the land of Virginny, O,
> Which made me for to know sorrow, grief and woe,
>   When that I was weary, weary, weary, weary, O. . . .
>
> I have played my part both at Plow and Cart,
>   In the Land of Virginny, O;
> Billets from the Wood upon my back they load,
>   When that I am weary, weary, weary, weary, O. . . .
>
> Then let Maids beware, all by my ill-fare,
>   In the Land of Virginny, O;
> Be sure to stay at home, for if you here do come,
>   You all will be weary, weary, weary, weary, O. . . .[9]

In 1643 a woman named Elizabeth Hamlin was sent to Newgate for "trapanning" girls in this manner. Another ballad tells the

---

by port of departure:

Occupation	Bristol	London
Farmers	47%	24%
Laborers	21%	28%
Artisans	30%	33%
Gent. & Prof.	2%	12%
Other	0%	3%

James Horn, "Servant Emigration to the Chesapeake in the Seventeenth Century," in Tate and Ammerman, eds., *The Chesapeake in the Seventeenth Century,* 51–95; similar findings appear in Anthony Salerno, "The Character of Emigration from Wiltshire to the American Colonies, 1630–1660" (unpub. diss., Univ. of Virginia, 1977), 55; Galenson, *White Servitude in Colonial America* 34–64.

[8]The sex ratio among Bristol servants (1654–86) was 308; among London servants it was 642. See Moller, "Sex Ratios and Correlated Culture Patterns."

[9]"The Trappan'd Maiden," in C. H. Firth ed., *An American Garland: Being a Collection of Ballads Relating to America, 1563–1759* (Oxford, 1915), 51–53.

Virginia's immigrants in the late seventeenth century were mostly indentured servants whose families had been poor tenant farmers and country laborers. The last remnants of this class still survive today in remote rural villages of southern England. As recently as 1985, two tenant-laborers named Jack and Roy French were suddenly thrust into the national limelight by the death of their landlord. They lived in the Cotswold village of Great Tew (Oxfordshire), in old stone cottages without electricity or water, and were tenants of a local squire named Major Eustace Robb. The death of Major Robb caused a furious controversy in the West Oxfordshire District Council about the disposition of the cottages and occupants.

tale of an "honest weaver" who sold his wife to Virginia. This practice, bizarre as it may seem, actually occurred in England during the seventeenth century.[10]

Most of Virginia's servant-immigrants were half-grown boys and young men. Three out of four were between the ages of fifteen and twenty-four. Only 3 percent were under fifteen, and less than 1 percent was over thirty-five—a sharp contrast with Massachusetts.[11] More than a few of these youngsters were "spirited" or kidnapped to Virginia. Parliament in 1645 heard evidence of gangs who "in a most barbarous and wicked manner steal away many little children" for service in the Chesapeake colonies.[12] Others were "lagged" or transported after being arrested for petty crime or vagrancy. Another ballad tells the story of a London apprentice was who "lagg'd" by a "hard-hearted judge," and "sold for a slave in Virginia":

> Come all you young fellows wherever you be,
> Come listen awile and I will tell thee,
> Concerning the hardships that we undergo,
>   When we get lagg'd to Virginia . . .
>
> When I was apprentice in fair London town,
> Many hours I served duly and truly,
> Till buxom young lasses they led me astray,
> My work I neglected more and more every day,
>   By that I got lagg'd to Virginia.
>
> But now in Virginia I lay like a hog,
> Our pillow at night is a brick or a log,
> We dress and undress like some other sea hog,
>   How hard is my fate in Virginia.[13]

The character of Virginia's great migration thus differed in almost every important way from the Puritan exodus to Massachusetts. From the start, immigrants to the Chesapeake colony were more highly stratified, more male-dominant, more rural, more agrarian, less highly skilled, and less literate. Many came from the south and west of England; few from East Anglia or the

---

[10]"A Net for a Night-Raven; Or, A Trap for a Scold," in *ibid.*, 54–56.

[11]Horn, "Servant Emigration," 61.

[12]Peter Wilson Coldham, "The 'Spiriting' of London Children to Virginia, 1648–1685," *VMHB* 83 (1975), 280–88.

[13]"The Lads of Virginia," in Firth, ed., *An American Garland*, 72–73.

north. These patterns did not develop merely by chance. Virginia's great migration was the product of policy and social planning. Its royalist elite succeeded in shaping the social history of an American region partly by regulating the process of migration.

❧ Virginia's Great Migration: Religious Origins

Religion was not as central to the origins of the Chesapeake colonies as it had been in New England. But the founders of Virginia shared the religious obsessions of their age, and they were sent upon their way with an abundance of spiritual exhortation. John Donne, the poet dean of St. Paul's Cathedral, called himself "an adventurer; if not to Virginia, then for Virginia". He preached a sermon to departing planters, and told them:

> Your principal end is not gain, nor glory, but to gain souls to the glory of God. This seals the great seal, this justifies itself, this authorises authority, and gives power to strength itself. . . . you shall have made this island, which is but the Suburbs of the old world, a Bridge, a Gallery to the new; to join all to that world that shall never grow old, the kingdom of heaven.[1]

John Donne had mainly in mind the salvation of Indian souls. Others suggested that the founding of Virginia might also be a means of redeeming a few unregenerate Englishmen. The Reverend William Crashaw delivered another departure sermon for the Virginia Company, in which he declared:

> As long as we have wise, courageous and discreet *Governours,* together with the preaching of God's word, we much care not what the generality is of them that go in person, considering we find that the most disordered men that can be raked up out of the *superflaitie,* or, if you will, the very *excrements* of a full and swelling state, if they be removed . . . from the licentiousness and too much liberty of the states where they have lived, into a more base and barren soil, as every country is at first, and to a harder course of life, wanting pleasures, and subject to some pinching miseries, and

---

[1]John Donne, *A Sermon . . . to the Honourable Company of the Virginian Plantation* (London, 1622). The same arguments appeared in William Symonds, a fellow of Magdalen College, Oxford, in *Virginia: A Sermon Preached at White Chappel, in the Presence of . . . the Adventurers and Planters of Virginia* (London, 1609). Symonds was a ghost-writer of Captain John Smith's general history of Virginia.

to a strict form of government and severe discipline, do often become new men, even as it were cast in a new mold.[2]

This advice was addressed to one "discreet governor" in particular, Lord De la Warr, who did as he was urged. One of his first acts in the New World was to open a "pretty chapel" decorated every day with fresh flowers, complete with a chancel of Virginia cedar, a communion table of black walnut, and a font in the shape of an Indian canoe. Lord De la Warr required every Virginian to assemble for prayers twice a day "at the ringing of a bell." Every Sunday all the settlers were compelled to attend two services conducted with high ceremony. The governor himself sat on a splendid green velvet throne, surrounded by "all the Councilors, Captains, other officers, and all the gentlemen, and with a guard of Halberdiers in his Lordship's Livery."[3]

For more than a century, the religious life of Virginia developed along these lines. It was ceremonial, liturgical, hierarchical, ritualist—and very different from New England. Each individual was not expected to share the same opinions. But all were compelled to join in the same rituals. The gentry who came from southwestern England had long favored "an uniform government of the Church in all points."[4]

During its first few decades, Virginia's immigrants held many varieties of Protestant belief. A few laymen and clergy had puritanical leanings. The marriage of Pocahontas and John Rolfe was performed by Richard Buck, a staunch Puritan. But Virginia did not attract many of that persuasion. In 1613, one clergyman marveled that "so few of our English ministers that were so hot against the surplice and subscription, come hither, where neither are spoken of."[5]

After Virginia became a royal colony, an ideal of Anglican conformity began to be more actively pursued. In 1632 the Assembly

[2]William Crashaw, *A Sermon Preached in London before the Honourable the Lord Lawarre* [*sic*], *Lord Governour and Captain Generall of Vergenea* (London, 1610), folio L, F.

[3]William Strachey, "A True Repertory . . . ," in Samuel Purchas, ed., *Hakluytus Posthumus of Purchas His Pilgrimes* (Edinburgh, 1906), xix, 56–57.

[4]This is from a petition dated 5 March 1603/04, and signed by a larger number of Sussex gentry, including Thomas La Warre himself and many families who appeared in Virginia, such as the Wests, Culpepers, Newtons, Goreings, Parkers and Palmers. See T.W.W. Smart, "Extracts from the Mss. of Samuel Jeake," *SAC* 9 (1857), 45–60.

[5]Alexander Whitaker to William Gough, 18 June 1614, George M. Brydon, *Virginia's Mother Church* (2 vols., New York, 1947), I, 24; see also Whitaker, *Good News from Virginia* (1613), ed. Wesley Frank Craven (New York, 1937).

enacted seventeen laws which required "uniformity throughout this colony, both in substance and circumstance to the canons and constitutions of the Church of England." Each minister was compelled to preach every Sabbath, to give communion three times a year, to "examine, catechise and instruct" all the children in his parish, and to "excel all others in puritie of life." Parishioners were required to attend church on Sundays and holidays, or to pay a shilling for each absence. They also had to pay tithes, and were forbidden to "disparage" their ministers.[6]

After 1642 Governor William Berkeley added other laws which required "all nonconformists . . . to depart the colony with all conveniency." Several small Puritan communities had been founded before he arrived, and nonconformist ministers had been sent to serve them. Berkeley scattered these settlements, and banished the Puritans from Virginia. More than 300 fled to Maryland, and others departed for New England. After the Civil War, the Protectorate was unable to break the Anglican establishment in Virginia. The Book of Common Prayer was specially permitted in the colony, as long as prayers to the King and Royal family were omitted.[7]

When Quakers began to appear the authorities moved quickly against them. A law in 1658 ordered all Quakers to be banished. Shipmasters who brought them were required to remove them in close confinement. One defiant female Friend was ordered to be whipped twenty strokes upon her bare back, and (more painful to a Quaker conscience) she was also required to confess her error upon bended knee. The whipping was remitted when she promised to conform. Quakers were also fined for failing to attend Anglican services and for refusing to pay tithes. In 1661 other laws punished Anglicans who were merely "loving to Quakers."[8]

This persecution worked. Puritan congregations were virtually eliminated from Virginia, and Quakers were reduced to a few small meetings. By the end of the seventeenth century, religious belief was remarkably uniform in the colony. Robert Beverley reported in 1705 that dissenters were "very few," with "not more

---

[6]Hening, *Statutes at Large,* I, 184.
[7]Brydon, *Virginia's Mother Church,* I, 123.
[8]Philip A. Bruce, *Institutional History of Virginia in the Seventeenth Century* (2 vols., 1910, Gloucester, Mass., 1964), I, 222–51.

than five conventicles amongst them, namely three small meetings of Quakers, and two of Presbyterians."[9]

A religious survey of Virginia in 1724 showed that the Anglican establishment was strong and healthy throughout the colony— more so than in the mother country. Most clergy reported that their services were well attended every Sunday by most white adults in the parish, and that a larger proportion took holy communion than in England. Dissenters were reported to be few, and in some parishes nonexistent.[10]

Later in the eighteenth century, this pattern rapidly changed with the increase of Presbyterians, Baptists and Methodists. But

---

[9]Beverley, *The History and Present State of Virginia,* 65.

[10]The following parochial reports in 1725 show that the Anglican establishment was stronger in Virginia than many historians have believed:

Name of Parish	Number of Churches	Number of Families	Usual Size of Congregation	Average Number Communicants
St. Pauls, Hanover	4	1,200	no information	400
James City, Mulberry I.	2	78	130 and 200 "in cong."	75–90
Bristol	2	430	"pretty full attendance, often more than there are pews"	50
St. Peters	1	204	"170–180 attend usually"	40–50
Westover	3	233	"two-thirds attend"	75
Hungar's	2	365	"scarce one third attend"	80
Newport-Chuckatuck	4	400	1000 in church and 3 chapels	40
Stratton-Major	2	200	"300 attend on average"	220
Wilmington	3	180	"No dissenters; church well frequented"	100
Blissland	2	136	"Greater part attend"	60–70
York-hampton	2	200	"About ⅔ are commonly present"	80
Christ Church, Lancaster	2	300	"Almost all persons attend"	60–80
South Farnham	2	200	no information	100
Petsworth	1	146	"300 attend on average"	100
Lawne's Creek	2	165	no information	32–52
Washington	2	200	"churches crowded . . . 2 qts wine" used	
Elizabeth City	1	350	"most attend; few dissenters"	100
Upper Parish, Isle of Wight	1	165	"small proportion attend"	10–20
Christ Church, Middlesex	3	260	"200 [families] attend	230
Bruton	1	110	"full cong. on some days"	50
Accomack	3	400–500	"churches cannot contain all who come"	200
St. Stephens, King & Queen	2	300	"a good congregation"	60
Henrico	3	400	no information	20
Southwalk [sic]	3	394	"congregations very large"	40–80
Abingdon	1	300	"attendance generally good"	60–70
St. Mary's	1	150	"attendance 150 [families]	100
Overwharton	3	650	"full attendance at church"	80–100
St. Anne's, Essex	2	130	"between 100 and 180"	50–80

Source: Parochial returns in 1725, reproduced in Brydon, *Virginia's Mother Church,* I, 371–72.

through the Old Dominion's first six generations Anglican orthodoxy was strong, and growing stronger. Here was a fact of high
importance for the history of Virginia, for the culture of this colony, no less than Massachusetts, was shaped by its religion.

✿ Virginia's Great Migration: Regional Origins

Virginia's immigrants came from every county of England, and
from thousands of parishes. But a majority of Virginia's indentured servants hailed from sixteen counties in the south and west
of England—the same area that produced Virginia's elite. A case
in point was the population that settled in Virginia's Isle of Wight
County. A local historian found that "early Isle of Wight families
seem to have come mostly from the southwest of England, that is
the counties of Gloucester, Somerset, Devon, Dorset, Wiltshire
and Hampshire . . . their names appear to be more numerous
in the west country than in any other part of England. After the
west country, London and its surrounding counties seem to be
next."[1]

Another example was the population of Berkeley Hundred in
Virginia. Its historian found that "the majority . . . whether spon-
sors, tenants at labor or indentured servants, were . . . born and
bred in Gloucester, where many of them were natives of the
Berkeley vale, the Cotswold Edge, or the Winchcombe area."[2]

In yet another group of 1,200 immigrants to all parts of Virginia, it was observed that "most of them [were] choice men,
born and bred up to labor and husbandry. Out of Devonshire,
about an hundred men, brought up to husbandry; out of Warwickshire and Staffordshire, above one hundred and ten; and out
of Sussex about forty, all trained to ironworks; the rest dis-
persedly out of divers Shires of the realm."[3]

---

[1] Of families known to have settled in the Isle of Wight County during the 17th century, 50%
came from the five counties of Devon, Dorset, Gloucester, Somerset and Wiltshire. Another
40% were from London and its environs. The rest of England contributed 10%. The data appear
in John Bennett Boddie, *Seventeenth Century Isle of Wight County, Virginia* (Baltimore, 1959),
204.

[2] Eric Gethryn Jones, *George Thorpe and the Berkeley Company, a Gloucester Enterprise in Virginia*
(Gloucester, 1982).

[3] "A Declaration of the State of Virginia," in Peter Force, ed., *Tracts and Other Papers Relating
Principally to the Colonies in North America* (4 vols., 1843–46, rpt. New York, 1947), III, 5.

These regional patterns changed a little during the mid-seventeenth century. One historian has reckoned that before 1650 as many as 80 or 90 percent of Virginia's servants sailed from London, and the great majority came from "the southeastern part of the country, particularly London and the Home counties." Roughly half (52%) of these servants who sailed from the River Thames identified their homes as London itself—mostly the suburbs. Only about 2 percent came from the inner city. The other half came mostly from counties to the west of London—Middlesex, Buckingham, Surrey, Berkshire, Oxfordshire, Warwickshire and Northamptonshire. Few came from East Anglia.[4] After 1650, Bristol became more important in Virginia's servant trade. The great majority of emigrants from Bristol (87% in one sample) came from the west of England and South Wales. The most important place of origin was the Severn Valley.[5]

In the mid-seventeenth century, Virginia's recruiting ground in England might have been encompassed by two great circles around the cities of London and Bristol, each with a radius of roughly sixty miles.[6] To this rule, however, there were important exceptions. Comparatively few of Virginia's immigrants came from East Anglia, though parts of that region lay very near to London. Even fewer came from Cornwall, though that county lay

---

[4]Horn, "Servant Emigration to the Chesapeake," 70–71.

[5]The regional origins of 721 servants who sailed from Bristol for the Chesapeake were as follows: West Country, 29%, Severn Valley, 38%; South Wales, 20%; other parts of England, 13%; Horn, "Servant Emigration to the Chesapeake," 51–95.

[6]David Souden discovered the following patterns of recruitment for apprentices and servants who sailed from Bristol in the period 1654–79:

Distance from Bristol	Servants	Apprentices
0–10 miles	19.0%	54.5%
10–20 miles	16.3	16.3
20–40 miles	26.2	14.6
40–60 miles	16.3	7.4
60–80 miles	6.1	2.5
80–100 miles	6.5	2.0
100–150 miles	7.9	2.4
150–200 miles	1.4	0.2
200+ miles	0.3	0.0
Total	100.0	99.9

Source: David Souden, "Rogues, Whores and Vagabonds? Indentured Servant Emigrants to North America, and the Case of Mid-Seventeenth-Century Bristol," *SH* 3 (1978), 31; for other ports see David F. Lamb, "The Seaborn Trade of Southampton in the First Half of the Seventeenth Century" (thesis, Univ. of Southampton, 1971).

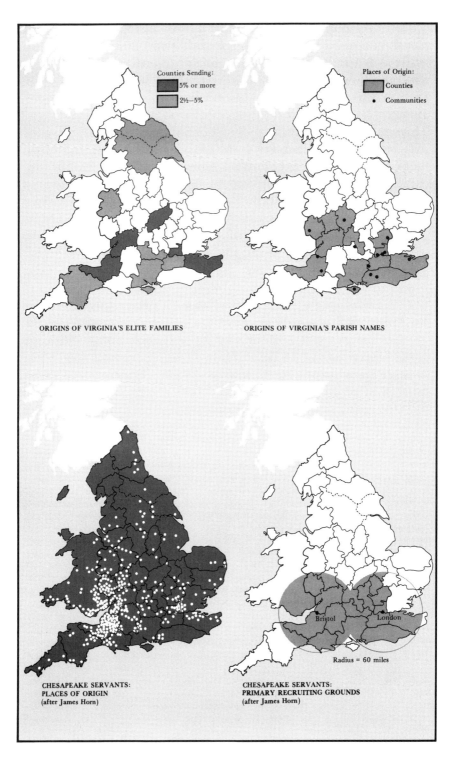

Counties Sending:
5% or more
2½–5%

Places of Origin:
Counties
• Communities

ORIGINS OF VIRGINIA'S ELITE FAMILIES

ORIGINS OF VIRGINIA'S PARISH NAMES

**CHESAPEAKE SERVANTS:
PLACES OF ORIGIN**
(after James Horn)

**CHESAPEAKE SERVANTS:
PRIMARY RECRUITING GROUNDS**
(after James Horn)

Bristol

London

Radius = 60 miles

within easy reach of Bristol.[7] The people of Cornwall, many of whom still spoke Gaelic in the seventeenth century, were culturally distinct from other counties of southwestern England. This pattern shows that for Virginia's indentured servants, the location of the seaport did not determine the region. It was more nearly the other way around—the region determined the seaport.[8]

The regional origins and social purposes of Virginia's English immigrants also appeared in the names that they gave to the new land—an important piece of evidence, for it is independent of registers and shipping lists. Altogether, twenty-five counties were created in Virginia by the year 1703. Two kept their Indian names—Accomac and Nansemond. Eight other names reflected the Royalist politics of the Virginians: James City County, Charles City County, Elizabeth City County, Henrico, Prince George, Princess Anne, King William, and King and Queen County. All the rest bore the names of British counties and towns. Only two names came from the east of England, and only four from the north. The remainder (8 of 14, or 57%) were drawn from the

---

[7]David Souden found the following counties of origin among 2,492 servants who sailed from Bristol during the years 1654–79, compared with apprentices in that town:

Area	Indentured Servants		Apprentices	
	n	%	n	%
Bristol	272	10.9	330	33.6
Somerset	395	15.9	158	16.1
Gloucester	287	11.5	201	20.5
Wiltshire	225	9.0	57	5.8
Monmouth	241	9.7	56	5.7
South Wales	225	9.0	52	5.3
Hereford, Salop, Worcs	283	11.4	54	5.5
Dorset, Hants., Sussex	74	3.0	18	1.8
Cornwall, Devon	87	3.5	9	0.9
London and Home Counties	135	5.4	15	1.5
East Anglia	18	0.7	0	0.0
Beds, Leics, Nhants, Notts, Oxon	32	1.3	2	0.2
Derby, Stafford, Warwick	26	1.0	4	0.4
Ches, Cumb, Lanc, Linc, Nhum, York	45	1.8	5	0.5
North Wales	106	4.3	12	1.2
Ireland	36	1.4	7	0.7
Other	5	0.2	1	0.1
Total	2,492	100.0	981	99.8

This emigration went mainly (86.1%) to Barbados and Virginia with no major differences in region of origin by colonial destination; Souden, "Rogues, Whores and Vagabonds," 31.

[8]Horn, in "Servant Emigration to the Chesapeake," suggests that most Virginia migrants came either from wood-pasture districts or from towns and cities—a hypothesis similar to that made by Anderson for the New England migration. I believe that this idea is mistaken, but firm evidence is lacking on both sides of the question.

same region in southwestern England which also dominated the shipping lists, servant registers and genealogies of the ruling elite. In southern Maryland and southern Delaware, county names also were drawn entirely from the south and west of England.[9]

A similar pattern also appeared in the names of Virginia's parishes. Of 54 parishes founded before 1726, most were given the names of Christian saints or Indian places. But fourteen parishes were named after English communities. All of them without exception were in the south and west of England—the same triangle of territory between Bristol, Warwick and Kent.[10]

✎ The Cradle of Virginia: The South of England

Virginia's recruiting ground was a broad region in the south and west of England, running from the weald of Kent to Devon and north as far as Shropshire and Staffordshire. This area was not defined by its physical features. It did not share the same soil resources or a single topography or a dominant agricultural regime. Its regional character was formed not by any of these material factors, but by its culture and history.

The heart of this territory was Wessex, Hardy country. Thomas Hardy's fictional Wessex included the counties of Wiltshire ("Mid Wessex"); Dorset ("South Wessex"); Somerset and Gloucestershire ("Outer Wessex"); Devon ("Lower Wessex"), Hampshire, West Sussex and Surrey ("Upper Wessex"), plus Berkshire,

---

[9]The 25 Virginia counties in being by 1703 were as follows: *Royalist names:* King and Queen, King William, Elizabeth City, Henrico, Prince George, Charles City, James City, Princess Anne; *southern and western names:* Surry, Isle of Wight, Gloucester, Northampton, Warwick, Stafford, Middlesex, New Kent; *eastern names:* Norfolk, Essex; *northern names:* York, Lancaster, Northumberland, Westmorland; *Indian names:* Accomac, Nansemond. Naming patterns in Maryland were similar, but not precisely the same. The name of the first county reflected the Roman Catholic religion of the founders. Many counties were given the surnames of families related to the lord proprietor of this colony, and a few bore royal names. Only a small minority were named after English counties. All these place names, without exception, were from the south and west of England: *Religious names:* St Mary's; *proprietary names:* Baltimore, Calvert, Cecil, Harford, Anne Arundel, Caroline; *Indian names:* Wicomico, Allegany; *Royalist names:* Prince George's, Charles, Frederick; *English counties and towns (all south and west):* Dorcester, Kent, Worcester, Somerset, Talbot; *Revolutionary leaders:* Washington, Montgomery, Howard, Carroll. The two counties of southern Delaware were named Sussex and Kent, both in the south of England.

[10]These parish names, and the English counties from which they came, were as follows: South Farnham (Surrey); Abingdon (Oxford); Petsworth (Sussex); Ware (Hertfordshire); Kingston (Worcester-Herefordshire); Bristol (Somerset); Bruton (Somerset); Newport (Isle of Wight); Sittenbourn [sic] (Kent); Whitechapel (London); Southwark (London); Warwick (Warwickshire); Washington (Sussex); Hampton (Middlesex); see Brydon, *Virginia's Mother Church,* I, 363–64.

Oxfordshire and Buckinghamshire ("North Wessex").[1] This area
sent large numbers of gentry and servants to the Chesapeake. The
first families of Virginia even included the Turbervilles from Bere
Regis (Hardy's Kingsbere) who were the originals for Hardy's fictional D'Urbervilles. In the court records of the Chesapeake colonies, one may also find the saga of many a tidewater Tess.[2] But
Virginia's recruiting ground was larger than Hardy's modern literary Wessex. It more nearly resembled the ancient historical
Wessex of Alfred and Athelred, which with its Mercian protectorate reached east as far as Canterbury, and north beyond Warwick and Northampton.

Through many centuries, this area developed its own distinctive culture. Its language and laws were those of the West Saxons,
rather than the Danes who settled East Anglia, or the Norse who
colonized the north country, or the Celts who held Cornwall and
Wales. Its shires were divided into hundreds rather than wapentakes; its tax units were reckoned in hides instead of carucates; its
weights and measures were old British rather than Scandinavian.[3]

The countryside of this region was divided into comparatively
large manors—larger than in the east of England—and dominated by a small landholding class. The boundaries of its estates
were very ancient. Historian J. H. Bettey writes that "the arrangement of the Wessex landscape and its administrative divisions and
estate boundaries had already been in existence for many centuries before the Norman conquest."[4]

During the early middle ages slavery had existed on a large
scale throughout Mercia, Wessex and Sussex, and had lasted
longer there than in other parts of England. Historian D.J.V.
Fisher writes that "the fate of many of the natives was not exter-
mination but slavery."[5] This was not merely domestic bondage,

---

[1]On Hardy's fictional map of Wessex, Casterbridge was Dorchester, Exonbury was Exeter,
Wintoncester was Winchester, and Christminster was Oxford, and Castle Royal was Windsor.
For the geography of Hardy's Wessex see David Daiches and John Flower, *Literary Landscapes
of the British Isles: A Narrative Atlas* (1979, New York, 1980), 158–71; Carl J. Weber, *Hardy of
Wessex* (rev. ed., New York, 1965); Merryn Williams, *Thomas Hardy and Rural England* (New
York, 1972); Ruth Firor, *Folkways in Thomas Hardy* (Philadelphia, 1951); Robert Gittings, *Young
Thomas Hardy* (Boston, 1975); *idem, Thomas Hardy's Later Years* (Boston, 1978).

[2]The Turbervilles intermarried with the Lees and Custis families; their genealogy and heraldry appears in Edmund J. Lee, *Lee of Virginia, 1642–1692: Biographical and Genealogical
Sketches of the Descendants of Col. Richard Lee* (1895, Baltimore, 1983), 93–95.

[3]David Hill, *An Atlas of Anglo-Saxon England*, maps 174–177.

[4]J. H. Bettey, *Wessex from AD 1000* (London, 1986) 6, summarizing much scholarship, notably D. Bonney, "Early Boundaries and Estates in Southern England," in P. Sawyer, ed., *Medieval
Settlement, Continuity and Change* (London, 1976), 72–81.

[5]D.J.V. Fisher, *The Anglo-Saxon Age, c 400–1042* (London, 1973), 44, 122, 333.

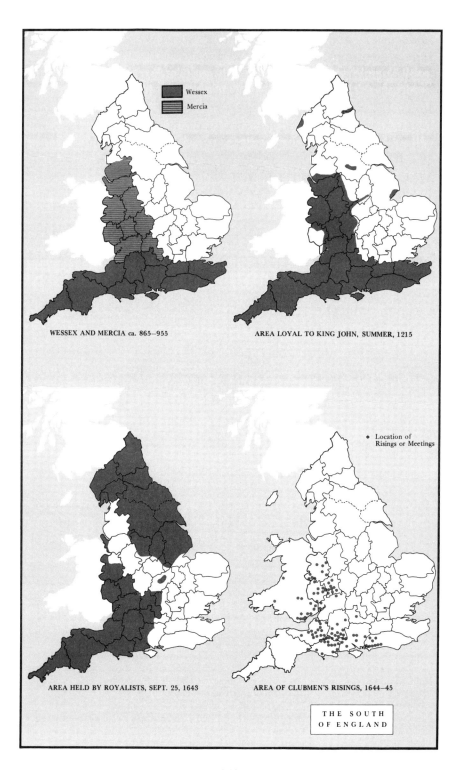

WESSEX AND MERCIA ca. 865–955

AREA LOYAL TO KING JOHN, SUMMER, 1215

AREA HELD BY ROYALISTS, SEPT. 25, 1643

AREA OF CLUBMEN'S RISINGS, 1644–45

Wessex

Mercia

• Location of
  Risings or Meetings

THE SOUTH
OF ENGLAND

but slavery on a larger scale. During the eighth and ninth centuries, the size of major slaveholdings in the south of England reached levels comparable to large plantations in the American South. When Bishop Wilfred acquired Selsey in Sussex, he emancipated 250 slaves on a single estate. Few plantations in the American South were so large even at their peak in the nineteenth century.[6] Serfdom also had been exceptionally strong in this region. Painstaking analysis of the Domesday book by historical geographers has shown that the proportion of *servi* was larger in Wessex than in other parts of England.[7]

By the time of American colonization, both slavery and serfdom were long gone from this region. But other forms of social obligation remained very strong in the seventeenth century. A smaller part of the population were freeholders in the south and west of England than in East Anglia.[8]

The political character of southwestern England was consistent with its social history. This was the territory that remained loyal to King John in 1215. It rallied to Richard II in 1381, and generally stood by the Tudors in the mid-sixteenth century. Most of this region supported the Stuarts during the Civil War.[9] With a few exceptions it was stony ground for Puritan proselytizers and dissenting denominations in the seventeenth century.[10]

In its religion this region leaned toward the orthodox side of the Anglican spectrum. Its churches and monasteries had nourished a rich tradition of liturgical Christianity for many centuries. In 1549, this region supported the Western Rebellion, a violent protest against Protestant innovations which spread through Hampshire, Dorsetshire, Devonshire, Warwickshire, Somerset-

---

[6]Eddius Stephanus, *The Life of Bishop Wilfrid*, ed. B. Colgrave, Cambridge, 1927); Fisher, *Anglo-Saxon Age*, 44.

[7]H. C. Darby and E.M.J. Campbell, *The Domesday Geography of South-East England* (Cambridge, 1962); H. C. Darby and R. Welldon Finn, *The Domesday Geography of South-West England* (Cambridge, 1967); H. C. Darby, *A New Historical Geography of England before 1600* (Cambridge, 1973).

[8]Even today habits of deference are stronger among older country people in Gloucestershire than in the north of England or East Anglia, in the experience of this historian. Elderly laborers in Gloucestershire still knuckle and tug their forelocks when met in remote country lanes. Manners in East Anglia and the north are distinctly different.

[9]The towns of Bath, Taunton, Poole and Bridgewater, and large parts of south Hampshire, supported Parliament during the Civil War. But the Cathedral towns were Royalist, as were many of the rural gentry.

[10]During the 19th century this region continued to vote for conservative candidates. It did so even in the 1880 election, which was a liberal landslide. In the late 20th century, the south of England is still a Tory stronghold, and the place of greatest popularity for the conservative policies of Prime Minister Margaret Thatcher.

shire and Leicestershire.[11] In 1655 it was also the place of Penruddock's Rebellion, the largest armed rising against Puritan rule
in England. The leader of this movement, Col. John Penruddock,
called himself "a free-born gentleman of England." His lieuten-
ants were drawn from the county gentry of Wessex. In the words
of the Roundhead who ordered their execution, they were "many
of good quality, many of ingenious education, some of better
parts than myself."[12]

In the early seventeenth century, the landscape of the south
and west of England differed in its appearance from East Anglia.
Much of it was a shaggy country, still very heavily wooded. The
county of Somerset in 1623 was described as "a great part of it
being forest and woodlands." Berkshire was "covered far and
wide with forests and woods." Similar statements were also made
about other counties in this part of England.[13]

A large part of this region were royal forests, some of enormous size—notably the Forest of Dean, Windsor Forest, and
New Forest where two sons of William the Conqueror were killed.
These vast tracts were governed by "forest law," a judicial system
of exceptional rigor.[14]

Much of the land was also kept as parks and chases for the
sport of country gentlemen. For many centuries, deer parks had
been more numerous in the south and west of England than in
the north and east. The Domesday survey, for example, listed
thirty-one deer parks in England—of which only three were in
East Anglia and none were in the Midlands or the North. Most
were in the south and west of England. In the sixteenth century,
deer parks continued to be more common in Gloucestershire,
Devonshire and Staffordshire than in other counties. They were
comparatively rare in Cambridgeshire, Lincolnshire and Huntingdonshire. As late as 1712, Northamptonshire was thought to

[11]Frances Rose-Troup, *The Western Rebellion of 1549* (London, 1913).

[12]John Penruddock, ms. notes dated 1655, Penruddock Mss 332/265/1–50, WILTRO; *The
Trial of the Honourable Col. John Penruddock, of Compton in Wiltshire and His Speech, which he Delivered the Day before He Was Beheaded in the Castle of Exon . . .* (n.p., 1655); a copy of this pamphlet
is in the Penruddock Mss. in the Wiltshire Record Office at Trowbridge.

[13]Christopher G. Dursten, "Berkshire & Its County Gentry, 1625–1629" (thesis, Univ. of
Sussex, 1977), 8; David E. Underdown, *Somerset in the Civil Wars and Interregnum* (Newton,
Abbott, 1973), 18; William Camden, *Britannia* (1586, Eng. tr., London, 1610); *A History of the
Worthies of England,* 81 (1662, ed. J. Freeman, London 1952).

[14]Charles R. Young, *The Royal Forests of Medieval England* (Philadelphia, 1979), 62, 152;
Philip A. J. Pettit, "The Royal Forest of Northamptonshire: A Study of the Economy, 1558–
1714," *NHANTRS* 23 (1968), 167.

have more deer parks than any county of England. The long continuity from the twelfth to the eighteenth century was very striking.[15]

Before 1700, the south and west was less densely settled than East Anglia. This was a cultural region without a capital. One of its modern historians writes that "the Wessex region has no natural center."[16] Between London and Bristol, there were no large towns and remarkably few little ones. In year 1600, for example, the entire county of Hampshire contained only two towns as large as 3,000 inhabitants—Winchester and Southampton, which were both about that size. Only six Hampshire villages were above 1,000 (Alton, Andover, Fareham, Basingstoke, Petersfield and Portsmouth). In Dorset, the largest town was Dorchester with only 1,500 souls; in the county of Sussex, only Chichester and Lewes had as many as 2,000 inhabitants.[17]

The population of the south and west was mostly scattered in manorial settlements. One local historian writes, ". . . the classic manorial system of medieval England decayed only very slowly in Berkshire."[18] The same statement could be made of every county in the south and west. The countryside was dominated by the great estates of the gentry, with their environing clusters of small houses inhabited by tenants and subtenants.[19]

The economy of this region was organized primarily around the production and sale of agricultural staples—principally grain and wool. The mid-seventeenth century was a dark period for this region. Its economy was as deeply depressed in the 1640s and 1650s as that of East Anglia had been in the 1620s and 1630s.[20] From 1642 to 1666, the Four Horsemen of the Apocalypse rode freely through this troubled countryside. It suffered much from

[15]The 31 deer parks in Domesday were distributed as follows: Sussex, Hampshire, Hertford and Kent, 3 each; Bucks, Hereford, Cambridge and Middlesex, 2 each; Surrey, Devon, Gloucester, Shropshire, Worcester, Bedford, Essex, Suffolk and Norfolk, 1 each; 1 of unknown location; the rest none. In later periods the pattern changed somewhat, as small deer parks increased in the counties round London, and diminished in the industrial midlands. In the 19th and 20th centuries shooting parks were founded in larger numbers in Essex and East Anglia by London exurbanites; this reversed the earlier distribution. See Evelyn Philip Shirley, *Some Account of English Deer Parks, with Notes on the Management of Deer* (London, 1867).

[16]Bettey, *Wessex from AD 1000*, 3.

[17]John Patten, *English Towns, 1500–1700* (Folkestone, Kent, 1978), 95–145, 114, 119, 120.

[18]Dursten, "Berkshire & Its County Gentry," 41 [permission needed to quote].

[19]For undertenants see Court Book of Coleshill Manor, in Wiltshire and Berkshire, ms. V219cD/Epbm6, BERKRO.

[20]C. E. Brent, "Employment, Land Tenure and Population in East Sussex, 1540–1640" (thesis, Univ. of Sussex, 1973), 51.

the violence of the Civil Wars, and labored severely under a cruel regime of martial law that was imposed by Parliament. The woolen trade was disrupted in this period; the old cloth towns of the west lost population and poverty rapidly increased. So also did epidemic disease, culminating in major epidemics of plague. Social anarchy became a serious problem. In 1644–45 the risings of the English Clubmen, who sought to restore order in their communities, corresponded almost exactly in their distribution with the region of emigration to the Chesapeake.[21]

There were many strong links between the character of the south and west of England and the culture of Virginia. Both regions were marked by deep and pervasive inequalities, by a staple agriculture and rural settlement patterns, by powerful oligarchies of large landowners with Royalist politics and an Anglican faith.

Even today, this historian who was born and raised in Maryland feels strangely at home when walking the country lanes of southwestern England. One finds much that seems familiar. Large brick manor houses are set back from the road behind hedges of privet or boxwood. Small farm cottages stand in isolation along the highways, surrounded by green rolling fields. Where two or three roads meet, there is apt to be a humble pub of the sort that seventeenth-century Englishmen called an "ordinary"—a word that long survived in Virginia.[22] In summer the roadside is white with Queen Anne's lace; and the air is heavy with the sweet smell of honeysuckle. The countryside is so shaggy and overgrown that the country roads sometimes become dark tunnels of dense foliage. As the traveler passes through these lanes, he has an eerie feeling that he has entered a tunnel through time. When he emerges into the light and the English landscape opens before him, this American from the Chesapeake Bay has a sense of coming home.

---

[21]J. Taylor, "Plague in the Towns of Hampshire: The Epidemic of 1665–6," *SH* 6 (1984), 104–22; David Palliser, "Dearth and Disease in Staffordshire, 1540–1670," in Christopher Chalk and Michael Havinden, eds., *Rural Change and Urban Growth, 1500–1800: Essays in English Regional History in Honour of W. G. Hoskins* (London, 1974), 54–75; Gary Lynch, "The Risings of the Clubmen, 1644–45," in *An Atlas of Rural Protest in Britain* (London, 1983), 123; *idem,* "The Risings of the Clubmen in the English Civil War" (thesis, Manchester Univ., 1973).
[22]*OED, s.v.,* "ordinary."

❧ The Chesapeake Environment

English folkways were not the only determinant of Virginia's culture. Another factor was the American environment. New England and Virginia were very different in their physical setting—more so than the distance between them would lead one to expect. Jamestown and Boston were separated by only five degrees of latitude (300 nautical miles). But they were much farther apart in their climate and geography.

The dominant feature of Virginia's environment was the Chesapeake Bay, always known to natives as *the* Bay. In ecological terms the Bay is an estuary, where fresh and salt water meet in a marine environment of exceptional fertility. The light of the sun reaches down through warm and shallow waters, rich in nitrogen and phosphorous, to nourish large populations of bacteria and plankton. The sandy bottom of the Bay is choked with eelgrass, sea lettuce and wild celery which support a great chain of marine life, culminating in the striped bass and shellfish that are an epicure's delight. For English colonists who settled on its shoreline, the teeming waters of the Bay held immense riches—and fatal dangers.

The surface of the Bay is a vast sheet of water, 200 miles long, 4 to 30 miles wide, and open throughout its length to ocean-going vessels. "No country can compare with it," wrote Hugh Jones, for "number of navigable rivers, creeks and inlets."[1] The Bay is fed by hundreds of streams and forty-eight navigable rivers, some of immense size. The James River is larger than London's Thames; the Potomac is longer than the Seine. The Bay and its tributaries hold many dangers for unwary navigators—treacherous shoals, shifting sandbanks, coastlines that rise and fall without warning, disastrous worms which can devour a ship's wooden bottom. But with care, a colonial captain could sail where he pleased in this vast waterway and find good anchorages for the largest vessel. Virginia planter Robert Beverley wrote that ocean-going ships could anchor directly "before that gentleman's door where they find the best reception, or where 'tis most suitable to their Business." Maryland's Dr. Charles Carroll observed that "planters can deliver their own commodities at their own back doors."

---

[1]Michael G. Kammen, ed., "Maryland in 1699: A Letter from the Reverend Hugh Jones," *JSH* 29 (1963), 368.

This fact led one visitor in the seventeenth century to predict that the Chesapeake would become "like the Netherlands, the richest place in all America."[2]

This watery maze of rivers and streams created vast tracts of rich alluvial soil. The best land was quickly appropriated by Governor Berkeley's Royalist elite for their large plantations. "Gentlemen and planters love to build near the water," wrote Hugh Jones, "though it be not so healthy as the uplands and barrens."[3] When William Hugh Grove sailed into the York River in 1732, he observed that it was "thick seated with gentry on its banks . . . the prospect of river render them very pleasant [and] equal to the Thames from London to Richmond, supposing the towns omitted."[4]

The "omission of towns" was encouraged by the structure of the Bay and its rivers. Their 6,000 miles of shoreline created an opportunity for dispersed settlement that did not exist in other environments. The people of the Bay were able to scatter themselves through a vast amphibious territory. Robert Beverley wrote that all the colonists on the Bay had "fallen into the same unhappy form of settlements, altogether upon country seats without towns."[5]

The shape of the terrain differs on the two sides of the Bay. On the eastern shore it tends to be as flat as a billiard table. The western shore is a more varied and rolling countryside that falls to the water's edge in gentle undulations. Captain John Smith accurately described it as a succession of "pleasant plain hills and fertile valleys, one prettily crossing another, and watered so conveniently with their sweet brooks and crystal springs, as if art itself had devised them." When cleared and cultivated, the western shore took on a quiet, pastoral beauty that reminded homesick colonists of southern and western England.[6]

Between the rivers were ridges or "necks" that tended to be thin and barren land. Here poor whites pitched their small houses and scratched out a miserable living from the earth. Upland soil sold for as little as five shillings an acre in the eigh-

---

[2]Beverley, *History and Present State of Virginia,* 120; Arthur Middleton, *Tobacco Coast; A Maritime History of Chesapeake Bay in the Colonia Era* (Newport News, Va., 1953), 31, 34.

[3]Jones, *Present State of Virginia,* 73.

[4]William Hugh Grove, "Virginia in 1732," *VMHB* 85 (1977), 26–28.

[5]Beverley, *History and Present State of Virginia,* 118.

[6]John Smith, "Description of Virginia," in Lyon G. Tyler, ed., *Narratives of Early Virginia,* (1907, New York, 1966), 83.

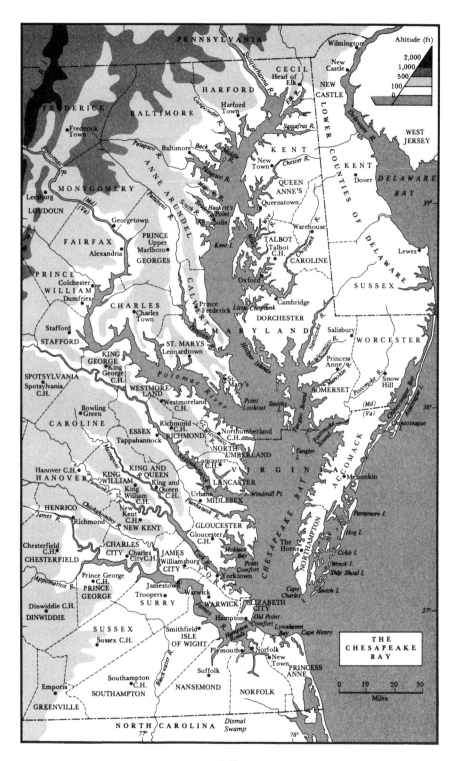

THE
CHESAPEAKE
BAY

249

teenth century. The price of rich bottom land was five pounds an acre—twenty times as much.[7]

The best river land was immensely fertile, and there was a great deal of it—vast tracts of virgin soil, which natives and visitors alike uniformly praised for its "extreme fruitfulness." It was farmed by primitive methods of husbandry, producing large yields until the late eighteenth century.

When Virginia was young, the tidewater was a lush, green country. "The whole country is a perfect forest," wrote Hugh Jones in 1724, "except where the woods are cleared for plantations, and old fields, and where have been formerly Indian towns." By the mid-eighteenth century more of the tidewater was cleared than today. The countryside around Williamsburg was described by the German traveller Johann Schoepf in 1784 as "a pleasant open plain." But he characterized the colony in general as an "eternal woods," broken by dense swamps and grassy uplands which the planters called "savannahs" or "barrens."[8]

The Chesapeake woodlands were magnificent stands of ancient trees, soaring "thirty, forty, fifty, some even sixty or seventy feet high without a branch or limb." There were towering tulip trees with gaudy yellow-orange flowers, and aromatic sweet gums with delicate star-shaped leaves, and majestic white oaks as much as five hundred years old. The variety of trees was astounding—as many as fifty varieties of oak alone. The swamps were dense with cypress and cedar; and the uplands were covered with sassafras and chinkapin.[9] Wild fruit trees flourished in profusion; among them, many wild plums and cherries ("the most delicious cherry in the world," wrote Robert Beverley); and persimmons which could be made into "an agreeable kind of beer." The open fields were choked with currants, raspberries, and delicate wild strawberries "so plentiful that few persons take care to transplant them, but can find enough to fill their baskets."[10]

To its first English colonists, the Chesapeake country appeared another Eden, demi-paradise. Captain John Smith thought that "heaven and earth never agreed better to frame a place for man's habitation."[11] It would have been so, were it not for one terrible

[7]Johann David Schoepf, *Travels in the Confederation* [1783–84] (1788, rpt. New York, 1968), II, 88.

[8]*Ibid.*, II, 88, 96.

[9]*Ibid.*, II, 124.

[10]Beverley, *History and Present State of Virginia*, 131.

[11]John Smith, *Works*, ed. Edward Arber and A. G. Bradley (2 vols., Edinburgh, 1910) I, 344.

defect. To colonists from northern Europe, the Chesapeake proved to be desperately unhealthy. The best lands on the water's edge became death traps in the summer and fall.

The climate of the Chesapeake in the seventeenth century was nearly as warm as in the twentieth. Such was the pattern of circulation in the "little ice age" that temperatures were about the same as today throughout the southern colonies while New England was colder. "The natural temperature of the inhabited part of the country, is hot and moist," observed Robert Beverley of Virginia. "The summer is as hot as Spain; the winter cold as in France or England," wrote Captain John Smith. The scientific traveler Johann Schoepf observed in the eighteenth century that "the Fahrenheit thermometer often stands at 80–90–95 degrees."[12]

This warm climate gave tidewater Virginia an asset in the length of its growing season, which was 210 days between heavy frosts—two months longer than in New England. But it also brought a liability in the relation between climate and disease. As the temperature rose, so did the death rate.

One part of the problem rose from the Bay itself. Fecal pollutants washed into swamps and stagnant pools. The estuary itself became an ideal breeding ground for typhoid fever and amoebic dysentery, trapping deadly organisms which ravaged the sickly population in the summer months. The "dying time" came mostly in the summer and early fall, when "fevers" took a heavy toll of young life. Every year this mortal season lasted much longer in Virginia than in New England.[13]

Another part of the problem was malaria. The tidewater was a perfect nursery for mosquitos. In the hot summers Robert Beverley wrote that "musketaes are a sort of vermin, of less danger [than others] but much more troublesome, because more frequent."[14] Malaria parasites were introduced at an early date by immigrants from Europe and Africa—first the comparatively mild *Plasmodium vivax* from southern England; then the more dangerous *Plasmodium falciparum* by which Africa had its revenge

[12]Schoepf, *Travels*, II, 72–73.

[13]An elegant essay on this subject is Carville Earle, "Environment, Disease and Mortality in Early Virginia," in Tate and Ammerman, eds., *The Chesapeake in the Seventeenth Century*, 96–125. Earle believes that the problem was most severe in the freshwater-saltwater transition zones, particularly on the left banks of rivers, because of the complex hydraulics of the estuary. A point of exceptionally high danger was unluckily the site of Jamestown, where health problems were compounded by salt-poisoning.

[14]Beverley, *History and Present State of Virginia*, 302.

for the slave trade. *P. vivax* was a great debilitator; *P. falciparum* was a killer. Particularly at risk were pregnant women, infants, small children, new immigrants and the chronically ill.[15]

Malaria, typhoid, dysentery, enteritis and other diseases took a terrific toll in that part of tidewater Virginia where the soil was richest, and where gentlemen liked to build their seats. A French visitor observed that the sallow faces of people in tidewater Gloucester County, "looked so sickly that I judged the neighborhood to be unhealthy." On higher ground in Rappahannock and Stafford counties, he remarked that complexions were "clear and lively."[16]

The heat and humidity of the tidewater, and its endemic summer diseases had other social consequences. Travelers and natives both remarked on the "idleness," "indolence" and "sluggishness" of the Virginians, as well as their irritability and quick tempers. Geographer Carville Earle has pointed out the similarity between this behavior and the symptoms of endemic diseases in the tidewater.[17]

The environment of the Chesapeake combined with the culture of Sir William Berkeley's Royalist elite to create the folkways of Virginia. The rich resources of the region supported a strong agricultural regime. But heavy mortality among European colonists disrupted nuclear households and discouraged immigration from Europe. Virginia's unique folkways emerged from the interplay of English culture and an American environment.

❧ The Colonial Mood: Virginia and the Mother Country

From an early date in the seventeenth century, Virginians began to speak affectionately of their new colony as the "Old Dominion" or even the "Ancient Dominion."[1] This curious phrase bespoke an attitude of mind that developed in many colonial envi-

---

[15]Darrett and Anita Rutman, "Of Agues and Fevers: Malaria in the Early Chesapeake," *WMQ3* 33 (1976), 31–60.

[16][Durand de Dauphiné], *A Huguenot Exile in Virginia, or the Voyages of a Frenchman Exiled for His Religion with a Description of Virginia & Maryland*, ed. Gilbert Chinard (New York, 1934), 130, 174. The book was first published as *Voyages d'un François exilé pour la Religion avec une description de la Virgine & Marilan [sic] dans l'Amérique* (The Hague, 1687).

[17]Schoepf, *Travels*, II, 49, 94; John F. D. Smyth, *Tour in the United States*, (2 vols., London, 1784) I, 41; Earle, "Environment, Disease and Mortality," 103.

[1]*Calendar of Virginia State Papers*, I, 63.

ronments. Throughout the New World, colonists far from home formed a strong attachment for what seemed old and even ancient in their culture.

This colonial mood became especially strong in Virginia, where it was reinforced by the values of an English culture that tended to be profoundly conservative in every sense—elitist, hierarchical, and strenuously hostile to social change. The writings of Sir Robert Filmer, the political philosopher whose family was so closely connected with Virginia, expressed these attitudes with exceptional clarity and force. One modern student of his thought observes that Filmer "succeeds in justifying the status quo in every little, almost accidental detail. He tried to prove that the slightest change in anything that went to make up the world as he knew it could be disastrous."[2]

Filmer was not alone in these opinions. Almost any Royalist diary or commonplace book revealed the same world view. The Hampshire gentleman Sir John Oglander warned others to "take heed of innovation, of bringing in any new device into our island." Words such as "innovation," "novelty" and "modern" were pejorative terms.[3]

This conservatism was deepened in Virginia by the mood of cultural nostalgia that developed in most new colonies. The Virginians long retained a sense of longing for the land they had left. Their children shared a common feeling of cultural loss that continued for many generations. As late as 1736, more than a century after settlement, William Byrd II wrote to an English correspondent, "Our lives are uniform without any great variety, till the season brings in the ships. Then we tear open the letters they bring us from our friends as eagerly as a greedy heir tears open a rich father's will." Byrd's choice of metaphor was specially revealing. Six generations after settlement, Virginians still perceived the culture of England as a precious inheritance to be protected from change, and passed intact from one generation to the next.[4]

For a very long time, the Chesapeake colonists thought of themselves as Englishmen apart from England—cultural exiles in a distant land. They often referred to their nation as "the mother

---

[2]Peter Laslett, "Sir Robert Filmer: The Man versus the Whig Myth," *WMQ3* 5 (1948), 545.
[3]Bamford, ed., *A Royalist's Notebook*, 132.
[4]William Byrd II to Mrs. Anne Taylor Otway, 30 June 1736, Tinling, ed., *Three William Byrds*, I, 482.

country," in maternal terms which implied a warm, nurturing, affective relationship—a very different idea from the Roman "patria" or the German "fatherland."

This consciousness of cultural exile created a curious melange of feelings: chief among them, an obsessive sense of colonial inferiority. In 1728, for example, Maryland's Governor Benedict Leonard Calvert wrote to the Earl of Litchfield, "We are at best but a feeble miniature of England."[5] The New World seemed a forlorn and empty place to these people. Henry Chicheley wrote home from Virginia in 1674, "For news I suppose you expect none from this barren part of the world."[6] As late as 1726, William Byrd wrote in the same deprecatory spirit of Virginia as "this silent country."[7]

This attitude did not merely exist among the colony's small elite. It was also shared by colonists of other ranks—perhaps by indentured servants most of all. One servant ballad sang:

> Old England, Old England, I shall never see you more,
> If I do it's ten thousand to twenty;
> My bones are quite rotten, my feet are quite sore,
> I'm parched with fever, and am at death's door,
> But if ever I live to see seven years more,
> Then I'll bid adieu to Virginia.[8]

Another side of this aching nostalgia for the "mother country" was a strenuous hostility to "strangers." In 1738, for example, William Byrd II in 1738 wrote, "I have learnt by long experience to be upon my guard against all strangers not well recommended, so that they can cheat me of nothing but my civilities."[9] This attitude deepened into a positive hatred of "foreigners," a category which included all people not English. The correspondence of the three William Byrds overflowed with virulent prejudices against

---

[5]Calvert added, "In short Sancho Pancha [sic] in his government, as described in Don Quixote, is the nearest description I can give you of myself and subjects. The country in itself is certainly kindly disposed by the author of Nature, to bless with kindly fruits the labour of man and beast, soil rich and various, and perhaps the greatest disposition of waters favorable to navigation, that any country has, but we as yet have only followed the planting of tobacco, which of late yields so little produce in England that without helps from the legislature in England, will not answer the Planters' pains. We must leave it off and turn to other manufactures." Benedict Leonard Calvert to Earl of Litchfield, 17 March 1728, Litchfield Mss, OXRO.

[6]Sir Henry Chicheley to his niece, 16 Feb. 1673/74, Lady Newton, *Lyme Letters, 1660–1760* (London, 1925), 64.

[7]Byrd to 5 July 1726, Tinling, ed., *Three William Byrds*, I, 355.

[8]"The Lads of Virginia," Firth, ed., *The American Garland*, 72–73.

[9]William Byrd II to John Bartram, 30 Nov. 1738, Tinling, ed., *Three William Byrds*, II, 530.

"foreigners." They detested every nation except England and despised all races except their own. They were intensely anti-Semitic. "As clamorous and unreasoning as any Jew," was a casual phrase that William Byrd II used without thinking. They also spoke ill of the French, Germans, Dutch, Spaniards, Portuguese, Italians, Roman Catholics, Calvinists, Puritans, Quakers, and Dissenters of every stripe.

These were the traditional prejudices of English gentlemen. The Duke of Wurtemberg, while traveling in England, observed that "they care little for foreigners, but scoff and laugh at them." The same attitudes were reinforced in Virginia by the colonial mood of anxiety, nostalgia, and cultural loss.[10]

Another symptom of the colonial *malaise* was a deep sense of uneasiness about present conditions and future events. These feelings grew steadily in mid-seventeenth-century Virginia, reaching a flash point in Nathaniel Bacon's Rebellion (1676), and the bloody repression that followed. The rebel Bacon himself was Governor Berkeley's kinsman and protégé. Both men came from the same rank and shared similar Royalist ideals. Bacon's "Declaration of the People" was far from a democratic document; he complained that Virginia was not hierarchical enough, and that its institutions had been corrupted by "vile" men. Both leaders expressed deep fears of external enemies and internal subversion. Bacon's Rebellion was a conflict that rose from a cultural mood that was widely shared in the colony.[11]

These emotions deepened the determination of Virginia planters to cling to their inherited folkways, but the cultural results of this effort were not always as they intended. A tenacious conservatism sometimes becomes a powerful engine of change. So it would be in Virginia. In an effort to preserve a cultural hegemony, for example, the gentry of Virginia would develop a novel type of race slavery on a large scale—a radical innovation with

[10]William Byrd to John Pratt, 24 June 1736, Tinling, ed., *Three William Byrds*, II, 480; Wurtemberg, "Travels," in Rye, ed., *England as Seen by Foreigners*, 7.

[11]On Bacon's Rebellion one finds four interpretations, very different in their sympathies. Thomas Jefferson Wertenbaker, *Torchbearer of the Revolution* (Princeton, 1940), sympathizes with Bacon; Wilcomb Washburn, *The Governor and the Rebel* (Chapel Hill, 1957), is more accurate, and sympathetic to Berkeley; Richard L. Morton, *Colonial Virginia* (2 vols., Chapel Hill, 1960), and Wesley Frank Craven, *The Colonies in Transition, 1660–1713* (New York, 1968), are balanced accounts by southern gentlemen who sympathize with both sides; Morgan, *American Slavery, American Freedom*, 251–70, is a view from New England, sympathetic to neither side. Yet to be written is a rounded cultural history which might capture the ideals, hopes, and fears that gave rise to this event.

profound consequences for the future. As we shall see in a subsequent volume, these new forms of slavery did not create the culture of the tidewater Virginia; that culture created slavery.

In any case, the culture of Virginia gradually took on its distinctive character during the second half of the seventeenth century, from 1640 to 1690. One may observe its emergence in the laws and court records of that period, in the accounts of travelers before 1690, in the correspondence of the Virginians themselves during the late seventeenth century.[12] By that date, this region had acquired distinctive habits of speech, special styles of architecture, settled norms of family life, and many other customs which set it apart from other parts of the English-speaking world. But these folkways were not unique. In some respects they were similar to habits and customs throughout the south and west of England. Let us examine this pattern in more detail, beginning with the speech ways of Virginia.

❧ Virginia Speech Ways: English Origins of the Southern Accent

Before the American Revolution, travelers from the northern colonies had begun to express surprise at the speech ways of the Chesapeake provinces. A Pennsylvania lady, for example, found herself strangely attracted to a Maryland gentleman, "who has the softest voice, never pronounces the R at all."[1]

Even more startling to northern travelers was the dialect of Virginians. In 1773, a young Princetonian named Philip Fithian came south to teach at Nomini Hall, the great Carter plantation

---

[12]This chronological fact must be stressed, because an opposite idea has become conventional—that Virginia's high elite and its classical culture were not firmly in place until the early or even mid-18th century. A problem of evidence exists here. Surviving sources for the study of Virginia's cultural history are more abundant for the 18th than the 17th century. But enough materials survive from the period 1650–90 to settle the question. They include the Fitzhugh letters and correspondence of the first William Byrd, and English materials including Filmer, Chicheley, Culpeper and Washington mss., together with the travel account of Durand of Dauphiné published in 1687. Further, the sources collected in Hening's *Statutes* (from manuscripts now lost) also establish that the institutional development of this culture happened mainly in the period 1643–90. The question of timing is important in its causal implications, for it shows that Virginia's classical culture emerged before the development of slavery on a large scale.

[1]The speaker was Major William Stoddard (1759–93), a rich Maryland planter who lived on the Potomac River; the incident appears in Kathyrn Zabelle Derounian, ed., *The Journal and Occasional Writings of Sarah Wister* (Rutherford, N.J., 1987), 47, 77 (26 Oct. 1777).

near Richmond. In his journal he described the language that he heard there:

> The people here pronounce Shower "Sho-er."—And what in New-Jersey we call a Vendue here they call a "sale"—All Taverns they call "Ordinarys"—When a horse is frolicsome and brisk, they say at once he is "gayly." . . . I piddled at my Exegesis, but (as they say here in Virginia) I did a mighty little. . . .[2]

Fithian discovered that Virginia speech ways differed from those of his native New Jersey in many ways at once. Where a northerner said, "I am," "You are," "She isn't," "It doesn't," and "I haven't," a Virginia even of high rank preferred to say "I be," "You be," "She ain't," "It don't," and "I hain't."[3] The people of the Chesapeake used "like" for "as if"— "He looks like he's dead." Boston's James Russell Lowell noted with an air of disdain that this construction was "*never* found in New England."[4]

The Virginia dialect also had its own vocabulary. Examples, recorded as early as the seventeenth century, include *bide* for stay, *howdy* for hello, *afterclap* for any unexpected event, *shuck* for husk, *porely* for unwell, *drag* for harrow, *craw* for throat, *afeared* for afraid, *cater-cornered* for crooked, *tarry* for stay, *tote* for carry, *passel* for pack, *woebegone* for wretched, *call* for cause ("no call to do it"), *chomp* for chew, *fresh* for flood, *grit* for courage, *lick* for beat, *links* for sausage, *bimeby* for by and by, *belly-ache* for pain in the stomach, *andirons* for firedogs, *flapjack* for pancake, *bandanna* for handkerchief, *botch* for blunder, *favor* for resemble, *unbeknownst* for unknown, *allowed* for admitted, *pekid* for unwell, *moonshine* for distilled liquor, *shock* for a sheaf of corn, *mess of greens* for a serving of vegetables, *laid off* for out of work, *skillet* for frying pan, *traipse* for walk, *disremember* for forget, *right good* for very good, *get shut of* for get rid of, *mighty* and *monstrous* for very, *proud* for happy or glad (as, "proud to know you"), *yonder* for distant, *cross-grained* for difficult, *innards* for insides, *pretend* for intend, *angry* for infected, *book-learning* for schooling, and *jeans* for cloth of a course twill weave (an old English corruption of Genoa, whence this fabric was imported). By the late eighteenth century these words had disappeared from polite usage in Britain. They are identified as archaic or provincial expressions

---

[2]Fithian, *Journal and Letters*, 235–36; Claude M. Newlin, "Philip Vickers Fithian's Observations on the Language of Virginia," *As* 4 (1928), 111.

[3]Hans Kurath, *A Word Geography of the United States* (Ann Arbor, 1949).

[4]George Philip Krapp, *The English Language in America* (2 vols., New York, 1925), 238.

in the *Oxford English Dictionary*. But they survived in Virginia for three centuries.

At the same time that these old words were preserved, new words were also created in the Chesapeake. Many terms were borrowed from the Indians and later from Africans. Novel expressions were necessary to describe the new Chesapeake environment, new techniques of tobacco farming, and the new institution of race slavery. This unique combination of continuity and change defined the vocabulary of an American region.[5]

The Virginia dialect was also distinctive in its pronunciation. In place of New England's harsh, rapid, rasping, metallic whine, Virginia's speech was a soft, slow, melodious drawl that came not from the nose but the throat. Virginians tended to add syllables where New Englanders subtracted them. Vowel sounds were prolonged, embellished and softened as in *ha-alf* for half, *gyarden* for garden, *ke-er* for care, *holp* for help, *puriddy* for pretty, *fuust* for first, *Aah'm* for I'm, *doo* for do, and the spectacular *wah-a-tah-mill-i-an* for watermelon. A conversation in Virginia about a watermelon could occupy an afternoon.[6]

Consonants were also softened and prolonged, as in *sebem* for seven, *chimbly* for chimney, *vahmint* for vermin, *holt* for hold, *mo'* for more, *flo'* for floor, *do'* for door, *fo'* for four, *dis* for this, *dat* for that, *dare* for there, *ax* for ask, *go-in'* for going, *perserve* for preserve, *foller* for follow, *yaller* for yellow, *acrost* for across, *wunnerful* for wonderful, *mistis* for mistress, and *wid* or *wud* for with. Redundancies were added, as in *you all* or *y'awl* for you.[7]

Proper nouns were pronounced in unexpected ways. The Carter family called itself *Cy'ah-tah*. Randolph was *Randall* in the tidewater, as it had been in the mother country. Armistead was pronounced *Um'sta-ed;* Berkeley remained *Barkly* as at home; and

---

[5]Bennett Wood Green, *Word-Book of Virginia Folk-Speech* (Richmond, 1889), is still the most comprehensive survey from historical materials; particularly useful as evidence of 17th-century Virginia speech are phonetic spellings in manuscripts, court records and especially the journals of non-English speaking visitors. See Gilbert Chinard, ed., *Un Français en Virginie* (Baltimore, 1932).

[6]Another example is *mushmillion* for muskmelon, which was used by Uncle Remus, and also by a Dorsetshire traveler in 1591; *OED*, s.v. "musk melon"; Cleanth Brooks, *The Language of the American South* (Athens, 1985), 8.

The Uncle Remus stories are very interesting for students of southern speech, especially with regard to the relative role of African and English contributions. Joel Chandler Harris gave a Gullah accent to Daddy Jack, but Uncle Remus himself spoke more in the manner of the old Sussex speech, as Brooks demonstrates in detail.

[7]"You all" appears in Virginia servant ballads recorded during the 17th century; see "The Trappan'd Maiden," line 60, in Firth, ed., *An American Garland*, 53

Blount was *Blunt.* The family of Lincoln's mad assassin John Wilkes Booth was called *Bowthe.* Botetourt was the rhythmic *Boat'a'tote,* Chisman was *Cheeseman,* Dinwiddie was *De-in-wood-y,* Fantleroy was *Fantilroy,* Fauquier was *Fawkeer,* Gooch was *Gouge,* Hackett was *Haa-yak-it,* Heyward was *Howahd,* Langhorne was *Langon,* Napier was *Napper,* Sclater was *Slaughter,* Semple was *Sarmple,* James was *Jems* or *Jims,* Yeardley was *Yardly,* and the family of Virginia playright Robert Munford was known as *Mumfud* to his contemporaries. Some of these tidewater pronunciations bore no recognizable resemblance to the written word. Crenshaw improbably became *Granger,* and Enroughty was somehow transformed into *Dahby.* A Florentine adventurer named Taliaferro so twisted Virginia tongues by the Tuscan rhythms of his name that he and his many descendants were always called *Toliver* in the tidewater.[8]

These Virginia speech ways were not invented in America. They derived from a family of regional dialects that had been spoken throughout the south and west of England during the seventeenth century. Virtually all peculiarities of grammar, syntax, vocabulary and pronunciation which have been noted as typical of Virginia were recorded in the English counties of Sussex, Surrey, Hampshire, Dorset, Wiltshire, Somerset, Oxford, Gloucester, Warwick or Worcester.[9]

In the mid-nineteenth century, for example, an English anti-

---

[8]Green, *Word-Book of Virginia Folk-Speech,* 13–16; see also "Virginia Names Spelt One Way and Called Another," *WMQ1* 3 (1894), 371; for the pronunciation of family names in the west of England, see R. Pearse Cheyne, *The Dialect of Hartland, Devonshire* (London, 1891, copy in the West Country Collection, Exeter Library, Exeter). Cheyne notes, for example, that Pennington was pronounced Tennent in his corner of Devon; Galsworthy was Gals'ry; Southward was Shaddick; Cookwood became Cookooda.

[9]Most but not all scholars agree. Bennett W. Green concluded from long study that "there seems to be a distinctly southern, southwestern and east midland character in the speech of the Virginians, little or none of the East-Anglian or Norfolk." Cleanth Brooks, who has studied this subject for fifty years, agrees that "the language of the South almost certainly came from the south of England." The dean of linguistic geographers, Hans Kurath, also concluded that "American regionalisms . . . are derived from British regional dialects," and that the speech of the American south came from southeastern and southwestern England. Also of the same opinion were Raven McDavid and Philip Bruce.

A small minority of radical and Marxist language-historians, of whom the most vocal is Joey L. Dillard, strenuously disagree, and insist that the southern accent came from Africanisms, Indian borrowings, and material conditions in America. There is an element of truth in this argument, but it is not an alternative to the prevailing view.

See Green, *Word-Book of Virginia Folk-Speech,* 9; Brooks, *The Language of the American South,* 13; Hans J. Kurath, *Studies in Area Linguistics* (Bloomington, 1972), 66; Bruce, *Social Life of Virginia,* 68–69; Raven I. McDavid, Jr., "Historical, Regional and Social Variation," *JEL* 1 (1967), 24–40; cf. J. L. Dillard, *Toward a Social History of American English* (Berlin, 1985), 52.

quarian published the Song of Solomon in a Sussex dialect which sounded remarkably like the speech ways of both whites and blacks in tidewater Virginia:

> De Song of songs, dat is Solomon's,
> Let him kiss me wud de kisses of his mouth;
>   for yer love is better dan wine
> Cause of de smell of yer good intments, yer naum is lik intment
>   tipped out; derefore de maidens love ye . . .
> Look not upan me, cause I be black, cause de sun has shouun
> upan me; my mother's childun was mad wud me; dey maud me
> kipper of de vineyards; but my own vineyard I han't kept . . .
>
> My beloved spoke, an said to me: Git up, my love, my fair un, an
> come away . . .
>
> Jest a liddle while ahter I passed by em, I foun him dat my soul
> loves . . .

This Sussex accent was reported to be "almost extinct" in 1860. In the twentieth century, *dis* and *dat* were rarely heard in any part of rural England, but they persisted among both poor whites and blacks in the American south.[10]

Thomas Hardy described the deliberate destruction of these dialects in *The Mayor of Casterbridge,* where Elizabeth says in a Wessex drawl, "Bide where you be a minute, father!"

> "Bide where you be," he echoed sharply. "Good God, are you only fit to carry wash to a pig-trough, to use such words as those?" She reddened with shame and sadness. "I meant, 'Stay where you are,' Father," she said in a low, humble voice. "I ought to have been more careful."[11]

Five generations of Wessex children learned to be "more careful," just as Elizabeth did. But traces of these archaic speech ways still survive in the American south.[12]

Much of Virginia's vocabulary (as well as its pronunciation) also appeared in word lists of Sussex speech, for example: *atwixt, bandanna, bimebye, bide, dis* and *dat, wud* for with, *fambly, favor, flapjack, fust, his'n, holp, holt, hotted up, innards, lay-off, leastways, such-*

---

[10]Brooks, *The Language of the American South,* 8–12.

[11]Thomas Hardy, *The Mayor of Casterbridge* (1886), chap. 20.

[12]Records of *dis* and *dat* in Sussex in the 19th century appear in W. D. Parish, *A Dictionary of the Sussex Dialect and Collection of Provincialisms in Use in the County of Sussex* (Lewes, Sussex, 1875, rpt. 1957). Other sources are brought together by Cleanth Brooks in *The Language of the American South,* 55–56.

like, mess of greens, moonshine, passell, pekid, shock, skillet, traipse, and *unbeknownst.*[13]

The dialect of rural Sussex in the nineteenth century startled American travelers by its resemblence to Virginia speech. One visitor from the United States wrote of a Sussex countryman that "but for his misplaced h's—and he dropped them all over the road in a most reckless and amazing manner—he might have been a Southern or Western American."[14]

Sussex speech belonged to a family of regional dialects in the south and west of England. Every county had its own linguistic peculiarities; so also did many small villages. But students of language have observed that these local speech ways throughout the south and west of England were closely related to one another. Sir William Cope concluded from long research that "the language or dialect of the counties which formed the kingdom of Wessex has in many respects great similarity. And of these the people of the district formed by West Sussex, Hampshire and Wiltshire have many words in common."[15]

This cluster of Wessex dialects bore a strong resemblance to Virginia speech ways. Hampshiremen, for example, used words such as *chitterlings* or *chittlins* for entrails, *no-count* for worthless, *dawg* for dog, *passel* for bunch, *poke* for thrust, and *whopper* (pronounced *whoppah* in Hampshire) for anything of large size. The people of that county also used the preterite instead of the participle in auxiliary verbs—*"he was took bad,"* or *"he was drove to it"*—much as in Virginia.[16] Devon folk said *ha'af* for half, *marster* for master, *keer* for care, *yaller* for yellow, and *a-go-in* for going. Natives of Somerset had a way of saying *bide, taters, porkers* and *holler.*[17] Wiltshire people used words such as *craw, cross-grained, drag, handy,* and *purserve.* In counties around Oxford, countrymen said *holt, gyarden, sebem, vahmint, priddy* and *chimbly.* All of

---

[13]Parish, *A Dictionary of the Sussex Dialect.*

[14]*Sussex Pilgrimages* (1927), 99.

[15]William H. Cope, *A Glossary of Hampshire Words and Phrases* (London, 1883), vi; see also William D. Cooper, *A Glossary of Provincialisms in Use in Sussex* (1852), and John George Akerman, *A Glossary of Words in Use in Wiltshire* (1842). On common elements in the dialects of Somersetshire, Wiltshire and parts of Devonshire see Frederic T. Elworthy, *The West Somerset Word-Book* (London, 1886), and *An Outline of the Grammar and Dialect of West Somerset* (London, 1877). These early glossaries show stronger resemblances to the southern accent than do the surveys of English rural speech by scholars in the 20th century. An excellent collection of materials on this question is in the West Country Room of the Exeter Library, adjacent to the Devonshire Record Office.

[16]Cope, *A Glossary of Hampshire Words and Phrases.*

[17]"Selected Poems in Somerset Dialect," *SFS* I (1922), 54–90.

these usages were carried to the Chesapeake during the seventeenth century.[18]

The Virginia dialect as it developed through the years was not
merely a simple replication of Wessex speech. The transfer of language was a dynamic process of linguistic selection and recom-
bination. Moreover, the speech ways of southern and western
England were not monolithic, but comprised a complex family of
local dialects. A Sussex countryman commonly dropped his h's;
but neighboring counties tended to sound that consonant clearly.
Somerset folk had a way of turning *s* into *z*, and *o* into *u*, so that
their county name became *Zumerzet.* This usage did not occur in
other parts of southern England.[19]

Other linguistic differences existed even between English villages and even neighborhoods. A case in point was Berkeley
Hundred in Gloucestershire, where an antiquarian wrote in the
seventeenth century,

> In this hundred of Berkeley are frequently used certain words,
> proverbs and phrases of speech which we hundreders conceive of
> as we do of certain market moneys, to be not only native but con-
> fined to the bounds and territories thereof; which if found in the
> mouths of foreigners we deem them as leapt over the wall, or as
> strayed from their proper pasture and dwelling place.[20]

"Berkeley Hundreders" as he called them preserved many old
Saxon words such as *geboren* for born and *wenchen* for girls. An
initial *v* was pronounced *f* in the Saxon way, so that venison
became *fenison;* at the same time *f* became *v,* so that folks were
volks. In the same fashion, a hard *c* became a *g,* as *grabs* for crabs.
This and *that* became *thicke* and *thucke,* and a *y* was commonly
inserted between words and especially names that ended and
began with consonants, so that a name such as Bill Carter became
Bill-y Carter in England's Vale of Gloucester.[21] Some of these
Berkeley speech habits became part of the American southern
accent—the nominal *y* between consonants, for example. But it
is interesting to observe that most of Berkeley Hundred's special
speech ways did not survive in Virginia, despite the fact that so
many inhabitants migrated there.

[18]Green, *Word-Book of Virginia Folk-Speech,* 7–8.
[19]"Selected Poems in Somerset Dialect," *SFS* I (1922), 21–90.
[20]John Smyth, *The Berkeley Manuscripts* (3 vols., Gloucester, 1883–85), III, 22–23.
[21]*Ibid.,* III, 23.

Here is an important clue to the dynamics of linguistic transmission, and to the complex process by which the Virginia accent was born. From a mixed family of dialects in southern and western England, local peculiarities tended to disappear and general characteristics survived. The dropped *h* of Sussex and the hard *s* Somerset did not take root in Virginia. But most countrymen throughout the south and west of England said *Ah be* for *I am*, and that usage became an important part of the Virginia accent. In this manner, a new speech way was manufactured out of old materials.

Other types of change also occurred. In the New World, English country accents tended to be overprinted with a layer of London uniformity—a common tendency in many parts of British America. "In general," observed the German traveler Johann Schoepf, "the dialects of the English speech in the several American colonies are not as sharply distinct as those of the sundry districts and counties of England itself."[22] Differences between a southern drawl and a Yankee twang became more muted than those between the Wessex broad and the Norfolk whine, in part because they added a common element of London speech.[23]

Another complexity appeared in the development of subregional dialects in America. Virginia speech ways rapidly created their own local variations in such number and variety that by the nineteenth century the birthplace of a native could be located within a few miles by subtle distinctions in the way that he sounded *a* and *r*. Other variations also developed between Virginians of different ranks; the speech ways of Virginia's first families were closest to educated London speech.

Yet another layer of complexity was added later when African expressions began to enrich southern speech. Africanisms were adopted throughout the southern colonies, especially in the Carolina lowcountry. In Virginia the borrowings were not so numerous, but as early as 1783, a German traveler observed that "here and there a few negroisms have crept in, and the salmagundy of the English language has here been enriched even by words of African origin." The major features of the Virginia accent, how-

[22]Schoepf, *Travels*, II, 62.

[23]In the Byrd correspondence, for example, one finds London expressions such as "dining with Duke Humphrey," a reference to a statue in London which was a gathering place for beggars (Tinling, ed., *Three William Byrds*, 273). For general discussions of London speech ways in the Chesapeake colonies, see Hugh Jones, *The Present State of Virginia* (1724), 80; and William Eddis, *Letters from America*, ed. Aubrey Land (Cambridge, 1969), 33.

ever, were established before African slaves could possibly have
had much impact on language.[24]

Altogether, the creation of this speech way was a cultural process of high complexity. On balance, one may conclude that the
southern drawl developed in a new American environment from
the dialects of southern and western England, just as the Yankee
twang evolved from the speech ways of the East Anglia.

❧ Virginia Building Ways: English Origins of Chesapeake Houses

Similar patterns also appeared in the vernacular architecture of
Virginia. During the governorship of Sir William Berkeley, a distinctive building style developed there. By the mid-seventeenth
century, homes and barns had become so standard throughout
the colony that when the Burgesses ordered a structure to be
built in 1647, they merely insisted that its construction should be
"according to the form of Virginia houses." No further specifi-
cations were thought necessary.[1]

Virginia's building ways, like its speech ways, were not created
de novo in the New World. They grew out of the vernacular architecture of southern England in a process that was guided by cultural purposes, environmental conditions and the inherited memory of an English past.[2]

---

[24]Schoepf, *Travels,* II, 62; Cleanth Brooks, *The Relation of the Alabama-Georgia Dialect to the
Provincial Dialects of Great Britain* (Baton Rouge, 1935), cf. J. L. Dillard, Black English (New
York, 1972). This question has given rise to an absurd academic controversy so typical of our
times, in which scholars of radical politics stress African origins of the southern accent and
conservatives take the other side. Both interpretations contain important elements of truth, and
are in fact complementary. The dialect of the tidewater south was an English regional dialect,
with an overlay of old London speech and the later addition of Africanisms.

[1]Hening, ed., *Statutes at Large,* III (1647), 340.

[2]"The Virginia house was a transplanted English house," wrote Henry C. Forman in *The
Architecture of the South: The Medieval Style, 1585–1650* (Cambridge, 1948). Most scholars agree;
see Thomas Waterman and John A. Barrows, *Domestic Colonial Architecture of Tidewater Virginia*
(1932, rpt. New York, 1969); Fiske Kimball, *Domestic Architecture of the American Colonies and the
Early Republic* (1922, rpt. New York, 1966); Cary Carson, "Settlement Patterns and Vernacular
Architecture in Seventeenth Century Tidewater Virginia" (thesis, Univ. of Delaware, 1969); Dell
Thayer Upton, "Early Vernacular Architecture in Southeastern Virginia," (thesis, Brown,
1980); Henry Glassie, *Pattern in the Material Folk Culture of the Eastern United States* (Philadelphia,
1969); *idem, Folk Housing in Middle Virginia* (Knoxville, 1975).

In the architectural historiography of Virginia, the first generation of Forman, Waterman,
Barrows and Kimball stressed great houses and public buildings as ideal types. The second generation of Carson, Glassie and Upton rejected this emphasis as a "cavalier myth." Upton writes
(p. 1), ". . . the large houses and public buildings of early Virginia are exceptional and unrep-

The vernacular architecture of Virginia was a complex hierarchy of styles, plans, materials and techniques. Its highest expression was the "great house"—a handsome, brick-built structure, surrounded by outbuildings, gardens and fields. It tended to be one and a half or two storys high and perfectly symmetrical, with a great central passage, or "summer hall," running through the house from front to back. The hall was flanked by large, lofty living spaces on the first floor, and small, low-ceilinged chambers below stairs. William Hugh Grove wrote in 1732, "The manner of building is much alike. They have a back staircase with a passage through the house in the middle which is the summer hall and draws the air; and two rooms on each hand."[3]

Interior plans were designed for congregate living. Even the largest houses had comparatively few rooms. "They always contrive to have large rooms," wrote Robert Beverley, "that they may be cool in the summer."[4] In the grandest houses, small private rooms called closets were constructed for the master and mistress of the house. But few Virginians had private spaces of their own in the mid-seventeenth century.[5]

The first great house in Virginia was Green Spring, a brick mansion built by Sir William Berkeley in 1646. The cost of its construction was supported by a special tax which the assembly levied with "an eye to the honor of the place." No longer in existence, Green Spring stood on an estate of 1,000 acres near Jamestown. In its own time it was the largest house in Virginia, with an imposing facade one hundred feet in breadth. Its central block, 48 feet wide by 43 feet deep, was flanked by two symmetrical wings, each extending 26 feet. The interior consisted of six large rooms and a long central hall. Later an elevated loggia and curious double dormers were added—fashions which did not catch on. But the general plan of this building set the fashion to which plantation architecture conformed for two centuries.[6]

---

resentative in almost every respect. Until the twentieth century, the characteristic rural eastern Virginia building was a single-pile frame house, one or two rooms long, with end chimneys." Both groups of scholars have enlarged our knowledge of this subject, but neither have encompassed it. Great houses and smaller ones were both part of the vernacular.

[3]Gregory Stiverson and Patrick H. Butler III, "Virginia in 1732: The Travel Journal of William Hugh Grove," *VMHB* 85 (1977), 18–44.

[4]Beverley, *History and Present State of Virginia*, 290.

[5]Darrett B. and Anita H. Rutman, *A Place in Time: Middlesex County Virginia, 1650–1750* (2 vols., New York, 1984), 154.

[6]Louis B. Caywood, "Green Spring Plantation," *VMHB* 65 (1957), 67–83; Jesse Dimmick, "Green Spring," *WMQ2* 9 (1929), 129–30; Henry C. Forman, *The Architecture of the Old South: The Medieval Style, 1585–1650* (Cambridge, Mass., 1948).

Green Spring, the home of Sir William Berkeley, was Virginia's first great house. It set the example for plantation architecture in generations to come. Built in 1646 with the aid of a special appropriation by the colonial assembly, it was originally a large symmetrical brick structure, with a central entrance and great hall flanked by "public" spacious rooms on the main floor. In 1796, British architect Benjamin Latrobe visited Green Spring and sketched the house shortly before it was pulled down. "It is a brick building of great solidity, but no attempt at grandeur," Latrobe wrote. "The lower story was covered with an arcade which is fallen down. The porch has some clumsy ornamental brickwork about it of the style of James the 1st." This drawing shows the building without its arcade (a later addition) as perhaps it might have looked in the time of Berkeley himself. The source is Edward C. Carter, ed., The Virginia Journals of Benjamin Henry Latrobe *(2 vols., New Haven, 1977), I, 181–82, 247, plate 21.*

Much has been written of this architecture as an adaptation to the Chesapeake environment. Long halls open at both ends caught refreshing summer breezes. High ceilings retained cool morning temperatures throughout a summer day. Massive brick fireplaces and chimney stacks repelled the winter chill. Steep-pitched slate roofs proved useful in heavy summer storms, and were more durable than in New England.

This was indeed an American architecture, but it was also English in its roots. In most respects Virginia's plantation houses were exactly like middle-sized manors in south and west of England during the seventeenth and early eighteenth centuries. One study of manorial architecture in this part of England found that the following general characteristics were typical of the genre: broad fronts of 70 to 100 feet; symmetrical plans; a first floor with a modest number of large rooms, generous proportions and high ceilings; a large central hall open at both ends; and a low "ground floor" with bed chambers. The great house was set far back from the road, with a cluster of small outbuildings for kitchens, stables, servants, and elaborate gardens in front. This description of manor houses in the south and west of England fits the great houses of Virginia exactly.[7]

The plans of these great country houses were highly symmetrical on both sides of the water, sometimes in surprising ways. The plan of the great plantation house at Shirley in Virginia, for example, looked at first sight to be a simple arrangement of boxes. It was in fact a complex mathematical structure, conceived with great care. Every dimension in the main block and wings was a multiple of the cabalistic Christian numbers of three and twelve. The design of Shirley became an act of architectural liturgy in this Anglican culture.[8]

The great hall running through the center of the house was not a Virginia invention. G. C. Tyack found that this feature was "universally popular" in larger country houses throughout the south and west of England during the seventeenth century.[9]

---

[7]Joan Thirsk, ed., *Agricultural History of England and Wales* vol. 5.2, p. 604–8; see also Wolesley, *Some of the Smaller Manor Houses of Sussex* (London, 1925).

[8]Theodore Reinhart and Judith Habicht, "Shirley Plantation in the Eighteenth Century," *VMHB* 92 (1984), 29–49; see also Henry Glassie, *Folk Housing in Middle Virginia* (Knoxville, 1975); William Kelso, "Impermanent Architecture in the Southern American Colonies," *Winterthur Portfolio* 16 (1981), 135–96.

[9]G. C. Tyack, "Country House Building in Warwickshire, 1500–1914" (unpub. thesis, Oxford, 1970), 41.

Large country houses were also set in much the same way in England and Virginia, surrounded by "gardens, stewponds, bowling-greens, terraces, and other natural concomitants of baronial residences." Recalcitrant American shrubs and trees were ruthlessly cut and pruned into imitations of English flora. On very large and rich plantations even the land itself was laboriously rearranged by sweating servants until it provided English vistas to please nostalgic masters.[10]

Plantation buildings in Virginia were also similar to English country houses in their architectural details. Virginia planters, like West Country gentry, ornamented their houses with emblems of royalism. In the twentieth century, archeologists have found plaster fragments of royal arms and other monarchical motifs which were used as ceiling decorations.[11]

In both England and Virginia, these structures were mainly designed not by professional architects but by local gentlemen. Their remarkable similarities were evidence that tastes were very much the same among the gentry on both sides of the Atlantic.[12]

There were also important differences between the country houses of England and America. Many changes were required by the American environment. Stone, for example, had been a common building material in a belt of territory that extended from Dorsetshire north across the Wiltshire Downs to the Cotswolds. During the seventeenth century, Virginians tried to build with a local yellow sandstone which seemed similar to Cotswold limestone. But in practice it proved too soft for general use, and nothing better was available. Thereafter, stone was generally abandoned in Virginia except for embellishments.[13]

The taste for stone survived, however, and found expression in curious ways. An example was Mount Vernon, the pretentious home of George Washington. Its exterior consisted of wooden weatherboards which were carved to resemble masonry and sprinkled with sand to give the look and feel of stone. The effect was somewhat spoiled by the dampness of Virginia's climate, which caused wooden seams to show through their gritty camouflage. But when Mount Vernon was seen in a haze of nostalgia

---

[10]H. A. Wyndham, *A Family History* (2 vols., Oxford, 1939–50), II, 72.

[11]Forman, *The Architecture of the Old South*, 122–27.

[12]J. Alfred Gotch, *The Old Halls and Manor Houses of Northamptonshire* (London, 1936), 27.

[13]For experiments in stone, see Henry C. Forman, *Jamestown and St. Mary's: Buried Cities of Romance* (Baltimore, 1938), 83.

after a bottle or two of madeira, the woodwork turned to stone in the eyes of homesick Englishmen.

With stone unavailable and craftsmen in short supply, Virginians were forced to adapt English building customs to the material realities of the New World. But they did so in ways that showed a strong continuity of cultural purposes. For the best tidewater buildings, the preferred building material was brick, which had rapidly gained popularity in England during the late sixteenth and early seventeenth centuries. Brick was used for foundation walls, cellar floors, building columns, curtain walls, and chimney stacks. Specially cut or moulded bricks were employed as window mullions, door frames, rounded cornices and corbelled parapets.

Brick building developed slowly in Virginia during the seventeenth century. Most houses even on large plantations continued to be made of wood for many years. But handsome brick of good quality was the ideal. It was made from local clay which fired to warm and beautiful colors that ranged from dark red to pale orange. The size of bricks in England was regulated by royal proclamation—precisely 9 by 4¼ by 2⅜ inches in Elizabeth's reign, and 9 by 4⅜ by 2¼ inches under Charles I. Virginians generally conformed to these standards; the size of bricks in seventeenth-century Virginia houses tended to be the same as in England.[14]

Techniques of bricklaying in Virginia were also very English for many generations. During the period 1625–50, Flemish bond (alternating stretchers and headers in every course) had been especially popular in the south of England. It also came to be widely used in Virginia, together with English bond (alternate courses of headers and stretchers) and various Garden bonds (which increased the proportion of stretchers in various combinations). Other patterns peculiar to the north or east of England (Yorkshire bond, Monk's bond) rarely appeared in the Chesapeake colonies.[15]

These great houses were of course few in number. Most houses in the Chesapeake were very modest. From an early date in the

---

[14] *Ibid.*

[15] Anthea Brian, "A Regional Survey of Brick Bonding in England and Wales," *VA* 3 (1972), 11–15; *idem*, "The Distribution of Brick Bonds in England up to 1800," *VA* 11 (1980), 3–11; R. J. Brown, *The English Country Cottage* (London, 1979), 194–205; Norman Davey, *A History of Building Materials* (London, 1961); Nathaniel Lloyd, *A History of English Brickwork* (London, 1925); J. Wight, *Brick Building in England* (London, 1972); Herbert A. Claiborne, *Comments on Virginia Brickwork before 1800* (Portland, Me., 1957).

Stratford, the ancestral home of the Lees, was one of many gentlemen's houses built in the half-century after the death of Sir William Berkeley. Constructed about the year 1725 for Thomas Lee, Stratford was the birthplace of Richard Henry Lee, Francis Lightfoot Lee and Robert E. Lee. It stands today in West-moreland County, surrounded by outbuildings, and shaded by huge beech trees. The plan is H-shaped, with a large central hall flanked by "public" rooms few in number but large in scale. On the ground floor are smaller low-ceilinged bedrooms and workrooms which stay comfortably cool in the summer. The brick exterior is dominated by two massive chimney clusters. The architecture creates a feeling of austerity, solidity, integrity, seriousness and permanence—a suit-able symbol of the family who lived there for two centuries. Grand houses of this sort were few in number before 1690, but many were constructed after that date. Their appearance changed in many superficial ways with the whirl of architectural fashion, but their structure and function remained the same for many generations.

seventeenth century smaller houses were also highly stylized in their design, and continued to be built in the same way for many years. They ran heavily to a single type called the hall and parlor house by architectural historians. These were humble structures of one or one and a half storys, divided into two large rooms. Exterior chimneys stood on one or both gable ends, and a corner staircase led to a sleeping loft which was sometimes lighted by gable windows.[16]

The French visitor Durand noted of the Virginians in 1687, "whatever their rank, and I know not why, they build only two rooms with some closets on the ground floor, and two rooms in the attic above. But they build several like this according to their means. They build also a separate kitchen, a separate house for the Christian slaves, one for the negro slaves, and several to dry the tobacco."[17] This design was carried from the southern and western counties of England, which contributed so heavily to the colonization of Virginia. The cultural continuities were as strong for smaller buildings as for larger ones.[18]

The typical size of a small farm house in Virginia was sixteen by twenty feet—a little smaller than in England. Furnishings were very sparse. Many Chesapeake houses lacked even beds in the mid-seventeenth century; families slept on piles of straw and leaves.[19] Building materials were modest as well. In Virginia as in England, smaller houses were rarely built of brick. Eric Mercer writes of English vernacular architecture that "small brick houses were nowhere erected before the second half of the 17th century." They remained uncommon for many years thereafter. Small Virginia houses were also constructed mostly of wood, but in a style very different from the prevailing East Anglian fashions of Massachusetts. They tended to be simple frame structures, one story high or a story and a half, with a steep pitched roof. Walls were sometimes strengthened by a technique in which clay filling

---

[16]For the hall-and-parlor house see Allen G. Noble, *Wood, Brick and Stone; The North American Settlement Landscape* (2 vols., Amherst, 1984), 48–49; Paul E. Buchanan. "The Eighteenth Century Frame Houses of Tidewater Virginia, in Charles E. Petersson, ed., *Building in Early America* (Radnor, Pa., 1976), 54–73; Dell Upton, "Toward a Performance Theory of Vernacular Architecture: Early Tidewater Virginia as a Case Study," *Folklore Forum* 12 (1979), 170.

[17]Durand, *A Huguenot Exile in Virginia,* 119.

[18]Raymond B. Wood-Jones, *Traditional Domestic Architecture in the Banbury Region* (Manchester, 1963).

[19]Specially helpful is the work of Cary Carson: "The 'Virginia House' in Maryland," *MDHM* 69 (1974), 185–96; "Segregation in Vernacular Buildings," *Vernacular Architecture* 7 (1976), 24–29; also Lorena Walsh in *MDHM* 67 (1972).

was rammed between the studs, and protected from the damp by oak clapboards.[20]

Methods of house carpentry were much simplified—more so than in Massachusetts. Virginians typically gave minimal attention to the foundations of their houses, which stood two or three feet above the ground on irregular posts or blocks. Walls were framed with as much simplicity as possible. Roofs were made of light collars and common rafters, which were mortised at the top and nailed at the bottom into ingenious false plates that allowed a great deal of play in the structures of these insecure buildings.[21] These patterns reflected economic realities in Virginia, where lumber was cheap and labor was costly. In 1687, William Fitzhugh warned a correspondent that "labor is so intolerably dear, and workmen so idle," that framing costs were at least a third higher than in London, "and near three times as long preparing." Material conditions made a major difference in colonial building.[22]

In the hierarchy of Virginia's vernacular architecture, there was also a third level of housing which consisted of rough one-room shacks or shanties, made of whatever materials came to hand. By the end of the seventeenth century, many of these structures were made of "puncheons," or timbers which had been crudely split. The quarters of servants and slaves were often puncheon houses. But they were not log cabins. Their plan and style followed the conventions of English architecture.[23]

None of these architectural forms was static. During the late seventeenth and eighteenth centuries, building styles changed on both sides of the Atlantic. New tastes ran to neo-classical proportions, pediments, pillars, quoins, bands, and hipped roofs. But through all of these changing fashions, strong continuities persisted in Virginia architecture. In an environment where firewood remained comparatively abundant, massive fireplaces and broad chimney stacks remained in fashion. Brick continued to be the building material of choice, rather than stone or stucco which became more fashionable in rural England. The result was a strong and vibrant combination of austere neoclassical forms with

[20]Eric Mercer, *English Vernacular Houses* (London, 1975), 130.
[21]Upton, "Early Vernacular Architecture in Southeastern Virginia," 96.
[22]*Fitzhugh Letters,* 202.
[23]George Washington, *Diary,* 20 Sept. 1704.

The Hall and Parlor House was typical of middling farmhouses in Virginia. It was commonly a small, simple building, more often built of wood than brick, with chimneys and fireplaces on the gable ends. Historian Dell Upton has found that half of all houses in Virginia inventories had only two rooms on the ground floor: often a hall and parlor, sometimes a hall and kitchen, or a kitchen and parlor, plus several small chambers above. This was the modal house type in Virginia for many generations. The average number of rooms remained constant at approximately five per house from 1646 to 1720.

vivid red walls, grey slates, and painted wooden trim. In all of these ways, the plantation architecture of Virginia was derived from the English rural forms but it became a unique provincial style, with its own distinct identity.

❧ Virginia Family Ways:
The Anglican Idea of the Patriarchal Family

The family customs of the Virginians were as distinctive as their architecture and speech ways.[1] The gentry of southern and western England brought to this colony a sense of family which was as strong as that of Puritan Massachusetts. The political theory of Robert Filmer, for example, has been described as "above all things an exaltation of the family. It made the rules of domestic society into the principles of political science."[2] The same attitude routinely appeared among the English gentry. An example was Sir John Oglander, a Royalist gentleman with Virginia connections who lived on the English Isle of Wight. It was observed of him that "family pride indeed was the ruling passion of his life."[3]

Among Virginians and New Englanders, ideas of the family were similar in strength, but different in substance. Virginians gave more importance to the extended family and less to the nuclear family than did New Englanders. Clear differences of that sort appeared in quantitative evidence of naming practices and inheritance patterns. The language of familial relationships differed too. The word "family" tended to be a more comprehensive term in Virginia than in Massachusetts.[4] Virginians addressed rel-

---

[1]Outstanding in a very large literature on the family in the 17th-century Chesapeake are the works of Lorena Walsh, especially "'Till Death Us Do Part': Marriage and Family in Seventeenth-Century Maryland," in Tate and Ammerman, eds., *The Chesapeake in the Seventeenth Century*, 126–52. Also of high quality are many publications by Lois Green Carr, including "The Development of the Maryland Orphans Court," in Aubrey Land et al., *Law, Society and Politics in Early Maryland*, (Baltimore, 1977), 41–62; other major works include Rutman and Rutman, *A Place in Time*, 94–127; Gloria Main, *Tobacco Colony, Life in Early Maryland, 1650–1720* (Princeton, 1982), 9–47, 167–239; Allan Kulikoff, *Tobacco and Slaves* (Chapel Hill, 1986), 165–204; and on the 18th century there are Daniel Blake Smith, *Inside the Great House: Planter Family Life in Eighteenth-Century Chesapeake Society* (Ithaca, 1980), and Jan Lewis, *The Pursuit of Happiness: Family and Value in Jefferson's Virginia* (Cambridge, 1984).

[2]Laslett, "Sir Robert Filmer," 544.

[3]Bamford, ed., *A Royalist's Notebook*, xxi.

[4]Michael Zuckerman, "William Byrd's Family," *Perspectives in American History* XII (1979), 255–311.

atives of all sort as "coz" or "cousin," in expressions that were heavy with affective meaning; but the term "brother" was used more loosely as a salutation for friends, neighbors, political allies, and even business acquaintances. It is interesting to observe that an extended kin-term tended to be more intimate than the language of a nuclear relationship. The reverse tended to be the case in Massachusetts.[5]

Individuals in Virginia were stereotyped by traits that were thought to be hereditary in their extended families. Anglican clergyman Jonathan Boucher believed that "family character both of body and mind may be traced thro' many generations; as for instance every Fitzhugh has bad eyes; every Thornton hears badly; Winslows and Lees talk well; Carters are proud and imperious; and Taliaferros mean and avaricious; and Fowkeses cruel." Virginians often pronounced these judgments upon one another. The result was a set of family reputations which acquired the social status of self-fulfilling prophecies.[6]

For most Virginians the unit of residence tended to be a more or less nuclear household, but the unit of association was the extended family, which often flocked together in the same rural neighborhoods. Jonathan Boucher noted that "certain districts are there known and spoken of . . . by there being inhabited by the Fitzhughs, the Randolphs, Washingtons, Carys, Grimeses or Thorntons." These kin-neighborhoods developed gradually during the late seventeenth and early eighteenth century by continuing subdivision of estates.[7]

From an early date in the seventeenth century, extended families were also buried together in Virginia—a custom that was uncommon in Massachusetts. Hugh Jones noted, " . . . it is customary to bury in gardens or orchards, where whole families lye interred together in a spot generally handsomely enclosed, planted with evergreens." This had also been the practice of country gentry in England for many centuries. In New England, extended family cemeteries rarely existed; people of every rank

---

[5]Many examples of this usage appear in the correspondence of the Byrds and Fitzhughs; see for example William Fitzhugh to Nicholas Hayward, 30 Jan. 1686/87; and William Fitzhugh to Mrs. Mary Fitzhugh, 30 Jan. 1686/87; Richard Beale Davis, ed., *William Fitzhugh and His Chesapeake World 1676–1701: The Fitzhugh Letters and Other Documents* (Chapel Hill, 1963), 197–201.

[6]Jonathan Boucher, ed., *Reminiscences of an American Loyalist* (Boston, 1925), 61.

[7]*Ibid.*

were normally interred in a common burying ground near the
meetinghouse—and were not grouped by family until the late
eighteenth century.[8]

Relations within Virginia's extended families were not always
harmonious. John Randolph, for example, looked with contempt
upon many of his uncles and cousins. He wrote:

> It was not necessary or even desirable that the descendants of
> these families should be learned or shining men, but they might
> have been better than mere Will Wimbles. Ah! I wish they were no
> worse than humble Will. But some are what I will not stain my
> paper with.[9]

The actual unit of residence in Virginia was not the extended
family, but a more or less nuclear unit. Its physical constitution
differed very much from those of Massachusetts. Many of these
households (more than in New England) included servants, lodg-
ers, and visitors, sometimes on a scale that did not exist in New
England. The northern tutor Philip Fithian was astonished to
learn from the wife of his employer, Mrs. Robert Carter of Nomini Hall, that "this family one year with another consumes 27,000
pounds of pork and twenty beeves, 550 bushels of wheat, besides
corn, four hogsheads of rum, and 150 gallons of brandy."[10] In
winter, 28 large fires were kept burning constantly at Nomini
Hall, and six oxen were needed every day to haul in the wood.
The pattern of consumption was very similar to great country
houses in the south and west of England. No household in Massachusetts operated on such a scale.[11]

Chesapeake households also tended to include more step-rela-
tives and wards, fewer children in the primary unit and also many
more servants than in New England. This was largely because the
southern colonies had higher rates of illness and death. Children
died young, and marriages were cruelly shattered at an early
age.[12]

---

[8]Jones, *The Present State of Virginia*, 97; for the custom in England see records of a court
case (ca. 1706) in Warwickshire, where a family refused to part with a manor "because it is so
ancient an estate and has been the burying-place of the Family for above 400 years." Ms.
B1309G, WARO.

[9]Bruce, *John Randolph*, I, 12.

[10]Fithian, *Journal and Letters*, 100.

[11]Morton, *Robert Carter of Nomini Hall*, 210.

[12]Family size (mean numbers of children) in the Chesapeake colonies was as follows for all

In tidewater Virginia during the seventeenth century, most children—more than three-quarters in fact—lost at least one parent before reaching the age of eighteen. One consequence was to enlarge the importance of other kin; for when a nuclear family was broken in Virginia the extended family picked up the pieces. Another consequence was to change the structure of the household in a fundamental way. Historians Darrett and Anita Rutman observe that in "just about any" household one might find "orphans, half-brothers, stepbrothers and stepsisters, and wards running a gamut of ages. The father figure in the house might well be an uncle or a brother, the mother figure an aunt, elder sister, or simply the father's 'now-wife,' to use the word frequently found in conveyances and wills."[13]

Yet another consequence was to increase the emotional complexity of domestic life. The courts of the Chesapeake colonies

---

families, and for completed families (which remained intact through the wife's child-bearing years):

Place	Population	Cohort	All Fams.	Compl. Fams.
Somerset Co. (Md.)	immigrant whites	1665–95m	3.9	6.1
	native whites	1665–95m	6.1	9.4
Prince George's Co. (Md.)	all whites	1700–24m	n.a.	7.5
		1725–49m	n.a.	7.6
Middlesex Co., Virginia	all whites	1650–54b	n.a.	7.0
		1655–59b	n.a.	8.1
		1660–64b	n.a.	9.6
		1665–69b	n.a.	6.2
		1670–74b	n.a.	6.2
		1675–79b	n.a.	5.9
		1680–84b	n.a.	7.3
		1685–89b	n.a.	7.3
		1690–94b	n.a.	7.4
		1695–99b	n.a.	7.2
		1700–04b	n.a.	7.3
		1705–09b	n.a.	6.2
		1710–14b	n.a.	4.7
Virginia	elite whites	pre-1700m	n.a.	8.5
		1701–20m	n.a.	6.7

Note: Cohorts are defined by date of marriage (m), or by date of the wife's birth (b); sources include Rutman and Rutman, *A Place in Time*, 73; Allan Kulikoff, "Tobacco and Slaves: Population, Economy and Society in Eighteenth-Century Prince George's County, Maryland" (thesis, Brandeis, 1976), chap. 12; Russell R. Menard and Lorena S. Walsh, "The Demography of Somerset County, Maryland: A Progress Report," *Newberry Papers in Family and Community History* 81-2 (1981), 33; Susan Simmons, unpublished research on Virginia elites.

[13]Darrett B. and Anita H. Rutman, "'Now-Wives and Sons-in-Law': Parental Death in a Seventeenth-Century Virginia County," in Tate and Ammerman, eds., *The Chesapeake in the Seventeenth Century*, 153–82; Rutman and Rutman, *A Place in Time*, 79–82; Kulikoff, *Tobacco and Slaves*, 170.

heard many complaints of cruel step-parents, who often lived up to their reputation. The courts also dealt with bitter conflicts over step-children. In 1696, for example, one Thomas Price was presented to a county court "by the information of Hannah Price his wife for selling a child of the said Hannah which she had by another husband in the colony of Virginia."[14]

There were also large numbers of servants in these households. Throughout tidewater Maryland, Virginia and the Carolinas, the number of servants in an average household was always much greater than in New England. As early as 1667, in Middlesex County, Virginia, male heads of households held as many as five servants and slaves on the average.[15]

On both sides of the Atlantic, these large households were very complex in their internal structure. Masters and house servants lived close together—often sleeping in the same room. "I called up my man, who lay in my room with me," one English gentleman noted in his diary.[16] Things were the same in Virginia, where masters, servants and visitors often shared the same room and sometimes even the same bed.[17]

The doors of these houses were rarely closed to strangers. A bed and a meal were offered to visitors of every rank, from the governor of the colony who was received as a royal personage to the most wretched beggar who was given a mat before the kitchen fire. There was a class of impoverished gentlemen in England and America who made "visiting" their profession. The Yankee tutor Philip Fithian met one of these threadbare gentry, who lived almost entirely upon the hospitality of others, and became a semi-permanent fixture in other men's houses. Fithian wrote:

> To day about twelve came to Mr. Carter's Captain John Lee, a gentleman who seems to copy the character of Addison's Will

---

[14]Walsh, "Till Death Us Do Part," 144.

[15]The mean number of servants and slaves per household declined a little in the late 17th century, and increased in the early 18th, fluctuating in the range of 4 to 7. The median number of slaves and servants per male household head was smaller, but most householders owned at least one. By the American War of Independence, the proportion of tidewater Virginia householders who owned servants or slaves had risen above two-thirds; in the Peninsula it was as high as 78%; Rutman and Rutman, *A Place in Time, Explicatus* (vol. 2), 123; Kulikoff, *Tobacco and Slaves,* 137.

[16]Wilbraham Diary, 2 Jan. 680, Ms. DDX 210/2, CHESRO.

[17]Field slaves were forbidden to enter the house; entering the house after dark was a capital offense. Col. Robert Carter announced that "if anyone be caught in the House, after the family are at rest, on any pretence what ever, that person he will cause to be hanged." But house slaves slept in the same chamber with the Carters. Fithian, *Journal and Letters,* 242 (5 Sept. 1774).

> Wimble. When I was on my way to this place I saw him up in the country at Stafford; he was then just sallying out for his winter's Visit, & has got now so far as here, he stays, as I am told about eight, or ten weeks in the year at his own house, the remaining part he lives with his waiting man on his Friends.[18]

A gentleman of Virginia took pride in his hospitality, and gained honor by its display. Those who accepted his invitation tacitly agreed to place themselves under his protection and authority. This custom had long existed in England, but in the seventeenth century English country houses were rapidly closing their doors to all but invited guests, much to the regret of those who remembered the old way. In 1709, one gentleman wrote in his diary:

> Died Sir Richard Brooke of Norton, Bart., an honest friendly gentleman whose hospitality justly gained him the prayers of the poor & applause of the rich . . . that good and ancient way of housekeeping has decayed to bring in new and more pernicious fashions.[19]

In Virginia the "good and ancient way" of open hospitality continued to flourish for a longer time. While it survived, a Virginia patriarch extended the word "family" to include all the people who slept under his roof—his nuclear family, visiting relatives, impecunious friends, tutors and clerks, servants and house slaves, and even total strangers who accepted his hospitality. When George Washington was at Valley Forge, he referred to his wife, servants, aides, staff and visitors as his "family," for they had placed themselves under his fostering hand. Here was yet another clue to the meaning of "family" in Virginia. In the great houses of the Chesapeake, as in the works of Filmer, "family" was fundamentally a sphere of authority, in which everyone was placed under a patriarch's protection.

These Virginia families tended to be more hierarchical than those of New England. Fathers and fathers-in-law were addressed not merely as "Sir" but "Worthy Sir."[20] The head of the family thought of himself as a patriarch, a word that often occurred in their self-descriptions, but was not much used in Massachusetts.

---

[18] *Ibid.,* 78.

[19] Wilbraham Diary, 3 Feb. 1709, ms.DDX 230/2, CHESRO.

[20] William Byrd I to Warham Horsmanden, 8 March 1685/86, in Tinling, ed., *Three William Byrds,* I, 56.

William Byrd liked to compare himself with the biblical patriarchs. He wrote, "Like one of the Patriarchs, I have my flocks
and my herds, my bondsmen & bond women and every sort of
trade amongst my own servants so that I live in a kind of Independence of every one but Providence."[21] On another occasion,
Byrd wrote, "Our comforts, like those of the good patriarchs are
mostly domestique. . . ." Patriarchy was a word that came to be
much used in Virginia, as it had been by English Royalists such as
Filmer. It was rarely employed by the Puritans, and sometimes
actually condemned.[22]

This patriarchal idea also appeared in the law of the family. The
courts of Virginia regarded the slaying of a father by his son, or
the killing of a husband by his wife, or the murder of a master by
his servant not as homicide but treason. The penalty was to be
burnt to death—a sentence which was actually inflicted upon a
woman who murdered her common-law husband in Maryland.
Even these laws were thought to be insufficently severe by Robert
Filmer, who wished to extend the law of petty treason to include
adultery by the wife.[23]

The laws of Virginia added a material base to the patriarchal
idea by requiring the "masters of the several families" to "detain
and keep within their hands and custody the crops and shares of
all freemen within their families," so as to ensure the payment of
taxes.[24]

The hard realities of life in the Chesapeake colonies tended to
reinforce these ideals in unexpected ways, and to make the family
ways of Virginia more extended and patriarchical than they might
otherwise have become. Altogether, the family ways of Massachusetts and Virginia were two distinct cultural systems. Even as they
shared important qualities in common, they rose from different
English roots, and responded to different American
environments.

---

[21]Byrd to Lord Orrery, 5 July 1726, *ibid.,* I, 354–55.

[22]Byrd to Anne Taylor Otway, 30 June 1736, *ibid.,* I, 482.

[23]Laslett, "Sir Robert Filmer," 545.

[24]Further, this law specified that "it shall be understood where they make a joynt cropp, that
he which hath the command shall be adjudged the master of the family." Hening, *Statutes at
Large,* I, 286 (1644).

❧ Virginia Marriage Ways:
The Anglican Idea of Marriage as a Sacred Union

Marriage in Virginia was a social condition which everyone was expected to achieve. Bachelors and spinsters were condemned as unnatural and even dangerous to society. When William Byrd II was slow to remarry after the death of his wife, his female relatives urged him forward in no uncertain way. "At night," he wrote, "the girls put a drawn sword and common prayer book open at the matrimony on my bed."[1]

Virginia and New England were alike in their ideas of universal marriage; both rejected the ideal of celibacy which was so strong in Catholic countries. But these two Protestant cultures of British America also differed in many ways as to their ideas of marriage, and their matrimonial institutions. In Massachusetts, as we have seen, marriage was thought to be a covenant which could be terminated when its terms were not fulfilled. In Virginia, matrimony was regarded as an indissoluble union—a sacred knot that could never be untied by mortal hands. Divorce in the modern sense did not exist. Only permanent separation and maintenance could be obtained, and even that release was rarely granted. In 1681 the Virginia lawyer William Fitzhugh wrote that his colony had allowed no divorces and only a single permanent separation during the previous sixty years. The sole exception was a decree given to the wife of Giles Brent after acts of physical cruelty so extreme that her life was thought in danger.[2]

Social rituals of matrimony reflected these ideas of marriage. Virginians followed the Church of England's elaborate five-step process of espousal, publication of banns, religious ceremony, marriage feast, and sexual consummation. The clergy of Virginia were forbidden to conduct any marriage without the prior publication of banns. In order to marry, children under age were compelled to obtain the written permission of parents or guardians. Clandestine marriages were punished by imprisonment.[3]

---

[1]William Byrd, *The London Diary (1717–1721) and Other Writings,* (New York, 1958), 469, 1 Nov. 1720.

[2]William Fitzhugh to Kenelm Chiseldine, 8 June 1681, Davis, ed., *Letters of Fitzhugh,* 97.

[3]Archibald Burnett of Maryland (1688) married an eleven-year-old heiress without permission of her guardian, and landed in jail. *Archives of Maryland* VIII, 32–34; for a clandestine child marriage in Northampton County, Va., where the bride was under the age of twelve, see Bruce, *Social Life in Virginia,* 224, 233.

The favored periods of marriage in Virginia were early November and late December after Christmas. In the Church of England, vows could not be exchanged during Lent (the forty weekdays from Ash Wednesday to Easter), or Advent (the four Sundays before Christmas), or the three weeks prior to the Feast of St. John. These customs were generally kept in the Chesapeake colonies.

The bride and groom in Virginia were often united in two ceremonies—both of which were condemned in Puritan New England. The first was a Christian ceremony, which was solemnized sometimes in a church or more often in the bride's home, but always by a minister according to the laws of the Anglican Church and the Book of Common Prayer. The other ceremony was an ancient pagan practice in which the bride and groom were made to jump over a broomstick. This ritual had long been observed throughout Britain and much of western Europe, and especially in the kingdoms of Wessex and Mercia. The custom of the broomstick marriage came to be widely practiced by white families throughout the southern colonies in addition to the Christian ceremony. For black slaves, it was the only type of marriage ceremony that was permitted, and rapidly acquired a special meaning in Afro-American culture.[4]

The marriage ceremony was followed by a feast, which among the great planters included a fancy ball and a house party that went on for days. Expensive gifts were given by the groom to his guests. At one marriage in Devon, six dozen guests received watches and silver ribbons as "favors."[5] Families of yeoman farmers celebrated on a smaller scale, but their customs were much the same. They appeared in Virginia during the mid-seventeenth century and persisted to the nineteenth and early twentieth. In the year 1686, the French traveler Durand was invited to a wedding feast in Gloucester County, Virginia:

> There were at least a hundred guests, many of social standing & handsome, well-dressed ladies. Although it was November, we ate under the trees. The day was perfect. We were twenty-four at the first table. They served us so copiously with meats of all kinds that I am sure there would have been enough for a regiment of five

[4]*North Carolina Folklore* I, 224.
[5]John Haynes, Household Expences 17 April 1635, Ms. 36, DEVRO.

hundred soldiers, even entirely made up of men from Langue-doc. . . . It is the custom to take only one meal upon such occa-sions, at two o'clock in the afternoon. . . . they caroused all night long & when it was day . . . I did not see one who could stand straight.[6]

Before the marriage ceremony took place, espousal was also a complex social ritual which involved many people in addition to the intending couple. Amongst landed families, marriage was regarded as a union of properties as well as persons, and the des-tinies of entire families were at stake. One English gentleman advised another to "marry thy daughters betimes, lest they marry themselves."[7]

Love was not thought to be a necessary precondition for these unions. Moralists insisted that love should follow marriage, but they did not believe that it would normally precede it. An English gentlemen recommended that one should "take a wife thou canst love." He did not think in terms of marrying a woman whom one loved already. Love was not thought to be special or exclusive bond between two unique personalities—a romantic idea that did not develop until a later era. The prevailing male attitude in the seventeenth century was summarized by Sir John Oglander, who believed that "any woman may be won, and almost by any man . . . importunity and opportunity overcometh all women. *Exper-ientia docet* [Experience teaches]."[8]

The parents had an active role in the marriage decision. Many Virginians owned an English marriage manual which commented, "Children are so much the goods, the possessions of their par-ents, that they cannot without a kind of theft, give away them-selves without the allowance of those that have the right in them." These ideas were carried into practice. Children who defied their parents were denied dowries and inheritance.[9]

Children were rarely made to marry against their will, but nei-

[6]Durand, *A Huguenot Exile in Virginia*, 138–39.

[7]Bamford, ed., *A Royalist's Notebook*, 235.

[8]*Ibid.*, 70–71, 201.

[9]*The Whole Duty of Man* (London, 1684); quoted in Smith, *Inside the Big House*, 140; Smith describes an episode when William Byrd's daughter Evelyn wished to marry a British baronet of whom he disapproved. The angry father ordered his daughter "never more to greet, speak or write to that gentleman"; and if she refused to obey she was warned "not to look for one brass farthing. . . . Figure then to yourself my dear child how wretched you will be with a pro-voked father and a disappointed husband."

ther were they left to decide the question for themselves. Parents
and guardians entered into complex negotiations to settle the size
of the marriage portion or "dot" which a couple needed to make
its way in the world. Written prenuptial agreements of high complexity were common not only among members of the gentry but
also among yeomen and husbandmen.[10] Many people were sometimes involved in these agreements. One English marriage agreement in the county of Hampshire (1676) was executed among five
sets of parties—the bride, the bride's relatives, the groom, the
groom's kinfolk, and the tenants of lands that were given to the
couple. Agreements in Virginia were similar in every important
way.[11]

In both England and Virginia, many of these unions were cou-
sin-marriages that had been arranged by elders. In England,
for example, Francis Carew sent a letter to his kinsman Sir Nicholas Carew:

> I have a daughter who for handsomeness, education, and compe-
> tency of portion, shall be a wife for any Gentleman in England. If
> you propose to marry a young woman, I shall be willing to treat
> with you therein & shall wish good success thereto.[12]

The marriage of first cousins was condemned by New England
Puritans as violating the law of consanguinity. But many an Anglican lady "changed her condition but not her name."[13] The same
custom was common in Virginia, and fundamentally important to
the cohesion of the tidewater elite. The culture of New England
created a different set of matrimonial priorities.

One consequence of these customs appeared in the pattern of
age at marriage. Male Virginians married at nearly the same age
as in New England, twenty-five or twenty-six on the average. But
brides in the Chesapeake colonies were much younger than in
Puritan Massachusetts. Before 1700, most Virginia girls found a
husband by the age of seventeen. Mean age at marriage was a

---

[10]Marriage agreements of Nicholas Wheeler (yeoman) and Isabel Wright, 1649, Ms., HAM-
PRO; for parallels in 17th-century Virginia, see Bruce, *Social Life of Virginia*, 230–31.

[11]Marriage agreement of Nicholas Hasted, Thomas Jaynes, Richard Shaloff, Edward Rooks
and Elizabeth Hasted, 1676, HAMPRO.

[12]Francis Carew to Sir Nicholas Carew, n.d., Ms. S/EL1/C1/81 BERKRO.

[13]"My eldest sister Alice [Wilbraham] changed her condition but not her name, being married in Wrenbury [sic] Church to Cousin Ralph Wilbraham," Wilbraham Diary, 26 May 1709,
Ms. DDX 230/2, CHESRO.

little higher—eighteen to twenty—but below the Massachusetts
average.[14]

Another consequence was a large difference in the ages of husbands and wives. In Virginia's Middlesex County before 1670,
grooms tended to be nearly ten years older than brides: 28.4
against 18.7. That disparity diminished to about five years in the

[14]Mean age at first marriage in the Chesapeake colonies was as follows:

Place	Population	Cohort	Males	Females
Charles Co., Md.	native whites	1640–79b	24.1(n = 40)	17.8 (15)
Somerset Co., Md.	native whites	1648–69b	23.1(30)	16.5 (44)
	native whites	1670–1711b	22.8(25)	17.0 (32)
	native whites	1710–40b	24.1(25)	19.0 (13)
Prince George's Co., Md. and Lower Western Shore	native whites	1680–99b	23.1(48)	18.2 (29)
		1710–19b	23.7(72)	18.5 (72)
		1720–49b	25.9(100)	21.4 (64)
Southern Maryland	slaves (age at 1st conception)	1725–34		17.8
		1735–47		17.3
		1748–57		18.1
		1758–67		18.5
Middlesex County, Va.	former servants	thru 1669b	29.5(70)	22.8 (21)
		1670–79b	28.9(21)	23.9 (6)
		1680–89b	27.2(22)	22.9 (8)
	all others	thru 1669b	28.4(105)	18.7 (86)
		1670–79b	26.7(53)	18.8 (59)
		1680–89b	25.2(92)	20.3 (97)
		1690–99b	24.7(90)	19.6 (94)
		1700–09b	25.0(108)	20.6 (118)
		1710–19b	24.4(109)	20.5 (119)
		1720–29b	25.0(48)	20.9 (53)
Virginia	elites	1725–34b	27.0	18.3
		1735–44m	28.2	19.8
		1745–54m	30.1	19.5

Sources include Russell R. Menard, "Immigrants and Their Increase . . .," in Aubrey Land, Lois
Carr and Edward Papenfuse, eds., *Law, Society and Politics in Early Maryland* (Baltimore, 1977),
100; "The Demography of Somerset County, Maryland: A Preliminary Report"; Lorena S.
Walsh, "Charles County, Maryland, 1658–1705: A Study of Chesapeake Social and Political
Structure" (thesis, Michigan State Univ.), ch. 2; Michael J. Kelly, "Family Reconstitution of
Stepney Parish, Somerset County, Maryland" (thesis, Univ. of Md., 1971), 18–25; Kulikoff,
"Tobacco and Slaves," chap. 3; Rutman and Rutman, *A Place in Time, Explicatus,* 65; Susan
Simmons, unpublished research on Virginia elites; R. B. Outhwaite, "Age at Marriage in
England from the Late Seventeenth to the Nineteenth Century," *RHST* 23 (1973), 55–70;
Stone, *The Family, Sex and Marriage in England,* 46–54; Michael W. Flinn, *The European Demo-
graphic System, 1500–1820* (Baltimore, 1981), 19–29.

mid-eighteenth century, but it remained much greater than in Massachusetts, where only a year or two separated the average ages of men and women at first marriage.[15]

Other inequalities appeared in the proportion of Virginians who married at all. Though the ideal was universal marriage, the reality was very different in seventeenth-century Virginia, because so few immigrants were females. Nearly all women were able to marry, but for men the pattern was very different. One study of estate-inventories in southern Maryland from 1658 to 1708 finds that one-quarter of men died without ever marrying. A man's chances of finding a wife were a function of his social rank. Here was yet another system of inequality in this hierarchical society.[16]

The Virginia pattern developed within a culture where marriage was regarded as something to be arranged between families, something that did not require love as a precondition, something that could never be dissolved, and something that joined husband and wife in an organic and patriarchal hierarchy. Given such an idea of matrimony, it seemed right and fitting in this culture that a typical Virginia marriage in the seventeenth century should join a man of maturity to a miss in her teens. These Virginia customs were very different from the marriage ways of Massachusetts.

❧ Virginia Gender Ways:
True-born Englishmen and Spirited "She-Britons"

On the subject of marital relations between husbands and wives, Virginia's governor Sir William Berkeley set his colony a high example of marital felicity and domestic peace. His will testified to his love for his wife and to the happiness of their married life together. Governor Berkeley left all his property to his "dear and most virtuous wife," declaring that "if God had blessed me with a far greater estate, I would have given it all to my most dearly beloved wife."[1]

The tone of this document captured the ideal of conjugal relations in both England and the Chesapeake—a devoted husband,

---

[15]This difference was partly a consequence of distorted sex ratios in Virginia, but not entirely so; even after sex ratios reached near normal levels, the pattern persisted.

[16]Walsh, "Till Death Us Do Part," 131n.

[1]*Minutes of the Council and General Court of Virginia,* 165.

a virtuous wife, and a loving life together. Many successful marriages came close to realizing these goals. Much domestic correspondence survives to tell us how deeply English-speaking men and women on both sides of the Atlantic valued a happy and loving marriage.

An outward expression of affection was also much encouraged in this culture. In the seventeenth century, husbands and wives addressed each other as "dearest heart," "sweet spouse," "my most sweet heart." The language of love changed during the eighteenth century, but the custom remained the same.[2]

Domestic realities, unhappily, were often different. In every culture there are happy marriages and unhappy ones. But historians of the family have remarked upon the extent of marital discord among the gentry of Virginia and southern England. One leading historian, Julia Cherry Spruill, testified that her sources "reveal a surprisingly large amount of general domestic dissatisfaction" throughout the southern colonies—more than in New England. Much strife also occurred within marriages that were generally happy.[3]

A case in point was the successful but very stormy marriage between William Byrd II and Lucy Parke Byrd. In this relationship, which lasted ten years (1706–16), Byrd acted the role of the domestic patriarch. He disposed of his wife's estate without consulting her, kept all his property in his own hands, and forbade her even to borrow a book from his library without permission. He also interfered in her domestic management, and infuriated her by dictating the smallest details of her appearance even to the shape of her eyebrows, which she was compelled to pluck according to his pleasure. At table one day, he and his male guests entirely consumed the best dish and left nothing for his wife to eat. She did not hide her outraged feelings.

Lucy Byrd, for her part, was the daughter of Colonel Daniel Parke, a high-born Virginia gentleman who later became governor of the Leeward Islands. By all accounts she was an exceptionally beautiful, proud and headstrong lady, with strong passions, a stubborn will, and a mind of her own. She did not submit meekly

---

[2]Many touching examples appear in the correspondence of the condemned leader of Penruddock's rising, John Penruddock, with his "virtuous lady," whom he routinely addressed as "my dearest heart," added many other *basciamani* which were conventional in this period. The correspondence is in the Wiltshire Record Office, Trowbridge.

[3]Julia Cherry Spruill, *Women's Life and Work in the Southern Colonies* (1938, rpt, New York, 1969), 184.

William Byrd II (1674–1744) of Westover came of an armigerous family of London goldsmiths who were connected by marriage to elites in counties near the English metropolis. These ties were reinforced by the marriage between Byrd's parents, William Byrd I and Mary Horsmanden Filmer Byrd, which anchored the family firmly at the center of the Chesapeake elite. His secret diary, kept in shorthand for many years, is a major source for the cultural history of Virginia, and especially enlightening on the subject of gender, sex, marriage and domestic life. It records in elaborate detail the acts and prejudices of a Virginia patriarch throughout his mature life in both England and America.

Lucy Parke Byrd, beautiful, sensual, imperious and high-spirited, was the daughter of Colonel Daniel Parke and the first wife of William Byrd II. Her domestic life is known in more intimate detail than that of any woman in early Virginia, mainly through the medium of her husband's diary. That source describes a stormy union, but one that was also loving and supportive. It ended prematurely when Lucy Byrd died of smallpox in 1716. "How proud I was of her," her grieving husband wrote, "and how severely am I punished for it. . . . All pronounced her an honor to Virginia." This sketch follows an unfinished painting which was interrupted by her death.

to her husband's rule. In consequence, Lucy Byrd and her husband quarreled frequently, as William Byrd confided in his secret shorthand diary:

> [April 5, 1709] I was ill treated by my wife, at whom I was out of humor. . . .
>
> [April 6] My wife and I disagreed about employing a gardener. . . . My wife and I continued very cool.
>
> [April 7] I reproached my wife with ordering the old beef to be kept and the fresh beef used first, contrary to good management, on which she was pleased to be very angry . . . then my wife came and begged my pardon and we were friends again. . . .
>
> [April 8] My wife and I had another foolish quarrel about my saying she listened on top of the stairs . . . she came soon after and begged my pardon.
>
> [April 9] My wife and I had another scold about mending my shoes, but it was soon over by her submission.[4]

The most violent quarrels were about the house servants, whom Mrs. Byrd abused with a sadistic cruelty that shocked even her husband, who was no humanitarian. One domestic battle occurred when Lucy Byrd ordered a little slave girl named Jenny to be burned with a hot iron for a minor fault. On another occasion, William Byrd wrote:

> I had a terrible quarrel with my wife concerning Jenny [whom] I took away from her when she was beating her with the tongs. She lifted up her hands to strike me but forbore to do it. She gave me abundance of bad words and endeavored to strangle herself, but I believe in jest only. However, after acting the mad woman for a long time she was passive again.[5]

These terrible scenes often ended as suddenly as they began, and within moments husband and wife became "good friends" again, strolling arm and arm in the garden, and talking so merrily together that in one such *tête à tête* with her husband Mrs. Byrd

---

[4]Louis B. Wright and Marion Tinling, eds., *The Secret Diary of William Byrd of Westover, 1709–1712* (Richmond), 17–20.

[5]*Ibid.*, 494 (2 Mar. 1712); Susan Irwin, in unpublished research on slave autobiographies, found that the mistress was more commonly feared and hated than the master. A cyclical relationship was obviously at work here. The husband-patriarch treated his wife with something less than equality of esteem. She in her frustration lashed out against those beneath her. Those acts of cruelty in turn brought down upon her the wrath of her husband, and her frustration increased once more.

"burst herself laughing—" splitting open the seams of her dress in high hilarity.[6]

Often a bitter quarrel ended in a bout of love-making. One furious battle began when Mrs. Byrd flogged a slave in the presence of a house guest—a major breach of etiquette in Virginia where slaves were supposed to be beaten after the guests had gone home. It ended in bed the next morning, when Byrd noted, "I lay abed till 9 o'clock this morning to bring my wife into temper again and rogered her by way of reconciliation."[7]

The rhythm of love-making in the Byrd household was less *legato* than *staccato*. For long periods, husband and wife abstained from sex with one another—sometimes because of pregnancy or childbirth; more commonly because one or the other was ill with malaria, dysentery, enteritis or some endemic Chesapeake complaint. But when both husband and wife were in good health, they made love frequently and spontaneously—once on top of a billiard table after an afternoon game. Sex seems to have been deeply satisfying to them both. Byrd noted once in his diary that "I gave my wife a flourish, in which she had a good deal of pleasure."[8]

There were also moments of quiet affection, which they cherished best of all. When Byrd fell ill with malaria, his wife gave him his quinine bark, and "looked after me with a great deal of tenderness."[9] After a painful episode of dysentery, William Byrd recorded that his wife "anointed my bum with hot linseed oil," and made him feel much better.[10] When Mrs. Byrd fell seriously ill (as frequently she did), and when her son died and she suffered paroxysms of grief, her husband was constantly at her side. He wrote that "I comforted her as well as I could." This was a stormy but happy marriage. It ended suddenly in 1716, when Lucy Byrd died of smallpox in London. William Byrd was shattered by her loss.[11]

Every Virginia marriage had its own history, and no two were quite alike. But many of these chronicles were filled with strife—some much more so than the Byrds. These domestic conflicts were elaborately patterned. The trouble commonly arose from deep contradictions in the gender ways of Virginia. Perhaps the

---

[6]Wright and Tinling, eds., *Secret Diary of William Byrd*, 483 (10 Feb. 1712).
[7]*Ibid.*, 463 (1 Jan. 1712).
[8]*Ibid.*, 253 (4 Nov. 1710).
[9]*Ibid.*, 401 (6 Sept. 1711).
[10]*Ibid.*, 197 (28 June 1710).
[11]*Ibid.*, 187 (June 5, 1710).

most common cause of trouble was money. Men were taught to believe that they were masters of their households. But women often possessed property of their own, and wished to make economic decisions independent of their husbands. An example was the disastrous marriage of Colonel John Custis of Arlington, one of the most powerful men in Virginia, and Frances Parke Custis, the daughter of Colonel Daniel Parke and the sister of Lucy Parke Byrd. The strife in this union seems to have arisen mainly from disputes over property. Mrs. Custis was a woman of wealth, which her husband had the right to manage as he wished. But he also had the duty to pass her property intact to her children. An elaborate marriage contract existed, but it became an invitation to struggle between husband and wife. So bitter was this strife that Col. Custis ordered that a record of his domestic misery should be carved upon his gravestone.[12]

For years, this unhappy couple refused to speak to one another, communicating only through their slaves. Long silences were punctuated by outbursts of rage so wild and violent as to border upon madness. After one such tempest, Col. Custis surprised his lady by inviting her to go driving with him. They rode in sullen silence through the Virginia countryside, until suddenly the colonel turned his carriage out of the road, and drove straight into Chesapeake Bay.

"Where are you going, Mr. Custis?" the lady asked, as the horses began to swim.

"To hell, Madam," he replied.

"Drive on," said she, "any place is better than Arlington."[13]

Domestic conflicts over property were common in this culture. In Virginia, as in England, it was not unusual for husbands and wives to keep written cash accounts with one another. Colonel and Mrs. Custis bound themselves to do so by their marriage contract. So also did English gentlemen such as the Dorset Squire John Richards of Warmwell, who gave his wife an annual allowance, and often found himself in the humiliating position of having to borrow money back from her:

Borrowed of my Alice 15 Guineas	16.2.6
I owe her last year's allowance money	10.0.0
	23.2.6
Received of her 10 Guineas	10.10.0[14]

---

[12]*VMHB* IV (1897), 64–66.
[13]Spruill, *Women's Life and Work*, 168.
[14]John Richards of Warmwell, Diary II, 16 Sept. 1699, DORSRO.

Altogether property appears to have been the leading source of marital discord in seventeenth-century Virginia—in conflicts that rose directly from contradictions in the gender ways of this culture.

A second source of marital strife was sex, on which there were cultural contradictions of another kind. Men were bound to fidelity by their marriage vows. But the unwritten customs of that culture created a different standard of behavior, as we shall see below. The diaries of the English gentleman John Richards and the Virginia patriarch William Byrd documented in melancholy detail the domestic conflicts that arose when both men engaged in sexual adventures. Richards, for example, had a liaison with a lady called M. in his diary. One day he wrote:

> This evening A [his wife Alice] was angry as usual about M telling me that I loved her more than her, and that because of ill-treatment in this house she had often thought of killing herself.[15]

Richards' diary became a running record of domestic strife between husband and wife. His wife Alice did not meekly accept her lot. She was "enraged to the last degree, and roared all the while," forcing her husband to sleep in the dining room, and some nights even in the cellar. The journal which recorded these events was normally kept in English, but when things went wrong, Richards switched to French, and when they went very wrong he wrote in Italian.[16]

Another cause of domestic conflict rose from the politics of family life. Here again, the gender ways of this culture were contradictory. A wife was bound by her marriage vows to obey her husband. An apparently male essayist in the Virginia *Gazette* laid down rules of "matrimonial felicity" for the instruction of wives: "Never dispute with him . . . if any altercation or jars happen, don't separate the bed, whereby the animosity will increase . . . read often the matrimonial service, and overlook not the important word OBEY."[17]

But the unwritten customs of the culture encouraged women to demand more freedom and respect. In 1687, for example, a spirited lady named Sarah Harrison married Dr. James Blair, the future founder of William and Mary College. When the minister

---

[15]*Ibid.*, 12 Sept. 1699.

[16]"Q[ues]ta notte dormis in Cellar Chamber per esser in repose dal Ecla [Alice spelt backwards]." John Richards Diary, 21 July 1700, DORSRO.

[17]Williamsburg *Virginia Gazette*, 20 May 1737.

Sarah Harrison disrupted her own wedding ceremony in 1687. When asked if she would love, cherish and obey her husband, she responded firmly, "No obey," and persisted in that answer until her husband agreed to marry on her own terms. Few women in Virginia were prepared to go quite so far, but many had a strong sense of their English liberties, and a determination to defend them. At the same time, the men of Virginia were raised to a tradition of high patriarchy. The domestic results were often explosive.

recited the marriage vows, she startled the congregation by responding, "No obey!" Three times the vows were repeated. Three times Sarah Harrison answered with increasing firmness "NO OBEY," until Dr. Blair finally agreed to take his chances and the wedding went forward without any promise of obedience. Their married life together proved to be deeply unhappy. Some years later, William Byrd noted in his diary:

> Went to the Commissary's, where . . . I was very much surprised to find Mrs. Blair drunk, which is growing pretty common with her, and her relations disguise it under the name of consolation.[18]

Few women were as outspoken as Sarah Harrison. But many resisted by other means. Yet most were compelled to obey their husbands, often much against their will, in matters which they cared deeply about. Thus William Byrd compelled his wife to send her sick baby Otway to her mother-in-law, who lived at a plantation which was thought to be more healthy. The wife replied,

> I am very sorry you have limited Poor, sweet Otway, so that he has but a short time to stay with me. Poor dear babe . . . But Sir, your Orders must be obeyed whatever reluctance I find thereby.[19]

Here was a fertile source of domestic strife.

A particular cause of trouble was the use of physical violence and verbal abuse by husbands against wives, and sometimes by wives against husbands as well. Here again the customs of the country were inconsistent. Men were expected to exercise authority over their wives, and were encouraged by custom to use moderate "chastisement" from time to time. But wife-beating was thought to be dishonorable and was punished in both England and American by practices variously called "rough music," the "charivari," and "riding skimmington." A Berkshire gentleman explained:

> A custom almost universally prevails in villages and rural districts, whenever a quarrel takes place between a man and his wife and the husband resorts to violence against his wife, for the laborers and the idle inhabitants of the parish and neighborhood to assemble together with flags, horns, bells, pieces of iron and all kinds of sonorous instruments with which they resort to the house where

---

[18]Wright and Tinling, eds., *Secret Diary of William Byrd,* 11 (2 March 1709); *VMHB* 7 (1900), 278; 31 (1929), 84.
[19]*VMHB* 37 (1930), 246–47.

the unfortunate couple resides and create all the noice and disturbance in their power, much to the chagrin of the unhappy husband and greatly to the annoyance of the quiet and orderly inhabitants. . . . This recreation among the country people is called
"rough music."

The sound of this "rough music" carried for miles across the
countryside. Sometimes it continued every night for several
weeks.[20]

Precisely the same punishment was also used against wives who
abused their husbands. In one such case, a Wiltshire mob punished both spouses by rough music, and then assaulted both the
man and wife together. In this instance, the local gentry prevented the mob from ducking the woman, but by and large country gentlemen looked upon rough music with approval. At Mon-
tacute Hall, one of the great Wessex houses, Sir Edward Phelips
ordered for the central decoration of the great hall a plaster relief
of a "Skimmington ride." This was not a device which arose spontaneously from rural communities; it was nourished by rural
elites.[21]

Yet another tension in gender roles developed from ideas
about love. Husbands and wives were expected to love one
another—but not overmuch. Landon Carter complained of a
Virginia lady who was "more fond of her husband perhaps than
the politeness of the day allows for."[22] Even in happy marriages,
the love that men felt for their wives was not a love between
equals, and sometimes it seemed to be less a love for a person
than for a valuable piece of property. One gentleman wrote when
his wife died:

> All grief will allow me to say of her is, that she was known to be a
> humble pious, virtuous, discreet woman, an ornament to her sex,
> and a crown to her husband. But woe is me the crown has fallen
> from my head.[23]

A further source of conflict arose from a confusion of roles for
women in Virginia. They were expected to be feminine, refined,

---

[20]*In Re Goble,* Ms. D/EW1/L3, BERKRO; see also Joan R. Kent, "Folk Justice and Royal
Justice in Early 17th Century England: A Charivari in the Midlands," *MH* 8 (1983), 70–85;
there is now a vast literature on rough music in England, Europe and America.

[21]Bettey, *Wessex from AD 1000,* 176; M. Ingram, "Ridings, Rough Music nd the Reform of
Popular Culture in Early Modern England," *PP* 105 (1984), 79–113.

[22]Lewis, *The Pursuit of Happiness,* 37.

[23]Mainwaring Diary, n.d., 1675 Ms. DDY/394/1/26r, CHESRO.

delicate, gracious, modest, virtuous. At the same time, all but the most privileged of women were also expected to do farm work and even field labor as well as housewifery. Women of every estate were required to be resourceful but self-effacing. Sir John Oglander celebrated his "most careful, thriving wife, who wore no splendor, never wore a silk gowne, but for her credit when she went abroad in company and never to please herself."[24]

There were even theological disputes in Virginia on questions of gender. Some members of this culture shared a deeper sense of spiritual inequality between men and women than commonly existed in Massachusetts. At a rich planter's table as late as 1773, the northern tutor Philip Fithian was startled to hear an argument on the question of whether women had souls. That ancient conundrum had long since been laid to rest among the Puritans. But it still remained a topic of debate in Virginia.[25]

All of these conflicts had a common denominator. In this society of English-speaking people, the rights which Christian Englishmen claimed for themselves were a standing reproach to the status of women in their society. A free-born English gentleman was in many ways the unfittest of all males to argue his wife into a condition of dependency. By an early date in the eighteenth century some of the ladies of Virginia were thinking of themselves as "She-Britons," and demanding a share of the rights that their husbands enjoyed. As early as 1736, the Virginia *Gazette* published an angry poem called "The Lady's Complaint," which captured the deepest contradiction in the genderways of Virginia:

> They plainly can their Thoughts disclose,
>> Whilst ours must burn within:
> We have got Tongues, and Eyes, in vain,
>> And Truth from us is sin. . . .

> Then Equal Laws let Custom find,
>> And neither Sex oppress;
> More Freedom give to Womankind,
>> Or give to Mankind less.[26]

---

[24]Bamford, ed., *A Royalist's Notebook* xxv.
[25]Fithian, *Journal and Letters,* 111.
[26]Williamsburg *Virginia Gazette,* 22 Oct. 1736.

❧ Virginia Sex Ways:
Male Predators and Female Breeders

Sexual relations between men and women tended to be less strictly regulated in the Chesapeake than in Puritan New England. They were also regulated in a different way. Rates of prenuptial pregnancy during the seventeenth and early eighteenth century were comparatively high in the Chesapeake region—higher than in the Puritan colonies, particularly among indentured servants. In Somerset County, Maryland, more than a third of immigrant brides were pregnant before they married. Overall, about a fifth of all women who married in that county, immigrants and natives together, were carrying a child on their wedding day.[1]

Despite this tendency, or perhaps because of it, fornication was not punished as frequently or as severely in the Chesapeake colonies as it had been in New England. In Maryland, the courts did not often hear cases of this sort, despite very high rates of illegitimacy and prenuptial pregnancy. When they did so, the female was punished severely, usually by whipping. But the male either escaped with a token penalty such as a bond for good behavior, or in most cases was not punished at all. This pattern of discrim-

[1]Rates of prenuptial pregnancy in the Chesapeake colonies were as follows:

Place	Cohort	Percent of First Births Within			
		7 mos.	8 mos.	8.5 mos.	9 mos.
Somerset County, Md. Immigrants	1665–95	23.7%	32.9%	34.2%	36.8%
Somerset County, Md. Natives	1665–95	9.5%	19.0%	19.0%	20.6%
Middlesex County, Va. Christ Church Parish	1720–36	9.4%		15.2%	16.8%
Gloucester County, Va.	1749–60	2.8%		13.9%	13.9%
Kingston Parish	1761–70	12.1%		22.7%	24.2%
Richmond County, Va.	1710–19		18.7%		
	1720–29		9.8%		
	1730–39		33.3%		
	1740–49		33.3%		
	1750–59		38.5%		

Sources: Menard and Walsh, "Demography of Somerset County," 23; Lois Green Carr and Lorena Walsh, "The Planter's Wife: the Experience of White Women in Seventeenth Century Maryland," *WMQ3* 34 (1977), 547–48; Daniel Scott Smith and Michael S. Hindus, "Prenuptial Pregnancy in America, 1640–1971: An Overview and Interpretation," *JIH* 5 (1975), 537–70; Robert V. Wells, "Illegitimacy and Bridal Pregnancy in Colonial America," in Peter Laslett et al., eds., *Bastardy and Its Comparative History* (Cambridge, 1980), 349–61; Lee Gladwin, "Tobacco and Sex: Factors Affecting Non-Marital Sexual Behavior in Colonial Virginia," *JSOCH* 12 (1978), 57–78.

ination against women in fornication cases was the reverse of New England customs, which penalized the male more harshly than the female during the early and mid-seventeenth century.[2]

Bastardy was punished with savage ferocity in the Chesapeake. When an unmarried woman gave birth outside of wedlock, a heavy fine was levied upon her. If the fine could not be paid (as often happened), she was trussed up like an animal, her dress was ripped open to the waist, and she was publicly whipped in the sight of a shouting mob until the blood flowed in rivulets down her naked back and breasts. Further, if she was a servant, she was also required to compensate her master for the time lost in her pregnancy by serving an additional term, even in some cases when he was the father of the child. Bastardy was regarded as an offense of the utmost seriousness in Virginia—not because it was a sexual transgression, but because it threatened to place a burden of support on the parish poor rolls, and to deprive a master of work that was thought due to him.[3]

Other sexual offenses were also punished in seventeenth-century Virginia, but not in the same way as in New England. Adultery was a case in point. In both New England and Virginia, adultery was defined as extramarital sex involving a married woman (not necessarily a married man). One study has found that in Massachusetts, men and women found guilty of adultery in most cases received similar punishments. In the Chesapeake, however, adul-

---

[2]This offense was dealt with more frequently in Virginia than in Maryland, but less so than in Massachusetts. The most frequent prosecutions were in Lower Norfolk County, a center of Puritanism in Virginia until Sir William Berkeley enforced his policy of religious uniformity. See Bruce, *Institutional History of Virginia*, I, 48–49; for cases of fornication in Maryland, I have drawn from Sheri Keller, "Adultery and Fornication in Massachusetts and Maryland, the 1600s" (paper, Brandeis, 1987).

[3]Illegitimate births in two counties of southern Maryland were very common:

		Annual Rates of Illegitimate Births		
Place	Date	Per 1000 Total Births	Per 1000 Population	Per 1000 Single Women 15–44
Prince George's Co., Md.	1696–99	26	1.7	17.2
Somerset Co., Md.	1666–70	63	2.5	32.1
	1671–75	68	2.8	34.7
	1676	75	3.3	38.3
	1683	68	3.1	34.7
	1688–94	118	5.9	60.2

Sources: Menard and Walsh, "Demography of Somerset County," 35; Wells, "Illegitimacy and Bridal Pregnancy in Early America," and Daniel Scott Smith, "The Long Cycle in American Illegitimacy and Prenuptial Pregnancy," in Laslett et al., eds., *Bastardy and Its Comparative History*, 349–61, 362–78.

terous women were punished more harshly than adulterous men. For that offense, women were flogged severely or dragged through the water behind a boat until they nearly drowned. Men were treated leniently.[4]

This difference was not the result of mindless or instinctive sexism. It rested upon the assumption that the bloodline within a family was threatened by a wife's adultery, but not by the husband's. That way of thinking was more important in Anglican Virginia than in Puritan New England. Here again we find evidence that Virginians held themselves to different standards of behavior according to their rank, gender and standing in society.[5]

A multiple standard of sexual behavior (not merely a double standard) appeared not only in the laws of Virginia but also in its customs. Women, especially gentlewomen, were held to the strictest standards of sexual virtue. Men, especially gentlemen, were encouraged by the customs of the country to maintain a predatory attitude toward women. A famous example was the secret diary of William Byrd II, an exceptionally full and graphic record of one planter's very active sex life. In its attitude toward sex, this work was very different from any diary that was kept in Puritan New England. William Byrd was a sexual predator. Promiscuous activity was a continuing part of his mature life, and in some periods an obsession. With very mixed success, he attempted to seduce relatives, neighbors, casual acquaintances, strangers, prostitutes, the wives of his best friends, and servants both black and white, on whom he often forced himself, much against their wishes.

In the period 1709 to 1712, for example, when Byrd was more or less happily married, he was frequently engaged in sexual adventures:

> 2 [November 1709] I played at [r-m] with Mrs. Chiswell and kissed her on the bed till she was angry and my wife also was uneasy about it, and cried as soon as the company was gone. I neglected to say my prayers, which I ought not to have done, because I ought to beg pardon for the lust I had for another man's wife.

---

[4]Miriam Hibel, "Adultery in New England and the Chesapeake," (essay, Brandeis n.d.,); Bruce, *Institutional History of Virginia*, I, 48.

[5]The idea that a woman's adultery polluted the family more than a man's was not absent from New England. One finds it expressed in Puritan sermons on this subject, and also in the law of adultery, which was defined as extramarital coitus involving a married woman. But Hibel found that men and women were punished more nearly equally in New England than in the Chesapeake.

It is important to note that the remorse he felt on this occasion had to mainly to do with his sense of violating another gentleman's property. More often, he felt no remorse at all.

Sometimes Byrd and his Virginia gentleman-friends went on collective woman hunts:

> 11 Mar. 1711. After church Mr. Goodwin invited us to dinner and I ate fish. Here we saw a fine widow Mrs. O-s-b-r-n who had been handsome in her time. From hence we went to Mr. B's where we drank cider and saw Molly King, a pretty black girl.

> 20 [October 1711] Jenny, an Indian girl, had got drunk and made us good sport.

> 21 [October 1711] At night I asked a negro girl to kiss me.[6]

During this period in his life, Byrd's sexual adventures were comparatively restrained. After his wife died, he sometimes engaged in this activity on a daily basis. An example comes from a visit to London in the month of September 1719:

> 7 September . . . went to see Mrs. S-t-r-d but she was from home . . .

> 8 September . . . saw two women, a mother and daughter who stayed about two hours and then came Mrs. Johnson with whom I supped and ate some fricasee of rabbit and about ten went to bed with her and lay all night and rogered her twice . . .

> 9 September . . . the two Misses Cornish called on us to go to Southwark Fair. We were no sooner there but Sally Cornish was so ill she was forced to go away to her sister and Colonel Cecil and I gallanted them to G-v-n [Covent] Garden

> 11 September . . . I wrote some English till nine and then came Mrs. S-t-r-d. I drank a glass of wine to our good rest and then went to bed and rogered her three times. However, I could not sleep and neglected my prayers. . . .

> 12 . . . went to the coffeehouse . . . after supper I was very sleepy and about nine went home in a chair. It rained hard.

> 14 . . . About eight I went to Mrs. Smith's where I met Molly and had some oysters for supper and about eleven we went to bed and I rogered her twice . . .

> 17 . . . about seven I went to Mrs. FitzHerbert's where I ate some boiled pork and drank some ale. About nine I walked away and picked up a girl whom I carried to the bagnio and rogered her twice very well. It rained abundance in the night.

---

[6]Wright and Tinling, eds., *Secret Diary of William Byrd*, 169, 313, 425.

October was a lean month.

> 1 October . . . we went to Will's and from thence to the play, where was abundance of company and particularly Mrs. [Cambridge], as pretty as an angel. After the play I walked home and said my prayers.
>
> 2 October . . . went to meet Molly H-r-t-n at Mrs. Smith's in Jermyn Street where I went to bed with her and lay till 9 o'clock but could do nothing. Then we had chicken for supper and I gave her two Guineas and about twelve walked home and neglected my prayers . . .
>
> 6 October. . . . endeavored to pick up a whore but could not. I neglected my prayers, for which God forgive me . . .
>
> 7 October . . . picked up a whore and carried her to a tavern where I gave her a supper and we ate a broiled fowl. We did nothing but fool and parted about 11 o'clock and I walked home and neglected my prayers . . .

Within a few weeks he was well again.

> 16 October picked up a woman and went to the tavern where we had a broiled fowl and afterwards I committed uncleanness for which God forgive me. About eleven I went home and neglected my prayers.
>
> 17 October . . . to the play where was but indifferent company . . .
>
> 20 October . . . to the play where I saw nobody I liked so went to Will's and stayed about an hour and then went to Mrs. Smith's where I met a very tall woman and rogered her three times . . .

In November, William Byrd and his English gentleman-friends were prowling in packs.

> 11 November, went with Lord Orrery to Mrs B-r-t-n where we found two chambermaids that my Lord had ordered to be got for us and I rogered one of them and about 9 o'clock returned again to Will's where Betty S-t-r-d called on me in a coach and I went with her to a bagnio and rogered her twice, for which God forgive me . . .
>
> 12 . . . sat a little with Mrs. Perry . . .
>
> 13 . . . took my ways towards Mrs. Southwell's but she was from home. Then I walked in the park and went to Ozinda's . . . After we went to Will's . . . then . . . to Mistress B-r-t and stayed about an hour
>
> 14 . . . went away to Will's where a woman called on me . . . then went to a bagnio where I rogered my woman but once. Her name was Sally Cook. There was a terrible noise in the night like a woman crying. . . .

22 . . . walked home and by the way picked up a woman and committed uncleanness with her, for which God forgive me . . .

27 . . . We sat and talked till ten and then retired and I kissed the maid and neglected my prayers

28 . . . I ate some boiled milk for supper and romped with Molly F-r-s-y and about 9 o'clock retired and kissed the maid so that I committed uncleanness, for which God forgive me.

29 . . . After dinner it rained, that I could not walk so was content to romp with Molly F-r-s-y. In the evening we drank tea, and then sat and talked till seven, when I ate some boiled milk for supper. After supper we sat and talked and romped a little. About ten I retired and kissed the maid and said my prayers . . .[7]

Sexual predators such as William Byrd have existed in every society. But some cultures more than others have tended to encourage their activities, and even to condone them. This was the case in tidewater Virginia, with its strong ideas of male supremacy and masculine assertiveness. William Byrd's behavior differed only in degree from Thomas Jefferson's relentless pursuit of Mrs. Walker, or George Washington's clumsy flirtation with Mrs. Fairfax. These men represented the best of their culture; the sexual activities of other planters made even William Byrd appear a model of restraint. An old tidewater folk saying in Prince George's County, Maryland, defined a virgin as a girl who could run faster than her uncle.[8]

The sexual predators of Virginia found many opportunities among indentured servant girls during the seventeenth century. The journal of John Harrower described free and easy fornication with female servants in Virginia. Exceptionally high rates of prenuptial pregnancy and illegitimacy among English female immigrants to Virginia was in part due to this cause. There is evidence in the records that some masters deliberately impregnated their servants as a way of extending their indentures.[9]

In the eighteenth century, race slavery created other opportunities for planter predators, some of whom started at an early age to exercise a *droit du seigneur* over women in the slave quarters. Philip Fithian noted that the master's son, Bob Carter, one Sunday morning took "a likely Negro girl" into the stable and was for

[7]Louis B. Wright and Marion Tinling, eds., *William Byrd of Virginia, The London Diary, 1717–1721, and Other Writings* (New York, 1958, passim.

[8]Personal communication by a lady of an old Prince George's County family; for an actual case see *VMHB* 14 (1896–97), 185–97.

[9]Edward M. Riley, ed., *The Journal of John Harrower,* (New York, 1963), 144.

a "considerable time lock'd . . . together." Bob was sixteen years old.[10]

The abolitionist indictment of slavery for its association with predatory sex had a solid foundation in historical fact. One thinks of Mary Boykin Chesnut's response to the antislavery movement in the nineteeenth century:

> Like the patriarchs of old our men live in one house with their wives and their concubines, and the mulattoes one sees in every family exactly resemble the white children—and every lady tells you who is the father of all the mulatto children in everybody's household, but those in her own she seems to think drop from the clouds. . . . You see, Mrs. Stowe did not hit on the sorest spot. She makes Legree a bachelor.[11]

Mrs. Chesnut knew whereof she spoke, and was haunted by her knowledge of sexual predators within her own family. But she (and the abolitionists, and many historians too) were very much mistaken in thinking that the "peculiar institution" of race slavery itself was the first cause of this behavior. The same pattern had appeared in Virginia before slavery was widespread. It had also existed in rural England.

The cultural idea of the predatory male was carried very far in early Virginia—even to the point of condoning rape. The diaries and commonplace books of Anglo-American gentlemen often recorded a complaisant and even jocular attitude toward rape that differed very much from prevailing mores in Puritan New England. The founders of New England made rape a hanging crime. In the courts of the Chesapeake colonies, it was sometimes punished less severely than petty theft—a different attitude from the Puritan colonies.[12]

The sex ways of the southern colonies differed from New England in other ways as well. Virginians had a way of thinking about fertility which set them apart from New England Puritans. The people of Virginia thought less of the biblical commandment to increase and multiply and replenish the earth which so obsessed the Puritans, and more of breeding stocks and blood-lines. Children of the elite were bred to one another in a manner not unlike dogs and horses. Much interest was shown in blood

---

[10]Fithian, *Journal and Letters*, 115, 246.
[11]C. Vann Woodward, ed., *Mary Chesnut's Civil War* (New Haven, 1981), 28, 168–69.
[12]See, for example, the Bennett Pedigree Book, Ms. 413/389, WILTRO.

lines. The gentry of Virginia studied one another's genealogies as closely as a stockman would scrutinize his stud books.

Gentlemen took pride in the fertility of their women and their animals—sometimes in the same breath. A seventeenth-century gentleman named William Blundell expressed delight in his *ménage,* when within 24 hours his wife was delivered of a son, his prize cow produced a calf, a sow dropped fifteen piglets, a bitch gave birth to sixteen puppies, a cat had four kittens, and his hens laid fifteen eggs.[13]

Women in the Chesapeake were called "breeders," a word not unknown in New England, but decidedly uncommon.[14] A great planter, Landon Carter, complained of Virginia ladies, "I do believe women have nothing general in view, but the breeding contests at home. It began with poor Eve and ever since then has been so much of the devil in woman."[15]

Little girls were encouraged to think of themselves in these terms. The Presbyterian tutor at Nomini Hall, Philip Vickers Fithian, was shocked to discover Fanny Carter (aged ten) and Harriet (aged six) playing at pregnancy. "Among the many womanish Fribbles which our little Misses daily practise," he wrote in his diary, "I discovered one today no less merry than natural; *Fanny* and *Harriet* by stuffing rags and other Lumber under their Gowns just below their Apron-Strings, were prodigiously charmed at their resemblance to Pregnant Women! They blushed, however, pretty deeply on discovering that I saw them."[16]

There was little prudery in this society—less than in New England. A visitor to Virginia was startled to see ladies buying naked male slaves after carefully examining their genitals.[17] The earthiness of this culture appeared in a case of adultery heard by the court of Accomack and Northampton counties in 1643. Two witnesses, John Tully and Susanna Kennett, heard a "great snoring" on a house. John Tully testified that "there was a hogshead of tobacco in the entrie directly agynst the door, so this deponent and the said Susanna stood upon the said hogshead," and peered inside. They saw Goodwife Mary West and Richard Jones lying abed, "both arm in arm," Jones asleep and snoring lustily into

[13]T. Ellison Gibson, *A Cavalier's Notebook . . .* (n.p., n.d.,), 179.
[14]Spruill, *Women's Life and Work in the Southern Colonies,* 46.
[15]Landon Carter, *Diary,* II, 713, 1103 Smith, 70.
[16]Fithian, *Journal and Letters,* 254 (20 Sept. 1774).
[17]Grove, in *VMHB* 85 (1732), 31.

Mary West's plackett. Susanna Kennett testified that she saw
Mary West

> put her hand in his codpiece and shake him by the member,
> whereupon this deponent could not forbear from laughing. And
> then this deponent and the said Tully did run away from the place
> where they stood.[18]

What was striking about this episode was not merely the event
itself, but the spirit in which it was described, which was far
removed from the tone (if not the substance) of prevailing sexual
attitudes in Puritan New England.

❧ Virginia Naming Ways: Anglican Onomastics

After a baby was born in Virginia, a complex set of cultural rituals
was put in motion. Among them was the naming of the infant—
an intricate process which tells us many things about ethical values, family structure, and ideas of childhood itself. The naming
ways of Anglican Virginia were different from those of Puritan
Massachusetts, and similar to naming customs throughout the
south and west of England.

The leading features of this onomastic system might be summarized by a single English example. In 1737, the historian
Edward Gibbon was born into an armigerous Surrey family with
a strong Virginia connection. He was the eldest of six brothers,
and received the name of his paternal grandfather. So important
to the family was the survival of the name that the future historian
wrote, "in the baptism of each of my brothers my father's pru-
dence successively repeated my Christian name of Edward, that,
in case of the departure of the eldest son, this patronymic appel-
lation might still be perpetuated in the family." That precaution
proved to be necessary, for of the six brothers named Edward
Gibbon, only one survived childhood.[1]

---

[18]Susie M. Ames, ed., *County Court Records of Accomack-Northampton, Virginia, 1640–1645*
(Charlottesville, 1973), 290–91.

[1]One of the historian's Royalist ancestors emigrated to Virginia in 1659. He was John Gibbon, an eccentric English gentleman whose passion was heraldry. He observed that the Indians
painted their shields in armorial designs, and wrote a curious book which argued that "heraldry

Edward Gibbon's forename came not from the Bible, but from the king list of ancient Wessex. Three West Saxon monarchs had borne the name of Edward including Edward the Confessor, the last of the line, who personified the values of Royalists and High Anglicans in the seventeenth century. In old English, the name Edward meant "lucky leader" (*ead*, fortunate; *weard*, guardian or leader). It remained a favorite in Wessex for a thousand years, and would be heavily used in Virginia for many generations. But in New England the name was very rare; Harvard College enrolled only one student called Edward in its first forty undergraduate classes.[2]

The onomastic customs which Edward Gibbon personified were widely imitated in Anglican Virginia, both as to the choice of forenames, and the descent of names within the family. Biblical names were less common in Virginia than in Massachusetts. Only about half of all forenames in the Chesapeake colony came from the Scriptures, compared with 90 percent in New England. But the proportion of biblical names in Virginia was almost exactly the same as in the parish of Colyton, Devon. It was broadly similar to naming patterns among both the gentry and the general population in south and west of England.[3]

Virginians preferred to name their sons after Teutonic warriors, Frankish knights and English kings. Special favorites included William, Robert, Richard, Edward, George and Charles—choices rarely made in Massachusetts during the seventeenth century. The daughters of Virginia received the names of Christian saints who did not appear in the Bible and also traditional English folk names—Margaret, Jane, Catherine, Frances and Alice—as well as the universal English favorites of Mary, Elizabeth, Anne and Sarah. This distribution of names was much the

---

was ingrafted naturally into the sense of the human race." It is interesting that the Puritans regarded the Indians as a lost tribe of Israel, the Quakers saw them as Children of Light, the borderers regarded them as rival warriors, and royalist gentlemen such as John Gibbon saw them as natural aristocrats with an inborn taste for heraldry.

The Gibbon heraldry, by the way, had a bizarre history. An ancestor named Edmund Gibbon quarreled incessantly with three female relatives, and was given permission to change family's coat of arms from three scallop shells to "three ogresses or female cannibals." After his death, the scallop shells returned. Edward Gibbon, *Autobiography*, ed. M. M. Reese (London, 1970), 7, 17.

[2]George R. Stewart, *American Given Names*, 106.

[3]Daniel Scott Smith, "Child-Naming Practices, Kinship Ties, and Change in Family Attitudes in Hingham, Massachusetts, 1641–1880," *JSOCH* 18 (1985), 543.

same among native-born Virginians and English emigrants in the seventeenth century.[4]

This onomastic system was also distinctive in the descent of names. In Massachusetts, as we have seen, eldest children were named after their parents, and younger children after grandparents and other relatives. That pattern was reversed in Virginia: first-born children were named for their grandparents, and second-born for parents. One study of naming patterns in Middlesex County, Virginia finds that only 27 percent of eldest sons and 19 percent of first-born daughters were given their parents' forenames, compared with more than 67 percent in Massachusetts. But 60 percent of eldest sons in Virginia received their grandparents' names, compared with 37 percent in Massachusetts. The nuclear naming strategies of New England were subordinated to a stronger concern for the extended lineage in Virginia.[5]

Once again, the Virginia pattern closely followed the con-

[4]One study of Middlesex County, Virginia, found both native-born colonists and immigrants favored the same forenames in the 17th century:

Rank	Virginia Immigrants 1650–1699		Virginia Natives 1650–1699	
1	John	Mary	John	Elizabeth
2	Thomas	Elizabeth	William	Mary
3	William	Ann	Thomas	Ann
4	Richard	Sarah	Richard	Sarah
5	Robert	Margaret	George	Catherine
6	James	Jane	Robert	Margaret
7	George	Catherine	James	Frances
8	Edward	Frances	Henry	Alice
9	Henry	Alice	Charles	Jane
10	Samuel	Dorothy	Edward	Rebecca

Source: Rutman and Rutman, *A Place in Time, Explicatus,* 86–88.

[5]This test understates the difference. The researches of the Rutmans on Middlesex County, Virginia, and Daniel Scott Smith on Hingham, Massachusetts, show a strong contrast when controls are introduced for names shared by the parents and grandparents and by grandparents on both sides. For the descent of names to the eldest male child they obtained the following result:

Place	Period	Percent with Same Forenames as				
		Father	Grandfather	Both	Neither	N
Hingham, Mass.	pre-1721	47%	17%	20%	17%	155
Middlesex Co, Va.	1651–1750	11%	44%	16%	29%	197

For the first-born daughters, the pattern was much the same:

Place	Period	Percent with Same Forenames as				
		Mother	Grandmother	Both	Neither	N
Hingham, Mass.	pre-1721	56%	18%	15%	11%	156
Middlesex Co., Va.	1651–1750	15%	46%	4%	34%	177

Source: Smith, "Child-Naming Practices," 550; Rutman and Rutman, *A Place in Time, Explicatus,* 90.

ventions of Anglican families in the south and west of England. Among the Filmers of East Sutton, every first-born son in the male line of the Filmer family was named for his paternal grandfather, and every second-born son for his father:

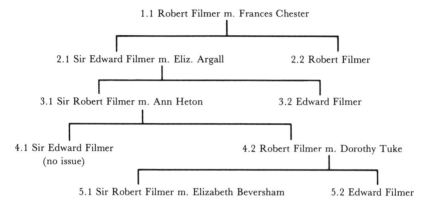

1.1 Robert Filmer m. Frances Chester

2.1 Sir Edward Filmer m. Eliz. Argall   2.2 Robert Filmer

3.1 Sir Robert Filmer m. Ann Heton   3.2 Edward Filmer

4.1 Sir Edward Filmer   4.2 Robert Filmer m. Dorothy Tuke
(no issue)

5.1 Sir Robert Filmer m. Elizabeth Beversham   5.2 Edward Filmer

In the fourth generation, the eldest male Filmer had no issue, and the title descended through a younger brother. Even so, the rhythm of three generation-naming was carefully preserved.[6]

These naming customs were very common among armigerous Anglican families in both southern England and tidewater Virginia. Another example was the Peyton family of Bedfordshire, Suffolk and Gloucestershire. Its younger sons settled in Virginia during the seventeenth century. For many generations, the Peytons used the same three-generational rhythm as did the Filmers:

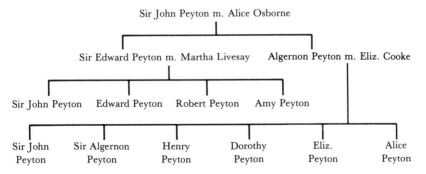

Sir John Peyton m. Alice Osborne

Sir Edward Peyton m. Martha Livesay   Algernon Peyton m. Eliz. Cooke

Sir John Peyton   Edward Peyton   Robert Peyton   Amy Peyton

Sir John   Sir Algernon   Henry   Dorothy   Eliz.   Alice
Peyton   Peyton   Peyton   Peyton   Peyton   Peyton

The Peytons, like the Filmers, were normally patrilineal in the descent of names. But that tendency varied in different families according to relative social standing of paternal and maternal

[6]William Berry, *County Genealogies; Pedigrees of the Families in the County of Kent* (London, 1830), 186–87.

lines. When Sir Algernon Peyton married Frances Sewster, daughter of Sir Robert Sewster, their first-born son was named Sewster Peyton.[7] Here was yet another naming-custom in that culture—the use of surnames as forenames to reinforce connections between families and strengthen the solidarity of the elite. As early as 1634, for example, William Gray of Middlesex County, Virginia, left his land to a nephew called Hugh Stewart on the condition that "the said Hugh Stewart shall name the first male child lawfully begotten of his body Gray Stewart."[8] This custom of using surnames as forenames was mostly used for boys, but it was not unknown for girls. The wife of the leader of Penruddock's Rising was named Arundel Penruddock.[9]

Complex patterns of cousin naming also appeared in Virginia, as they also did among the gentry of the south of England. Lateral ties were added to linear ties, to create a complex grid of naming customs. Godparents were closely involved in the choice of names in both Virginia and the south and west of England.

The naming of children was not entirely determined by this calculus of social rank and material interest. Names were also chosen for magical properties. Astrologers were consulted in an attempt to find a fortunate name. The "fortune books" of the first gentlemen of England and Virginia were full of astrological lore on this question.[10] This search for a lucky name tempered the use of necronyms in this culture. The Virginians, like New Englanders, tended to repeat forenames whenever children died. But they did so with some reluctance, for when children died young, their fathers feared to use names which had seemed unlucky. Thus, Sir John Oglander discussed in his diary the use of a necronym for his second-born son:

> I also named him John, the eldest being also by me named of the same name and died 12 months before, and if this dieth, I will never Christen any of that name more. Sir Richard Dillington and my lady Richards were the other gossips with me.[11]

In many ways, the onomastic customs of Anglican Virginia were far removed from the naming patterns of Puritan New England. The contrast of cultures began in the first years of life.

---

[7]For the Peyton genealogy in England see Robert E. C. Waters, *Genealogical Memoirs of the Extinct Family of Chester of Chicheley* (London, 1878).

[8]Rutman and Rutman, *A Place in Time*, 85.

[9]*The Trial of the Honorable John Penruddock* (n.p., 1655), 8.

[10]See, for example, the Diary and Fortune Book of Henry Sturmy, ms. D2375, GLOCRO.

[11]Bamford, ed., *A Royalist's Notebook*, 105.

❧ Virginia Child-rearing Ways: Bending the Will

"An infant coming into the world in Virginia during the eighteenth century," writes Edmund Morgan, "had a good deal more reason to cry about it than one who arrives in any part of the United States today."[1] Roughly one-third of newborn babies perished within the first twenty months of life, and nearly half were dead before they reached adulthood.[2] Those who survived also faced another ordeal, which was not physical but cultural in its nature. Growing up in Virginia was a process full of pain and difficulty for the young.

At first sight, it did not appear to be so. Visitors commonly remarked that Virginians seemed to be exceptionally indulgent toward their children—an observation that was never made in New England during the seventeenth century. The Calvinist doctrine that children were inherently evil rarely appeared in the writings of Anglican parents in Virginia. In consequence the Puritan custom of will-breaking was not much practiced in the Chesapeake colonies.[3]

But growing up in Virginia was in some ways even more difficult than in New England. The culture of the Chesapeake colonies placed two different and even contradictory demands upon its young. On the one hand youngsters were compelled to develop strong and autonomous wills. On the other hand, they were expected to yield willingly to the requirements of an hierarchical culture. These psychic tensions took a heavy toll.

In place of the Puritan will-breaking, young Virginians at a very early age were actively encouraged to exercise their wills. Parents took pride in their youngsters' childish acts of psychic autonomy. In 1728, a planter named Thomas Jones boasted that his infant nephew "struts around the house and is as noisy as a bully." The same man expressed delight at the antics of his own two-year-old son, Tom Junior. A sister-in-law complained that little Tom's wild

[1]Morgan, *Virginians at Home*, 5.

[2]Kulikoff, *Tobacco and Slaves*, 61, estimates the proportion dying before age 20 as 39% in the 17th century and 33% in the 18th.

[3]Daniel Blake Smith writes, " . . . anyone who reads through the family letters and diaries from the eighteenth-century Chesapeake will discover an abundance of evidence of parental tenderness and affection toward young children. These sources clearly suggest that children were not treated as sinful beings whose willfulness and sense of autonomy had to be controlled, if not quashed, by age two or three—as children were apparently seen in much of Puritan New England. Rather, parents in Virginia and Maryland during the eighteenth century seemed to delight in the distinctively innocent and playful childhood years of their offspring" (*Inside the Great House*, 40).

behavior in the house was "enough to distract all about him except his papa, and to him I believe all his [son's] noise is music. If he can't have and do everything he has a mind to, he is ready to tear the house the down."[4]

For boys, this regime of parental permissiveness commonly continued through childhood to adolescence. The German traveler Johann Schoepf observed that "a Virginia youth of fifteen years is already such a man as he will be at twice that age. At fifteen, his father gives him a horse and a negro, with which he riots about the country, attends every fox-hunt, horse-race and cockfight, and does nothing else whatever; a wife is his next and only care."[5]

Boys especially were required to develop strong wills and boisterous emotions. Not to possess them was thought to be unmanly. Philip Fithian was struck by the passionate nature of his young male charges at Nomini Hall: he described the elder son as "of a warm, impetuous disposition," and the younger son as "extremely volatile and unsettled in his temper."[6] Foreign travelers repeatedly noticed a clear difference in that respect between children in the northern and southern colonies. One English visitor in Maryland and Virginia observed that "the youth of these more indulgent settlements, partake pretty much of the *Petit Maître* kind, and are pampered much more in softness and in ease than their neighbors more northward."[7]

But these descriptions could mislead a reader in the twentieth century. Child rearing in the Chesapeake was not indulgent in the modern sense. By comparison with New England, it was not so much a method of freedom as a different system of constraint.

A primary goal of socialization in Virginia was to prepare the child to take its proper place in the social hierarchy. The child's

---

[4]Thomas Jones to Elizabeth Jones, 10 Nov. 1736; Rachel Cocke to Elizabeth Jones, 17 Sept. 1728; Jones papers LC; quoted in Smith, *Inside the Big House,* 51.

[5]Schoepf, *Travels,* II, 95.

[6]Fithian, *Journal and Letters,* 65.

[7]Morgan, *Virginians at Home,* 7. Another difference between Massachusetts and Virginia was in the degree of daily intimacy between parents and small children. In both cultures, adolescents were often placed in other families. To this common English practice, called "sending out" in New England and "putting out" in the Chesapeake, Virginians added the segregation of small children as well. Nomini Hall had separate dining rooms for adults and children, so that youngsters would not intrude upon the conversation of their elders. The master's children on that plantation also slept in outbuildings, away from their parents and under doubtful authority of nurses and tutors. This custom had long been practiced in the great country houses of England. It still survives today within upper-class families.

will was not broken, but in a phrase that Virginians liked to use, it was "severely bent against itself." This end was accomplished primarily by requiring children to observe elaborate rituals of self-restraint.

Child rearing in Virginia included many rituals of restraint which did not appear in New England. An example was the dance, which children of good family were compelled to study with close attention. Dancing was discouraged in the Puritan and Quaker colonies, and in some instances even forbidden outright. But in Virginia, children were compelled to dance. The Presbyterian tutor Philip Fithian was astonished by the seriousness with which Virginians applied themselves to dancing. He described an all-day dancing lesson at Nomini Hall, taught by a sadistic martinet ironically named Mr. Christian—one of many professional dancing masters who found employment in the colony:

> After breakfast, we all retired into the dancing-room, and after the scholars had their lesson singly round Mr. Christian. . . . There were several minuets danced with great propriety, after which the whole company joined in country-dances; and it was indeed beautiful to admiration, to see such a number of young persons, set off by dress to the best advantage, moving easily, to the sound of well-performed music, with perfect regularity, tho' apparently in the utmost disorder.
>
> The dance continued til two; we dined at half after three. Soon after dinner we repaired to the dancing room again. I observe in the course of the lessons, that Mr. Christian is punctual, and rigid in his discipline, so strict indeed that he struck two of the young Misses for a fault in the course of their performance, even in the presence of the mother of one of them!
>
> And he rebuked one of the fellows so highly as to tell him he must alter his manner, which he had observed through the course of the dance to be insolent, and wanton, or absent himself from the school—I thought this a sharp reproof, to a young gentleman of seventeen, before a large number of Ladies. . . .
>
> When the candles were lighted we all repaired for the last time into the dancing room. First each couple danced a minuet. Then all joined as before in the country dances, these continued till half after seven, when Mr. Christian retired.[8]

Altogether, the lesson lasted nine hours, from ten o'clock in the morning till after seven at night. As the exacting Mr. Christian

[8]Fithian, *Journal and Letters*, 44–45 (18 Dec. 1773).

insisted, dance was a form of discipline for young ladies and gentlemen of Virginia. The complex rhythms of minuet and country dance became metaphors for an entire cultural system. Governor Gooch boasted of Virginia's ruling elite that there was "not a bad dancer in my government." He had more in mind than merely their "easy movements" on the ballroom floor.

By the third quarter of the seventeenth century, the social ritual of the dance had become an important part of Virginia's culture, and also an instrument of the socialization process. Professional dancing teachers were employed in the colony as early as the 1660s. In the course of the eighteenth century, these customs changed mainly in an involutionary way by becoming more elaborately the same. In the process, they preserved their primary cultural functions. For many generations in Virginia, the ritual of the dance became a school of manners where young people learned to bend gracefully in more than merely a physical sense.[9]

Another closely related child-rearing custom was the careful instruction of young people in formal rules of right conduct. In Virginia, youngsters of every rank were required to master these rules, and they were punished severely for failing to respect them. All children without exception—even orphans, apprentices and slaves—were compelled to learn them. The higher a child's social rank, the more elaborate and constraining the rules became. During the late seventeenth and early eighteenth century, these rules were much more than an "etiquette" in the modern trivializing sense. They comprised an entire grammar of cultural ethics.

In substance, these rules were very much the same in Virginia and the south of England. One schoolmaster in the English county of Somerset, for example, compelled his students to memorize no fewer than 96 of these cultural axioms. A selection will suggest their quality:

1. Fear God
2. Honour the King
3. Reverence thy Parents
4. Submit to thy Superiors
5. Despise not thy Inferiors

[9]Bruce observes, " . . . the taste for dancing did not content itself with such skill as could be acquired by the ordinary participation in this form of amusement. There is some evidence of the presence in the colony of dancing masters who gave lessons in the art professionally. One of these was Charles Cheate, who was accompanied by his servant Clason Wheeler, a fiddler . . . it is quite probable that they were also able to secure large fees by serving as musicians at the entertainments so frequently given in the planters' residences" (*Social Life of Virginia,* 184–85).

   6. Be courteous to thy Equals
   7. Pray daily and devoutly
   8. Converse with the good
   9. Imitate not the wicked . . .
 22. Approach near thy parents at no time without a bow . . .
 28. Never speak to thy parents without some title of respect—
     viz.—Sir, madam, etc. according to their Quality . . .
 32. Ask not for anything but tarry till it be offered thee . . .
 38. Stare not in the face of anyone (especially thy superiors) . . .
 60. Laugh not aloud, but silently smile upon occasion . . .
 62. Be not among Equals forward or fretful but gentle and
     affable . . .
 67. Boast not in discourse of thy wit or doings.
 68. Beware thou utter not anything hard to be believed . . .
 78. Affront no one, especially thy elders by word or deed . . .
 80. Always give the wall to thy superiors that thou meetest, or if
     thy walkest with thy elder give him the upper hand . . .
 87. Give always place to him that excelleth thee in quality, age
     or learning . . .
 89. Be not selfish altogether; but kindly, free and generous to
     others . . .
 96. Let thy words be modest and about those things only which
     concern thee.[10]

This list was drawn from a book called *The School of Manners*, which went through many editions in the early eighteenth century, and circulated widely in Europe and America. Many similar works were published in England, France and Italy during the seventeenth century.[11]

The children of Virginia were required to learn these rules by rote. Among the earliest writings by George Washington was a list of 110 "rules of civility and decent behaviour in Company and conversation," which the young scholar had been compelled to inscribe in his best copybook hand:

    1st   Every action done in Company ought to be with some sign of respect to those that are present . . .
  19th   Let your countenance be pleasant but in serious matters somewhat grave . . .
  26th   In pulling off your Hat to Persons of Distinction, as Noblemen, Justices, Churchmen &c make a reverence, bowing more or less according to the custom of the better bred . . .

[10]John Cannon Memoirs, Ms., 161–64, SOMERO.
[11]Cannon followed the fifth edition of Garretson's *The School of Manners* (London, 1726).

31st   If any one far surpasses others, wither in age, Estate, or
       merit [yet] would give place to a meaner than himself the
       one ought not to accept it . . .

37th   In speaking to men of Quality do not lean nor Look them
       full in the Face, nor approach too near them. At least
       keep a full pace from them . . .

39th   In writing or Speaking, give to every person his due Title
       According to his Degree & the Custom of the Place . . .

40th   Strive not with your superiors in argument, but always
       submit your judgment to others with modesty . . .

42d   Let thy ceremonies in Courtesie be proper to the Dignity
       of his place with whom thou conversest for it is absurd to
       act the same with a Clown and a prince . . .

46th   Take all admonitions thankfully [even when not culpable
       for them] . . .

57th   In walking up and down in a House, only with one in com-
       pany if he be greater than yourself, at the first give him
       the right hand and stop not till he does and be not the
       first that turns and when you do turn let it be with your
       face towards him, if he be a man of great quality, walk not
       with him cheek by jowl, but somewhat behind him; but yet
       in such a manner that he may easily speak to you . . .

110th Labour to keep alive in your breast that little spark of
       celestial fire called conscience.

These lists were given to children not merely as copybook exercises. They were instruments of a larger purpose, which was to
discipline the will.[12]

Young gentlemen of Virginia were given "freedom of the will"
not as an end in itself, but as a means of achieving virtue—that
is, of living in harmony with reason, nature, and fortune. This
idea was very far from the restless striving of New England Puritans. It was a stoic ideal which cultivated a calm acceptance of life.
It taught that one must fear nothing and accept whatever fate
might bring with courage, honesty, dignity and grace. The mastery of this stoic creed was one of the central goals of socialization
in Virginia.

A case in point was the childhood of George Washington,
whose upbringing is full of clues about the culture of Virginia.[13]

---

[12]A facsimile appears in Charles Moore, ed., *George Washington's Rules of Civility and Decent
Behaviour in Company and Conversation* (Boston, 1926), 2–21. Washington's rules were largely
taken from Francis Hawkins, *Youths' Behaviour, or Decency in Conversation Amongst Men* (London,
2d ed., 1646).

[13]Here I follow a neglected classic of Virginia's historiography, Samuel Eliot Morison, "The
Young Man Washington," *By Land and By Sea* (New York, 1953), 161–80.

Washington had little formal schooling. When he was eleven years old, his family was shattered by the death of his father. The usual institutions of child rearing functioned very badly for him, as they did for many children in this world. Society itself became his schoolroom; in it he mastered a complex system of social ethics which was widely shared among the Anglican gentry in England and Virginia.

This social creed was fundamentally a form of stoicism—not quite the same as that of the ancient world, but directly derived from classical authorities. One of the few books that young George Washington is known to have owned and read was an English summary of Seneca's dialogues. The chapter titles of this work comprised another set of rules to be learned by a Virginia gentleman:

> An honest man can never be outdone in courtesy.
> A good man can never be miserable, nor a wicked man happy.
> A sensual life is a miserable life.
> Hope and fear are the bane of human life.
> The contempt of death makes all the miseries of life easy to us.

Washington was never much of a reader. But in company with his friend Sally Fairfax he read Addison's tragedy *Cato,* which became one of his favorite works. That Augustan classic, with its prologue by the poet Pope, celebrated the stoic virtues of the great Roman patrician who became a model for young George Washington. In the play, one character declaims:

> Turn up they eyes to Cato!
> There mayst thou see to what a godlike height
> The Roman virtues lift up mortal man.
> While good, and just, and anxious for his friends,
> He's still severely bent against himself.

At Valley Forge, Washington ordered that Addison's *Cato* should be performed for all his officers, and he attended the production himself. He quoted *Cato* in his presidential papers, and in his last years returned again and again to this work. Washington's character and conduct embodied Cato's creed. This was Virginia's ideal of an autonomous gentleman, with a character that was "severely bent against himself."

The inner stresses were sometimes very great. A gentleman of Virginia was expected to have boisterous feelings and manly passions and a formidable will. But at the same time he was also expected to achieve a stoic mastery of self. This vital tension became a coiled spring at the core of Virginia's culture, and a source of its great achievements during the eighteenth century. In the personality of George Washington, Virginia's system of child rearing had a spectacular success. Here was a character who seemed to be perfectly in harmony with his cultural environment. But other gentlemen of Virginia personified the inner tensions which were created by this culture.

A leading example was Colonel Daniel Parke (1669–1710), whose daughters Frances and Lucy we have already met. Daniel Parke was a fantastic figure, whose exploits made him a legendary character throughout the English-speaking world. He was also a typical product of Virginia's socialization process. As a young gentleman, he gained a reputation for pride and "willfulness." Commissary James Blair described him as a

> handsome young man . . . who, to all the other accomplishments that make a complete sparkish gentleman, has added one upon which he infinitely values himself, that is, a quick resentment of every the least thing that looks like an affront or injury. He had learned, they say, the art of fencing, and is as ready at giving a challenge, especially before company, as the greatest Hector in the town.[14]

Parke once challenged the visiting Governor of Maryland to a duel at a public gathering—an act which doubly shocked respectable opinion in the Chesapeake. Challenges were properly delivered in private, and governors were thought to be exempt. He also caused another scandal when on a visit to England he eloped with a gentleman's beautiful wife and brought her to Virginia as a thrall of love. This act prompted Commissary James Blair to thunder against adultery from the pulpit of Bruton Parish Church, which led the hot-blooded young Daniel Parke to challenge even his clerical critic—another grievous breach of the rules. In later life, Colonel Parke openly kept a mistress as his consort—and ordered that she should inherit his coat of arms, which was the most shocking impropriety of all in armigerous Virginia.

But even as he behaved so badly by the standards of his own culture, there was also another side to Daniel Parke's personality. At an early age he imbibed the stoic creed of a Virginia gentle-

---

[14]Langhorne Washington, "Virginia Gleanings in England," *VMHB* XX (1912), 373.

The troubled life and violent death of Colonel Daniel Parke expressed the ten-sion between the stoic ideas of Virginia gentlemen and the turbulent reality of their world. In an old painting Daniel Parke wears as a badge of honor on his breast a pearl-encrusted miniature that Queen Anne gave him when he was chosen for his gallantry to bring her the news of the great British victory at Blenheim. Colonel Parke honorably refused all material reward for that service except a picture of his sovereign, and an engraved silver service of the sort that Virginians loved to display. A few years after this likeness was painted, Colonel Parke became governor of Antigua, where he was captured by rebels and tor-tured to death. His last words, long admired in Virginia, were "Gentlemen, you have no sense of honor left, pray have some of humanity," and he died "recommending his soul to God, with some pious ejaculations."

man, and tried to live according to its precepts. To one of his daughters, Daniel Parke wrote,

> Mind your writing and everything else you have learnt, and do not learn to romp, but behave yourself soberly and like a gentlewoman. Mind reading, and carry yourself so that everybody may respect you. Be calm and obliging to all the servants, and when you speak, do it mildly, even to the poorest slave.[15]

Colonel Parke was long remembered in Virginia for his gallantry. In 1697 he returned to England and was commissioned a colonel in the British Army. He became aide-de-camp to the Duke of Marlborough in the Wars of Louis XIV, and was ordered to carry home the report of the great English victory at Blenheim. Offered a gift of £500 by Queen Anne, Colonel Parke refused the money and asked only a small picture of his sovereign—an act of gallantry which was praised even by his enemies.[16]

The most memorable scene in Colonel Parke's life was its remarkable ending. Sent as Royal Governor to the Leeward Islands, he was captured by rebels in Antigua and tortured to death. In an extremity of pain and suffering, Colonel Parke's behavior became a model of stoic virtue. "Insulted and reviled by every scoundrel, in the agonies of death," he made "no other return but these mild expressions, 'Gentlemen, you have no sense of honor left, pray have some of humanity,'" and died "recommending his soul to God, with some pious ejaculations."[17]

Here was a spectacular example of a Virginia gentleman, sternly bent against himself. Altogether, the process of socialization was less successful for Colonel Parke than for General Washington. In Daniel Parke's life, the inner tensions of this culture were outwardly expressed with exceptional clarity and force. For two hundred years, the example of his troubled life and noble death was held up for the moral instruction of young gentlemen in Virginia.

[15]*Ibid.*, 373–75.
[16]Louis B. Wright, *The First Gentlemen of Virginia; Intellectual Qualities of the Early Colonial Ruling Class* (San Marino, Calif., 1940), 80.
[17]*Ibid.*

❧ Virginia Age Ways:
The Anglican Idea of the Elder-Patriarch

Attitudes toward age, and actual experiences of aging, were not the same in Virginia and Massachusetts. Respect for age was very strong in both cultures—but not in the same way. In place of the Puritan ideal of the venerated elder-saint, Virginians organized a system of age deference around the paternal figure of the elder-patriarch.

In seventeenth-century England, a vital principle of Royalist political thought had been what Sir Robert Filmer called "the agreement of paternal and regal power." In his treatise *Patriarcha*, Filmer explained:

> If we compare the natural duties of a Father with those of a King, we find them to be all one, without any difference at all but only in the latitude and extent of them. As the Father over one family, so the King, as Father over many families, extends his care to preserve, feed, clothe, instruct and defend the whole commonwealth. His wars, his peace, his courts of justice, and all his acts of sovereignty tend only to preserve and distribute every subordinate and inferior father, and to their children, their rights and privileges, so that all the duties of a King are summed up in an universal fatherly care of his people.[1]

This argument worked two ways. It invested a king with the legitimacy of a father, and endowed a father with the authority of a king. Further, Royalist writers such as Filmer also identified elders with father-kings. In *Patriarcha* Filmer quoted with approval Aristotle's axiom that "the eldest in every house is King."[2]

This patriarchal principle of respect for age was very strong in gentry families throughout the south of England. Elders were normally treated with deference. In a Warwickshire family, Richard Newdigate II in his mature years routinely addressed his father as "Honored Sir," and signed himself "your truly obedient son." The letters were studded with sentences such as "your direction in this business which shall most readily be obeyed by, most dear father, your ever obedient son." Letters from sons to

---

[1]Sir Robert Filmer, *Patriarcha and Other Political Works*, ed. Peter Laslett (Oxford, 1949), 63.

[2]*Ibid.*, 79.

their fathers were couched in language so elaborately submissive that one modern scholar describes them as "priggish," "stiff," and "pompous." But the same phrases rang differently in seventeenth-century ears.[3]

The submission of youth to age was more than merely an empty ritual. It was also accompanied by substantive acts. When John Oglander was offered a knighthood, for example, he refused to accept it because his living father had not preceded him in that honor. "Sir John Oglander," a friend wrote, "might have been knighted before all the gentleman of the Island [of Wight] but out of too much niceness, as his father, then living, refused it."[4]

Respect for age was strongest when elders were men of high rank in society. But the same principle also extended to people of humble stations. In the west and south of England during the seventeenth century, elders who were not gentlemen received the honorific title of Gaffer, and older women were called Gammer. These salutations were used as genuine titles of respect even by young noblemen when they addressed elders of low rank. They were also accompanied by acts of highly complex mutual deference from young men of high rank to elders of a lower order. When, for example, the Dorset gentleman John Richards had a falling out with a young servant named Arthur Cryde, the boy was sent home "to take his father's advice." When the father supported his son, the master himself deferred to the judgment of "father Cryde."[5]

This rule of respect for age was not confined to private affairs. It also appeared in public life during the seventeenth century. In the south of England, young gentleman-justices routinely deferred to senior colleagues. Sir John Oglander, for example, when appointed to the Commission of Peace in England's Isle of Wight at the exceptionally early age of twenty-two, described a sense of "shame" that he felt because of his youth. "I was put into the Commission of peace at the age of 22 years," he wrote, "when I not well understood myself or place, and was ashamed

[3]Richard Newdigate II to Richard Newdigate I, 19 Sept., 30 Sept. 1674; Newdigate Papers, CR 136/B349, WARRO; the modern judgment is Vivienne M. Larminie, "The Life Style and Attitude of the Seventeenth Century Gentleman, with Special Reference to the Newdigates . . ." (thesis, Univ. of Birmingham, 1980), 238.

[4]Bamford, ed., *A Royalist's Notebook,* xiv.

[5]Many examples of "gaffering" and "gammering" appear in the Dorset diary of John Richards, Ms. D320/F65, DORSO; the saga of Arthur Cryde is in an entry dated 15 Sept. 1692.

to sit on the bench as not having then any hair on my face and less wit."[6]

The same principle of a patriarchal respect for age was carried to the Chesapeake. In the county courts of Virginia, justices were ranked and seated by seniority. When openings occurred, older men were preferred over younger ones. The court of Essex County as late as 1787 stated the common belief that "senior magistrates would keep more order and decorum on the bench."[7] The laws of Virginia gave special responsibilities to the justice who was "the eldest in every commission." In actual practice, the eldest was sometimes not very old; high rates of mortality rapidly promoted the young. But seniority remained the rule.[8]

The patriarchal principle was also very strong in family relationships throughout tidewater Virginia. Historian Daniel Blake Smith, in a general survey of family correspondence throughout the Chesapeake colonies finds a "general pattern of paternal dominance and deferential conduct in sons that prevailed in most gentry families until the late eighteenth century."[9]

This Virginia habit of deference to elder-patriarchs was different from the New England practice of veneration for elder-saints. Empirical evidence appears in patterns of age-heaping: that is, the systematic distortion of ages reported to a census taker. In twentieth-century America, with its intense youth bias, people tend to make themselves a little younger than they actually are; many choose to remain 39, or 49, or 59. In early America a very different sort of age bias appeared: people of mature age tended to make themselves a little older. This was the case both in New England and Virginia. But in the Puritan colonies the tendency to inflate one's age was strongest in later life, and comparatively weak in early adulthood. In Virginia, on the other hand, people tended to make themselves a little older in every stage of adulthood. The explanation may be found in cultural ideals. In the Puritan colonies, which made long life into a Calvinist "Sign," the status of elder saint applied only to people of advanced age. But in Virginia, the idea of patriarchy applied to senior adult males

---

[6]Bamford, ed., *A Royalist's Notebook,* xiv.

[7]Quoted by A. G. Roeber, "Authority, Law and Custom: The Rituals of Court Day in Tidewater Virginia, 1720 to 1750," *WMQ3* 37 (1980), 33.

[8]See, for example, an "Act Concerning Styllyards," 1654, in Hening, *Statutes at Large,* I, 391.

[9]Smith, *Inside the Big House,* 101.

of any age. One culture exalted old age; the other rewarded seniority—two very different systems.[10]

In Virginia, this patriarchal system of respect for seniority made a major difference in family relations—particularly between fathers and sons. As fathers grew older, they commonly kept at least one son beside them. Thus, George Hume, of Spotsylvania County, in 1751 wrote, "I thank God I have now a son who does my business for me, and when he leaves me I hope to have another ready."[11]

These relationships were often full of tension. A few sons rebelled outright against this treatment. An example was the strife that developed between the great planter Landon Carter of Sabine Hall (1710–78), and his son Robert Wormeley Carter (1734–97). In the year 1766, the son was thirty-two years old and married, with money of his own but not enough for independence. He was forced to live under his father's roof, still subject to paternal authority. The two men quarreled endlessly. The son called his father a "bashaw," an Oriental despot, and at the age of forty protested that "he was not a child to be controlled." So

---

[10]Age-heaping ratios are not available for Virginia. But in 1776, a census of exact ages was taken in Prince George's County, Maryland, on the north bank of the Potomac River, and culturally similar to Virginia. The pattern of age heaping was as follows, in comparison with data for early New England and the modern United States (1950):

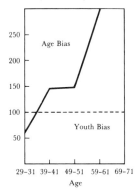

Age	Prince George's Co., Md. (1776)	New Haven, Conn. (1787)	United States (1950)
29–31	.60	n.a.	.94
39–41	1.46	.87	.93
49–51	1.47	1.58	.93
59–61	2.99	1.72	.92
69–71	n.a.	n.a.	.91

These ratios measure the relative strength and direction of bias in age reporting. Where no net bias exists, the ratio is 1.0. Where a youth bias exists, the age-heaping ratio falls below 1.0; a bias toward older ages causes the ratio to rise above 1.0. For further discussion, see D. H. Fischer, *Growing Old in America* (rev. ed., New York, 1978), 82–86; sources of New England data appear in part I, above; Maryland data are from John Modell, unpublished compilation from Gaius Marcus Brumbaugh, *Maryland Records* (2 vols., Baltimore, 1915, 1967), 1–89; data for the United States in 1950 are from Ansley J. Coale and Melvin Zelnik, *New Estimates of Fertility and Population in the United States* (Princeton, 1963), 90–138.

[11]Smith, *Inside the Big House,* 124.

heated did these quarrels become that the father began to fear for his life. "Surely it is happy our laws prevent parricide," he wrote, ". . . Good God! That such a monster is descended from my loins!"[12]

Open hostility of this sort was very much an exception in Virginia. But tensions so commonly existed that Philip Fithian advised another tutor in Virginia to "place yourself, according to your most acute calculation, at a perfect equidistance between the father and the eldest son."[13]

Relations between patriarchal fathers and sons, even when not so stormy, were often laden with emotional complexity. William Byrd II in his mature years was literally haunted by the memory of his dead father. In 1710, he ordered his father's corpse to be dug up, so that he could look his sire in the face. "I had my father's grave opened to see him," Byrd wrote, "but he was so wasted there was not anything to be distinguished."[14]

William Byrd's secret diary reveals many other things about age-relations, and also about the process of aging in that society. A secret shorthand notebook that he kept from 1739 to 1741 (age 65–67) exposes the inner feelings of a Virginia patriarch in his sixties, who was feeling his age in many ways. He was plagued by illness and worried about the decline of his mental faculties. "God preserve my head," he wrote in 1740, "and grant I may not lose my memory and sense." Yet his diary showed little loss of activity in the last years of his life, by comparison with our own world. To the end of his life he continued his career in politics, reaching his highest office in the last year of his life when he was elected president of the Virginia council. This was an important office in the colony, and it came to Byrd because of his age. He was senior councilor and had been so for many years. But the incumbent president James Blair clung stubbornly to life, dozing in his chair of state for many years until the end finally came at the age of eighty-seven; and Byrd, a mere stripling of seventy, inherited the office.[15]

In his last years, Byrd's private life continued to be as crowded as his public career. He began each morning with lessons in

[12]Jack P. Greene, ed., *Diary of Colonel Landon Carter of Sabine Hall* (2 vols., Charlottesville, 1965), 250, 310, 315, 713, 763, 1004, 1102; this relationship is discussed at greater length in Fischer, *Growing Old in America*, 73–76.

[13]Fithian to John Peck, 12 Aug. 1774, *Journal and Letters*, 212.

[14]Wright and Tinling, eds., *Secret Diary of William Byrd*, (24 Jan. 1710).

[15]Fischer, *Growing Old in America*.

Latin, Hebrew and Greek, and took his exercise almost every day. In the evenings he proved himself a mighty trencherman, and at any hour of the day he could be dangerous to unwary housemaids who came within reach. Even in his seventies, William Byrd continued to be a sexual predator:

> 9 May 1741 I played the fool with Sally . . .
> 15 June 1741 In the evening I played the fool with Marjorie. God forgive me.

In old age Byrd moved more slowly, and rarely caught his prey. But he preserved most activities in his life even as he approached the end of it.[16]

❧ Virginia Death Ways:
The Anglican Idea of Stoic Fatalism

On the dark subject of death in Virginia, a curious double paradox presents itself. The most striking fact about death in the Chesapeake was how much there was of it, compared with New England and western Europe. Rates of mortality may have been at least twice as high in tidewater Virginia as in rural Massachusetts, and higher also than in many parts of England during the seventeenth century. Illness and death were constant companions in this "pestered country."

A second fact was equally striking. Virginians appeared, on the surface at least, to have been remarkably nonchalant about the mortal dangers that surrounded them. They showed comparatively little of the anxiety about death that was so much a part of Puritan culture. They did not observe the rituals of "daily dying" which became standard spiritual exercises in Massachusetts. Neither did they drag their children screaming to the open grave. By comparison with other people, the Virginians responded to sudden and terrible mortality with a cultivated *sang-froid* that could not have been more different from the manic behavior of Massachusetts Calvinists.

In the year 1720, for example, William Byrd II traveled to Williamsburg on public business. "About 12 o'clock," he wrote in his diary, "I went to the Capitol and in court the Secretary was

---

[16]Maude H. Woodfin, ed., *Another Secret Diary of William Byrd of Westover, 1739–1741* (Richmond, 1742), 50.

struck with the fit of an apoplexy and died immediately and fell upon me. This made a great consternation. About two I dined at [illeg.] and ate some wild duck." Byrd added no reflections on the frailty of life, or the omnipotence of God. Immediately after this event he sat down to a heavy dinner with no sense of incongruity or loss of appetite.[1]

Subsequent passages in his diaries suggest, however, that this show of unconcern was merely a facade. A few months after the courtroom death of Secretary Cocke, Byrd began to be deeply troubled by dreams of his own impending demise. On December 2, he wrote,

> Colonel Harrison came to us and we played at cards and I lost ten shillings and about 11 o'clock went home and said my prayers. I dreamed that I had notice given me that I should die suddenly in six or seven days.

The next day, he was horrified when his friend Colonel Harrison told him "he dreamed there was a funeral at Westover, which agreed with my dream last night and made me begin to think there was something to it."

The day after, Byrd went to church twice, and was careful to say his prayers morning and night. When a housemaid incautiously entered his bedroom he showed unusual restraint. "After I was in bed," he wrote, "the maid of the house came into my chamber and I felt her and committed uncleanness but did not roger her."

Seven days later William Byrd awoke to discover that his dream was false. He hurled himself back into the business of life. When a young slave girl came within reach, he forced himself upon her. "I felt the breasts of the negro girl, which she resisted a little," he noted. Then he went out and visited his friends and in the evening "walked a little to pick up a woman and found none." He dined with his friends, gambled at cards, and was delighted to have a winning streak. While his luck continued at the gaming table, all thoughts of death disappeared.[2]

Another outlet for the fears that lurked below the surface in Virginia was elaborate death ritual—much more elaborate than in early New England. After Secretary Cocke died, for example, there was a splendid service at Bruton Church, with Governor

[1]Byrd, *London Diary and Other Writings*, 465 (22 Oct. 1720).
[2]Wright and Tinling, eds., *Secret Diary of William Byrd*, 481–85; 2–11 Dec. 1720.

Spotswood in attendance. A table was erected which proclaimed that "the principal gentlemen of the country attended his funeral, and, weeping, saw the corpse interred. . . ."[3]

State funerals made a great show in Virginia—more so in the eighteenth century than the seventeenth. When Governor William Botetourt died in 1770, an elaborate procession was staged in Williamsburg. The street was lined with militia from York and James City counties, and the bells of the town tolled mournfully. The funeral parade was led by the hearse surrounded by six mutes and eight pallbearers, followed by the governor's servants in "deep mourning," and the chief mourners in white hatbands and white gloves. The aisle of Bruton church was carpeted in black; the altar, pulpit and governor's throne were hung with black cloth. The sermon was heard by a large crowd who wept copiously through the ceremony, in an open and extravagant display of grief which was also customary at Virginia funerals, and very different from the grim restraint of New England burials.

Interments were conducted with high ceremony even for Virginians of modest rank. The minister and pallbearers wore mourning gloves, love scarves, ribbons and other tokens of grief. A common part of the proceedings was a *fusillade* which by the quantity of gunpowder indicated the status of the deceased. Thomas Wall in 1650 in his will requested "three volleys of shot for the entertainment of those who came to bury him." As many as ten pounds of black powder were expended on these occasions—enough for many volleys.[4]

Even more lavish was the consumption of food and liquor. At the funeral of Mrs. Elizabeth Eppes, the assembled mourners consumed three entire sheep and a steer, plus five gallons of wine and two gallons of brandy. That was a comparatively abstemious event; at other funerals as many as fifty or sixty gallons of alcoholic beverages were drunk by a crowd of mourners who were highly volatile and heavily armed. More than a few Virginians requested in their wills that weapons and alcohol be omitted from their funerals, in hopes of preventing "excess."[5]

The place of burial in Virginia was normally not a public burying ground as in New England, but a private family plot in some

[3] *WMQ1* 16 (1907), 16.
[4] Bruce, *Social Life of Virginia*, 219.
[5] *Ibid.*

secluded corner of a farm or plantation. Hugh Jones described the prevailing customs:

> The parishes being of great extent (some sixty miles long and upwards) many dead corpses cannot be conveyed to the church to be buried: So that it is customary to bury in gardens or orchards, where whole families lye interred together, in a spot generally handsomely enclosed, planted with evergreens, and the graves kept decently: Hence likewise arises the occasion of preaching funeral sermons in houses, where at funerals are assembled a great congregation of neighbours and friends; and if you insist upon having the sermon and ceremony at church, they say they'll be without it, unless performed after their usual custom.[6]

Indentured servants who died in appalling numbers were hurried into the ground with little ceremony. Black slaves were often buried in unmarked graves, apart from their masters. Public funerals for slaves were forbidden by order of the Virginia Council in 1687.[7] Great planters noted the death of slaves without even bothering to record their names:

> 18 August 1739 several people sick above, God preserve them.
>
> 22 August . . . my sick people continued bad, God preserve them.
>
> 23 August . . . My people were still ill: God save them if it be his good pleasure. . . . After dinner I was a little out of order myself but visited my sick people again who were better, thank God. I had a negro girl die. God's will be done.[8]

There were a great many deaths to record in the Chesapeake, but Virginians never really became hardened to them. They mourned their losses as deeply as people in other times and places. The death of infants caused parents to suffer as grievously as in our own time. An example was the death of William Byrd's infant son Parke Byrd in 1710:

> 3 [June 1710] . . . news was brought that the child was very ill. We went out and found him just ready to die and he died about 8 o'clock in the morning. God gives and God takes away; blessed be the name of God. Mrs. Harrison and Mr. Anderson and his wife and some other company came to see us in our affliction. My wife

---

[6]Jones, *The Present State of Virginia*, 96–97.
[7]*Executive Journals, Council of the Colony of Virginia*, I, 85–87.
[8]Woodfin, ed., *Another Secret Diary of William Byrd*, 6–8.

was much afflicted but I submitted to His judgment better, notwithstanding I was very sensible of my loss, but God's will be done. . . . My poor wife and I walked in the garden . . .

4 . . . my wife had several fits of tears for our dear son but kept within the bounds of submission . . .

5 . . . my wife continued very melancholy, notwithstanding I comforted her as well as I could . . .

6 . . . we prepared to receive company for the funeral . . . we gave them burnt claret and cake. About 2 o'clock we went with the corpse . . .

7 . . . my wife continued to be exceedingly afflicted for the loss of her child, notwithstanding I comforted her as well as I could . . .

8 . . . my wife continued disconsolate . . .

9 . . . my wife continued melancholy . . .

11 . . . my wife was still disconsolate . . .

14 . . . my wife began to be comforted, thank God . . .

18 . . . In the afternoon my wife told me a dream she had two nights. She thought she saw a scroll in the sky in form of a light cloud with writing on it. It ran extremely fast from west to east with great swiftness. The writing she could not read but there was a woman before her that told her there would be a great dearth because of want of rain and after that a pestilence . . . [9]

In the twentieth century, the death of an infant is an exceptional event. But in Virginia households during the late seventeenth and early eighteenth century it happened very freqently. Even so, the psychic cost of these losses was very great. Their cumulative effect was greater still.

Virginians found a way of coming to terms with death by cultivating a spirit of stoic fatalism which was in keeping with other aspects of their culture. This attitude was not invented in America, but carried out of England in the seventeenth century. In Warwickshire, for example, when a father was grieving deeply for the death of a young child, a friend sent a typical letter of condolence:

Noble Sir,
    I am very sorry that I am not able to give sufficient comfort to one, that hath such cause of sorrow as now you have, but we all

[9]Wright and Tinling, eds., *Secret Diary of William Byrd*, 188–92.

knowing that all things happen according unto the will of God, the best remedy I think is ever for all things with patience to give praise unto him, and no doubt but he that took away that child, which now to you justly doth bring great grief, can and will in his good time give more children that then will yield more cause of rejoicing then this now of sorrowing, so that I know your wisdom is such that it will not let you give yourself ever too much unto sorrow's yoke, and for your bedfellow, who hath an equal if not a greater part in this sorrow than yourself, I am sorry that I am neither worthy nor able to send her sufficient comfort for her now too much greaved and discontented mind, but I pray you let my best service be remembered unto her. . . .

> Your always well-wisher
> and true affectionate friend.[10]

Virginians shared the same attitude, and found frequent opportunity to express it. An example was Frances Bland Randolph (1752–88), who lost her husband when she was twenty-three, and followed him to the grave when barely thirty-six. When she was fifteen, the death of a much-loved sister prompted her brother to write, "Alas, Fanny, 'tis in vain for us to grieve at misfortunes." She agreed, "It is of little use to dwell on melancholy subjects."[11]

The children of the Chesapeake were taught this stoic fatalism at an early age. William Fitzhugh in 1698 wrote to his mother, "Before I was ten years old . . . I look'd upon this life here as but going to an inn, no permanent being by God's will . . . therefore always prepared for my certain dissolution, which I can't be persuaded to prolong by a wish." The death of one's children, he wrote, could be "cheerfully and easily borne" if one cultivated the proper attitude of resignation.[12]

Here was a way of thinking about mortality that was far removed from the cultivated death-obsessions of Calvinist New England. The Virginia attitude of stoic fatalism rested upon a belief that people were not personally responsible for their misfortunes, and that they must accept what fate might bring. That brave defense, alas, did not always work for them. In 1720, Robert Carter wrote to a friend after losing his wife, " . . . after we have preached up all the lessons of resignation we are masters of, so long as we carry flesh and blood about us . . . all our philoso-

[10]Edward Holt to John Newdigate, 21 Jan. 1621, Newdigate Papers, CR 136/B224, WARRO.

[11]Lewis, *The Pursuit of Happiness,* 72.

[12]William Fitzhugh to Mrs. Mary Fitzhugh, 30 June 1698, Davis, ed., *Fitzhugh Letters,* 261.

phy will sometimes recoil and give ground under such severe trials. I remain a mourner to this day."[13]

❧ Virginia Religious Ways: The Anglican Devotional-Liturgical Style

In a world that was haunted by death, religion became urgently important to the Virginians—more urgent then their worldly business, and more important than many secular historians have believed. When Sir William Berkeley sat down to write his will, for example, his first thought was not for his material wealth, but his spiritual estate:

> First, I desire God, who gave it, to take my soul into his mercy; and that, for the only merits and mercies of my *blessed Saviour Christ Jesus*. My body I give to the earth, from whence it came.[1]

This concern was typical of its time and place. Another example was the will of Colonel John Stringer, which began with an elaborate declaration of faith. He wrote:

> I bequeath my soul to God, who first gave it to me, Father, Son and Spirit in Unity and Trinity, and Trinity and Unity, who hath redeemed and preserved me by and through Jesus Christ, and also died for my sins, and for the sins of all peoples that truly believe in Him by unfeigned faith and repentance, for whose sake and loving kindness I hope to entertain everlasting life, wherefore, Dear Father, have mercy upon my soul.[2]

The spontaneity of this devotional creed revealed the depth of feeling that lay behind it.

Other wills testified not only to the religion of their makers, but also to their concern for its continuing support. In Surry County, for example, George Jordan insisted that his kin could inherit his estate only if they paid for a sermon to be preached every year in memory of his dead daughter. He also required that Holy Communion should be celebrated if the day fell on Sunday, and that all the neighborhood should be given food and drink. He demanded that this ritual should continue every year until the

[13]Wright, *Letters of Robert Carter*, 18; Smith, *Inside the Big House*, 267.
[1]Hening, *Statutes at Large*, I, 559.
[2]Bruce, *Institutional History of Virginia*, I, 19.

"destruction of the world," and that any owner who failed to honor it should lose the estate, "though it be a thousand generations hence."[3]

Still more striking were the many wills in which Virginians provided for the religious education of their children, often at great trouble and expense. Historian Philip Bruce has published large numbers of these provisions, which show the breadth of Christian belief in Virginia during the seventeenth century.[4]

Virginia wills sometimes expressed their religious feeling in unpuritanical ways. An eminent gentleman of Westmoreland County, Colonel Richard Cole, ordered that the following words should be engraved upon his tombstone:

> Here lies Dick Cole, a grievous sinner,
> That died a little before dinner,
> Yet hoped in Heaven to find a place
> To satiate his soul with grace.[5]

Even these light-hearted words tell us that religion was important to the cavaliers of Virginia, as it had been to the Puritans of Massachusetts; but it was important in a different way. Strong contrasts appeared in the vernacular religions of these colonies—that is, in ordinary rituals of common worship, and also in the individual exercise of faith.

The vernacular religion of Virginia was closely linked to its official Anglican creed, which had been imposed upon the colony partly by persuasion and partly by force. Private eccentricities were tolerated, but open dissenters were harassed and driven out. The leading architect of this policy was once again Sir William Berkeley. By the end of the seventeenth century, religious belief was remarkably uniform in Virginia. Robert Beverley wrote in 1705, "There are very few dissenters . . . they have not more than five conventicles amongst them, namely three small meetings of Quakers, and two of Presbyterians." Through the first century of Virginia's history, Anglican orthodoxy was strong—and growing stronger.[6]

Governor Berkeley also worked to support this orthodoxy by actively recruiting an Anglican clergy for Virginia. Before he took

[3] *Ibid.*, I, 20.
[4] *Ibid.*, I, 3–27, 293–315 *passim.*
[5] Bruce, *Institutional History of Virginia*, I, 21. This will was proved between 1665 and 1677.
[6] Beverley, *The History and Present State of Virginia*, 65.

office, a few of its ministers were thought to have a low-church
bias and even a tincture of Puritanism in their beliefs. Berkeley
recruited churchmen of a different cast, and urged them to "pray
oftener and preach less." The Royalist elite also tried to attract
what William Fitzhugh called "able, painfull and sober Pastors"
for the colony. This effort was successful. By the late seventeenth
century many of Virginia's clergy were able and pious men of
good family and education. Several were younger sons of noble
families; many were graduates of the more Royalist Oxford colleges, in particular Christ Church, Corpus Christi, Merton, Oriel
and Queens.[7]

Led by these men, the vernacular religion of Virginia reached
deeply into the lives of ordinary people. The Christian faith of
the Chesapeake planters was not the central purpose for the
founding of their colony, but many were men and women of deep
piety.[8] Henry Filmer called his plantation *Laus Deo,* and in 1672
left a large legacy to the parish of Mulberry Island for the purchase of communion silver. Bequests of that sort were very common in the colony.[9]

Family libraries gave special attention to Bibles, prayer books
and religious tracts of various kinds, which were very common in
Virginia households. In the library of Ralph Wormeley of Rosegill, as many as 123 of 391 works were religious or moral in their
nature—a smaller proportion than in New England, but large by
comparison with other times and places.[10]

One of the books in Ralph Wormeley's library was Richard
Allestree's *The Whole Duty of Man* (London, 1660), a devotional
work which was found more often in Virginia libraries than any
other book. Its ideal of quietism and practical piety contrasted
sharply with the restless striving of the New England Puritans.
Other favorites were Richard Allestree's *The Gentleman's Calling*
(1660), Jeremy Taylor's *The Rule and Exercises of Holy Living* and
Holy Dying (1650, 1651), Lewis Bayly's *Practice of Piety* (1613),
and Edward Synge's *A Gentleman's Religion* (1693).[11]

---

[7]William Fitzhugh to Capt. Roger Jones, 18 May 1685, Davis, ed., *Fitzhugh Letters,* 168; for
the origins of Virginia's clergy, which have been much misunderstood by historians, see Bruce,
Institutional History of Virginia, I, 194–207.

[8]Cf. Perry Miller, "Religion and Society in the Early Literature: The Religious Impulse in
the Founding of Virginia," *WMQ3* 6 (1949), 24–41.

[9]"A Release for the Parish of Mulberry Island in Virginia," 1672, Filmer ms., KAO.

[10]Bruce, *Institutional History of Virginia,* I, 25.

[11]George K. Smith, "Private Libraries in Colonial Virginia," *AL* 10 (1938), 24–52.

Bruton Church in Williamsburg is a classic example of Anglican architecture. The first building in this parish (ca. 1674) was a temporary wooden structure. The second (1681–83) was a small gabled brick building with five buttresses on a side. The third (1711) still stands, and claims to be the oldest church in continuous use in the southern colonies. It is in the shape of a long Latin cross, with the altar, rail and crucifix on the east wall, flanked by the pulpit and the governor's throne. The baptismal font is said to have been brought from the old church at Jamestown; George Washington stood as godfather to at least fourteen slaves who were baptized here. A gallery was added in 1715 for unruly students from the College of William and Mary. Their graffiti still appear in the gallery railing. This church was the scene of many funerals where the first gentlemen of Virginia were mourned in high pomp. In 1720, after Secretary Cocke suddenly fell dead at the Capital, "the principal gentlemen of the country attended the funeral, and weeping saw the corpse interred." For state funerals, the aisle, altar, pulpit and governor's throne were draped in black cloth. Bruton Parish was named for the town of Bruton, Somerset, the English home of Governor William Berkeley, Philip Ludwell and John Page.

In place of the Puritans' conversion journals and spiritual auto-biographies, Anglican gentlemen kept devotional diaries which placed heavy emphasis on rituals of prayer and acts of exemplary piety. They showed less concern about salvation than did the Puritans, but gave more attention to liturgy and devotion such as morning and evening prayers.[12]

The religious differences between Virginia and Massachusetts were visible in the physical setting of public worship. The Anglican ideal was a small parish church, solidly constructed on a cruciform plan, with an altar and cross at the eastern end of the building and a pulpit tucked into a corner. At least forty-nine pre-revolutionary churches still stand in Virginia, of which forty-three were built by Anglicans. In southern Maryland, twenty-eight survive, of which twenty-three were erected by the Church of England.[13]

The church architecture of Virginia was designed on the assumption that Christian worship was mainly a devotional act. Every part of the Anglican service had a liturgical quality which distinguished it from the "meeting and lecture" style of New England. The order of worship in morning and evening services, and also the administration of the sacraments, was strictly defined by the Book of Common Prayer. The exquisite cadences of this beautiful work celebrated moderation, proportion, refinement and restraint. Virginians commonly used an edition of the Book of Common Prayer which included the "Black Rubric" or "Declaration on Kneeling," which was specially disliked by the Puritans.

Sermons were a secondary part of Anglican worship, and in tone and substance they were also very different from Puritan preaching. Northern visitors observed that Virginia sermons were much shorter than in New England, less theological, more pietistic and "all in the forensic style." Philip Fithian was astonished to find that they were "seldom under and never over twenty minutes, but always made up of sound morality or deeply studied metaphysicks."

---

[12]An English example is John Newdigate's Commonplace Book, 1609, Ms. B 632C WARRO.

[13]Surviving examples of cruciform or T-shaped Virginia churches built before 1775 include Blandford Church, Petersburg; St. Paul's Church, Norfolk; St. John's Church, Hampton; St. John's Church, Richmond; Abingdon Church, Gloucester; Mattapony Church, King and Queen County; Vauter's Church, Essex County; St. John's Church, King William County; and Yeocomico Church, Westmoreland County; St. Paul's Church, King George County, and Aquia Church in Stafford County.

T Yeocomico Church (Westmoreland County, 1706), is the oldest surviving T-form church in Virginia. A leading member of the vestry
was Colonel William Ball, the grandfather of George Washington.
The northern tutor Philip Fithian often worshiped here in 1773–74. He heard
the parish clergyman Thomas Smith, a man of great wealth, preach on "the
uncertainty of riches and their insufficiency to make us happy." It was also at
Yeocomico that Fithian was "surprised when the psalm began to hear a large
collection of voices singing at the same time, from a Gallery, entirely contrary
to what I had seen before."

For all their brevity, these twenty-minute Anglican sermons had rhetorical structures of high complexity. They developed in fixed and regular stages from the opening *praecognito* to *partitio, explicatio, amplificatio, applicatio,* and *peroration.* The composition was cast in a belletristic style which made much use of tropes and flowers and figures of speech. The religion of the cavaliers celebrated the holiness of beauty as well as the beauty of holiness.[14]

Anglican church music was more important than in New England, and very different from that of the Puritans. Philip Fithian visited Yeocomico Church one morning and was amazed by the sound of a choir which he had never heard before. "I was surprised when the psalm began," he wrote, "to hear a large collection of voices singing at the same time, from a Gallery, entirely contrary to what I had seen before." It is not clear what most astonished this northern visitor—the existence of the choir itself, or the fact (surprising to a Calvinist) that they were all "singing at the same time." This was very different from the traditional rote singing in Puritan meetinghouses.[15] Bruton Parish Church also had an organ, and even a professional organist. Virginians enjoyed singing complex four-part hymns and anthems, and gave employment to as many as seven professional singing masters before 1711.[16]

On a Sunday in Anglican Virginia, these liturgical structures of common prayer, religious rhetoric and sacred harmony were joined to yet another set of secular rituals which preceded and followed the service itself. At Christ Church, Lancaster County, Virginia, built by the great planter Robert "King" Carter, the act of worship began with a grand entrance by the patriarch himself. "On the sabbath," writes historian Louis Morton, "no member of the congregation dared to enter Christ Church until Carter's carriage, drawn by six lively horses, drew up before its entrance. 'King' Carter would then alight and enter the place of worship, the others following respectfully. After he had taken his seat, the service would start."[17]

This beautiful church still stands today, a fitting symbol of the style of worship that inspired it. The plan of the church is a per-

---

[14]Fithian, *Journal and Letters,* 38 (13 Dec. 1773); 220 (12 Aug. 1774).

[15]*Ibid.,* 256 (25 Sept. 1774).

[16]Robert Stevenson, *Protestant Church Music in America,* (New York, 1966), 54; Norman A. Benson, "The Itinerant Music Masters of Eighteenth Century America" (thesis, Univ. of Minnesota, 1963); Wright and Tinling, eds., *Secret Diary of William Byrd,* 272, 276, 292.

[17]Morton, *Robert Carter of Nomini Hall,* 20–21.

✚ *Christ Church (Lancaster County, 1732–35), with its elegant swag roof and opulent detail, is built in the shape of a symmetrical Greek cross, 68 feet on each side. The walls are three feet thick, and the round window arches are of rubbed brick with masonry keystones. Its construction was paid for by the first gentleman of the parish, Robert "King" Carter of Corotoman (d. 1732). A special road, bordered with cedar trees, ran three miles from Corotoman Plantation directly to the churchyard. Every Sunday the congregation waited outside the church until "King" Carter arrived in his six-horse coach, entered the large front door and walked to his large pew which was decorated with damask curtains on heavy brass rods. The entire north transept was reserved for Carter servants and tenants. Many generations of Carters headed the vestry list of this parish from as early as 1654. Outside the church are the large sarcophagi of "King" Carter himself and his wives, embellished with the Carter arms and Latin epitaphs, to which one disgruntled parishioner added a chalk inscription:*

> *Here lies Robin, but not Robin Hood*
> *Here lies Robin that was never good*

fect Greek cross sixty-eight feet on a side, with massive walls three feet thick, a pilastered entrance, oval windows, and an elegant swag roof. The interior still contains the original walnut table, a marble font, a handsome wineglass pulpit and other trappings of Anglican ritual.

Every Sunday the congregation of Christ Church joined in its devotions before that magnificent table, and heard a short sermon from the pulpit. After the formal service was over, the Sunday ritual continued in the churchyard. "Over three-quarters of an hour spent strolling round the Church among the Crowd," Fithian noted in his journal, "in which time you will be invited by several different gentlemen home with them to dinner."[18] Altogether, Philip Fithian concluded, "a Sunday in Virginia don't seem to wear the same dress as our Sundays to the northward."[19]

❧ Virginia Magic Ways:
The Cavalier Obsession with Fortune

In most seventeenth-century cultures, religion was closely linked to what the modern world calls magic. Virginians were deeply interested in magic—even obsessed by it. But the quality of their obsession was not the same as in Massachusetts. In the Chesapeake colonies, there as nothing like the Puritans' concern with witchcraft. No person was ever executed in Virginia for that offense.[1] Instead, the courts actively punished false accusations of witchcraft, often assessing heavy fines and costs against those who denounced their neighbors as minions of the Devil. Many denunciations were indeed brought forward by people of low estate, particularly during the decade of the 1650s which was a painful and uncertain period in the colony. But Virginia's ruling elite had little sympathy for witchcraft prosecutions, and actively discouraged them in a manner very different from the ministers and magistrates of Massachusetts.[2]

---

[18]Fithian, *Journal and Letters,* 38 (13 Dec. 1773); 220 (12 Aug. 1774).

[19]*Ibid.,* 10 July 1774.

[1]In 1659, an "old woman" named Katharine Grady was accused of witchcraft and summarily hanged from a yardarm on board an immigrant ship bound for Virginia. The authorities in the colony, far from approving the action, hauled the captain into court to answer for the affair. Bruce, *Institutional History of Virginia,* I, 280–81.

[2]Judicial punishment for witchcraft was not unknown in Virginia. In 1655, a case appeared

This distaste for witchcraft persecutions had also appeared among the Royalist gentry of southern England. As early as 1653, Sir Robert Filmer published a polemic against capital punishment for witchcraft. He argued that the biblical injunction, "thou shalt not suffer a witch to live," had no jurisdiction in England but applied only to Jewish witches. The Manichean conception of the world which so haunted the Puritans had comparatively little part in Filmer's thinking, or in that of Virginia's gentry.[3]

At the same time, however, Virginians were much interested in other forms of magic which had comparatively little meaning (or a different meaning) for the people of New England. The gentlemen of Virginia were deeply absorbed in the study of stars, planets, spheres, and portents—not as signs of God's purpose but as clues to their own fate. They believed that every man possessed a certain fixed quality called fortune, which could be understood by knowledge of these things. This idea had been widely accepted in Elizabethan England.[4]

Many gentlemen kept "fortune books," which were collections of magical and astrological lore for good luck in love, marriage, sex, health, travel. One such fortune book included an entire chapter on marriage with entries on "whether a man shall marry, the time of marriage, how many husbands a woman shall have, who shall be master of the two, how they shall agree after marriage, and whether the man or his wife shall die first, and the time when."[5]

This cult of *fortuna* implied that life was a game of chance in which the odds were rigged by mysterious powers in the universe.

---

in the prosecution of William Harding of Northumberland County, by a clergyman recently arrived from Scotland. Harding was found guilty of sorcery by a jury and sentenced to banishment. Bruce concludes that "whilst accusations of witchcraft brought into court for investigation were numerous enough, there seems to have been little disposition on the part of justices or juries to affirm them by a favorable judgment or verdict." Many defamation suits, however, were brought successfully by people denounced for witchcraft. For a review of the evidence, see Bruce, *Institutional History of Virginia*, I, 276–89.

[3]Robert Filmer, *An Advertisement to the Jurymen of England, Touching Witches; Together with a Difference betywen an English and a Hebrew Witch* (Royston, 1653); see also H[enry] F[ilmer], *A Prodigious and Tragicall History of the Arraignment, Tryall . . . of Six Witches at Maidstone* (1652). Similar attitudes appear in gentlemen-justices who sat on the Somerset bench. See T.G. Barnes, ed., "Somerset Assize Orders, 1629–1640," *SOMERSRS* 65 (1959), 28.

[4]David Woodman, *White Magic and English Renaissance Drama* (Rutherford, N.J., 1973).

[5]An example of an English gentleman's "fortune book" is the Henry Sturmy Fortune Book (1646), Ms. D 2375, GLOCRO; see also William Gregory, "Speculum Navitates," Gainsborough Collection ms. 1655, LAO. Many other examples of this genre are to be found in English archives and country houses.

A Devon gentleman named Samuel Watts noted in his common-place book:

> Love is a play at table where the dye
> Of maides affection doth by fancy fly
> If that you take her fancy at a blot
> Tis ten to one, if straight you enter not[6]

Another example was the English autobiography of John Holden (1691–1730), a fascinating chronicle in which entries for each year culminated in an anniversary verse that testified to the sway of fortune over individual life:

> Something presents itself in ev'ry year
> That puts so often between hope and fear;
> Makes so uneasy in a doubtful state
> To know how fortune will decree or fate. . . .

> Great things were moved this septinary year
> Tho' little but the fruits of love appear
> Yet time may soon produce some great event
> That nothing but ill fortune can prevent.[7]

This interest in fortune was linked to another striking characteristic of Virginians—their obsession with gambling. Virginians were observed to be constantly making wagers with one another on almost any imaginable outcome. The more uncertain the result, the more likely they were to gamble. They made bets not merely on horses, cards, cockfights and backgammon; but also on crops, prices, women and the weather. "They are all professional gamesters . . . ," a French traveler observed of Virginia's gentry, "Colonel Byrd is never happy but when he has the box and dice in his hand."[8]

Gambling had many meanings in the lives of Virginia planters. Historians have demonstrated that it was an expression of social status and a form of social bonding. But it was also something else. The cabalistic patterns that the dice made as they tumbled out of the box represented something more than merely an idle amusement, and something other than a form of status-striving. A gentleman's dice were like the soothsayer's bones from which they had descended—a clue to the cosmos, and a token of each

---

[6]Samuel Watts Commonplace Book, 1610, Watts mss., SOMERO.
[7]John Holden, Autobiography, 1694, Ms. D 1371, GLOCRO.
[8]"Journal of a French Traveler in the Colonies: 1765," *AHR* 26 (1920–21), 746.

individual's place within it. If the Puritans searched desperately for signs of God's redeeming providence in the world, the Virginians sought another sort of assurance about *fortuna* in their incessant gambling.

In Massachusetts gambling was strictly forbidden by law, and severely punished by the magistrates. It was condemned by Puritan moralists as not merely idleness but blasphemy. To John Cotton and Cotton Mather, gambling made a mockery of God's presence in the world. The attitudes of Virginians were very different. Gambling was formally recognized and regulated by law. Betting was prohibited to those with "no visible estate, profession or calling to maintain themselves." Courts enforced wagers as a form of contract, and required that gambling debts should be faithfully paid. Fraudulent gaming was ferociously punished, and the highest powers in the colony were invoked to secure honest games. This common law of wagering was an indication that gambling was more than merely a game in Virginia. It was a way of testing one's *fortuna*.[9]

These attitudes were not invented in the New World. They had long existed among the gentry of the south and west of England, with whom gambling was also an obsession. The diary of the Dorset gentleman John Richards was also a betting book which became a running record of many small wagers with friends and acquaintances. Richards often set down the results of bets in which he had no personal stake, by other gentlemen who engaged compulsively in heavy and even ruinous wagers. He was as much interested in the *fortuna* of others as of himself.[10]

Virginians of all ranks also showed still another interest in magic. On their house, they carved signs which were thought to bring the occupants good fortune. Some of these signs were very old—older than the sign of the cross. They had long appeared on buildings in the south and west of England, from whence so many Virginians came. These signs might be thought of as a sort of liturgy—that is, a ritual which was thought to be a way of propitiating the powers of fortune.[11]

---

[9]Timothy Breen, "Horses and Gentlemen: The Cultural Significance of Gambling Among the Gentry of Virginia," *Puritans and Adventurers* (New York, 1980), 148–63.

[10]John Richards Diary II, 24 Jan. 1697; 11 Feb., 24 March 1699, DORSRO; on white magic in England, see Keith Thomas, *Religion and the Decline of Magic* (New York, 1971); Katherine M. Briggs, *The Anatomy of Puck* (London, 1959); Charles Grant Loomis, *White Magic* (Cambridge, 1948).

[11]Henry C. Forman, *The Architecture of the Old South: The Medieval Style, 1585–1850* (Cambridge, 1948), 76.

The magic of the Virginians was closely linked to their vernacular religion. To a modern mind these spheres of thought seem opposed, but in the seventeenth century they tended to blur into one another. In respect to both magic and religion, the beliefs of the Virginians tended to be less Manichean than did those of New Englanders. They were also less instrumental. The prevailing cosmology of the Chesapeake colony minimized man's responsibility for his fate. The idea of fortune lay very near the heart of this culture.

✎ Virginia Learning Ways:
Anglican Traditions of Hierarchical Learning

Virginia's folkways also appeared in its patterns of learning and literacy. In the year 1643, for example, an illiterate farmer named Robert Lawson lay dying in his home on Virginia's eastern shore. He had a substantial property but no family, and in his last hours the neighbors gathered around his deathbed. After a few perfunctory inquiries about his health, they began to ask pointed questions about his property.

"If thou dyest, who shall have thy cow," one neighbor asked bluntly.

"George," whispered the dying man.

"George Smith?" the neighbor persisted.

"Yea," he answered.

"Who shall have your Bulchin?"

"George Smith."

"Who shall have your sow—shall George Smith have it?

"Yea," came the reply.

"Who shall have your match coat?"

"Robert West is a knave," the dying man inexplicably answered. Then he turned from his questioners and "did most fearfully rattle in the throat" and passed away.

The neighbors were much concerned about the disposition of his estate. "This will by word of mouth . . . is worth nothing," one of them observed, "the king will have all because there was no literate fellow to the making of it."

Their fears proved to be well founded. Two shady characters called Mr. Thomas Parks and Robert West suddenly appeared in court with a sealed paper which they represented to be Robert Lawson's will. The document was written in Thomas Parks' hand

and signed by mark. It left everything to Robert West, except a few choice items that went to Parks.

The neighbors were outraged. They swore up and down that this document was false, and the very opposite of Robert Lawson's intention. But they failed to convince the court, because there had been "no literate fellow" among them who could provide written proof. The court accepted the document of "Mr. Parks," who had the rank if not the character of a gentleman.[1]

This episode reveals an important truth about Virginia. It tells us that literacy was an instrument of wealth and power in this colony, and that many were poor and powerless in that respect.

The proportion of adults who could read and write in Virginia was significantly lower than in Massachusetts. In the seventeenth century, most adult Virginians (white and black, male and female altogether) were unable to sign their own names. Disparities by wealth, race, class and gender were very great. Among Virginia's gentry, literacy approached 100 percent. But of male property holders in general, about 50 percent were able to write. Among tenants and laborers that proportion fell to about 40 percent. Even the minority who could spell their own names often did so in a clumsy and trembling script which suggested that writing was an alien act.[2] Indentured servants in the Chesapeake had even

---

[1]Ames, ed., *County Court Records of Accomack-Northampton*, 307, 311, 320, 350, 382, 287, 407 (1643).

[2]The most comprehensive quantitative study is still that of Philip Bruce, who obtained the following results from wills and depositions:

		Proportion Signing by Mark		
		Total Population		Women Only
County	Period	Deeds	Depositions	All Documents
Lower Norfolk	1646–98	48.4	51.8	80.3
Isle of Wight	1643–1700	45.3	53.7	89.4
Surry	1652–84	48.8	63.2	83.0
Henrico	1677–97	50.7	63.3	67.1
Elizabeth City	1693–99	32.3	66.7	64.4
York	1657–1700	44.9	63.5	75.1
Middlesex	1673–1700	34.6	n.a.	66.6
Essex	1692–99	46.7	53.8	84.1
Lancaster	1652–97	32.3	37.9	56.3
Rappahannock	1654–99	49.3	n.a.	77.8
Northumberland	1652–77	47.6	52.4	83.0
Westmoreland	1653–77	36.6	68.4	67.3
Northampton	1647–98	38.2	53.3	68.5
Accomac	1641–97	49.3	61.7	73.7
All Counties	1641–1700	45.3	57.6	75.3

The sample was 13,135 for deeds; 2,376 for depositions; and 3,066 women; computed from data in Bruce, *Institutional History of Virginia*, I, 458.

lower rates of literacy; only about 25 to 30 percent were able to sign their names in the seventeenth century.[3] And of African slaves, less than 1 percent were literate in the seventeenth and early eighteenth century. These disparities were larger than in New England.[4]

Large differences in literacy also existed between men and women. Before 1641–1700, less than 25 percent of women could sign their names on legal documents. Even women of the highest rank in Virginia were unable to write their names. The wives of Colonel John Washington, Colonel George Mason and Colonel John Ashton all signed by mark. More women could read than write in Virginia—a condition of passive literacy which was the common lot of females in the seventeenth century.[5]

Altogether, the pattern of literacy in seventeenth century Virginia differed from that of Massachusetts in many ways, but it was similar to those parts of rural England from whence the colonists came. It is interesting to note that the incidence of literacy in the rural south and west of England was markedly lower than in East Anglia.[6]

---

[3]Galenson, *White Servitude in Colonial America*, ch. 5. Literacy of servants tended to be higher in East Anglia, and during the 18th century increased markedly.

[4]Advertisements for runaway slaves in Virginia during the mid-18th century reported that less than one in a hundred were able to read and write. That proportion rose a little from 1750 to 1790, but remained at very low levels—much below rates of literacy among slaves in northern colonies. Literacy rates among 678 runaway slaves (according to published descriptions by their masters) was as follows:

Period	Able to Read	Able to Write	Able to Read and Write	Total	N	%
1750–59	0	0	1	1	135	0.7
1770–79	0	0	4	4	253	1.6
1790–99	5	4	5	14	189	7.4

Compiled by Donna Bouvier, Susan M. Irwin, Marc Orlofsky and the author from fugitive slave advertisments in the holdings of the *Virginia Gazette*.

[5]The Rutmans' study of literacy in Middlesex County, Virginia, yields estimates of literacy by gender and father's status through time:

Literacy by Gender, Status and Period of Maturity

Status of Father	1650–1699		1700–1719		1720–1744	
	m	f	m	f	m	f
High	100.0	100.0	100.0	100.0	100.0	100.0
High Middle	87.5	80.0	100.0	100.0	100.0	83.3
Middle	80.0	17.8	81.4	17.9	78.7	17.8
Lower Middle	44.4	20.0	66.7	20.0	95.7	20.0
Low	50.0	5.3	47.5	0.0	45.8	14.3

Source: Rutman and Rutman, *A Place in Time, Explicatus,* 169

[6]David Cressy, *Literacy and the Social Order; Reading and Writing in Tudor and Stuart England* (Cambridge, 1980), 73–74.

During the eighteenth century, literacy rapidly increased on both sides of the Atlantic. As it did so, differences between people of high and low status tended to diminish in New England and Britain. But in Virginia the opposite was the case. Disparities in literacy between rich and poor actually grew greater. Here was yet another system of inequality in the cultural life of the colony.[7]

As it was with literacy, so also with learning. There was a striking paradox in attitudes toward schools and schooling in Virginia. The elite was deeply interested in the education of gentlemen. "Better be never born than ill-bred," wrote William Fitzhugh in 1687. By "ill-bred" in that passage, he meant "unschooled."[8]

At the same time, visitors and natives both agreed that schools were few and far between, that ignorance was widespread, and that formal education did not flourish in the Chesapeake. This condition was not an accident. It was deliberately contrived by Virginia's elite, who positively feared learning among the general population. The classic expression of this attitude came from Governor William Berkeley himself. When asked in 1671 by the Lords of Trade about the state of schools in Virginia, he made a famous reply: "I thank God," he declared, "there are no free schools nor printing, and I hope we shall not have these [for a] hundred years; for learning has brought disobedience, and heresy, and sects into the world, and printing has divulged them, and libels against the best government. God keep us from both!"[9]

This remark has earned Governor Berkeley a place of infamy in the history of education. But it was not merely the isolated absurdity of an eccentric reactionary. Precisely the same policy was adopted by Berkeley's kinsman and successor, Lord Culpeper, who actively suppressed printing in the colony. When John Buckner set up a press, he was "prohibited by the governor and council from printing any thing, till the King's pleasure should be known." An historian observes that the King's pleasure was "very tardily communicated, as the first evidence of printing thereafter in Virginia was . . . 1733."[10]

Berkeley and Culpeper were not unique. Many English Royalists were of the same mind in the seventeenth century. William Cavendish wrote to Charles II in the 1650s, "The Bible in English under every weaver and chambermaid's arm hath done us much

[7]Kenneth Lockridge, *Literacy in Colonial New England* (New York, 1974), 73–87.
[8]William Fitzhugh to Nicholas Hayward, 30 Jan. 1687, Davis, ed., *Fitzhugh Letters*, 203.
[9]Hening, *Statutes at Large*, II 517.
[10]*Ibid.*, II, 518.

hurt."[11] This fear of learning in the general "populace" was shared even by gentlemen who are remembered for their devotion to scholarship. Francis Bacon wrote to James I in 1611 that England was in danger of educational "excess," at a time when three-quarters of adult men and women were illiterate. Bacon feared that if schools were expanded, "Many persons will be bred unfit for other vocations and unprofitable for that in which they are brought up, which fills the realm full of indigent, idle and wanton people." This attitude was carried to Virginia by "distressed Royalists" in the mid-seventeenth century, and became a persistent part of Chesapeake culture for many generations.[12]

These hierarchical attitudes toward learning also appeared in the distribution of books in Virginia. The libraries of great planters William Byrd and Robert Carter were among the best in British America, superior to the holdings of most colleges in the northern colonies. But the yeomanry of Virginia owned few books, and servants nearly none. Slaves were forbidden to read at all, on pain of savage punishment. The penalty for a slave who tried to learn how to write was to have a finger amputated. The riches of great plantation libraries made a dramatic contrast with the inaccessibility of books for ordinary people.[13]

The same duality also appeared in regard to schooling. Virginia gentlemen cultivated the arts, sciences and education among themselves, but did not encourage schools for the general population. They hired private tutors for their own youngsters, sponsored schools of high quality for children of the elite, founded the College of William and Mary at Williamsburg, and sent their sons to Oxford.[14] Altogether, the proportion of planters' sons who were sent to college in England and America was similar to that of the gentry of southern England. But these same county oligarchies were largely responsible for the miserable condition of parish schools throughout Virginia, and for the long absence of printing in the colony.[15]

---

[11]Cressy, *Literacy and the Social Order,* 45.

[12]*Ibid.,* 187.

[13]John R. Barden, "Reflections of a Singular Mind: The Library of Robert Carter of Nominy Hall," *VMHB* 96 (1988), 83–94.

[14]As early as 1658 John Lee of Virginia presented to The Queen's College a silver cup which bears the piquant inscription, "Coll. Regi. Oxon. D.D. Johanes Lee Natus in Capohowasick Wickacomoco in Virginia Americae, Filius Primogenitus Richardi Lee Chiliarchae Orundi de Morton [orig. Coton?] Regis in Agro Salopiensi 1658." This branch of the Lee family came from Coton in Shropshire; the error was probably made in re-engraving.

[15]A survey of education among the gentry of Warwickshire by Ann Hughes finds that roughly

It might be noted that Virginia learning ways were not the product of slavery, or of rural poverty. They were fully developed before slaves appeared in large numbers, and when that colony was one of the richest in British America. They were rooted in a culture which came out of England in the seventeenth century, and persisted in the southern states for three hundred years.[16]

∾ Virginia Food Ways: Origins of Southern Cooking

Also carried out from England was the material structure of this culture—that is, its methods of managing physical things. A case in point was its food ways. As early as the mid-seventeenth century, the dietary habits of the Virginians were distinctly different from those of New Englanders, particularly in what might be called the sociology of food. From the start, Virginia's culinary customs were more highly stratified than in the Puritan colonies.

Prosperous planters kept the same food ways as did the gentry of southwestern England. Both of these elites consumed red meat in large quantity. Roast beef was so closely identified with English *milords* that in Italy and Spain it was called *rosbif.* Gentlemen of Virginia also had a taste for game, and particularly for animals of the chase. William Byrd paid others to supply his table with venison, blue-winged teal, pigeon and partridge. But even the succulent shellfish and waterfowl of the Chesapeake were not esteemed as highly as the roast beef of old England. Byrd complained of having to eat oysters and geese too often when away from his own table.

Rich planters also consumed large quantities of fresh vegetables and fruits throughout the year. Again, their favorites were very English. Byrd ate asparagus and strawberries every day when he could get them. But native American plants such as potatoes and tomatoes rarely appeared on the best colonial tables until they had become fashionable in the mother country. Culinary

---

18% had some university training, mostly at Oxford. Another 13% had attended the Inns of Court; two-thirds had no higher education. Ann Hughes, *Politics, Society and Civil War in Warwickshire, 1620–1660* (Cambridge, 1987), 44.

[16]Particularly valuable for the history of education in this region are the "Memoirs of the Birth, Education, Life and Death of Mr. John Cannon" (1684–1742), a sometime excise officer and school keeper in the West Country. The manuscript is in the Somerset Record Office, Taunton.

tastes of gentlefolk in Virginia remained English in all of these ways.[1]

Colonists of humble rank commonly ate a one-dish meal, which was called a "mess" in the old English sense of a "dish of food."[2] It often consisted of greens and salt meat, seasoned with wild herbs. Another staple was hominy or the corn porridge called mush in the south, served in a common bowl or cup. The diet of ordinary Virginians in the seventeenth century was similar to black "soul food" in the twentieth. With the addition of Indian corn it was much like the diet of farm workers in the south and west of England.[3]

Among both high-born and humble folk, eating was a more sensual experience in Virginia than in Massachusetts. There was nothing in the Chesapeake colonies to equal the relentless austerity of New England's "canonical dish" of cold baked beans. Poor whites improved their simple food with high seasonings and delicate flavors. Slaves supplemented their basic rations of corn and salt fish with American and African foodstuffs that added spice and variety to their meals. Great planters carefully cultivated the only true *haute cuisine* in British America before the nineteenth century. William Byrd took a special interest in imaginative and highly seasoned dishes. His diary recorded memorable meals of stewed swan, spiced udder and roast snipe.[4] These elaborate dishes were similar to others recorded in cookery books of country houses throughout the south and west of England.[5]

If baked beans were the canonical dish of Massachusetts, a special favorite among middling and upper ranks in Virginia was the

---

[1]In William Byrd's diary, 43 references to meat appeared within a period of three months, from 1 Dec. 1709 to 1 March 1710. Beef was mentioned twenty-four times, pork five times, mutton three times, fish, goose, turkey and chicken twice each, and venison, pigeon and duck once each; in other periods Byrd abstained from meat. Main, *Tobacco Colony*, 209.

[2]*OED, s.v.* "mess," I.1, a "prepared dish. . . ." In England, this usage was identified as "now only *archaic*" as early as the 19th century, but it continued in the American south until the 20th century and is still current in black culture throughout the United States, as a "mess of greens."

[3]Main, *Tobacco Colony*, 220–21; for English diet in the records of Berkshire farmers, see G. E. Fussell, ed., "Robert Loder's Farm Accounts, 1610–1620," *CS* 3d series 53 (1936), passim; Cicely A. H. Howell, "The Social Condition of the Peasantry in South East Leicestershire, AD 1300–1700" (thesis, Univ. of Leicester, 1974), 193.

[4]Byrd, *London Diary and Other Writings*, 462, 248, *passim.*

[5]Many English cookery books survive in ms. from the 17th century, both in country houses and county record offices. One of them, from a Berkshire household circa 1650, included recipes for artichoke pie, almond pudding, roast pullet stuffed with oysters, buttered lobster, boiled carp in blood, potted lamprey, marinated cherries, hartshorn jelly, blow pudding ("the lights and heart of a hog") carrot pudding, gooseberry fool, blanc mange, marrow pudding and many fricassees. See "Book of Cookery. . .," ms. D/ED F37, BERKRO.

"frigacy" or "fricassee." One English recipe called for chicken, veal, or rabbit to be simmered in an open pan, with "a good handful of sweet herbs as of marjoram, a little thyme, savory or sprig of penny royal." Sometimes a pint of claret was added, and a pint of oysters, and a dozen egg yolks. William Byrd often ordered a fricassee of chicken, veal or game for his dinner. Virginia cooks had broad repertory of these dishes. There were brown fricassees of beef or venison, white fricassees for "small fowls, rabbits, lamb, veal and other white meats," and clear fricassees of calves' feet or cod sounds.[6]

Byrd also enjoyed fried chicken, often cooked with bacon or ham—a dish different from fricassees, which tended to be simmered in the pan rather than fried. As early as the first decade of the eighteenth century, fried chicken had become a distinct regional favorite in Virginia. Later in the eighteenth and early nineteenth century, some Virginia cookery books dismissed fried chicken as a vulgar dish. But that view was not shared by the Byrds and Carters, who tucked into their fried chicken with high enthusiasm.[7]

This style of Virginia cooking became the basis of a distinctive regional food way in America—highly seasoned, with much roasting, simmering and frying. It was very similar to the regional cuisine of southern and western England, where frying, simmering and sautéing in a skillet were methods of preparation called "Dorset fashion" or "Dorset cooked."[8]

In the twentieth century, quantitative surveys of regional cooking in England have found that frying, roasting and grilling continue to be specially characteristic of the south and west of England, as baking is of East Anglia and boiling of the North. The same survey also reported that a taste for spicy food was more developed in the south and west than elsewhere in England. Merchants in the early twentieth century stocked more salty bacon, pungent cheese and peppery sausage in the south and west than elsewhere in Britain.[9] In both southwestern England and the Chesapeake colonies, methods of cooking varied by social rank.

[6]Jane Carson, *Colonial Virginia Cookery; Procedures, Equipment, and Ingredients in Colonial Cooking* (Williamsburg, 1985), 98–99.

[7]"Book of Cookery Hints," D/ED/F37 BERKRO; Wright and Tinling, *Secret Diary of William Byrd*, 487, 514 (18 Feb., 14 April 1712).

[8]Dorothy Hartley, *Food in England* (London, 1954) 174.

[9]David Ellerton Allen, *British Tastes: An Inquiry into the Likes and Dislikes of the Regional Consumer* (London, 1968), 75, 34.

One study finds that virtually every household had kettles for boiling and pans for frying. But very poor families tended not to have roasting equipment such as spits, which were commonplace in households of higher rank. Most middling and upper families practiced a great variety of cooking methods. Boiling, stewing, frying, braising, grilling, broiling and roasting were all highly developed in Virginia.[10]

But another form of cooking tended to lag behind. Baking, which was central to New England cuisine, developed very slowly in the Chesapeake. One historian of cooking in Virginia writes that "a built-in brick oven for baking breads and cakes, apparently came late to Virginia kitchens; certainly most of the surviving ones date from the eighteenth century." Outdoor ovens appeared at an early date, as did cast-iron Dutch ovens. A good deal of open baking was also done directly on the hearth. But baking in general had a less prominent place in Virginia cooking than in Massachusetts. Here again the differences between the Chesapeake and New England were similar to those between Wessex and East Anglia.[11]

Customs of eating, as well as cooking, also differed by region in British America. Virginians dined; New Englanders merely ate. "Dining was a fine art in Virginia," writes historian Edmund Morgan. In households of even middling rank, meals were highly developed rituals. The major repast of the day was served at two or three o'clock in the afternoon, in a dining room that was one of the most important spaces in the house. Chesapeake epicure Frederick Stieff writes, ". . . in all my Maryland meanderings, I have yet to see an unimportant dining room in an important Maryland manor."[12]

Men and women in prosperous households were expected to primp for dinner—to dress their hair, to change their clothing

---

[10]Horn, "Social and Economic Aspects of Local Society in England and the Chesapeake," 183, 185, 205, reports the following frequencies of roasting equipment (spits), by total wealth of inventoried estates, in the late 17th century:

Total Wealth	Gloucestershire	Maryland	Virginia
less than £10	29.7%	6.7%	0.0%
£10–£49	63.2	24.6	34.8
£50–£99	73.8	44.9	68.3
£100–£249	77.5	73.1	78.9
£250 and up	81.1	77.6	91.7

[11]Carson, *Colonial Virginia Cookery,* 11.

[12]Frederick P. Stieff, *Eat, Drink and Be Merry in Maryland* (New York, 1932), xiv.

and generally to make a pleasing appearance. The table and side-board in a great house were set with a great display of silver, all engraved with the family arms. Even small farmers proudly put out a piece or two of plate, investing their hard-won tobacco profits not in agricalatural improvements, but in this form of consumption. Even very poor families in Virginia had tablecloths in their inventories, as did English families in Gloucestershire. In prosperous houses, an abundance of food was set upon the table, and Virginians cultivated the art of conversation in which all adults were expected to join. When Philip Fithian, the Princeton tutor at Nomini Hall, once neglected to appear for dinner, he was chastised by his employer for his churlishness. He wrote in his journal:

> I took a whim in my head and would not go to dinner. My head was not dressed, and I was too lazy to change my clothes. Mrs. Carter, however, in the evening lashed me severely. I told her I was engaged in reading a pleasant novel, that I was not perfectly well. But she would not hear none [sic], and said I was rude, and censurable.[13]

This ritual of dining has persisted for three centuries in the country houses of England and the Chesapeake—even to our own time. A pleasant conversation was thought to be an indispensable part of a social existence. A gentleman of Virginia who somehow survived into the twentieth century put it this way:

> Salt yo' food, suh, with humor . . . season it with wit, and sprinkle it all over with the charm of good-fellowship, but never poison it with the cares of life. It is an insult to yo' digestion, besides bein' suh, a mark of bad breedin'.[14]

Southern food ways were also special in another way. Feasting was an important part of the culture of Virginia—more so than in Massachusetts. The people of New England did a good deal of heavy eating and drinking from time to time, particularly after the death of a neighbor or townsman. But feasts in Virginia happened very frequently—at weddings and christenings, at Christmas and Easter, the return of a family member or the visit of an interesting stranger—and they were very much more festive.

A Virginia feast could be staged on short notice, or no notice

[13]Fithian, *Journal and Letters,* 15 June 1774.
[14]F. Hopkinson Smith, *Col. Carter of Cartersville;* Stieff, *Eat, Drink and Be Merry in Maryland,* 181.

at all. A French traveler in the seventeenth century was present at one impromptu occasion in the year 1686, when twenty mounted cavaliers suddenly descended on William Fitzhugh's plantation, and a feast was instantly improvised for them: "We rode twenty strong to Colonel Fichous [Fitzhugh's]," he wrote, "but he has such a large establishment that he did not mind. We were all of us provided with beds, one for two men. He treated us royally, there was good wine and all kinds of beverages, so that there was a great deal of carousing. He had sent for three fiddlers, a jester and a tight-rope dancer, an acrobat who tumbled around, and they gave us all the entertainment one could wish."[15]

These feasts occurred among both rich and poor—sometimes rich and poor together. A funeral feast would bring together everyone in the neighborhood. "Planters drank to the memory of the poorest man," Gloria Main writes, "when his estate could foot the bill."[16] Slaves were allowed special feast days after Easter and Christmas. Easter Monday was a day of wild celebration in black communities, a custom that continued for two centuries, even into the Chesapeake childhood of this historian. These customs of feasting had long been traditional in the south and west of England, even among families of modest means. On harvest homes and holy days, the usual fare of bread, soup, lard and garden greens yielded to "boiled beef, bacon, puddings, apple pie, hot cakes and ale" even in laborers' cottages.[17]

All of these various customs of feasting, dining and cooking were fully established in Virginia by the late seventeenth century. They became the basis of inherited food ways which still flourished in the Chesapeake during this historian's youth, and set that region apart from other cultures in British America.

~ Virginia Dress Ways: Cavalier Ideas of Clothing and Rank

This culture was also highly distinctive in its habits of dress. "These Virginians are a very gentle, well-dressed people, and look perhaps more at a man's outside than his inside," a writer observed in the year 1737. From the beginning, Chesapeake

---

[15]Chinard, ed., *A Huguenot Exile in Virginia*, 158.

[16]Main, *Tobacco Colony*, 211.

[17]Keith Wrightson, *English Society, 1580–1680* (London, 1982), 32–33, citing Everitt, "Farm Labourers," in Thirsk, ed., *Agrarian History of England and Wales*, IV, 438–553.

elites tended to dress more opulently than did the builders of Massachusetts Bay Colony. The tone was set by the gentry of southern England, whose costume was designed to display their riches and refinement, their freedom from manual labor, and their dominion over others.[1]

The costume of this elite was made of fragile fabrics, perishable colors, and some of the more impractical designs that human ingenuity has been able to invent. An example was the wardrobe of Sir Walter Raleigh, who walked, or rather teetered, through a world of filth and woe in a costume that consisted of red high heels, white silk hose, a white satin doublet embroidered with pearls, a necklace of great pearls, a starched white ruff, and lace cuffs so broad as to bury his hands in fluffy clouds of extravagant finery. His outfit was completed by a jaunty plume of ostrich feathers that bobbed above his beaver hat, and precious stones in high profusion. The jewels that Raleigh wore on one occasion were said to be worth £30,000—more than the capital assets of some American colonies.

High fashions of this sort were never static. The "traditional" world of the seventeenth century was as changeable in that respect as our "modern" society would be. Fashions whirled constantly from one generation to another—even from one season to the next. In the reign of James I, when political conditions were dangerously unstable throughout Europe, gentlemen wore quilted doublets and breeches for protection against a dagger's thrust. This cloth armor was encrusted with precious stones, and trimmed with ribbons, and interwoven with gold and silver thread.[2]

During the reign of Charles I, fashions changed again. Opulence was increasingly displayed in many layers of dress. Outer coats were cut and slashed to expose intricate underwear that had consumed many hours in the making. Contempt for labor was expressed in a fad for gossamer gloves so fragile that the slightest effort would ruin them. Wealth was displayed by necklaces, brooches and even earrings for men. Charles I went to the scaffold in 1649 with a huge tear-shaped pearl in his ear.

The costume of country laborers was very different—an expression of poverty, dependency and incessant toil. Farm work-

---

[1]Peter Collinson to John Bartram, 17 Feb. 1737, *WMQ2*, 6 (1926), 304.

[2]The conventional sources for costume are inventories of estates; even better evidence is to be found in household account books. A particularly rich trove of information for this subject is the John Haynes Book of Household Expences, 1631–43, Ms. 36 DEVRO.

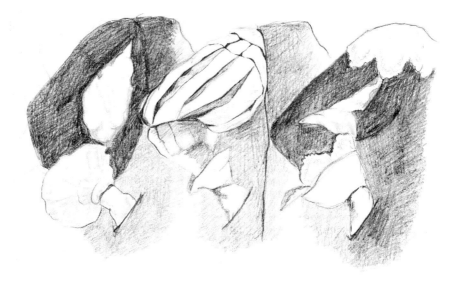

Slashed sleeves were merely one of many methods of conspicuous display in the dress ways of Stuart England and seventeenth-century Virginia. Slashes were designed to reveal undergarments of extravagant beauty, and to make a show of wealth and rank. The Puritan founders of New England did not approve of them. The General Court of Massachusetts forbade men and women of all conditions to "make or buy any slashed clothes, other than one slash in each sleeve and another in the back." Further, the magistrates also ordered that heavily slashed garments acquired before the prohibition should be discarded. They insisted that "men and women shall have liberty to wear out such apparel as they now are provided of except the immoderate great sleeves and slashed apparel." Attitudes were very different in Virginia. Excess was prohibited in the poor, and the first assembly assessed people according to apparel. But elaborate costumes were thought to honor their wearers, and were encouraged in the elite, who followed the latest London fashions with close attention.

ers dressed in worn and tattered garments which had been patched in the parti-colored cloth that harlequins and clowns took as their inspiration; the word "clown" was a synonym for a rustic laborer in the seventeenth century. Other workers dressed in rough leather garments, crudely stitched together with rawhide thongs. Many wore long frocks and loose baggy trousers of coarse cloth. Some had nothing to wear but filthy rags; there are descriptions of laborers who were unable to attend church because they lacked clothing to cover their nakedness.

Still another sort of dependency appeared in the costume of servants and apprentices. In the seventeenth century, English servants and apprentices commonly wore blue. "Blue cloaks in winter, blue coats in summer," wrote Alice Morse Earle, "Blue was not precisely a livery; it was their color, the badge of their condition of life, as black is now a parson's."[3]

Virginians copied most of these customs, but introduced some important differences. Extremes of dress became rather more muted in the New World. No gentleman of Virginia ever contrived to be quite as elegant as Sir Walter Raleigh. At the other extreme, many planters insisted that their slaves were better clothed than the laboring poor of England.

But distinctions of dress by rank and condition were carefully preserved in Virginia. The elite copied the styles of the southern gentry as best they could. Thomas Warner, a mechant who died in Virginia circa 1630, left "a pair of silk stockings, a pair of black hose, a pair of red slippers, a sea green scarf edged with gold lace, a felt hat, a black beaver, a doublet of black camlet, a gold belt and sword." This was not the sort of outfit which commonly appeared in New England. Wills and inventories tell us that the first gentlemen of Virginia strutted through the muddy streets of Jamestown and Williamsburg in gaudy costumes which for opulence and display much exceeded those in Massachusetts.

The servants and "commons" of Virginia, on the other hand, tended to dress in doublets of canvas and frieze rather than the leather and kerseys of New England. Black slaves were dressed not in African costumes—which were actively suppressed and even forbidden outright—but in the ordinary costume of country laborers throughout the south and west of England.

Costume thus covered a broader range in Virginia than in Massachusetts. But by comparison with England both colonies

[3]Alice Morse Earle, *Two Centuries of Costume in America* (New York, 1903).

showed a middling tendency. From an early date, Virginia gentlemen often complained that social distinctions of dress were not
sufficiently respected in the colony. John Pory wrote home of a
cowkeeper in Jamestown who went to church in "fresh flaming
silk," and a collier's wife who wore a "rough beaver hat with fair
pearl hatband, and a silken suit."

To deal with this problem, Virginia enacted sumptuary laws
which had a different purpose from the dress codes of New
England. Their primary object was not to restrain display, but to
support a spirit of social inequality. In the eighteenth century,
these sumptuary laws were not actively enforced by the courts of
Virginia. But sumptuary customs played a stronger role in regulating patterns of dress according to rank. Ladies, for example,
wore cloaks of red camlet, a fine strong cloth of silk and camel's
hair. The color, cut and fabric of this garment was reserved for
people of high estate. Philip Fithian in 1773 wrote, " . . . almost
every lady wears a red cloak, and when they ride out they tie a
white handkerchief over their head and face, so that when I first
came to Virginia I was distressed whenever I saw a lady, for I
thought she had the toothache!" Ladies also wore riding masks
when abroad, as if in purdah.[4]

In the early eighteenth century the social distinction between
gentlemen and "simple men" expressed itself in almost every
imaginable article of apparel: hats versus caps, coats versus jack-
ets, breeches versus trousers, silk stockings versus worsted, red
heels versus black heels. In chilly weather, high-born Virginia
gentlemen carried great fur muffs which demonstrated their freedom from manual labor. They continued to pierce their ears for
pearls or elegant black earstrings, and adorned their persons with
silver buckles, snakeskin garters, gold buttons, lace cross clothes,
and silver hatbands. Men of lower orders wore none of these
things.[5]

The gentry also displayed their standing by wearing swords—a
custom which continued among Virginians into the late eighteenth century.[6] As late as 1733, gentlemen of Virginia were said
to be "naked" when they went in public without their swords.[7]

---

[4]Fithian, *Journal and Letters*, 38–39.

[5]For gold and silver hatbands see Massingbird Diary, 1648, Ms. MM10/1 LINCRO; ribands
and laces frequently appear in John Haynes Household Account Book, 3 Sept. 1638, Ms. 36
DEVRO.

[6]Carter, *Diary*, II, 938.

[7]"Gentlemen appear in all places naked (i.e. without their swords) . . . from a polite decla-

They appear not to have gone naked in this sense very often. Some owned special black or purple sword belts to be worn in mourning.[8]

Horses were used not only for transportation but also as part of costume by an elite which thought of itself as an equestrian order. Hugh Jones wrote, "I have known some to spend the morning in ranging several miles in the woods to find and catch their horses, only to ride two or three miles to church, or to the court house, or to a horse race, where they generally appoint to meet on business."[9]

Gentlemen also made much display of coats of arms. Planters made major efforts to obtain the sanction of the College of Heralds in London, and displayed their arms on silver, books, buildings, furniture, and rings. The Fitzhughs trained one of their slaves to work as a silver engraver.[10] Gentlemen also had family colors, which were displayed with much ceremony. When they could afford to do so, they dressed their house slaves in livery. George Washington's slaves were gorgeous in the family livery of white coats, scarlet facings, scarlet waistcoats and cheap trimmings called "livery lace"—the same colors as the Washington arms. Well into the nineteenth century, the Tylers kept a barge crew of black slaves dressed in dashing blue uniforms of the family color, their broad collars embroidered with their master's initials.

In all of these many ways, the costume of Virginia closely resembled that of southwestern England, both in style and social function. Elites in the Chesapeake attended carefully to changing fashions in the mother country. A visitor in 1732 observed that the great planters "dressed mostly as in England and affected London dress."[11] A few grudging concessions were made to the American climate. In the summer, gentlemen of Virginia dressed in white holland, and ladies wore "thin silk or linen."[12] But English tastes remained strong in the Chesapeake, just as they

---

ration that in places of public resort all distinctions ought to be lost in a general complaisance." Arthur Rowntree, *History of Scarborough,* 256.

[8]John Haynes Household Account Book, 13 June 1639, ms. 36, DEVRO.

[9]Jones, *Present State of Virginia,* 24.

[10]William Fitzhugh to Capt. Henry Fitzhugh, 30 Jan. 1686/87, Davis, ed., *Fitzhugh Letters,* 192.

[11]Gregory A. Stiverson and Patrick H. Butler III, "Virginia in 1732: The Travel Journal of William Hugh Grove," *VMHB* 85 (1977), 44.

[12]*Ibid.*

had done in New England in very different ways. Despite many attempts at historical revision, the old images of the Roundhead and cavalier had a solid foundation in sartorial fact—complete even to the legendary "gauntlet and glove."

❧ Virginia Sport Ways: The Great Chain of Slaughter

Another part of the cavalier legend also had a foundation in fact. This was its association with amusements of a certain type. Here again, the sporting life of Virginia differed very much from that of New England, both as to sports actually played in the Chesapeake colony, and the general relationship between sport and society.

The most striking fact about sport in Virginia was its stratification. From an early date in the mid-seventeenth century, a hierarchy of sports was deliberately created by high authority and actively enforced by law. A special class of recreations was reserved exclusively for the colony's ruling elite. In 1691, for example, Virginia's governor Sir Francis Nicholson ordered the establishment of annual tournaments or field days, with prizes for feats of strength and skill. Competition was carefully restricted to "the better sort of Virginians only." Gentlemen competed for honor among themselves, in a manner that set them apart from the rest of the population.[1]

By law and custom, horse-racing and betting were also reserved for gentlemen alone. People of "lower estate" were forbidden to compete, and punished when they did so. A famous example was the fate of an unfortunate artisan who failed to keep his station: "James Bullock, a Taylor, having made a race for his mare to run with a horse belonging to Mr. Matthew Slader for two thousand pounds of tobacco and cask, it being contrary to law for a laborer to make a race, being a sport only for gentlemen, is fined for the same one hundred pounds of tobacco and cask."[2]

At the same time, the gentry themselves were strongly encouraged by the custom of the country to make extravagant and even ruinous bets on horses. Wagers of hundreds and even thousands of pounds of tobacco were not uncommon. In 1693, one bet

[1] Wright, *First Gentlemen of Virginia,* 87; Mary Newton Stanard, *Colonial Virginia: Its People and Customs* (Philadelphia, 1917), 257.
[2] *WMQ1* 3 (1894), 136.

between two planters in Northumberland County amounted to £22 sterling at a time when an average planter realized a net profit of only about £8 a year from the sale of his tobacco. It was this excess that caused the courts to intervene, and to insist that only the gentry could play the horses. Poor servants and slaves were permitted to look on, but only gentlemen could place bets.[3]

Virginia horse races were apt to be spontaneous affairs. In Rappahannock, for example, a race ground lay next to the church. On Sunday mornings, the congregation would commonly adjourn to this field, in hopes that the young bloods of the congregation might challenge each other on the spur of the moment. Even the clergy were in attendance. On at least one occasion the court summoned the testimony of the Reverend James Blair to decide a disputed wager.[4]

Races also occurred on court days. The gentry of the county liked to gather round a jug of peach brandy, and brag about their horses. When a wager was made, the company would shout "Done! Done!" and adjourn to an open field. The gentleman-justices themselves would sometimes leave the bench and volunteer to decide the winner. The race tracks were only ten or twelve feet wide and a quarter-mile long. At one end of the field the horses would be brought together, wild with excitement, backing and rearing as their riders struggled to turn their heads in the general direction of the finish line. A gun would be fired, and in a billowing cloud of white smoke the race was on. The awkward riders (their old-fashioned horsemanship was much despised by European visitors in the eighteenth century) sat nearly upon their horses' necks, legs dangling straight down in long stirrups. The animals were compact and wiry—the ancestors of the American quarter horse which was bred for these races. Virginia horses lost about six inches in height during the first century of American history.[5] Their heads were small in proportion to their bodies, but their powerful hindquarters allowed them to spring forward with tremendous acceleration. Thomas Anburey wrote that "If you happened to be looking the other way, the race is terminated before you can turn your head."[6]

Early Virginia horse races often became brutal bloodsports in

---

[3]Breen, "Horses and Gentlemen," 159.
[4]Bruce, *Social Life in Virginia*, 201.
[5]Jane Carson, *Colonial Virginians at Play* (Charlottesville, 1965), 113.
[6]Thomas Anburey, *Travels through the Interior Parts of America* (London, 1789), 227.

which gentlemen-jockeys lashed at one another with whip and spur, in a flying tangle of elbows and feet. Now and again, the riders might agree to a "fair race," in which no blows were to be exchanged. But Chesapeake races were apt to be wild melees.[7]

Similar customs surrounded English horse races, which were run with scant regard for people of lesser rank who happened to get in the way. In Northamptonshire, for example, one gentleman wrote of another, ". . . he rode down a man and the poor fellow fell from his horse." No sympathy was shown for the unlucky plebeian who was trampled beneath the galloping hooves. Concern was expressed only for the gentleman-jockey who lost his seat.[8]

Horse-racing in the Chesapeake was part of a complex culture of sport, which contrasted sharply with the customs of New England.[9] The Virginians looked with contempt upon the town games of Massachusetts. Thomas Jefferson wrote to his nephew Peter Carr, "Games played with the ball, and others of that nature, are too violent for the body and stamp no character on the mind." The master of Monticello preferred a gentleman's traditional recreations of riding and shooting. "As to the species of excrcise," he wrote, "I advise the gun. While this gives a moderate exercise to the body, it gives boldness, enterprize and independence to the mind."[10]

Virginia's favorite amusements were bloodsports. There was an entire hierarchy of these gory entertainments. Virtually every male in Virginia could be ranked according to the size of animals that he was allowed to kill for his pleasure. At the top was the noblest of bloodsports—the hunting of the stag. This was the sport of kings and noblemen in the seventeenth century. It was staged in Virginia with the same elaborate pomp and ritual that had occurred in Europe.

Lesser gentry chased the fox—a quarry that the high nobility despised as low and vulgar until the sport came to be elaborately rationalized by the Meynell family in the eighteenth century. English fox hunting was not easily introduced to the New World. Then, as now, *Vulpes americanus* made a more elusive quarry than his Old World cousin. At great trouble and expense, the gentry

[7]Carson, *Colonial Virginians at Play*, 120–22.
[8]*Diary of Thomas Isham*, 5 Sept. 1672; James Rice, *History of the British Turf* (n.p., 1879), 151.
[9]Fairfax Harrison, "Racing in Colonial Virginia," *VMHB* 2 (1895), 293.
[10]Thomas Jefferson to Peter Carr, 19 Aug. 1785, *Jefferson Papers*, ed., Boyd, VIII, 407.

of Virginia imported the red fox from England for their sport in the eighteenth century.

Before that date, fox hunting was an impromptu affair on both sides of the water. It was commonly done with the gun in the seventeenth century, and sometimes culminated in scenes of high savagery. "When they hunted last in Laxton wood," one English gentleman wrote, "Mr. K. shot a fox before the hounds after they had run him sharply for some time, which they tore to pieces and it has given them very good blood."[11]

"Very good blood" was also the object of another entertainment which was followed by the yeomanry and parish clergy on both sides of the water. This was the sport of coursing—an afternoon's diversion, in which hares, rabbits and small vermin were hunted on foot with the aid of specially trained dogs. Such was the enthusiasm for this pedestrian slaughter that it was not uncommon to have several courses in a single day.[12]

Husbandmen and laborers amused themselves in a more humble manner, by murdering birds of various sizes in social rituals of high complexity. One favorite bloodsport of farmers in Virginia was called ganderpulling. By an irony of the Christian calendar, this savage event was commonly staged on Easter Monday—a day of riotous celebration in the eighteenth-century Chesapeake. An old male goose was suspended upside-down by his feet from the branch of a tree, and the neck of the bird was lathered with grease. The contestants mounted their horses and galloped past the goose, endeavoring to tear off the bird's head by brute force as they rode by. The game was dangerous to the galloper as well as the goose. More than one contestant was pulled backward off his speeding horse and succeeded only in snapping his own neck while the goose cackled in trumph. Others lost fingers or thumbs in the gander's angry beak. But as the contest continued, the bird's neck was slowly stretched and torn by one contestant after another, until some rural champion finally succeeded in ripping off the head, claiming the body as his prize. In early Virginia, one man remembered that a good ganderpull was "anticipated with rapture." The scene was a lively one— shouting crowds, a swirl of violence, the goose twisting in agony, dismounted riders rolling in the dust, and finally the climax when

---

[11]Daniel Eaton to 3rd Earl of Cardigan, 12 Aug. 1725, "Letters of Daniel Eaton," *NHANTRS* 24 (1971), 38.

[12]John Richards Diary, 26 Oct. 1698, DORSRO.

the carotid artery gave way and the winner rode in triumph through a shower of crimson gore.[13]

Apprentices enjoyed still another sort of bloodsport called cockshailing, which they played at Shrovetide. A cock or chicken was tethered to a stake, and crowd of youths tried to torture and kill it by throwing dangerous objects. The Puritans detested this barbarous amusement, and did all in their power to suppress it in New England—without entirely succeeding in doing so. But it flourished in Virginia, as it had done in the south and west of England, where one countryman wrote to another in 1668, "I cannot but give some touch of public affairs—what with the throwing at shrovetide and fighting this Lent time there's a great mortality of Cocks."[14]

Smaller boys amused themselves in yet a different way by the juvenile bloodsport of annihilating songbirds. In Devon, one of these diversions was called "muzzling the sparrow." A local historian described it thus: "A boy had his hands tied together behind him, and the tip of one wing of a sparrow or other small bird was placed in his mouth. He then tried by the action of his teeth and lips gradually to draw the wing of the bird into his mouth and bite off its head, the bird in the meantime pecking at his cheeks and eyes and endeavoring to escape."[15]

At the bottom of this hierarchy of bloody games were male infants who prepared themselves for the larger pleasures of maturity by torturing snakes, maiming frogs and pulling the wings off butterflies. Thus, every red-blooded male in Virginia was permitted to slaughter some animal or other, and size of his victim was proportioned to his social rank. Sport became a great chain of slaughter in this society. A European tourist observed with wonder, ". . . everything that is called fighting is a delicious pleasure to an Englishman."[16]

[13]For descriptions of ganderpulling in Virginia, Kentucky, Tennessee, North Carolina and Georgia, see Henry Fearon, *Sketches of America* (London, 1818), 243; A. B. Longstreet, *Georgia Scenes* (New York, 1957), 97–105; J. P. Young, "Happenings in a White Haven Community, Shelby County, Tennessee, Fifty or More Years Ago," *THM* 7 (1923), 97; Guion G. Johnson, *Antebellum North Carolina: A Social History* (Chapel Hill, 1937), 111–12.

[14]Thomas Aldrich to Thomas Isham, 4 March 1668, ms. 596, Isham Papers, NHANTSRO.

[15]Cheyne, *The Dialect of Hartland, Devonshire*, 17.

[16]Marlow, ed., *Diary of Thomas Isham, 1658–1681*, 30.

**๛ Virginia Work Ways:
The Ambivalence of the Cavalier Ethic**

Attitudes toward pleasure in this culture were related to its ideas about work. The Wessex Royalist Sir John Oglander summarized the cavalier work ethic in a sentence. "I scorn base getting and unworthy penurious saving," he wrote, "yet my desire is to lay up somewhat for my poor children."[1]

Here was a paradox that commonly appeared in the attitudes toward work and trade among English gentlemen and Virginia planters. To characterize these workways in rounded and accurate terms is not an easy task. Most Virginia gentlemen worked harder than they cared to admit. They engaged in raising crops for the market, and as a consequence found themselves deeply engaged in trade. The great planters also functioned as merchants and bankers for their neighbors. Many owned shops, stores, ships and warehouses.[2] But even as Virginians did all of these things, they did not value the doing of them as highly as did the people of Massachusetts or Pennsylvania. The work ethic in Virginia thus became a classical study in cultural ambivalence.[3]

Many people who actually visited the colony of Virginia— natives, immigrants and casual travelers alike—testified that the ethic of work was very weak in this society. As early as 1622, John Martin observed that in the Chesapeake, even the Indians "work better than the English."[4] The Virginians themselves commonly agreed with this assessment. From the planter's perspective, William Byrd wrote, "Nature is very indulgent to us, and produces its good things almost spontaneously. Men evade the original curse of hard labour, and sweat as much with eating their bread as getting it. . . . if plenty and a warm sun did not make us lazy and hate motion and exercise."[5]

Robert Beverley shared this view. In a book that generally cel-

---

[1]Bamford, ed., *A Royalist's Notebook*, 230.

[2]A very large literature on this subject is surveyed in John J. McCusker and Russell R. Menard, *The Economy of British America, 1607–1789* (Chapel Hill, 1985), 117–43.

[3]Here again the historiographical literature has gone through broad swings. Three generations ago, Virginia gentlemen were perceived as hostile to commerce and removed from it. The next generation reversed this interpretation, and argued that the first gentlemen of Virginia were descended from merchants, and actively and even centrally engaged in commercial activity. The truth lies in between.

[4]Kingsbury, *Records of the Virginia Company*, III, 706.

[5]William Byrd II to Charles Boyle, Earl of Orrery, 2 Feb. 1727, Tinling, ed., *Correspondence of the Three William Byrds*, I, 350.

ebrated the virtues of Virginians, he wrote, "I must . . . reproach
my countrymen with a laziness that is unpardonable."[6] Beverley
believed that the problem developed not from the climate but
from the culture, and particularly from the inability of Virginians
to think in what he called "oeconomic" terms. "Nay," he
declared, "they are such abominable ill husbands, that though
their country is overgrown with wood, yet they have all their
wooden ware from England."[7]

These judgments did not accurately describe material conditions in Virginia. But in company with other evidence they
revealed an important truth about cultural attitudes in that society. Many Virginians of middle and upper ranks aspired to behave
like gentlemen. In the early seventeenth century an English gentleman was defined as one who could "live idly and without manual labor."[8] The words "gentleman" and "independent" were
used synonymously, and "independence" in this context meant
freedom from the necessity of labor.[9] But in Virginia, independence could be achieved or maintained only by labor of the sort
that a gentleman was trained to despise. Here was the root of an
ambivalence toward "base getting" which became part of the
folkways of Virginia.

These ideas about labor were closely linked with attitudes
toward commerce. The gentlemen-planters of Virginia repeatedly
expressed an intense contempt for trade, even as they were compelled to engage in it on a daily basis. They were even more con-
temptuous of traders, at the same time they were forced to deal
with them. Governor William Berkeley, for example, raged
against the greedy materialism of merchants. "We cannot but
resent," he wrote, "that forty thousand people should be impoverished to enrich more than forty merchants."[10] It did not trouble
him that forty thousand people should enrich forty landed gentlemen. On another occasion he collectively described merchants
as "avaricious persons, whose sickle hath bin ere long in our harvest already."[11]

But Berkeley also recognized the necessity of these mercenary

---

[6]Beverley, *The History and Present State of Virginia*, 296.

[7]*Ibid.*, 295.

[8]Thomas Smith, *De Republica Anglorum*, ed. Mary Dewar (Cambridge, 1982), 63.

[9]The earliest American directories in the 18th century used the words "independent" and
"gentleman" as synonyms.

[10]Berkeley, *Discourse and View of Virginia*, 6–7.

[11]Morgan, *American Slavery, American Freedom*, 147.

people whom he so despised. He actively recruited them for the colony, and encouraged the creation of markets and entrepôts. One of his statutes provided that if any "particular persons shall settle any such place whither the merchants shall willingly come for the sale or bringing of goods, such men shall be looked upon as benefactors to the publique." The wording of this law did not suggest that the merchants themselves were "benefactors to the publique," but that any man who attracted them and their wares to Virginia might be thought of in such a way.[12]

The same ambivalence also appeared in attitudes toward money, which Virginians liked to have, but hated to handle. The writings of William Byrd provided many examples. To his friend the Earl of Orrery, William Byrd boasted (far beyond the material fact) that he lived apart from the market: "Half a crown will rest undisturbed in my pocket for many moons together," he wrote. But Byrd often manifested an obsessive interest in money, and shared a tendency (more common in Virginia than in New England) to rank people in proportion to their riches.[13]

There was a deep ambivalence in attitudes toward wealth, which was much valued by Virginians, but not for its own sake. Wealth was regarded not primarily as a form of capital or a factor of production, but as something to be used for display and consumed for pleasure. A gentleman could never appear mean-spirited (in the old-fashioned sense of niggardly and grasping) without losing something of his rank. The display of wealth was important to Virginians not only as a way of demonstrating material riches but also as a means of showing a "liberal" spirit, which was part of the ideal of a gentleman.[14]

The economic consequence of this attitude was debt. Most great families of Virginia fell deep into indebtedness. Even the richest planters were permanent debtors. Robert Carter of Nomini Hall had heavy debts to British creditors. In 1758, he wrote that "the produce of my land and negroes will scarcely pay the demand requisite to keep them." He was often compelled to sell capital in order to stay afloat.[15] The magnitude of private debt was greater in Virginia than in other parts of British America. After

---

[12]"An Act for the repealing the Act for Markets and regulating trade." Hening, *Statutes of Virginia,* I (March 1655–56), 397.

[13]Byrd to Lord Orrery, 5 July 1726, Tinling, ed., *Correspondence of the Three William Byrds,* I, 355.

[14]Collinson to Bartram, 17 Feb. 1737, *WMQ2* VI (1926), 304.

[15]Morton, *Robert Carter of Nomini Hall,* 262.

the War of Independence, it was officially determined that Americans owed about three million pounds to British creditors. Of that total, nearly half (£1.4 million) was due from the planters of Virginia, and a large part of the remainder from the neighboring colony of Maryland. In 1776, at least ten gentlemen of Virginia owed more than £5,000 to British creditors, a very large sum. Many owed in excess of £1,000, among them George Washington and Thomas Jefferson.[16]

Some economic historians believe that the chronic debts of Virginian gentlemen arose mainly from the difficulties of tobacco growing, and also from the structure of credit in the British empire. But it is interesting to note that chronic indebtedness had long been part of the life style of country gentry in the south and west of England. One study of the Warwickshire gentry found that heavy debts were a common and continuing part of their economic condition. In Warwickshire, as in Virginia, some men were more prudent than others, and some seasons were better than the next. Debt was sometimes an instrument of growth, and sometimes of decline. But chronic indebtedness itself was a normal condition of life.[17] Among both English gentry and Virginia planters it arose not so much from a material but a cultural imperative.

✎ Virginia Time Ways:
The Cavalier Idea of "Killing the Time"

In the year 1732, William Byrd was visiting his lands in a "retired part of the country," and stayed the night at Tuckahoe, the home of the Randolph family. After supper another guest brought out a copy of *The Beggar's Opera* and the assembled company amused themselves by reading the play aloud. "Thus," Byrd wrote in his diary, "we killed the time."[1]

This notion of "killing the time" set the Virginians apart from the people of Massachusetts. The destruction of time was not an idea which sat well with the builders of the Massachusetts Bay Colony. Whenever the hours hung heavily upon a New England

---

[16]An excellent discussion of planter debt appears in Timothy Breen, *Tobacco Culture: The Mentality of the Great Tidewater Planters on the Eve of Revolution* (Princeton, 1985), 128.

[17]Vivienne M. Larmine, "The Lifestyle and Attitudes of the Seventeenth Century Gentleman with Special Reference to the Newdigates" (thesis, Univ. of Birmingham, 1980).

[1]Byrd, "A Progress to the Mines," in *London Diary and Other Writings*, 627.

conscience, the people of that northern region attempted to "improve the time"—an attitude far removed from the temporal folkways of Virginia.

The temporal differences between these two English cultures were remarkable in their complexity. By comparison with New England, the time ways of the Chesapeake were in some ways more relaxed, but in other respects more rigid. The people of Virginia were less obsessed than New Englanders with finding some godly purpose for every passing moment, but their lives were more tightly controlled by the rhythms of a rural life.

Time in seventeenth-century Virginia meant mainly the pulse of nature and the organic processes of life itself. Even among great planters the language of time was sometimes closer to that of American Indians than to English Puritans. William Byrd reckoned the passing of time in expressions such as "many moons together." The rhythms of nature played a significant part in his own way of reckoning time.[2]

The most important of these natural rhythms might be called crop time, which in the Chesapeake arose primarily from the growing season of tobacco. In 1800, a merchant named William Tatham described in detail the tobacco cycle in Virginia. It began "as early after Christmas as the weather will permit," with the sowing of seedbeds. The seedlings sprouted slowly, and were not ready for the fields until five months had passed. Then the farmer awaited a "planting season." Tatham explained:

> the term, season for planting, signifies a shower of rain of sufficient quantity to wet the earth . . . these seasons generally commence in April, and terminate in what is termed the long season in May; which (to make use of an Irishism) very frequently happens in June. . . . when a good shower or season happens at this period of the year . . . the planter hurries to the plant bed, disregarding the teeming element which is doomed to wet his skin.[3]

Once planted, tobacco required unremitting care. The young plants needed "hilling" and "weeding until the lay-by," which was the happy moment when that heavy work could cease. At precisely the right moment, the plants also had to be "primed," "topped" and "suckered." Always they needed watching for the

---

[2]Wm. Byrd to Earl of Orrery, 5 July 1726, Tinling, ed., *Correspondence of the Three William Byrds*, I, 354–55.

[3]William Tatham, *An Historical and Practical Essay on the Culture and Commerce of Tobacco* (London, 1800), 16–17, 119.

"rising" of the worm. When these dreaded enemies appeared, Tatham noted, then the "whole force is to be employed in searching round each plant, and destroying this worm." Then came the harvest—another difficult moment. If the leaf was cut a week too early it could rot in the cask; if only a few days late it might not be cured properly. In the eighteenth century, expectant planters waited anxiously for a moment when the leaves took on a slightly greyish cast, and began to feel thick and brittle between the fingers. When these signs appeared, the crop was instantly harvested. Next the curing began, another long and arduous cycle with disaster lurking at every turn.

This tobacco cycle exercised a complete temporal tyranny over the lives of Virginians. It created alternating periods of crisis and calm, and culminated in climactic moments of frantic intensity. Major events such as the lay-by and the harvest were celebrated with high enthusiasm by masters and slaves alike. For many years, Chesapeake planters kept the ancient custom of *largesse* or *harvest-home* when servants paid homage to the master and mistress, and carried round the house a pair of painted ram's horns, trimmed with flowers.[4]

Natural rhythms were not the only determinants of Virginia's time ways. Imposed upon the crop cycle was a cadence of cultural time which was regulated by the Christian calendar. Accounts were settled and rents were due on Lady Day (March 25), Midsummer's Day (June 24), Michaelmas (September 29), and Christmas Day, in both Virginia and southern England. Events such as Twelfth Night, Shrovetide, Lent, Easter, Ascension and Lady Day were also times of high celebration. Whitsunweek was a long holiday. So also was Easter Monday and Hock Tuesday, the second Tuesday after Easter. Many saints' days were also observed in the Chesapeake.[5] The climax of the year was Christmas, a happy season of parties, dances, visits, gifts and celebration. On Christmas Eve, for example, Philip Fithian noted that "Guns were fired this Evening in the Neighborhood, and the negroes seem to be inspired with new Life."[6]

The most elemental acts of life were regulated by these rhythms. The season of marriage in Virginia, for example, was

---

[4]John Gage, *The History and Antiquities of Hengrave in Suffolk* (London, 1822), 6.

[5]For the actual settling of annual accounts in England, see John Meriwether Diary, 25 Dec. 1711, ms. 2220, WILTRO; for the Chesapeake, see Carville Earle, *The Evolution of a Tidewater Settlement System: All Hallow's Parish, Maryland, 1650–1783* (Chicago, 1975), 158.

[6]Fithian, *Journal and Letters*, 52.

determined by the Anglican calendar and the crop cycle. The favored time for marriage fell in the period between Christmas and Ash Wednesday when Lent began. Few Virginians married during Lent; the eight weeks from Ash Wednesday to Easter Sunday were a period when marriage had long been prohibited to Anglicans. After Easter, the number of marriages rose moderately, but remained far below the winter peak. They continued at a low level in the planting season, revived after the harvest, and then fell again in the weeks before Christmas, which was another period when marriage was prohibited in the Church of England. This rhythm was different from the marriage cycle in Puritan Massachusetts and Quaker Pennsylvania, but it was the same as in the south and west of England. In the Chesapeake it was highly stable, recurring every year from the mid-seventeenth century to the late eighteenth. In this historian's Maryland family, it has persisted even into the mid-twentieth century.[7]

Fertility also had a distinctive rhythm in Virginia. Babies were made in the spring, more than in any other season. This pattern also appeared in most parts of British America, but its magnitude was exceptionally large in the Chesapeake colonies—larger than in Puritan Massachusetts or Quaker Pennsylvania. In one parish

---

[7]The index of marriages in All Hallow's Parish, Anne Arundel County, Maryland, was as follows (1700–1776):

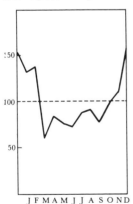

Month of Marriage	Percent of All Marriages	Marriage Index $\bar{m} = 100$
Jan.	11.0	132
Feb.	12.4	149
March	5.1	61
April	7.1	85
May	6.4	77
June	6.1	73
July	7.3	88
Aug.	7.7	92
Sept.	6.6	79
Oct.	8.1	97
Nov.	9.2	110
Dec.	13.0	156

Computed from data in Earle, *The Evolution of a Tidewater Settlement System*, 159; similar patterns are reported for other parts of Maryland and Virginia in Darrett B. Rutman, Charles Wetherell and Anita Rutman, "Rhythms of Life: Black and White Seasonality in the Early Chesapeake," *JIH* 11 (1980), 29–53; and Kulikoff, *Tobacco and Slaves*, 256; see also David Cressy, "The Seasonality of Marriage in Old and New England," *JIH* 16 (1985), 23; for similarities between Virginia and the south of England (which was very different from the north) see Ann Kussmaul, "Time and Space, Hoofs and Grain: The Seasonality of Marriage in England," *JIH* 15 (1985), 755–79.

of tidewater Maryland, twice as many babies were conceived in the peak months of May, June and July as in February, March or April when conceptions fell to their lowest level through the year. The cause was a complex interplay of many factors—nutrition, morbidity, the crop cycle and the Christian calendar. The amplitude of this fertility cycle demonstrates that the people of Virginia lived closer to the seasons than did the Puritans in New England or Quakers in Pennsylvania.[8]

The Virginians regulated their lives more by these natural and cultural rhythms than by mechanical clocks or mathematical calendars. They also thought in much the same way about the life cycle itself. In a generation when Puritan ministers in Massachusetts normally defined old age in quantitative terms as life after sixty, Virginians took a very different view of the subject. "Age," wrote William Byrd II, "should be dated from the declension of our vigor, and the impairing of our faculties, rather than from the time we have lived in the world."[9]

These general time ways in Virginia were marked by many variations. In particular, the temporal lives of individuals varied according to their social rank. Time was hierarchical in Virginia. Gentleman demonstrated their status by making a great show of temporal independence. The diaries of gentry in Virginia and England during the seventeenth century displayed a cultivated

[8]On the conception cycle, Carville Earle's research on All Hallow's Parish yields the following pattern for the period from 1700 to 1776:

Month of Conception	Month of Baptism	Percent of Annual Births	Monthly Index (Monthly Mean = 100)
Dec.–Jan.	Oct.	9.6%	115
Jan.–Feb.	Nov.	4.9%	59
Feb.–March	Dec.	4.3%	52
March–April	Jan.	3.3%	40
April–May	Feb.	8.6%	103
May–June	March	10.0%	120
June–July	April	11.0%	132
July–Aug.	May	8.6%	103
Aug.–Sept.	June	10.2%	122
Sept.–Oct.	July	8.1%	97
Oct.–Nov.	Aug.	11.8%	142
Nov.–Dec.	Sept.	9.6%	115

Computed from data in Earle, in *The Evolution of a Tidewater Settlement System,* 159; similar but not identical cycles are reported in Rutman, Wetherell and Rutman, "Rhythms of Life," 30–31; and Kulikoff, *Tobacco and Slaves,* 256. These data refer to the white population only; as will be discussed in volume 3, the rhythm of seasonality among blacks was different.

[9]William Byrd to John Custis, 29 July 1723, Tinling, ed., *Correspondence of Three William Byrds,* I, 346.

contempt for temporal regularity. An example was the time of rising from bed. The diary of Bullen Reynes, kept alternately in French and English, was very interesting in that respect. One morning he might rise at six or earlier; on another he would stay abed till noon or even later. Early risings tended to be recorded in English; late sleepings were noted in a fractured French:

> Je dormi tout le matin [*sic*].
>
> Je dormi jusqua deux heures [*sic*].[10]

This English gentlemen kept his insouciant schedule not merely because it pleased him. It also demonstrated his independence— a condition fundamental to the status of a gentleman.

Very different was the temporal condition of servants and slaves. Their time was not their own. It belonged to their masters, who decreed that a field slave must work from "day clean" to "first dark." A slave had very little control over daylight time except on Sundays and holidays which were days of riotous cele-bration. Some such hierarchy of time has existed in most cultures, but rarely has it been as stark as in Tidewater Virginia.[11]

The temporal hierarchy of Virginia ranked people largely by their ability to regulate their own time whenever and however they pleased. Time-killing thus became an expression of social rank. Through many centuries, when the people of Virginia found a moment of leisure, they "killed the time" with any lethal weapon that came to hand. A dice box did nicely, or a pack of playing cards, or a book of dramatic readings, or long conversa-tion at table in the gathering dusk of a Chesapeake "evening"— a word which was enlarged in this culture to include the entire afternoon. The progeny of the New England Puritans, on the other hand, preferred to "improve the time" by inventing alarm clocks and daylight saving time and by turning every passing moment to a constructive purpose. Here were two distinctly dif-ferent time ways which lay very near the heart of regional cultures in British America.

---

[10]Bullen Reynes Diary, 8 Sept. 1632, 5 April 1632, 27 Nov. 1632; Ms. 865/392, WILTRO; see also Richard Newdigate Diary, 12 May 1682, Ms. B 1306a-C, WARRO.

[11]Kenneth Stampp, *The Peculiar Institution* (New York, 1956), chap. 2.

❧ Virginia Wealth Ways:
Cavalier Ideas of the Material Order

"Praised be to God," wrote a gentleman of Virginia in 1686, "I neither live in poverty nor pomp, but in a very good indifferency, and to a full content." This ideal of material moderation was widely shared by Virginians.[1] The reality, however, was very different. From the outset, the distribution of wealth was profoundly unequal. During the late seventeenth and early eighteenth century it became even more so. Magnitudes of material inequality varied from one part of the colony to another, but the general trend was very much the same throughout the tidewater region.

In terms of their possessions, the adult male population of Virginia was divisible into several groups. At the top were the planters, who owned much of the land, most of the servants and nearly all of the slaves in the colony. The size of this tidewater elite was relatively large by comparison with other ruling groups. In point of numbers, the Chesapeake gentry were more like a large continental nobility than the exceptionally small aristocracy of England. As many as 10 percent of adult males belonged to this group. Together they owned 50 to 75 percent of productive assets in Virginia.

Below them was a stratum of yeomen who owned their own land and tilled it with their own hands, often with the help of a servant or two. This group of small freeholders was always a minority of Virginia's population from 1680 to 1760—in many counties, a very small minority. Overall, it ranged from 20 to 30 percent of the population.

The bottom 60 to 70 percent of Virginia's male population owned no land at all, and very little property of any other sort. This landless majority included a large number of tenant farmers, who worked the land of others and owned no real estate. Their numbers varied from one part of Virginia to another; in some neighborhoods they were the great majority. Below these tenants were poor white laborers, servants and black slaves. They were a rural proletariat who in most cases owned next to nothing—not even themselves.[2]

---

[1]William Fitzhugh to William Fitzhugh, 22 April 1686; David, ed., *Fitzhugh Letters*, 174.

[2]In Surry County, Virginia, historian Kevin Kelly finds that male tithables were distributed

Overall, the Gini ratio for wealth distribution in Virginia was in the range of .60 to .75 during the late seventeenth and early eighteenth century. It was rising in the direction of still greater inequality.[3] This typical pattern of wealth stratification in the

---

as follows by material status in 1703/04:

Status	Number (%)
Free landowners	96 (11.1%)
Great landowners (950 acres+)	8
Upper middling landowners (650–949 acres)	6
Lower middling landowners (350–649 acres)	15
Small landowners (1–349 acres)	67
Free non-landowners	344 (39.8%)
Non-free non-landowners	425 (49.2%)
Dependent sons of landowners	74
White male servants	131
Black slaves	220
Total tithables	865 (100.1%)
Total population	2,230

Surry was a low, swamp-filled county directly across the James River from Jamestown. Inventoried estates in 1690 showed a Gini ratio of .55, which was exceptionally egalitarian by Virginia standards at that date. Tithables in this county included males from 16 to 60, and widows who held property, plus male servants and slaves. See Kelly, "Economic and Social Development of Seventeenth Century Surry County, Virginia" (thesis, Univ. of Washington, 1972), 19, 111, 135.

[3]Many studies of wealth distribution in the Chesapeake colonies report the following results.

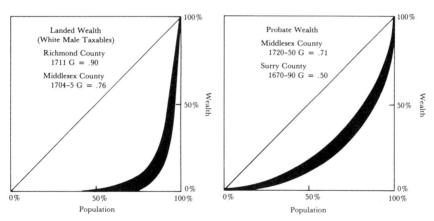

Sources include Kelly, "Surry County"; Rutman and Rutman, *A Place in Time, Explicatus,* 117–32; Main, *Tobacco Colony,* 55; Robert E. and B. Katherine Brown, *Virginia, 1705–1786: Democracy or Aristocracy?* (East Lansing, 1964), 13, 75; Lee Gladwin, "Tobacco and Sex," *JSH* 12 (1978), 57. The Browns omitted tenants, whose numbers may be computed from data in Evarts B. Green and Virginia D. Harrington, *America Population before the Federal Census of 1790* (1932, rpt. New York, 1966), 150–51. This has been done here.

Chesapeake was much less equal than to Massachusetts, where Gini ratios ranged from .40 to .60 in most New England towns. Throughout the Puritan colonies, the middle class of yeoman farmers and artisans made up the great majority of the population. Slaves, servants and tenants were comparatively few.[4]

The Virginia pattern was, however, much the same as in the south and west of England during the seventeenth century. Historian J.P.P. Horn has made a comparative study of wealth distribution in Gloucestershire and the Chesapeake colonies. He concludes that "one is immediately struck by the similarity. Both had large numbers of poor, both had middling groups making up about 30 to 40 per cent of the population, and both had a small elite of rich comprising 10 to 12 per cent." In both Gloucester-

---

The Rutmans found the following patterns for Middlesex County, Virginia:

Wealth Type	Period	Gini	SSTT	SSBT	n
Personal wealth	1650–59	.62	50.0	4.2	23
	1700–19	.78	71.6	2.0	120
	1720–50	.71	58.7	2.7	192
Servants and slaves	1668	.74	58.4	0.0	83
	1687	.85	73.5	0.0	231
	1724	.77	60.5	0.0	254
Land	1668	.61	47.5	4.0	83
	1687	.74	60.5	0.1	215
	1724	.74	58.5	0.0	242

Gini = Gini Ratio; SSTT = size share top tenth; SSBT = size share bottom tenth.

Gloria Main's research on Maryland inventories yielded much the same findings: a Gini ratio of .59 for gross personal wealth in 1656–83; rising to .65 in 1694–1705 and to .73 in 1715–19.

Probate records understate inequality in Virginia (more so than in Massachusetts or Pennsylvania), and yield results very different from land lists and tax assessments when the latter are adjusted for the large number of landless adult males. In Middlesex County (1704–5), the Gini ratio of land distribution among adult white males was .76; the proportion owning no land was above 43%. When black males are included, the Gini ratio rises to .81 and zero holding to 58%. In Richmond County (1711), wealth was even more concentrated: the Gini ratio was .90 among white males and .94 when blacks are included. In a population of approximately 2,500 people, 13 planters possessed 61% of taxable acreage and only 72 others owned any land at all; most white male adults were landless. In Lancaster County (1750–55) nearly half of the adult male population were slaves; another quarter were landless white tenants, and 21 great planters owned between 500 and 2,000 acres apiece.

[4]The richest families in New England were only middling prosperous by comparison with the great tidewater planters. Most towns in Massachusetts knew nothing like the dominion of great landed families that existed throughout the Chesapeake. The closest parallel in New England was the town of Springfield, where the Pynchon family was exceptionally rich and powerful. But even at the peak of their power, the Pynchons owned only about 20% of taxable wealth in that town. By most quantitative measures, the distribution of wealth even in Springfield was closer to the New England average than to Virginia's. Stephen Innes, *Labor in a New Land: Economy and Society in Seventeenth Century Springfield* (Princeton, 1983), 44–47.

shire and Virginia, the middling ranks were minorities, and wealth was largely concentrated in the hands of a small elite.[5]

The leading cause was the method of land distribution, which was managed in a manner very different from Massachusetts. In Virginia, the land belonged to the Crown. Access was carefully controlled by the Royal Governor and Council. This narrow oligarchy of great planters was able to dominate the distribution of land for the better part of two centuries. The result was a pattern of ownership opposite to that of New England in a great many ways. Only a few tracts of land in Virginia went to corporate groups; most were given directly to individuals. One basis for distribuiton was the headright system in which a "privilege" of fifty acres was given for every person transported to Virginia—another device by which a large part of Virginia's land was controlled by a few great holders.[6]

The average size of individual land patents in Virginia was always larger than in New England. They reached their peak in the last years of Governor Berkeley's administration, at 890 acres on the average. Some grants were as large as 20,000 acres, or more than thirty square miles—an area larger than entire towns in Massachusetts.[7]

A few were of even greater size. The leading example was Virginia's "northern neck," a vast area of more than two million acres bounded by the Rappahannock and Potomac rivers. This enormous tract, three times larger than the colony of Rhode Island, was granted by Charles II to his Royalist supporters after the Restoration. Title was acquired by Thomas Lord Culpeper, and later passed by inheritance to Thomas Lord Fairfax, whose family held it until after the War of Independence. Many other holdings were similar in structure, though not in size Beverley

---

[5]Horn, "Social and Economic Aspects of Local Society in England and the Chesapeake," 126–28; see also *idem*, "The Distribution of Wealth in the Vale of Berkeley, Gloucestershire, 1660–1700," *SH* 3 (1981), 81–110.

[6]On the nexus of land, family and politics see John Randolph to Sir Justinian Isham, 7 March 1660, Isham Mss. 499, NHANTSRO.

[7]Bruce computed the size of land grants as follows:

Year	Mean	Maximum
1607–50	442	5,350
1650–1700	674	20,000

Source: Philip A. Bruce, *Economic History of Virginia in the Seventeenth Century* (2 vols., 1895, New York, 1935), I, 532.

manor, for example, was an area of 118,000 acres which had been given to William Beverley in 1736 for an annual rent of one pound for every thousand acres.[8]

A large proportion of land grants in Virginia were awarded by the Council to its own members and their kin—Carters, Byrds, Wormeleys, Beverleys, Fitzhughs and others. The contrast with New England could scarcely have been more complete. In Massachusetts, access to the land was controlled by men of middling status who used it to reproduce families of their own rank. In Virginia, the distribution of land was dominated by an elite who employed it to maintain their own hegemony. The authority of Virginia's first families rested in part upon this material base.

Virginia's planting elite owned not merely a large proportion of arable farmland in the tidewater, but also much of what little urban real estate there was in the colony. A case in point was a little trading town optimistically called Urbanna, which stood on Rosebud Creek across from Rosegill, the great house of the Wormeley family. The entire town was built on fifty acres of Wormeley land. For many years the Wormeleys dominated the affairs of Urbanna—by law when possible, by force if need be. When a building project displeased Ralph Wormeley, he simply sent his servants across Rosebud Creek with orders to pull it down.[9]

Other planters also behaved as if they owned the Anglican churches near their estates. In 1747, an Anglican minister named William Kay infuriated the great planter Landon Carter by preaching a sermon against pride. The planter took it personally, and sent "his kindred relations, or such as were subject to him" and ordered them to nail up the doors and windows of all the churches in which Kay preached.[10]

These great tidewater families also controlled much undeveloped land on the western frontier of Virginia. The Byrd family, for example, acquired vast tracts of virgin territory in the Piedmont and the Southside. So also did many other great planters. The frontier in the southern colonies never functioned as an engine of equality; its effect on wealth distribution was to reinforce dominant tendencies in the material culture that was carried to it.

In some parts of Virginia a very large proportion of the white

[8]Edward Ingle, *Local Institutions in Virginia* (Baltimore, 1885), 32.

[9]Rutman and Rutman, *A Place in Time*, 216–17.

[10]Wyatt-Brown, *Southern Honor*, 102.

population were tenants of these great landed families. Many white householders owned no land at all, and not even the roofs over their heads. This was the especially the case in the Northern Neck, where the Fairfax family had vast proprietary holdings and the great majority of all householders were its tenants. The Northern Neck was exceptional in that respect, but the number of tenant-farmers was also large throughout many tidewater counties, and in the Piedmont as well.[11]

Entire estates such as Beverley Manor on the Rappahannock were worked by leaseholders who paid rent in money, labor and a share of their crops. Southern share-cropping was not an invention of the post-Civil War period. Before the end of Governor Berkeley's administration, it was well established in tidewater Virginia, where it had been introduced from southern England.[12] As late as 1724, the word "farming" in Virginia still meant "tenant farming" in the English sense—a meaning it had already lost in Massachusetts.[13] This was an echo of something very old in the Western world, and at the same time the beginning of something new—a material order destined to spread throughout the American south from the seventeenth century to the twentieth.

This material system supported the cultural achievements of Virginia gentlemen. It also produced a degraded caste of poor whites and an exploited black proletariat. There were large numbers of desperately poor farm workers in seventeenth-century Virginia. Some were indentured servants; others were tenants; a

---

[11]Allan Kulikoff has brought together the results of many research projects on tenancy in the Chesapeake colonies:

Place	Year	Percent of Households Owning Land	Number of Households Altogether
Prince George's Co., Md.	1705	65%	459
	1733	58%	1,204
	1755	56%	1,337
	1776	45%	1,669
Charles and Calvert Cos., Md.	1783	47%	2,805
Northern Neck, Va.	1787	42%	n.a.
Fairfax Co., Va.	1782	36%	831
Richmond Co., Va.	1782	70%	511
	1790	56%	655
James City Co., Va.	1768	70%	268
Tidewater Virginia	1787	64%	n.a.

Source: Kulikoff, *Tobacco and Slaves,* 135, citing research by Lois Green Carr, Gregory Stiverson, Jackson Turner Main and Norman Risjord, in addition to his own inquiries.

[12]Andrews, *Colonial Folkways,* 35.
[13]Willard F. Bliss, "The Rise of Tenancy in Virginia," *VMHB* 58 (1958), 427–41.

few were free laborers who wandered from job to job. The condition of the working poor in the Chesapeake was as harrowing
as it had been in England. They were required to work from sun-
up to sun-down. They slept wherever they could find shelter in
sheds, barns and filthy lofts. They dressed in rough, baggy linsey-
woolsey trousers, with ill-fitting shirts tied at the waist with a bit
of yarn, or perhaps a piece of green vine. Their diet consisted
mainly of a gruel made of corn. And on top of all else they were
despised as the refuse of the earth by the people who exploited
them. In all of this, Virginia and England were similar; Massachusetts was a world apart.[14]

The working poor of Virginia, miserable as they may have been,
were not the lowest stratum of the white population in this colony. At the very bottom were dependent paupers who were supported by the Anglican parishes. Pauper poverty was a persistent
problem in Virginia, as it had been throughout the south of
England. Where New England towns spent most of their taxes for
the support of churches and schools, southern parishes were
compelled to contribute the bulk of their hard-won public funds
to poor relief. Here again, they resembled southwestern England
in the seventeenth century.[15]

Another part of Virginia's wealth ways was its system of inheritance. From an early date the laws of the colony insisted that
primogeniture and entail must apply in all intestate estates.
Whenever a Virginian died without a valid will, the eldest son
inherited the homestead and all the lands, in fee tail rather than
fee simple. This law had a genuine impact upon inheritance practices, for many Virginians died intestate.[16]

Planters who prepared their own testaments were permitted to
do as they pleased. In the early and mid-seventeenth century, few
of them observed the rules of primogeniture. Most divided their
lands and chattels amongst their several children. The greater
abundance of land in the New World allowed parents more latitude in that respect. As late as 1724, Hugh Jones wrote that this
practice was customary in Virginia, "the tracts being divided
every age among several children not unlike gavelkind in Kent."[17]

[14]Rutman and Rutman, *A Place in Time*, 130; Morgan, *American Slavery, American Freedom*,
338–43.
[15]Rutman and Rutman, *A Place in Time*, 201; cf. Virginia Bernhard, "Poverty and the Social
Order in Seventeenth Century Virginia," *VMHB* 85 (1977), 141–55.
[16]C. Ray Keim, "Primogeniture and Entail in Colonial Virginia," *WMQ3* 25 (1968), 545–86.
[17]Jones, *Present State of Virginia*, 93.

But these divisions were not equal, and the eldest son tended to be specially favored. Often he inherited the "great house," if the family was fortunate enough to own one. Younger sons commonly received less, and youngest sons got least of all. In 1699 Virginia planter John Washington (himself a youngest son) testified to the custom of the country. "I had not the value of twenty shillings of my father's estate," he wrote bitterly, "I being the youngest and therefore the weakest which generally comes off short."[18]

As time passed, the custom of primogeniture grew stronger in Virginia. The proportion of testators who gave their land to a single child increased steadily. In western Albemarle County, for example, during the 1750s less than 8 percent of property owners with two or more children left all or most of their real estate to a single heir. That proportion rose to 19 percent in the 1760s, and 26 percent in the 1770s. The same trend appeared much earlier in tidewater counties. When land ran short, parents quickly abandoned the principle of partibility.[19]

The primary purpose of these customs was not to serve the interest of individuals, but to promote the welfare of the family and even the estate. When, for example, a member of the Newdigate family disposed of his lands in Warwickshire, he wrote, ". . . my wife shall have the possession of the whole during her life, not only thereby the better to maintain my children, but also for the better increase of the profits of my lands." The land itself seemed more in his mind than his own kin. More than one English gentlemen believed that his estate did not exist to serve posterity; but that posterity existed to serve the estate.[20]

The same concern also appeared in the Chesapeake colonies where even very rich men were forced to choose between the interest of individual children and the welfare of the family. When every child was given an equal share, the family tended to decline in status. In Maryland, for example, when a Huguenot gentleman named Mareen Duvall divided his large estate equally amongst twelve children, only three were able to marry into fam-

---

[18]John Washington to his sister 22 June 1699, Ms. P1700a, NHANTSRO.

[19]Smith, *Inside the Great House,* 245.

[20]Half of this estate went to the eldest son at his majority, with the stipulation that he would provide marriage portions for his sisters. The smallest portions in the Newdigate family went to the younger sons. This was a common pattern in the south and west of England. Younger sons did not do as well as their sisters. Newdigate testament and inventory, 10 July 1610, Newdigate Mss. CR 136, C19, WARRO.

ilies of their fathers' rank. The rest were wed to yeomen or husbandmen. The entire family lost status as a consequence of partible inheritance.[21] In general, inheritance customs were very
similar in the Chesapeake and southwestern England. They were
an important factor in maintaining social hierarchies on both
sides of the Atlantic.[22]

Altogether the wealth ways of Virginia were similar to those of
southern England in many ways—in the small and very powerful
class of landed gentry, in the large majority of landless tenants
and laborers, in the minority status of its middle class, in the general level of wealth inequality (Gini ratios of .60 to .75), in the
magnitude of poverty and in the degradation of the poor. The
rise of this wealth system cannot be explained merely in terms of
market relationships or material factors. It was shaped by the values of Virginia's ruling elite, and transmitted through social institutions from one generation to the next.

❧ Virginia Rank Ways: A System of Extended Orders

Virginia's wealth ways developed within a system of stratification,
which is not easily translated into the social language of a later
age. Even in its own time, it was commonly described in meta-
phorical terms—which may still be the best way to approach it.
In the year 1699, for example, an English landowner named
Richard Newdigate explained his idea of society by a metaphor
that came readily to the mind of a country gentleman. Society, he
wrote, was like the landscape of his native Warwickshire. The
common people were the grass that grew in the fields. The nobles
and gentry were the trees that shaded the grass. And the clergy
were the cherries that hung from the trees.[1]

That curious image was not unique to its author. Many similar
metaphors of social stratification were carried outward to the
Chesapeake by English emigrants in the seventeenth century.
These ideas were similar in some respects to those that went to

---

[21]Kulikoff, *Tobacco and Slaves,* 267; Harry Wright Newman, *Mareen Duvall of Middle Plantation* . . . (Washington, 1952).

[22]For another study which finds broad similarities in the inheritance customs of Gloucestershire and the Chesapeake, see Horn, "Social and Economic Aspects of Local Society in England
and the Chesapeake," chap. V.

[1]Richard Newdigate, ms. dated 15 July 1699, Newdigate Papers, B 1308 a–c, WARRO.

Massachusetts. Both Anglo-American cultures preserved many forms of inequality which had existed in the mother country. Neither had modern class systems in which rank was determined by riches. In those respects, Virginia and Massachusetts were the same.

In other ways, however, these two ranking systems were different. New England, as we have seen, had a truncated system of social orders. The Virginians, on the other hand, extended the full array of English social orders, and reinforced them. There was much discussion of this ranking system among English country gentlemen during the period when Virginia was founded. Most described it as a hierarchy of "orders" and "degrees." In the year 1630 one observer who signed himself "Thomas Westcote, Gent." wrote that in Devon "there are (as I conceive it) but four degrees of difference." He labeled them "1. nobility or gentility; 2. yeomanry and husbandmen; 3. merchants; 4. day laborers and hirelings."[2] Others offered more elaborate descriptions. Camden in his *Britannia,* and Dugdale in his Diary, enumerated no fewer than six ranks of "esquires" alone, plus many shadings of "gentility." The authors of these various taxonomies differed in many details. In particular, country gentlemen were never very clear about the proper place of merchants in the scheme of things. Thomas Westcote ranked them below the "husbandmen" who were his tenant farmers; but others put them closer to the top; and some set them to the side in another social dimension altogether. Despite these differences, nearly everyone agreed on the fundamental fact that rural England was a layered society of high complexity—a hierarchy of orders and estates.[3]

Many twentieth-century historians have tried to translate these social orders into materialist terms. But most conceptions of social rank in the seventeenth century were not materialist. Westcote, for example, wrote that gentlemen and nobles were "not only such as by descent from ancient and worthy parentage are so, but those also as by their own proper virtues, valiant actions, travels, learning and other good deserts, have been and are by their sovereign advanced thereto."[4] In the same vein, William Harrison wrote that "gentlemen be those whom their race and blood, or at least their virtues, do make noble and known." In

[2]Thomas Westcote, Gent., *A View of Devonshire in 1630* (Exeter, 1845).

[3]William Camden, *Britannia* (1586, 6th ed. 1606, Eng. tr. London, 1610); William Dugdale, *Life, Diary and Correspondence* (London, 1827).

[4]Westcote, *A View of Devonshire.*

both England and Virginia gentility was normally defined in terms of ancient and worthy descent, virtue and valor, reputation and fame. Most of all, gentility was a matter of honor.[5]

This ranking system was more rigid than a modern class system. In the twentieth century, status changes instantly with one's material possessions; in consequence, many studies find that social mobility (in small steps) is a common and even normal part of the ranking system. In a world of social orders movement was more constrained in some respects, and less so in others. But status was also more brittle, and more easily shattered—by loss of honor for example.

All of these characteristics were carried to Virginia. In the period from 1650 to 1775, few men in that colony succeeded in rising above the social order in which they were born. Many servants became freemen, but comparatively few rose to the rank of freeholder. Further, historian Martin Quitt finds that "not a single indentured servant who arrived after 1640 appears to have won a seat in the assembly before 1706." Further, Quitt also discovered that "apparently none of the burgesses from 1660 to 1706 was descended from indentured servants who emigrated after 1640." Virginia's social system had been more fluid before the arrival of Governor Berkeley. But by 1676, the rigidity of social orders was very great. It was exceptionally difficult to cross the great divide that separated "common folk" and "gentle folk" in that colony.[6]

The psychological cement of this system was a culture of subordination which modern historians call deference. Country gentlemen in England and Virginia normally expected a display of social deference from their inferiors, and by and large they received it. "Everybody offered me abundance of respect," William Byrd entered in his diary on more than one occasion.[7] Gen-

---

[5]William Harrison, *A Description of England*, ed. George Edelen (New York, 1968), 149; on honor see Wyatt-Brown, *Southern Honor*, chap. 2.

[6]Quitt adds the word "apparently" because he was unable to discover the origins of 13 burgesses out of 345. Arguments to the contrary have been made about the Chesapeake, but they tend to draw their evidence from Maryland, which was more open than Virginia in the late 17th and early 18th century. The social system of Virginia had been more fluid in the early years of the colony, but after the arrival of Sir William Berkeley, it became very much more rigid. Quitt's evidence shows that the major change occurred in the 1640s and 1650s, not in 1676 or 1690. See Martin H. Quitt, "Virginia House of Burgesses, 1660–1706: The Social, Educational and Economic Bases of Political Power (thesis, Washington Univ. 1970), 274.

[7]Byrd, *Secret Diary*, 410, 411, 413: Rhys Isaac, *The Transformation of Virginia, 1740–1790* (Chapel Hill, 1982), 108.

tlefolk and common folk agreed on the fundamental fact that social deference was normal in Virginia. The classical account, often quoted by historians, is the autobiography of Devereux Jarrett, who was born in the lowest order. "We were accustomed to look upon, what were called *gentle folks,* as beings of a superior order," he remembered. "For my part, I was quite shy of *them,* and kept off at a humble distance."[8]

This relationship created intense feelings of anxiety and fear among the "common folk," in a manner that is not easy for people of another world to understand. A clergyman named James Ireland remembered an encounter with a Virginia gentleman: "When I viewed him riding up, I never beheld such a display of pride in any man. . . . arising his deportment, attitude and gesture; he rode a lofty elegant horse . . . his countenance appeared as bold and daring as satan himself."[9]

Social rank in Virginia was an extended hierarchy of deferential relationships. Even the greatest planters were conscious of a rank above them, which was occupied by the King himself and the royal family. Distant as the sovereign may have been, the gentry of Virginia thought much about him. William Byrd even dreamed about imaginary intimacies with members of the royal family, as did many English-speaking people in the seventeenth and early eighteenth century. "I . . . dreamed the King's daughter was in love with me," he wrote in his diary on one occasion—a common fantasy in the minds of seventeenth-century Englishmen, who were obsessed with the feelings of those above them.[10]

Just as the gentlemen of Virginia deferred to their King, so the yeomanry were expected to defer to gentlemen, servants were required to defer to their yeoman masters, and African slaves were compelled to submit themselves to Europeans of every social rank. These rules were generally obeyed in Virginia. Acts of criminal violence, for example, were rarely committed on people of higher rank by social inferiors.

Deference also had a reciprocal posture called condescension—a word which has radically changed its meaning in the past two hundred years. To condescend in the seventeenth and eigh-

---

[8] *The Life of the Rev. Devereux Jarratt, Rector of Bath Parish, Dinwiddie County, Virginia, Written by Himself* (Baltimore, 1806), 39.

[9] Isaac, *The Transformation of Virginia,* 161.

[10] Byrd, 27 Aug. 1720, *London Diary and Other Writings,* 444; similar dreams appear in the diary of the English astrologer Simon Forman; see A. L. Rowse, *Sex and Society in Shakespeare's Age: Simon Forman the Astrologer* (New York, 1974), 20–21.

The iconography of deference in Royalist England appears in a self-portrait by the court painter Anthony Van Dyck. This work had a very different purpose from self-portraiture in our own time. Van Dyck sought to celebrate a spirit of subordination, obligation and deference in his hierarchical world. The artist's right hand points to an enormous sunflower, while his left hand fingers a heavy gold chain. In Thynne's Emblems and Epigrams presented to Sir Thomas Egerton *the sunflower was made to represent the bond between king and people, for "just as the sunflower turns to the sun for strength and sustenance, so the subject turns toward his monarch." The same symbol also appeared in* The Mirror of Majestie *(1618), where the courtier is compared to a sunflower, "waiting upon the sonne of his Majestie" (Brown,* Van Dyck, *147). Another symbol of obligation was Van Dyck's golden chain, which had been given to him by Charles I, together with a portrait medallion of the king. These hierarchical relationships were thought to exist not merely between the king and his loyal subjects, but between superiors and inferiors of every rank.*

teenth centuries was to treat an inferior with kindness, decency and respect. The gentlefolk of Virginia were taught to "condescend" in this special sense, and many of them tried to do so. St. George Tucker recalled that in colonial Virginia "the rich rode in Coaches, or Chariots, or on fine horses, but they never failed to pull off their hats to a poor man whom they met, and generally appeared to me to shake hands with every man in a Court-yard, or a Church-yard." Gentlemen and ladies were taught to "condescend" graciously to their inferiors in this manner.[11]

But not all of them learned to do so. The social reality was sometimes very far from this ideal. The darker side of deference was a common attitude of contempt for the poor and weak and unlucky. This was a world without pity. Charles Woodmason described an encounter in the low country of South Carolina with the vestrymen of St. Mark's parish—many of whom were transplanted tidewater Virginians:

> When I first came over, they advis'd me to marry—a circumstance I am wholly unfit for, as being both old and impotent for many years past, 'thro a fall received from an horse, and a kick received in the scrotum. . . . I told our vestry my unfitness, which they laughed at as a joke.[12]

In all of these respects, Virginia's system of stratification was very similar to that in the south and west of England. In another way, however, the rank ways of that colony were profoundly different from those of the mother country. To the English system of social orders, Virginians added the even more rigid category of race slavery. Sir William Berkeley himself played a major role in its development. He tried first to establish an Indian slave trade. In 1666, he wrote:

> I think it is necessary to destroy all these northern indians. . . . 'Twill be a great terror and example and instruction to all other Indians . . . it may be done without charge, for the women and children will defray it.[13]

When these efforts failed, Berkeley encouraged the development of African slavery. It is important to remember the timing of its appearance. Slavery came late to Virginia. The first Africans

---

[11]"Notes of St. George Tucker on Manuscript Copy of William Wirt's *Life of Patrick Henry* (September 25, 1815)," *WMQ1* 22 (1914), 252; Breen, *Tobacco Culture*, 34.

[12]Charles Woodmason, *The Carolina Backcountry* (Chapel Hill, 1953), 198.

[13]Sir William Berkeley to Maj. Gen. Smyth, 22 June 1666, *WMQ2* 16 (1936), 591.

appeared in the colony as early as 1619; a census of 1625 enumerated 23 blacks.[14] But when Sir William Berkeley first arrived,
there were fewer Africans in the Chesapeake than in New
England or New Netherlands. Their legal status remained very
unclear. The concept of chattel slavery was defined very gradually
in a series of statutes through the late seventeenth and early eighteenth century. Several of the major statutes were probably written by Sir William Berkeley himself.[15]

The development of slavery in Virginia was a complex process—one that cannot be explained simply by an economic
imperative. A system of plantation agriculture resting upon slave
labor was not the only road to riches for Virginia's royalist elite.
With a little imagination, one may discern a road not taken in
southern history. In purely material terms, Virginia might have
flourished as did her northern neighbors, solely by complex spec-
ulations in land and trade, and by an expansive system of freehold
farming. But Virginia's ruling elite had other aims in mind. For
its social purposes, it required an underclass that would remain
firmly fixed in its condition of subordination. The culture of the
English countryside could not be reproduced in the New World
without this rural proletariat. In short, slavery in Virginia had a
cultural imperative. Bertram Wyatt-Brown writes, " . . . the South
was not founded to create slavery; slavery was recruited to perpetuate the South."[16]

But this solution created another set of problems. The harsh
reality of slavery undercut the cultural ideal that it was meant to
serve. The result was an elaborate set of subterfuges, in which
Virginia planters tried to convince themselves, if no one else, that

---

[14]The number of Africans in Virginia was reckoned at 500 in 1649 by an anonymous pam-
phleteer, 2,000 in 1671 by Sir William Berkeley, and 3,000 in 1681 by Thomas Culpeper. Philip
Bruce estimated that there were 6,000 blacks in Virginia by 1700. Wesley Frank Craven put the
number in that year at "somewhat larger but not greatly in excess of six thousand." Edmund
Morgan guessed that the total number of blacks was between 1,000 and 3,000 in 1674 and
between 6,000 and 10,000 in 1700—with the lower estimates being more likely. The *Historical
Statistics of the United States* are grossly inaccurate on this issue. See Bruce, *Economic History of
Virginia,* II, 108; Craven, *White, Red and Black,* 98–103; Morgan, *American Slavery, American
Freedom,* 423.

[15]The black population changed as follows in the four colonies:

	New England	New York	Chesapeake	Maryland	Virginia
1640	195	232	160	10	150
1680	470	1,200	5,438	1,438	4,000

Source: Russell R. Menard, "Population, Economy and Society in Seventeenth Century Maryland," *MDHM* 79 (1984), 71–92.

[16]Wyatt-Brown, *Southern Honor,* 16.

their peculiar system was little different from that which had existed in rural England. As early as 1727, William Byrd II wrote to the Earl of Orrery, "Our poor negroes are freemen in comparison of the slaves who till your ungenerous soil; at least if slavery consists in scarcity, and hard work."[17]

Other subterfuges were also resorted to. A slave was rarely called a slave in the American south by his master. Slaves were referred to as "my people," "my hands," "my workers," almost anything but "my slaves." They were made to dress like English farm workers, to play English folk games, to speak an English country dialect, and to observe the ordinary rituals of English life in a charade that Virginia planters organized with great care.

In the end, these fictions failed to convince even their creators. William Byrd, in a more candid mood, confessed to the Earl of Egmont in 1736 that slavery was a great evil. It was typical of him (and others of his rank) to believe that it was hateful not so much because of its effect on the slave but because of what it did to their masters. "They blow up the pride, and ruin the industry of our white people," he wrote, ". . . another unhappy effect of my negroes is the necessity of being severe."[18]

William Byrd, in company with many large planters, came to favor a parliamentary prohibition of the slave trade. But this was after his status as a country gentleman was secure. If slavery was not quite what Virginians really wanted, it carried them closer to their conservative utopia than any alternative which lay within reach.[19]

❧ The Virginia Comity:
Patterns of Migration, Settlement and Association

In the year 1754, a planter of high rank named Peter Fontaine gave his brothers a prescription for social happiness in Virginia. "The most happy state this life affords," he wrote, "is a small estate which will . . . set him above the necessity of submitting to

---

[17]William Byrd II to Charles Boyle, Earl of Orrery, 2 Feb. 1727, Tinling, ed., *Correspondence of the Three William Byrds*, III, 358.

[18]William Byrd II to John Perceval, Earl of Egmont, 12 July 1736, *ibid.*, I, 487.

[19]The history of slavery and African folkways in America is discussed at length in volume 2 of this book. Here only two points are to be made. First, the culture of Virginia came before slavery. Second, slavery developed not merely from an economic but a broadly cultural imperative.

the humors and vices of others. . . . One thousand acres of land will keep troublesome neighbors at a distance."[1]

Few Virginia families were able to achieve this material goal, but many shared the same dream. In consequence, patterns of settlement in the Chesapeake colonies were very different from those in Massachusetts. Despite strong official efforts to encourage the growth of towns and cities, the people of Virginia preferred to scatter themselves across the countryside. Many visitors remarked upon the Virginians' taste for "living solitary and unsociable . . . confused and dispersed." But their houses were not scattered at random across the countryside. By the mid-seventeenth century, a distinct system of settlement had developed in Virginia—small market villages straggling along major streams, large plantations and little farms.[2]

This pattern was not invented in the New World. English travelers commonly recorded an impression that they had seen it all before. The little towns of Virginia reminded them of small market centers in the south and west of England. William Hugh Grove, for example, thought that the market town of Yorktown resembled Richmond Hill in Surrey.[3] Tidewater plantations were often compared to English manorial communities. Grove observed that the great houses, with their surrounding servant quarters "shew like little villages." A French traveler in Virginia thought that they had "the appearance of a small town." Other tourists in the mother country had recorded similar impressions of larger manors throughout southwestern England.[4] The small dispersed farms of Virginia also reminded observers of settlement patterns in southern England. Robert Beverley wrote, "'the neighborhood is at much the same distance as in the country in England. . . . The goodness of the roads and the fairness of the weather bring people together."[5]

In the absence of townships, local attachments were not as strong in Virginia as in New England, and rates of geographic migration were much higher. Persistence rates (by decade) for the

---

[1]Peter Fontaine to John and Moses Fontaine, 15 April 1754, in Ann Maury, *Memoirs of a Huguenot Family* (New York, 1853), 340–42; quoted in Jan Lewis, *The Pursuit of Happiness,* (Cambridge, 1983), 12.

[2]Thomas Glover, "The Account of Virginia," *The Philosophical Transactions and Collections to the End of the Year 1700 . . .* , ed. John Lowthrop (London, 1716), III, 569.

[3]Stiverson and Butler, "Virginia in 1732," 18–44.

[4]*Ibid.,* 26; see also Isaac, *Transformation of Virginia,* 35.

[5]Beverley, *The History and Present State of Virginia,* 308.

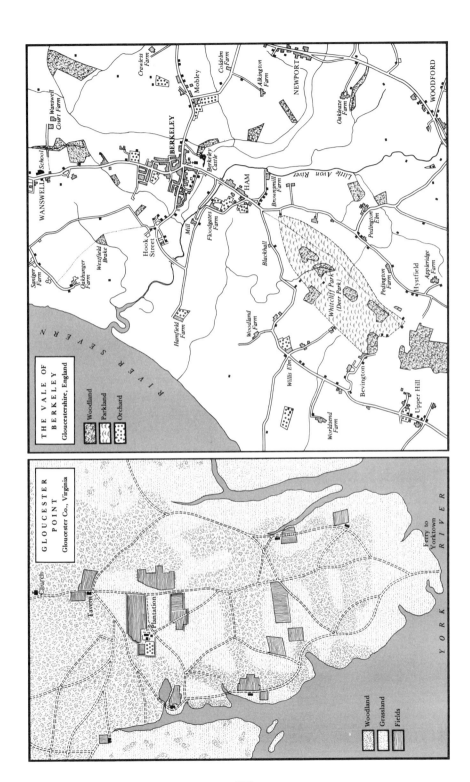

THE VALE OF BERKELEY
Gloucestershire, England

Woodland
Parkland
Orchard

RIVER SEVERN

Crawless Farm
Mobley
Coldelm Farm
Alkington Farm
NEWPORT
WOODFORD
Oakleaze Farm
Wanswell Court Farm
BERKELEY
School
Berkeley Castle
Little Avon River
HAM
Brownsmill Farm
Pedington Elm
WANSWELL
Hook Street
Mill
Floodgates Farm
Blackhall
Pedington Farm
Aystfield
Appleridge Farm
Saniger Farm
Westfield Brake
Oakhunger Farm
Whitcliff Park (Deer Park)
Hamfield Farm
Woodland Farm
Willis Elm
Bevington
Upper Hill
Worldsend Farm

GLOUCESTER POINT
Gloucester Co., Virginia

Woodland
Grassland
Fields

Church
Tavern
Plantation
Ferry to Yorktown
YORK RIVER

free whites were only about 40 to 50 percent in seventeenth-century Virginia, compared with 60 to 70 percent in most Massachusetts towns.[6] Migration in Virginia tended to be more hierarchical than in New England. A study of geographic mobility in Massachusetts found remarkably little difference between rich and poor in rates of persistence. But in the Chesapeake colonies, that disparity was very great.[7]

Studies of migration in England have not been done by methods which permit exact comparison. But the best available evidence suggests that persistence rates in the Chesapeake colonies were similar to those in those parts of England from which the most Virginians came. Rates of migration in Northampton County, Virginia, for example, were almost exactly the same as in the parish of Cogenhoe, Northamptonshire.[8]

This system of migration and settlement had an impact upon patterns of association in Virginia. The primary units of belonging were the family and the rural "neighborhood," a word often used in the seventeenth and eighteenth centuries to describe a group of ten or twenty households which were close enough to think of themselves as neighbors. The size of these rural neighborhoods was much the same in the Chesapeake and the west of England.[9]

[6]Crude rates of persistence for tithables were as follows in Northampton Co., Va.: 1664–74, 45%; 1665–75, 43%; 1666–76, 46%; 1667–77, 42%. In Surry Co., Va., they were: 1668–78, 46%; 1678–88; 47%; 1688–98, 45%. Comparisons with rates of persistence in New England are problematical. The unit of study is the county in Virginia and the town in New England. The county tended to be larger than the town. As the analytic unit increases in size, the persistence rate rises too, *ceterus paribus*. In consequence, the difference between Massachusetts and Virginia in rates of crude persistence was actually greater than appears here. But mortality was higher in the Chesapeake than in New England; refined persistence rates (which cannot yet be computed for Virginia) would be closer in the two regions than crude persistence rates tended to be. Sources include Kevin Kelly, "Economic and Social Development of Seventeenth Century Surry County, Virginia" (thesis, Univ. of Washington, 1972); Edmund S. Morgan, *American Slavery, American Freedom* (New York, 1975), 427.

[7]Allan Kulikoff reports the following refined migration rates for Prince George's County, Maryland, 1733–43: householders owning land and slaves, 15%; householders owning land or slaves, 29%; long-term residents, owning neither, 39%; recent immigrants, owning neither, 58%; sons of tenants, 65%; laborers without kin ties in county, 75%; Kulikoff, *Tobacco and Slaves*, 93.

[8]Peter Laslett discovered two population lists for the parish of Cogenhoe, Northamptonshire, an area that contributed heavily to the peopling of Virginia. The crude persistence rate in Cogenhoe from 1618 to 1628 was 48%, almost exactly the same as in Northampton County, Virginia. See Peter Laslett and John Harrison, "Clayworth and Cogenhoe," in H. E. Bell and R. L. Ollard, eds., *Historical Essays Presented to David Ogg* (1963); a revised and expanded edition appears in Peter Laslett, *Family Life and Illicit Love in Earlier Generations; Essays in Historical Sociology* (Cambridge, 1977), 50–101.

[9]For evidence that the size of the neighborhood was similar in the Chesapeake and the west of England, see Horn, "Social and Economic Aspects of Local Society in England and the Chesapeake," 286.

As one generation succeeded another, neighborhoods tended to become kin-groups. Ties of blood and marriage created a web of increasing density. The members of these kin-neighborhoods worked together, played together, and went to church and court days together. They borrowed from one another, becoming also a network of credit and barter relationships. Gifts were frequently exchanged within these groups. The most important time for gift-giving was the new year. Cousins and neighbors exchanged presents such as sugar loafs, pomegranates, capons, spices, tobacco pipes, porcelain dishes. This tradition had been specially strong in the south of England—stronger than in the North or East Anglia. "Sussex is the freest place in England for the giving of New Year's gifts," one gentleman observed in 1622. The custom was also stronger in Virginia than in New England.[10]

Among the high elite, patterns of association were a little different. Virginia's elite tended to mix with others of their own rank at a greater distance through the colony. But in other respects, the structure of these relationships was the same as within small neighborhoods of middling farmers. The gentry also increasingly became a cousinage, working and living together in unitary relationships of increasing intensity.[11]

Diaries on both sides of the Atlantic recorded the density of this associative pattern:

> 10 April 1649 [visiting with] Sir Thomas Wilbraham, my cozen Thomas, my cozen Roger Wilbraham of Derfold & my cozen Peter, my cozen John Bellot, Mr. Morgell & my cozen Ed. Nyonhall with divers others.
>
> 11 April at Baddesley, nothing remarkable
>
> 12 April at Baddesley. That day my cozen Peter Wilbraham and his wife, my cozen Rachel Lothian and my cozen Alice Wilbraham were here.
>
> 13 April at Stoke; in the afternoon my cozen Roger Wilbraham and old cozen Bellot came thither.[12]

These neighborhoods were intensely curious about strangers. When one West Countryman was traveling in England from

---

[10]Bamford, ed., *A Royalist's Notebook,* 4.

[11]John Richards Diary, DORSRO, is particularly full in descriptions of credit relations among cousins and neighbors, and also of the constant entertaining. See especially entries for 1692 and 1697.

[12]Manwaring Diary, 10 April 1649, ms. DDY 384/1, CHESRO.

Somerset to Berkshire, he recorded many instances of this attitude. At Castle Cary in Somerset he wrote, "A crowd gathered and asked of what country I was," though he was only a few miles from home. The same thing happened to him at Andover in Hampshire and Reading in Berkshire. A similar attitude also existed in Virginia.[13]

In southwestern England and tidewater Virginia, the rhythm of association was much the same. Through the week, people worked on their farms and plantations, mixing mostly with their own families and neighbors. But on church days and court days, the scale of association suddenly changed. Virginians of all ranks and conditions met and mingled at their parish churches and county courthouses, which were favorite places for buying and selling, racing and gambling, meeting and gossiping.

This tidewater pattern followed the prevailing customs in southwestern England. The seventeenth-century diary of an affluent Devon yeoman named William Honeywell, for example, detailed very much the same sort of life in the West Country of England, near the town of Exeter. Most days, Honeywell labored on his land. He had daily contacts with what he called his "principal friends" in his rural neighborhood, and he remembered them all in his will:

> To my principal friend Mrs. Staplehill forty pounds, to my delighted sure friend Mr. Estchurch, thirty pounds, to my singular great friend Mr. Simon Clifford twenty pounds, to my constant friend Mr. Bollen twenty pounds, to my fast friend and cousin Mr. Bagwell of Exon twenty pounds, to my trusty friend Mr. Augustine Rackley five pounds, to my ancient and loving friend Mr. Simons five pounds.

Several times a year William Honeywell traveled to the shire town on court day:

> August 6 [1602].—I did reap my rye. . . . August 10.—I rode to Exeter at the Assize and staid at Hole's myself and horse, and spent there xvid. . . . August 11, 12, 13.—I remained at the Assizes. I bought a pair of shoes, and paid 2s. 6d. I bought a pair of boots, and a pair of shoes, and am to pay 9s. I spent there this week in horse and self 15s. . . .

[13]Cannon Memoirs, 1707, SOMERO.

William Honeywell's diary also showed that Sundays were a time for recreation in rural Devon:

> August 22—I went to Trusham Church. After evening prayers went to bowles.[14]

These patterns of association were closely interwoven with the structure of material life in southwestern England. The inhabitants of that region were not isolated subsistence farmers. A large part of its social life consisted of market relationships. Our Devon yeoman William Honeywell accumulated an estate of several hundred pounds sterling. His wealth did not sit idle in a strong chest. It was loaned in sums of ten or twenty pounds to neighbors of all ranks and conditions. Most lenders charged a fixed interest of a shilling on a pound (5.0%), the custom of the country. A few were allowed to borrow without interest. Most loans were short-term transactions, settled at Christmas, Candlemas or Lady Day.

Altogether, a large part of this Devon yeoman's wealth was liquid capital which was carefully invested in a local money market and brought handsome returns. In the year 1600, for example, Honeywell reckoned his total assets at £440, of which £220 were stock and household goods, and £211 were loaned to his neighbors. At the same time he also owed £80 to others.[15]

Here was a capital market without capitalists, a financial market without banks, and a money market without middlemen of any kind. It was a web of many small transactions among family, friends and neighbors. Most countrymen participated in proportion to their wealth without distinctions of rank or station. Agreements were not reduced to writing but made orally in the presence of witnesses. The memory of the community thus became the record of its transactions. An oral contract was thought to be binding:

> Jan. 14 [1599]. I agreed with Hugh Clampitt and Arthur Horne's son-in-law to build the barn at Riddon . . . I must pay him 56 shillings 8 pence and if I bring the water to the place, then he is to abate five shillings. Hugh Clampitt hath given his word to see it finished . . . and this agreement was between us in the presence of George Murch, and I gave him fourpence in earnest.[16]

---

[14]F. J. Snell, "A Devonshire Yeoman's Diary," *A* 26 (1892), 254–59.
[15]*Ibid.*, 257.
[16]*Ibid.*, 256.

Some of the transactions became triangular exchanges, in which debts and credits passed current to a third party.

> June 23, 1601. I lent to Dick Drake of Morchard, on the 23rd of June five pounds in old gold, 2 Royals and 5 angels, and one piece of twenty shillings. He engaged himself with a great many oaths not to exchange it, but he would deliver it to his Aunt and have silver for it: he promised on his soul's health to bring it whole, in the presence of my sister Elisabeth.[17]

In the margin next to this entry, Honeywell later noted, "paid by Mrs. Thomas Clifford."

When William Honeywell's loans were not repaid, he went to law to recover them even from members of his own family. The result was a vast tangle of litigation in the country courts of southern England. Large numbers of little cases were tried without lawyers, and settled quickly by a member of the local gentry. The diaries of Chesapeake planters described precisely the same patterns as did the journals of southwestern England.[18]

This system of association was linked to a special idea of social bonding and belonging, in which reputation played a large part. Much depended on one's "standing" in the eyes of neighbors, friends and family. Particularly important was that form of reputation which Virginians called honor.

Honor in Virginia was compounded of two ideas. One of them was what historian Bertram Wyatt-Brown calls "primal honor," which meant physical courage and tenacity of will—in short, honor as valor. This was the meaning that Nathaniel Bacon had in mind when he cried out to his followers in 1676: "Come on, my hearts of gold! He that dies in the field lies in the bed of honor."[19] The other idea had to do with gentility, breeding, character and good conduct. This was honor as virtue. One English moralist in 1616 wrote, ". . . honor in [its] true definition is a certain reverence, which one man yieldeth to another extraordinarily, for his virtuous merit, and worthy desert, so that it should not be wealth but virtue, which should make an honorable man." An honorable person never lied, cheated, stole, or betrayed his

---

[17]*Ibid.*, 257; see also Christopher M. Gerrard, "Taunton Fair in the Seventeenth Century: An Archaeological Approach to the Historical Data," *SANHSP* 128 (1985), 65–74.

[18]Francis Taylor Diary, SHCUNC.

[19]"Bacon's Speech at Green Spring," *WMQ1* 3 (1894), 121; Wyatt-Brown, *Southern Honor,* 82.

family or friends. He was not disloyal, cowardly or mean-spirited.[20]

These two ideals of honor-as-valor and honor-as-virtue were interwoven in a creed that had great force in the culture of Virginia. Honor was a hierarchical principle. A high-born gentleman had great honor. A yeoman had less honor, but was thought capable of behaving honorably. A servant had little honor, and a slave had none at all. But people of every rank were mindful of reputation, in a way that does not exist in our modern world.

When Virginians misbehaved, they were punished by rituals of public humiliation. The common punishments were meant to shame them, sometimes by the same devices that were used in Puritan New England. One miscreant in Virginia was ordered to stand "several Sundays in time of divine service . . . in a white sheet with a white wand in his hand." This custom had long been kept in English parish churches, where people were required to appear "barehead, barefoot and barelegged," with a white sheet wrapped around a body "from the shoulder to the feet" and a white wand in one's hand."[21]

Shame had an emotional power which it has lost today. In a seventeenth-century suit for slander, it was said of a woman that:

> She lives forever in eternal shame
> That lives to see the death of her good name.[22]

The image of mortality was appropriate, for loss of reputation was a form of social death in this culture. In the comity of both Virginia and New England, rituals of honor and reputation, shame and humiliation were highly important during the seventeenth century, but in very different ways.

---

[20]Wright, *First Gentlemen of Virginia,* 10.

[21]Clara Ann Bowler, "Carted Whores and White-Shrouded Apologies: Slander in the County Courts of Seventeenth Century Virginia," *VMHB* 85 (1977), 411–26; William Andrews, *Old-Time Punishments* (1890, rpt. Williamstown, 1977), 164–75.

[22]*Charles County Court Proceedings,* 1662, *MDA* LIII, 319.

❧ Virginia Order Ways:
The Anglican Idea of Order as Hierarchy

In seventeenth-century Virginia, order was fundamentally a hierarchical conception. The classical expression of this idea was the
Anglican Homily of Obedience, which was read in the churches
of the colony:

> Almighty God hath created and appointed all things in heaven,
> earth and waters, in a most excellent and perfect order. In heaven
> he hath appointed distinct and several orders and states of arch-
> angels and angels. In earth he hath assigned and appointed kings,
> princes and other governors under them, all in good and neces-
> sary order. . . . The sun, moon, stars, rainbows, thunder, light-
> ning, clouds and all the birds in the air do keep their order. The
> earth, trees, seeds, plants, herbs, corn, grass, and all manner of
> beasts keep themselves in order. . . . And man himself hath all his
> parts . . . members of his body in a profitable, necessary and pleas-
> ant order. Every degree of people in their vocations, calling and
> office, hath appointed to them their duty and order. Some are in
> high degree; some in low, and every one have need of the other.[1]

This hierarchical idea of order had its antithesis in "confusion"
or "conmingling," two words which were used as synonyms. In
the neighboring province of Maryland, for example, the Royalist
writer George Alsop defined order as the opposite of confusion;
and confusion as "ranging in contrary and improper spheres."[2]

The ordering institutions of Virginia were as hierarchical as the
idea of order itself. The most important order-keepers were not
town constables who had been elected by the people, as in New
England, but county sheriffs who had been appointed in the
name of the Crown. In the seventeenth century, this office was
established in Virginia, and it has survived throughout the southern and western United States even to our own time. By law, a
sheriff was required to reside in the county where he served. By
custom, he was also expected to be a landed gentleman. In 1623,

---

[1] "An Exhortation to Obedience," *Book of Homilies* (1562). This was still read in Anglican
churches in Virginia as late as the mid-17th century. For a helpful discussion see Terence R.
Murphy, "The Early Tudor Concept of Order," in Emilio C. Viano and Jeffrey H. Reiman, eds.,
The Police in Society (Lexington, Mass., n.d.), 75–87; Keith Wrightson, "Two Concepts of Order
. . . ," in John Brewer and John Styles, eds., *An Ungovernable People; The English and Their Law
in the Seventeenth and Eighteenth Centuries* (London, 1980), 21–46.

[2] George Alsop, "A Character of the Province of Maryland" (1666), rpt. in Clayton C. Hall,
ed., *Narratives of Early Maryland,* 340–87.

Michael Dalton dedicated his essay on the duties of the sheriff "to the better encouragement of the gentry, upon whom the burthen of the office lyeth."[3]

In some Virginia counties the office of sheriff was held in rotation by the gentlemen justices. In others it became a patronage appointment. The justices of York County recommended one of their number, Captain Ralph Langley, on the ground that the "sheriff's office may be a great help to him in his present suffering condition."[4]

But the job was no sinecure. The sheriff was the leading executive officer of the county. His duties were to organize the courts, impanel juries, issue writs, call elections, read royal proclamations, maintain the peace, protect the church, administer judicial punishments, run the jail, and keep the county's records.

The sheriff was not expected to do these things himself. A gentlemen did not work with his hands, but guided the hands of others. Just as a physician did not cut open a body (a barber/surgeon's work) and a barrister did not actually engross a will (the task of a scrivener), so a sheriff was not actually required to lay hands upon a dirty felon. This was the work of under-sheriffs, deputies, jailers, county whippers, and clerks who did the dangerous manual labor of order-keeping in Virginia. The gentlemen-justices sometimes compelled one criminal to punish another. One convict was sentenced to serve as a hangman; another was ordered to cut off the ears of a culprit in the pillory.[5]

The same hierarchical ideas also appeared in treatment of the disorderly. Convicted felons in Virginia received very different punishments according to their rank. For all but the most serious crimes, literate criminals could plead "benefit of clergy." By reading aloud the "neck verse"[6] from the Bible they escaped a hanging, and were sentenced to be branded on the brawn of the thumb. Gentlemen-felons were sometimes sentenced to be branded with a "cold iron" which left no mark that might destroy their honor. But the poor and illiterate went to the gallows.[7]

---

[3]Michael Dalton, *The Office and Authoritie of the Sherifs* (London, 1623, rpt. 1682, 1700).

[4]Cyrus H. Karraker, *The Seventeenth-Century Sheriff: A Comparative Study of the Sheriff in England and the Chesapeake Colonies, 1607–1689* (Chapel Hill, 1930), 77–78.

[5]Arthur P. Scott, *Criminal Law in Colonial Virginia* (Chicago, 1930), 316.

[6]The neck verse ran, "Have mercy upon me, O God, according to thy loving kindness; according unto the multitude of thy mercies blot out my transgressions."

[7]Benefit of clergy rarely occurred in New England. Only two cases have been found in that region—in York County, Maine (1736), and in the trial of British soldiers after the Boston

The death penalty was very common in Virginia. As in the mother country, hundreds of felonies were capital crimes— which was not the case in the Puritan colonies. In a sample of forty-seven Virginia court sessions from 1737 and 1772, 164 people were convicted of a felony and not allowed to plead benefit of clergy. Of that number, 125 were actually executed.[8]

The method of execution was the same as in England. The convict was carried in a cart to the gallows which were sometimes erected at the scene of the crime. The condemned man was made to stand in the cart with a rope around his neck, and was invited to speak his last words before a huge crowd. Then the cart was driven forward, and he was left kicking and choking in the air. Death sometimes came slowly. In 1738, when a confessed murderer named Anthony Ditton dangled alive at the end of his rope, the hangman grabbed his legs in an effort to strangle him, and succeeded only in breaking the rope. Ditton fell unconscious to the ground; when he revived he mounted the cart once more and was hanged yet again.[9]

Punishment did not end with death. The body was given to physicians for dissection, or for the most heinous crimes was hung in chains on the public highway as a warning to others. The bodies of pirates were hung in chains at a river's edge. In another process called "corruption of blood," the convicted felon also forfeited his property to the Crown. This was done in the colony of Virginia.[10]

In addition to the violence of law, there was also customary violence, which occurred in many forms. These were not random or promiscuous acts. The use of nonjudicial violence was sanctioned and regulated by the unwritten rules of this society, more or less as follows. First, Virginia's system of customary violence was hierarchical in its nature. It was often used by superiors against inferiors, and sometimes by equals against one another, but rarely by people of subordinate status against those above them. Violence was thought to be the legitimate instrument of masters against servants, husbands against wives, parents against

---

massacre (1770). Hundreds of cases have been found in Virginia; see Arthur Lyon Cross, "Benefit of Clergy in American Criminal Law," *MAHSP* 61 (1928), 154–81; George W. Dalzell, *Benefit of Clergy & Related Matters* (Winston-Salem, 1955); Hugh F. Rankin, "Criminal Trial Proceedings in the General Court of Colonial Virginia," *VMHB* (1964), 50–71.

[8]Rankin, "Criminal Trial Proceedings," 50–74.

[9]*Virginia Gazette*, 24 Nov. 1738.

[10]Rankin, "Criminal Trial Proceedings," 71.

children, and gentlemen against ordinary folk. But violent acts by servants against masters, or common folk against gentle folk was followed by savage punishment.

Second, this legitimate social violence in Virginia was usually a response to some social or moral offense which affronted either the authority of a superior or the honor of an equal. In its customary forms it was meant to be measured violence. It tended to be proportionate to the seriousness of the offense, to the social status of the offender, and to the rank of the offended. But sometimes it exceeded these bounds.

The diary of William Byrd recorded many examples of customary violence:

> 4 April 1720 My maid Rose had endeavored to steal a sheep from Jack, for which reason I caused her to be whipped . . .

> 26 April 1720 I walked home and by the way beat my man for being drunk and saucy . . .

> 4 August 1720 Jenny B-s-n was whipped for several faults . . .

> 7 August 1720 My people almost all got drunk with cider I had given them, for which I was very angry with them and threatened to punish them that I should ever see drunk again.

The use of violence and even torture against servants and slaves occurred very frequently. An example was Byrd's treatment of a house boy named Eugene in the year 1709:

> 8 February 1709 Jenny and Eugene were whipped

> 10 June 1709 Eugene was whipped for running away and had the [bit or boot] put on him. I said my prayers and had good health, good thoughts and good humor, thanks be to God.

> 30 November 1709 Eugene was whipped for pissing in bed

> 1 December 1709 Eugene was whipped

> 3 December 1709 Eugene pissed abed again for which I made him drink a pint of piss.

> 10 December 1709 Eugene had pissed in bed for which I gave him a pint of piss to drink

> 16 December 1709 Eugene was whipped for doing nothing[11]

---

[11] Byrd, *London Diary and Other Writings*, 435; Wright and Tinling, eds., *Secret Diary of William Byrd*, 2, 46, 112, 113, 117, 119.

This treatment continued for years:

> 18 September 1712 I found Eugene asleep instead of being at
> work, for which I beat him severely

Occasionally a servant resisted—not by violence of his own,
which would have brought terrific punishment, but by announc-
ing that he would not agree to be whipped. Some masters acquiesced in this resistance, or found another mode of punishment.
But the usual response was that of William Byrd, who summoned
reinforcements and increased the punishment, without reflecting
very much about it.

> 17 June 1720 I found my man Johnny drunk, for which I threat-
> ened to beat him. He said I should not, so I had him whipped and
> gave him thirty lashes. I danced my dance. Read some Latin till
> dinner, then ate some cold ham and sallet. After dinner I took a
> nap . . .[12]

It is interesting to observe that William Byrd also used the same
customary violence against wives, children, servants, slaves, and
animals—especially animals:

> 2 July 1720 I took a walk about the plantation and shot an old dog
> with an arrow for flying at me but did not kill him.

> 23 July 1720 I talked with my people and Jack told me of some
> horses that had destroyed a hogshead of tabacco and I gave him
> orders to shoot them as not being fit to live. I said my prayers and
> retired.[13]

William Byrd thought of himself as the patriarchal master of his
animals as well as of his people. Here was an old English folk attitude, related to the ancient feudal law of deodand that ordered
the death of any animal which caused mortal injury.

These forms of heirarchical violence were carried to Virginia
from England, where they had long existed in the same form.
One famous example involved Lord Lovelace in a horrific chain
of violence:

> Lord Lovelace seeing a maid in his kitchen pursue a dog with a
> spit snatched it from her and killed her on the spot. The girl's
> lover revenged her death by similarly killing Lord Lovelace.[14]

---

[12]*Ibid.*, 419.
[13]*Ibid.*, 424, 431.
[14]Mary Isham to Sir Thomas Isham, 9 Dec. 1677, Isham Mss. 1007, NHANTSRO.

A similar chain of violence appeared in a letter by a little girl in Virginia, Sally Fairfax, who described her feelings when a cat scratched a slave, and the slave killed the cat. Little Miss Fairfax was moved not to sadness for the cat but rage against the bondsman:

> That vile man Adam at night killed a poor cat of rage, because she eat a bit of meat out of his hand and scratched it. A vile wretch of new negroe, if he was mine I would cut him to pieces, a son of a gun, a nice negroe, he should be killed himself by rights.[15]

Other acts of social violence had a different context. When any neighbor, stranger or even kinsman invaded the property of a landed gentleman without leave to do so, he could expect a violent response. One English country gentleman described such an event in Dorset:

> I espied a pack of hounds with a man on horseback in my green lands, about my chalk hills . . . I scolded him very passionately, whipped off his dogs and forbade him coming any more on pain of having all his dogs killed and himself hanged, whereupon he packed away in haste and promised to come that way no more.[16]

Virginia gentlemen behaved in exactly the same way—responding violently to interlopers on their lands.[17]

Hierarchical violence of this sort was commonplace in Virginia. But there was remarkably little violence by the poor against the rich, or by the humble against the elite. William Byrd wrote to an English friend, "We all lye securely with our doors unbarred, and can travel the whole country without arms or guard."[18] Even small acts of symbolic protest against superiors brought down horrific punishments of unimaginable savagery. When, for example, Richard Barnes made "base speeches" against Governor Wyatt, he was sentenced to have his weapons broken, to be bored through the tongue, to "pass through a guard of 40 men" and be "butted by everyone of them," to be "knocked down and footed out of the fort," to pay £200 and to be banished from the colony.[19]

---

[15]Morgan, *Virginians at Home*, 19.

[16]John Richards Diary, 13 Oct. 1701, DORSRO.

[17]Byrd, *London Diary and Other Writings*, 433.

[18]William Byrd II to William Beckford, 6 Dec. 1735, Tinling, ed., *Correspondence of the Three William Byrds*, II, 464.

[19]Scott, *Criminal Law in Colonial Virginia*, 150.

In that respect, the first gentlemen of Virginia were the same as the English gentry, savagely punishing anyone who used violence against them. In Wiltshire during the year 1631, for example, a shoemaker convicted of highway robbery hurled a brickbat at the judge. Instantly the shoemaker was seized. His hand was cut off and nailed to the gibbet from which he was hanged. There all could see the penalty for threatening a superior.[20] Altogether, this system of violence was itself an order, as elaborately hierarchical in Virginia as it had been in southern England. In both places its social function was very much the same.

The criminal courts of the Chesapeake colonies were less active than in New England. Rates of criminal prosecuton were less than half as high as in New England.[21] The distribution of criminal offenses in the Chesapeake was also different from New England. In five Maryland county courts crimes against order were less than half their proportion in New England, but crimes of violence were more than twice as high.[22]

Individual offenses also differed in their frequency. Prosecutions for sexual morality commonly consisted of fornication in Massachusetts and bastardy in Maryland. Crimes against order in Puritan colonies were often sabbath violations, profane speech, blasphemy, idleness and lying; in the Chesapeake this category consisted almost entirely of disturbing the peace, disorderly conduct and drunkenness, which often involved acts of violence.[23] In the punishments meted out to defendants, Chesapeake courts were more apt to discriminate by social status. Masters were treated leniently; servants were punished harshly. Men received lighter sentences than women in the Chesapeake colonies. These practices were very different from New England, where discrimination by rank was more muted, and in most cases men and

---

[20]W. S. Holdsworth, *A History of English Law* (13 vols., London, 1922–52), V, 348.

[21]In five Maryland county courts (1658–79), annual rates of criminal prosecution averaged 248 per 100,000; in four New England courts, 561 per 100,000. Saloman, "Community and Hierarchy," 42.

[22]Mark Saloman obtains the following results for criminal prosecutions in Maryland courts:

Crimes against	Maryland total	Charles Co. 1658–74	Talbot Co. 1662–74	Kent Co. 1668–71	Somerset Co. 1665–71	Pr. George's Co. 1696–99
Order	52 (31%)	6 (13.6%)	3 (10.3%)	15 (50.0%)	1 (16.7%)	27 (46.5%)
Sexual Morality	60 (35.9%)	19 (43.2%)	18 (62.1%)	7 (23.3%)	3 (50.0%)	13 (22.4%)
Property	29 (17.4%)	9 (20.5%)	5 (17.2%)	3 (10.0%)	1 (16.7%)	11 (19.0%)
The Person	26 (15.6%)	10 (22.7%)	3 (10.3%)	5 (16.7%)	1 (16.7%)	7 (12.1%)

Source: Saloman, "Community and Hierarchy," 43–51.

[23]*Ibid.*, 43–44.

women were treated equally. Altogether, historian Mark Saloman concludes that systems of criminal justice in Massachusetts and Maryland had two different purposes—the former primarily to preserve comity; the latter mostly to maintain hierarchy.

❧ Virginia Power Ways: The Politics of Court and Vestry Government

In the year 1685 a French Protestant nobleman named Durand de Dauphiné was forced to flee his native Languedoc on account of his religion. In his flight he had many adventures—a hair's-breadth escape from the dragoons of King Louis XIV, an intimacy with a beautiful Italian widow, a chase by Turkish pirates, a terrific storm in the English Channel, a desperate illness in London, starvation on a transatlantic voyage, and shipwreck on the coast of Virginia where he landed with his belt drawn in sixteen inches and his "clothes all covered in pitch and tar." To his surprise this ragged French aristocrat was welcomed by the first gentlemen of Virginia, who instantly accepted him as one of themselves. Durand de Dauphiné wrote a book about his experiences among Virginia's ruling elite in the late seventeenth century, a few years after Governor Berkeley had left office.

"The gentlemen called cavaliers," Durand wrote, "are greatly esteemed and respected, and are very courteous and honorable. They hold most of the offices in the country." Durand was invited to dine with the governor and councilors, and to sit with the Assembly which like his hosts he called the Parliament of Virginia. "I saw there fine-looking men, sitting in judgment booted and with belted sword," he reported.[1]

This oligarchy of "gentlemen called cavaliers," who bestrode Virginia booted and spurred, was no novelist's dream. It actually existed, and played a role of high importance in the political history of the colony.

The distinctive polity which Durand observed in Virginia had developed during the governorship of Sir William Berkeley. By and large it was not imposed upon an unwilling population by imperial authorities, but created within the colony by Virginia gentlemen from materials which had been familiar to them at home. The result was a political culture that proved to be remark-

---

[1]Chinard, ed., *A Huguenot Exile in Virginia,* 111, 148, *passim.*

ably stable for more than a century, from its emergence in the mid-seventeenth century to the American War of Independence.

In this Virginia polity, the leading local institutions were the parish and county. Both were dominated by self-perpetuating oligarchies of country gentlemen—the parish through its vestry, and the county through its court. They were more complex in their structure than the town meeting system of new England, but less active in the life of the community. Levels of per capita public spending in Virginia tended to be less than half that of Massachusetts.[2]

The vestry system was established by law in 1643, shortly after Governor Berkeley arrived in Virginia. A law passed in that year required every parish to have a vestry. By 1665 or earlier, these vestries had become closed oligarchies, and control was securely in the hands of a small group of "the most selected and sufficient men." Their responsibilities extended far beyond the affairs of the parish church itself, to include the administration of the poor law, and much other secular business. By 1670, there were approximately forty parishes in the colony. Each vestry looked after a population of about two or three hundred families.[3]

The vestry was a familiar institution in southern England. But it was not very old as English institutions went—not nearly as old as the town or folkmoot. The word vestry itself came from the Norman French *vestiarie,* which was introduced to England after the Conquest. The vestry was an imposition from above; the town was an emanation from below. By the seventeenth century, these two institutions tended to blur into one another in some parts of England. But they were distinctly different in their origins, and they were put to very different uses in Massachusetts and Virginia.

Another unit of local government in Virginia was the county. Its principal officers were the county justices, the county sheriff and the county surveyor, who were nominally appointed from above rather than elected from below. In practice they were controlled by the county gentry, who regarded these offices as a species of property which they passed on to one another. William Fitzhugh in 1685 proposed that High Sheriffs should be appointed "in fee or for life." He explained that "for the sheriff's place to be granted in fee, has been anciently practicable in

[2]R. R. Palmer, *The Age of the Democratic Revolutions* (2 vols., Princeton, 1959), I, 155.

[3]Hening, *Statutes at Large,* I, 240; Wm. H. Seiler, "The Anglican Parish Vestry in Colonial Virginia," *JSH* 22 (1956), 310–37.

England, and in one county is still retained in the family of Cliffords." Fitzhugh's suggestion was not adopted, but local offices often became a form of property in fact if not in law.[4]

On court days a large part of the county came together in a great gathering which captured both the spirit and substance of Virginia politics. Outside the courthouse, the county standard flew proudly from its flagstaff, and the royal arms of England were emblazoned above the door. The courthouse in Middlesex County actually had two doors which symbolized the structure power in that society—a narrow door at one end of the building for the gentry, and a broad double door at the other for ordinary folk. Inside, on a raised platform at one end of the chamber sat the gentlemen-justices, their hats upon their heads, and booted and spurred just as Durand observed them. To one side sat the jury, "grave and substantial freeholders" who were mostly chosen from the yeomanry of the county. Before them stood a mixed audience who listened raptly to the proceedings. Outside on the dusty road, and peering in through the windows was a motley crowd of hawkers, horse traders, traveling merchants, servants, slaves, women and children—the teeming political underclass of Virginia.[5]

Any expression of disorder in the courtroom, or of disrespect for the court itself, was punished instantly, sometimes with savage severity. Deference was routinely demanded and received. It was repaid in the coin of "condescension," a special form of courtesy that was reserved for inferiors throughout the English-speaking world.

These county oligarchies were not sovereign bodies. Above them sat the Assembly, Council and Royal Governor. The status of these institutions was in dispute until the American War of Independence. The Assembly was understood by Imperial officials as the colonial equivalent of a municipal council in England. They called it the House of Burgesses, a name which brought to mind the Burgesses of Bristol and other British towns. But Virginians had a different idea of their Assembly. In 1687, William Fitzhugh called it "our Parliament here," a representative body which knew no sovereign except the King himself.[6]

Whatever their parliamentary standing, the Assembly repre-

---

[4]Fitzhugh to Roger Jones, 18 May 1685, Davis, ed., *Fitzhugh Letters*, 168.

[5]A. G. Roeber, "Authority, Law and Custom: Rituals of Court Day in Tidewater Virginia," *WMQ3* (1980), 29–52; for the architecture of the Middlesex County court house see Rutman and Rutman, *A Place in Time*, 129.

[6]William Fitzhugh to Robert Fitzhugh, 30 Jan. 1687, Davis, ed., *Fitzhugh Letters*, 201.

sented not the people at large, but the county oligarchies who really ran Virginia. Most of its members had served for many years in public office, rising slowly through the vestries and courts of their counties.[7]

At the pinnacle of this system was the royal governor. For thirty-five years this office was held by Sir William Berkeley. Until the disaster of Bacon's Rebellion at the end of his tenure, he was very popular—"the darling of the people," one Virginian described him. Berkeley was removed from office by the English Puritans, and forcibly retired to the privacy of his plantation at Green Spring. But after the fall of the Protectorate, the Virginians themselves "unanimously chose him their governor again."[8]

Young Governor Berkeley was an outspoken royalist, a high Anglican and a staunch prerogative man who demanded of the colonists the same unquestioning loyalty that he gave to the King above him. In his prime he was also a leader of exceptional intellect and ability. From the start he was so popular that the Virginia assembly, "with an eye to the honor of the place," levied an extra tax of two shillings on every tithable specially for his support, payable in country produce. The people of Virginia made an act of homage of this obligation. They arrived at Green Spring bearing tribute of "corn, wheat, malt, beef, pork, peas, capons, calves, goats, kids, turkeys, geese, butter and cheese" until the governor's estate looked like a fairground.[9]

Berkeley dominated the colony through the Assembly, which sat for many years without an election in what was described as the governor's "long Parliament." He despised popularity, and once acidly observed that "never any community of people had good done to them, but against their wills."[10] But a large part of Governor Berkeley's power derived from his standing with the county oligarchies that ran Virginia. William Byrd later wrote to a friend, "Our government . . . is so happily constituted that a governor must first outwit us before he can oppress us. And if he

---

[7]Strong similarities between the English county courts and those of the west of England may be observed by comparing American materials with sources such as T. G. Barnes, *Somerset Assize Orders, 1629–1640,* and J. S. Cockburn, ed., *Somerset Assize Orders, 1640–1659, SOMERSRS* 71 (1971); for a helpful comparative study of one local officer, see Cyrus H. Karraker, *The Seventeenth Century Sheriff; A Comparative Study of the Sheriff in England and the Chesapeake Colonies, 1607–1689* (Chapel Hill, 1930).

[8]Beverley, *The History and Present State of Virginia,* 65.

[9]From the ruins of the house, antiquarians reckoned that the main part was 48 feet broad by 43 feet deep, with two wings each measuring 26 feet by 16. The massive walls were 2 1/2 feet thick.

[10]Berkeley, *Discourse and View of Virginia,* 8.

ever squeezes money out of us he must first take care to deserve it."[11]

Popular elections were a part of this system, just as they had been in England. From time to time, the "freeholders" were invited to choose their county burgesses in elections that resembled those in the south and west of England. The electors voted for men rather than measures, picking the most congenial gentleman-candidate from several who "stood" for election.

In the elections of 1755 about 40 percent of tithables voted in most tidewater counties. The pattern of participation differed from New England town meetings. Average levels of turnout tended to be higher on the average in Virginia than in Massachusetts, but without the sudden surges of participation that occurred in New England town meetings when controversial questions were introduced.

Many free whites, and all servants and slaves, were disfranchised by property qualifications. These restrictions tended to increase rather than to diminish before 1776. Through more than a century, the trend in Virginia did not move toward an enlargement of democracy. Before 1776, the only elections in Virginia were those for Burgesses, which occurred at very infrequent intervals. These occasional events were great social happenings which attracted the planter elite and many taxable males, but were not democratic in any meaningful sense.[12]

---

[11]William Byrd II to William Beckford, 6 Dec. 1735, Tinling, ed., *Correspondence of the Three William Byrds*, II, 464.

[12]In the elections of Burgesses during the year 1755, turnout in tidewater Virginia was as follows:

	Percent of White Adult Males Voting:				
County	1742	1752	1755	1758	1771
Accomac Co.	49%	43%	48%	50%	
Amelia Co.				50%	
Brunswick Co.	46%				
Elizabeth City Co.				45%	
Essex Co.	53%	44%	53%	53%	33%
Fairfax Co.	42%		36%		
Henrico Co.		58%			
King George Co.		34%	45%		
Lancaster Co.	58%	50%	39%	60%	46%
Northumberland Co.				45%	39%
Prince Edward Co.			27%	45%	
Prince George Co.				55%	
Richmond Co.		45%	37%	40%	37%
Spotsylvania Co.	46%	35%	42%		49%
Surry Co.				44%	
Westmoreland Co.	53%	57%	48%		

Sources include Robert J. Dinkin, *Voting in Provincial America* (Westport Conn., 1977), 148–

This system of government developed in Virginia by a process of prescription. As early as the year 1679 it was spoken of as "the constitution of the country," in the traditional British sense of unwritten customs and established institutions, rather than the future American sense of fundamental written law. This "constitution" was radically different from the polity of Massachusetts. But the gentlemen oligarchs of Virginia thought of it as the ordinary and natural way in which English-speaking people ordered their political affairs.[13]

William Fitzhugh wrote in 1684, "The laws we have made amongst us here since our first settlement, are merely made for our own particular Constitution, when the laws of England were thought inconvenient in that particular, and rather disadvantageous & burdensome . . . Our continual usage and practice since the first settlement, hath been according to the laws and customs of England."[14] Any other idea of "laws and customs" was not merely uncongenial to Virginia gentlemen. It was literally inconceivable.

ॐ Virginia Freedom Ways:
The Anglican Idea of Hegemonic Liberty

"How is it," Dr. Samuel Johnson asked, "that we hear the loudest yelps for liberty among the drivers of negroes?" That famous question captured a striking paradox in the history of Virginia. Like most other colonists in British America, the first gentlemen of Virginia possessed an exceptionally strong consciousness of their English liberties, even as they took away the liberty of others.[1] Governor William Berkeley himself, notwithstanding his reputation for tyranny, wrote repeatedly of "prized liberty" as the birthright of an Englishman. The first William Fitzhugh often wrote of Magna Carta and the "fundamental laws of England," with no sense of contradiction between his Royalist politics and

---

49; Lucille Griffith, *The Virginia House of Burgesses, 1750–1774* (revised ed., University, Ala., 1970), 168. These may be understood as upperbound estimates, which require correction for under-enumeration of tithables, a problem as yet unsolved.

[13]William Fitzhugh to Thomas Clayton, 7 April 1679, Davis, ed., *Fitzhugh Letters,* 72.

[14]William Fitzhugh to Ralph Wormeley, 10 June 1684, *ibid.,* 157–59.

[1]Samuel Johnson, *Taxation No Tyranny: An Answer to the Resolutions and Address of the American Congress* (London, 1775).

libertarian principles. Fitzhugh argued that Virginians were both "natural subjects to the king" and inheritors of the "laws of England," and when they ceased to be these things, "then we are no longer freemen but slaves."[2]

Similar language was used by many English-speaking people in the seventeenth and eighteenth century. The fine-spun treatises on liberty which flowed so abundantly from English pens in this era were rationales for political folkways deeply embedded in the cultural condition of Englishmen.

These English political folkways did not comprise a single libertarian tradition. They embraced many different and even contradictory conceptions of freedom. The libertarian ideas that took root in Virginia were very far removed from those that went to Massachusetts. In place of New England's distinctive idea of ordered liberty, the Virginians thought of liberty as a hegemonic condition of dominion over others and—equally important—dominion over oneself.

The Virginia idea of hegemonic liberty was far removed from the New England system of communal restraints which a town meeting voluntarily imposed upon itself. The English traveler Andrew Burnaby observed that "the public and political character of the Virginians corresponds with their private one: they are haughty and jealous of their liberties, impatient of restraint, and can scarcely bear the thought of being controlled by any superior power."[3]

Virginia ideas of hegemonic liberty conceived of freedom mainly as the power to rule, and not to be overruled by others. Its opposite was "slavery," a degradation into which true-born Britons descended when they lost their power to rule. The idea was given its classical expression by the poet James Thomson (1700–1748) in a stanza that everyone knows without reflecting on its meaning:

> When Britain first, at Heaven's command,
>   Arose from out of the Azure main,
> This was the charter of the land,
>   And guardian angels sang this strain:
> Rule, Britannia, rule the waves;
>   Britons never will be slaves.[4]

---

[2]Fitzhugh to Thomas Clayton, 7 April 1679, Davis, ed., *Fitzhugh Letters*, 72.
[3]Burnaby, *Travels* (1812), 715; quoted in Breen, *Tobacco Culture*, 244.
[4]James Thomson, *Alfred* (1740), act 2, scene 5.

In Thomson's poetry, which captured the world view of the Virginians in so many ways, we find the major components of hegemonic liberty: the concept of a "right to rule"; the notion that this right was guaranteed by the "charter of the land"; the belief that those who surrendered this right became "slaves"; and the idea that it had been given to "Britain first, at heaven's command."

It never occurred to most Virginia gentlemen that liberty belonged to everyone. It was thought to be the special birthright of free-born Englishmen—a property which set this "happy breed" apart from other mortals, and gave them a right to rule less fortunate people in the world. Even within their own society, hegemonic liberty was a hierarchical idea. One's status in Virginia was defined by the liberties that one possessed. Men of high estate were thought to have more liberties than others of lesser rank. Servants possessed few liberties, and slaves none at all. This libertarian idea had nothing to do with equality. Many years later, John Randolph of Roanoke summarized his ancestral creed in a sentence: "I am an aristocrat," he declared, "I love liberty; I hate equality."[5]

In Virginia, this idea of hegemonic liberty was thought to be entirely consistent with the institution of race slavery. A planter demanded for himself the liberty to take away the liberties of others—a right of *laisser asservir,* freedom to enslave. The growth of race slavery in turn deepened the cultural significance of hegemonic liberty, for an Englishman's rights became his rank, and set him apart from others less fortunate than himself. The world thus became a hierarchy in which people were ranked according to many degrees of unfreedom, and they received their rank by the operation of fortune, which played so large a part in the thinking of Virginians. At the same time, hegemony over others allowed them to enlarge the sphere of their own personal liberty, and to create the conditions within which their special sort of libertarian consciousness flourished.

To a modern mind, hegemonic liberty is an idea at war with itself. We think of it as a contradiction in terms. This is because we no longer understand human relationships in hierarchical terms, and can no longer accept the proposition that a person's status in the world is determined and even justified by his fortune. But in Virginia during the seventeenth and eighteenth cen-

---

[5]Bruce, *John Randolph,* II, 203.

The noblest product of Virginia's culture was the idea of a gentleman, here represented by Thomas Lee, who was so renowned for his character that his portrait hung in a place of honor at Badminton, home of the Dukes of Beaufort. When he suffered a fire a purse was contributed by the Queen herself.

The code of a Virginia gentleman made moral absolutes of truth, candor, fidelity, courage, manners, courtesy, and responsibility. Most of all, a gentleman treated others decently and was true to his own convictions. He was required to lead others of lower rank, and they were expected to follow his high example. The moral authority of a gentleman derived from his material independence. So important was this condition that in occupational lists of the eighteenth century, "independent" and "gentleman" were used as synonyms. Freedom was the necessary condition of a Virginia gentleman's existence, but others in that society lived in various degrees of unfreedom and many had no freedom at all. Their bondage supported a gentleman's freedom and independence, which thus became a hegemonic idea, very different from libertarian thinking in New England and Pennsylvania.

tury, and throughout much of the American south until 1865, this idea of hegemonic liberty was entirely in harmony with its environing culture.

One acute English observer in the eighteenth century clearly perceived the special meaning of hegemonic liberty in what he called the "southern colonies." Edmund Burke declared in Parliament:

> a circumstance attending these colonies . . . makes the spirit of liberty still more high and haughty than in those to the northward. It is, that in Virginia and the Carolinas, they have a vast multitude of slaves. Where this is the case in any part of the world, those who are free are by far the most proud and jealous of their freedom.
>
> Freedom is to them not only an enjoyment, but a kind of rank and privilege. Not seeing there that freedom, as in countries where it is a common blessing and as broad and general as the air, may be united with much abject toil, with great misery, with all the exterior of servitude, liberty looks amongst them like something that is more noble and liberal.
>
> I do not mean, Sir, to commend the superior morality of this sentiment, which has at least as much pride as virtue in it; but I cannot alter the nature of man. The fact is so; and these people of the southern colonies are much more strongly, and with a higher and more stubborn spirit, attached to liberty than those to the northward. . . . In such a people, the haughtiness of domination combines with the spirit of freedom, fortifies it, and renders it invincible.[6]

Burke understood very well this system of hegemonic liberty in Virginia—perhaps because it was also shared by so many English gentlemen in the eighteenth century. He correctly perceived that liberty in Virginia was both a right and a rank, with a good deal of "pride" in it, and many contradictions. He also understood that this conception of hegemonic liberty contained larger possibilities which would expand in years to come.

One of these larger libertarian possibilities lay in its conception of self-government and minimal government. Hegemonic liberty was not an anarchical idea, opposed to all government. The preservation of liberty was thought to require the protection of the state. But the function of the state was largely limited to that minimal role. These ideas were introduced at the very beginning of

---

[6]Edmund Burke, Speech on Conciliation with the Colonies, 22 March 1775, in *Speeches and Letters on American Affairs* (London, 1908), 94.

Virginia's history. In the critical years from 1649 to 1652 the people of Virginia agreed to stand by Governor Berkeley and the Royalist cause only on condition that light taxes and loose restraints would be guaranteed to them. This wish was granted. Berkeley agreed to a general reduction of taxes, to the abolition of poll taxes altogether, to the principle of no taxation without representation, and to the idea of equitable assessments—"proportioning in some measure payments according to men's abilities and estates." Berkeley's tax policy lay at the root of his popularity. The burgesses acknowledged a debt of gratitude for themselves and their descendants. "This is a benefit descending unto us and our posterity," they declared, "which we acknowledge [is] contributed to us by our present governor."[7]

Another important possibility within hegemonic liberty lay in its principle of the rule of law. In that regard, Governor Berkeley also made a change in the constitution of his colony. In the year 1643, he agreed to a statute which allowed appeals to be taken from the courts to the Assembly. This reform established the rule of law in a way which made the gentlemen-burgesses of Virginia the masters of their own world. Later the Assembly lost their appellate role, but the Council continued to function in Virginia as the court of last resort, and this body remained firmly in the hands of the planter elite of Virginia. It created for them a condition of cultural hegemony which continued for more than two centuries. At the same time, it also provided a firm base for the rule of law through two turbulent centuries of Virginia's colonial history.[8]

Yet another expansive possibility in hegemonic liberty existed in its conception of freedom as a condition of social independence. This also was originally an hierarchical idea. The higher a person's social status, the more independent he was thought to be. Great planters took special pride in their independence. Thus, Landon Carter characterized his estate which he called Sabine Hall as an "excellent little fortress . . . built on a rock of *Independency*." Peyton Randolph used precisely the same formulation. In a quarrel with his British creditors, he wrote, "I shall never be affected with any reply that can be made, having an excellent little fortress to protect me, one built on a Rock not

---

[7]Hening, *Statutes at Large,* I, 236–37; Steven D. Crow, "Your Majesty's Good Subjects," *VMHB* 87 (1979), 158–73.

[8]Hening, *Statutes at Large,* I, 235.

liable to be shaken with Fears, that of Independency."[9] Foreign travelers also commented upon this condition of "independence" among the great planters. A French visitor to Virginia in the seventeenth century observed that "there are no lords, but each is sovereign on his own plantation."[10]

The largest possibility in this idea of hegemonic liberty lay in its conception of dominion over self. A gentleman of Virginia was trained to be, like Addison's Cato, "severely bent against himself." He was taught to believe that a truly free man must be the master of his acts and thoughts. At the same time, a gentleman was expected to be the servant of his duty. "Life is not so important as the duties of life," said John Randolph, in one of the best of his epigrams.[11]

So exalted was this ideal of hegemony over self that every gentleman fell short. But the ideal itself was pursued for many generations. At its best, it created a true nobility of character in Virginia gentlemen such as George Washington, Robert E. Lee and George Marshall. The popular images of these men are not historical myths. The more one learns of them, the greater one's respect one becomes. Their character was the product of a cultural idea.[12]

Hegemonic liberty was a dynamic tradition which developed through at least three historical stages. In the first it was linked to Royalist cause in the English Civil War. The Virginia gentleman Robert Beverley boasted that the colony "was famous, for holding out the longest for the Royal Family, of any of the English Dominions."[13] Virginia was the last English territory to relinquish its allegiance to Charles I, and the first to proclaim Charles II king in 1660 even before the Restoration in England.[14] Speeches against the Stuarts were ferociously punished by the county courts.[15] The Assembly repeatedly expressed its loyalty to the Crown, giving abundant thanks for "his Majesty's most gracious

<hr>

[9] *The Diary of Landon Carter,* I, 19; Peyton Randolph, *A Letter to a Gentleman in London, from Virginia* (Williamsburg, 1759); both quoted in Breen, *Tobacco Culture,* 86, a work to which I am much indebted in this section.

[10] Chinard, ed., *A Huguenot in Exile in Virginia,* 110.

[11] Bruce, *John Randolph,* II, 205.

[12] Even the most cynical scholars have felt the force of their character. An example was Rupert Hughes, who intended to write a "debunking" biography of George Washington, and before he was finished, had become an enthusiastic admirer.

[13] Beverley, *The History and Present State of Virginia,* 287.

[14] Bruce, *Social Life of Virginia,* 31.

[15] Bruce, *Institutional History of Virginia,* I, ch. V.

favors towards us, and Royal Condescensions to anything requisite."[16]

In the second stage, hegemonic liberty became associated with Whiggish politics, and with an ideology of individual independence which was widely shared throughout the English-speaking world. In Virginia, many families who had been staunch Royalists in the seventeenth century became strong Whigs in eighteenth century; by the early nineteenth century they would be Jeffersonian Republicans. Their principles throughout tended to be both elitist and libertarian—a clear expression of a cultural ethic which was capable of continuing expansion.

In Britain, this Whiggish idea of hegemonic liberty was taken up by English landed families who had tended to be Royalists in the seventeenth century, and became Whigs in the eighteenth. The classical examples were England's great aristocratic families such as the Russells and Cavendishes. Both had been Royalist in the Civil Wars of the seventeenth century. William Cavendish, the third Earl of Devonshire, lost his fortune in the service of Charles I. His brother Charles Cavendish lost his life in the same cause, and became the *beau ideal* of a gallant cavalier. The poet Waller celebrated the loyalty of these royalist Cavendishes:

> Two loyal brothers took their Sovereign's part,
> Employed their wealth, their courage and their art;
> The elder did whole regiments afford,
> The younger brought his courage and his sword.[17]

In the 1680s, another William Cavendish, the fourth Earl and first Duke of Devonshire, in the words of a family historian, removed "the politics of his race from a Cavalier to a Whig foundation."[18] The Cavendishes and Russells supported the Revolution of 1688, and became staunch Whigs for a century, until the French Revolution divided them. Late in the eighteenth century, the Cavendish connection stood with Burke, and the Russells went with Fox. But through the eighteenth century, many of the great landed families of England were as staunchly Whiggish as they had been Royalist a century before. Among them were the

---

[16]H. R. McIlwaine, ed., *Journals of the House of Burgesses, 1659/60–1693*, (Richmond, 1914), 110.

[17]Quoted in Bernard Holland, *The Life of Spencer Compton, Eighth Duke of Devonshire* (2 vols., New York, 1911), I, 4.

[18]*Ibid.*, I, 5.

Berkeley family, who were among the most extreme Royalists in the seventeenth century, and would become decided Whigs in the eighteenth.

In the nineteenth and twentieth centuries, the tradition of hegemonic liberty entered a third stage of development, in which it became less hierarchical and more egalitarian. Such are the conditions of modern life that this idea is no longer the exclusive property of a small elite, and the degradation of others is no longer necessary to their support. The progress of political democracy has admitted everyone to the ruling class. In America and Britain today, the idea of an independent elite, firmly in command of others, has disappeared. But the associated idea of an autonomous individual, securely in command of self, is alive and flourishing.

NORTH MIDLANDS TO THE DELAWARE

❧ The Friends' Migration, 1675–1725

> My friends, that are gone or are going over to plant
> and make outward plantations in America, keep
> your own plantations in your hearts.
>
> —George Fox

O N A BRIGHT SPRING DAY in the year 1677, "the good ship
Kent," Captain Gregory Marlowe, Master, set sail from
the great docks of London. She carried 230 English
Quakers, outward bound for a new home in British North
America.

As the ship dropped down the Thames she was hailed by King
Charles II, who happened to be sailing on the river. The two vessels made a striking contrast. The King's yacht was sleek and
proud in gleaming paintwork, with small cannons peeping
through wreaths of gold leaf, a wooden unicorn prancing high
above her prow, and the royal arms emblazoned upon her stern.
She seemed to dance upon the water—new sails shining white in
the sun, flags streaming bravely from her mastheads, officers in
brilliant uniform, ladies in court costume, servants in livery, musicians playing, and spaniels yapping. At the center of attention was
the saturnine figure of the King himself in all his regal splendor.

On the other side of the river came the emigrant ship. She
would have been bluff-bowed and round-sided, with dirty sails
and a salt-stained hull, and a single ensign drooping from its halyard. Her bulwarks were lined with apprehensive passengers—
some dressed in the rough gray homespun of the northern Pennines, others in the brown drab of London tradesmen, several in

the blue suits of servant-apprentices, and a few in the tattered motley of the country poor.

As the two ships passed, the King shouted a question across the water.

"Are all aboard good Quakers?" he asked.

"Yes," came the reply, "we are all Friends."

The King wished them godspeed for America, and the two vessels drew rapidly apart—two different parts of England sailing on their separate ways.[1]

Many months later, the emigrant ship *Kent* reached her destination and dropped anchor in the River Delaware. Her weary passengers splashed ashore and planted a new settlement which they named Bridlington, after a village in Yorkshire from whence many of them had come. It is now the city of Burlington, New Jersey.

❧ The Friends' Migration: Numbers and Proportions

The colonization of West Jersey marked the start of yet another English folk-wandering, which might be called the Friends' migration. Individual Quakers had begun to appear in the American colonies as early as the 1650s, only a few years after the Society of Friends had been founded in England. The earliest American Friends were mostly wandering evangelists and missionaries who were punished cruelly in the Puritan and Anglican colonies, just as they had been at home.[2]

The larger movement called the Friends' migration began in earnest during the year 1675 when the first full shipload of Quakers disembarked in West Jersey, at a place which they named

---

[1] For this encounter, there are several accounts, varying in detail; some place the King in his barge, others in his royal yacht. See "Emigration from Yorkshire to West Jersey, 1677," *AHR* II (1897), 472–74; Samuel Smith, *History of the Colony of Nova Caesaria, or New Jersey* (Burlington, 1765), 93; Amelia Mott Gummere, "Friends in Burlington," *PMHB* 7 (1883), 249–67, 353–76; *New Jersey Archives*, II, 239; the details of the royal yacht are taken from her builder's model in Frank C. Bowen, *From Carrack to Clipper; A Book of Sailing-Ship Models* (London and New York, 1948), plate 20.

[2] Not all Quaker emigrants came to the Delaware. Others went to the West Indies, and a few to the Chesapeake colonies and New England. Many also found their way to Carolina, encouraged by the great Quaker colonizer John Archdale, a country gentleman from Buckinghamshire. Quakers became an important part of North Carolina's population until the 19th century, when most left the state in a flight from slavery. See Stephen Weeks, *Southern Quakers and Slavery* (Baltimore, 1896), and Kenneth Carroll's articles on Maryland Quakers in *MDHM* 47 (1952), 297–313; 53 (1958), 326–70.

Salem (from the Hebrew Shalom) "for the delightsomenesse of the land." Other ships soon followed carrying some 1,400 people called Quakers to West Jersey by 1681.[3]

In the year 1682 the scale of this migration suddenly increased when twenty-three ships sailed into Delaware Bay with more than 2,000 emigrants who founded the colony of Pennsylvania. One of these vessels was the ship *Welcome*, which carried William Penn himself and 100 other Quakers on a ghastly voyage where smallpox was also a passenger and thirty died at sea of that dread disease. The *Welcome* was followed by ninety shiploads of settlers in three years from 1682 to 1685.[4]

The Friends' migration continued into the early eighteenth century. Altogether, as many as 23,000 colonists moved to the Delaware Valley during the forty years from 1675 to 1715.[5] The

---

[3]Arrivals included the ships *Griffen* [sic] with 150 settlers who founded Salem in 1675; *Kent*, with 230 passengers who established Burlington in 1677; *Willing Mind*, with 60 or 70 and *Martha* with 114 to Burlington in 1677; *Mary* and *Shield* to Burlington in 1678. In 1677, the deputy lieutenant of the West Riding of Yorkshire reported that "some 200 men, women and children from Sheffield and nearby parts of Derbyshire and Nottinghamshire had sailed from Hull to 'an island in America called West Jersey.'" Most authorities agree that 1,400 Quakers migrated to West Jersey by 1681. A few other Quakers may have settled in what is now Pennsylvania and Delaware before 1680. See John E. Pomfret, *The Province of West New Jersey, 1609–1702* (Princeton, 1956), 75, 102–3, 106–7; Amelia M. Gummere, "The Early Quakers in New Jersey," in Rufus Jones, ed., *The Quakers in the American Colonies* (rpt. ed., New York, 1966), 357.

[4]These estimates were made by William Penn himself, who recorded the arrival of "about ninety sail of ships," each carrying about 80 passengers each, or 7,200 immigrants in all from 1682 to 1685. He also noted that "not one vessel designed to the Province, through God's mercy, hitherto miscarried," but many emigrant ships to Pennsylvania suffered severely from shipboard epidemics. See William Penn, "A Further Account of the Province of Pennsylvania," in Albert Cook Myers, ed., *Narratives of Early Pennsylvania, West New Jersey and Delaware, 1630–1707* (1912, rpt. New York, 1967).

[5]The growth of population was as follows:

Year	West Jersey	Pennsylvania	N. Delaware	Total
1670	100	000	500	600
1680	1,700	700	700	3,100
1690	2,500	11,500	1,000	15,000
1700	4,000	18,000	2,000	24,000
1710	7,000	25,000	3,000	35,000
1720	10,000	31,000	4,000	45,000
1730	16,000	52,000	6,000	74,000
1740	24,000	86,000	9,000	119,000
1750	36,000	120,000	14,000	170,000

Census returns in West Jersey enumerated 14,380 people in 1726; 20,900 in 1737–38; and 31,931 in 1745. Pennsylvania conducted no census before 1776, because of Quaker hostility to "numbering the people." Immigration to the Delaware Valley (both transatlantic and intercolonial) may be estimated by decade as follows: 1,500 (1670–80), 11,000 (1680–90), 3,000 (1690–1700), 2,500 (1700–1710), 5,000 (1710–20), for a total of 23,000 from 1670 to 1720. Only a small minority of these emigrants carried certificates from Quaker meetings, but many were sympathetic to the Society of Friends.

majority of these emigrants were either Quakers or Quaker sympathizers. So large were their numbers that in some parts of Britain's North Midlands the number of Friends declined rapidly because of migration to America. In Derbyshire, for example, the Quaker population reached its peak in the 1690s and fell sharply thereafter for several generations. The leading historian of the Society of Friends in that county concludes that emigration was the primary cause of this depopulation.[6] In parts of Wales the impact of the Friends' migration was even greater. Monthly meetings of Welsh Quakers expressed deep concern about "runnings to America." The historian of one small community in Penllyn, Wales, writes of the exodus for America that "It is not sufficient to say that Quakerism declined in Penllyn; it received a mortal blow."[7]

During the early eighteenth century, the number of American Quakers increased very rapidly—doubling every generation. By the year 1750 Quakers had become the third largest religious denomination in the British colonies. Their 250 meeting houses were more numerous than the churches of any other faith except Congregationalists (465) and Anglicans (289). After the mid-eighteenth century the number of Quakers in British America continued to rise in absolute terms, but began to fall relative to other religious groups. Among all American denominations, Quakers slipped to fifth place by 1775 (with 310 meetings); ninth place by

---

The conclusion adopted here mediates between Joseph Illick's standard estimate that "some 8,000 people, almost entirely English, Welsh and Irish Quakers, migrated to Pennsylvania by 1685" out of a British population of 60,000 to 80,000 Quakers in 1680; and Richard Vann's revisionist argument that the number of Pennsylvania immigrants who were "Quakers in good standing . . . could not have been much greater than 1,000 in the 1680's and another 1,000 in the 1690's," from a British population of approximately 50,000 to 60,000 Quakers ca. 1681–85. See Joseph E. Illick, *Colonial Pennsylvania* (New York, 1976), 7, 21; Richard T. Vann, "Quakerism: Made in America?," in Richard S. Dunn and Mary Maples Dunn, eds., *The World of William Penn* (Philadelphia, 1986), 164–65; *HSUS* (1976), series Z1-19; Evarts B. Greene and Virginia D. Harrington, *American Population before the Federal Census of 1790* (New York, 1932); Robert V. Wells., *The Population of the British Colonies in America before 1776* (Princeton, 1975); Henry A. Gemery, "Emigration from the British Isles to the New World, 1630–1700: Inferences from Colonial Populations," *Research in Economic History* V (1980), 179–233.

[6]An estimate of numbers of Quakers belonging to Derby Meeting (extrapolated from numbers of marriages) was as follows: 1660–69, 216; 1670–79, 446; 1680–89, 533; 1690–99, 573; 1700–1709, 400; 1710–19, 493; 1720–29, 340; 1730–39, 240; 1740–49, 153. Helen Forde, "Derbyshire Quakers, 1650–1761" (thesis, Univ. of Leicester, 1977), 31.

[7]J. Gwynn Williams, "The Quakers of Merioneth during the Seventeenth Century," *Journal of the Merioneth Historical and Record Society* 8 (1978), 335–36.

1820 (350 meetings); and sixty-sixth place by 1981 (532 meetings). But in early America, the Friends were not a small sect.[8]

These Quaker immigrants were accompanied by many other colonists who were not members of the Society of Friends, but sympathized with the values of the sect.[9] Throughout the Delaware Valley, in eastern Pennsylvania, West Jersey, northern Delaware and northeastern Maryland, travelers noted that Quaker meetings attracted a large attendance from neighbors who did not choose to join in any formal way or to subject themselves to its rigorous discipline. In 1742, for example, an English Quaker observed in West Jersey that "the meetings were very large and [with] great comings in of other people besides Friends, for 20 or 30 miles around in the country."[10] In Maryland's Cecil County (the northeastern corner of that colony), the same traveler attended another Quaker meeting and noted that "abundance of people besides Friends were there."[11] Quaker schools throughout

---

[8]Several quantitative studies of religion in early America yield the following estimates of churches or meetings:

Denomination	1650	1750	1775	1820	1850
Congregationalist	62	465	668	1,096	1,706
Episcopalian	31	289	495	600	1,459
Quaker	1	250	310	350	726
Presbyterian	6	233	588	1,411	4,824
Lutheran	4	138	150	800	16,403
Baptist	2	132	494	2,885	9,375
German Reformed	0	90	159	389	2,754
Catholic	6	30	56	124	1,221
Methodist	0	0	65	2,700	13,280
Disciples	0	0	0	618	1,898

Sources include: (1650): Edwin S. Gaustad, *Historical Atlas of Religion in America* (rev. ed. New York, 1976), 21–26; (1750 and 1820): unpublished research by Edward Richkind and Janice Bassil for the author; Howard K. Macauley, Jr., "A Social and Intellectual History of Elementary Education in Pennsylvania to 1850" (thesis, Univ. of Pa., 1972), II, 895–927; (1775): research directed by Marcus W. Jernegan for Charles O. Paullin, *Atlas of the Historical Geography of the United States* (New York, 1932), 50; (1850): U.S. Census of 1850.

[9]Historian Richard Vann finds that only one-third of English and Welsh emigrants to Pennsylvania carried certificates from Quaker meetings in Britain, and that less than 40% of Pennsylvania's First Purchasers could be found in Quaker registers of vital events, or books of sufferings. He concludes that there were only about 2,000 "British Quaker emigrants in good standing" to Pennsylvania in the period 1681–99, but that many others were "attenders" or "sympathizers." This estimate, as Vann himself is careful to point out, must be used with caution. It derives from records which were underregistered and regionally skewed. Most Quaker meetings kept no formal membership lists and the lines between "members," "attenders" and "sympathizers" were very thin; see Vann, "Quakerism: Made in America?," 157–72.

[10]Edmund Peckover Journal, 1742–44, ms. HAV.

[11]*Ibid.*

the Delaware Valley drew many children of other denominations. As late as 1795 Joshua Evans visited New Brunswick, New Jersey, and noted in his diary that "many of the people hereabouts have had an education among Friends, and are Friendly."[12]

Together, these two groups of Quakers and Quaker sympathizers came to constitute a majority of English-speaking settlers in the Delaware Valley by the end of the seventeenth century. In 1702, James Logan reckoned that half the people of Pennsylvania were Quakers, and the rest were divided among many smaller groups. That guess, together with general estimates of population in these colonies suggests that at least 13,000 people were either Friends or "Friendly" in the Delaware Valley by 1700. This population increased very rapidly. By 1766, Benjamin Franklin estimated that between 60,000 and 70,000 Quakers lived in Pennsylvania alone. Many more dwelled in the neighboring colonies of West Jersey, northern Delaware and northern Maryland.

Other people who settled in the Delaware Valley were distinctly "un-Friendly" and showed no sympathy with Quaker beliefs and customs. This category included a large part of the population in Philadelphia, which attracted the human flotsam and jetsam that washed ashore in every seaport city during the eighteenth century. These "un-Friendly" immigrants appeared in growing numbers after 1716, and moved quickly to the interior of the colony. By the mid-eighteenth century, meetings of the Society of Friends were outnumbered by churches of other denominations throughout Pennsylvania and New Jersey. But in the Delaware Valley, the dominion of Friends and "Friendly" continued long enough to imprint a large part of their culture and institutions upon this region.

～ The Friends' Migration: Religious Origins

The central truth about the Friends' migration was its religious purpose and inspiration. In large part this movement was a flight from persecution by a people who had suffered severely for their faith. Quaker monthly meetings in England kept special "Books of Sufferings" which recorded the many acts of oppression against them. After 1675 some of the worst abuses of physical violence had come to an end, but persecution of another kind

---

[12]Joshua Evans, Journal, 29.vii.1795 to 17.xii.1796, ms., SWAR.

continued—much of it at the hands of Anglican clergy whose income was threatened by Quaker refusal to pay church taxes. Friends were jailed in large numbers, and many had their property seized in amounts far beyond the tithes themselves.[1]

Persecution played a major part in driving Quakers to America, but it was never the leading cause. The primary religious goals of the Friends' migration were positive rather than negative. An historian observes that the founders of the Delaware colonies wished "to show Quakerism at work, freed from hampering conditions."[2]

The great majority of leaders in Pennsylvania and West Jersey shared this sense of collective inspiration, but among ordinary immigrants religious motives tended to be more personal and individual. Many came to America as a direct result of spiritual experiences. In the year 1711, for example, a sixteen-year-old London Quaker of humble rank named Jane Hoskins fell desperately ill of a fever. As she lay delirious in "a sore fit of sickness nigh unto death," the image of God appeared before her and said, "If I restore thee, go to Pennsylvania." Jane Hoskins later wrote, ". . . the answer of my soul was, wherever thou pleasest." On her recovery, she borrowed passage money from another Friend and boarded an emigrant ship for the Delaware.[3]

For Quakers such as Jane Hoskins the Friends' migration became a spiritual pilgrimage that differed very much from the secular movements of our own time. Jane Hoskins did not count the material costs and benefits of coming to America, except in the most incidental way. She thought of herself as a servant of God's will, and embarked upon her westward voyage in a mood of optimistic fatalism, perfectly secure in the spiritual values of her faith.

To understand the culture that developed in the Delaware Val-

[1]These judgments (which run contrary to some secondary authorities) rest upon a reading of Books of Sufferings for Derbyshire and Nottinghamshire, principally in the Nottinghamshire Record Office. Many Quakers continued to suffer severely for refusal to pay "steeple taxes."

[2]Gummere, "Friends in Burlington"; historians of this movement do not agree on the importance of persecution as a stimulus for migration. Rufus Jones and William Braithwaite believed it to be a major factor. Frederick Tolles showed, on the other hand, that some Quakers condemned emigration to escape persecution as "shunning the cross." Joseph Illick and Richard Vann took a mediating position, arguing that persecution created a sense of a collective purpose which led to emigration; cf. Tolles, *Meeting House and Counting House: The Quaker Merchants of Colonial Philadelphia, 1682–1783* (Chapel Hill, 1948), 34–37; Illick, *Colonial Pennsylvania*, 11; Vann, "Quakerism: Made in America?" 163.

[3]Jane Hoskins, "The Life of That Faithful Servant of Christ Jane Hoskins . . .," *Friends Library*, I, 461.

ley, one must know something of the religious beliefs of Quakers such as Jane Hoskins. Quakerism, as we call it today, was a highly articulated form of Christianity, very different from Puritan and Anglican beliefs in its theology, ecclesiology and biblical exegesis.

To understand those differences one might begin with the way that Quakers read the Bible. All Protestants were children of the Book. The Bible was the foundation of their faith. But Quakers, Calvinists and Anglicans drew very differently upon that common source. The beliefs of the Quakers came from the New Testament. One of the most important Quaker texts, Robert Barclay's *Apology* (1675), contained 821 biblical citations, of which 656 (80%) referred to the New Testament. In Barclay's *Catechism,* 93 percent of biblical references were to the New Testament, and only 7 percent to the Old. This pattern differed very much from that of Anglicans and especially Puritans, who made heavy use of both books.[4]

Closely linked to the Quakers' biblicism was their theology, which also set them apart from Puritans and Anglicans. The Society of Friends always maintained an official hostility to formal doctrine, and never required subscription to a creed. But Quakers developed what Barclay called a "system of religion," which repudiated the Five Points of Calvinism, and many Anglican dogmas as well. At the center of this Quaker "system" was a God of Love and Light whose benevolent spirit harmonized the universe. One American Quaker copied the following couplet into his commonplace book:

> For love in all things doth Oneness call,
> Thinking no evil, but pure good to all,
> Yea, love is God, and God is love and light.
> Fullness of pleasure, joy and great delight.[5]

The Puritans worshiped a very different Deity—one who was equally capable of love and wrath—a dark, mysterious power who could be terrifying in his anger and inscrutability. Anglicans, on the other hand, knelt before a great and noble Pantocrator who ruled firmly but fairly over the hierarchy of his creatures.

A central tenet of Quaker theology was the doctrine of the inner light, which held that an emanation of divine goodness and virtue passed from Jesus into every human soul. They believed

---

[4]J. William Frost, *The Quaker Family in Colonial America* (New York, 1973), 24.
[5]Caleb Raper, Commonplace Book, 1711, HAV.

that this "light within" brought the means of salvation within reach of everyone who awakened to its existence. Most Quakers rejected the Calvinist principle of limited atonement. They believed that Christ died not merely for a chosen few, but for all humanity. Quakers also rejected the Calvinist ideas of inexorable predestination, unconditional election and irresistible grace. They agreed that people could spurn the spiritual gift that was given to them. "Man's destruction is of himself," wrote Thomas Chalkley, "but his salvation is from the Lord."[6]

Quakers were twice-born Christians. They believed that salvation was attained through a process of spiritual conversion. Many were deeply troubled in their youth until they felt themselves to be born again. David Cooper recalled that "when very young, I experienced two spirits in strife in me." Benjamin Ferris remembered that "when I was about four or five years old I had many solitary hours alone by myself thinking of an endless world after death."[7]

The psychology of conversion among Quakers was similar in some respects to that of Calvinists. But it was not precisely the same. Most Quakers had little doubt that salvation could be achieved by individual effort, and that the instruments had been placed by God in their hands. Once converted, they felt a sense of optimistic fatalism about the world to come. There was less of the brooding salvation-angst and violent mood-swings of hope and despair that troubled so many Puritans.

The ecclesiology of the Quakers was an extension of their theology. They invented a system of church government which differed radically from those of Anglicans and Puritans. Quakers condemned what they called a "hireling clergy," and "steeple house ways." They repudiated all sacraments, ceremonies, churches, clergy, ordinations and tithes, and maintained no ministers in the usual sense—only lay missionaries and exhorters whom they were sometimes called ministers. But the Quakers were not Christian anarchists. Of the many radical sects who appeared in seventeenth-century England, they were one of the few to survive beyond the era of their birth, largely because they also created an exceptionally strong set of religious institutions.

---

[6]Thomas Chalkley, "Concerning Personal Election and Reprobation," *Works* (Philadephia, 1749), 544; quoted in David R. Kobrin, *The Saving Remnant: Intellectual Sources of Change and Decline in Colonial Quakerism, 1690–1810* (Philadelphia, 1968), 80.

[7]David Cooper, Memoir, ca. 1777, Haverford; Benjamin Ferris Journal, n.d., Swarthmore.

The Society of Friends was organized as a complex structure of meetings—men's meetings and women's meetings, meetings for worship and meetings for business, monthly meetings, quarterly meetings and yearly meetings. They recognized a need for leadership by elders and overseers, whose task was to teach, counsel and support. But authority belonged to the society itself; Quakers created a rigorous system of collective discipline which regulated marriage, sex, business ethics, dress, speech, eating and drinking, politics, and law. Special attention was given to the rearing of the young—an important factor in the survival of Quakerism, and in the culture that it created in the Delaware Valley.[8]

These Quaker beliefs were not static. They changed in many ways through time. Four distinct stages might be distinguished in the history of this Christian denomination. The first was the seedtime of a revolutionary sect (ca. 1646–66), when Quakerism tended to be radical, primitive, militant, aggressive, evangelical and messianic. The second stage (ca. 1666–1750) was the time of flowering, when the Society of Friends became increasingly institutional, rational, progressive, optimistic, enlightened, liberal, moderate, political and actively engaged in world, without losing its piety and godly purposes. The third stage (ca. 1750–1827) was an era when Quakers turned inward upon themselves and grew increasing sectarian, exclusive, quietist and perfectionist. A fourth stage of denominational division and maturity followed the Hicksite separation of 1827.[9]

Of these four stages, the most important for American history was the second (ca. 1666–1750), when the cultural institutions of the Delaware Valley were created. The guiding principles of Quakers in this period were not the revolutionary, messianic ideas of the first stage, nor the inward-looking ideas of the third stage, but something in between. In this second stage, Quaker

---

[8]The leading study of Quaker discipline is Jack D. Marietta, *The Reformation of American Quakerism, 1748–1783* (Philadelphia, 1984), 6–7.

[9]Still the standard history of Quakers is the "Rowntree series," including William C. Braithwaite, *The Beginnings of Quakerism* (London, 1912); *idem, The Second Period of Quakerism* (London, 1919); Rufus Jones, *The Later Periods of Quakerism* (London, 1921); *idem*, ed., *The Quakers in the American Colonies*. Specially helpful on the first period of Quakerism are Hugh Barbour, *The Quakers in Puritan England* (New Haven, 1964); W. A. Cole, "The Quakers and the English Revolution," in Trevor Aston, ed., *Crisis in Europe* (New York, 1967), 358–76; Barry Reay, *The Quakers and the English Revolution* (London, 1985). For the second period see Richard T. Vann, *The Social Development of English Quakerism* (Cambridge, Mass., 1969); Jones, ed., *Quakers in the American Colonies;* and Tolles, *Meeting House and Counting House*. On the third period, a short but excellent overview appears in Tolles, *Meeting House and Counting House*, 230–43. Also valuable are Marietta, *The Reformation of American Quakerism;* Sydney V. James, *A People Among Peoples; Quaker Benevolence in Eighteenth-Century America* (Cambridge, Mass., 1963); and Kobrin, *The Saving Remnant.* (Philadelphia, 1968).

ideals were exceptionally open, outgoing, and liberal in an eighteenth-century sense.

The special teachings of Quakerism in this second period entered deeply into the culture of the Delaware Valley. Friends and neighbors alike embraced the idea of religious freedom and social pluralism. They favored a weak polity and strong communal groups. Most came to share the Quakers' concern for basic literacy and their contempt for higher learning. They also accepted Quaker ideas of the sanctity of property, equality of manners, simplicity of taste, as well as their ethic of work, their ideal of worldly asceticism, their belief in the importance of the family and their habits of sexual prudery. All of these attitudes became exceptionally strong in the folkways of an American region.

After 1750, the Society of Friends turned inward, and distanced itself not merely from other people in the present, but also from its own past. It increasingly developed ideas of unyielding pacifism, withdrawal from politics, extreme sectarian discipline, and extravagant ways of "going plain" in the world. But the more open and liberal spirit of Quakerism's second period survived apart from the Friends themselves, in the culture of an American region which they did so much to create.

The Friends' Migration: Ethnic Origins

The Quaker idea of a universal "inner light" within all humanity encouraged a spirit of fraternity with other people. They addressed everyone as "Friend," and welcomed others of many different backgrounds to live beside them. From the start, European settlers in the Delaware Valley were very mixed in their ethnicity. Even before the first English Quakers arrived, a diverse population had already gathered there. William Penn wrote in 1685, ". . . the people are a collection of Divers Nations in Europe: as, French, Dutch, Germans, Swedes, Danes, Finns, Scotch, French and English, and of the last equal to all the rest." By 1700, the proportion of English and Welsh colonists had risen from one-half to about two-thirds of the population. But a pattern of ethnic diversity persisted throughout the colony's history. It was actively encouraged by William Penn himself, and accepted by his co-religionists.[1]

---

[1] Penn, "A Further Account of the Province of Pennsylvania, 260.

The Quakers, unlike Puritans and Anglicans, were comfortable with ethnic pluralism. In the seventeenth century, the Society of Friends was an evangelical movement which sent missionaries in search of converts throughout the world. From its birthplace in England, it spread rapidly to Wales, Ireland and many parts of Protestant Europe. In the seventeenth century, the Quakers had nothing like the Puritans' Hebraic idea of a chosen people, nor anything comparable to the Anglican gentry's fierce pride of rank and nationhood. They looked upon all humanity as their kin.

This attitude was reinforced in the Delaware colonies by a diversity of origins among the Quakers themselves. Most were English, but many came from other nations. A sizable minority were Irish. Nearly 10 percent of immigrants registered in Philadelphia County were from Ireland. Among Quaker missionaries who were recognized by the Philadelphia Yearly Meeting, 16 percent were Irish. The proportion of Irish Quakers was smaller in rural Chester and Bucks counties, but even larger in other localities. The town of Newton, West Jersey, was largely settled by Friends from Ireland; surrounding lands were called the "Irish Tenth."[2]

Also numerous were Quakers from Wales, who colonized a broad area called the "Welsh Tract" west of the Schuylkill River. They came mainly from comparatively prosperous parts of Merioneth, and also from Radnor and Montgomeryshire in east Wales. Few were from poor and backward regions such as Anglesey and Carnarvon. Many spoke Welsh and took great pride in their ethnic origins, even as they were also strong converts to the Society of Friends.[3]

Dutch and German Quakers were also recruited actively by William Penn, who had traveled as a missionary in the Rhine Valley. As early as 1683 thirteen families settled Germantown, north of Philadelphia, where their leader Francis Daniel Pastorius founded the first non-English-speaking Quaker meeting in Pennsylvania. These people came mostly from Protestant communities in the lower Rhineland such as Krefeld and Kriegsheim, and spoke a mixed German-Dutch Rhenish dialect called "Krefeld-

---

[2]John Clement, *Sketches of the First Emigrant Settlers in Newton Township, Old Gloucester County, New Jersey* (Camden, 1877), 51; Nicholas Canny, "The Irish Background to Penn's Experiment," in Dunn and Dunn, eds., *The World of William Penn*, 139–56.

[3]T. M. Rees, *A History of Quakers in Wales and the Emigration to North America* (Carmarthen, 1925), 178; J. Ambler Williams, "The Influence of the Welsh in the Making of Pennsylvania," *PH* 10 (1943), 120; Charles H. Browning, *Welsh Settlement of Pennsylvania* (Philadelphia, 1912), 27; A. H. Dodd, *The Character of Early Welsh Emigration to the United States* (Cardiff, 1953).

Hollandisch."[4] The Germantown district (a cluster of small communities) became exceptionally diverse in its religion and ethnicity. Within a two-mile stretch of Germantown's Great Road, churches were built by Lutherans, Mennonites, Moravians, Quakers, Dunkards and Calvinists. But within this mixture, Quakers were two-thirds of the population in 1690. During that year a Dutch Reformed clergyman came to Germantown and wrote that "this village consists of forty-four families, twenty-eight of whom are Quakers, the other sixteen of the Reformed [including] the Lutherans, the Mennists [Mennonites] and the Papists who are very much opposed to Quakerism."[5]

After 1715, non-Quaker colonists began to arrive in growing numbers. Among them were North British Borderers who have been called Scotch Irish (inaccurately, as we shall see). The Quakers heartily disliked these people and hurried them on their westward way. Other non-Quaker immigrants also arrived from Protestant communities in western Germany, Switzerland and Alsace mostly during the mid-eighteenth century; half of all German-speaking colonists in Pennsylvania arrived within a period of five years from 1749 to 1754.[6]

By 1760, English Quakers were a minority in the colonies they had founded, and the Delaware Valley had become a cultural mosaic of high complexity. Some of these other ethnic groups, however, shared much in common with Quaker culture. Many had been recruited by William Penn because of this affinity, and had remained in the Delaware Valley because the Quaker colonies were congenial to their own ways.[7]

---

[4]William Hull, *William Penn and the Dutch Quaker Migration to Pennsylvania* (Swarthmore, 1935).

[5]Stephanie Grauman Wolf, *Urban Village: Population, Community and Social Structure in Germantown, Pennsylvania, 1683–1800* (Princeton, 1976), 12, 129.

[6]Marianne Wokeck, "Promoters and Passengers: The German Immigrant Trade, 1683–1775," in Dunn and Dunn, eds., *The World of William Penn*, 259–78.

[7]The ethnic composition of Pennsylvania's population changed as follows in the 18th century:

Year	English-Welsh	Scots-Irish	German	Other	Total
1726	60%	12%	23%	5%	100%
1755	28%	28%	42%	2%	100%
1790a	35%	23%	33%	9%	100%
1790b	29%	30%	38%	3%	100%

Source: 1726 and 1755 from Alan Tully, *William Penn's Legacy; Politics and Social Structure in Provincial Pennsylvania, 1726–1755* (Baltimore, 1977), 53; 1790a from ACLS, "Report of the Committee on Linguistic and National Stocks," *AHAR for 1931* I (1932), 107–441; 1790b from Thomas L. Purvis, "The European Ancestry of the United States Population, 1790," *WMQ3* 41 (1984), 98–101.

There was little conflict between German Pietists and English Quakers. Benjamin Franklin's slur upon the Germans as a race of "Palatine Boors" was the attitude of a transplanted New England Yankee—not a member of the Society of Friends. Quakers by and large welcomed German settlers and lived comfortably beside them. German-speaking elites, for their part, rapidly assimilated English culture. Daniel Pastorius wrote to his sons, "Dear Children, John Samuel and Henry . . . though you are of high Dutch Parents, yet remember that your father was naturalized, and you born in an English Colony, consequently each of you [is] *anglus natus,* an Englishman by Birth." Many Pennsylvania Germans anglicized their names. In Germantown, for example, the family of Zimmermann became Carpenter, Rittinghuysen became Rittenhouse and Schumacher became Shoemaker. Intermarriage frequently occurred between children of different nationalities who shared the same religious faith. English, Irish, Welsh, Dutch and German Quakers rapidly became an extended cousinage.[8]

Germans of other Christian denominations did not intermarry with Quakers so freely, but they came to terms with the Quaker establishment in different ways. Germans did not run for the Pennsylvania Assembly; they cast their votes for Quaker candidates and supported the "Quaker Party." For many years, German Protestants and English Quakers tended to stand together in the politics of Pennsylvania. This cultural alliance dominated the Delaware Valley for nearly a century.[9] It also supported the dominion of an English-speaking Quaker elite, which firmly maintained its cultural hegemony in the Delaware Valley for seventy years. Of the first generation, Rufus Jones writes that "we hear nothing of any men of prominence in these early days except Friends."[10]

From 1675 to 1745, the dominion of this elite tended to grow stronger rather than weaker. An indicator was the composition of the Pennsylvania Assembly. In the year 1730, British Quakers made up 60 percent of that body. That proportion rose to 80 percent in 1740, and reached its peak in the year 1745 at 83 percent. It was 75 percent as late as 1755 when many Quakers with-

---

[8]Wolfe, *Urban Village,* 140; Harry Tinkcom, Margaret Tinkcom and Grant Simon, *Historic Germantown* (Philadelphia, 1955).

[9]James O. Knauss, *Social Conditions among the Pennsylvania Germans in the Eighteenth Century* (Lancaster, 1922).

[10]Jones, ed., *Quakers in the American Colonies,* 422.

drew from politics. Even after that event, the proportion of Quakers in the Assembly as high as 50 percent until 1773.[11]

In short, the English Friends who founded West Jersey and Pennsylvania welcomed immigrants of different national origins, but remained firmly in control of their colonies long enough to shape the character of the region. For eighty years, they wrote the laws, distributed the land, decided immigration policy and created institutions which still survive to the present day. Most important, the Quakers also established the rules of engagement among people of different ethnic groups. These governing principles developed from Quaker ideals of association, order, power and freedom. Even as the Quakers became a minority of the population, their values remained embedded in the institutional structure of the Delaware Valley for centuries to come.

It is easy to misunderstand the culture that the Quakers created in the Delaware Valley. Alan Tully warns us that "because of the dynamic nature of Pennsylvania society, observers have mistakenly described the social organization of the colony as fragmentary and weak. In fact, Pennsylvania possessed a strong, coherent and flexible community structure. . . . Because different individuals identified with, and felt they belonged to, the local community as they perceived it, Pennsylvania society had a cohesiveness that appearances belied."[12]

Further, the Delaware Valley appeared at first sight to be a melting pot which attracted many different ethnic and religious groups. But the Quaker founders deliberately created a coherent cultural framework which allowed this pluralism to flourish. They

---

[11]The religious composition of the Pennsylvania legislature was as follows in these years:

Denomination	1729–30	1739–40	1745–46	1749–50	1754–55
Quaker	18	24	25	24	27
Anglican	3	5	2	1	1
Presbyterian	3	1	2	3	2
Baptist	2				
Dutch Reformed	1			1	1
Moravian					1
Deist					1
Non-Quaker				2	3
Unknown	3		1	1	
Total	30	30	30	32	36
% Quaker (Tully)	60%	80%	83%	75%	75%
% Quaker (Ryerson)	63%	90%	87%	75%	75%

This table comes from Tully, *William Penn's Legacy*, 170–73; a second estimate comes from Richard Ryerson, "The Quaker Elite in the Pennsylvania Assembly," in Bruce C. Daniels, ed., *Power and Status; Officeholding in Colonial America* (Middletown, Conn., 1986), 106–35.

[12]Tully, *William Penn's Legacy*, 53.

did so in a highly principled way, and their organizing principles survived long after the Quakers themselves dwindled to a small minority.

∿ The Friends' Migration: Social Origins

Every year from 1681 to 1686, more than a thousand English emigrants arrived in West Jersey and Pennsylvania. The annual numbers were roughly the same as in the Puritan migration to Massachusetts, and not unlike the movement to Virginia. But the social origins of the Delaware settlers differed from those of other colonists.

The Friends' migration was not as much of a family affair as in New England, but more so than in Virginia. In Pennsylvania, two early immigrant registers show that the proportion who arrived in nuclear families was 39 percent in Philadelphia, and 58 percent in Bucks County. In that respect, the movement to the Delaware was intermediate between migrations to Massachusetts and the Chesapeake.[1]

As to social rank, the same sources show that Pennsylvania's immigrants tended to be men and women of humble origin, who came from the lower middling ranks of English society. Their social status was similar to that of English Quakers in general.[2]

---

[1]Much of this movement was a chain migration. In Derbyshire for example two brothers called Adam and John Rodes emigrated to Pennsylvania in 1684. They were followed by their father John Rodes, and by their brothers Joseph and Jacob. This pattern of chain migration sometimes continued over many decades. The first Bunting emigrated from Derbyshire to Chesterfield, New Jersey, before 1680; other Buntings of the same family were still coming over in the 1720s. Family units were thus stronger than the statistics cited above would suggest. But large numbers of servants came to Pennsylvania—larger than in Massachusetts, though smaller than in Virginia. The comparative generalizations would therefore survive a correction for chain migration. See Forde, "Derbyshire Quakers," 40.

[2]A learned controversy continues on the social origins of English Quakers. Alan Cole, in "The Social Origins of the Early Friends," *FHSJ* 48 (1956–58), 103–14, argues that Quakers tended to be "petty bourgeois" traders and artisans. Richard T. Vann, in *The Social Development of English Quakerism*, finds that Quakers in Norfolk and Buckingham were of the "upper bourgeoisie," with an overrepresentation of yeomen and traders, and an underrepresentation of laborers and artisans. David Heber Pratt concludes that occupational patterns shifted from yeomen and artisans in the 17th century to middle-class traders in the 18th. Helen Forde reports that the Quakers of Derbyshire were of "middling status," being mostly husbandmen, yeomen and artisans, with very few gentlemen or laborers ("Derbyshire Quakers," 81–99). Barry Reay believes that "Quakerism was essentially an affair of the middling sort. It was more plebeian than Vann's pioneering work suggested. It was also, above all, rural." See Reay, *Quakers and the English Revolution*, 25; see also Alan Anderson, "The Social Origins of Early Quakers, *QH* 68 (1979), 133–40; J. J. Hurwich, "The Social Origins of the Early Quakers," *PP* 48 (1970), 156–

Bishop Sheldon observed in 1669 that most Quakers were "very mean, the best scarce worth the title of Yeomen."[3] This opinion, shorn of its pejoratives, was true in one sense and false in another. In registers of immigration kept for the counties of Bucks and Philadelphia, only a few people called themselves yeomen, and not one described himself as a gentleman. Most were husbandmen, craftsmen, laborers and servants. Bishop Sheldon was correct in thinking that very few Quakers were high-born, but he was mistaken in his belief that they were mostly of "the meanest sort"—a common error of perception among Anglican clergy who were the Quakers' most impassioned enemies.[4]

Marriage registers kept by Friends in both England and Pennsylvania showed similar patterns of social rank. In rural neigh-

---

61; Barry Reay, "The Social Origins of Early Quakerism," *JIH* 11 (1970), 55–72; David Heber Pratt, "English Quakers and the First Industrial Revolution: A Study of the Quaker Community in Four Industrial Counties: Lancaster, York, Warwick and Gloucester, 1750–1830" (thesis, Univ. of Neb., 1975).

[3]Tolles, *Meeting House and Counting House*, 39.

[4]Ranks and occupations in these two lists were as follows:

Occupation	Philadelphia	Bucks
Yeoman	0	9
Freeman	17	0
Husbandman	9	12
Merchant	2	0
Seller of Small Wares	0	1
Chapman	0	1
Schoolmaster	1	0
Grocer	1	1
Glover	2	1
Shoemaker	2	2
Feltmaker	1	0
Blacksmith	2	2
Carpenter	2	1
Mason	1	1
Joyner	1	1
Taylor	2	0
Tanner	1	0
Glassmaker	1	0
Brickmaker	1	0
Brazier	1	0
Vilemonger (?)	0	1
Weaver	0	1
Fruiterer	0	1
Callenderer	0	1
Wheelwright	0	1
Servant	185	78

These data are computed from "A Partial List of the Families Who Resided in Bucks County, Pennsylvania, Prior to 1687, with the Date of Their Arrival," *PMHB* 9 (1886), 223–33; and "A Partial List of the Families Who Arrived at Philadelphia between 1682 and 1687," *PMHB* 8 (1885), 328–40.

borhoods, most male Quakers called themselves husbandmen. A majority in urban areas tended to describe themselves as manual workers, artisans, tradesmen and small shopkeepers of various kinds. In the marriage records of Philadelphia, for example, only one man in ninety called himself a gentleman, and only one a laborer. The rest were mainly craftsmen, tradesmen and merchants.[5]

Welsh Quakers who came to Pennsylvania appear to have been of higher social rank than their English brethren—or at least these Welshmen thought of themselves in more exalted terms. Of 163 emigrants from Merioneth, 14 (8.5%) called themselves gentlemen, and 42 (26%) described themselves as yeomen. But most gave no rank or occupation; probably the majority were husbandmen or laborers. Few appear to have been artisans.[6]

Altogether, this evidence confirms the carefully balanced conclusion of historian Frederick Tolles that the majority of immigrants to Pennsylvania were "persons in moderate or humble circumstances, some of them on the edge of destitution." Even the leaders were of comparatively modest beginnings. Here was a pattern very different from Massachusetts and Virginia.[7]

This difference in social origins was partly due to the structure of migration to the Quaker colonies. Meetings of Friends in England subsidized the passage of at least a few poor families. Thus, when Richard Torr asked for money to carry his family to America, the Yorkshire Quarterly Meeting agreed that "he only

---

[5]Quaker marriage records in Philadelphia showed a remarkable variety of urban occupations: merchants, 16; cordwainers, 8; tailors, 7; carpenters, 5; bricklayers, bakers and weavers, 4 each; coopers, joiners and shipwrights, 3 each; mariners, chandlers, turners, brickmakers, sawyers, wheelwrights, husbandmen and yeomen, 2 each; clothier, saddler, glassmaker, tanner, glover, winedresser, worsted-comber, combmaker, blacksmith, bodicemaker, vintner, locksmith, tobacco pipemaker, clerk, physician and gentlemen, 1 each. Quaker marriage records in London showed much the same patterns; Tolles found that three fifths were artisans and manual workers; the rest were mostly tradesmen and shopkeepers. See Tolles, *Meeting House and Counting House,* 41.

[6]Williams, "The Quakers of Merioneth," 122–56, 312–39. Controversy exists on the social origins of Welsh Quaker emigrants. Charles H. Browning argued that they were "the highest social caste of the landed gentry in Wales." J. Ambler Williams, on the other hand, thought that they tended to be "the most impecunious brethren." Subsequent inquirers tended to take a middling position. Cf. Browning, *Welsh Settlement of Pennsylvania,* 27; Williams, "The Influence of the Welsh in the Making of Pennsylvania," 120; F. B. Tolles, *Quakers and the Atlantic Culture* (New York, 1960), 113; Dodd, *Character of Early Welsh Emigration to the United States.*

[7]Tolles, *Meeting House and Counting House,* 40; in another study, Richard Vann found that Quaker emigrants from Bristol were mostly textile workers (35.7%) and artisans, servants and laborers (42.9%); only one emigrant was identified as a gentleman and only two were merchants or tradesmen. Vann, "Quakerism: Made in America?," 161.

sojourns here in the city of York & scarce owned as members any Meeting in this County, yet in pity to them this meeting is willing to give 40 shillings. . . . He is only to have it if he goes, and not for any other purpose."[8] The Chester Quarterly Meeting in 1699 paid £8.12.2, "the charge of Barbara Janney & her daughter's passage into Pennsylvania with other expences." This support was not undertaken on a large scale. But it provided passage money for at least a few Quakers who must otherwise have stayed home.[9]

Other Quakers were supported by private arrangements with individual friends. A case in point was the Quaker servant girl Jane Hoskins whose passage to Pennsylvania in 1712 was paid by another Friend:

> One Robert Dane, Welchman with his wife and two daughers, were going to settle in Philadelphia; a friend told me of their going, and went with me to them. We soon agreed, that he should pay my passage and wait until I could earn the money on the other side of the water, for which he accepted my promise without note or bond, or being bound in indenture.[10]

The Quaker founders of Pennsylvania showed no hostility to servants, such as had existed among the leaders of Massachusetts Bay. As a consequence, people too poor to pay their own way came in larger numbers to the Delaware than to New England.

The social filter of the Friends' migration also tended to screen out English elites, mainly because Quaker principles had little appeal to families of high rank. An exception serves to illustrate the rule. The rich and well-born English Quaker Mary Penington described the tension that existed between her rank and her religion. She wrote:

> One night as I lay in my Bed it was said in me, "Be not hasty to join with these people called Quakers." For many months I was under some exercise of Mind, not that I disputed against the Doctrines they held, but I set myself against taking up the cross to the language, fashions, customs and honours of the world—for indeed my station and connections in life made it very hard.[11]

---

[8]W. Pearson Thistlethwaite, ed., *Yorkshire Quarterly Meeting* (privately published, Harrogate, 1979), 160; These requests were not always granted. When Robert Thompson asked for help in 1683, the Yorkshire Quarterly Meeting decided that it was "not free to yield him any assistance upon that accompt to further his transportation . . . but rather desires him to rest contented in his own country"; but recognizing his poverty, it gave him one pound. *Ibid.*, 160.

[9]Chester Quarterly Meeting Records, 1699, EFC 1/1, CHESRO.

[10]Hoskins, "The Life of That Faithful Servant," I, 461.

[11]Mary Penington Abstract, md., n.d., HAV.

William Penn was often reprimanded by other English gentlemen for mixing with Quakers. In 1671 Sir John Robinson told him:

> I vow Mr. Penn I am sorry for you. You are an ingenious gentle-man, all the world must . . . allow you that, and you have a plen-tiful estate. Why should you render yourself unhappy by associat-ing with such a simple people?

To this complaint, Penn answered that he favored "honestly sim-ple" people above the "ingeniously wicked." In the Friends' migration, he found the company that he preferred to keep.[12]

❧ The Friends' Migration: Regional Origins

The Quaker founders of Pennsylvania and West Jersey came from every part of England. But one English region stood out above the rest. The Friends' migration drew heavily upon the North Midlands, and especially the counties of Cheshire, Lancashire, Yorkshire, Derbyshire and Nottinghamshire. In one list of English immigrants who arrived at Philadelphia between the years 1682 and 1687, more than 80 percent came from these five con-tiguous counties. Only a few came from the south and west, and none were from East Anglia.[1]

The same pattern also appeared among immigrants who settled in Pennsylvania's Bucks County before 1687. Two-thirds came from the counties of Yorkshire, Lancashire, Cheshire, Derby-shire, Nottinghamshire and Staffordshire. The rest were mainly from the vicinity of London and Bristol. None were East Angli-ans; the region which was so important to the settlement of Mas-sachusetts was entirely absent from the list of Bucks County settlers.[2]

---

[12]" . . . Brief Relation of the Illegall Committment of William Penn by Him Called Sr John Robinson, Lt. of the Tower . . ." (Feb. 1671), *Papers of William Penn*, I, 199.

[1]In 1684 the government of Pennsylvania required immigrants to register on arrival. The law was not strictly enforced; in Philadelphia only 410 people registered and many did not give their place of origin. For those who did so, the results were as follows: England, 115; including Lancashire, 52; Yorkshire, 20; Cheshire, 18; London, 7; Sussex, 6; Worcestershire, 5; Derby-shire, 3; Shropshire, 3; and Gloucester, 1; also Wales, 34; including Montgomeryshire, 14; Rad-norshire, 13; Merioneth, 5; Carmarthen, 2; and Ireland, 39; Germany, 71; Holland, 2; origin unknown, 142; total, 410; see "A Partial List of the Families Who Arrived at Philadelphia between 1682 and 1687," 328–40.

[2]In the Bucks County list, which in a few cases duplicated the list of Philadelphia arrivals, patterns of origin were as follows: English immigrants, 234; including Cheshire, 89; York, 32; Lancashire, 18; Staffordshire, 13; Dorset, 12; London, 11; Wiltshire, 10; Middlesex, 10; Sussex,

A similar distribution also appeared in many other lists, including land grants, marriage records, meeting certificates, ministerial rosters, servants' registers and shipping lists. Of Quaker missionaries who were recognized by the Philadelphia Yearly Meeting, for example, half came from five northern counties in England: Cumberland, Westmorland, Durham, Lancashire and Yorkshire. A sizable number also came from English settlements in Ireland. But only 10 percent came from East Anglia and barely 5 percent came from those counties of southwestern England which contributed so heavily to the peopling of Virginia. Less than 10 percent came from the city of London. The evangelical side of this movement was strongest in the northern counties of England.[3] That pattern also appeared among Quakers whose journals were published in the *Friends' Library*, a massive anthology of spiritual autobiographies. The authors of these evangelical works came mostly from what one called the "north country."[4]

A variant pattern appeared among Quakers who carried certificates from their meetings in England to Philadelphia. Approximately 300 of these documents recorded places of origin in England, of which one-third came from London, and another third were from the north of England. The rest were widely scattered. This source represented the institutional strength of the Society of Friends, and had a pronounced urban bias. Even so, one historian who has studied these certificates concludes that "the greatest stronghold" was in "the North of England." Once again, few came from the eastern counties or the southern coast.[5]

7; Somerset, 6; Berkshire, 5; Devonshire, 4; Oxfordshire, 3; Buckinghamshire, 3; Gloucestershire, 3; Worcestershire, 1; Wales, 7; including Denby, 6; Montgomeryshire, 1; also Ireland, 6; unknown, 13; total, 260; compiled from "A Partial List of the Families Who Resided in Bucks County, Pennsylvania," 223–33.

[3] The geographic origins of 111 Quaker ministers engaged by the Philadelphia Yearly Meeting from 1684 to 1773 were as follows: Cumberland, 5; Westmorland, 7; Durham, 2; Yorkshire, 21; Lancashireshire, 5; Nottinghamshire, 2; Hertfordshire, 2; London, 8; Essex, 5; Norfolk, 3; Lincolnshire, 2; Cornwall, 1; Somerset, 1; Wiltshire, 1; Oxfordshire, 1; England, unspecified, 24; Ireland, 18; Barbados, 1; America, 2; total, 111; tabulated from lists in Jones, ed., *Quakers in the American Colonies*, 540–43.

[4] The birthplaces of Quaker autobiographers in this source were as follows: Westmorland, 10; Yorkshire, 8; Cumberland, 8; London, 7; Wales, 4; Gloucestershire, 3; Somerset, 3; Cornwall, Sussex, Nottingham, Lincoln, Norfolk, Essex, Worcestershire, 2 each; Leicestershire, Buckinghamshire, Hertfordshire, Durham, Bedford, Cheshire, Kent, Oxfordshire, Hampshire, Staffordshire, Devon and Berkshire, 1 each. Another 10 were born in America, 6 in Ireland, 1 in the West Indies, 1 in the Netherlands, and 5 were of unknown origin. Compiled from William and Thomas Evans, eds., *Friends' Library* (14 vols., Philadelphia, 1837–50).

[5] Albert Cook Myers, *Quaker Arrivals in Philadelphia, 1682–1750* (Philadelphia, 1902); "The district least affected by Quakerism was the tier of counties forming the south midlands." Tolles, *Meeting House and Counting House*, 30. The numbers were as follows: London, 96; Yorkshire,

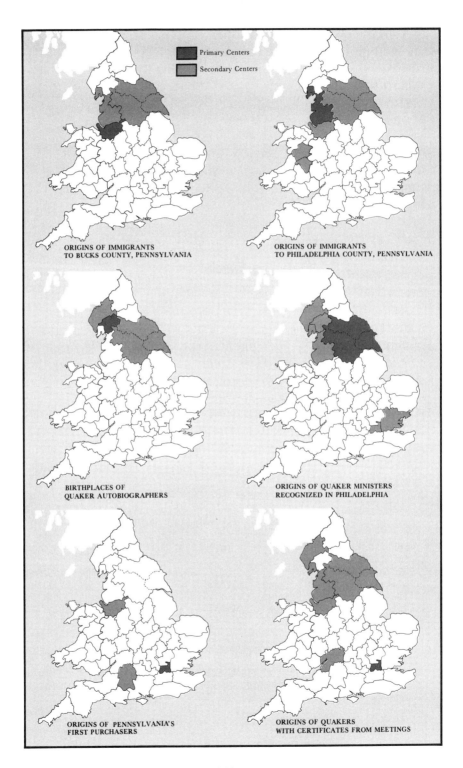

Primary Centers

Secondary Centers

ORIGINS OF IMMIGRANTS
TO BUCKS COUNTY, PENNSYLVANIA

ORIGINS OF IMMIGRANTS
TO PHILADELPHIA COUNTY, PENNSYLVANIA

BIRTHPLACES OF
QUAKER AUTOBIOGRAPHERS

ORIGINS OF QUAKER MINISTERS
RECOGNIZED IN PHILADELPHIA

ORIGINS OF PENNSYLVANIA'S
FIRST PURCHASERS

ORIGINS OF QUAKERS
WITH CERTIFICATES FROM MEETINGS

A different distribution appeared among the "First Purchasers" among Pennsylvania—the 589 people who bought land from William Penn before 1686. This list was not an accurate guide to the origin of actual settlers in Pennsylvania. Many who bought land from William Penn did not emigrate but sold it again to "underpurchasers" who actually took possession. Still, the list of First Purchasers was an important guide to Pennsylvania's investors. The great majority (88%) were English, and were concentrated in major financial centers. The largest group (35) came from London and the home counties. The next biggest concentration was from the North Midlands and the county of Cheshire in particular (11% were from Cheshire alone). A third group lived in the city of Bristol and its environing counties. Scarcely any came from East Anglia, and, except for a few counties close to London and Bristol, comparatively few came from the rural south or west of England which had been so important in the founding of Virginia.[6]

These six population lists all referred primarily to the province of Pennsylvania. In the Quaker colony of West Jersey, the pattern of regional origins was much the same. The colonists who founded West Jersey before 1681 were about 1,400 altogether. Nearly all were reported to be Quakers. Half were said to come from London and Middlesex and half from Yorkshire, Derbyshire and Nottinghamshire.[7] The settlement at Burlington was built on two sides of a stream, and the bridges across it were called London Bridge and York Bridge.[8] Burlington's founders combined

---

27; Gloucester, 18; Wales, 15; Lancashire, 14; Cumberland, 13; Bristol, 13; Cheshire, 11; Worcestershire, 8; Essex, 7; Middlesex, 7; Somerset, 7; Staffordshire, 6; Berkshire, 6; Durham, 6; Oxfordshire, 6; Leicestershire, 5; Wiltshire, 5; Kent, 5; Nottingham, 4; Sussex, 4; Derby, 4; Devon, 4; Suffolk, 3; Herefore, 2; Shropshire, 2; Dorset, 2; Westmorland, 2; Northampton, 2; Hampshire, Surrey, Warwickshire, Bedfordshire, Huntingdon, Hertfordshire, Norfolk, 1 each; unidentified, 8. Also, 81 came from Ireland and 3 from America. Compiled for the author by Jonathan Schwartz.

[6]The distribution of 589 First Purchasers was as follows: *London Area,* 185 (35%), including London 107, Middlesex 20, Berkshire 13, Buckinghamshire 17, Surrey 11, Kent 10, Hertfordshire 7; *Bristol Area,* 110 (21%), including Bristol 36, Wiltshire 53, Somerset 21; *North Country,* 113 (22%), including Cheshire 55, Yorkshire 13, Derbyshire 7, Worcestershire 6, Nottinghamshire 6, Westmorland 5, Lancashire 5, Staffordshire 5, Shropshire (fm Salop) 5, Northumberland 4, Durham 2, Cumberland 0; *East,* 3 (1%), including Essex 2, Suffolk 1, Lincolnshire 0, Norfolk 0, Huntingdonshire 0, Cambridgeshire 0; *S. and W.,* 31 (6%), including Huntingdon 7, Sussex 25, Dorset 0, Devon 0, Cornwall 0; *S. Midlands,* 24 (4%), including Oxfordshire 18, Gloucestershire 2, Herefordshire 2, Warwickshire 0, Northamptonshire 2, Leicestershire 0, Rutland 0; *Other,* 61 (11%), including Ireland 28, Wales 23, Scotland 2, Germany 3, France 2, Holland 1, Barbados 1, New York 1; *Unknown,* 58. Source: *Papers of William Penn,* II, 630–64.

[7]John E. Pomfret, "West New Jersey . . . ," 8 *WMQ3* (1951), 493–519.

[8]Amelia Gummere, "London Bridge, Burlington, N.J.," *PMHB* 8 (1884), 1–16.

two distinct groups—poor farmers and craftsmen from the north of England, and tradesmen and artisans from London.

On both banks of the Delaware River, these Quaker immigrants distributed themselves in small settlements according to their places of origin in Britain. Country Quakers from Cheshire, Lancashire and Yorkshire settled mainly in Chester and Bucks counties. "The farmers among them, poverty stricken dalesmen from the moors of northern England," writes Frederick Tolles, "headed straight for the rich uplands of Bucks and Chester."[9] The lands around Trenton were occupied by emigrants from the Peak District of Derbyshire and Nottinghamshire.[10] London Quakers preferred the city and county of Philadelphia. Emigrants from Bristol founded a town of the same name on the Delaware River. Dublin Quakers occupied Newton, West Jersey.[11] Emigrants from Wales colonized the "Welsh Tract," west of the Schuylkill River.[12]

The origins of these immigrants may also be observed in the names that they gave to the new land. A few Quaker place names expressed their social ideals—Philadelphia, Salem, Concord, Upper Providence and Nether Providence. Other settlements preserved their Indian names: Tinicum, Shackamaxon, Shamokin. The counties were mostly given English place names, of which more than half came from the north: Chester, York and Lancaster in Pennsylvania; Burlington, Cumberland and Monmouth in New Jersey; and Newcastle in northern Delaware. This pattern made a striking contrast with northeastern New Jersey, where the county settled mainly by New England Puritans was called Essex. It differed also from southern Delaware, which was settled from Virginia and Maryland and culturally akin to those colonies, and where the counties were named Sussex and Kent.[13]

---

[9]Tolles, *Quakers and the Atlantic Culture*, 118.

[10]Reuben Pownall Ely, *An Historical Narrative of the Ely, Revell and Stacye Families* (New York, 1910).

[11]Clement, *Sketches of the First Emigrant Settlers in Newton Township*, 51.

[12]T. M. Rees, *A History of Quakers in Wales and the Emigration to North America*, 178; J. Ambler Williams, "The Influence of the Welsh in the Making of Pennsylvania," 120; Browning, *Welsh Settlement of Pennsylvania*, 27; Dodd, *Character of Early Welsh Emigration to the United States*.

[13]In 1775 the counties (and county seats) of Pennsylvania were named Philadelphia (Philadelphia), Bucks (Newtown), Chester (Chester), Northamptom (Easton), Berks (Reading), Lancaster (Lancaster), York (York), Cumberland (Carlisle), Northumberland (Sunbury), Bedford (Bedford), and Westmorland (Hannah Town). Of eleven counties, six bore northern names; the rest were scattered through the center of England. None bore East Anglian names and only one (Berks) was from the south and west. A secondary center lay in three contiguous counties north of London (Buckinghamshire, Bedfordshire and Northamptonshire).

The names of townships in Pennsylvania and West Jersey also betrayed the northern and North Midland origins of many settlers. Towns were named Aston, Billton, Birmingham, Bradford, Bristol, Burlington, Carlisle, Chester, Chesterfield, Darby, Durham, Edgemont, Kennet, Leeds, Liverpool, Marple, Morland, Newcastle, Ridley, Sheffield, Trenton and York. Most of these names were from the North Midlands.

Quaker immigrants from Wales tended to flock together in what was called Cambry or the Welsh Tract. The earliest village names of this district defined the region of origin in the mother country: Flint, Montgomery, Bala, Tredyffrin, Radnor, Haverford, Denbigh. These place names came mostly (not entirely) from northern and eastern Wales, just across the River Dee from Cheshire.[14]

In the eighteenth century, other towns throughout the Delaware Valley were given the names of individual settlers. This practice rarely occurred in New England or Virginia during the early seventeenth century—an indicator of an increasing individuation of social consciousness a half-century later. Many individuals and families whose names still appear on the map of the Delaware Valley were emigrants from the North Midlands. The hamlet of Recklesstown, New Jersey, for example, was named after Joseph Reckless, a Quaker immigrant from a prominent Nottingham family. His ancestor was John Reckless, sheriff of Nottingham and a rich ironmonger and maltster who became a Quaker convert when George Fox was imprisoned in Nottingham Gaol in 1649.[15] Other town names of the same sort included Dilworthtown, Shippensburg, Pennsbury, Norristown, Morristown, Smithville, Allentown, Mifflintown, Wrightstown, Harrisburg and Walnford; most of these families came from the North Midlands.

The Low Dutch and High German Quakers from the Rhineland who founded the township of Germantown named their settlements Cresheim, Crefeld and Sommerhausen, after the com-

---

[14]For an early account of these towns, "where the Welchmen do abide," see Richard Frame, "A Short Description of Pennsylvania," in Myers, ed., *Narratives of Pennsylvania,* 304. Some of the Welsh names on Philadelphia's "main line" were later picked by a railroad president. But Radnor, Haverford, Merion, Gwynedd, Bala and many others were named before 1695. Bryn Mawr was the home of Rowland Ellis; Berwyn was taken from the high country between Merioneth and Montgomery in Wales; see Browning, *Welsh Settlement of Pennsylvania;* J. J. Levick, "John Ap Thomas and His Friends," *PMHB* 4 (1880), 301–28.

[15]James Lomax, "Early Organization of Quakers in Nottingham," *Thoroton Society Transactions* 48 (1944), 40–51; Henry Charlton Beck, *More Forgotten Towns of Southern New Jersey* (1937, rpt., New Brunswick, 1963), 199–206.

munities very near the present German-Dutch border which had expelled them. After 1730, other ethnic groups entered at a rapid rate, and also left their names upon the new land. A few Swedish names survived (Christiana). And in the mid-eighteenth century, Scots and Irish would leave their names upon the landscape. But the north midland origins of the Quaker colonists may still be seen in the place names of the Delaware Valley, even to our own time.

❧ "The Quaker Galilee": England's North Midlands

These emigrants came not from North Midlands in general, but mainly from the Pennine moors and uplands which ran in a northerly way from the Peak District of Derbyshire to the Fells of Yorkshire and Cumbria. This was the highest ground in England. It encompassed the six counties of Derbyshire, Nottinghamshire, Lancashire, east Cheshire, west Yorkshire and southern Westmorland. The Pennine Moors are Brontë country. *Wuthering Heights* and *Jane Eyre* were set in the West Riding of Yorkshire, where Charlotte, Anne and Emily Brontë had grown up in the village of Haworth. Their writings are uncertain guides to the culture of dissent in this region, but powerful evocations of its climate and terrain.

Later in the modern era, this area became the industrial heartland of Britain, a vast ganglion of gritty industrial cities such as Manchester, Bradford, Sheffield and Leeds, where large urban proletariats are now packed into close-built brick tenements that stretch mile after mile across the rolling countryside. In the seventeenth century this was a very different place—one of England's most rural regions, thinly settled and desperately poor. The population consisted mostly of small farmers and shepherds who struggled to feed themselves and to produce a small surplus of wool for the market. Every year the wool was loaded on packhorses and sent to markets as far distant as Southampton. Even in good years there was barely enough to get by; in bad years famine lay heavy upon the land.

During the seventeenth century the north of England had the reputation of being a dangerous place. The English antiquary William Camden felt "a kind of dread" when he came to the borders of Lancashire—an apprehension shared by other travelers. There was a strong sense of insecurity in this sparsely settled land.

Isolated houses were attacked and robbed by roving nocturnal bands, and sometimes all the victims were brutally murdered to hide the crime.[1] As late as the year 1680 a Yorkshire diarist recorded one such event, when a gentleman of that county, together with his mother and servants, was robbed and killed, and the house set ablaze to hide the crime: "The old gentlewoman was most burnt," the diarist wrote, "her face, legs and feet quite consumed to ashes; the trunk of her body much burnt, her heart hanging as a coal out of the midst of it. . . . Some observe that all of their skulls were broken, as it were in the same place."[2]

This region shared a common cultural condition, and also a common history. The North Midlands, more than any other part of England, had been colonized by Viking invaders. Historian Hugh Barbour writes, ". . . in the central region of the North, the Pennine moorland, where Quakerism was strongest, the villages were mainly Norse in origin and name, and Norse had been spoken there in the Middle Ages. From the Norsemen came the custom of moots, or assemblies in the open at a standing-stone or hilltop grave, which may have influenced the Quakers' love for such meeting places. The Norse custom was individual ownership of houses and fields: the Norman system of feudal manors imposed in the twelfth century was always resented."[3]

The Norman conquest of the north had been particularly brutal, and had left a region bitterly divided against itself. Its governing families were culturally distinct from the governed, and long remembered their Norman-French origins. Many remained Roman Catholic more than a century after Henry VIII broke with the Pope. In the seventeenth century many of this elite became Royalist. But shepherds and farmers of the north thought of themselves as a race apart from their overlords. Their religion was evangelical and Protestant. They felt themselves to be aliens from the schools and churches and courts and political institutions of the region—all of which remained securely in the hands of the ruling few. This attitude entered into the theology of the Quakers, and profoundly shaped their social purposes. In some respects, the Quaker culture was that of its native region; in others it was a reaction against it.[4]

---

[1] Joan Parkes, *Travel in England in the Seventeenth Century* (London, 1925).

[2] Ralph Thoresby Diary, 24 Jan. 1680, ms. 31, YAS.

[3] Barbour, *The Quakers in Puritan England*, 74.

[4] William Kapelle, *The Norman Conquest of the North: The Region and Its Transformation* (Chapel Hill, 1979).

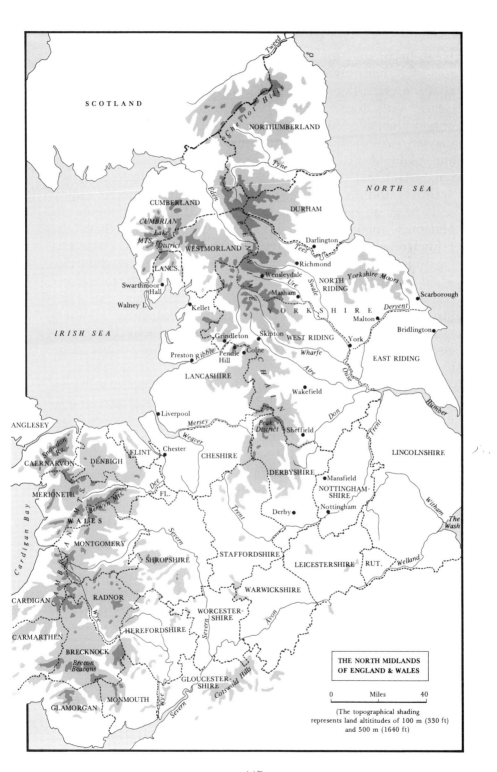

THE NORTH MIDLANDS
OF ENGLAND & WALES

0   Miles   40

(The topographical shading
represents land altititudes of 100 m (330 ft)
and 500 m (1640 ft)

The farmers and herdsmen of this region, in the words of Hugh Barbour, "had a reputation for independence" and a custom of equality among themselves. The "family and farmhands all ate together," at simple meals of "boiled porridge and oatcakes." They dressed alike, in simple homespun suits and dresses of a distinctive color called "hodden gray." Their houses were sparsely furnished, and their culture made a virtue of simplicity and plain speech. All of these folkways became a part of Quakerism.[5]

During the disturbances of the seventeenth century, radical sects in great variety multiplied rapidly throughout the North Midlands—Baptists of many types, Muggletonians, Familists, Fifth Monarchy Men, Ranters, Seekers and Quakers. These various movements were all part of a common impulse. In 1656, when England was ruled by Puritan major-generals, the officer responsible for the north wrote to John Thurloe, "Our Fifth Monarchy men have many of them turned Anabaptist . . . others have renounced that and other ordinances and are termed seekers, and . . . sober people [fear they] will soon profess to be Quakers."[6]

This was the region where the Quakers first appeared. It long remained their strongest base. The founder, George Fox (1624–91), was a Leicestershire weaver's son who developed his doctrine of the Inner Light by 1646 and made his early converts mostly in the North Midlands. By the year 1654, 85 percent of Quaker meetings were in the northern counties of England.[7]

The Quakers were most numerous in the poorest districts of this impoverished region. In Cheshire, for example, Quaker emigrants to Pennsylvania came not from the rich and fertile plains in the center and southwest of the county, but mostly from the high ridges and deep valleys on the eastern fringe of the county. This was rough country, with settlements that bore names such as Bosely Cloud and Wildboarclough. In the seventeenth century, much of this region was still densely wooded, the "last refuge in England of the wolf and the boar." The climate was more severe

---

[5]Barbour, *The Quakers in Puritan England,* 74.

[6]Quoted in Forde, "Derbyshire Quakers," vi.

[7]Pratt, "English Quakers and the First Industrial Revolution," 53–65; especially helpful is chap. 3, "The Geography of Nonconformity," which concludes that "the Quakers had always been a northern religion." By the end of the 17th century, there were Quakers in every English county and city. In the 18th century, many Quakers moved south to London and Birmingham. But the largest number remained north and west of the River Trent.

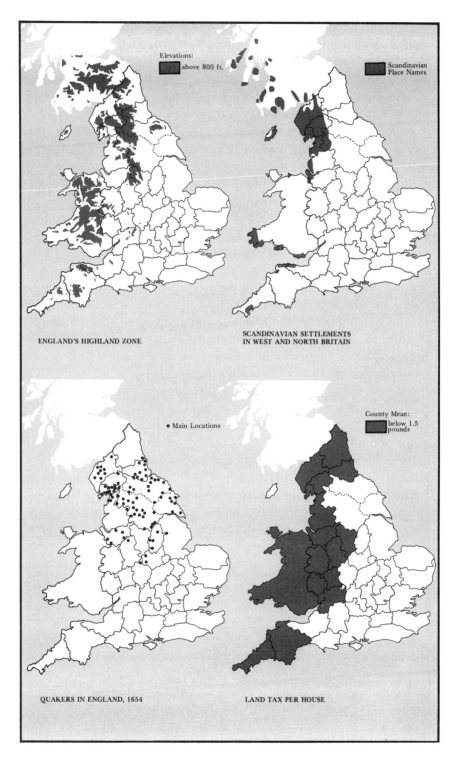

Elevations:
above 800 ft.

ENGLAND'S HIGHLAND ZONE

Scandinavian
Place Names

SCANDINAVIAN SETTLEMENTS
IN WEST AND NORTH BRITAIN

• Main Locations

QUAKERS IN ENGLAND, 1654

County Mean:
below 1.5
pounds

LAND TAX PER HOUSE

449

than in the lowlands—with bitter "close mists" that settled in the valleys, and the dreaded "wireglass" that glazed the ridges and killed many an unwary traveler. The sense of desolation was deepened by the forbidding appearance of small isolated farmhouses, constructed of a harsh gray-black millstone. On the steep slopes of eastern Cheshire, they may still be seen to this day.[8]

In Nottinghamshire, the Quakers came not from the rich alluvial lands of the Trent Valley, but from the craggy uplands. The men of the Monyash monthly meeting once wrote, ". . . we are a poor, unworthy and despised people, scattered amongst the rocky mountains and dern valleys of the high peak country."[9] In Derbyshire, the pattern was also much the same. Here the Quakers lived mostly in the "coal measures" on the east side of the county, and also in the Peak District. Comparatively few came from South Derbyshire.[10]

In the West Riding of Yorkshire, Quakers tended to be poor dalesmen who lived in places such as Lotherdale, a secluded valley on the border between Yorkshire and Lancashire. In the seventeenth century this area was described as "perfectly inaccessible by road." Remoteness was indeed one of its attractions. Some Quakers fled there to escape their persecutors.[11]

One of the great unanswered questions in Quaker historiography is to explain the regional origins of this sect. One scholar, Hugh Barbour, believes that the Scandinavian heritage of this region created an exceptionally fertile culture for Quaker evangelists. This ethnocultural interpretation has been adopted by some American scholars, while materialist explanations have found more favor among British historians. Both schools of thought are probably correct in some degree. The theology of Quakerism arose from an oppressed regional underclass which despised the foreign elite that exploited them. It also rejected the institutions of high culture that were visited upon them, and

---

[8]Parishes specially prominent in the emigration were Stockport, Wilmslow, Macclesfield, Gawsworth, Middlewich, Northwich, Nantwich, Great and Little Budworth, Cheadle and Prestbury. All but the Budworths lay along the eastern edge of Cheshire. Comparatively little emigration came from north Cheshire, which has been identified mistakenly as a major Quaker center in the 17th century. For a good description of the eastern part of the county see R. N. Dore, *Cheshire* (London, 1974), chap. VI, "The Pennine Border." On wind and wireglass and close mist, see William Bagshawe Diary, 1 Jan. 1697, DERBRO.

[9]Monyash Monthly Meeting Minutes, 21.xii.1672, ms. Q86/NRS, NOTTRO.

[10]Forde, "Derbyshire Quakers," 1–6.

[11]Humphrey Moore, *The Case of Lydia Davy* (York, 1983), 25–26.

made virtues of simplicity and hard work in a hostile environment.[12] The austere culture of this regional population became a fertile field for Quakerism. The values of both a region and a class were carried from England's North Midlands to the Delaware Valley.

❧ The Quaker Canaan: The Delaware Valley

European colonists in the Delaware Valley described the dimensions of their new world with a sense of awe. Even today, the great river startles the most jaded modern traveler by its breadth and majesty. In the seventeenth century it was thought to be a wonder of the world. Francis Daniel Pastorius wrote in 1700, ". . . the Delaware River is so grand that it has no equal in Europe." Inside its twin capes, the river opens to form a bay forty miles wide. One hundred miles upstream at Newcastle it is still nearly two miles across. The largest ships in the seventeenth century could sail inland as far as Trenton, 165 miles from the sea.[1]

The ecology of the Delaware Valley was exceptionally well suited to the cultural purposes of its Quaker colonists. Of all the environments of the Atlantic coast it was uniquely favorable to commercial and industrial development. The river and bay became a great common, lined with flourishing settlements. The Welsh Quaker Gabriel Thomas wrote that "between these towns, the watermen constantly Ply their Wherries, likewise all these towns have fairs in them."[2]

Both banks of the Delaware River were laced with small rivers and creeks "in number hardly credible," wrote Penn. On the western shore, the fall line lay only a few miles inland. Streams such as Brandywine Creek and Chester Creek offered many fine mill sites within easy reach of the sea. Close to Philadelphia were large deposits of building stone, coal, copper, iron ore, dense stands of oak, and walnut and chestnut. The soil was rich and

---

[12]Barbour, *The Quakers in Puritan England,* 74.

[1]Francis Daniel Pastorius, "Circumstantial Geographical Description of Pennsylvania," 1700, in Myers, ed., *Narratives of Pennsylvania,* 378; "Letter of Thomas Paschall," *ibid.,* 251.

[2]Gabriel Thomas, "An Historical and Geographical Account of Pensilvania and West-New-Jersey," in Myers, ed., *Narratives of Pennsylvania,* 318.

fertile, a "good and fruitful land," Penn called it, "in some places a fast fat earth, like to our best vales in England."

Another feature of the Delaware Valley was specially important to the Quakers. The natives were friendly, and very different from the more militant tribes of the lower Chesapeake and upper New England. The Delaware Indians as the English called them, or Lenni Lenape as they called themselves, were as distinct from the bellicose Abnaki, the ferocious Pequots and the warlike Powhatan Confederacy as the Quakers were unlike Puritans and cavaliers.[3] William Penn's Indian policy would have been a disastrous failure in Massachusetts or Virginia, just as it later failed in western Pennsylvania. In the valley of the Delaware, it succeeded splendidly, not only because of the Quakers themselves, but also because of the Indians.[4]

A third environmental factor was the temperate climate, which tended to be favorable to European settlement. Levels of mortality were high by modern standards, and also highly unstable, but the first generation found the Delaware Valley to be healthier than England or Virginia, and not much inferior to Massachusetts. This pattern changed for the worse during the eighteenth century when malaria infested the lower Delaware Valley, and yellow fever became a great killer in Philadelphia. Death rates rose generally throughout the region, but the higher ground of Pennsylvania remained exceptionally healthy. Throughout most of the Delaware Valley, moderate levels of mortality supported stable family life—a material fact of high importance for the Quakers.[5]

The settlement of the Delaware Valley by members of the Society of Friends did not happen merely by historical accident. The Quakers had long looked with interest upon this region. As early as the year 1660, George Fox and a consortium of English Friends dispatched an agent named Josiah Coale to buy land

---

[3]C. A. Weslager, *The Delaware Indians* (New Brunswick, 1972); *idem*, "The Delaware Indians as Women," *Journal of the Washington Academy of Sciences* 34 (1944), 381–88; Anthony F. C. Wallace, *King of the Delawares: Teedyuskung, 1700–1763* (Philadelphia, 1949); Albert C. Myers, ed., *William Penn, His Own Account of the Lenni Lenape or Delaware Indians* (Moylan, 1937); Daniel G. Brinton, *The Lenape and Their Legends* (Philadelphia, 1885); Frank H. Stewart, *The Indians of South Jersey* (Woodbury, 1932).

[4]Thomas, "An Historical and Geographical Account of Pensilvania and West-New-Jersey," 340.

[5]In 1768, a clergyman wrote of a colleague in southern Delaware, "from a ruddy robust young man, he looks like one just risen from the Dead; and prays, for God's sake, that he may be moved up to his native hills in Pennsylvania. Sussex on Delaware is as it were the Fens of Essex." John Duffy, *Epidemics in Colonial America* (Baton Rouge, 1953), 211.

from the Indians in what is now southeastern Pennsylvania. His mission failed, but he later informed William Penn about the region. George Fox himself also made a personal reconnaissance of the Delaware Valley in 1672 and found the Indians "very loving."[6] He urged Penn to plant his colony there.[7]

In this environment, English Quakers deliberately acquired no fewer than three American colonies—West Jersey, Pennsylvania and Delaware. For a time they also owned East Jersey, and parts of Carolina. Some of these acquisitions were made in very strange ways. In 1674, New Jersey had been given by the Duke of York (the future King James II) to his boon companions John Lord Berkeley and Sir George Carteret, who divided it in two parts which they inaccurately called East Jersey and West Jersey. In the same year, Lord Berkeley promptly sold West Jersey to Edward Byllinge, a London Quaker who may have been acting for the Society at large and later resold it to a consortium of Quakers. Much of the land in West Jersey was distributed to 1,400 Quaker colonists who arrived between 1677 and 1681.[8]

In 1682, the colony of East Jersey was bought at auction from the widow of Sir George Carteret by another group of Quakers who included the ubiquitous William Penn. The colonists of East Jersey were people of many faiths—including many Dutch settlers from New Netherlands, and a large number of New Englanders whose major settlement was named New Ark (now Newark). Largely as a consequence of incessant complaints by Puritan settlers against Quaker proprietors, imperial authorities in 1702 took over both provinces and combined them in a single royal colony called New Jersey.[9]

In 1681, the Duke of York was instrumental in the creation of Pennsylvania, the largest and most important of the Quaker colonies. This great province was granted to William Penn in nominal payment of a debt which the Crown had owed his father. But

---

[6]Fox, *Journal*, 619, 632 (9.iii.1672; 9.vii.1672).

[7]William Sewel, *The History of the Rise, Increase and Progress of the Christian People Called Quakers* (1717, 2 vols., London, 1811), I, 450; Josiah Coale, *The Books and Divers Epistles of the Faithful Servant of the Lord Josiah Cole* (London, 1671).

[8]These transactions were complex; West Jersey was actually sold by Berkeley to John Fenwick of Buckinghamshire, who was acting as an agent for Edward Byllinge. It is not clear whether Fenwick and Byllinge were mainly engaged in a commercial or a spiritual speculation. In any case, the colony passed quickly into the control of a group including William Penn, Gawen Laurie and Nicholas Lucas.

[9]The bill of sale for East Jersey was dated 2 Feb. 1681/82. Jones, ed., *Quakers in the American Colonies*, 368; Braithwaite, *Second Period of Quakerism*, 403.

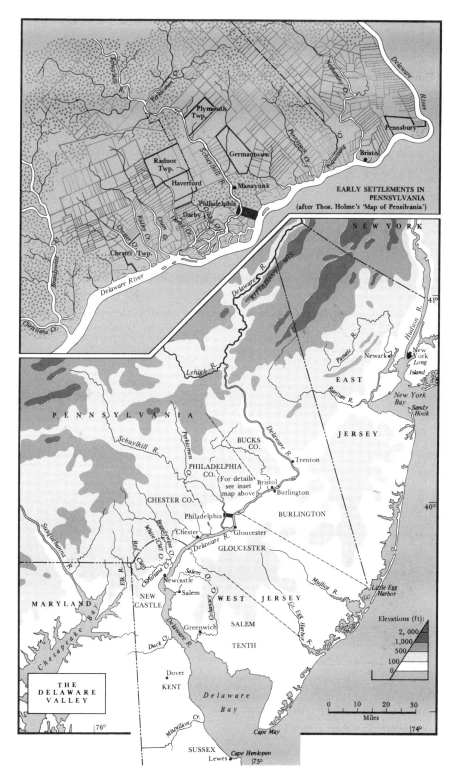

EARLY SETTLEMENTS IN
PENNSYLVANIA
(after Thos. Holme's 'Map of Pensilvania')

Schuylkill R.

Perkiomen R.

Plymouth
Twp.

Germantown

Radnor
Twp.

Haverford

Schuylkill R.

Manayunk

Philadelphia

Darby

Chester Twp.

Chester Cr.

Ridley Cr.

Crum Cr.

Darby Cr.

Brandywine

Christiana Cr.

Delaware River

Pennsbury

Bristol

Neshaminy Cr.

Pennypack Cr.

Poquessing Cr.

Delaware River

NEW YORK

Delaware R.

KITTATINNY MTS.

Lehigh R.

PENNSYLVANIA

Schuylkill R.

Perkiomen

BUCKS
CO.

PHILADELPHIA
CO.
(For details
see inset
map above)

CHESTER CO.

Philadelphia

Chester

Susquehanna R.

Brandywine Cr.

White Clay Cr.

Red Clay Cr.

Christiana Cr.

Elk R.

Newcastle

NEW
CASTLE

Salem

MARYLAND

Chesapeake Bay

Duck Cr.

Delaware R.

Dover

KENT

Mispillion Cr.

SUSSEX

Lewes

Cape Henlopen

Delaware R.

Gloucester

Delaware R.

GLOUCESTER

Greenwich

Cohansey R.

Salem Cr.

WEST JERSEY

SALEM

TENTH

Delaware
Bay

Cape May

Bristol

Burlington

BURLINGTON

Trenton

Delaware R.

Mullica R.

Gt. Egg Harbor R.

Little Egg
Harbor

Passaic R.

Raritan R.

Newark

EAST

JERSEY

New
York

Long
Island

New York
Bay

Sandy
Hook

Hudson R.

41°

40°

Elevations (ft):

2,000
1,000
500
100
0

0   10   20   30
Miles

THE
DELAWARE
VALLEY

|76°

|75°

|74°

that was not the leading motive. The founding of Pennsylvania was a serious effort to settle the "Quaker problem," by a monarch who sympathized with their plight. The original grant was larger than the present state of Pennsylvania. Altogether, Penn's province covered about 600,000 square miles, stretching from sea to sea between the 40th and the 43rd parallels, an area six times the size of Great Britain. It later grew a little larger when William Penn was allowed to buy the colony of Delaware from the Duke of York. For many years Delaware was governed as a separate part of Pennsylvania.

From the start, the Delaware colonies were generally perceived as parts of a single region. Quakers throughout the Delaware Valley organized themselves into a single yearly meeting which met alternately on each bank of the river. When the Anglicans attempted to rescue the inhabitants from "Quakerism or heathenism" in the eighteenth century, they organized the valley into a "single missionary field."[10] The valley also became an economic unit which sent its produce to Philadelphia.[11] Historian Frederick Tolles writes:

> The colonial Pennsylvanian knew without being told that he lived in the valley of the Delaware. He first saw his new home from the deck of a ship sailing up the great river. . . . The Delaware united West Jersey, Pennsylvania and the Lower Counties (which eventually became the state of Delaware) into a single economic province, and linked it with the rest of the Atlantic community. It also unified the valley into a single "culture area."[12]

❧ William Penn and the Delaware Valley: The Intent of the Founder

This "Delaware culture area," as Frederick Tolles called it, developed not by some random process of social selection, but from the conscious will and purpose of its Quaker founders. The leading role was played by one founder in particular, William Penn—who served Pennsylvania, Delaware and also West Jersey as lawgiver, social planner, organizer, tireless promoter, and regulator of the immigration process. The cultural history of this

---

[10]Tolles, *Quakers and the Atlantic Culture,* 116.
[11]James Weston Livingood, *The Philadelphia-Baltimore Trade Rivalry* (Harrisburg, 1947), 3.
[12]Tolles, *Quakers and the Atlantic Culture,* 117.

region cannot be understood without knowing something about the mind and character of this extraordinary man.[1]

William Penn was bundle of paradoxes—an admiral's son who became a pacifist, an undergraduate at Oxford's Christ Church who became a pious Quaker, a member of Lincoln's Inn who became an advocate of arbitration, a Fellow of the Royal Society who despised pedantry, a man of property who devoted himself to the welfare of the poor, a polished courtier who preferred the plain style, a friend of kings who became a radical Whig, and an English gentleman who became one of Christianity's great spiritual leaders.

William Penn's life began 14 October 1644, on London's Tower Hill, in the shadow of the great castle where he would later be imprisoned for his faith. He was born into a violent world and very nearly made violence his career. The great events of his early life were wars and revolutions in which his family was intimately involved. His father was a naval officer who served both Cromwell and the King, and was rewarded by both sides with large estates in Ireland.

Penn grew up in Ireland, and believed (mistakenly) that he was of Welsh descent. But by birth and breeding he was very much an English gentleman. His Anglo-Norman family (originally De La Penne) was kin to many of the gentry who went to Virginia. By marriage he was related to Frances Culpeper Berkeley (the wife of Sir William Berkeley) who knew him well and called him "cousin."[2]

---

[1]The historiography of William Penn is a fascinating story in its own right. In 1870 his papers were vandalized and sold for scrap paper, probably by an illegitimate and disinherited great-grandson. Fortunately, a dealer rescued much of the material. In the 20th century, 2,600 manuscripts have been microfilmed, and a generous selection issued in a letterpress edition of *The Papers of William Penn*. An interpretive bibliography of William Penn by Edwin Bronner and David Fraser has identified 135 works published in Penn's lifetime or shortly thereafter. A distillation of Penn's works in one volume by Frederick Tolles and E. Gordon Alderfer, *The Witness of William Penn* (New York, 1957), makes the best beginning for a modern reader.

Of more than 40 full-scale biographies of Penn, the most valuable are early works by Sewel (1722), Clarkson (1813) and Janney (1852), and later studies by Fisher (1900), Dobrée (1932), Pound (1932), Vulliamy (1934), Hull (1937) and Peare (1956, rpt. 1966). Specialized monographs of high quality include Mabel Brailsford, *The Making of William Penn* (London, 1930), Mary Maples Dunn, *William Penn: Politics and Conscience* (Princeton, 1967); Joseph Illick, *William Penn the Politician* (Ithaca, 1965); Edward C. O. Beatty, *William Penn as a Social Philosopher* (New York, 1939); Melvin Endy, Jr., *William Penn and Early Quakerism* (Princeton, 1973); and Dunn and Dunn, eds., *The World of William Penn*.

[2]The great-grandmother of William Penn's first wife Gulielma Springett was Lord Thomas Culpeper's great aunt. Culpeper's daughter Frances Berkeley, the wife of Sir William Berkeley, corresponded with Penn and called him cousin. See Penn to Lord Thomas Culpeper, 5.xii.1682/83; Lady Frances Culpeper Berkeley to Penn, 13 Oct. 1685, *Papers of William Penn*, II, 350; III, 64–65.

This portrait of William Penn as a young warrior was painted in 1666 (when he was 22 years old). It captures the improbable origins of the Quaker leader. He was raised in a military family, nearly became a professional soldier, and always cherished a warrior's virtues, even when he turned against war itself. This militant Christian would always be a fighter for God's truth, closer in spirit to St. George than to St. Francis. Penn appears in heavy armor such as he might have worn when he saw combat at Carrickfergus in the same year. The light falls upon his right arm and chest, bringing out a sense of strength. The neck cloth of fine lace adds a tone of refinement. A dark thick wig hides Penn's unfashionable thin blond hair. The face has a delicate beauty, a candid expression, and a firm jaw. The lines of composition converge upon the eyes which are exceptionally full, deep and thoughtful—adding a hint of detachment from the world. This drawing is from an eighteenth-century copy of a lost original in the Historical Society of Pennsylvania.

As a youth, William Penn was trained to arms. He became so
skillful a swordsman that once when attacked by a French duelist
he expertly disarmed his enemy, gallantly spared his life and went
upon his way, wondering if any "ceremony were worth the life of
any man." In 1666 Penn served in combat in the suppression of
an English mutiny at Carrickfergus, and so distinguished himself
that he was recommended for a military post.[3]

Penn was tempted to accept, but he was destined for a different
life. Raised in a pious Protestant household to be a "Christian
and a gentleman," he had begun to have deep mystic visions as
early as the age of twelve. His father sent him to Christ Church,
Oxford, to temper his faith. The effect was the reverse. Penn was
deeply shocked by what he called the "hellish darkness and
debauchery" of Oxford. He refused to wear a black gown or to
attend compulsory chapel, and was expelled for nonconformity.

Returning to Ireland, this restless young man heard the
Quaker preacher Thomas Loe and was converted to that faith.
His father tried to change his mind, first by "whipping, beating
and turning out of doors," then by sending him on a grand tour.
Penn wavered in his faith. But after his return, the diarist Samuel
Pepys (who knew him well and detested his piety) wrote cynically,
"Mr. Penn . . . is a Quaker again, or some such melancholy
thing."

Penn quickly became a leader among Friends. He preached
throughout Britain, published more than one hundred works,
and was often imprisoned by the alarmed authorities. In 1668 he
was locked in the Tower of London for writing a Quaker book.
Penn used his time in jail to write another book called *No Cross,
No Crown,* which many take to be his greatest work.[4] Soon after
his release, Penn was arrested again in 1670 for preaching outside a locked meetinghouse in London. In the trial that followed,
Penn conducted his defense so brilliantly that the jurors refused
to convict him even when threatened with prison themselves. The
case became a landmark in the history of trial by jury.[5]

In 1671 Penn was arrested once more. This time he was tried

---

[3]William Penn, *No Cross, No Crown* (London, 1682), 148.

[4]Penn was imprisoned for writing *The Sandy Foundation Shaken* (London, 1668), which
seemed to deny the divinity of Christ and the doctrine of atonement. In prison he wrote *Inno-
cency with an Open Face* (London, 1669), and his most successful work, *No Cross, No Crown* (London, 1669).

[5][Thomas Rudyard?], *The People Ancient and Just Liberties Asserted in the Tryal of William Penn,
and William Mead* . . . (London, 1670), reprinted at least nine times in 1670, and many times
thereafter.

secretly in the Tower and sent to Newgate, where he refused the privileges of his rank and lived in a common cell. There he finished *The Great Case of Liberty of Conscience,* one of the noblest defenses of religious liberty ever written.[6]

While suffering for his faith, Penn was treated with deference by his persecutors, and affection by many of his jailors. He maintained warm personal relations with Charles II and the future James II. From his cell he courted and won the hand of Gulielma Springett, a high-born lady who was celebrated for Quaker piety and for her blonde beauty (Penn's rivals included London's leading Restoration rakes). Her many connections gave Penn much influence in English society and helped him secure the charter of Pennsylvania. After her death, Penn married Hannah Callowhill, a rich Bristol heiress who brought him an income of £3000 a year—enough to keep his colony afloat.

In 1671 Penn traveled in Europe, and met with German Pietists who also suffered heavily from persecution. In company with them he began to think seriously about founding a colony in America—an idea which had been stirring in his mind since 1661. He became a trustee of West Jersey, and drew up the fundamental laws of that colony. But as the sufferings of Quakers and Pietists continued in western Europe, Penn felt the need of a larger sanctuary for oppressed Christians throughout the world. He petitioned his royal friend Charles II for a colony. In 1681, Charles overruled his advisors, and granted the request. The King himself named the colony, adding with his own hand the prefix "Penn" to the proposed "Sylvania."[7]

Pennsylvania and its neighboring provinces were intended to be in Penn's words a "colony of heaven" for the "children of Light." He did not think of his province as a retreat from the world, but as a model for general emulation. Like the Puritans of Massachusetts and the cavaliers of Virginia, Penn intended his American settlement to be an example for all Christians.

The cornerstone of this "holy experiment" was liberty of conscience—not for everyone, and never for its own sake. William Penn believed that religious liberty was an instrument of Christian salvation. It did not occur to him that liberty was to be desired as an end in itself. He excluded atheists and nonbelievers from his colony, and confined officeholding to believing Christians. Even so, Pennsylvania came closer to his goal of a non-coer-

---

[6] *The Great Case of Liberty of Conscience* (1670, rev. London, 1671).
[7] Fulmer Mood, "William Penn and English Politics in 1680–81," *FHSJ* 32 (1935), 1–19.

William Penn in maturity looks out upon us from this unfinished crayon sketch by Francis Place, which shows Penn as proprietor of Pennsylvania, aged 52 (ca. 1696). The face has grown very full, with fleshy cheeks and double chin. Even so, a lady called him "the handsomest best-looking, lively gentleman she had ever seen." (Hull, 301). There is a feeling of simplicity and goodness in this gentle, kindly Quaker face. But one sees also a hint of rank and authority; and the set of the mouth and the arch of the brow are those of a man accustomed to command.

cive society than any state in Christendom during the seventeenth century.

Another part of Penn's holy experiment was the renunciation of war. The Quaker colonies had no military establishment; Penn wrote to a Friend in 1685 that in the Delaware Valley there was "not one soldier, nor arm borne, or militia man seen, since I was first at Pennsylvania."[8]

Penn also intended the Quaker colonies to be a political experiment for his radical Whig principles. He was no democrat, but believed deeply in the "ancient English constitution" of mixed or balanced government. Most of all he believed in the rule of law. "For the matters of liberty and privilege," he wrote, "I propose . . . to leave myself and successors no power of doing mischief, that the will of one man may not hinder the good of an whole country."[9]

In economic terms, Penn was not interested in founding an agrarian utopia. From the start, he intended his colonies to be a hive of commerce and industry, with a "due balance between trade and husbandry." He recruited artisans and what he called "laborious handicrafts" more actively than other colonizers, and also with greater success.[10]

In social terms, Penn envisioned a society where people of different beliefs could dwell together in peace. His dream was not unity but harmony—and not equality but "love and brotherly kindness." Penn never imagined that all people were of the same condition. He expected "obedience to superiors, love to equals, and help and countenance to inferiors." There was to be no freedom for the wicked; Penn's laws against sin were more rigorous in some respects than those of Puritans or Anglicans.

Some of Penn's ideas for his colony have an aura of modernity about them. But he was not a modern man. He despised the material and secular impulses that were gaining strength around him, and dreamed of a world where Christians could dwell together in love. His vision for America looked backward to the primitive Church, and also to what he called England's ancient constitution. These were not progressive ideas.[11]

---

[8]Penn to Stephen Crisp, 28 Feb. 1685, *Papers of William Penn*, III, 28.

[9]Penn to Robert Turner et al., 12.ii. [Apr.] 1681, *Papers of William Penn*, II, 89.

[10]Penn, "Some Account of the Province of Pennsylvania," 197–254.

[11]Here I follow Mary Maples Dunn, *Politics and Conscience* (Princeton, 1967), with one difference. Penn's idea, I think, was not Christian unity but Christian harmony—a crucial distinction on which Penn's idea of reciprocal liberty was based.

The result of William Penn's holy experiment was not precisely as he intended, but he gave decisive shape to the culture of the Delaware Valley. To this day its customs still bear the imprint of his mind and personality. "An institution," Emerson remarked, "is the lengthened shadow of one man; as . . . Quakerism [is] of Fox." He might have said, "as Pennsylvania is of Penn."[12]

❧ "Our Mob": Origins of William Penn's Delaware Elite

For all his sense of humanity, William Penn never believed in social equality. "Tho' [God] has made of one blood all nations," Penn wrote, "he has not ranged or dignified them upon the *Level*, but in a sort of subordination or dependency."[1]

That spirit of "subordination" was introduced to West Jersey, Pennsylvania and Delaware in the seventeenth century. Within the first generation of settlement, a small elite appeared in all of these provinces. Its core was a group of Quaker families whom Deborah Norris of Philadelphia called "our mob."[2] So tight was this Quaker "connection" that of all the men who were admitted members of Philadelphia's Corporation (the oligarchy that ran the town) from 1727 to 1750, no fewer than 85 percent were related to one another.[3]

This Delaware elite had its English roots mainly in the North Midlands of England. Many of its members had emigrated from small northern villages to London and Bristol and seaports throughout the empire. After accumulating a capital, they moved again to Pennsylvania. An example was the Shippen family, who came originally from Hillam in the West Riding of Yorkshire. Edward Shippen (1639–1712) emigrated in 1668 to Boston, where he became a prosperous merchant, but was cruelly persecuted for his faith. He removed to Philadelphia, becoming one of

---

[12]Ralph Waldo Emerson, "Self Reliance," in *Essays: First Series,* in *The Selected Writings of Ralph Waldo Emerson* (New York, 1940), 154.

[1]William Penn, *Some Fruits of Solitude* (London, 1693); quoted in Tolles, *Meeting House and Counting House,* 110.

[2]Deborah Norris to Isaac Norris, 3 Nov. 1733, quoted in Tully, *William Penn's Legacy,* 81.

[3]This was a closed corporation called "the mayor and commonalty of Philadelphia," which controlled the city from the 1701 to 1776; see Judith Diamondstone, "The Philadelphia Corporation, 1701–1776" (thesis, Univ. of Pa., 1969), 258–68; and "Philadelphia's Municipal Corporation, 1701–1776," *PMHB* 90 (1966), 183–201; see also Daniel R. Gilbert, "Patterns of Organization and Membership in Philadelphia Club Life" (thesis, Univ. of Pa., 1952).

the leading merchants in the town, and also mayor, speaker of the assembly, chief justice and president of the provincial council. His children intermarried with the leading families of the Delaware elite.[4]

Many of those families came from the North Midlands of England. The Dilworth, Waln, Pemberton, Harris and Morris families all hailed from Lancashire. The Sharplesses, Janneys, Simcocks, Stanfields and Brasseys were from Cheshire. The Matlocks, Buntings and Bartrams came from Derbyshire; the Yardlys and Rudyards from Staffordshire; Hopkinsons from Nottinghamshire; Holmeses from Yorkshire; Whartons from Westmorland; Kirkbrides from Cumberland; and Fenwicks from Northumberland.

Another group of Quaker families came from Bristol and its surrounding countryside—the Budds, Emlens, Allens and the Proprietor's secretary James Logan who had Bristol connections. Many of these families were related to William Penn through his second wife Hannah Callowhill whom he had married when he lived in Bristol.

Also of high prominence was a Buckinghamshire connection consisting of the Coxe, Pennington (Penington) and Ford families—a rich and well-born Quaker gentry. They were related to Penn himself through his first wife Gulielma Springett, whose mother and stepfather were Isaac and Mary Penington. All of these families settled in West Jersey and Pennsylvania.

Yet another group consisted of Quakers from Wales—David Lloyd and his rival kinsman Thomas Lloyd, and also the Jones, Cadwalader, Owen, Meredith and Painter families. A few other elite families migrated individually from various English counties, and from every corner of the British empire—the Norrises from London by way of Jamaica, the Carpenters from Sussex by way of Barbados, the Dickinsons from Jamaica and the Rawles family from Cornwall. In the New World they were joined by German and Dutch Quakers.

Some of this elite had first settled in Burlington, West Jersey, before 1682—including the Biddle, Morris, Read and Robeson families. Others such as the Yeates family had established themselves in Newcastle County, Delaware. Both groups gravitated toward the city of Philadelphia, which became the seat of the Del-

---

[4]Randolph Shipley Klein, "The Shippen Family: A Generational Study in Colonial and Revolutionary Pennsylvania" (thesis, Rutgers, 1972).

aware Valley's "first families." The Philadelphia elite was linked
by blood and marriage to other families who remained in the
country, and dominated rural culture throughout the region,
long after other ethnic groups became more numerous. This was
so even in Pennsylvania's Lancaster County, which rapidly
acquired a large German population after 1720. By the mid-eighteenth century, only 100 Quakers were said to live in Lancaster
County, but they included the Wrights, Blunstons, Barbers,
Lindleys, Worrals, Webbs and Allens, who kept the government
of the county securely in their own hands. Rhoda Barber
remembered:

> the first proprietors being all connected or related to each other,
> there was an harmony and friendship among them beautiful to
> behold and pleasing to recollect. I well remember their being at
> my father's house in first day afternoon. Their entertainment was
> apples and cider, bread and butter and smoked beef.[5]

That Quaker connection, which met over apples and cider in the
Barbers' best room, dominated Lancaster for many years.

Similar Quaker elites existed in other parts of the Delaware
Valley. In Bucks County, there was a Quaker connection headed
by Jeremiah Langhorne which was very powerful in local affairs.
A third Quaker elite controlled public affairs in Chester County.
A fourth lived in the Welsh Tract. Yet another group of Quakers,
including the Cox, Pennington and Ford families, were very powerful in northeastern Maryland. All of these local elites came to
be connected in a great cousinage with Philadelphia's major families: Reads, Pembertons, Logans, Norrises, Lloyds, Carpenters,
Prestons, Smiths, Emlens, Powels, Morrises, Cadwaladers and
Shoemakers.

By the year 1750, most members of the Delaware elite were
linked to this connection in one way or another. Many were the
lineal or collateral kin of Sarah Read Logan, wife of James Logan,
who was to the first families of her region as Mary Horsmanden
Filmer Byrd had been to the "topping families" of Virginia and
Sarah Storre Cotton Mather would be to the ministers and magistrates of Massachusetts.

The Delaware elite was similar in its solidarity to those of New
England and Virginia, but very different in its origin and attitudes. A remarkably large proportion were of humble rank—

---

[5]Rhoda Barber Journal, HSP.

The Delaware Elite

I. The Core Connection: Burlington and Philadelphia
(Read–Pemberton–Logan–Norris–Lloyd–Carpenter–Preston–Smith– Emlen–Powel–Morris–Cadwalader–Shoemaker)

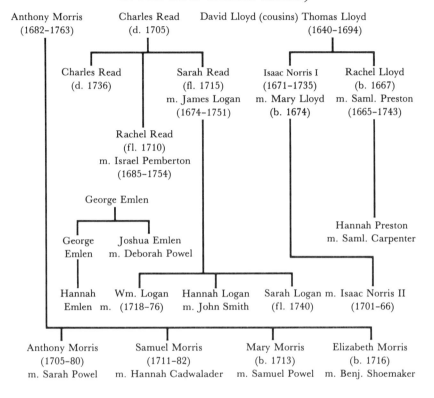

II. The Bristol Connection (Budd–Allen–Logan–Penn–Callowhill)

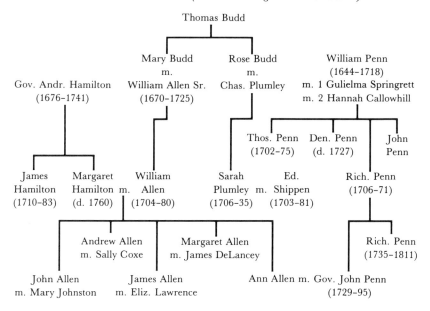

country artisans, petty traders, tenant farmers, servants and laborers. The first William Fisher was a cordwainer; the first John Fisher, a glazier; the first Allen, a cooper; the first Biddle, a shoemaker; the first Bringhurst, a cooper's apprentice; the first Harrison, a shoemaker; the first Hollingsworth, a servant; the first Kirkbride, a carpenter; the first Matlack, a carpenter; the first Stansfield, a farm laborer; the first West, a "girdler"; the first Wynne, a barber-surgeon; the first Zane, a sergemaker; the first Jenkins, an "emasculator of animals." Many were husbandmen (Langhornes, Nixons, Dilworths, Walns, Brasseys, Simcocks). Others were small traders and petty merchants. Scarcely any of this Quaker elite came from armigerous families. The English gentry who came to Virginia were conspicuous by their absence from the Delaware Valley. There were a few exceptions. Welsh Quaker Thomas Lloyd was of an old family which claimed fifteen quarterings on its escutcheon. But few leading Quakers had solid claims to such distinctions.

Even fewer had been to a university—William Penn himself, his secretary James Logan, and a few others. But Quakers were unable to attend Oxford and Cambridge without abjuring their faith. The formal learning that was so important in defining New England's elite had no place in the Delaware Valley.

The lack of heraldic arms and university degrees did not mean that the founders of the Delaware elite were poor. Many brought a substantial capital to the New World, and rapidly advanced from affluence to wealth, which they achieved in the Delaware Valley primarily by investing in land. "It is almost a proverb in this neighborhood," a traveler wrote in 1768, "that 'every great fortune made here within these 50 years has been by land.'"[6]

Even as this elite grew very rich, its members continued to identify themselves with their manual occupations in a manner that was very different from Virginia or New England. The first Samuel Powel was always called the "rich carpenter," even after he had acquired ninety houses in the city and large tracts of land in the country.[7] In the most affluent families young men were urged not to live in idleness. Thus, Edward Shippen of Lancaster instructed his son: "Avoid what the world calls pleasure. Pleasure

---

[6]"Extracts from Letters of Alexander Mackraby to Sir Philip Francis," *PMHB* 11 (1887), 277.

[7]Carl Bridenbaugh, *Rebels and Gentlemen; Philadelphia in the Age of Franklin* (1942, rpt. New York, 1962), 199.

is only for crowned heads and other great men who have their incomes sleeping and waking. . . . Go to your cousin Allen, opulent as he is, and you will find him up early and busily employed."[8]

Ties of industry and commerce united this elite. Edward Shippen formed a commercial partnership with James Logan, trading as the firm of Logan and Shippen. Later Shippen also formed another alliance with Thomas Lawrence, as Shippen and Lawrence. In the eighteenth century the pivotal firm was Morris and Willing, with whom many elite families did business. As time passed, merchants of other backgrounds found their way to Philadelphia, but the old families retained a moral and material hegemony even to the twentieth century.

In the early years, these families were also united by religion. Their founders were nearly all Quakers. Many had felt the lash of persecution before coming to the Delaware. The first Edward Shippen had twice been whipped severely by the Puritans, merely for attending Quaker Meeting. Others had been jailed in England—an experience that shaped their attitudes toward power and liberty for years to come.[9]

As time passed, some children of these founders fell away from the Society of Friends. In the eighteenth century, entire families, including the Shippens, Clymers, Mifflins, Bonds, Plumsteds, Redmans, Stretells and even the Penns themselves returned to the Church of England. Other religious divisions had earlier occurred among leading Quakers over the Keithian controversy, and later between strict Quakers and "wet Quakers."[10]

The Delaware elite also quarreled over politics, dividing into factions called the Proprietary and Quaker parties. But the leaders of both parties were related to one another. The Proprietary party was led by Thomas Lloyd; the Quaker party by his kinsman David Lloyd. Party rivalry pitted cousin against cousin within the narrow circle of a family argument.

This elite was more open than those of Massachusetts and Virginia. During the eighteenth century, it demonstrated strong powers of regeneration. It allowed newly rich families of old Quaker stock (Biddles, Clymers, Hollingsworth, Penrose) to move

---

[8]Edward Shippen of Lancaster to his son the future Chief Justice Edward Shippen, 20 March 1754, *PMHB* 30 (1906), 85–90.

[9]A graphic account of his sufferings appears in the Anthony Sharp Papers, Dublin Friends Meeting, microfilm in SWAR.

[10]Thomas Wendel, "The Keith-Lloyd Alliance," *PMHB* 92 (1968), 293.

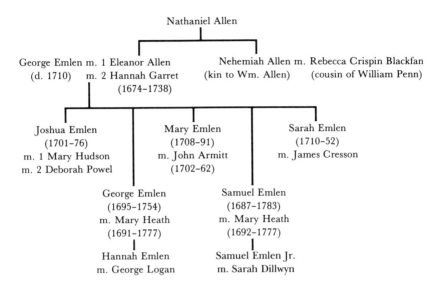

Nathaniel Allen

George Emlen m. 1 Eleanor Allen
(d. 1710)   m. 2 Hannah Garret
(1674–1738)

Nehemiah Allen m. Rebecca Crispin Blackfan
(kin to Wm. Allen)   (cousin of William Penn)

Joshua Emlen
(1701–76)
m. 1 Mary Hudson
m. 2 Deborah Powel

Mary Emlen
(1708–91)
m. John Armitt
(1702–62)

Sarah Emlen
(1710–52)
m. James Cresson

George Emlen
(1695–1754)
m. Mary Heath
(1691–1777)

Samuel Emlen
(1687–1783)
m. Mary Heath
(1692–1777)

Hannah Emlen
m. George Logan

Samuel Emlen Jr.
m. Sarah Dillwyn

IV. The Yorkshire Connection (Shippen-Plumley-Willing-Francis-MacCall-Yeates)

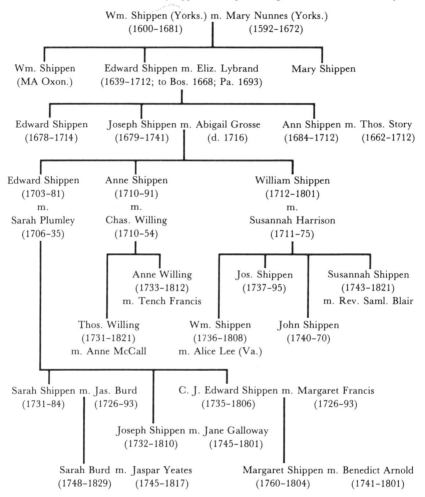

Wm. Shippen (Yorks.) m. Mary Nunnes (Yorks.)
(1600-1681)   (1592-1672)

Wm. Shippen   Edward Shippen m. Eliz. Lybrand   Mary Shippen
(MA Oxon.)   (1639-1712; to Bos. 1668; Pa. 1693)

Edward Shippen   Joseph Shippen m. Abigail Grosse   Ann Shippen m. Thos. Story
(1678-1714)   (1679-1741)   (d. 1716)   (1684-1712)   (1662-1712)

Edward Shippen   Anne Shippen   William Shippen
(1703-81)   (1710-91)   (1712-1801)
m.   m.   m.
Sarah Plumley   Chas. Willing   Susannah Harrison
(1706-35)   (1710-54)   (1711-75)

                   Anne Willing   Jos. Shippen   Susannah Shippen
                   (1733-1812)   (1737-95)   (1743-1821)
                   m. Tench Francis   m. Rev. Saml. Blair

          Thos. Willing   Wm. Shippen   John Shippen
          (1731-1821)   (1736-1808)   (1740-70)
          m. Anne McCall   m. Alice Lee (Va.)

Sarah Shippen m. Jas. Burd   C. J. Edward Shippen m. Margaret Francis
(1731-84)   (1726-93)   (1735-1806)   (1726-93)

          Joseph Shippen m. Jane Galloway
          (1732-1810)   (1745-1801)

Sarah Burd m. Jaspar Yeates   Margaret Shippen m. Benedict Arnold
(1748-1829)   (1745-1817)   (1760-1804)   (1741-1801)

V. The Lancashire Connection (Waln, Dilworth)

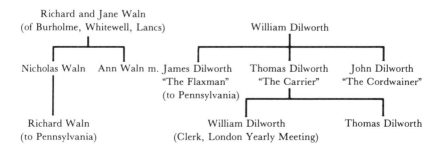

Richard and Jane Waln
(of Burholme, Whitewell, Lancs)   William Dilworth

Nicholas Waln   Ann Waln m. James Dilworth   Thomas Dilworth   John Dilworth
                         "The Flaxman"   "The Carrier"   "The Cordwainer"
                         (to Pennsylvania)

Richard Waln   William Dilworth   Thomas Dilworth
(to Pennsylvania)   (Clerk, London Yearly Meeting)

steadily from the periphery to core.[11] It also admitted new members who were Anglican or Presbyterian or Free Thinkers such as Benjamin Franklin and Benjamin Rush. But it expected them to marry suitably (as Franklin "married" a Read and Rush wed a Stockton). These newcomers were also expected to conform to established Delaware Valley customs of dress and demeanor.

For many years, this Delaware elite remained dominant in its region. From the late seventeenth century to the early twentieth, its core consisted of Quaker or lapsed-Quaker families who had arrived in the period from 1675 to 1695.[12] A close student of Pennsylvania politics finds that "members of the Society of Friends dominated elective offices, held large numbers of appointive positions, and constituted a majority of the colony's economic and social leaders," from its founding to the mid-eighteenth century. Its social hegemony in Philadelphia has survived even to our own time.[13]

[11]This Quaker elite of the Delaware Valley should not be confused with Gary Nash's "early merchants of Philadelphia," a different but overlapping group. Nash identifies 102 "first-generation" Philadelphia merchants, and 143 of the second generation. He finds that 111 or 112 of the second generation were not "related by birth" to the first and concludes that the "founding elite" failed to perpetuate itself. But in Nash's analysis, "not related by birth" means not sons of first-generation merchants; a test which takes no account of other degrees of kinship. Moreover, some members of elite families moved in and out of mercantile occupations; occupational mobility was not proof of the "disintegration of an elite." Further, many merchants (even rich merchants) in every generation were never members of Philadelphia's elite—e.g., Jewish merchants who arrived from New York and abroad after 1711. Their appearance was not evidence of a disintegrating elite. Many of Nash's merchants were modest traders with middling or even small estates; in the second generation, 21 left estates below £500, and 5 below £100. Altogether, Nash's "early merchants" and the Delaware elite were like overlapping circles in a Venn diagram. Cf. Gary B. Nash, "The Early Merchants of Philadelphia: The Formation and Disintegration of a Founding Elite," in Dunn and Dunn, eds., *The World of William Penn*, 337–62.

[12]Many scholars distinguish between Quaker and non-Quaker elites in mid-18th-century Philadelphia. Non-Quakers had their own institutional life—the College of Philadelphia, the Mount Regale Fishing Company, the Hand-in-Hand Fire Company, and the Dancing Assembly. The leaders of the non-Quaker elite are identified by Brobeck as the Penn, Shippen, Allen, Coxe, Dickinson and other families which had originally been Quaker. Some were of different origins—Richard Peters, for example, who had fled England to escape arrest for bigamy. But these "non-Quakers" were often ex-Quakers with many kin connections to the Quaker elite; see Stephen J. Brobeck, "Changes in the Composition and Structure of Philadelphia Elite Groups" (thesis, Univ. of Pa., 1974), 123–81.

[13]Tully, *William Penn's Legacy*, 141.

✎ The Colonial Mood:
Cultural Nostalgia in a New Environment

The founders of the Delaware colonies were religious radicals, but like most American immigrants they also became cultural conservatives who were full of nostalgia for the land they had left. A sense of loss and longing for the mother country was transmitted to their children and persisted many years in the Delaware Valley.

In 1725, this colonial mood was captured in a letter from a young Pennsylvanian named John Jones to a relative in Wales. The writer had been born in America, but he showed nothing of what historians of modern immigration in the twentieth century would call the "second generation syndrome." John Jones described his native American colony with an air of detachment, as "this woody region, this new world, . . . this distant and foreign land." He continued to speak and write in Welsh many years after his parents had come to America. To his kinsman in Wales he described his nostalgia for the mother country.

> I have heard my father speak much about old Wales. . . . I remember him frequently mentioning such places as Llanycil, Llanwchllyn, Llanfor, Llangwm, Bala, Llangower, Llyn Tegid, Arcnig Fawr, Fron Dderw, Brynllysg, Phenbryn, Cyffdy, Glanllafar, Fron Goch, Llaethgwm, Hafodfadog, Cwm Tir y Mynach, Cwm Glan Lleidiog, Trawsfynydd, Tai Hirion yn Mignaint and many others.
>
> It is probably uninteresting to you to hear these names of places; but it affords me great delight even to think of them, although I do not know what kind of places they are; and indeed I long much to see them, having heard my father and mother so often speak in the most affectionate manner of the kind-hearted and innocent old people who lived in them, most of whom are now gone to their long home.
>
> Frequently during long winter evenings, would they in merry mood prolong their conversation about their native land till midnight; and even after they had retired to rest, they would sometimes fondly recall to each other's recollection some man, or hill, house, or rock.
>
> Really I can scarcely express in words how delighted this harmless old couple were to talk of their old habitations, their fathers and mothers, brothers and sisters, having been now twenty–four years in a distant and foreign land, without even the hope of seeing them more.[1]

---

[1]John Jones to Hugh Jones, n.d., ca. 1725, Myers, ed., *Narratives of Pennsylvania*, 454–55.

This colonial mood became a cultural instrument of high importance in the Delaware Valley, as it had been in New England and the Chesapeake. It caused Quaker immigrants to cling to the culture which they had carried out of England.

Another part of the colonial mood was intense anxiety for the future, and a fear of cultural disintegration which so often appeared in new settlements. The ironic effect of this cultural angst was to cause much internal strife in Pennsylvania, just as it had done in Massachusetts and Virginia. Within a few years of settlement, the Delaware Quakers fell to quarreling furiously among themselves over the question of whether they needed a written creed to preserve their faith in the New World. For some, the absence of formal doctrines threatened the colony with chaos. For others, the very idea of such a creed betrayed the spiritual purposes which it was meant to protect. The result was a Quaker schism in Pennsylvania, the so-called Keithian controversy (1690–93), which took its name from George Keith, a Scottish Quaker who led the movement for a creed. Keith in turn was accused of "preaching two Christs," and "denying the sufficiency of the Light within." The strife caused deep divisions among the Quakers.

At the same time there were many other "wrangles" and "heats" in the early 1690s. When a gang of pirates stole a ship in Philadelphia and began to plunder the Delaware Valley, Quakers quarreled among themselves over the difficult question of how a society which renounced the use of violence could suppress crime in its midst. The leaders of Pennsylvania, after much soul-searching, decided to use force against the pirates. But the contrary-minded Mr. Keith denounced the use of arms, and another angry controversy developed in the Quaker colonies.

George Keith and his followers also published highly personal attacks upon the leaders of Pennsylvania accusing them of "spiritual and carnal whoredoms," and describing the colony itself as "a strumpet cohabiting in the wilderness." This assault caused Quakers who had spoken out for free expression in England to demand restraints in America. Printers were arrested for publishing "unlicensed books," and their press and types were seized, as

---

This letter was first published in its original Welsh in *Y Greal* V (1806), 210–14; it was reprinted with omissions in *PMHB* 14 (1890), 227–31.

The parents of John Jones came from Bala in North Wales to Pennsylvania in 1682. It is interesting to note that in the immigrant lists they are mistakenly identified as Londoners, for they boarded their ship in the metropolis and gave London as their place of origin. Here is more evidence of a London and Bristol bias in these documents.

Quakers struggled to preserve the cultural fabric of their colonies.[2] In the end, the dissenters were defeated and George Keith
left the colony in 1693. But the colonial mood continued for
many years.

The culture of the Delaware Valley differed in many ways from
the folkways of Massachusetts and Virginia, but the dynamics of
its historical development were in many ways the same. Here
again one finds strong continuities in the transit of culture from
England to America, and also similar patterns of change in a new
environment. Let us examine these processes in more detail, by
analyzing this culture in its constituent parts. We shall begin with
the speech ways of the Delaware Valley.

❧ Delaware Speech Ways:
English Origins of the American Midland Dialect

Students of American English recognize a linguistic region in the
United States today which they call the zone of "midland
speech." Its boundaries coincide exactly with the broad area of
settlement that expanded outward from the Quaker colonies in
the Delaware Valley. This American dialect developed largely
from the language of England's North Midlands—not from that
source alone, but from a complex process of mixing and merging,
in which the primary source was an English regional dialect.[1]

The dialect of England's North Midlands was itself a linguistic
hybrid which had evolved through many centuries from a mixture
of British and Scandinavian tongues. This was a muscular
speech—bluff, literal, direct, vivid, forceful and plain-spoken. It
had strong and simple ways of saying things, and little use for the

---

[2]Edwin B. Bronner, *William Penn's "Holy Experiment": The Founding of Pennsylvania, 1681–
1701* (New York, 1962), 134–53; Gary B. Nash, *Quakers and Politics: Pennsylvania, 1681–1726*
(Princeton, 1968), 127–80.

[1]Craig Carver, *American Regional Dialects: A Word Geography* (Ann Arbor, 1987), 248; Hans
Kurath, *A Word Geography of the Eastern United States* (Ann Arbor, 1949), v; Ashcom agrees:
". . . this Midland area which is linguistically distinct from the Northern and Southern areas and
is in part set off by sharp boundaries, corresponds to the Pennsylvania settlement area." B. B.
Ashcom, "Notes on the Language of the Bedford, Pennsylvania, Subarea," *AS* 28 (1953), 241;
see also Ann Louise Sen, "The Linguistic Geography of Eighteenth-Century New Jersey Speech
Phonology" (thesis, Princeton, 1973); Raven I. McDavid, Jr., *Linguistic Atlas of the Middle and
South Atlantic States* (Chicago, 1980).

learned niceties of Latin and French. It also had its own distinctive patterns of pronunciation, vocabulary and syntax.

Consider syntax, for example. In the early and middle years of the twentieth century, British linguists found strong regional patterns in syntactical structures throughout rural England. East Anglians tended to say *you are;* but the people of Wessex preferred *you be,* and northerners used *thee is* or *thou art.* An East Anglian even of high station said *I ain't,* but a northerner even of humble rank said *I'm not,* and Wessexmen of every class said *I be'ent.* Many verb forms were constructed differently in these regions: the past tense of the verb *to grow,* for example, became *he did grow* in East Anglia, *he growed* in Wessex, and *he grew* in the north.[2]

Similar regional differences also appeared in vocabulary and pronunciation. The southern *married* became *wed* in the north of England. An East Anglian would *stay* the night; a Wessexman would *bide* a while; a northerner would *stop over.* In the east, people were *scared;* in the south they were *afeared;* in the North Midlands they were *frightened.*[3]

In the seventeenth century, these English regional speech ways were transplanted to various parts of British America. Linguist Hans Kurath has turned up an amusing example in the onomatopoetic folk-words that are used to describe the sounds that horses make. East Anglian and New England horses *neighed,* a word related to the Dutch *neijen.* In southwestern England and the Chesapeake Bay, a cavalier's mount was thought to *whicker.* Along the British borders of Cumberland and Durham, and also in the Appalachians, horses *nickered.* In the midlands of England and America, they were said to *whinny.* These regional variations have persisted into the twentieth century. Kurath observes that

---

[2]Orton, *A Word Geography of England* (London, 1974), M28, 29, 59, 67.

[3]Many other examples appear in Orton, *Linguistic Atlas of England,* including:

Standard English	East Anglian Rural English	Southern Rural English	Northern Rural English
She isn't	She ain't	She ban't	She isn't
He doesn't	He don't	He don't	He doesn't
We are	We are	We be	We are
I haven't	I haint	I haint	I haven't
his	his	his'n	his
yours	yours	your'n	thine
himself	himself	hissell	hisself

they might be thought of as "marker-words" or "tracers" which help us to follow the pattern of folk migration.[4]

The Friends' migration brought the speech of England's North Midlands to the Delaware Valley, where it became the basis of an American regional dialect (though not precisely the dialect itself). The epicenter of this American speech-region was Burlington in New Jersey, and Bucks County and especially Chester County in Pennsylvania, where "as late as the middle of the eighteenth century, the people of Chester still spoke in a broad Yorkshire dialect."[5]

This accent did not remain static in the New World. As time passed, the rough edges of North Midland speech were rubbed off by constant friction with dialects from other parts of England. The broad northern *come* (pronounced *coom*) did not survive in Pennsylvania after the mid-eighteenth century. But less obtrusive North Midland vowels became standard in the Delaware Valley and still survive there to this day. The most familiar example is the *a* in *dance.* Here, the English north midlands and American midland speech are much the same, and different from many other pronunciations, such as the English elite *dahnce,* or the harsh, nasal Yankee-East Anglian *daance,* or the slow southern *day-ence.* Similar regional patterns also appear in the vowels of *caught, fast, calf, aunt, fertile, got, cover, crop, God, stock, frog, earth, firm, turn, cut* and *enough*—all much the same in North Midlands of England and the midland speech area of British America.

Other continuities also appeared in the stresses of these dialects—in *de'tail* for de-tail' and particularly in sharply articulated consonants such as the post-vocalic *r* and *t.* But other consonants were often lost at the ends of words—as in *learnin* for learning, which is common to the midlands of both England and America.

Not only the pronunciation but also the vocabulary of the England's North Midlands became part of American midland speech. In the word lists of Cheshire, Derbyshire, Lancashire and Yorkshire we find the following terms, all of which took root in the Delaware Valley: *abide* as in "can't abide it," *all out* for entirely, *apple-pie order* to mean "very good order," *bamboozle* for deceive, *black and white* for writing, *blather* for empty talk, *boggle* for take fright, *brat* for child, *budge* for move, *burying* for funeral,

---

[4]Hans Kurath, *Studies in Area Linguistics* (Bloomington, Ind., 1972), 66; *EDD, s.v.,* "nicker"; *OED, s.v.,* "neigh"; H. Orton and W. J. Halliday, *Survey of English Dialects: The Six Northern Counties* (Leeds, 1962–63).

[5]John F. Watson, *Annals of Philadelphia* (2 vols., Philadelphia, 1830, new ed., 1856), I, 129.

by golly as an expletive, *by gum* for another expletive, *cattails* for
the plants called bullrushes in the south of England, *catawumpus*
for a come down, *chuck* for toss, *chock-full* for completely full,
clean for entirely (as "clean gone"), *clump* for clod, *cotton* for
attach, as in "to cotton on," *cuddle* for caress, *crib* for a child's
bed called a cot in southern England, *dad* for father, *daddy long
legs* for an insect that is called a crane fly in the south of England,
dither for upset, *dresser* for chest of drawers, *drat* as an impreca-
tion ("drat that person"), *dumb-founded* for astonished, *egg on* for
urge on, *elbow grease* for industry, *expect* for suppose, as "I expect
that's so," *find* to provide for, *flabbergasted* for extremely surprised, *flare-up* for quarrel, *fuzzball* for puffball, *gab* for talk, *gal-
livant* for go about in search of pleasure, *gawk* for stare, *get shut
on* for attached to, *ginger snap* for a type of cookie, *good grief* for
an expression of surprise, *grub* for food, *gumption* for determination, *guts* for belly, *guzzle* for drink greedily, *heap* for a large
number, *home-coming* for a return, *howsomdever* for however, *kin-
dling* for light wood, *knuckle under* for give way, *lick* for try, as
"give it a lick," *mad* for angry, *nailed* for caught, *nap* for a short
sleep, *nice* as in "nice and short," *poke* for bag, *pummel* for beat,
quality folks for gentry, *rag* for tease, *road* for way, *rumpus* for
tumult, *scalawag* for a good-natured rascal, *scruff* for the back of
the neck, *shaggareen* for untidy person, *sick* for ill, *skimpy* for
slight, *slam* for put down with violence, *slugger* for a person who
beats, *sneezlepooak* for a hesitating person, *spuds* for potatoes,
sucker for a sugar candy, *swatch* for a fabric sample, *thingamajig*
for an article of unknown name, *tiff* for quarrel, *upsa daisy* as an
ejaculation for a child in play, *us* for me (as in "wake us up . . ."),
and *wallop* for beat. None of these words was invented in America, though many have been mistakenly identified as Americanisms. All were carried from the North Midlands of England to the
Delaware Valley, and became the basis of an American regional
vocabulary which is still in use today.[6]

The speech of England's north midlands became the primary
source of the midland American dialect. But it was not the only

[6]All of these words may be found in J. C. Atkinson, *A Glossary of the Cleveland Dialect* (London, 1868); Abel Bywater, *Sheffield Dialect* (Sheffield, 1839); W. H. Thompson, *Speech of Holderness and East Yorkshire* (Hull, 1890); John H. Wilkinson, *Leeds Dialect and Glossary* (2 vols.,
Leeds, 1924); Samuel Dyer, *Dialect of the West Riding, Yorkshire* (Brighouse, 1891); and also the
following anonymous compilations: *The Dialect of Craven* (London, 1828); *The Dialect of Leeds
and Its Neighborhood* (London, 1862); and *A Glossary of Yorkshire Words and Phrases Collected in
Whitby and the Neighborhood* (London, 1855).

source. Another important ingredient was the special language of the Society of Friends, which added a religious imperative to regional speech ways. The use of *thee* and *thou* as the standard second-person pronoun had long been customary in the North Midlands of England. It was taken up by Quakers and given a special egalitarian meaning. Among Quakers in the Delaware Valley, this usage was observed to be different from that of English friends in the nineteenth and twentieth century. Americans said "thee is" where London Quakers said "thou art." The American preference for "thee" rather than "thou" preserved a North Midland pattern. Historian Hugh Barbour found English Quakers in the North Midlands who wrote, "If thee will, thee may send it when thee finds freedom," much as their American posterity would continue to do. Barbour concludes that this was both a religious and a regional usage, which established itself in the Delaware Valley.[7]

"The witness of Friends on points of speech," writes historian William Braithwaite, ". . . touched some of the greatest issues of their life." They made a fetish of plain speech, and also of silence. "Let your words be few," was the counsel of one Friend to others. Quakers also cultivated what Richard Bauman has called the "rhetoric of impoliteness," deliberately purging their language of routine courtesies and ornaments which seemed "needless" in their special meaning of that word.[8] This linguistic austerity persisted among the speech ways of American Quakers for more than two centuries. Something of its spirit entered into the regional dialect of midland America.

In addition to Quaker speech ways, many other sources flowed into American midland speech. An exceptionally large number of words were taken from the Indians. The Quakers were more open to these borrowings than were other English-speaking settlers. William Penn himself took the trouble to learn Algonkian and tried to speak with the Indians in their own tongue. More Indian place names were preserved in Pennsylvania than in other colonies.[9]

---

[7]Barbour, *The Quakers in Puritan England*, 165.

[8]Richard Bauman, *Let Your Words Be Few: Symbolism of Speaking and Silence among Seventeenth Century Quakers* (Cambridge, 1983); T. Edmund Harvey, *Quaker Language* (Philadelphia, 1928).

[9]A test of regional bias toward Indian languages appeared in the naming of rivers throughout the colonies. Virtually all major rivers in the Quaker colonies kept their Indian names even when unpronounceable to English tongues (Susquehanna, Schuylkill, Juniata, Tioga, Kiskiminetas, Youghiogheny, Allegheny, Conemaugh, Monongahela, Kishecoquillas, Lackawanna); the only major exception was the Delaware which was named before the Quakers arrived.

In southern New England, on the other hand, most rivers were given English names

Other expressions were also taken from the language of Dutch, Swedish, German, and Welsh settlers. From German, for example, English-speaking Pennsylvanians borrowed not only individual words such as *hex, fresh* (for impudent), *bum, bub, spiel* and *phooey,* but also entire syntactical structures. A Pennsylvania German might say in English, "Throw your father down the stairs his hat." Some of these German constructions entered English usage in the Delaware Valley—for example, those involving *already, get, need,* and *still.*[10]

Other new words were spontaneously invented in response to novel conditions in the New World. In all of these various ways, the northern speech ways of English settlers gradually evolved into a major American dialect. But in the process they retained many fundamental characteristics of England's North Midland speech. The result was an American speech way in the Delaware Valley which by the mid-eighteenth century was distinct from the New England twang and southern drawl. It has preserved its character for three centuries.

❧ Delaware Building Ways: North Midland Origins of Quaker Houses

Similar regional patterns also appeared in the vernacular architecture of the Delaware Valley. Even today, as one travels south from Manhattan on the old highways of New Jersey, the ancient buildings that stand beside the road offer many clues to the cultural history of their region. In the neighborhood of Newark, for example, the older houses tend to be rambling wooden structures like those of Massachusetts and Connecticut, whence their builders came. But forty miles further south, as one passes through the township of Princeton, the architecture begins to change. The old houses are stone-built, and very different in their style and pro-

---

(Charles, Sudbury, Concord, Taunton, Farmington, Ware, Miller's, Swift, Deerfield, Westfield, Thames, Blackstone). The only major exceptions were the Merrimack, Pawtucket, Connecticut, Naugatuck and Housatonic. Many small ponds and creeks in southern New England which bear Indian names today received them in the nineteenth century. Thus, the sheet of water east of Worcester was named Long Pond by the Puritans; it was renamed Lake Quinsigamund in the nineteenth century.

In Virginia, the pattern was mixed (Potomac, Rappahannock, York, James, Blackwater, Shenandoah, Dan, Roanoke, Appomattox). Here were three distinct regional patterns of river naming.

[10]Albert H. Marckwardt, *American English* (1958, rev. ed. J. L. Dillard, Oxford, 1980), 59.

portions. These were the homes of Quakers who settled in the Delaware Valley. They represent a distinct regional vernacular.

These Quaker buildings were not the first European houses in the region. During the mid-seventeenth century, Swedish and Dutch building styles had been introduced to the Delaware Valley. But an architectural historian writes that "not until 1682, when English Quaker settlers began to arrive in numbers, did this cultural hearth assume its ultimate character."[1] In 1748, the Swedish traveler Peter Kalm observed of the Delaware Valley, ". . .the houses here are commonly built in the English manner." So they were. But the choice of English architectural models was very different from those in Massachusetts and Virginia.[2]

These differences were most visible in building materials. At first the houses of English settlers in the Delaware Valley were made mostly of wood. "For covering the house, ends and sides," one wrote home, "we use clapboard, which is rived feather-edged of five foot and a half long. . . . this may seem a mean way of building, but " 'tis sufficient and safest for ordinary beginners." There was nothing specially American about these early structures; they were "plastered and ceil'd, as in England."[3]

Within the first generation, houses in West Jersey and Pennsylvania began to be rebuilt of more durable materials. On both banks of the Delaware River, farm houses were constructed of the beautiful gray-brown fieldstone which give the vernacular architecture of this region its special character and enduring charm. These country houses of the Delaware Valley were similar in outward appearance to farm houses in the north of England. Methods of masonry in the Delaware resembled split-cobble and fieldstone farm buildings of the Lake counties, north Lancashire, west Yorkshire, east Cheshire and the Peak District of Derbyshire.[4]

In the New World a few changes in building materials were necessary. Lintels, doorways and window frames could not easily be made of stone, and so were constructed of wood in America. But in other ways the fieldstone farmhouses of West Jersey and southeastern Pennsylvania were fundamentally like domestic buildings in the North Midlands of England.

[1]Allen G. Noble, *Wood, Brick and Stone; The North American Settlement Landscape* (2 vols., Amherst, 1984), I, 40.

[2]Peter Kalm, *Travels in North America* (1770, New York, 1964), 98 (11 Oct. 1748).

[3]"Directions to Such Persons as Incline to America," *PMHB* 4 (1880), 335; "Present State of the Colony of West Jersey," Myers, ed., *Narratives of Pennsylvania*, 192.

[4]R. W. Brunskill, *Vernacular Architecture of the Lake Counties* (London, 1974), 53, 70, 110.

The vernacular architecture of the Delaware Valley was very different from that of New England and Virginia. Fieldstone walls, slate roofs and simple wood trim were all combined in a plain style that emerged from Quaker-Pietist values and North Midland traditions. Two distinctive building plans also developed in this region. One was the Quaker Plan House, which commonly had three rooms on the first floor, a corner stair, and a chimney stack with several fireplaces grouped economically together on one exterior wall. This design made efficient use of a limited space and materials, and was used in both urban and rural settings. Another was the Four-over-Four House, which tended to be a large symmetrical structure with four spacious rooms and central halls on both floors. These houses tended to appear wherever English Quakers made their homes. They were also adopted by other ethnic groups in the Delaware Valley.

*Pent roofs and door hoods contributed to the special character of Quaker archi-
tecture in Pennsylvania. Many houses and barns in the Delaware Valley were
built with these small coverings extending outward above doors and windows
on the ground floor. Pent roofs had been and still are common features of vernacular architecture in the North Midlands of England, from Cheshire and
Derbyshire north to Cumbria.*

Strong continuities also appeared in building motifs as well as materials. A striking feature of houses, meetings, and out-buildings in Pennsylvania and West Jersey were small pent roofs projecting outward from front walls above windows and doors. Some of these roofs ran the entire breadth of the house; others were no wider than the doors and windows that they protected. They were commonly supported by white-painted wooden timbers which made a pleasing contrast with the fieldstone walls. These pent roofs had been commonly found on barns, shops and houses of northern England—from the Midlands north to Lancashire and Yorkshire, where they are called "pentise" or "pentice" roofs.[5] Throughout Pennsylvania and West Jersey, houses without pent roofs were often given small gabled roof hoods which projected at right angles to the wall. Hooded roofs were covered with slate and supported by strong but simple wooden frames. The same custom may still be seen in the North Midlands of England.[6]

Houses in the Delaware Valley tended to be built on several distinctive plans. One is called by architectural historians the "Quaker-plan" house. This tended to be a simple cottage with three rooms on the first story, a corner stair leading to a full second story, and a chimneystack with several fireplaces on one wall. This plan often appeared in the North Midlands of England. It became common throughout West Jersey and Pennsylvania, and also appeared in other American regions where Quaker emigrants settled.[7]

Another common "Quaker plan" was the spacious "four over four" house in the Delaware Valley, which strongly resembled larger homes throughout the north of England.[8] Historian Barry

---

[5]For pent roofs, see Brunskill, *Vernacular Architecture of the Lake Counties*, 83; John and Jane Penoyre, *Houses in the Landscape: A Regional Study of Vernacular Architecture* (London, 1968), 139; K. R. Adey, "Seventeenth Century Stafford," *MH* II (1974), 161. Also widespread from northern Staffordshire to Westmorland was the hooded roof; see, e.g., *Some Westmorland Wills, 1686–1738* (Kendal, 1928), 5.

[6]Penoyre and Penoyre, *Houses in the Landscape*, 139.

[7]Many examples of these three-celled Quaker houses from Lancashire, the West Riding of Yorkshire, Cheshire and Derbyshire appear in Eric Mercer, *English Vernacular Houses* (London, 1975), 185, 220, 224, 227, 142, 146–47; for the Quaker plan in the Delaware, see Noble, *Wood, Brick and Stone*, I, 45; Henry Glassie, *Pattern in the Material Folk Culture of the Eastern United States* (Philadelphia, 1969), 56; Patricia Irvin Cooper, "A Quaker-Plan House in Georgia," *Pioneer America* 10 (1978), 14–34; "Postscript to a Quaker-Plan House in Georgia," *Pioneer America* 11 (1979), 143–50; Thomas T. Waterman, *The Dwellings of Colonial America* (Chapel Hill, 1950).

[8]Brunskill, *Vernacular Architecture of the Lake Counties*, 53; Eleanor Raymond, *Early Domestic Architecture of Pennsylvania* (Exton, Pa., 1977).

Levy has found that Quaker houses, though very plain, tended to be larger and more comfortable than homes built by Anglicans or Congregationalists. He also discovered that the homes of Quakers had more bedrooms (and beds) in proportion to living spaces. Levy concludes that Quaker homes gave more attention to privacy and domesticity than did the more "publicly oriented Anglican houses."[9]

The interiors of these buildings tended to be exceptionally bright, clean, austere and spacious. Walls were plastered with a mixture of lime and hair. The houses were furnished sparsely in an almost monastic style which Max Weber called worldly asceticism. The journals of American Friends expressed a strong and persistent hostility to what Joshua Evans called "superfluities of various sorts .such as fine houses, rich furniture and gaudy apparel."[10] Quaker meetings actively intervened in these questions; one of them admonished its members that kitchens should not be decorated with "flourishing needless pewter and brass."[11]

Inventories of Quakers on both sides of the Atlantic Ocean described in detail the same austerity of house furnishings—a few rush-bottomed ladderback chairs around a plain board table in the dining room; a cupboard, a few stools and a long seat in the parlor; bedsteads and benches in the bedroom; and nothing but the necessities in the kitchen.[12] Amelia Gummere remembered the simple pine tables of Burlington houses in her youth, their only decoration the golden grain of the wood itself, glowing with age.[13] Rugs were condemned as "vain" and "needless" decorations. Quakers called them floorcloths.[14]

To these building ways, other elements were later added. German Pietists introduced sturdy barns with a special style of *fachwerk* construction distinguished by heavy wall braces, massive floor joists and heavy roof purlins. German immigrants also used

[9]Barry Levy, "The Birth of the 'Modern Family' in Early America: Quaker and Anglican Families in the Delaware Valley, Pennsylvania, 1681–1750," in Michael Zuckerman, ed., *Friends and Neighbors: Group Life in America's First Plural Society* (Philadelphia, 1982), 26–64; since this book was written, Levy has also published *Quakers and the American Family; British Settlement in the Delaware Valley* (New York, 1988), a most helpful and stimulating work.

[10]Joshua Evans Journal, n.d., SWAR.

[11]Gummere, "Friends in Burlington," 354.

[12]An example is the inventory of George Hopkinson, dated 12 April 1700, ms. PRNW, NOTTRO.

[13]Gummere, "Friends in Burlington," 354, 357; Max Weber, *The Protestant Ethic and the Spirit of Capitalism* (1904–5, rpt. New York, 1958).

[14]Amelia Gummere, *The Quaker: A Study in Costume* (Philadelphia, 1901), 23.

distinctive house plans—such as the *flürkuchenhaus* (corridor-kitchen house), with a spacious kitchen that spanned the full length of the building, and the *kreuzhaus* (crosshouse) where the long kitchen was partitioned into a pantry.[15] Another ethnic style was the Swiss bank house, which was built into the side of a hill, with kitchens and workspaces on the ground floor.[16]

A distinctive style of urban architecture also developed in the Delaware Valley. Philadelphia quickly came to resemble parts of Bristol, London and Dublin in the late seventeenth and early eighteenth century—brick fronts with raised entries on one side and cellarways on the other, and chaste details which created an atmosphere of simplicity, dignity, serenity and grace.

These various building traditions shared many qualities in common. All of them cultivated the plain style in sturdy structures that were designed for use rather than display. They developed within a culture that was dominated by the values of English Quakers and German Pietists. As time passed, they tended to fertilize each other within a regional style that was fully developed as early as the mid-eighteenth century.

❧ Delaware Family Ways: The Quaker Idea of the Family of Love

Ideas of the family among the Quakers were as distinctive as their language and architecture—and deeply interesting to historians of domestic life. Some scholars believe that the origins of the "modern American family" are to be found in the folkways of the Delaware Valley. Historian Barry Levy argues that the Quaker settlements were "the first scene of a major, widespread, obviously successful assertion of the child-centered, fond-fostering, nuclear family in early America and most likely in the Anglo-American world."[1]

There is an important element of truth in this thesis. But the Quaker family must be understood in its own terms, not those of a later era. It is important to note that Quakers used the word

---

[15]Dell Upton, "Traditional Timber Framing," in Brooke Hindle, ed., *Material Culture of the Wooden Age* (Tarrytown, 1981), 35–96; Noble, *Wood, Brick and Stone*, I, 40–43.

[16]Robert C. Bucher, "The Swiss Bank House in Pennsylvania," *PF* 18 (1968–69), 2–11.

[1]Levy, "The Birth of the 'Modern Family,'" 56.

"family" in ways that differed fundamentally from modern meanings. They spoke of the Society of Friends itself as their "family."
George Fox characterized a Quaker meeting as "a Family of
God," and a "household of faith." Meetings both in England and
America routinely addressed each other as "brethren of one family." These were more than mere metaphors. Quakers considered
all Friends as their "near relations" and welcomed them to hearth
and home. In this respect, Quaker ideas of the family were not
more nuclear than those of other English colonists, but actually
less so.[2]

In every Anglo-American culture, the nuclear family was the
normal unit of residence, and the extended family was the conventional unit of thought. The Quakers were no exception to this
rule. They commonly lived in nuclear households, but thought of
grandparents, cousins, uncles, aunts, nephews and nieces as
members of their family. Relatives by marriage were not "in-
laws," but were called simply "father," "brother" or "sister." In
these respects, the family ways of the Quakers were similar to
most other English-speaking people in their own time. But the
Quakers submerged the nuclear and the extended family in a
larger sphere which was their "family of God."[3]

Quaker family customs were also distinctive in other ways.
Tests such as the descent of names show that the intensity of
nuclear consciousness in Quaker families was stronger than in
Anglican Virginia, but weaker than in Puritan New England. The
physical composition of households in the Delaware Valley also
showed a similar pattern, which was intermediate between the
northern and southern colonies. An average Quaker household
had smaller numbers of children than in New England, and larger
numbers of servants. But by comparison with Virginia, it had
more children and fewer servants.[4]

---

[2]Frost, *The Quaker Family*, 64.

[3]Judy Mann DiStefano, "The Concept of the Family in Colonial America: The Pembertons
of Philadelphia" (thesis, Ohio State Univ., 1970), 136–68.

[4]Mean household size in West Jersey (1772) was 6.4; in Massachusetts (1764) it was 7.2. The
mean number of children was 3.1 in West Jersey, and 3.4 in Massachusetts; but the number of
servants and slaves was larger in the Delaware Valley than in New England. Robert V. Wells,
The Population of the British Colonies in America before 1776 (Princeton, 1975).

Six family reconstitution studies also show that completed family size (except among Philadelphia elites) tended to be a little smaller in the Delaware Valley than in New England, but
much larger than in the Chesapeake during the 17th and early 18th century. Calvinist groups
in the middle colonies had fertility levels similar to New England Puritans:

Quaker ideas of the family were less hierarchical than those of New England Puritans or Virginia Anglicans. Even as many Friends continued to insist that children should obey their parents, and that the young should honor their elders, they tended to think of the family and the household as a union of individuals who were equal in the sight of God. A European visitor in the Quaker household of John Bartram was astonished to find that everybody dined together at the same table—parents, children, hired men, servants and slaves:

> There was a long table full of victuals: at the lowest part sat his Negroes; his hired men were next, then the family and myself; and at the head the venerable father and his wife presided. Each reclined his head and said his prayers.[5]

This not a system of strict equality, but it was more egalitarian than attitudes in other Western cultures.

Also, Quakers gave special emphasis to the ideal of love as the spiritual cement of the family. One first-generation Pennsylvanian wrote to his children, "There is so much beauty in beholding brothers and sisters living in Love, endeavoring to help one another, as occasion may require." Their family correspondence was commonly a testimony of love between parents and children, brothers and sisters, husbands and wives.[6]

Group	Cohort	All	Complete	Incomplete	n
Philadelphia Elites	m. 1700–75	7.5	9.2	6.0	42
	m. 1776–1825	7.9	9.1	5.8	46
N.J. and Pa. Quakers	b. before 1730	6.7	7.5	5.4	
	b. 1731–55	5.7	6.2	4.4	
	b. 1756–85	5.0	5.1	4.8	
	all cohorts	5.7	6.0	4.9	276
Germantown Quakers	first settlers	5.8			14
Pa. Schwenkfelders	m. 1735–64		5.3		28
	m. 1765–89		6.1		39
N.J. and N.Y. Dutch	m. 1685–89		8.9		34
	m. 1760–89		7.0		46
New Paltz Huguenots	m. 1750–74		7.3		28
	m. 1775–79		8.9		34

Sources: Louise Kantrow, "The Demographic History of a Colonial Aristocracy: A Philadelphia Case Study" (thesis, Univ.of Pa., 1976), 103–8; Robert V. Wells, "Family Size and Fertility Control in Eighteenth Century America: A Study of Quaker Families," PS 25 (1971), 73–82; Stephanie Wolf, *Urban Village* (Princeton, 1976), 269; unpublished family reconstitution studies of Schwenkfelder, Dutch and Huguenot families prepared for the author by Lawrence J. Kilbourne.

[5]Crèvecoeur, *Letters from an American Farmer,* letter XI.

[6]Joseph Oxley, "Joseph's Offering to His Children," ms. HSP; Abigail Pemberton to Israel Pemberton, 5 day, 4 mo 1700, ms. HAV.

Quakers repudiated the principle of fear as the cement of family relations. Puritans and Anglicans both regarded fear as a healthy emotion, and urged that it should be cultivated in relations between parents and children, and even husbands and wives. Members of the Society of Friends, however, actively condemned fear as an organizing principle of human relationships, except fear of God. They built their ideas of the family upon a radically different base.

In the words of founder George Fox, the Quakers, believed that the family should "outstrip and exceed the world, in virtue, in purity, in chastity, in godliness and in holiness; and in modesty, civility, and in righteousness and in love."[7] They tended to think of the family as a spiritual communion which was a sanctuary of goodness and love in a world of sin and hatred. Here was another belief that flowed from the sectarian thrust of their faith, with its idea of "gathering out" from a sinful world.

Moreover, Quakers believed that the members of a household should hold themselves apart from others who were not of their kin and faith. Meetings repeatedly urged Friends to insulate the family from other non-related people in the world. In 1682, for example, one Quaker meeting strongly advised "those who do not require them to guard against the admission of servants into their houses," if those servants were not Quakers themselves.[8] They were especially concerned about admitting elements of spiritual discord to the household.[9] Further, Quakers tended to believe that the primary role of the family was to raise its children and to promote the spiritual health of its various members. The special intensity of the Quaker family as a child-centered institution arose directly from a religious imperative. In many ways, these Quaker beliefs seemed very close to that shimmering ideal of a "child-centered, fond-fostering, nuclear family" which would dominate thinking about familial relations in our own time. But it is important to recognize the vast distance that separated their values and purposes from those of secular American families three centuries later. The importance that Quakers gave to the ideal of familial love, to the primacy of child rearing, and to the idea of the family as a spiritual sanctuary, all derived from a sys-

---

[7]Quoted in Frost, *The Quaker Family*, 187.

[8]Gummere, "Friends in Burlington," 354.

[9]*Ibid*. Note that the advice to "guard against the admission of servants" was applied not merely to non-believers, but to servants in general.

tem of Christian belief that belonged to the seventeenth century and not to the twentieth. The Quaker family was never thought to be an end in itself, but an instrument of God's holy purposes in the world.

Other family ways were also introduced to the Delaware Valley, by different ethnic groups—in particular by immigrants from Germany, Switzerland and the Netherlands. Ideas of the family among German Pietists tended to be more hierarchical than those of English Quakers, but in other respects were very much the same. In both groups one finds the same ideas of the "family of God," and similar conceptions of "the family of love." These ideas of the family had important implications for marriage, gender, sexuality, child rearing, age-relations and inheritance. On all of those questions, English Quakers and German Pietists together created a web of custom in the Delaware Valley which was distinctly different from prevailing practices in Massachusetts and Virginia.

❧ Delaware Marriage Ways: The Quaker Idea of Marriage as "Loving Agreement"

The Quakers also brought to America a strict set of marriage customs, which specified who one might marry, how and when and where and why. These questions were urgently important to the Society of Friends—so much so that its founder, George Fox, wrote no fewer than sixty epistles about marriage. Other leaders frequently addressed the same themes.

On the question of marriage partners, Quakers strongly condemned what they called "mongrel marriages" to "unbelievers."[1] Outmarriage caused many disciplinary proceedings by Quaker meetings. In 1706, for example, one English meeting recorded the disownment of a member named Bartholemew Mastin:

> [He] hath gone and joyned himself in marriage with one that is not one of our profession and that we are altogether strangers to . . . according to the holy writ that believers should not marry with unbelievers . . . we do deny and disown the said Bartholemew.[2]

---

[1] ". . .bitterness of spirit to them, and so indeed ought all such mungrel marriages to be to all godly parents." Ann Cooper Whitall Diary, 1st day, vii month, 1760, Haverford.

[2] Break Meeting Records, 10.v.1706, NOTTRO. This hostility to marriage with strangers had regional as well as religious roots. "Better to marry over the mixen than over the moor," was

This Quaker rule against outmarriage was strictly enforced in America. For nearly two centuries, half of all the disciplinary proceedings among Pennsylvania Quakers were about problems of courtship, and marriage with "unbelievers." The frequency of these cases increased with time.[3]

The rule against outmarriage was grounded not merely in a negative principle of sectarian exclusion, but in the positive idea that marriages should be founded in true Christian love. To the Quakers, love did not mean romantic attraction, sexual passion or even domestic affection. Their idea of "pure and true love" was not the Greek *eros* or Roman *amor* but the Christian *caritas* and *pietas* which were thought to be attainable only between true believers.

Quakers insisted that marriage should not be for lust. One Friend wrote in his Commonplace Book:

> If thou resolute [*sic*] to change a single life
> And hast a purpose to become a wife,
> Then chuse thy husband not for worldly gain,
> Nor for his comely shape or beauty vain.
> If money make the match or Lust impure
> Both bride and bridegroom too shall weep be sure.[4]

But Quaker moralists demanded that love must be a part of every marriage. They believed that marriage should be a union of "sweethearts," a word which they often used. Further, they insisted that love should precede marriage, and not merely follow it. But this was to be the pure and undefiled love between Christians, and not a carnal appetite for the flesh.[5]

Quakers also condemned dynastic marriages which were made for material gain. They forbade first-cousin marriages which were commonplace in Virginia. During the eighteenth century, many Quaker meetings even discouraged unions between second cousins—a major restriction in small rural communities, and an

---

an old Cheshire proverb. Here again, the religious attitudes of the Quakers added a religious imperative to customs and traditions which had long existed in the North Midlands. *Cheshire Proverbs* (Chester 1917), *q.v.* "Mixen"; see also *OED* and *EDD*, "Mixen."

[3] Jack D. Marietta, "Ecclesiastical Discipline in the Society of Friends, 1682–1776" (thesis, Stanford, 1968), 31–32.

[4] Caleb Raper Commonplace Book, 1711, HAV.

[5] "We were met to confirm the agreement between thy brother and his sweetheart. . . . She is really an agreeable girl and don't doubt they'll live happily together." James Pemberton to John Smith, 15.xi.1741/2, John Smith Correspondence, HSP.

exceptionally difficult problem for the Delaware elite.[6] They insisted that a marriage must be acceptable to the family, the meeting and the entire community of Friends. The formal consent of all parents was required; without it permission to marry was refused.[7] The approval of a large part of the community was also sought. One Quaker marriage certificate in England (1735) was signed by no fewer than twenty-three supporting witnesses. The marriage of William Penn and Gulielma Springett (1672) was supported by forty-six witnesses, who testified that the couple had "first obtained the good will and consent of their nearest friends and relations." These customs were also kept in America. Members of the Delaware elite had as many as fifty witnesses; ordinary country folk often had twenty or thirty.[8]

These various rules were strictly enforced by the Society of Friends. One result was that marriage came late among both English Quakers and German Pietists. Mean age at first marriage was higher than among Anglicans.[9]

---

[6]Cheshire Quarterly Meeting Records, 2.ii.1685, ms. EFC 1/1, CHESRO, see also Arnold Lloyd, *Quaker Social History, 1669–1738* (London, 1950), 58; Forde, "Derbyshire Quakers," 138.

[7]For two couples who were refused permission to marry for "not producing a Certificate from his relations of their consent," see Chesterfield Monthly Meeting Records, ms. Q62b, NOTT.

[8]Forde, "Derbyshire Quakers," 14, Low Laughton Monthly Meeting, ms. EFC 3/2, 1735, CHES; William Penn and Gulielma Springett, Marriage Certificate, [4 Apr. 1672], *Papers of William Penn* I, 238–39.

[9]Mean age at first marriage for Quakers in England and America, and also for other ethnic groups in New Jersey and Pennsylvania, was as follows in seven studies:

Sample	Marriage Cohort	Males	Females
Derbyshire Quakers	wed before 1710	31.0	27.0
(Forde)	wed after 1710	31.9	29.8
Nottinghamshire Quakers	wed before 1710	31.9	29.8
(Forde)		27.7	26.9
Pa. and N.J. Quakers	wives born by 1730	26.5	21.9
(Wells)	wives born 1730–55	25.8	22.8
	wives born 1756–85	26.8	23.4
Philadelphia Elites	1700–1775	26.2	23.3
(Kantrow)	1776–1825	26.1	24.0
	1826–75	28.2	26.6
Germantown Families	1750–59	29.8	25.0
(Wolf)			
Pa. Schwenkfelders	1735–64	n.a.	27.1
(Kilbourne)			
N.J. and N.Y. Dutch	1685–1759	n.a.	21.2
(Kilbourne)			

These estimates, it should be stressed, refer to the *mean* age at marriage; median age was lower. All studies are of age at first marriage except Wolf who included remarriages. Sources include Forde, "Derbyshire Quakers," 33; Wells, "Quaker Marriage Patterns in a Colonial Perspec-

Another consequence was that many Quakers never married at all. One study of the Society of Friends in New Jersey during the eighteenth century found that 16 percent of women were still single at the age of fifty. By comparison with other colonies, these numbers of spinsters were large. In New England and Virginia, 95 to 98 percent of women married during the same period. The difference cannot be explained in terms of sex ratios. It was caused by different cultural ideas of marriage.[10]

Quaker ideas of marriage were also expressed in wedding rituals, which differed in many curious details from matrimonial customs in Puritan Massachusetts and Anglican Virginia. These practices changed very little during the period of American colonization. A leading authority writes, "The Society of Friends had established its marriage customs in England and . . . the practices were transferred intact to the New World." The rituals of marriage within the Society of Friends developed in reaction to the complexities of Episcopal and Congregational observances. But Quaker marriages became so fantastically elaborate that Puritan and Anglican practices seemed simplicity itself.[11]

A proper Quaker wedding had no fewer than sixteen stages. When a man and woman agreed to marry, their first formal step was to consult their parents, which sometimes they did even before settling the question among themselves. When Pennsylvania Quaker Benjamin Ferris decided to marry, he asked his own parents first, then his future wife, and then her parents—a common sequence.[12]

If all agreed, the couple jointly announced their intention to marry before the women's meeting. After an interval which gave the community time to digest the news, a female Friend formally sent a notice to the men's meeting. The intending couple then presented themselves before the men's meeting and announced that "with the Lord's permission and Friends' approbation they

---

tive," *WMQ3* 29 (1972), 415–42; Kantrow, "The Demographic History of a Colonial Aristocracy," 71; Wolf, *Urban Village,* 257; Lawrence Kilbourne, unpublished research reports on Schwenkfelder and Dutch families prepared for the author.

[10]Wells, "Quaker Marriage Patterns."

[11]Frost, *Quaker Family,* 172.

[12]"It was now ripened in my mind, to go and see my dear Friend, Hannah Brown, having the free consent of my parents," he wrote in his diary. After she agreed he approached her parents. "I let them know the occasion of my being there, and that I thought Parents had a right timously [*sic,* in a timely fashion] to know any intention of that sort." Benjamin Ferris Diary, 1.vi.1765, SWAR.

intend to take each other in marriage." Thereafter, the men's meeting consulted the parents of both partners. Unless approval was given in writing a marriage could not proceed. If either partner came from another meeting, the men's meeting also solicited "certificates of cleanliness," from that body. This process required a second session of the men's meeting, so that overseers could report on their inquiries.

At this stage a waiting period was imposed—often two meetings in duration—while others were given time to make objections. After the prescribed period had passed, the men's meeting formally considered the question, and agreed either to approve or forbid the union. This was called "passing the meeting," and was a great event.

The wedding could now proceed. Another stage followed in which the formal preparations were made. A supper was organized for the families and close friends.[13] Then, invitations were sent for the wedding itself, and the date and hour of the wedding were made known. Without this formal announcement, the wedding could not occur. On the appointed day, the marriage at last took place. It proceeded very much like a meeting for worship. People entered quietly and sat in silence, sometimes for very long periods. Those who wished to speak could rise and say what they wished, and some were moved to speak at length. Then, almost as an anticlimax, the intended couple quietly declared their agreement to marry, and spoke promises to one another in words of their own invention. After this exchange, everyone sat silently for a while, and quietly went home.

The newly married couple went to the house of the bride's father, and lived there commonly for two weeks, receiving visitors every day. After that period had passed, the newly married couple settled in their own home, which was often built for them by friends and neighbors. Then a long period followed in which the newly married couple returned such visits as they wished. This visiting process was conducted with great care, for by returning

---

[13]There were Quaker controversies about what Thomas Chalkley called "great entertainments at marriages" ("Journal," 1714, *Friends' Library,* VI, 30). But great dinners were favored even by so pious a Quaker as Benjamin Ferris. This reclusive Friend had a curious motive for marriage. "I . . . marryed my wife thinking that I should have more opportunity for retirement." In the end, he was much disappointed. But on his wedding day, even Ferris had a dinner with "the company of about twenty-two Friends," including relatives "that came from Wilmington to dine with us." Ferris Diary, 24.x.1765, SWAR.

a visit the couple announced they wished to have a continuing association. By not doing so, associations came to an end.[14]

The actual Quaker wedding "ceremony" was very plain, but the entire process of marriage became exceptionally complex. It was an agreement not merely between a man and a woman, but between a couple and a community.

❧ Delaware Gender Ways:
The Quaker Idea of "Help-Meets for Each Other"

On subject of gender, the Quakers had a saying: "In souls there is no sex." This epigram captured one of the deepest differences between the founders of the Delaware colonies and their neighbors to the north and south.[1] Of all the English-speaking people in the seventeenth century, the Quakers moved farthest toward the idea of equality between the sexes. Their founder George Fox set the tone, writing in his journal as early as the year 1647:

> I met with a sort of people that held women have no souls, adding in a light manner, no more than a goose. I reproved them, and told them that was not right, for Mary said, "My soul doth magnify the Lord."[2]

---

[14]Frost, *Quaker Family,* chap 9; for descriptions of Quaker marriages see Peter Kalm, *Peter Kalm's Travels in North America: The America of 1750* (2 vols., New York, 1937), II, 677; Gottlieb Mittelberger, *Journey to Pennsylvania* (Cambridge, 1960), 69; Moreau de St. Méry, *Moreau de St Méry's American Journey, 1793–1798* (Garden City, N.Y., 1947), 286–87.

[1]Penn actually wrote, ". . . sexes made no difference; since in souls there is none." *Some Fruits of Solitude,* 33; for the proverb itself see Margaret Hope Bacon, *Mothers of Feminism: The Story of Quaker Women in America* (San Francisco and New York, 1986), 2; in a large literature on this subject, specially helpful works are Mary Maples Dunn, "Women of Light," in Carol Berkin and Mary Beth Norton, eds., *Women of America: A History* (Boston, 1979), 114–36; Jean R. Soderlund, "Women's Authority in Pennsylvania and New Jersey Quaker Meetings, 1680–1760,"*WMQ3* 44 (1987), 722–49; Joan M. Jensen, *Loosening the Bonds: Mid-Atlantic Farm Women, 1750–1850* (New Haven, Conn., 1986).

[2]In his ministry, George Fox labored repeatedly to reach the most miserable and abandoned female outcasts of English society. In 1649 he found a raving madwoman at Nottingham Jail. "The poor woman would make such a noise in roaring," he wrote, ". . . that it would set all the Friends in a heat . . . and there were many friends who were overcome by her with the stink that came out of her, roaring and tumbling on the ground." Fox comforted her and in his care she became calm and well. At Mansfield-Woodhouse, Fox found a "distracted woman under a doctor's hand, with her hair loose all about her ears." As the doctor was about to bleed her, "she being bound, and many people being about her holding her by violence." Fox intervened and set her free, and "bid her be quiet and still, and she was so. The Lord settled her mind, and she mended and afterwards received the Truth, and continued in it to her death." Fox, *Journal* 8, 43 (1647, 1649).

His followers developed this idea into a doctrine that differences of sex were merely carnal, that men and women were equal in the spirit, and that spiritual "power was one in the male and in the female, one spirit, one light, one life, one power, which brings forth the same witness."[3]

Most Quakers wholeheartedly subscribed to these principles. A leading historian of their faith writes that "the equality of men and women in spiritual privilege and responsibility has always been one of the glories of Quakerism."[4]

In consequence, the role of women within the Society of Friends differed fundamentally from other Protestant denominations. Most Christians followed Paul's teaching: "Let the woman learn in silence, with all subjection . . . suffer not a woman to preach."[5] The Quakers always went another way. From the start, female Friends preached equally with men, and became leading missionaries and "ministers" in their faith. The pattern was set by George Fox's first convert, a grandmother named Elizabeth Hooten (1600–1672) who also became the Quakers' first woman preacher and died on a mission to America at the age of seventy-two. In 1658, another Quaker missionary named Mary Fisher traveled alone through the Ottoman Empire, and even attempted to convert the Turkish Sultan Mehmed IV. Other female missionaries preached actively on both sides of the Atlantic, and shared the spiritual labor of their society.[6]

Quaker women suffered persecution equally with men. A serving maid named Dorothy Waugh was dragged through the streets of Carlisle with an iron bridle in her mouth to keep her from preaching to the men of that northern city. In Starford, another Quaker woman who preached to an Anglican congregation was seized by the church officers and locked in a cage, "and there she did sit seven hours, where she was pissed on, and spit on." Near Ormskirk in Lancashire, a Quaker minister named Rebecca Barnes was beaten to death by an angry mob. In Salem, Massachusetts, Puritan magistrates ordered that Quaker Cassandra Southwick should have her children taken and sold at public auction. In Cambridge, Massachusetts, aged missionary Elizabeth

---

[3]Sarah Blackborow [Blackbury], *The Just and Equal Balance Discovered* (London, 1660), 13; quoted in Bauman, *Let Your Words Be Few*, 36.

[4]Braithwaite, *The Second Period of Quakerism*, 270.

[5]I Timothy 2.11–12.

[6]Sewel, *History of the Rise, Increase and Progress of the Christian People Called Quakers*, I, 433; Braithwaite, *The Beginnings of Quakerism*, 421–24.

Hooten was severely flogged with a three-corded whip, then taken to Dedham and Watertown and whipped twice again and abandoned in the woods. Undaunted, she returned to Cambridge where she was assaulted by a mob of Harvard students and faculty, whipped severely at a cart's tail through four Puritan towns, and left lying in the New England woods once again—bloody, battered and half-naked. An even worse fate was in store for Quaker missionary Mary Dyer, a "comely woman and a grave matron," who defied a sentence of banishment from Massachusetts, and was hanged on a high hill in Boston, her skirt billowing in the wind "like a flag," as one Puritan observed.[7]

These acts of violence against Quaker women arose in part from their headlong challenge to an entire system of gender relations. In the seventeenth century, the mere appearance of a female preacher was enough to start a riot. As late as 1763 the spectacle of "she-preaching" seemed perverse and unnatural to many Englishmen, and gave rise to Dr. Samuel Johnson's famous canard, which was aimed specifically at female Quakers:

> Boswell: I told him I had been that morning at a meeting of the People called Quakers, where I had heard a woman preach.
>
> Johnson: Sir, a woman's preaching is like a dog's walking on his hind legs. It is not done well; but you are surprised to find it done at all.[8]

The Quakers themselves did not entirely escape these conventional prejudices. Their idea of spiritual equality between the sexes had its limits. The early Friends were not modern feminists, and normally expected female preachers to show a measure of modesty and restraint. It was said of Ann Camm, for example:

> She had wisdom to know the time and season of her service, in which she was a good example to her sex; for without extraordinary impulse and concern it was rare for her to preach in large meetings, where she knew there were brethren qualified for the service of such meetings; and she was grieved when any, especially of her sex, should be too hasty, forward, or unseasonable in their appearing in such meetings.[9]

---

[7] Joseph Besse, *Sufferings of the Quakers* (London, 1753), II, 228–31; Bauman, *Let Your Words Be Few,* 67.

[8] James Boswell, *The Life of Samuel Johnson* (1791, rpt. New York, Modern Library, n.d.), 279 (31 Jan. 1763).

[9] Braithwaite, *Second Period of Quakerism,* 286.

Quaker women played larger roles in the Society of Friends during the seven-teenth century than did females in any other Christian denomination. This scene from an old print shows a female "tub preacher" expounding Scripture to a rapt audience of both sexes. Puritans and Anglicans forbade women to preach before men.

Ann Camm was no shrinking violet. She was regarded as the "leading woman Friend in Westmorland," and a strident critic of church tithes. Her attitude suggests the distance between her world and that of modern feminism.[10]

The interplay of these ideas gave rise to a unique institutional structure within the Society of Friends, in which Quaker men and women came together for meetings of worship, but sat apart in separate meetings for business. George Fox explained the reason:

> There are some dark spirits that would have no women's meetings, but as men should meet with them, which women cannot for civility and modesty's sake speak amongst men of women's matters, neither can modest men desire it and none but Ranters will desire to look into women's matters.[11]

William Penn agreed:

> Why should women meet apart? We think for a very good reason. The church increaseth, which increaseth the business of the church, and women whose bashfulness will not permit them to say or do much, as to church affairs before men, when by themselves, may exercise their gift of wisdom and understanding, in a direct care of their own sex.[12]

Women's meetings were introduced to the Delaware Valley by 1681. They kept their own records, enforced their own discipline, exchanged epistles with other meetings throughout the world, ran their own system of charity, and managed their own funds, independent of male control. They became institutions of high importance in the Quaker colonies.[13]

In secular relations between the sexes, Quakers were unable to escape entirely the hierarchical beliefs that surrounded them. But the precept that "in souls there is no sex" proved to be an expansive principle which created a fundamentally different tone in the culture of the Quaker colonies. If the Quakers did not completely realize the ideal of gender equality, they came closer to it than

---

[10]One must be careful of anachronism here; 17th-century Quakers were not 20th-century feminists. They did not intend that women should possess material independence or social autonomy, and had no conception of their gender as an interest group.

[11]George Fox, *A Collection of Many Select and Christian Epistles, Letters and Testimonies . . .* (2 vols., London, 1698), 313; Braithwaite, *Second Period of Quakerism,* 274.

[12]William Penn, *Just Measures* (London, 1692).

[13]Margaret Hope Bacon, "A Widening Path: Women in the Philadelphia Yearly Meeting Move Toward Equality," in John M. Moore, ed., *Friends in the Delaware Valley: The Philadelphia Yearly Meeting, 1681–1981* (Haverford, 1981), 173–99.

any contemporary religious group in British America. Their continued striving toward that distant goal had important consequences for the regional culture of the Delaware Valley.

An example was the way in which Quakers struggled with the problem of authority within the family. Attitudes were mixed. One conservative Friend addressed husbands in the traditional Pauline language as those "who in the ordinances of God are placed to be a head over your wives." He urged men to "rule over your wives as the weaker vessel, not domineering over them in your own perverse will, but ruling them in the fear of the lord, as those who hope to be fellow heirs with them of eternal life."[14] Some Quaker meetings also recognized special responsibilities in male heads of families. In 1677, for example, the Morley Meeting in Cheshire agreed that "It is thought good and also judged meet that every man friend who is a ruler of a family do give in a public testimony against tithes and steeplehouse lands."[15] But the meetings explicitly included wives as "rulers." Their epistles addressed both parents as "heads of family," and spoke of "male heads" and "female heads." This differed from the customs of other people in the same period.[16] Quakers also modified another biblical precept in the book of Genesis where woman was created as the help-meet for a man. George Fox insisted that each gender was meant to help the other. "They are helps-meet, man and woman," he declared.[17]

As a rule, Quaker households were less male-dominant than those of Puritans or Anglicans. Men and women in Massachusetts and Virginia were apt to speak of their homes as "my father's house." Quakers spoke of "my father and mother's house." Father came first, but the values of the Quakers were reflected in this semantical equality among husbands and wives.

Similar attitudes also entered the institutional fabric of the Delaware colonies. The laws of the Quaker provinces were the first in America to use routinely the double pronoun "he or she." In the culture of the Delaware Valley, women had exceptionally high status, and sometimes much power and influence as well. A good

---

[14]"Epistle to Friends in Holland," 15.vii.1682, in "A Collection of Letters Dreams, Visions and Other Remarkable Occurrences of Some of the People Called Quakers," ms. Weeks v/1936, 8/6, FLL.

[15]Morley Monthly Meeting Records, 2.xi.1677, ms. EFC 2/1/1 CHESRO.

[16]Many examples are quoted by DiStefano, "Concept of the Family in Colonial America," 22–23.

[17]Soderlund, "Women's Authority in Quaker Meetings," 726.

example was Susannah Wright, who inherited the property of Samuel Blunston, one of the richest Quakers in the first generation. One who knew her wrote:

> Susanna Wright was a person of note in this place. Her education was superior to most in her day. She was consulted on all difficult matters, did the writings necessary in the place, was charitable to the poor in a great degree, gave medicine gratis to all the neighborhood. She lived and died in the principles of Friends.[18]

For a woman to be "consulted on all difficult matters" was very rare in New England and virtually unknown in Virginia. Here was another indicator that women did indeed have exceptionally high status in the Quaker colonies.

Actual practices in this region, of course, varied broadly from one ethnic group to another and even from one family to the next. Some Quaker women in Pennsylvania complained bitterly in their diaries of the soul-destroying drudgery of their lives. The Quaker Anne Cooper Whitall quoted the biblical lament:

> I am like a pelican of the wilderness. I am like an owl of the desert . . . and am as a sparrow alone upon the house top. Mine enemies reproach me all the day and they are all against me. My days are like a shadow that declineth. I am withered like the grass. . . . I think there is no comfort anywhere; nothing but sorrow at home . . . I was very unwell and often thinks I can't live long.[19]

Still more wretched was Anne Cooper Whitall's friend Alice Hayes, who suffered many indignities from her overbearing husband:

> Many trials she met with from her husband. She says sometimes when I have been going to dress my best to go to meeting, my husband would take away my clothes from me; but that I valued not and would go with such as I had, so that he soon left off that.[20]

Anne Cooper Whitall commented,

> I do believe there is much to met with now from the men as she met with, and where will the truth get to, or who will dare to say they have it.[21]

---

[18] Rhoda Barber, Journal, HSP.

[19] Anne Cooper Whitall Diary, 6.vii.1760, HAV; the diarist was born in 1716, married in 1739, and became the mother of nine children. She lived in Red Bank, New Jersey, and died in 1797; see John M. Whitall, *Story of Her Life, by Hannah Whitall Smith* (Philadelphia, 1879).

[20] Anne Cooper Whitall Diary, 31.i.1762, HAV.

[21] *Ibid.*

But other households came closer to the ideal. Some Quaker husbands actively supported their wives in social activities that were forbidden outright to women in other Christian cultures. In Wrightstown, Pennsylvania, for example, Samuel Bownas recalled a woman who "had something to say, though but little, as a minister, and her husband thought she did not give way to her gift as [often as] she ought." He encouraged her to speak out, and to take a leading role in her community. The range of custom was very broad in the Delaware Valley. But it was not the same range as in other English colonies.[22]

These gender ways arose not only from the religious beliefs of the Quakers, but also from the regional culture of England's North Midlands. In the mother country, Quaker teachings on gender (and many other questions) found their strongest following within an area which had a distinct ethnic character, as a consequence of having been heavily settled from Scandinavia. The coastline of Lancashire and Cheshire, with its many rivers and sheltered bays, provided easy access for Norse invaders who colonized the North Midlands more densely than any other part of England. Scholars have noted a striking spatial correlation between the north midland region where Quakers flourished and the area of Viking colonization.[23]

In Scandinavian culture, women enjoyed positions of high social status, with full legal rights. The burial mounds of females were on a par with males of the same rank. The Norse sagas were full of strong-minded and independent women who were not culturally equal to men in all respects but who expected to be treated with equality of esteem. A notable example in Njal's Saga was Hallgerd, a "hard-willed" and high-spoken Viking lady who talked with "confidence and ease" in the presence of men. In the Laxdaela Saga there was Unn the Deep Minded who led her male kin from Britain to Iceland. And there was the great Viking heroine Gudrun, "the loveliest woman in Iceland . . . the shrewdest and best spoken of women," who inspired men with her dreams.[24]

In many respects the Viking women who settled England's North Midlands were very different from the Quakers who came

---

[22]Samuel Bownas, "Life," *Friends' Library,* III, 57

[23]"Where Quakerism was strongest, the villages were mainly Norse in origin and name, and Norse had been spoken there in the Middle Ages." Barbour, *The Quakers in Puritan England,* 74.

[24]*Njal's Saga,* tr. Magnus Magnusson and Hermann Palsson (New York, 1960), 56, 66; *Laxdaela Saga,* tr. Magnusson and Palsson (New York, 1969), 51, 117–19.

after them. Before the arrival of Christianity, Norse females carried daggers in their dresses and did not hesitate to use them
when treated with disrespect. The sagas tell of more than one
Norse warrior who returned in triumph from some epic slaughter
only to be murdered by his Viking wife for a minor act of domestic incivility. But even as Quaker women turned against this violent past, they preserved the strength of character, independence
of mind, tenacity of purpose and high courage of their Scandinavian ancestors, and also demanded in their different way to be
treated with respect. If the Quaker doctrine that "in souls there
is no sex" arose from a religious belief, that religion in turn developed within an ethnic and a regional culture which had important
consequences for Anglo-American history.

❧ Delaware Sex Ways:
"Not to Go into Her but for Propagation"

The Quaker doctrine that "in souls there is no sex" also had
another meaning. Among Friends, the Inner Light was thought
to be the enemy of the carnal spirit. Quakers drew a sharp distinction between love and lust. William Penn wrote, "It is the difference betwixt lust and love that this is fixed, that volatile. Love
grows, lust wastes by enjoyment."[1]

The meetings of Friends, often very active in the discipline of
their members, heard sexual offenses less frequently than did
Puritans or Anglicans; but when they did so, the punishments
were severe. Fornication before marriage, a venial sin for Puritans of Massachusetts and the Anglicans of Virginia, was sometimes cause for disownment, the heaviest penalty in the power of
a meeting to inflict. The Leeds preparative meeting, for example,
heard only three cases of fornication in twenty years (1692–
1712)—all males. But two cases ended in disownment; the third
offender was allowed to remain only after receiving condemna-
tion in two successive meetings.[2]

---

[1]Tolles and Alderfer, eds., *The Witness of William Penn,* 174; others accused the Quakers of
being sexual "libertines," but this opinion arose from a confusion of the Friends with other
radical sects; for one such episode in New England see Christine Leigh Heyrman, *Commerce and
Culture, The Maritime Communities of Colonial Massachusetts, 1690–1750* (New York, 1984), 99–
103.

[2]Daniel Langstaff was disowned for many offenses, among them, making his wife "great with
child by fornication." Joseph Siddall was punished in the same way for "taking his wife before

Quakers were specially interested in ending the sexual exploitation of social inferiors. George Fox in 1672 insisted that any master who had sexual relations with a female servant must marry her, "no matter what the difference in outward rank or race."[3] The meetings of Friends also specifically condemned the predatory attitude toward sexuality which had been so much a part of Virginia's sexual customs. The Marsden monthly meeting agreed that

> All men who hunt after women, from woman to woman, and also women whose affection runs some time after one man and soon after to another and so . . . draws out the affection one of another and after a while leaves one another and goes to others and do the same things and the doing makes them more like sodomites than the saints and is not of God's moving nor joyning together.[4]

In addition to these actions by Quaker meetings, the public laws of Pennsylvania were very harsh in their repression of sexual offenses. That colony's Law Code of 1683 included a statute against fornication which specified that both single men and women should be punished "by enjoying marriage, or fine, or corporal punishment, or any or all of these." This statute was more rigorous than those of Massachusetts, Virginia or England. After 1700 it was disallowed by the Crown as "unreasonable."[5]

For adultery, the penalty in Pennsylvania after 1682 was a year's imprisonment for the first offense and life imprisonment for the second. A revision in 1700 required that adulterers on the third offense should be branded on the forehead with the letter A. They were not merely required to sew the letter to their clothing as in New England. Quakers decreed that the faces of adulterers should be disfigured permanently for their crime. Quakers did not hang people for adultery, as did the Puritans, but this was because of a difference in attitudes toward capital punishment rather than toward the crime itself.[6]

For the offenses of sodomy and bestiality, the laws of Pennsyl-

---

a priest, and his evill practice of knowing her before marriage." A "troubled friend" named Emanuel Lapage was chastised for "not taking due care" in his "evil actions to commit fornication with his servant." See Jean and Russell Mortimer, eds., *Leeds Friends' Minute Book, 1692–1712* (Leeds, Publications of the Yorkshire Archaeological Society, vol. 139, 1980), 38, 63, 107–10.

[3]George Fox, *Works* (Philadelphia, 1831), 7, 338–39; Frost, *Quaker Family,* 181.
[4]Marsden Monthly Meeting, Book of Sufferings, 1679, ms. FRM 1/739, LANCRO.
[5]Frost, *Quaker Family,* 181.
[6]*Ibid.*

vania ordered single men to be imprisoned for life, and whipped every three months. Married men were ordered to be divorced and castrated. Imperial authorities also disallowed this statute as "unreasonable" and excessively severe. The Quakers were not libertarian in matters of the flesh.[7]

On the question of sex within marriage, Quakers were not of one mind. Some carried their sexual asceticism to the point of condemning all carnal relations between husband and wife. This was actually a prevailing view among Friends in New England for a brief period. When the missionary couple Joseph Nicholson and his wife came to Salem in 1660, they reported that most Quaker couples totally abstained from sexual relations; one couple had done so for four years; others for a year or more. The Quaker Mary Dyer who was hanged at Boston believed in total celibacy within marriage.[8] This attitude survived among radical Quakers even to the late eighteenth century, and gave rise to a sect of Quaker heretics called Shaking Quakers or simply Shakers, who seceded largely on the question of marital celibacy.

Most Quakers did not believe in celibacy, but many tried to restrain sexual activity within marriage. In 1795 a Quaker named Joshua Evans had an interesting conversation with a Shaker on the morality of sex within marriage. The Shaker declared: "The manner you gratify yourselves with your wives when they are not in a capacity of conception but to gratify your lust is fornication, as it is not for multiplying." To this the Quaker replied:

> I told him if others erred they [the Shakers] did on the other hand in forbidding what Christ did not, but taught to leave father and mother and cleave to his wife. And though I did see they were in error, his remarks are worthy of serious thought, that none may abuse that privilege of marriage by gratifying lustful inclinations, with no design of multiplying, and though they carry the matter to an extreme the other way, yet in beholding the sins committed by men and women I do not wonder some are raised up who will not touch women that way. Though I told him the right path lay between us viz. to marry but not to go into her but for propagation and asked if he did not believe the same. He said yea.[9]

---

[7] *Ibid.,* 185–86.

[8] Joseph Nicholson to Margaret Fell 2.iii.1660, Swarthmore Mss., FLL; Frost, *Quaker Family,* 179.

[9] Joshua Evans Journal, 1794–96, 28.ix.1795, SWAR; this passage is omitted from the transcript of this journal and must be consulted in the original manuscript.

That rule of sexual restraint was often carried into practice. Abstinence for extended periods seems to have been common and even normal in Quaker families. Even between husbands and wives, the Quakers urged restraint in the exercise of "animal passions." When English Quaker Robert Dudley married for the third time, he was visited by two Quaker spinsters of advanced age.

> He was warned by one of them against too fondly indulging in conjugal delights, lest, (like Sampson formerly) he should lose the means of his strength, whilst reposing in the lap of his Delilah. The other minister felt (or thought that she felt) a like concern for *both*, and my friend assured me, alluded to some things about which they (as old maids) could not have been supposed to know anything. And all this too in the presence of a youth, the son and stepson of the parties![10]

Behind this attitude lay an assumption that sex was sinful in itself, and that a strong physical relationship between a husband and wife threatened to weaken the spiritual foundation of a proper marriage.

Here again the tone was set by William Penn. As early as 1671, when he prepared to marry the beautiful Gulielma Springett, Penn began to be tormented by stirrings of "lust" and "lewd thoughts." To restrain them, he wrote a paper for the men's meeting on the eve of his marriage, in which he prayed that he and his wife "may not give way to the inordinate aboundings of affection, for that dishonors the marriage bed, yea that is a defiled bed, as well as grosser pollutions."[11]

One unintended consequence of this attitude was that Quakers became the first people in Anglo-America who succeeded in controlling fertility within marriage. In the beginning, birth rates were very high in the Delaware Valley. A Welsh Quaker immigrant named Gabriel Thomas observed before 1690 that there was "seldom any young married woman but hath a child in her belly, or one upon her lap."[12] But as early as the mid-eighteenth century— perhaps even earlier—Quakers in the Delaware Valley

---

[10]J. William Frost, ed., *The Records and Recollections of James Jenkins* . . . (New York, 1984), 205.

[11]William Penn, "Right Marriage," 1671, *Papers of William Penn*, I, 232–37.

[12]Thomas, "An Historical and Geographical Account of Pennsylvania and of West-New-Jersey," 333.

and also on the island of Nantucket were practicing some method of birth limitation within marriage. How they managed to do so remains unknown, perhaps unknowable. No evidence survives of coitus interruptus in any Quaker family, or contraceptive technology. But much quantitative evidence testifies to a regime of sexual abstinence, single beds, separate rooms and the control of physical contact between husbands and wives.

From an early date, Quakers also encouraged the practices that would be called prudery in the nineteenth century. Quaker meetings carefully monitored female dress and sternly forbade even the slightest hint of sensuality. In 1718 the London yearly meeting went so far as to condemn "naked necks."[13] Ordinary language was carefully purged of carnal connotation. A French traveler in the eighteenth century was startled to discover that respectable ladies of Pennsylvania could not bring themselves to speak plainly about their bodies even to their physicians, but delicately described everything from neck to waist as their "stomachs," and anything from waist to feet as their "ankles."[14] This prudery had an important function. It lowered the general level of sexual tension in social relationships, even between husbands and wives. The Quakers of the Delaware Valley were very different in that respect from both the New England Puritans and Virginia Anglicans, but very similar to their co-believers in England.

A similar spirit of sexual asceticism was shared by many groups of German Pietists, some of whom practice it to this day. It also became part of the official culture of Philadelphia, which was very different from New York or Baltimore. For many generations, what Digby Baltzell calls "mild sexlessness in the Quaker tradition" set a tone for the sexual ideology of an American region.[15]

❧ Delaware Child-naming Ways: Quaker Onomastics

Another clue to the character of this culture appeared in the ways that it named its children. Among Friends, there were no godparents and christening ceremonies as in Anglican Virginia, and no baptisms as in Puritan Massachusetts. Quakers condemned these "needless" practices as corruptions of Christianity. They

---

[13]Frost, *Quaker Family*, 180.
[14]*Ibid.*, 48.
[15]E. Digby Baltzell, *Puritan Boston and Quaker Philadelphia* (Boston, 1979), 102.

put their own babies through another sort of onomastic ritual which was called the "nomination." The infant's name was carefully selected by the parents, certified by friends, witnessed by the neighbors, and solemnly entered in the register of the meeting. By the late seventeenth century, this event gradually became a typical Quaker anti-ceremony of the most elaborately studied simplicity. In 1694, William Penn described the custom of "nomination" as follows:

> The parents name their own children, which is usually some days after they are born, in the presence of the midwife if she can be there, and those that were at the birth, who afterward sign a certificate, for that purpose prepared, of the birth and name of the child or children, which is recorded in a proper book in the Monthly meeting to which the Parents belong, avoiding the accustomed ceremonies and festivals.[1]

Delaware Quakers also differed from other English-speaking people in the descent of names from one generation to the next. Unlike New England Puritans, Quakers named their first-born children after grandparents. Unlike Virginia Anglicans, they were careful to honor maternal and paternal lines in an even-handed way. An example was the family of Thomas and Rachel Wharton, who came to Pennsylvania from Westmorland and Wales. They named their first-born children after grandparents on both sides of the family, and later arrivals after themselves in the following order:

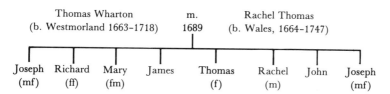

The eldest son was named after the mother's father, and the eldest daughter after the father's mother.

A son born of that union, John Wharton, married Mary Dubbins, daughter of James Dubbins. Their children were named as follows:

[1]William Penn, *The Rise and Progress of the People Called Quakers* (London, 1694), chap. xi; for other evidence see Frost, *Quaker Family*, 70.

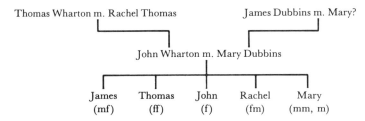

Here again, the grandparents were commemorated before the parents themselves. Further, the mother's father and father's mother were the first to be honored.[2]

Yet another example was the family of John and Elizabeth Woolston, who married at Middletown, Bucks County, Pennsylvania, in 1735. The eldest children were three daughters, who were named after the father's mother, the mother's mother and the mother herself in that order. The first-born son received a forename common to his father and his maternal grandfather; the second son was named for his father's father. Once again, the descent of names was carefully balanced between maternal and paternal sides of the family.[3]

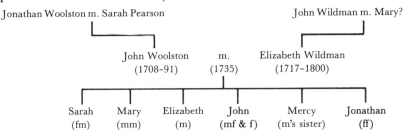

A fourth example was the family of Nathan and Hannah Sharples (var. Sharpless), also of Bucks County, Pennsylvania.[4]

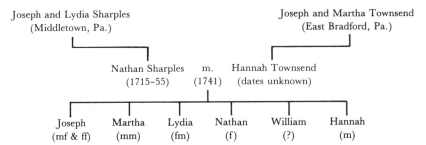

[2]Anne Wharton, "The Wharton Family," *PMHB* I (1877), 324–26.

[3]Jane W. T. Brey, *A Quaker Saga: The Watsons of Strawberyhowe, the Wildmans and Other Allied Families from England's North Counties and Lower Bucks in Pennsylvania* (Philadelphia, 1967).

[4]Joseph Sharpless, *Family Record: Containing the Settlement and Genealogy to the Present Time of the Sharples Family in North America* (Philadelphia, 1816).

This bilateral descent of names was not universal among Quaker families. But it was very common in the Delaware Valley—more so than in Massachusetts or Virginia. An onomastic equality between husband and wife was more evident in the naming customs of Quaker families than in other Anglo-American cultures. This concern for equality was carried to the point of double-reversing the naming order for children of different genders, so that the first-born female commemorated the father's line, and the eldest male followed the maternal line. This custom appeared in all but one of the examples listed above. In both the Wharton and Woolston families, boys were named first for the mother's father; girls were named first for the father's mother.

Quaker onomastics were also distinctive in the choice of names. Favored forenames often came from the Bible, but the proportion of biblical names was not nearly as strong as among the Puritans. In England only about 50 percent of male Quakers received biblical names, compared with 90 percent in Calvinist families. The leading favorites were John, Joseph and Samuel. Traditional English and Teutonic names continued to be popular among Friends. The extravagant biblicism of the Puritans was tempered by the plain style among the Quakers.[5]

Biblical namesakes were more common for females than for males. Mary, Elizabeth and Sarah accounted for a large part of all Quaker names, as they did among other English-speaking people. Also popular among Friends were the names Anne-Anna-Hannah, and Esther-Hester, which commemorated two of the strongest feminine characters in the Bible—an outspoken female prophet, and a consort of the Persian King Xerxes. Esther would

---

[5]Among English Quakers, the most popular names were as follows:

Derbyshire Quakers, 1680–1750		Cheshire Quakers, 1680–1750	
John	Mary	John	Mary
Joseph	Sarah	Thomas	Elizabeth
William	Anne	Samuel	Sarah
Samuel	Elizabeth	Jacob	Martha
Thomas	Hannah	Joseph	Hannah
George	Hester/Esther	Richard	Anne
Francis	Phoebe	Daniel	Catherine
Henry	Martha	Benjamin	Ellen
Benjamin	Margaret	James	Hester
Elihu	Ruth	David	Phoebe
		Isaac	

Compiled from vital records of Chesterfield Monthly Meeting, DERBRO; and Cheshire and Staffordshire Meeting Records, CHESRO.

seem at first sight to have been an unlikely Quaker namesake—reveling as that Jewish lady did in an epic slaughter of the Gentiles. But she also appears in the Bible as a woman of strong and independent character who was devoted to helping the people of God.

These naming choices were not invented in the New World. They were virtually identical among Quakers in England's North Midlands and America's Delaware Valley. Through the eighteenth century, males received the same combination of biblical and teutonic names—with John, Thomas, William, Joseph and George the leading favorites among Friends on both sides of the water. Quaker females were mostly named Mary and Sarah in England and America, with Hannah, Anne, Elizabeth, Hester, Esther and Deborah strong secondary favorites. Plain English names such as Jane, and traditional Christian favorites such as Catherine and Margaret preserved their popularity among Quakers, more so than among Puritans. Also exceptionally popular among Quakers in England and America was the name of Phebe, which rarely appeared in Puritan and Anglican families.[6]

Many Quaker families also made occasional use of grace names for their daughters, with particular favorites being Patience, Grace, Mercy and Chastity. A few families gave them to male children as well. All the names chosen by Richard and Abigail Lippincott for their eight children could be combined into a prayer:

Remember
John

---

[6]Three Quaker genealogies, centered on the Watson, Smedley and Sharples/Sharpless families yielded the following results for children born between 1675 and 1750:

Male Names	Female Names
1. John	1. Mary
2. Thomas	2. Sarah
3. William	3. Ann
4. Joseph	4. Jane
5. George	5. Hannah
6. James	6. Elizabeth
7. Samuel	7. Lydia
8. Jacob	8. Esther
9. Robert	9. Martha
10. Daniel	10. Rebecca

The next ten names for males were Benjamin, Nathan, Joshua, Richard, Caleb, Henry, Amos, Ezra, Edward and Adam; and for females, Rachel, Margaret, Grace, Phebe, Susanna, Abigail, Alice, Edith, Patience, Mercy and Deborah (the last three tied). The sources are Sharpless, *Family Record;* Gilbert Cope, *Genealogy of the Smedley Family* (Lancaster, 1901).

Restore
Freedom
Increase
Jacob
Preserve
Israel

The Lippincotts were a Calvinist family who converted to the Society of Friends.[7]

Altogether, Quaker names were much the same on both sides of the Atlantic. In its choice of forenames this onomastic system was similar to the Puritans in some respects; but in the descent of names its three-generational rhythm was closer to Anglicans; and its even-handed bilateral descent of names was *sui generis*. Altogether, the Quaker culture of the Delaware Valley was unique in its customs of child naming.

❧ Delaware Child-rearing Ways: Bracing the Will

On the subject of child rearing, Quaker ideas took form very slowly during the seventeenth century. The founder George Fox continued for many years to endorse the Calvinist idea that "all children should be brought into, and kept in subjection . . . through the breaking of the stubborn will within."[1] But many Quakers rejected the idea that children were born evil, and some also denied the doctrine of original sin. Robert Barclay condemned this cardinal belief of Calvinism as an "unscriptural barbarism."[2] By the early eighteenth century, Quakers in both England and America had come to believe that small children were "harmless, righteous and innocent creatures."[3] Many members of the Society of Friends believed that children were incapable of sin until old enough to understand their acts. Others suggested that youngsters continued in a state of innocence until they were as old as eleven or twelve.[4]

---

[7]Brey, *A Quaker Saga.*"Notes on the Lippincott Family," ms. FLL.
[1]Fox, *Works,* VIII, 23.
[2]Walter Joseph Homan, *Children and Quakerism* (Berkeley, 1939), 32.
[3]John Hepburn, *The American Defense of the Christian Golden Rule . . .* (Philadelphia, 1714?).
[4]Frost, *Quaker Family,* 67.

These ideas about child nature created distinctive Quaker customs of child nurture which differed very much from those of Puritans and Anglicans. The first and most important difference was in the special intensity of Quaker interest in the young. One Quaker parent wrote in her diary, "My chief concern is about my children. O if they may be preserved out of wickedness . . . there is so much wickedness in this place on every side."[5] Others expressed the same interest in a happier way. Isaac Norris wrote of his own children,

> I have two daughters yet alive, delightful children. . . . They are a constant care as well as a great amusement and diversion to me to direct their education aright and enjoy them truly in the virtuous improvement of their tender minds.[6]

This concern was shared not merely by parents but by the entire community. One historian concludes from long acquaintance of meeting records that "the Quaker yearly meetings for nearly three centuries have drawn attention to the welfare of young people more frequently than any other topic."[7]

Quaker autobiographers testified to the constant attention of their parents. "I was not 'christened' in a church," wrote Rufus Jones, "but I was sprinkled from morning till night with the dew of religion." Even in the late seventeenth century, the environment of a Quaker family was more child-centered than home life in other cultures.[8]

For the first years of infancy, Quakers believed in what they called a "guarded education." They thought that small children should be sheltered from the world and raised within a carefully controlled environment. Behind this idea lay an empiricism which held that children could be "trained up" by control of their surroundings. "Virtue passes not by lineal succession, nor piety by inheritance," said the London meeting.[9]

The second stage of Quaker child rearing began with what was perceived to be "the dawn of reason" in the child. One Philadelphia mother wrote candidly:

> I acknowledge with truth that I am not so dotingly fond of very young infants, as some are, I have no idea of kissing every little

---

[5]Anne Cooper Whitall Diary, 3.vii.1760, HAV.
[6]Isaac Norris to Sampson Lloyd, 27.x.1746, Isaac Norris Letterbook, HSP.
[7]Lloyd, *Quaker Social History*, 166.
[8]Rufus Jones, *Finding the Trail of Life* (New York, 1926), 21–22.
[9]Frost, *Quaker Family*, 76; Homan, *Children and Quakerism*, 48, 55.

dirty mouth, that is held up for notice, and I wou'd quite as leave, indeed, should prefer playing with a good large rag baby, than with a child of two or three months. But when the dawn of reason begins to make its beautiful appearance, and they can take notice; I think them the most engaging little creatures in the world.[10]

When this stage was reached, Quaker parents were urged to raise their children mainly by working through their reason. William Penn put it thus:

> If God give you children, love them with wisdom, correct them with affection: never strike in passion, and suit the correction to their age as well as fault. Convince them of their error before you chastise them . . . punish them more by their understandings than the rod.[11]

Travelers of other faiths also often commented upon the permissiveness of child rearing among Quakers—of children who said "I will not" to their parents with impunity. These travelers commented also on the extent to which Quaker households appeared to be, in the modern phrase, child-centered. They observed accurately an important truth about child-rearing customs in this culture.[12]

Quaker parents made heavy use of rewards rather than punishments, and promises rather than threats. One father, while on a trip to England, wrote home to his daughter in America, "If when I return I hear thee has been a good Girl, there is not a little girl in Burlington shall have what I intend for thee."[13]

Corporal punishment was used with moderation by some Quaker parents and masters, and others forswore it altogether. David Cooper wrote in his memoir that he could "never remember receiving but one stroak from a master." The ideal and often the reality was a different method. Cooper himself wrote:

> A strict obedience is so important that no head of a family can support their station with any degree of peace and satisfaction, without [it], and by timely and steady care is easily maintained, whereby a great deal of jarring, scolding and correcting is avoided.[14]

---

[10]Hannah Pemberton to Thomas Parke, 29 Aug. 1780; quoted in DiStefano, "Concept of the Family in Colonial America," 95.

[11]Penn, *Works* I, 901; Frost, *Quaker Family,* 77.

[12]Joseph Oxley, "Joseph's Offering to His Children" (1770), 357, HSP.

[13]William Dillwyn to Susannah Dillwyn, 21 Dec. 1774, Dillwyn Papers, HSP.

[14]David Cooper, "Some Memoirs . . . Intended for the Use of His Children," 1725–95, HAV.

Child-nurture among Friends, however, should not be confused with a modern permissive system. Quaker children were trained to strict ideals of "silence and subjection"—not so much to parents or elders, but to the meeting. The individuality of the Quaker child was subordinated to the entire community, even as it was protected against the relentless will-breaking of the Puritans and the hierarchical will-bending of the Virginians.[15]

Child rearing was a communal process, which collectively involved many people besides the parents themselves. "In learning about goals for raising children," an historian of one Quaker family writes, "the Pembertons largely relied upon the exchange of ideas among family and friends. . . . in the main, parents expected to raise children in much the same way as they had been raised."[16]

Children also actively socialized each other, from a very early age. This process happens in every culture, but among Quakers, it took on a special quality. The Quaker journalist John Kelsall, for example, wrote, "As I remember about the sixth year of my age, my brother and I would have got under some hedge, wall or such like place, and there have kept a meeting in imitation of Friends."[17]

Further, Quaker children were trained from an unusually early age to think in terms of serving the community. William Dillwyn wrote to his daughter Sukey, "Good girls always love to serve the poor, and make their lives happy—it is much better than romping about with rude children."[18]

By precept and example, and also by the structure of socialization, Quaker children were taught subordination not so much to other individuals as to a community of values. Here was an important part of the process by which cultures were maintained from one generation to the next.

The third stage of life was one which the Quakers called youth, and which we know as adolescence—a period they defined as life from fourteen to twenty-one.[19] One Quaker called this "the slippery and dangerous time of life."[20] In this stage, Quaker parents tended to be more active and constraining than Puritans and

---

[15]Frost, *Quaker Family*, 81.
[16]DiStefano, "Concept of the Family in Colonial America," 81.
[17]John Kelsall Journal, ms. 3/194, FLL, ca. 1690.
[18]William Dillwyn to Susannah Dillwyn, 21 Dec. 1774, Dillwyn Papers, HSP.
[19]Frost, *Quaker Family*, 133–49.
[20]John Smith to Dr. William Logan, 2 June 1750, J. Smith Papers, HSP.

Anglicans had been. Quakers argued that young people should remain within their families. "I think it is better," one wrote, "for children to be at home than a gadding abroad."[21] Many strenuously condemned the custom of "sending out" which was widely practiced among the Puritans. William Penn wrote angrily against those who "do with their children as with their souls, put them out at livery for so much a year."[22] Where apprenticeship was necessary, Quakers were careful to find members of their faith to serve as masters. When they were unable to do so, the question was carried as high as the quarterly meeting—a serious business indeed.[23]

Quakers encouraged their children to remain at home even to adulthood. Others of different sects suspected that the motives were not entirely spiritual. Henry Muhlenberg wrote in 1748 that young people in Pennsylvania were "almost in bondage" to their parents. Whatever the reason, youngsters in Quaker families tended to stay at home in a way that Puritan children did not.[24]

Quakers were also very strict in other ways with their teenage children. An example was their attitude toward dancing. A Quaker preacher, traveling in the more complaisant colony of Maryland, came upon a party of young people who were dancing merrily together. He broke in upon them like an avenging angel, stopped the dance, and demanded to know if they considered Martin Luther to be a good man. The astonished youngsters answered in the affirmative. The Quaker evangelist then quoted Luther on the subject of dancing: "as many paces as the man takes in his dance, so many steps he takes toward hell." This, the Quaker missionary gloated with a gleam of sadistic satisfaction, "spoiled their sport."[25]

In some ways, Quakers could be very repressive of their young. But they never created the same hierarchy of age that was so strong in other cultures. They cultivated an ideal of equality among children. William Penn urged Quaker parents to take great care to be even-handed with all of their off-spring. "Be not unequal in your love to your children, at least in the appearance

---

[21] Anne Cooper Whitall Diary, 10 day of 6 month, 1760, Haverford.

[22] Penn, *Works*, I, 901; Frost, *Quaker Family*, 144.

[23] "Ellen Chapman being a place for her cannot be found where she may be bound as an apprentice among friends." The monthly meeting agreed to "lay it before the quarterly meeting"; Marsden Monthly Meeting Records, 7.iv.1686.

[24] Henry Muhlenberg, *Journal* (Philadelphia, 1958), I, 197.

[25] Thomas Chalkley, *Journal* (New York, 1808), 93.

of it; it is both unjust and indiscreet; it lessens love to parents, and provokes envy among children." In a later generation, this advice would become a cliché of child-rearing literature. But the Quakers were far ahead of others in their concern for sibling equality.[26]

The Quakers also extended this ideal of equality to relations between children and adults. People of other faiths were startled to observe Quaker children giving moral and religious instruction to their elders. We have one account of a ten-year-old child who interrupted a gathering of adults to deliver a spontaneous speech on salvation. The adults listened respectfully, and after the child was done speaking, a grandmother offered a prayer, and said, "Oh lord! That this young branch should be a teacher unto us old ones."

Another young Friend, Thomas Chalkley, at the age of ten regularly reprimanded adults in his own family—condemning their swearing, breaking up their card parties, preaching to them about sin and salvation. To people of other cultures, the behavior of these Quaker *infants terribles* seemed to turn the world upside down. But among Friends, they appeared to put things right side up again.[27]

Other ethnic groups in the Delaware Valley introduced their own customs of child rearing. It is interesting to observe that many German pietists were remarkably similar to the Quakers in this respect. Among the Amish, for example, customary ideas of child nature and nurture had many qualities in common with those of English Friends. In both groups one finds the same belief in the innocence of the young, the same intensity of love and concern for their upbringing, the same combination of permissiveness in infancy and restraint in adolescence, the same hostility to "sending out," and the same insistence upon strict subordination to a spiritual community.[28]

---

[26]William Penn, *Fruits of a Father's Love,* 50–51; quoted in DiStefano, "Concept of the Family in Colonial America," 97.

[27]Frost, *Quaker Family,* 43, 80. Conservative Quakers complained bitterly of this practice. One wrote, "I reckon among all the delusions of the Notionists it is not the least that of pretending and publishing that great numbers of children of Six years old and upwards are brought under deep convictions, Nay are converted by their Ministry. I have seen a boy younger imitate a preacher very nicely, use unexceptional words, and deliver himself, as if he was affected with what he said. But I count it no miracle. Who does not know that children of that age, by example and tuition, are capable of imitating almost anything. . . . Even a parrot may be taught to speak some few words, but he cannot [give] any rational account of the cause of those words." John Smith to James Pemberton, 20.v.1741, Pemberton Papers, HSP.

[28]John A. Hostetler, *Amish Society* (rev. ed., Baltimore, 1968), 108–9, 153–57. The Amish

There were also many similarities in the child-rearing customs of German Pietists and English Quakers, which became the basis of a regional culture in the Delaware Valley, and the means of its transmission from one generation to the next.

◆ Delaware Age Ways:
Quaker Elders as "Nursing Fathers and Mothers"

When the Quaker missionary Mary Dyer was about to be hanged in Boston, her Puritan executioners asked if she wished an elder to pray for her. "Nay," said she, "first a child, then a young man, then a strong man before an elder." In her response, one may observe how radical was her challenge against conventional attitudes. Mary Dyer did not merely challenge the prevailing system of age-stratification. She turned it upside down.[1]

The second generation of Quakers took a different view. They revived something of the traditional respect for age, but tempered it by the tenets of their faith. Meetings and moralists in the Delaware Valley routinely urged honor and respect for elders, citing the same biblical injunctions and rewards that were so often mentioned in Massachusetts and Virginia. "Honour your father and your mother, that your days may be long," the Burlington Friends' meeting quoted from Scripture, just as their New England neighbors did. Further, elders within the Society of Friends were thought to be entitled to the same honor that was due to parents.[2]

In other respects, however, ideas of age relations were different among the Quakers. Their notion of respect for age did not rest upon principles of veneration as in New England, or on ideas of patriarchy as in the Chesapeake. Quakers did not think of elders as Abraham's seed who had been specially chosen by God to live a long life. Nor did they believe that older people were Adam's heirs who had been specially ordained to rule the young.

In the Society of Friends, older people were thought of in another way—mainly as "nursing fathers and mothers to the

---

were not representative of Swiss and German immigrants in general, but the author can testify from the experience of his own family that similar ideas about child nature and nurture also existed among German Lutherans. Different practices prevailed in German Reformed households, which were closer to English Puritans.

[1]Jones, *Quakers in the American Colonies,* 87.

[2]Frost, *Quaker Family,* 64, 40.

young," and teachers (in the Christian sense) who were assigned
a special sort of nurturing role which the Quakers called "eldering." This idea developed in the late seventeenth century, when
the young Quaker radicals of the 1650s had become "ancient
solid friends," with a special standing in their sect. In Richard
Bauman's phrase, they were highly respected as "weighty veterans of the Lamb's war." When they spoke to the young, their
words seemed to rise from the very roots of the movement. As a
consequence, they had a special eminence as prophetic ministers
whose role was to "feed the flock of God." Thereafter, this status
passed to subsequent generations of elders.[3]

One women's meeting described the function of elders in the
following way:

> Elder women in the truth were not only called Elders but Mothers
> and likewise mothers in Israel; now a mother in the church of
> Christ and a mother in Israel is one that gives suck and nourishes,
> feeds and dresses and washes and rules, [and] is a teacher in the
> church and . . . an admonisher and instructor and exhorter. . . . so
> the elder women as mothers are to be teachers of good things and
> to be teachers of the younger and the trainers up in virtue, holi-
> ness and Godliness, in wisdom and in the fear of the Lord.[4]

Men's meetings used different metaphors, but the organizing
principle was much the same. Quaker elders were not saints or
patriarchs, but nursing mothers and even "nursing fathers" who
supported, exhorted, admonished and when necessary also corrected the young. In turn, youngsters were urged to respect their
elders, and to follow their advice. Instruments of this purpose
included the memoirs which elderly Quakers produced in large
number for the instruction of the young. One example was
Joseph Oxley's huge manuscript called "Joseph's Offering to His
Children." Another was David Cooper's autobiography which he
called "Some Memoirs . . . Intended for the Use of His
Children."[5]

This ideal of a nurturing relationship became a living reality in
the Delaware Valley. Autobiographers warmly remembered the
support they had received from elders in difficult moments of
youth. Thus, Benjamin Bangs wrote, ". . . there was a tender care

---

[3]Bauman, *Let Your Words Be Few*, 139.
[4]Marsden Monthly Meeting, Womens Meeting Book, 1678–1738, ms. FRM 1/24, LANCRO.
[5]Oxley, "Joseph's Offering to His Children"; David Cooper, "Some Memoirs."

in the elders over me, who often would be dropping some seasonable cautions to me, by which I was greatly benefited."[6] Israel Norris remembered of his father:

> In the latter part of his life his great care was to consider the difference between Age and Youth ... his innocent cheerfulness to ... his children ... deservedly merited their respect and duty due a parent, and his pleasure in their company and the ease and cheerfulness of his conversation made them choose him as a companion and friend.[7]

That "difference between age and youth" also had another side. Elders made themselves very busy in the way of admonition—so much so that among Quakers the word "elder" was not merely a noun but a verb which meant to scold or correct the young. One Quaker wrote of another that "she gave her friend a good eldering."[8]

In the first years of the Quaker movement, elders did not have a special status. But as time passed, they became a separate "station" or quasi-office in the meeting—"pillars in the House of our God," Barclay called them.[9] Friends began to be formally selected to serve as elders—a process that was full of pain and difficulty for Quakers.[10] As early as 1686, the Philadelphia monthly meeting asked its elders to talk with those "professing truth that walk not according to it."[11] In 1727, the York quarterly meeting in England appointed four elders to correct "a growing evil of pride ... [and] other vain and pernicious practices run into by some of the youth among Friends, which notwithstanding the frequent and repeated advice given in that respect. . . ."[12] Elders were also made responsible for organizing the affairs of the meeting, and maintaining order. It was their task to deal with mentally disturbed people in meetings.[13] During the early eighteenth century, they were also given the task of advising ministers.

On difficult and doubtful questions, young and even middle-aged Friends were actually compelled by their meetings to consult

---

[6]Benjamin Bangs, *Memoirs* ... (London, 1798), 19; quoted in Bauman, *Let Your Words Be Few*, 139.

[7]Israel Norris to Sampson Lloyd, 12.vi.1736, Israel Norris Letterbook, HSP.

[8]Harvey, "Quaker Language," 19.

[9]Bauman, *Let Your Words Be Few*, 145.

[10]*Ibid.*, 139–44.

[11]Frost, *Quaker Family*, 53.

[12]Thistlethwaite, ed., *Yorkshire Quarterly Meeting*, 238.

[13]*Ibid.*, 39.

elders. Thus, the York quarterly meeting in 1708 issued a minute on "unnecessary and extravagant wigs," which required that any Quaker who needed to wear a wig should "acquaint" the elders with his problem and get their advice.[14] This process of consulting with elders was common in that culture. Anne Cooper Whitall remembered the Quaker community where she grew up as a place where

> the old governed the young, and those of them that obeyed not . . . were punished—it was a shame not to hear reproof among the youth and among the aged a matter of punishment not to give it. . . . the youth mixed with the aged to awe them, and give them examples.[15]

When elders fell out among themselves, communities were deeply riven. George Churchman described the shattering effect of "a difference between two members not in low stations, and advanced in age," much to the distress of "younger branches of our heavenly father's family."[16]

There were limits, however, to the authority of elders in Quaker culture. Their roles were not as authoritarian as those in Puritan Massachusetts or Anglican Virginia. The young had an obligation to listen, but not always to obey. Further, elders were entitled to respect only when Truth was with them. Not all elders were honored among the Quakers. And the young were also to be respected when truth was on their side. Ministers were apt to be Quakers of any age: some were as young as ten; others of ripe years. Elders themselves were not always very old; meetings were often instructed not to choose their elders merely according to age, though normally they did so.[17]

In daily affairs, younger Quakers commonly waited for their elders to take the lead. But when elders failed to do their duty, then youth itself stepped into the breach. John Woolman remembered one such incident. It arose from a disturbance at a public house in Mount Holly, New Jersey, about the year 1742, when "many people, both in town and from the country," were "spending their time in drinking and vain sports." Woolman was then a young man in his twenty-third year. He waited for his seniors to do something. "I considered I was young," he wrote,

---

[14]*Leeds Friends Meeting Book*, xxxviii.
[15]Anne Cooper Whitall, Diary, 10.vi.1760, HAV.
[16]George Churchman, Diary, 26.ii.1761, HAV.
[17]Frost, *Quaker Family*, 46–47.

"and that several elderly friends in town had opportunity to see these things." When they did nothing, the young man himself reproved the master of the drinking house.[18]

But elderly Quakers were often very active in their nurturing and teaching role. An example was Susannah Morris, a Quaker missionary. In 1746 at the age of sixty-four she "found drawings in my mind to go to and fro in visiting meetings." Leaving her husband and children at home, she sailed from Pennsylvania to Europe on her fourth Atlantic crossing to proselytize for her faith. Two years later she was traveling in America on another mission. Even in the coldest months when the Delaware was frozen, she was busy visiting "much at home in winter," though she wrote that "for my age could not well bear cold." In the year 1752 (aged 70) she made still another transatlantic missionary trip, and continued her work until she died at the age of seventy-three.[19]

Quaker age ways, in summary, were less hierarchical than in Virginia or Massachusetts. The precepts of patriarchy and veneration were condemned within the Society of Friends. But elders were honored by this culture in other ways, and they served actively until the end of life—which leads to another question about attitudes toward death.

~ Delaware Death Ways: The Quaker Idea of Optimistic Fatalism

By the standards of the age, rates of mortality in the Delaware Valley were in a middling range during the late seventeenth and early eighteenth century—lower than in Virginia, but higher than in Massachusetts. From 1675 to 1750, death rates increased and also became increasingly unstable—with sudden surges caused by the spread of epidemic disease.[1]

In that setting the Quakers no less than Puritans and Anglicans frequently reminded themselves of what John Woolman called "the uncertainty of temporal things." They cultivated an attitude

---

[18]Phillips B. Moulton, ed., *The Journal and Major Essays of John Woolman* (New York, 1971), 32.

[19]Susannah Morris, Travels, 1746, HSP.

[1]This was the general trend throughout British America and is discussed in D. H. Fischer and Mary Dobson, "The Dying Time," chaps. 2, 3.

of fatalism which was nearly universal in this era. But the substance of their fatalistic thinking was not the same as that of other people. The Quaker attitude might be described as optimistic fatalism—optimistic in more ways than one. They regarded death as the climax of life—an event not to be feared or abhorred but welcomed and embraced. Death for a believing Quaker was an act of Christian apotheosis—the extinction of the mortal self.

Quakers were deeply interested in deathbed scenes, which had a very different texture from those of Puritan Massachusetts. A favorite book among Friends was *Piety Promoted,* an anthology of Quaker deathbed events which was published in at least thirty editions during the eighteenth century. This genre was not unique to Quakers; Puritans and Anglicans also produced many collections of the same sort. But the Quakers had different ways of thinking about mortality.[2]

An example was the death of a twenty-eight-year-old Quaker named Sybil Matlock Cooper, in 1759. Her husband recorded the event. As the end approached she said:

> Give me one drop more of cold water, then let me go if it be thy will, Father, divers times repeating Come Death, Come Death. . . . The blood now retired from her face, and it was thought she was expiring, but it returned and she came to her natural colour as in a time of health and opening her eyes asked to be raised up. She seemed to admire to find herself still with us . . . I said My Dear, it may be the almighty will please to restore you to us again. She replied, I have not desired it.[3]

Many others not merely accepted death but welcomed it in this manner. Mary Penington wrote that since she came to be "settled in the truth," she lived "free from the sting of death and without the least desire to live."[4] Yet another example was William Dillwyn's description of his wife's death:

> Her sense continued to the last and free from pain. . . . [she] resigned her breath in a happy frame of mind and humble assurance of eternal rest—which even in that solemn hour her coun-

---

[2]Specimens of this literature include John Tomkins, ed., *Piety Promoted; in a Collection of the Dying Sayings of Many of the People Called Quakers* (1701, 2d ed., London, 1703); also *A Seasonable Account of the Christian and Dying-Words, of Some Young Men Fit for the Considerations of All; But Especially the Youth of This Generation* (Philadelphia, 1700); and Hannah Hill, *A Legacy for Children; Being Some of the Last Expressions and Dying Sayings of Hannah Hill* (Philadelphia, 1717).

[3]David Cooper, Diary, 16.iv.1759, HAV.

[4]Mary Penington, "Abstract," HAV.

tenance sweetly testified—an innocent smile remaining on it, when a corpse.[5]

Male Quakers showed the same attitude. Joseph Oxley wrote:

> I am now pretty far advanced in years, waiting daily until my change shall come, having no desire to stay longer than is my Master's good will and pleasure; in this state of resignation I desire to live, and to live so as to be fit to die.[6]

Quakers often dreamed about death, as did New England Puritans and Anglican Virginians, and published their dreams in hundreds of journals. Many of these accounts were elaborate death fantasies in which the writers, after an initial feeling of revulsion, embraced death and glorified it. The classical example was a dream that came to John Woolman as he lay upon his sickbed:

> In a time of sickness, with the pleurisy a little upward of two years and a half ago, I was brought so near the gates of death that I forgot my name. Being then desirous to know who I was, I saw a mass of matter of a dull gloomy color between the south and the east, and was informed that this mass was human beings in as great misery as they could be and live, and that I was mixed with them, and that henceforth I might not consider self as a distinct or separate being.
>
> In this state I remained several hours. I then heard a soft melodious voice, more pure and harmonious than any I had heard with my ears before; I believed it was the voice of an angel who spake to other angels. The words were, "John Woolman is dead." I soon remembered that I once was John Woolman, and being assured that I was alive in the body, I greatly wondered what that heavenly voice could mean. I believed beyond doubting that it was the voice of an holy angel, but as yet it was a mystery to me. . . .
>
> The song of the angel remained a mystery; and in the morning, my dear wife and some others coming to my bedside, I asked them if they knew who I was, and they telling me I was John Woolman, thought I was only light-headed, for I told them not what the angel said. . . .
>
> At length I felt a Divine power prepare my mouth that I could speak, and I then said, "I am crucified with Christ, nevertheless I live; yet not I but Christ that liveth in me. . . ." Then the mystery was opened, and I perceived there was joy in heaven over a sinner

---

[5]William Dillwyn to Susannah Dillwyn, 5.i.1770, Dillwyn Papers, HSP.
[6]Oxley, "Joseph's Offering to His Children." HSP

who had repented, and that the language, "John Woolman is dead," meant no more than the death of my own will.[7]

In the face of death, Quakers cultivated an attitude not merely of resignation but confident expectation. For believing Quakers, death became the fulfillment of life. It was an escape from the corruptions of the world, and the final transcendence of the mortal self.

When death actually came to a Quaker household, the entire family assembled, and shared an experience of the highest solemnity. The last words were heard with loving attention. The dying Friend lay at the very center of his friends and relations. Visitors crowded into the room, and children were also required to watch, listen and reflect. But once "the spirit had flown," Quakers showed comparatively little interest in the physical remains of the deceased. Burial, funeral and mourning customs were exceptionally austere in this culture. Quakers grieved over the deaths of their loved ones as deeply as other people. But they condemned a show of mourning as "proud" and "vain" and "needless." The yearly meeting in 1728 condemned "wearing black or black and white cloathes at Burials."[8] Funerals were kept very plain and simple. Large processions were discouraged. There were no palls, bearers, mutes, rings or gloves. Meetings issued strict rules of restraint for these occasions. One meeting urged its members "to keep out all needless and ayery [airy] discourses and to behave themselves soberly and in a weighty mind as becomes Truth; and not to be hasty to put the corpse in the ground, but pause a little that all may be done in a very solemn manner."[9]

The act of interment itself was also very simple among the Quakers. When Richard Cooke was buried at Chester, the total expenses were six shillings for a plain wood coffin, and four shillings for all other charges.[10] John Woolman asked that his coffin be made without any ornament from ash instead of oak, because "Oak . . . is a wood more useful than ash."[11] The corpse was wrapped in a simple shroud, woven of wool in England and of linen in America.

---

[7]Moulton, ed., *Woolman Journal,* 185–86.
[8]Bacon, "A Widening Path," 178.
[9]Thistlethwaite, ed., *Yorkshire Quarterly Meeting,* 63.
[10]Chester Mens Quarterly Meeting Minutes, 4.x.1683, ms. EFC1/1/120, CHESRO.
[11]Frost, *Quaker Family,* 43.

The issue of gravemarkers was, as Pearson Thistlethwaite has written, a special "stone of stumbling" for Quakers.[12] The London yearly meeting recommended in 1766 that all markers should be removed from Quaker graves. Many meetings refused to agree, and Quakers quarreled about this practice for years. Not until 1850 were gravestones approved by the London yearly meeting—a plain flat marker without ornament or elaborate inscriptions.[13]

Wakes were also discouraged. George Fox called them a "heathen custom." In the year 1700 the York quarterly meeting agreed that:

> This meeting having under their weighty consideration the practice that is used in many places among Friends at burials (vizt.) of giving Cakes, and providing much meat and drink for the neighbors and friends which may come to such burials, it is the sense of this meeting that the providing too much meat and drink and cakes or such like things in the Method and manner aforesaid, tends to the prejudice and hurt of Truth's testimony.

Shortly thereafter, cakes and "such like" things were forbidden outright by the York meeting, and "two weighty and faithful Friends" were appointed to "inspect and see into the practice." But they continued to occur, despite official disapproval.[14]

Wakes were also discouraged in America, but never entirely suppressed. According to tradition, Quakers throughout the Delaware Valley worked out a compromise. Cakes and wine were served before a burial, and a full meal thereafter—but with a spirit of self-restraint. The bottle was allowed to circulate only twice.[15]

As time passed, mourning customs grew more elaborate among the Quaker colonies. Thomas Chalkley complained as early as 1714 that "funerals began to be growing thing among us."[16] As late as 1782, a child's elaborate burial in a Quaker graveyard inspired one disapproving Friend to write:

> The child's father had been disowned for paying a military fine. His mother, a worthy public friend, was not present. His wife and

---

[12]Thistlethwaite, ed., *Yorkshire Quarterly Meeting*, 63.

[13]*Ibid.*, 63–64.

[14]*Ibid.*, 63.

[15]Frost, *Quaker Family*, 44.

[16]Chalkley, "Journal," *Friends' Library*, VI, 30.

children were members. The corpse was carried by four young
women. Three of them did not belong to Friends, the other a disowned widow's daughter. [They] were dressed in white, their
hands white with powder, without bonnets, etc. To see this show
enter our graveyard, and the corpse a member of a society that
professed so much plainness and self-denial affected me much and
occasioned disagreeable observations.[17]

As this comment suggests, old attitudes toward death lingered for
a century in the Delaware Valley.

Among the other ethnic groups in this region, similar death
customs were also kept by German Pietists. The Amish, for example, tended to share the same optimistic fatalism, the same death-
watches until the flying of the spirit, the same austere burials, and
the same emotional restraint. There were differences of detail.
The Amish carefully washed the corpse, and always dressed it in
white. But with these exceptions German Pietists, English Quakers and other Protestant "Spiritists" were very similar in their
mortuary customs. In general, the death ways of these English
and German cultures in the Delaware Valley had a very special
texture that rose from their religious beliefs.

❧ Delaware Religious Ways: The Quaker Spiritist Style

"As to religion," Delaware Quaker David Cooper told his children in 1772, ". . . Let it have the chief and principal place in thy
heart." He explained, "I mean real religion, not ceremonious
attendance at meetings, and talking God and Godliness."[1]

David Cooper's "real religion" was far removed from practices
in Puritan Massachusetts and Anglican Virginia. It gave rise to a
unique ritual of worship that centered on the Inner Light and the
movement of the Spirit.

Members of the Society of Friends met in meetings, sometimes
once a week, or even several times a week. These meetings for
worship normally went through a strict sequence of ritual stages.
First was the gathering. Quakers quietly arrived, either as individuals or in small family groups. They were urged to cultivate a
gravity of demeanor on their journey to the meeting. "Frivolous"
conversation was condemned, as was laughter, smoking, spitting

---

[17]David Cooper, Memoir, 1782, HAV.
[1]David Cooper, Memoir, HAV.

and chewing. Men and women entered the meeting by different doors, and were expected to take seats nearest the front in order of their arrival, and not by rank or wealth or age, except for the special honor done to elders.

Then the second stage began—a time of expectant silence called "turning the mind to the light." The English Quaker Alexander Parker wrote in 1660:

> So Friends, when you come together to wait upon God, come orderly in the fear of God; the first that enters into the place of your meeting, be not careless, nor wander up and down, either in body or mind; but innocently sit down in some place, and turn in thy mind to the light, and wait upon God singly, as if none were present but the Lord. . . . Then the next comes in, let them in simplicity of heart, sit down and turn in the same light, and wait in the Spirit; and so all the rest coming in, in the fear of the Lord, sit down in the pure stillness and silence of all flesh, and wait in the light.[2]

Sometimes no words were ever spoken, and yet the meeting was thought to have been highly successful. Many Quakers believed that the best meetings happened when no outward words needed saying.

But most meetings passed to another stage when people began to rise and speak, either in the form of preaching (if the words were addressed to one another) or prayer (if to the Lord). Usually, the elders spoke first, and others followed. The manner of speaking was different from ordinary discourse. Visitors in the eighteenth century remarked upon its strange cadence and accent. The Swedish traveler Peter Kalm attended a meeting for worship in Philadelphia's Bank Meeting House, on 7 December 1750, and described it thus:

> We sat and waited very quietly from ten o'clock to a quarter after eleven. . . . Finally, one of the two . . . old men in the front pew rose, removed his hat, turned hither and yon, and began to speak, but so softly that even in the middle of the church, which was not large, it was impossible to hear anything except the confused murmur of the words. Later he began to talk a little louder, but so slowly that four or five minutes elapsed between the sentences; finally the words came both louder and faster. In their preaching the Quakers have a peculiar mode of expression, which is half

---

[2]A. R. Barclay, *Letters &c of Early Friends* (London, 1841), 365; quoted in Bauman, *Let Your Words Be Few*, 121.

singing, with a strange cadence and accent, and ending each
cadence, as it were, with a half or . . . a full sob. Each cadence
consists of two, three or four syllables, but sometimes more,
according to the demand of the words and means; e.g. my friends/
put in your mind/ we/do nothing/ good of ourselves// without
God's //help and assistance. . . . When he stood for a while using
his sing-song method he changed his manner of delivery and spoke
in a more natural way . . . at the end, just as he was speaking at his
best, he stopped abruptly, sat down, and put on his hat.[3]

Anyone could speak in meeting—Friends and strangers, elders
and youngsters, men and women. One diarist recorded every
speaker in meetings he attended; both men and women spoke frequently, but a small number of individuals accounted for most
contributions. Elders were responsible for dealing with disturbed
or disruptive speakers. The meeting itself sometimes responded
to unwelcome remarks by standing silently in protest.[4]

The last stage of the meeting was often a return to silence.
Then worship would end when one member, usually an elder,
rose and shook hands with another, and everyone departed in
quiet dignity. A Quaker meeting for worship was thus conducted
in a manner very different from an Anglican liturgical service and
the Puritans lecture day.

Other differences also appeared in the physical setting of
Quaker worship. Meetinghouses in both England and the Delaware Valley tended to be simple rectangular buildings, with massive stone walls and plain white shutters. Double doors for men
and women were sheltered beneath a projecting hood.[5]

A striking feature of Quaker meetinghouses was the intensity
of their illumination. Interiors were very bright. Windows were
large, numerous, and set high in the walls. Interior walls and ceilings were frequently "whitened" for additional effect. Quakers
preferred to worship in a room that was suffused with light—a
symbol of their beliefs, and a sharp contrast with the gloom of
Anglican churches and especially Puritan meetinghouses which
were sometimes so dark that ministers complained they were
unable to read their sermons.[6]

---

[3]Quoted in Frost, *Quaker Family,* 36–37.

[4]*Ibid.*

[5]Photographs of 73 surviving Quaker meetinghouses, all built before 1789, appear in Harold Wickliffe Rose, *The Colonial Houses of Worship in America* (New York, 1963).

[6]A 19th-century treatise on the design of meetinghouses gave much attention to "atmospheric light." See William Alexander, *Observations on the Construction and Fitting Up of Meeting
Houses . . .* (York, 1820).

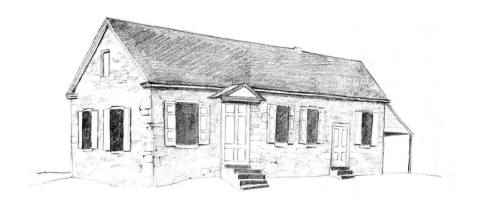

Quaker meetinghouses in the Delaware Valley were very different from Puritan meetinghouses in New England and Anglican churches in Virginia, and much the same as Quaker buildings in the North Midlands of England. These patterns of similarity and difference were defined both by religious beliefs and regional traditions. In the Delaware Valley, the church architecture of other Christian denominations was influenced by the customs of the hegemonic culture. The churches of Lutherans and Presbyterians in parts of Pennsylvania during the eighteenth century sometimes resembled Quaker meetinghouses in exterior design.

Inside the meetinghouse, all "vain" and "needless" furniture was ruthlessly stripped away. Quakers had no need for pulpits and altars, but often there was a raised platform called the "stand" where the elders sat in a place of special honor. Everyone else took a seat on the simple benches, men on one side and women on the other. There was no assigned seating as in Anglican and Puritan churches. A gallery called the loft was reserved for children and youths. Other furnishings included a sliding partition which separated men and women during their business meetings, and a cabinet where records were kept, including a locked deed-box which could be opened only in the presence of three Friends.[7]

American meetinghouses differed in a few details from those of England. Stonework in the Delaware Valley consisted of random walls, rather than cut stone blocks. Doors were placed differently in America and large stables were constructed for Friends who had to travel longer distances than was the case in England. But in most important ways, architecture of the meetinghouses changed very little in the New World.[8]

It is interesting to observe that Quaker meetinghouses set the fashion for religious architecture in rural communities throughout the Delaware Valley. Other denominations built many of their country churches in the same plain style throughout this region. The exteriors of some Calvinist and Lutheran churches were sometimes indistinguishable from Quaker buildings. Here was yet another way in which the religious customs of the Quakers had an impact upon the culture of an entire region.

∾ Delaware Magic Ways:
    The Quaker Obsession with Spiritualism

"We have not hoofs nor horns in our religion," Quakers liked to say.[1] But even the Children of Light were not without some belief in the supernatural. The history of magic in the Delaware Valley was a two hundred years' war between old fears and a new faith—

---

[7]For the locked deed box, see Chesterfield Meeting Records, ms. Q61a, 1.xi.1690.

[8]Hubert Lidbetter, *The Friends Meeting House* (2d ed., York, 1979), examines architecture on both sides of the Atlantic. See also David M. Butler, *Quaker Meeting Houses of the Lake Counties* (London, 1978); and on America, Horace Mather Lippincott, *Quaker Meeting Houses, and a Little Humor* (Jenkintown, 1952).

[1]Watson, *Annals of Philadelphia*, I, 266.

a running conflict between ancient superstition and the magic of the Inner Light. Many traditional forms of folk magic were carried to West Jersey and Pennsylvania by individual settlers. But the Quaker leaders of those colonies had no use for these "needless" beliefs and did their best to discourage them, without ever succeeding entirely in doing so. The old magic continued to be practiced and opposed in the Quaker colonies for many years.

As early as 1683 two elderly women named Margaret Mattson and Yeshro Hendrickson were accused of witchcraft, and brought to trial before the Proprietor himself. Both were Swedish, and required an interpreter in the English court. One of them, Margaret Mattson, was accused by her own daughter. Of the witnesses who appeared against them, one complained that the accused had bewitched his cattle. Another testified that while he was boiling the heart of a calf which he believed to have been killed by magic, Margaret Mattson came into his house looking visibly discomposed. A third declared that his wife "had awakened him in a great fright, alleging that she had just seen a great light, and an old woman with a knife at her bed's feet." On examination, the witnesses could not link any of their misfortunes directly to the accused Margaret Mattson herself, and the Proprietor's court delivered a curious verdict which captured the ambivalence of attitudes toward witchcraft in Quaker Pennsylvania. Margaret Mattson was found guilty of "having the common fame of a witch," but not guilty of practicing witchcraft. She was set free.[2]

This witchcraft trial was an exceptional event in the Quaker colonies. Pennsylvania had no laws against witchcraft in the seventeenth century. Its Quaker leaders showed great hostility to accusations, and actively suppressed persecutions of the sort that raged in New England with much encouragement from ministers and magistrates during the late seventeenth century.[3]

Popular belief in witchcraft was so strong in Pennsylvania that the governing elite felt compelled to act from time to time. In 1719, the justices of Chester County were specifically empowered to inquire into "witchcrafts, enchantments, sorceries and magic arts." But the purpose of that order was mainly to discourage belief in magic itself, rather than to punish alleged malefactors.[4]

[2]Lawrence Lewis, Jr., "The Courts of Pennsylvania in the Seventeenth Century," *PMHB* 5 (1881), 141–90.

[3]Amelia Mott Gummere, *Witchcraft and Quakerism* (Philadelphia, 1908).

[4]*Ibid.*

Still, ancient beliefs survived to the end of the eighteenth century. When the courts failed to act, mobs found other means to
punish eccentric people who were feared as witches. In 1749,
when a court refused to punish a man accused of wizardry, a riot
occurred in Philadelphia. As late as 1787, an old woman was
dragged from her house by a mob of youths, and stoned to death
for witchcraft in the streets of Philadelphia.[5] In Burlington, New
Jersey, a gigantic sycamore of great age was long remembered as
the "witch tree," after an old woman was allegedly hanged from
its branches by a mob.[6]

Here was a paradox that ran deep in the Quaker colonies.
Friends who founded Pennsylvania were unwilling to persecute
witches themselves, but unable to prevent persecutions by others.
No witch was ever ordered to be executed by the courts of any
Quaker colony. But witches continued to be mobbed, hanged and
even stoned to death as late as 1787.

Prophecy and divination were also practiced by the ordinary
people of Pennsylvania. In 1695, Robert and Philip Roman were
brought before the monthly meeting, and later Robert Roman
was presented by the grand inquest of Chester County, "for practicing geomancy according to Hidon, and divining with a stick."
For those offenses he was fined five pounds, and ordered to
deliver to the court his learned books—"Hidon's *Temple of Wisdom,* Scott's *Discovery of Witchcraft,* and Cornelius Agrippa's *Geomancy.*" There were also at least a few conjurers, witch doctors
and fortune tellers among the Teutonic immigrants who founded
Germantown. Their services were in demand by people seeking
the recovery of stolen goods, the whereabouts of buried treasure
or the removal of spells.[7]

But Quakers had no need of the devil to explain the existence
of evil in the world, nor any use for geomancy to predict the
future. Few believing Christians of any faith have ever shown so
little interest in the black arts. Quakers commonly regarded the
wrongs of the world as the work of man rather than the Devil—

---

[5]George Winthrop Geib, "A History of Philadelphia, 1776–1789" (thesis, Univ. of Wis.,
1969), 23; citing Philadelphia *Pennsylvania Packet,* 16 July 1787; *Pennsylvania Herald,* 21 July
1787.

[6]Gummere, "Friends in Burlington," 259.

[7]These books were John Heydon, *Theomagia: or, The Temple of Wisdom* (1644), and Agrippa
[a false attribution], *The Fourth Book of Occult Magic* (1655). Reginald Scot, *Discoverie of Witchcraft* (1584), argued that witches did not exist. A discussion of this episode appears in Jon Butler,
"Magic, Astrology and the Early American Religious Heritage, 1600–1760," *AHR* 84 (1979),
333–34.

and especially as the product of carelessness, ignorance and human error.[8]

Members of the Society of Friends, particularly in the second period of their history, believed that error would be overcome by the magic of the inner light. Historian Frederick Tolles writes that there was a strong "tendency of the Friends to delimit the area of supernatural action and thus to widen the realm in which natural causes operated."[9]

White magic, no less than black magic, was equally condemned by them. A Friend who turned to a conjurer or fortune teller could be disowned by the meeting. Quakers were also intensely hostile to astrology. For a believing Friend, the brightest heavenly stars paled against the shining of the light within.[10]

But the Quakers were not entirely liberated from magic. One particular variety of supernatural belief came to be very widely shared among them. The idea of the Inner Light led them to that form of superstition which is commonly called spiritualism today. In the seventeenth century there were repeated instances of attempts by Quakers to communicate with the dead, and even to raise them from the grave. In Worcestershire, for example, one English Quaker dug up the body of another, and "commanded him in the name of the living God to arise and walk." There were many similar events in which Quakers attempted to resurrect the dead.[11]

They also believed in the healing power of the holy spirit. Keith Thomas writes that "for the performance of spectacular miracles there was no sect to rival the Quakers. Over a hundred and fifty cures were attributed to George Fox alone, and many other Friends boasted similar healing powers. . . . The early days of Quakerism had been marked by healing miracles on a scale comparable to those of the early church; they helped to make the Friends numerically the most successful of the sects."[12] One historian observes that "there are traces too of the Hermetic tradition, a belief that man has fallen out with the creation but that in a state of perfection (of restoration) unity can once more be achieved and nature's secrets revealed."[13]

---

[8]I am told that in England's Oxford Friends meeting, after the assassination of John F. Kennedy, the only prayer offered was for the assassin.

[9]Tolles, *Meeting House and Counting House*, 213.

[10]Keith Thomas, *Religion and the Decline of Magic*, (New York, 1971), 261.

[11]Reay, *The Quakers and the English Revolution*, 37.

[12]Thomas, *Religion and the Decline of Magic*, 127.

[13]Reay, *The Quakers and the English Revolution*; G. F. Nuttall, "Unity with the Creation: George Fox and the Hermetic Philosophy," *Friends Quarterly* I (1947).

Quakers also believed in reincarnation. Their concern for the welfare of animals was sometimes connected to this belief. It was written of Isaac Hopper that:

> One day when he saw a man beating his horse brutally he stepped up to him and said, very seriously, "Dost thou know that some people think men change into animals when they die?"
>
> The stranger's attention was arrested by such an unexpected question and he answered that he never was acquainted with anybody who had that belief. . . .
>
> "But some people do believe it," rejoined Friend Hopper; "and they also believe that animals may become men. Now I am thinking that if thou shouldst ever be a horse, and that horse should ever be a man, with such a temper as thine, the chance is thou wilt get some cruel beatings."[14]

In consequence of these various beliefs, two very different and even hostile sets of attitudes toward magic coexisted in the Quaker colonies, sometimes within the same head. That ambivalence continued for many centuries—even to our own time.

❧ Delaware Learning Ways:
Quaker Ideas of Learning and the Light Within

The faith of the Society of Friends, for all its heavy stress upon the spirit, was also solidly grounded in reason. "Since nothing below a man can think," Penn wrote, "man in being thoughtless must needs fall below himself."[1] Quakers believed that reason was part of the inner light. This idea of the "light within" led them to think about learning in a special way. Their attitudes toward knowledge, books, reading and schooling were curiously mixed—a classical study in cultural ambivalence. Even that most literate of Friends, William Penn, warned the young members of his family that "much reading is an oppression of the mind, and extinguishes the natural candle, which is the reason of so many senseless scholars in the world."

---

[14]Isaac T. Hopper, *A True Life*, ed. Lydia Maria Child (Cleveland, 1853), 92; Howard H. Brinton, *Quaker Journals: Varieties of Religious Experience among Friends* (Wallingford, Pa., 1972), 92.

[1]Penn, *Some Fruits of Solitude*, preface.

This idea of reason as a "natural candle" led Penn to advise his own children not to read too much:

> Have but few books, but let them be well chosen and well read, whether of religious or civil subjects . . . reading many books is but taking off the mind too much from meditation. Reading yourselves and nature, in the dealings and conduct of men, is the truest human wisdom.[2]

That opinion must be taken in context. It was typical of William Penn to declare his dislike of "much reading" by writing a book against it. He clearly expressed a conflict within Quaker minds between the light within and the enlightenment of learning.

Another ambivalence about reading in this Protestant culture arose from the central place of one book in particular, which diminished the relative importance of all others in the minds of Friends. Thus, Thomas Chalkley in 1727 scolded his son-in-law, "I perceive thou art inclined to read pretty much: I pray thee, that thy chief study in books may be in the holy Scriptures. Let all other books (tho' of use and good in their places) be subservient to them."[3]

Yet a third sort of ambivalence also appeared in Quaker attitudes toward the act of reading itself. In 1744, an American Friend named Elizabeth Hudson rended herself for "having some taste of books, and indeed found I had too high a relish for them, they being very engrossing of our time." Elizabeth Hudson found books to be curious, interesting, even enticing. But she regarded them as "needless" distractions from the serious business of life.[4]

All of this was very different from normative attitudes in both Massachusetts and Virginia. The Quakers never shared the obsessive interest in learning which was so strong in puritan New England. At the same time, they disagreed with the first gentlemen of Virginia, who favored higher learning but feared common literacy. The Quakers reversed these judgments. By and large they favored literacy and feared learning but were painfully ambivalent about both attainments.

Those Quaker attitudes were transplanted to the Delaware colonies, and entered deep into the cultural grain of middle America. Their operation may be observed in actual levels of literacy

---

[2]William Penn, "The Advice of William Penn to His Children," *Works,* I, 898–99.
[3]Chalkley, "Journal," 210; Tolles, *Meeting House and Counting House,* 146.
[4]"Abstract of the Travels of Elizabeth Hudson from 22.i.1743," HAV.

and schooling in the Delaware Valley. For the entire population, rates of literacy in the Quaker colonies ranked below Massachusetts, but above Virginia. In Chester County and also Lancaster County, Pennsylvania, roughly half of all adults were unable to sign their own names, a proportion intermediate between New England and the Chesapeake colonies. Similar patterns appeared among German pietists and English Quakers. Historian Alan Tully finds that rates of literacy among these two ethnic groups were "not radically different," and very slow to change through the first century of settlement.[5]

The distribution of literacy in the Delaware Valley showed large differences by gender; surprisingly so, given the Quakers' concern for the spiritual equality of the sexes. The proportion of women who were unable to write their own names was twice that of males in the Pennsylvania counties of Chester and York. In urban Philadelphia, the disparity between men and women was not so great, and rates of literacy were generally higher than in the rural counties. But inequalities of gender were striking even there.[6]

Large differences also appeared in literacy by social rank. At the top were Quakers such as James Logan, an enthusiastic bibliophile who collected one of the largest libraries in the British America. "Books are my disease," he once confessed. Logan lovingly assembled a collection of 3,000 volumes which were left as

[5]Alan Tully obtained the following results from Pennsylvania wills (1729–1774):

		Percent Signing by Mark			
Place	Period	Male	Female	Mean	Number
Chester Co.	1729–44	32%	54%	43%	312
	1745–54	27%	81%	54%	328
	1755–64	31%	73%	52%	333
	1765–74	27%	56%	42%	413
Lancaster Co.	1729–44	37%	100%	68%	63
	1745–54	40%	86%	63%	182
	1755–64	35%	85%	60%	273
	1765–74	36%	62%	49%	412

Source: Alan Tully, "Literacy Levels and Educational Development in Rural Pennsylvania, 1729–1775," *PH*, 39 (1972), 304.

[6]Lawrence Cremin reported the following results for Philadelphia:

	Percent Signing by Mark		
Period	Male	Female	N
1699–1706	20%	40%	50
1773–1775	18%	29%	136

Source: Cremin, *American Education: The Colonial Experience* (New York, 1974).

a public trust called the Loganian Library in a special building near the State House. One scholar who has studied this collection writes that "no collection of books in colonial America . . . was better chosen for breadth and catholicity; none was nearly so rich in rare editions of the classics, or the great works of the scientific tradition."[7]

In lower ranks, however, illiteracy was very common, and also highly persistent in the Delaware Valley. As late as 1837, long after literacy was universal in New England, a legislative committee in Pennsylvania found that among factory children throughout the state, "not more than one third can either read or write."[8]

Here was a social paradox which rooted itself in the regional life of the Delaware Valley. The egalitarian ideas of the Inner Light and liberty of conscience weakened the formal institutions of literacy. That weakness in turn created cultural inequalities— for the rich had many resources and the poor had few. This paradox of egalitarian inequality became a central part of the culture of middle America.[9]

Another expression of this paradox were the rural school ways of the Delaware Valley, which were a product of Quaker ideas and English experiences in the American environment. In England's North Midlands, as we have seen, many humble people who became Quakers regarded educational institutions as alien growths. Throughout that region, churches and schools were in the hands of a foreign elite. As a consequence, ordinary people tended to be strongly hostile to institutions of formal education. This attitude contributed to the Quakers' suspicion of a learned clergy, and indeed of learning itself. It was reinforced by their religious beliefs. Historian Frederick Tolles observes that the Quakers made "all men bearers of the Inward word, a belief which diminished the importance of outward words."[10]

These beliefs shaped the school ways of the Quaker colonies in an extraordinarily persistent way. Pennsylvania and West Jersey had nothing like New England's school laws, or the comparatively

---

[7]Frederick B. Tolles, *James Logan and the Culture of Provincial America* (Boston, 1957), 194.

[8]Macauley, "A Social and Intellectual History of Elementary Education in Pennsylvania," I, 671.

[9]One may observe here the operation of an historical law. Egalitarian movements which take the form of "leveling down" commonly create substantive inequalities, despite their own intention, because the few will always find their own way up, against the general trend. This was equally true of dachas in Soviet Russia and learning in Quaker Pennsylvania. Movements which seek equality by "leveling up" tend to be more successful.

[10]Tolles, *Meeting House and Counting House*, 3–11.

high rates of enrollment that existed in Massachusetts. But at the same time, there was nothing comparable to the Virginia elite's fear of education. Schooling was perceived in Pennsylvania as a matter of conscience which every sect, family and individual was expected to work out in its own way.

This is not to say that Quakers were hostile to schooling. Both William Penn and Thomas Budd wrote at length about education—a subject on which they had strong views. They did not like the prevailing practices in English schools. "We press their memory too soon," Penn himself wrote, "and puzzle and strain and load them with words and rules to know grammar and rhetoric and a strange tongue or two that it is ten to one may never be useful to them; leaving their natural genius to mechanical, physical or natural knowledge uncultivated and neglected, which would be of exceeding use and pleasure to them through the whole course of their lives."[11]

Pennsylvania's "Frame of Government" empowered the governor and council to "erect and order all public schools" in the province. An act of 1683 required that all children must be taught to read and write by the age of twelve and trained in a useful trade or skill, no matter where rich or poor. Stiff fines were threatened for noncompliance, and a "Friends Public School" was opened to poor children without fee.[12]

Some Quakers wished to go much farther. Thomas Budd in 1698 proposed a system of Quaker schools in Pennsylvania and New Jersey, and a requirement that all children attend every day (half session on Sunday) for seven years. Budd also proposed that both girls and boys should be educated (in separate classes), and that the schools should offer vocational training "in all the most useful arts and sciences. . . ." The boys were to be "instructed in some mystery or trade, as the making of mathematical instruments, joinery, turnery, the making of clocks and watches, weaving, shoemaking or any other useful trade." The girls were to learn "spinning of flax and wool, and knitting of gloves and stockings, sewing, and making of all sorts of useful needlework, and the making of straw work, as hats, baskets, etc." Budd believed deeply in educational equality. "To the end that the children of the poor people, and the children of Indians, may have good

---

[11]Penn, *Some Fruits of Solitude,* in Tolles and Alderfer, eds., *The Witness of William Penn,* 169.
[12]This school still exists as Penn Charter Academy.

Hexagonal schoolhouses were commonly used in the Delaware colonies by both English Quakers and German Pietists. They were smaller than New England schoolhouses and different in their interior design. The children were seated in circles rather than rows—an arrangement that by its very nature was less hierarchical and more communal and an expression of different attitudes toward learning, authority and children in the Quaker colonies. Many of these hexagonal schools were constructed of wood, and have disappeared. This example was made of stone, and survived to the twentieth century near Newtown, in Chester County. The drawing follows an old photograph made before 1930 by Eleanor Raymond, and published in Early Domestic Architecture of Pennsylvania *(1930, rpt. Exton, Pa., 1977).*

learning with the children of the rich people," he wrote, "let them be maintained free of charge to their parents."[13]

This plan failed to find broad support in the Quaker colonies. On the subject of education, no public laws of any importance were passed in Pennsylvania from 1700 to 1776. John Woolman observed, ". . . meditating on the situation of schools in our provinces, my mind hath at times been affected with sorrow." But the remedy that he recommended—private charity in place of public support—was itself part of the problem.[14]

The result of these Quaker attitudes was a profusion of sectarian schools, supported by the private efforts of individual religious groups. Quaker education itself developed as a series of local schools, which were attached to individual meetings and neighborhoods. A great many of these schools were founded. One historian estimates that approximately 60 regular schools were run by Quaker meetings by 1776, and an equal number of neighborhood schools were also supported by Quakers.[15] As other ethnic and religious groups were invited to settle in the Delaware Valley, they were encouraged to found their own church-related educational institutions. In the process, many sectarian school systems developed in Pennsylvania. They were less comprehensive than New England's town schools, but more so than Virginia's hierarchical system which created one track for the elite, another for ordinary English people, and a third for black slaves.[16]

Another consequence of these Quaker attitudes was a cultivated disinterest in higher education. Of all the major Christian denominations in early America, the Quakers were the slowest to found colleges. Every major Protestant denomination was more active in this field. Congregationalists, Presbyterians, Anglicans, Baptists, Dutch Reformed and Methodists all founded colleges before 1800. The Quakers had no requirement for a learned ministry, and little respect for higher learning.

This also became part of Pennsylvania's folkways. Of all the

---

[13]Thomas Budd, *Good Order Established in Pennsylvania and West New Jersey in America* (Philadelphia, 1685); a discussion of Budd's work appears in Thomas Woody, *Early Quaker Education in Pennsylvania* (New York, 1920), 36–37.

[14]Woolman, *Works*, 305–6.

[15]Woody, *Early Quaker Education in Pennsylvania;* and his *Quaker Education in the Colony and State of New Jersey: A Source Book* (Philadelphia, 1923). See also Macauley, "A Social and Intellectual History of Elementary Education in Pennsylvania," II, 388–415, 908–12.

[16]A quantitative survey of Pennsylvania schools appears in Macauley, *ibid.*, II, 895–928.

northern colonies, Pennsylvania, Delaware and West Jersey were comparatively inactive in the field of higher education. Before the American War of Independence four colleges were founded in New England, and three in New York and East Jersey. But only one existed in the Delaware Valley—the present University of Pennsylvania, which had little support from Quakers. Higher learning was regarded with suspicion even by Quakers as erudite as William Penn. His aphorisms often returned to this subject:

> [Universities are] signal places for idleness, looseness, prophaneness, prodigality and gross ignorance.

> We are at pains to make them scholars but not men, to talk rather than to know, which is true canting.

> We pursue false knowledge and mistake education extremely.

> Children had rather be making of tools and instruments of play, shaping, drawing, framing, etc., than getting some rules of propriety of speech by heart.

> If man be the index or epitome of the world, as philosophers tell us, we have only to read ourselves well to be learned in it.[17]

At the same time, Penn gave strong support to practical education:

> Let their learning be liberal. Spare no cost, for by such parsimony all is lost that is saved, but let it be useful knowledge such as is consistent with truth and godliness, not cherishing a vain conversation or an idle mind; but ingenuity mixed with industry is good for the body and mind too. I recommend the useful parts of mathematics, as building houses, or ships, measuring, surveying, dialing, navigation; but agriculture especially is my eye. Let my children be husbandmen and housewives.[18]

These opinions could easily be misunderstood. They developed not from an absence of concern for education, but from the very opposite. Anne Whitall Cooper wrote in 1761, "as the right education of children and the nurture of youth is of good consequence to them and the succeeding generations, we pressingly exhort Parents and Heads of Families to preserve such useful learning for their children, as their abilities will admit, and to encourage them, as well by example as Precept."[19]

[17]Tolles and Alderfer, eds., *The Witness of William Penn,* 167–99.
[18]William Penn, *A Letter from William Penn to Wife and Children* (London, 1761).
[19]Anne Whitall Cooper Diary, 1.ii.1761, HAV.

That attitude gave more encouragement to families and meetings than to schools and the state. It also supported sectarian
schools better than public schools, and lower schools more than
higher education. It rested upon the belief that education like
politics was a matter of conscience. These priorities had a central
place in the pantheon of Quaker values, and entered deeply into
the culture of an American region.

❧ Delaware Food Ways:
Quaker Ideals and North Midland Traditions

This regional culture was both a mind-set and a material order.
It strictly regulated most ordinary acts of everyday life—even
waking and sleeping, cooking and eating.

Consider food for an example. Quaker food ways seemed at
first sight to be exceptionally plain and simple. But historian William Weaver observes from long study of this subject that "in
Quaker terms, there is nothing so complex as simplicity." Here
again, the plain style became almost baroque in its cultural
elaboration.[1]

Quaker food ways began to take form in the first period of this
religious movement. The founder George Fox himself categori-
cally condemned all "feastings and revellings, banquetings and
wakes."[2] Indulgence of the appetite was thought to be a "pam-
pering the lower self."[3] A simple diet was recommended on the
highest Christian authority. Margaret Fell wrote: "Christ Jesus
saith that we must take no thought what we shall eat."[4] The plain
style was further reinforced by Quaker principles of Christian
charity. "Is this the Saints' practice," asked Nayler, ". . . living in
excess of apparel and diet . . . when your brethren want food and
raiment?"[5]

In the second period of Quakerism, William Penn and others

---

[1] William W. Weaver, *A Quaker Woman's Cookbook: The Domestic Cookery of Elizabeth Ellicott Lea* (Philadelphia, 1982), xvi.

[2] Thomas J. Wertenbaker, *The Founding of American Civilization: The Middle Colonies* (New York, 1938), 193.

[3] Braithwaite, *Second Period of Quakerism*, 556.

[4] Lloyd, *Quaker Social History*, 73.

[5] James Nayler, *A Collection of Sundry Books, Epistles and Papers . . .* (London, 1716), 46; quoted in Barbour, *The Quakers in Puritan England*, 170.

of his generation developed this doctrine of culinary asceticism in copious detail. "Luxury has many parts," he warned, "and the first that is forbidden by the self-denying Jesus is the belly."[6] Penn's advice to his children devoted an entire chapter to this theme, and revealed how very indulgent a Quaker's thoughts could become on the subject of self-restraint. He wrote:

> Eat therefore to live and do not live to eat. That's like a man, but this below a beast.

> Have wholesome but not costly food, and be rather cleanly than dainty in ordering it.

> The recipes of cookery are swelled to a volume, but a good stomach excels them all, to which nothing contributes more than industry and temperance.

> If thou rise with an appetite, thou are sure never to sit down without one.

> The proverb says that "enough is as good as a feast," but it is certainly better, if superfluity be a fault, which never fails to be at festivals.

> The luxurious eater and drinker who is taken up with an excessive care of his palate and belly. . . . so full is he fed that he can scarce find out a stomach, which is to force hunger rather than to satisfy it.

Penn offered the same advice on the subject of drink.

> Rarely drink but when thou art dry; nor then, between meals, if it can be avoided.

> The smaller the drink, the clearer the head and the cooler the blood, which are great benefits in temper and business.

> Strong liquors are good at some times and in small proportions, being better for physic than food, for cordials than common use.

> All excess is ill, but drunkeness is of the worst sort: it spoils health, dismounts the mind, and unmans men; it reveals secrets, is quarrelsome, lascivious, impudent, dangerous, and mad. In fine, he that is drunk is not a man, because he is so long void of reason, that distinguishes a man from a beast.[7]

[6]Penn, *No Cross, No Crown,* in Tolles and Alderfer, eds., *The Witness of William Penn,* 54.
[7]Penn, *Some Fruits of Solitude; ibid.,* 172.

These epigrams were conceived within an ontology of sensual restraint which lay very near the center of Quaker values:

> It is a cruel folly to offer up to ostentation so many lives of creatures as make up the state of our treats, as it is a prodigal one to spend more in sauce than in meat.

> The most common things are the most useful, which shows both the wisdom and goodness of the great Lord of the family of the world.

> What therefore he has made rare, don't thou use too commonly, lest thou shouldst invert the use and order of things, become wanton and voluptuous, and they blessing prove a curse.

> "Let nothing be lost," said the Saviour; but that is lost is misused.

> Neither urge another to that thou wouldst be unwilling to do thyself, nor do thyself what looks to thee unseemly and intemperate in another.

The central theme in this philosophy was clear and consistent. Food and drink were not to be consumed for pleasure but only for subsistence. Common things were best, and moderation was to be cultivated in their consumption.[8]

Quaker meetings sternly enforced this idea of temperance in diet and drink. Lapses were punished severely, and offenders were required to stand before the meeting and to take shame upon themselves, as William Kay was made to do in Morley meeting:

> Having a weight upon my spirit because of my miscarriages at thy house in being overtaken with wine. This testimony I now give out against myself that I did that which was evil in the sight of the Lord . . . . I take to myself the shame, and clear the people of God and their way.[9]

Excess was prohibited in everything except moderation itself, which was recommended without reserve by the moralists of Pennsylvania. Feasting, which had so large place in the folkways of Virginia, was condemned by Delaware Quakers. The result of these injunctions was a spirit of culinary austerity that persisted

---

[8] *Ibid.*, 54.

[9] Testimony of William Kay, 28.v.1685, Morley Monthly Meeting Records, ms. EFC 2/1/1, NOTTRO.

in the folkways of the Delaware Valley until the twentieth century. "It is better to go to the house of mourning than to the house of feasting" wrote Anne Cooper in 1762.[10]

Quakers also refused to touch foods that were tainted by social evil. Some did not use sugar because it had been grown by slave labor. Others banned salt from their tables, because it bore taxes which paid for military campaigns.[11] Benjamin Lay, a Quaker eccentric who lived in a cave, refused to drink tea or wear animal skins or even to use wool. Joshua Evans refused to eat the flesh of any creature, and drank only broth and gravy. Few Quakers were as radical as Lay and Evans, but many practiced some small act of symbolic sacrifice. Anne Mifflin, for example, gave up butter because she believed that it was "corrupting" to the spirit.[12]

This Quaker austerity was severely tested by the cornucopia that opened before them in America. One wrote home in 1677 that there was "plenty of fish and fowl, and good venison very plentiful, and much better than ours in England, for it eats not so dry, but is full of gravy, like fat young beef."[13] Others reported "peaches in such plenty that some people took their carts a peach-gathering," and "great store of wild fruits, as strawberries, cranberries, hurtleberries which are like our billberries in England but for sweetness; they are very wholesome fruits. The cranberries [are] much like cherries for color and bigness . . . an excellent sauce is made of them for venison, turkeys and other great fowl, and they are better to make tarts than either gooseberries or cherries."[14]

The rivers of the Delaware Valley teemed with fish, especially "fine rock and perch, caught with hook and line." Shad choked the streams in their spring spawning runs.[15] The sky was darkened by flocks of fowl, that were captured easily in nets and carried to market by the cartload. In 1829, an early historian of Philadelphia informed his incredulous contemporaries that "his forefathers . . . saw a flock fly over the city so as to obscure the sun for two or three hours, and many were killed from the tops of the

---

[10]Anne Whitall Cooper Diary, 26.iii.1762, HAV.

[11]*Ibid.*, 110.

[12]Marietta, *Reformation of American Quakerism,* 110.

[13]John Kips to Henry Stacy, 28 Aug. 1677, in Harry B. Weiss, *Life in Early New Jersey* (Princeton, 1964).

[14]Mahlon Stacy to Henry Stacy, 1680, *ibid.,* 21.

[15]Watson, *Annals of Philadelphia,* I, 26.

houses."[16] As late as 1763 a Jersey Quaker brought down thirty pigeons with a single round of bird-shot.[17]

But Quaker austerity was more than a match for American abundance. Edward Shippen wrote, "We eat so moderately . . . that the whole day seems like a long morning to us."[18]

At an early date in the eighteenth century the cuisine of the Delaware Valley began to settle into a fixed pattern, in which the Quaker ideal of simplicity combined with a style of traditional cooking by humble folk in England's North Midlands which has persisted in that region even to the twentieth century.

A quantitative survey of regional food ways in Britain finds that just as baking was specially characteristic of East Anglia, and frying of southern and western England, so boiling has been predominant in the north. The leading British expert on this subject writes, ". . . today, the northerner still prefers to boil where the southerner roasts or grills—the cooking pot as always, resisting the advance of the oven."[19]

These boiled breakfasts and dinners became an important part of Delaware food ways. John F. Watson remembered from his childhood in the Delaware Valley during the mid-eighteenth century that "in the country, morning and evening repasts were generally made of milk, having bread boiled therein, or else thickened with pop-robbins—things made up of flour and eggs into a batter, and so dropped in the boiling milk."[20]

Other important parts of Quaker cuisine were boiled dumplings and puddings. So often did they appear on the table that Israel Acrelius called them "Quakers' food."[21] Peter Kalm also observed that boiled apple dumplings were a daily dish in the Delaware Valley. Pot-puddings of many kinds were also prominent in this diet. The cookery books of this region made a specialty of puddings and dumplings.[22]

The Quaker colonists also introduced from England a special form of food-preservation which came to be characteristic of the

[16] *Ibid.,* I, 260.

[17] Isaac Decow, Journal, 8.xi.1763, SWAR.

[18] Edward Shippen of Lancaster to C. J. Edward Shippen, 20 March 1754, *PMHB* 30 (1906), 85–90.

[19] Allen, *British Tastes,* 23.

[20] Watson, *Annals of Philadelphia,* I, 179.

[21] J. Thomas Scharf, *History of Delaware 1609–1888* (Philadelphia, 1888) I, 158; Weaver, *A Quaker Woman's Cookbook,* xxix.

[22] Kalm, *Travels in North America,* I, 66; Weaver, *A Quaker Woman's Cookbook,* xlv; Evelyn A Benson, ed., *Penn Family Recipes* (York, Pa., 1966).

Delaware Valley. This was a method of dehydration by boiling, simmering or standing. The classical example was the foodstuff that became famous throughout America as Philadelphia cream cheese. In its traditional form, it was not truly a cheese in the usual sense, for it was made without rennet or curds. Cream or milk was warmed gently over a slow heat and allowed to stand between cloths for several weeks, until it had lost much of its moisture and become semi-solid. "True cream cheese," writes William Weaver, was "nothing more than partially dehydrated sour cream." He writes that "the technique for making cream cheese was brought to Pennsylvania on a large scale during the late 1600s by the English and Welsh settlers."[23]

Fruits and vegetables were also preserved in a similar way. The Quakers were fond of "apple cheese" as they called it, which was much like apple butter. The pulp of the fruit was thickened and partly dried by slow cooking, and seasoned with sugar and spices. "Cheese" in the Delaware Valley as in the North Midlands became a generic term for "any sort of food thickened or partially dehydrated by slow cooking or pressing." Special favorites were plum cheese, pear cheese, walnut cheese and lemon cheese.[24]

Lemon cheese, also called lemon butter, was in Weaver's words "perhaps the one dish that Quakers in the Middle-Atlantic States identify as a symbol of their cookery." It was a heavy custard which appeared on Delaware tables not as a desert but as part of the main course. A variant called orange cheese or orange butter was (and is) a Christmas dish in Quaker households.

Dehydration was also used by the Quakers to preserve their meats. A favorite staple was dried beef, which when properly prepared would keep for several years.[25] Weaver writes that "Quaker dried beef could be purchased in country stores almost every-

---

[23]Weaver, *A Quaker Woman's Cookbook*, lix; recipes for cream cheese appear in Mary Smith, *The Complete House-Keeper* (New Castle, Eng., 1786); and Elizabeth E. Lea, *Domestic Cookery, Useful Receipts and Hints to Young Housekeepers* (Baltimore, 1853). The latter work, in its recipe for "Pennsylvania Cream Cheese," calls for the use of rennet and curds.

Quaker housewives also preserved dairy products in other ways. They simmered milk over a slow heat until it was as thick as cream, and then they bottled it; a recipe for condensed milk appeared in Margaret Hill Morris Recipe Book, 26.iii.1762, HAV.

[24]Weaver, *A Quaker Woman's Cookbook*, xliii.

[25]"Take a spoonful of salt petre to each piece of beef—mixed with salt and as much molasses as will make it like brown sugar—rub it well and let it lay three days; then make a cold pickle to bear an egg, pour it on the meat and let it lay ten days, drain it from the pickle and smoke it"; this recipe for dried beef appears in Margaret Hill Morris Recipe Book, ca. 1750, HAV.

where in Maryland and Pennsylvania, and . . . became . . . firmly labeled as a Quaker food in the Middle Atlantic region." Dried beef was often served as a "sauce" on puddings and dumplings; in the eighteenth century it was called "Quaker gravy."[26]

Quaker cooking was not, of course, the only food way in the Delaware Valley. Earlier occupants kept their own customs, and German immigrants introduced another culinary tradition in the eighteenth century. There was much borrowing back and forth among these various ethnic groups. Quaker cooks quickly adopted compatible German dishes such as scrapple—a boiled pot pudding of meat and buckwheat which became a part of the regional cuisine. But the Quakers themselves and their English customs set the tone for a distinct style of Delaware food ways, which persisted in this region for many generations.[27]

✌ Delaware Dress Ways:
The Quaker Idea of "Going Plain in the World"

"The Calico! O the Calico!" wrote Anne Cooper in 1762. "I think tobacco and tea and calico may all be set down with the [keeping of] negroes, all one as bad as another."[1]

To strangers, the cultural values of the Quakers were most visible in these distinctive attitudes toward dress, which became a vital part of Quaker identity and an important expression of their faith. The idea of "going plain in the world" made its appearance during the first period of Quakerism, as part of George Fox's gospel. His followers took up this teaching with high enthusiasm. In many a North Midland town the visit of a Quaker evangelist was followed by an event called the "burning of the braveries," in which the people made a bonfire of their ribbons and silks.[2]

During the second period of Quakerism, the Society of Friends developed George Fox's taste for simple clothing into dress codes of fantastic complexity. Quakers believed that clothing in all its forms was an emblem of Adam's fall—a "badge of lost inno-

[26] *Ibid.,* xxix.

[27] Susan J. Ellis, "Traditional Food in the Commercial Market: The History of Pennsylvania Scrapple," *PF* 22 (1973), 10–21.

[1] Anne Whitall Cooper Diary, 18.iii.1762, Haverford.

[2] Braithwaite, *The Beginnings of Quakerism,* 72.

cence." William Penn argued that "guilt brought shame, and shame an apron and a coat":

> [As] sin brought the first coat, poor Adam's offspring have little reason to be proud or curious of their clothes, for it seems their original was base, and the finery of them will neither make them noble nor man innocent again . . . our first parents . . . were then naked and knew no shame, but sin made them ashamed to be no longer naked.
>
> Since therefore guilt brought shame, and shame an apron and a coat, how low are they fallen that glory in their shame, and that are proud of their fall. For so they are that use care and cost to trim and set off the very badge and livery of that lamentable lapse. . . . if a thief were to wear chains all his life, would their being gold and well made abate his infamy? To be sure, his being choice of them would increase it.[3]

This idea was reinforced by another principle. Quakers believed that clothing should be only what was "needful" "to cover their shame" and "fence out the cold." Every ornament not "needful" was systematically searched out and condemned. Quakers generally agreed that excess of dress was "unscriptural." Penn asked:

> How many pieces of ribbon, feathers, lace bands and the like had Adam and Eve in paradise or out of it? What rich embroideries, silks, points, etc., had Abel, Enoch, Noah and good old Abraham? Did Eve, Sarah, Susanna, Elizabeth and the Virgin Mary use to curl, powder, patch, paint, wear false locks of strange colors, rich points, trimmings, laced gowns, embroidered petticoats, shoes and slip-slaps laced with silk or silver lace and ruffled like pigeons' feet?[4]

To all of these reasons for "going plain," Quakers added yet another argument that a primary purpose of fashion was to arouse the sexual passions which they feared and despised. "It's notorious," Penn wrote, "how many fashions have been and are invented on purpose to excite to lust, which . . . enslaves their minds to shameful concupiescence."[5]

As if these objections were not enough, Quakers added the argument that costly costumes created envy in the world and divided one Friend from another. They also believed (in company

---

[3]Penn, *No Cross, No Crown,* 54–55.
[4]*Ibid.,* 56.
[5]*Ibid.,* 55.

with most others of their age) that the stock of wealth was fixed, and that one person's extravagance caused the impoverishment of another. "If thou art clean and warm, it is sufficient," wrote William Penn, "for more doth rob the poor."[6]

Further, Quakers argued that attention to superficial things diminished a deeper concern for the life within. Isaac Norris of Philadelphia in 1719 instructed his son in London: "Come back plain. This will be a reputation to thee and recommend thee to the best and most sensible people—I always suspect the furniture of the inside where too much application is shewn for a gay or fantasticall outside."[7]

Moreover, it was important to Quakers that they should simply be different from others in the world. In 1726, the female Friends of the Philadelphia yearly meeting drafted an open letter to all women of their persuasion, condemning "vain conversations, customs and fashions in the world. "Dear Sisters," they wrote, "These things we solidly recommend to your care and notice, . . . that we might be unto the Lord, a Chosen Generation, a Royal priesthood, an Holy Nation, a Peculiar People."[8]

When Quakers translated their ideal of "going plain" into actuality, they adopted a special form of simple dress which derived from the folk costume of England's North Midlands. George Fox himself wore the costume of a North Country shoemaker, including heavy leather breeches and a doublet of distinctive cut which became a symbol of both the man and his movement. Fox was called "the man in the leather breeches," and was thought to wear them all the time, "except a little one hot summer."[9]

George Fox's costume was widely imitated by other male Quakers for many years. Ancient leather breeches were handed down from father to son. A Yorkshire Friend in the nineteenth century recalled, ". . . when I was a lad there was a vast [many] still sitting in their fathers' leather breeches and more than one I kenned had breeks their grandfathers had had for their best and there was a vast of good wear in 'em yet."[10]

[6]Penn, *Some Fruits of Solitude,* 174.

[7]Isaac Norris to Joseph [?] Norris, April [?] 1719; quoted in Tolles, *Meeting House and Counting House,* 58.

[8]Epistle of Women Friends at Burlington Yearly meeting, 21.vii.1726, Alice Morse Earle, *Two Centuries of Costume in America, 1620–1820* (1903, rpt. Rutland, 1971), II, 595.

[9]Quoted in Joan Kendall, "The Development of a Distinctive Form of Quaker Dress," *C* 19 (1985), 59.

[10]*Ibid.,* 59.

Other humble people in the North Midlands wore simple trousers of a broad cut, with a wide leather apron in front. This costume was brought to the Delaware Valley and was worn by farmers for many years. A European visitor found Quaker farmer John Bartram dressed in "wide trousers and a large leather apron."[11]

The conventional costume of male Quakers also derived in other ways from the dress of farmers and artisans in the north of England. The common fabric in the north was a plain homespun called "Hodden gray."[12] One variety, called penistone, was a course woolen fabric named after a village in Yorkshire. In the Delaware Valley, penistone was one of the first textiles to be manufactured on a large scale. Its soft gray color set the tone for Quaker clothing through generations.[13] So normal did this costume seem that when Mary Penington had a vision of Jesus, the Saviour appeared before her as "a fresh lovely youth, clad in grey cloth, very plain and neat."[14]

Quaker meetings in England and America enforced the rule of simplicity in dress with regulations of high complexity. The Pennsylvania Council entertained a proposal for restricting all men to only two sorts of dress through the year.[15] Male Friends were forbidden to wear "cross pockets" on their coats and "needless" pockets of any sort. They were warned against broad hems, deep cuffs, false shoulders, superfluous buttons, fashionable creases, wide skirts and cocked hats.[16] The refusal of Quakers to use tricks of tailoring created a garment of curious profile called the "shadbelly coat" in the Delaware Valley. The question of male headgear was much debated among Quakers. Men were encouraged to wear plain broad brimmed beaver hats, undyed and uncocked. So many adopted this fashion that American Quakers in the early eithteenth century were called "broadbrims" or "men with broad hats and no pockets."[17]

Many meetings also wrestled with the difficult question of wigs. Hairless Friends were permitted to wear modest periwigs, but

[11]Crèvecoeur, *Letters from an American Farmer*, 178.

[12]For "the well-known hodden gray of the Cumberland yeoman," see Walter McIntire, *Lakeland and the Borders of Long Ago* (Carlisle, Eng., 1948), 240–42; Barbour, *The Quakers in Puritan England*, 74.

[13]"Letter of Thomas Paschall," 1683, in Myers, ed., *Narratives of Pennsylvania*, 250.

[14]Thomas, *Religion and the Decline of Magic*, 475; quoting *Some Account of the Circumstances of Mary Penington* (1821), 24.

[15]J. W. Frost, "Religious Liberty in Pennsylvania," *PMHB* 105 (1981), 419–51.

[16]On cross pockets, see David Cooper, Memoir, 1777, HAV.

[17]*PMHB* 92 (1968), 318.

only after they had consulted with elders and solemnly affirmed that "necessity and not voluptuousness has brought them to the use of them." Even these "needful" wigs were expected to be "such as in color and shape resemble their former hair as need be," and were not to be excessively long, full, bushy, proud or powdered. Quakers who kept their own hair were generally discouraged from wearing any wigs at all.[18]

For women, even more elaborate dress codes were recommended. The women's meetings discussed at length every imaginable aspect of feminine costume. Fashionable hair styles and fancy hats were condemned. Women of all ages were encouraged to wear plain hoods, which in the eighteenth century were replaced by bonnets of extreme severity. Handkerchiefs were worn modestly over the top of the bodice. Quaker women were expected to wear aprons when they appeared in public—"either of green or blue or other grave cloth colours and not white . . . nor any silk aprons."[19] Dresses were to be of simple cut and plain colors. Special warnings were issued against "the wearing of stript or branched stuff or silk, or long scarves, or any other things which may lead us into the fashions of the World."[20]

In the eighteenth century, Quakers discouraged the use of dyes, particularly indigo, because it was produced by slave labor. Bright dyes were condemned as excessively proud, and dark dyes were forbidden because they were thought to hide dirt. The New Jersey Quaker John Woolman conducted a lifelong campaign against the use of dye-stuffs on this ground:

> I have been where much cloth hath been dyed [he wrote in his journal], and have, at sundry times, walked over the ground where much of their dye-stuffs has drained away. This hath produced a longing in my mind that people might come into cleanness of spirit, cleanness of person, and cleanness about their houses and garments. . . .
>
> Real cleanliness becometh a holy people; but hiding that which is not clean by coloring our garments seems contrary to the sweetness of sincerity. Through some sorts of dyes, cloth is rendered less useful. And if the value of dye-stuffs, and expense of dyeing, and the damage done to cloth were all added together, and that cost applied to keeping all sweet and clean, how much more would real cleanliness prevail.[21]

[18]Lloyd, *Quaker Social History*, 73.
[19]Braithwaite, *Second Period of Quakerism*, 514.
[20]Thistlethwaite, ed., *Yorkshire Quarterly Meeting*, 237.
[21]Moulton, ed., *Woolman Journal*, 220.

This Quaker wedding dress was made in the mid-eighteenth century and still survives in Philadelphia. It had no buttons, belt, sash, decorations or adornments of any kind; but it was designed with grace and refinement and cut from fine silk. The dress was worn with a handkerchief folded modestly over the bodice in accordance with the recommendation of the many women's meetings. The source is John A. Gallery, ed., Philadelphia Architecture *(Cambridge, Mass., 1984), 17.*

Neatness and cleanliness were also encouraged in other ways. Amelia Gummere remembered that Friends were "as notable for the neatness as for the old-fashioned cut of their garments. Their linen was always fine and clean."[22]

Quakers were also forbidden to have commerce in clothing that was denied to them. This was the case in both England and America. The Cheshire quarterly meeting as early as 1699 agreed to very strict rules in that respect:

> A question having been proposed to this meeting whether any friend may make, sell or buy anything which it is not consistent with truth or that friends cannot wear, which matter came to this result—that the making, buying or selling striped, figure, printed silks, stuffs or cloths or anything else that friends cannot wear is altogether inconsistent with truth and for future to be avoided. Liberty being only given that such as have any such by them do dispose thereof and for the future buy no more.[23]

Quaker hostility to changing fashion caused them to cling to the clothing styles of the past. Amelia Gummere wrote that "it may be set down as a safe rule, in seeking for a Quaker style or custom at any given time, to take the worldly fashion or habit of the period preceding."[24]

Always, some rebelled against these rules. A few restless souls called "gay Quakers" wore whatever pleased them. But most Friends, even the most affluent, attempted to preserve something of "going plain." One who allowed himself the luxury of silver buttons insisted they should not be "wrought" (engraved). In 1724 a German printer noted that affluent Quakers in Pennsylvania wore plain clothing "except that the material is very costly, or even is velvet."[25] "Plain" did not mean cheap. Many Quakers, including William Penn himself, combined exceptionally refined taste with the plain style, and were willing to spend large sums for clothing of good quality.[26]

Quaker dress ways were invented in the North Midlands of England. But they survived longer in the New World than the Old, and became more uniform in the Delaware Valley than they had been in any part of Britain. As early as 1770, an English

---

[22]Gummere, *The Quakers: A Study in Costume*, 33.

[23]Cheshire Quarterly Meeting, 14.i.1699, ms. EFC 1/1. CHESRO.

[24]Gummere, *The Quakers: A Study in Costume*, 195.

[25]Rayner Kelsey, ed., "An Early Description of Pennsylvania," *PMHB* 45 (1921), 252–53; Tolles, *Meeting House and Counting House*, 127.

[26]Richard S. Dunn, "Penny Wise and Pound Foolish: Penn as a Businessman," in Dunn and Dunn, eds., *The World of William Penn*, 37–54.

Quaker was startled by the sight of his first American meeting—
"such as I had not seen before—so consistent in appearance of
dress and uniformity," he wrote. He noted that conformity in
dress was much stronger among Quakers in America than in
England.[27] When Brissot de Warville visited Philadelphia yearly
meeting in 1788, he also observed that 90 percent of the Quakers
were dressed in plain homsepun.[28] As late as 1985, long after
Quaker costume was generally abandoned in England, one historian observed that "stylized plain dress only lingers now within
certain groups of Friends in the United States of America."[29]

The Quakers were not the only people who adopted the plain
style in the Delaware Valley. Many German pietists had similar
dress ways. Mennonite men of various sects were required to
wear simple clothing, dark colors, plain suits, and broad-brimmed
hats. Women were expected to wear modest dresses with an
apron, a triangular *Bruschttuch* (breast cloth) folded over the bodice and a little *kapp* on the back of the head. The fabric and pleats
of the *kapp* were unique to each little sect and local community.
Many Pennsylvania Germans adopted plain clothing of some sort
or other, similar in tone and feeling to the costume of English
Quakers.

During the eighteenth century, the plain dress of the Quakers
was much admired by others. In the year 1784, for example, a
Latin adventurer named Francisco de Miranda was traveling
through the United States. One Sunday he amused himself by
attending a Quaker meeting, and was captivated by the women he
saw there. In his journal he wrote:

> At three o'clock went to the temple of the Quakers, in whose com-
> pany I remained for two hours, without anybody speaking a single
> word. I entertained myself all this time by examining slowly the
> dress and the countenances of the female concourse and I can
> assure you with all ingenuousness that neither more simplicity,
> cleanliness and taste in the first nor more natural and simple
> beauty in the second can be imagined. I am firmly persuaded that
> the coloring of Rubens and the carnations of Titian can never imi-
> tate what nature offers here in the hue and complexion of these
> simple Quaker women, who have not a grain of powder or drop
> of oil on their persons.[30]

[27]Oxley, "Joseph's Offering to His Children."

[28]Brissot de Warville, *New Travels*, 301; Frost, *Quaker Family*, 195.

[29]Kendall, "The Development of a Distinctive Form of Quaker Dress," 72.

[30]Francisco de Miranda, *The New Democracy in America: Travels . . .* (Norman, Okla., 1963),
5 Sept. 1784, 140.

Many Pennsylvanians who were not themselves Quakers or German Pietists tended to imitate these dress ways. Benjamin Franklin, an immigrant from Puritan Massachusetts, adopted the Quakers' idea of "going plain," and conformed to so many articles of their dress that he was often mistaken for a Quaker himself. So also did the Presbyterian Benjamin Rush, the Freethinker Thomas Paine, and others of various denominations. In more moderate forms, the ideal of simple dress spread westward from the Delaware Valley into the American midlands, and for many generations became part of the culture of an American region.

~ Delaware Sport Ways:
The Quaker Idea of Useful Recreation

Libertarian as the Quakers may have been on many questions, they were exceptionally intolerant on the subject of sport. The statutes of Pennsylvania forbade many forms of sport outright, under threat of severe criminal punishment. Its laws agreed upon in England banned "all prizes, stage plays, cards, dice, may games, masques, revels, bull-baitings, cock-fightings, bear-baitings and the like."[1]

Most colonies in British America enacted laws on the subject of sport, but none were quite as strict as those of Pennsylvania. The legendary blue laws of New England paled by comparison with those of the Quaker province, which gave their courts unlimited power to punish any sort of amusement "which excites the people to rudeness, cruelty, looseness and irreligion."[2]

Quaker meetings also acted to restrain their members from idle pursuits of every kind. The Yorkshire quarterly meeting warned its members "to shun all publick diversion (of the bowling green, long room or any other places for plays, gaming or dancing) or any vain sights and shows whatsoever not agreeable to the gravity of our profession."[3] Morley meeting added an anathema against the "running of races" as "unfruitful works of darkness."[4]

Quakers also deeply disliked the ball games that flourished in New England. Anne Cooper Whitall was much provoked when

---

[1]*Pennsylvania Colonial Records,* I (1838), xxxiii.
[2]*Ibid.*
[3]Thistlethwaite, ed., *Yorkshire Quarterly Meeting,* 238.
[4]Morley Meeting, 5.viii.1681, ms. EFC 2/1/1, CHESRO.

the men in her family amused themselves with a ball. "O how I have been grieved this day because of their playing at ball," she wrote in her diary, "[I] do believe that they [don't know what] 'tis to be a Quaker."[5]

Much as they detested these "needless" games, the Quakers reserved their deepest disapproval for blood sports. They insisted that no person had the "right to make a pleasure of that which occasions pain and death to animal-creation."[6] Killing for the pot was permitted; killing for pleasure was absolutely condemned. The York quarterly meeting delivered a testimony against unnecessary hunting as "not only vain but cruel . . . inconsistent with the feelings of humanity and the duties of Christians." It warned darkly that Friends who continued to hunt would be "dealt with."[7]

Quakers also opposed horse racing, mainly on the grounds that this sport was cruel to the animals by "over-forcing creatures . . . beyond their strength."[8] They condemned even exhibitions of captive animals as hurtful to their feelings. When a traveling showman exhibited a baboon in a barrel to the people of Pennsylvania, Quaker diarist Elizabeth Drinker took a peep and wrote, ". . . it looked so sorrowful, I pity'd the poor thing, and wished it in its own country."[9]

During the eighteenth century, underground blood sports began to appear in Philadelphia. Butchers in the Northern Liberties even introduced bullbaiting. But that brutal sport was stopped by a courageous mayor of Quaker upbringing, "Squire" Wharton, at some considerable risk to his own skin:

> He went out to the intended sport seemingly as an intended observer . . . when all was prepared for the onset of the dogs he stepped suddenly into the ring, and calling aloud, said he would, at the peril of his life, seize and commit the first man who should begin; at the same time calling on names present to support him at their peril, he advanced to the bull and unloosed him from the stake. He then declared that he would never desist from bringing future abettors of such exercises to condign punishments. They have never been got up since.[10]

---

[5] Ann Cooper Whitall Diary, 2.v.1760, HAV.

[6] Frost, *The Quaker Family*, 207.

[7] Thistlethwaite, ed., *Yorkshire Quarterly Meeting*, 238.

[8] Keith Thomas, *Man and the Natural World* (New York, 1983), 158.

[9] Elizabeth Drinker Diary, 16.x.1793, HSP.

[10] Watson, *Annals of Philadelphia*, I, 279.

For all their hostility to blood sports and needless games, the Quakers were not totally opposed to physical diversion. Though they generally condemned the idea of "sport," they encouraged other forms of "recreation" which they regarded as "useful" and "needful."

Quakers gave much encouragement to recreation as a form of physical exercise. William Penn urged that "children can't well be too hardy bred: for besides that it fits them to bear the roughest Providences, it is more masculine, active and healthy."[11] Quaker schools required physical exercise as part of the curriculum. George Fox at his death left the Philadelphia meeting sixteen acres, partly to be used "for a playground for the children of the town to play on."[12]

For similar purposes, Quakers also encouraged "needful" and "useful recreation" among adults. They were among the first people in America to take up swimming and bathing. They also cultivated ice-skating in the winter, a recreation which became immensely popular on the Schuylkill and Delaware rivers. "During the old fashioned winters," Watson wrote, ". . . the river surface was filled with skaters of all colours and sizes mingled together and darting about here and there."[13]

Quakers also allowed hunting and fishing for subsistence, and made a point of extending opportunities to the entire population. The "laws made in England" guaranteed to all inhabitants "liberty to fowl and hunt upon the lands they hold, and all other lands therein not enclosed; and to fish in all waters in the said lands . . . with liberty to draw his fish on shore on any man's lands."[14]

Perhaps the most characteristic form of recreation among the Quakers was gardening, a "gentle recreation" which attracted many members of this culture. They argued amongst themselves in their accustomed way about the comparative morality of raising vegetables, fruits and flowers, but many devoted themselves to horticulture with an extraordinary passion. Historian Keith Thomas writes that "the early Quakers were often buried in their gardens" and that the Society of Friends produced "a quite disproportionate number of botanists, plant-collectors and nursery-

[11]Frost, *Quaker Family*, 83.
[12]Ulysses P. Hedrick, *A History of Horticulture in America* (New York, 1950), 84.
[13]Watson, *Annals of Philadelphia*, I, 280.
[14]*Ibid.*

men." Quakers such as Peter Collinson and John Bartram became leading horticulturalists in both England and America.[15]

But even with their interest in "needful" and "useful" diversions, Quakers never imagined that avocations were the important things in life. William Penn, as always, summarized their attitudes in an epigram. "The best recreation," he wrote, "is to do good."[16] These people also found their higher forms of "re-creation" in activities which other cultures called work.

❧ Delaware Work Ways:
Quaker Ideas of Cumber and Calling

If Quakers made play into work, they also made work into a form of worship. Their attitudes toward work in general, and also their accustomed work ways were as distinctive as their ideas on most other subjects. Here again, their customs were introduced to the Delaware Valley within the first generation of settlement. In conjunction with similar folkways among German pietists, these practices became the basis of a regional economy which differed from New England and the Chesapeake.

One important component of this regional culture was an attitude which strongly encouraged industry and condemned idleness. William Penn, visiting an Irish prison in 1669, found that the Quakers confined there were toiling away in their cells at work of their own devising—and the rhythm of their work was interrupted only for worship. "The jail," he wrote, "by that means became a meeting-house and a work-house, for they would not be idle anywhere."[1]

This ethic of industry was reinforced by the idea of serving God with one's best talents. John Woolman wrote, ". . . our duty and interest are inseparably united, and when we neglect or misuse our talents, we necessarily depart from the heavenly fellowship." This idea had developed from Martin Luther's concept of the calling *(beruf)*, which had an important place in the cultural thinking of many Protestant denominations. It was exceptionally strong among the Quakers.[2]

---

[15]Thomas, *Man and the Natural World*, 237; see below, "Land Ways."
[16]Penn, *No Cross, No Crown*, 56.
[1]Tolles, *Meeting House and Counting House*, 57.
[2]Moulton, ed., *Woolman Journal*.

Yet another important idea was "discipline," a word which often appeared in Quaker writings. The diaries of Friends in England and America tended to take the form of spiritual exercises in which Quakers attempted to acquire absolute dominion over their acts. An example was a young English lad named John Kelsall, who at the age of fourteen had "a great conflict concerning sleeping and a drowzy spirit in meetings. I was sometimes sorely beset with it, and much adoe I had to get over it. . . . Sometimes I would take pins and prick myself, often rise up and sometimes go out of doors, yea I would set myself with all the strength I could get against it."[3]

Also important was an attitude which encouraged extreme austerity. The Quakers, more than any major Protestant denomination, fostered a style of life which Max Weber called worldly asceticism—the idea of living in the world but not of it. Work itself became a sacrament, and idleness a deadly sin. Wealth was not to be consumed in opulent display, but rather to be saved, invested, turned to constructive purposes. Restraints were placed upon indulgence. The most extended form of this belief was to be found not among the Puritans with whom it is often associated, but among the Quakers.

But the Weber thesis is much too simple to capture the complexity of Quaker thinking about work. An important theme in Quaker journals, even of highly successful merchants and manufacturers, was that business should not be overvalued. This had been the warning of George Fox:

> There is the danger and temptation to you of drawing your minds into your business, and clogging them with it, so that ye can hardly do anything to the service of God, but there will be crying, my business, my business! And your minds will go into the things and not over the things.[4]

Quaker diarists were constantly reminding themselves to "live more free from outward cumbers," as John Woolman phrased it. The idea of "cumber" was an interesting one, which often recurred in Quaker thinking. Thomas Chalkley tried to strike the balance in a sentence. "We have liberty for God, and his dear Son, lawfully, and for accommodation's sake, to work or seek for

---

[3]John Kelsall Journal, n.d., ms. s/194, FLL.
[4]Brinton, *Quaker Journals*, 69.

food or raiment; tho' that ought to be a work of indifferency, compared to the first work of salvation."[5]

These attitudes may on balance have provided a more solid ethical foundation for capitalist enterprise than the more monistic attitudes that Max Weber attributed to the Quakers.[6]

Further, Quakers also insisted that business ethics must be maintained at the highest level of honesty. Monthly meetings appointed committees to monitor the business ethics of members. In 1711, for example, the York quarterly meeting agreed:

> It is desired by this meeting that each monthly meeting take care that two honest friends be appointed in every particular meeting to inspect friends' faithfulness to truth in the several testimonies thereof, and especially touching friends dealings in commerce and trading, in order to prevent any from contracting and running into more or greater debts than they can make payment of in due time, or launch out into matters in the world beyond their abilities, nor be overmuch going with their desire for earthly things.[7]

Members of Quaker meetings on both sides of the Atlantic were disciplined for "dishonest dealing." In Break meeting, a Friend named Luke Hanks was disowned for "breaking his word time after time in his trade." Many of these proceedings dealt with members who failed for one reason or another to pay their debts. The Quakers had a horror of debt, which they felt to be a palpable evil in the world. Falling into debt beyond one's ability was regarded as a moral failing of the first degree.[8]

At the same time, Quakers also condemned the spirit of avarice in creditors. William Penn gave much attention to this in his advice to his children—who stood specially in need of it. "Covetousness is the greatest of monsters," wrote Penn. "A man . . . [who] lived up to his chin in [money]bags . . . is *felo de se* and deserves not a Christian burial." It is interesting that Penn also condemned the miser as "a common nuisance, a weir across the stream that stops the current, an obstruction to be removed by a purge of the law."[9]

[5]Chalkley, *Journal.*

[6]Brinton, *Quaker Journals,* 69–75. This work includes a chapter on "restriction of business," which is a helpful corrective to the Weber thesis.

[7]Thistlethwaite, ed., *Yorkshire Quarterly Meeting,* 358–59.

[8]Monyash Monthly Meeting, 1672–1735, ms. Q86; Break Monthly Meeting Records, 1701–64, ms. Qxx, NOTTRO.

[9]Penn, *Some Fruits of Solitude,* 175.

In all of these ways, the ethics of the Quakers condemned unrestrained capitalist enterprise, and put narrow limits upon its operation. Nevertheless, Quaker beliefs provided a strong support for industrial and commercial activity. So also in more tangible ways did the structure of the Society of Friends. Quakers tended to help one another. They loaned money at lower rates of interest to believers than to nonbelievers, and sometimes charged no interest at all "to those who have no capital of themselves and may be inclined to begin something."[10] It is interesting that Quakers also developed systems of insurance against commercial risks, and played a major role in the development of the insurance industry. The oldest business corporation still existing in America was the Philadelphia Contributionship for the Insurance of Houses from Loss by Fire—founded in 1752, and incorporated in 1768.[11]

International ties throughout the Atlantic world also gave Quaker merchants many advantages in the eighteenth century. "By virtue of their commercial, religious, personal and family contacts," historian Frederick Tolles writes, "the Philadelphia Quakers were in close touch with the entire north Atlantic world from Nova Scotia to Curacao and from Hamburg to Lisbon."[12]

In all of these ways, the Quakers provided an ethical and cultural environment which strongly supported industrial and capitalist development. Frederick Tolles writes from long acquaintance with the records of Quaker capitalists, "One is probably justified suggesting that in the conduct of business, the Quaker merchants were extremely cautious and prudent, meticulously accurate in details, and insistent upon others being so. It is not difficult to understand how men who exhibited these traits in their commercial dealings (no matter how generous and sympathetic as individuals and friends) should have acquired a reputation for driving a hard bargain."[13]

In England Quakers played a role far beyond their numbers in the industrial revolution. The great banking houses of England were those of Quakers. The largest private bank in Britain was developed by descendants of the great Quaker writer Robert Barclay. Lloyd's Bank was also owned by Quakers, together with

---

[10]"A Collection of Divers Letters," 15. vii.1682, ms. Weeks Colls/1936/8/6, FLL.

[11]N.S.B. Gras, "The Oldest American Business Corporation in Existence," Business Historical Society *Bulletin* 10 (1936), 21–24.

[12]Tolles, *Meeting House and Counting House,* 91.

[13]*Ibid.,* 95.

Attitudes toward time, work, and land among English Quakers and German Pietists appeared in the buildings that still stand on many Pennsylvania farms. Settlers in other cultural regions threw together temporary wooden buildings with the utmost economy of time and materials. On Pennsylvania farms, even the smallest outbuildings were built for the ages, with heavy stone walls and strong slate roofs. These structures combined simplicity of design with a concern for permanence that was very rare in other cultures of Anglo-America. Quakers and Pietists took a long view of their temporal condition. They husbanded their land, which today after three centuries of cultivation is still the most fertile acreage in the eastern United States. Their solid stone houses, barns and even small outbuildings still stand as monuments to a world view that was an important part of their folkways.

many financial houses in the City of London. Industrial enterprise in the north of England was also often organized and run
by Quakers.[14]

The same thing happened in the New World. Quakers founded
the first bank in British America, and made Philadelphia the most
important capital market in the New World until the emergence
of New York in the early nineteenth century. From the beginning,
the Delaware Valley also became a hive of industry—more so
than New England. Even before the founding of Pennsylvania,
the Quakers who settled in New Jersey created an extraordinarily
complex industrial economy within a few years of their arrival.
One observer reported in 1681, ". . . they have also coopers,
smiths, bricklayers, wheelwrights, plowrights and millwrights,
ship carpenters and other trades, which work upon what the
country produces for manufactories. . . . There are iron-houses,
and a Furnace and Forging Mill already set up in East-Jersey,
where they make iron."[15] Another wrote in 1698 that in the
Quaker communities of Burlington and Salem, "cloth workers
were making very good serges, druggets, crapes, camblets,
plushes and other woolen cloths. Entire families [are] engaged in
such manufactures, using wool and linen of their own raising."[16]
Both the North Midlands of England and the middle colonies of
Pennsylvania and New Jersey became the industrial heartlands of
their nations.

❧ Delaware Time Ways:
The Quaker Idea of "Redeeming the Time"

Closely related to these attitudes toward work were Quaker ways
of thinking about time. In place of the Puritan idea of "improving
the time," and the Anglican notion of "killing the time," the
Quakers thought in terms of "redeeming the time." This concept
of temporal redemption had a complex meaning. Fundamentally,
Quakers tried to purge time of sin and corruption. They also
sought to raise time above the world.[1]

[14]Pratt, "English Quakers in the First Industrial Revolution."
[15]"Present State of the Colony of West Jersey," in Myers, ed., *Narratives of Early Pennsylvania*, 191–95.
[16]Weiss, *Life in Early New Jersey*, 21.
[1]Winton Solberg, *Redeem the Time: The Puritan Sabbath in Early America* (Cambridge, 1977), 231.

The Quaker idea of "redeeming the time" began with a reform in the way that time was reckoned. One of the distinguishing features of the Society of Friends was the special way in which it recorded the passing of the months and days. Quakers abolished the ancient calendar of the Christian West, and adopted a new system which was carefully purged of every vestige of what they regarded as pagan corruption. The traditional names of months and days were abolished as "needless" and "unscriptual." In Quaker calendars (after the Gregorian reform was adopted), January became merely "First Month," and December was simply "Twelfth Month."[2] The week began not with an Anglican Sunday or a Puritan Sabbath but a Quaker "First Day," and it ended on "Seventh Day." In Quaker diaries and letters, events were dated with the utmost simplicity by this method. "Eleventh of eleventh month, 1758, this day I set out," wrote John Woolman, in a typical passage.[3]

During the seventeenth century, these customs had been kept by many sects of Christians, including English Puritans, who disliked the pagan origin of the calendar and found a warrant for their numbering system in the Book of Genesis.[4] But this custom of numbering rather than naming the months and days took root specially among the Quakers. For many years after the founding, court records and other public documents in Pennsylvania and West Jersey continued to be dated in this manner.[5]

In company with other groups of radical Christians, including the Puritans in New England, Quakers also abolished many religious holidays. They did so partly because these celebrations seemed corrupt and "needless" to them, and also for a deeper reason. "All days are alike holy in the sight of God," Robert Barclay declared. William Penn agreed, ". . . we utterly renounce all special and moral Holiness of Times and Days."[6]

Quakers also condemned traditional English folk festivals such as May Day, which they regarded as a corrupt and pagan event, inconsistent with "Truth." Even Christmas was excised from the Quaker calendar, as it had been by the Puritans. The Leeds meet-

---

[2]Before the adoption of the Gregorian Calendar by Parliament in 1752, the first day of the year was Lady Day, March 25, and the Quakers' "First Month" was March.

[3]Moulton, ed., *Woolman Journal*, 94.

[4]George Fox argued that the number-system was the manner in which "they were given forth and called by God from the beginning," in the book of Genesis. See Bauman, *Let Your Words Be Few*, 44.

[5]Many examples appear in the *Chester County Court Records*.

[6]Solberg, *Redeem the Time*, 231.

ing, for example, urged its members in 1702 not to keep Christmas as a family holiday:

> Friends of this meeting having under their serious consideration
> of days and times set up in the times of darkness and ignorance,
> which since we were a people we have born testimony against; but
> whereas some amongst us have not been so cleare in their testi-
> mony against the observation thereof as they ought: Therefore in
> the love of god and zeal for the Truth we advise all friends of our
> meeting that they be zealous in their testimony against the holding
> up of such days. And that they keep their servants at work, as also
> they do not go themselves nor suffer their servants to visit their
> relations at such times.[7]

The redemption of time had yet another meaning. Like the Puritans, Quakers were deeply interested in making the best use of time, which they regarded as a precious and perishable gift. They marveled at the ways in which other people squandered time. William Penn's writings included many disquisitions on the value of time. On one occasion, he wrote:

> There is nothing of which we are apt to be so lavish as of time, and
> about which we ought to be more solicitous, since without it we
> can do nothing in this world. Time is what we want most, but what,
> alas, we use worst, and for which God will certainly most strictly
> reckon with us when time shall be no more.[8]

On another occasion he argued:

> What would such be at? What would they do? And what would they
> have? They that have trades have not time enough to do the half
> of what hath been recommended. And as for those who have noth-
> ing to do, and indeed do nothing (which is worse) but sin (which
> is worst of all), here is variety of pleasant, of profitable, nay, of
> very honorable employments and diversions for them. Such can
> with great delight sit at a play, a ball, a masque, at cards, dice, etc.,
> drinking, reveling, feasting, and the like, an entire day; yes, turn
> night into day and invert the very order of the creation to humor
> their lusts. And were it not for eating and sleeping, it would be
> past a doubt whether they would ever find time to cease from
> those vain and sinful pastimes till the hasty calls of death should
> summon their appearance in another world. Yet do they think it
> intolerable and not possible for any to sit so long at a profitable
> or heavenly exercise?[9]

---

[7]*Leeds Friends Minute Book*, 23 Dec. 1702, 80.

[8]Penn, *Some Fruits of Solitude* (1693), Tolles and Alderfer, eds., *The Witness of William Penn*, 166.

[9]Penn, *No Cross, No Crown*, 57.

Like the Puritans, the Quakers tended to seek precision in their reckoning of clock time. In the inventory of Edward Astell, a Cheshire Quaker who died in 1680, the most valuable item of personal property was a "brass clock" worth two pounds ten shillings—twice the total value of his plate.[10] From as early as 1670, Quakers in the Pennines were making wooden clocks for households unable to afford any other instrument.[11]

More than their neighbors, the Quakers were morning people. They carefully organized their daily routines and kept schedules which contrasted sharply with the time ways of Virginia gentlemen. Edward Shippen in 1754 described the temporal routine of his household as follows:

> My son Jo [Joseph Shippen] and myself rise every morning at about Sun rising, having prepared over night some dry hickory for a good fire—we then sit close to our business til close to 9 o'clock and we find that we can do more by that time than in all the rest of the day. . . .
>
> We eat so moderately, without tasting a drop of liquor, that the whole day seems like a long morning to us. . . .
>
> That we may be sufficiently refreshed with sleep, we have agreed upon ten o'clock at night for going to bed and so after eating a light supper and drinking a little wine we lay ourselves down with light stomachs, cool heads and quiet consciences.[12]

This Quaker idea of a routine which made "the whole day seem like a long morning" would have filled many an English gentleman with horror.

In some of these temporal attitudes, Quakers and Puritans were very much alike. But there were also important differences between the two Protestant denominations. Quakers were at special pains to avoid what they called the idolatry of time. It was not a Quaker who said that "Time is Money," but the Boston-born son of New England Puritans. To become totally absorbed in the affairs of the world was for a Quaker to lose sight of the main thing. They often reminded themselves of "the uncertainty of temporal things."[13]

They did not believe that one should devote every possible minute to one's calling. A Quaker naturalist named John Rutty often

[10]Hodson, *Cheshire, 1660–1780,* 81.

[11]M. L. Baumber, *A Pennine Community on the Eve of the Industrial Revolution: Keighly and Hawworth between 1660 and 1740* (Keighly, n.d.), 89.

[12]Edward Shippen of Lancaster to C. J. Edward Shippen, 20 March 1754, *PMHB* 30 (1906), 85–90.

[13]Moulton, ed., *Woolman Journal,* 101.

upbraided himself in his diary for devoting too much time to his work. One day he wrote: "Instituted an hour's retirement every evening, as a check to the inordinate study of nature."[14]

Quaker aphorisms also generally condemned haste. William Penn's proverbs had a distinctly different tone from those of Poor Richard:

> Have a care therefore where there is more sail than ballast.

> It were happy if we studied nature more in natural things. . . . Let us begin where she begins, go her pace, and close always where she ends.

> Be not rash, but firm and resigned.

> Busyness is not our Business.

> Choose God's Trades before men's.

> So soon as you wake, retire your mind into a pure silence, from all thoughts and ideas of worldly things.[15]

Time, for Quaker moralists, was too important to be squandered on haste. The American Quaker John Woolman, on a visit to England, was shocked by the obsession with speed which he observed in that society:

> Stagecoaches frequently go upwards of one hundred miles in twenty-four hours; and I have heard Friends say in several places that it is common for horses to be killed with hard driving. . . . Some boys who ride long stages suffer greatly in winter nights, and at several places I have heard of their being frozen to death. So great is the hurry in the spirit of this world, that in aiming to do business quickly and to gain wealth the creation at this day doth loudly groan.[16]

Quakers took a longer view of their temporal condition. They were deeply conscious of their place in the continuum of generations, and described themselves as "trustees" of the world.

> Do we feel an affectionate regard to posterity? And are we employed to promote their happiness? Do our minds, in things outward, look beyond our own dissolution? And are we contriving for the prosperity of our children after us? Let us then, like wise builders, lay the foundation deep. . . .[17]

[14]Brinton, *Quaker Journals*, 73.
[15]*Ibid.*, 180–202.
[16]Moulton, ed., *Woolman Journal*, 183.
[17]*Ibid.*, 101.

The time ways of the Quakers were closely linked to their faith, and to the forms of a culture which they planted in the New World. The rhythms of life among Friends in the Delaware Valley differed from those of Massachusetts Puritans and Virginia Anglicans, but were similar to the time ways of England's North Midlands.

A leading example was the season of marriage. In the seventeenth century, every Western culture had its "marrying time," which was deeply embedded in its temporal folkways. In New England, as we have seen, the season of marriage showed a single peak in the late fall and winter—much as in East Anglia and the south of England. But the Quakers came in large numbers from the North Midlands, where the pattern of marriage had long been different, with two peak periods in the spring as well as the fall.[18] This Midland pattern was transplanted to the Delaware Valley, where the marriage cycle also became bimodal, with two high seasons from March to May and September to November.[19]

Other differences in Delaware time ways appeared in the conception cycle. In the households of New Jersey Quakers, fertility varied less through the year than among Virginia Anglicans or New England Puritans. Magnitudes of monthly variance in conceptions (and probably in coitus) were much lower than in other cultures, with only a vestigial trace of the spring peak and summer nadir which appeared throughout Christian Europe. In the jargon of social science, Quakers "deseasonalized" fertility

[18]Ann Kussmaul, "Time and Space, Hoofs and Grain: The Seasonality of Marriage in England," *JIH* 15 (1985), 775–79.

[19]R. V. Wells discovered this bimodal pattern in the season of marriage among Quakers of Rahway, Plainfield and Chesterfield, New Jersey:

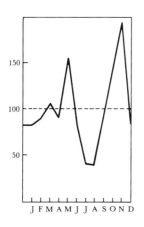

Month	Index of Marriages	Index of Conceptions
January	81.7	96.9
February	89.1	89.0
March	106.0	88.4
April	89.0	117.5
May	155.0	114.9
June	82.3	102.3
July	41.2	105.7
August	40.6	93.9
September	90.8	77.2
October	147.0	99.2
November	194.9	111.7
December	82.3	103.3
Total	1199.9	1200.0
	(n = 447)	(n = 1,542)

Source: R. V. Wells, "A Demographic Analysis of Some Middle Colony Quaker Families of the Eighteenth Century" (thesis, Princeton, 1969), 66, 99.

before other people. This pattern was connected to Quaker attitudes toward sex within marriage: particularly to sexual asceticism and to their exceptionally early adoption of fertility control.
Here again, the Quakers differed from their neighbors to the
north and south.

❧ Delaware Wealth Ways: Quaker Ideas of the Material Order

The wealth ways of the Quakers revealed a deep irony in their
system of social values. On the one hand, these good people had
an abiding belief in spiritual equality. On the other, their ideals
and institutions slowly created a system of material inequality
which was increasingly at war with their own intentions.

Throughout the Quaker colonies, land was distributed in a
manner very different from that of Massachusetts and Virginia.
In Pennsylvania and Delaware, William Penn's land policy was
meant to serve two purposes. The first was to provide a source of
capital for the founding of his colony—even a "holy experiment"
needed a matcrial base. The second purpose was to create a rural
society of independent farming families without great extremes
of wealth or poverty. Despite many difficulties and defeats along
the way, Penn succeeded remarkably in that design.[1]

To capitalize his colony, William Penn hoped to sell land in
large blocks of 5,000 or 10,000 acres to rich English buyers. Most
of these tracts came with strings attached. Residence was normally required for continued possession. Absentee owners were
compelled to subdivide their tracts into smaller holdings for individual settlers. A proprietary Land Office and a Board of Property were made responsible for managing the system.

Between 1681 and 1685, Penn actually sold about 715,000
acres to 589 "First Purchasers," many of whom were affluent
Quakers in London and Bristol. Perhaps half of these buyers did
not come to America, and a large number of purchases were forfeited for nonpayment or nonresidence.[2] Many tracts were subdivided among "underpurchasers" who actually occupied the

[1]Two exceptionally good studies of land policy in Pennsylvania appear in Edwin Bronner,
William Penn's "Holy Experiment," 39–60, and in James T. Lemon, *The Best Poor Man's Country:
A Geographical Study of Early Southeastern Pennsylvania* (Baltimore, 1972).

[2]"The First Purchasers of Pennsylvania, 1681–1685," *Papers of William Penn,* II, 630–64.

land. Most holdings in Pennsylvania were between 100 and 500 acres. The average was about 250 acres—twice as large as town grants to individual families in Massachusetts, but less than half the average size of land patents in Virginia during the seventeenth century.[3]

William Penn's system proved to be a highly efficient way of promoting settlement. As early as the year 1715, it was reported that no unsettled land remained within fifty miles of Philadelphia. The proprietor and his agents distributed their land very rapidly, at the same time that they prevented the growth of a small landowning oligarchy. The proprietor explained:

> The regulation of the country being a family to each five hundred acres. . . . many that had right to the land were at first covetous to have their whole quantity without regard to this way of settlement, tho' by such wilderness vacancies they had ruined the country, and then our interest of course. I had in my view, society, assistance, busy commerce, instruction of youth, government of people's manners, conveniency of religious assembling, encouragement of mechanicks, distinct and beaten roads, and it has answered in all those respects, I think, to an universal content.[4]

For a long period, the distribution of wealth in the Delaware Valley continued to be more egalitarian than any other region of British America. Tax lists in rural Chester County showed that the richest 10 percent held only 23.8 percent of assessed taxable wealth in 1693—an unusually small share by comparison with other cultures. In the Chesapeake colonies, as we have seen, the richest 10 percent held more than two-thirds of the taxable wealth.[5]

The pattern of wealth-holding was not perfectly uniform throughout the Delaware Valley. Wealth was more concentrated in urban Philadelphia than in rural Chester County. But even the metropolis of the Delaware Valley was remarkably egalitarian by comparison with other seaport cities in the American colonies. The richest 10 percent held only 36 percent of the wealth in Philadelphia during the late seventeenth century, according to the evidence of probate records. In Boston, by comparison, the top

---

[3]Lemon, *Best Poor Man's Country*, 65; John R. Stilgoe, *Common Landscape of America, 1580 to 1845* (New Haven, 1982), 79.

[4]Penn, "A Further Account of Pennsylvania," in Myers, ed., *Narratives of Pennsylvania*, 263.

[5]James T. Lemon and Gary B. Nash, "The Distribution of Wealth in Eighteenth Century America," *JSH* 2 (1968), 1–24; for similar patterns of wealth distribution in Germantown, Pa., see Wolf, *Urban Village*, 108–9, 120–24.

10 percent owned more than half of the assets in the town. In Virginia, they possessed two-thirds or more.[6]

This pattern of wealth distribution was maintained in part by inheritance customs. In cases of intestacy, the laws of West Jersey and Pennsylvania at first followed the biblical pattern of double partible inheritance, widows' thirds, and small shares for prodigal children. But in subsequent statutes, the double partible rule yielded to the principle of equal shares for all children. This law of intestacy in the Quaker colonies conformed to actual practices which were more egalitarian than in New England or the Chesapeake. The norm in Quaker families was equal division of the estate—not only between the first-born son and his brothers but also (for personal property) between brothers and sisters. By and

[6]Patterns of wealth distribution in tax assessments and inventories of estates were as follows, for urban Philadelphia and rural Chester County from 1684 to 1750.

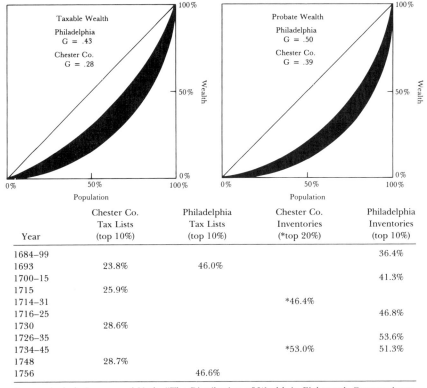

Year	Chester Co. Tax Lists (top 10%)	Philadelphia Tax Lists (top 10%)	Chester Co. Inventories (*top 20%)	Philadelphia Inventories (top 10%)
1684–99				36.4%
1693	23.8%	46.0%		
1700–15				41.3%
1715	25.9%			
1714–31			*46.4%	
1716–25				46.8%
1730	28.6%			
1726–35				53.6%
1734–45			*53.0%	51.3%
1748	28.7%			
1756		46.6%		

Sources include Lemon and Nash, "The Distribution of Wealth in Eighteenth Century America"; G. B. Nash, "Urban Wealth and Poverty in Pre-Revolutionary America," *JIH* 6 (1976), 545–84; G. B. Nash, "Poverty and Poor Relief in Pre-Revolutionary Philadelphia, *WMQ3* 33 (1976), 3–30; Duane Ball, "Population and Wealth in Pennsylvania," *JIH* 6 (1976), 545.

large, daughters did not inherit land. But they were given "portions" at marriage and a share of the personal estate.[7]

Similar patterns also appeared in the wills of English Quakers. Thus, Dionnis Davy, a Quaker of Steeton, Yorkshire, left one-third of his property to his wife Alice, and the rest he "did give unto his children equally."[8] There were many variations. Other Quakers assigned small landholdings to a single heir, but divided their personal estate equally; James Sanderlands of Cheshire in 1692 left his house to his wife, his lands to a son, and his personal estate to be equally divided among all his sons and daughters.[9] Quakers often remembered their grandchildren, who shared equally in small gifts of esteem. John Hart of Nottingham in 1712 left equal legacies to his grandchildren to be paid when they reached the age of twenty-four; if any died, the remaining share was to be divided equally among the survivors.[10] Edmund Gibson left all his estate to "Hannah my loving wife," for her lifetime, and then to be sold and the proceeds divided equally among all grandchildren, both male and female.[11] There were many other arrangements: sometimes a surviving son received all real estate, and a surviving daughter the personal estate.[12] Quakers who owned small rural properties would leave the farm to one child with instructions that payments must be made to other children.[13]

While inheritance practices among English Quakers varied in detail from one family to another, there were also strong general trends. First, widows usually received their "third" (sometimes adjusted to a quarter or a half) "according to the custom," as many documents noted. Second, primogeniture was uncommon and partible inheritance was the general rule. Third, daughters normally received their inheritance in forms other than land. Fourth, grandchildren were often remembered in at least token ways. This pattern developed not merely from Quaker beliefs but from a fusion of those religious ideas with inheritance customs in the North Midlands of England. Among families of middling and lower ranks throughout that region, partible inheritance had long

---

[7]George Staughton et al., *Charter to William Penn, and Laws of the Province of Pennsylvania, Passed between the Years 1682 and 1700 . . .* (Harrisburg, 1879).

[8]Moore, *Case of Lydia Davy*.

[9]Will of James Sanderlands, 6 April 1692, ms. 546/253/viii, CHESRO.

[10]Will of John Hart, Nottingham, 23 Oct. 1712, ms. PRNW, NOTTRO.

[11]John Somervell, *Some Westmorland Wills, 1686–1798* (Kendal, 1928), 80; this volume is a collection of wills drawn by Quakers of Kendal and the surrounding countryside.

[12]Will of Thomas Wilson, *ibid.*, 69.

[13]Will of Thomas Braithwaite, *ibid.*, 74.

been a common practice. To this tradition, Quakers added the extra weight of a religious imperative.[14]

In the New World, Quakers moved even farther away from primogeniture and closer to the partible ideal. One study finds that no fewer than 87 percent of English and Welsh Quaker families in Pennsylvania with more than one son practiced simple partible inheritance.[15]

Quakers in both England and America deliberately used inheritance as an instrument of communal control over the young, specially in regard to the problem of outmarriage. Some meetings required members to disinherit children who wed nonbelievers, or at least to refuse to give marriage portions. Thus, the Cheshire Quarterly Meeting agreed:

> If any friends child marry any that's no friend the parents of such child shall not communicate by way of a portion unto such without the advice and consent of the Quarterly Meeting, or whom they shall depute excepting at their decease at which time the said parents are at liberty to do as they shall see meet.[16]

American Friends also did not hesitate to disinherit children who left the fold. The affluent Quaker William Wynne, for example, ordered that half of his large personal estate should go to his wife, and that the other half should be divided equally among all his children except his daughter Tabitha Wynne who had "fallen away from friends." Tabitha received only a token legacy of fifty shillings; her brothers and sisters each got more than fifty pounds. In 1748, an observer noted that disinheritance for religious reasons was very common among Quaker families in the Delaware Valley.[17]

The execution of a will was a social event that involved many more people than the testator alone. Quakers often consulted some learned Friend in the neighborhood, who helped them to prepare the document and to shape its contents. John Woolman remembered "an ancient man of good esteem in the neighborhood who came to my house to get his will written." This neighbor owned slaves, and Woolman refused to draw up the will until their freedom was assured.[18]

---

[14]Cunliffe Shaw, "The Townfields of Lancashire," *HSLCT* 114 (1962).

[15]This differed from Anglican families who "tended to invest in the family line rather than individual children." See Levy, "The Birth of the 'Modern Family' in Early America," 44, 37.

[16]Cheshire Quarterly Mens Meeting Records, 10.vii.1689, ms. EFC 1/1/ CHESRO.

[17]G. H. Jenkins, "Thomas Wynne," ms. 61, FLL.

[18]Moulton, ed., *Woolman Journal*, 50–51.

Quaker wills often included charitable bequests. This occurred in small estates as well as large ones. Philanthropy was an important part of this culture—more so than in New England or Virginia. In all of these various ways, the inheritance customs of Quakers in the Delaware Valley were an instrument of equality.

As time passed, the pattern of wealth distribution in the Delaware Valley began to change, moving slowly in the direction of greater inequality. The trend was very gradual until after 1750. In some rural areas of the Delaware Valley it did not begin until the nineteenth century; a few remote counties actually shifted in the opposite direction. But in most parts of the Delaware Valley, inequality of material condition increased after 1750.

Tenancy also tended to increase throughout the Delaware Valley after the mid-eighteenth century. Comparatively few tenants had lived in that region during the first and second generations. But by 1760, perhaps one-third of families in older counties of Pennsylvania did not own the land they farmed.[19] In cultural terms, however, the institution of tenancy was not the same in the Delaware Valley as in the Chesapeake colonies. Rhoda Barber remembered that tenancy was not a permanent but a transitional status in the Quaker colonies. She wrote:

> The people who had served a time with the owner of the land or had been employed to work for them seemed to claim a kind of patronage from their master. They seldom left the place but contrived to get a little dwelling in the neighborhood, often on the land of their former master. They had a little garden and potato patch, their rent was so many day's work in harvest.[20]

Tenancy in Chester County rose to a peak circa 1760, then leveled off and declined until the War of Independence. This was so because land was easier of access for small holders in Pennsylvania than in the Chesapeake.[21]

Even so, the central tendency in the Delaware Valley was toward increasing inequality. Quaker moralists complained bitterly of this trend. John Woolman warned tirelessly against the concentration of riches, and argued that "Large possessions in the hands of selfish men have a bad tendency, for by their means too small a number of people are employed in things useful . . .

---

[19]Various estimates appear in Main, *Social Structure of Revolutionary America,* 180; Lemon, *Best Poor Man's Country,* 94; Lucy Simler, "Tenancy in Colonial Pennsylvania: The Case of Chester County," *WMQ3* (1986), 542–69.

[20]Rhoda Barber, Journal, HSP.

[21]Simler, "Tenancy in Colonial Pennsylvania," 555.

while others would want business to earn their bread, were not
employments invented which, having no real use, serve only to
please the vain mind."[22] Joshua Evans wrote angrily of prosperous Haverford and Merion, "Here they build large farms but little meeting houses."[23]

Ironically, Quakers such as Joshua Evans and John Woolman
were themselves the principal beneficiaries of the trend which
they condemned. The leading victims were immigrants who
arrived at a later date. At the bottom of society in the Delaware
Valley a proletariat slowly began to form—a growing underclass
of very poor people.[24]

The Quakers always showed much solicitude for the poor.
Probably no other English culture was so strongly committed to
philanthropy. From the start, charity for the poor had been a
deep concern of the Society of Friends. This sect did more to
relieve poverty in proportion to their numbers than did their
more affluent Anglican and Calvinist neighbors. In England,
monthly meetings maintained a "publick stock" for the support
of those in need, and collections were also taken for a "national
stock" which was maintained by the London yearly meeting.
Women's meetings were specially active in this work. Each month,
every member was expected to pay something, if only a penny or
two. Among the Quakers, charity became an engrained cultural
habit.[25]

Charity was always an important part of their world, perhaps
because so many of them had been poor themselves. Studies of
American philanthropy repeatedly find that the poor give a larger
proportion of their assets to charity than do the rich. Among
Friends, charity also arose from their exceptionally strong sense
of responsibility toward other "creatures." Most Quaker charity
in the seventeenth and eighteenth centuries went to indigent
Friends. But as early as 1683, the Philadelphia meeting was
actively relieving the needs of non-Quakers.[26] Where possible, an
attempt was made to put people to work rather than merely to
give them alms. The Chesterfield monthly women's meeting in
1698, for example, invited the men's meeting to "assist them in

---

[22]Woolman, "A Plea for the Poor," in Moulton, ed., *Woolman Journal*, 238–39.
[23]Joshua Evans Diary, 4.x.1796–29.vi.1798, 81, SWAR.
[24]Tolles, *Meeting House and Counting House*, 109–143.
[25]Chester Quarterly Meeting Records, 3.iv.1684, ms. EFC 1/1 CHESRO; Break Meeting,
1701, ms. Q59, NOTTRO.
[26]James, *A People Among Peoples*, 40.

raising some money to buy some tow . . . to set some poor friends to work so they may not be burdensome to friends as they have been." But among Quakers there was an exceptionally strong sympathy for the unfortunate, and a determination to relieve their needs.[27]

Here was yet another irony. The Quakers created a social system in Pennsylvania which gave them increasing opportunity to exercise their charitable impulses. They became deeply concerned about a class of paupers which their own values and institutions had helped to create. Some Quakers understood this system very well. John Woolman observed that "the money which the wealthy receive from the poor, who do more than a proper share in raising it, is frequently paid to other poor people."[28]

This intricate cultural system of wealth and poverty was constructed in the Delaware Valley during the first decade of settlement. It survives to this day.

❧ Delaware Rank Ways:
Stratification Within a Single Order

On the subject of property, Quakers tended to be highly conventional and even conservative. But on questions of social rank, they were radical and revolutionary. In the early stages of this movement, Quaker pronouncements about rank sent a thrill of horror through the possessing classes. "Woe unto you that are called *Lords, Ladies, Knights, Gentlemen, and Gentlewomen* . . . ," English Quaker James Parnell warned in 1655, "Woe unto you . . . who are called *Mister* and *Sir* and *Mistress*. . . . Because of your much earth, which by fraud, deceit and oppression you have gotten together, you are exalted above your fellow-creatures, and grind the faces of the poore. And they are as slaves under you, and must labour and toyle under you, and you must live at ease."[1]

In the second generation of Quakerism, the rhetoric became more muted, but underlying attitudes remained the same. Even a Quaker as high-born as William Penn published gentle polemics

---

[27]Chesterfield Women's Meeting Records, 1698, ms. Q62b, NOTTRO.
[28]Woolman, "A Plea for the Poor," 225.
[1]James Parnell, "The Trumpet of the Lord," [1655] in *A Collection of the Several Writings of James Parnell* (London, 1675), 28–29; Barbour, *The Quakers in Puritan England*, 171.

against the idea of social orders in general and aristocracy in particular. "What a podder [pother] has this noble blood made in the world . . . ," he declared, "methinks nothing of man's folly has less show of reason to palliate it."[2]

William Penn detested distinctions of "blood" and "birth." He insisted that England's structure of hereditary social orders was an organized absurdity, and a contradiction in terms. He argued:

> Since virtue comes not by generation, I neither am the better nor the worse for my forefather, to be sure. . . . To be descended of wealth and titles fills no man's head with brains nor heart with truth. . . .
>
> Oh, says the person of blood, it was never a good world since we have had so many upstart gentlemen. But what should those have said of that man's ancestor when he first started up into the knowledge of the world? For he, and all men and families, aye, and all states and kingdoms too have had their upstarts, that is, their beginnings. . . .[3]

Deep as was his disdain for aristocracy, William Penn reserved his strongest contempt for plutocracy, "Never esteem any man or thyself the more for money," he wrote, "nor think the meaner of thyself or another for want of it."[4]

But Penn was no egalitarian. He believed that a society should be run by an aristocracy of Christian virtue. "Pray let nobility and virtue keep company, for they are the nearest of kin," he wrote.[5] Most of all, he believed that every individual should be judged for what he was and did. "A man, like a watch, is to be valued for his goings," he declared.[6]

Many Quakers shared Penn's thinking on social rank. They expressed their hostility to England's system of social orders most eloquently not in words but acts. The ritual displays of social deference required in Anglican Virginia were actively discouraged in the Delaware Valley. Old customs such as "capping" and "kneeing" were condemned by Quakers. Many steadfastly refused to give "hat honor" to those of high social rank. In place of bowing, curtseying, scraping, and uncovering, Quakers substi-

---

[2]Penn, *No Cross, No Crown*, 50.
[3]*Ibid.*, 51.
[4]*Ibid.*
[5]*Ibid.*
[6]Penn, *Some Fruits of Solitude*, 180.

tuted the ritual of the universal handshake—a decency which Friends extended to everyone—even their social superiors.[7]

In England, the stubborn refusal of the Quakers to give "hat honor" was punished with a brutal force which tells us that these rituals had deep meaning in the seventeenth century. In 1655, for example, the high sheriff of Lancashire, John Parker, routinely bullied and beat Quakers who did not bare their heads to him. While out riding one day, Sheriff Parker met a Quaker tenant named James Smithson who refused to remove his hat.

"Knowest then me not?" the sheriff demanded.

"I know thee," the Quaker replied.

"Who am I?"

"Thou art my Landlord."

"Am I so!" the sheriff said. "But I will teach thee."

The Sheriff swung his heavy rod and struck James Smithson full in the head. Then he pulled off the Quaker's hat, and "did continue striking him on the head till his rod broke off so short that he cast away what was left of it and stroke him with his hands while he pleased."

A little later Friend Smithson met the sheriff again, and once more refused to give hat honor. "Is there no honor belongs to a landlord?" the sheriff asked plaintively.

"I honor thee with my rent," Smithson replied, "other honor I have not for thee."

Once again the sheriff "struck him in the head with a rod, and pushed off his hat and did strike him in the head and face til the blood came."[8]

"Hat honor" was merely one of many rituals of subordination which Quakers denied to their social superiors. Another was the use of the second person plural, the pronoun "you," which in many European languages implied deference. When Quakers used "thee" and "thou" in place of "you" they sometimes set off exceptionally violent reactions. A Quaker servant named Richard Davies remembered that his master did not much mind, but his mistress was infuriated:

> When I gave it [thee and thou] to my mistress, she took a stick and gave me such a blow upon my bare head, that it made it swell and sore for a considerable time; she was so disturbed at it, that she

[7]Bauman, *Let Your Words Be Few*, 45.
[8]Marsden Monthly Meeting Records, 1655, ms. FRM 1/39, LANCRO.

swore she would kill me, though she would be hanged for me; the enemy so possessed her, that she was quite out of order; though beforetime she seldom, if ever, gave me an angry word.[9]

Quakers also refused to use social titles. They did not call any mortal "master," "mister," "sir," or "ma'am." They would not address titled aristocrats as "my Lord," for they recognized only one Lord. They disdained to call dukes "Your Grace," for they believed that England's ducal families were deficient in the only grace that mattered. They also resisted calling gentlemen and high officeholders "your honor," or "your excellency." In America, as in England, they insisted that "all these titles and styles of honor are to be rejected by Christians because they are to seek the honor that comes from above, not the honor that comes from below."[10] Everyone was addressed simply as "Friend" without distinctions of age, estate, gender, office or rank.

Quakers also objected to other ranking customs—in particular to the fulsome language of courtesy which flourished in the seventeenth century. A famous example was set in 1656 by George Fox while a prisoner at Launceston Castle. One morning, while taking his exercise on the castle green, the great Quaker was greeted by his jailor, an English gentleman named Major Ceely, who swept off his hat and said civilly: "How do you do, Mr. Fox? Your servant, Sir." This courtesy brought a rude reply. "Major Ceely," said the Quaker, "take heed of hypocrisy and a rotten heart, for when came I to be thy master and thee my servant? Do servants use to cast their masters in prison?"[11]

The Quakers found many reasons for condemning these courtesies—because they were literally false, lying, deceitful, hypocritical; because they rewarded evil and made a ceremony of sin; because they gave attention to empty honors; and because they distracted people from important distinctions that were not of this world.[12]

Quakers made this challenge in a generation which raised these rituals of social inequality to their highest level. Historians of

---

[9]Richard Davies, *An Account of . . . Richard Davies* (Philadelphia, 1832), quoted in Bauman, *Let Your Words Be Few*, 51.

[10]Frost, *Quaker Family*, 192; Staughton George et al., *Charter to William Penn and Laws of the Province of Pennsylvania* (Harrisburg, 1896), 111.

[11]Bauman, *Let Your Words Be Few*, 47.

[12]*Ibid.*

manners believe that in no other period did elites demand so rigorous an etiquette of inequality as in the sixteenth and seventeenth centuries.[13]

In the Delaware Valley, Quaker rank ways rapidly became part of an American regional culture, and set it apart from both New England and the Chesapeake colonies. In the words of historian Gary Nash, traditional "patterns of elitism, hierarchy and deference had tended to decay" in the early decades of Pennsylvania's history.[14] In terms of the England's hereditary ranking system, the Quaker ideal was a society with a single order. In their own terms, they did not seek to create a world of social equality, but rather to maintain a new system of moral distinctions in which men and women were ranked according to virtue and merit.

◆ The Delaware Comity:
Patterns of Migration, Settlement and Association

On the day after William Penn arrived in Pennsylvania, he called his colonists together, and solemnly pledged to protect their full "spiritual and temporal rights." In return, he asked only two things. The first was that they should try to stay sober. The second was that they should keep up a "loving neighborhood" with one another.[1]

This notion of "loving neighborhood" was an ideal of high importance in the Delaware Valley. It became the cultural cement of a special type of comity which combined Quaker ideas and North Midland traditions. This Delaware comity differed from those of New England and the Chesapeake in many ways—in patterns of settlement, migration, association and social bonding.

The ideal settlement in the Delaware Valley was one where every family lived separately upon its farmstead, but was not entirely isolated from others. Houses were to be built in small clusters which became the nuclei of rural neighborhoods—a pattern still to be seen throughout the Pennsylvania countryside.

---

[13]Joan Wildeblood and Peter Brinson, *The Polite World: A Guide to English Manners and Deportment from the Thirteenth to the Nineteenth Century* (Oxford, 1965).

[14]Nash, *Quakers and Politics*, 327.

[1]Philip Ford, *A Vindication of William Penn* (London, 1683); Jean R. Soderlund, ed., *William Penn and the Founding of Pennsylvania* (Philadelphia, 1983), 188.

This form of settlement had long existed in the north of England—a pattern equally distinct from the town life of East Anglia and the manorial villages of Wessex. Nucleated towns were comparatively rare in the North Midlands. So also were landed estates with a great house surrounded by a cluster of close-built cottages. The economy of the northern counties required smaller units and more open settlements.[2]

In America, this North Midland pattern was modified and reinforced by Quaker ideals. William Penn intended that homesteads should be grouped in "townships" of five or ten "for near neighborhood." The houses were to be close-built on lots of ten acres, and surrounded by individual farmlands of 450 acres each. The purpose was to combine material autonomy with spiritual community. "Before the doors of the houses," Penn explained, "lies the highway, and cross it every man's 450 acres . . . so that conveniency of neighborhood is made agreeable with that of the land."[3] Near the center of each township, he ordered common meadows and pasturelands.

Penn's idealized townships were different in scale from New England towns, which tended to be at least six miles on a side and 20,000 acres in area—sometimes much larger. The townships of Pennsylvania were originally intended to cover only about 5,000 acres, and to include only about fifty people. They were not self-governing. The vision of the founder was a quiet open countryside dotted with small clusters of independent farms. By 1685, more than fifty of these little townships had actually been planted in Pennsylvania.

The proprietor's official policy received a mixed reception from his fellow Quakers. Most liked the idea of private property, fee simple tenure, moderate land grants of approximately the same size, and restriction of ownership to actual residents. But they did not favor nucleated farming towns, communal pastures or common meadows. Against the wishes of their Proprietor, the people of Pennsylvania proceeded to create their own pattern of land distribution: small farms scattered in clusters across the countryside without the common lands that Penn had wished to

---

[2]"In Yorkshire and Cumberland, the mainly pastoral economy and lower population levels required [sic] a much thinner scattering of market towns." Peter Clark and Paul Slack, *English Towns in Transition, 1500–1700* (Oxford, 1976), 18.

[3]Penn, "A Further Account of Pennsylvania," in Myers, ed., *Narratives of Pennsylvania*, 263.

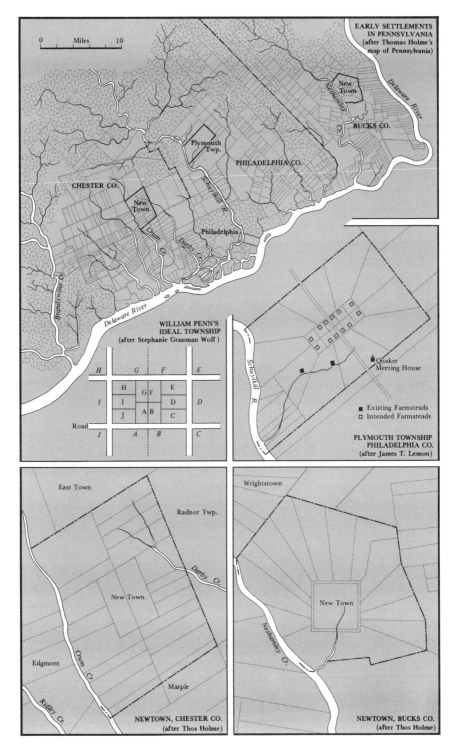

EARLY SETTLEMENTS
IN PENNSYLVANIA
(after Thomas Holme's
map of Pennsylvania)

Delaware River

New
Town

Neshaminy

BUCKS CO.

Plymouth
Twp.

PHILADELPHIA CO.

CHESTER CO.

New
Town

Schuylkill R.

Philadelphia

Crum Cr.

Darby Cr.

Brandywine Cr.

Delaware River

WILLIAM PENN'S
IDEAL TOWNSHIP
(after Stephanie Grauman Wolf)

H	G	F	E
	H	G	F	E	
I				D
	I	G	F	D	
	J	A	B	C	
Road				
J	A	B	C

Schuylkill R.

Quaker
Meeting House

■ Existing Farmsteads
□ Intended Farmsteads

PLYMOUTH TOWNSHIP
PHILADELPHIA CO.
(after James T. Lemon)

East Town

Radnor Twp.

Darby Cr.

New Town

Crum Cr.

Edgmont

Ridley Cr.

Marple

NEWTOWN, CHESTER CO.
(after Thos Holme)

Wrightstown

New Town

Neshaminy Cr.

NEWTOWN, BUCKS CO.
(after Thos Holme)

see. In the process, historian James T. Lemon observes that "the Quakers firmly established the pattern for all who followed in the eighteenth century, indeed well into the twentieth.[4]

Within a generation Penn's colonists had moved beyond the Delaware Valley into the interior of Pennsylvania where rolling hills and valleys followed one another like waves of the sea. Across this corrugated countryside, the steep and barren hillsides remained uninhabited. Many stand empty even to this day. Each fertile valley became a unit of settlement with a distinct cultural character. A case in point is Big Valley, a beautiful crescent of fertility near the present geographical center of Pennsylvania. Today Big Valley is Pennsylvania Dutch territory. The names on the mailboxes are Zook and Peachey and Hostetler. An eighteenth-century Swiss-German dialect is still spoken from one end of the valley to the other. North of Big Valley across Stone Mountain lies Nittany Valley, which has a very different culture. In the eighteenth century its settlers were Presbyterians and Anglicans who came mainly from the borderlands of North Britain. Today, the young people of Nittany Valley still unconsciously pronounce some of their vowels in the old north British way. Very few Quakers settled in either of these places but patterns of settlement in Big Valley and Nittany Valley were similar to those that English Friends had planted on the banks of the Delaware. This Pennsylvania pattern became typical of an entire American region.

A similar tendency also appeared in patterns of internal migration. A distinctive "migration regime" was introduced to the Delaware Valley by English Quakers. Rates of geographic mobility were higher in this region than in Massachusetts or even Virginia. Most of this incessant movement consisted of local, short-distance migration.[5]

Here again, the Delaware Valley resembled England's North Midlands. Studies of migration in England do not easily admit of controlled comparison with America. But comparable evidence exists for the parish of Clayworth (Nottinghamshire) in the midland region which contributed so heavily to the peopling of Penn-

---

[4]Lemon, *Best Poor Man's Country*, 220.
[5]One study reports the following crude rates of persistence for adult males:

Place	Period	Annual	Decennial
Chester County, Pa.	1774–85	94%	38%
Lancaster County, Pa.	1771–82	95%	n.a.

Source: Lemon, *Best Poor Man's Country*, 74–75, 249.

sylvania. It is interesting to observe that rates of persistence in Clayworth were almost exactly the same as in Pennsylvania's Chester and Lancaster counties.[6]

These patterns of migration and settlement also supported a distinctive system of association. The comity in Pennsylvania was not as close or interactive as in New England, or as intense as the court days and county meetings of the Chesapeake colonies. Quaker meetings cautioned their members against "needless" socializing. The Morley women's meeting urged that "friends keep clear in needless visits to the World, or to one another, in their childbed or other times, in giving or receiving [visits] where there is no need."[7] The Cheshire quarterly meeting agreed:

> A question being put to this meeting whether frequenting christenings, gossipings, housebringings and such like festivals justifiable or allowable, the Answer is no, and the judgment of the meeting is that no such thing ought to be practised that if any friend be found in the practice thereof that care be taken speedily to deal with them.[8]

The diaries of individual Quakers showed similar attitudes. John Kelsall entered into his journal, circa 1700, "I could not endure to see people take too much liberty in talk, laughter and such like things."[9] In the same spirit, American Quaker Anne Cooper Whitall wrote:

> Converse as much as may be with God, with his holy Angels, with thy own conscience: and complain not for want of company. . . . Decline you may crowds and company, for frequent discourse, even of news or indifferent things, which happens upon such occasions, is sometimes destructive to virtue.[10]

---

[6]Laslett and Harrison report the following rates of persistence:

Place	Period	Annual	Decennial
Clayworth, Notts.	1676–88	95%	39%

These crude persistence rates were within one percentage point of those in Chester and Lancaster counties, Pa. See Peter Laslett, *Family Life and Illicit Love in Earlier Generations; Essays in Historical Sociology* (Cambridge, 1977), 79; This finding was first reported by Laslett and John Harrison, "Clayworth and Cogenhoe," in H. E. Bell and R. L. Ollard, eds., *Historical Essays Presented to David Ogg* (1963), 157–84; the evidence is taken from an extraordinary rector's book kept by William Sampson and published under the title of *Sparrows of the Spirit*, Harry Gill and Everard L. Guilford, eds. (London, 1961).

[7]Morley Womens Meeting, 4.vii.1706, ms. EFC 2/3/1, CHESRO.

[8]Cheshire Monthly Meeting, 1.vii.1686, ms EFC/1/1, CHESRO.

[9]John Kelsall Journal, n.d., [circa 1700], p. 35; ms. S/194, FLL.

[10]Anne Cooper Whitall Diary, 28.viii.1760, HAV.

Many Quakers were uncomfortable about "keeping company," even with other Friends.

Still, Penn's idea of "good neighborhood" was held in high esteem. "Useful" gatherings were encouraged. "Raisings" of meetinghouses and barns and homes were common among both English Quakers and German Pietists from an early date in the eighteenth century. These raisings were a classic form of "needful" association.[11]

Rhoda Barber also remembered from her youth in early eighteenth-century Pennsylvania the affection that existed among the Quaker families of her neighborhood:

> The place not being as closely settled as now people seemed more affectionate to each other. I well remember when a death anywhere in the neighborhood seemed to cast a gloom over all even if it was the lowest class, and some of every family must attend the funeral. The neighbors for many miles around all were known to each other. A person from a distance was easily recognized and excited curiosity to know who they were and from whence they came.[12]

The Quaker comity, as historian Sydney James has taught us, was conceived as a system of association for "a people among peoples"—that is, "an organized segment of the population which kept morality and good order in its own ranks, expected no special favor from the government, and thought other elements should do likewise." This pluralistic ideal came to be generally accepted throughout the Quaker colonies. It was not the product of ethnic expediency, but a highly principled idea, supported by strong moral imperatives.[13]

Local comities multiplied rapidly in Pennsylvania. The countryside, in consequence, took on an exceptionally open character. But the internal structure of each comity was tightly closed and strictly regulated. Reputation became all important in this system. For Quakers, a good reputation was a matter of "honor." Loss of honor created intense feelings of shame.

Quaker ideas of honorable behavior were far removed from what historian Bertram Wyatt-Brown calls "primal honor." They had nothing to do with the celebration of valor, or virility, or the

---

[11] For reference to a meetinghouse "raising," see John Bernard Diary, x.1775, HSP.

[12] Rhoda Barber, Journal, HSP.

[13] James, *A People Among Peoples*, 332–33.

exaltation of rank. Honor in that sense was the opposite of Quaker values.[14] But in another way Quakers were as deeply mindful of "honor" and "reputation" as others of their age. Thomas Mifflin was set to writing in his copybook about "the sense of honor, by which we regard the approbation of men, and are uneasy under censure."[15] Isaac Norris explained his hesitation in a business transaction by writing, "I can't tell if it would be accounted honorable if we should be concerned in shipping upon your order."[16]

A Quaker's honor was far removed from the code of chivalry that existed among Virginia gentlemen. It was also not the same as the contractual code that was kept by New England's specially elected saints. Instead it was a reputation for Christian love, peace, "good neighborhood," godliness, and doing good to others. As such, it became profoundly important to their comity. Joseph Oxley instructed his children:

> There is much beauty in beholding brethren and sisters living in love, endeavoring to help one another, as occasion may require . . . in so doing, my children, your peace will flow in upon you abundantly, and your reputation and honour will be renowned among men. The Lord will delight himself in you.[17]

In this culture, as in every other of the same era, "reputation and honor" were urgently important. When a Quaker lost honor, he was compelled to stand before his brethren and to "take shame upon himself," or be expelled from their association. The social operation of honor, reputation and shame was similar in some respects among Quakers, Puritans and Anglicans in the seventeenth and early eighteenth century. But the substance of these social ideas differed very much from one group to another.[18]

---

[14]Bertram Wyatt-Brown, *Southern Honor* (Oxford, 1982), 17, 75–78, 150–51.

[15]Thomas Mifflin, "Abridgement of Metaphysicks," 1759, HSP.

[16]Isaac Norris to Moses Gainsborough, 8 Oct. 1735, Norris Letterbook, HSP.

[17]Oxley, "Joseph's Offering to His Children," HSP.

[18]For an excellent discussion of the contrast between Pennsylvania Quakers and Virginia gentlemen on this point, see Wyatt-Brown, *Southern Honor,* 77.

Wyatt-Brown notes that "honor was not merely a noun but a verb in these cultures." Here again, Quakers were different from Virginia gentlemen. A young English Quaker named Thomas Ellwood wrote after his conversion in 1659 that "the honour due to parents did not consist in uncovering the head and bowing the body to them, but in ready obedience to their lawful commands, and in performing all needful services unto them." His Anglican father Thomas Ellwood had a very different idea of honor, and was so outraged by his son's argument that "the old man fell upon his son with both fists, 'plucked off the headgear,' and 'threw it away.'" *Ibid.*

In all of these many ways, the interplay of North Midland experiences, Quaker ideals and the values of a generation combined to create a very special comity in the Delaware colonies. The topography of Pennsylvania imposed its physical frame; North Midland experiences defined different orbits of association and levels of internal migration; Quaker beliefs contributed a pluralistic ideal of "a people among peoples," and also an austere conception of comity in which a special conception of honor, reputation and shame played a major role. Many of these characteristics persisted in midland America for many generations. Some survive even today.

❧ Delaware Order Ways: The Quaker Idea of Order as Peace

Quaker ideas of comity called into being a special conception of social order, which was defined not in terms of unity (as among Puritans) or of hierarchy (as by Anglicans) but in another way. Order, in their thinking, was a condition of social peace.

This notion did not exist among Quakers in the earliest stages of the movement. The first English Friends were not a people of peaceable disposition. Nor were their principles pacifistic. But in 1651 the Puritans locked George Fox in a dungeon for refusing to fight at the battle of Worcester. Thereafter, the testimony of peace became an important part of Quaker teachings. In 1659, when England appeared to be hovering on the brink of yet another Civil War, George Fox sent this epistle to his friends:

> Ye are called to peace, therefore follow it . . . seek the peace of all men, and no man's hurt . . . keep out of plots and bustling and the arm of the flesh, for all these are amongst Adam's sons in the Fall, where they are destroying men's lives like dogs and beasts and swine, goring, rending and biting one another and destroying one another, and wrestling with flesh and blood. From whence arise these wars and killing but from the lusts?[1]

From these teachings the Quakers created a new idea of social order which they carried to the Delaware Valley. This idea was thought by others to be impossibly utopian, and doomed to failure in the New World. In some respects it did fail. But in other

---

[1]George Fox, *Journal* (Cambridge, 1952), 357.

ways it succeeded beyond the intention of the founders, and became the framework for a system of social order throughout the American midlands.

As always, the leading exponent was William Penn himself. He defined order as a system which "enjoins men to be just, honest, virtuous; to do no wrong, to kill, rob, deceive, prejudice none; but to do as one would be done unto."[2] The same idea was written into the laws of West Jersey, Pennsylvania and Delaware, which made their officers responsible for maintaining "good order," by which was meant a condition of social peace in which each individual was forbidden to intrude upon the quiet of another person.[3]

This was a revolutionary idea in its own time—a conception of order in which everyone did not have to believe the same creed or to fit into a single hierarchy. Here was an open idea of order, grounded in the golden rule and the doctrine of the "light within." To Anglicans this Quaker idea of order appeared to be dangerously permissive; to Puritans it seemed a contradiction in terms. But an idea of order as mutual forbearance defined its own obligations, which the Quakers enforced very strictly in their colonies. Their conduct of this experiment was more tough-minded than either their admirers or their critics have believed.

To keep the peace and to guarantee mutual forbearance, the Quaker founders of the Delaware colonies created a novel set of ordering institutions which were compatible with their ideals. The most important orderkeepers in Pennsylvania were county sheriffs and coroners. These officers were not controlled by a small clique of county gentry as in Virginia, nor elected by the consensus of a local community as were the constables of New England. Pennsylvanians selected their sheriffs by a more complex method. Each county held a popular election in which more than one candidate was required to appear. Of the two leading vote-getters, the governor appointed one as sheriff. Terms of office were short—normally one year. After 1730 rotation in office was required; a sheriff could serve no more than three years running, and then became ineligible for another three years. These elections were often sharply contested. In 1764, one member of the Proprietary party wrote to another about Lancaster County, "I wish the unhappy contests about Sheriff could be reduced to two

---

[2]William Penn, *The People's Ancient and Just Liberties Asserted* (London, 1670).
[3]*Colonial Records of Pennsylvania*, I, 96.

Competitors on our side . . . it would unite our friends to act with
more spirit."[4]

Implicit in this method of selection was a sense of separation
between the state and society, an idea of distance between central
and local government, and also an assumption of diversity of
interests and values. The Pennsylvania sheriff became a sort of
social referee whose task was to maintain the peace among different groups.

Sheriffs were not the only orderkeepers in the Delaware Valley.
County justices were also appointed by the Proprietor. As a deliberate act of proprietary policy, these justices were mostly Quakers, long after that religious denomination had ceased to be a
majority of the population. As late as 1764, Richard Peters wrote
to the Proprietor Thomas Penn, "By your having always given the
Preference to the Quakers in the Commissions of Peace, and
every favour you could bestow on them, they have obtained great
influence in the Country."[5]

These justices were assisted by another set of public officers
who were unique to the Quaker colonies. They were called peace
makers. Disputes of a noncriminal nature were referred to them
for arbitration under the direction of the court.[6] Disputes
between Quakers themselves were arbitrated in a different way,
under the direction of their meetings. Members of the Society of
Friends were generally forbidden to "go to law" against one
another. If they insisted upon doing so, they were sometimes
punished by expulsion from meeting. This combination of orderkeepers—sheriffs, justices, peace makers and arbitrators—was
unique to the Delaware Valley.

Forms of disorder in the Delaware colonies also differed from
other regions of British America. There were no crimes of conscience in the Quaker colonies before 1755, and comparatively
few crimes against morality or order.[7] In the court of Chester
County, crimes against authority consisted mainly in acts of defiance to peace officers in the performance of their duty. These
cases were punished severely; Quakers had no illusions about the

---

[4]The term of office was extended to three years in 1701, but reduced to one year again in
1706. The limit on length of service did not apply to coroners. See Wayne L. Bockelman, "Local
Government in Colonial Pennsylvania," in Bruce C. Daniels, ed., *Town and Country: Essays on
the Structure of Local Government in the American Colonies* (Middletown, Conn., 1978), 219–20.

[5]*Ibid.*, 232.

[6]For Peacemakers see *Record of the Courts of Chester County*, 34, 39;14.x.1683.

[7]After 1755, Quakers began to be punished in Pennsylvania for refusing to pay war taxes.
But this irony belongs to the history of a subsequent period.

need to maintain the authority of their ordering institutions. Abraham Effingwell, for the offense of "menacing the Majestracy [sic] of this County" was ordered to receive "twenty one lashes at the Public whipping post on his bare back well laid on and 14 days imprisonment at hard labour in the house of correction."[8]

But if crimes against public morality were comparatively uncommon in Pennsylvania, a great many people were punished for violating the private rights of others. The court docket of Chester County was crowded with cases of trespass, trover and case, in which these old forms of common-law pleading were turned to new purposes by a pluralistic culture.[9] In the Delaware Valley, crimes against property and crimes against persons tended to be roughly equal in their incidence, unlike New England where property crime predominated and the southern colonies where personal crimes were more common.[10]

Treatment of the disorderly also differed in the Quaker colonies from other parts of British America. The founders broke decisively with the harsh capital laws of England.[11] In Pennsylvania and West Jersey the number of hanging offenses was reduced from more than two hundred in English law to merely two—treason and willful murder. When the Quakers lost control of their

---

[8] *Record of the Court of Chester County,* 56 (3.iv.1685); Winthrop, *Journal,* 14 June 1631.

[9] *Record of the Court of Chester County,* 5, 9, 10, 12, 15.

[10] Alan Tully found the following patterns in cases heard by the court of quarter sessions in Chester County, 1726–55:

	number	percent
Crimes against persons	(192)	(27.7%)
Assault and battery	192	27.7%
Crimes against property	(158)	(22.8%)
Larceny	144	20.8%
Forgery and counterfeiting	8	1.1%
Forcible entry	6	0.9%
Crimes against morality	(167)	(24.1%)
Sexual offenses	159	22.9%
Keeping a disorderly house	8	1.2%
Crimes against order and authority	(56)	(8.1%)
Riot and disturbing the peace	31	4.5%
License violations	16	2.3%
Contempt of authority	9	1.3%
Crimes unidentified	93	13.4%
Crimes miscellaneous	28	4.0%
Total	694	100.1%

Source: Tully, *William Penn's Legacy,* 190–91; a study of Philadelphia County in a later period found a higher incidence of property crimes; see A. H. Hobbs, "Criminality in Philadelphia, 1790–1810, Compared with 1937," *ASR* 8 (1943), 198–200.

[11] For the testimony of George Fox and John Bellers against capital punishment, see Herbert W. K. Fitzroy, "The Punishment of Crime in Provincial Pennsylvania," *PMHB* 60 (1936), 244.

colonies the number of capital crimes increased, but their number remained small by comparison with other colonies. After the Revolution, Pennsylvania led the Western world in the cause of penal reform. As early as 1794 it abolished the death penalty for all offenses except murder in the first degree.[12]

At the same time that the laws of the Quaker colonies were comparatively mild as regards capital punishment, they punished very harshly acts of disorder in which one citizen intruded upon the peace of another. In Pennsylvania, penalties for crimes of sexual violence against women were exceptionally severe. The lash was used abundantly in that colony, and such was its shame and horror that in 1743 a man who was brought to the whipping post took out a knife and cut his throat before the assembled crowd, rather than submit to a public flogging.[13] Samuel Breck remembered the terrible spectacle of public punishments in Philadelphia during the eighteenth century:

> The large whipping-post, painted red, stood conspicuously and permanently in the most public street in town. It was placed in State street, directly under the windows of a great writing-school which I frequented, and from them the scholars were indulged in the spectacle of all kinds of punishments. . . .
>
> Here women were taken from a huge cage, in which they were dragged on wheels from prison, and tied to a post with bare backs, on which thirty or forty lashes were bestowed amid the screams of the culprits and the uproar of the mob.
>
> A little further in the street was to be seen the pillory, with three or four fellows fastened by the head, and standing for an hour in that helpless posture, exposed to gross and cruel insult from the multitude, who pelted them incessantly with rotten eggs and every repulsive kind of garbage that could be collected. These things I have often witnessed.[14]

In these customs of lash and whipping post, the order ways of the Delaware Valley superficially resembled those of Massachusetts

---

[12]Fitzroy, "The Punishment of Crime in Provincial Pennsylvania," 242–69; Harry and Grace Weiss, *An Introduction to Crime and Punishment in Colonial New Jersey* (Trenton, 1960); Albert Post, "Early Efforts to Abolish Capital Punishment in Pennsylvania," *PMHB* 68 (1944) xxx; Harry Elmer Barnes, *The Evolution of Penology in Pennsylvania: A Study in American Social History* (Indianapolis, 1927); Harry Elmer Barnes, A History of the Penal, Reformatory and Correctional Institutions of the State of New Jersey (Trenton, 1918); Kathryn Preyer, "Penal Measures in the American Colonies: An Overview," *AJLH* 26 (1982), 326–53.

[13]Watson, *Annals of Philadelphia*, I, 309.

[14]Samuel Breck, *Recollections* (Philadelphia, 1877) 36–37.

and Virginia. But the same instruments served different ideas of social order.

Further, the Quakers adopted penal practices which were designed not to punish the offender but to rehabilitate him. The object was not to isolate the criminal from society, but to restore him as rapidly as possible. In the 1690s, prisoners in Philadelphia's house of correction were allowed to leave their cells during hot weather.[15] The courts of Pennsylvania and West Jersey also used peace bonds in a special way, issuing them in lieu of an indictment as an alternative to a criminal proceeding.[16]

Something of this Quaker testimony of peace and order entered permanently into the cultural fabric of the Delaware Valley. After the Revolution, the people of that region were persuaded to adopt many Quaker ideas on the subject of crime and punishment. Rates of violent crime remained comparatively low. Orderkeepers continued to function as referees between different cultural groups. The idea of order continued to be defined in terms of peace and mutual forbearance, rather than unity or hierarchy.

Through many vicissitudes, there was a sense in Pennsylvania that peace was the inexorable will of Providence. Thus, one Quaker wrote to a friend, "The blessings of plenty and peace which we hitherto enjoy should thankfully engage us in the returns of gratitude to that good providence which protects us, without the assistance of the sword."[17] The reality of life in the Delaware Valley appeared to confirm this mood of optimism. A Portuguese visitor to eighteenth-century Philadelphia wrote, ". . . the quiet that reigns in the midst of this infinity of people is worthy of note."[18] In all of these ways, the customs of the Delaware Valley owed much to the interplay of Quaker values and English traditions in a new American environment.

[15]Lewis, "The Courts of Pennsylvania in the Seventeenth Century," 176.

[16]Paul Lermack, "Peace Bonds and Criminal Justice in Colonial Philadelphia," *PMHB* 100 (1976), 173–77.

[17]I. Norris to Richard Partridge, 31.v.1744, Norris Letterbook, HSP.

[18]Robert C. Smith, ed., "A Portuguese in Philadelphia," *PMHB* 78 (1954), 86–87.

❧ Delaware Power Ways:
The Politics of Commission Government

Quakers generally controlled the government of Pennsylvania for a period of sixty-seven years (1682–1755). During that era, they created a political system which differed very much from New England and Virginia. Many institutions in this polity were formed as early as the year 1725; some continued to exist for more than two centuries. Long after the Quakers relinquished the reins of power to other groups, their legacy survived in the political institutions and folkways of an American region.[1]

The English Quakers brought to America a habit of intense public activity, and a highly developed set of political principles. Despite the accusations of their enemies, they were not a sect of seventeenth-century anarchists. "Certainly," wrote Isaac Norris in 1710, "every thinking man must believe that government [is] absolutely necessary; daily experience proves it whenever any number of people are got together."[2]

In William Penn's words, the Quakers believed that politics was "a part of religion itself, a thing sacred in its institution and its end."[3] The Philadelphia yearly meeting repeatedly reminded its members that they were bound by the principles of their religion in public affairs as well as private business.[4]

The political meaning of these religious principles was, however, a matter of dispute. Quakers quarreled furiously among themselves on public questions. On one occasion, William Penn beseeched them, "For the love of God, me, and the poor country, be not so *governmentish!*"[5]

So deep did these disagreements become in Pennsylvania, that to James Logan it seemed as if the "powers had brake loose from their center," and the vessel of sovereignty had shattered into its separate shards of individual conscience.[6] Quakers insisted that a believing Christian had a sacred duty to stand against evil in government, and that individual conscience was the arbiter of God's

---

[1]There was a brief period of royal control from 1692 to 1694.

[2]Isaac Norris, *Friendly Advice to the Inhabitants of Pennsylvania* (n.p., n.d., (Philadelphia, 1710?); a copy is in the Pemberton Papers, HSP.

[3]Tolles, *Meeting House and Counting House*, 10.

[4]For an example by the Philadelphia Yearly Meeting in 1711, see Richard Bauman, *For the Reputation of Truth*, 2.

[5]William Penn to Thomas Lloyd et al., 15 Aug. 1685, Penn Papers, HSP.

[6]Nash, *Quakers and Politics*, 241.

truth. The ideology of Quakerism justified political opposition in a way that was not the case in other English cultures. The political culture of Pennsylvania was defined not only by Quaker principles themselves, but also by a prolonged quarrel over their purposeful application.

One consequence was the emergence of political parties in Pennsylvania at an early date. By 1701, two stable parties were functioning in that province. Both consisted mainly of Quakers. The Country party found its following mainly among farmers and artisans in the counties. The Proprietary party was closely linked to the Penn family and was led by their agent James Logan in alliance with leading Quaker merchants in the city of Philadelphia.

These parties nominated candidates, contested elections, issued manifestos, recruited stable followings and defended positions of high principle. The major issues that divided them would be the classical constitutional questions of American politics: the powers of the Proprietor and the Assembly, the relative importance of property rights and personal liberties, the control of the judiciary. Both parties claimed to be defending their liberties in a classical conflict between two Whig ideologies.

After the death of William Penn in 1718 this first American party system disintegrated. A brief period of partisan inactivity followed. By the mid-1720s Pennsylvania politics were dominated by two new parties, called the Quaker party and the Gentlemen's party. The Quaker party drew its support from English Friends and German Pietists who shared many values and purposes in common. The Gentlemen's party won the support of Anglican merchants, rough seamen and Scots-Irish immigrants as well as the non-Quaker bourgeoisie of Philadelphia. These parties also nominated candidates and contested elections for many years. Altogether, the first and second party systems of colonial Pennsylvania lasted longer than either the first or second party systems in American national politics.

Another part of this political culture was the politics of ethnicity. This arose among the Quakers as early as the 1680s in tensions between Welsh and English Quakers. So suspicious were these two groups of one another that the English majority deliberately drew the county boundaries of Pennsylvania so as to split the Welsh settlements. The townships of Haverford and Radnor were made part of Chester County, while Merion was placed in Philadelphia County. This was done to keep the Welsh Quakers

from controlling an entire county—the earliest instance of ger-
rymandering in American history.[7]

In the eighteenth century, when William Penn's agents
recruited German Pietists to Pennsylvania, and the unwelcome
Scots-Irish also began to arrive in large numbers, ethnic factors
became increasingly important in Pennsylvania politics. Once
again, an institutional framework already existed. The legitimacy
of ethnic pluralism was recognized by the Quakers, many of
whom thought of themselves as "dissenters in their own land."
This idea encouraged the rapid development of political pluralism in Pennsylvania.

Another part of the Quaker legacy was a special set of local
institutions. The founders of Pennsylvania drew selectively upon
traditional English institutions in ways which were consistent with
their Quaker principles. For purposes of local government, they
abolished the Anglican parish, but preserved the English county
and adapted it to their own goals. At first, the founders placed
most local administration into the hands of county justices who
were appointed by higher authority.

That system did not last very long, for it was unacceptable to
the Country party. In a series of statutes (1718, 1725, 1728) the
Assembly created a new system of local government by county
commissions. These officers were at first appointed by the legislature, and after 1725 chosen by the people. Every county had
three commissioners, one of whom was elected each fall, together
with nominees for sheriff and coroner. The power to tax was
vested in the county commission, in conjunction with county
assessors who were annually elected.[8]

Pennsylvania's system of county commissions worked very differently from New England's town meetings and Virginia's government by court and vestry. The polity of Pennsylvania lacked
the institutional machinery to enforce conformity as in New
England.[9] It also did not develop the strong oligarchical tendencies of Virginia's politics. Popular elections occurred very frequently in Pennsylvania. By 1775, voters were being asked to cast

[7]Tolles, *Quakers and Atlantic Culture*, 124.

[8]Clair W. Keller, "The Pennsylvania Commission System, 1712 to 1740," *PMHB* 93 (1969),
372–82; this essay summarizes a dissertation by the same author, "Pennsylvania Government,
1701–1740" (thesis, Univ. of Wash., 1967).

[9]Tully, *William Penn's Legacy*, develops this point.

their ballots as often as five times each year. The result was a culture where "residents were actively and constantly involved in the political process" in a way that differed from other colonies.[10]

Turnouts of taxable adult white males in Pennsylvania tended to be lower than in Virginia, but higher than in New England on the average. Rates of participation fluctuated from year to year, rising perceptibly during heated party battles in the 1740s and 1760s. But on the whole, participation was comparatively stable, with nothing like the *staccato* rhythm of surge and decline that happened in small New England towns.[11]

Another component of this political culture was the Whig ideology of England's Restoration era which rooted itself more firmly in Pennsylvania than in either Massachusetts or Virginia. William Penn was himself a staunch English Whig who supported

[10]Bockelman, "Local Government in Colonial Pennsylvania," 216–37.

[11]In various elections of legislators and local officers throughout the Delaware Valley, the following levels of turnout were recorded (as a percentage of adult white males):

Place	Year	Turnout	Place	Year	Turnout
Bucks Co., Pa.	1738	26%	Philadelphia Co., Pa.	1727	28%
	1739	19%		1728	33%
	1740	22%		1730	19%
	1765	46%		1732	26%
	1742	38%		1734	22%
Chester Co., Pa.	1737	29%		1735	28%
	1738	37%		1736	18%
	1739	32%		1737	21%
	1742	32%		1738	29%
	1765	22%		1739	12%
Lancaster Co., Pa.	1737	31%		1740	38%
	1738	40%		1741	23%
	1740	34%		1742	34%
	1741	37%		1743	19%
	1742	45%	Philadelphia City, Pa.	1737	15%
	1749	32%		1742	32%
	1757	14%		1751	37%
	1765	48%		1757	23%
Middlesex Co., N.J.	1754	49%		1758	7%
Kent Co., Del.	1751	48%		1764	42%
				1765	62%
				1766	46%
				1774	36%
				1775	27%

Sources: Robert J. Dinkin, *Voting in Provincial America* (Westmont, Conn., 1977), 158–59; Tully, *William Penn's Legacy*, 93; Chilton Williamson, *American Suffrage from Property to Democracy* (Princeton, 1960), 34; Richard P. McCormick, *History of Voting in New Jersey* (New Brunswick, 1963), 63; David P. Peltier, "Border State Democracy: A History of Voting in Delaware, 1682–1897" (thesis, Univ. of Del., 1967), 36.

the election of Algernon Sydney, and was said to have rescued Locke and Trenchard from imprisonment. The leaders of all political parties in Pennsylvania called themselves Whigs. Historians Caroline Robbins and Frederick Tolles found in their studies of Quaker libraries repeated proof of a "persistent fondness" for the classical works of what Robbins called the commonwealth tradition: Trenchard's and Gordon's *Independent Whig*, and *Cato's Letters*.[12]

Elements of this ideology came to be shared widely throughout the American colonies. But in Pennsylvania it took a special form. Among its features were a unicameral legislature, and annual assemblies which met upon their own adjournment. Another component was the ideal of minimal government. Andrew Hamilton wrote in 1739, ". . . we have no officers but what are necessary, none but what earn their salaries, and those generally are either elected by the people or appointed by their representatives."[13] To this idea was added minimal taxes, which tended to be lighter in Pennsylvania than in most other colonies. In 1692 a proposed tax of a penny on the pound, which amounted to four-tenths of 1 percent of assessed wealth, was rejected as "a great tax," ruinous of "liberties and properties."[14]

The idea of minimal government was carried farther in Pennsylvania than in any other colony. There was no legally established militia until after the 1750s. In one period, when interest from a land bank provided an alternative source of revenue, there were nearly no taxes at all. The legislature of Pennsylvania passed fewer laws before 1750 than any other assembly in British America, and its courts were less active in the work of enforcement than most provinces. In each of these practices the Quaker colonies differed from most other parts of British America.[15]

This system of institutionalized dissent, organized parties, political pluralism, commission government, light taxes, and minimal government was firmly constructed before 1740. It was the work of Quakers, and the combined product of their Christian beliefs, English traditions and generational experiences in the late seventeenth century. In 1756 many leading Quakers withdrew from politics, and nominal control of the colony passed into

---

[12]Tolles, *Meeting House and County House*, 178.

[13]Jones, *Quakers in the American Colonies*, 487.

[14]"An Early Petition of the Freemen of the Province of Pennsylvania to the Assembly, 1692," *PMHB* 38 (1914), 495.

[15]Jones, *Quakers in the American Colonies*, 487.

other hands. But the political culture which they created still flourishes. It is one of the Quakers' enduring legacies to the American Republic.

❧ Delaware Freedom Ways:
The Quaker Idea of Reciprocal Liberty

In 1751 the Assembly of Pennsylvania celebrated an anniversary. The Charter of Privileges, which William Penn had granted his settlers in 1701 to guarantee their liberty, was exactly half a century old. To mark the occasion, the legislature ordered that a great bell should be purchased for the Pennsylvania State House.

Today, that building is better known as Independence Hall, and the great Quaker bell is called the Liberty Bell. Both of these symbols are associated in the popular mind with the American Revolution. But in fact they were the products of an earlier period of Anglo-American history; and they were meant to celebrate a special idea of liberty which was unique to the Quaker founders of Pennsylvania.

The original resolution to purchase the great Quaker bell was voted by members of the Society of Friends, who made up 70 percent of the Pennsylvania Assembly in 1750. The inscription was selected by the Quaker speaker, who chose a passage from the book of Leviticus which seemed particularly meaningful to Christians of his denomination. The quotation referred to the liberty that God had given not merely to a chosen few, but to all his children, so that they might be safe in the sanctity of their families and secure in the possession of their property. The full biblical text seemed perfectly suitable to the anniversary of William Penn's Charter of Privileges:

> Ye shall hallow the fiftieth year, and proclaim liberty throughout *all* the land unto all the inhabitants thereof: and ye shall return every man unto his possession, and ye shall return every man unto his family.[1]

Here was a libertarian idea that differed very much from the Puritan conception of ordered liberty for God's chosen few, and also from the cavalier notion of hierarchical liberty for the keepers of

---

[1] *Leviticus* 25:10; italics original in the King James version.

The Great Quaker Bell was purchased by the Pennsylvania Assembly many years before the American Revolution. It was rung on July 8, 1776, to celebrate the adoption of the Declaration of Independence, and thereafter called the Liberty Bell. Even after it cracked while tolling the death of Chief Justice John Marshall in 1835, it continued to be used on great libertarian occasions. This historian remembers hearing it on D-Day, June 6, 1944, when its sound was carried throughout the world by radio to mark the impending liberation of western Europe. This great bell of freedom has become a universal symbol, but it was originally intended to commemorate a very special idea of liberty that was unique to the radical Protestants, both British Quakers and German Pietists, who settled Pennsylvania. The bell bears a biblical inscription, "Proclaim Liberty throughout all the Land unto all the inhabitants thereof." It symbolized an idea of reciprocal liberty that differed profoundly from other conceptions of freedom in British America.

slaves. Quakers believed in an idea of reciprocal liberty that embraced all humanity, and was written in the golden rule.

This Christian idea was reinforced in Quaker thinking by an exceptionally strong sense of English liberties. As early as 1687, William Penn ordered the full text of the Magna Carta to be reprinted in Philadelphia, together with a broad selection of other constitutional documents. His purpose was to remind the freeholders of Pennsylvania to remember their British birthright. He urged them:

> not to give anything of liberty that at present they do enjoy, but take up the good example of our ancestors, and understand that it is easy to part with or give away great privileges, but hard to be gained if lost.[2]

On the subject of liberty, the people of Pennsylvania needed no lessons from their Lord Proprietor. Few public questions were introduced among the colonists without being discussed in terms of rights and liberties. On its surface, this libertarian rhetoric seemed superficially similar to that of Massachusetts and Virginia. But the founders of Pennsylvania were a different group of Englishmen—a later generation, from another English region, with a special kind of Christian faith. Their idea of liberty was not the same as that which came to other parts of British America.

The most important of these differences had to do with religious freedom—"liberty of conscience," William Penn called it. This was not the conventional Protestant idea of liberty to do only that which is right. The Quakers believed that liberty of conscience extended even to ideas that they believed to be wrong. Their idea of "soul freedom" protected every Christian conscience.

The most articulate spokesman for this idea was William Penn himself. Of nearly sixty books and pamphlets that Penn wrote before coming to America, half were defenses of liberty of conscience. Some of these works were among the most powerful statements ever written on this subject. One ended with a revealing personal remark: ". . . tis a matter of great satisfaction to the author that he has so plainly cleared his conscience in pleading for the liberty of other men's."[3]

---

[2]Tolles, *Meeting House and Counting House*, 12.
[3]William Penn, *The Great Case of Liberty of Conscience* (London, 1670).

Penn's idea of liberty of conscience was a moral absolute. It was summarized in many of his epigrams:

> Conscience is God's throne in man, and the power of it his prerogative.

> Liberty of conscience is every man's natural right, and he who is deprived of it is a slave in the midst of the greatest liberty.

> There is no reason to persecute any man in this world about anything that belongs to the next.

> No man is so accountable to his fellow creatures as to be imposed upon, restrained or persecuted for any matter of conscience whatever.

> For the matters of liberty and privilege, I propose . . . to leave myself and successors no power of doing mischief, that the will of one man may not hinder the good of the whole country.

These ideas of liberty of conscience were grounded in Penn's Quaker faith. He once remarked that there was an "instinct of a deity" within every human soul which needed no forcing from the hand of mortal man. Further, the idea of the inner light led him to believe that everyone possessed the power of telling truth from error. The optimistic fatalism of Quaker faith persuaded him that truth would inevitably overcome error if it were left free to do so. Penn's "liberty of conscience" was not a secular liberalism that valued freedom for its own sake. It was a means to a greater end: the triumph of Christian truth in the world.

William Penn's personal experience of religious persecution gave him other reasons for believing in religious liberty. His own sufferings convinced him that the coercion of conscience was not merely evil but futile, and deeply dangerous to true faith. "They subvert all true religion," Penn wrote, ". . . where men believe, not because 'tis false, but so commanded by their superiors."[4]

These memories and experiences were not Penn's alone. In the period from 1661 to 1685, historians estimate that at least 15,000 Quakers were imprisoned in England, and 450 died for their beliefs. As late as the year 1685, more than 1,400 Quakers were still languishing in English jails. Most "books of sufferings" recorded punishments that continued well into the eighteenth

---

[4]Braithwaite, *Second Period of Quakerism*, 114. This is a conservative estimate. Others are much higher. Besse's *Sufferings* list 366 Quaker martyrs by name; Braithwaite raises that total to "at least 450." Various editions of Besse also list by name 12,406 Quakers who were made victims for their Christian beliefs. The true number was undoubtedly much higher. Jeremy White reckoned it at 60,000 imprisonments and 5,000 deaths in prison.

century—mostly fines and seizures for nonpayment of tithes. These records also revealed that the cruelest persecutors of the Quakers were Anglican clergy:

> John Lingard of Stockhall [Derbyshire] the younger was imprisoned Darby Gaols at the suit of William White priest of Chapell of Fritt [*sic*] who himself seized upon him as he was reaping his own corn the last corn harvest and detayned him until the officers came who carried him straightaway to Derby gaol. . . .

> The said priest had formerly himself broke into the said John Lingard the elder's house forcing the outward door from the hooks and broke an inward door at the same time in pieces and hath taken his corn by his own hands, carrying it away on horseback.[5]

For their refusal to pay tithes, Quakers were often fined far beyond the amount in question; sometimes all of their property was confiscated. In 1672, English Quaker William Cooper refused to pay a few shillings in tithes, and was fined five pounds fifteen shillings, "for which they sold his cow, corn, hay and household goods to the coat he should have worn."[6]

Many Quaker immigrants to Pennsylvania had experienced this religious persecution; they shared a determination to prevent its growth in their own province. The first fundamental law passed in Pennsylvania guaranteed liberty of conscience for all who believed in "one Almighty God," and established complete freedom of worship. It also provided penalties for those who "derided the religion of others." The Quaker founders of Pennsylvania were not content merely to restrain government from interfering with rights of conscience. They also made it an instrument of positive protection. Here was a reciprocal idea of religious liberty which they actively extended to others as well as themselves.[7]

Liberty of conscience was one of a large family of personal freedoms which Quakers extended equally to others. William Penn recognized three secular "rights of an Englishman": first, a "right and title to your own lives, liberties and estates; second, representative government; third, trial by jury."[8] In Pennsylvania, these liberties went far beyond those of Massachusetts, Virginia and old England itself. In regard to the right of trial by jury, Penn insisted that every free-born Englishman had a right to be tried

---

[5]Book of Sufferings of Friends in Derby, 1672, ms. Q/62a/1, NOTTRO.
[6]*Ibid.*, 1670.
[7]Bronner, *William Penn's "Holy Experiment,"* 264.
[8]Tolles, *Meeting House and Counting House*, 13.

by his peers; that a jury had the right to decide questions of both fact and law; and that the law could not be used to punish a jury for its verdict. The laws of Pennsylvania also guaranteed the right of every freeman to a speedy trial, to a jury chosen by lot in criminal cases, and to the same privileges of witnesses and counsel as the prosecution. These ideas went far beyond prevailing practices in England and America.[9]

The protection of property was also a principle of high importance to William Penn. The seizure of Quaker estates for non-payment of tithes was condemned not merely as an infringement of rights of conscience, but also as a violation of the rights of property. Others have seen a conflict between personal rights and property rights. William Penn did not. The laws of the Quaker colonies reflected his belief that the two rights were both part of one libertarian heritage. The Charter of Privileges in 1701 decreed that no person could be "at any time hereafter, obliged to answer any complaint, matter or thing whatsoever relating to property before the governor and council," except in "the ordinary course of justice."[10]

As regards the right of representative government, the Quaker colonies also went beyond other provinces in British America. One of the fundamental laws of Pennsylvania required that taxes could be imposed only by consent of the governed, and that all tax laws expired automatically after twelve months. These rules expressed the Quaker principle of reciprocal liberty, and their libertarian application of the golden rule, in the idea that no taxes should be levied upon the people except those which they were willing to impose upon themselves.

In all of these ways, the Quakers extended to others in America precisely the same rights that they had demanded for themselves in England. Many other libertarians have tended to hedge their principles when power passed into their hands. That sad story has been reenacted many times in world history, from New England Puritans to French Jacobins to Israeli Jews who have cruelly denied to others the rights they demanded for themselves. The Quakers behaved differently. They always remained true to their idea of reciprocal liberty, to the everlasting glory of their denomination.

---

[9]Penn, *The People's Ancient and Just Liberties Asserted;* "Injustice Detected . . . ," *Papers of William Penn,* I, 194–204; Dunn, *William Penn, Politics and Conscience,* 13–19.

[10]Bronner, *William Penn's "Holy Experiment,"* 267–68.

The Quakers of the Delaware Valley also differed from other English-speaking people in regard to race slavery. The question was a difficult one for them. The first generation of Quakers had been deeply troubled by slavery, but many were not opposed outright. The problem was compounded in the Delaware Valley by the fact that slavery worked well as an economic institution in this region. Many Quakers bought slaves. Even William Penn did so. Of the leaders of the Philadelphia Yearly Meeting for whom evidence survives, 70 percent owned slaves in the period from 1681 to 1705.[11]

But within the first decade of settlement a powerful antislavery movement began to develop in the Delaware Valley. As early as 1688, the Quakers of Germantown issued a testimony against slavery on the ground that it violated the golden rule.[12] In 1696, two leading Quakers, Cadwalader Morgan and William Southeby, urged the Philadelphia Yearly Meeting to forbid slavery and slave trading. The meeting refused to go that far, but agreed to advise Quakers "not to encourage the bringing in of any more Negroes." As antislavery feeling expanded steadily among Friends, slaveowning declined among leaders of the Philadelphia yearly meeting—falling steadily from 70 percent before 1705, to only 10 percent after 1756.[13]

The Pennsylvania legislature took action in 1712, passing a prohibitive duty on the importation of slaves. This measure was disallowed by the English Crown, which had a heavy stake in the slave trade. In 1730 the Philadelphia yearly meeting cautioned its members, but still a few Friends continued to buy slaves. Other Quaker antislavery petitions and papers followed in increasing number. A close student of this material finds that Quaker "antislavery reformers never contended that slavery was economically unsound." They insisted that it was morally corrupt, and at war with the deepest values of Christianity. The argument came down to the reciprocal principle of the golden rule. Quakers argued that if they did not wish to be slaves themselves, they had no right to enslave others.[14]

Delegations from Quaker meetings throughout the Delaware Valley were sent to slaveholders, urging a policy of compensated

[11]Jean R. Soderlund, *Quakers and Slavery* (Princeton, 1985), 34.
[12]"The Germantown Protest," *PMHB* IV (1880), 28–30.
[13]Soderlund, *Quakers and Slavery*, 34.
[14]*Ibid.*, 137.

manumission. The evidence of private journals and public testimony shows that many Quaker slaveholders were profoundly
troubled by this question, which haunted them even in their
dreams. But a few continued to hold out, and the near unanimity
that was needed for agreement could not be obtained.

The turning point came in 1758. The Philadelphia Yearly
Meeting recorded a "unanimous concern" against "the practice
of importing, buying, selling, or keeping slaves for term of life."[15]
This was the first success for the cause of abolition anywhere in
the Western world. "The history of the early abolitionist movement," writes historian Arthur Zilversmit, "is essentially the
record of Quaker antislavery activities."[16]

Quakers also took an active interest in the welfare of former
slaves. Many masters helped to support their slaves after manu-
mitting them. Others compensated them for their labor during
slavery. When Abner Woolman (the brother of John Woolman)
in 1767 freed two slaves his wife had inherited, he decided to pay
them a sum equal to the amount that the estate had been
increased by their labor, and asked the Haddonfield (New Jersey)
meeting to help him compute a just sum.[17]

The antislavery ideas of the Quakers were shared by others
throughout the Delaware Valley. Attitudes of German Pietists
were similar to those of English Friends. Quaker abolitionists
such as John Woolman and Anthony Benezet carried the cause to
others in the Delaware Valley. In 1773, non-Quakers joined
Friends within the Pennsylvania legislature in trying to stop the
trade in human flesh by imposing a prohibitively high duty on
slaves. Once again it was disallowed by British imperial authorities. In January 1775, one of the first acts of Pennsylvania's Provincial Convention, when freed from British oversight, was to
prohibit the importation of slaves. After a protracted legislative
process, the Assembly also passed a bill in 1780 for the gradual
abolition of slavery. Here was yet another expression of the idea
of reciprocal liberty which Quakers made a part of the political
folkways of the Delaware Valley.[18]

The Quakers were among the most radical libertarians of their

---

[15]Arthur Zilversmit, *The First Emancipation: The Abolition of Slavery in the North* (Chicago, 1967), 74–75.

[16]*Ibid.*, 3.

[17]Soderlund, *Quakers and Slavery*, 179.

[18]For southern Quakers and slavery see Hiram H. Hilty, *Toward Freedom for All: North Carolina Quakers and Slavery* (Richmond, Ind., 1984).

age. But they were not anarchists. Penn himself wrote in his *Frame of Government* that "liberty without obedience is confusion, and obedience without liberty is slavery."[19] Penn instructed his governor to "rule the meek meekly, and those that will not be ruled, rule with authority."[20]

The Quakers radically redefined the "rights of Englishmen" in terms of their Christian beliefs. But they never imagined that they were creating something new. Penn and others in the colony wrote always of their rights as "ancient" and "fundamental" principles which were rooted in the immemorial customs of the English-speaking people and in the practices of the primitive church.

In the conservative cast of their libertarian thinking, the Quakers were much the same as Puritans and Anglicans. But in the substance of their libertarian thought they were very different. In respect to liberty of conscience, trial by jury, the rights of property, the rule of representation, and race slavery, Quakers genuinely believed that every liberty demanded for oneself should also be extended to others.

One leading student of this subject summarizes the vital principle of Quaker liberty in a sentence: "Men will reciprocate if treated kindly and justly." This, he writes, was "the basis of Quaker dealings with other men."[21]

This idea of reciprocal liberty continues to exist in the United States. It has changed in many ways, becoming more procedural and less substantive in its conception. It has been appropriated by those who believe that the republic itself should not associate itself with any creed other than that of secular liberty itself. This idea of ethical neutrality is profoundly different from the purposes of the Quakers. But in that modern form, the idea of reciprocal liberty still flourishes in healthy competition with other principles of freedom in America today.

---

[19]William Penn, *Frame of Government* (1682).

[20]Bronner, *William Penn's "Holy Experiment,"* 266.

[21]William Comfort, *The Quakers, A Brief History of Their Influence on Pennsylvania* (rev. by F. B. Tolles, Harrisburg, 1955), 6.

BORDERLANDS TO THE BACKCOUNTRY

❧ The Flight from North Britain, 1717–1775

> Whole neighborhoods formed parties for removal;
> so that departure from their native country is no
> longer exile. He that goes thus accompanied . . . sits
> down in a better climate, surrounded by his kindred
> and his friends: they carry with them their language,
> their opinions, their popular songs, and hereditary
> merriment: they change nothing but the place of
> their abode.
>
> —Dr. Samuel Johnson on the emigration
> from North Britain to America, 1773

EARLY IN THE SUMMER OF 1717, the Quaker merchants of Philadelphia observed that immigrant ships were arriving in more than their usual numbers. By September, as the first hint of autumn was in the air, the Delaware River was crowded with vessels. They came not only from London and Bristol, but from Liverpool and Belfast, and small northern outports with strange-sounding names—Londonderry and Carrickfergus in northern Ireland, Kirkcudbright and Wigtown in Scotland, Whitehaven and Morecambe on the northern border of England.

In October of the same year, a Philadelphia Quaker named Jonathan Dickinson complained that the streets of his city were teeming with "a swarm of people . . . strangers to our Laws and Customs, and even to our language."[1] These new immigrants dressed in outlandish ways. The men were tall and lean, with hard, weather-beaten faces. They wore felt hats, loose sackcloth shirts close-belted at the waist, baggy trousers, thick yarn stockings and wooden shoes "shod like a horse's feet with iron." The young women startled Quaker Philadelphia by the sensuous appearance of their full bodices, tight waists, bare legs and skirts as scandalously short as an English undershift. The older women came ashore in long dresses of a curious cut. Some buried their faces in full-sided bonnets; others folded handkerchiefs over their heads in quaint and foreign patterns.[2]

The speech of these people was English, but they spoke with a lilting cadence that rang strangely in the ear. Many were desperately poor. But even in their poverty they carried themselves with a fierce and stubborn pride that warned others to treat them with respect.[3]

The appearance of these immigrants in the streets of Philadelphia marked the start of yet another great folk migration from Britain to America. The magnitude of this movement was very large—more than a quarter-million people altogether. This was truly a mass migration, on a scale altogether different from the movements that had preceded it. Its rhythm was different too—not a single migration but a series of wavelike movements that continued though much of the eighteenth century. It also drew from a different part of Britain. Many of these people came from territories that bordered the Irish Sea—the north of Ireland, the lowlands of Scotland, and the northern counties of England. Together they introduced still another variety of British culture to the New World.

The first slow trickle of emigration from North Britain to America had actually begun much earlier, in the seventeenth century. In Virginia, headrights had been granted for Irish servants before 1630. In New England, a group of 140 Irish Calvinists had arrived from Belfast as early as the year 1636, on board an immigrant ship nicely named *Eagle's Wing*.[4] A small flow of population continued through the seventeenth century. Then, after the end of Queen Anne's War in 1713, this movement began to accelerate in a strong wavelike rhythm that continued to the outbreak of the American Revolution. Peak periods occurred in the years 1718, 1729, 1741, 1755, 1767 and 1774. Two-thirds of this

---

[1]Jonathan Dickinson to John Aiken, 22 Oct. 1717; Dickinson to brother, 22 Aug. 1718; Dickinson to cousin, 17 Oct. 1719, Jonathan Dickinson Letterbook, 1715–21, HSP.

[2]For details of dress and appearance, see *GM* 36 (1766), 582; also Robert Ferguson, *Northmen in Cumberland and Westmorland* (London, 1856), 144–45.

[3]*GM* 36 (1766), 582.

[4]The name was inspired by Exodus xix:4–5, where the Lord said to Moses, "Ye have seen what I did unto the Egyptians, and how I bare you on eagles' wings, and brought you to myself. Now therefore, if ye will obey my voice indeed, and keep my covenant, then ye shall be a peculiar treasure unto me above all people: for all the earth is mine."

ORKNEY

CAITHNESS

SUNDERLAND

ROSS AND
CROMARTY

Outer Hebrides

North

MORAY

NAIRN

BANFF

INVERNESS

Skye

SCOTTISH

HIGHLANDS

ABERDEEN

KINCARDINE

Inner Hebrides

PERTH

ANGUS

ARGYLL

FIFE

D

STIR-
LING

C K

R

BUTE

W M E

Edinburgh

LOWLANDS

BERWICK

LANARK

PEEB

Ayr

AYR

SEL

ROX-
BURGH

Coleraine   Portrush
Londonderry
DONEGAL   DERRY
NORTHERN   Larne
TYRONE   ANTRIM
I R E L A N D   Belfast
Sligo   FERMA-   MO-   AR-   DOWN
NAGH   NA-   MAGH
SLIGO   GHAN   Newry
ROS-   LEI-
COMMON   TRIM   CAVAN   Dundalk
LONG-   LOUTH
FORD   WEST-   MEATH
MEATH

Wigtown   Kirkcud-
bright

KIRK-   DUMFRIES
CUDBRIGHT

WIGTOWN

NORTH-
UMBERLAND

Newcastle-on-Tyne

Maryport   CUMBERLAND   DURHAM
Whitehaven
WEST-
MORLAND

Whitby

N O R T H E R N

Scarborough

Isle of
Man

E N G L A N D

Morecambe

I r i s h   S e a

Y O R K S H I R E

Bridlington

Hull

LANCA-
SHIRE

DUBLIN

Dublin

KING'S   KIL-
DARE

QUEEN'S

WICKLOW

ANGLESEY FLINT

Liverpool

CAERNARVON DENBIGH

CHESHIRE

DERBY

LINCOLN-
SHIRE

TIPPE-
RARY

KIL-
KENNY

CAR-
LOW

MERIONETH

NOTTING-
HAM

WEXFORD

MONT-
GOMERY

SHROP-
SHIRE
(SALOP)

STAF-
FORD

LEICES-
TER

RUT.

NORFOLK

WATERFORD

CARDIGAN   RADNOR

St. George's Channel

WORCES-   WAR-
TER   WICK

NORTH
ANTS

HUNTS

PEMBROKE
CAR-   BRECK-
MARTHEN   NOCK

HERE-
FORD

CAMBS

SUFFOLK

BEDS

MON-   GLOUCESTER
MOUTH

OXON

BUCKS

HERTS

ESSEX

GLAMORGAN

Bristol

BERK-
SHIRE

MDX London

WILT-
SHIRE

SOMERSET

HAMPSHIRE

SURREY

KENT

DEVON

DORSET

SUSSEX

CORNWALL

North Channel

T H E   F L I G H T
F R O M   N O R T H   B R I T A I N

traffic was concentrated in the decade from 1765 to 1775. As much as one-third of it may have occurred in the four years preceding American Independence.

❧ Motives for Migration

As the flight from North Britain approached its climax, Dr. Samuel Johnson and his faithful friend James Boswell were touring the west coast of Scotland. At Armadale they were invited to a country dance which captured the spirit of this great folk movement. Boswell remembered:

> We had again a good dinner, and in the evening a great dance . . . we performed a dance which I suppose the emigration from Skye has occasioned. They call it "America." A brisk reel is played. The first couple begin, and each sets to one—then each to another— then as they set to the next couple, the second and third couples are setting; and so it goes on till all are set a-going, setting and wheeling round each other, while each is making the tour of all in the dance. It shows how emigration catches till all are set afloat.[5]

Boswell asked a lady to explain the dance, and recorded her reply:

> Mrs. Mackinnon told me that last year when the ship sailed from Portree [a small village on the Isle of Skye] for America, the people on shore were almost distracted when they saw their relations go off; they lay down on the ground and tumbled, and tore the grass with their teeth. This year there was not a tear shed. The people on shore seemed to think that they would soon follow.[6]

Through the long period from 1718 to 1775, the annual number of immigrants from Ireland, Scotland and the north of England averaged more than 5,000 a year. At least 150,000 came from northern Ireland, sailing mostly from the ports of Belfast Lough, Londonderry, Newry, Larne and Portrush.[7] Another

---

[5]James Boswell, *Journal of a Tour to the Hebrides with Samuel Johnson, LL.D.* (1785, New York, 1936), 242 (2 Oct. 1773).

[6]*Ibid.* Dr. Johnson noted in his journal, "I inquired the subjects of the songs, and was told of one, that it was a love song, and of another, that it was a farewell composed by one of the Islanders that was going, in this epidemical fury of emigration, to seek his fortune in America." Samuel Johnson, *A Journey to the Western Islands of Scotland* (1775), ed. Mary Lascelles (New Haven, 1971), 59, 67, 95.

[7]The "Scotch-Irish" emigration to Anglo-America before 1775 has been variously estimated as follows:

75,000 departed from seaports in the west of Scotland, from the Clydebank to Solway Firth.[8] At least 50,000 (probably more) left from coastal towns of northern England from Maryport to Merseyside. These are conservative estimates. The true magnitude may have been much larger.[9]

Period	Number	Area or Population	Date and Source
1733–73	400,000	Ireland "mainly Ulster"	*Dublin Journal,* 1773
1750–99	200,000	Ireland	Newenham, 1805
1718–75	250,000	Scotch-Irish	Dunaway, 1944
1718–75	200,000	Scotch-Irish	Leyburn, 1962
1718–75	114,000	Ulster Scots	Dickson, 1966

More recently, the American historian Bernard Bailyn has reckoned that 155,000 to 205,000 people left Ulster for the New World from 1718 to 1775. In the period 1760–75, he also estimates the number of emigrants at 55,000 from the north of Ireland, 40,000 from Scotland and 30,000 from England. See Bailyn, *Voyagers to the West* (New York, 1986), 26; *Faulkner's Dublin Journal,* 10–13 April 1773; Thomas Newenham, *A Statistical and Historical Inquiry into the Progress and Magnitude of the Population of Ireland* (London, 1805), 59–60; James G. Leyburn, *The Scotch-Irish: A Social History* (Chapel Hill, 1962), 180; R. J. Dickson, *Ulster Emigration to Colonial America, 1718–1775* (London, 1966), 23, 34, 59, 64; Forrest McDonald and Ellen Shapiro McDonald, "Commentary," *WMQ3* 41 (1984), 95.

[8] Estimates of emigration from Scotland itself remain very doubtful. One contemporary observer reckoned that 20,000 left in the decade from 1763 to 1773; Another guessed that 30,000 Scots may have sailed in the years 1773–75. A modern estimate has been made by I.C.C. Graham, who found actual records of 15,989 departures Scotland in the years 1768–75, and an additional 4,256 arrivals culled from American records. He concludes that the emigration totaled 20,245 from 1768 to 1775. A leading Scottish historical demographer, Michael Flinn, agrees that "it seems very unlikely . . . that emigration from Scotland in the 18th and early 19th century ever sustained an average of much more than about 2,000 per year for more than a few years at a time." An American scholar, T. L. Purvis, reckons that emigration from Scotland was approximately 62,500 in the period 1707–75. If the annual flow was between 1,200 and 1,500 a year, then the magnitude of Scottish migration to America in the period from 1717 to 1775 was probably in the range of 70,000 to 80,000. Cf. Ian C. C. Graham, *Colonists from Scotland: Emigration to North America, 1707–1783* (Ithaca, 1956,); Michael Flinn, ed., *Scottish Population History* (Cambridge, 1977), 443; Thomas L. Purvis, "The European Ancestry of the United States Population, 1790," *WMQ3* 41 (1984), 85–101.

[9] Recent and authoritative estimates of Scottish and Irish migration by Dickson, Graham and Flinn are too low to square with estimates of the population identified as Scotch Irish, Scottish and Irish in studies of the U.S. Census of 1790 by the McDonalds (above 25%), Purvis (21.6%) or even Barker (14.3%). These estimates by American historians can be reconciled with the findings of Irish and Scottish demographers only if many immigrants called "Scotch-Irish" in the United States were Anglo-Irish, Anglo-Scots, or English borderers.

It is important to bear in mind that the entire population of Scotland was only about one million in 1650, increasing to 1.5 million by 1800. Ireland's population was 2.5 million in 1650, rising to 5.25 million in 1800; England's was about 5.75 million in 1700, rising to 9.25 million in 1800.

Migration from the north of England and Wales to the backcountry has not been estimated with precision in this period. Scattered evidence suggests that it may have been roughly equal to the flow from the north of Ireland and much larger than from Scotland. One statistical straw in the wind is a study of servants from Britain and Ireland mentioned in the Charleston *Gazette* from 1733 to 1773, which found the following numbers from Britain and Ireland: Irish and Scotch-Irish, 38.6%; English and Welsh, 40.0%; "Scotch," 21.4%. See Warren B. Smith, *White Servitude in Colonial South Carolina* (Columbia, S.C., 1961), 44–48.

In one respect, this folk wandering from North Britain was similar to other migrations that preceded it. It was mainly a movement of families. A study of British records (1773–76) finds that 61 percent of emigrants from northern England traveled in family groups. From the border counties of Scotland, 73 percent also did so.[10] From northern Ireland, 91 percent of 405 Ulster emigrants who came to the Shenandoah Valley of Virginia during the year 1740, arrived in families. Only 37 traveled as individuals.[11]

Many of these emigrants were women and girls. The sex ratio of those who left Scotland in the 1770s was 149 males for every 100 females—an unusually even-handed distribution in an emigrant population. The mix of genders was less equal than in New England's great migration, but more so than in the movement to the Chesapeake colonies.[12]

The age distribution of men and women was also remarkably broad in this moving population. A large proportion were adolescents and young adults. But 25 percent were children under fifteen, and nearly 40 percent were over twenty-five. All age-cohorts were represented in large numbers except the elderly. Here again, the pattern was intermediate between the migration to New England and the Chesapeake.[13]

In other respects, however, this fourth great migration differed

---

[10]These estimates are a weighted average of Bailyn's data for six counties: Cumberland, Westmorland, Northumberland, Durham, Lancashire and Yorkshire. His data for the Scottish borders includes the seven counties of Berwick, Roxburgh, Peebles, Selkirk, Dumfries, Kirkcudbright and Wigtown. For other parts of Scotland, Bailyn reports a more mixed pattern; overall, 48% came in family groups. From the south of England, the proportion traveling in families was very low—approximately 7% in the period from 1773 to 1776, ranging from 2 to 14% by region. See Bailyn, *Voyagers to the West,* 140.

[11]Of these 405 immigrants, 379 (93.5%) were from northern Ireland; 20 (4.9%) were from Great Britain or Ireland; and 6 (1.5%) were from Germany. The rest were not identified. Of the 379 from northern Ireland, 93% had taken ship to Philadelphia, and traveled overland to the backcountry. The rest arrived in Virginia ports. The majority reported that they had traveled at their own expense. Robert David Mitchell, "The Upper Shenandoah Valley of Virginia during the Eighteenth Century: A Study of Historical Geography" (thesis, Univ. of Va., 1969), 68.

[12]Bailyn, *Voyagers from the West,* 129–34.

[13]The distribution of ages among Scottish emigrants in the period from 1773 to 1776 appears as follows in an analysis of migration records of Bernard Bailyn:

Age Cohort	Emigrants from Scotland 1773–1776	Population of Scotland 1755
1–14	24.7%	33.1%
15–24	35.8%	18.0%
25–59	38.7%	41.1%
60+	0.8%	7.8%

Source: Bailyn, *Voyagers to the West,* 128. Data are not available for emigrants from northern Ireland and northern England.

very much from all of its predecessors. The motives of these emigrants were fundamentally unlike those of New England Puritans, Delaware Quakers and even Virginia cavaliers. Among the North Britons, there was no talk of holy experiments, or cities on a hill. These new emigrants came mainly in search of material betterment. In the early eighteenth century, many surveys of their motives found the same pattern of concern about high rents, low wages, heavy taxes and short leases. In northern Ireland, conditions were so very hard that famine and starvation were often mentioned as a leading cause of migration.[14]

The same material motives also appeared fifty years later, when this movement was nearing its end. In the year 1774, four shiploads of emigrants to Nova Scotia were individually asked why they had come to America. Their answers were more positive than before, but still strongly materialist. Once again, they spoke about the rapacity of English landlords, the shortage of food, and their dreams for a better life in the New World.[15]

An important stimulus to emigration was correspondence from family and friends who had already made the journey. In 1729, two clergymen wrote that members of their congregations received "many letters from their friends and acquaintances . . .

---

[14]R. J. Dickson tabulated six surveys of motives for emigration from northern Ireland and northern England in the year 1719. The following causes were mentioned in positive or negative terms.

Cause	English Judges	Presbyterian Ministers	Anglican Bishops	Dublin Essayist	Landowner	Emigrants
Famine	yes	yes	yes	yes		yes
High rents	yes	yes	yes	yes	yes	yes
Church taxes	yes	yes	no	yes	yes	yes
News from America	yes	yes			yes	yes
Short leases	yes	yes			yes	yes
Little coin				yes	yes	yes
Luxuries of the rich					yes	yes
Fall of linen trade	yes					yes
Too little tillage			yes		yes	
Absentees and pensions					yes	yes
To escape creditors	yes					
Oppression by JPs		yes				
Overpopulation						yes
Sacramental tests		yes	no			

Source: Dickson, *Ulster Emigration*, 46; rearranged by frequency; for similar findings see Bailyn, *Voyagers to the West*, 189–93.

[15]A total of 518 emigrants in this group mentioned the following motives for migration (some giving more than one): to seek a better livelihood, or find employment, 298; excessive rents, 156; scarcity and dearness of provisions, 67; the engrossing of small farms, 4; other (to visit relatives, see the country, etc.). 19. Dickson, *Ulster Emigration*, 81.

[in the] plantations, inviting them to transport themselves thither, and promising them liberty and ease as the reward of their honest industry, with a prospect of transmitting their acquisitions and privileges safe to their posterity, without the imposition of growing rents and other burdens."[16]

The process of migration itself also became more materialist in the eighteenth century. Much of it was organized for profit by shipping agents who scoured the countryside in search of likely prospects. The Atlantic crossing also tended to pass into the hands of greedy entrepreneurs, with horrific human consequences. Ships were laden beyond their capacity. In 1767, an epidemic broke out on board a crowded emigrant vessel sailing from Belfast to South Carolina; the unscrupulous owners had packed 450 people into its hold and more than 100 died at sea. Another ship bound from Belfast to Philadelphia ran out of food in midpassage. Forty-six passengers starved to death; the survivors were driven to cannibalism and some even consumed the flesh of their own families. The transatlantic journey became more dangerous in the eighteenth century than it had been in the seventeenth. Mortality in ships sailing from North Britain approached that in the slave trade.[17]

When these people arrived in the New World, they faced intense prejudice from other ethnic groups. "I was looked upon as a barbarian," wrote Lieutenant James MacMichael.[18] But so desperate were conditions at home that few chose to return to the world that they had left. One Scots-Irish immigrant wrote from Pennsylvania in 1767, "I do not know one that has come here that desires to be in Ireland again."[19]

---

[16]C.M.L. Bouch and G. P. Jones, *A Short Social and Economic History of the Lake Countries, 1500–1830* (1961, rpt. New York, 1968), 897.

[17]Transatlantic insurance rates declined during the 18th century, but human cargo was more roughly handled. See James F. Shepherd and Gary Walton, *Shipping, Maritime Trade and Economic Development of Colonial North America* (Cambridge, 1972).

[18]James MacMichael, "Diary . . . ," ed. William P. MacMichael, *PMHB* 16 (1892), 145–46.

[19]A. C. Davies, "'As Good a Country as Any Man Needs to Dwell In': Letters from a Scotch Irish Immigrant in Pennsylvania, 1766, 1767, and 1784," *PH* 50 (1983), 313–22.

❧ Social Origins: Poverty and Pride

On the question of social origins in this migration, contemporary opinion was divided. Some observers believed that most emigrants came from the middling ranks of their society. Reports from three different Irish ports in 1774, for example, agreed that the majority were "paying passengers of the middle class."[1] Others, however, formed a different impression. One writer unkindly described the Scots-Irish emigrants as "the scum of two nations." An outspoken Anglican clergyman, not to be outdone, called them, "the scum of the universe." Another estimated that no more than "one man in ten is a man of substance." A fourth remarked that most seemed "very poor."[2]

All of these observers accurately described some parts of the North British migration, but none of them comprehended the whole of it. This large flow was very mixed in its social composition. A small but important minority of Irish and North British migrants were gentry who came from the ruling order of this region. This narrow elite was destined to become eminent in American affairs. But in quantitative terms it accounted for no more than 1 or 2 percent of all emigrants.

A somewhat larger group were independent yeomen who had achieved a measure of independence from the great landlords who dominated the border region. In Cumberland and Westmorland these yeomen were called the "statesman" class. Their numbers were comparatively small throughout this area, and even smaller in the emigrant stream.

Most emigrants came from ranks below that of the gentry and statesmen. In the border counties of England and Scotland and northern Ireland as well, the majority were farmers and farm laborers who owned no land of their own, but worked as tenants and undertenants. A large minority were semiskilled craftsmen and petty traders. In northern Ireland, many had worked in the linen trade—impoverished handloom weavers, unemployed agents, traders and entrepreneurs. This was especially the case in

---

[1]Dickson, *Ulster Emigration*, 97.

[2]Boulter to Newcastle, 23 Nov. 1728, Wayland F. Dunaway, *The Scotch-Irish of Colonial Pennsylvania* (Chapel Hill, 1944), 20; John Stewart, "Letter," 3 May 1736, *PMHB* 21 (1897), 485–86; S. F. Warren to Dr. Warren, 22 Jan. 1766, in H. Roy Merrens, ed., *The Colonial South Carolina Scene: Contemporary Views, 1697–1774* (Columbia, S.C., 1977), 233–34.

the period from 1772 to 1774, when the linen industry suffered a contraction of great severity.[3]

Remarkably few came in bondage. From 1773 to 1776, indentured servants were only 1 percent of Scottish border emigrants, and less than 20 percent of those who had left the six northern counties of England.[4] Among emigrants from northern Ireland, the proportion of servants was somewhat higher, but even there a majority were free. This was so in part because Irish servants were not much wanted in America. They were thought to be violent, ungovernable and very apt to assault their masters. Buyers were discouraged by lurid accounts of Irish servants who rioted in Barbados, "straggled" in Bermuda or ran away on the mainland, sometimes with their masters' wives and daughters in tow. In the Leeward Islands, 125 unruly Irish servants were deliberately marooned on the desolate Isle of Crabs. Throughout British America, purchasers complained of the "proud" and "haughty" spirit of these people.[5]

The social origins of these emigrants were more humble than those of New England Puritans or Delaware Quakers. But they did not come from the bottom of British society. Only a minority were unskilled laborers. As always in a voluntary migration, desperately poor people were excluded by the fact of poverty itself. The cost of a family's passage to America was high enough to keep the poorest people at home. An even greater obstacle was an impoverished spirit which robbed the poor of their hope, their pride and even their dreams of betterment.

---

[3]A quantitative analysis of British emigrant registers (1773–76) by American historian Bernard Bailyn yields the following occupational data for those who came from the borders:

Occupation	Emigrants from Northern England	Emigrants from Scottish Borders
Gentry	1.0%	0.6%
Merchandising	4.8%	3.3%
High skilled crafts and trades	4.6%	7.8%
Ordinarily skilled crafts and trades	37.5%	27.2%
Farming	40.0%	26.7%
Laborers	12.1%	34.4%
Total	100.0%	100.0%

Note: Northern England includes the six counties of Cumberland, Westmorland, Northumberland, Durham, Lancashire and Yorkshire; the Scottish Borders include the seven counties of Wigtown, Kirkcudbright, Dumfries, Roxburgh, Selkirk, Peebles, and Berwick. The source is Bailyn, *Voyagers to the West,* 162–63.

[4]*Ibid.,* 170–71.

[5]Cheesman A. Herrick, *White Servitude in Pennsylvania* (Philadelphia, 1926), 164–66; Abbot E. Smith, *Colonists in Bondage: White Servitude and Convict Labor in America, 1607–1776* (Chapel Hill, 1947), 171, 289.

The Scots-Irish who came to America in the eighteenth century were not poor in any of these senses. Their pride was a source of irritation to their English neighbors, who could not understand what they had to feel proud about. It was said of one Scots-Irishman that "his looks spoke out that he would not fear the devil, should he meet him face to face. . . . He loved to talk of himself, and spoke as freely and encomiastically as enthusiastic youths do of Alexander and Caesar. . . . Qualities united in him which are never found in one person except an Irishman."[6]

This combination of poverty and pride set the North Britons squarely apart from other English-speaking people in the American colonies. Border emigrants demanded to be treated with respect even when dressed in rags. Their humble origins did not create the spirit of subordination which others expected of "lower ranks." This fierce and stubborn pride would be a cultural fact of high importance in the American region which they came to dominate.

❧ Religious Origins: Militant Christianity

The borderers of North Britain were mixed in their religious beliefs. Those who came from Scotland and the north of Ireland tended to be Presbyterian, with a scattering of Roman Catholics among them. The English border folk were mostly Anglican, with a sprinkling of small Protestant sects. Border emigrants of the two leading denominations, Anglican and Presbyterian, both showed a strong tendency toward what was called New Light Christianity in the eighteenth century. Many Scottish and Irish Presbyterians called themselves People of the New Light before coming to America. They believed in "free grace," and before emigrating they had formed the habit of gathering in "field meetings" and "prayer societies," a custom which they carried to America and established in the backcountry. In Scotland, these New Light Presbyterians were specially numerous on the edges of the Irish Sea.[7]

---

[6]George R. Gilmer, *Sketches of Some of the First Settlers of Upper Georgia* . . . (rev. ed., Baltimore, 1965), 62.

[7]T. C. Smout, *A History of the Scottish People, 1560–1830* (London, 1969), 213–22; J. D. Mackie, *A History of Scotland*, eds. Bruce Lenman and Geoffrey Parker (2d ed., Harmondsworth, 1978), 298–305; W. L. Mathieson, *The Awakening of Scotland, 1747–1797* (Glasgow, 1910); *idem, Church and Reform in Scotland* (Glasgow, 1916), P.W.J. Riley, *The English Ministers and Scotland* (London, 1964).

In Protestant Ireland, similar religious tendencies also appeared—a deep interest in reformed religion, a settled hostility to the established church, a belief in "free grace," a habit of field meetings and a bias toward New Light Christianity. An Anglo-Irish archbishop in 1714 wrote that "the people of the north have a particular aversion to curates and call them hirelings."[8]

The same religious attitudes also existed among the English borderers. Though they were mostly Anglican, an increasing number had joined small Protestant sects, or were converted to more evangelical forms of Christianity by Methodist and Baptist missionaries. They also were hostile to the "hireling clergy" which the Church of England had settled upon them.

In Scotland some were of a militant sect called "Society People" or "Cameronians." Their founder, Richard Cameron, was a field preacher who advocated a particularly uncompromising form of covenanted Christianity. The Cameronians grew very strong in the south and west of Scotland, where they engaged in a practice called "rabbling," or forcibly removing "unregenerate" clergy from their livings, sometimes with much violence. The authorities hunted the Cameronians like animals across the countryside, and hanged several of their leaders. But many survived, worshipping defiantly with a Bible in one hand and a weapon in the other, and slaughtering the forces that were sent to suppress them. After 1689, the authorities conceded defeat, and adopted the typically North British solution of recruiting these Protestant rebels to fight against Roman Catholic Jacobites in the Highlands. The result was the creation of a great fighting regiment in the British army called the Cameronians, the only regiment in the army list to bear the name of a religious leader. It appointed an Elder in every company of infantry, and required each enlisted man to carry a Bible in his kit. Even in the twentieth century this Presbyterian regiment carried arms to worship and posted sentries at the four corners of the church. It quickly became known for the ferocity of its fighting. In its first battle in 1689, 1,200 recruits of this regiment broke a veteran force of 5,000 Jacobites and burnt many in their fortifications.[9]

In 1743, the followers of Richard Cameron reorganized themselves as the Reformed Presbyterian Church. Many found their

---

[8]Charles K. Bolton, *Scotch Irish Pioneers in Ulster and America* (Baltimore, 1967), 68.

[9]R. M. Barnes, *The Uniforms and History of the Scottish Regiments* (London, 1960), 37, 42–45, *passim.*

way to the American backcountry, with other North British sects. The Anglican missionary Charles Woodmason complained in 1765 that "Africk never more abounded with new Monsters, than Pennsylvania does with the New Sects, who are continually sending out their emissaries around. One of these Parties, known by the title of *New Lights* or *Gifted Brethren* (for they pretend to inspiration) now infest the whole Back Country."[10]

Sectarian conflicts became commonplace in the backcountry. Many denominations were planted in the wilderness, but various groups of Presbyterians outnumbered all others, and outrivaled them in religious bigotry.[11] The journal of the English missionary Charles Woodmason was a running chronicle of religious strife. When Woodmason tried to conduct an Anglican sermon in the back settlements, Presbyterians disrupted his services, rioted while he preached, started a pack of dogs fighting outside the church, loosed his horse, stole his church key, refused him food and shelter, and gave two barrels of whiskey to his congregation before a service of communion. One Baptist tried to discredit the Anglican missionary by stealing a clerical dressing gown, climbing into bed with a woman in the dark, and "making her give out next day the Parson came to bed with her."[12]

Their victim complained bitterly that "the perverse persecuting spirit of the Presbyterians displays itself much more here than in Scotland. . . . the sects are eternally jarring among themselves." He quickly learned the border variant of the golden rule—do unto others as they threatened do unto you. He preached furiously against the Presbyterians, and tried to start legal actions against them, but all in vain. "As all the magistrates are Presbyterians, I could not get a warrant," he wrote, and further, "if I got warrants, as the constables are Presbyterians likewise I could not get them served."[13]

This sectarian strife continued for many generations in the backcountry. In the year 1846, Allen Wiley remembered, "the preachers and people of the present day can form no estimation of the asperity of feeling and language which prevailed in those

[10]Charles Woodmason, "An Account of the Churches in South Carolina, Georgia, North Carolina and the Floridas," in *The Carolina Backcountry on the Eve of the Revolution: The Journal and Other Writings of Charles Woodmason, Anglican Itinerant* (Chapel Hill, 1953), 78.

[11]Carl Bridenbaugh, *Myths and Realities, Societies of the Colonial South* (Baton Rouge, 1952), 183.

[12]Woodmason, *Carolina Backcountry*, 20, 30–31, 39, 45.

[13]*Ibid.*, 45, 53.

days of bitter waters, even among good men and able ministers."[14] Military metaphors abounded in backcountry sermons
and hymns. Prayers were invoked for vengeance and the destruction of enemies. When these Christian warriors were not battling
among themselves they fell upon the Indians with the same
inplacable fury. Their militant faith flourished in the environment
of the back settlements, just as it had done on the borders of
North Britain for many generations before.

❧ Ethnic Origins: "We Are a Mixed People"

Some historians describe these immigrants as "Ulster Irish" or
"Northern Irish." It is true that many sailed from the province
of Ulster in northern Ireland, but these labels are not accurate
when applied to the movement as a whole. The emigration from
Ulster was part of much larger flow which drew from the lowlands
of Scotland, the north of England, and every side of the Irish Sea.

Many scholars call these people "Scotch-Irish." That expression is an Americanism, rarely used in Britain and much resented
by the people to whom it was attached. "We're no Eerish bot
Scoatch," one of them was heard to say in Pennsylvania.[15] Some
preferred to be called Anglo-Irish, a label that was more commonly applied to them than Scotch-Irish during the eighteenth
century. Others were called "Saxon-Scotch."[16] One scholar
writes: ". . . some Ulster Protestants derived from families that
were not Scottish at all, but English or Irish," He adds, ". . . some
immigrant groups that historians have labeled as Scots-Irish
never lived in Ireland but came directly from Scotland."[17]

A student of Appalachian culture in the early twentieth century
reached the same conclusion:

> Inquiries . . . as to family history and racial stock rarely bring a
> more definite answer than that grandparents or great-grandpar-
> ents came from North Carolina or Virginia or occasionally from
> Pennsylvania, and that they "reckon" their folks were "English,"
> "Scotch," or "Irish," any of which designations may mean Scotch-
> Irish.[18]

[14]T. Scott Miyakawa, *Protestants and Pioneers* (Chicago, 1964), 128.
[15]Dunaway, *Scotch Irish in Colonial Pennsylvania*, 10.
[16]Gilmer, *First Settlers of Upper Georgia*, 173.
[17]Ned C. Landsman, *Scotland and Its First American Colony, 1683–1765* (Princeton, 1985), 8.
[18]John C. Campbell, *The Southern Highlander and His Homeland* (New York, 1921), 51.

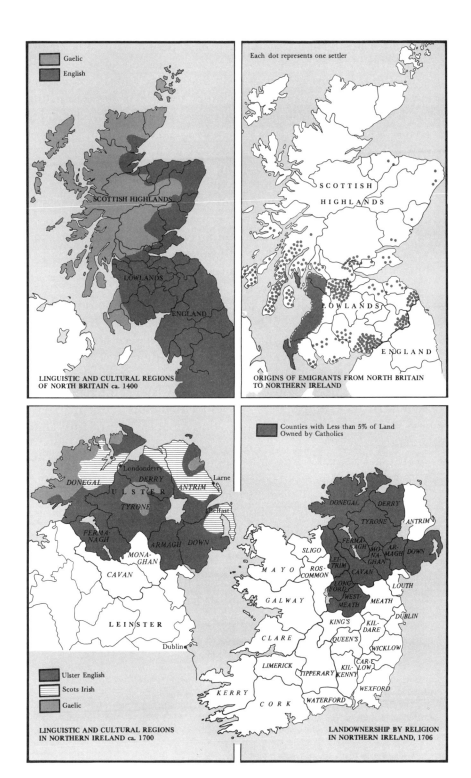

Gaelic

English

LINGUISTIC AND CULTURAL REGIONS
OF NORTH BRITAIN ca. 1400

Each dot represents one settler

ORIGINS OF EMIGRANTS FROM NORTH BRITAIN
TO NORTHERN IRELAND

Ulster English

Scots Irish

Gaelic

LINGUISTIC AND CULTURAL REGIONS
IN NORTHERN IRELAND ca. 1700

Counties with Less than 5% of Land
Owned by Catholics

LANDOWNERSHIP BY RELIGION
IN NORTHERN IRELAND, 1706

619

Two historians have characterized these people as "Celts." But this label is also very much mistaken as a rounded description of their ethnic origins. Some among them were indeed of Celtic descent. Before the Roman invasion of the north, the dominant people in the north of England were a loose confederacy of Celtic warrior tribes called in Latin *Brigantes.* The ruined ramparts of their hill forts may still be seen at Carrock Fell in Cumbria and many other places throughout the region.[19] The *Brigantes* were broken by the Romans about the year A.D. 80. Thereafter, many other people invaded and colonized the region—the Romans themselves in the first century, the Saxons in the sixth century, the Vikings and Irish in the tenth century, and the Norman French in the eleventh and twelfth centuries. All of these groups contributed to the growth of this regional culture.[20]

By the eighteenth century, the culture of this region bore little resemblence to the customs of the ancient Celts. The dominant language was English—unlike that of Gaelic-speaking Irish Catholic peasants, Scottish highlanders, Welsh cottagers, and Cornish miners. The borderers had comparatively little contact (much of it hostile) with these Celtic people. In the seventeenth and eighteenth centuries, it was observed that "the Ulster settlers mingled freely with the English Puritans and Huguenots," but married very rarely with the Gaelic-speaking people of Ireland and Scotland.[21]

Few Gaelic-speaking people emigrated from Ireland, Cornwall or Wales to the American colonies before the nineteenth century. Celtic Irish immigrants were excluded by law from some American colonies. A South Carolina statute of 1716 forbade "what is commonly called native Irish, or persons of known scandalous character or Roman Catholics."[22]

Gaelic-speaking Scottish highlanders also were ethnically distinct from the borderers. There was no love lost between lowland and highland Scots, who differed in language, politics, religion

---

[19]R. G. Collingwood, "The Hill Fort on Carrock Fell," *CWAAS* ns 10 (1910), 342–53.

[20]Much of the archaeology of this region, including excavations at Carrock Fell, was done by W. G. Collingwood and his philosopher-son R. G. Collingwood. Two surveys of high quality are Nick Higham, *The Northern Counties to AD 1000* (London, 1986), and Roy Millward and Adrian Robinson, *The Lake District* (rev. ed., London, 1974).

[21]The "Celtic" interpretation appears in Forrest McDonald and Grady McWhiney, "The Antebellum Southern Herdsman: A Reinterpretation," *JSH* 41 (1975), 147–66, and many other essays; a contrary interpretation appears in Landsman, *Scotland and Its First American Colony,* 282–83, *passim.*

[22]William A. Schaper, *Sectionalism in South Carolina,* (1901, rpt. New York, 1968), 66.

and culture. In America, Scottish highlanders tended to settle apart in North Carolina's Cape Fear Valley, where Gaelic continued to be spoken even into the late twentieth century. Many of these transplanted highlanders became Tories in the American Revolution, largely because their border neighbors were Whig. The fighting between them was as savage as any conflict in North Britain.[23]

"We are a mixed people," a border immigrant declared in America during the eighteenth century. "We are a mix'd medley," said another. So they were in many ways. They were mixed in their social rank, mixed in their religious denominations, and most profoundly mixed in their ancestry, which was Celtic, Roman, German, English, Scandinavian, Irish and Scottish in varying proportions. They were also very mixed in their place of residence—coming as they did from England, Scotland and Ireland.[24]

But in another way, these immigrants were very similar to one another. No matter whether rich or poor, Anglican or Presbyterian, Saxon or Celt, they were all a border people. They shared a unique regional culture which was the product of a place in time.

❧ The Borders of North Britain

Early in the twentieth century the English folklorist Cecil Sharp left his home in Stratford-on-Avon and spent many months in America's Appalachian highlands, collecting the songs and dances of the back settlers. After careful comparison with British materials, he wrote of these people:

> From an analysis of their traditional songs, ballads, dances, singing-games, etc. . . . they came from a part of England where the civilization was least developed—probably the North of England, or the Border country between Scotland and England.[1]

This border region included six counties in the far north of England: Cumberland, Westmorland and parts of Lancashire on

---

[23]Duane Meyer, *The Highland Scots of North Carolina, 1732–1776* (Chapel Hill, 1961), Graham, *Colonists from Scotland*, 188; Bailyn, *Voyagers to the West*, 110–11.

[24]Woodmason, *Carolina Backcountry*, 6.

[1]Cecil Sharp to John Campbell, n.d., in Campbell, *The Southern Highlander and His Homeland* (New York, 1921), 70; see also Olive Campbell and Cecil J. Sharp, *English Folk Songs from the Southern Appalachians* (New York, 1917).

the western side of the Pennines; Northumberland, Durham and parts of Yorkshire to the east. It also embraced five counties of southern Scotland—Ayr, Dumfries, Wigtown, Roxburgh and Berwick. During the seventeenth century, its culture was carried westward across the Irish Sea to five counties of Ulster—Derry, Down, Armagh, Antrim and Tyrone.[2]

Within this region the North British emigration to America drew heavily from counties that touched upon the Irish Sea— Ayr, Dumfries and Wigtown in Scotland; Cumberland and Westmorland in England; Derry, Antrim and Down in Ireland. The sea itself united its surrounding lands in a single cultural region.[3]

To a traveler who enters this border region from the south of England, the landscape seems strange and forbidding even today. As one drives northward on the M6 motorway, the first impression is of a bare and empty country, which by comparison with the teeming English Midlands appears almost uninhabited. The terrain is uneven—a stark succession of barren hills and deep valleys. West of Kendal, a handsome stone-built shire town in the old county of Westmorland, the countryside begins to change. Here one enters the Lake District, with its romantic scenery and beautiful views. Westward beyond Lake Windermere lies the Fell country, a sparsely settled mountain district with peaks rising to 3,000 feet, and high moorlands of almost lunar bleakness. Still farther to the west, the houses grow more numerous as one approaches the close-built coastal towns on the Irish sea.

Forty-five miles north of Kendal lies the city of Carlisle, the metropolis of the English marches. This town is still dominated by its castle with massive walls of crimson stone which brood ominously above the busy traffic on Castle Way. To wander through the damp dungeons of Carlisle Castle, and to study the strange graffiti carved in its walls by captives many centuries ago, is to feel once again the violence of life upon the border. Everywhere in the region one still discovers ruined walls and crenellated towers which are memorials to its violent past. At Penrith, a market town

---

[2]By tradition this region is called the border in England and the borders in Scotland.

[3]Here is another application for the Palmer-Godechot thesis, about the relative permeability of land and sea in the eighteenth century. Maritime communications had much improved since the middle ages, but travel over land was not much better than in the world of the Romans. The argument of Palmer and Godechot about the borders of the "Atlantic world" also applies to the edges of the Irish Sea. See Jacques Godechot and R. R. Palmer, "Le problème de l'Atlantique du XVIIIe au XXe siècle," *Relazioni del X Congresso Internazionale di Scienze Storiche (Roma 4–11 Settembre 1955)* (Florence, 1955), V, 175–239.

halfway between Carlisle and Kendal, there is a great red sandstone beacon high on a barren hill, where warning fires were
lighted when the Scots came over the border.[4]

The border derived its cultural character from one decisive historical fact. For seven centuries, the kings of Scotland and
England could not agree who owned it, and meddled constantly
in each other's affairs. From the year 1040 to 1745, every English
monarch but three suffered a Scottish invasion, or became an
invader in his turn. In the same period, most Scottish kings went
to war against England, and many died "with their boots on," as
the border saying went. Scotland's first king, Duncan (1034–40),
was murdered by Macbeth after losing a war to the Northum-
brians. In 1057, Macbeth himself suffered the same fate after his
defeat by another English army in the forest fight at Dunsinane.
The next Scottish king, Malcolm Canmore (1058–93), invaded
England five times in hopes of conquering its northern provinces,
and was at last slain in Northumberland. After 1093 the Normans
attacked northward in their turn and when Scotland's king Donald Bane (1093–97) resisted, they took him captive and their
Scottish allies put out his eyes to quiet him.

An interval of peace followed, but in 1136 Scotland's King
David led an army into England and the fighting began again. In
the course of the next century most towns on both sides of the
border were brutally sacked and burned, and the countryside was
ravaged from Newcastle to Edinburgh. Churches and monasteries became favorite targets; one Scottish army struggled home so
laden with loot that soldiers drowned in the river Eden beneath
the weight of plundered chalices and crucifixes.

These wars continued for many generations. In the year 1215,
England's King John marched north on a mission of revenge. The
Scottish burghers of Berwick were put to death by torture; the
English king set fire to their houses with his own hand. During
the late thirteenth century, Scotland was forced to accept English
overlordship, which brought another interval of sullen peace.
Conditions improved in the reign of Alexander III (1249–86), a
golden age for Scottish culture. But on a dark night in 1286,
Alexander fell to his death over a cliff—or perhaps was pushed—
and the slaughter began again. England's King Edward I (1272–

[4]The Penrith beacon was built in 1719, within a year of the beginnings of the American
migration. It was used in 1745, and repaired as late as 1780. Nikolaus Pevsner, *The Buildings
of England: Cumberland and Westmorland* (Harmondsworth, 1967), 178.

1307) captured the border town of Berwick and put to death every male of military age. For three centuries Scottish soldiers in their bloodlust cried "Remember Berwick!"

The lowlands remained in English hands until about 1297, when Scotland's national hero William Wallace invaded Cumberland. His soldiers flayed the bodies of English officers who fell into their hands. When Wallace himself was captured, his body was drawn and quartered, and his head impaled atop an English pike. England's warrior King Edward I (1272–1307) then harried the north with such violence that he was called the "Hammer of the Scots"; as he lay dying in Cumberland, Edward ordered his bones to be carried into Scotland by an avenging English army. His hapless son Edward II (1307–27) tried to obey, but was beaten at Bannockburn (1314) by the Scottish hero Robert the Bruce, whose followers looted, burned and raped the northern counties of England, and part of Ireland for good measure. England's Edward III (1327–77) took his revenge in the campaign which is still remembered as the "burnt Candlemas"—a systematic destruction of the Scottish lowlands as far north as Edinburgh. The act of savagery led to new atrocities by the Scots, and new expeditions by England's Richard II (1377–99) and Henry IV (1399–1413).

All the while, private fighting continued between warlords on both sides of the border. Through the fifteenth century, North Britain was reduced to anarchy. Scotland's James I (1406–37) was assassinated by his own henchmen; James II "of the fiery Face" (1437–60) was blown to pieces while attacking the English at Roxburgh; James III (1460–88) was murdered by a family of rampaging border warlords; and James IV (1488–1513) died fighting the English on Flodden Field. English vengance reached its bloody climax when Henry VIII (1509–47) ordered the ruin of hundreds of border villages in a retribution that Scots remember as "the Rough Wooing."

The border fell quiet after 1567, when James VI became King of Scotland and later King of England as well. But in the reign of Charles I, English and Scots went to war again, and hostilities continued under the Commonwealth and Protectorate. Major raids and border risings also occurred in 1680, 1689, 1715 and 1745. Altogether, two historians of the border write that "until after 1745, the region never enjoyed fifty consecutive years of quiet." This endemic violence caused heavy loss of life on both sides of the border. It was written that "a Scots raid down toward

Penrith Beacon stands high on a hill near the Cumbrian town of the same name. Its purpose was to warn the English countryside when Scottish raiders were over the border. Many such beacon towers were constructed throughout this turbulent region. Several had earlier stood on the site where this one was constructed of a local red sandstone in 1715, the year of the Scottish Jacobite rising. It was used in 1745 during the last Scottish invasion of England. The Penrith Beacon still stands today, a monument to many centuries of violence in the borderlands. This drawing follows two illustrations, kindly supplied by the Penrith Library.

the Tyneside often did as much killing in relation to the local population as the plague did nearly everywhere."[5] The cultural effect
of violence was magnified by a climate of fear which continued
even in periods of peace. Long after the "Forty-five," English diaries often recorded rumors that the Scots were "over the borders." Fear itself remained a social fact of high importance after
so many centuries of strife.[6]

Dynastic stuggles between the monarchs of England and Scotland were only a small part of the border's sufferings. The quarrels of kings became a criminal's opportunity to rob and rape and
murder with impunity. On both sides of the border, and especially in the "debatable land" that was claimed by both kingdoms,
powerful clans called Taylor, Bell, Graham and Bankhead lived
outside the law, and were said to be "Scottish when they will, and
English at their pleasure."[7] They made a profession of preying
upon their neighbors—"reiving," it was called along the border.[8]
Other families specialized in the theft of livestock—"rustling"
was its border name. Rustling on a small scale was endemic
throughout the region. Large gangs of professional rustlers also
"operated on a scale more reminiscent of the traditional American model than any English equivalent," in the words of an
historian.[9]

This incessant violence shaped the culture of the border
region, and also created a social system which was very different
from that in the south of England. On the border, forms of tenancy were designed to maintain large bodies of fighting men.
Lord Burghley noted, " . . .there is no lease in that country, but
with provision to find horse and arms, to be held by an able
man."[10] In the great manors of Wark and Harbottle, it was
observed that "customary tenure was very secure . . . descent was
by partible inheritance, so that potential fighting men were guaranteed subsistence."[11]

[5]Bouch and Jones, *Economic and Social History of the Lake Counties,* 2, 11, 16.

[6]George Williams Diary, Ms. DX 124, CUMROC.

[7]George M. Fraser, *The Steel Bonnets,* (New York 1972), 65.

[8]The word *reiving* is from the ME *reven,* to take by force; for the Debateable Land, see
T.H.B. Graham, "The Debateable Land," *CWAAS* n.s. 12 (1912), 33–58.

[9]It would, of course, be chronologically more correct to say that American rustling was reminiscent of the traditional northern English model. See R.A.E. Wells, "Sheep Rustling in Yorkshire," *NH* 20 (1984), 127–84; J. G. Rule, "The Manifold Causes of Rural Crime: Sheep Stealing in England, *circa* 1740–1780," in J. G. Rule, ed., *Outside the Law* (Exeter, 1983).

[10]Robert Newton, "The Decay of the Borders: Tudor Northumberland in Transition," in
Christopher Chalkin and Michael Haveden, eds., *Rural Change and Urban Growth, 1500–1800*
(London, 1977), 2–31.

[11]Joan Thirsk, ed., *Agrarian History of England and Wales,* (Cambridge, 1967), IV, 49.

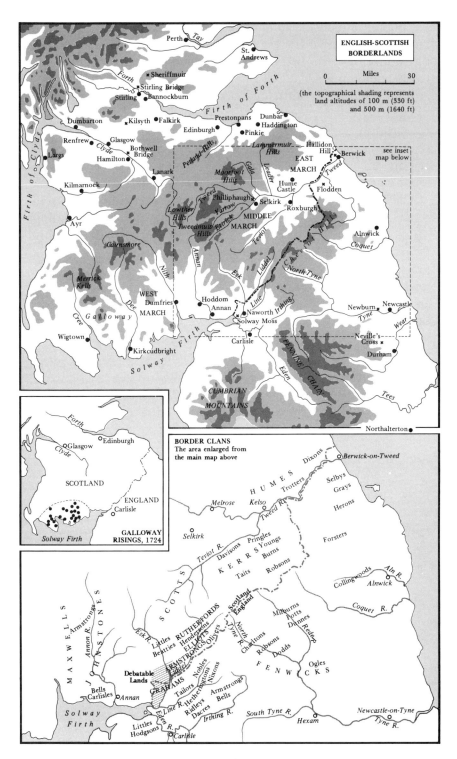

ENGLISH-SCOTTISH BORDERLANDS

0   Miles   30

(the topographical shading represents
land altitudes of 100 m (330 ft)
and 500 m (1640 ft)

Perth   *Tay*

St. Andrews

Sheriffmuir

Forth   Stirling Bridge
Stirling   Bannockburn

Dumbarton   Kilsyth   Falkirk   Prestonpans   Dunbar
Edinburgh   Haddington
Firth   *of*   *Forth*
Renfrew   Glasgow   Pinkie
Clyde   Bothwell
Largs   Hamilton   Bridge   *Lammermuir*   Hallidon
Firth of Clyde   *Hills*   Hill   Berwick
Kilmarnock   Lanark   *Pentland Hills*   **EAST**
  Gala   **MARCH**
  Moorfoot   *Leader*   *Tweed*
  Hills   Hume   Flodden
  Tweed   Castle
Ayr   Phlliphaugh   Selkirk
Lowther   *Yarrow*   Roxburgh
Cairnsmore   *Hills*   **MIDDLE**
  Tweedmuir   *Ettrick*   **MARCH**   Alnwick
  Hills   *Teviot*   *Coquet*
Merrick   *Nith*   *Ann*
Kells   *Esk*   *Liddel*   *North Tyne*
  WEST   Hoddom   *Line*   Newburn   Newcastle
Dee   Dumfries   Annan   Naworth   *Irthing*
Cree   *Galloway*   **MARCH**   Solway Moss   *Tyne*   *Wear*
Wigtown   Carlisle   Neville's
Kirkcudbright   *Solway*   *Firth*   Cross
  Eden   Durham
  PENNINE   *CHAIN*
  CUMBRIAN
  MOUNTAINS   *Tees*
  Northalterton

see inset
map below

**GALLOWAY
RISINGS, 1724**

Forth
Glasgow   Edinburgh
Clyde
SCOTLAND
  ENGLAND
  Carlisle
Solway Firth

BORDER CLANS
The area enlarged from
the main map above

  Dixons   Berwick-on-Tweed
  H U M E S   Selbys
  Trotters   Grays
Melrose   Kelso
  Tweed R.   Herons
  Pringles
Selkirk   Davisons   Youngs
  K E R R S   Burns   Forsters
  Teviot R.   Taits   Robsons
  S C O T T S   Collingwoods   *Aln R.*
  Alnwick
  Milburns   *Coquet R.*
M A X W E L L S   Armstrongs   RUTHERFORDS   Potts
  Annan R.   Littles   Hendersons   *Scotland*   Charltons   Dunnes
J O H N S T O N E S   Beatties   ELLIOTS   Olivers   *England*   Robsons   Redep
  Esk R.   ARMSTRONGS   *North Tyne R.*   Dodds
Debatable   *Liddel*   Nobles   F E N W I C K S   Ogles
Lands   Tailors   Hetheringtons   Nixons
  GRAHAMS   Armstrongs
Bells   Ridleys   Bells
Carlisles   *Annan*   Hetheringtons   Dacres
Solway   *Line R.*   *South Tyne R.*   Newcastle-on-Tyne
Firth   *Eden R.*   *Irthing R.*   Hexam   *Tyne R.*
Littles   Carlisle
Hodgsons

627

Endemic violence also had an effect upon the economy, which lagged far behind other parts of England in the pace and pattern of its development. In 1617 the Venetian ambassador noted that the border country "at a distance of forty miles from the frontier, and especially the county of Northumberland was very poor and uncultivated and exceedingly wretched . . . from the sterility of the ground and also from the perpetual wars with which these nations have savagely destroyed each other." For centuries the region remained in the grip of a vicious cycle. Poverty and violence caused much poverty and more violence.[12]

The insecurity of the borders created a unique style of architecture throughout this region. The gentry lived in buildings called *peles,* stone towers three or four stories high. The ground floor was a windowless storeroom with walls ten feet thick. Stacked above it was a hall for living, a bower for sleeping and a deck for fighting. Camden wrote that "there is not a man amongst them of the better sort that hath not his little tower or pele."[13] Some of these structures were begun as early as the twelfth century; others as late as 1586. A few still stand today.[14] Poor tenants dealt with danger in another way, by erecting rude "cabbins" of stone or wood or beaten earth "such as a man may build within three or four hours." The destruction of these temporary buildings was not a heavy loss, for they could be rebuilt almost as rapidly as they were wrecked.[15]

Border violence also made a difference in patterns of association. In a world of treachery and danger, blood relationships became highly important. Families grew into clans, and kinsmen placed fidelity to family above loyalty to the crown itself. One officer, who was charged with the thankless task of keeping the King's peace among the borderers, reported in despair in 1611:

> They are void of conscience, the fear of God; and of all honesty, and so linked in friendship by marriage, and all or most of them of one flesh, ending to make their gain by stealing, that of a hundred felonies scarcely one shall be proved.[16]

---

[12]*Calendar of State Papers, Venetian, 1615–1617,* 150.

[13]Douglas L. W. Tough, *The Last Years of a Frontier; A History of the Borders During the Reign of Elizabeth* (Oxford, 1928), 38; Bouch and Jones, *Economic and Social History of the Lake Countries,* 123.

[14]Pevsner, *Cumberland and Westmorland,* 29.

[15]Tough, *Last Years of a Frontier,* xvi; R. T. Spence, "The Pacification of the Cumberland Border, 1593–1628," *NH* 13 (1977), 62.

[16]Sir William Hutton to the Earl of Cumberland, Dec. 1611, quoted in Spence, "The Pacification of the Cumberland Border," 123.

Borderers placed little trust in legal institutions. They formed the custom of settling their own disputes by the *lex talionis* of feud violence and blood money. There was also a system which the borderers called "blackmail," involving the payment of protection money to powerful families.[17]

As we shall see, endemic violence shaped the culture of this region in many other ways—in attitudes toward work, sport, time, land, wealth, rank, inheritance, marriage and gender. This culture was much the same on both sides of the border. "English and Scots Borderers had everything in common except nationality," writes historian George Fraser. "They belonged to the same small, self-contained, unique world, lived by the same rules and shared the same inheritance."[18]

This border culture was carried across the Irish Sea to Ulster by the settlers who would be called Scotch-Irish and Anglo-Irish. Those immigrants came from many parts of Scotland and England, but an historian observes that "the greatest numbers came from the Borders." In Ireland they found another environment of endemic violence. There the old folkways survived for centuries after they had disappeared on the border itself, and still go on today in northern Ireland, with its Protestant drums and Catholic bombs and savage knee-cappings and tortures in the Maze. In the unceasing torment of that beautiful ravaged land, the long legacy of border violence still bears its bitter fruit.

But in the borderlands themselves, the old culture began to be transformed in the seventeenth century—mainly by new political conditions. The two warring kindgoms gradually became one, in a long consolidation that began when Scotland's James VI inherited the English throne in 1603, and ended in the Act of Union in 1706–7.

In this process, the borders experienced a sweeping social revolution. There are many truths to be told about this event. One was the truth of its agents, who saw it as a process of "pacification." Another was the truth of its objects, who thought of themselves not as villains but victims. In any case, this ordering process was as violent as the world that it destroyed. The pacification of this bloody region required the disruption of a culture that had been a millennium in the making. Gallows were erected on hills

---

[17]The term *blackmail*, from the French *mail* for rent, is defined by the *OED* as "a tribute formerly exacted from farmers and small owners in the border counties of England and Scotland . . . in return for protection or immunity from plunder."

[18]Fraser, *The Steel Bonnets*, 66.

throughout the English border counties, and put busily to work. Thrifty Scots saved the expense of a rope by drowning their reivers instead of hanging them, sometimes ten or twenty at a time. Entire families were outlawed *en masse,* and some were extirpated by punitive expeditions. Many were forcibly resettled in Ireland, where officials complained that they were "as difficult to manage in Ireland as in north Cumberland," and banished them once again—this time to the colonies. The so-called Scotch-Irish who came to America thus included a double-distilled selection of some of the most disorderly inhabitants of a deeply disordered land.[19]

The pacification of the border transformed its social system. The old border warlords were deprived of their income and fell deep in debt, losing their properties to the merchants of expanding towns. A romantic account of their fate was the history of the Osbaldistone family, in Scott's great border novel *Rob Roy*. An actual example was Sir William Chaytor, seized for debt in his ancient pele and carried off to London's Fleet Prison raging helplessly, "From Hell, Hull, Halifax and York, Good Lord deliver us."[20]

The old warrior families were replaced by a new class of entrepreneurs who saw the future of their region in commerce and coal. Arable lands along the border passed into the hands of agricultural capitalists. Most great landlords in Cumberland and Westmorland were absentees who never knew their tenants and rarely visited their estates. One of the largest holders, the Duke of Somerset (1682–1748), saw his Cumbrian lands only once in sixty-six years. These properties were run by stewards and bailiffs. The income that they extracted from the tenantry was sent to southern England. The distribution of wealth, always unequal in the borderlands, now became still more so.[21]

Some middling families of the class called statesmen were able to improve themselves. Even these small holders were technically tenants, but in fact they owned everything except the mineral

[19]A case in point was the "robber clan" of Graham, forcibly "transported beyond the seas." See J. Nicolson and R. Burn, *The History and Antiquities of Westmorland and Cumberland* (2 vols., 1977), I, cxviii–cxxi; and Spence, "The Pacification of the Cumberland Border," 59–160.

[20]Edward Hughes, *North Country Life in the Eighteenth Century: The North East, 1700–1750* (London, 1952), 1, 3, 5, 11, xx; see also J. D. Marshall, "The Rise and Transformation of the Cumbrian Market Town, 1660–1900," *NH* 19 (1983), 128–209; and *idem*, "Kendal in the Late Seventeenth and Eighteenth Centuries," *CWAAS* 75 (1975), 188–257.

[21]J. V. Beckett, "Absentee Land Ownership in the Later 17th and Early 18th Centuries: The Case of Cumbria," *NH* 19 (1983), 87–107.

rights to their lands for the payment of nominal rents. Some enlarged their holdings, and were able to pass them to their children for the payment of a fine equal to two years' rent, plus a piece of silver called "God's Penny."[22]

Others were not so lucky. When the borders were pacified, changes were made in the form of tenure. "When fighting men were no longer needed," one historian has written, "landlords began to argue that customary tenants were in fact tenants of the will of the lord."[23] In the process, both tenants and undertenants became vulnerable to exploitation. The cruelties of rack renting became commonplace throughout the region, and evictions were widespread. Many emigrants brought to America an indelible memory of oppression which shaped their political attitudes for generations to come.[24]

Some tenants resisted by going to law against the landlords. Others took the law into their own hands. This was specially the case in southwestern Scotland, where the rural population rose against their oppressors and leveled the stone walls that landlords were building for livestock. The largest of these insurrections was the so-called Galloway Levellers' Revolt of 1724. In northern Ireland, tenants banded together in violent vigilante groups called Hearts of Steel and Hearts of Oak against rack-renting landlords. The absentee proprietors themselves were safe in London or Dublin, but many an agent was brutally assassinated.[25]

More violence occurred when new roads began to be built throughout the region, and were forcibly resisted. A custom called "pulling up the ways" became a common form of rural protest against encroaching civilization. England's new standing army was called out to suppress road riots along the border.[26]

As if these miseries were not enough, the people of the borders were also afflicted by famine and epidemic disease, which so often accompanied rapid change in the early modern era. A large part of the population lived close to the edge of subsistence, and

[22]S. H. Scott, *A Westmorland Village: The Story of the Old Homesteads and "Statesman" Families of Troutbeck by Windermere* (Westminster, 1904), 21. A statesman whose papers survive in the Cumbria Record Office at Kendal was Benjamin Browne of Westmorland (1664–1748).

[23]Paul Brassley, "Northumberland and Durham," in Thirsk, ed., *Agrarian History of England and Wales*, Vol. 5, Part 1, 49.

[24]Robert V. Remini, *Andrew Jackson and the Course of American Empire, 1767–1821* (New York, 1977), 15; T.G.F. Darby, "The Agrarian Economy of Westmorland" (thesis, Univ. of Leicester, 1965).

[25]J. Leopold, "The Levellers' Revolt of Galloway in 1724," *SLHSJ* 14 (1980), 4–29.

[26]Hughes, *North Country Life in the Eighteenth Century: The North East, 1700–1750*, 16.

became highly vulnerable to harvest fluctuations. Major crop failures occurred repeatedly in the eighteenth century—notably in the years 1727, 1740, and 1770. Each scarcity was followed by a surge of emigration.

These trends also occurred in Ireland, where Calvinist colonists were caught between a rapacious Anglican elite on the one hand, and a fast-growing Catholic majority on the other. They were increasingly exploited by rack-renting landlords, bullied by county oligarchies, and taxed by a church to which they did not belong. Another factor in Ireland was the depression of the linen trade. This industry suffered a prolonged decline throughout the period of emigration, and experienced a major collapse in the early 1770s.

The cause of these various troubles was a social transformation of high complexity. Their consequence was a surge of emigration so strong that observers compared it to an "epidemic" or "rage" or "distemper." Authorities were appalled by the loss of population, but could find no way to stop it. One of them wrote in 1728:

> The whole north is in a ferment at present, and people every day engaged one another to go next year to the West Indies. The humour has spread like a contagious distemper, and the people will hardly hear of anybody that tries to cure them of their madness. The worst is, it affects only Protestants.[27]

In Ireland, so desperate did people become that some attempted to escape in open boats across the Irish Sea and drowned in those treacherous waters.[28]

These people were refugees from a great historical transformation which had caught them in its complex coils. Some wished only to keep their own customs; others thought more of the future than the past. For both groups, the New World held the promise of a happiness which eluded them at home. In their teeming thousands they fled to America.

---

[27]Hugh Boulton to Duke of Newcastle, 23 Nov. 1728, in *Letters Written by His Excellency Hugh Boulton, D.D.* (2 vols., Dublin, 1770), I, 225–26.

[28]Dickson, *Ulster Emigration*, 76.

❧ The American Backcountry

The borderers entered America principally through the ports of Philadelphia and Newcastle. They moved quickly into the surrounding countryside, and in the words of one official, simply squatted wherever they found "a spot of vacant land." The Quakers were not happy about this invasion. "Our people are in pain," wrote Jonathan Dickinson in 1717, "From the north of Ireland many hundreds [have come]."[1] The North Britons brought with them the ancient border habit of belligerence toward other ethnic groups. As early as 1730, Pennsylvania officials were complaining of their "audacious and disorderly manner." One of them wrote, "I must own from my own experience in the land office that the settlement of five families from Ireland gives me more trouble than fifty of any other people. Before we were now broke in upon, ancient Friends and first settlers lived happily; but now the case is quite altered."[2]

Among Quakers there was talk of restricting immigration as early as 1718, by "laying a Duty of £5 a head on some sorts and double on others."[3] But this idea cut against the grain of William Penn's holy experiment, and was not adopted. Instead, the Quakers decided to deal with the problem in a different way, by encouraging the borderers to settle in the "back parts" of the colony. In 1731, James Logan informed the Penns in England that he was deliberately planting the North Britons in the west, "as a *frontier* in case of any disturbance." Logan argued that these people might usefully become a buffer population between the Indians and the Quakers. At the same time, he frankly hoped to rid the east of them.[4]

With much encouragement from Quaker leaders, the North Britons moved rapidly westward from Philadelphia into the rolling hills of the interior. Many drifted south and west along the mountains of Maryland, Virginia and the Carolinas. They gradually became the dominant English-speaking culture in a broad belt of territory that extended from the highlands of Appalachia

[1]Jonathan Dickinson to John Asher, 22 Oct. 1717, Dickinson Letterbook, 1715–1721, HSP.

[2]Charles A. Hanna, *The Scotch-Irish; or the Scot in North Britain, North Ireland and North America* (2 vols., New York, 1902), II, 63.

[3]Jonathan Dickinson to John Asher, 22 Oct. 1717, Dickinson Letterbook, 1715–1721, HSP.

[4]James Logan to John, Thomas and Richard Penn, 17 April 1731, Penn Papers, Official Correspondence, Historical Society of Pennsylvania; Frederick B. Tolles, *Quakers and the Atlantic Culture* (New York, 1960), 126.

through much of the Old Southwest. In the nineteenth century, they moved across the Mississippi River to Arkansas, Missouri, Oklahoma and Texas. By the twentieth century, their influence would be felt as far west as New Mexico, Arizona and southern California.

The area of their settlement may be observed in the first U.S. Census of 1790. The distribution of surnames shows that immigrants from North Britain found their way into every part of the American colonies. But by far the largest concentration was to be found in the backcountry region that included southwestern Pennsylvania, the western parts of Maryland and Virginia, North and South Carolina, Georgia, Kentucky and Tennessee.[5]

Throughout that broad area, more than half of the population came from Scotland, Ireland and northern England. Other ethnic minorities also moved into the backcountry, but their numbers remained comparatively small. The largest of the non-English-speaking groups were the Germans, who swarmed into the west-central parts of Pennsylvania and Maryland, and also in

---

[5]Two studies yield the following estimates of Scottish and Irish surnames in the census of 1790.

State	McDonald	Purvis
Me.	20.8	17.4
N.H.	20.8	15.7
Vt.	18.6	14.5
Mass.	15.0	10.5
R.I.	16.9	13.1
Conn.	11.3	8.3
N.Y.	21.0	17.1
N.J.	n.a.	14.3
Pa.	36.9	29.8
Del.	n.a.	21.8
Md.	31.6	26.5
Va.	32.2	24.4
N.C.	40.9	32.3
S.C.	44.6	36.5
Ga.	n.a.	26.9
Ky.	n.a.	33.8
Tenn.	n.a.	35.3

In addition, during the mid-18th century at least one-fourth (or more) of all English settlers in the backcountry came from six northern counties. If we average the estimates of Purvis and McDonald and add 25% of the English population, then the combined total of Scottish, Protestant Irish and northern English settlers was more than 51% of whites in North Carolina, and more than 53% in South Carolina, ca. 1790. These data refer to entire colonies including coastal districts; in the backcountry, the proportion was above 60%. See Forrest McDonald and Ellen Shapiro McDonald, "The Ethnic Origins of the American People, 1790," *WMQ3* 38 (1980), 179–99; Purvis, "The European Ancestry of the United States Population, 1790," 85–101; John B. Sanderlin, "Ethnic Origins of Early Kentucky Land Grantees," *KSHSR* 85 (1987), 103–10.

the northern reaches of the Valley of Virginia. But altogether, the Germans made up only about 5 percent of the population in North and South Carolina, Georgia, Tennessee and Kentucky in 1790. They remained a very small minority in the southern highlands.[6]

Other ethnic groups also included scattered settlements of French Huguenots, Swiss Protestants, Welsh Baptists, West Indians and even a colony of Greeks. But 90 percent of the backsettlers were either English, Irish or Scottish; and an actual majority came from Ulster, the Scottish lowlands, and the north of England. North Britons were 73 to 80 percent of the population in Virginia's Augusta, Rockbridge, Fayette and Lincoln counties; 75 percent in Pennsylvania's Washington County, 90 percent in some counties of Tennesses and Kentucky, nearly 100 percent in the Hillsboro district of North Carolina and a large majority in much of the South Carolina upcountry. These areas would become the seed settlements of the southern highlands.

Numbers alone, however, were not the full measure of their dominion. These emigrants from North Britain established in the southern highlands a cultural hegemony that was even greater than their proportion in the population.[7] An explanation of this fact may be found in the character of this American environment, which proved to be exceptionally well matched to the culture of the British borderlands.

The southern backcountry was a vast area roughly the size of western Europe, extending 800 miles south from Pennsylvania to

---

[6]The evidence supports the McDonalds' conclusions that comparatively few Germans migrated more than 300 miles from Philadelphia. See McDonald and McDonald, "Commentary," 134. Other scholars have replicated these results. John Campbell (*The Southern Highlander*, 63) concluded from surnames in pension lists, muster rolls and census tracts that in North Carolina and Tennessee, the English and Scots-Irish were each about one-third of the population; in Kentucky, the English were 40% and the Scots-Irish 30%; in Georgia, English and Scots-Irish were each about 40% of all names. He reckoned that Germans accounted for one-fifth of names in North Carolina, one-seventh in Tennessee and one-twelfth in Kentucky. Even this estimate overcounts the number of Germans. H. Roy Merrens (*Colonial North Carolina in the Eighteenth Century* (Chapel Hill, 1964), 53–81) reckons that Germans were between 2.8 and 4.7% of the population of North Carolina as a whole, but 22.5% of two counties near the Moravian Tract.

[7]Bridenbaugh, who thought of them as Scotch-Irish, wrote, "Of all the national groups the Scotch Irish were the most numerous, and it is not surprising that in the long run they came to dominate" the backcountry. McDonald and McWhiney thought of them as Celts and concluded that they were dominant in North Carolina, South Carolina, and other settlements to the south and west. See Bridenbaugh, *Myths and Realities*, 132; McDonald and McDonald, "Ethnic Origins," 199; *idem*, "Commentary," 133; Schaper, *Sectionalism in South Carolina*, 43; Mitchell, "Upper Shenandoan Valley," 218.

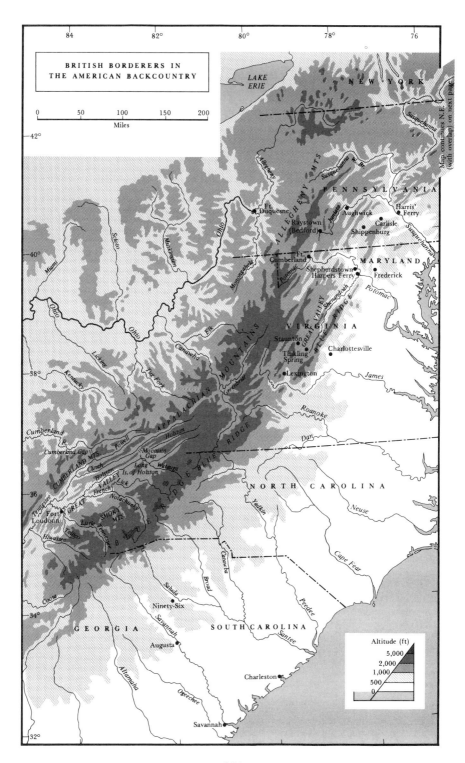

BRITISH BORDERERS IN
THE AMERICAN BACKCOUNTRY

0   50   100   150   200
Miles

Altitude (ft)

5,000
2,000
1,000
500
0

636

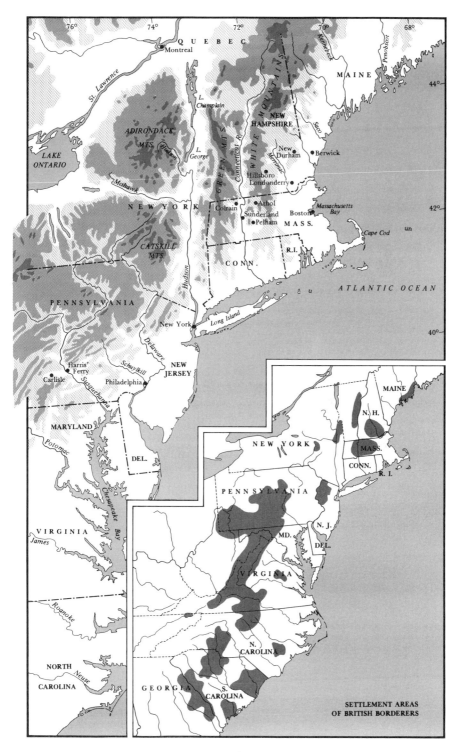

SETTLEMENT AREAS
OF BRITISH BORDERERS

637

Georgia, and several hundred miles west from the Piedmont plateau to the banks of the Mississippi. The terrain consisted of corrugated ridges and valleys, rising from the coastal plain to the
crest of the Appalachians (the highest point was Mt. Mitchell in
North Carolina at 6,684 feet), then falling away to the western
rivers.

In the mid-eighteenth century this area was a great deciduous
forest of oak, hickory and chestnut. In the mountains, the forest
changed to birch, evergreens and maple. On the banks of the Mississippi it turned into stands of tupelo, red gum and cypress; and
further south it became the "pineywoods" of loblolly and long
leaf pine. Scattered throughout the region were canebreaks and
grassy openings such as the Kentucky bluegrass which attracted
early settlement by their fertility.

The backcountry was a beautiful land in every season of the
year. On sunny spring days the woods were dappled with a golden
light that filtered through the trees. The undergrowth was bright
with blooming dogwood, mountain laurel, wild azaleas and trail-
ing arbutus. In summer mornings, the countryside was shrouded
by a mist that rose like a white cloud from the hollows; the author
can remember how it awakened a sense of mystery even in the
mind of a child. On summer afternoons, the distant hills were
masked in a shimmering haze that gave the mountains their
names: Great Smoky, Blue Ridge, Purple Mountain. When fall
came to the southern highlands, the hills were as colorful as New
England—a riot of red maples, yellow hickories and russet oaks
beneath a bright October sky. Even winter brought an austere
beauty to the landscape when its gothic tracery of bare branches
showed black against the setting sun.

The climate of the backcountry was very moist, with forty or
fifty inches of rain a year, rising as high as eighty inches on the
mountain slopes of North Carolina. The land was laced by falling
waters and mountain springs that never ran dry. This abundance
of water became a social fact of high importance in the backcountry, for it allowed small family farms to flourish independently without the aid of any earthly power, and encouraged a
sense of stubborn autonomy among the farming folk who settled
there.

Temperatures tended to be moderate throughout the region—
another important fact. By seventeenth-century standards, the
southern highlands proved to be healthy for Europeans during
the first years of settlement, before the malaria parasites followed

their human hosts into the interior, and the disease called the "milk sick" came to be a major problem. Even at their worst, mortality rates in the upcountry were much lower than the tidewater, and far below the fever-ridden valleys of the old southwest. Low levels of endemic illness made the backsettlers highly vulnerable to epidemics which struck with deadly force, but families increased rapidly and were not so often shattered by death as in other parts of British America.

Before the borderers arrived, the backcountry was occupied by strong and warlike Indian nations, from the Shawnee in the north, to the Cherokee, Creek, Choctaw and Chickasaw in the south. These proud people did not give way easily before white settlement. Savage warfare began in the late seventeenth century, and continued to the early nineteenth century in some of the fiercest Indian wars of American history.

To the first settlers, the American backcountry was a dangerous environment, just as the British borderlands had been. Much of the southern highlands were "debateable lands" in the border sense of a contested territory without established government or the rule of law. The borderers were more at home than others in this anarchic environment, which was well suited to their family system, their warrior ethic, their farming and herding economy, their attitudes toward land and wealth and their ideas of work and power. So well adapted was the border culture to this environment that other ethnic groups tended to copy it. The ethos of the North British borders came to dominate this "dark and bloody ground," partly by force of numbers, but mainly because it was a means of survival in a raw and dangerous world.

✎ Border Names for the New Land

The cultural hegemony of the borderers appeared in the names that were given to the new land. In the southern highlands one rarely met the Royalist names that were so common in tidewater Virginia. There were a few exceptions, such as *Charlotte* and *Mecklenberg County* and an occasional *Orange County* (North Carolina) or *Orangeburg* (South Carolina), which had a special meaning for Scotch-Irish Presbyterians. But as a rule, these settlers cared little for the trappings of English monarchy. One western river which a tidewater Virginian named after Princess Louisa quickly degenerated into *Levisa* among the backsettlers. High-toned names in general did not flourish in this environment; a place originally called *Mont Beau,* North Carolina, became *Monbo.* The settlers of Appalachia also made little use of the hortatory names which had been common in Massachusetts and Pennsylvania. But when they did so, their choices ran not to *Concord* or *Contentment* as in New England, but to *Liberty* (West Virginia, Georgia), *Soldier's Delight* (Maryland), *Barbacue* [sic], *Frolicsome, Faro, Bacchus,* and *Calypso* (all in North Carolina).[8]

A large proportion of Appalachian place names were drawn from the geography of Britain—with a heavy bias toward the border region. The most common British county name in Appalachia was Cumberland—the extreme northwestern county in England. There was a *Cumberland* town in western Maryland, a *Cumberland River* in Tennessee, the *Cumberland Mountains* in Kentucky, *Cumberland Knob* in North Carolina, *Cumberland Gap* through the Appalachians, and *Cumberland counties* in most states throughout this region. The name had a double appeal to English borderers, for it also commemorated the Duke of Cumberland who broke their ancient highland enemies at the battle of Culloden.

Other border place names also frequently recurred in the backcountry. In North Carolina alone, one finds a *Galloway Creek, Galloway Crossroads, Galloway Mountain* and a *Galloway town* in six different counties. There is also *Durham Branch,* several *Durham Creeks, Durham County* and *Durham Township* as well as the city of *Durham,* which were named at various dates between 1705 and 1855.[9] Counties in Pennsylvania were also called *Westmoreland* [sic] and *Northumberland.*

A specially popular place name was *Londonderry* or *Derry,* which was given to the leading Scots-Irish settlement in New Hampshire, and also to townships and hamlets in southwestern Pennsylvania, Virginia and the Carolinas. A Scots-Irish settlement in New Hampshire was named *Antrim,* and interior towns in Massachusetts and Maine were called *New Glasgow, Colerain, Belfast* and *Newcastle.* Other settlements throughout the backcountry were named *Aberdeen, Abernethy, Ayr, Balfour, Balgra, Blantyre* and *Dalkeith* (all in North Carolina), *Donegal* (Pennsylvania), *New Dublin* (Virginia), *Hillsboro* (North Carolina) and *Lochaber* (South Carolina). There were many *New Scotlands, Caledonias* and *Little Britains* and *Scotchtowns.*

[8]Hanna, *Scotch-Irish,* II, chap. 5, "The Settlements Enumerated."
[9]William S. Powell, *The North Carolina Gazetteer* (Chapel Hill, 1968).

Immigrants from North Britain also liked to name their settlements after individuals and clans—an uncommon practice in Puritan New England and Anglican Virginia. Many of these names also came from the borderlands. In North Carolina alone, for example, there are more than 130 place names beginning with *Mc* or *Mac,* and many *Alexanders, Jacksons, Robertsons, Williamsons,* and *Grahams.* Other examples included *Harper's Ferry, Graham's Meeting House, Gordon's Meeting House, McAden's Church, Craig's Creek* and *Jackson River* in Virginia; *Hobkirk's Hill* and *Lynch's Creek* in South Carolina; *Bryan's Station, Logan's Fort* and *McAfee's* in Kentucky; *McMinnville, Johnston's Fork, Sullivan* and *Knoxville* in Tennessee.

The names of backcountry places reflected many other aspects of border culture. Its food ways appeared in place names such as *Clabber Branch, Frying Pan, Corncake, Whiskey Springs* and *Hangover Creek.* Its religion was evident in settlements called *Campground* and *New Light.* The material bias in this culture was evident in the villages of *Ad Valorem* and *Need More,* both in North Carolina. The disappointment of dreams was registered in *Hardbargain Branch, Pinchgut Creek, Lousy Creek, Worry, Noland, Big Trouble, Hell's Half Acre* and *Devil's Tater Patch.* The violence of this culture appeared in *Bloody Rock, Bloodrun Creek, Breakneck Ridge, Brokeleg Branch, Cutthroat Gap, Gallows Branch, Hanging Rock, Killquick, Scream Ridge, Lynch's Creek, Whipping Creek, Skull Camp Mountain, Scuffletown, Grabtown* and *See-off Creek,* also in North Carolina. Names of that sort were very rare on the New England Frontier.[10]

Backcountry place names were the products of a period as well as of a place. In North Carolina, there was a *Whigg Branch,* and a distinctively Whiggish spirit appeared in the towns of *Enterprise, Improvement,* and *Progress.* Kentucky has a creek called *Lulbegrud,* after the capital city of Brodingnag in *Gulliver's Travels.* It was named by one of Daniel Boone's explorers who carried a copy of Jonathan Swift's book into the wilderness and read it aloud in the evening around the campfire.[11]

Other backcountry names showed a spirit of improvisation which differed from naming customs in other regions. Back settlements were called *Thicketty* and *Saltketcher* (both in South Carolina), *Licking Creek* (Tennessee), *Big Sandy, Kerless Knob, Tater*

[10] *Ibid.*
[11] George R. Stewart, *Names on the Land* (new ed., San Francisco, 1982), 113, 151.

Knob and Teeny Knob. A relaxed attitude toward naming in general appeared in *Aho,* whose founders were unable to agree upon a choice, and decided to take the first sound that was made in the new community. Other names in the same vein included *Why Not, Odear, Shitbritches Creek, Naked Creek, Cuckold's Creek, Stiffknee Knob, Big Fat Gap, Ben's Ridge* and *Bert's Creek* and *Charlie's Bunion Mountain.* This casual nomenclature was far removed from the naming ways of Puritans, Quakers and Cavaliers.[12]

The distribution of these place names defined the cultural boundaries of a region that was called the "back settlements" or the "backcountry" or simply the "back parts" in the eighteenth century. Scarcely anyone thought of it as a "frontier" in Frederick Jackson Turner's sense during the first two centuries of American history. The fact that it was thought to be "back" rather than "front" tells us which way the colonists were facing in that era.[13]

❧ The Backcountry "Ascendancy": Border Origins of an American Elite

Not all of these backcountry settlers were people of humble origins. Some had held high rank in the Old World. Their motive in moving to America was not to rise higher in society, but to keep from falling below the status which they had already achieved. A case in point was the family of Andrew Jackson, the first of many American Presidents to spring from border stock. Jackson's campaign biographies have stressed the plebian origins of this popular leader. But in fact he did not come from poor or humble people. In his earliest youth, he was taught to think of himself as a gentleman. President Jackson's Irish grandfather, Hugh Jackson, was a rich man who called himself a "weaver and merchant of Carrickfergus, Ireland, and left his American grandson a legacy later reckoned at three or four hundred pounds sterling. The future President's immigrant father had been a well-to-do farmer who held a large property near the town of Castlereagh in northern Ireland, and led an entire party of emigrants to America in 1765. Andrew Jackson's wife, Rachel Donelson, also came from

---

[12]*Ibid.,* 150.

[13]Some called it "the frontiers" in the conventional 18th-century sense of a boundary between governments—a very different meaning from the Turnerian usage. An exception was Benjamin Franklin, who developed his own frontier thesis before 1760.

The archetypical backcountry leader was Andrew Jackson, the son of Scots-Irish immigrants who became the seventh President of the United States. Historians and social scientists have suggested many ways of making sense of this man and his movement. To study him in the context of his time and place is to discover that he was the carrier of a special folk culture which was brought from the borders of North Britain to the American backcountry.

an eminent family. Her father, Colonel John Donelson, was one of the most powerful men in the southern backcountry. She was the grandniece of Dr. Samuel Davies, a learned Presbyterian minister who became president of Princeton College.[1]

Still other immigrants came from even higher ranks, and had belonged to a narrow elite who were known in Ireland and along the borderlands as the "Ascendancy." These people were few in numbers among the flood of immigrants. But they quickly established a cultural hegemony in the American backcountry, and kept it for many generations. An example of this backcountry "Ascendancy" was the Polk family. Its American progenitor was Captain Robert Polk (d. 1699), who emigrated from County Donegal, Ireland, ca. 1680. He had been highly placed in Anglo-Scots-Irish society. His wife, Magdalen Tasker Porter Polk, was the daughter of the Lord Chancellor of Ireland, who had lived at Bloomfield Castle near Londonderry, and inherited an Irish estate called Moneen. Robert and Magdalen Polk had seven sons. One of them was David Polk who settled in Maryland where his offspring intermarried with the Chesapeake gentry—Tilghmans, Fords, Coxes and Hacketts. Another son, William Polk, made his way to Virginia, and his five children settled mostly in Mecklenberg County, North Carolina. By the end of the eighteenth century, the Mecklenberg Polks had intermarried with leading backcountry clans throughout North Carolina and Tennessee—Alexanders, Ashes, Caldwells, Campbells, Donelsons, Hawkinses, Gilchrists, Knoxes, Shelbys, Spratts and many others. One member of this family was the extraordinary Bishop-General Leonidas Polk, who managed to be both Episcopal bishop of Louisiana and lieutenant general in the Confederate Army. Another descendant was a future president of the United States, James Knox Polk. Two other Presidents, Andrew Jackson and Zachary Taylor, were related by marriage to this clan, as were many political leaders of North Carolina and Tennessee.[2]

A third example of the backcountry Ascendancy was the Calhoun clan, which moved from Scotland to Ireland in the seventeenth century, and thence to America in 1733. The immigrants included Patrick and Catherine Calhoun, and their four sons

---

[1]Remini, *Andrew Jackson*, 2; Marquis James, *The Life of Andrew Jackson* (unabr. one-vol. ed., Indianapolis, 1938), 31.

[2]Mrs. Frank M. Angellotti, "The Polks of North Carolina and Tennessee," *NEHGR* 77 (1923), 133–45, 250–70; 78 (1924), 33.

Political leaders in the southern highlands for many generations traced their descent from elite families of North Britain's border "ascendancy." An example of this persistence was the eleventh President of the United States, James Knox Polk (1795–1849). He was called "Young Hickory" and was elected as a Democratic leader, but in fact his ancestors had come from the uppermost strata of North British society. President Polk's public acts and personal values, and his ideals of honor and loyalty, were shaped by the culture of his border forebears.

James, William, Ezekiel and Patrick. These four brothers lived and worked closely together. In 1746 all were named in a single indictment as "divulgers of false information."[3]

The Calhouns settled first in Lancaster County, Pennsylvania, then moved south and west to the Carolina upcountry, where they made their home on Long Cane Creek, intermarrying with other North British families along the way—Montgomerys, Nobles, Pickenses—with whom they had been allied even before coming to America. They also intermarried with themselves. The most eminent member of this clan, John C. Calhoun, married his cousin Floride Calhoun, the daughter of John E. Calhoun (or Colhoun). Most of their matrimonial alliances were with other border families—Scottish, Irish and English.

The Calhouns were pioneers in the Carolina backcountry, settling so near the frontier that in 1760 the Cherokees killed twenty-three of them, including the family matriarch Catherine Montgomery Calhoun, who was seventy-six years old.[4] By the end of the eighteenth century, there were hundreds of Calhouns in the Carolina upcountry.

From the start the Calhouns were people of substance. The family patriarch Patrick Calhoun was called "squire" even before he settled in South Carolina. As early as the mid-eighteenth century, the four Calhoun brothers owned thousands of acres, and rapidly acquired large numbers of slaves as well. They also held many high offices. Four of them represented South Carolina in the federal Congress before 1815.

Yet another example was the Henry family. Its progenitor was an Anglo-Scottish gentleman named John Henry, who emigrated about the year 1730. He was related to leading families on both sides of the border. Among his cousins was David Henry, publisher of *Gentleman's Magazine,* and on his mother's side he was connected to William Robertson, the historian who became principal of Edinburgh University. Yet another cousin was Eleanor Syme, a famous Edinburgh beauty who married Henry Brougham of Brougham Hall in Westmorland and raised one of England's great political families.

In Hanover County, the immigrant John Henry met and married one of his own relatives, a beautiful backcountry widow named Sarah Syme. The ubiquitous William Byrd stayed a night

---

[3] *SCHGM* 7 (1906), 81.
[4] A. S. Salley, "The Grandfather of John C. Calhoun," *SCHGM* 39 (1938), 50.

In old portraits and early photographs, the baleful faces of backcountry leaders often bear a striking resemblance to verbal descriptions of the North British borderers who settled the Appalachian highlands. Contemporary observers described these men as tall, lean and sinewy, with hard, angry, weatherbeaten features. The strong emotions that were so actively cultivated in this society left indelible marks upon them. A case in point was John Caldwell Calhoun, whose physiognomy in many ways resembled his enemy Andrew Jackson. Both of these men were descended from the backcountry ascendancy. The compelling portraits of these men testify to their strength of character and force of will, and also to their courage and cruelty. Their vices and virtues had been nourished by the environment of the British borderlands and the American backcountry.

in the home of this lady, and described her in his diary as "a portly handsome dame . . . of a lively and cheerful conversation. . . ." Byrd wrote:

> we tost off a bottle of honest port, which we relished with a broiled chicken. At nine I retired to my devotions, And then slept so sound that Fancy itself was stupified, else I should have dreamed of my most obliging Landlady. . . . the courteous Widow invited me to rest there the next day, and go to Church with her, but I excused myself by telling her she would certainly spoil my Devotion. Then she civilly entreated me to make her House my Home whenever I visited my Plantations, which made me bow very low.[5]

A little later, Mistress Syme married John Henry, and in 1736 became the mother of Patrick Henry. That great revolutionist liked to appear as a tribune of the people, but by birth he was a high-born backcountry gentleman with connections to the English border gentry. Patrick Henry was the cousin of the great English Whig Lord Brougham of Brougham Hall, Westmorland.[6]

Yet another example of the backcountry ascendancy was John Houston, who arrived in America with his wife and six children in 1730. He signed himself "John Houston, Gent.," and was of a family of border baronets. He did not come penniless to the New World. According to family legend he arrived with a small keg of gold sovereigns. In passage to America, a rapacious captain and crew discovered the wealth of their passenger, and made the fatal mistake trying to steal it. John Houston promptly organized the passengers, seized the ship, and sailed it himself to America. In the backcountry, he instantly assumed the station of county justice and acquired vast holdings of rich land in the Valley of Virginia. At the age of sixty-five, he was killed by a falling tree. One of his descendants was Sam Houston, the future governor of Tennessee and president of Texas.[7]

Other elite groups in the backcountry included three of the most prominent raiding, reiving and rustling families on England's northwestern frontier: the Grahams, Bells and Bankheads. All were expelled from England and forcibly resettled in Ireland. Many members of these clans came to America, and joined the elite of the southern highlands. The Bankheads became specially eminent in Alabama—producing leaders in

---

[5]Moses Coit Tyler, *Patrick Henry* (Boston, 1887), 2.

[6]Both families were aware of this connection; Patrick Henry's grandnephew was received by Lord Brougham on a visit to Britain in the 19th century; Tyler, *Patrick Henry*, 4.

[7]Marquis James, *Sam Houston* (New York, 1929), 3–6.

The Backcountry Elite: The Polks of Mecklenberg

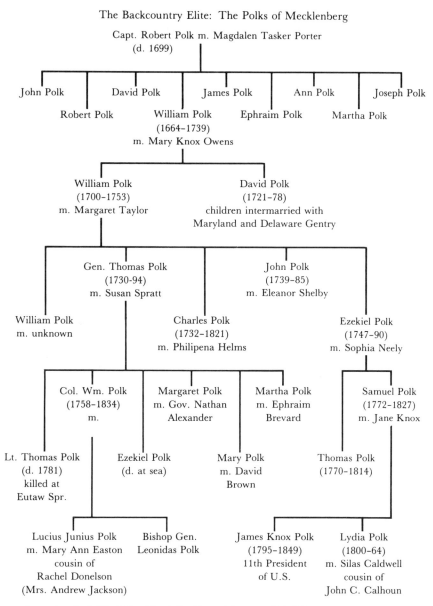

Source: Angellotti, "The Polks of North Carolina and Tennessee," *NEHGR* 77 (1923), 133-45; 78 (1924), 33.

The Backcountry Elite: The Calhouns of Long Cane

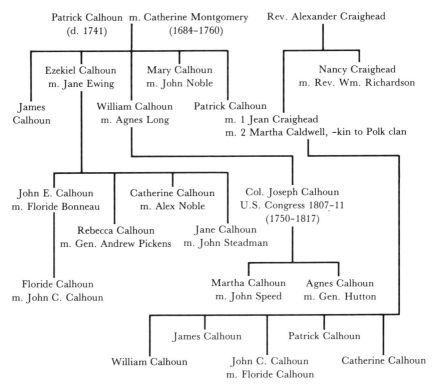

Patrick Calhoun m. Catherine Montgomery   Rev. Alexander Craighead
(d. 1741)   (1684–1760)

Ezekiel Calhoun   Mary Calhoun   Nancy Craighead
m. Jane Ewing   m. John Noble   m. Rev. Wm. Richardson

James   William Calhoun   Patrick Calhoun
Calhoun   m. Agnes Long   m. 1 Jean Craighead
                                         m. 2 Martha Caldwell, –kin to Polk clan

John E. Calhoun   Catherine Calhoun   Col. Joseph Calhoun
m. Floride Bonneau   m. Alex Noble   U.S. Congress 1807–11
                                                      (1750–1817)
          Rebecca Calhoun   Jane Calhoun
          m. Gen. Andrew Pickens   m. John Steadman

Floride Calhoun   Martha Calhoun   Agnes Calhoun
m. John C. Calhoun   m. John Speed   m. Gen. Hutton

                James Calhoun   Patrick Calhoun

        William Calhoun   John C. Calhoun   Catherine Calhoun
                                 m. Floride Calhoun

Source: A. S. Salley, Jr., "The Calhoun Family of S.C.," *SCHGM* 7 (1906), 81–98, 153–69; *idem*, "The Grandfather of John C. Calhoun," 50; Charles M. Wiltse, *John C. Calhoun, Nationalist* (Indianapolis, 1944), 18.

many fields, including U.S. Senator John Bankhead, his brother William Bankhead, Speaker of the U.S. House of Representatives, and the Speaker's actress daughter Tallulah Bankhead. Even to our own time, Bankheads occupy many positions of eminence throughout the southern highlands. Also present in even greater number were the Grahams and Bells, two of the earliest border clans to settle in western North Carolina. They held many high offices, and gave their name to counties and towns throughout the southern highlands.

The Calhouns, Polks, Jacksons, Henrys, Houstons, Bells, Grahams and Bankheads were typical of the backcountry elite. The founders of these families in America had all been people of substance in North Britain. They tended to emigrate during the early eighteenth century. Some came a generation earlier or later, but most arrived in the backcountry during the 1730s. They moved quickly to the top of backcountry society, and preserved their eminence for many generations.

These elite families firmly established their hegemony in the backcountry before the American War of Independence. Other ethnic elites also appeared in that region, but the North British borderers reigned supreme. An example of their dominion was the pattern of leadership at the battle of King's Mountain in 1780, a decisive event in the southern highlands during the American Revolution. The victorious backsettlers fought under ten commanders. One of those officers came from southwest of Scotland, another from northern Ireland, three from the north of England, two from the marches of Wales. One was from Germany, one was from a mixed Huguenot and border family, and one was from parts unknown. The first impression is one of ethnic diversity. But of nine whose regional origins are known, seven came from the borderlands of North Britain. None came from East Anglia or from southwestern England. Further, of eight families whose dates of emigration are known, all arrived in America between 1726 and 1740, the critical period for the formation of the backcountry elite.[8]

---

[8]The nine commanders, plus another relieved shortly before the action, were William Campbell (b. Augusta County, Va., 1745), whose ancestors were connected with the Scottish aristocracy and emigrated ca. 1726; Benjamin Cleveland (b. Prince William Co., Va., 1738), whose his parents emigrated in the 1730s from the North Riding of Yorkshire where they were an old armorial family; Frederick Hambright (b. in Germany, 1727), emigrated to America ca. 1738 and married Sarah Hardin of Border stock; William Graham, of a leading Cumbrian family; Edward Lacey (b. Shippensburg, Pa., 1742), of English descent, region unknown; Joseph McDowell (b. Winchester, Va., 1756), his father was a Scots-Irish weaver who emigrated ca. 1740; John Sevier (b. Rockingham County, Va., 1745), his father emigrated from England ca.

These border families, no matter whether English, Scots, Scots-Irish, Anglo-Irish or even Anglo-Welsh, shared many values and beliefs in common. They intermarried among themselves, and rapidly became an integrated elite throughout the southern highlands. For two centuries the public life of this region has been dominated by names that first appeared in the backcountry during the middle decades of the eighteen century.

❧ The Colonial Mood:
Anxiety and Insecurity in the Back Settlements

A backcountry gentleman was once heard to pray, "Lord, grant that I may always be right, for thou knowest I am hard to turn."[1] This supplication captured the prevailing cultural mood in the back settlements, which were profoundly conservative and xenophobic. The people of this region were intensely resistant to change and suspicious of "foreigners." One student of the Appalachian dialect found that "the word foreigner itself is used here [in Appalachia] in its Elizabethan sense of someone who is the same nationality as the speaker, but not from the speaker's immediate area." All the world seemed foreign to the backsettlers except their neighbors and kin.[2]

The people of the southern highlands would become famous in the nineteenth century for the intensity of their xenophobia, and also for the violence of its expression. In the early nineteenth century, they tended to detest great planters and abolitionists in equal measure. During the Civil War some fought against both sides. In the early twentieth century they would become intensely negrophobic and antisemitic. In our own time they are furiously hostile to both communists and capitalists. The people of the southern highlands have been remarkably even-handed in their antipathies—which they have applied to all strangers without regard to race, religion or nationality.

1740, the son of a French Huguenot who married into a family from the north of England; Isaac Shelby (b. North Mountain, now Washington County, western Md., 1750) whose father emigrated from Wales, ca. 1735; James Williams (b. Hanover County, Va., 1737), his father emigrated from Wales ca. 1730; Joseph Winston (b. Louisa County, Va., 1746), his family emigrated from Yorkshire at an unknown date, and his father was a kinsman of Patrick Henry's mother.

[1]Bridenbaugh, *Myths and Realities*, quoting Dunaway, *Scotch Irish*, 182.
[2]Wylene P. Dial, "The Dialect of the Appalachian People," *WVAH* 30 (1969), 463–71.

Behind these attitudes lay the same deep feelings of cultural anxiety and insecurity that had existed in most other colonial societies. These emotions were specially intense among the first generation. They reached their climax in the violent movement called the Regulation, which swept through the back settlements of North and South Carolina from 1765 to 1771. In both colonies, the Regulators were backcountry vigilantes who sought to impose order by force upon their region, and also attacked outsiders. Their actions were part of a cultural process which was common to all new colonies—an expression of feelings of cultural danger and loss.[3]

Another symptom of this attitude was a strong mood of cultural conservatism. From the seventeenth century to the twentieth, travelers in the backcountry often remarked upon the intensity of its attachment to ancestral ways. The Anglican missionary Charles Woodmason wrote in disgust, "They delight in their present low, lazy, sluttish, heathenish, hellish life, and seem not desirous of changing it."[4] That statement, without its pejoratives, described an instinctive conservatism which was also noted by other travelers and acknowledged by the backsettlers themselves. "We never let go of a belief once fixed in our minds," wrote an Appalachian woman with an air of pride.[5]

This mood caused the backsettlers to cling tenaciously to the customs that they had carried from the borderlands of North Britain. The result was a complex process of continuity and change, similar in its form to that which occurred in other cultural regions of the New World, but different in its substance. Let us examine this subject in more detail, beginning with the speech ways which were carried to the American backcountry.

---

[3]Historians first perceived the Regulation as a political event; other scholars have interpreted it as a social movement. It was both of these things, but also a cultural movement; see Richard M. Brown, *The South Carolina Regulators* (Cambridge, 1963); Rachel N. Klein, "Ordering the Backcountry: The South Carolina Regulation," *WMQ3* 38 (1981), 661–80; Ronald Hoffman et al., eds., *An Uncivil War: the Southern Backcountry during the American Revolution* (Charlottesville, 1985).

[4]Woodmason, *Carolina Backcountry*, 14, 31, 52; Bridenbaugh, *Myths and Realities*, 177.

[5]Emma Miles, *The Spirit of the Mountains* (1905, rpt. Knoxville, 1975), 137.

✍ Backcountry Speech Ways:
Border Origins of Southern Highland Speech

In the United States, a distinctive family of regional dialects can still be heard throughout the Appalachian and Ozark mountains, the lower Mississippi Valley, Texas and the Southern Plains. It is commonly called southern highland or southern midland speech.[1]

This American speech way is at least two centuries old. It was recognized in the colonies even before the War of Independence, and identified at first in ethnic rather than regional terms, as "Scotch-Irish speech." In the backcountry, it rapidly became so dominant that other ethnic stocks in this region adopted it as their own. As early as 1772, a newspaper advertisement reported a runaway African slave named Jack who was said to "speak the Scotch-Irish dialect."[2]

The earliest recorded examples of this "Scotch-Irish" speech were strikingly similar to the language that is spoken today in the southern highlands, and has become familiar throughout the western world as the English of country western singers, transcontinental truckdrivers, cinematic cowboys, and backcountry politicians.

This southern highland speech has long been very distinctive for its patterns of pronunciation. It says *whar* for where, *thar* for there, *hard* for hired, *critter* for creature, *sartin* for certain, *a-goin* for going, *hit* for *it*, *he-it* for hit, *far* for fire, *deef* for deaf, *pizen* for poison, *nekkid* for naked, *eetch* for itch, *boosh* for bush, *wrassle* for wrestle, *chaney* for china, *chaw* for chew, *poosh* for push, *shet* for shut, *ba-it* for bat, *be-it* for be, *narrer* for narrow, *winder* for window, *widder* for widow, and *young-uns* for young ones.[3]

---

[1]Hans Kurath, *A Word Geography of the Eastern United States* (Ann Arbor, 1949); Craig M. Carver, *American Regional Dialects; A Word Geography* (Ann Arbor, 1987); Robert F. Dakin, "South Midland Speech in the Old Northwest," *JEL* 5 (1971), 31–48; C. Williams, "Appalachian Speech," *NCHR* 55 (1978), 174–79.

[2]Virginia *Gazette*, 22 Oct. 1772; Bridenbaugh, *Myths and Realities*, 169.

[3]An early description of backcountry speech ways—so early as to capture the language of the immigrants who had arrived in the 18th century—was made by the American traveler Anne Royall, after a visit to the region which she fancifully called "Grison republic," and is now the state of West Virginia:

"To return to my Grison republic," she wrote, "their dialect sets orthography at defiance, and is with difficulty understood; for instance, the words *by, my, rye,* they pronounce as you would *ay.* Some words they have imported, some they have made out and out, some they have swapped for others, and nearly the whole of the English language is so mangled and mutilated by them, that is hardly known to be such. When they would say *pretence,* they say *lettinon,* which

Its grammar also differs in many details from other English dialects. Verb forms include constructions such as *he come in, she done finished, they growed up,* the plural *they is judged,* the interrogative *you wasn't there, was you,* the emphatic *he done did it,* and the use of *hoove* as a past participle of heave. The indefinite article as *she had a one* frequently occurred in the southern highlands, as did the emphatic double negative, *he don't have none.*[4] It also used prepositions in a curious ways. In the early nineteenth century, James Parton recorded examples such as "He went *till* Charleston" and "there never was seen the *like* of him for mischief." Parton wrote, ". . . these are specimens of their talk."[5]

Southern highland speech also has its own distinctive vocabulary in words such as *fornenst* (next to), *skift* (dusting of snow), *fixin* (getting ready to do something), *brickle* (brittle), *swan* (swear), *hant* (ghost), *hate* (it ain't worth a hate), *nigh* (near), *man* (husband), *cute* (attractive), *scawmy* (misty), *lowp* (jump), *lettin'on* (pretend), *sparkin* (courtin), *hippin* (a baby's diaper), *bumfuzzled* (confused), *scoot* (slide) and *honey* as a term of endearment.[6]

This was an earthy dialect. The taboos of Puritan English had little impact on Southern highland speech until the twentieth century. Sexual processes and natural functions were freely used in figurative expressions. Small children, for example, were fondly called "little shits" as a term of endearment. A backcountry granny would say kindly to a little child, "Ain't you a cute little shit."[7] Sexual terms also frequently appeared in backcountry place names, before the Victorians erased them from the maps of

---

is a word of very extensive use amongst them. It signifies a jest, and is used to express disapprobation and disguise; 'you are just lettinon to rub them spoons—Polly is not mad, she is only lettinon.' Blaze they pronounce *bleez,* one they call *waun,* sugar *shugger;* 'and is this all it ye got?' handkerchief *hancorchy,* (emphasis on the second syllable); and 'the two ens of it comed loose'; for get out of the way, they say, get out of the road: Road is universally used for way; 'put them cheers, (chairs) out of the road.' But their favorite word of all, is *hate,* by which they mean the word thing; for instance, *nothing,* 'not a hate—not wann hate will ye's do.' What did you buy at the stores ladies? 'Not a hate—well you hav'nt a hate here to eat.' They have the *hickups,* and corp, (corpse), and are a (*cute*) people. Like Shakespeare they make a word when at a loss: *scawm'd* is one of them, which means spotted." Anne Royall, *Sketch of the History, Life and Manners in the United States* (New Haven, 1826), I, 53; for other early descriptions of this dialect see "Skitt," [H. E. Taliaferro], *Fisher's Rover (North Carolina) Scenes and Characters* (New York, 1859); and Ralph Steele Boggs, "North Carolina Folktales . . . ," *JAF* 47 (1934), 268–88.

[4]Dial, "The Dialect of the Appalachian People," 463–71.

[5]James Parton, *Life of Andrew Jackson* (3 vols., New York, 1859), I, 47.

[6]*Honey* as a term of endearment was also occasionally heard in New England and the Chesapeake. But it was specially associated with North British and Irish speech, and in the 18th century came to be regarded as an "hibernianism."

[7]Dial, "The Dialect of the Appalachian People," 470.

this region. In Lunenberg County, Virginia, two small streams were named Tickle Cunt Branch and Fucking Creek.[8]

Scholars generally agree that this language developed from the "northern" or "Northumbrian" English that was spoken in the lowlands of Scotland, in the North of Ireland, and in the border counties of England during the seventeenth and early eighteenth century.[9] Every vocabulary word which we have noted as typical of American backcountry speech also appears in word lists collected in the English border counties of Cumberland and Westmorland during the nineteenth century. W. Dickson observed, for example, that *man* was "the term by which a Cumbrian wife refers to her husband," as in "stand by your man." He noted that *honey* was "a term of endearment expressive of great regard" in the English border counties, northern Ireland and the southern lowlands. Dickson and others recorded in Cumbria usages such as *let on* for tell, *scawmy* for thick or misty, *cute* for attractive, *nigh* for near, *fixin* for getting ready, and *lowp* for jump, *hoove* as a past participle for heave, and *lang sen* or *langseyne* for long since. This emphatic double negative had long been common in border speech. One Northumbrian gentleman wrote to another, "I assure your honour I never sold none."[10]

In North Britain, this speech way tended to be broadly similar on both sides of the border. One early nineteenth century student of speech in Cumberland and Westmorland observed that "in the Border and all along the verge of the old Marches or debateable lands the speech of the people is completely Scotch, in everything, excepting that there is but little tone."[11] North of

---

[8]Richard R. Beeman, *The Evolution of the Southern Backcountry: A Case Study of Lunenburg Country, Virginia, 1746–1832* (Philadelphia, 1984), 18.

[9]J. H. Combs, "Old, Early and Elizabethan English in the Southern Mountains," *DN* 4 (1913–17), 283–97; Thomas Pyles, *The Origins and Development of the English Language* (New York, 1964).

[10]W. Dickson, *Glossary of Words and Phrases Pertaining to the Dialect of Cumberland* (London, n.d.); see also an anonymous compilation, *Westmorland and Cumberland Dialects, Dialogues, Poems, Songs & Ballads by Various Writers in the Westmorland and Cumberland Dialect Now Collected with a Copious Glossary* (London, 1839); and see W. Dickinson and E. W. Prevost, *A Glossary of the Words and Phrases Pertaining to the Dialect of Cumberland* (London, 1879); and Ann Wheeler, *Westmorland Dialect . . .* (London, 1840), 130. Also valuable are writings in dialect by the 18th century "Cumberland Bard," Robert Anderson. Early descriptive sources are more helpful for an historian's purposes than 20th-century speech studies, which, though more refined in their analytic tools, are less useful as a guide to past patterns.

Patterns of grammar were also very much the same. Hughes notes, for example, that the borderers "used the indefinite article freely, e.g., 'he had *a* one.'" See Hughes, *North Country Life in the Eighteenth Century: The North East*, 37. An example of the Northumbrian double negative appears in Fraser, *Steel Bonnets*, 72.

[11]*Westmorland and Cumberland Dialect*, vi.

the border, another speech-scholar described the accent of the Scottish lowlands as "nothing more than a corruption of that which is now spoke . . . in all the northern counties of England."[12]

This border dialect became the ancester of a distinctive variety of American speech which still flourishes in the southern highlands of the United States. The process of transmission was complex. Southern highland speech was not merely an archaic North British form—this was not a simple story of stasis and replication. New words were required to describe the American environment, and many were coined in the backcountry. Other expressions were borrowed from Indians, Spanish, French and Germans. But the strongest ingredients were the speech ways of North Britain in the seventeenth century.

❧ Backcountry Building Ways: Border Origins of Cabin and Cowpen

As early as the mid-eighteenth century, travelers also found a characteristic style of vernacular architecture in the Appalachian highlands. "These people live in open log cabins with hardly a blanket to cover them." Charles Woodmason observed in 1767.[1]

Log cabins had not been much used by English colonists in Massachusetts, Virginia or the Delaware Valley during the seventeenth century and were not invented on the American frontier. The leading authority on this subject, H. B. Shurtleff, concludes after long study that the log cabin was first introduced by Scandinavians, and popularized mainly by Scots-Irish settlers in the eighteenth century. "The log cabin did not commend itself to the English colonists," Shurtleff wrote. "The Scotch Irish who began coming over in large numbers after 1718 seem to have been the first . . . to adopt it."[2]

---

[12]Ferguson, *Northmen in Cumberland and Westmorland*, 152–53; see also Dickinson and Provost, *A Glossary of the Words and Phrases Pertaining to the Dialect of Cumberland*, xxv.

[1]Woodmason, *Carolina Backcountry*, 16.

[2]See H. B. Shurtleff, *The Log Cabin Myth* (Cambridge, Mass., 1939). Log houses of various types appeared at an earlier date throughout the colonies, often for special purposes such as forts and jails and garrison houses, where walls of unusual thickness were desired. Instances appear in the *Archives of Maryland*, II (1884), 224; *North Carolina Colonial Records*, I (1886), 300.

Germans also introduced log buildings, but these structures differed from the classical log cabin in many ways. See C. A. Weslager, *The Log Cabin in America* (New Brunswick, N.J., 1969); Henry Glassie, "The Appalachian Log Cabin," *MLW* 39 (1963), 5–14; *idem*, "The Types of Southern Mountain Cabin," in *The Study of American Folklore*, ed. Jan H. Brunvand (New York, 1968), 338–70; Fred Kniffen, "Folk Housing: Key to Diffusion," *AAAG* 55 (1965), 549–77;

The historiography of the log cabin has centered mostly on the history of the *log*, but at least equally important is the history of the *cabin*. The trail of that topic leads from the American back-country to the British borderlands. In the seventeenth and eigh-teenth centuries, cabin architecture was commonplace through-out the Scottish lowlands and northern Ireland, and also in the English counties of Cumberland, Westmorland and Northumber-land, but not often in the south of England. Travelers in the bor-der country expressed surprise at the state of housing they found there. One soldier from the south of England, marching north near Duns a few miles beyond the river Tweed, noted that the "husbandmen's houses . . . resemble our swine coates, few or none of them have more storeys than one, and that very low and covered usually with clods of earth, the people and their habits are suitable to the dwellings."[3]

Small and impermanent houses were common throughout North Britain, in part because the system of land tenure gave no motive for improvement. An historian of Scotland wrote in 1521:

> In Scotland, the houses of the country people are small, as it were, cottages, and the reason is this: they have no permanent holdings, but hired only, or in lease for four or five years, at the pleasure of the lord of the soil; therefore do they not dare to build good houses, though stone abound, neither do they plant trees or hedges for their orchards, nor do they dung their land; and this is no small loss and damage to the whole realm.[4]

On the borders, this factor was compounded by chronic insecur-ity. There, cottages became cabins of even more primitive con-struction. The word "cabin" itself was a border noun that meant any sort of rude enclosure, commonly built of the cheapest mate-

---

Fred Kniffen and Henry Glassie, "Building in Wood in the Eastern United States," *GR* 56 (1966), 40–66.

[3]John Aston, "Diary," in "Six North Country Diaries," *Publications of the Surtees Society* 118 (1910), 31; for modern discussions, see R. W. Brunskill, "The Clay Houses of Cumberland," *AMST* 10 (1962), 57–80; Christopher Stell, "Pennine Houses," *FL* 3 (1965), 5–24; James Wal-ton, "Upland Houses: The Influence of Mountain Terrain on British Folk Building," *AA* 30 (1956), 142–48; Caoimhín ó Danachair, "The Combined Byre-and-Dwelling in Ireland," *FL* 2 (1964), 58–75; Alan Gailey, "The Peasant Houses of the South-west Highlands of Scotland: Distribution, Parallels, and Evolution," *G* 3 (1962), 227–42; M. W. Barley, *The English Farm-house and Cottage* (London, 1961); Henry Glassie, *Pattern in the Material Folk Culture of the Eastern United States* (Philadelphia, 1968); *idem, Folk Housing in Middle Virginia* (Knoxville, 1975); Carl Linsberg, "The Building Process in Antebellum North Carolina," *NCHR* 60 (1983), 431–56.

[4]John Major, *Historia Majoris Britanniae tam Angliae q. Scotiae . . .* (Paris, 1521); tr. in P. Hume Brown, ed., *Scotland before 1700 from Contemporary Documents* (Edinburgh, 1893), 44.

rials that came to hand: turf and mud in Ireland, stone and dirt in Scotland, logs and clay in America.[5]

Within these structures, raised beds were uncommon as late as 1582, when George Buchanan wrote of his fellow Scots, "In their houses, also, they lie upon the ground; strewing fern or heath, on the floor, with the roots downward, and the leaves turned up. In this manner they form a bed so pleasant that it may vie in softness with the finest down, while in salubrity it far exceeds it."[6]

In the American backcountry, the first emigrants from the borderlands began by building earthen cabins which one of them described as "dirt houses or rather like potato houses, to take their families into." Roofs were made of poles and sand, with catastrophic consequences in a heavy storm. "The rain quickly penetrated through between the poles and brought down the sand that covered over, which seemed to threaten to cover us alive . . . I believe we all sincerely wished ourselves again at Belfast."[7] These cabins of dirt and stone soon yielded to log cabins which were better suited to the climate and resources of the New World. But no matter what the materials happened to be, the cabin idea remained much the same.[8]

The interior design of these cabins was similar on both sides of the Atlantic. Rectangular walls enclosed a single room in which an entire family lived together. The floors were usually of hard-packed dirt. The walls had a few simple openings for windows, and doors were placed on both the front and back walls for quick exits. Some of these structures had a firepit and a hole in the roof; others had a rough open fireplace on the gable end.[9]

Backcountry cabins had a standard size. Many were between sixteen and seventeen feet long. This dimension had been com-

---

[5]The *OED* defines a cabin as "a permanent human habitation of rude construction. Applied especially to mud or turf-built hovels of slaves or impoverished peasantry, as distinct from the comfortable cottages of working men." Most examples of usage in the 17th and 18th centuries are from Scotland, Ireland and the English border counties. The *EDD* identifies the area of most common English usage as Northumberland, Durham and Yorkshire.

[6]George Buchanan, "Description of Scotland," in Brown, ed., *Scotland before 1700 from Contemporary Documents*, 235.

[7]Robert Witherspoon, "Recollections," in Merrens, ed., *Colonial South Carolina Scene*, 126.

[8]E. Estyn Evans, "Cultural Relics of the Ulster-Scots in the Old West of North America," *Ulster Folklife* 11 (1966), 33–38.

[9]Interesting ethnic variations existed in interior design. Germans preferred to divide their cabins into three small rooms with a sleeping loft above. The borderers preferred one large open space, rectangular dimensions and opposed front and rear doors. See Evans, "Cultural Relics of the Ulster Scots"; Glassie, "The Appalachian Log Cabin," 5–14; *idem, Pattern in the Material Folk Culture of the Eastern United States*, 78.

mon in northern England, where it was taken from an old unit of
measure variously called a rod, lug, pole, or perch, normally five
and a half yards long. It had been used in the mother country for
"coppice cutting" of saplings which were carefully regulated by
local folk law. Those customs were preserved in log-cabin building for many years in the New World.[10]

Methods of construction also tended to be much the same on
both sides of the water. The spaces between the logs or other
materials were "daubed" with clay. In the English border county
of Cumberland, this was done in a communal event called a "clay-
daubin" where neighbors and friends of a newly married couple
came together and built them a cabin with weathertight walls. The
work was directed by men called *daubers*.[11] The same technique of
wattle and clay daubing (sometimes called wattle and funk) was
widely used in the American backcountry. In 1753, for example,
James Patton had two "round log houses" on his Shenandoah
farm, with "clapboard roofs, two end log chimnies, all funcked
and daubed both inside and out."[12]

Larger dwellings in the backcountry tended to be several small
cabins built close together, rather than buildings of a different
type. The traveler Johann Schoepf observed in 1784:

> Thus are built gradually a good many small houses and cabins,
> commonly without the assistance of carpenters, patched together
> by the people themselves and their negroes; this being an easier
> method than to put together a large house all at once. One often
> sees such little houses growing up where there is neither material
> nor capital for bringing them together in one solid house.[13]

A common practice was to raise two log structures side by side,
with an open breezeway covered by a simple roof. In Appalachia,
this was called a dog-trot cabin. The same plan had long been
used in Britain, where breezeways were widely known.[14] Other

---

[10]*OED*, *s.v.* "rod", "perch" and "pole." The length varied according to local tradition. In
Ireland a perch was 21 feet long. On the use of this measure in the American backcountry,
Noble writes, " . . . the dimensions of the log pen house averaged about sixteen or seventeen
feet by twenty-one through twenty-four feet. . . . a sixteen to seventeen foot length had long
been a standard dimension in both English houses and barns"; Allen G. Noble, *Wood, Brick and
Stone* (2 vols., Amherst, Mass., 1984), I, 114.

[11]*Westmorland and Cumberland Dialect,* 339.

[12]Mitchell, "Upper Shenandoah Valley," 294.

[13]Johann David Schoepf, *Travels in the Confederation* [1783–84] (1911, New York, 1968), II,
33.

[14]The dog-trot cabin was similar to the design that has been called the statesman house in
Britain; see Bouch and Jones, *Economic and Social History of the Lake Country,* 108–9.

The log house did not spring spontaneously from the American forest. It was a type of vernacular architecture that had been carried out of Europe by Scandinavians, Germans and especially North British borderers. Log-building was common to all of these ethnic groups, but the idea of the cabin was brought from the borderlands. The choice of materials changed in the forests of the New World, where log walls and wooden roofs replaced stone and thatch. But the cabin plans and proportions remained very much the same. Many other forms of log architecture also appeared in America—solid New England garrison forts, fragile Swedish log houses, dovetailed Finnish plank buildings, and big German Blockhausen—*but the classic American log cabin came from North Britain.*

plans were the saddle-bag, in which two adjacent cabins shared a single chiminey stack; and the "double pen," in which they had a wall in common. These also had been known in Britain.[15]

Cabin architecture was striking for its roughness and impermanence. It was a simple style of building, suitable to a migratory people with little wealth, few possessions and small confidence in the future. It was also an inconspicuous structure, highly adapted to a violent world where a handsome building was an invitation to disaster. In that respect, cabin architecture was an expression of the insecurity of life in the northern borders.[16]

The cabin was also the product of a world of scarcity. It was a style of vernacular architecture created by deep and grinding poverty through much of north Britain during the late seventeenth and early eighteenth century. In that barren country, cabins made of earth and stone were an adaptation to an environment in which other building materials were rare.

Cabin architecture was also a style of building well suited to a people who had a strong sense of family and a weak sense of individual privacy. Travelers from the south of England expressed horror at the lack of respect for privacy. Much the same observations were also made in the American backcountry. "They sleep altogether in common in one room, and shift and dress openly without ceremony," Woodmason wrote, ". . . nakedness is counted as nothing." Sometimes there was not even a bed. Wil-

---

[15]Martin Wright, "The Antecedents of the Double Pen House Type," *AAAG* 48 (1958).

[16]Leyburn has collected impressive evidence of continuities in the vernacular architecture of the Scottish lowlands, quoting Froissart in the 15th century that "after an English raid, the country-folk made light of it, declaring they had driven their cattle into the hills, and that with six or eight stakes they would soon have new houses."

Of the 16th century, MacKenzie wrote that throughout Galloway, cottages and cabins were "constructed of rude piles of [drift]wood, with branches interwoven between them, and covered on both sides with a tenacious mixture of clay and straw."

A report in 1670 noted that "the houses of the commonalty are very mean, mud-wall and thatch, the best; but the poorer sort live in such miserable huts as never eye beheld. . . . In some parts, where turf is plentiful, they build up little cabins thereof, with arched roofs of turf, without a stick of timber in it; when the house is dry enough to burn, it serves them for fuel, and they remove to another."

Of the 18th century it was written that the houses were "little removed from hovels with clay floors, open hearths . . . only the better class of farmers had two rooms, the house getting scant light by two tiny windows."

Leyburn, *The Scotch-Irish: A Social History,* 18; P. Hume Brown, *Early Travelers in Scotland* (Edinburgh, 1891), 12–16; William Mackenzie, *History of Galloway from the Earliest Period to the Present Time* (2 vols., Kirkcudbright, 1841), I, 232; *Harleian Miscellany,* VI, 139; H. G. Graham, *The Social Life of Scotland in the Eighteenth Century* (London, 1899), 182–83.

liam Byrd described one backcountry family that "pigged lovingly together" on the floor.[17]

In the eighteenth century, these cabins began to rise throughout the American backcountry wherever migrants from North Britain settled. The strong resemblance of these houses to the vernacular architecture of the borders was noted by travelers who knew both places. One English traveler noted of a Scots-Irish settlement in the backcountry of Pennsylvania that the people lived in "paltry log houses, and as dirty as in the north of Ireland, or even Scotland."[18]

Cabin architecture was not static in its new environment. Folklorists have studied in fascinating detail the hewing of cabin logs, the notching of corners, the development of floor plans and the refinement of fenestration. This was mostly a form of cultural involution, in which things changed by becoming more elaborately the same.[19]

The architecture of the cabin itself was merely one part of an entire regional vernacular which also included other structures. Barns and stables were crude, impermanent shelters, often made of saplings and boughs—a method widely used in the border country.[20] Cattle were kept in simple enclosures called cowpens, descended from border "barmkins" which had been built for centuries in North Britain. Historians Bouch and Jones note that "the basis of medieval settlement appears to have been the 'barmkin,' a sort of corral or stockade, where behind a timber fence, cattle and dependents could shelter, defended by menfolk." Cowpens became very common throughout the southern highlands in the eighteenth century. One such area in the Caro-

[17]Woodmason, *Carolina Backcountry*, 31; William Byrd, *The London Diary (1717–1721) and Other Writings* (New York, 1958), 588–89; Edmund Morgan, *Virginians at Home* (New York, 1952), 73; similar observations were made two centuries later of Appalachian families in industrial cities such as Baltimore and Detroit.

[18]Leyburn, *The Scotch-Irish; A Social History*, 151.

[19]Michael J. O'Brien and Dennis E. Lewarch, "The Built Environment," in M. J. O'Brien, ed., *Grassland, Forest and Historical Settlement* (Lincoln, Neb., 1984), 231–65; Terry Jordan, *Texas Log Building: A Folk Architecture* (Austin, 1978); Wilbur Zelinsky, "The Log House in Georgia," *GR* 43 (1953), 173–93; Eugene M. Wilson, *Alabama Folk Houses* (Montgomery, Ala., 1975); Donald A. Hutslar, *The Log Architecture of Ohio* (Columbus, 1977); Charles McRaven, *Building the Hewn Log House* (New York, 1978); Fred Kniffen, "Louisiana House Types," *AAAG* 26 (1936), 179–93.

[20]Amos Long, "Fencing in Rural Pennsylvania," *PF* 12 (1961), 30–35; Arthur Dobbs in *Colonial Records of North Carolina*, V, 262.

lina upcountry became the site of the battle of Cowpens during the American War for Independence.[21]

In North Britain the architecture of cabin and cowpen began to be abandoned during the seventeenth and eighteenth centuries, as violence diminished and prosperity increased. The vernacular architecture that one finds throughout the region today was a later development. "In the seventeenth century," one local historian writes, "the statesmen had begun to build better houses, in imitation of Jacobean manor halls, and evolved a type of their own—the low, rough-cast building with porch and pent-house, a dead-nailed door and massive threshwood, mullioned windows, and behind the rannel-balk a great open fire-spit where peat burned on the cobble-paved hearth."[22]

But the architecture of cabin and cowpens persisted for many generations in the American backcountry. As late as 1939 there were 270,000 occupied log cabins in the United States. Many were in the southern highlands. In the county of Halifax, Virginia, 42 percent of all houses were log cabins as recently as World War II.[23]

Even today an architecture of impermanence survives in new forms such as prefabricated houses and mobile homes, which are popular throughout the southern highlands. The mobile home is a cabin on wheels—small, cheap, simple and temporary. The materials have changed from turf and logs to plastic and aluminum, but in its conception the mobile home preserves an architectural attitude that was carried to the backcountry nearly three centuries ago.

❧ Backcountry Family Ways: Border Ideas of Clan and Kin

The family ways of the backcountry, like its speech and building ways, were also brought from the borderlands of North Britain and adapted to a new American environment with comparatively little change. "The conquest of the back parts," writes Carl Bri-

---

[21]Bouch and Jones, *Economic and Social History of the Lake Countries,* 33; Eugene Cotton Mather and John Fraser Hart, "Fences and Farms," *GR* 44 (1954), 201–23.

[22]Ernest Hudson, *Barton Records* (Penrith, 1951), 56; W. G. Collingwood, *The Lake Counties* (London, 1902), 144; Scott, *A Westmorland Village,* 64–65, Bouch and Jones, *Economic and Social History of the Lake Countries,* 108.

[23]Shurtleff, *Log Cabin Myth,* 185.

denbaugh, "was achieved by families. . . . The fundamental social unit, the family, was preserved intact . . . in a transplanting and reshuffling of European folkways."[1]

From the perspective of an individual within this culture, the structure of the family tended to be a set of concentric rings, in which the outermost circles were thicker and stronger than among other English-speaking people. Beyond the nuclear core, beyond even the extended circle, there were two rings which were unique to this culture. One was called the derbfine. It encompassed all kin within the span of four generations. For many centuries, the laws of North Britain and Ireland had recognized the derbfine as a unit which defined the descent of property and power. It not only connected one nuclear family to another, but also joined one generation to the next.

Beyond the derbfine lay a larger ring of kinship which was called the clan in North Britain. We think of clans today mainly in connection with the Scottish Highlands. But they also existed in the lowlands, northern Ireland and England's border counties where they were a highly effective adaptation to a world of violence and chronic insecurity.

The clans of the border were not precisely the same as those of the Scottish Highlands, and very different from the Victorian contrivances of our own time. They had no formal councils, tartans, sporrans, bonnets or septs. But they were clannish in the most fundamental sense: a group of related families who lived near to one another, were conscious of a common identity, carried the same surname, claimed descent from common ancestors and banded together when danger threatened.

Some of these border clans were very formidable. The Armstrongs, one of the largest clans on the Cumbrian border in the sixteenth century, were reputed to be able to field 3,000 mounted men, and were much feared by their neighbors. The Grahams held thirteen towers on the western border in 1552, and bid defiance to their foes. The Rutherfords and Halls were so violent that royal officials in 1598 ordered no quarter to be given to anyone of those names. The Johnston-Johnson clan adorned their houses with the flayed skins of their enemies the Maxwells in a blood feud that continued for many generations.[2]

The migration from North Britain to the backcountry tended

---

[1] Bridenbaugh, *Myths and Realities*, 135.
[2] Fraser, *Steel Bonnets*, 55–65 passim.

to become a movement of clans. A case in point was the family of Robert Witherspoon, a South Carolinian of Border-Scots descent. Witherspoon recalled:

> My grandfather and grandmother were born in Scotland about the [year] 1670. They were cousins and both of one name. His name was John and hers was Janet. They lived in their younger years in or near Glasgow and in 1695 they left Scotland and settled in Ireland in the county of Down . . . where he lived in good circumstances and in good credit until the year 1734, [when] he removed with his family to South Carolina.

When Witherspoon used the word "family" he meant not merely a nuclear or extended family but an entire clan. His grandparents, their seven children, at least seventeen grandchildren and many uncles and cousins all sailed from Belfast Lough to America and settled together in the same part of the southern backcountry. Witherspoon described their exodus in detail:

> We did not all come in one ship nor at one time. My uncles William James and David Wilson, and their families with Uncle Gavin left Belfast in the beginning of the year 1732 and Uncle Robert followed us in 36.[3]

Here was a classic example of serial migration or stream migration which was common in the peopling of the backcountry. A few clan members opened a path for others, and were followed by a steady stream of kin.

These North British border clans tended to settle together in the American backcountry. An example was the Alexander clan. In North Carolina's Catawba County, the first United States Census of 1790 listed 300 nuclear families named Alexander. Most were blood relations. Similar concentrations appeared throughout the backcountry—the Polks of Mecklenburg, the Calhouns of Long Cane, the Grahams of Yadkin, and the Crawfords of upper Georgia, to name but four examples.

These concentrations of kinsmen, all bearing the same surname, created endless onomastic confusion. We are told that in Catawba County, "so numerous were the tribe of the Alexanders that they had to be designated by their office, their trade or their middle name." The most eminent Alexander was called "Gover-

---

[3]Robert Witherspoon, "Recollections," in H. Roy Merrens, ed., *The South Carolina Scene: Contemporary Views, 1697–1774* (Columbia, S.C., 1977), 124. For another description of clan migration, see Parton, *Life of Andrew Jackson*, I, 46.

nor Nat" to distinguish him from "Red Head Nat" and "Fuller Nat." This became a common custom throughout the southern highlands.[4]

The clan system spread rapidly throughout the southern highlands, and gradually came to include English and German settlers as well as North Britons, because it worked so well in the new environment. When George Gilmer compiled his classic history of upper Georgia, he organized his book by clans, beginning with the Gilmers and moving to others in order of their kinship with the author. He specifically described these groups as clans, and wrote that their members "called each other cousin, and the old people uncle and aunt. They lived in the most intimate social way—meeting together very often."[5]

The internal structure of the clan was not what some modern observers have imagined. Historian Ned Landsman writes, ". . . among the distinctive features of clan organization was the emphasis on collateral rather than lineal descent. In the theory of clan relationships, all branches of the family—younger as well as older, female as well as male—were deemed to be of equal importance. This fit in well with the mobility of the countryside, which prevented the formation of 'lineal families' in which sons succeeded to their fathers' lands."[6]

Admission by marriage was a process of high complexity. "When a Scottish man or woman took a spouse who was not of Scottish descent," Landsman writes, "the whole family could be absorbed into the 'Scottish' community."[7] But when the bride had belonged to a rival clan, then the question of loyalty became more difficult. Generally a new bride left her own kin, and joined those of her husband. Elaborate customs regulated the relationship between the wife and the family she had joined by marriage. These customs were highly complex, but by and large they established the principle that marriage ties were weaker than blood ties. One marriage contract in Westmorland explicitly stated that a newly married wife could never sit in her mother-in-law's seat.[8]

In many cases the husband and wife both came from the same clan. In the Cumbrian parish of Hawkshead, for example, both the bride and groom bore the same last names in 25 percent of

[4]Charles G. Sellers, *James K. Polk, Jacksonian, 1795–1843* (Princeton, 1957), 8–9.
[5]Gilmer, *First Settlers of Upper Georgia,* 168.
[6]Landsman, *Scotland and Its First American Colony,* 46.
[7]*Ibid.,* 160.
[8]Bouch and Jones, *Economic and Social History of the Lake Countries,* 30.

all marriages from 1568 to 1704. Marriages in the backcountry, like those on the borders, also occurred very frequently between kin.[9]

Within these family networks, nuclear households were highly cohesive, drawing strength from the support of other kin groups round about them. Landsman writes: "The patterned dispersal of the Scots, rather than isolating individual settlers from their homes and families, served instead to bind together the scattered settlements through a system of interlocking family networks. Rather than a deterrent, mobility was an essential component of community life." The effect was reinforced by exchanges of land, by rotations of children, and by chain migrations.[10] The clan was not an alternative to the nuclear family, but its nursery and strong support. The pattern of cohesion was different from the nuclear families of Puritans and Quakers which had exceptionally strong internal bonds, powerfully reinforced by ethical and religious teachings. Among the North Britons the clan system provided an external source of cohesion—supporting each nuclear family from the outside like a system of external buttresses.

Nuclear households were large in the backcountry—among the largest in British America during the eighteenth century. The Anglican missionary Charles Woodmason wrote with his usual mixture of fact and prejudice, ". . . there's not a cabin but has ten or twelve young people in it . . . in many cabins you will see ten or fifteen children—children and grand children of one size—and the mother looking as young as the daughter."[11]

Woodmason's account was exaggerated, but other evidence confirms the same general pattern. North Carolina's governor Arthur Dobbs, who had served as surveyor general of Ireland, took his own informal census of household size in the backcountry, and found that of thirty households on Rocky River, near the boundary of North and South Carolina, there were "not less than from five or six to ten children in each family."[12]

In the first comprehensive census of the backcountry, taken in 1800, fertility ratios in the southern highlands were 40 percent higher than in the Delaware Valley, and higher also than on the

[9]G. E. Braithwaite, "The Braithwaites," 10, LANCSRO.

[10]*Ibid.,* 153.

[11]Woodmason, *Carolina Backcountry,* 39.

[12]Arthur Dobbs to Board of Trade, 24 Aug. 1755, *Colonial Records of North Carolina,* V, 355; somewhat smaller households are reported in Alan D. Watson, "Household Size and Composition in Pre-Revolutionary North Carolina," *MQ* 31 (1978), 551–69.

northern frontier. An unusually large proportion of backcountry households were intact, with both husband and wife present. Many were also joint households, with more than one nuclear family living under the same roof. As late as 1850 one-third of all households in the southern highlands included members who were not of the primary nuclear group.[13]

There was no "emergence of the modern nuclear family" in this region, through its first two hundred years. The very opposite was the case. As time passed, clans became stronger rather than weaker in the southern highlands. In the early twentieth century, a mountain woman wrote:

> All the children in the district are related by blood in one degree or another. Our roll-call includes Sally Mary and Cripple John's Mary and Tan's Mary, all bearing the same surname; and there is, besides, Aunt Rose Mary and Mary-Jo, living yon side the creek. There are different branches of the Rogers family—Clay and Frank, Red Jim and Lyin' Jim and Singin' Jim and Black Jim Rogers—in this district, their kin intermarried until no man could write their pedigree or ascertain the exact relation of their offspring to each other. This question, however, does not disturb the children in the least. They never address each other as cousin; they are content to know that uncle Tan's smokehouse is the resource of all in time of famine; that Aunt Martha's kind and strong hands are always to be depended on when one is really ill; that Uncle Filmore plays the fiddle at all the dances, and Uncle Dave shoes all the mules owned by the tribe.[14]

These clans fostered an exceptionally strong sense of loyalty, which a modern sociologist has called "amoral familism," from the ethical perspective of his own historical moment.[15] In its own time and place, it was not amoral at all, but a moral order of another kind, which recognized a special sense of obligation to kin. That imperative was a way of dealing with a world where violence and disorder were endemic. Long after it had lost its reason

---

[13]Yasukichi Yasuba, *Birth Rates of the White Population in the United States, 1800–1860* (Baltimore, 1962), 61–62, 131–32; Colin Forster and G.S.L. Tucker, *Economic Opportunity and White American Fertility Ratios, 1800–1860* (New Haven, 1972), 40–41; for the persistence of large and complex households in this region during the nineteenth century, see William M. Selby, Michael J. O'Brien and Lynn M. Snyder, "The Frontier Household," in Michael J. O'Brien, ed., *Grassland, Forest and Historical Settlement* (Lincoln, Neb., 1984), 266–316. There is evidence of large families in Ulster, with as many as five males each on the average; see Raymond Gillespie, *Colonial Ulster: The Settlement of East Ulster, 1600–1641* (Cork, 1985), 55.

[14]Miles, *The Spirit of the Mountains*, 13–14.

[15]Edward C. Banfield, *The Moral Basis of a Backward Society* (New York, 1958), 110.

for being, family loyalty retained its power in the American backcountry.

An example was the persistence of the family feud, which continued for many centuries in the southern highlands. These feuds flowed from the fact that families in the borderlands and backcountry were given moral properties which belonged mainly to individuals in other English-speaking cultures. Chief among them were the attributes of honor and shame. When one man forfeited honor in the backcountry, the entire clan was diminished by his loss. When one woman was seduced and abandoned, all her "menfolk" shared the humiliation. The feuds of the border and the backcountry rose mainly from this fact. When "Devil Anse" Hatfield was asked to explain why he had murdered so many McCoys, he answered simply, "A man has a right to defend his family." And when he spoke of his family, he meant all Hatfields and their kin. This backcountry folkway was strikingly similar to the customs of the borderers.[16]

Historians of a materialist persuasion have suggested that the feud was a modern invention in the southern highlands. One has called it a "response to industrialism." Another has interpreted it as the product of changes in the means of production. These modern processes would indeed provide many occasions for feuds.[17] But they were not the cause of the feuding itself, which had deeper cultural roots. Other historians have argued that southern feuds were mainly a legacy of the Civil War. But feuds occurred in the backcountry before 1861. They were part of the brutal violence of the American Revolution in the backcountry. Strong continuities in family feuding may be traced from the borders of North Britain to the American backcountry—a pattern that persisted throughout the southern highlands even into the twentieth century.[18]

---

[16]W. D. Weatherford and Earl D. C. Brewer, *Life and Religion in Southern Appalachia* (New York, 1962), 9.

[17]Otis K. Rice, *The Hatfields and McCoys* (Lexington, 1978).

[18]Charles G. Mutzenberg, *Kentucky's Famous Feuds and Tragedies* (New York, 1917); S. S. McClintock, "The Kentucky Mountains and Their Feuds," *AJS* 7 (1901), 1–28, 171–87; O. O. Howard, "The Feuds in the Cumberland Mountains," *I* 56 (1904), 783–88; Jenny Wormald, "Blood Feud, Kindred and Government in Early Modern Scotland," *Past and Present* 87 (1980), 54–97.

❧ Backcountry Marriage Ways: Border Origins of Bridal Customs

Marriage customs among the people of the backcountry also derived from border roots. An ancient practice on the British borders was the abduction of brides. In Scotland, Ireland and the English border counties, the old custom had been elaborately regulated through many centuries by ancient folk laws which required payment of "body price" and "honor price." Two types of abduction were recognized: voluntary abduction in which the bride went willingly but without her family's prior consent; and involuntary abduction in which she was taken by force.[1] Both types of abduction were practiced as late as the eighteenth century. It was observed of the borderlands and Ulster during this period that "abductions, both 'under the impulse of passion and from motives of cupidity,' were frequent."[2]

The border custom of bridal abduction was introduced to the American backcountry. In North and South Carolina during the eighteenth century, petitioners complained to authorities that "their wives and daughters were carried captives" by rival clans.[3]

Even future President of the United States Andrew Jackson took his wife by an act of voluntary abduction. Rachel Donelson Robards was unhappily married to another man at the time. A series of complex quarrels followed, in which Rachel Robards made her own preferences clear, and Andrew Jackson threatened her husband Lewis Robards that he would "cut his ears out of his head." Jackson was promptly arrested. But before the case came to trial the suitor turned on the husband, butcher knife in hand, and chased him into the canebreak. Afterward, the complaint was dismissed because of the absence of the plaintiff—who was in fact running for his life from the defendant. Andrew Jackson thereupon took Rachel Robards for his own, claiming that she had been abandoned. She went with Jackson willingly enough; this was a clear case of voluntary abduction. But her departure caused a feud that continued for years.[4]

For a cultural historian, the responses to this event were more

---

[1] Patrick C. Power, *Sex and Marriage in Ancient Ireland* (Dublin and Cork, 1976), 42–47.

[2] Leyburn, *The Scotch-Irish: A Social History*, 32; R. Chambers, *Domestic Annals of Scotland* (Edinburgh, 1858–61), I, 5.

[3] Woodmason, *Carolina Backcountry*, 207.

[4] There are many versions of this tangled affair; an authoritative account appears in Remini, *Andrew Jackson*, I, 40–58.

*The old border custom of bridal abduction continued in the American back-
country. The petitions of the Regulators complained of frequent abductions, and
even members of the border ascendancy resorted to this practice. The leading
example was Andrew Jackson and Rachel Donelson. This was a case of voluntary abduction; Rachel went willingly. But her departure started a feud that
continued many years. It later became an electioneering issue in other parts of
the United States, but in the backcountry, Rachel and Andrew Jackson were not
condemned by their own culture. Most backcountry marriages, of course, were
not abductions, but abduction rituals long remained an important part of marriage customs in this region.*

important than the act itself. In later years, Jackson's methods of courtship became a campaign issue, and caused moral outrage in other parts of the republic; but in the backcountry he was not condemned at the time. Historian Robert Remini writes, "One thing is certain. Whatever Rachel and Andrew did, and whenever they did it, their actions did not outrage the community."[5]

Most backcountry courtships were not as primitive as this. The strict Protestantism of Scottish and Ulster Presbyterians created a heavy overlay of moral restraint. But many backcountry marriages included mock abduction rituals that kept the old customs alive in a vestigial way. A wedding in the back-settlements was apt to be a wild affair. On the appointed day, the friends of the groom would set out for the wedding in a single party, mounted and heavily armed. They would stop at cabins along the way to fire a volley and pass around the whiskey bottle, then gallop on to the next. Their progress was playfully opposed by the bride's friends, also heavily armed, who felled trees along the road, and created entanglements of grape vines and branches to block the passage of the groomsmen.

> Sometimes an ambuscade was formed by the way side, an unexpected discharge of several guns took place, so as to cover the wedding company with smoke. Let the reader imagine the scene which followed this discharge, the sudden spring of the horses, the shriek of the girls, and the chivalric bustle of their partners to save them from falling. Sometimes, in spite of all that could be done to prevent it, some were thrown to the ground; if a wrist, elbow or ankle happened to be sprained, it was tied with a handkerchief, and little more was thought or said about it.[6]

The two parties then came together and staged a contest in which their champions raced for a beribboned bottle of whisky. The results were celebrated with another explosive *feu de joie.*

> Two young men would single out to run for the bottle; the worse the path, the more logs, brush and deep hollows, the better, as obstacles afforded an opportunity for the greatest display of intrepidity and horsemanship. The English fox chase, in point of danger to their riders and their horses, was nothing to this race for the bottle. The start was announced by an Indian yell, when logs, brush, mud holes, hill and glen, were speedily passed by the

[5] *Ibid.,* I, 66.
[6] Samuel Kercheval, "The Wedding," in *A History of the Valley of Virginia* (1833, 3d ed., rev. and extended, Woodstock, Va., 1902), 58, 266–69.

rival ponies. The bottle was always filled for the occasion, so that there was no use for judges; for the first who reached the door was presented with the prize, with which he returned in triumph to the company. On approaching them he announced his victory over his rival by a shrill whoop. At the head of the troop he gave the bottle to the groom and his attendants, and then to each pair in succession, to the rear of the line, giving each a dram, and then putting the bottle in the bosom of his hunting shirt, took his station in the company.

Finally, both parties would assemble with invited guests from the neighborhood. These were "bidden weddings," which could be attended only by invitation. "It often happened," Kercheval remembered, "that some neighbors or relations, not being asked to the wedding, took offence; and the mode of revenge adopted by them on such occasions, was that of cutting off the manes, foretops and tails of the horses of the wedding company."[7]

When all were assembled, the bride would be brought into the room by the best man—not, significantly, by her father. The bride and groom put their right hands behind their backs, and their gloves were ceremonially removed by the best man and the bridesmaid, who took care to do so at exactly the same moment.

After the ceremony, there were more volleys, much whooping, and an abundance of kissing, drinking and high hilarity. Then a dinner and dance would take place, with everyone joining in wild reels, sets and jigs while a fiddler scraped frantically in the corner. Before the wedding dinner, another mock-abduction was staged indoors; the bride was stolen by one party and "recovered" by the other. During the dinner itself the party played still another abduction-game called stealing the shoe. While dinner went on, the young people crawled about beneath the table and some of the groomsmen tried to steal the bride's shoe while others sought to stop them. Four of the most beautiful girls and the most handsome men were appointed "waiters" and had the honor of protecting her while at the same time they served the dinner. Their badge of office was an exquisitely embroidered white apron, on which the bride and her family had labored for many weeks before the wedding. If the bride lost her shoe, she could not dance until it was recovered by her champions in mock combat.

As the sun set upon this turbulent scene, the couple retired to their chamber, while hordes of well-wishers crowded round the

[7] *Ibid.*, 269

bed and offered ribald advice. Yet another contest was staged at the foot of the marriage bed. After the couple was placed beneath the covers, the bridesmaids took turns throwing a rolled stocking over their shoulders at the bride. Then the groomsmen did the same, aiming at the groom. The first to hit the mark was thought to be the next to marry. These games continued well into the night. When the wedding party finally left the chamber, a "cali-thumpian serenade" took place outside—the bells and whistles punctuated by uninhibited gunplay that sometimes caused a back-country wedding to be followed by a funeral.[8] As morning approached, a bottle of Black Betty was sent to revive the bride and groom and the merriment continued, sometimes for several days.[9]

All this was very similar to marriage customs in the borders of north Britain, as appears in a poetic description by the "Cumberland bard" Robert Anderson:

> They sing of a weddin' at Worton
>   Where aw was fehgt, fratchin' and fun,
> Feegn! sec a yen we've hed at Codbeck
>   As niver was under the sun.
> The breydegruim was weaver Joe Beyley
>   He com' frae about Lowther Green;
> The breyde Johnny Dalton's h'sh dowter,
>   And Betty was weel to be seen.[10]

In this scene, "Betty" was Black Betty, the whisky bottle.

A good deal of wealth changed hands on these occasions. Affluent families in Cumbria kept the custom of marriage portions, often very large, which were paid over a period of several years.[11] In families too poor to afford a portion, other marriage customs were carried from the border to the backcountry—the "bidden

---

[8]For a virtually identical description of Scots-Irish wedding customs in Londonderry, New Hampshire, see Alice Morse Earle, *Customs and Fashions in Old New England* (1893, Rutland, Vt., 1973), 74; see also *North Carolina Folklore*, II, 238.

[9]Kercheval, *Valley of Virginia*, 266–69; John Lewis Peyton, *History of Augusta County, Virginia* (Staunton, Va., 1882), 44–46; Julia Cherry Spruill, *Women's Life and Work in the Southern Colonies*, (1938, New York 1972), 110–11.

[10]Robert Anderson, "The Codbeck Weddin'," in *Westmorland and Cumberland Dialect*, 262–63.

[11]One Cumberland man recorded in much detail the dowry for his daughter; "Sep. 20 [1677], paid unto my son in law [Edward] Wilson in part of his wife's portion £10 . . . March 18 [1678] paid my son [in law] Wilson more of his wife's portion 9/0/0 . . . May 17 [1678] more of his portion £20. . . . June 28 [1678] more of his portion £20. . . ." Danlie Fleming Accounts, WD/R/box 199, CUMROK.

wedding," and "bridewain." The former was explained by a Cumbrian antiquarian:

> Some of the Cumbrians, particularly those who are in poor circumstances, have, on their entrance into the married state, what is called a BIDDING (invitation) or BIDDEN WEDDINGS, at which a pecuniary collection is made among the company for the purpose of setting the wedded pair forward in the world. It is always attended with music & dancing; and the fiddler when the contributions begin takes care to remind the assembly their duties, by notes imitative of the following couplet:
> Come my friends, and freely offer
> Here's a bride that has no toucher.[12]

Another custom called bridewain had a similar social function in this culture:

> In Cumberland . . . the friends of a new married couple assemble and are treated with cold pies, fermenty and ale; at the close of the day the bride and bridegroom are placed in two chairs in the open air, or in a large barn, the bride with a pewter dish on her knee, half covered with a napkin. The company put offerings into a dish—offerings often amount to a considerable sum. The word wain was said to be ancient custom in the north.[13]

Even in poor border families, much was spent on weddings. One antiquarian wrote of the borderers, "They intermarry one with another, and will spend all they have in the wedding week, and then go begging."[14]

Marriage customs in the American backcountry bore a striking resemblance to those of the British border lands—complete even to the abductions and mock abductions, the competitions and mock combats, bidden weddings and bridewain, the wild feasts and heavy drinking, wedding reels and jigs, the rituals of the wedding chamber, and the constant presence of Black Betty. Some of these customs were shared by other cultures. But in their totality the backcountry wedding was a unique adaptation of ancient border customs to the conditions of an American region.

The distinctiveness of this system also appeared in quantitative indicators. Age at marriage in the backcountry was different from

---

[12]"Toucher" was the border word for a dowry; see *Westmorland and Cumberland Dialect,* 330.

[13]*Ibid.*

[14]Jane M. Ewbank, *Antiquary on Horseback: The First Publication of the Collections of the Reverend Thomas Machell, Chaplain to Charles II, towards a History of the Barony of Kendal* (Kendal, 1963).

every other American region. Both brides and grooms were very young. South Carolinian David Ramsay wrote of the backcountry, ". . . marriages are early and generally prolific. In one district, containing upwards of 17,000 white inhabitants, there is not one woman at the age of twenty-five who is neither wife or widow."[15] That impression has been solidly confirmed by statistical fact. Historian Mark Kaplanoff finds that in three districts of upcountry South Carolina during the eighteenth century, women married at the average age of nineteen; men at twenty-one. In no other region of British America did both sexes marry so early. Nowhere else were the ages of males and females so nearly the same.[16]

This was partly the result of a frontier environment, but not entirely so. Other frontiers were very different. And it is interesting to observe that of all the regions of England, age at marriage was lowest in the north—as much as three years below southern England. Here again, the backsettlers followed their ancestral ways.[17]

❧ Backcountry Gender Ways: Border Rituals of Love and Violence

In his account of backcountry marriages, Samuel Kercheval recorded another curious custom called the wedding toast. After dinner, as Black Betty passed from hand to hand, each male guest raised the bottle in his right fist and cried: "Here's to the bride, thumping luck and big children!" Kercheval explained:

> Big children, especially big sons, were of great importance, as we were few in number and engaged in perpetual hostility with the

---

[15]David Ramsey, *History of South Carolina from Its First Settlement in 1670 to the Year 1808* (2 vols., Charleston, 1809), II, 600.

[16]Mark Kaplanoff obtained the following estimates of mean age at marriage from an ingenious analysis of the South Carolina census of 1800, for marriages contracted in the population living at that time.

District	Males	Females
Greenville	22.3	19.4
Newberry	21.4	19.1
Sumter	20.9	19.8

Source: Unpublished research, communicated by the kindness of Mark Kaplanoff.

[17]In England before 1750, mean age at first marriage of women was 26.9 in twenty-six southern parishes, and 23.5 in sixteen northern parishes. Age at marriage was generally higher in all British regions than in the American colonies, but relative differences were much the same. See Michael W. Flinn, *The European Demographic System, 1500–1820* (Baltimore, 1981), 124–25.

Indians, the end of which no one could foresee. Indeed many of
them seemed to suppose war was the natural state of man, and
therefore did not anticipate any conclusion of it; every big son was
therefore considered a young soldier.[1]

Here was the basis of gender relationships in the backcountry.
The first principle was that men were warriors. The second was
that women were workers. These ideas had long flourished on the
borders of north Britain. When they were combined with the ethics of Christianity, the result was a gender system of high complexity which might best be described as a bundle of paradoxes.

One paradox concerned gender distinctions. In the backcountry, work roles were not as sharply divided by sex as in other
English cultures. But at the same time, the people of the backcountry had exceptionally clear-cut ideas of masculinity and fem-
inity in manners, speech, dress, decorum and status.[2]

Travelers in the backcountry often reported that women and
men routinely shared the heaviest manual labor. Both sexes
worked together in the fields, not merely at harvest time but
through the entire growing season. Women not only tended the
livestock but also did the slaughtering of even the largest animals.
Travelers were startled to observe delicate females knock down
beef cattle with a felling ax, and then roll down their sleeves,
remove their bloody aprons, tidy their hair, and invite their visitors to tea. Females also helped with the heavy labor of forest-
clearing and ground-breaking. William Byrd noted that women in
the back settlements were not merely "up to their elbows in housewifery," but also busy with what other English cultures took to
be a man's work.[3]

Those customs have sometimes been explained as a response to
the frontier environment. But they did not exist in quite the same
way on the Puritan frontier, and the same patterns had long been
observed by travelers in the borderlands of North Britain. One
anonymous visitor to the counties of Cumberland and Westmorland wrote that wives of even landowners were expected to share
equally in the heavy farm work. "These petty landowners work

---

[1] Kercheval, *Valley of Virginia*, 268.

[2] Alan D. Watson, "Women in Colonial North Carolina . . . ," *NCHR* 58 (1981), 1–22.

[3] John Oldmixon also wrote that, throughout the backlands, "the ordinary women take care
of cows, hogs, and other small cattle, make butter and cheese, spin cotton and flax, help to sow
and reap corn, wind silk from the worms, gather fruit and look after the house"; *The History of
the British Empire in America* in Alexander S. Salley, Jr., *Narratives of Early Carolina* (1911, New
York, 1967), 372.

like slaves," one traveler observed in 1766. "They cannot afford to keep a manservant, but husband, wife, sons and daughters all turn out to work in the fields."[4] An historian of Galloway wrote that on women "devolved almost every task of mean and painful drudgery."[5]

In other respects, there was very little equality between husbands and wives in the British borderlands or the American backcountry. The historical myth that the frontier created a spirit of equality among the sexes could not be farther from the truth. Backcountry families were decidedly male-dominant—much more so than in New England or the Delaware Valley. The male was expected to be the head of the household; his consort was required to do his bidding quietly, cheerfully and without complaint. This was a traditional folkway among the border people. Of a woman's place in Ulster, Leyburn writes, "the status of women, whether legal or actual, improved not a whit during the seventeenth century. . . . they were disciplined in the churches, but their life must otherwise have been the traditional one of subordination to men in a patriarchal society."[6] Precisely the same patterns appeared in the American backcountry families. Arthur Calhoun remembered from the experience of his own Appalachian childhood that "the Scots-Irish . . . were marked by family loyalty. The women led hard lives but were patient and submissive. The person familiar with the backcountry of western Pennsylvania today [c. 1917] will note apparent survivals of the last two primitive features."[7]

More than in other English-speaking cultures, the identity of backcountry women was submerged in the status of their husbands. An example appeared on a gravestone. When Patrick Calhoun erected a memorial to his wife, the name he placed at the top was not hers but his. The inscription read:

Patk Calhoun Esq

In memory of Mrs. Catherine Calhoun
Aged 76 years who with 22 others
was here murdered by the Indians. the
First of February 1760.[8]

[4] *Gentleman's Magazine* 36 (1766), 582.
[5] Mackenzie, *History of Galloway*, I, 236.
[6] Leyburn, *The Scotch-Irish: A Social History*, 148.
[7] Arthur W. Calhoun, *The American Family, the Colonial Period* (rpt. New York, 1960), 207.
[8] A. S. Salley, "The Grandfather of John C. Calhoun," *SCHGM* 39 (1938), 50.

George Gilmer remembered many similar vignettes of gender relations in this society. He told one such story about John Marks and his pretty bride Mary Tomkins. One day the husband was building a log cabin:

> His wife came to the place, and began objecting to the manner in which he was fashioning what he was doing. He listened to her for some time, and reasoned the matter with her; but she still insisted upon having the house made according to her own notions. He pulled off his breeches, and threw them down to her, telling her to put them on and wear them."[9]

There was yet another paradox in the tone of these relations—which were filled with love and violence both at the same time. Gilmer told another tale of a hard-drinking backsettler who called himself Colonel Nicholas Johnson. One day, Colonel Johnson got drunk and assaulted his daughter and wife:

> Col. Johnson threw one of his daughters on the floor, and made such a plausible feint that he intended to take her life, by sticking his knife into the floor near her head, that his wife interfered to save her child. He immediately let go his daughter, and attempted to seize his wife. She fled from the house to Broad River, about half a mile distant. Whilst seated over the water, considering the question whether it were better to be or not to be, she was suddenly precipitated into the river, and turning her head, saw that her husband's hand had done the deed. As soon as he perceived that his wife's life was in imminent peril, his whole nature underwent a sudden revulsion. He was sober in a moment. Unable to swim, to have jumped into the water would have been certain destruction to both. He looked around with the quickness of thought for means to save her. He found nothing at hand, but a long weed. Extending it at once towards her, he spoke gently, and begged her to take hold. The voice of love never fails to find a vibrating chord in a woman's heart. Her clothes held her up for a moment. She saw the change in her husband's feelings, and did as she was implored to do.[10]

Love and violence together were common ingredients of backcountry marriages—both expressed with an emotional intensity that rarely appeared in Massachusetts or the Delaware. Gilmer

[9]Gilmer, *First Settlers of Upper Georgia*, 117.
[10]*Ibid.*, 95.

told another tale of love and violence in the backcountry family of Mr. and Mrs. Thomas Meriwether:

> His love for his wife was without intermission, and . . . his gallantry equalled his love. When she tired of sleeping on one side, and turned on the other, he always crossed over, if awake, that they might be ever face to face.

But Thomas Meriwether did not hesitate to use violence to dominate the woman he loved so deeply. Once he and his wife attended a camp meeting, and she began to be caught up in the process of conversion. "Tom Meriwether," we are told, "became alarmed, lest his wife's love might be drawn away from him, and placed upon what he took no interest in. He seized her by the arm, and led her forcibly away," dragging her violently from the camp meeting.[11]

Despite these expressions of love, there was a great distance between men and women of the backcountry. A mountain woman wrote from hard experience of her own marriage:

> A rift is set between the sexes at babyhood that widens with the passing of the years, a rift that is never closed even by the daily interdependence of a poor man's partnership with his wife. Rare is a separation of a married couple in the mountains; the bond of perfect sympathy is rarer. . . . The pathos of the situation is none the less terrible because it is unconscious. They are so silent. They know so pathetically little of each other's lives.
>
> Of course the woman's experience is the deeper; the man's gain is in breadth of outlook. His ambition leads him to make drain after drain on the strength of his silent wingless mate. Her position means sacrifice, sacrifice and every sacrifice, for her man first, and then for her sons.[12]

Gender relations in the backcountry, like those of the borderlands, combined elements which have often coexisted in warrior cultures—clear-cut ideas of men as fighters and women as workers; exceptionally sharp distinctions between masculine and feminine roles; extreme male domination and female dependence within the family; intense expressions of love and violence between wives and husbands; and sometimes a great aching silent distance that kept them apart.

[11] *Ibid.*, 78.
[12] Miles, *The Spirit of the Mountains*, 70.

One is occasionally tempted to abandon the role of the historian and to frame what social scientists call a theory. Whenever a culture exists for many generations in conditions of chronic insecurity, it develops an ethic that exalts war above work, force above reason, and men above women. This pattern developed on the borders of North Britain, and was carried to the American backcountry, where it was reinforced by a hostile environment and tempered by evangelical Christianity. The result was a distinctive system of gender roles that continues to flourish even in our own time.

❧ Backcountry Sex Ways: The Border Celebration of Sensuality

On the subject of sex, the backsettlers tended to be more open than were other cultures of British America. Sexual talk was free and easy in the backcountry—more so than in Puritan Massachusetts or Quaker Pennsylvania, or even Anglican Virginia. So too was sexual behavior.

The Anglican missionary Charles Woodmason was astounded by the open sexuality of the backsettlers. "How would the polite people of London stare, to see the Females (many very pretty) . . . ," he wrote. "The young women have a most uncommon practice, which I cannot break them of. They draw their shift as tight as possible round their Breasts, and slender waists (for they are generally very finely shaped) and draw their Petticoat close to their Hips to show the fineness of their limbs—as that they might as well be *in puri naturalibus*—indeed nakedness is not censurable or indecent here, and they expose themselves often quite naked, without ceremony—rubbing themselves and their hair with bears' oil and tying it up behind in a bunch like the indians— being hardly one degree removed from them. In a few years I hope to bring about a reformation."[1]

The backsettlers showed very little concern for sexual privacy in the design of their houses or the style of their lives. "Nakedness is counted as nothing," Woodmason remarked, "as they sleep altogether in common in one room, and shift and dress openly without ceremony . . . children run half naked. The Indians are

[1]Woodmason, *Carolina Backcountry*, 30, 61.

better clothed and lodged."[2] Samuel Kercheval remembered that young men adopted Indian breechclouts and leggings, cut so that "the upper part of the thighs and part of the hips were naked. The young warrior, instead of being abashed by this nudity, was proud of his Indian-like dress," Kercheval wrote. "In some few places I have seen them go into places of public worship in this dress."[3]

Other evidence suggests that these surface impressions of back-country sexuality had a solid foundation in fact. Rates of pre-nuptial pregnancy were very high in the backcountry—higher than other parts of the American colonies. In the year 1767, Woodmason calculated that 94 percent of backcountry brides whom he had married in the past year were pregnant on their wedding day, and some were "very big" with child. He attributed this tendency to social customs in the back settlements:

> Nothing more leads to this than what they call their love feasts and kiss of charity. To which feasts, celebrated at night, much liquor is privately carried, and deposited on the roads, and in bye paths and places. The assignations made on Sundays at the singing clubs, are here realized. And it is no wonder that things are as they are, when many young people have three, four, five or six miles to walk home in the dark night, with convoy, thro' the woods? Or perhaps staying all night at some cabbin (as on Sunday nights) and sleeping together either doubly or promiscuously? Or a girl being mounted behind a person to be carried home, or any wheres. All this contributes to multiply subjects for the king in this frontier country, and so is wink'd at by the Magistracy and Parochial Officers.[4]

Another factor was a scarcity of clergy to perform marriages in the backcountry. But there was also a different explanation. Rates of illegitimacy and prenuptial pregnancy had long been higher in the far northwest of England than in any other part of that nation. The magnitude of regional differences was very great. Rates of bastardy in the northwest were three times higher than in the east of England during the sixteenth and seventeenth centuries. Regional disparities persisted from the beginning of parish registers to the twentieth century. Historian Peter Laslett notes that "in early Victorian times Cumberland . . . had the highest recordings [of bastardy] in the country." Westmorland was very

[2] *Ibid.*, 32.
[3] Kercheval, *Valley of Virginia*, 257.
[4] Woodmason, *Carolina Backcountry*, 7, 100.

similar. High rates of illegitimacy and prenuptial pregnancy in the backcountry were not the necessary consequences of frontier conditions. Puritans also moved onto new lands in the northern colonies and continued to behave in puritanical ways. The same continuities appeared among the Quakers when they moved to the frontier. The sexual customs of the southern backcountry were similar to those of northwestern England.[5]

When prenuptial pregnancy occurred, customary responses in the backcountry differed from other regions. Where Puritans, Quakers and cavaliers launched formal prosecutions for fornication, the back settlers had a merry game and a good laugh. Kercheval remembered that a backcountry custom "adopted when the chastity of the bride was a little suspected, was that of setting up a pair of horns on poles or trees, on the route of the wedding company."[6]

Another sort of sexual deviance was very rare in the backcountry. There were not many cases of seduction and abandonment, which was regarded not merely as a violation of a woman's virtue but of her entire family's honor. Such an act was thought to be a high crime, and any man who committed it was lucky to escape a lynching. Kercheval could remember but a single instance of this offense, in which reactions were so violent that "the life of the man was put in jeopardy by the resentment of the family to which the girl belonged . . . this crime could not take place without great personal danger from the brothers or other relations of the victim seduced, family honor being then estimated at a very high rate."[7] Some cases of this sort were settled by cash payments, without intervention of church or court. In 1770, for example, one backcountry diarist noted, "George Johnson made up with

---

[5]Peter Laslett supplies the following regional data for illegitimacy ratios in England by period from 1581 to 1820:

Region	1581–1640	1661–1720	1721–80	1781–1820
West and northwest	3.6	1.4	4.6	6.2
North	2.9	1.3	3.5	4.2
South	2.1	1.4	4.0	4.5
Midlands	1.6	1.3	2.9	3.1
East	1.2	1.0	3.3	4.0

The "west and northwest" included much of the border country. As late as 1842–45, Cumberland had the highest recorded rates of illegitimacy of any county in England. See Peter Laslett, "Long Term Trends in Bastardy in England," in *Family Life and Illicit Love in Earlier Generations* (Cambridge, 1977), 142–46.

[6]Kercheval, *Valley of Virginia*, 269.

[7]*Ibid.*, 294.

Pegg Wright for ten pounds I hear." Such a sum was sufficient to
preserve the honor of a family, if not the virtue of its wayward
daughter.[8]

The sexual customs of backcountry, like those of the North
British borderers, were rigid in this respect. But in others, they
were much more relaxed. An example was a sexual game called
cockle bread, which were played by nubile girls in Westmorland.
It was described by a disapproving Victorian folklorist as a "wanton sport of young wenches," who would "get upon a Tableboard
and then gather-up their knees and their coates as high as they
can, and then they wabble to and fro with their buttocks," singing
'Up with your heels, down with your head; that is the way to make
cockeldy bread.'"[9]

Here was an earthy and unrestrained celebration of animal sexuality that was distinctly different from the ways of Puritans,
Quakers and even cavaliers. Once again we find another strong
similarity between the British borderlands and the American
backcountry.

❧ Backcountry Child-naming Ways: Border Onomastics

Another important clue to backcountry culture was the naming
of its children. The onomastic customs of these people were
unique. Favored forenames in the backcountry included a mixture of biblical names (John was the top choice), Teutonic names
(such as Robert or Richard), and the names of border saints
(especially Andrew, Patrick, David). This combination did not
exist in any other English-speaking culture.

Popular namesakes in the backcountry included Saint Andrew,
an apostle who became the patron saint of Scotland. Also much
in vogue was David, a name associated not only with its biblical
bearer, but also with a seventh-century archbishop who became
the patron saint of Wales, and with two early Scottish kings. Yet
another favorite namesake was Saint Patrick, the legendary mis-
sionary-priest who converted Ireland to Christianity; his name
was often used by Protestant as well as Catholic families throughout northern Ireland.

---

[8]Dyer Journal, 9 Nov. 1770, HSP.
[9]Alice B. Gomme, *The Traditional Games of England, Scotland and Ireland* (1894–98, new ed.,
London, 1984), 75

These saints' names were rare in the other regional cultures of British America. Davids were few and far between in New England and the Delaware Valley; Puritans and Quakers were not amused by King David's biblical antics. Patricks were uncommon in Anglican Virginia and nearly unknown in Puritan New England. Harvard College did not admit a single undergraduate named Patrick in all the years from 1636 to 1820. But in Cumberland Country, Pennsylvania, Patrick was the fourth most popular name on military muster rolls during the eighteenth century.[1]

The backsettlers sometimes used Celtic names such as Ewan (var. Ewen, Owen), Barry and Roy. They also had a taste for Scandinavian and Teutonic names unknown to other English-speaking cultures, such as Archibald and Ronald. Particular favorites in the American backcountry were the names of Scottish kings Alexander, Charles and James. Also popular were the names of brave warriors on both sides of the border, notably Wallace, Bruce, Percy and Howard. Nostalgic parents even named their children for border places such as Ross, Clyde, Carlisle, Tyne, Cumberland and Derry.[2]

These backcountry naming patterns had long existed on the borders of North Britain. But they were different from onomastic patterns in the south of England, and also from naming practices in the Gaelic-speaking parts of the Scottish Highlands and Catholic Ireland. The borderers did not often use forenames such as Douglas, Donald, Kenneth, Alan, Ian, Neil or Stewart which were favored by highlanders. Neither did they make much use of Gaelic Irish names such as Sean, Kathleen, Maureen or Sheila.[3] Altogether, a complex border and backcountry combination of biblical names, Celtic names, Teutonic names, saints' names, folk names, Scottish kings' names and border warriors' names was unique to this regional folk culture.

In another respect, however, backcountry naming customs were not unique. The descent of names from one generation to

---

[1] The ten most popular names on backcountry militia lists were as follows, ca. 1776: John, William, James, Patrick, Robert, Thomas, Charles, Samuel, Edward, and Joseph. See George R. Stewart, *American Given Names* (New York, 1979), 25, 208–9.

[2] *Ibid.*

[3] Border onomastics should not be confused with the romantic inventions of Victorian border poets and novelists. Enid was popularized by Tennyson, Lorna by Blackmore and Cedric by Sir Walter Scott.

the next was very similar to the folkways of Virginia and the south of England, but different from Puritan and Quaker customs. Eldest sons in the backcountry tended to be named after grandfathers, and second or third sons after fathers, much as in tidewater Chesapeake families. An example was the family of Andrew Jackson (1767–1845). The future President was the second son of a Scots-Irish immigrant also named Andrew Jackson (1730–67), and grandson of Hugh Jackson (d. 1782), a weaver in the Irish town of Castlereagh. The naming rhythm ran as follows through three generations:

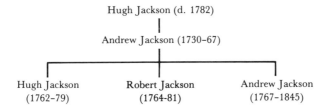

Precisely the same pattern had long prevailed in the northwestern counties of England, as well as in Scotland and northern Ireland. Another example was a Cumberland family (originally from the Isle of Man) which variously called itself McChristen and Christian:

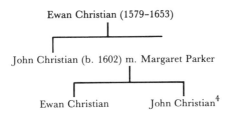

This naming rhythm was much the same in every part of the border region—in the English counties of Cumberland and Westmorland, in the Scottish lowlands and also in northern Ireland. It was introduced to the American backcountry in the eighteenth century and persisted for a long time.[4]

A good example of this persistence was another presidential family, that of Zachary Taylor. His ancestors were an English border family from Carlisle in the county of Cumberland, who first

[4]William Hutchinson, *History of the County of Cumberland* (Ilkley, Yorkshire, 1974), 146.

settled in Virginia, and then moved west to Kentucky. The descent of names in the Taylor family ran as follows:[5]

Zachary Taylor (1707–66)
(Virginia farmer of Cumbrian descent)
|
Richard Taylor (1744–1829)
(settled in Kentucky)
|
Zachary Taylor (1784–1850)
(12th U.S. President)
|
Richard Taylor (1826–79)
(Lt. General, Confederate Army)
|
Zachary Taylor (1857–died young)

In this respect, backcountry onomastics were much like those of the tidewater south. But in another curious naming custom, the backsettlers went their own way. From an early date they cultivated a spirit of onomastic individualism, sometimes with bizarre results. One famous border family of high status in the backcountry were the Hoggs, who later became one of richest and most cultivated families in Texas. One daughter, a lady of taste and refinement, was named Ima Hogg by her proud parents. Another example of onomastic individualism occurred in Oklahoma City, during the 1940s, where a woman named Hoyette White named her daughters Hoyette, Norvetta, Yerdith, Arthetta, Marlynne and Wilbarine White. A reporter was dispatched by the local newspaper to ask why she made those choices. Mrs. White explained, "When my mother saw I looked so like my father, she made a girl's name out of the family name Hoyt and called me Hoyette. That started the names. When I named my own girls, I wanted names no one had ever had, and names that nobody would ever want. So I made them up."[6]

---

[5] *Burke's Presidential Families of the United States of America* (London, 1981), 235–46.

[6] Oklahoma City *Oklahoman,* 19 May 1947; as quoted in Thomas Pyles, "Bible Belt Onomastics; or, Some Curiosities of Antipedobaptist Nomenclature," in *Selected Essays on English Usage* (Gainesville, 1979), 152.

❧ Backcountry Child-rearing Ways: Building the Will

Backcountry families also had special ways of raising their young. Child-rearing customs in the southern highlands tended to be very different from those of New England Puritans, Pennsylvania Quakers and Virginia Anglicans—and yet similar to the folkways of the British borderlands.

This system of child rearing was also far removed from modern thinking on the subject. In cultural terms, one of its most important stages occurred before the baby was born. A world of extreme uncertainty required that the fates should be propitiated with the same care and attention that a suburban mother today studies the latest treatises on infant science. The entire community joined in these precautions, and the old grannies were consulted as urgently as a modern pediatrician:

> What a plucking of herbs, what a consulting of signs and omens, both before and after the event! . . . The baby must wear a strong of corn-beads round its neck to facilitate teething, and later a bullet or coin to prevent nose-bleed. Its wee track must be printed in the first snow that falls, to ward off croup. The first woodtick that fastens itself to the little body is an omen, too; you must kill it on an axe or other tool if you wish baby to grow into a clever workman. If it be killed on a bell or banjo, or any clear-ringing substance, he will develop a voice for singing; if on a book, he will learn to speak "all kind o' proper words," all gifts highly esteemed in the mountains.[1]

No self-respecting mother neglected this form of prenatal and postnatal care.

After the baby was born, parents began the process which the modern world calls socialization. For backcountry boys, the object was not will-breaking as among the Puritans, or will-bending as in Virginia. The rearing of male children in the back settlements was meant to be positively will-enhancing. Its primary purpose was to foster fierce pride, stubborn independence and a warrior's courage in the young. An unintended effect was to create a society of autonomous individuals who were unable to endure external control and incapable of restraining their rage against anyone who stood in their way.

A case in point was the childhood of young Andrew Jackson, the future seventh President of the United States. Important

[1]Miles, *The Spirit of the Mountains*, 100–101.

parts of his socialization in this oral culture were the stories that
his mother told him. They were old border tales that celebrated
courage, pride and independence. The games of his youth were
contests for dominion—wrestling, running and fighting. A childhood friend remembered, "I could throw him three times out of
four, but he would never stay throwed."[2]

As a small boy, Jackson was remembered as "wild, frolicsome,
mischievous, daring and reckless." His upbringing left him quick
to take offense, and with a mighty rage that burst upon its objects
with explosive violence. As a young militiaman, he was described
as "bold, dashing, fearless and mad upon his enemies." That style
of behavior was widely admired in the backcountry, where small
boys were routinely taught to conduct themselves in the same
way.[3]

This system of child rearing began by being highly indulgent
and permissive. In both the British borderlands and the American
backcountry, parents doted upon male children, with an intensity
of feeling that startled observers. An example of this attitude was
recorded in North Britain in the eighteenth century:

> Harry Potts has got a son of which he's very fond. . . . He got it in
> his arms the morning it was born, which was yesterday and said,
> "Honey, thou's my darling and shalt want for nothing as long as I
> am able to work for thee."[4]

This custom was carried to the back settlements, where infants
received the same indulgent attention from both sexes—more
than at any other stage of life. This tendency was remarked upon
as early as 1782 by the Marquis de Chastelleux, who found child
rearing in the southern highlands to be very different from that
in his own nation. "They are very fond of their *little ones,* and care
much less for their *children,*" he wrote after a tour of the back
settlements. The same pattern continued to be observed even
into the twentieth century.[5]

In the eighteenth and nineteenth centuries, travelers such as
Charles Woodmason complained constantly about the forward-

---

[2]Remini, *Andrew Jackson,* I, 9.

[3]*Ibid.,* 9.

[4]Quoted in Hughes, *North Country Life in the Eighteenth Century: The North East,* 36–37.

[5]Marquis de Chastelleux, *Travels in North America in the Years 1780, 1781 and 1782* (2 vols.,
Chapel Hill, 1963), II, 442; these generalizations referred explicitly to "Americans" and to
"Virginians," but they were framed in the backcountry; for similar modern descriptions see
Miles, *The Spirit of the Mountains,* 3; Margaret J. Hagood, *Mothers of the South: Portraitures of the
White Tenant Farm Women* (New York, 1977); Bertram Wyatt-Brown, *Southern Honor* (New York,
1982), 159.

ness and freedom of backcountry children. His remarks were repeated by many other observers in the southern highlands. One wrote, "for three centuries . . . parents often look on it as evidence of spirit and smartness to see their children rudely insulting the quiet and often humble citizens of the country." Similar descriptions were also written in the nineteenth and twentieth centuries, by travelers and by the southern highlanders themselves. A mountain woman wrote in 1905, ". . . most of the children hereabout run free as the fawns and cubs that they often capture for playmates."[6]

After a small boy "dropped slips" and put on his first pair of breeches, he toddled after his parents and was allowed great freedom on the farm. At an early age, male children were given their own miniature weapons—an axe, a knife, a bow, even a childish gun. Daniel Drake recalled that as a child he was given a hatchet to "hack down saplings," while his father did the "heavy chopping." More than fifty years later, Drake remembered the joy that he felt in annihilating his first tree. "I loved it in proportion to the facility with which I could destroy it," he wrote.[7]

Corporal punishment of children was condemned in the abstract, but much practiced in an intermittent way. A backcountry church in Lunenburg County, Virginia, considered the question, "Is it lawful to beat or whip servants or children . . . before the method that Christ laid down in the 18th Matthew?" and decided the issue in the negative by majority vote. Another doctrine of St. Matthew was explicitly ratified by this congregation: "Take heed that ye despise not one of these little ones."[8]

But backcountry autobiographers also remembered terrific beatings received from frustrated fathers and mothers who found themselves equally incapable of controlling their children or restraining their own parental rage. These autobiographers also recalled their feelings of anger against what seemed to be parental tyranny. The result was a highly volatile process of child rearing: extremely permissive most of the time, but punctuated by acts of angry and illegitimate violence.

This problem of promiscuous violence in child rearing was compounded by alcohol. The diary of a school boy in Tennessee described the terror that the entire family felt whenever "papa was groggy." All the members of the household conspired to

[6]Johnson, *Antebellum North Carolina,* 254; Miles, *The Spirit of the Mountains,* 3.

[7]Daniel Drake, *Pioneer Life in Kentucky, 1785–1800* (New York, 1948), 37.

[8]Beeman, *The Evolution of the Southern Backcountry,* 109.

dilute his whisky in hopes of diminishing the fury that caused "Papa" to beat and kick even his own infant children.[9]

Youngsters responded by running away, fighting back, or sometimes even trying to murder their parents. In 1805, when one North Carolina mother attempted to control her "large family of children," they rose en masse and tried to kill her.[10] From an early age, small boys were taught to think much of their own honor, and to be active in its defense. Honor in this society meant a pride of manhood in masculine courage, physical strength and warrior virtue. Male children were trained to defend their honor without a moment's hesitation—lashing out instantly against their challengers with savage violence.

This method of child rearing was used mainly for boys. The daughters of the backcountry were raised in a different way. Mothers were expected to teach domestic virtues of industry, obedience, patience, sacrifice and devotion to others. Male children were taught to be self-asserting; female children were trained to be self-denying.

These backcountry child ways were not the product of slavery or the frontier. They were transplanted from the borders of North Britain, where they were yet another cultural adaptation to the endemic violence of that region. They were also similar to systems of socialization which have existed in warrior castes throughout the world.

This system of child rearing flourished in its new American environment. This backcountry held a different set of dangers, but they operated in the same way. Indians, bandits, regulators, weak governments and wars all combined to reinforce the warrior ethic of the backsettlers. That ethic in turn promoted a system of child rearing which was designed to make boys into warriors and girls into their consorts and helpmeets. The backcountry environment reinforced these border customs in relations between young people and their elders.

[9]William B. Little Diary, ms., NYPL.
[10]Raleigh *Register,* 16 Sept. 1805.

❧ Backcountry Age Ways:
The Border Idea of the Elder-Thane

Not many elderly emigrants moved to the back settlements during the first few years. This was a country for young people. In the eighteenth century, less than 1 percent of the population were over sixty-five—a very small minority. But a few older folk were to be found in even the newest settlements. The manner of their treatment tells us many things about this regional culture. Even more than in most societies, the status of elders in the backcountry tended to vary from one older person to the next. Some received deference and deep respect. A case in point was Patrick Calhoun, "Squire Calhoun" as he was called, the founder and family patriarch of the Calhouns of Long Cane, and also his wife Catherine Calhoun. This aged couple sat in the seats of honor on public occasions. Their wisdom was routinely consulted on domestic questions, and their word was law in the community.[1]

Similar attitudes of respect for age often appeared in the Presbyterian churches of Appalachia. Congregations were normally seated by age, and the oldest were given the best and most comfortable places. "Women with little children were seated nearest the fireplace—the old men were honored with seats near the wall where they could lean back—the young men and young ladies next in front of them, and the boys of restless, unruly age were placed in the center, where batteries of eyes could play on them from all quarters."[2]

Old women, as well as old men, were often treated with special respect in this culture. Emma Miles has left us a memorable portrait of a backcountry granny named Geneva Rogers, "Aunt Genevy" to all the neighborhood. Her ancient profile was deeply lined with a lifetime's suffering. Her manner was gentle, but she was a force to be reckoned with in the community. Emma Miles recalled:

> For all her gentleness and courtesy, there is something terrible about old Geneva Rogers. . . . At an age when the mothers of any but a wolf-race become lace-capped and felt-shod pets of the household . . . she is able to toil almost as severely as ever. She takes wearisome journeys afoot, and is ready to do battle upon occasion to defend her own. Her strength and endurance are

[1] Salley, "The Grandfather of John C. Calhoun," 50.
[2] William Stuart Fleming, *Historical Sketch of Maury County* (Columbia, Tenn., 1876), 26.

beyond imagination to women of the sheltered life. . . . I have learned to enjoy the company of these old prophetesses almost more than any other. The range of their experience is wonderful; they are, moreover, repositories of tribal lore—tradition and song, medical and religious learning. They are the nurses, the teachers of practical arts, the priestesses, and their wisdom commands the respect of all. An old woman usually has more authority over the bad boys of a household than all the strength of man. A similar reverence may have been accorded to the mothers of ancient Israel, as it was given by all peoples to those of superior holiness. . . . It is not the result of affection, still less of fear.[3]

The authority of these mountain grandmothers was very great, and their wrath was terrible to behold. Emma Miles observed a scene between one of these old women and a backcountry preacher called Elisha Robbins who preached that even his own mother would be eternally damned without baptism in his own small sect. This doctrine brought upon him the full wrath of a mountain granny:

> "Lishy," she shrilled at him, unheeding the crowd, "Lishy Robbins, I held you in my arms before you was three hours old, and . . . you ought to be slapped over for preaching any such foolishness about your mother, and I'm a-gwine to do it!" And forthwith she did. Her toil hardened old fist shot out so unexpectedly that the young preacher went down like a cornstalk. Angry? Of course he was angry, but she was a grandmother of the mountains. There was nothing for it but to pick himself up with as much dignity as remained to him.[4]

The rule of deference to the old was widespread throughout the backcountry, but it was far from universal. If some old people were respected and obeyed, others were deeply degraded and treated with extreme contempt. One backcountry traveler came upon a toothless "old man" in the woods, who might have been only fifty years of age, but seemed much older. He was a helpless dependent, who was kept alive by his daughter in a small sylvan "hut." The traveler described him as "an Indian-like animal . . . in mien and feature, as well as ragged clothing; and having lit [his pipe], made an awkward scratch with his Indian shoe and . . . fell to sucking like a calf without speaking for near a quarter of an hour."[5]

---

[3] Miles, *The Spirit of the Mountains*, 37, 54.

[4] *Ibid.*, 136.

[5] Vernon L. Parrington, *Main Currents of American Thought: The Colonial Mind, 1620–1800* (New York, 1927), 138.

Other travelers recorded similar descriptions of solitary old women who wandered alone through the American forest—the outcasts of their culture. In the Pennsylvania backcountry, Rhoda Barber remembered an aged female named Mary Pitcher. "I have heard my mother describe her as wandering through the woods leading an old horse, her only property her knitting in her hand and her dress mostly sheepskin," Barber wrote.[6]

Many sad accounts exist of lonely, weak and impoverished old people in the backcountry. Daniel Drake, for example, recorded his vivid memory of another despised old backsettler:

> Old Mr. Rhodes, or "Grand-daddy" as the children called him, was a man of large frame, very meanly dressed, with a rude and extensive white beard. When I most frequently saw him, he must have been, as it now appears to me, nearly ninety years of age. He stayed constantly in the little cabin, and much of the time in bed. He was silent, childish and morose, seemed to have no sympathy with those around him, and they appeared to have but little care or affection for him, who was their terror. His aspect, and the relations of the family with him, made on my feelings and memory an ineffaceable impression. I had never before, nor scarcely since, seen the forlorn and repulsive character of extreme old age so impressively illustrated. I believe that to the sad spectacle which he exhibited to me 53 or 4 years ago, I may trace up much of my dread of falling, at that advanced period of life, out of communion of mind and heart with children, grandchildren, and great grandchildren. When an old man is found in this desolate isolation— those around him praying that he would die, instead of laboring to make him comfortable and cheerful—the fault is generally, I presume, in himself; for it is more reasonable to believe one person to be wrong in feeling and conduct, than a whole family.[7]

The degradation of these unfortunate older people in the backcountry made a dramatic contrast with the deference given to patriarchs such as Patrick Calhoun, and to mountain grannies such as Aunt Genevy Rogers. Similar dualities have existed in many cultures, but in the backcountry this disparity was exceptionally strong. It derived from an ancient custom deeply embedded in the culture of North Britain, where it was called the rule of tanistry.

In North Britain, from time immemorial, the rule of tanistry (or thanistry, as in thane) had long determined the descent of authority within a clan. It held that "succession to an estate or

[6]Rhoda Barber Journal, Ms. HSP.
[7]Drake, *Pioneer Life in Kentucky*, 219.

dignity was conferred by election upon the 'eldest and worthiest' among the surviving kinsmen.'"[8] Candidates for this honor were males within the circle of kin called the derbfine—all the relatives within the span of four generations. By the rule of tanistry, one man among that group was chosen to head the family: he who was strongest, toughest and most cunning. This principle became an invitation to violent conflict, and the question was often settled by a trial of strength and cunning. The winner became the elder of his family or clan, and was honored with deference and deep respect. The losers were degraded and despised—if they were lucky. In ancient days they were sometimes murdered, blinded or maimed.

This rule of tanistry had long existed throughout parts of Ireland and Scotland. For many centuries, it had been formally invoked to decide the descent of the Scottish crown.[9] Tanistry caused much violence in the history of North Britain. It was also a product of that violence, for it was a way of promoting elders who had the strength and cunning to defend their families, and command respect. But those elders who were unable to do so became a danger to their people. They were degraded and even destroyed. Here was yet another custom by which the culture of North Britain adapted itself to conditions of chronic disorder. By the rule of tanistry, families, clans and even kingdoms gained strong leaders who were able to protect them.

The principle of tanistry operated in North Britain on two levels. It was used in a formal way to settle the descent of high office—in Scotland, even the monarchy. At the same time it also existed as a broad principle of eldership which sorted the old into two categories—the strong who were respected and honored; and the weak who were degraded and despised. In some other cultures, the respect given to age tended to be a form of ascription. In the borders and the backcountry it had more to do with achievements of a special kind that stressed cunning, force, power and the manipulation of others.

These customs were reflected in quantitative indicators of age-heaping. A census in 1776 of exact ages in Maryland's Frederick County (which then included all of the backcountry region in that colony) showed an interesting pattern of age heaping. An exceptionally large proportion of the population rounded their ages to years ending in zero or five. This bias grew stronger beyond

[8]*OED, s.v.,* "tanistry."
[9]Mackie, *A History of Scotland,* 33, 42, 65.

The familiar features of Andrew Jackson are an image of aging in the back settlements. Even in his middle years, the leathery face of this tough old warrior was ravaged by age. Jackson's gaunt cheeks were deeply scarred by pain, his brow was lined and furrowed by constant care, and his deep-set eyes were marked by an ineffable sadness. Yet, this was the face of power, strong in the habit of command. The marks of age deepened its air of authority.

Old age also had another face in the back settlements. For every border chieftain who grew old in authority and all the mountain grannies who bullied the young bucks of the neighborhood, there were other men and women for whom old age brought a kind of social death. This had long been the cruel rule of tanistry in the British borderlands, where the strong were treated with deference and the weak were despised and abandoned.

thirty, and was very strong after fifty. In these patterns we may ask what proportion rounded their ages up and down—that is, how many made themselves older, and how many younger.

The evidence showed nothing like the extravagant youth bias of Americans in the twentieth century. But neither did it show the strong age bias of New England or the Chesapeake in the seventeenth and eighteenth centuries. Attitudes of backcountry men and women toward age were very mixed. Except when they approached twenty-one, backcountry men and women tended to show a strong youth orientation into their fifties, and also a pronounced age bias in the later years of life.[10]

These border and backcountry age ways differed from the customs of other regions in British America, and also from attitudes in our own time. But they were not unique. Similar patterns have also appeared in many human cultures which survive precariously on the edge of insecurity. It was this factor that lay behind the principle of tanistry in North Britain, and that also caused Patrick Calhoun to be honored in the Long Cane, and Aunt Genevy to be instantly obeyed, whilst the "silent, childish and morose" old man in his cabin and the wandering old women of the woods were neglected and despised until death at last overtook them.

[10]The following pattern occurred in a census of Lower Potomack Hundred, Frederick County, Md., 1776: A ratio of 1.0 is age-neutral; the proportion who rounded their ages down and those who rounded up were precisely the same. Lower ratios are biased toward youth; higher ones are biased toward age:

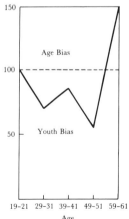

Reported Ages	Backcountry Age Bias (1776)	Modern U.S. Age Bias (1950)
19–21	1.00	1.04
29–31	.67	.94
39–41	.83	.93
49–51	.53	.93
59–61	1.50	.92

Computed from data in Gaius M. Brumbaugh, ed., *Maryland Records* (2 vols., Baltimore, 1915, rpt. 1967), 181–92. Onomastic evidence indicates that a large proportion of this hundred were from North Britain; 20th-century data is from Ansley J. Coale and Melvin Zelnik, *New Estimates of Fertility and Population in the United States* (Princeton, 1963), 127–29.

❧ Backcountry Death Ways:
The Border Idea of Nescient Fatalism

In the borderlands of North Britain, death had long been the constant companion of life. Warfare and raiding took a heavy toll of the population on both sides of the border. Communities shattered by violence also suffered much from famine, and their weakened inhabitants became easy prey for epidemic disease. This pattern changed during the eighteenth century, when the toll of epidemics diminished, and the worst excesses of violence were also suppressed. But life remained precarious upon the borders, and death was still its dark companion.

The American backcountry, for all its romantic reputation as a "bloody ground," was healthier than the British borderlands had been. Rates of morbidity were higher in the southern highlands than in the northern colonies—largely as a consequence of the malaria which the colonists themselves introduced, and later of other environmental illnesses such as the "milk sick." But rates of mortality were lower than in the Chesapeake country, and below those of North Britain as well.[1]

Even so, there were dangers enough in the formative years of this region. Settlers and Indians warred constantly upon one another. Bandit gangs roamed the wilderness, and many an unwary traveler disappeared without a trace. Regulators enforced order with vigilante violence as savage as the acts they condemned. Major wars broke out at least once in every generation from 1689 to 1865. These bloody events did not drive death rates as high in the backcountry as in the Chesapeake region, or other places in British America. But they created a climate of danger and uncertainty that kept old border customs alive. Attitudes toward death in the backcountry long remained very much the same as they had been in the borderlands.

There was a curious way of thinking about dying in these cultures—as if death were itself an act of lawless violence against the living. Images of death in border poetry were strikingly different from those in the south of England. Robert Burns, in a poetic

---

[1] In the year 1806, Samuel Blodget estimated that annual crude death rates per thousand by region as follows: Southern highlands, 20–22; Boston, 20–21; Philadelphia, 20–23; Tidewater south, 26–29. Samuel Blodget, *Economica: A Statistical Manual for the United States of America* (Washington, 1806), 76.

epitaph for a friend, described death as a murderer:

> Whoe'er thou art, O reader know
> That death has murdered Johnny! . . .[2]

Another poem by Burns compared death to a border warlord:

> Ae day, as Death, that gruesome earl,
> Was driving to the tither warl' . . .[3]

Yet another of his verses made death into a corrupt, illegitimate and violent ruler over uncertain life:

> O Death! thou tyrant fell and bloody!
> The meikle devil wi' a woodie.[4]

The poetry of Robert Burns, so bright and sunny and good-humored on most subjects, was filled with rage on the subject of mortality—anger, darkness and despair.

> I've seen yon weary winter-sun
> Twice Forty Times return,
> And ev'ry time has added proofs
> That Man was made to mourn.[5]

The people of this culture were very superstitious about death. They searched the world for signs and portents. When, for example, Daniel Drake was writing his autobiography, both his candles suddenly burned out at the same moment. That event instantly turned his thoughts to the subject of his own death:

> My candles both burnt out at the same moment; an emblem of the beautiful termination in old age, by death, at the same hour, of husband & wife. I have lit two others; which indicates that I am likely to keep on, though it is not far from midnight.[6]

Daniel Drake's two guttering candles inspired a morbid midnight fantasy about his death-bed scene. "When that solemn event shall come," he wrote, "I hope to see female faces round my bed,

> And wish a woman's hand to close
> My lids in death, and say—Repose![7]

---

[2]"Epitaph on Wee Johnny," *The Poetical Works of Robert Burns* (Oxford, 1904, 1960), 316.
[3]"Epitaph to J. Rankine," *ibid.,* 310.
[4]"Elegy on Captain Matthew Henderson," *ibid.,* 102. A translation from the Scots is:

> O Death! thou tyrant cruel and bloody!
> The very devil with his hanging tree.

[5]"Man Was Made to Mourn," *ibid.,* 111.
[6]Drake, *Pioneer Life in Kentucky,* 35.
[7]*Ibid.,* 35.

Drake's melancholy night thoughts and Burn's strident poetry were far apart in mood, but to one another in similar one important way. Drake was only mildly interested in what lay in store in the next world, but he was obsessed with the question of how death should come to him in this one. This question, for a Puritan or a Quaker, was a mere triviality compared with the great business of salvation. But for Daniel Drake, as for Robert Burns, the secular circumstances of death loomed as large as its sacred nature. Both men were fatalistic about the inevitability of death, but they were deeply affected by its uncertainties.

This is an attitude that commonly exists in the face of endemic violence. In the twentieth century the same paradox of nescient fatalism—that is, of fatalism without foreknowledge—may be observed among men at war. It has also existed in entire cultures where sudden, violent and senseless death was a constant fact of life—as in the British borders and the American backcountry.

A woman of the Bell clan who understood this backcountry culture very well, tried to explain the special quality of its fatalism to outsiders:

> The fatalism of this free folk is unlike anything of the Far East; dark and mystical though it be . . . it is lighted with flashes of the spirit of the Vikings. A man born and bred in a vast wild land nearly always becomes a fatalist. He learns to see nature not as a thing of field and brooks, friendly to man and docile beneath his hand, but as a world of depths and heights and distances illimitable, of which he is a tiny part. He feels himself carried in the sweep of forces too vast for comprehension, forces variously at war, out of which are the issues of life and death. . . . Inevitably he comes to feel, with a sort of proud humility, that he has no part in the universe save as he allies himself, by prayer and obedience, with the order that rules.[8]

Here was a fatalism very different from those of Puritan Massachusetts, Quaker Pennsylvania and Anglican Virginia. Many backsettlers were stern Calvinists, and they shared a concern for salvation. But they rarely expressed the same obsessive angst which had appeared among the Puritans, and did not engage in rituals of "daily dying." Backcountry folk, like their border ancestors, had no need of those spiritual calisthenics. They knew death intimately as the cruel and violent destroyer of life, and they also knew how capricious it could be. The main thing was to cultivate courage in the face of these cosmic uncertainties. One wrote,

[8]Miles, *The Spirit of the Mountains,* 140.

"Courage seems to me the keynote of our whole system of religious thought." This was a courage that could triumph not only over danger, violence and evil, but most of all over the uncertainty of the world:

> "You can't foretell nothing in this world certainly," said a hard-headed man to a valley preacher who was arguing certain prophecies of his own. "Didn't Christ refuse to give them Pharisees a sign? Didn't he tell 'em, 'Ye say when ye see the sky red at morning,' and so on?—I fergit the words, but he never even told 'em, 'Ye say' thus and so. He knowed the weather does just as it pleases!"[9]

The rituals of dying in the backcountry also differed from those of other English-speaking people, in ways that were connected to these attitudes and to the conditions which produced them. When the last moment came, the dying man or woman was gently lifted from the bed and lowered to the floor, where the spirit was thought to be in touch with the mysterious forces of the earth. Then the corpse was laid upon a board and watched constantly by friends and relations. A platter of salt was mixed with earth and placed on the stomach of the corpse. The salt was a symbol of the spirit; earth represented the flesh.[10]

Everyone in the neighborhood was expected to pay a visit, friend and foe alike. All were compelled to touch the corpse. This practice derived from an ancient belief that when a murderer laid hands upon the body of his victim, the corpse would begin to bleed again. Every "touching" was closely watched, for on the borders foul play was often suspected.[11]

The death watch was followed by a wake in which many folk rituals were performed by family, friends and neighbors:

> On the death of a person, the nearest neighbors cease working till the corpse is interred. Within the house where the deceased is, the dishes and all other kitchen utensils are removed from the shelves or dressers; looking-glasses are covered or taken down, clocks are stopped, and their dial-plates covered. Except in cases deemed

---

[9]*Ibid.*, 143.

[10]"It is customary yet in some parts of the north of England to place a plate filled with salt on the stomach of a corpse after death." Charles Hardwick, *Traditions, Superstitions and Folklore* (London, 1872), 181; see also Lowry C. Wimberly, *Death and Burial Lore in the English and Scottish Popular Ballads* (Lincoln, Neb., Univ. of Nebraska Studies in Language, Literature and Criticism, no. 8, 1927).

[11]William Rollinson, *Life and Tradition in the Lake District* (London, 1974), 56.

very infectious, the corpse is always kept one night, and sometimes two. This sitting with the corpse is called the Wake, from *Like-Wake* (Scottish), the meeting of the friends of the deceased before the funeral. Those meetings are generally conducted with great decorum; portions of the Scriptures are read, and frequently a prayer is pronounced, and a psalm given out fitting for the solemn occasion. Pipes and tobacco are always laid out on a table, and spirits or other refreshments are distributed during the night. If a dog or cat passes over the dead body, it is immediately killed, as it is believed that the first person it would pass over afterwards, would take the falling sickness. A plate with salt is frequently set on the breast of the corpse.

These customs were recorded in Carrickfergus, northern Ireland, during the eighteenth century. They continued to be kept in Appalachia for two hundred years.[12]

In North Britain, the corpse was carried to the burying ground while the church bells were rung in a complex rhythm that announced many things about the deceased. The cadence of the bells told the age, gender, estate and reputation. The funeral itself was a great event; guests were "bidden" to attend in large number. The Cumbrian "statesman" Benjamin Browne invited 271 guests to the funeral of his first wife. His own funeral was attended by 258. The service and burial were followed by an elaborate ritual of dining and drinking. Small cakes called "arval bread" were served to the guests. These were taken home by the mourners, as "a parting gift from the deceased."[13] Most wills in the border country contained a provision for these presents, which often consumed a large portion of a small estate. The will of a Cumberland statesman named John Wilson declared, "I hereby order that all persons that shall attend my funeral shall be treated with ale and bread according to the custom."[14]

People of wealth distributed presents to the entire community on a lavish scale. An example was the funeral which a rich Cumbrian gentleman named Daniel Fleming of Rydal Hall arranged for his wife, who died 13 April 1675, two days after having given birth to her fourteenth child. Her grieving husband ordered six quires of paper (150 large sheets) for folding "sweetmeats." He also ordered that the poor of Cumberland should receive four

[12]Parton, *Andrew Jackson,* I, 42–43.
[13]Scott, *A Westmorland Village,* 78.
[14]Will of John Wilson of Rosthwaite, 23 March 1763, ms. DX 241/108, CUMROC.

pennies apiece, and for that purpose he set aside the sum of 30 pounds, ten shillings, and four pence—enough for 1,831 poor people.[15]

Daniel Fleming also spent another large sum on ringing, singing, sermons, gravemaking,and a "coffin and clasp." But this was an exceptional event. Coffins were not generally used in this impoverished region. Borderers were buried in cloth sacks. A statue of 1678 required that south of the Scottish border, only English wool could be used. The Scots and Irish preferred linen, but in most respects the customs were much the same.[16]

These border customs were carried to the American backcountry in the eighteenth century. The same process of death-watching and laying-out was followed. Even the smallest details were observed in the New World. The corpse was laid out on an open board, and touched by the mourners, just as on the border.[17] A plate of salt and earth was placed on the body in the back settlements, as it had been in North Britain. One North Carolinian told a folk-lore collector in the twentieth century: "The corpse is stretched on a board. On it is placed a platter of salt and earth, unmixed. The salt is an emblem of the immortal spirit, the earth of the flesh."[18]

A backcountry funeral was a great event which brought large crowds together. When a North British immigrant named Robert Stuart and his three sons were killed by sulphur vapors in a well that they were digging, their burial attracted a great throng. "They were buried in one ground, where was judged to be a thousand people," one neighbor noted in 1767. This was not an unusual attendance. In the same neighborhood, two years later, an ordinary funeral of a borderer named John Scarborough drew "above a thousand people."[19]

Death rituals which had long existed in the borderlands of North Britain were preserved in the southern highlands for two hundred years. Even in the twentieth century, folklore collectors were astonished by the continuities which they observed in the death ways of this American region.[20]

---

[15]Daniel Fleming, Book of Accounts, 15 April 1675, ms. 386, WD/R/box 199, CUMROK.

[16]Hudson, *Barton Records*.

[17]"If the murderer touches the corpse of a murdered man, it will purge; therefore, have the suspect touch the corpse." *North Carolina Folklore,* VI, 490.

[18]*North Carolina Folklore,* I, 258.

[19]Dyer Journal, 24 Aug. 1767, 7 June 1769, Ms. HSP.

[20]Johnson, *Antebellum North Carolina,* 145–48.

❧ Backcountry Religious Ways:
The North British Field-Meeting Style

Strong continuities also existed in the religious customs of this culture. The Anglican missionary Charles Woodmason learned about their power the hard way. In 1766, he packed his saddle-bags with prayerbooks and a pint of rum, and "heavy loaded like a trooper," rode bravely into the Carolina backcountry to convert the heathen. His self-appointed task was a heavy one, for Wood-mason's idea of the heathen was as spacious as the land itself, embracing Indians, Africans, Presbyterians, Congregationalists, Quakers, Baptists, Irish of any denomination, and even Anglicans of "low church" opinions.

Traveling into the interior of Carolina, Woodmason met a reception which was very mixed, to say the least. Some settlers welcomed him to their cabins. Others drove him away by force. One family of Scottish Presbyterians told him plainly that "they wanted no damned black gown sons of bitches among them," and threatened to use him as a backlog in their fireplace. Others stole his horse, rifled his clothing, drank his rum and even purloined his prayer books.

After many adventures which might have flowed from the pen of Swift or Fielding, the grand climax came when this missionary fell into an "ambuscade," and was captured by a gang of old-fashioned border reivers. They carried him captive to a secret set-tlement where they lived with their women and children. The clergyman prepared himself for Christian martyrdom, but when he arrived at their cabins his treatment suddenly changed. To his astonishment, the reivers began to treat him with "great civility," returned his property and promised to restore his freedom on one condition: that he preach a hellfire-and-damnation sermon, which he heartily agreed to do.[1]

That curious experience expressed a central paradox in back-country Christianity—its intense hostility to organized churches and established clergy on the one hand, and its abiding interest in religion on the other. This version of militant Christianity did not fit well with the plans of Britain's imperial authorities, who intended that the backcountry should become an Anglican gar-den. Governor William Bull of South Carolina observed in a gen-teel manner that "tho I charitably hope every sect of Christians

---

[1]Woodmason, *Carolina Backcountry*, 29.

will find their way to the kingdom of heaven, yet I think the
Church of England best adapted to the kingdom of England"—
in which he included the provinces of British North America.

Governor Bull's desire was doomed to frustration, even within
his own English colony. By 1770, he was complaining that the
Anglicans had already lost the backcountry to what he called
"illiterate enthusiasm." He wrote:

> Our toleration comprehends every denomination of Christians
> but the Roman Catholic, and these are subdivided ad infinitum in
> the back parts, as illiterate enthusiasm or wild imagination can mis-
> interpret the Scripture. . . . I am informed that between the Con-
> garees, the Indian boundary and the Saludy River, where there are
> fourteen hundred fencible men, there are not less than six meet-
> ing houses built and ministers maintained by the poor inhabitants,
> besides the French Protestants at Hillsborough and German
> Lutherans at Londonburgh, and not one Church of England
> congregation.[2]

The backcountry was indeed very mixed in its religious denominations—much as the borders of North Britain had been. But
most visitors observed that Presbyterians generally predominated
by the middle decades of the eighteenth century.[3] The English
also tended to include growing numbers of dissenters of many
different sects. Even members of the Church of England behaved
like dissenters in the backcountry, as they had often done in the
north of England. On both sides of the British border there had
been a strong antipathy to state churches, religious taxes and
established clergy.[4]

Throughout the backcountry and borderlands, Anglican
priests were held in special contempt for their lack of personal
piety, and for their habit of subservience to landed elites. Clerical
diaries from the late seventeenth and early eighteenth century
suggest that there was truth in these complaints. The diary of an
Anglican clergyman named George Williamson in the English
county of Cumberland was an extraordinarily secular document,

[2]Governor William Bull to Board of Trade, 30 Nov. 1770; reprinted in Merrens, ed., *Colonial
South Carolina Scene,* 254–70.

[3]"The Presbyterians are the most numerous," *Informations Concerning the Province of North
Carolina, Addressed to Emigrants from the Highlands and Western Isles of Scotland* (Glasgow, 1773);
reprinted in Wm. K. Boyd, ed., *Some Eighteenth Century Tracts Concerning North Carolina*
(Raleigh, 1927), 450.

[4]Thomas P. Ford, "Status, Residence and Fundamentalist Religious Beliefs in the Southern
Appalachians," *SF* 39 (1960), 41–49.

full of detail about his hunting, fishing, coursing, drinking and gambling but with little mention of spiritual questions. One of the few references to church affairs was the record of a bet on whether a colleague would continue as rector of a parish. Established clergymen such as Williamson were regarded as corrupt and alien presences on the borders. That prejudice was carried to the backcountry where Anglican missionaries met with much hostility, not only from Scots and Scots-Irish, but from English settlers as well.[5]

There was, however, no hostility to learned and pious ministers of acceptable opinions. Presbyterian settlers sent home to Scotland and Northern Ireland for their own college-trained clergy who came out to serve them. As early as 1736, it was written that "about this time, the people began to form into societies and sent back to Ireland for a minister."[6] These Presbyterian ministers were proud of their learning. One of them infuriated a Quaker by allegedly arguing that "the most ignorant College learnt man could open the true meaning of the Scriptures better then the best and wisest of God's children that had not College learning."[7]

These ministers were valued for their skill at preaching, which combined appeals to reason with strong emotions. In the backcountry, before the end of the eighteenth century, a familiar form of evangelical religion was the camp meeting. This was an outdoor gathering, commonly convened in some sylvan setting, where a large number of people worshiped together for several days. Many historians have mistakenly believed that the camp meeting was invented on the American frontier. In fact it was transplanted to America from the border counties of Britain, where it was well established by the eighteenth century. Even the Anglican population of that region often met in outdoor "field meetings" during the eighteenth century. So also did Scottish Presbyterians who held frequent "Holy Fairs," which were camp meetings by another name.

The following hostile description of a Scottish Holy Fair dates from the year 1759:

> At the time of the administration of the Lord's supper, upon the Thursday, Saturday and Monday, we have preaching in the fields

[5]"I wager 5 shillings a side Mr. Graham is not the Rector of Arthuret for two years longer," George Williamson Diary, 18 Jan. 1745, ms. CUMROC.

[6]Witherspoon, "Recollections," 127.

[7]Benjamin Ferris Journal, ca. 1777, ms. HSP.

near the church. Allow me then, to describe it as it really is: at first
you find a great number of men and women lying upon the grass;
here they are sleeping and snoring, some with their faces toward
heaven, others with their faces turned downwards, or covered with
their bonnets; there you find a knot of young fellows and girls
making assignations to go home together in the evening, or to
meet in some ale-house; in another place you see a pious circle
sitting around some ale-barrel, many of which stand ready upon
carts for the refreshment of the saints. . . . In this sacred assembly
there is an odd mixture of religion, sleep, drinking, courtship, and
a confusion of sexes, ages and characters. When you get a little
nearer the speaker, so as to be within reach of the sound, tho' not
of the sense of his words, for that can reach only a small circle . . .
you will find some weeping and others laughing, some pressing to
get nearer the tent or tub in which the parson is sweating, bawling,
jumping and beating the desk; others fainting in the stifling heat,
or wrestling to extricate themselves from the crowd; one seems
very devout and serious, and the next moment is scolding or curs-
ing his neighbours for squeezing or treading on him; in an instant
after, his countenance is composed to the religious gloom, and he
is groaning, sighing and weeping for his sins: in a word, there is
such an absurd mixture of the serious and comick, that were we
convened for any purpose than that of worshipping the God and
Governour of Nature, the scene would exceed all power of farce.[8]

Many borderers deeply believed in this form of worship and
had been persecuted for it in Great Britain and Ireland. Robert
Witherspoon remembered that his father had been "one of the
sect that followed field meetings, some of his kindred and himself
were much harassed."[9]

Presbyterian emigrants such as the Witherspoons introduced
field meetings to the American backcountry as early as 1734,
probably earlier. Outdoor assemblies of the same sort were held
by Presbyterians and Baptists before the Revolution. Woodmason
recorded many instances of "big meetings," as they were called,
as early as 1768.[10] After the Revolution, Presbyterians and Methodists began to sponsor large "field meetings" on a regular basis.

---

[8]"A Letter from a Blacksmith to the Ministers and Elders of the Church of Scotand," 1759,
quoted in Robert T. Fitzhugh, *Robert Burns* (Boston, 1970), 72.

[9]Witherspoon, "Recollections," 127.

[10]Woodmason, *Carolina Backcountry*, 95; Guion Griffis Johnson, "The Camp Meeting in
Ante-bellum North Carolina," *NCHR* X (1933), 1–20; Robert B. Semple, *A History of the Rise
and Progress of Baptists in Virginia* (1810, rpt. 1894), 23–24.

At Mabry's Chapel, Brunswick circuit, Virginia, a quarterly meeting was thought to have drawn 4,000 souls, black and white together, on 25 and 26 July 1785. An even larger one was held at Jones Chapel, 17–28 July 1785. On the first day, 5,000 people attended; on the second day, the meeting was so large that nobody could count it. More startling than the size of the crowd was the intensity of its behavior. The shouting was heard half a mile away, and on the ground there were wild displays of emotion. "Such a sight," wrote one observer, "I never had before. Numbers were saints in their ecstasies, others crying for mercy, scores lying with their eyes set in their heads, the use of their powers suspended, and the whole congregation in animation."[11]

The Methodist itinerant Francis Asbury preached at many such meetings in the 1780s—500 people at Bayside Chapel, on Maryland's eastern shore (1783); 400 gathered round a great sycamore in western Virginia (1784); 1,000 in an urban meeting at Baltimore (1785).[12] Most were held for two days. These assemblies began with prayer and preaching, reached their climax in what was called a "great shout," and ended in a Christian "love feast."

Other camp meetings followed in a series of waves, spreading south into the Carolinas and west to the far frontier. There they developed into something called the "Kentucky style" which was marked by close cooperation among denominations, careful preparation and much advance work, a battery of skillful preachers, the use of anxious seats, and fellowship meetings.[13]

The borderers also introduced another form of worship which had spread widely among reformed Christians throughout Europe. This was a ceremony of fellowship which in North Britain was called the "Feast of Fat Things" or the "Love Feast." A backsettler named Benjamin Ferris wrote, in the year 1726,

> I came into communion with the Presbyterian Church and ate bread and drank wine with them at that feast of fat things as they often called it and many times they used to call it a love feast. But I could not see it to be so; for many of the members was often in contention and quarreling, back-biting and slandering.[14]

---

[11]Wesley M. Gewehr, *The Great Awakening in Virginia, 1740–1790* (Durham, 1930), 170.

[12]Francis Asbury, *Journal* I, 444, 447, 461, 493, 612.

[13]John B. Boles, *The Great Revival, 1787–1805; Origins of the Southern Evangelical Mind* (Lexington, 1972); Dickson D. Bruce, *They All Sang Hallelujah: Plain-Folk Camp-Meeting Religion* (Knoxville, 1974);

[14]Benjamin Ferris Journal, 1726, Ms., SWAR.

Ferris later became a Quaker and rejected this form of worship. But for many it was a profoundly moving experience, and also came to be practiced by Methodists and Baptists and many small sects. It has remained part of the religious folkways of the southern highlands for two centuries. Here were the major ingredients of backcountry religion: the camp meeting, the Christian fellowship, the love feast, the evangelical preacher, the theology of Protestant fundamentalism and born-again revivalism. All of them had appeared in that region by the mid-eighteenth century.

Altogether, this form of reformed religion—intensely emotional, evangelical and personal—was a central part of backcountry culture. Robert Witherspoon wrote of his family:

> As I have had an opportunity of having personal knowledge of their lives and deaths, I bear them this testimony, that they were servers of God, that they were well acquainted with the Scriptures, they were much in prayer, they were strict observers of the Sabbath, in a word, they were a stock that studied outward piety and inward purity.[15]

This form of Christianity was not invented on the frontier. It was an adaptation of religious customs which had long existed on the borderlands of North Britain.

❧ Backcountry Magic Ways: The Border Obsession with Sorcery

As recently as 1920 a traveler in the Ozark mountains observed a startling sight. Early on a spring morning as the birds began to sing, he watched in astonishment as a farmer and his wife hurried from their cabin to a new-ploughed field, stripped off their clothing, began "chasing each other up and down like rabbits," and then copulated on the ground. The couple were known as "quiet, hardworking folk," who came of good family and went to the local church.

In southwestern Missouri, Ozark ethnographer Vance Randolph collected many similar reports:

> A very old woman said that before sunrise on July 25, four grown girls and one boy did the planting. "They all stripped off naked," she told me, "The boy started in the middle of the field patch with

---

[15]Witherspoon, "Recollections," 128.

them four big gals a-prancin 'round him. It seems like the boy throwed all the seed, and the girl kept a-hollering 'Pecker deep! Pecker deep.' And when they got done, the whole bunch would roll in the dust like some kind of wild animals. There ain't no sense to it," the old woman added, "but them folks always raised the best turnips on the creek."[1]

This type of magic has persisted in the backcountry even to our own time. It may serve to remind us of an important theme in this history. Each Anglo-American folk culture was the product not merely of a place but of a period. The people of the backcountry brought with them the magic that existed on the borders of North Britain in the early and middle decades of the eighteenth century. These beliefs included an interest in witchcraft, wizardry and other forms of diabolical magic—but not the same sort of witchcraft obsession that had flourished among the Puritans a century earlier.

Witchcraft still survived in this culture. Daniel Drake remembered meeting a borderer in the American backcountry named Old Billy Johnson who was "an implicit believer in witchcraft, and 'raising' and 'laying' the Devil."[2] The folklore of the southern mountains was full of witches and goblins for many generations. As late as the 1930s, collectors of folk beliefs in the southern mountains were told of many witch-beliefs:

If an old woman has only one tooth, she is a witch.

If a warm current of air is felt, witches are passing.

If you are awake at eleven, you will see witches.

The twitching of an eye is a sign that one is bewitched.

If there are tangles in your hair early in the morning, the witches have been riding you.

The howling of dogs shows the presence of witches.

If your shoestring comes untied, the witches are after you.

If you see a cross-eyed person you must cross your fingers to ward off the evil eye.[3]

---

[1]For these and many other accounts, see Vance Randolph, "Nakedness in Ozark Folk Belief," *JAF* 66 (1953), 333–34.

[2]Drake, *Pioneer Life in Kentucky*, 216.

[3]Proverbs in this chapter, unless otherwise cited, are drawn from Newman Ivey White, ed., *The Frank C. Brown Collection of North Carolina Folklore* (7 vols., Durham, 1952–64), I, 329–502.

Many backcountry folk dabbled in witchcraft themselves.

> Wet a rag in your enemy's blood. Put it behind a rock in the chimney. When it rots your enemy will die.

> To work evil upon one, get the person's picture.

> Take seven hairs from a blood snake, seven scales from a rattlesnake, seven bits of feathers from an owl, add a hair from the person you desire, a bit of nail paring, and cook these for seven minutes over a hot fire in the first rainwater caught in April. Sprinkle the concoction on the clothes of the person to be charmed. It cannot fail.

> To point an index or dog finger of the right hand at a person will give that person bad luck.

In early settlements, there was apt to be a specialist in superstition called the witchmaster whose services were much in demand. Samuel Kercheval recalled: "I have known several of these witchmasters, as they were called, who made a public profession of curing these diseases, inflicted by the influence of witches." The practice of witchmasters was often as fixed and regular as those of physicians in the twentieth century. Witchmasters were expected to make house calls. When their services were not available, the backsettlers were trained to administer a sort of magical first-aid.

> If you want to keep witches away, lay a straw broom in the doorway.

> To kill a witch, draw a heart on a holly tree, and drive a spike into her heart for nine mornings.

But these practices had nothing like the urgency that had existed in seventeenth-century New England. No person is known to have been executed for witchcraft anywhere in the southern highlands, though a goodly number were hanged for other crimes. Here was an important difference from the culture of an earlier period.

Backcountry folk also showed an intense interest in astrology and divination. It was widely believed that the stars and planets had a power over earthly events:

> Plant flowers in the blooming days [under the sign of Virgo].

> Never castrate stock when the sign of the zodiac point to the loins. Bleeding will be profuse. . . . Altering hogs is best when the zodiac sign is in the head [Pisces].

> Zinnias should be planted when the sign is in the scales [Libra].
>
> Never gather fruit in the watery signs, or in the new moon, because the fruit will spoil.

These beliefs were never cultivated with the same degree of refinement that had existed among Virginia planters or Renaissance gentlemen throughout western Europe. In its highest pitch of development, this also had been the obsession of an era which was passing when the back settlements were born. But it persisted in more popular forms.

The folk culture of the backcountry ran strongly to another category of magic, which might be called experimental sorcery or secular superstition. It consisted mainly in the pragmatic use of conjuring, sorcery, charms, omens, spells, potions, incantations and popular astrology to change the course of events, or to predict them.[4]

This magic contained a vast repertory of practices for any imaginable occasion—for troubles with animals, crops, neighbors, children, weather, illness. It recommended actions for the control of any possible emotion, and for the execution of any imaginable purpose in the world. In the early twentieth century, one group of folklorists collected nearly 10,000 of these prescriptions in North Carolina, from which a few examples might be selected. A few of these prescriptions have been confirmed by science:

> Eating cornbread causes pellagra.
>
> For scurvy, apply uncooked potatos sliced and soaked in vinegar.
>
> To cure snake bite, if no wound is in the mouth, suck out the poison and spit it out; cauterize, cut so as to make the place bleed freely.

Others were positively lethal:

> A cure for homesickness is to sew a good charge of gunpowder on the inside of the shirt near the neck.
>
> To cure a fever, climb a tall tree with your hands (do not use feet), and jump off.

---

[4]Conjuring originally referred to rites in which spirits were summoned by secret oaths and rituals. Sorcery in the 17th century meant mainly black magic, and in particular the science of poisoning. Superstition in its original Latin meant an exaggerated fear of the Gods. All of these words later took on the broad and general meaning which is used here—a practical belief in the power of charms, omens, spells, potions and incantations to change the course of events.

Many were contradictory:

> It is lucky for a bird to come into the house.
>
> If a bird flies into the house there will be bad luck.
>
> It is bad luck to kill a cat.
>
> For good luck, boil a black cat alive.

Many charms and potions showed a spirit of extreme brutality:

> Against epilepsy wear a bit of human cranium.
>
> A piece of rope by which a person has been hanged will cure epilepsy by its touch.
>
> For fever, cut a black chicken open while alive, and bind to the bottom of a foot. This will draw the fever.
>
> The blood of a bat will cure baldness.
>
> Eating the brain of a screech owl is the only dependable remedy for headache.
>
> For rheumatism, apply split frogs to the feet.
>
> To reduce a swollen leg, split a live cat and apply while still warm.
>
> Bite the head off the first butterfly you see, and you will get a new dress.
>
> Open the cow's mouth and throw a live toad-frog down her throat. This will cure her of hollow horn.

These good–luck charms, whatever they may have done for their human users, brought very bad luck to large numbers of backcountry cats, bats, frogs, owls, snakes, chicks and puppy dogs. Samuel Kercheval remembered that the first glassblowers in the backcountry "drove the witches out of their furnaces by throwing live puppies into them." He also recalled that "there was scarcely a black cat to be seen, whose ears and tail had not been frequently cropped off for a contribution of blood."[5]

Other magical folk-beliefs shaped the manners, dress, diet and appearance of backcountry folks in ways that startled visitors from other cultures:

> Some old people let the nails of their little fingers grow very long, and they called it "a luck nail."

---

[5]Kercheval, *Valley of Virginia*, 288, 281.

It is good luck to put a garment on wrong side out and leave it that way all day.

It is bad luck to say thank you.

It is bad luck to bathe on your wedding day.

A small piece of shit worn in a bag round the neck will keep off disease.

Water is poisonous during dog days.

Some of these customs tell us about conditions of life in crowded backcountry cabins.

When three people wake up abed together, the oldest will die first.

If two people wash their hands in the same water, they will be friends forever.

Others were often desperate attempts to control one's destiny.

If a woman is pregnant, and drinks some of her own urine, she will miscarry.

To sit over a pot of stewed onions will cause a miscarriage.

But most were innocent omens and harmless charms.

To cure sore eyes, kiss a red-head.

To take away freckles, wash your face in cobweb dew.

If a butterfly comes into the house, it means a stranger is coming to visit.

Three drops of your own blood, fed to another, is an effective love charm.

If you carry a lock of hair of a person, you will have power over that person.

Get the ugliest person you know to look in the cream jar so you can churn it.

Potatoes should be planted on St. Patrick's Day.

Much of this folklore was brought from Ireland, Scotland and the north of England. But backcountry magic was an eclectic body of beliefs, constantly growing by borrowings from Indians, Africans, Germans, and other cultures. Novel folk practices were continuously invented within this culture. It is important to note that when these "traditional" backcountry prescriptions were recorded in the twentieth century, some were not very old. The people of Appalachia endowed many modern industrial products with magical properties. A particular favorite was kerosene:

> Take kerosene for asthma.
>
> To stop a wound from bleeding, pour kerosene on it.
>
> To cure a burn use kerosene oil.
>
> Rub your feet with kerosene and salt for chilblain.
>
> Take a teaspoonful of sugar wet with kerosene, and it will cure a bad cold.
>
> Take kerosene as a cure for the colic.
>
> Kerosene will prevent swelling in a snake bite.
>
> It is bad luck to leave a kerosene lamp burning until all the oil is burned out.
>
> Hang up a bottle of kerosene in a tree to prevent blight.

Umbrellas were also endowed with special powers:

> If you open an umbrella in the house, you will not get married that year.
>
> If you drop an umbrella, let someone else pick it up, or disappointment will come to you.
>
> Raising an umbrella in the house is bad luck.
>
> To put an umbrella on a bed causes disputes.

The railroad and the motor car acquired a magic of their own:

> If one walks sixteen railroad ties without falling off, any wish made will come true.
>
> [If] a cat cross[es] the road in front of your automobile, make a crossmark on the windshield.

This self-renewing backcountry magic needed none of the institutional apparatus which the Puritans of New England brought to bear upon witchcraft. It did not require any of the intellectual refinement which country gentlemen in Virginia devoted to the study of fortune. The magic of the backcountry was a simple set of homespun superstitions, designed for use by small groups of unlettered people.

The magic of the backcountry was remarkably secular in its nature and purposes. It retained vestigial beliefs in the Devil, witches, stars and planets. But mainly it sought to control worldly events by the manipulation of worldly things.

Backcountry magic was highly materialist, experimental and empirical in its nature. Its ancient rituals and homespun remedies were mainly a device by which these people struggled to understand and control their lives in the midst of many uncertainties of their world.

Any modern social scientist might be able to "explain" the persistence of backcountry magic in half a dozen ways—Marxian, Freudian, Hegelian, Aristotelian, structuralist, empiricist. But mainly this folk magic flourished because none of those other "explanations" was intellectually available or acceptable within this culture. Active and highly intelligent backcountry minds had no better system of accounting for the secular uncertainties that surrounded them. A mountain woman has written:

> Speaking for my own people, I am sure that almost every one has had some experience he can not explain away. Perhaps he has heard a warning of some one's death, a strange noise, a shriek on the roof. Perhaps a man has passed him in the open road and disappeared suddenly, leaving no tracks. . . . My people, like the Hindoos and the Scotch Highlanders, have the faculty of dealing with the occult, of seeing and hearing that which is withheld from more highly educated minds. Always there is some souvenir of the spirit-world in a nook of the mountainer's brain. He is unwilling to accept it, never believes quite all that it seems to imply. Still, there it is.[6]

❧ Backcountry Literacy

On the subject of literacy, backcountry folk liked to tell a tall tale about themselves. They bragged that one interior county of North Carolina had so little "larnin" that the only literate inhabitant was elected "county reader." That story is apocryphal, but in Moore County, North Carolina, a battered book has survived with an inscription on its flyleaf: "David Kennedy his Book he may read good but God knows when."[1]

---

[6]Miles, *The Spirit of the Mountains*, 118.
[1]Blackwell P. Robinson, *A History of Moore County, N.C., 1747–1847* (Southern Pines, N.C., 1956), 140.

These colorful examples have misled unwary historians into thinking that levels of literacy were uniformly low in the backcountry. This was not the case. Throughout the southern highlands as a whole, the pattern was very mixed. Charles Woodmason in 1767 observed of one settlement that "few can read—fewer can write. . . . these people despise knowledge." Similar impressions were recorded by many travelers.[2] But in other communities a different pattern appeared. In the backcountry settlement of Williamsburg, South Carolina, which was planted by Scots-Irish Presbyterians, historian William Boddie finds that "not more than one man out of the first hundred [signers of] wills and transfers or property had to make his mark." Further, Boddie discovered that 98 percent of Revolutionary soldiers from Williamsburg were able to write their own names: a remarkably large proportion.[3]

Rates of literacy varied broadly throughout the backcountry, not only by place, but also by wealth and rank. Many men without property were unable to write; but most large wealthowners could sign their names to wills and deeds. Differences of this sort appeared in many parts of British America, but were exceptionally great in the backcountry. Large variations in literacy also existed from one ethnic group to the next. Several studies have found that German Protestant and French Huguenot settlers were the most literate: more than 90 percent could write their names. Scottish highlanders were the least so among the free population; of highland Scots who made their wills in Cumberland County, North Carolina during the late eighteenth century, 50 percent signed by mark. Between these broad extremes were immigrants from the north of England, the lowlands of Scotland and northern Ireland, of whom approximately 20 to 30 percent signed by mark in the mid-eighteenth century—a level which was very near the average for the region as a whole.[4]

This pattern of backcountry literacy was similar to that in the borderlands of North Britain in both its central tendency and its variations. Recent revisionist historical research has found that rates of literacy were much the same in the lowlands of Scotland

---

[2]Woodmason, *Carolina Backcountry*, 49, 52; Arthur K. Moore, *The Frontier Mind* (1957, New York, 1963), 192–193, passim.

[3]William W. Boddie, *History of Williamsburg* (Columbia, S.C., 1923), 543.

[4]Robert L. Meriwether, *The Expansion of South Carolina, 1729–1765* (Kingsport, Tennessee, 1940, rpt. Phila., 1974), 177; Duane Meyer, *The Highland Scots of North Carolina, 1732–1776* (Chapel Hill, 1961), 119.

and the northern counties of England.[5] On both sides of the border, the proportion of male tenants and craftsmen who signed by mark was in the range of 20 to 30 percent—almost exactly the same as in the backcountry. This was the lower-middling class that produced the majority of emigrants to America.[6]

Variations by social rank were very great in the borderlands, as they would be in the backcountry. Nearly all the gentry were literate as early as the seventeenth century. But less than 15 percent of laborers could write their names in the lowlands of Scotland and in the north of England as late as 1770. These differences also were carried to America.[7]

The British borderlands and the American backcountry were also similar in the distribution of books and libraries. A few exceptional individuals and families owned remarkably large libraries. An outstanding example in the county of Westmorland was the Brownes of Troutbeck, a highly literate "statesman" family who owned 2,000 volumes in 1700.[8] A few major collections were also to be found in the American backcountry. But in North Carolina before 1783, forty to fifty volumes were thought to be

---

[5]The most detailed study, which radically revises previous estimates, concludes that the "levels and the profile of illiteracy in Lowland Scotland [were] extremely close to those for northern England . . . literacy over Lowland Scotland as a whole was not particularly high compared to northern England." R. A. Houston, *Scottish Literacy and the Scottish Identity* (Cambridge, 1985), 41, 34; *idem*, "Illiteracy in the Diocese of Durham, 1663–89 and 1750–62: The Evidence of Marriage Bonds," *NH* 18 (1982), 229–51.

[6]Houston finds the following rates of occupational illiteracy for craftsmen and traders in the borderlands during the period of emigration:

Decade	Northern England	Lowland Scotland
1710s	n.a.	22%
1720s	44%	14%
1730s	23%	15%
1740s	22%	17%
1750s	31%	21%

Source: Houston, *Scottish Literacy and Scottish Identity*, 40.

[7]Houston's research yields the following levels of illiteracy by occupation for the period 1700–1770:

Occupation	England	Scotland
Professional	0%	1%
Gentry	0%	3%
Craft and Trade	26%	18%
Yeoman and Tenant	26%	32%
Laborer	64%	68%

Source: Houston, *Scottish Literacy and Scottish Identity*, 41, 34.

[8]Scott, *A Westmorland Village*, 70.

a large library.[9] Most estates in probate included at least a few books—primers, prayer books, and practical handbooks on farming and medicine. But by comparison with New England, Pennsylvania and even Virginia, private libraries in North Carolina were remarkably secular. Before 1753, only about one in five titles was religious. In the late eighteenth century, that ratio fell to one in nine—an exceptionally small proportion.[10] These backcountry libraries tended to be entirely vernacular collections. One survey of more than 500 North Carolina inventories from 1733 to 1783 found not a single work in Latin or Greek. Typical of the backcountry elite was Andrew Jackson, who was said to have read only two books in his lifetime, the Bible and Goldsmith's *Vicar of Wakefield.*[11]

These patterns must be seen in perspective. By comparison with other parts of the world, the backcountry was not illiterate. At a time when 20 to 30 percent of males in the southern highlands were unable to read and write, the proportion of illiteracy in Italy and Spain was 70 to 80 percent.

Even so, the backcountry was an oral culture in which writing was less imporant than the spoken word. The backsettlers maintained an attitude of cultivated contempt for orthography. The future President Andrew Jackson once declared that he could never respect a man who knew only one way to spell a word. He was not entirely joking. This attitude was widely shared in the backcountry, as it had been in the British borderlands, where it was observed that "the spelling even of well-educated people was highly variable," for a much longer period than in other regions.[12]

This culture was impoverished in its written literature, but it was rich in ballads and folktales which were carefully handed down from one generation to the next. Samuel Kercheval remembered that a favorite entertainment of the backsettlers during the eighteenth century was the singing of old folksongs. "The tunes

[9]Ralph L. Rusk, *The Literature of the Middle Western Frontier* (2 vols., New York, 1925, 1962), I, 51–76.

[10]The ratio of religious titles to all books was 1:4 in Edgecombe County (1733–53), and 1:6 in Bertie County (1720–74); it later fell to 1:8 in Edgecombe (1765–83), and 1:10 in Bertie (1775–83); these data are from Helen R. Watson, "The Books They Left: Some 'Liberies' in Edgecombe County, 1733–1783," *NCHR* 46 (1971), 245–57.

[11]Others testified that Jackson read only *Tristram Shandy* and a pamphlet on the South Sea Bubble. For two different views cf. Parton, *Life of Andrew Jackson,* and Remini, *Andrew Jackson,* I, 7; see also Arda Walker, "The Educational Training and Views of Andrew Jackson," *ETHSP,* 16 (1944), 22.

[12]Hughes, *North Country Life in the Eighteenth Century: The North East,* 37.

were rude enough to be sure," he wrote. "Robin Hood furnished a number of our songs; the balance were mostly tragical, and were denominated 'love songs about murder.'" Another popular pastime was what he called "dramatic narration":

> Many of those tales were lengthy, and embraced a considerable range of incident . . . and were so arranged as to the different incidents of narration, that they were easily committed to memory. They certainly have been handed down from generation to generation from time immemorial.[13]

One of the earliest recorded folktales was a memoir published in 1859 by H. E. Taliaferro, a native of Surry County in western North Carolina.[14] One of these tales told of a backcountryman named Walker who felt the call to preach, and asked his pastor for a license. The following exchange took place:

PASTOR: Do you believe, brother Walker, that you are called of God to preach, "as was Aaron?"

WALKER: Most sartinly I does.

PASTOR: Give the Church, that is, the bruthering, the proof.

WALKER: I was mightily diffikilted and troubled on the subjeck, and I was detarmined to go inter the woods and wrastle it out.

PASTOR: That's it, Brother Walker.

WALKER: And while there wrastlin, Jacob-like, I hearn one ov the curiousest voices I uver hearn in all my borned days.

PASTOR: You are on the right track, Brother Walker. Go on with your noration.

WALKER: I couldn't tell for the life ov me whether the voice was up in the air ur down in the sky, it sounded so curious.

PASTOR: Poor creetur! how he was diffikilted. Go on to norate, Brother Walker. How did it appear to sound unto you?

WALKER: Why, this a-way: "Waw-waw-*ker*—Waw-waw-*ker*! Go *preach*, go preach, go *preach*, go *preachee*, go *preach-ah*, go *preach-uh*, go *preach-ah-ee-uh-ah-ee*."

PASTOR: Bruthering and sisters, that's the right sort of a call. Enough said, brother Walker. That's none ov yer college calls, nor money calls. No doctor ov divinity uver got sich a call as that. Brother Walker must have license, fur sartin.[15]

---

[13]Kercheval, *Valley of Virginia*, 285–86.

[14]Taliaferro, *Fisher's River (North Carolina) Scenes;* an analysis appears in Ralph Steele Boggs, "North Carolina Folktales Current in the 1820's," *JAF* 47 (1934), 268–88.

[15]Taliaferro, *Fisher's River (North Carolina) Scenes*, 233.

This tale was recorded in the Appalachian highlands before 1830, and published in 1859. The man who told it had been born in the eighteenth century, perhaps in the English border country. He spoke a dialect that is still heard among older people in Appalachia. And his contempt for "college-calls," doctors of divinity, learned professions, and book learning of every kind became an important part of backcountry culture.[16]

The importance of oral communication in the backcountry created a special form of knowing, in which testimony had a peculiar importance. The power of testimony, in turn, gave a special importance to truth-telling, which was defined in the biblical sense as not bearing false witness—an idea different from other cultures. The memoirs that come to us from this culture spoke often of the problem of truth. Thomas Meriwether in Georgia was remembered as "a man who never prevaricated . . . he had the greatest reverence for truth, and never violated its spirit, knowingly at least."[17] A lawyer named Thomas Gilmer was described as "a man of good sense, aided but little by reading . . . he was truthful and upright."[18]

This obsession with truth created a curious custom in the backcountry—the "lye bill," as it was called. "If you speak of a libel in a crowd of old Georgia people," Gilmer wrote, "they suppose that you are using a dandy phrase for lye bill . . . in old times a writing acknowledging that the writer had told a lie." These curious documents were entered into the court records of the backcountry.[19]

An oral culture placed an exceptionally high value on speaking the truth. The penalty for lying or breaking one's "word of honor" was ostracism from the society, and even from one's kin. One twentieth-century lawman in the southern highlands reported from long experience that "no matter how hardened a criminal a hillman may be, those who know him insist that his word of honor would never be broken."

This oral culture also put a high value on memory, which was often strong in proportion to the weakness of the written word. A case in point was George Mathews, a backcountry governor of

---

[16]James T. Pearce, "Folk Tales of the Southern Poor-White," *JAF* 63 (1950), 398–411.
[17]Gilmer, *First Settlers of Upper Georgia*, 78.
[18]*Ibid.*, 13.
[19]An example is given in *ibid.*, 146; see also *North Carolina Folklore*, I.

Georgia, who was barely able to read and write. "He was unlearned," an acquaintance recalled:

> when he read it was always aloud, and with the confidence which accompanies the consciousness of doing a thing well. He pronounced full the *l* in "would," "should," &c, &c, and *ed* at the termination of compound words with a long drawling accent. He spelt "coffee," Kaughphy. He wrote "congress" with a k. When Governor, he dictated messages to his secretary, and then sent them to James Mason Simmons, the Irish schoolmaster, to put them into grammar.

At the same time, Governor Mathews was a highly intelligent man, capable of heroic feats of memory:

> His memory was unequalled. Whilst he was a member of Congress, an important document which had been read during the session, was lost. He was able to repeat its contents verbatim.

As sheriff of Augusta County before the revolution, Mathews kept the county tax lists in his head, and "recollected for a long time the name of every taxpayer."[20]

The oral culture of the backcountry had an epistemic structure that set it apart from other Anglo-American folkways. It gave great importance to experience, memory, testimony and truth-telling. It also showed an actual antipathy to fixed schemes of grammar, orthography and punctuation. Here again the four folkways of early America did not merely know different things. They also knew them differently.

❧ Backcountry Learning Ways: North British Rituals of Schooling

Throughout the southern highlands, average levels of formal schooling were very low—in fact, the lowest in British America. When enrollment data first became available in the early decades of the nineteenth century, the proportion of white children enrolled at school in one county of North Carolina amounted to less than 10 percent of the school-age-population. This dismal statistic meant that children in this culture went to school only

---

[20]Gilmer, *First Settlers of Upper Georgia*, 62.

about 1.5 years on the average. Given the annual length of school sessions in the backcountry, they received only a few weeks of formal education during their entire lives. Other evidence suggests that the pattern in North Carolina was not very different from upcountry South Carolina, Tennessee, Kentucky and Georgia.[1]

Education increased with length of settlement, but low rates of school enrollment remained a regional tradition throughout the southern highlands for many generations. Levels of schooling were lower here than in any other part of the United States from the early nineteenth century to the late twentieth.[2]

This pattern cannot be explained merely as the reflex of poverty alone, for poor communities in other regions gave strong support to schools. It was not primarily the product of frontier conditions, for other frontiers behaved very differently. It was not caused by that *diabolus ex machina* of southern historiography—the ethos of race slavery—for rates of school enrollment were lowest in those parts of the southern highlands where slavery did not exist. A more satisfactory explanation might combine these three factors with a fourth: the weight of cultural tradition that was carried from the borders of North Britain.

In northern Ireland, the north of England, and parts of rural Scotland which were largely untouched by the educational reforms of the Scottish Reformation and the Edinburgh Enlightenment, formal education was very limited. There were many some exceptions in Scotland, which had founded a system of parish schools supported by taxes on landowners and centrally controlled by the Presbyterian church. These Scottish schools have been much celebrated—by Scottish scholars. But they were not strong in areas of the southwest which contributed much to the American migration. In Ayrshire, whence many backsettlers came, half the parishes had no schools at all at the beginning of the eighteenth century. Further, where parish schools existed, their primary purpose was to seek out exceptionally gifted boys and send them on to higher places, rather than to provide mass

---

[1]Here again, as in other regional cultures, mean years of schooling are derived from total enrollment data by the following equation: $Y_s = Y_p (E/P)$ where Y_s is mean years of schooling, Y_p is the range in ages of enrolled children. E is the number enrolled, and P is the population of school age. The result may be thought of as a total education rate, comparable in its epistemic status to a total fertility rate. Data are drawn from A. R. Newsome, "Twelve North Carolina Counties in 1810," *NCHR* 6 (1929), 17–99; this subject will be discussed in more detail in volume II.

[2]*SAUS* (1984), 145.

education. For children of modest means, levels of schooling were very low on both side of the border. This was especially the case for females.[3]

These border patterns were transplanted to the American backcountry, where there were no institutions comparable to New England's town schools, or even to Virginia's system of parish education. Charles Woodmason wrote, ". . . through the non-establishment of public schools, a great multitude of children are now grown up, in the greatest ignorance of ev'ry thing save vice—in which they are adepts."[4] This judgment was repeated in less pejorative terms by others who lived in the colonies. Governor Bull of South Carolina wrote in 1770, "Literature is but in its infancy here. We have not one good grammar school, tho' foundations for several [exist] in our neighbouring parishes. All our gentlemen, who have anything of a learned education, have acquired it in England."[5]

Backcountry education occurred mostly in small "neighborhood schools" maintained by private subscription and taught by itinerant masters for a few weeks each year. These humble institutions were similar to schools in the British borderlands where masters were hired *ad hoc* by local gentry.[6] Individual parents in the backcountry and the borderlands sometimes made heroic efforts to obtain a little schooling for their children. Wills often expressed deep concern about the education of the young, and set aside large sums for that purpose. But the cultural circumstances which created these anxieties also conspired to defeat them.[7]

---

[3]A radical revision of this historical problem appears in Houston, *Scottish Literacy and Scottish Identity*, 110–61; see also Rosemary O'Day, *Education and Society, 1500–1800* (London, 1982); D. J. Witherington, "Education and Society in the Eighteenth Century," in N. T. Phillipson and R. Mitcheson, eds., *Scotland in the Age of Improvement* (Edinburgh, 1970); idem, "Schools in the Presbytery of Haddington in the Seventeenth Century," *ELAST* 9 (1963), 90–111; T. C. Smout, *A History of the Scottish People*, 424; W. Boyd, *Education in Ayrshire through Seven Centuries* (London, 1961). For education in the north of England see Hughes, *North Country Life in the Eighteenth Century: Cumberland and Westmorland*, 293–333; and idem, *North Country Life in the Eighteenth Century: The North East*, 341–79.

[4]Woodmason, *Carolina Backcountry*, 26.

[5]Gov. Wm. Bull to Board of Trade, 30 Nov. 1770, Merrens, ed., *Colonial South Carolina Scene*, 265.

[6]"Given yesterday at Ambleside unto William Baxter to drink—having then hired him to be schoolmaster, for a year from the 3rd day of May next at 40s. and his diet, and to suffer others to come unto him—the sum 1s." Daniel Fleming, Book of Accounts, 19 Feb. 1663, ms. WD/R/Box 199, CUMROK.

[7]Alan Watson finds in North Carolina wills the same concern for education that Bruce discovered in Virginia; see Alan D. Watson, "Society and Economy in Colonial Edgecombe County," *NCHR* 50 (1973), 231–55.

To this general rule of educational poverty in the back settlements, there was an important exception in the growth of Presbyterian academies. These institutions were modeled on dissenting academies in Ireland and North Britain during the seventeenth century. Their primary purpose was to prepare candidates for the ministry. The American prototype of these academies was founded in 1727/28 by Presbyterian minister William Tennent at Little Neshaminy Creek, in Pennsylvania. Tennent was a graduate of the University of Edinburgh. His object was to create what he called a "converted ministry" in America. George Whitefield visited Tennent's school in 1739 and wrote, "The place wherein the young men study now is in contempt called *the College*. It is a log-house, about twenty feet long and near as many broad, and to me it seemed to resemble the schools of the old Prophets."[8]

At least twelve of these Presbyterian academies were founded in the backcountry by the year 1750. More than thirty-three had opened their doors by 1770. Some were flourishing institutions. David Caldwell's academy in Guilford County, North Carolina, survived from 1767 to 1820, and was faithfully attended by fifty or sixty students a year. But most were small and struggling institutions which collapsed after few years. Still, they helped to supply the need of the back settlements for an educated ministry and a literate elite.[9]

We tend to think of formal education as the enemy of folkways. But most societies have a folklore of learning which might be called their school ways. The backcountry was a case in point. It adopted educational folk customs which had long existed in North Britain. One example was the curious custom called "barring out." This was a ritual of rebellion which occurred regularly before Christmas and sometimes at other seasons of the year. The larger students would forcibly bar the master from the schoolroom, until he granted them a long vacation. When he did so, the master commonly received small presents in return.[10]

---

[8]Douglas Sloan, *The Scottish Enlightenment and the American College Ideal* (Columbia, 1971), 45.

[9]*Ibid.*, 36–72; Sloan's list of Presbyterian academies founded before 1800 appears on pp. 281–84.

[10]The account books of Daniel Fleming in Cumbria recorded most years a sum of one shilling, or 1/6d., "given to the children at their barring out." The dates varied from 24 Nov. to 10 Dec. He also gave his children larger sums, from ca. 30 Jan. to 24 March, for "cock pennies to the master." See Daniel Fleming Account Books, 9 Dec. 1664, 6 Feb. 1665, 26 Feb., 26 March, 10 Dec. 1666; 24 Nov. 1668, 25 Nov. 1670, 30 Jan. 1675; Ms. WD/R/box 199, CUMROK.

In England this custom had many names—barring out, shutting out, penning out, or merely "the exclusion." Its origins were described as "ancient" as early as the year 1558. In the seventeenth and eighteenth centuries, barring out was a regional custom in the northernmost counties of England, and in the lowlands of Scotland and northern Ireland. It was most common in the English border counties of Cumberland, Westmorland, Durham, Northumberland and Yorkshire.[11]

This curious custom was transplanted to America, where it also became a backcountry folkway. Barring out was not unknown in other colonies, but it happened very rarely in New England, and was uncommon in the coastal south.[12] Mainly it occurred in the backcountry, where it spread from Pennsylvania into the southern highlands, and west to the Ohio and Mississippi valleys. It was specially common among American descendants of the British borderers in the back settlements.[13]

Sometimes barring out ceased to be merely a ritual, and devel-

[11]Keith Thomas has mapped the incidence of barring out, and concludes that "the ninety or so schools for which I have so far collected definite evidence of the ritual are all situated north of the line from the Severn to the Wash, which marks so many fateful divisions in English history. Instances occur in almost every English county above that boundary, with a particularly heavy concentration in what is now called Cumbria, but never outside the North and the midlands"; *Rule and Misrule in the Schools of Early Modern England* (Reading, 1976), 30; and conversation with the author.

Whitehead observed that barring out occurred in most Cumberland villages; "the master, who always expected the barring out at the proper time, used to adjourn to the village ale-house, & treat the biggest boys to mulled ale, for in the winter season plenty of big fellows 18–20 years in age attend school"; see *Talks about Brampton* (Selkirk, 1907), 171–72.

Rollinson describes barring out in Westmorland as a "good natured, . . . school riot." Most lasted "a day and a night and the next [day] till one in the afternoon." But the custom of Brampton was a three-day barring out; see *Life and Tradition in the Lake District*, 60.

In the north of Ireland, barring out was also very common. "Within memory," writes an historian of Carrickfergus, "it was common with boys to assemble early at their school-house on the morning before Christmas, and to bar out the master, who was not admitted till he promised a certain number of days' vacation. Early on Christmas day, the boys set out to the country in parties of eight or twelve, armed with staves and bludgeons, killing and carrying off such fowl as came in their way. They were taken to their respective school-rooms, and dressed the following day. To this feast many persons were invited, who furnished liquors, or other necessaries; the entertainment usually continued for several days." Parton, *Andrew Jackson*, I, 44.

[12]Barring out occurred in the grammar school at Williamsburg in 1702 and again in 1705; Commissary James Blair wrote that Lt. Gov. Francis Nicholson was "the author and contriver of this business." Nicholson was a Yorkshireman, who came from the north of England where this custom was very common. The documents are brought together in Edgar W. Knight, ed., *A Documentary History of Education in the South Before 1860* (5 vols., Chapel Hill, 1949), I, 474–88.

[13]The classical description appears in Edward Eggleston, *Hoosier School-master* (1872, rpt. New York, 1957), 73–74; also *idem, Transit of Civilization*, 270; for other accounts see H. M. Brackinridge, *Recollections of Persons and Places in the West* (Philadelphia, 1834), and J. P. Wickersham, *History of Education in Pennsylvania* (Lancaster, 1886), 207.

oped into a pitched battle between older scholars and the teacher's friends:

> At our first common school we had a contest, which I mention
> here, because it shows the habits of the times. The schoolboys
> determined to turn out William P. Culbertson, the schoolmaster,
> for a day's holiday. They assembled early in the morning, and
> barred the entry into the school-house by filling the door with
> benches and other heavy things. The school-master was then
> boarding with Abram's father. He and all his brothers took part
> with him against the boys. They got to the school-house before
> Culbertson, and commenced threatening the boys inside with the
> master's hickory. They dared any boy inside to come out. Those
> inside shoved me through the opening cut in a log for lighting the
> writing bench, to accept Abram's banter. At it we went. I made a
> missing blow, slipped, or somehow else got down on the ground,
> and Abram on me. His brothers surrounded us, urging Abram to
> give it to me well. This was too much for the boys inside to bear.
> They tore away the fastenings from the door, and rescued me from
> my perilous position, put me upon my feet, and secured a fair
> fight.[14]

The custom of barring out was consistent with many aspects of
border and backcountry culture. In this warrior society, even the
most able scholar was literally compelled to fight for the esteem
of the community. Even where barring out became merely a ritual, it preserved the old spirit of violence in a vestigial form.

The ritual of barring out was also an expression of restlessness
under institutional restraint—an act which was sometimes violent
in its form and always libertarian in its spirit. In one early instance
of barring out (1587), Scottish schoolboys taunted their teacher:

> Liberty, liberty under a pin
> Six weeks holiday or never come in![15]

This was, as we shall see, a very special conception of liberty, far
removed from the ordered liberty of the Puritans, the reciprocal
liberty of the Quakers and the hierarchical liberty of the cavaliers.
It was an act deeply rooted in backcountry culture.

Barring out was merely one of many educational folkways in
the backcountry. Another was what might be called educational
magic. When Appalachian children went to school they adopted

---

[14]Gilmer, *First Settlers of Upper Georgia*, 133.
[15]Quoted in Thomas, *Rule and Misrule*, 21.

(and continuously reinvented) a system of scholastic superstition which developed from the culture of their ancestors. Folklorists recorded many of these beliefs in Pennsylvania, Maryland, Kentucky, Tennessee, and the Carolinas:

> If you sleep with your books under your pillow, you will know your lesson the next day.
>
> If you sleep with your book under your head the night before an examination, you will pass successfully.
>
> Put a willow leaf in the book that you are to pass an examination on, and you will pass successfully.
>
> If you drop a book, you will miss that lesson unless you kiss the pages at which it opened.
>
> Never write on the first sheet of a pack of paper. If you do your work will be poor.
>
> The first lizard that you see running in the spring is a sign that you'll be smart.
>
> Put a stick in your book and you can walk a footlog without becoming dizzy.[16]

Educational magic flourished in the backcountry, as part of an inherited pattern of school ways which were carried from North Britain to the New World.

꙳ Backcountry Food Ways:
   North British Origins of Southern Highland Cooking

In regard to diet, the southern back settlements differed fundamentally from other regions of British America. Samuel Kercheval recalled that the "standard" supper dish in the mid-eighteenth century was a wooden bowl of milk and mush—seasoned with a splash of bear oil. The Anglican missionary Charles Woodmason regarded these backcountry meals with horror, and complained incessantly about what he was expected to eat. "Clabber, butter, fat mushy bacon, cornbread," he wrote, "as for tea and coffee they know it not ... neither beef nor mutton nor beer, cyder or anything better than water." When he visited a community of Ulster emigrants, Woodmason noted that "the people

---

[16]*North Carolina Folklore*, VI, 69–70.

are all from Ireland, and live wholly on butter, milk, clabber and what in England is given to hogs."[1]

Many visitors remarked that backsettlers ate food which other English-speaking people fed to their animals. This observation was repeated so often that it became a cliché of travel literature in the southern highlands. It is interesting to discover that precisely the same statements were made by English travelers in the borderlands of North Britain.[2]

Backcountry food ways are sometimes thought to be the product of frontier conditions. So they were, in some degree. But mainly they were an expression of the folk customs that had been carried from the borders of North Britain. Strong continuities appeared in favored foodstuffs, in methods of cooking and also in the manner of eating.

One important staple of this diet was clabber, a dish of sour milk, curds and whey which was eaten by youngsters and adults throughout the backcountry, as it had been in North Britain for many centuries. In southern England it was called "spoiled milk" and fed to animals; in the borderlands it was "bonny clabber" and served to people. Travelers found this dish so repellent that some preferred to go hungry.[3]

Another important foodstuff in the borderlands and the back settlements was the potato. This American vegetable had been widely introduced to western Europe during the seventeenth and eighteenth centuries, and became especially popular in Ireland, Scotland and the north of England. Despite its American origins, the potato had been uncommon in the English colonies until the North Britons arrived during the eighteenth century, and made it an important part of backcountry diet.[4]

Yet another staple was a family of breadstuffs variously called "clapbread," "haverbread," "hearth bread," "griddle cakes," and "pancakes." Sometimes they were also called scones, after an

[1]Kercheval, *Valley of Virginia,* 196, 253; Woodmason, *Carolina Backcountry,* 34, 173.

[2]Woodmason, *Carolina Backcountry,* 34, 173, 176, 196; Thomas Anburey, *Travels* (2 vols., London, 1789), 340, 376; William Eddis, *Letters from America* (1792, Cambridge, 1969), 57; "Observations on Several Voyages and Travels to America," *WMQ3* 15 (1958), 146.

[3]John Gough, *The Manners and Customs of Westmorland* (Kendal, 1827), 20; also *Ulster Journal of Archaeology* II (1854), 204; Woodmason, *Carolina Backcountry,* 176, 34, passim.

[4]Redcliffe N. Salaman, *The History and Social Influence of the Potato* (Cambridge, 1985); for a first-hand account of the introduction of the potato to the backcountry by North British immigrants, see James Ellerton, Journal, 19 March 1740, in Merrens, ed., *Colonial South Carolina Scene,* 132; potatoes were not unknown in other food-cultures of British America, but they were not staples.

old Norse word for crust. Ingredients varied, but methods of cooking were often the same: small cakes of unleavened dough were baked on a flat bakestone or a circular griddle in an open hearth. These breadstuffs were brought from the borderlands to the backcountry, where they remained a major part of regional cuisine for many generations.[5]

In other respects, backcountry food ways necessarily departed from the customs of North Britain. Oats yielded to maize, which was pounded into cornmeal and cooked by boiling. But this was merely a change from oatmeal mush to cornmeal mush, or "grits" as it was called in the southern highlands. The ingredients changed, but the texture of the dish remained the same.

Another change occurred in the consumption of meat. The people of North Britain had rarely eaten pork at home. Pigs' flesh was as loathesome to the borderers as it had been to the children of Abraham and Allah. But that taboo did not survive in the New World, where sheep were difficult to maintain and swine multiplied even more rapidly than the humans who fed upon them. Pork rapidly replaced mutton on backcountry tables, but it continued to be boiled and fried in traditional border ways.[6]

New American vegetables also appeared on backcountry tables. Most families kept a "truck-patch," in which they raised squashes, cushaws (a relative of squash), pumpkins, gourds, beans and sweet roasting ears of Indian corn. Many families also raised "sallet" greens, cress, poke and bear's lettuce. Here again, the ingredients were new, but the consumption of "sallet" and "greens" was much the same as in the old country.[7]

The distinctive backcountry beverage was whiskey. A taste for liquor distilled from grain was uncommon in the south and east of England. But it was highly developed in north Britain, and was brought to the American backcountry by the people of that region. "'Wheyski,'" the Marquis de Chastelleux wrote in backcountry Virginia, "was our only drink, as it was on the three days following. We managed however to make a tolerable towdy [toddy] of it."[8]

A change of ingredients was made necessary by the new envi-

---

[5]Ferguson, *Northmen in Cumberland and Westmorland,* 149; Rollinson, *Life and Traditions in the Lake District,* 38–40, 49.

[6]Sam Bowers Hilliard, *Hog Meat and Hoecake: Food Supply in the Old South, 1840–1860* (Carbondale, Ill., 1972).

[7]Kercheval, *Valley of Virginia,* 253.

[8]Chastelleux, *Travels,* II, 409, 19 April 1782.

ronment. In the back settlements Scotch whiskey (which had been distilled from barley) yielded to Bourbon whiskey (which was made mainly from corn and rye). But there was no other change from the borders, except perhaps in the quantity of consumption. Whiskey became a common table drink in the backcountry. Even little children were served whiskey at table, with a little sugar to sweeten its bitter taste.[9] Temperance took on a special meaning in this society. Appalachia's idea of a moderate drinker was the mountain man who limited himself to a single quart at a sitting, explaining that more "might fly to my head."[10]

Other beverages were regarded with contempt in the backcountry. "Tea and coffee were only slops," Kercheval remembered, ". . . they were designated only for persons of quality who did not labor, or the sick. A genuine backwoodsman would have thought himself disgraced by showing a fondness for these slops. Indeed many of them have to this day very little respect for them."[11]

Methods of food preparation also showed strong continuities from the borderlands to the back settlements. In the southern highlands, backcountry cooking ran more to boiling than to baking or roasting. This had also been the case in North Britain. Studies of regional cooking methods in Britain, as we have seen, find that the south and west of England had a taste for frying; East Anglia, a preference for baking; and the North, a penchant for boiling. The "simmering pot" became a cliché of border poets and antiquarians. John Gough observed that border breakfasts consisted "chiefly of porridge . . . boiled in milk." Many travelers to the backcountry noted the taste for "mush boiled in milk." Both borderers and backcountry people also consumed soups, stews and potpies for their second meal.[12]

Backcountry cuisine was less fastidious than that of other Anglo-American cultures—"all the cooking of these people being exceedingly filthy and most execrable," Woodmason grumbled.[13] This observation was made by many travelers in the American back settlements, and in the British borderlands. One visitor was astonished when his hostess proceeded to wash her feet in

[9]Hudson, *Barton Records,* 56; John C. Campbell, *The Southern Highlander and His Homeland* (New York, 1921), 203.

[10]Campbell, *The Southern Highlander,* 203.

[11]Kercheval, *Valley of Virginia,* 255.

[12]Allen, *British Tastes,* 75 passim; see also Gough, *Manners and Customs of Westmorland,* 20; Bouch and Jones, *Economic and Social History of the Lake Counties,* 243.

[13]Woodmason, *Carolina Backcountry,* 173.

the cookpot. Another was given the tablecloth for a bedsheet. The folklore of that region actively discouraged cleanliness. To wash a milk churn was thought to be unlucky. Frogs were dropped into the milk to make it thicken. The quality of butter was believed to be improved in proportion to the number of human hairs embedded in it. "The mair dirt the less hurt," Appalachian housewives liked to say.[14]

The backsettlers also differed from other cultures in their eating habits. They tended to take only two meals a day—a plain breakfast and a hearty meal in mid-afternoon. "These people eat twice a day only," Woodmason declared, and complained that he was unable to find a proper English breakfast, lunch and dinner. The rhythm of two daily meals was a North British custom, carried to the interior of America by the border people.[15]

Tables were set with trenchers and noggins of wood and pewter. The utensils were two-tonged forks, heavy spoons and hunting knives. Kercheval remembered that the use of china was actively opposed. "The introduction of delft ware was considered by many of the backwoods people as a culpable innovation," he wrote. "It was too easily broken, and the plates of that ware dulled their scalping and clasp knives."[16]

There was much feasting in the back settlements. On these grand occasions, the major dishes were not baked as in New England, or roasted as in Virginia, but boiled in black-iron cooking pots which hung over backcountry hearths. Kercheval remembered that "the standard dinner dish" for a "log-rolling, or house-raising and harvest-day" was a "pot-pie, or what in other countries is called sea-pie."[17] There was little of the dietary asceticism that marked the food ways of Puritans and Quakers. When backsettlers and borderers could eat and drink abundantly they did so with high enthusiasm. Altogether, the food ways of these people were the product of a cultural tradition which had a long past in the British borderlands, and a long future in America's southern highlands.[18]

[14]Leyburn, *The Scotch Irish: A Social History,* 25; Graham, *The Social Life of Scotland in the Eighteenth Century,* 179–80.

[15]*Ibid.,* 196.

[16]Kercheval, *Valley of Virginia,* 255.

[17]*Ibid.,* 253.

[18]The account book of a Cumbrian "statesman" Benjamin Browne recorded many feasts and special meals. See the Browne Account Book, 1719, Browne mss., WD/TE box 8, CUMROK. For the persistence of these food ways in Appalachia during the twentieth century, see Campbell, *The Southern Highlander and His Homeland,* 198–203.

❧ Backcountry Dress Ways:
Border Origins of Country Western Costume

Travelers also expressed surprise at the costume of the backsettlers. Men, women and even children tended to adorn themselves in a manner that seemed fundamentally alien to other English-speaking people.

Backcountry women dressed in what Anglican clergyman Charles Woodmason called "shift and petticoat," which were its nearest equivalents in the south of England. But in fact it was a different style of clothing altogether—a full bodice with deep décolletage, tight-fitted waist, short full skirt and a hem worn high above the ankle. The Anglican missionary thought it scandalously revealing.

Married women covered themselves more modestly in long dresses, with heavy woolen shawls draped across their head and shoulders. Elderly women wore heavy-hooded bonnets made of what was called "six or seven hundred" linen, and covered their feet with coarse shoes or heavy "shoepacks" as they were called in the eighteenth century.[1]

Backcountry women of all ages normally wore homespun linsey-woolsey garments, often of exquisite beauty and refinement. Even the acidulous Anglican Charles Woodmason was moved to admiration by the sight of fifty Presbyterian ladies, "all dressed in white of their own spinning."[2] These dresses were not shut away in closets but draped upon the cabin walls as a form of decoration. A backcountry writer remembered that in the eighteenth century:

> The coats and bedgowns of the women . . . were hung in full display on wooden pegs around the walls of their cabins, so that while they answered in some degree the place of paper hangings or tapestry, they announced to the stranger as well as neighbor the wealth or poverty of the family in the articles of clothing. This practice has not yet been laid aside among the backwoods families.[3]

Male backsettlers also had a style of dress that startled strangers. They commonly wore shirts of linen in the summer and deer-

[1] Woodmason, *Carolina Backcountry*, 61.
[2] *Ibid.*, 21.
[3] Kercheval, *Valley of Virginia*, 257.

skin in the wintertime. Kercheval recalled,

> The hunting shirt was universally worn. This was a kind of loose frock, reaching halfway down the thighs, with large sleeves open before, and so wide as to lap over a foot or more when belted. The cape was large, and sometimes handsomely fringed with a raveled piece of cloth of a different color. The bosom of this dress served as a wallet to hold a chunk of bread, cakes, jerk, tow for wiping the barrel of the rifle, or any other necessary for the hunter or warrior. The belt, which was always tied behind, answered for several purposes. . . . The hunting shirt was generally made of linsey, sometimes of coarse linen and a few of dressed deerskins.[4]

This upper garment was cut full in the chest and shoulders, with broad seams that ran horizontally across the front and back, and was drawn or "cinched" tightly at the waist. The effect was to enlarge the shoulders and the chest. Much as female costume created an exceptionally strong sense of femininity, male dress in the backcountry put equally heavy stress on masculinity. The dress ways of the backcountry were designed to magnify sexual differences.

The men of the backcountry also wore loose, flowing trousers or breeches or "drawers" as Kercheval called them. The lower legs were sometimes sheathed in gaiters called "leather stockings," which writers such as James Fenimore Cooper in his Leatherstocking Tales made the hallmark of the backcountryman.

Children in the backcountry also dressed differently from youngsters in other parts of British America. They were allowed great freedom in articles of clothing. "No shoes or stockings," Charles Woodmason wrote, with his accustomed air of disapproval. "Children run half-naked. The Indians are better cloathed and lodged."[5]

These backcountry dress ways were often compared with those of the Indians. But in fact the costume of adult backwoodsmen and women was very different from the breechclouts, tight leggings, and matchcoats of the eastern tribes. It was also highly impractical in the eastern woodlands—"very cold and uncomfortable in bad weather," Kercheval remembered, and was put aside in time of military campaigning, when according to Ker-

---

[4]*Ibid.*, 256.
[5]Woodmason, *Carolina Backcountry*, 176.

cheval young Europeans tended to copy the more functional clothing of their Indian counterparts.[6]

Later generations remembered this backcountry costume as aboriginally American—the pioneer dress of the frontier. But it was not worn on most frontiers, and was not invented in America. It was similar to dress ways described by travelers in the north of England, the lowlands of Scotland and northern Ireland. This male costume in the British border country was very similar to that which would be worn in the American backcountry—the same linsey or leather shirts, the same broad cut across the shoulders and chest, the same horizontal seams, the same heavy stress on masculinity, the same "drawers" and trowsers, the same leather stockings. Leather shirts and leggings were not frontier inventions. They were commonly worn throughout the borders in the eighteenth century. The account books of one Cumbrian yeoman recorded the cost of covering his legs in sheepskin leggings.[7] Another bought gaiters which he called "leather stockings" at Carlisle in 1742. That phrase, which American writers such as Cooper tied to the frontier, was in fact a common north border expression. The distinctive dress of the American frontiersman was adapted from the customs of the British borderlands in all respects except the moccasins and coonskin cap.[8]

Equally striking were the similarities in women's costume. One English traveler from Cheshire noticed on a trip to the lowlands of Scotland in 1639 that older women wore a "garment of the same woolen stuff whereof our saddlecloths in England are made: which is cast over their heads, and covers their faces on both sides." He also observed that "young maids not married are bareheaded," and "ancient women" wore "a broad boungrace coming over their brows." A boungrace was a cloth shade or curtain attached to the front of a woman's bonnet. It was also worn in the northern counties of England, and called an "Ugly" in Northumberland.[9]

Children's costume on the borders was also much the same as in the backcountry. On the borders, children normally went barefoot, just at they did in the back settlements. One observer wrote

[6]For a discussion of the differences between this costume and that of the Indians, see Kercheval, *Valley of Virginia*, 256.

[7]Rollinson, *Life and Traditions in the Lake District;* Scott, *A Westmorland Village,* 91–93.

[8]For leather stockings see George Williams Diary, 22 May 1742, ms. DX/124, CUMROC.

[9]Journal of Sir William Brereton, *SSP* 124 (1914) 30.

that they tended to leap "as if they had hoofs, but it is almost the same all over the north."[10]

These various dress ways spread through the southern highlands and onto the southwestern frontier. Many elements survive to this day, in the clothing style that is called "western dress" in the United States. Derivative forms also appear in the stage costumes of country-western singers, and in the wardrobes of backcountry presidents such as Lyndon Johnson and Ronald Reagan. They may still be seen in the ordinary dress of men and women throughout a broad region from Nashville to Dallas. The whirl of fashion has modified this costume in many ways with the introduction of Spanish elements in the nineteenth century and a touch of Hollywood *glitz* in the twentieth. But strong continuities linked the costume of North Britain in the seventeenth century to backcountry dress ways in the eighteenth century, frontier fashions in the nineteenth century, and "country western" clothing today.

❧ Backcountry Sport Ways: North British Origins of Southern Highland Games

The people of the backcountry also brought their own folk games which had long been popular on the borders of north Britain. These entertainments were often very violent—as many folk amusements had been throughout England in the seventeenth and eighteenth centuries. But the games of the border country had a special quality which derived from the endemic fighting in that region. "Scots and English," for example, was a favorite game on both sides of the border. Two teams of boys faced each other with their hats and coats in piles behind them. The object was to make a raid across the line, and to plunder the other team of its possessions without being captured. The boys shouted the ancient war cries of their region.[1]

Border folk-games, like so many other parts of its culture, not

---

[10]Roger North, *Lives of the Right Hon. Francis North* . . . (3 vols., London, 1826); quoted in Hughes, *North Country Life in the Eighteenth Century: The North East*, 14.

[1]Gomme, *Traditional Games of England, Scotland and Ireland*, 183; William Dodd, ed., *Edenhall and People Who Have Lived There* (n.p., 1974), 19, CUMBROC; Ferguson, *Northmen in Cumberland and Westmorland*, 150; Scott, *A Westmorland Village*, 18.

only reflected the insecurity of life in that region. They also prepared men to deal with it. More than other parts of England, the
sports of the border were contests of courage, strength and
violence.

Special importance was given to wrestling—an ancient sport
on the borders, commonly pronounced "wrasslin" or "russlin."
There were two types of wrestling in this region. One was carefully regulated and elaborately staged in annual tournaments.
The burly contestants commonly dressed in sleeveless vests, long
tights tucked into stockings, and velvet trunks incongruously
embroidered with delicate flowers. Each man stood facing the
other, arms locked around the opponent's body and chins tucked
into each other's right shoulder:

> When both men have taken hold, the bout begins, slowly at first
> as competitors move crab-like, sizing each other up, but suddenly
> with a flutter of legs there is action as one man is thrown. If any
> part of his body other than his feet touches the ground, the bout
> is lost; similarly if a competitor loses his hold he forfeits the bout.
> Clearly such a sport calls for not only great reserves of strength
> but also for skill, stamina and physical fitness.[2]

This sport was brought to Appalachia where wrestling tournaments were regularly held. A North Carolina settler named Cyrus
Hunter recalled that "wrestling and jumping [were] two of the
most prominent sports" of that early period.[3]

The borderers also engaged in another sort of combat called
"wrassling" or "fighting." This was a wild struggle with no holds
barred that continued until one man gave up—or gave out.[4]
These events often began with a contest in "bragging and boast-
ing" between men who had been drinking heavily beforehand. In
the Lake District of England, one gentleman justice witnessed
such a happening, and put a stop to it. "On Thursday," he wrote,
"I went again to Ambleside . . . to see the wrestling. It was very
good. A man from Cumberland with a white hat and brown shirt
threatened to fling everybody, and fight them afterwards. The
fighting I put a stop to."[5]

The border sport of bragging and fighting was also introduced
to the American backcountry, where it came to be called "rough

[2]Rollinson, *Life and Tradition in Lake District*, 161–62.
[3]Parton, *Andrew Jackson*, I, 66.
[4]Jacob Robinson and Sidney Gilpin, *Wrestling and Wrestlers* (n.p., 1893).
[5]Hugh W. Mackell, *Some Records of the Annual Grasmere Sports* (Carlisle, 1911), 15.

and tumble." Here again it was a savage combat between two or more males (occasionally females), which sometimes left the contestants permanently blinded or maimed. A graphic description of "rough and tumble" came from the Irish traveler Thomas Ashe, who described a fight between a West Virginian and a Kentuckian. A crowd gathered and arranged itself into an impromptu ring. The contestants were asked if they wished to "fight fair" or "rough and tumble." When they chose "rough and tumble," a roar of approval rose from the multitude. The two men entered the ring, and a few ordinary blows were exchanged in a tentative manner. Then suddenly the Virginian "contracted his whole form, drew his arms to his face," and "pitched himself into the bosom of his opponent," sinking his sharpened fingernails into the Kentuckian's head. "The Virginian," we are told, "never lost his hold . . . fixing his claws in his hair and his thumbs on his eyes, [he] gave them a start from the sockets. The sufferer roared aloud, but uttered no complaint." Even after the eyes were gouged out, the struggle continued. The Virginian fastened his teeth on the Kentuckian's nose and bit it in two pieces. Then he tore off the Kentuckian's ears. At last, the "Kentuckian, deprived of eyes, ears and nose, gave in." The victor, himself maimed and bleeding, was "chaired round the grounds," to the cheers of the crowd,[6]

Sporadic attempts were made to suppress "rough and tumble." Virginia's tidewater legislators passed a general statute against maiming in 1748, and in 1772 added a more specific prohibition against "gouging, plucking or putting out an eye, biting, kicking or stomping."[7] In 1800 the grand jury of Franklin Country, Tennessee, in the manner of American juries, generally indicted the "practice of fighting, maiming and pulling out eyes, without the offenders being brought to justice."[8]

But in the southern highlands, rough and tumble retained its popularity. During the War of Independence, and English prisoner named Thomas Anburey witnessed several backcountry gouging contests. "An English boxing match," he wrote, ". . . is humanity itself compared with the Virginian mode of fighting," with its "biting, gouging and (if I may so term it) Abelarding each other."[9] Anburey described "a fellow, reckoned a great adept in

[6]Thomas Ashe, *Travels in America, Performed in 1906* (New York, 1811).
[7]Hening, *Statutes*, VI, 250; VIII, 520.
[8]Greenfield *Gazette*, 12 July 1800.
[9]Anburey, *Travels*, II, 217–18.

gouging, who constantly kept the nails of both his thumbs and second fingers very long and pointed; nay, to prevent their breaking or splitting . . . he hardened them every evening in a candle." Bloodsports have existed in many cultures, but this was one of the few that made an entertainment of blinding, maiming, and castration.[10]

Also very popular on the borders of North Britain were individual competitions in running, jumping, leaping, throwing axes and spears. An example in the Lake District of Cumbria were annual gatherings at Ferry, Ambleside and later Grasmere.[11] Some of these tournaments were very ancient. One of them was held in a ruined earthwork of great antiquity called Stone Carr near Greystoke. Wrestlers competed for a leather belt, leapers for a pair of gloves, and footracers for a handkerchief. These tournaments were great festivals, with large crowds, heavy drinking, food stalls, brandy booths, tambourine girls and accordion boys.[12]

These athletic contests were also brought to the American backcountry by emigrants from North Britain. The young Andrew Jackson first came to eminence for his skill in running and leaping. Other contestants competed in sledge-throwing and "long bullets," in which young sportsmen hurled iron cannonballs—sometimes at each other. Large crowds gave these contests the same carnival air that had existed in border tournaments.[13]

Athletic competitions of this sort were introduced to America mainly by borderers and Scots, whose traditional "Caledonian Games" became the ancestor of track and field in the United States. These meets commonly included the shot-put, hammerthrow, running broad jumps and high jumps, pole-leaping, hop-step-and-jump, hurdles, a "long race" of one mile, a walking match, sack races, wheelbarrow races, three-legged races, highland dancing, and tossing the caber. All of this activity occurred within a ring 500 feet in circumference.[14]

"Caledonian games" became very popular in America, and were gradually opened to non-Scottish competitors. As early as

[10] *Ibid.,* II, 201–2.

[11] Mackell, *Some Records of the Annual Grasmere Sports;* Robinson and Gilpin, *Wrestling and Wrestlers.*

[12] Collingwood, *Lake District,* 150; Rollinson, *Life and Tradition in the Lake District,* 162.

[13] Johnson, *Antebellum North Carolina,* 111.

[14] "Caledonian games" had not been confined to the highlands. The leading historian writes, ". . . similar games were held in other parts of Scotland as well, and Lowlanders and Borderers often disputed the alleged superiority of the Highlanders." Gerald Redmond, *The Caledonian Games in Nineteenth-Century America* (Rutherford, N.J., 1971), 30.

1836 the New York Highland Society held a "sportive meeting" in the Elysian Fields across the Hudson River. Other athletic clubs, schools and colleges began to sponsor them, eliminating the competitions which were thought to be too strenuous for undergraduates (caber-tossing), or not strenuous enough (sack-races), or not in keeping with the ideology of masculine athletics (male dancing). The first college in North America to sponsor these games in a formal way was McGill University in Montreal. In the United States, the leader was Scots Presbyterian Princeton, with its Scottish president James McCosh and its sports-loving Scottish teacher George Goldie. By the mid-nineteenth century, Caledonian games were being held in 125 American cities, and the field sports of North Britain had become the foundation of track and field throughout the United States.[15]

Many other folk games were also carried from the border to the backcountry. An example was the ancient and primitive game called *shinny*.[16] This ancestor of hockey had originally been played with the long bones of a sheep. The game was known throughout the British Isles. In the west of England, it was called *not;* in London it was named *hockey;* on the borders it was known as *shinny*. Of the Scots Irish it was said that "great numbers of men and boys resorted to the fields on this day to play at shinny." The backsettlers preserved the northern name, and played the game in a ritual way at Christmastime. This custom persisted throughout Appalachia into the twentieth century. Here again, there were strong continuities from the borders of North Britain to the American backcountry, and to Appalachia in our own time.[17]

The sport ways of the back settlements were not a static set of inherited customs but a dynamic folk tradition. Amusements unknown to the British borderlands were invented in the American backcountry within the framework of an existing sport culture.

A case in point were games involving guns. "Shooting at marks was a common diversion among the men, when their stock of ammunition would allow it," Kercheval remembered. Backcoun-

[15] *Ibid.*, 37; Rowland Berthoff, *British Immigrants in Industrial America* (Cambridge, 1953), 151.

[16] *PA* 2 series XV, 175–78.

[17] Many instances of shinny were recorded by folklorists throughout Derby, Lancashire, Cumberland, Cheshire, Derby, the lowlands of Scotland and northern Ireland. See Gomme, *Traditional Games of England, Scotland and Ireland*, II, 190; Parton, *Andrew Jackson*, I, 45; Don K. Price tells the author that he remembers playing shinny as a child at Middlesboro, Kentucky, where he was born in 1910.

try gunnery games were very different from the casual snap shooting of English country gentlemen who competed in the slaughter of prodigious quantities of half-domestic birds by off-hand hip and shoulder shots at point blank range, with prodigious expenditures of ammunition. In the Appalachians, a marksman had to make every bullet count at great distances. Kercheval recalled that "shooting off-hand was not then in practice; it was not considered as any trial of the value of the gun, nor indeed as much of a test of the skill of a marksman." The backsettlers achieved astounding feats of marksmanship by firing very carefully and slowly at distant marks, their rifles resting in a cushion of moss on a branch or tree trunk.[18]

Another backcountry amusement was throwing the tomahawk. Samuel Kercheval remembered that "a little experience enabled the boy to measure the distance with his eye, when walking through the woods, and strike a tree with his tomahawk in any way he choose."[19] Competitions were also held in imitating the cries of animals. "The bleating of the fawn brought its dam to death," Kercheval recalled, "the cries of turkeys and owls were requisite as a measure of precaution in war." Altogether, Kercheval observed that "the sports of the early settlers of this country were imitative of the exercise and stratagems of hunting and war." In this respect, they were much the same as the war games of the British borderlands. Only the nature of war itself had changed.[20]

❧ Backcountry Work Ways:
Border Attitudes toward War and Work

Where the warrior ethic is strong, the work ethic grows weak. This was so among the borderers and backsettlers, on both sides of the water. A traveler in North Britain remarked that the inhabitants were "indolent in high degree, unless roused to war."[1] In the American backcountry, other travelers frequently repeated

---

[18]Kercheval, *Valley of Virginia*, 285.

[19]*Ibid.*, 284.

[20]*Ibid.*, 283.

[1]Thomas Pennant, *A Tour of Scotland* (London, 1790); qtd. in Grady McWhiney and Perry D. Jamieson, *Attack and Die: Civil War Military Tactics and the Southern Heritage* (University, Ala., 1981), 183.

similar observations. "They are very poor owing to their extreme indolence," wrote an itinerant clergyman. A Philadelphia Quaker wrote: ". . . the Irish are mostly poor beggarly idle people."[2]

This "indolence" was in some ways more apparent than real. The impression of idleness rose in part from the fact that men and women in this culture worked differently from others. Most of them lived by a combination of farming and herding which required heavy labor in some seasons and little effort in others. In their new American environment the backsettlers adopted an old North British system of agriculture called the "infield-out-field" farming. The "infields" were given over to the most valuable crops, and cultivated with the light plows that were common in North Britain or with hoes that became more common in the backcountry. The outfields were allowed to lie fallow. The land was fertilized by confining animals in movable enclosures called "cowpens."[3]

Crop farming remained very primitive in Appalachia. It was mainly a system of hoe-husbandry that was also introduced from North Britain. In the 1730s, the tools for each hand in one settlement were "one axe, one broad hoe and one narrow hoe," with very little use of the plow.[4] Except for the abandonment of the plow, this system of farming had been followed very generally throughout the English border counties, the Scottish lowlands and northern Ireland. It was introduced to the American backcountry at an early date.[5] A traveler in the backcountry noted, "A fresh piece of ground . . . will not bear tobacco past two or three years unless cow-penned; for they manure their ground by keeping their cattle . . . within hurdles, which they remove when they have sufficiently dunged one spot."[6]

At some seasons of the year, large herds of grazing animals were allowed to browse freely in the forests and canebreaks of the old southwest, and later on the open range of Texas. In 1773, a surveyor for South Carolina described this system in detail. He

[2]Woodmason, *Carolina Backcountry*, 49; J. Dickinson to John Harriot, 10 Nov. 1719, Jonathan Dickinson Letterbook, 1715–21, HSP.

[3]A. R. H. Baker and R. A. Butlin, eds., *Studies of Field Systems in the British Isles* (Cambridge, 1973), has chapters on English borders, Scotland and Ireland; also relevant are chapters in Thirsk, ed., *Agrarian History of England and Wales*, vols. 4 and 5; these works summarize an immense literature and include extensive bibliographies.

[4]Witherspoon, "Recollections," 125.

[5]For cowpens in Northumberland see Thirsk, ed., *Agrarian History of England and Wales*, IV, 17, 27.

[6]OED, "cowpens."

reported that vast herds of cattle, often more than a thousand animals, were raised in the woods throughout the backcountry between the Savannah and Ogechee rivers. They were tended by "gangs under the auspices of cow-pen keepers, which move (like unto the ancient patriarchs or the modern Bedouins in Arabia) from forest to forest in a measure as the grass wears out or the planters approach them." Once a year, these animals were rounded up, penned and driven to market on the hoof.[7]

This system of herding had also been practiced in the North British borderlands, and was transferred to the American backcountry. A few important changes were made necessary by the new environment. Sheep, which had been the main support of British animal husbandry, became an easy prey for predators in the American wilderness. They were replaced by swine which were allowed to breed freely on the range, rapidly reverting to the wild species from which they had descended. This process of devolution produced the backcountry razorback, which was more like a wild boar than a barnyard pig. It became so wild that it was hunted with a rifle.

A similar process also created tough and dangerous Texas Longhorn cattle, which were American descendants of similar animals that had flourished in Scotland, northern Ireland, and the north of England during the seventeenth and eighteenth centuries.[8]

For both swine and cattle, this system of herding was fully developed in the backcountry by the mid-eighteenth century. Robert Witherspoon remembered that "as the range was good, they had no need of feeding creatures for some years."[9] A petition of the inhabitants in 1767 made reference to "our large stocks of cattle," and described the system of "cowpens" and infield-outfield husbandry. This method of farming was land-consuming, but labor-saving. By one estimate, each head of range

[7]Schaper, *Sectionalism in South Carolina*, 59; Forrest McDonald and Grady McWhiney, "The Antebellum Southern Herdsman: A Reinterpretation," *JSH* 41 (1975), 147–66; *idem*, "The South from Self-Sufficiency to Peonage: An Interpretation," *AHR* 85 (1980), 1095–118; *idem*, "The Celtic South," *History Today* 30 (1980), 11–15; Grady McWhiney, "Antebellum Piney Woods Culture: Continunity Over Place and Time," in Noel Polk, ed., *Mississippi's Piney Woods: A Human Perspective* (Jackson, Miss., 1986), 40–59.

[8]Grady McWhiney and Forrest McDonald, "Celtic Origins of Southern Herding Practices," *JSH* 51 (1985), 165–82, traces the continuities from Britain and Ireland to the American backcountry; Terry G. Jordan, *Trails to Texas: Southern Roots of Western Cattle Ranching* (Lincoln, Neb., 1981). Here again the McWhiney-McDonald thesis grows stronger if it is recast from racial to regional terms.

[9]Witherspoon, "Recollections," 126.

cattle in the southern backcountry required fifteen acres of piney woods—a total of 1,500 acres for a herd of 100 cattle.[10]

The backsettlers also sought to introduce a mixed economy of domestic manufacturing. The raising of flax and the weaving of linen became a flourishing cabin industry throughout the southern highlands, as it had been for many generations on the borders of North Britain. Governor William Bull of South Carolina wrote in 1770, "The Irish from Belfast have now raised flax for their own wear, and barter the superfluous linen to supply their wants with their neighbours." A correspondent in 1768 reported that in the back settlements the "inhabitants now manufacture most of their linens (such as cost in England from 12d to 18d a yard) linsey-woolsey and even coarse cloths: that it has been proposed shortly to establish a stocking manufactory amongst them." This movement toward a factory system was abandoned in Appalachia during the nineteenth century, and not revived until the twentieth. But in the eighteenth century it was developing strongly. In this way as in so many others, the people of the backcountry transplanted the work ways of their kin on the borders of North Britain.[11]

❧ Backcountry Time Ways: The Border Idea of "Passing the Time"

The backsettlers were also distinctive in their ways of thinking about time. Like others of their age, they believed in the ancient rule of Ecclesiastes that "to everything there is a season, and a time to every purpose." But backcountry seasons and times were not the same as in other regional cultures of British America. The rhythms of life in the southern highlands differed from those of New England, tidewater Virginia, and the Delaware Valley.

A case in point was the season of marriage. In Congregational New England, as we have seen, the "marrying time" came in the autumn—especially in November and December. In Anglican Virginia, on the other hand, the favorite season of marriage fell between Christmas and Lent. The Quakers of the Delaware Valley kept a third custom, in which the rhythm of marriage showed

---

[10]Remonstrance presented to the Commons House of Assembly by the Upper Inhabitants, 1767, reprinted in Woodmason, *Carolina Backcountry*, 213.

[11]Boston *Chronicle*, 5–12 Dec. 1768; Gov. Wm. Bull to Board of Trade, 30 Nov. 1770; reprinted in Merrens, *The Colonial South Carolina Scene*, 265.

two annual peaks in spring and autumn. All of these American patterns followed regional folkways in England.

In the backcountry a fourth rhythm appeared: a single predominant season of marriage in April, May, June and July. Among Scots-Irish settlers of Augusta County, Virginia, the favorite month for marriage was May. Two-thirds of all recorded marriages occurred in the spring and summer; the least active period was the fall.[1]

This rhythm was not invented in America, nor was it the product of frontier conditions. It had long appeared on the borders of north Britain, where weddings were normally held in the spring during the late seventeenth and eighteenth century.[2]

The rhythms of backcountry life were different in other ways as well. The backsettlers organized their lives by events in the Christian calendar, but not in the same way as other cultures of British America. They preserved ancient Christian rituals which had lingered in the borderlands of North Britain long after they had been abandoned in other regions.

[1]The season of marriage in Augusta County, Va., from 1749 to 1773 was as follows:

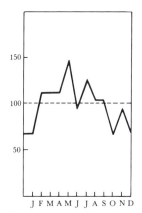

Month	Marriage Index ($\overline{m}$ = 100)	Percent of all Marriages
January	68.09	5.7
February	110.64	9.2
March	110.64	9.2
April	110.64	9.2
May	144.68	12.1
June	93.62	7.8
July	127.67	10.6
August	102.13	8.5
September	102.13	8.5
October	68.09	5.7
November	93.62	7.8
December	68.09	8.5
Total	1200.04	

Source: Computed from data in William A. Crozier, *Early Virginia Marriages* (Baltimore, 1968), 85–88.

[2]In eight English border parishes scattered through the counties of Cumberland and Westmorland, all showed a peak season of marriage in the months of April, May, June and July. See E. A. Wrigley and R. S. Schofield, *The Population History of England, 1541–1871* (Cambridge, 1981), 302; and Ann Kussmaul, "Time and Space, Hoofs and Grain: The Seasonality of Marriage in England," *JIH* 15 (1985), 755–79.

This North British pattern differed from that of East Anglia, which showed a strong autumn peak, and the Midlands, which tended to be mixed or bimodal. Marriages in Roman Catholic countries of western Europe, including France, Italy and Belgium, generally showed a January-February peak similar to that in Anglican Virginia. The Cambridge Group offer a materialist explanation for these variations, in terms of systems of production and agricultural regimes (arable, wood pasture), but their own evidence does not support them.

For example, many borderers kept a day which they called the "Old Christmas" on January 6 when there was a feast in even the poorest houses, and bonfires at night with much gunplay and fireworks. This had also been a folk custom in North Britain, where the revelry of "Old Christmas" reached its climax in a practice called "stanging," a rough and sometimes violent ceremony in which a victim was hoisted on a long pole and made to dangle in the air until he bought himself free.[3] In America's southern highlands, these customs survived for many generations. Even in the twentieth century, folklore collectors were startled to find that the custom of the "Old Christmas," with its roaring bonfires and gunplay, still flourished in Appalachia. In the highlands of North Carolina, one noted:

> In some parts of this county it is the custom to observe what is known as Old Christmas. Opinion varies as to the date; some believe it is the fifth and some the sixth of January. This day is believed by the people who keep it to be the real Christmas, the birthday of Christ. They say the Christmas we regularly keep is the "man-made" Christmas.[4]

Another folklorist observes that "the shooting of firecrackers and the discharging of firearms at Christmastime are customs rarely, if ever, observed anywhere north of the Mason-Dixon line."[5]

Other ancient Christian customs also came from North Britain to the backcountry. The borderers celebrated Easter in a special way, with "pace-egging," and the ritual performance of a folk play called St. George and the Black Morocco Dog. Easter Monday was a day of wild revelry, with much cockfighting. Whitsuntide was a time for hiring laborers. In late summer English borderers kept the ritual of Rushbearing, when they collected

---

[3]January 6, the twelfth day after Christmas, is the feast of the Epiphany in the Christian calendar. In the eastern church it is celebrated in honor of the baptism of the infant Jesus. In the western churches it is usually taken to mark the adoration of the Magi; that is, the first manifestation of Christ to the Gentiles. In England, even to this day, the sovereign marks the occasion by special offerings of gold, myrrh and frankincense, in ceremonies of great beauty and antiquity.

The evening before Epiphany is Twelfth Night, a happy event celebrated differently in various parts of the English-speaking world. The people of Herefordshire, for example, light twelve bonfires at once, in honor of the Apostles.

Other Christians, however, have celebrated January 6 as the actual birthday of Jesus. This still is the case in the Armenian Church, and was so in some parts of the Appalachian highlands as recently as the 1930s.

[4]Newman, I. White, Frank C. Brown, et al., *The Frank C. Brown Collection of North Carolina Folklore* (7 vols., Durham, N.C., 1952–64), I, 2416.

[5]*Ibid.*, I, 224.

bundles of rushes "to carpet the muddy floors of the churches afresh." The fall was celebrated by Halloween customs of exceptional extravagance. At various appointed times the borderers also observed "young folks days" and "old folks nights," "bidden weddings," wrestling tournaments, field days and various other events.[6]

Some of these rituals did not survive in the New World. Quickly abandoned were events such as rushbearing which had been tied to the established church. But folk rituals which centered on the family and neighborhood became an established part of back-country culture. The folk custom of wild revelry on Easter Monday survived in the southern highlands, together with cockfighting and heavy drinking on that day. Most of these customs were kept in the backcountry for a longer time than in other parts of British America.[7]

The backsettlers also kept other temporal customs of high complexity. Their culture assigned many fixed seasons for doing things. Their folklore told them, for example:

> Never mix April 30th milk with that of May 1st or the butter will be slow in coming.

> Make soap on the full of the moon or else it won't set.

> A swarm of bees in June is worth a silver spoon
> A swarm of bees in July is not worth a fly.

> As slow as Christmas coming.

> Sprinkle ashes on animals and fowl on Ash Wednesday.

The flow of life was regulated by many of these rhythms—annual, monthly, weekly, even daily. Sunday, of course, was a day of worship. Mondays and Tuesdays were favorite days for visiting. Fridays were days for going to market. But Friday and Saturday were thought to be unlucky for new enterprises. President Andrew Jackson, "to the end of his life, never liked to begin any thing of consequence on Friday, and would not if it could be avoided."[8]

At the same time that these folk rules were kept with great care, the people of the back settlements startled travelers from other

[6]Collingwood, *Lake District*, 152; T. E. Lones, ed., *British Calendar Customs (England)* (London, 1938); M. Macleod Banks, *British Calendar Customs (Scotland)* (London, 1937).

[7]Johnson, *Antebellum North Carolina*, 180.

[8]Parton, *Andrew Jackson*, I, 45–46; James Elerton, Journal, 1740, published in Elizabeth Poyas, *Olden Time of Carolina* (Charleston, 1855), and excerpts in Merrens, ed., *The Colonial South Carolina Scene*, 130–37.

cultures by their complaisant attitudes toward the use of time. The proverbs of the backcountry showed a strong spirit of temporal fatalism in a world of insecurity:

> To-day's to-day and tomorrow's tomorrow.
>
> Come day, go day, God send Sunday.
>
> You can't rush God.
>
> Never trouble trouble, 'til trouble troubles you.
>
> Do not argue with the wind.

These were not a people who took time by the forelock. The folkways of the backcountry differed very much in that respect from the attitudes of New England, the Delaware, and even tidewater Virginia. Of all the inhabitants of British America, the back settlers were the most conservative and the least instrumental in their time ways. By and large the people of the backcountry tended to believe that the rhythms of life were inexorable and ineluctable, and beyond the capacity of mere mortals to change in any fundamental way. In place of the more instrumental attitudes of improving time, or redeeming time, or even killing time, the backsettlers had a fatalistic idea of passing the time—letting it happen in its ineluctable way. Here was another striking paradox of backcountry culture. The more these people moved through space, the more rooted they became in time.

❧ Backcountry Wealth Ways: Border Ideas of the Material Order

Across so vast a global space, the great magnet that drew the British borderers to American backcountry was land—the dream of fertile farmland to be had for the taking. This motive dominated the settlement of the southern highlands for many generations. In the year 1796, Moses Austin observed the steady stream of settlers moving west along the Wilderness Road. As they passed by he asked why they were traveling, and recorded their replies in the backcountry dialect.

> Ask these Pilgrims what they expect when they git to Kentuckey the Answer is Land. have you any. No, but I expect I can git it. have you any thing to pay for land. No. did you Ever see the Country. No but Every Body says its good land. can any thing be more

> Absurd than the Conduct of man, here is hundreds travelling
> hundreds of miles, they know not for what Nor Whither, except
> its to Kentucky . . . and when arrived at this heaven in idea what
> do they find? a goodly land I will allow but to them forbiden Land.
> Exhausted and worn down with distress and disappointment they
> are at last Obliged to become hewers of woods and drawers of
> water.[1]

Their frequent disappointment was caused by the pattern of land
distribution in the southern backcountry, which differed very
much from that in Massachusetts, Pennsylvania and tidewater
Virginia.

In the southern highlands, many different sovereignties created a chaos of conflicting claims that "overlapped like shingles
on a roof," as one historian has written. Small tracts of land were
given out on a headright or bounty system. Individual patents of
a few hundred acres that were sold for small sums.[2] At the same
time, huge tracts were granted to a few great landowners with
connections in London and colonial capitals. A majority of adult
males in the southern highlands owned no land at all. The result
was a system of landholding characterized by a large landless
underclass of tenants and squatters, a middle class that was small
by comparison with other colonies, and a few very rich landlords.

By far the largest individual holding in the backcountry was
Granville District in North Carolina, which had been granted to
John Carteret, Earl of Granville (1690–1763) in settlement of a
proprietary claim. The Granville District was so vast that it was
measured not in acres or miles but degrees of latitude and lon-
gitude. North Carolina's Governor William Tryon described it in
a letter to the Earl of Shelburne in 1767:

> His Lordship's District contains nearly one Degree of Latitude,
> and better than five Degrees of Longitude, from Currituck Inlet
> to . . . the western boundary. . . . There is thirteen counties in his
> Lordship's District, the two westernmost of which counties con-
> tain a tract more than ten times the contents of Rhode island.

One county alone (of thirteen) was sixty miles square; another
measured 60 by 150 miles. Altogether, Granville District encom-

---

[1]"A Memorandum of M. Austin's Journey from the Lead Mines in the County of Wythe in
the State of Virginia to the Lead Mines in the Province of Louisiana West of the Mississippi,
1796–1797," *AHR* 5 (1899–1900), 525–26.

[2]In South Carolina, from 1760 to 1765, there were about 2,500 applications for land, a total
of 525,000 acres. The average grant was a little larger than 200 acres. But many of these grants
went to petitioners who were already landowners. See Robert L. Meriwether, *The Expansion of
South Carolina* (1940, rpt. Philadelphia, 1974), 257–59.

passed approximately twenty million acres—and all of it was the property of one Englishman. Granville was able to defend his title, and by the 1760s he was collecting rents from backsettlers who had moved upon his land.

Many of these settlers had very modest estates. There was a class of small landowners in the backcountry who have been called the southern yeomanry. Their numbers were relatively smaller than in New England or the middle colonies. At the same time, large numbers of backsettlers owned no land at all, but merely squatted on the lands of others. Many remained poor and landless for generations. This pattern of land distribution—a few large absentee owners, a small class of yeomanry, and many landless families, was characteristic of the southern highlands.

One of the most stubborn myths of American history is the idea that the frontier promoted equality of material condition. This national folk legend is, unhappily, very much mistaken. With some exceptions, landed wealth was always highly concentrated throughout the southern highlands, as it would be in the lower Mississippi Valley, Texas and the far southwest. Inequality was greater in the backcountry and the southern highlands than in any other rural region of the United States.

In this respect, as in so many others, the southern backcountry resembled the borderlands of North Britain. Every region of Great Britain has been marked by deep and pervasive inequalities. But some regions have been more unequal than others, and among the most inegalitarian of all were the borderlands of North Britain. Throughout the northern counties of England, and the lowlands of Scotland and northern Ireland, a large part of the best land was owned by a small number of people—many of them absentees.

During the late seventeenth and early eighteenth century, England's richest peers owned a large part of productive resources in Cumberland and Westmorland, but in the year 1680, not a single peer of the realm actually lived in either of those counties.[3] The majority of adult males in Cumberland and Westmorland owned no land of their own. Most were tenants or subtenants who held their farms on terms that were increasingly exploitative. On Cumberland manors the majority of tenants (55% by one historian's count) paid arbitrary rents which could

---

[3]John Vincent Beckett, "Landownership in Cumbria, c. 1680–c. 1750" (thesis, Univ. of Lancaster, 1975); Charles F. Searle, "The Odd Corner of England: A Study of Rural Social Forms in Transition: Cumbria, 1700–c. 1924" (thesis, Univ. of Essex, 1983).

be raised at will by the owner. Tenants were also required to pay many feudal dues and fines. "Fines," writes historian Charles Searle, "were the principal means by which the lords pumped the surplus out of Cumbria."[4] Between great landlords and humble tenants, there was also a small middling order of "statesmen," as they were called in Cumbria. Some of these middling families did very well for themselves during the seventeenth century. But many were hard pressed, and the general drift was toward greater inequality.[5]

In Scotland and northern Ireland, the concentration of wealth was even more extreme. One historian writes that "except for parts of southwestern Scotland, virtually the whole of the Lowland countryside belonged to wealthy landowners. There were very few small owners in Scotland, and freeholding as a status did not exist. In many areas all landed property was in the hands of as little as one or two percent of the population . . . an extreme stratification probably greater than any other rural area of England."[6]

This system of inequality was rooted in the conditions of life which shaped so many other parts of border culture. An historian of Northumberland and Durham observes that "forms of land tenure long outmoded further south had been maintained by the crown, which owned many of the border manors, in order to retain a sufficient supply of fighting men. . . . Customary tenure was very secure, and in the larger manors of Wark and Harbottle descent was by partible inheritance, so that potential fighting men were virtually guaranteed enough land for subsistence. . . . The resultant overpopulation had deleterious effects."[7]

The pacification of the borders was followed by the eviction of tenants in both England and Scotland. Large numbers of landless poor were created by this process. Local officeholders were compelled to devote much of their attention to this problem of poverty in their region. Many emigrants who sailed from North Britain to America had been the victims of this social process.[8]

Ironically, parts of the same exploitative system were also car-

---

[4]In Westmorland most customary manors had fixed rents. See Searle, "The Odd Corner of England," 43.

[5]*Ibid.,* 45.

[6]Landsman, *Scotland and Its First American Colony,* 21.

[7]Paul Brassley, "Northumberland and Durham," in Thirsk, ed., *Agrarian History of England and Wales,* I, 49.

[8]"Disbursed for conveying vagrants through the county . . . three man and three horses and a cart two days and their meat and wages, and myself four days." Benjamin Brown Accounts, 2 Dec. 1731, Brown mss. WD/TE/wI CUMROK.

ried to the New World. Before the end of the eighteenth century, the distribution of landed wealth had become highly unequal in the southern highlands. There were, of course, many local variations, but the same general pattern appeared in seventeen out of nineteen counties of western North Carolina, Tennessee and Kentucky where distribution of wealth could be measured for the eighteenth century.

Throughout this great region where virgin land existed in abundance, most men were landless. At the same time, a few families owned very large tracts. By the last decade of the eighteenth century, Gini ratios for landed wealth were in the range of .60 to .88 throughout many counties in this region—the highest levels of concentration in any rural part of the United States at that time. The top decile of wealthholders owned between 40 and 80 percent of the land. In many areas, one-third to one-half of taxable white males owned nothing. This was the case in eight counties of East Tennessee, from the eighteenth to the mid-nineteenth century.[9]

[9]The distribution of taxable wealth in East Tennessee was as follows:

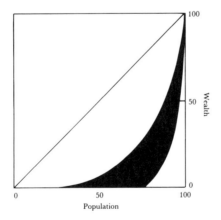

Place	Year	Total Wealth			Wealth in Land			Wealth in Slaves		
		SSTT	Gini	Zero	SSTT	Gini	Zero	SSTT	Gini	Zero
Washington Co.	1778	46	57	10	na	na	na	na	na	na
Washington Co.	1787	47	64	28	42	60	29	100	94	89
Sullivan Co.	1796	50	67	30	39	60	33	87	92	83
Carter Co.	1796	73	83	39	72	83	41	100	95	91
Grainger Co.	1799	85	86	53	79	88	57	89	92	87
Jefferson Co.	1800	61	75	38	59	74	41	92	92	88
Hawkins Co.	1809–12	63	79	47	68	82	50	82	89	82
Cooke Co.	1836–37	62	77	38	59	75	39	100	95	90

na = not available
SSTT = Size share of the upper decile of wealth holders

A similar pattern also appeared in eleven counties of Kentucky from 1792 to 1819, where Gini ratios ranged from .66 to as high as .92 for property in land and slaves. A few of these counties (Cumberland and Christian) were more equal than others. But by comparison with rural parts of New England and the Delaware, most counties were highly unequal.[10]

As time passed, inequalities diminished in some of these coun-

---

Gini = Gini ratio of wealth inequality

Zero = percent of taxables owning no taxable property, and paying only a poll tax.

These data are calculated from tax lists published in Polyanna Creekmore, ed., "Early East Tennessee Taxpayers," *ETHSP* 27 (1955), 100–119; 23 (1963), 121–51. Landed wealth refers to acres; slaves, to black polls; total wealth to property weighted by the Tennessee assessment act of 1805: 100 acres = 1.0; town lots = 0.5; taxable slaves = 1.00. The author wishes to thank Mark Orlofsky for his help with data processing.

[10]The distribution of taxable wealth in Kentucky was as follows:

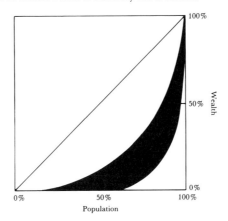

Place	Date	Total Wealth			Wealth in Land			Wealth in Slaves		
		SSTT	Gini	Zero	SSTT	Gini	Zero	SSTT	Gini	Zero
Madison Co.	1792	68	83	59	69	84	68	82	89	81
Washington Co.	1792	64	79	44	58	79	52	81	89	79
Nelson Co.	1792	na	na	na	72	83	48	na	na	na
Lincoln Co.	1792	na	na	na	na	na	na	73	87	77
Logan Co.	1795	86	92	78	99	97	88	91	92	86
Campbell Co.	1795	86	92	73	92	94	78	100	95	90
Mercer Co.	1795	na	na	na	na	na	na	76	87	74
Montgomery Co.	1799?	na	na	na	96	96	81	na	na	na
Cumberland Co.	1799	42	67	47	40	61	45	100	95	90
Christian Co.	1800	50	66	34	37	55	37	80	88	80
Hart Co.	1819	na	na	na	60	77	51	na	na	na

na = not available

SSTT = Size share of the upper decile of wealth holders

Gini = Gini ratio of wealth inequality

Zero = percent of taxables owning no taxable property

Source: Calculated from Kentucky tax lists with the assistance of Marc Orlofsky.

ties and increased in others, but the general pattern persisted throughout much of the region into the nineteenth century for many years. The United States Census in 1850 and 1860 found evidence of extreme rural inequalities throughout the old southwest. Studies of eight sample counties of Tennessee in 1850 showed that more than half of all adult males (free and slave altogether) owned no land at all. The top 20 percent owned 82 percent of improved land and 99 percent of the slaves. In between was a rural middle class of yeoman farmers who were a minority of the adult male population of Tennessee in 1850.[11]

The same patterns persisted into the twentieth century, when an elaborate study of wealth distribution in eighty counties of Appalachia came to this conclusion:

> The image of Appalachia as the land of rugged individuals, owning and working relatively small family holdings, is strong in the literature about the region. But . . . the reality is a region where the ownership of land is concentrated in relatively few hands.[12]

In 1983, the top 1 percent of owners possessed half of the land in Appalachia. The top 5 percent owned nearly two-thirds. This pattern of wealth distribution in the southern highlands in the twentieth century was much like that which had existed two hundred years earlier.[13]

---

[11]This conclusion rests upon the same data used by Harriet and Frank Owlsley, as carefully reworked in Donald L. Winters, "'Plain Folk" of the Old South Reexamined: Economic Democracy in Tennessee," *JSH* 53 (1987), 565–86. As Winters himself points out, his own computations understate wealth concentration, and an attempt is made to refine them here. His data are limited to farm operators listed in the agricultural schedules of the Census of 1850. This source omitted many landless freemen who appeared in the population schedules of the census but not in the agricultural schedules. From the research of Blanche Clark, we know that, when they are included, landlessness in the eight Tennessee counties rises to 35% of the free population. Further, it also omits slaves as potential wealthowners, who made up 25% of the Tennessee population in 1850. These two large landless groups were a majority of the population. Without them Winters obtained a Gini ratio of .58 for improved acres. If they are included, the Gini ratio rises to .8, and even this estimate understates concentration, for the Census of 1850 missed many poor farmers, migrant farm laborers and squatters.

[12]Charels C. Geisler et al., *Who Owns Appalachia?* (Lexington, Ky., 1983), 14; another study that obtained similar results is Lee Soltow, "Kentucky Wealth at the End of the Eighteenth Century," *JEH* 43 (1963), 617–33.

[13]*Ibid.*, 14–40.

❧ Backcountry Rank Ways:
A System of Stratification Without Orders

As these patterns of wealth and inheritance suggest, social stratification in the backcountry was a system of high complexity.
Extreme inequalities of material condition were joined to an
intense concern for equality of esteem.

Visitors of exalted rank complained that they were not treated
with the same respect as in other parts of British America. The
Anglican missionary Charles Woodmason filled his journal with
angry accounts of "ill treatment" by "insolent" and "impudent"
settlers who stubbornly refused to display the deference which he
thought his due. He complained that these people were "the
most audacious of any set of mortals I ever met with."[1] William
Byrd, on his various backcountry rambles, also complained of
undue "familiarity," and a lack of deference to age, wealth, birth
and breeding. Militiamen in the backcountry commonly refused
to obey orders from their officers, unless persuaded to do so.
Colonel David Stokes of backcountry Lunenburg, Virginia, characterized the militia of his county as marked by "unruly
licentiousness."[2]

These complaints rose from fundamental differences in social
manners and expectations. In the backcountry, rich and poor
men dealt with one another more or less as social equals. They
wore similar clothing, and addressed each other by first names.
They worked, ate, laughed, played, and fought together on a foot-
ing of equality. Many backcountry proverbs captured the equality
of manners that coexisted with inequalities of material condition
in this culture:

> The rain don't know broadcloth from jeans.
>
> No man can help his birth.
>
> Poor folks have poor ways, and rich folk damned mean ones.
>
> Any fool can make money.
>
> Don't care keeps a big house.
>
> As Black as the Earl of Hell.
>
> A falling master makes a standing man.

---

[1] Woodmason, *Carolina Backcountry*, 43, 47, 53.
[2] Beeman, *Evolution of the Southern Backcountry*, 132.

He who is at the bottom can fall no lower.

All Stuarts are not kinsmen of the king.[3]

These attitudes were not invented on the frontier. They had long been characteristic of the borderers. Travelers in this region frequently described the manners of the natives in terms such as "insolence," "impudence," "forwardness," "familiarity," "unruliness," "licentiousness" and "pride." The authorities complained for example that the famous border reiver Sandie Scott was worse than a thief—he was a "proud thief" who not only stole from his superiors, but believed himself to be their equal. Here was another border pattern that came to the American backcountry.[4]

Despite this equality of manners, a clear-cut system of social status existed in both the borderlands and the backcountry, which differed from ranking customs in other parts of British America. At the top of this system was the "ascendancy" whom we have already noticed. These families cherished the memory of immigrant-ancestors who had been highly placed in North British society—not at the very top, but high enough to have a coat-of-arms on the silverware, or to send a younger son to the university, or to marry a daughter to a good family, or at least to dress and act like a gentleman. In the American backcountry this elite rapidly acquired a firm hold on wealth and power throughout the region. They owned a large part of the best lands and held most of the top military and political offices. Their manners tended to be very rough, and were not much refined by their new environment. But they knew who they were, and instantly recognized one another, and cemented their status by ties of marriage and friendship. Andrew Jackson's violent courtship of Rachel Donelson, for example, was not a spontaneous event, but a calculated act of high consequence. Jackson thought of himself as a gentleman, and took a wife who was appropriate to his rank. She was described as "the daughter of a man of considerable prestige, one of the richest and most distinguished of the western Virginians, but she went into the forest when a young girl, and the result was that she was barely literate, and she smoked a pipe on occasion."[5]

This backcountry elite was not distinguished by learning,

[3]*North Carolina Folklore*, I, 371, 374, 399, 402, 410, 443, 465, 482.
[4]Fraser, *Steel Bonnets*, 42, 236; passim.
[5]Thomas P. Abernethy, *From Frontier to Plantation in Tennessee* (Memphis, 1955), 160.

breeding, intellect or refinement. In consequence, its eminence
was always directly contingent upon its wealth and power. In the
southern highlands (and indeed on the southern rim to this day)
one rarely finds the tattered respectability of old families in Massachusetts, or the threadbare gentility of tidewater Virginia. A
backcountry family that lost its property fell instantly to a lower
level of society, and disappeared from the ascendancy without a
trace. The result was a highly materialistic system of social rank.
Wealth alone became more important as a determinant of status
than in New England, Pennsylvania or Virginia.

Below the ascendancy was a middle class which has sometimes
been called the "yeomanry" of the southern highlands. Most
were small farmers who owned their own land. A native of the
region writes:

> Differences in the status of families at either end of the group are
> striking, but often such disparity as exists is not noticeable save in
> the size of the houses and the land holdings. One may remark a
> less bountiful table. . . . He may note, too, if he is observing, less
> stock and scantier farm equipment; but the life of this class is
> homogeneous, and the absence of some things noted in the homes
> of the more well-to-do is not of necessity an indication of greater
> poverty. It may be merely a sign of greater simplicity in the taste
> of a family.[6]

Below this comparatively small backcountry middle class was a
large rural proletariat, who owned no land and few personal possessions. Most were either tenants or squatters. Their property
ran on four legs—consisting mostly of cattle and swine which
they raised in the woods. Their pride was heavily invested in these
animals. The Hatfield-McCoy feud, in which more than twenty
people were killed, started as an argument over two hogs.

In the eighteenth century, this backcountry underclass was
called by many names which have become a permanent part of
the American language. By and large these words connoted a
stubborn combination of poverty and pride which had existed on
the borders of north Britain. The words themselves, though now
thought of as Americanisms, were also carried from the borderlands. One such term was *hoosier*. Everitt Dick writes that

> before it was used to designate the citizens of Indiana, the term
> "Hoosier" was used in the South to describe a rough or uncouth

---

[6]Campbell, *The Southern Highlander*, 86.

*Crackers, Rednecks, Hoosiers—words that described the largest social class in
the American backcountry—were not coined in the New World. They were carried out of North Britain. For three centuries these terms were variously used
as praise words and pejoratives, according to context and occasion. But always
they described the same paradox of poverty and pride. Something of that spirit
was captured by the American painter Frederic Remington in a sketch from
which this drawing is taken.*

person. . . . the name "hoosier" was often applied to these back-woodsmen even as far south as northern Louisiana and southern Arkansas. Everywhere the general characteristics of this tribe were the same, east to Georgia and from Mississippi and Alabama north to Illinois and Indiana.[7]

The word *hoosier* comes from *hoozer* or *hoozier* in the old Cumberland dialect, which meant something or someone who was unusually large and rough—in W. J. Cash's phrase, "a hell of a fellow." After coming to America in the eighteenth century, the noun migrated north to Indiana with so much of backcountry culture, and was attached to the citizens of that state to distinguish them from their Yankee neighbors.[8]

Another term for this rural proletariat was *redneck,* which was originally applied to the backsettlers because of their religion. The earliest American example known to this historian was recorded in North Carolina by Anne Royall in 1830, who noted that "red-neck" was "a name bestowed upon the Presbyterians." It had long been a slang word for religious dissenters in the north of England.[9]

A third word for this rural proletariat which also came from Britain was *cracker,* which derived from an English pejorative for a low and vulgar braggart. In 1766, an informant wrote the Earl of Dartmouth about the American backcountry,

> I should explain to your Lordship what is meant by Crackers; a name they have got from being great boasters; they are a lawless set of rascals on the frontiers of Virginia, Maryland, the Carolinas and Georgia, who often change their abode.[10]

This distinctive backcountry underclass was in being by the mid-eighteenth century. Its call names had originated in North Britain. So also had its character and culture, which still survive today.

---

[7]Everett Dick, *The Dixie Frontier: A Social History of the Southern Frontier from the First Trans-montane Beginnings to the Civil War* (New York, 1948), 24, 310.

[8]*EDD,* "Hoozer;" cf. Mitford Mathews, *A Dictionary of Americanisms on Historical Principles* (1951, Chicago, 1956), "Hoosier."

[9]"Red-neck," Matthews, *Dictionary of Americanisms,* 1373; Anne Royall, *Mrs. Royall's Southern Tour* (3 vols., Washington, 1830–31), I, 148; for an earlier example in the north of England, see *OED,* "redneck," under "red," 18.a.

[10]"Cracker," Matthews, *Dictionary of Americanisms;* for earlier English examples, see "Cracker," *OED.* Other suggestions that cracker is short for "corn-cracker" or for "whip-cracker" are contradicted by the earliest examples.

❧ The Backcountry Comity:
Patterns of Migration, Settlement, and Association

The borderers were a restless people who carried their migratory ways from Britain to America. There had been many folk movements in their history before the Atlantic crossing, and many more were yet to come. The history of these people was a long series of removals—from England to Scotland, from Scotland to Ireland, from Ireland to Pennsylvania, from Pennsylvania to Carolina, from Carolina to the Mississippi Valley, from the Mississippi to Texas, from Texas to California, and from California to the rainbow's end.

Rates of geographic migration were very high in this culture. In Britain, some of the highest rates of rural migration were to be found on the northern borders. The Scottish village of Fintray, for example, had a turnover of 75 percent in five years (1696–1701)—a rate much above the parishes of southern England.[1] Similar patterns also appeared in the American backcountry, where rates of internal migration were also higher than in the rural communities of New England, the Delaware and tidewater Virginia. In backcountry Lunenburg County, Virginia, for example, one historian found what he called "phenomenal movement" of the population. From 1750 to 1769, 80 percent of the population disappeared from the county; 40 percent did so in five years from 1764 to 1769. These rates of movement were exceptional by eighteenth-century standards.[2]

The backsettlers thought about moving in a way that was different from more sedentary people. There was a folk-saying in the southern highlands: "When I get ready to move, I just shut the door, call the dogs and start." This was the footloose way in which Andrew Jackson was said to have come into the backcountry, with nothing but two riding horses, a gun at his side, and a pack of hunting dogs at his heel.[3]

Most geographic migration in both the British borderlands and the American backcountry consisted of short-distance movements that covered only a few miles, as families searched for slightly better living conditions. Frequent removals were encour-

---

[1] Landsman, *Scotland and Its First American Colony*, 31, 44; Gillespie, *Colonial Ulster*, 60.

[2] Those statistics do not include movement within the county, nor were they much affected by mortality; Beeman, *Evolution of the Southern Backcountry*, 29–30, 67–70, 81–82.

[3] Miles, *The Spirit of the Mountains*, 177; Remini, *Andrew Jackson*, I, 37.

aged by low levels of property-owning and by characteristic attitudes toward wealth and land and work in this culture.

During the first few years of settlement, backcountry folk settled close to one another for mutual protection. The result was
the planting of "stations" in Tennessee, and "forts" in Kentucky.
But as the backcountry gradually became more secure, another
pattern appeared—one that was very different from the comities
of Massachusetts, Virginia and Pennsylvania.

The backcountry ideal was a scattered settlement pattern in isolated farmsteads, loosely grouped in sprawling "neighborhoods"
that covered many miles. The German traveler Schoepf in 1784
observed that in North Carolina the farms were "scattered about
in these woods at various distances, three to six miles, and often
as much as ten or fifteen or twenty miles apart."[4] North Carolina
Congressman Nathaniel Macon startled his Yankee colleagues by
arguing that "no man ought to live so near another as to hear his
neighbor's dog bark."[5] That attitude was widely shared in the
backcountry. In this culture, a house became a hermitage,
beyond sight and sound of every human habitation. Once again,
Andrew Jackson personified his culture. Jackson's home in Tennessee was actually called the Hermitage. When he was away from
it he wrote home to his wife expressing his longing for "sweet
retirement," apart from other people.[6]

There were, of course, physical limits to the realization of this
idea. But the idea itself became an important reality in the culture
of the backcountry. It persisted for many generations in the isolated homes that were built in the hollows of the Appalachians,
the canebreaks of Kentucky, the flatlands of Texas and the
ravines of southern California.

Samual Kercheval described the common settlement pattern.
"The greater number of farms in the western parts of Pennsylvania and Virginia," he wrote, "bear a striking resemblence to an
amphitheater. The buildings occupy a low situation, and the tops
of the surrounding hills are the boundaries of the tract to which
the family mansion belongs. Our forefathers were fond of farms
of this description, because, as they said, they are attended with
this convenience, "that everything comes to the house down
hill."[7]

[4]Schoepf, *Travels,* II, 103.
[5]John Hill Wheeler, *Historical Sketches of North Carolina* (rpt. Baltimore, 1964), 438.
[6]Andrew Jackson to Rachel Jackson, May 9, 1796, *Papers of Andrew Jackson,* I, 91.
[7]Kercheval, *Valley of Virginia,* 250.

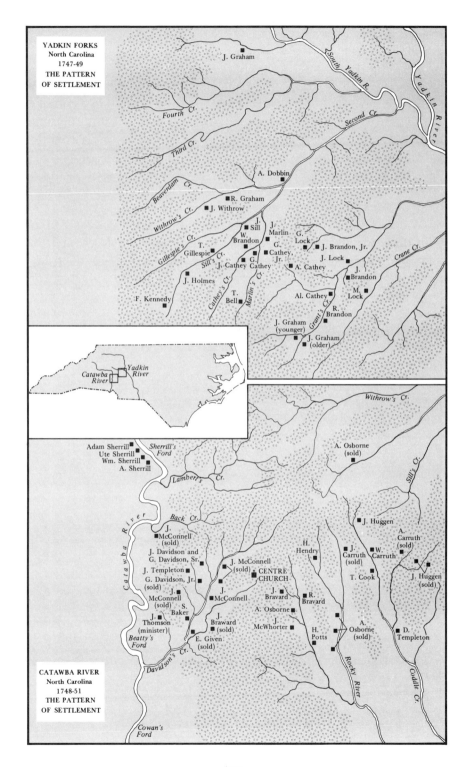

YADKIN FORKS
North Carolina
1747-49
THE PATTERN
OF SETTLEMENT

J. Graham

South Yadkin R.

Yadkin River

Fourth Cr.

Second Cr.

Third Cr.

Beaverdam Cr.

A. Dobbin

R. Graham
J. Withrow

Withrow's Cr.

J.
Sill
W.
Brandon
J.
Marlin
G.
Lock
J. Brandon, Jr.

Crane Cr.

T.
Gillespie
Gillespie's Cr.

Sill's Cr.
G.
Cathey,
Jr.
J. Lock

J. Cathey
J. Cathey Cathey
A. Cathey
J.
Brandon

J. Holmes

Cathey's Cr.

Martin's Cr.

Al. Cathey
M.
Lock

F. Kennedy

T.
Bell

Grant's Cr.

R.
Brandon

J. Graham
(younger)

J. Graham
(older)

Catawba
River

Yadkin
River

CATAWBA RIVER
North Carolina
1748-51
THE PATTERN
OF SETTLEMENT

Withrow's Cr.

A. Osborne
(sold)

Adam Sherrill
Ute Sherrill
Wm. Sherrill
A. Sherrill

Sherrill's
Ford

Lambert's Cr.

Sill's Cr.

Catawba River

Back Cr.

J. Huggen

J.
McConnell
(sold)

H.
Hendry

A.
Carruth
(sold)

J. Davidson and
G. Davidson, Sr.

J. McConnell
(sold)

J.
Carruth
(sold)

W.
Carruth

J. Templeton
G. Davidson, Jr.
(sold)

CENTRE
CHURCH

T. Cook

J. Huggen
(sold)

J.
McConnell
(sold)

J.
McConnell

J.
Bravard

R.
Bravard

S.
Baker

A. Osborne

J.
Thomson
(minister)

J.
Braward
(sold)

J.
McWhorter

A.
Osborne
(sold)

D.
Templeton

Beatty's
Ford

E. Given
(sold)

H.
Potts

Davidson's Cr.

Rocky River

Coddle Cr.

Cowan's
Ford

761

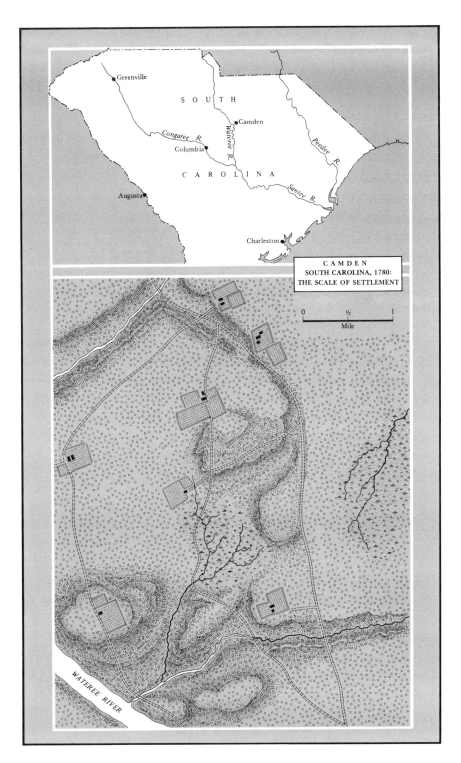

CAMDEN
SOUTH CAROLINA, 1780:
THE SCALE OF SETTLEMENT

0   ½   1
Mile

Greenville

S O U T H

Congaree R.

Camden

Columbia

Wateree R.

Peedee R.

C A R O L I N A

Santee R.

Augusta

Charleston

WATEREE RIVER

This pattern of settlement had often occurred on the borders of North Britain, where even today one finds isolated farmsteads nestled in valleys, with barren hillsides rising high above them on every side. One geographer observes that "The Scotch-Irish brought the Celtic dispersed farm with cattle-grazing and kitchen garden common in Ireland and Scotland. Members of each group moved in single family units onto the uplands. The Scotch-Irish often squatted on land in forested coves and mountainsides."[8]

Unlike the road-bound settlements of New England or the fluvial patterns of Virginia, the backsettlers built their houses near creeks or springs. Emma Miles wrote:

> The site of a cabin is usually chosen as near as possible to a fine spring. No other advantages will ever make up for the lack of good water. There is a strong prejudice against pumps . . . cisterns are considered "dead water," hardly fit to wash one's face in. The mountaineer takes the same pride in his water supply as the rich man in his wine cellar, and is in this respect a connoisseur. None but the purest and coldest of freestone will satisfy him.[9]

This also had been a border habit, where a safe supply of water could be a matter of life or death.

This pattern of settlement engendered a distinctive style of association. Family, friends and neighbors visited one another over long distances, staying in each other's houses, sleeping in the same beds, eating from the same dish. Few homes were so humble as not to have some accommodation for visitors, even if only a mattress, a stool and a spoon.

There was always a welcome for kin and friends, but an intense suspicion of strangers. This cultural attitude had deep roots in the borderlands of North Britain; one Cumbrian observed that anyone from a neighboring district was looked upon as a "'foreigner.'"[10] Precisely the same outlook long existed in the backcountry, where there were many bizarre proverbs on the subject:

> Put the stranger near the danger.
>
> Let the blame of every ill be on the stranger.
>
> The bad and no good on the back of a stranger.
>
> The stranger is for the wolf.[11]

[8]Karl B. Raitz, *Appalachia, A Regional Geography: Land, People and Development* (Boulder, Colo., and London, 1984), 115.

[9]Miles, *The Spirit of the Mountains*, 19–20.

[10]T. W. Carrick, *History of Wigton (Cumberland)* (Carlisle, 1949), 25.

[11]*North Carolina Folklore*, I, 482.

The backsettlers had little tolerance for those who broke their own rules. They dealt harshly with social deviance by a ritual which they called "hating out." Kercheval explained "the punishment for idleness, lying, dishonesty and ill-fame generally was that of 'hating the offender out,' as they expressed it . . . a general sentiment of indignation against such as transgressed the moral maxims of the community." Hating out could take many forms. Sometimes it was the "silent treatment," or a form of ritual abuse called "tongue-lashing," or petty harassment, or whipping, or banishment outright.[12]

These punishments derived their force from the importance of reputation in this culture. The backsettlers were as sensitive to questions of honor as the gentlemen of Virginia—but not in precisely the same way. In the backcountry, honor had very little to do with gentility. An Alabama planter summarized the prevailing attitude in a simple verse:

> Honor and shame from all conditions rise;
> Act well your part and their [sic] the honor lies[13]

Backcountry ideas of honor were understood more in terms of valor and virility. To behave dishonorably was to commit an "unmanly act." Folk punishments in the backcountry were designed to inflict humiliation by depriving an offender of his manhood—sometimes in a direct and literal sense. One common penalty was called "riding the stang." James Parton explained:

> A kind of punishment was formerly inflicted occasionally, called *Riding the Stang,* meaning riding upon a sting, that is, receiving chastisement for some offense of which the common law did not take any cognizance. On these occasions, some low fellow, who represented the delinquent, was mounted on a long pole carried on men's shoulders, and in this way he was taken about the streets, the bearers occasionally halting, and making loud proclamation of the person's real or alleged offense, the crowd huzzaing. They afterwards repaired to the residence of the offender, where a grand proclamation was made of his crime, or misdemeanor; after which the common dispersed, giving three hearty cheers.[14]

Altogether, reputation in the back settlements was very much a matter of what historian Bertram Wyatt-Brown calls "primal honor."[15]

---

[12]Kercheval, *Valley of Virginia,* 292.
[13]Wyatt-Brown, *Southern Honor,* 147.
[14]Parton, *Andrew Jackson,* I, 42.
[15]Wyatt-Brown, *Southern Honor,* 34, 50, 388, 390.

In all of its many aspects, this backcountry comity has some-times been interpreted by historians as a product of "the fron-tier." But it did not develop on other frontiers, and was remark-ably similar to patterns of settlement, migration, association, and belonging on the borderlands of north Britain. Here again, the pattern of cultural persistence was very strong.

❧ Backcountry Order Ways: The Border Idea of Order as *Lex Talionis*

Within this comity, personal relations between backsettlers were often brutally direct. The mother of President Jackson prepared her son for this world with some very strong advice. "Andrew," said she, "never tell a lie, nor take what is not your own, nor sue anybody for slander, assault and battery. Always settle them cases yourself."[1]

That folk saying was a classical expression of backcountry atti-tudes toward order, which differed very much from other regions of British America. In the absence of any strong sense of order as unity, hierarchy, or social peace, backsettlers shared an idea of order as a system of retributive justice. The prevailing principle was *lex talionis,* the rule of retaliation. It held that a good man must seek to do right in the world, but when wrong was done to him he must punish the wrongdoer himself by an act of retribu-tion that restored order and justice in the world.

This backcountry idea of order rested upon an exceptionally strong sense of self-sovereignty. Something of the same principle had also existed in tidewater Virginia, where the gentry were fond of quoting the old English cliché that every man's home was his castle. But the people of the backcountry went a step farther. A North Carolina proverb declared that "every man should be sher-iff on his own hearth."[2] That folk saying had been brought to the backcountry from the borderlands of North Britain, where it existed in almost the same words: "Every man is a sheriff on his own hearth."[3] This idea implied not only individual autonomy, but autarchy. Further, it narrowly circumscribed the role of gov-ernment, for if every man were sheriff on his own hearth, then

---

[1] Andrew Jackson to Martin Van Buren, 4 Dec. 1838, *Jackson Correspondence,* V, 573; W. H. Sparks, *The Memories of Fifty Years* (Philadelphia, 1882) 147–48; Remini, *Andrew Jackson,* I, 11–12, 429.

[2] *North Carolina Folklore,* I, 472.

[3] Selwyn G. Champion, *Racial Proverbs* (London, 1938), 59.

there was not very much work for a county sheriff to do, except to patrol the roads that lay in between.

The same ideas also appeared in the ordering institutions of the backcountry. There were official sheriffs and constables throughout that region, but the heaviest work of order-keeping was done by ad hoc groups of self-appointed agents who called themselves regulators in the eighteenth century, vigilantes in the nineteenth, and nightriders in the twentieth. This was not a transitional phenomenon—unless one wishes to think of a transition five centuries long. Nor was it the reflexive product of a frontier environment, for other frontiers experienced little or none of it. It rose instead from a tradition of retributive folk justice which had been carried from the British borderlands to the American backcountry.[4]

During the eighteenth century the back settlements suffered much from "banditti" whose depredations were punished by the summary justice of these self-styled "regulators." When, for example, one robber gang grew so bold that it tried to steal the horses of an entire congregation as they sat in church, the backcountry rose spontaneously. In retaliation, a "posse" of regulators reported it had "pursued the rogues, broke up their gangs, burnt the dwellings of all their harborers and abetters—whipped 'em and drove the idle, vicious and profligate out of the province, men and women without distinction."[5] Conflicts between bandits and "regulators" continued on the southwestern frontier for many generations. But it was not characteristic of the frontier itself. Nothing quite like it occurred on most parts of the northern frontier in New England or in the upper northwest.[6]

Vigilante movements began in the southern backcountry during the 1760s.[7] Their legitimacy rested upon a doctrine called

---

[4]The tradition still exists. A vigilante killing occurred in the small town of Maryville, Missouri, as recently as the 1980s, when Kenneth McElroy, a typical backcountry bully who "for most of his years . . . terrorized many of the town's 440 citizens," shot a grocer in town. When he continued to threaten his neighbors, he was surrounded by a crowd of sixty townspeople and shot to death "by person or persons unknown." *NY Times,* 26 Sept. 1986.

[5]Woodmason, *Carolina Backcountry,* 28.

[6]The leading survey has found evidence of 326 American vigilante movements, of which 211 occurred in the southern highlands and the southern rim. Most of the remainder were on the fringes of that region, in the lower middle west and the mountain states. Not a single case was recorded in New England, New York, or the Yankee part of the old northwest. There were none in the Delaware Valley, and only two cases in tidewater Virginia and the Carolina low country. Other cases can be found in all of these regions, but they were very rare compared with the southern highlands and the southwestern rim. See Richard M. Brown, "The American Vigilante Tradition," in *The History of Violence in America,* 154–226.

[7]This is Brown's judgment in *ibid.,* 158–59.

"Lynch's law," which probably took its name from Captain William Lynch (1742–1820), of Pittsylvania County, Virginia, and later Pendleton District, South Carolina. Captain Lynch was a backcountry settler of border descent. "Lynch's Law" began as a formal agreement among his neighbors:

> Whereas, many of the inhabitants of Pittsylvania have sustained great and intolerable losses by a set of lawless men ... we will inflict such corporal punishment on him or them, as to us shall seem adequate to the crime committed or the damage sustained.[8]

Lynch's law was swift and violent. Its victims were often flogged and sometimes killed without much attention to due process, or even to the evidence. One backcountry gravestone read: "George Johnson, Hanged by Mistake."[9]

This system of justice captured the two vital principles of backcountry order ways—the idea that order was a system of retributive violence and that each individual was the guardian of his own interests in that respect. Even sheriffs in the backcountry shared the same ideal of retributive violence, and often took the law into their own hands. Alabama's Tombigbee County, for example, had five justices of the peace in 1810, of whom three were themselves fugitives. Two were wanted on charges of murder, and a third for helping an accused murderer break jail.[10]

The idea of retributive justice was also reflected in common forms of disorder throughout the southern backcountry. One example was the prevalence of the blood feud in the southern highlands. The custom of feuding had been very common on the borders of North Britain. Bloody strife continued for many generations between families on both sides of the border.[11]

During the eighteenth century, this custom of the blood feud was introduced to the backcountry. In that new environment it flourished for more than two hundred years. Feuds occurred in many forms—between individuals, families, clans and communities. They began in a variety of ways—loss of property or reputation, political rivalries, sexual jealousies, moral insults and

---

[8]Mathews, *Dictionary of Americanisms*, 1010; A. Matthews in *CSM*, 27, 256–71.

[9]Charles L. Wallas, *Stories on Stone* (n.p., n.d.), 62.

[10]*ALAR* 12 (1959), 92; Clarence E. Carter, *Territorial Papers of the United States* (27 vols., Washington, D.C., 1934–69), VI, 243–46, 268–69.

[11]For many examples, see D.L.W. Tough, *The Last Years of a Frontier: A History of the Borders during the Reign of Elizabeth* (Oxford, 1928), 14, 16, 12, 117, 131, 141, 156, 173–74, 180, 225; also, Fraser, *Steel Bonnets*, passim.

material injuries.[12] In the classical feud between the Hatfields and the McCoys, the *casus belli* was a dispute over two razorback hogs which led to the killing of twenty people and the wounding of at least twenty more. Both families were of border stock; their feud arose more generally from an entire culture and its concept of order as retributive justice.[13]

Another expression of *lex talionis* was the heavy preponderance of crimes against persons over crimes against property. One study of criminal indictments in Ohio County, Virginia (1801–10), found that murders and assaults were more common than all other crimes and misdemeanors combined, and more than five times as common as property offenses.[14] This pattern persisted for two centuries. In the 1930s, an Appalachian lawyer wrote:

> Our people . . . are as a rule only charged with crimes of impulse, such as assault and battery, homicides of the different degrees, etc., or crimes against prohibitory statutes which they think inter-fere with their personal freedom, such as moonshining, and offenses of that nature. Seldom do you find them accused of crimes such as larceny, burglary or what are known as social crimes.[15]

Treatment of the disorderly was also different from other regions of British America. Backcountry courts tended to punish property crimes with the utmost severity, but to be very lenient with crimes of personal violence. In Cumberland County, Virginia, during the eighteenth century, a court administered the following punishments: for hog stealing, death by hanging; for scolding, five shilling fine; for the rape of an eleven-year-old girl, one shilling fine.[16] This structure of values continued for many

---

[12]For general accounts see Charles G. Mutzenberg, *Kentucky's Famous Feuds and Tragedies* (New York, 1917); Noah and John Reynolds, *History of the Feuds of the Mountain Parts of Eastern Kentucky* (Whitesburg, Ky., n.d.); S. S. McClintock, "The Kentucky Mountains and Their Feuds," *AJS* 7 (1901), 1–28, 171–87.

[13]Otis K. Rice, *The Hatfields and the McCoys* (Lexington, Ky., 1978).

[14]Edward M. Steel obtained the following pattern of indictments for crimes and misdemeanors in Ohio County, Va., 1801–10: Crimes against persons (125): Murder, 3; Assault and battery, 91; Peace action (abortive assaults), 31. Crimes against property (24): Larceny, 16; Robbery, 1; Counterfeiting, 2; Forgery, 2; Breaking and entering, 2; Trespass, 1. Crimes against morality (29): Profanity, 24; Bastardy, 4; Sabbath breaking, 1. Crimes against order and authority (62): Riot, 8; Affray (unpremeditated riot), 2; Unlawful assembly, 2; Disturbing public assembly, 1; Misfeasance (failure to lay out roads), 36; Unlawful distilling and retailing, 8; Obstructing highway, 2; Contempt, 3. Total: 240. Source: Edward M. Steel, "Criminality in Jeffersonian America—A Sample," *Crime and Delinquency*, 18 (1972), 154.

[15]Campbell, *The Southern Highlander,* 119.

[16]Garland F. Hopkins, *Cumberland County, Virginia* (Winchester, 1942), 31.

generations in the backcountry. Historian Edward Ayers finds that in the southern upcountry during the nineteenth century, county courts "treated property offenders much more harshly than those accused of violence."[17]

This system of order created a climate of violence in the American backcountry which remained part of the culture of that region to our own time. The proverbs of the backcountry are full of the spirit of violence: "A word and a blow and the blow first," Carolinians would say. "Evil words cut mair than swords."[18] This ethic of violence in the backcountry was far removed from the chivalric ideals of the tidewater elite. It is interesting that the proverbs of the backcountry justified the use of violence only when it promised to succeed. The backsettlers said:

> Better a coward than a corpse.

> Better a living dog than a dead lion.

> He that fights and runs away
> Will live to fight another day.

Backcountry proverbs did not glorify fighting for its own sake, but fighting for the sake of winning. Here was an ethic of violence which had been formed in ambuscades and border-raiding. It had nothing to do with combats of chivalry or the idea of war as a gentleman's game. The classical example of this instrumental attitude toward violence was Andrew Jackson. A friend who knew him well for forty years said that "no man knew better than Andrew Jackson when to get into a passion and when not." James Parton commented that Jackson's anger was "a Scotch-Irish anger. It was fierce, but never had any ill effect upon his purposes; on the contrary, he made it serve him, sometimes, by seeming to be much more angry than he was; a way with others of his race."[19]

But backcountry violence also had another side. Andrew Jackson's strategy of controlled anger worked because most rage was genuine in this culture. Violence often consisted of blind, unthinking acts of savagery by men and women who were unable to control their own feelings. Much backcountry violence occurred within the family. Visitors recorded with horror the vio-

---

[17] Edward L. Ayers, *Vengeance and Justice: Crime and Punishment in the Nineteenth-Century American South* (New York, 1984), 111.

[18] *North Carolina Folklore*, I, 500.

[19] Parton, *Andrew Jackson*, I, 112–13.

lence of parents against children, husbands against wives, and friends against neighbors.[20]

An example was Russell Bean, the first white child born to permanent settlers in what is now the state of Tennessee. He was of Scottish border stock—the family name was originally Baines— and he became a figure of high eminence in the backcountry. His life was filled with violence. In 1789 he was found guilty of beating and kicking the wife of a neighbor. In 1801 he went to New Orleans for a long period, and on his return found that his wife had given birth to an infant who could not have been his own. In a rage, Russell Bean took the child from its cradle, drew out his hunting knife and cut off its ears, declaring that he "had marked it so that it would not get mixed up with his children." A warrant was issued for Russell Bean's arrest. He was brought to justice, found guilty of maiming an infant, and sentenced to be branded with the letter M on the brawn of the thumb. Justice was swift in the backcountry. Bean's hand was instantly lashed to the bar, and the red-hot branding iron was applied. But the defendant remained as violent as ever. When his hand was released, he bit out the brand with his teeth, and spat the charred and bleeding flesh defiantly on the courtroom floor.[21]

These backcountry order ways created an exceptionally violent world. In the eighteenth century, travelers often commented upon the frequency of murders and assaults in that region. Backcountry bandits were as brutal and sadistic as border raiders had been. In 1767, for example, Carolina newspapers reported that robbers seized a man named Davis and tortured him at his own hearth with red-hot irons until he told them where his money was hidden. Then they burned his farm for their amusement, and "left the poor man tied to behold all in flames." This gang included members of the infamous Moon family and the Black brothers, who sometimes mutilated their victims for sport. These backcountry bandits often worked in family groups. Some of the most violent members were women.[22]

Violence continued to be characteristic of the southern highlands for many years. An example was Edgefield District, South Carolina, a backcountry area which was known for its extraordinary violence from the eighteenth century to the twentieth. Par-

[20] Woodmason, *Carolina Backcountry,* 133.
[21] Paul M. Fink, "Russell Bean, Tennessee's First Native Son," *ETHSP* 37 (1965), 35, 39.
[22] Charleston *South Carolina Gazette and Country Journal,* 28 July, 4 Aug. 1767; quoted in Rachel Klein, "The Rise of the Planters in the South Carolina Backcountry, 1767–1808" (thesis, Yale, 1979), 66.

son Weems made its violence the subject of a chapbook called *The Devil in Petticoats,* in which one character exclaims, "What! Old Edgefield again! Another murder in Edgefield! . . . for sure it must be pandemonium itself, a very district of devils." In 1850, the South Carolina legislature found a "vast number of crimes in Edgefield," and a homicide rate twice the average of the state. After the Civil War, the congressional investigation of the Ku Klux Klan found that Edgefield was "the most violent region in the state." The mayhem continues even to our own time.[23] Similar patterns also appeared in Hardin County, Kentucky, in parts of East Texas, and in Williamson County, Illinois, which, with the area of that state called Little Egypt, is culturally part of the backcountry.[24]

This world of endemic violence and retributive justice was very similar to the British borderlands, where for many centuries people had been forced to conquer their own peace. Well into the eighteenth century, the borders remained "a region notorious for its continuing lawlessness."[25] As late as 1714, Sir Henry Liddell presented his friend William Cotesworth with a pair of pocket pistols and advised him "never to travel without them."[26] In Cumberland, justices carried arms on the bench, and the public expenditures of the county included daggers for use of the judges.[27]

This border violence was highly instrumental in its nature, and was often encouraged by local elites. In 1712, for example, the board of directors of a powerful coal cartel in the North of England, "including gentlemen and citizens of the highest repute," openly exhorted their tenants to "cut-up" a "wagonway" that belonged to a rival group.[28]

Here was yet another continuity which extended from the border country of North Britain to the backcountry in the eighteenth century, and to the southern highlands in our own time.[29]

---

[23]Jack Kenny Williams, *Vogues in Villainy: Crime and Retribution in Ante-bellum South Carolina* (Columbia, 1959), 4; Allen Trelease, *White Terror: The Ku Klux Klan Conspiracy and Southern Reconstruction* (New York, 1971), 72, 349.

[24]Paul M. Angle, *Bloody Williamson: A Chapter in American Lawlessness* (New York, 1973); Henry P. Lundsgaarde, *Murder in Space City: A Cultural Analysis of Houston Homicide Patterns* (New York, 1977).

[25]Hughes, *North Country Life: The North East,* 12–25.

[26]*Ibid.,* 19; see also expenditures for pistols and holsters in Daniel Fleming Account Books, 16 March 1661, passim; ms. WD/R/199, CUMROK.

[27]Fleming Account Book, 25 April 1665, ms. WD/R/199, CUMROK.

[28]Hughes, *North Country Life,* 16.

[29]Tough, *The Last Years of a Frontier,* 147–86.

❧ Backcountry Power Ways:
The Politics of Personal Government

This system of order gave rise to a special style of backcountry politics which was far removed from classical ideas of democracy and aristocracy. It was a highly distinctive type of polity which Charles Lee appropriately called "macocracy"—that is, "rule by the race of Macs."[1] This system of macocracy was a structure of highly personal politics without deference to social rank. In that respect it was very different from Virginia. In the early eighteenth century, William Byrd observed of the back settlements, "They are rarely guilty of flattering or making any court to their governors, but treat them with all the excesses of freedom and familiarity."[2] It was also a polity without strong political institutions, and in that regard very far removed from New England. There was comparatively little formal structure to local government— no town meetings, no vestries, no commissions, and courts of uncertain authority. But within the same broad tradition of self-government common to all English-speaking people, the borderers of North Britain easily improvised their own politics.

In the year 1770, an instance occurred aboard an emigrant ship which carried Major Pierce Butler, a high-born Anglo-Irish aristocrat who was destined to become part of the South Carolina elite. Soon after they sailed, Major Butler and his fellow travelers, in cabin and steerage alike, improvised a government of English laws and liberties for the duration of their voyage. One of them wrote:

> Being so many we found it necessary to form ourselves into an assembly, and meet from time to time as occasion required. We made rules and established order amongst ourselves, for future regulation, and one of the first concerns that came before us was the due observation of the first day of the week. The assembly came to this result, viz that the first day of the week shall be set apart . . . for the performance of religious worship; and whereas men differ in their opinions as to the mode of religious worship, that everyone may enjoy liberty of conscience and have an opportunity of performing religious worship according to the mode and opinion of that particular church or people of which he or she is a member. . . . to give Major Butler his due, he interested himself much in behalf in setting up these meetings.[3]

[1] Bridenbaugh, *Myths and Realities*, 132.
[2] William Byrd, *History of the Dividing Line*, ed. William Boyd (Raleigh, 1929), 207.
[3] Joseph Oxley, "Joseph's Offering to His Children," ms. memoir, 377–78 (1770), HSP.

Many American historians have observed this same process of political improvisation at work on the frontiers of settlement. Some attribute it to the frontier itself. But as Pierce Butler and British companions demonstrated, the process was fully at work before they reached the American shore. Their spontaneous shipboard polity rose not from the American environment but from their British culture, and it became an important ingredient of backcountry politics.

Another feature of this backcountry "macocracy" was strong personal leadership. The politics of the back settlements were dominated by leaders who possessed a quality called "influence" or 'interest." David Caldwell, one of the leaders of Lunenberg County in backcountry Virginia, was described as "a man of great interest in the county."[4] Colonel Thomas Fletchall of Fair Forest Creek in Carolina was described as having "great influence in that part of the country." Another wrote, "Col. Fletchall has all of those people at his beck, and reigns among them like a little king."[5] Another example was Colonel Richard Richardson, of St. Mark Parish, South Carolina. He had moved south from Virginia, married into the backcountry ascendancy, acquired a large property called Big Home, commanded a regiment of militia in the Cherokee War of 1760, and became the leading man in his part of the country. It was said that he was:

> judge and arbiter of most . . . feuds, bickerings and dissensions, and possessed an equity jurisdiction from the Santee to the North-Carolina boundary. . . . His family residence frequently presented the appearance of the assizes, and few, if any, even of the disappointed parties, ever left his hospitable board and cordial welcome with an inclination to dispute his position, or appeal to law.[6]

These "men of influence" could be found in most parts of the backcountry. They tended to be large landowners, magistrates, merchants, surveyors, millers and speculators—often all at once. But the "influence" and "interest" of these men had narrow limits. The authority of office or rank counted for very little, as many travelers observed:

> Of what dignity is a North Carolina Justice in these times the following incident will show, which happened immediately after our

---

[4]Beeman, *Evolution of the Southern Backcountry*, 92.

[5]Oliver Hart, "Diary . . . ," *Journal of the South Carolina Baptist Society* I (1975), 94; quoted in Klein, "Rise of Planters," 94.

[6]Joseph Johnson, *Traditions and Reminiscences of the American Revolution in the South* (Charleston, 1851), 158–60; as quoted in Richard Maxwell Brown, *The South Carolina Regulators* (Cambridge, 1963), 26, whose account I follow on Richardson.

arrival. A young man who rode up after us, offered his hand to another whom he found here but it was not accepted, because the latter fancied the man had injured him on some former occasion.

After a brief exchange of words, there was a challenge, and both young men, laying aside their coats and shirts, hurriedly prepared themselves for a boxing-match, which took place on the spot, in front of the house and in the presence of the Justice of the peace. Women, children and blacks gathered around, the women exclaiming at the contempt shown for the officer's house.

The Justice himself stepped forward with folded arms and tranquil demeanor, and once, twice, three times bade the combatants to keep the peace, withdrew with the same measured step, and looked on in cold blood. Outraged at the disobedience, the Justice's wife appeared and repeated the commands of her husband, but was received with derision. Finally the antagonists cooled, shook hands by the fighting code, and each rode on his way.

"By the law, must they not give obedience to your commands," I asked the squire, "and abstain from their squabbling in your presence?"

"They should," was the answer.

"Well! and could you not bring them into court for their behavior, and have them punished?"

"I could," was the second laconic answer of the good-natured Justice, who seemed to make far less of the matter than his indignant wife, and was of the opinion that it was more in keeping with his official worth to pass over an apparent slight.[7]

Worse indignities were suffered by other backcountry magistrates. In 1767, when several gentlemen justices in South Carolina tried to bring some "banditti" to trial, the magistrates themselves were seized and tried before a kangaroo court by the intended defendants. One justice was dragged eighty miles at a horse's tail.[8]

Men who rose to positions of leadership in this culture commonly did so by bold and decisive acts. An example comes from the life of Andrew Jackson. In the late eighteenth century, Jackson was in the backcountry hamlet of Jonesboro, Tennessee, for a court day. At midnight, fire suddenly broke out in a stable, and ignited a large quantity of hay. An eyewitness recalled:

The alarm filled the streets with lawyers, judges, ladies in their nightdresses, and a concourse of strangers and citizens. General Jackson no sooner entered the street than he assumed the com-

---

[7]Schoepf, *Travels*, II, 124.
[8]South Carolina *Gazette*, 19 Oct. 1767, quoted in Klein, "Rise of Planters," 66.

mand. It seemed to be conceded to him. He shouted for buckets, and formed two lines of men reaching from the fire to a stream that ran through the town; one line to pass the empty buckets to the stream, and the other to return them full to the fire. He ordered the roofs of the tavern and of the houses most exposed to be covered with wet blankets, and stationed men on the roofs to keep them wet. Amidst the shrieks of the women, and the frightful neighing of the burning horses, every order was distinctly heard and obeyed. In the line up which the buckets passed, the bank of the stream soon became so slippery that it was difficult to stand. While General Jackson was strengthening that part of the line, a drunken coppersmith, named Boyd, who said he had seen fires at Baltimore, began to give orders and annoy persons in the line.

"Fall into line!" shouted the General.

The man continued jabbering. Jackson seized a bucket by the handle, knocked him down, and walked along the line giving his orders as coolly as before. *He saved the town!*[9]

The politics of the backcountry consisted mainly of charismatic leaders and personal followings, cemented by strong and forceful acts such as Jackson's behavior at Jonesboro. The rhetoric that these leaders used sometimes sounded democratic, but it was easily misunderstood by those who were not part of this folk culture. The Jacksonian movement was a case in point. To easterners, Andrew Jackson looked and sounded like a Democrat. But in his own culture, his rhetoric had a very different function. Historian Thomas Abernethy observes that Andrew Jackson never championed the cause of the people; he merely invited the people to champion him. This was a style of politics which placed a heavy premium upon personal loyalty. In the American backcountry, as on the British borders, loyalty was the most powerful cement of political relationships. Disloyalty was the primary political sin.

Andrew Jackson's political style was explicitly drawn from the borders of North Britain. He required his wards to read the history of the Scottish chieftains whom he deeply admired and made the models for his own acts. The memory of the great border captains continued to inspire leaders in the backcountry for many generations.[10] This system of politics was nourished on its mem-

[9]Parton, *Andrew Jackson*, I, 163.

[10]Remini, *Andrew Jackson*, I, 8; on politics in the British borderlands see Robert Hopkinson, "Elections at Appleby, 1700/01–1714/15" (B.A. dissertation, Univ. of Newcastle-upon-Tyne, 1968); *idem*, "Elections in Cumberland and Westmorland, 1695–1713" (thesis, Univ. of Newcastle-upon-Tyne, 1973).

ories. Andrew Jackson always remembered the stories that his mother told him about aristocratic oppression and the cruelties of rack-renting landlords in the old country.[11] The result was a very strong tradition which John Roche has called "retrospective radicalism." The folk memory operated as a powerful political amplifier when triggered by symbolic events.

There were many different ethnic groups in the backcountry. But it is interesting that this region never developed anything like the ethnic politics of Pennsylvania. For many generations, back-country politics were mainly a collision of highly personal factions and followings, rather than ethnic blocs or ideological parties or social classes. Charismatic appeals carried elections, which tended to be decided on questions of personal style.

Voting qualifications were highly permissive in this region, and even more permissively enforced. One bizarre bylaw in the bor-ough of Campbellton, North Carolina, allowed any man to vote who came within two miles of the polls on election day.[12] Turn-out, however, tended to be low. In those parts of the Virginia backcountry where elections were held, participation was com-monly in the range of 15 to 25 percent—the lowest in British America before 1776.[13]

This polity was in part the consequence of frontier condi-tions—of sparse settlements and a new territory. But it also reflected a political spirit which had existed on the borders of North Britain.

---

[11] *Ibid.*, I, 15.

[12] Chilton Williamson, *American Suffrage from Property to Democracy* (Princeton, 1960), 18.

[13] Turnout in the backcountry Virginia counties was as follows, as a percentage of adult white male tithables:

Year	County	Turnout
1755	Frederick Co., Va.	18.9%
1786–89	Albemarle Co., Va.	23.2%
	Culpeper Co., Va.	16.7%
	Orange Co., Va.	20.7%

Source: Charles S. Sydnor, *Gentlemen Freeholders* (Chapel Hill, 1952), 142, corrected for pop-ulation growth; and Lucille Griffith, *The Virginia House of Burgesses, 1750–1774* (University, Ala., 1968), 168.

❧ Backcountry Freedom Ways: The Border Idea of Natural Liberty

The backsettlers, no less than other colonists in every part of British America, brought with them a special way of thinking about power and freedom, and a strong attachment to their liberties. As early as the middle decades of the eighteenth century their political documents contained many references to liberty as their British birthright. In 1768, the people of Mecklenberg County, North Carolina, declared, "We shall ever be more ready to support the government under which we find the most liberty."[1]

No matter whether they came from the England or Scotland or Ireland, their libertarian ideas were very much alike—and profoundly different from notions of liberty that had been carried to Massachusetts, Virginia and Pennsylvania. The traveler Johann Schoepf was much interested in ideas of law and liberty which he found in the backcountry. "They shun everything which appears to demand of them law and order, and anything that preaches constraint," Schoepf wrote of the backsettlers. "They hate the name of a justice, and yet they are not transgressors. Their object is merely wild. Altogether, natural freedom . . . is what pleases them."[2]

This idea of "natural freedom" was widespread throughout the southern back settlements. But it was not a reflexive response to the "frontier" environment, nor was it "merely wild," as Schoepf believed. The backcountry idea of natural liberty was created by a complex interaction between the American environment and a European folk culture. It derived in large part from the British border country, where anarchic violence had long been a condition of life. The natural liberty of the borderers was an idea at once more radically libertarian, more strenuously hostile to ordering institutions than were the other cultures of British America.

In 1692, for example, a British borderer named Thomas Brockbank, who had been born and raised in the county of Westmorland, sent a letter to his parents on the subject of natural liberty. "Honored parents," he wrote, "liberty is a thing which every animate creature does naturally desire, yea and even vegetables

---

[1]Norris W. Preyer, *Hezekiah Alexander and the Revolution in the Backcountry* (Charlotte, 1987), 66.

[2]Schoepf, *Travels*, 238–39.

themselves also seem to have a great tendency towards it. But man, the perfection of the vast creation, who is endowed with a rational soul, does more eagerly pursue freedom, because he has knowledge and can give a just estimate of the true value thereof."[3]

In North Britain this idea of natural liberty as something which "every animate creature does naturally desire, yea and even vegetables themselves," was rapidly in process of decay during the eighteenth century. But in the hour of its extinction, it was carried to the American back settlements, where conditions conspired to give it new life. The remoteness of the population from centers of government and the absence of any material necessity for large-scale organization created an environment in which natural liberty flourished.

A leading advocate of natural liberty in the eighteenth century was Patrick Henry, a descendant of British borderers, and also a product of the American backcountry. Throughout his political career, Patrick Henry consistently defended the principles of minimal government, light taxes, and the right of armed resistance to authority in all cases which infringed liberty.

In the first great issue that brought him to notice—the court case called the Parsons Cause—Patrick Henry amazed his audience in the backcountry courthouse of Hanover County, Virginia, by arguing that the King, in disallowing an obscure act of 1758, had "degenerated into a tyrant and forfeit[ed] all rights to his subjects' obedience."[4] The tidewater gentry were astounded by this argument. An eyewitness on that occasion remembered that "amongst some gentlemen in the crowd behind me, was a confused murmur of 'treason, treason!'" But the backcountry jury was "highly pleased with these doctrines."[5]

The fame that Patrick Henry won by this address carried him to a prominent career in the House of Burgesses, where he made an even greater reputation by arguing that Virginia was too much governed, and by leading a crusade against the "spirit of favoritism" that lay at the center of Virginia's oligarchical tidewater government.

He is even better remembered for his headlong assault upon

---

[3]Richard Trappes-Lomax, "The Diary and Letterbook of the Rev. Thomas Brockbank, 1671–1719," *CHSP* n.s. 89 (1930), 44.

[4]Tyler, *Patrick Henry*, 418.

[5]*Ibid.*

*Patrick Henry gave classic expression to backcountry ideals of natural liberty.
This great revolutionary leader, who is still remembered as a tribune of the
people, was in fact a high-born backcountry gentleman whose forebears were
closely related to powerful and highly cultivated North British families. Patrick
Henry himself was the nephew of William Robertson, the Scottish historian and
rector of the University of Edinburgh. He was also the cousin of Lord
Brougham of Brougham Hall, Westmorland, the great English Whig reformer
who was educated at Edinburgh, and whose home lay very near the North British border. Patrick Henry's idea of natural liberty was itself a border folkway
that took root in the American back settlements and still flourishes in the United
States today. His mother described the American Revolution as another set of
"lowland troubles."*

the Stamp Act, in a speech that threatened the King of England with tyrannicide: "Caesar had his Brutus," he declaimed, "Charles the First his Cromwell, and George the Third . . ."— and he was stopped short by the tidewater gentry who had felt Henry's lash upon their own backs. Patrick Henry went on to introduce the Virginia Resolves, which ended by declaring that all who dissented from his view of the question should be treated as an "enemy to this his Majesty's Colony"—a classical expression of the intolerance for contrary opinions which was part of the backcountry's idea of natural liberty.[6]

A decade later, Patrick Henry was a member of the first Continental Congress, and startled that body by arguing that as a result of the passage of Parliament's Intolerable Acts, "Government is dissolved." Henry insisted that "we are in a state of nature, sir!"[7] Congressmen from Pennsylvania and Massachusetts were as shocked as Virginia's Burgesses had been. One described Patrick Henry as "in religious matters a saint; but the very Devil in politics."[8]

In 1788, Patrick Henry led the opposition to the new national Constitution, primarily on the grounds that strong government of any sort was hostile to liberty:

> When the American spirit was in its youth, the language of America was different: liberty, sir, was then the primary object. We are descended from a people whose government was founded on liberty; our glorious forefathers of Great Britain made liberty the foundation of everything. That country is become a great, mighty and splendid nation; not because their government is strong and energetic, but sir because liberty is its direct end and foundation. We drew the spirit of liberty from our British ancestors; by that spirit we have triumphed over every difficulty. But now, sir, the American spirit, assisted by the ropes and chains of consolidation, is about to convert this country into a powerful empire. . . .[9]

[6]For two versions of this event, see *American Historical Review* 26 (1921) 745–46; and Leon G. Tyler, *Letters and Times of the Tylers* (3 vols., New York, 1884–96), I, 56; four versions of the Virginia resolves are printed in Edmund S. Morgan, ed., *Prologue to Revolution: Sources and Documents of the Stamp Act Crisis* (Chapel Hill, 1959), 46–50.

[7]Tyler, *Patrick Henry*, 111.

[8]William Meade, *Old Churches, Ministers and Families of Virginia* (2 vols., 1857, rpt. Baltimore, 1966), I, 220.

[9]Jonathan Elliot, *Debates in the Several State Conventions on the Adoption of the Federal Constitution* (5 vols., 1836–45), III, 53–54.

These attitudes were broadly shared in Appalachia. "The Friends of Liberty will expect support from the back people," Patrick Henry wrote in 1787. They got it.[10]

Patrick Henry's ideas of natural liberty were not learned from treatises on political theory. His idea of a "state of nature" was not the philosophical abstraction that it had been for Locke. Thomas Jefferson said of Patrick Henry with only some exaggeration that "he read nothing, and had no books."[11] Henry's lawyer-biographer William Wirt wrote, "Of the science of law he knew almost nothing; of the practical law he was so wholly ignorant that he was not only unable to draw a declaration or a plea, but incapable, it is said, of the most common or simple business of his profession, even of the mode of ordering a suit, giving a notice, or making a motion in court."[12]

Patrick Henry's principles of natural liberty were drawn from the political folkways of the border culture in which he grew up. He embibed them from his mother, a lady who described the American Revolution as merely another set of "lowland troubles."[13] The libertarian phrases and thoughts which echoed so strongly in the backcountry had earlier been heard in the borders of North Britain. When the backcountry people celebrated the supremacy of private interests they used the same thoughts and words as William Cotesworth, an English borderer who in 1717 declared: ". . . you know how natural it is to pursue private interest even against that Darling principle of a more general good. . . . It is the interest of the Public to be served by the man that can do it cheapest, though several private persons are injured by it."[14]

This idea of natural liberty was not a reciprocal idea. It did not recognize the right of dissent or disagreement. Deviance from cultural norms was rarely tolerated; opposition was suppressed by force. One of Andrew Jackson's early biographers observed that "It appears to be more difficult for a North-of-Irelander than for other men to allow an honest difference of opinion in an oppo-

[10]Patrick Henry to Thomas Madison, 21 Oct. 1787, NYPL; quoted in Robert Douthat Meade, *Patrick Henry, Practical Revolutionary* (Philadelphia, 1969), 334.

[11]Tyler, *Patrick Henry,* 12.

[12]William Wirt, *Sketches of the Life and Character of Patrick Henry* (Hartford, n.d.), 18.

[13]J. Lewis Peyton, *History of Augusta County, Virginia* (2d ed., Bridgewater, Va., 1953), 345.

[14]Hughes, *North Country Life: The North East,* 39.

nent, so that he is apt to regard the terms opponent and enemy as synonymous."[15]

When backcountrymen moved west in search of that condition of natural freedom which Daniel Boone called "elbow room," they were repeating the thought of George Harrison, a North Briton who declared in the borderlands during the seventeenth century that "every man at nature's table has a right to elbow room." The southern frontier provided space for the realization of this ideal, but it did not create it.[16]

This libertarian idea of natural freedom as "elbow room" was very far from the ordered freedom of New England towns, the hegemonic freedom of Virginia's county oligarchs, and the reciprocal freedom of Pennsylvania Quakers. Here was yet another freedom way which came to be rooted in the culture of an American region, where it flourished for many years to come.

[15]Ayers, *Vengeance and Justice*, 22.
[16]George Harrison, "Every Man at Nature's Table Has a Right to Elbow Room," *FHSJ* 21 (1924), 27–30.

CONCLUSION

❧ Four British Folkways in American History:
The Origin and Persistence of Regional Cultures in the
United States

> Colonies then are the Seeds of Nations, begun and
> nourished by the care of wise and populous Coun-
> tries; as conceiving them best for the increase of
> Humane Stock.
>
> —William Penn, 1681

INDEPENDENCE DID NOT MARK THE END of the four British folkways in America, or of the regional cultures which they
inspired. The history of the United States is, in many ways the
story of their continuing interaction. Most broad areas of consensus in American life have grown from values that these cultures
shared in common. Many major conflicts in American history
have developed primarily from their differences. Every presidential election shows their persistent power in American politics.
Every decennial census finds that cultural differences between
American regions are greater in some ways than those between
European nations.

The persistence of regional culture in the United States
explains many things about American history. In particular, it
helps to answer the question which led to this inquiry, about the
determinants of a voluntary society. By way of a summary and
conclusion, it might be useful to examine in a general way the
origins and development of the four British folkways, and their
relationship with the main lines of American history from the
great migrations of the seventeeth century, to our own time.

❧ Genesis: The British Reconnaissance of North America

In the beginning, there was a neglected half-century of Anglo-American history which preceded the four great migrations. From 1580 to 1630, more than thirty English settlements were planted in what is now the eastern United States. Many survived, and a few remain culturally distinctive even today.[1]

On Smith and Tangier islands in the Chesapeake Bay, for example, immigrants from the far southwest of Britain founded a culture which still preserves the dialect of seventeenth century Cornwall and Devon (*zink* for sink, *noyce* for nice). At Plymouth in southeastern New England, another variety of English culture

[1]Atlantic settlements planted in the present United States between 1606 and 1625 include:

State	Date by	Settlement	Location	Leader
Me.	1607	Sagadahoc	Kennebec River	George Popham
	1612	St. Croix	St. Croix Island	Jesuit Mission
	1612	St. Johns	near Calais	Men of St. Malo
	1613	St. Sauveur	Mt. Desert Island	Pierre Biard
	1613	Matinicus	near Mt. Desert I.	Fishermen
	1616	Winter Harbor	Saco River	Richard Vines
	1622	Damariscove	Damariscove Island	Sir Ferd. Gorges
	1622	Monhegan	Monhegan Island	Fishermen
	1622	Isle of Shoals	Isle of Shoals	Fishermen
	1623	Quack	York	Chris. Levett
	1623	Cape Newagen	Boothbay	Fishermen
	1623	Pemaquid	Pemaquid Point	Fishermen
N.H.	1623	Rendezvous Pt.	Odiorne's Point	David Thomson
	1623	Cochecho	Dover	Wm. and Ed. Hilton
Mass.	1620	New Plymouth	Plymouth	John Carver
	1622	Wessagusset	Weymouth	Thos. Weston
	1622	Natascot	Hull	John Lyford
	1623	Nantasket	Nantasket	Thomas Gray
	1623	Cape Ann	Gloucester	Thos. Gardner
	1623	Wessagusset	Weymouth	Robert Gorges
	1624	Conant's I.	Mass. Bay	Roger Conant
	1624	Winnissimmet	Chelsea	Samuel Maverick
	1624	Shawmut	Boston	Wm. Blackstone
	1624	Mishawum	Charlestown	Thos. Walford
	1625	Passonagessit	Quincy	Thos. Wollaston
	1626	Naumkeag	Salem	John White
	1625?	Thompson's I.	Mass. Bay	David Thomson
Conn.	1624	E. Settlement	Connecticut River	Dutch W.I. Co.
N.Y.	1624	Fort Nassau	Castle Island	Dutch W.I. Co.
	1624	Fort Orange	Hudson River	Dutch W.I. Co.
	1624	Governors I.	Governors I.	Dutch W.I. Co.
	1625	Fort Amsterdam	Manhattan I.	Dutch W.I. Co.
N.J.	1624	W. Settlement	Hudson River	Dutch W.I. Co.
Pa.	1624	S. Settlement	Delaware River	Dutch W.I. Co.
Md.	by 1625	Kent Island	Chesapeake Bay	Wm. Claiborne
Va.	1607	Jamestown	James River	Virginia Co.
	by 1629	Smith I.	Chesapeake Bay	Eng. Fishermen
	by 1629	Tangier I.	Chesapeake Bay	Eng. Fishermen

was introduced by the *Mayflower* Pilgrims who were very different from the Massachusetts Puritans; even today this small sub-region still calls itself the "Old Colony," and speaks a strain of English which is subtly distinctive from other Yankee accents. On New England's north shore from Marblehead to Maine yet another culture was planted by fishermen from Jersey, Guernsey and English channel ports; their folkways still survive in small towns and offshore islands from Kittery to the Cranberry Islands.[2]

In Massachusetts Bay, an eccentric Devon family called Maverick settled the present town of Chelsea and an island in Boston harbor that still bears their name. They had trouble with the Puritans and moved away, keeping one jump ahead of the larger cultures that threatened to engulf them. By the nineteenth century, the Mavericks had found their way onto the western plains. Their name was given to range cattle that bore no man's brand, and became a synonym for independent eccentricity in American speech.[3]

Many such "mavericks" settled America before 1630. The Balch and Conant families, to name but two, both arrived in Massachusetts before the Winthrop fleet and are still known in New England for going their own way. Altogether these earliest English settlers added color and variety to the cultural mosaic of early America. But their primary role was to prepare the way for larger groups that followed. They were the reconnaissance parties of British America.[4]

❧ Exodus: The Four Great Migrations, 1629–1750

After 1629 the major folk movements began to occur, in the series of waves that are the subject of this book. As we have seen, the first wave (1629–40) was an exodus of English Puritans who came mainly from the eastern counties and planted in Massachusetts a very special culture with unique patterns of speech and

[2]There is much manuscript material on early Maine in the Devon Record Office and the Exeter City Library. Some of it has been published in Robert E. Moody, ed., *The Letters of Thomas Gorges, Deputy Governor of the Province of Maine, 1640–1643* (Portland, Me., 1978); see also Daniel Vickers, "Work and Life on the Fishing Periphery of Essex County, Massachusetts, 1630–1675," *CSMP* 63 (1984), 83–118; Edwin A. Churchill, "The Founding of Maine, 1600–1640: A Revisionist Interpretation," *MEHSQ* 18 (1978), 21–54; Charles E. Clark, "The Founding of Maine, 1600–1640, A Comment," *MEHSQ* 18 (1978), 55–62.

[3]"Maverick," *NEHGR* 69 (1915), 146–59.

[4]Clifford K. Shipton, *Roger Conant* (Cambridge, 1945).

architecture, distinctive ideas about marriage and the family, nucleated settlements, congregational churches, town meetings, and a tradition of ordered liberty.

The second wave brought to Virginia a different set of English folkways, mainly from a broad belt of territory that extended from Kent and Devon north to Northamptonshire and Warwickshire. This culture was characterized by scattered settlements, extreme hierarchies of rank, strong oligarchies, Anglican churches, a highly developed sense of honor and an idea of hegemonic liberty.

The third wave (ca. 1675–1715) was the Friends' migration, which carried yet another culture from the England's North Midlands to the Delaware Valley. It was founded on a Christian idea of spiritual equality, a work ethic of unusual intensity, a suspicion of social hierarchy, and an austerity which Max Weber called "worldly asceticism." It also preserved many elements of North Midland speech, architecture, dress and food ways. Most important, it deliberately created a pluralistic system of reciprocal liberty in the Delaware Valley.

The fourth great migration (1717–75) came to the backcountry from the borderlands of North Britain—an area which included the Scottish lowlands, the north of Ireland and England's six northern counties. These emigrants were of different ethnic stocks, but shared a common border culture which was unique in its speech, architecture, family ways and child-rearing customs. Its material culture was marked by extreme inequalities of condition, and its public life was dominated by a distinctive ideal of natural liberty.

Each of these four folk cultures in early America had a distinctive character which was closer to its popular reputation than to many academic "reinterpretations" in the twentieth century. The people in Puritan Massachusetts were in fact highly puritanical. They were not traditional peasants, modern capitalists, village communists, modern individualists, Renaissance humanists, Victorian moralists, neo-Freudian narcissists or prototypical professors of English literature. They were a people of their time and place who had an exceptionally strong sense of themselves, and a soaring spiritual purpose which has been lost beneath many layers of revisionist scholarship.

The first gentlemen of Virginia were truly cavaliers. They were not the pasteboard protagonists of Victorian fiction, or the celluloid heroes of *Gone with the Wind*. But neither were they self-made bourgeois capitalists, modern agro-businessmen, upwardly mobile yeomen or "plain folk." Most were younger sons of proud armigerous families with strong Royalist politics, a devout Anglican faith, decided rural prejudices, entrenched manorial ideals, exalted notions of their own honor and at least the rudiments of an Aristotelian education. The majority of Virginia's white population were indentured servants, landless tenants and poor whites—a degraded rural proletariat who had no hope of rising to the top of their society. Not a single ex-servant or son of a servant became a member of Virginia's House of Burgesses during the late seventeenth century. The mythical figures of Virginia cavaliers and poor whites were solidly founded in historical fact.

The culture of the Delaware Valley was dominated by British Quakers and German Pietists whose Christian beliefs had a special moral character. Here again, their culture has been distorted

Four English Folk Migrations: Modal Characteristics

Region of origin	East Anglia	South and West	North Midlands	Borderlands
American destination	Massachusetts	Virginia	Delaware Valley	Backcountry
Period of migration	1629–40	1642–75	1675–1715	1717–75
Duration of migration	11 years	33 years	40 years	57 years
Size of migration	21,000	ca. 45,000	23,000	ca. 250,000
Control of migration	Corporate	Royal Colony	Proprietary	Fragmented
Religion of migrants	Congregational	Anglican	Friends	Presbyterian and Anglican
Origin of immigrant elites	Puritan ministers and magistrates	Royalist younger sons of gentry and aristocracy	Quaker traders artisans and farmers	Border gentry and statesmen
Elite kin, nets and links	E. Anglian kin Cambridge net North Sea links	S. W. Eng. kin Oxford net London links	N. Midland kin Quaker net Atlantic links	Border kin Glasgow net Irish Sea links
Modal ranks of immigrants	Yeomanry and artisans	Laborers and servants	Farmers, artisans and traders	Tenants and cottagers
Occupation (% farmers)	33%	60%	40%	60%
(% artisans)	54%	30%	40%	30%
Residence: (% urban)	65%	35%	30%	20%
Sex ratio (males per 100 females)	140	500	250	160
Age composition (% 0–14)	31%	3%	24%	25%
(% 15–24)	26%	70%	35%	36%
(% 25–59)	42%	27%	38%	39%
(% 60 and up)	1%	0%	1%	1%
Family structure (% coming in families)	90%	20%	50%	70%

by historical revisionists who have variously "reinterpreted" them as utopian cranks, manipulative materialists, secular pluralists and the "first modern Americans." The modernity of the Delaware Valley has been much exaggerated, and the primitive Christian roots of William Penn's "holy experiment" have too often been forgotten.

The backsettlers also possessed a strong and vibrant culture which also has been much misunderstood. They were not ancient Celts, or wild Scotch-Irish savages, or innocent children of nature. Neither were they rootless pluralists, incipient entrepreneurs, agents of the Edinburgh enlightenment or heralds of the New South. The majority, no matter whether northern Irish, lowland Scots or North Country English, shared a culture of high integrity which had been tempered in fire of the British borderlands. The more we learn by empirical research about these four cultures of British America, the more distinctive they appear from one another, and the closer to historical "myths" which they inspired.

❧ British Origins: The Regional Factor

The origins of these cultures were highly complex, involving differences of British region, religion, rank, and generation, as well as of the American environment, and the process of migration. Let us briefly examine each of these determinants, beginning with British regions—not because this factor was more important than any other, but because it has been less clearly understood.

The idea of a region creates few practical problems for American historians, who tend normally to think in regional terms without reflecting very much about them. In English historiography, however, region remains an alien concept. The history of England is highly developed on national and local levels, but a third level is missing in between. So little has been written about the history of English regions that in a formal sense there is no regional historiography at all—that is, no established set of regional *problematiques*.[5]

---

[5]Signs of change appear in the founding of English journals called *Northern History* (1966), *Midland History* (1971), and *Southern History* (1979). But few articles in these journals are truly regional in nature; most run to national or local history. Even the manifestos that called these journals into being were reluctant to make strong claims for regional history. One called it "provincial history," and argued that it should be "outward looking" rather than "inward look-

Regional history has long flourished in France, Germany, Italy, Spain and even in smaller countries such as Belgium, Switzerland, Sweden and the Netherlands. England is unique in the exceptional riches of its national and local historiography and the poverty of its regional research.[6]

This has been so not because England is more uniform than other nations, but because its internal differences are more complex. To travel across the English countryside is to be continuously surprised by the complexity of its cultural terrain. One meets many different ideas of spatial discrimination which have the collective effect of blurring regional perceptions. The leading regional ideas might be summarized in a few sentences:

Zones are topographical units popularized by Cyril Fox, who divided England into a "highland zone" (the north and west) and a "lowland zone" (the south and east), each supporting different cultures.[7]

Pays in English usage are soil regions and agricultural regimes. Leading examples are David Underdown's elegant essay on "the chalk and the cheese," and Joan Thirsk's meticulous studies of wood pasture and open pasture, "fielden, forest, fell and fen."[8]

---

ing" (see Asa Briggs, "Themes in Northern History," *NH* I (1966)). Only in the 1980s did the number of genuinely regional essays increase.

Other harbingers of change are centers for regional history at the universities of East Anglia, Exeter and Leeds. But again much of their work is not regional but local or national in its conception. The oldest and strongest of these centers is the Centre of East Anglian Studies at the University of East Anglia. But comparatively little of its research is devoted to the region as a unit. The largest project under way at the Centre of East Anglian studies is a building survey of Norwich—a very useful project, but not an exercise in regional history. See Janice Henney, ed., *East Anglian Studies: Theses Completed* (Norwich, 1982).

Still, the important beginnings have been made. A new series of monographs on English regional history began to appear in 1986—another sign of growing interest in this field.

[6] John Langton, an English geographer who is swimming against the tide, writes that "relatively little regional geography has been written about England"; see "The Industrial Revolution and the Regional Geography of England," *IGBT*, n.s. 9 (1984), 145–67. Strong arguments against regional models have come from British geographers and historians, at the same time that colleagues in other nations have been moving the other way. See G.H.T. Kimble, "The Inadequacy of the Regional Concept," in L. D. Stamp and S. W. Wooldridge, eds., *London Essays in Geography* (London, 1951). This antiregional bias is especially strong among middle-class Londoners (as it also tends to be in New Yorkers and Parisians) who divide their country into the "metropolis" and the "provinces."

[7] Cyril Fox, *The Personality of Britain* (Cardiff, 1932); Joan Thirsk, "The Farming Regions of England and Wales," in Thirsk, ed., *The Agrarian History of England and Wales: IV, 1500–1640* (Cambridge, 1967), 1–112; John D. Gay, *The Geography of Religion in England* (London, 1971); R. T. Mason, *Framed Buildings of England* (Horsham, 1974); Eric Mercer, *English Vernacular Houses* (London, 1975).

[8] David Underdown, "The Chalk and the Cheese," *PP* 85 (1979), 129–54; Thirsk, "The Farming Regions of England and Wales," 1–112. Thirsk asks, "Was it generally true that pastoral regions were also the most fertile seedbeds for Puritanism and dissent?" In the 17th cen-

Principates refer to ancient sovereignties, which tend to be strong sources of regional identity throughout Europe. They are weaker in England where national unity came early, but the ancient kingdoms of East Anglia, Wessex, Mercia and Northumbria still survive as regional conceptions.

Counties are more than administrative units; many of England's collective memories are organized by counties. Its archives are lodged in county offices, its military traditions are kept by county regiments, its gentry were defined by county visitations, and its scholarship is written in county histories. County consciousness was even stronger in the past; one historian asserts that "when an Englishman of the early seventeenth century said, 'my country' he meant 'my county.'"[9] Most regional taxonomies in English scholarship today are county-clusters.[10]

---

tury, antiquarians such as John Aubrey used soil types to explain differences in dialect in Wiltshire. "In North Wiltshire and the Vale of Gloucestershire (a dirty clayey country)," he wrote, "the Indigenae or Aborigines speak drawling. They are phlegmatique, skins pale and livid, slow and dull, heavy of spirit." *The Natural History of Wiltshire* (1862, rpt. New York, 1969), 11.

[9]Lawrence Stone, *The Causes of the English Revolution, 1529–1642* (New York, 1972), 106; Many historians have argued that the "county community" was the most important unit of identity in Civil War. The seminal work was done by A. M. Everitt, "The County Community," in E. W. Ives, ed., *The English Revolution, 1600–1660*, (London, 1968), 49; *idem, The Local Community in the English Civil War*, Historical Association Pamphlet G70 (1969); *idem, Change in the Provinces: The Seventeenth Century* (Leicester University Department of Local History, Occasional Papers, 2d ser., I, 1969).

Other "county community" studies include W. B. Willcox, *Gloucestershire, 1590–1640* (New Haven, 1940); Thomas Garden Barnes, *Somerset 1625–1640: A County's Government during the Personal Rule* (Cambridge, Mass., 1961); C. W. Chalkin, *Seventeenth Century Kent: A Social and Economic History* (London, 1965); Alan Everitt, *The Community of Kent and the Great Rebellion, 1640–1660* (Leicester, 1966); J. S. Morrill, *Cheshire 1630–1660: County Government and Society during the English Revolution* (Oxford, 1974); Anthony Fletcher, *Sussex 1600–1660: A County Community in Peace and War* (London, 1975); J. T. Cliffe, *The Yorkshire Gentry from the Reformation to the Civil War* (1969); B. G. Blackwood, *The Lancashire Gentry and the Great Rebellion, 1640–1660* (1978); Clive Holmes, *Seventeenth Century Lincolnshire* (Lincoln, 1980).

A second generation of studies, as yet unpublished but made available to the author in manuscript, tends to stress the permeability of county communities and the importance of connections that carried across county lines—thus opening a quasi-regional consciousness.

[10]In a pioneering regional history of England, series editors Barry Cunliffe and David Hey write, "English regional identities are imprecise, and no firm boundaries can be drawn . . . any attempt to define a region must be somewhat arbitrary, particularly in the midlands . . . yet regional differences are nonetheless real. . . . People still feel that they belong to a particular region within England as a whole." Their taxonomy uses the following county-clusters:

Northern Counties (Cumb., Dur., Nhumb., Tyne and Wear, N. Cleve.); *Lancashire/Cheshire* (Lancs., Ches., Mersey, Gr. Mancs.); *Yorkshire* (N., S., W. Yorks.; S. Cleve., N. Humberside); *West Midlands* (Salop, Staffs., W. Mid., Here. and Worcs., Warw., Glocs.); *East Midlands* (Derby, Notts., S. Humber, Lincs., Leics.); *South Midlands* (Northants., Oxon., Beds., Bucks., Herts., NW London); *Eastern Counties* (Norf., Suff., Essex, Cambs., NE London); *South West* (Devon., Cornwall); *Wessex* (Avon, Wilts., Berks., Hants., Dorset, Somerset); *South East* (Surrey, Kent, E. and W. Sussex, S. London); see Nick Higham, *The Northern Counties to AD 1000* (London, 1986), xv.

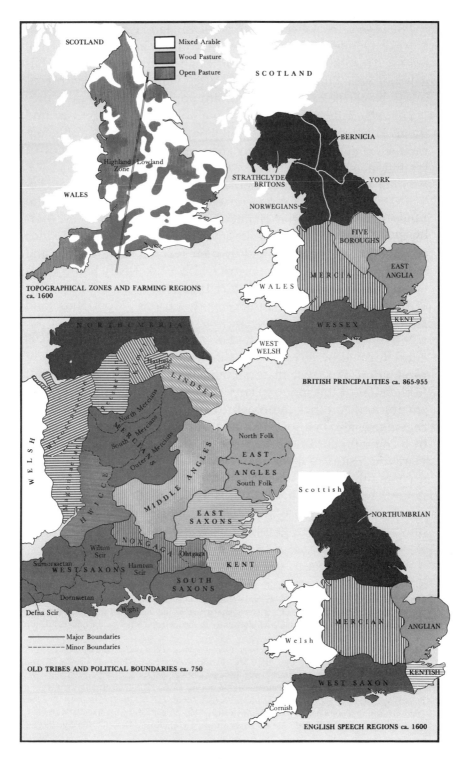

SCOTLAND

Mixed Arable
Wood Pasture
Open Pasture

SCOTLAND

Highland / Lowland
Zone

WALES

BERNICIA

STRATHCLYDE
BRITONS

YORK

NORWEGIANS

FIVE
BOROUGHS

EAST
ANGLIA

MERCIA

WALES

TOPOGRAPHICAL ZONES AND FARMING REGIONS
ca. 1600

WEST
WELSH

WESSEX

KENT

BRITISH PRINCIPALITIES ca. 865-955

N O R T H U M B R I A

Hatfield
land

LINDSEY

W E L S H

North Mercians

South Mercians

Outer Mercians

M E R C I A

North Folk

EAST

ANGLES

South Folk

MIDDLE ANGLES

H W I C C E

EAST
SAXONS

Scottish

NORTHUMBRIAN

NORFOLK

Wilton
Scir

Ohtgaga

KENT

Sumorsaetan

WEST SAXONS

Hamtun
Scir

SOUTH
SAXONS

Dornsaetan

Wight

Defna Scir

MERCIAN

ANGLIAN

——— Major Boundaries
------- Minor Boundaries

Welsh

OLD TRIBES AND POLITICAL BOUNDARIES ca. 750

WEST SAXON

KENTISH

Cornish

ENGLISH SPEECH REGIONS ca. 1600

Provinces refer collectively to all of England except London, in a great disjunction between the metropolis and the rest of the nation. This idea is very strong in English scholarship today, but it is not very old—perhaps not older than the eighteenth century.[11] Nevertheless, many historians apply it to earlier periods.[12]

Hinterlands include both individual towns and the areas around them. This spatial unit is especially popular among English geographers, and has been highly developed in general studies of migration and trade.[13]

Other quasi-regional ideas include *river systems* which are ecological units of increasing conceptual prominence in England today; one thinks of the Thames Valley, the Severn Valley, Merseyside, Humberside and Tyneside. Also much in use is the idea of ecological *districts*, defined by their terrain, climate, flora and fauna—such as the Lake District, the Peak District, the Cotswolds, the Chilterns, the Yorkshire Dales, the Norfolk Broads, the Weald of Kent and Sussex, and various Moorlands and Downlands.

What, after all, is a region? For many scholars it is a physical entity formed by terrain, soil, climate, resources and systems of production. But these material models of English regions do not fit the facts of this inquiry. They do not coincide with patterns of emigration. Another approach to the problem works better. A region may also be thought of as a cultural phenomenon, created by a common customs and experiences. It might be defined primarily in historical terms, as a place in time whose people share a common heritage that sets them apart from others of their nation. A major conclusion of this work is that regions, so understood, have been more important in the history of Britain than they are in its historiography. But they have not always been the

---

[11]"The earliest use so far discovered of the expression 'the provinces' to describe England outside London places it significantly in the context of the Industrial Revolution"; Donald Read, *The English Provinces, 1760–1790: A Study in Influence* (London, 1964), 2. The idea of "provinces" and "provincial" as a collective alternative to the metropolis was imported from France, and was rarely used as collective alternative to the metropolis before the mid-eighteenth century.

[12]John Morrill, *The Revolt of the Provinces: Conservatives and Radicals in the English Civil War, 1630–1650* (London, 1976, 1980). Both Morrill and Everitt use the idea of "provinces" and "provincialism" to mean local attachments of many kinds.

[13]General works include John Patten, *English Towns, 1500–1700* (Folkestone, Kent, 1978); Peter Clark and Paul Slack, *Crisis and Order in English Towns, 1500–1700* (London, 1972); *idem, English Towns in Transition, 1500–1700* (Oxford, 1976). Individual studies include Wallace T. MacCaffrey, *Exeter, 1540–1640* (2d ed., Cambridge, 1976); Roger Howell, *Newcastle-on-Tyne and the Puritan Revolution* (Oxford, 1967); and many other works.

same regions, nor have they always been important in the same way. Regional boundaries have changed with historical conditions.[14]

This inquiry was not about English regions in general, but historical regions that existed at a particular point in time, during the seventeenth and the early eighteenth century. They appear most clearly not in evidence collected after the industrial revolution, but in maps of cultural processes and political events through the preceding seven hundred years—in the jurisdiction of the Dane Law and the ancient boundaries of British kingdoms before King Edred; in the English earldoms of 1066 and the areas of support and opposition to King John in 1215; in the Peasants' Rebellion of 1381 and Jack Cade's Revolt in 1450; in the distribution of Marian martyrs in the sixteenth century and the incidence of Elizabethan Puritanism; in the areas that rallied to Parliament and to the Crown in the seventeenth century; and not least in patterns of emigration to the American colonies.

All of this evidence shows strong and consistent regional patterns that do not conform to the boundaries of topographical zones, soil types, field systems, farming regimes, hinterlands, river systems or ecological districts. The regions of seventeenth-century England were defined primarily by broad ethnic, cultural and historical processes.[15]

Four historical regions in seventeenth-century Britain were specially important to this inquiry. The first of them lay in the east of England, and included the three peninsulae of East Anglia itself, eastern Lincolnshire and the northeastern fringe of Kent. The boundary of this territory ran through the old counties of Rutland, Huntingdon and Hertford. In the seventeenth century, this area was commonly called the "East" or "eastern England." With the addition of Kent it corresponded roughly to the area of the "Eastern Association" which supported Parliament in the

[14]An example is the changing role of communications in defining regional identities. In the early 17th century, water was a medium more permeable than land. Areas which are now held apart by the arms of the sea were joined together in close embrace. East Lincolnshire, East Anglia and East Kent, for example, were united by the North Sea. In the same way, English Cumbria, Scottish Galloway and the Irish provinces of Antrim and Down were all linked by the Irish Sea. In these terms, British regions in the 17th century were not the same as those we know today. The idea of "permeability" comes from R. R. Palmer and Jacques Godechot, "Le problème de l'Atlantique du XVIIe au XXe siècle," *Relazioni del X Congresso Internazionale di Scienze Storiche* (Rome, 1955), 5, 175–239; for a similar argument as regards the Irish Sea, see Innes Macleod, *Discovering Galloway* (Edinburgh, 1986), 5.

[15]These maps appear below.

English Civil War. This region produced approximately 60 percent of emigrants to Massachusetts.[16]

A second historical region, which sent many sons to Virginia, was a broad belt of territory through the south of England, extending from Kent to Devon, and north as far as Warwick. It encompassed the ancient kingdom of Wessex and its Mercian protectorates—the realm of Alfred and Aethelred. This area had the least articulated sense of regional identity because it believed itself to be the heartland of the country—in Henry James's phrase, "midmost England, unmitigated England." Nevertheless, it had a cultural existence which was defined by its history, in ways that made it distinct from East Anglia, the North Country and the Celtic cultures of Wales and Cornwall to the west. Roughly 60 percent of Virginia gentlemen and servants came from this region.[17]

A third historical region lay in the North Midlands of England. It included a broad belt of territory from Cheshire and Derbyshire north through Lancashire and the West Riding of Yorkshire to southern Cumbria. This area was called "the North Country" in the seventeenth century. Thus a Quaker named John Crock wrote, "I was born in the North Country." Another wrote that "he heard of a people in the North of England, who preferred the light. . . ." And a third described Quakerism as "glad tidings brought out of the north." This area was the source of approximately 60 percent of the Quaker population which settled in the Delaware Valley.[18]

The fourth historical region was an area which included the English counties of Westmorland, Cumberland, Northumberland, Durham, and the North Riding of Yorkshire, together with the southern counties of Scotland. As early as the fifteenth century this region was called the "border," or "borders," and its inhabitants called themselves "borderers."[19] These people of Scotland and northern England, together with their transplanted cousins in Ulster, were very mixed in their ethnicity, but they

[16]Clive Holmes, *The English Association in the English Civil War* (Cambridge, 1974).

[17]Henry James, *English Hours* (1905, rpt. New York, 1960), 724; James Bishop, ed., *The Illustrated Counties of England* (London, n.d.), 124; evidence of the common historical experience of this region appears in part 2, below.

[18]John Crock, "Memoirs"; Charles Marshall, "Journal . . ."; and Edmund Chester, "Narrative," in William and Thomas Evans, eds., *Friends' Library* (14 vols., Philadelphia, 1837–50), XIII, 207; IV, 123; III, 71.

[19]*OED, s.v.* "Border," 3.a; "Borderer," 1.

shared a common culture which was shaped by the history of their region. More than 60 percent of settlers in the American back-country were immigrants or the children of immigrants from northern Ireland, the lowlands of Scotland, and the six northern counties of England.

The origin of regional differences between East Anglia, south-western England, the North Country and the borderlands is a problem that carries far beyond the subject of this book. A search for their beginning leads back a thousand years before American history to ethnic movements as early as the seventh century—and even that date is not early enough to mark the beginning of dif-ferences between these cultural regions in the east and south and north of England, which had important consequences for Amer-ican history.

❧ British Origins: The Religious Factor

Of all the determinants which shaped the cultural character of British America, the most powerful was religion. During the sev-enteenth century, the English-speaking people were deeply divided by the great questions of the Protestant Reformation. These divisions in turn created a broad spectrum of English denominations in the New World.

The "right wing" of the British Reformation was the party of Anglican Episcopacy which favored an inclusive national church, a hierarchy of priests, compulsory church taxes and a union of church and crown. Its worship centered on liturgy and ritual, its theology became increasingly Arminian in the seventeenth cen-tury, and its creed was defined by the Book of Common Prayer. This denomination was specially strong in the south and west of England. It was destined to dominate Virginia for more than a century.

Next to the Episcopalians on Britain's spectrum of religious belief were Presbyterians. They also favored a broad national church, but one which was ruled by strong synods of ministers and elders rather than by bishops and priests. The theology of Presbyterianism was Calvinist; its worship centered on preaching and conversion. The Presbyterians were numerous in North Brit-ain, where they made much use of evangelical field meetings and prayer meetings. They became very strong in the American backcountry.

Near the center were Congregationalists, who defined their position as the "middle way." Their church government was a mixed confederacy of independent congregations and weak synods. Their theology took a middle ground between Arminianism (which tended toward rationalism and free will) and Antinomianism (the dominion of the spirit). Their formal beliefs were defined by the Synod of Dort (1618–19) in the five points of Calvinism (total depravity, limited atonement, unconditional election, irresistible grace and the final perseverance of the saints)— a Christian creed of extreme austerity. This group was strong in the eastern counties of England. It founded the colonies of Massachusetts and Connecticut.

To the left of the Congregationalists were the Separatists, who believed in the autonomy of each congregation, and wished to separate themselves from the corruption of an unreformed national church. Their theology was broadly Calvinist, and their classical text was Robert Browne's *Reformation without Tarrying for Any* (1583). This denomination included the *Mayflower* Pilgrims who founded Plymouth Colony.

Farther left were various sects of Anabaptists, many of whom subscribed to the five points of Calvinism, but added a "sixth principle" that baptism should be restricted to regenerate Christians. Their theology stressed the working of the Holy Spirit more than the teaching of divine law. Their church was a fellowship in which worship was a sharing of the spirit of Grace. Most Baptists also believed in the separation of church and state, primarily to preserve the church from spiritual pollution. They founded the colony of Rhode Island.

Beyond the Baptists were the Quakers, who believed that Jesus died not merely for a chosen few but for everyone, and that a Holy Spirit called the Inner Light dwelled within all people. Their beliefs rose from the teachings of George Fox and received their classic statement in Robert Barclay's *Apology for the True Christian Religion*. Quakers rejected the legitimacy of established churches, ordained clergy and formal liturgy. Their meetings for worship centered upon the movement of the spirit. This denomination first appeared in the North Midlands of England. It founded the colonies of West Jersey, Pennsylvania and Delaware.

Because religion touched so many parts of life in the era of the reformation, these denominational divisions created deep cultural differences which have survived in American regions long after their original purposes have been lost.

British Protestantism in the Seventeenth Century: The Spectrum of Practice and Belief

Denomination	Quakers	Baptists	Separatists	Congregationalists	Presbyterians	Anglicans
Ecclesiology	Hierarchy of Meetings	Small Sects and Fellowships	Separate Congregations	Weak Synods Strong Congregations	Strong Synods	Episcopal
Polity	Consensual	Communal	Democratic	Mixed	Oligarchic	Monarchic
Sect-Church typology	Sect-type	Sect-type	Sect-type	Mixed	Church-type	Church-type
Forms of worship	Spirit-centered	Fellowship-centered	Sermon-centered	Sermon-centered	Sermon-centered	Liturgy centered
Church state Relations	Extreme Separation	Extreme Separation	Moderate Separation	Moderate Separation	Moderate Union	Strong Union
Theology	Inner Light	Six Points and Mixed	Five Points of Calvinism	Five Points of Calvinism	Five Points of Calvinism	Arminian and Mixed
Creed	None	Many	Browne's Booke	Cambridge Platform	Westminster Confession	Book of Common Prayer
Texts	Barclay's Apology	Many	Brown's Reformation without Tarrying	Ames's Marrow of Sacred Divinity	Knox's Discipline	Hooker's Laws of Ecclesiastical Polity
Colonies	West Jersey Pennsylvania	Rhode Island	Plymouth	Massachusetts Connecticut	Backcountry	Virginia
Leaders	William Penn	Roger Williams	William Bradford	John Winthrop	Francis Makemie	William Berkeley

❧ British Origins: The Factor of Social Rank

Another determinant of cultural differences in British America was the social rank of the colonists. This factor worked in two ways. First, the founders of America's various regional cultures came from different strata of British society. Second, major changes occurred in England's ranking system during the era of colonization. Emigrants in the early seventeenth century had one way of thinking about social status; those who arrived in the mid-eighteenth century had another. This process of change added another dimension to regional differences in America.

To understand this problem we must study the ranking systems of earlier periods in their own terms. Between 1577 and 1600, this subject was discussed by three English writers: Thomas Smith (1583), William Harrison (1587), and Thomas Wilson (1600).[20] None of these authors thought in terms of modern social classes, or even used the word "class." Sir Thomas Wilson wrote of "estates"; Harrison, of "conditions" and "degrees"; Smith, of "orders." These categories were defined not by material possessions or by the means of production, but by access to power. In Smith's phrase they were "orders of authority . . . annexed to the blood and progeny."[21]

The three authors agreed in their description of the upper orders. At the top of every list came the King himself, who was quaintly called the "first gentleman" or "chief gentleman" of England. Then came the princes and the *"nobilitas major,"* an order so small in England that Harrison could list every member on a single page: he counted one marquis, twenty earls, two viscounts and forty-one barons, plus twenty-four bishops who were the "lords spiritual" of England. Smith's list in 1600 was even smaller—sixty-one noblemen altogether. This was England's high aristocracy; it contributed much to the capitalization of British America but little to its population.[22]

Next came the *nobilitas minor,* who were identified as knights,

---

[20]Sir Thomas Smith, *De Republica Anglorum* (1583), ed. Mary Dewar (Cambridge, 1982); William Harrison, *The Description of England* (1587), ed. Georges Edelen (Ithaca, 1968); Sir Thomas Wilson, "The State of England, 1600," ed. F. J. Fisher, *CS* 3d ser. 52 (1936), 18–25. Some parts of Harrison's account (which appeared earlier in another form) were copied by Smith; parts of Smith and Harrison were borrowed by Wilson. Each author added many passages of his own invention.

[21]Smith, *De Republica Anglorum,* 64, 76.

[22]*Ibid.,* 20.

esquires, and gentlemen. Wilson reckoned that there were about 500 knights and 16,000 esquires whom he defined as "gentlemen whose ancestors are or were knights, or else they are the heirs and eldest of their houses and of some competent quantity of revenue." This order or estate also included a residue of undifferentiated gentlemen who were defined in different ways. Smith identified them as "those whom their blood and race doth make noble and known," or "whose ancestor hath been notable in riches or for his virtues, or (in fewer words) old riches."[23] Wilson, on the other hand, defined them in an interesting way as "younger brothers," and added:

> their state is of all stations for gentlemen the most miserable, for . . . my elder brother forsooth must be my master. . . . This I must confess doth us good someways, for it makes us industrious to apply ourselves to letters or to arms, whereby many times we become my master elder-brothers' masters, at least their betters in honour and reputation, while he lives at home like a mome [a fool].[24]

This group, particularly the younger sons, played an important role in the creation of a Virginia elite.

Beneath the rank of gentlemen were clergy, lawyers and learned professions. There was general agreement that professional men were "made good cheape in England," and had become too numerous for the good of the realm. Below the professions, all writers recognized an estate of "citizens" who had been admitted to the liberties of England's towns and boroughs—"a commonwealth among themselves," Wilson wrote.[25]

Next came the yeomanry. Wilson divided this rank into "great yeomanry" (10,000 strong), whom he thought much "decayed," but often with estates larger than "some covetous mongrel gentleman." Below them came "yeomen of meaner ability which are called freeholders," whom he reckoned to have been 80,000 strong, after having studied the sheriffs' books in which they were listed.[26] Smith noted that the rank of yeoman, though mainly defined by possession of a freehold, also implied a certain age. "Commonly, he wrote, "we do not call any a yeoman till he be married, and have children, and as it were have some authority

---

[23] *Ibid.*, 70.
[24] Wilson, "The State of England."
[25] Smith, *De Republica Anglorum*, 72.
[26] Wilson, "The State of England."

among his neighbours. . ."[27] Harrison wrote that "this sort of people have a certain pre-eminence . . . live wealthily, keep good houses and travail [work] to get riches." This rank, with lawyers, clergy and citizens, was important in the formation of New England's elite.[28]

Below the rank of yeoman, all of these lists became very thin as they reached the "lower orders" who included the great majority of England's population. Wilson's taxonomy ended in a single broad category which embraced "copyholders who hold some land and tenements of some other lord," and "cottagers," who "live chiefly upon country labour, working by the day for meat and drink and some small wages." He noted that "the number of this latter sort is uncertain because there is no books or records kept of them." Smith also had a catch-all category at the bottom for "day laborers, poor husbandmen, merchants or retailers which have no free land, copyholders, all artificers." To a modern mind this lower order seems a very mixed group, but all shared a quality in common. Smith called them "men which do not rule." Harrison explained, "These have no voice or authority in our common wealth, and no account is made of them but only to be ruled."[29]

This was England's system of social rank at the beginning of the seventeenth century—a complex set of orders, degrees, estates or conditions which were more rigid than modern classes. It was a way of thinking that persisted through the period of the English Civil War. The poll tax of 1660, for example, recognized the same taxonomy.

By the late seventeenth century, however, new ideas of social rank were stirring in England. A case in point was a famous analysis of English society by Gregory King. At first sight, his list of "ranks, degrees, orders and qualifications" seemed similar to those of Harrison, Smith and Wilson nearly 100 years earlier. But on closer examination, important differences appeared. King's social orders were less distinct than those a century earlier. Between the *nobilitas major* and *nobilitas minor,* the rank of baronet had been introduced as a fund-raising device by cash-poor Stuart kings. The professions had grown more numerous and

[27]Smith, *De Republica Anglorum,* 76.
[28]Harrison, *Description of England,* 117.
[29]Smith, *De Republica Anglorum,* 64, 76; Harrison wrote that they "have neither voice nor authority in the commonwealth, but are to be ruled and not to rule other." *Description of England,* 118.

Three Taxonomies of Social Rank in England, 1577–1600

I. Harrison, 1577 "Of Degrees of People in the Commonwealth of England"	II. Smith, 1583 "Of the Parties of the Commonwealth of Englande"	III. Wilson, 1600 "The Ability and State of . . . the People of England"
Gentlemen of the Greater Sort The King "first gentleman" Princes Dukes Marquises Earls Viscounts Barons Bishops	**Nobilitas Major** The King "chiefe gentleman" Princes Marquises Earls Viscounts Barons	**Nobilitas Major** King Princes Marquises Earls Viscounts Barons Bishops
Gentlemen of the Lesser Sort Knights Esquires Gentlemen	**Nobilitas Minor** Knights Squires Simple Gentlemen	**Nobilitas Minor** Knights Esquires (elder brothers) Gentlemen (younger brothers) **Professors** **Ministers, Archdeacons** **Prebends and Vicars** **Lawyers**
Citizens or Burgesses Officers Merchants	**Citizens and Burgesses**	**Citizens** Aldermen and Burgesses Great Merchants Meaner Merchants
Yeomen Farmers Artificers	**Yeomen**	**Yeomanry** Great Yeomen Meaner Yeomen or Freeholders
Labourers Day labourers Poor Husbandmen Retailers Meaner Artificers	**Men Which Do Not Rule** Day labourers Poor Husbandmen Merchants or retailers that have no free land Copiholders All Artificers, as Taylors, Shoemakers, Carpenters, Brickmakers, Bricklayers, Masons, &c	**Copyholders and Cottagers**
Idle Servingmen		
Beggars		

more complex, and two new ranks were added for "persons in office." Merchants had advanced from the bottom to near the top—above even the clergy. The lower ranks had become elaborately subdivided by occupation.[30]

In the early eighteenth century, this new way of thinking about stratification began to develop rapidly. Rank was defined increasingly not by origins, but by possessions. One finds this new ranking system in the writings of Daniel Defoe, who used the word "class" in its modern sense as early as the year 1705.[31] In 1709, Defoe described English society as follows:

1. The great, who live profusely.
2. The rich, who live very plentifully.
3. The middle sort, who live well.
4. The working trades, who labour hard, but feel no want.
5. The country people, farmers, &c., who fare indifferently.
6. The poor, that fare hard.
7. The miserable, that really pinch and suffer want.[32]

Here was a modern class model in which people were assigned a place according to their material possessions. Thereafter, this idea developed steadily through the eighteenth century. Raymond Williams writes that the "development of *class* in its modern social sense, with relatively fixed names for particular classes (lower class, middle class, upper class, working class) belongs essentially to the period between 1770 and 1840."[33]

This transformation had important consequences for American history. The four waves of British emigrants came not only from different ranks, but also from different periods in the history of ranking systems. The older system of orders came to Massachusetts where it survived in a truncated form, and also to Virginia where it was extended by the development of servitude and slavery. But the founders of the Quaker colonies and especially the back settlements came from a later era in which orders and estates were yielding to social classes. This fact made a difference in the development of regional cultures throughout British America.

[30]This question is separate from that of the accuracy of King's estimates. It is thought by some historians that King undercounted the upper ranks and underestimated incomes of those at the bottom. See G. S. Holmes, "Gregory King and the Social Structure of Pre-Industrial England," *RHST* (1977).

[31]Daniel Defoe, *Review,* 14 April 1705.

[32]*Ibid.,* 25 June 1709, quoted in Dorothy George, *London Life in the Eighteenth Century* (New York, 1965), 370n.

[33]Raymond Williams, *Keywords: A Vocabulary of Culture and Society* (New York, 1976), 51.

✏ British Origins: The Factor of Generations

The four migrations came not only from different regions, ranks and religions, but also from different generations. The key concept here is that of an *historical* generation—not a demographic cohort but a cultural group whose identity is formed by great events. In the turbulence of the twentieth century, for example, everyone recognizes the "generation of the Great Depression," the "generation of World War II," and the "generation of the '60s." Seventeenth-century England had similar historical generations, which were defined by the same events that set the major folk migrations in motion.

Each of these migrations created a culture which preserved something of the moment when it was born. The Puritans settled Massachusetts within a period of eleven years from 1629 to 1640—an epoch in English history which is remembered by Whig historians as the "eleven years' tyranny." This was the time when Charles I tried to rule without a Parliament and Archbishop William Laud attempted to purge the Anglican Church of Puritans. The great constitutional and religious issues of this epoch were carried to the Puritan colonies and became central to the culture of New England—persisting as intellectual obsessions long after they had been forgotten in the mother country.

A large part of Virginia's migration of cavaliers and indentured servants occurred between 1649 and 1660, an unstable era of English history called the interregnum. In this period of disorder the dominant elite was an oligarchy of English Puritans, and their victims included a group of defeated Royalists, some of whom carried to Virginia a culture which was defined not merely by their rank and party but also by their generation—in its fascination with constitutional questions, its obsession with honor, and its contempt for the arts of peace. The culture of America's tidewater south was to retain these characteristics long after England had moved beyond them.

The Friends' migration to the Delaware Valley happened mainly in the years from 1675 to 1689. This was part of an historical epoch which began with the Restoration, and continued through the reigns of Charles II (1660–85) and his Catholic brother James II (1685–88). In this period of English history, the great questions were about how people of different beliefs could live in peace together. That question was central to the cultural history of the Delaware colonies, and remained so for many years.

Another period of English history followed the Glorious Rev-

A Short Chronology of Anglo-American History, 1558–1760

Reign	Events in Britain		Events in America	
Elizabeth I (1558–1603)			1583	Gilbert in Newfoundland
			1584–87	Raleigh founds Roanoke
	1587	War with Spain; colonization ceases		
			1590	Roanoke found abandoned
James I (1603–25)	1604	Spanish War ends; colonization revives		
	1606	Virginia Companies of Plymouth and London		
			1607	Jamestown founded
				Sagadahoc founded
			1620	Plymouth founded
Charles I (1625–49)	1629–40	**Eleven Years' Tyranny**	1630–41	**Puritan Great Migration**
		Charles rules without Parliaments	1630	Massachusetts founded
	1633–40	Archbishop Laud purges Puritans from Church of England	1634	Laud's Commission on Plantation
			1634	Maryland founded
			1636	Connecticut and Rhode Island founded
			1638	New Haven founded
	1640	Parliament called / Laud impeached and later executed		
	1642–47	First Civil War	1642	Sir Wm. Berkeley to Virginia
	1649	Charles I executed		
Interregnum	1649–60	**England Becomes a Commonwealth**	1649–65	**Royalist Migration to Virginia**
	1653	Oliver Cromwell becomes Protector	1655	Protectorate seeks to curb colonial autonomy
	1658	Richard Cromwell succeeds father / Protectorate disintegrates		
Charles II (1660–85)	1660	Restoration of Charles II / Declaration of Breda promises Religious liberty to all Christians		
	1661–65	Clarendon Code penalizes Dissenters and Quakers in particular	1663	Carolina granted to eight Royalists
	1665–67	Anglo-Dutch War	1664	New Netherland granted Duke of York
	1672	Declaration of Indulgence suspends Penal laws against dissenters		
	1673	**Test Act; Tithe Persecution of Quakers Continues**	1675–95	**Friends' Migration to West Jersey and Pa.**
James II (1685–88)	1685	King seeks repeal of Test Act and is defeated; prorogues Parliament	1685	James creates Dominion for New Eng. to curb colonies
	1688	Glorious Revolution;	1688–89	Revolutions in colonies
Wm. & Mary (1689–1702)	1689	Declaration of Rights		
			1696	Board of Trade founded
	1701	Act of Settlement defines descent		
Anne (1702–14)	1702–13	War of Spanish Succession	1702–13	Queen Anne's War
	1707	**Union of England and Scotland**	1715–75	**North Britons Move to Backcountry**
George I (1714–27)	1715	The '15 Rebellion in Scotland		
	1721	Walpole's ministry		
George II (1727–60)			1729	NC and SC royal colonies
	1745	The '45 Rebellion in Scotland	1733	Georgia founded

olution of 1688, when a pattern of political stability formed "as suddenly as water becomes ice," in historian J. H. Plumb's words.[34] The government of England passed firmly into the hands of an oligarchy of country gentlemen. This solution created new problems which concerned the relationship between England's governing elite and others—in particular, the people of Ireland, Scotland, America, the London mob and the rural poor. Violent conflicts set in motion yet another wave of emigration which brought to America the great question of whether the rights of English gentlemen belonged to other people. These issues took root in the American interior, where they survive even to our own time. All four folk cultures of Anglo-America preserved the dominant themes in English history during the years when they began.

✒ American Development: The Environment

British culture was not the only determinant of regional differences. The American environment also played an important role—not by "breaking down" or "dissolving" European culture (as the frontier thesis suggested) but by more complex material pressures which modified European cultures in some respects and reinforced them in others.

In New England, the Puritans selected a rigorous environment which was well suited to their purposes. The climate (colder and more changeable than today) proved exceptionally healthy to Europeans, but high mortality among African immigrants reinforced a Puritan ambivalence toward the growth of slavery. The configuration of New England's coastline and the distribution of soil resources in small pockets of alluvial fertility encouraged town settlement. The Indians of Massachusetts Bay had been nearly destroyed by disease before the Puritans arrived; conflicts remained at a comparatively low level for nearly fifty years except during the Pequot War.

The Virginians encountered a very different environment. The Chesapeake Bay, with its 6,500 miles of tidal shoreline, its hundreds of rivers and creeks, and its abundance of good soil, encouraged scattered settlement and plantation agriculture. The climate (about the same as today) produced bountiful staple crops. But the Chesapeake estuary was unhealthy, and European

[34]J. H. Plumb, *The Growth of Political Stability in England, 1675–1725* (London, 1967), 13.

death rates were twice as high as in New England. Africans had lower mortality rates than in the northern colonies, and slavery developed rapidly from the late seventeenth century. The large Indian population of the Powhatan Confederacy strongly resisted English settlement, with much bloody fighting.

The Delaware Valley offered yet a third set of environmental conditions. This area proved more salubrious than the Chesapeake, but less so than Massachusetts. Its climate was mild and its soil endowment was the richest of the eastern colonies, producing crop yields above all other coastal regions for three centuries. An abundance of mineral resources and a fall line only a few miles from the sea supported rapid industrial development. The Delaware Indians were not warlike in the early years of settlement. Altogether this environment was perfectly suited to the purposes of the Quakers, as they well knew when they chose to settle there.

Regional Cultures of Anglo-America: Environmental Conditions

Hearth Area	Massachusetts	Virginia	Delaware Valley	Backcountry
Temperature (1950–1980)				
January mean	25°F	40°F	31°F	37°F
January average low	18°F	32°F	24°F	30°F
Temperature (1950–1980)				
July mean	72°F	78°F	76°F	77°F
July average high	82°F	88°F	86°F	87°F
Temperature (18th Century)				
Coastal sea surface deviation from 20th-century norms				
January mean	−5.4°F	0	−1.8°F	n.a.
July mean	−3.6°F	0	−1.8°F	n.a.
Precipitation (1950–1980)				
Annual inches	40	45	42	48
Annual wet days	118	113	116	120
Percent daily sunshine	57%	62%	58%	61%
Snow, annual inches	55	8	21	15
Water Access				
Sources	Riverine	Estuarine	Riverine	Springs
Bay areas (sq. mi.)	959	3,237	665	0
Tidal shoreline (mi.)	2,484	6,505	1,512	0
Salubrity (ca. 1700)				
Death rate, whites	25	50	37	35
Death rate, blacks	65	50	n.a.	n.a.
Dying time, whites	Aug.–Oct.	June–Oct.	July–Oct.	July–Oct.
Dying time, blacks	Jan.–May	May–Sep.	n.a.	n.a.
Woodlands				
Forest types	Boreal to temperate	Temperate to subtropical	Temperate	Mixed by elevation
Growing season	150 days	210 days	180 days	180 days

For many years it supported their "holy experiment" in prosperity and peace.

The southern backcountry was a densely forested highland region of enormous proportions. Markets were distant and travel difficult, but the abundance of land and water encouraged the rapid growth of family farming and herding. The climate was comparatively mild and healthy. The Indians were numerous and very hostile to European settlement. The backcountry became a cockpit of international rivalry, and was ravaged by major wars in every generation from 1689 to 1815. The climate, resources and dangers of this American environment were well matched to the culture of the British borderlands.

✌ American Development: The Indians

In every region, English colonists met an indigenous population of American Indians. The collision of these groups was a cultural process of high complexity, which can only be discussed here in a summary way. In brief, the Indian populations of North America were not a cultural monolith. Even within the eastern woodlands, the Indians of New England, the Delaware Valley, the Chesapeake Bay and the Appalachian highlands were at least as diverse in their folk customs as were the British themselves—in many ways, much more so. Moreover, the demography of these various Indian populations also tended to be very different from one to another. Further, Indian cultures were changing through time. Each had its own history, which scholars are only beginning to reconstruct.

The founders of the British colonies were aware of this diversity, and deliberately selected the sites of their own settlements in part because of the special character of the Indians in the vicinity. This was very much the case among New England Puritans and Delaware Quakers. All four major British groups also invented their own distinctive policies toward the Indians. They tended to treat the Indians in profoundly different ways, and were treated differently in their turn.

The results were distinct regional processes of interaction, involving at least four causal variables: Indian culture, Indian demography, white culture and white demography. A result was that relations between Indians and Europeans reinforced regional differences in a complex web of cause and consequence.

The larger outlines of this process have never been described comprehensively, though various monographic findings are beginning to come in. The author has been collecting his thoughts and materials on this subject for many years and hopes to find an opportunity to set them forward in more detail than is possible here.

❧ American Development: Imperial Politics

The growth of regional folk cultures in British America was also fostered by a unique political environment which was very different from other European colonies. New France and New Spain were more closely controlled by imperial authorities than were England's American provinces, which had more freedom to manage their own affairs.

This condition did not develop by design. English statesmen looked upon the empires of France and Spain with admiration, and even with envy. The authorities in London often tried to impose similar controls upon their own colonies. But for many years these efforts failed and regional cultures of British America were left to go their own way. The first important English attempt to control the American colonies was made by Charles I, who created a Commission for Foreign Plantations in 1634. Its head was Archbishop William Laud, the great Anglican enemy of Puritanism, whose assignment was to curb New England's independence. For that purpose, a "great ship" was ordered in England, while the people of Massachusetts made ready to defend themselves. But before the great ship sailed, Parliament rose against Charles I and one of its first acts was to execute Archbishop Laud. New England continued to govern itself for many years.

During the Civil War, King and Parliament both claimed the right to regulate the colonies, but neither was able to do so. A Parliamentary Commission for Plantations was appointed in 1643, but before it began to act effectively, Parliament itself was overthrown by Oliver Cromwell. The colonies continued to go their own way.

After 1653 the Protectorate also tried to organize the colonies into a coherent imperial system. To that end, Oliver Cromwell and his Protector's Council created two new bodies—a Committee for Foreign Plantations (1655), and a Committee for America (1656). An expedition was sent against the Royalist regime in Virginia, but after Cromwell's early death in 1658, these bodies also disbanded. The colonies continued to control their own affairs.

The restoration of Charles II in 1660 was followed by a more sustained effort to create an imperial system—this time through the Privy Council's Committee for Trade and Plantations, called the Lords of Trade (1660). Various other councils and committees also functioned in a fitful way from 1660 to 1685, but none gained effective control over the colonies. The fragility of England's restored monarchy, the poverty of the new regime, and the caution of the King himself all prevented strong measures, except in Virginia after Bacon's Rebellion. The colonies retained much of their independence.[1]

After the year 1685, England's King James II tried to impose a consolidated government called the Dominion of New England upon all the colonies from Maine to Delaware. He appointed a viceregal figure named Sir Edmund Andros to govern it. The result was an American Revolution of 1688 which began before the accession of William and Mary, and ended with Sir Edmund Andros a prisoner in Boston. The colonies narrowly survived yet another imperial challenge.[2]

After the Glorious Revolution, the new Protestant regime of William and Mary also tried to bring the colonies to heel, and at last succeeded in doing so. It created a new body called the Board of Trade, and a complex machinery of imperial government. But the delicate relationship between King and Parliament prevented either from asserting itself as forcefully as did imperial authorities in France and Spain. After 1714, Britain was ruled by German kings who cared little about America, and English ministers who knew less. One of them believed that Massachusetts was an island. There was in London a profound ignorance of American conditions.

Throughout the empire, colonial assemblies continued to claim parliamentary status, even though officials in London regarded them as comparable to municipal councils. This constitutional

[1] The Lords of Trade might be thought of as a transitional institution, which began to assert effective control over the American colonies; see Winfred T. Root, "Lords of Trade and Plantations, 1675–1696," *American Historical Review* 23 (1917), 20. A strong case has recently been made for the mid-1670s as the pivot point, rather than the 1680s or 1690s. See Stephen S. Webb, *1676: The End of American Independence* (New York, 1984).

[2] The revolution began in Boston on 19 April 1689, after news that William had landed in England, but before the outcome was known. See David S. Lovejoy, *The Glorious Revolution in America* (New York, 1972).

question was not resolved before 1775. While it continued, England's American provinces remained more nearly autonomous than other European colonies, and regional cultures developed with less interference from above.

❧ American Development: Immigration and Race

British America also differed from other empires in another way. It was settled mainly by voluntary migration. Most British men and women made their own way to the New World. Many raised the price of their own passage, and freely chose to settle in a colony which was congenial to their culture. This pattern changed in the eighteenth century when large numbers of involuntary immigrants appeared: transported felons, soldiers under orders, and more than 250,000 African slaves. But even when this traffic was at its peak, most people came to America as volunteers.[3]

This voluntary migration was unique to the British colonies. In New France, a large part of the population was descended from conscripts, soldiers, sailors, basket women, "king's girls," civil servants, priests and nuns, and others who had been ordered to America, sometimes much against their will.[4] Once arrived, these immigrants tended to be more closely controlled, except on the fringes of the colony. In Quebec, a secret organization of females called the Congregation of the Holy Family kept watch by a system of domestic espionage which had no counterpart in the English colonies.[5] In New Spain, colonists were screened for religious and social orthodoxy, and kept under continuing surveillance by imperial authorities. The Spanish Inquisition became more active in Mexico than it had been in Iberia. Its worst excesses of cruelty and persecution were committed in the New World.[6]

---

[3]A subsequent volume in this series will examine this question.

[4]The "king's girls" were collected from orphanages, alms-houses and various other places, and sent by the shipload to Quebec. More than 1,000 arrived in the eight years from 1665 to 1673.

[5]Francis Parkman turned up the manuscript sources and reported them in *The Old Regime in Canada* (Cambridge, 1974), 418.

[6]The leading works are still those of José Toribio Medina, *Historia del tribunal del Santo oficio* . . . (6 vols., Santiago, 1887–1905), and Henry C. Lea, *The Inquisition in the Spanish Dependencies* . . . (New York, 1908); see also Cecil Roth, *The Spanish Inquisition* (1937, London, 1964), 208–26; Richard E. Greenleaf, *Zumárraga and the Mexican Inquisition, 1536–1543* (Washington, 1961).

British America's voluntary migration encouraged religious diversity rather than uniformity. It also allowed like-minded colonists of various sects to settle together and to transplant their own folkways to the New World.

Immigration also promoted regional development in another way. For many years, the American colonies effectively became their own gatekeepers. They were able to control the process of immigration themselves, and did so in very different ways.

The Puritan colonies stubbornly enforced a policy of strict exclusion despite imperial opposition. The homogeneity of New England's population was not an historical accident; it arose from the religious purposes and social values of a regional culture.

The founders of Pennsylvania had very different ideas about immigration. William Penn and the Quaker elite of the colony made a special effort to attract European Protestants whose values were compatible with their own. English Quakers, German Pietists and Swiss Anabaptists all believed deeply in the doctrine of the inner light, religious freedom, the ethic of work and the evil of violence. The immigration policy of the Quakers expanded the community of Christian values beyond the boundaries of their own sect, and deliberately encouraged a diversity of national stocks in the Delaware Valley.

The rulers of Virginia adopted still a third immigration policy. Puritans and Quakers were not welcome; many were banished or driven out. But the Virginians actively recruited a servile underclass to support their manorial ideal, first by bringing in large numbers of English servants, and then by importing African slaves. Their object was not merely to solve a problem of labor scarcity (which might have been done in many other ways) but to do so in a manner consistent with their hierarchical values.

The backsettlers were not able to control immigration to the southern highlands in any formal way. But local neighborhoods had other methods of deciding who would go or stay. The old folk custom of "hating out" was used when necessary. The prevailing cultural climate also had a similar effect; in the late eighteenth and early nineteenth century, for example, Quakers and Congregationalists left the southern backcountry, moving north to a more congenial cultural environment.

Local control of immigration thus tended to reinforce cultural differences between regions. Even as most parts of British America became more diverse during the eighteenth century, they did so in very different ways, according to purposes and values of their founders.

One effect of immigration was to change the racial composition of the four major regions of British America. African slaves were imported to every colony, but in very different proportions. In many parts of New England blacks were never more than 1 percent of the population before 1760; in some southern coastal counties, blacks were more than a majority by that date.

To understand the relationship between race and regional culture in British America, one must study carefully the timing and sequence of historical change. An important and neglected fact about race slavery in British America is that it developed very slowly. Africans did not begin to arrive in large numbers until the late seventeenth century. The presence of blacks did not begin to have a major cultural impact on British America until the late seventeenth and early eighteenth century. Then, the impact was profound. The problem of race relations moved rapidly to the center of cultural history in the plantation colonies. African folkways also began to transform the language and culture of Europeans, and the "peculiar institution" of slavery created new folkways of its own.

These great and complex processes will be studied in the second volume of this work, "American Plantations." In this first volume, the major conclusion is that race slavery did not create the culture of the southern colonies; that culture created slavery.

∾ The Expansion of Four Regional Cultures

By the year 1770 the four folk cultures had taken firm root in British America. All expanded rapidly. Emigrants from Massachusetts founded colonies with similar cultures in Connecticut, New Hampshire, southern Maine, eastern Vermont, Long Island, East Jersey, upstate New York and northern Ohio. The culture of tidewater Virginia expanded into southern Maryland, southern Delaware, coastal North Carolina and west beyond the mountains to parts of Kentucky. The folkways of the Delaware Valley spread through West Jersey, eastern Pennsylvania, parts of northeastern Maryland and central Ohio. After 1740 the borderers of North Britain rapidly occupied the Appalachian highlands from Pennsylvania to the Georgia, and moved west to the Mississippi.

The people of these four cultures shared many traits in common. Nearly all spoke the English language, lived by British laws, and cherished their ancestral liberties. Most dwelled in nuclear households, and had broadly similar patterns of marital fertility.

Four Regional Cultures in Anglo-America; A Summary of Cultural Characteristics, ca. 1700–50

	Massachusetts Greater New England	Virginia Tidewater South	Delaware Valley N.J., Pa., Del., N. Md.	Backcountry Southern Highlands
Location				
Hearth				
Region	Greater New England	Tidewater South	N.J., Pa., Del., N. Md.	Southern Highlands
Language and Literacy				
Dialect	Northern	Southern coastal	Midland	Southern highland
Literacy (S) (m/f)	80%/50%	50%/25%	65%/33%	n.a.
Architecture				
Materials	Wood frame	Wood and brick	Stone and brick	Earth and log
Style	Saltbox, Stretched Box	Hall and parlor	Quaker plan	Cabin style
Family				
Identity	Strong nuclear	Extended	Moderate nuclear	Clan and derbfine
Cohesion	High	Low	Moderate	Moderate
Completed size (F)	7	3	5	n.a.
Servants (mean)	0–1	4–5	2	n.a.
Marriage, Gender and Sex				
Ceremony	Civil contract	Sacred ceremony	Meeting and agreement	Abduction Rituals
Mean Age (Ma) (m/f)	26/23	24/18	27/24	20/19
Adults, never wed (m/f)	2%/6%	25%/2%	12%/16%	n.a.
Male dominance	Moderate	High	Moderate	Very high
Prenuptial Pregnancy Rate (PPR)	Low (10–20%)	High (20–40%)	Very Low (5–15%)	Very high (40%)
Bastardy rates (B)	Low (7–10)	High (26–118)	Low (1–7)	Unknown
Penalty bias	Even	Against females	Even	n.a.
Child Naming, Child Nature and Child Nurture				
Origin of names	Biblical	Norman/Teuton	Mixed Biblical	Saints Names
Bible names (Nb)	90%	50%	70%	65%
Descent of names	2 generation nuclear	3 generation extended	3 generation bilateral	3 generation
Parent names (Np)	60–70%	20–30%	20–30%	20–30%
Child nurture	Will-breaking	Will-bending	Will-bracing	Will-building
Sending out	Yes	Mixed	No	Mixed
Old Age, Death				
Age ideals	Elder-Saint	Elder-Patriarch	Elder-Teacher	Elder-Thane
Age ideology	Veneration	Patriarchy	Eldering	Tanistry
Age heaping (A)	Old age bias	Seniority bias	no census data	Mixed
Death ways	Activist-Fatalist	Stoic-Fatalist	Optimist-Fatalist	Nescient-Fatalist
Burial customs	High austerity	High ceremony	Extreme austerity	Folk ritual

Four Regional Cultures in Anglo-America; A Summary of Cultural Characteristics, ca. 1700–50 (continued)

Religion and Magic				
Denomination	Congregational	Anglican	Quaker	Presbyt. etc.
Worship	Lecture-centered	Liturgy-centered	Spirit-centered	Field Mtg. and Fellowship
Magic Obsession	Witchcraft	Fortune	Spiritualism	Sorcery
Learning and Literacy				
Schools	Town schools	Parish schools	Meeting schools	Private schools
Common education	Strong	Weak	Strong	Weak
Higher education	Strong	Strong	Weak	Weak
Years enrolled (E)	4–5 years	1–3 years	3–4 years	1–2 years
Foodways				
Distinctive Dishes	Beans and brown bread	Fricasees	Cream cheese and dry beef	Clabber and potato
Cooking bias	Baking	Roasting and frying	Boiling	Boiling and frying
Eating Patterns	Age-dominant	Rank-dominant	Communal	Gender-dominant
Dress				
Class display	Moderate	High	Moderate	Moderate
Color display	Sad colors	Bright colors	Neutral colors	Folk colors
Sexual display	Moderate to low	Moderate to high	Very low	Very high
Sport, Work and Time				
Amusements	Town and team games	Blood sports	Useful recreations	Field contests
Work ethic	Puritan work ethic	Leisure ethic	Pietist work ethic	Warrior ethic
Economic bias	Mixed commercial	Staple farming	Mixed industrial	Farming & Herding
Time ethic	Improving the time	Killing the time	Redeeming the time	Passing the time
Seasonality (Tm)	Fall peak	Winter peak	Bimodal peaks	Spring peak
Rank and Wealth				
Rank system	Truncated	Hierarchical	Egalitarian	Segmented
Deference	Moderate	High	Low	Mixed
Wealth (G)	.4 to .6	.6 to .75	.3 to .5	.7 to .9
Inheritance	Double partible	Primogeniture	Single partible	Mixed
Land grants (L)	90–120 acres	674 acres	250 acres	n.a.
Settlement and Association, Honor and Shame				
Ideals	Towns	Manorial villages	Farm communities	Hermitage
Realities	Hamlets	Plantations	Farm clusters	Isolated
House location	Roadside	Setback	Corner-clusters	Creek & Spring
Intl. migration	Low	Moderate	High	Very high
Persistence (rPr)	75–96%	50–75%	40–60%	25–40%
Honor	Grace-centered	Rank-centered	Holiness-centered	Primal honor

Power, Order and Freedom

	Town meeting	Parish and court	Commission	Court
Local polity	Town meeting	Parish and court	Commission	Court
Taxes per cap.	12d (1765)	12d (1765)	5d (1765)	4d (1765)
Voting (%AWM)	20–30% and surges	40–50% and stable	20–45% and stable	15–25%
Violence	Very low	Moderate	Low	High
Crime index (C)	0.4	0.9	1.2	5.2
Order index (O)	.51	.31	.08	.25
Freedom ways	Ordered liberty	Hegemonic liberty	Reciprocal liberty	Natural Liberty

Definitions of Quantitative Indicators:

A	Age bias, computed as a ratio of the reported age to expected age
AWM	Voting participation as a proportion of adult white males
B	Bastardy rate, illegitimate births per 1000 total births
C	Crime index, ratio violent crimes against persons to crimes against property
E	Mean years enrolled
F	Completed family size, mean number of children born to all families
G	Gini ratio, ranging from .00 (perfect equality) to .99 (perfect inequality, the uppermost percentile owns all)
L	Land grants, mean size in acres
Ma	Mean age at first marriage
Nb	Naming patterns, proportion of biblical names
Np	Proportion of first-born children named for parents
O	Crimes against order, as a proportion of all crimes
PPR	Prenuptial pregnancy rate, proportion of first births within 8 months of marriage
rPr	Refined persistence rate, percent of living adults persisting through ten years
S	Signature/mark literacy rates, percent signing by mark.
Tm	Season of marriage, the timing of major peaks in the annual marriage cycle

815

Their prevailing religion was Christian and Protestant. Their lands were privately owned according to peculiar British ideas of property which were adopted throughout much of the United States. But in other ways these four British cultures were very different from one another. The more we learn empirically about them, the less similar they appear to be. The skeptical reader is invited to review the evidence of this inquiry, which is summarized in the preceding table.

❧ Other Colonial Cultures

The four major cultures did not embrace all of British America. Other cultural areas also existed. Some were of considerable size, though smaller than the major regions. The largest of these other cultures was New Netherland, which occupied much of the Hudson Valley. In 1700 Dutch burghers and boers were two-thirds of the population in Dutchess and Ulster counties, three-quarters in Orange County, five-sixths in Kings County and nine-tenths in Albany. They also colonized part of East Jersey, where as late as 1790 they were 75 percent of the population in Bergen County, and 80 percent in Somerset County.[7]

This was a very conservative culture. Its old-fashioned Dutch dialect survived even into the mid-nineteenth century. Its architecture remained distinctive for broad barns, hay barracks, step-gabled town houses, and low, narrow farmhouses with half doors. Settlement patterns retained a special character, with homes built in distinctive irregular clusters around a reformed church. Rates of internal migration were exceptionally low, and Dutch households had a different demographic profile from those of English neighbors, with fewer children and more slaves. In 1738, most Dutch families in King's County were slave-owners.[8]

This culture developed its own special ways of dealing with other ethnic groups. It combined formal toleration, social dis-

[7]Patricia U. Bonomi, *A Factious People* (New York, 1971), 22.

[8]Recent historical writing has been more interested in commercial and material processes; see Thomas J. Condon, *New York Beginnings: The Commercial Origins of New Netherland* (New York, 1968); and Van Cleaf Bachman, *Peltries or Plantations* (Baltimore, 1969). The work of historical ethnography is only beginning; see Peter O. Wacker, "The Dutch Culture Area in the Northeast, 1609–1800," *NJH* 104 (1986), 1–21; *idem, Land and People; A Cultural Geography of Preindustrial New Jersey* (New Brunswick, 1975); Sophia Hinshallwood, "The Dutch Culture Area of the Mid-Hudson Valley" (thesis, Rutgers, 1981); David S. Cohen, "How Dutch Were the Dutch of New Netherland?," *NYH* 38 (1981), 43–60.

tance and inequality in high degree. The result was an ethnic pluralism that became more atomistic than in the Delaware Valley and more hierarchical than in New England. The peculiar texture of life in New York City today still preserves qualities which existed in seventeenth-century New Amsterdam—and Old Amsterdam as well.[9]

The culture of New Netherland did not expand far beyond its original boundaries. Its population remained small. In 1664, only 7,000 Dutch settlers (and 3,000 non-Dutch) were living in New Netherland. By 1790 only about 98,000 people of Dutch descent were living in the United States—less than one-tenth the population of New England, and a small fraction of the other major regional populations.[10]

Another distinctive colonial culture developed on the coast of South Carolina. Some of its founding families came from the West Indies; others were French Huguenots, and more than a few were emigrants from tidewater Virginia. Three-quarters of the low-country population in 1790 were slaves who came mostly from the Congo basin and the coast of Angola. These groups rapidly developed their own unique customs and institutions, which were closer to the Caribbean colonies than to the Chesapeake. Speech ways were heavily influenced by the "Gullah" (Angola) dialect of the black majority. Building ways were a unique amalgam of Caribbean, French, African and English elements. Patterns of settlement were marked by the highest level of urbanization in colonial America: nearly 25 percent of low-country whites lived in Charleston. The wealth of its white families was the greatest in the colonies (£450 in 1740), and highly concentrated in a few hands. The annual rhythm of life was regulated by a pattern of transhumance that did not exist in other mainland colonies.[11] This area became a distinct cultural region, but it never

---

[9]Differences between Dutch and English Calvinists prefigured those between Yankees and Yorkers. Besides the familiar texts such as Bradford's *Plymouth Plantation,* much manuscript material exists in English archives such as the Ralph Thoresby diary in the York Archeological Society. In 1678, Thoresby was in Rotterdam. "I could not but with sorrow observe one sinful custom of the place," he wrote, "it being customary for all sorts to profane the Lord's day by singing, playing, walking, sewing, etc., which was a great trouble to me, because they profess the name of Christ, and are of the Reformed churches." Ralph Thoresby Diary, 14 July 1678, ms. 21, YASL.

[10]The preferred estimate of 98,000 is from Thomas L. Purvis, "The European Ancestry of the United States Population, 1790," *WMQ3* (1984), 98. Other estimates by Wacker, Hansen and Swierenga are a little higher—in the range of 100,000 to 110,000. The doubling time of the old Dutch population in the Hudson Valley was approximately 35 years, compared with 25 to 28 years for New England and the Delaware colonies.

developed into a major cultural hearth. As late as 1790 less than 29,000 whites lived in the South Carolina low country, compared with more than 300,000 whites in eastern Virginia and 450,000 in the southern back settlements (of whom 112,000 were in the South Carolina upcountry alone).[12]

Yet another colonial culture developed in North Carolina's Cape Fear Valley, where Highland Scots began to arrive circa 1732. Many followed after the '45 Rebellion, and by 1776 their numbers were nearly as large as the white population in the South Carolina low country.[13] Other ethnic groups also settled in the Cape Fear Valley, but so dominant were highlanders that Gaelic came to be spoken in this region even by people who were not Scots. There is a story of a newly arrived Highland lady who heard two men speaking in Gaelic:

> Assuming by their speech that they must inevitably be fellow High-landers, she came nearer, only to discover that their skin was black. Then she knew that her worst foreboding about the climate of the South was not unfounded and cried in horror, "A Dhia nan fras, am fas sinn vile mar sin?" (O God of mercy, are we all going to turn black like that?)[14]

Even in the twentieth century, the Cape Fear people sent to Scotland for ministers who were required to wear the kilt, play the pipes, and preach in Gaelic.[15]

The political history of this culture was very different from its border neighbors. During the American Revolution the borderers were mostly Whig; Scottish highlanders were mainly Tory. In the new republic, the backsettlers tended to vote Democratic-Republican, and the highlanders of the Cape Fear Valley voted Federalist. Historian Duane Meyer writes that these people were "remarkably consistent in choosing the losing side." They never

---

[11]M. Eugene Sirmans, *Colonial South Carolina: A Political History, 1663–1763* (Chapel Hill, 1966); Peter H. Wood, *Black Majority: Negroes in Colonial South Carolina from 1670 through the Stono Rebellion* (New York, 1974); Charles Joyner, *Down by the Riverside: A South Carolina Slave Community* (Urbana, 1984).

[12]The low country in 1790 was normally defined as the districts of Beaufort, Charleston and Georgetown. See John H. Wolfe, *Jeffersonian Democracy in South Carolina* (Chapel Hill, 1940), 5; Robert Mills, *Statistics of South Carolina* (Charleston, 1826).

[13]Duane Meyer, *The Highland Scots of North Carolina, 1732–1776* (Chapel Hill, 1961).

[14]*Ibid.*, 119; Charles W. Dunn, *Highland Settler: A Portrait of the Scottish Gael in Nova Scotia* (Toronto, 1953), 138.

[15]Personal conversation with Charles Joyner.

became part of the solid south; in 1900 they cast their ballots for McKinley rather than Bryan. Here was another culture that preserved its separate identity into the twentieth century.[16]

❧ Rhythms of Regional Development

Every regional culture had its own history, which unfolded in its own way. But all of them passed through a similar sequence of stages which created a powerful rhythm in colonial history. The first stage was the transit of culture from Britain to America, in which individual actors played decisive roles. In Massachusetts, for example, Puritan leaders such as John Winthrop and John Cotton shaped the future of their region when they decided to bring the charter of the Massachusetts Bay Company to the New World, to define church membership in a rigorous way, to create a standard model for town government, and to block the growth of a Puritan aristocracy in New England. In Virginia, Sir William Berkeley made many critical decisions when he recruited a colonial elite, encouraged the growth of slavery, drove out Puritans and Quakers, and discouraged schools and printing. In Pennsylvania, William Penn's decisions transformed the history of a region—in the design of local institutions, the recruitment of German immigrants, and the content of libertarian laws. In the southern highlands the backcountry "ascendancy" played a seminal role. All of these cultural leaders gave a direction to regional development.

The second stage was a cultural crisis of great intensity. It always began as an internal conflict among immigrant elites who supported the founding purposes of their colony, but disagreed on issues of authority, order, and individual autonomy. In Massachusetts, the crisis came with the Separatist challenge of Roger Williams (1635–36) and the Antinomian Crisis of Anne Hutchinson (1638–39). In Virginia, the critical period was that of Bacon's Rebellion (1676) and the violent repression that followed

[16]Many other colonial cultures in British America maintained separate identities and close relations with various parts of England. The longest and strongest of these associations was that between Newfoundland and the Dorset seaport of Poole, which may have begun as early as 1528 and survived into the twentieth century. F. W. Mathews, *Poole and Newfoundland* (Poole, 1936), copy in DORSRO.

(1676–77). Pennsylvania's crisis occurred in the 1690s, when William Penn briefly lost control of the colony (1692–94) and the Quaker colonists were deeply divided by the "Keithian schism" (1692). The critical time in the back settlements was the Regulation (1768–70). In each case a new clarity was brought to regional cultures by these events.

These crises were followed by a period of cultural consolidation which occurred in Massachusetts during the 1640s, in Virginia during the 1680s, in Pennsylvania during the early decades of the eighteenth century, and in the backcountry during the late eighteenth century. In every case, the dominant culture of each region was hardened into institutions which survived for many years. In Massachusetts, for example, courts, churches, towns, schools, and militia all were given their definitive shape in laws which were passed within the span of a few years, mostly in the period from 1636 to 1648. Something similar happened in most other colonies at comparable stages in their development.

This period of consolidation was followed by a complex and protracted process of cultural devolution. In New England, that trend occurred in the half-century from 1650 to 1700, when Puritans became Yankees. It happened in Virginia from 1690 to 1750, when Royalists became Whigs. It took place in the Delaware Valley during the transition from the second to the third stage of Quakerism, and the development of a more inward-looking faith in an increasingly pluralistic society. In the backcountry, it happened as backsettlers evolved into frontiersmen. In every instance, founding purposes were lost, but institutions were preserved and regional identities were given new life.[17]

---

[17]In New England, some historians of the Puritans understood this process as a great declension. But this captures only one part of a complex transformation, which included strong continuities and positive developments; the best accounts include Richard L. Bushman, *From Puritan to Yankee: Character and the Social Order in Connecticut, 1690–1765* (Cambridge, 1967); Robert G. Pope, *The Half-Way Covenant* (Princeton, 1969). A large literature has also been written on Pennsylvania, including Frederick Tolles, *Meeting House and Counting House* (Chapel Hill, 1948); and Gary Nash, *Quakers and Politics: Pennsylvania, 1681–1726* (Princeton, 1968); Alan Tully, *William Penn's Legacy: Political and Social Structure in Provincial Pennsylvania, 1726–1755* (Baltimore, 1977); on Virginia, Rhys Isaac, *The Transformation of Virginia, 1740–1790* (Chapel Hill, 1982), deals with a different subject. The transformation from Royalists to Whigs in the Chesapeake, and from backsettler to frontiersman in the southern highlands, still await their historians.

❧ Regional Conflict in the Colonies

From the start, the four major cultures of British America did not get on well with one another. Long before collisions of material interest developed, they were divided by conflicts of value. Puritan New Englanders detested the people of Virginia. As early as 1651 one Puritan observed of Virginians in general, "I think they are the farthest from conscience and moral honesty of any such number together in the world."[1] This attitude of moral disapproval toward the Chesapeake settlers was shared by the Delaware colonists. When a young gentleman of New Jersey was preparing to take a job in Virginia, friends warned him that "the people there are profane, and exceeding wicked."[2]

Virginians equally despised New England Puritans and Delaware Quakers. In 1736, William Byrd II expressed his contempt in a letter to the Earl of Egmont. "The saints of New England," Byrd wrote, "I fear will find out some trick to evade your Act of Parliament. They have a great dexterity in palliating a perjury so as to leave no taste of it in the mouth, nor can any people like them slip through a penal statute. . . . A watchful eye must be kept on these foul traders."[3]

One of the few points of agreement between Anglican Virginians and Puritan New Englanders was their common loathing of Quakers. However inoffensive the Society of Friends may seem today, they were genuinely hated in their own time as dangerous radicals, disturbers of the peace, and pious frauds and hypocrites who were said to "pray for their fellow men one day a week, and on them the other six."[4]

Many Quakers in turn not unreasonably developed an intense hatred of Puritans. Members of this sect which preached the idea of universal salvation made an exception for the people of New England. As late as 1795, a Pennsylvania Quaker collectively reviled all Yankees as "the flock of Cain."[5]

The North British borderers who came to the backcountry were heartily disliked by Puritans, cavaliers and Quakers alike. New Englanders regarded them as savages and barbarians. A Pennsylvania Quaker called them the Goths and Vandals of

[1]George Gardiner, *A Description of the New World* (London, 1651), 92.
[2]Fithian, *Journal and Letters,* 62 (2 Jan. 1774).
[3]William Byrd II to the Earl of Egmont, 12 July 1736, Tinling, ed., *Three Byrds,* I, 487.
[4]Caleb Raper Commonplace Book, 1711, HAV.
[5]Joshua Evans Journal, 24.vi.1795, SWAR.

America; another described them as the "unlearned and uncivil-
ized part of the human race." Tidewater Virginians doubted that
they were part of humanity at all; one cavalier defined them as "a
spurious race of mortals."[6]

The backsettlers reciprocated these opinions. In the Pennsylvania interior, the Paxton Boys slaughtered a group of peaceable
Indians, and "made boast how they had gotten so many scalps
they would go to Philadelphia and the Quakers should share the
same fate." There was also very bad blood between backcountry
folk and the tidewater gentry in Virginia and the Carolinas, and
between the North British backsettlers and New England
Yankees.[7]

Familiarity did not improve these attitudes. On close acquaintance, various members of the four folk cultures were startled to
discover how very different they were from one another. The
New Jersey tutor Philip Fithian wrote to a Yankee friend about
the Virginians, "their manner of living, their eating, drinking, diversions, exercise &c, are in many ways different from any thing
you have been accustomed to."[8]

On many occasions these antipathies gave rise to acts of violence. Fighting broke out repeatedly between Puritans and Quakers in central New Jersey. The inhabitants of the Delaware Valley
and the people of Chesapeake region met in armed combat along
what is now the Mason-Dixon Line. Backsettlers and tidewater
folk came to blows in Virginia, North Carolina, South Carolina
and Pennsylvania. North Britons fought New Englanders in
northeastern Pennsylvania and the Connecticut Valley after the
Revolution.

These tensions were reduced by the simple expedient of physical separation. In the great American spaces, the four British
folk cultures found room enough to protect their differences
merely by moving apart. This process of spatial separation created a curious paradox in colonial America. "Early America,"
observes John Roche, "was an open country dotted with closed
enclaves."[9]

To this general rule, there were many exceptions—notably in
the seaport cities which collected very mixed populations. But in

[6]Charles M. Andrews, *Colonial Folkways* (New York, 1919), 235; Joshua Evans Journal,
24.ii.1797, SWAR.
[7]Rhoda Barber Journal, HSP.
[8]Fithian, *Journal and Letters*, 220.
[9]Conversation with the author.

relative terms, the urban population of early America actually declined during the period from 1720 to 1775. At the same time, many rural parts of British America grew more uniform rather than less so, and more fixed in their traditional ways.

❧ Regional Cultures and the Coming of Independence

In the mid-eighteenth century, the four cultures of British America suddenly faced a major challenge from a new imperial elite in London. This small ruling class developed its own special variety of English culture, which differed very much from the older folkways of British America. In the late seventeenth and eighteenth century, it invented its own distinctive language which is still the hallmark of England's upper class. To American ears, the salient feature of this speech was its very broad *a,* which is sometimes said to have been popularized by David Garrick on the London stage. That story may be apocryphal, but the broad *a* became fashionable during Garrick's life (1717–79). With other refinements of idiom and intonation, it created an elite dialect which promoted the integration of England's ruling few.[10] It also increased the cultural distance between the few and the many.[11]

This new dialect of England's ruling class differed markedly from the speech ways of American colonists, to whom it seemed contrived and pretentious. On the other hand, British officers who came to the colonies remarked that natives even of high rank seemed to be speaking in archaic accents of the seventeenth century. Loyalists who fled to Britain after the Revolution were startled to discover that their old-fashioned speech and manners were far removed from the latest affectations of London drawing rooms.[12]

The new speech ways of England's governing class were only one part of a complex elite culture which was also distinctive in its ideas of family life, marriage practices and especially its child-rearing customs. It also had its own ideas about order, freedom

---

[10]Another part of this speech way, now long forgotten, was the slurred *s* which came to be called the cavalryman's lisp. Perhaps borrowed from Castilian Spanish, this curious mannerism was adopted by England's equestrian class, and persisted in fashionable cavalry regiments even into the twentieth century.

[11]Raymond Williams, "The Growth of 'Standard English,'" in *The Long Revolution* (rev. ed., New York, 1966), 214–29.

[12]Henry Van Schaack, *The Life of Peter Van Schaack* (New York, 1842), 162–63.

and power which became major threats to the cultures of British America.

In the century from 1660 to 1760 England's elite created many new institutions which still dominate the life of their nation. The regimental traditions of the British army were formed in this period. The Royal Navy, despite its claims to be the "senior service" founded by King Alfred, was largely a creation of this era. So also were many legal institutions; the rituals, ceremonies, architecture and costumes of English law still preserve the fashions of the century in which they were elaborately developed. In this period the Church of England created new institutions of evangelical Anglicanism, notably the Society for the Propagation of the Gospel in Foreign Parts. The Bank of England and many great commercial institutions were founded in the same time. A new national bureaucracy began its inexorable growth in Whitehall's neoclassical buildings. Above all these various institutions hovered the King-in-Parliament, an elaborately integrated idea of sovereignty that had scarcely existed before 1689.

These new ideas and institutions were no sooner formed than they were brought to bear upon the American colonies, whose independent ways appeared to be archaic survivals from an earlier and less happy age of strife and social confusion. As late as 1903, an English historian of high rank was still raging against the narrowness and provincialism of the American colonies. "There was not one of these communities," wrote Sir John Fortescue, "not even the tiniest of the Antilles, but possessed its little legislature on the English model, and consequently not one but enjoyed facilities for excessive indulgence of local feeling, local faction and local folly."[13]

England's governing elites mounted a major effort to bring the American colonies into line with the new national institutions. This challenge was not only political, but broadly cultural. It included proposals for an American aristocracy on the model of the Irish peerage; an American bureaucracy like that in Whitehall; and an American religious establishment like the Church of England. The folkways of British America were deeply threatened by these policies.

Shortly before the American Revolution, for example, the Anglican Society for the Propagation of Gospel sent missionaries to Massachusetts for the conversion of the "heathen." They built

[13]John W. Fortescue, *A History of the British Army* (13 vols. in 20, London, 1902), III, 3.

one of their missions not on the frontier but across the street from Harvard College and labored to convert the sons of Congregational New England. The head of this Anglican organization, Bishop Thomas Secker, made no secret of his contempt for the colonists, whom he collectively characterized in 1741 as "wicked, and dissolute and brutal in every respect."[14] In 1758, this man became Archbishop of Canterbury and tried to create uniform Anglican establishments in the colonies. His grand design simultaneously posed a mortal threat to the Congregational orthodoxy of New England, the Quakers' regime of religious freedom of Pennsylvania, the powerful lay-vestries of Virginia, and Presbyterians in the backcountry.[15]

The new imperial elite also tried to force educational institutions and social structures in the colonies into line with its own ideas. The authors of the Stamp Act believed that

> the Duties upon admissions to any professions or to the University degees should be certainly as high as they are in England; it would indeed be better if they were raised both here and there in order to keep mean persons out of those situations in life which they disgrace.[16]

They imposed a heavy stamp tax of two pounds on matriculation papers, and two pounds more on diplomas "in any university, academy, college, or seminary of learning within the said colonies" (compared with two shillings, eighteen pence in England). To restrict the growth of professions, they placed a duty of ten pounds on papers of admission to practice law.[17]

They also attempted to restrain the institutional growth of regional cultures in even more direct ways. In 1769, for example, backcountry Presbyterians in Mecklenberg County, North Carolina, founded an institution (which still exists) called Queen's College. A charter was reluctantly granted by the North Carolina legislature, only after a "considerable body" of backsettlers marched on the colonial capital. When Queen's College began to operate it was the only such institution south and west of Williamsburg,

[14]Thomas Secker, *A Sermon Preached before the Society* (1741); reprinted in Frank J. Klingberg, *Anglican Humanitarianism in Colonial New York* (1940), 213–233.

[15]Arthur Lyon Cross, *Anglican Episcopate and the American Colonies* (1902, rpt. Hamden, Conn., 1964); Carl Bridenbaugh, *Mitre and Sceptre* (New York, 1962).

[16]Edmund S. Morgan, *Prologue to Revolution: Sources and Documents on the Stamp Act Crisis* (Chapel Hill, 1953), 57.

[17]D. Pickering, *The Statutes at Large . . .* (46 vols., Cambridge, 1762–1807), XXVI, 179–87, 201–4. (5 George III, chap. 12).

but it was one too many for imperial authorities. In 1773 after long delay, the charter of Queen's College was disallowed in London on the ground it gave preference to Presbyterians. At the same time, the Crown also disallowed an amended North Carolina Marriage Act which permitted Presbyterian ministers to solemnize marriages, on the ground that it did not give preference to the Church of England. These decisions became symbolic issues which infuriated the backsettlers and deepened their determination to "support the Government under which we find the most liberty," as one Mecklenberg petition ominously threatened.[18]

While Bishop Secker was trying to change the religious life of the colonies, others of the imperial elite reformed its legal institutions. Each cultural region had its own system of courts which had long remained in their own hands. Now Americans were given an expanded system of vice admiralty courts which operated without juries under Roman Civil Law which was alien to American customs. The colonists were also forced to deal with novel legal doctrines, and new hierarchies of barristers and legal officers.

England's imperial elite also mounted another assault on the political institutions of British America. The result was a decline in the power and autonomy of regional cultures. As late as 1660, for example, five out of seven mainland colonies in British North America had elected their governors. By 1760, only two out of thirteen colonies did so. The rest were ruled by royal governors, who had been appointed in London from the ranks of England's ruling class. One of these men, Governor Francis Bernard, was chosen governor of Massachusetts solely because he had married the cousin of a powerful peer. In 1774, Bernard formally proposed the creation of an American aristocracy. "A nobility appointed by the King for life, and made independent," he wrote, "would probably give strength and stability to the American governments, as effectually as an hereditary nobility does to that of Great Britain."[19]

These various challenges threatened all four American cultures at the same time. In response to a common danger, they forgot

---

[18]The leaders of this agitation were the Alexander and Polk clans. See Norris W. Preyer, *Hezekiah Alexander and the Revolution in the Backcountry* (Charlotte, 1987), 58, 72, 88.

[19]*Select Letters on the Trade and Government of America, and the Principles of Law and Polity, Applied to the American Colonies* (London, 1774); Edmund S. Morgan and Helen M. Morgan, *The Stamp Act Crisis* (New York, 1953), 14–18.

their differences and joined together in the movement that led to the American Revolution. The indigenous elites of New England, Virginia and the backcountry were united in that struggle. Only the Delaware elite was divided—not so much by their views of British policy as by their reluctance to use force against any provocation.

❧ The Revolution as a Rising of Regional Cultures

The Revolution was not a single struggle, but a series of four separate Wars of Independence, waged in very different ways by the major cultures of British America. The first American Revolution (1775–76) was a massive popular insurrection in New England. An army of British regulars was defeated by a Yankee militia which was much like the Puritan train bands from which they were descended. These citizen soldiers were urged into battle by New England's "black regiment" of Calvinist clergy. The purpose of New England's War for Independence, as stated both by ministers and by laymen such as John and Samuel Adams, was not to secure the rights of man in any universal sense. Most New Englanders showed little interest in John Locke or Cato's letters. They sought mainly to defend their accustomed ways against what the town of Malden called "the contagion of venality and dissipation" which was spreading from London to America.

Many years later, historian George Bancroft asked a New England townsman why he and his friends took up arms in the Revolution. Had he been inspired by the ideas of John Locke? The old soldier confessed that he had never heard of Locke. Had he been moved by Thomas Paine's *Common Sense?* The honest Yankee admitted that he had never read Tom Paine. Had the Declaration of Independence made a difference? The veteran thought not. When asked to explain why he fought in his own words, he answered simply that New Englanders had always managed their own affairs, and Britain tried to stop them, and so the war began.

In 1775, these Yankee soldiers were angry and determined men, in no mood for halfway measures. Their revolution was not merely a mind game. Most able-bodied males served in the war, and the fighting was cruel and bitter. So powerful was the resistance of this people-in-arms that after 1776 a British army was never again able to remain in force on the New England mainland.

The second American War for Independence (1776–81) was a more protracted conflict in the middle states and the coastal south. This was a gentlemen's war. On one side was a professional army of regulars and mercenaries commanded by English gentry. On the other side was an increasingly professional American army led by a member of the Virginia gentry. The principles of this second American Revolution were given their Aristotelian statement in the Declaration of Independence by another Virginia gentleman, Thomas Jefferson, who believed that he was fighting for the ancient liberties of his "Saxon ancestors."

The third American Revolution reached its climax in the years from 1779 to 1781. This was a rising of British borderers in the southern backcountry against American loyalists and British regulars who invaded the region. The result was a savage struggle which resembled many earlier conflicts in North Britain, with much family feuding and terrible atrocities committed on both sides. Prisoners were slaughtered, homes were burned, women were raped and even small children were put to the sword.

The fourth American Revolution continued in the years from 1781 to 1783. This was a non-violent economic and diplomatic struggle, in which the elites of the Delaware Valley played a leading part. The economic war was organized by Robert Morris of Philadelphia. The genius of American diplomacy was Benjamin Franklin. The Delaware culture contributed comparatively little to the fighting, but much to other forms of struggle.

The loyalists who opposed the revolution tended to be groups who were not part of the four leading cultures. They included the new imperial elites who had begun to multiply rapidly in many colonial capitals, and also various ethnic groups who lived on the margins of the major cultures: notably the polyglot population of lower New York, the Highland Scots of Carolina and African slaves who inclined against their Whiggish masters.

ᴥ Regional Cultures in the New Republic: The Constitutional Coalition, 1787–95

After the achievement of independence, the four regional cultures found themselves in conflict with one another. Even during the war, the Continental Congress divided into factions which were not primarily ideological or economic, but regional and cultural in their origin. Three voting blocs appeared: an "eastern" bloc of colonies settled by New Englanders; a southern bloc centered on tidewater Virginia; and a midland bloc which consisted mainly of delegations from the Delaware Valley. A leading historian of the Continental Congress has found that regional conflicts among these cultures were the leading determinants of Congressional voting on major issues from 1777 to 1785, such as oversight of the army, the taxing power of Congress and navigation of the Mississippi River.[20]

So strong were these regional identities in the new Confederation that the British secret agent Paul Wentworth reported that the American states comprised not one but three republics: an "eastern republic of Independents in church and state"; a "middle republic of toleration in church and state"; and a "southern republic or mixed government copied nearly from Great Britain." Wentworth asserted that the differences among these American republics were greater than those between European states. "There is hardly any observation, moral or political, which will equally apply," he believed.[21]

The Constitution of 1787 was an attempt to write the rules of engagement among these regional "republics" of British America. The purpose of the Constitutional Convention was to create an institutional consensus within which four regional cultures could mutually agree to respect their various differences. In the Great Convention itself, some of the most important compromises were not between states or sections or ideologies, but between cultural regions.

A case in point was the question of representation in the new government. Edmund Randolph's "Virginia plan" was accepted as a basis for discussion, but required major modification before it was generally acceptable. The result was a series of compromises between big states and little ones on the two branches of Congress. Not so familiar, but equally important was another compromise between cultural regions. Randolph's plan envisioned a national polity such as Virginia possessed—an oligarchy of country gentlemen who dominated the legislature by long ten-

---

[20] In the new nation, "eastern" usually meant New England. Not affiliated with any of these blocs were a few independent Congressmen mostly from Rhode Island, Maryland and the Carolina low country—the boundary cultures of British America. See H. James Henderson, "The Structure of Politics in the Continental Congress," in Stephen G. Kurtz and James H. Hutson, eds., *Essays on the American Revolution* (Chapel Hill, 1973), 157–196; and *idem, Party Politics in the Continental Congress* (New York, 1974); cf. Joseph L. Davis, *Sectionalism in American Politics, 1774–1787* (Madison, 1977).

[21] Paul Wentworth, "Minutes Respecting Political Parties in America and Sketches of the Leading Persons in Each Province," in Benjamin F. Stevens, ed., *Facsimiles of Manuscripts in European Archives Relating to America, 1773–1783* (25 vols., 1889–95), XVII, 487.

ure and infrequent elections. This system was alien to New
England. Roger Sherman explained to the Virginians, ". . . in
Connecticut, elections have been very frequent, yet great stability
and uniformity both as to persons and measures have been experienced from its original establishment to the present time; a
period of more than 130 years."[22]

On this question the little state of Connecticut and the large
state of Massachusetts voted together against Virginia. The result
was a regional compromise of high complexity. Several generations of political scientists have misled us into thinking that the
"great compromise" was mainly intended to mediate between
large states and little ones. But the more serious task was to reconcile different political cultures in the four regions of British
America. Regional compromises were also necessary on questions
of representation, taxation, economic policy, slavery and ideas of
law and liberty. In the great convention, as in the Continental
Congress, the strongest voting patterns were regional in nature.

One region, the backcountry, was largely unrepresented in the
convention. The federal Constitution was enacted mainly by a
coalition of cultural elites from New England, Virginia and the
Delaware Valley. It was generally opposed by the backsettlers,
and by dissenting minorities in the various regions. Opposition
came from boundary cultures between the major regions—notably the Clintonian elite of New York, the Chase faction in Maryland and Rhode Islanders of every description. But the dominant
coalition of three regional elites supported the Constitution, and
secured its ratification.

In 1789, the coexistence of the regional cultures was further
protected by the Bill of Rights. A case in point was the first sentence of the First Amendment, "Congress shall make no law
respecting an establishment of religion, or prohibiting the free
exercise thereof." This deceptively simple statement was another
regional compromise of high complexity. Its intent was to preserve religious freedom of Virginia and Pennsylvania, and at the
same time to protect the religious establishments of New England
from outside interference. As time passed its meaning was
enlarged; a measure which was written to protect regional pluralism became a basis for national libertarianism.[23]

---

[22]James Madison, *Notes of Debates in the Federal Convention of 1787*, ed. Adrienne Koch (Athens O., 1966), 195.

[23]Madison's first draft of this clause embodied attitudes that prevailed in Virginia and Penn-

❧ The Persistence of Old British Cultures in the New Republic

After the revolution, foreign travelers in the United States continued for many years to remark on what one called the "essential Englishness" of its culture. The agricultural reformer William Strickland wrote, ". . . the predilection of these northern states for everything that is English, and their attachment to the *Old Country*, as they call England, is truly remarkable, of the New England states in particular . . . it is not quite so strong in N. York, which is inhabited by a mixed people."[24]

Another commentator remarked in 1818, "Whoever has well observed America cannot doubt that she still remains *essentially English*, in language, habits, laws, customs, manners, morals, and religion. . . . the great mass of our people is of *English* origin, and *not* made up, originally, of convicts, mendicants and vagabonds, according to the vulgar but erroneous opinion."[25]

Well into the nineteenth century, foreign travelers were still repeating these remarks. In 1835, French visitor Michel Chevalier described the people of New England as not merely English, but "double distilled English."[26] Alexis de Tocqueville added, "In spite of the ocean that intervenes, I cannot consent to separate America from Europe. I consider the people of the United States as that portion of the English people who are commissioned to explore the forests of the new world."[27]

In the Appalachian highlands, nineteenth-century travelers were even more startled by the patterns of cultural persistence which they discovered there. George Flower, in the mountains of western Pennsylvania, was surprised in 1816 to find "a style of

---

sylvania: "The civil rights of none shall be abridged on account of religious belief or worship, nor shall any national religion be established, nor shall the full and equal rights of conscience be in any manner, or on any pretext, infringed." It was strenuously opposed by New England congressmen (Sherman and Huntington of Conn., Gerry of Mass., Livermore of N.H.), who protested that it would be "extremely hurtful to the cause of religion" in "congregations to the Eastward." The opposition was regional rather than ideological; it included both Federalists and Antifederalists, or as Elbridge Gerry preferred to call them, "rats and anti-rats." The final wording was a regional compromise. *Annals of Congress* 1st Cong., 1st Session, cols. 434–35, 729–32 (8 June, 15 Aug. 1789).

[24]William Strickland to J. Robinson, 5 Dec. 1794, Strickland Papers, NYHS.

[25]John Bristed, *Aermica and Her Resources* (London, 1818) 377, 386.

[26]Michel Chevalier, *Society, Manners and Politics in the United States* (1961, New York, 1969), 139.

[27]Alexis de Tocqueville, *Democracy in America* (2 vols., New York, 1951), II, 36.

conversation that prevailed in England about Cromwell's time."[28]
That same discovery would often be made by others through the
next two centuries. A student of American language, Albert
Marckwardt, has written that "on the average of once every five
years some well meaning amateur in the field of folklore or cultural history 'discovers' that either the Kentucky or Virginian or
Ozark mountaineers . . . speak the undefiled English of Chaucer
or Shakespeare."

In fact, this impression of cultural stasis was not correct. What
appeared at first hearing to be merely a linguistic archaism was
produced by a complex pattern of continuity and change. Nevertheless, each of the four folkways of English speaking America
retained its linguistic identity for many years after independence.[29]

The Hegemony of Four Cultural Regions

After independence, all four Anglo-American cultures began to
expand very rapidly. Each of the original areas in Massachusetts
Bay, tidewater Virginia, the Delaware Valley and the Appalachian
highlands were what folklorists call "cultural hearths" or
"seedbeds" from which four different populations overspread
the nation.

These various groups intermingled very little, except along the
edges of the great migration-streams. Even there, they tended to
settle in homogenous communities, and regarded one another as
aliens. In south-central Illinois, for example, an area settled
mostly from the southern highlands, a New Englander named
Lucy Maynard wrote, "Our neighbors are principally from Indiana and Kentucky, some from Virginia, all friendly but very different from our people in their manners and language and every
other way." An English traveler William Oliver observed in 1843
that pioneers from the various cultural regions were as unlike one
another "as if they were different nations."[30]

[28]George Flower, *History of the English Settlement in Edwards County, Illinois. . . .* (Chicago, 1882), II, 24.

[29]Marckwardt, in company with many linguists, heaped ridicule upon this idea. But ridicule is not a form of refutation, and as Marckwardt himself observed, these persistent "impressions of archaism remain to be accounted for." Albert H. Marckwardt, *American English* (2d ed., rev. by J. L. Dillard, New York, 1980), 70–71.

[30]John Mack Faragher, *Sugar Creek: Life on the Illinois Prairie* (New Haven, 1986), 45–46.

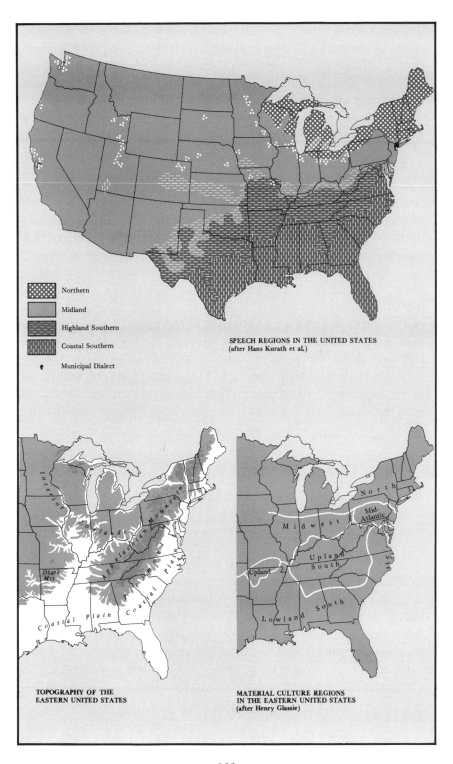

Northern

Midland

Highland Southern

Coastal Southern

♪ Municipal Dialect

SPEECH REGIONS IN THE UNITED STATES
(after Hans Kurath et al.)

TOPOGRAPHY OF THE
EASTERN UNITED STATES

MATERIAL CULTURE REGIONS
IN THE EASTERN UNITED STATES
(after Henry Glassie)

Traces of these separate migrations are still visible today in the regional patterns of American speech. During the mid-twentieth century, linguistic geographers discovered four major dialect regions in the continental United States. They are the areas in which the four English folkways expanded after independence.

One area, the "northern speech region," included New England, upstate New York, northern Ohio and Indiana, much of Michigan and Wisconsin, the northern plains, and the Pacific North West, together with islands of urban speech at Denver, Salt Lake City and San Francisco. A second area of "midland speech" covered the middle states, the middle west, and the middle latitudes from Pennsylvania to the Pacific coast, broadening outward in the Mississippi Valley; its cultural hearth was the Delaware Valley. The third speech region, called "coastal south," extended from Virginia to Florida along the Atlantic coast and the Gulf of Mexico. Its soft southern drawl of this region was carried from the Chesapeake. The fourth speech region was "highland southern," from the Appalachia and the old southwest across the lower Mississippi Valley to Texas, New Mexico, Arizona and Southern California. Similar patterns also appeared in material culture, vernacular architecture, onomastic customs, folklore and many other indicators. All of this evidence describes an historical process by which four regional cultures expanded throughout the United States.

❧ The Presidency as a Case Study

For two centuries after 1789, the four major regions controlled the national politics of the United States as completely as they dominated its language and its culture. Not until the late twentieth century did this pattern begin to change. An indicator of this hegemony may be seen in the cultural origins of American Presidents. In two centuries from 1789 to 1989, the highest office has been held by forty men, of whom thirty-eight were descended from one or another of the four folk migrations.

Of those four cultural groups, this historian was surprised to discover that the largest number of Presidents, eighteen in all, were descended in whole or in part from North British borderers, most of whom had settled in the backcountry during the eighteenth century. They included Andrew Jackson, James Knox Polk, James Buchanan, Andrew Johnson, Ulysses Grant, Rutherford Hayes, Chester Arthur, Grover Cleveland, Benjamin Harrison, William McKinley, Theodore Roosevelt (who was nearly three-quarters North British), Woodrow Wilson, Harry Truman, Lyndon Johnson, Richard Nixon, Gerald Ford, Jimmy Carter and Ronald Reagan.[31]

The next largest group of Presidents, sixteen altogether, traced their American ancestry wholly or partly to Puritans who had landed in Massachusetts during the great migration (1629–1640). They included John and John Quincy Adams, Millard Fillmore

---

[31]Andrew Jackson was entirely of North British stock; his parents emigrated from Carrickfergus, northern Ireland, in 1765.

James Knox Polk was descended from William and Margaret Pollock [shortened to Polk], emigrants from Londonderry in 1698; the future President's mother was Jane Knox and his maternal grandmother was Mary Wilson; both were of North British origin.

James Buchanan's father emigrated from County Donegal to the backcountry in 1783.

Andrew Johnson's parents were Jacob and Mary (McDonough) Johnson; his paternal grandfather was Andrew Johnson, who migrated from Ulster to the backcountry ca. 1759.

Zachary Taylor's progenitor James Taylor emigrated from Carlisle, Cumberland County.

Rutherford Hayes's namesake came from Scotland, ca. 1680.

Chester Arthur was the son of Ulster emigrant Alan Arthur who had been born in Dreen, County Antrim (the house is now an historic site), and after attending college in Belfast came to Quebec, ca. 1818 (Sam Henry, "The Ulster Background of Chester Alan Arthur . . .," *Ulster-Irish Society Year Book* (1939), 38–46).

Grover Cleveland's mother Ann Neal was the daughter of an Anglo-Irish immigrant to the backcountry.

Benjamin Harrison's mother was Elizabeth Irwin, of a rich and powerful Anglo-Scottish border family in backcountry Westmoreland County, Pa.; his paternal grandmother was Anna Symmes, of New England ancestry; his paternal father was John Scott Harrison, of Virginia.

William McKinley's father, and also his mother Nancy Campbell Allison, came mostly from border immigrants who settled in Pennsylvania, ca. 1740; but an important family influence was great-grandmother Mary Rose, an English Quaker whose forbears came to Pennsylvania with William Penn (Robert P. Porter and James Boyle, *Life of William McKinley* (Cleveland, 1897)).

Theodore Roosevelt's mother Martha Stewart Bulloch was of border Scots ancestors who came to South Carolina in the 18th century; his paternal grandparents were Cornelius Van Schaik Roosevelt (entirely Dutch) and Margaret Barnhill of Pennsylvania.

Woodrow Wilson's father, Joseph Ruggles Wilson, was the son of an immigrant from northern Ireland. His mother, Jessie Woodrow, had been born in Carlisle, on the Cumbrian border of England. The future President identified strongly with what he called "the stern covenanter tradition that is behind me" (Arthur Link, *Wilson: The Road to the White House* (Princeton, 1947).

Harry S. Truman's parents were of English and Scots backcountry stock; genealogists later found a thin link to the Tylers of tidewater Virginia, which was unknown to the President.

Lyndon Johnson was the great-great-grandson of John Johnson, an English borderer who was in Georgia by 1795. The Johnsons intermarried with eminent backcountry families including the Polks and Buntons. His mother, Rebekah Baines, was of lowland Scots descent on her father's side and German on her mother's side.

Gerald Ford was originally named Leslie Lynch King. His natural father was of mixed English and Scots-Irish stock. The future President was an adopted child, raised by Gerald R. Ford, Sr., a businessman in Grand Rapids, Michigan.

Jimmy Carter was mostly of border and backcountry stock; his Carter forbears had lived in the interior of Georgia for eight generations; the future President's mother also came from border Scots who had lived in the backcountry since the 18th century.

Ronald Reagan's Irish Catholic forbear Michael O'Regan entered the United States without papers in the 1840s. The future President's mother was of mixed Anglo-Scottish Protestant border and backcountry descent; her culture was dominant in his upbringing.

and Franklin Pierce, Abraham Lincoln and Ulysses Grant, James
A. Garfield and Chester A. Arthur, Rutherford Hayes and Grover
Cleveland, Benjamin Harrison and William Howard Taft, Warren
Harding, Calvin Coolidge and George Bush.[32] Also in this group
was Franklin Delano Roosevelt, who was three-quarters New
England Yankee despite his Dutch name.[33]

New England ancestry was important to the self-identities of
these men. All but one of them took a suitably solemn pride in
their Puritan forbears. The exception was Abraham Lincoln, who
made a typically Lincolnian joke about his Puritan past. "The first
ancestor that I know anything about," he told a friend, "was Tom
Lincoln who came over in 1634 and settled at a place [called]
Hingham—or perhaps it was Hanghim. Which was it, judge?"[34]

[32]The first Adams was a Puritan maltster who came to New England in 1638; both John and
John Quincy Adams were entirely descended from families who arrived in the great migration.
    Millard Fillmore was entirely of old New England stock. He was the son of Nathaniel and
Phebe (Millard) Fillmore, whose ancestors had arrived in the great migration.
    Franklin Pierce was descended from Thomas Pierce, who emigrated to Charlestown, Mas-
sachusetts, in 1634–35; his mother, Anna Kendrick, was also of an old New England family
which came in the great migration.
    Rutherford Hayes was of mixed ancestry; he was descended from George Hayes, who emi-
grated from Scotland to New England, ca. 1680, and on his mother's side from John Birchard,
who settled in New England ca. 1635. Despite these Scottish and Huguenot names, his biog-
rapher notes that the "majority of his forefathers were English on both sides," mostly
descended from the great migration (H. J. Eckenrode, *Rutherford B. Hayes* (Port Washington,
N.Y., 1963), 4). Hayes identified strongly with his New England forbears (letter to Harriet
Moody, 24 Feb. 1838, *Diary and Letters*, I, 19).
    James Garfield's American roots began with Edward Garfield, who came to Massachusetts
Bay in 1630. The future President's mother was Eliza Ballou, also of an old Massachusetts
family.
    Chester Arthur was half-Yankee; his Ulster emigrant father married Malvina Stone, of old
New England stock.
    Grover Cleveland was also of mixed origins; the first Cleveland came from East Anglia to
Massachusetts in 1635; his father was a Congregational (later Presbyterian) minister who wed
Ann Neal, who was the daughter of an Anglo-Irish immigrant and an Anglo-German Quaker
mother from Germantown, Pennsylvania.
    William Howard Taft was entirely of New England stock. An ancestor named Robert Taft
appeared in the records of Braintree, Massachusetts, by 1678; the date of his emigration is
unknown. The president's paternal grandmother, Sylvia Howard, was descended from forbears
originally called Hayward who settled in Braintree by 1642. His mother, Louisa Maria Torrey,
was descended from Capt. William Torrey, who emigrated to Massachusetts in 1640.
    John Calvin Coolidge traced his descent from John Coolidge, who had migrated from Cam-
bridgeshire to Massachusetts ca. 1635. The future President's mother, Victoria Moor, was of
an eminent Connecticut Valley family. Her father Hiram Dunlap Moor was of mixed English
and Scottish descent; her mother, Abigail Franklin, came from forbears who had migrated to
Massachusetts during the 1630s.
[33]Franklin Roosevelt's Dutch grandfather Isaac Roosevelt married Mary Aspinwall, of a New
England family who arrived in Boston ca. 1630. His mother Sara Delano came entirely from
old New England stock; his maternal grandmother was a Lyman, whose forbears had come to
Massachusetts in 1631.
[34]He was descended from Samuel Lincoln, a weaver who migrated from East Anglia to Massachusetts in 1637; several Lincolns moved to Berks County, Pennsylvania, marrying with Quak-

Except for Lincoln, the others strongly identified with their New England roots, even far beyond the genealogical fact. Ulysses Grant, for example, was only one-quarter New Englander, but he was taught by his genealogist-father to think of himself as mainly of New England stock.[35] Even Warren Harding, the least puritanical of American Presidents, made a hobby of his New England genealogy, and devoted many proud hours to tracing his Calvinist forbears.[36]

A third group of ten Presidents were descended from Virginia's "distressed cavaliers." They were George Washington, Thomas Jefferson, James Madison, James Monroe, William Henry Harrison, John Tyler, Zachary Taylor (part), Benjamin Harrison (part), Harry Truman (part) and Jimmy Carter (part).[37]

---

ers. "The family were originally Quakers," the President wrote, "though in later times they have fallen from the peculiar habits of that people." The ancestry of Lincoln's mother Nancy Hanks is unknown; she may have come from one of many Quaker Hanks families who went from Cheshire and Derbyshire to Pennsylvania during the 1680s. Lincoln was raised by a stepmother of part New England stock, Sarah Bush Johnston, who became a strong influence upon the future President. See Abraham Lincoln, "Autobiography Written for John L. Scripps, 1860," Abraham Lincoln to Solomon Lincoln, 6 March 1848; and Abraham Lincoln to Jesse W. Fell, 20 Dec. 1859, in *The Collected Works of Abraham Lincoln,* ed. Roy P. Basler (New Brunswick, 1953), IV, 60–61; I, 456; II, 511; cf. William E. Barton, *Lineage of Lincoln* (Indianapolis, 1929), 316–18.

[35]Grant was mostly of border stock, but identified primarily with his Puritan forbears, Matthew and Priscilla Grant, who came to Massachusetts ca. 1630. Matthew Grant's Puritan diary survives in the Connecticut State Library. Grant's mother was Hannah Simpson, from a Pennsylvania family whose origin was unknown to the future President. He wrote in his memoirs, "I have little information about her ancestors . . . her family took no interest in genealogy. . . . on the other side my father took a great interest in the subject" (I, 22). His mother was in fact the granddaughter of John Simpson, who emigrated from northern Ireland to Pennsylvania in 1763. Grant's New England father married Rachel Kelly of Westmoreland County, Pennsylvania.

[36]He was descended from Richard Harding, who came with his brothers to Massachusetts before 1640, and whose children and grandchildren intermarried with Puritan families and moved west to New York and Pennsylvania. His mother, Phoebe Dickerson, was of a Quaker family who settled in West Jersey before 1680.

[37]The first Washingtons were two Royalist brothers of an old Northampton gentry family who came to Virginia, ca. 1656. The President's mother, Mary Ball Washington, was descended from Col. William Ball, the second son of an armigerous Berkshire family who emigrated in 1650.

Thomas Jefferson's paternal origins are unknown; his mother, Jane Randolph, was the daughter of Isham Randolph of a Royalist gentry family in Warwickshire which appeared in Virginia ca. 1650.

James Madison's roots reached to an emigrant from Gloucestershire who patented 600 acres in 1653 and whose children intermarried with the Catlett, Conway and Taylor families.

James Monroe was descended from Capt. Andrew Monroe, a cavalry commander who emigrated after the battle of Preston in 1648.

William Henry Harrison was the son of Virginia's governor Benjamin Harrison (1726–91), and grandson of Robert (King) Carter. His mother was Elizabeth Bassett, a relative of Washington.

Three of these lineages were very thin. Benjamin Harrison was only one-quarter Virginian through his presidential grandfather. Truman had only a tenuous tidewater connection which was discovered after he became President and had no part in forming his cultural identity. Jimmy Carter also had a distant connection to the old Virginia family of the same name. But that relationship was of less significance than his deep roots in the southern backcountry. As chief executive Carter formally changed his official forename from the royal James to the proletarian Jimmy—a specimen of backcountry onomastics which descendants of Puritans and cavaliers alike observed with surprise.

The fourth folk culture contributed comparatively little to the presidency. The English Quakers and German Pietists who settled the Delaware Valley did not approve of politics. Nevertheless, seven American Presidents had a connection with this culture. Abraham Lincoln's Puritan ancestors intermarried with Pennsylvania Quakers. Grover Cleveland had a German Quaker grandmother from Pennsylvania. William McKinley had a Quaker great-grandmother. Warren Harding was of Quaker descent on his mother's side. Herbert Hoover was descended from mixed German and English Quakers and Dwight Eisenhower came from German Mennonites whose experiences and beliefs were similar to English Quakers in many ways.[38] The black sheep of the presidential flock, Richard Nixon, also traced his ancestry to Quakers who migrated to Pennsylvania before 1730.[39]

These lists count several Presidents more than once if they

John Tyler was the descendant of Henry Tyler, a Royalist who emigrated to Virginia ca. 1650. His maternal grandmother was Anne Contesse, a French Huguenot; all other American ancestors were armigerous English gentry who emigrated in the mid-17th century.

[38]Hoover's ancestor Andreas Huber came from the Rhineland to Lancaster Co., Pennsylvania, in 1738. His wife and son became Quakers. The family lived in North Carolina, then moved to Ohio and Iowa because of slavery and the violence of backcountry culture. There they intermarried with Quakers of English origin.

Eisenhower was descended from Hans Nicol Eisenhauer, a German Mennonite who came in 1741 to Lancaster County, Pennsylvania. The president's mother, Ida Stover, was in her son's words a "passionate pacifist" who traced her origins from Germans who emigrated from the Rhineland to Pennsylvania in 1730. The president's parents were Mennonite River Brethren.

[39]His father, a "Black Irishman" named Francis Nixon, was descended from James Nixon, who emigrated from Ireland to the Delaware in 1731 and settled in the Pennsylvania backcountry. His mother, Hannah Milhous, was a Quaker descended from Friends who settled in Pennsylvania by 1729. Nixon was born in a Quaker household, grew up in the Quaker community of Whittier, California, and attended Quaker Whittier College.

Another wayward lamb, by the way, wore a fleece that was not black but Confederate grey. Jefferson Davis traced his descent from a family of Welsh Quakers who originally settled in Pennsylvania and then moved south and intermarried with the elite of another culture.

were of mixed ancestry. There is an interesting pattern in that respect. Before the year 1856, every American President but one came from a single cultural stock. The sole exception was John Tyler, who had a Huguenot grandmother. Here is another indicator of cultural homogenity in regional elites through the first two centuries of early American history.

With the election of 1856, that pattern began to change. American Presidents began to combine two or even three cultures in their own ancestry. The first to do so was James Buchanan (b. 1791). The second was Abraham Lincoln (b. 1809), whose father's forbears had been both Puritan and Quaker, and whose mother's ancestry was largely unknown even to the President himself. Six Presidents in the late nineteenth century had plural origins, and eight Presidents did in the twentieth. There was a good deal of intermarrying among British elites, French Huguenots, Dutch Calvinists and German Protestants. But British culture remained predominant in most of these mixed unions.

In summary, during the first two centuries of American history (1789–1989), every President except two was descended from one or more of the four hearth cultures of Anglo-America. All but two Presidents were also descended from ancestors who arrived in the four major folk migrations. The only exceptions were Martin Van Buren (a Dutch Calvinist from New York), and John F. Kennedy (an Irish Catholic from New England).[40] No Presidents came from the South Carolina low country, Maryland, Rhode Island or Maine. For two centuries the dominion of the four major regional cultures has remained remarkably strong.

❧ Four Regional Cultures in Washington's Presidency: The Constitutional Coalition vs. the Backcountry, 1789–97

During the first years of George Washington's administration (1789–93), regional elites in New England, the Delaware Valley and the coastal south strongly supported the new federal government. The unanimity of Washington's election was produced not

---

[40]Martin Van Buren was entirely of Dutch descent, without "a single intermarriage with one of different extraction from the time of arrival of the first emigrant to that of the marriage of my eldest son, embracing a period of over two centuries and including six generations" (*Autobiography* (ed. J. C. Fitzpatrick, Washington, 1920), 8).

John F. Kennedy was completely Irish Catholic; his great grandfather, Patrick Kennedy, came from County Wexford, ca. 1848–50.

by his personal popularity alone, but by a fundamental consensus on the frame of government among the leaders of three major regions.

These groups did not agree in every respect. Intense regional conflicts arose over the location of the national capital, and the regulation of foreign trade. Major differences also developed from the fiscal policies of Alexander Hamilton, a native West Indian, naturalized New Yorker and extreme nationalist who had no roots in any regional culture.[1]

These questions were full of trouble for the ruling coalition through the First and Second Congresses (1789–93). But the major cultural regions were able to resolve most of their differences. In a complex series of regional compromises, a home was found for the national capital, a fiscal policy was agreed upon, a foreign policy was adopted and foreign trade was regulated in a manner acceptable to leaders from three regions.

The fourth region, however, remained stubbornly opposed to this coalition. The backcountry did not support the federal government. Throughout the interior parts of Pennsylvania, Maryland, Virginia and the Carolinas, hostility to the new regime grew stronger as it began to function. In 1794, after a federal excise tax was enacted, the backcountry rose in an armed insurrection which has been miscalled the Whiskey Rebellion—a label which has trivialized a regional movement of high seriousness and danger to the republic.[2]

The rebellion broke out in mountain counties of Pennsylvania (Allegheny, Cumberland, Westmoreland, Washington) which had been settled by British borderers. It was much more than merely a protest against a whiskey tax. Behind it lay a culture which felt its ideal of natural liberty to be deeply threatened by the new Federal system. One North Carolinian expressed his feeling in cadences that called to mind the border poets of North Britain, and many earlier conflicts in the American backcountry:

> The country's a' in a greetin mood
> An some are like to rin wud blud:
> Some chaps whom freedom's spirit warms

[1]This historian has discussed Hamilton's special angle of vision, which was very different from most other Federalists, in *The Revolution of American Conservatism* (New York, 1965).

[2]Leland D. Baldwin, *Whiskey Rebels: The Story of a Frontier Uprising* (Pittsburgh, 1939), was a close study of Pennsylvania sources, and one of the first to take this movement seriously; Thomas P. Slaughter, *The Whiskey Rebellion* (New York, 1986), discovered in other materials its regional breadth and depth.

> Are threatening hard to take up arms . . .
> Their liberty they will maintain.
> They fought for't, and they'll fight again.[3]

The violent acts of the backcountry rebels were similar to risings in North Britain. Federal officers (themselves often borderers with names such as Graham, Johnson, Boyd, Wilson and Connor) were brutally beaten, tortured, and mutilated just as many a North British exciseman had been.

The rising spread swiftly throughout the back settlements of Maryland, Virginia, the Carolinas, Kentucky and Tennessee. Backcountry leaders approached the governments of Britain and Spain, with plans for their own separate republic. Only President Washington's instant application of overwhelming force prevented a major crisis which might have ended in disaster for the new republic. The backcountry rebellion ended in scenes that were also reminiscent of North Britain: marching armies, fortified houses, small skirmishes, and hundreds of ragged, barefoot captives held at bayonet-point by uniformed troops from other regions.

Separatist movements continued to flourish in the back settlements—the Blount conspiracy, Wilkinson's intrigue and the Burr affair. These were not marginal movements; many leading figures of the backcountry Ascendancy were involved. The restlessness of the back settlements was alarming to contemporaries, who feared that the separatist spirit might spread throughout America, and every region would become a nation. The balkanization of British North America (as happened in Latin America) would have been catastrophe for the cause of freedom in the modern world.

❧ A National Experiment in Ordered Liberty: New England's Hegemony in the Adams Presidency, 1797–1801

The constitutional coalition survived this danger, but it did not long remain intact. The French Revolution caused a major realignment in American politics by raising urgent new questions about the nature of liberty and republican government—questions to which every regional culture had its own range of

[3]Slaughter, *Whiskey Rebellion,* 132.

answers. During the era of the French Revolution, voting patterns in Congress on both domestic and foreign policy were primarily partisan in nature, but party pluralities were regional in
their base.

A leading example was Jay's Treaty with Great Britain, which
became the major issue of Washington's second term. More than
any other question, Jay's Treaty caused two new political parties
to form in the national capital—the Federal Republicans (a different group from the Federalists of 1787) against the Democratic Republicans. New England and the Delaware Valley solidly
supported Jay's treaty; the coastal south and backcountry were
strongly opposed.[4]

After the retirement of George Washington, the new President
was New Englander John Adams, who was narrowly elected by a
plurality of three electoral votes. In office, he surrounded himself
with men from his own region. So complete was New England's
hegemony that in 1800 the President, Secretary of State, Secretary of the Treasury and Secretary of War (more than half of the
entire Cabinet) came from Massachusetts and Connecticut alone.

During the presidency of John Adams, New Englanders and
their allies responded to the great questions of the French Revolution by attempting to create a national system of ordered liberty, such as had long existed in their own region. This idea meant
an active role for government, increased taxation, a strong navy,
an expanded national judiciary with broad common law jurisdiction, a more active regulation of commerce, narrow restriction of
immigration, an active attempt to suppress dissent, and a moralistic tone of government that was deeply resented by others of
different persuasions. All of these policies were enacted by the
Fifth and Sixth Congresses in the Alien and Sedition Acts, the
Naturalization Act of 1798, the Navy and Army acts of 1798, the
Bankruptcy Act of 1800, the Judiciary Act of 1801 and many new
federal taxes, including a direct tax, a salt tax and even a stamp

---

[4]On the critical question of appropriations to implement Jay's treaty, regional votes were as
follows:

	Aye	Nay
New England	23	4
Delaware and Susquehanna	12	1
Coastal South	0	15
Backcountry	3	26

Votes in the Hudson Valley were divided. The roll call appears in *Annals of Congress,* 4th Cong.
1st Session, 30 Apr. 1796.

tax. New England's idea of ordered liberty was very different from the ideology of the French Revolution, which Federalists condemned for its violence, its corruption and its hostility to religion.

After 1797, the American republic found itself embroiled in a "quasi-war" with France, which briefly caused an interesting realignment in regional politics. With war fever at its height in 1798, voters in the coastal south and the backcountry suddenly rallied to the government. In the Congressional elections of 1798, Federalists carried 63 out of 106 seats, including 20 seats below the Potomac and in the back settlements. Even counties that gave rise to the Whiskey Rebellion now voted Federalist.[5]

The war fever of '98 marked the beginning of a consistent pattern in American military history. From the quasi-war with France to the Vietnam War, the two southern cultures strongly supported every American war no matter what it was about or who it was against. Southern ideas of honor and the warrior ethic combined to create regional war fevers of great intensity in 1798, 1812, 1846, 1861, 1898, 1917, 1941, 1950 and 1965. Here is another subject that remains to be studied in detail.

But in the Delaware Valley, Quaker and German voters turned against the Federalist administration in 1798. So strong was this feeling that it led to an insurrection in Bucks, Montgomery and Northampton counties of eastern Pennsylvania. Historians call this event Fries Rebellion after a German who forcibly opposed a federal marshal in the town of Bethlehem, Pennsylvania. Contemporaries knew it as the Hot Water War, after the weapon which angry farm wives used against federal troops and tax assessors.

President John Adams observed the growth of this war fever with increasing alarm. The effective head of the new national army was Alexander Hamilton, whom the President distrusted. Conservative military officers interfered in elections and assaulted civilians of other political views; a captain and lieutenant of marines even attacked Congressman John Randolph of Roanoke. Suddenly it appeared that the "Friends of Order," as they called themselves, were beginning to become a greater danger to Adams's ideal of balanced government and ordered liberty than the specter of revolution from the left.

---

[5]Manning Dauer, *The Adams Federalists* (Baltimore, 1953), 339; James Broussard, *The Southern Federalists* (Baton Rouge, 1978) 14.

In February 1799, John Adams suddenly reversed the foreign policy of his administration, and sent a peace mission to France. By that act, he instantly stopped the war movement, but also shattered his party and wrecked his chances for reelection. As the war fever rapidly cooled, southerners abandoned against the administration. Adams's decision led to a regional realignment in 1799, and an electoral revolution in 1800.

The Jeffersonian Coalition: Virginia, Pennsylvania and the Backcountry against New England, 1801–25

In 1800, Thomas Jefferson was elected President by the combined votes of the middle states, the coastal south and the southern highlands, against the entrenched opposition of New England which still strongly supported Adams.[6] This new Jeffersonian coalition of Virginia, Pennsylvania and the backcountry was destined to dominate American politics for a quarter-century (1801–25). Its ideology was a complex and highly unstable combination of three different ideas of liberty, which derived not from "classical republicanism" in Europe but from the inherited folkways of British America. Jeffersonians in the middle and northern states believed in reciprocal liberty; the backcountry thought more in terms of natural liberty; tidewater Virginians drew upon their heritage of hegemonic liberty. The Republican leaders—Jefferson himself, Madison and Gallatin—had their own highly developed principles. Together they created a pluralist libertarian movement.[7]

But even as Jeffersonians espoused different libertarian ideals, they all opposed New England's idea of ordered liberty, which most Americans regarded as a contradiction in terms. The major legislation of the Adams presidency was repealed: the Alien Friends Act, the Sedition Act, the Naturalization Act, the Bankruptcy Act of 1800, the Judiciary Act of 1801, and the new tax measures all were overturned. Support for the Federal party

---

[6]For an analysis of the voting patterns in 1800, see Fischer, *The Revolution of American Conservatism,* appendix.

[7]Cf. Lance Banning, *The Jeffersonian Persuasion* (Ithaca, 1978); Drew McCoy, *The Elusive Republic* (Chapel Hill, 1980), and Joyce Appleby, *Capitalism and a New Social Order* (New York, 1984).

dwindled everywhere except New England. The purchase of Louisiana (1803) and the annexation of West Florida (1810) vastly enlarged the backcountry, and promised to shift the balance of regional power toward the south and west.

Now it was New England's turn to think about disunion. In the period from 1804 to 1814, a separatist movement gathered strength in that region. It was very different from backcountry separatism. In place of mobs and lynchings there were sermons and town meetings which talked of God's Providence for his chosen people. Yankee children were taught to sing (to the tune of Rule Britannia): "Rule, New England! New England rules and saves!"[8] One little girl stitched this sentiment into a sampler:

> Amy Kittredge is my name,
> Salem is my dwelling place
> New England is my Nation.
> And Christ is my salvation.[9]

The Federalist leader Fisher Ames believed that New England was "of all colonies that were ever founded, the largest, the most assimilated, and to use the modern jargon, nationalized, the most respectable and prosperous, the most truly interesting to America and to humanity, more unlike and more superior to other people (the English excepted)."[10]

New England Republicans shared this nascent sense of Yankee nationalism. James Winthrop, for example, praised the determination of New Englanders to "keep their blood pure." He added, ". . . the eastern states have, by keeping separate from the foreign mixtures, acquired their present greatness in a century and a half, and have preserved their religion and morals."[11]

These feelings were most intense from 1807 to 1814, when the American republic was caught up in a bitter conflict between Tory Britain and Napoleonic France. The Jefferson administration desperately sought a way of defending national honor by the Great Embargo, an "experiment in peaceful coercion" which vir-

---

[8]James M. Banner, *To the Hartford Convention* (New York, 1970), 87.

[9]Samuel Eliot Morison, *Maritime History of Massachusetts* (Boston, 1921, rpt. 1979), 211.

[10]Fisher Ames, "To New England Men," *Works of Fisher Ames,* ed. Seth Ames (2 vols., Boston, 1854), II, 134.

[11][James Winthrop], "Agrippa IX," in Cecilia Kenyon, ed., *The Antifederalists* (Indianapolis, 1966), 135.

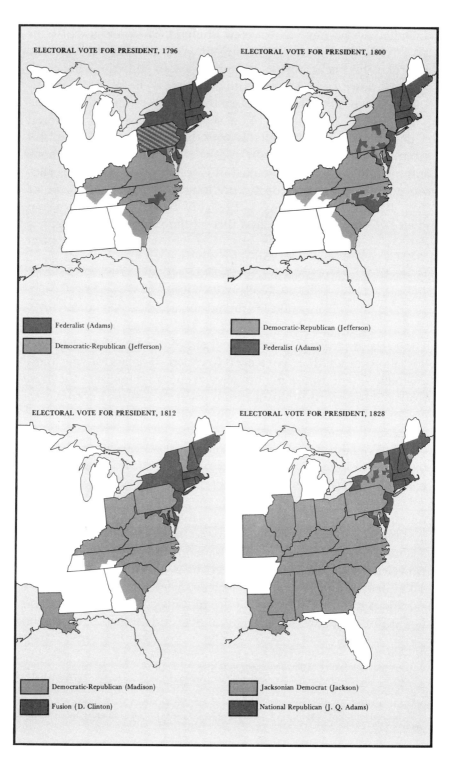

ELECTORAL VOTE FOR PRESIDENT, 1796

Federalist (Adams)
Democratic-Republican (Jefferson)

ELECTORAL VOTE FOR PRESIDENT, 1800

Democratic-Republican (Jefferson)
Federalist (Adams)

ELECTORAL VOTE FOR PRESIDENT, 1812

Democratic-Republican (Madison)
Fusion (D. Clinton)

ELECTORAL VOTE FOR PRESIDENT, 1828

Jacksonian Democrat (Jackson)
National Republican (J. Q. Adams)

tually stopped America's foreign trade from 1807 to 1809. The effect of this policy was greatly to increase material disparities between American regions. Jefferson's embargo was an economic disaster which fell hardest on his own region; it shattered the staple agriculture of the coastal south, and encouraged industrial development in New England and the Delaware Valley.[12]

The War of 1812 divided the nation more deeply than any event since the Revolution, on both regional and party lines. Once again, the coastal south and backcountry strongly supported the war: of 60 Congressmen from those regions, 52 voted for it, and only 8 against. New England and the middle states were internally divided, and experienced an unprecedented growth of organized political parties, and a revolutionary surge in popular participation in democratic politics. These divisions prevented disunionist movements from developing in the northern states, but the democratization of politics increased the cultural differences between the north and south—adding another dimension to regional disparities.[13]

❧ The Jacksonian Coalition:
A Border Chieftain in the White House, 1829–37

After the defeat of Napoleon in 1815, the great questions of a revolutionary age suddenly lost their urgency in American politics. The immediate result was the collapse of the first party system. The Federalist party disappeared and the Jeffersonian coalition rapidly disintegrated in a post-war period inaccurately remembered as the Era of Good Feelings. During the presidency of James Monroe (1817–25), national politics became a conflict of personal cliques and followings. One of those factions gained the presidency in 1825 for New Englander John Quincy Adams in a series of complex and highly controversial parliamentary maneuvers.

The presidency of John Quincy Adams attained few of its own goals, but it had an unintended consequence of high importance

---

[12]Louis M. Sears, *Jefferson and the Embargo* (Durham, 1927).

[13]On the declaration of war in 1812, a map of voting by Congressional district appears in Charles O. Paullin, *Atlas of the Historical Geography of the United States* (Washington, 1932), 113a; and residence of Congressmen in Bardford Perkins, *Prologue to War: England and the United States, 1805-1812* (Berkeley and Los Angeles, 1961), 409.

in American history. Once again, the New England spirit of ordered freedom was brought to Washington by a moralistic President who favored an active role for the national government in economics, education and morality. These measures were strongly supported in New England. But Americans from three regions deeply disliked the policies of the Yankee President, and detested his political style. In the elections of 1828, John Quincy Adams won every electoral vote except one in his native region of New England. He also ran well in boundary states which had voted Federalist in the early republic.[14]

But Adams was deeply unpopular in other regions. Once again, Pennsylvania, the coastal south and the highland south joined together against New England in a new coalition which governed the nation for twelve years, from 1829 to 1841. Its structure was similar to the Jeffersonian coalition; voting patterns in 1828 and 1832 were much the same as in 1804 and 1808. But its style was very different. Its leader was not a Virginia planter but a back-country border captain, Andrew Jackson. The values of Jacksonian democracy varied broadly from one cultural region to another, but the dominant purposes of Andrew Jackson himself owed much to the folkways of his ancestors.[15]

President Jackson was deeply conscious of cultural differences between American regions. In his Farewell Address he declared:

> In a country so extensive as the United States and with pursuits so varied, the internal regulations of the several States must frequently differ from one another in important particulars; and this difference is unavoidably increased by the varying principles upon which the American colonies were originally planted; principles which had taken deep root in their social relations before the Revolution, and, therefore, of necessity influencing their policy since they became free and independent states. But each state has an unquestionable right to regulate its own internal concerns.[16]

[14]Adam's support included Delaware, Maryland, parts of North Carolina.

[15]The Jacksonians have been interpreted as a class movement, (Schlesinger), a frontier phenomenon (Turner), yeomen farmers (Beard), small capitalists and "incipient entrepreneurs" (Hofstadter-Hammond), nostalgic neo-Jeffersonians (Meyers), "Old Republicans," (McCormick *fils*), moral crusaders for honesty in government (Remini), professional politicians on the make (White), and as an ethno-religious group (Benson, Formisano). Every one of these interpretations adds something to our understanding of this complex phenomenon. But there is room for another idea of the Jacksonians as a coalition of regional cultures.

[16]Andrew Jackson, *Farewell Address of Andrew Jackson to the People of the United States . . .* (Washington, 1837).

Jackson's goals for the government of an "extensive republic" were the preservation of honor abroad and the protection of liberty at home. By liberty, he had in mind the natural freedom of the backcountry—minimal government, maximal autonomy for each individual and no "unwarrantable interference" by the people of one region in the customs of any other.

The Jacksonian coalition was built upon principles which most Americans accepted, but many voters were deeply troubled by the behavior of President Jackson himself—a political style characterized by intensely personal leadership, charismatic appeals to his followers, demands for extreme personal loyalty, and a violent antipathy against all who disagreed with him. This style of leadership had long been rooted in the political folkways of the backcountry, but it was alien to other American cultures. In some ways it seemed merely absurd to others—as in the Peggy Eaton affair (1831), when a petty quarrel among Cabinet wives grew into a test of personal loyalty which became a matter of the highest moment to a border chieftain. To the astonishment of Americans from other regions, this tempest ended in the disruption of the administration, the discharge of the Cabinet, and political feuds that continued for many years.

If the Peggy Eaton affair amused Jackson's critics, other events genuinely alarmed them. In the Nullification crisis, Jackson's proclamations and force bills challenged southern ideas of hegemonic liberty. In his battle with Nicholas Biddle and the "Monster Bank," and the removal of federal deposits from the Bank of the United States, the President badly frightened the elite of Philadelphia. His refusal to respect a ruling of the Supreme Court in *Worcester v. Georgia* and his trampling of Indian rights outraged moral opinion in New England.

During Andrew Jackson's presidency, voting returns were mainly regional in nature. Patterns of partisan allegiance to the Jacksonian Democratic Republicans and anti-Jacksonian National Republicans in 1828 and 1832 were very similar to those in the early republic. Jackson was deeply distrusted in greater New England and in the Delaware Valley. He was generally supported in central and western Pennsylvania, in the Mississippi Valley, the coastal south and the highland south. These regional patterns were so strong that in 1828 Jackson carried the electoral votes of every southern and western state, and lost virtually all of New England. Congregationalists, Quakers, Mennonites and Moravians were strenuously hostile to him. Most large denominations—

Presbyterian, Methodist, Episcopal, and Baptist—divided on regional lines.

Regional culture was the primary determinant of party allegiance in this period. The backcountry rallied to the idea of natural freedom under the banners of Jackson's Democratic Republican party. Greater New England supported the idea of ordered liberty and the National Republicans. The coastal south held to its idea of hegemonic liberty. Other regions and ethnic groups aligned themselves with one group or another, according to their customs and beliefs.[17] In the election of 1832, the pattern was a little different as a consequence of the defection from the Democratic party of South Carolina and Kentucky, caused by feuds between Andrew Jackson and his rival border chieftains Henry Clay and John C. Calhoun. Otherwise, the Jacksonian coalition continued to dominate the republic from 1824 to 1840, against the minority opposition of greater New England.

∾ The Whig Omnibus, 1840–52

In 1834, Andrew Jackson's many enemies joined together to found the Whig party. The name they chose revealed the root of their distrust of his border-chieftain politics. But coming as they did from every cultural region in the United States, they found it difficult to stand together. In consequence, during the election of 1836, the Whigs ran not one but three presidential candidates, in hopes of winning pluralities within each region and forcing the election into the House of Representatives. They simultaneously supported Daniel Webster in New England, Hugh Lawson White in the highland south, and William Henry Harrison, a Virginia gentlemen who had moved to Ohio.

This stratagem failed. Webster won only the votes of New England, and White carried only Tennessee and Georgia. Enough of the Jacksonian coalition held together to carry Jackson's lieutenant Martin Van Buren into the White House. But one of the Whig candidates, William Henry Harrison, proved to be unexpectedly popular in many regions. Thus was born a new strategy in presidential politics—the omnibus candidate. William Henry Harrison was an aged military hero: an unknown soldier in poli-

---

[17]Burton W. Folsom, Jr., "The Politics of Elites: Prominence and Party in Davidson County, Tennessee, 1835–1861," *JSH* 39 (1973), 359–79; Ronald Formisano, *The Birth of Mass Political Parties* (Princeton, 1971), 192, passim.

tics with few discernable opinions to divide the electorate. An omnibus image was carefully created for him. In 1840, Harrison was nominated as the only Whig candidate, and won 80 percent of the electoral vote.

The election of 1840 was something new in American politics—the triumph of an omnibus campaign carefully designed to appeal to all cultural regions, not by issues but by symbolic identities. Harrison was a Virginia gentleman, a backcountry settler and the candidate of a political party which showed some sympathy for New England ideas of ordered liberty and moral reform. His party mounted its classic "log cabin and hard cider campaign," by combining many different cultural symbols: the western log cabin, the *gravitas* of the Virginia gentleman, and hard cider which was a temperance alternative to hard liquor.

This omnibus strategy succeeded brilliantly for the Whigs, not only in 1840 with William Henry Harrison's election, but again in 1848 for Zachary Taylor. Both men were military heroes, Virginia gentlemen, western settlers and unknown soldiers who ran strongly in every cultural region.

Meanwhile, Democratic leaders struggled to keep alive the memory of Old Hickory. In 1844, they won the presidency for another border captain from Appalachia, James Knox Polk, who was called Young Hickory. Polk's Jacksonian foreign policy led to the Mexican War, a war of conquest which was immensely popular in the coastal south and southern highlands, and strongly opposed in the Delaware Valley and New England. Northern critics of the war invented a new form of politics called civil disobedience, which in substance and form expressed the values of those cultures.[18]

The omnibus candidates of both Whigs and Democrats reached across regional lines. In the 1840s New England was divided in its party allegiance. The state of Massachusetts voted Whig in every presidential election from 1836 to 1852; so also did Vermont and Connecticut throughout the 1840s. But New Hampshire and Maine were Democratic, and Rhode Island went its own way.

The southern states were also split. Virginia consistently produced Democratic pluralities in every presidential election from 1836 to 1852; as did Alabama, Missouri and Arkansas. Kentucky

---

[18]Robert W. Johannsen, *To the Halls of the Montezumas* (New York, 1985), 270–301; John Q. Anderson, "Emerson on Texas and the Mexican War," *Western Humanities Review* 13 (1959), 191–99; John H. Schroeder, *Mr. Polk's War: American Opposition and Dissent* (Madison, 1973).

and Tennessee, on the other hand, voted Whig throughout the period. Three other states (North Carolina, Louisiana and Georgia) were divided, and South Carolina as always was *sui generis.*

The midland states were equally divided. New York and Pennsylvania changed their party allegiance in every presidential election—Democrat in 1836, Whig in 1840, Democrat in 1844, Whig in 1848 and Democrat in 1852. These reversals were caused by the shift of only a few votes. The states of the old northwest were also bitterly contested.

The period from 1840 to 1848 was the only era in American history when every major cultural region and most states were deeply divided in their party allegiance. This extraordinary effect was produced by the breadth of the Jacksonian appeal and also by the success of the Whigs' omnibus strategy. Individual voting patterns became highly complex—compounded of class, ethnicity, and religion. Regional patterns became more muted in this era than in any other period of American history.

In the presidential election of 1852, the Whigs tried their omnibus strategy yet again. They put up General Winfield Scott, a Virginia gentleman, a long-time resident of the west, and a hero of two wars. But Scott was also highly intelligent, intensely conservative and outspoken in his political opinions—not at all what was wanted in an omnibus candidate.

Against this formidable figure, the Democrats tried an omnibus strategy of their own. They adopted the ingenious expedient of nominating a New England Jacksonian and gentleman-Democrat named Franklin Pierce. His party called him "Young Hickory from the Granite Hills," and his ticket was perfectly tailored to attract support in every political culture. This Democratic omnibus succeeded brilliantly. "Young Hickory" from New Hampshire carried all the states in the union except the Whig bastions of Massachusetts, Vermont, Kentucky and Tennessee.[19]

---

[19]Roy Nichols, *Franklin Pierce* (2d ed., Philadelphia, 1969), 189–215.

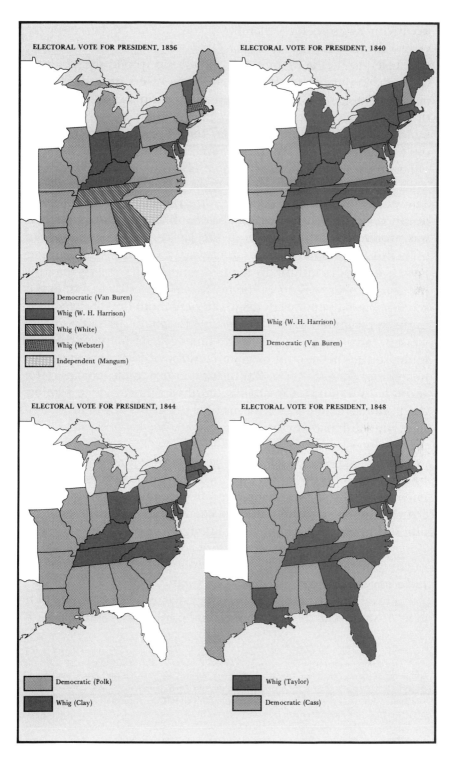

ELECTORAL VOTE FOR PRESIDENT, 1836

ELECTORAL VOTE FOR PRESIDENT, 1840

Democratic (Van Buren)

Whig (W. H. Harrison)

Whig (White)

Whig (Webster)

Independent (Mangum)

Whig (W. H. Harrison)

Democratic (Van Buren)

ELECTORAL VOTE FOR PRESIDENT, 1844

ELECTORAL VOTE FOR PRESIDENT, 1848

Democratic (Polk)

Whig (Clay)

Whig (Taylor)

Democratic (Cass)

853

❧ From Regions to Sections

Ironically, while the omnibus politics of the second party system were disguising regional differences, the effect of cultural and material change in the early nineteenth century was to reinforce them—and also to change their nature. New England and the middle states became more similar to one another, and increasingly different from the coastal and southern highlands. The effect of these tendencies was to combine regions into sections. That pattern had not existed in the United States before 1820. The words "north" and "south" were rarely used in a sectional sense during the early years of the republic. But they developed very rapidly.[20]

In the late eighteenth century, every part of the nation had been heavily agricultural. By the mid-nineteenth century, the proportion of farm workers in the north was only 40 percent; in the south it was 84 percent. By 1860, 26 percent of northerners lived in cities, compared with 10 percent of the south. In that year, the value of farmland per acre was 2.6 times greater in the north than in the south; the amount of manufacturing capital per capita was nearly four times as great. But in another economic indicator, the south led the north. Concentration of wealth was greater below the Potomac than above it. With only one-third of white population, the south had nearly two-thirds of its richest men and a large proportion of the very poor.

The national communications network also developed on sectional lines; both the north and the south created dense railroad networks by 1860, but the rail links between them were very thin. Patterns of internal migration occurred mainly within sections, and not between them. Foreign immigration also become a sectional process. In 1860 seven-eighths of immigrants came to the north. The effect of ethnic diversity was not to diminish sectional differences, but actually to increase them.[21]

Cultural disparities were also very great. In the north, 94 percent of the population was found to be literate by the census of

---

[20]There were occasional exceptions. In 1791, for example, a traveling Quaker stopped the whipping of a slave boy in South Carolina; he noted in his journal that the master was "full of horrid execrations and threatenings upon all the northern people; but I did not spare him, which occasioned a bystander to express an oath that I should be 'popped over.'" William Savery, "Journal," *Friends' Library*, I, 331.

[21]James M. McPherson, *Ordeal by Fire* (New York, 1982), 23–25; *idem, Battle Cry of Freedom* (New York, 1988), 40.

1860; in the south, barely 54 percent could read and write. Roughly 72 percent of northern children were enrolled in school compared with 35 percent of the same age in the south. The average length of a school year was 135 days in the north and 80 days in the south.

From 1800 to 1852, the northern states dominated the many reform movements that developed in this era—education, temperance, penology, care for the insane and the blind, feminism, pacifism and especially abolitionism. Most leaders of these reform movements came from New England and Quaker stock. A majority were descended from families who had arrived in the Puritan great migration of 1629–40, and the Friends' migration of 1675–95.[22]

One of these movements, antislavery, gradually became a political movement of increasing power. Its electoral strength was especially strong among Quakers, German Pietists and New Englanders. In the states of Ohio and New York, for example, votes by county for the Liberty party and black suffrage correlated more strongly with the proportion of the population who were of New England origin than with any other variable.[23] At the same time, most reform movements—not merely abolitionism but "isms" of every kind—found few followers in the coastal south, and even fewer in the southern highlands. The Richmond *Enquirer* roundly attacked what it called "Our Enemies, the Isms." Modern ideologies in general were regarded as hostile to southern folkways.[24]

---

[22]A path-breaking essay, David Donald, "Toward a Reconsideration of Abolitionists," in *Lincoln Reconsidered* (New York, 1956), 19–37, has been confirmed in its description of regional origins of abolitionist leaders, but refuted in its argument for "downwardly mobile" social origins. See John L. Hammond, *The Politics of Benevolence: Revival Religion and American Voting Behavior* (Norwood, N.J., 1979), 92–93.

[23]John L. Hammond finds the following zero-order r values between New England origins and voting for the Liberty Party and Black Suffrage:

Year	Ohio Liberty Party	New York Liberty Party	New York Black Suffrage
1840	.539	.349	
1842	n.a.	.419	
1844	.521	.521	
1846	.374		.697

The author himself points out that this association is stronger than other social variables. See John L. Hammond, *The Politics of Benevolence*, 90–91.

[24]Clement Eaton, *The Freedom-of-Thought Struggle in the Old South* (rev. and enl. ed., New York, 1964), 347

❧ Regional Cultures and the Republican Coalition: Greater New England and the Midlands against the Coastal and Highland South, 1856–1924

During the decade of the 1850s, a revolution of parties occurred in American politics. The Whig party disintegrated after the election of 1852, and eight years later the Democratic party came to pieces as well. The critical factor was the emergence of a new issue which shattered both the Whig and the Democratic omnibus strategies and polarized sectional opinion.

That issue of course was slavery and particularly the question of its expansion into new territories, which threatened to upset delicate sectional balances. The question had been compromised many times before—in the Constitutional Compromises of 1787, the Missouri Compromise of 1819–21, the Compromise of 1850, and the admission of almost every new state. In 1854, Stephen Douglas tried compromise once again. He introduced the Kansas-Nebraska Bill, which proposed to preserve sectional balances and regional autonomy by adopting the doctrine of popular sovereignty, which held that the question of slavery in the territories would be left for local populations to settle in their own way.[25]

The result was political disaster—for Douglas himself, his party and his nation. By 1854 slavery was increasingly regarded in many parts of the north and south as a moral issue which could not be compromised. This perception defeated Douglas's proposal. It shattered the Democratic party, destroyed the Whigs, gave birth to the new Republican party and revived regional and sectional voting in American politics.

In presidential politics, these new regional and sectional patterns first clearly emerged in the election of 1856. The new Republican party swept every state in the northern tier from New England to upstate New York, Ohio, Michigan, Wisconsin and Iowa. This pattern of Republican support in 1856 was a map of

---

[25]The motives which led Stephen Douglas to introduce his disastrous Kansas-Nebraska Bill have been much debated by historians. Without reviving that learned controversy here, it might be noted that Douglas meant his bill to be the basis of a new regional compromise, within which omnibus coalitions would continue to function.

Stephen Douglas himself aspired to be an omnibus candidate for his party. He was a native New Englander and a long resident of the west, who was closely tied by politics and marriage to leaders in both the coastal south and the southern highlands. His wife was related to Jefferson Davis. At the same time he was a leader of the movement called Young America, whose spread-eagled rhetoric appealed to voters in every region. Douglas's motives were expressed in a regional calculus and compounded of both altruism and interest.

greater New England. Every state that voted Republican had been colonized by descendants of the Puritan migration. Within those states, votes by county for Republican candidates correlated more closely with the proportion of the population who sprang from New England stock than with any other variable.[26]

But the support of one cultural region was never enough to carry a national election. In 1856, the Democrats nominated an omnibus candidate named James Buchanan, a Pennsylvanian of border ancestry with strong ties to the south. Buchanan's candidacy attracted the electoral votes of three cultural regions of midland America, the coastal south and the southern highlands. He won every electoral vote outside the northern tier except the boundary state of Maryland, and promised to build a new coalition of midland and southern cultures.

The events of Buchanan's presidency quickly shattered this emerging coalition. Chief Justice Roger B. Taney's proslavery and negrophobic decision in the Dred Scott case deeply outraged opinion in the north, and John Brown's raid at Harpers Ferry polarized opinion in every region. One by one, the national institutions of the republic divided on sectional lines. Churches such as the Presbyterians, Methodists and Baptists who had been able to recruit members in many regions broke apart into northern and southern wings. After Harpers Ferry, northern colleges lost their southern students. And in 1860 the Democratic party itself disintegrated.

At the same time, a new coalition of northern regional cultures began to form—the first time since Washington's administration that the north had been firmly united. In the election of 1860, the Republican candidate Abraham Lincoln was himself a fitting personal symbol of this new coalition. On his father's side, Lincoln was descended from New England Puritans who had intermarried with Pennsylvania Quakers and migrated to Appalachia and the Ohio Valley. He represented every regional component of the Republican coalition.

---

[26]Here again, Hammond reports strong and robust zero-order r correlations for the association between Republican voting and New England origins:

Year	Ohio	New York
1856	.534	.560
1860	.569	.732

He finds negative correlations of nearly equal strength between Know-Nothing voting and New England origins. See *The Politics of Benevolence*, 132–33.

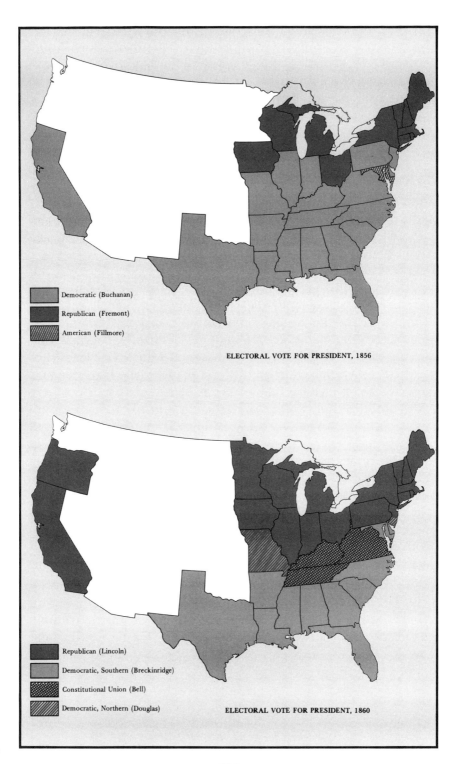

Democratic (Buchanan)

Republican (Fremont)

American (Fillmore)

ELECTORAL VOTE FOR PRESIDENT, 1856

Republican (Lincoln)

Democratic, Southern (Breckinridge)

Constitutional Union (Bell)

Democratic, Northern (Douglas)

ELECTORAL VOTE FOR PRESIDENT, 1860

The election of 1860 was carried by this new sectional alliance. Lincoln won every New England county, most of the northern tier, and all but three electoral votes in the middle tier from the Delaware Valley west to the Pacific. At the same time, he lost every electoral vote in the southern states. This pattern became the basis of a Republican coalition that dominated American politics from the Civil War to the New Deal.

In the elections of 1864 and 1868, the Republican coalition grew a little stronger with the addition of non-slaveholding parts of the highland south—West Virginia, eastern Kentucky, eastern Tennessee, western North Carolina, north Georgia and northern Alabama. This region was courted in 1864 by a presidential ticket composed of Abraham Lincoln and Andrew Johnson, a back-country Democrat from East Tennessee. Upper Appalachia began to vote Republican in that year, and continued to do so for more than fifty years. With its accession in 1864, the Republican coalition was complete. It governed the nation from the inaugural of Abraham Lincoln in 1861 to the retirement of Herbert Hoover in 1933, with only occasional intermissions. Throughout that long period, the hearth states of Massachusetts and Pennsylvania voted together in every presidential election from 1860 to 1924 except one (1912).

❧ The Civil War as a Conflict of Regional Cultures

With the success of the Republican coalition in 1860, the southern regions lost control of the Senate, House of Representatives and presidency altogether for the first time since the eighteenth century. New England had often been in that position before, but its culture had discouraged violent responses. Southern folkways caused a different reaction. The Republican victory was seen not only as a challenge to southern interests, but as an affront to southern honor and a threat to southern freedom—that is, to its special ideas of hegemonic liberty and natural liberty. Without consciousness of contradiction, southern masters cast their defense of slavery in libertarian terms, and demanded the freedom to enslave.

The Republican coalition promised not to interfere with slavery where it already existed, but proposed to halt its expansion into new territories, and to protect its own ideas of ordered liberty and reciprocal liberty. Both the north and south began the

Civil War in a defensive mood, determined to preserve two different ways of life.

The war was not a contest of equals. In 1861, the Union outnumbered the Confederacy in total population by 2.5 to 1, and in free males of military age by 4.4 to 1. So different had been the pattern of economic growth in the two sections that the north exceeded the south in railroad mileage by 2.4 to 1, in total wealth by 3 to 1, in merchant ships by 9 to 1, in industrial output by 10 to 1, in firearms production by 32 to 1, and in coal mining by 38 to 1. A much smaller proportion of northern workers were farmers, but the Union outreached the Confederacy in farm acreage by 3 to 1, in livestock by 1.5 to 1, in corn production by 2 to 1 and in wheat production by 4 to 1.

But the south was superior to the north in the intensity of its warrior ethic. The southern states produced a larger proportion of regular army officers than did the north. There were many military academies below the Mason-Dixon line and few above it. Militia units were more popular in the south; in 1852, for example, Massachusetts had one militia officer for every 216 men; North Carolina had one officer for every sixteen men. By 1864, 90 percent of southern freemen were fighting, compared with 44 percent in the north.[1]

In defense of their different cultures, the two sections also fought differently. The armies of the north were at first very much like those of Fairfax in the English Civil War; gradually they became another New Model Army, ruthless, methodical and efficient. The Army of Northern Virginia, important parts of it at least, consciously modeled itself upon the *beau sabreurs* of Prince Rupert. At the same time, the Confederate armies of the southwest marched into battle behind the cross of St. Andrew, and called themselves "Southrons" on the model of their border ancestors.[2]

The regional cultures of the northern and southern states also

---

[1] John Hope Franklin, *The Militant South* (Cambridge, 1956), 189.

[2] A controversy has developed on the question of cultural differences in the military conduct of the war. Some historians have insisted that strong cultural differences existed. Others have strongly denied them. This historian believes that the Celtic thesis of Grady McWhiney and Perry D. Jamieson requires conceptual revision, and that the counterargument of Richard E. Beringer et al. has not settled the question. There are persistent quantitative and qualitative differences in the combat records of Union and Confederate armies which cannot be explained in material or strategic terms. Cf. Grady McWhiney and Perry D. Jamieson, *Attack and Die: Civil War Military Tactics and the Southern Heritage* (University, Ala., 1982); Richard E. Beringer et al., *Why the South Lost the Civil War* (Athens, Ga., 1986).

appeared in the politics of the Civil War. The greatest figure of
the war, Abraham Lincoln, perfectly represented the Republican
coalition of regional cultures. Lincoln's abiding sense of morality
in politics, his lifelong defense of ordered liberty, the simplicity
and strength of his biblical prose, his plain style and egalitarian
manner were all derived from the folkways of his Puritan and
Quaker ancestors, and personified the high moral ideals that lent
power and seriousness to the Union cause.[3]

Below the Mason-Dixon line, the leaders of the Confederacy
were also products of their regional folkways. Their ideals were
personified in the character of Robert E. Lee—himself the direct
descendant of an English gentleman who had moved to Virginia
in the mid-seventeenth century. Lee's nobility of conduct symbolized an ethic of honor which had existed in his region for
many generations. The symbolic qualities of Lincoln and Lee
were often far removed from the sordid realities of the Civil War.
But symbols themselves became realities of high importance in
this great and terrible strife.[4]

Within the Confederacy, southern folkways were also the
source of major weaknesses in the war effort. The Confederacy
did not die of democracy, as some conservative scholars have
argued, but suffered much from the vices of its old oligarchical
ways—in particular from the extreme restlessness of southern
gentlemen under any sort of restraint, their exaggerated sense of
personal honor and their lack of sympathy for the rights of others. The same cultural values which caused secession were also
partly responsible for its eventual defeat.

The events of the war itself radically transformed northern attitudes toward southern folkways. As casualty lists grew longer
northern war aims changed from an intention merely to resist the
expansion of southern culture to a determination to transform it.
As this attitude spread through the northern states the Civil War
became a cultural revolution.

The results were mixed. The southern armies were broken by
the north, and southern slavery was abolished. But southern cul-

---

[3]The Puritan idea of ordered liberty may be traced through Lincoln's earliest public
speeches. I am thinking particularly of his "Address before the Young Men's Lyceum of Springfield, Illinois," first printed in the *Sangamo Journal,* 3 Feb. 1838, and reprinted in Basler, ed.,
The Collected Works of Abraham Lincoln, I, 108–15.

[4]Edmund Jennings Lee, *Lee of Virginia, 1642–1892: Biographical and Genealogical Sketches of
the Descendants of Colonel Richard Lee* (1895, rpt. Baltimore, 1974, 1983); Thomas L. Connely,
The Marble Man: Robert E. Lee and His Image in American Society (New York, 1977).

ture survived the war, and so did its animus against the north. An
extreme but not untypical example of this attitude was the Virginia secessionist Edmund Ruffin, who was said to have fired one
of the first shots of the war in 1861, pulling the lanyard on a
cannon aimed at Fort Sumter in Charlestown harbor. After the
Confederate surrender at Appomattox in 1865, he fired the last
shot of the war into his own brain, committing suicide after com-
posing a defiant epitaph for himself and his cause. "With what
will be my last breath," he wrote, "I here repeat and would willingly proclaim my unmitigated hatred to Yankee rule—to all
political, social and business connections with Yankees, and the
perfidious, malignant and vile Yankee race."[5] Many Confederates
shared his attitudes, which did not bode well for the prospects of
postwar Reconstruction.

❧ Regional Cultures in Reconstruction, 1865–77

After the War, old regional patterns briefly disappeared from voting maps of national elections, but in no period of American history was regional consciousness more intense, or regional hegemony more complete. The Republican coalition dominated
national politics by its electoral majorities in the north, and by
military occupation of the south. Radical reconstruction was an
attempt to impose by force the cultures of New England and the
midlands upon the coastal and highland south. The southern
states were compelled to accept Yankee constitutions and Yankee
judges, Yankee politics and Yankee politicians, Yankee schools
and Yankee schoolma'ams, Yankee capitalists and a Yankee labor
system.

This cultural revolution continued in some parts of the south
until 1876. It succeeded for a time in modifying many southern
institutions—its labor system, its politics and its schools. But with
the exception of slavery itself, most of these effects lasted only as
long as they were supported by northern bayonets. In the end,
Radical Reconstruction was a revolution that failed.[6]

Some historians believe that this failure occurred primarily
because freedmen were not given land. This materialist explanation is very much mistaken. The fundamental cause of failure was

---

[5]Bertram Wyatt-Brown, *Southern Honor*, (New York, 1983), 35.
[6]Cf. Eric Foner, *Nothing but Freedom: Emancipation and its Legacy* (Baton Rouge, 1983).

not narrowly material but broadly cultural. Reconstruction regimes collapsed because they were unable to change southern folkways. Such a truly radical reconstruction of southern culture was impossible in 1868, for it would have required acts of a sort that were forbidden by the culture of the north. And as long as the old folkways survived in the south, it was inevitable that the material and institutional order of southern life would rapidly revive when Yankee soldiers went home.

The experiment of reconstruction continued for a decade. After the elections of 1876, a weary north finally gave up its attempt to transform the south, and Union troops were withdrawn. Southern whites quickly recovered control of their regions and rapidly undid the reforms of Reconstruction. Yankee school systems were abolished; Yankee schoolma'ams were shipped back to New England; Yankee constitutions were rewritten. Former slaves were rapidly reduced to a condition of economic exploitation, political dependency and social degradation which was only one step removed from slavery. Despite talk of a "new South" after 1876, young southerners (both white and black) continued to learn the old folkways. Material differences between American regions grew greater than ever before—as great as the disparities between the richest and poorest European nations. Historian C. Vann Woodward discovered that in 1880 the relative difference in per capita wealth of the southern states ($376) and the northeastern states ($1,353) was almost exactly that of Russia and Germany.[7]

❧ The Republican Coalition versus the Solid South, 1880–96

When the southern states returned to the union, sectional voting patterns instantly reappeared in national politics, stronger than ever. In every presidential election from 1880 to 1908, the south voted as a single bloc, casting virtually all of its electoral ballots for candidates of the Democratic party. The expression "solid South" was popularized in this period.[8]

In these years, the great majority of electoral votes in the northern states were also united behind the Republican candi-

---

[7]C. Vann Woodward, *Origins of the New South* (Baton Rouge, 1951), 111.
[8]Mathews, *Dictionary of Americanisms*, s.v. "South."

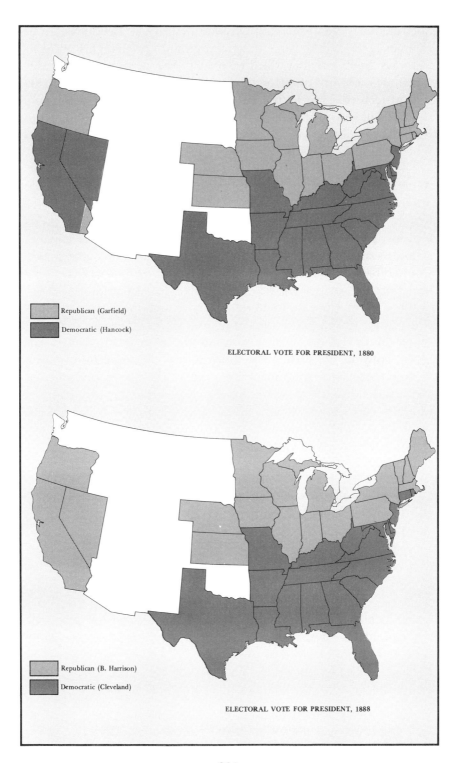

Republican (Garfield)

Democratic (Hancock)

ELECTORAL VOTE FOR PRESIDENT, 1880

Republican (B. Harrison)

Democratic (Cleveland)

ELECTORAL VOTE FOR PRESIDENT, 1888

864

date. The only exception occurred in 1892 when Populists carried electoral votes in six western states, and Democrat Grover Cleveland ran strongly in the north. Otherwise, regional identities were absolutely the decisive factor in every presidential election from 1880 to 1908.

Regional voting patterns were even stronger and more persistent in Congress. The most detailed study of Congressional voting in this period concludes that "sectional competition . . . has been and remains the dominant influence on the American political system." Social scientist Richard Bensel finds evidence in roll-call analyses that "the geographical alignment of sectional competition has undergone very little change in the last one hundred years [1880–1980]."[9]

Bensel discovered that Congressional voting was primarily regional on most leading questions in this era, including tariffs, military pensions, contested elections, admission of new states, imperialism and foreign policy. Other scholars also discovered strong regional patterns in other issues. On the Bland Free Coinage Bill (1892), and the Gold Standard Act (1899), for example, New England Congressmen voted as a bloc, and the south was almost equally united. The middle states were rather more mixed.[10] These major Congressional issues were not merely collisions of material interest. They were also conflicts of cultural value.[11]

Regional identity was not, of course, the only determinant of political behavior in this period. Ethnicity, class and party loyalty also made a difference. But these other factors were closely interlocked with cultural regionalism. In terms of class, for example, the dominant elite in one section tended to ally itself with the proletariat in the other. Republican Speaker Thomas Reed of New England declared that it was "just as fair for the Republicans to poll ignorant Negroes in the South as for Democrats to poll ignorant immigrants in the North."[12]

Partisan allegiance was also very strong in this era. Party battles between Democrats and Republicans were exceptionally hard-fought, and often decided by paper-thin pluralities. The domi-

[9]Richard Franklin Bensel, *Sectionalism and American Political Development, 1880–1980* (Madison, 1984) xix.

[10]Paullin, *Atlas of the Historical Geography of the United States*, plate 119.

[11]Bensel, *Sectionalism and American Political Development*, xix.

[12]*Ibid.*, 76.

nant Republican coalition could not afford to lose any of its regional components—not New England and the northern tier, or the midland states, or even Appalachia. It is interesting to observe that most Republican Presidents in this period had backgrounds which included more than one cultural region. Lincoln, Grant, Hayes, Arthur, McKinley, Theodore Roosevelt, Harding and Hoover all in various ways symbolized the union of New England, the midlands and parts of Appalachia which together constituted the Republican coalition.

✎ Regional Responses to Imperialism

During the presidency of William McKinley, the American republic joined the ranks of the imperial powers. It annexed Hawaii in 1897, seized the Spanish possessions of Puerto Rico, Guam and Philippines in 1898, sent 5,000 troops to China in 1900 and made Cuba a protectorate in 1901. The Spanish-American War was one of the most popular conflicts in American history. Every region supported it—especially the south. Of four new major generals, two were aging Confederate veterans who in combat referred to the Spanish as "the Yankees."

But during the war there were rumblings of dissent, and later a full-fledged anti-imperialist movement which opposed the acquisition of territory against the wishes of their inhabitants, and protested against the American suppression of popular insurrections in the Philippines and Cuba. Anti-imperialism was a regional movement, centered in New England. Its leading spokesmen in the Senate were George Hoar of Massachusetts and Eugene Hale of Maine. The Anti-imperialist League was founded in Boston. There was support from other parts of the nation, but historian Frank Friedel found that New England was its stronghold. This regional pattern has appeared many times in American history, from the War of 1812 and the Mexican War to the Vietnam War and the nuclear freeze movement of the 1980s.[13]

---

[13]Samuel Eliot Morison, Frederick Merk and Frank Friedel, *Dissent in Three American Wars* (Cambridge, 1970), 78–79; Robert Beisner, *Twelve Against Empire: The Anti-Imperialists, 1898–1900* (New York, 1968); E. Berkeley Tompkins, *Anti-Imperialism in the United States: The Great Debate, 1890–1920* (1970).

❧ Regional Origins of Populism and Progressivism

Regional cultures also defined the reach of reform impulses during this period. Two very different reform movements developed in the United States during the late nineteenth and early twentieth century—Populism and Progressivism. Both were national in their aspirations, but regional in their appeal. The Populist movement was strong in the south and west, but weak in the north and east and nearly nonexistent in New England. The emotional violence of its rhetoric, the intensity of its agrarian reforms and the flamboyant individuality of its leaders brought success in one region and failure in another.

The Progressive movement was very different from Populism in its political style and cultural base. Progressivism developed mainly in the northern and northeastern states. A large proportion of its leaders were men and women of Yankee stock, who traced their ancestry to the Puritan great migration. Progressivism tended to be rationalist and moralist. Its approach to social problems was intellectual; its solutions were institutional. Generally it adopted an idea of ordered liberty which was consistent with New England's Puritan past. The cultural style of the Progressive movement made it strong in one part of America, and weak in others.

Both Populism and Progressivism developed great power in American politics, but neither was able to transcend its regional limits. The descendants of the Puritans looked with horror upon Populist leaders such as Leonidas Polk of North Carolina, James H. "Cyclone" Davis of Texas, "Sockless Jerry" Simpson of Kansas and Davis H. "Bloody Bridles" Waite. In 1896, the Populist rhetoric of Democratic candidate William Jennings Bryan attracted strong support in the south and west, but failed to carry a single county in New England.

The Progressives, on the other hand, drew their support mostly from the north and northeast, and ran poorly below the Mason-Dixon line. In 1904, the Progressive presidential candidate Theodore Roosevelt carried every county in New England, and all but a handful in New York, New Jersey, Pennsylvania and the Old Northwest. But he lost every county except one in the southern states of South Carolina, Mississippi, Florida, Louisiana, and Alabama.

✍ Woodrow Wilson: The Omnibus Reformer, 1913 –20

Only one reformer ran well in every region. He was Woodrow Wilson, the southern-born Progressive governor of New Jersey who came of border stock. His Georgia and Virginia roots made him attractive to the south, and his Presbyterian morality had strong appeal in greater New England. In national elections, Wilson proved to be an omnibus reformer with exceptional breadth of support throughout the nation.

In 1912, a division in Republican ranks gave Wilson his opportunity. Former President Theodore Roosevelt indulged in a style of highly personal politics which were akin to the ways of his border ancestors. His antics split his party and alienated the normally Republican voters of the northern states. The Republican coalition disintegrated, and regional voting patterns disappeared beneath the Democratic landslide, which put a southern-born President in the White House for the first time since 1865. Wilson's exceptionally broad personal popularity gave him a victory in 1916 as well.

But Wilson's national popularity did not attach to Progressivism in general. Votes for and against leading Progressive measures continued to be primarily regional. A case in point was women's suffrage. The Congressional suffrage resolution of 1919 was strongly supported in the northern states, and strenuously opposed in the south. The suffrage amendment failed of ratification in ten states—all southern. These regional patterns cannot be explained by any material factor. Here was a question that turned primarily on cultural values. Many other Progressive measures showed similar voting patterns.[14]

✍ The High Tide of Regional Politics, 1920–28

After Woodrow Wilson retired from politics, the old regional voting patterns immediately reappeared. They were very strong in the election of 1920, and even stronger in 1924, when a solid northern bloc supported Calvin Coolidge and an even more solid south voted for West Virginian John W. Davis. In 1928, the Democratic party nominated Alfred Smith, the first Roman Catholic

---

[14]Paullin, *Atlas of Historical Geography of the United States*, 128a.

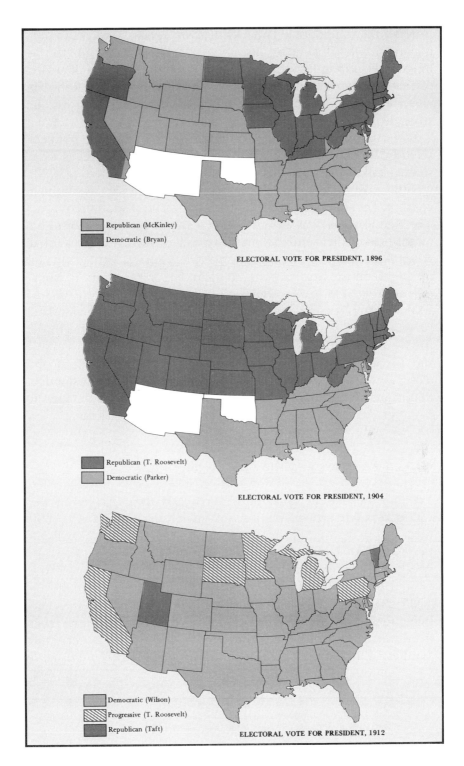

Republican (McKinley)
Democratic (Bryan)

ELECTORAL VOTE FOR PRESIDENT, 1896

Republican (T. Roosevelt)
Democratic (Parker)

ELECTORAL VOTE FOR PRESIDENT, 1904

Democratic (Wilson)
Progressive (T. Roosevelt)
Republican (Taft)

ELECTORAL VOTE FOR PRESIDENT, 1912

presidential candidate in American history, and a Manhattan politician closely linked to Tammany Hall. He proved to be immensely unpopular throughout the nation. The result was a divided southern Democratic vote, and a landslide for Republican Herbert Hoover. The Republicans won the Congress, in strongly sectional voting.

Within Congress during the decade of the twenties, political scientist Richard Bensel finds that sectional voting patterns were stronger than ever. The Sixty-seventh Congress (elected in 1920) was the most deeply divided on sectional lines of any session in a century. Democrats held all but two seats in ten southern states. The Republicans won all but one seat in the rural northern and middle states. The northern cities were divided. Congressional votes were intensely sectional on Henry Ford's Muscle Shoals proposal, on the first McNary-Haugen bill, on prohibition, women's suffrage and many other questions.[15]

Many years earlier, historian Frederick Jackson Turner had predicted that sectionalism would disappear after the closing of the frontier. But as he watched the politics of the 1920s, Turner was forced to revise his own thesis. "That sectionalism is not dying away in the United States," he wrote, "will be clear enough to anyone who examines the newspapers and reads the debates in Congress, not to speak of analyzing the votes in that body."[16]

❧ Old Folkways and the New Immigration

Even as the old sectional politics reached their apogee in the 1920s, a major transformation was taking place in the ethnocultural character of American society. As late as 1900 nearly 60 percent of Americans had been of British stock. The old English-speaking cultures still firmly maintained their hegemony in the United States. But that pattern was changing very rapidly. By 1920 the proportion of Americans with British ancestry had fallen to 41 percent. Still, three-quarters of the nation came from northwestern Europe, but other ethnic stocks from eastern and southern Europe were growing at a formidable rate.

---

[15]Bensel, *Sectionalism and American Political Development*, 375.

[16]Wilbur R. Jacobs, ed., *America's Great Frontiers and Sections* (Lincoln, Neb., 1969) 63; quoted in Bensel, *Sectionalism and American Political Development*, 8.

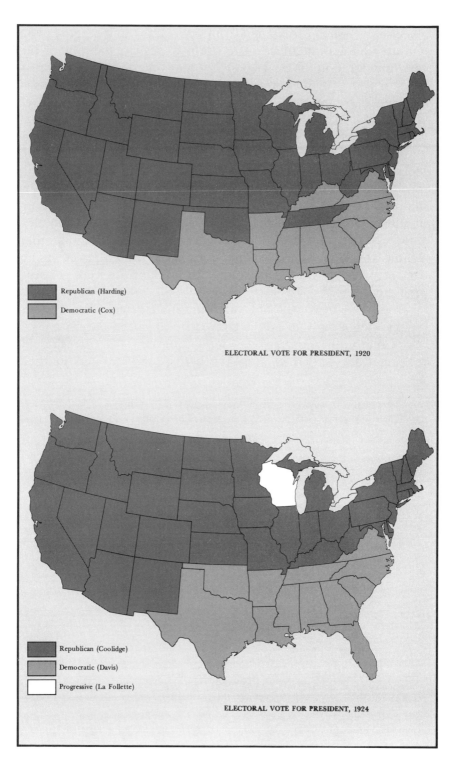

Republican (Harding)
Democratic (Cox)

ELECTORAL VOTE FOR PRESIDENT, 1920

Republican (Coolidge)
Democratic (Davis)
Progressive (La Follette)

ELECTORAL VOTE FOR PRESIDENT, 1924

As always when threatened from abroad, the four Anglo-Saxon cultures joined together in the 1920s to restrict the flow of the new immigration. Every region voted as one on this question— so much so that the immigration restriction bill of 1921 passed the Senate by a margin of 78 to 1. The House of Representatives approved it in a few hours without even bothering to take a roll call.[17]

By these measures, Congress succeeded in reducing the numbers of new immigrants during the twenties. But the ethnic composition of the United States continued to change very rapidly by natural increase. By 1980, the proportion of the American population who reported having any British ancestors at all had fallen below 20 percent. Nearly 80 percent were descended from other ethnic stocks. The largest ethnic stock in the United States was no longer British but German. Many other minorities were growing at a great rate.[18]

In the northeast, the new and old ethnic groups found themselves increasingly in conflict on cultural questions. In a New York referendum on pari-mutuel betting in 1939, for example, communities settled by Yankees before 1855 united in their

---

[17]John Higham, *Strangers in the Land* (New Brunswick, N.J., 1955), 311.

[18]The changing ethnic composition of the American Population has been estimated as follows in the 20th century:

"Ancestry Group"	1920–24	1970–71
British	41.4%	21.4%
German and Austrian	15.4	19.1
Irish	10.0	11.2
Scandinavian	4.3	8.5
Italian	3.2	6.0
French	2.5	3.6
Polish	2.6	3.4
Dutch	1.8	1.9
Russian	1.6	1.5
Czech	1.6	1.1
Swiss	1.0	1.1
Other European groups	3.0	7.0
Total European groups	88.4%	82.8%
African	9.8	11.4
Latin American	1.2	4.4
American Indian (1970)	0.2	0.4
Asian (1970)	0.3	0.7
Other non-European (1970)	0.1	0.3
Total non-European groups	11.6%	17.2%
Grand total	100.0%	100.0%

Source: U.S. Bureau of the Census, *Current Population Reports,* series P-20; and *SAUS* (1976), table 40; estimates of non-European ethnic stocks as indicated are drawn from the Census of 1970.

opposition. The new immigrants were equally solid in support. The lines of conflict between the older communities and the new immigrants were sharply drawn on these issues.[19]

But these ethnic collisions were only one part of a complex process of acculturation, which had an important regional dimension. The growth of ethnic pluralism did not diminish regional identities. On balance, it actually enhanced them. This was so because the new immigrants did not distribute themselves randomly through the United States. They tended to flock together in specific regions. Ethnic pluralism itself thus became a regional variable.

Further, the new immigrants did not assimilate American culture in general. They tended to adopt the folkways of the regions in which they settled. This was specially the case among immigrant elites. This process of regional assimilation might be illustrated by a few individual examples. A familiar case in point was President John Fitzgerald Kennedy, whose ancestors came from Ireland to the United States in the mid-nineteenth century. Kennedy was raised within a distinctive Irish Catholic culture and acquired many of its values. At the same time, he was also a New Englander in his education, associations, prejudices, dress ways and even his speech ways ("Cuber"). Kennedy's social and political identity combined ethnic and regional elements.

A second example was one of the most powerful politicians in the city of Washington during the late twentieth century. He was an Afro-American, a descendant of black slaves, and a leader of the black power movement in American politics. At the same time, his attitudes, beliefs, and speech were in many ways those of a Virginia gentleman. So also was his name, Walter Fauntroy, which derived from one of the proudest Royalist families in the ancient dominion. The thoughts and acts of this prominent American politician, like those of John F. Kennedy, were shaped both by his ethnic and regional heritage.

Another representative of this process was Barry Goldwater, an American of Jewish descent who lived his formative years in the southwest. He became deeply interested in the history of that region and collected a library of western history which was one

---

[19]On pari-mutuel betting in 1939, John L. Hammond found zero-order r values of negative .523 for communities founded by Yankees before 1855; for immigrant populations the correlation was a positive .700 on the other side. He reported similar patterns in voting on state lotteries in 1966; *The Politics of Benevolence,* 169.

of the best in private hands. His speech, dress, attitudes, political principles, and his idea of natural liberty were drawn from the culture of the backcountry and the southwestern frontier. His manners and behavior conformed to old border and backcountry folkways.

A fourth instance was Grace Kelly, the American film actress who was deeply conscious of her Irish Catholic heritage, and so active in maintaining it that one of the most important centers of Irish Studies today is improbably to be found in the principality of Monaco. At the same time, Grace Kelly was also a loyal Philadelphian, and very much a product of its culture. Her dignity of manner, simplicity of appearance, and directness of speech all owed much to the culture of the Delaware Valley. Grace Kelly was also the product of both an ethnic and a regional culture.

These were not isolated examples. Black culture throughout the United States tended generally to be an amalgam of African and southern folkways. Hispanic Americans in Texas and southern California combined the legacy of Latin America with the culture of the backcountry. Irish, Italian, Greek and French Canadian immigrants in Massachusetts all joined their special ethnic heritage to the customs of New England. The Germans and Scandinavians who settled the middle west learned the folkways which had spread outward from the Delaware Valley. Similar patterns of regional acculturation appeared in most major American ethnic groups. The author's Protestant stereotypes about the culture of Judaism were utterly exploded by his Brandeis students who have included Yankee Jews, Philadelphia Jews, southern Jews and, most startling of all, backslapping Texas Jews in cowboy boots and ten-gallon hats. Here again, their culture was a product of ethnicity and region.

❧ The New Deal Coalition: Ethnic and Regional Cultures

The new immigrants were slow to move into positions of leadership in the United States. A complex system of discrimination by licensing, quotas and covenants kept their numbers small in prestigious professions, the strongest schools and the best neighborhoods. But by 1932 their voting strength made a powerful difference in American politics and produced a major realignment of ethnic and regional groups which put Franklin Roosevelt in the White House.

During the Great Depression, the sufferings of southern farmers and northern workers created the basis for a new coalition which was destined to dominate national politics for nearly twenty years. This New Deal coalition united disparate cultural groups who shared little more than their common revulsion to the cultures, policies and moral purposes of the Republican coalition that had failed so dismally during the Great Depression. The political economy of laissez-faire and the Protestant ethic had been discredited by the Depression. The "noble experiment" of ordered freedom in national prohibition was regarded as a social disaster. This was a period when "puritanism" became a pejorative term in American speech. Descendants of the great migration were ridiculed as absurd and pathetic figures in Sinclair Lewis's *Main Street* and Grant Wood's *American Gothic*.

The old Republican coalition still remained strong, especially in the northern and midland rural regions which had been settled from New England and Pennsylvania. The states of Maine and Vermont voted Republican in every presidential election but one from 1856 to 1960.[20] Republican candidates also ran strongly in the parts of the old northwest (Ohio, Indiana, Michigan, and Wisconsin), in the many northern plains states (Iowa, Nebraska, Kansas and the Dakotas), and in the Pacific northwest state of Oregon. In the depths of the Depression, the old Republican coalition still remained the strongest single culture in American politics. But the growing pluralism of American society now made it impossible for that cultural bloc to dominate national politics as it had done from 1860 to 1932.

The New Deal coalition was a response to this development. It united the many enemies of the old Puritan ethic: Catholic immigrants, Jewish intellectuals, southern gentlemen, black sharecroppers, Appalachian mountain folk, Texas stockmen and California hedonists. All joined in one movement improbably led by a patrician Democrat of New England stock from New York.

The various groups who supported Roosevelt all believed that the national government should play a larger economic role. But they did not share the same moral values and cultural purposes. The policies of New Deal reflected this diversity of cultural origins. It was an American middle way, "slightly left of center" in Franklin Roosevelt's favorite phrase—a series of pragmatic

---

[20]The sole exception was the presidential election of 1912, when Maine went Democratic, largely as a result of the Republican divisions.

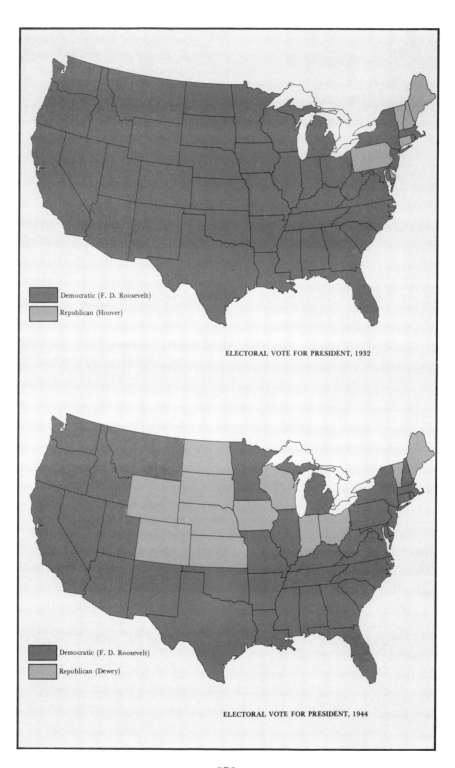

Democratic (F. D. Roosevelt)

Republican (Hoover)

ELECTORAL VOTE FOR PRESIDENT, 1932

Democratic (F. D. Roosevelt)

Republican (Dewey)

ELECTORAL VOTE FOR PRESIDENT, 1944

experiments designed to preserve the capitalist and democratic fabric of American society by increasing public intervention in the material life of the nation. At the same time, the New Deal also opposed public legislation on questions of private morality. It abolished national prohibition, and rejected the moral activism of the Republican coalition.

Here was the central paradox of the New Deal—material intervention and moral non-intervention. It increased the economic role of government, but diminished its role as the instrument of any single system of ethnic or regional culture. The south received strong material support, but was not required to change its folkways. The ethnic cultures of new immigrants in northern cities were given economic aid in many forms, but legislative challenges to their culture were abandoned. The cultural hegemony of the Republican coalition was finally destroyed.

ᖷ Regional Cultures in World War II

When the Second World War began, many Americans wished not to be involved in quarrels of the Old World. But as the fascist juggernaut crushed the infant democracies of Europe until only Britain stood alone, America slowly awakened to a mortal danger. All doubts were removed when Japan launched its surprise attack against Pearl Harbor, and Germany and Italy declared war against the United States. Americans forgot their differences, and rallied together as never before—or since—on any public question.

Each American culture had its own motives for supporting the war. Northeastern liberals joined it as a crusade against fascism and militarism—an idea that gained strength as the full horror of German and Japanese regimes was gradually revealed. Southern conservatives, always more internationalist than the nation as a whole, were drawn into the conflict by their kinship with Britain. The backcountry, bellicose as ever, fought for national honor— and also for the joy of fighting. Even Quakers and pacifists nonviolently supported a war against the warrior spirit.

These various cultures also contributed in different ways to the conduct of the war. The behavior of the nation's major military leaders reflected the regional origins. A case in point was George S. Patton, Jr., America's most brilliant field commander. Patton was descended from North British immigrants who had settled in the backcountry during the eighteenth century, and whose progeny had found their way to southern California. They thought of themselves as a warrior race. George Patton as a little child was told the hero tales of the borders and the martial deeds of his forebears. Many Pattons had fought in the Revolution, and at least fourteen had served in the Civil War. "Men of my blood . . . have ever inspired me," he once remarked. "Should I falter, I will have disgraced my blood." Patton believed that his ancestors literally hovered over him on the battlefield. Of combat during World War I he wrote, "I was trembling with fear when suddenly I thought of my progenitors and seemed to see them in a cloud over the German lines looking at me. I became calm at once, and saying aloud, 'It is time for another Patton to die,' called for volunteers and went forward to what I honestly believed was certain death."

Patton's method of making war was also true to the customs of his ancestors. Even in an age of mechanized war he led from the front. American prisoners of war at Mooseberg, Germany, were astounded when an armored spearhead fought its way into their camp, and General Patton himself emerged from one of the lead tanks. The victories of his Third Army owed much to Patton's aggressive spirit and brilliant battlefield improvisations. Behind the front, however, his volatile emotions and uncontrollable rages nearly led to his removal.[1]

Patton's long-suffering superior was a soldier of another stripe. Dwight David Eisenhower, born in Abilene, Texas, was descended from Swiss Mennonites and German Pietists who had settled in Quaker Pennsylvania before 1733. His forebears had refused to bear arms in the Revolution and the Civil War, and his parents were of a pietist sect called River Brethren who raised their children to believe in hard work, simplicity, decency and strict self-discipline. Eisenhower remembered his mother quoting the Bible: "He that conquereth his own soul is greater than he who taketh a city."[2] He went to West Point primarily for a free education, rose in the army as a staff officer and never served in combat during his entire military career. As Allied commander, Eisenhower rarely ventured even as far forward as army group

[1]Martin Blumenson, *Patton, The Man Behind the Legend, 1885–1945* (New York, 1985), 20–21, 113, *passim;* George S. Patton, Jr., *War As I Knew It* (Boston, 1947); Martin Blumenson, *The Patton Papers* (2 vols., 1972–74); Kenneth W. Simmons, *Kriegie* (New York, 1960).
[2]Stephen Ambrose, *Eisenhower* (2 vols., New York, 1983–84), I, 30.

headquarters, and preferred to toil at his desk far in the rear. He was a soldier who hated fighting and thought of war as a business in which the object was to succeed with all possible economy of human life.

Eisenhower's boss, General George Catlett Marshall, came from yet another Anglo-American culture. Though Marshall had been born in Pennsylvania, he was by breeding a gentleman of Virginia. The first Catletts and Marshalls in America were Royalist officers who had settled in the Chesapeake about the year 1650. George Marshall graduated not from West Point but from the Virginia Military Institute; his first wife was a Virginian, Lily Carter. Those who knew him testified to "terrific influence and power" which flowed mainly from a force of character that reminded others of Washington and Lee. The same words were invariably used to describe him—honor, dignity, integrity, character. Even the intrepid George Patton once declared that he "would rather face a whole Nazi Panzer army single-handed than be called to an interview with General Marshall."[3]

Marshall's commander-in-chief was Franklin Delano Roosevelt, who had still a fourth style of leadership. Roosevelt was Dutch only in name. By birth and breeding he was a Yankee. More than three-quarters of his ancestors were New Englanders, and he had been educated in New England schools (Groton and Harvard). As President, Franklin Roosevelt contributed a special quality of leadership which combined high moral purpose, clarity of vision, toughness of mind, tenacity of purpose, flexibility of method and an implacable will to win. That pattern of leadership was not only a set of personal attributes. It was also a cultural artifact which owed much to the folkways of New England. So also were his statements of war aims and his vision of the future—which expressed an ideal of ordered liberty that owed much to the freedom ways of his ancestors. Even phrases such as "freedom from want" and "freedom from fear" had appeared in the records of the Massachusetts Bay Colony.

America's regional cultures made a difference not only in styles of leadership, but also in the substance of command decisions, sometimes in a way that caused trouble for the Allied war effort. In 1944, for example, while American soldiers and Marines were fighting the Japanese on the island of Saipan, Marine General Holland M. Smith relieved the army's General Ralph C. Smith for

[3]Leonard Mosley, *Marshal, A Hero for Our Times* (New York, 1928), 107.

"lack of aggressiveness." That decision caused a "war of the Smiths" which is remembered by military historians mainly as a clash of personalities and institutions, and also conflict between Marine doctrines of frontal assault, and army tactics of fire and envelopment. But it was also a collision of cultures. General Holland M. Smith was a product of the southern backcountry, born and raised in rural Alabama. In battle he was brave, aggressive, violent and profane. Fellow Marines called him "Howlin' Mad" Smith.

The army's Ralph Corbett Smith came from old New England stock. His ancestors had arrived in the Puritan great migration, and his grandparents had moved to the middle west where he became a national guard officer. After a distinguished record in World War I he made the army his career. Smith was quiet, calm, serious, soft-spoken and exceptionally self-possessed. An aide recalled, "I have never, never seen him angry. . . . I have never heard the level of his voice go up any more than in normal conversation. As a matter of fact, I don't recall the old man ever saying even a 'God Damn.'" General S.L.A. Marshall, who knew him well, wrote that "his extreme consideration for other mortals would keep him from being rated among the great captains; he is a somewhat rarer specimen, a generous Christian gentleman."

This affair was more than merely a tactical dispute between soldiers and Marines. The "war between the Smiths" was also a clash of cultures. But strife of that sort was fortunately rare in the American war effort. The regional pluralism of the United States was on balance a source of strength rather than weakness.

❧ The Postwar Revival of Regional Politics, 1945–60

The Second World War kept the New Deal coalition together. But in the first presidential election after the peace, northern liberals and southern conservatives parted ways. There were many divisive issues—primarily the problem of race, on which the two wings of the Democratic party deeply disagreed. The result was the revolt of the Dixiecrats, a bloc of southern conservatives who seceded from the Democratic party in 1948 because of their opposition to civil rights for blacks. In the presidential election of that year, four southern states gave their presidential votes to a regional politician, Strom Thurmond and his States' Rights Democratic party.

In this election, Republican nominee Thomas E. Dewey also proved to be a regional candidate. Dewey was a New Yorker of old Yankee and Puritan stock—narrow-featured, neatly dressed, bland, remote, restrained and rational. He carried every northeastern state except Massachusetts, and ran powerfully in the northern plains and the Pacific northwest.

The Democratic incumbent Harry Truman made a dramatic contrast with both his Dixiecrat and Republican rivals. Truman was a cultural product of the Missouri backcountry. His campaign was high-spirited, coarse-grained, aggressive, informal, emotional, personal and profane. Its spirit was captured in a rallying cry, "Give 'em Hell, Harry!" Its substance appeared in its slogan, "Vote your own interests!" Truman managed to be liberal on race and conservative on property, pro-union and pro-farm, pro-producer and pro-consumer. His combination of strong words and moderate acts had powerful appeal in the American midlands.

When the ballots were counted, Truman, no less than his challengers, also proved to be a regional candidate, who drew his electoral majority mainly from the southern highlands, the middle west, border states, the great basin and the far west. He lost greater New England and the northern tier to Dewey and much of the south to Dixiecrat Strom Thurmond.

❧ The Eisenhower Omnibus

As the presidential elections approached in 1952, the frontrunners in both parties were classical regional candidates—the backcountry Tennessee Democrat Estes Kefauver, and the Ohio Republican of old New England stock Robert Taft. But both parties rejected these men in an effort to broaden their appeal. Democrats turned to Adlai Stevenson, a patrician progressive who promised to run well in the northeast. The Republicans adopted the omnibus strategy so often used by conservative parties, and nominated a folksy military hero with few discernable opinions on controversial questions. The omnibus strategy succeeded brilliantly. In 1952 and again in 1956, Eisenhower carried every American state outside the south. The success of the Republican omnibus dealt a crushing blow to the New Deal coalition.

❧ The Revolution in Regional Alignments, 1960–68

During the decade of the 1960s, a revolution occurred in regional voting patterns. For a century, New England, Pennsylvania, Ohio and Michigan had voted Republican in nearly every presidential election except when Woodrow Wilson and Franklin Roosevelt had drawn them away. In the same period, the coastal and highland south had gone Democratic in every presidential contest except during the Reconstruction era. This general pattern had persisted from 1856 to 1956.[4]

Then, during the 1960s, new trends of great strength and stability began to appear. The leading tendency was the growth of a new Democratic voting bloc in New England and New York, Pennsylvania, Michigan, Wisconsin and Minnesota. These states had been the core of the Republican coalition in the nineteenth century. Now they became the new base of the Democratic party; in the elections of 1960, 1964 and 1968, most of them voted for liberal Democratic candidates.

At the same time, southern states turned toward the Republican party. A new conservative coalition united the coastal and highland south, the mountain states, the great basin and the far southwest. In 1964, the candidate of this alliance was Republican Barry Goldwater. Many conservative Democrats throughout the south changed parties to vote for him. The pattern of support for Republican Goldwater was strongest in the south and west.

Behind this change in regional alignments lay a striking continuity in their environing cultures. Political scientist Walter Dean Burnham made an interesting discovery in that respect. While studying the election returns of New York in 1964, he found that the counties which voted Democratic and supported civil rights in 1964 were the same as those which had voted Republican and opposed slavery in the mid-nineteenth century. They were also the counties which had been settled from New England during the late eighteenth century. Burnham concluded that voting in this region was determined by "durable community norms which have their historical origins in the values of the original settlers and their descendants."[5]

---

[4]This generalization refers to New England as a bloc. Democratic presidential candidates carried Connecticut in 1876, 1884, 1888 and 1892; Rhode Island in 1928 and 1948; Ohio in 1948; and Pennsylvania in 1856.

[5]Walter Dean Burnham, "American Voting Behavior and the 1964 Election," *Midwest Journal of Political Science* 12 (1968), 1–40.

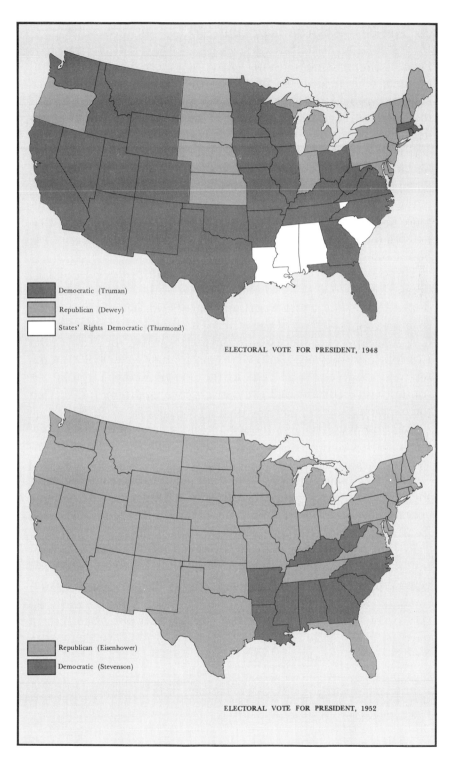

Democratic (Truman)

Republican (Dewey)

States' Rights Democratic (Thurmond)

ELECTORAL VOTE FOR PRESIDENT, 1948

Republican (Eisenhower)

Democratic (Stevenson)

ELECTORAL VOTE FOR PRESIDENT, 1952

～ The New Regionalism, 1968–86

Dean Burnham's conclusions were not widely shared by his colleagues, who repeatedly predicted the imminent extinction of regional voting in American politics.[6] But once again, reports of the death of regionalism proved to be premature. In the presidential elections of 1968 and 1972, voting patterns were strongly regional. Conservative Republican candidate Richard Nixon won his largest pluralities in the coastal south, the highland south and Great Basin. He was less successful in the midlands, and least so in the north. The only state that voted against him was Massachusetts. His smallest pluralities were in the northern tier that extended through southern New England, Wisconsin, Minnesota, South Dakota and Oregon.[7]

These new regional patterns in American politics tended to break down from time to time, just as earlier alignments had done. They came apart when one party nominated a candidate from the regional base of the other. The Democrats, for example, had their strongest successes in this period when they ran Texan Lyndon Johnson (1964) and Georgian Jimmy Carter (1976). Carter won every electoral vote in the south except Virginia; his southern strength divided the conservative coalition and carried the election.

Regional patterns also tended to disappear when either party chose a candidate who seemed to be outside the cultural mainstream. Republican Barry Goldwater in 1964 and Democrat George McGovern in 1968 were both made to appear radicals of the right and left, respectively. In substantive terms neither was very far from the center, but their rhetoric appeared radical with disastrous results for their parties.

Regional ties were also disrupted when the conservative coalition put up an omnibus candidate. In 1980, this device was tried again in a novel form. No victorious generals had emerged from

---

[6]V. O. Key, *Politics, Parties and Pressure Groups* (New York, 1964).

[7]Nixon was re-elected by the following pluralities:

Northern: 52–55%	Southern: 68–70%
New England 52%	South Atlantic 68%
Northern Plains 56%	East South Central 70%
Pacific Northwest 55%	West South Central 68%
Midland: 59–60%	Great Basin: 68%
Mid-Atlantic 59%	California: 55%
E.N. Central 59%	
W.N. Central 60%	

the Vietnam War, but the Republican party discovered that a professional actor made a highly acceptable substitute. Ronald Reagan proved to be a perfect omnibus candidate. In the election of 1980 he carried every cultural region and all but six states.

In 1984, Reagan won an even more commanding victory when Democrats made the fatal mistake of nominating Walter Mondale, a candidate from their only strong region. Mondale's political style was reminiscent of many northern candidates in the past; it did not attract voters from other parts of the country. The resulting Reagan landslide buried regional patterns. Once again journalists and political scientists predicted that regions were disappearing from American life. But in the Congressional and gubernatorial elections of 1986, regional voting became visible once again.

On most substantive issues of the mid-1980s, regional patterns were also very strong. The nuclear freeze, for example, was supported by all but a few New England Congressmen, and opposed by most Representatives from the south and west. In attitudes toward military affairs, foreign policy, capital punishment and many domestic questions, regional attitudes are still powerful.

These regional patterns were also evident in the presidential campaign of 1988. Among Democratic contenders, Massachusetts Governor Michael Dukakis combined his Greek and Yankee heritage in a manner reminiscent of the Irish Yankee John Kennedy; Dukakis's managerial style was in the tradition of New England ideas of ordered liberty. Jesse Jackson also combined an ethnic and a regional identity—a black minister and politician, who had been born in upcountry South Carolina, and christened with an old border name—his style was descended from three centuries of field preaching in the region of his birth. Richard Gephardt was a backcountry politician who ran heavily on a single issue, which was to apply the old border rule of *lex talionis* to foreign affairs; his message was well received in his own region, but found little support outside it. Among Republicans, Robert Dole of Kansas was also a midland candidate who did well in his region and badly everywhere else; Pat Robertson came from the "backcountry ascendancy" and had a very strong regional identity. The candidates who did worst in both parties (Hart, Babbitt, Schroeder, Kemp, Haig, Dupont) had no firm base in any cultural region. The one who did the best, Republican George Bush, had a base in more regions than one—with his old New England origins, his long residence in Texas, and an accent that combined

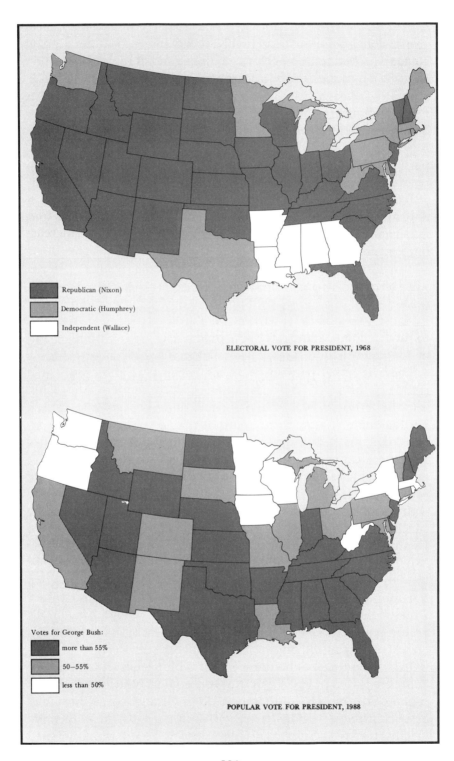

Republican (Nixon)

Democratic (Humphrey)

Independent (Wallace)

ELECTORAL VOTE FOR PRESIDENT, 1968

Votes for George Bush:

more than 55%

50–55%

less than 50%

POPULAR VOTE FOR PRESIDENT, 1988

886

both a Yankee twang and a southern drawl—an extraordinary feat of political linguistics.

The presidential election of 1988 was marked by cynical manipulation of cultural symbols—which were perceived very differently in various regions. Democrat Michael Dukakis did best in the northern tier from Massachusetts to Washington and Oregon, but his ideas of ordered liberty alienated voters in every region except his own. Republican George Bush carried every southern state plus the conservative Great Basin by very large margins. The American midlands were divided. Bush carried this region too, but often by paper-thin pluralities—51 percent in Pennsylvania, Maryland, and Illinois. The final result showed that the new regional voting patterns were very strong, and increasingly stable.

❧ Regional Identities: America's Mental Maps

These cultural regions were not static in their structure. By 1988, the original four regions of British America had greatly expanded, and were also joined by other regional cultures which did not exist two centuries earlier. Altogether, there were now at least seven cultural regions in the continental United States:

1. *The Northern Tier,* including New England, the upper old northwest, the northern plains and the Pacific northwest, all settled by Yankees but now dominated by other ethnic groups who are Roman Catholic in New England, Lutheran in the middle west.
2. *Greater New York,* small in area but 10 percent of the national population, and a very heavy infusion of middle European and Jewish culture grafted on the old Dutch root.
3. *Midland America,* extending from Pennsylvania west through the Ohio Valley and the middle west to the Rocky Mountains, marked by a diversity of European immigrant groups; the leading religion in many midland counties is Methodist.
4. *The Great Basin,* a predominantly Mormon culture in Utah, and parts of Idaho, Nevada, Arizona, Colorado and Wyoming; a mix of New England, midland and highland southern culture.
5. *The Coastal South,* from southern Maryland to Florida and the Texas coast near Houston. Its culture is tempered by large numbers of northern immigrants.

6. *The Southern Highlands,* including Appalachia, the old southwest, the Ozark Plateau, and much of Texas and Oklahoma
   which are still dominated by the old ethnic groups; the leading
   religion is Baptist.
7. *Southern California,* a hybrid of highland southern, midland,
   Hispanic and Jewish culture, spreading into Nevada, Arizona
   and New Mexico.

Each of these seven cultures is a complex mixture of old regional
patterns with new ethic and religious groups. Each has its own
speech ways. In addition to the old dialects of northern, midland,
coastal southern and highland southern speech, three others have
appeared in the twentieth century. New York English developed
from a distinctive mixture of northern and midland speech,
enriched by central European and Jewish languages. California
English combines highland southern and midland speech with
many Hispanic expressions. Great Basin English brings together
northern, midland and highland southern speech ways in a syn-
cretist accent which is beginning to emerge as American standard
speech. In the late twentieth century, national television broad-
casters are trained to use the accent of Salt Lake City—the American equivalent of BBC English.

Within these cultural regions, new ethnic groups and religious
denominations have emerged; but the old regional identities
themselves remain remarkably strong. In the mid-1960s, cultural
geographers Peter Gould and Rodney White measured American
attitudes in that respect, by the ingenious method of constructing
"mental maps" in which spatial judgments are represented in
topographical terms. They found that the mental maps of most
Americans shared a few topographical features in common, notably a "California high" and a "Dakota low." But attitudes also
differed profoundly from one historical region to another. Ala-
bamans despised New England; northerners disliked Alabama.
Gould and White were surprised by the persistence of these historical attitudes, which they regarded as temporary aberrations
caused by the Civil War. "By the year 2000," they wrote, "we may
hope that the mental maps of Americans, northerners and southerners, will no longer reflect the wound established over a century ago." But these regional antipathies had appeared long
before the Civil War and they remained remarkably strong in the
twentieth century.[8]

[8]Peter Gould and Rodney White, *Mental Maps* (New York, 1974), 175.

During World War II, for example, three German submariners escaped from Camp Crossville, Tennessee. Their flight took them to an Appalachian cabin, where they stopped for a drink of water. The mountain granny told them to "git." When they ignored her, she promptly shot them dead. The sheriff came, and scolded her for shooting helpless prisoners. Granny burst into tears, and said that she would not have done it if she had known they were Germans. The exasperated sheriff asked her what in "tarnation" she thought she was shooting at. "Why," she replied, "I thought they was Yankees!"[9]

❧ Regional Patterns of Cultural Behavior

The persistence of American regionalism also appeared in every federal census, which continues even today to yield evidence of greater differences between American regions than among European nations. Further, these patterns show remarkably strong linkages with the distant colonial past.

A case in point are statistics of order and violence in the United States. In 1982, the murder rate in the nation as a whole was 9.1 per 100,000. This level of violence was four times higher than most western countries. But within the United States, the homicide rate differed very much from one region to another. The northern tier, from New England across the northern plains to the Pacific northwest, tended as always to have the lowest rates of homicide: 3.8 in Massachusetts, 2.1 in Maine, 3.1 in Wisconsin, 2.3 in Minnesota, 0.9 in North Dakota, 4.4 in the state of Washington. The middle states, on the other hand, had murder rates that were moderately higher, but below the national average: 5.7 in Pennsylvania, 7.2 in the middle west, 5.7 in Kansas, 6.0 in Colorado. Homicide rates were much higher in the upper coastal south. The south Atlantic states averaged 10.9 murders per 100,000 in 1982. The southern highlands and the southwestern states had extremely high murder rates—14.7 in the west south-central states, and 16.1 in Texas. Homicide rates were also high in northern cities with large populations of southern immigrants, both black and white. But southern neighborhoods occupied by migrants from the north tended to have low homicide rates. These patterns are highly complex; many ethnic and material fac-

[9]Arnold Krammer, *Nazi Prisoners of War in America* (New York, 1979), 133.

tors clearly have an impact. But in ecological terms, homicide rates throughout the United States correlate more closely with cultural regions of origin than with urbanization, poverty, or any material factor.

One may ask why this is the case. Why have American regions preserved these differences for so long a time? The pattern is particularly striking in New England, because it has persisted in the face of sweeping ethnic changes. Three centuries ago, New England was Congregationalist; today it is mostly Roman Catholic.[10] In 1650, its white population was almost entirely English; it has become heavily Irish, Italian and French Canadian. Even so, levels of social violence remain low in New England, just as they have stayed high in the southern highlands. Why?

Some scholars offer a materialist explanation: the comparative wealth of New England against the poverty of the southern highlands. But many a hardscrabble Yankee hill town is poor and orderly, and more than a few southwestern communities are rich and violent.

Others argue that southern violence is mainly a legacy of ethnic or racial diversity. But some of the most violent communities in the southern highlands have no black residents at all, and are in ethnic terms among the most homogeneous in the nation. At the same time, many New England communities are ethnically diverse and yet comparatively peaceful.

A few scholars have explained southern violence in terms of its frontier legacy. But New England was once a frontier too. An occasional explanation of southern violence refers to the Civil War, or to the hot climate or even to human necessity. When one southerner was asked why so many people were killed in his region, he answered that "there were just more folks in the South that needed killing."[11]

A less colorful but more promising explanation is cast in institutional terms. At an early date, each regional culture developed its own institutions of order and violence which have persisted powerfully through time. The laws of New England have always given little latitude to violence. This pattern began in Puritan Massachusetts during the seventeenth century; it still existed in the 1980s when Massachusetts enacted the toughest gun-control statutes in the nation.

---

[10] Edwin S. Gaustad, *Historical Atlas of Religion in America* (rev. ed., New York, 1976).
[11] Sheldon Hackney, "Southern Violence," *AHR* 74 (1969), 906–25.

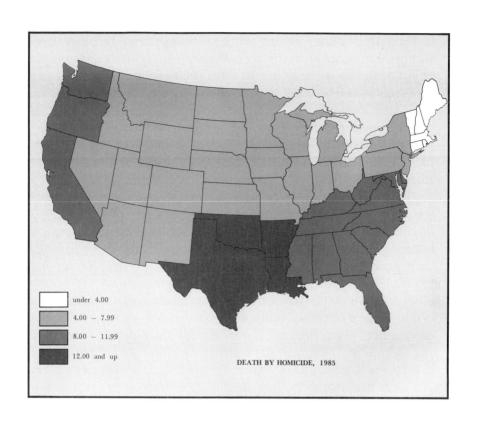

under 4.00

4.00 – 7.99

8.00 – 11.99

12.00 and up

DEATH BY HOMICIDE, 1985

The laws of New England are actively supported by other institutions. For more than three centuries, town schools have taught children not to use violence to solve their social problems. Town meetings strongly condemn internal violence. Town elites teach others by example that violence is not an acceptable form of social behavior in New England. In short, violence "isn't done" in the prescriptive sense. And when it is done, the regional culture of New England has little tolerance for violent acts, and punishes them severely.

All of these tendencies run in reverse throughout the old southwest and southern highlands. The principle of *lex talionis* is still part of Texas law, which allows a husband to kill his wife's lover *in flagrante delictu*. Texas places comparatively few restraints on the ownership of firearms. Texas schools and schoolbooks glorify violence in a way that those of Massachusetts do not. Texas elites still live by the rule of retaliation, and murder one another often enough to set an example. Texas is entertained by displays of violence; Massachusetts is not amused. In short, violence simply *is* done in Texas and the southern highlands, and always has been done in this culture—since before the Civil War and slavery and even the frontier—just as it had been done in the borderlands of North Britain before emigration.[12]

Similar regional disparities, also inherited from the distant past, appeared in other social indicators. A good example is education. By 1980, elementary education was universal in the United States. But large regional differences existed in patterns of secondary schooling and higher education. The proportion of youngsters who graduated from high school varied broadly from one region to another. The highest graduation rates were in the northern tier: the top three states were Minnesota (91%); Connecticut (90%) and North Dakota (90%). Midland states were in an upper middling range (Pennsylvania, 78%, New Jersey 78%, Ohio 80%), and the upper south was in a lower middling position (Maryland, 76%, Virginia, 74%). The lowest states were in the deep south (Georgia, 63%, Louisiana, 63%, and Florida, 62%), and the southwest was also very low (Arizona, 63%, Nevada, 65%, California, 67%), as were northern or midland cities with heavy

---

[12]Texas humor continues to be full of vicarious violence against humanity in general, and Yankees in particular. During the oil crisis of 1973–81, for example, a Texas bumper-sticker read, "Drive at 90; Freeze a Yankee."

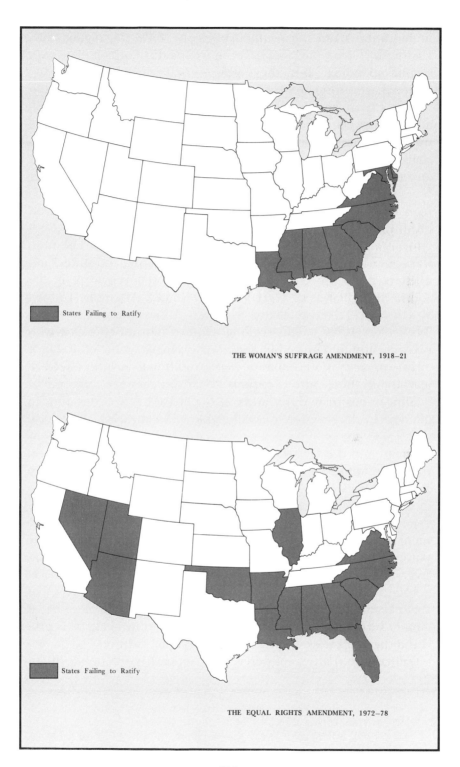

States Failing to Ratify

THE WOMAN'S SUFFRAGE AMENDMENT, 1918–21

States Failing to Ratify

THE EQUAL RIGHTS AMENDMENT, 1972–78

immigration from the south (New York, 64%, Michigan, 68%, District of Columbia, 57%). These trends did not correlate with school spending. But they were closely linked to inherited regional attitudes toward education.[13]

Similar patterns also appeared in higher education. Exceptionally high levels of college attendance were to be found in the northern states originally settled by New England Puritans and Yankees. In Massachusetts, Connecticut, Maine, and Vermont approximately 20 percent of the population had completed four years of college by 1980. The proportion was also comparatively high across the northern tier and in the Great Basin—17 percent in Minnesota, 19 percent in the states of Washington and Oregon, 20 percent in Utah and 23 percent in Colorado. The ratio, was lower in other regions: 16 percent in the midland states, and 15 percent in the coastal south. The lowest levels were in the southern highlands of West Virginia (10.4%), Arkansas (10.8%), Kentucky (11.1%), Alabama (12.2%), Mississippi (12.3%) and Tennessee (12.6%). This regional pattern did not correlate with urbanization or with public spending on higher education. Once again, primary determinants were traditional attitudes toward learning in these various regions.[14]

Similar regional differences also persist in attitudes toward gender. In the seventeenth and eighteenth centuries, as we have seen, the status of women was comparatively high in New England and the Delaware Valley, low in Virginia, and lowest in the backcountry. These regional differences persisted through four centuries. The northern states supported women's suffrage in the nineteenth and twentieth centuries, while the South and especially the southwest consistently opposed the enfranchisement of women. In the late twentieth century, precisely the same pattern appeared in voting on the Equal Rights Amendment. Every state in the northern tier voted in favor of this measure. All states in the southern highlands voted against it. The fact that this pattern has persisted for so long a time is evidence that it cannot be explained merely as a temporary cultural lag. It is produced by deep-seated differences in regional cultures.

Yet another pattern of persistence appears in the public life of

---

[13]*New York Times*, 1 March 1988.

[14]*SAUS* (1984), 145; exceptionally high was the District of Columbia (27.5%), and contiguous states of Maryland and Virginia.

the major cultural regions. In every region, the dominant forms of local government are descended from institutions which were introduced in the seventeenth and early eighteenth century. Most New England communities still govern themselves through town meetings. This system has spread through the northern tier to New York, Ohio, Michigan, Wisconsin, Minnesota and the Dakotas. Pennsylvania preserves its county commissions. Virginia and the coastal south are still controlled by county courthouse elites. The tone of government in these regions has remained remarkably stable through many generations.

Further, levels of governmental activity (measured by public spending) have remained relatively the same for three centuries. In the mid-eighteenth century, levels of taxation for state and local governments were roughly twice as high in New England as in Virginia, with the Delaware Valley somewhere in between, and the backcountry below all other regions. Precisely the same patterns still appear today, even when controlled by population and wealth. In 1981, for example, a family of four with an income of $75,000 paid state and local taxes of $10,900 in Boston, $7,000 in Philadelphia, $5,700 in Norfolk, $4,800 in Louisville and $4,600 in Houston. Relative levels of taxing and spending by region have changed remarkably little in many generations.[15]

❧ Persistent Regionalism: Problems of Cause

Why have regional cultures persisted for so long a period in Anglo-America? How does any culture persist? This problem has long been neglected by historians and social scientists. Barrington Moore observes:

> There is a widespread assumption in modern social science that social continuity requires no explanation. Supposedly it is not problematical. Change is what requires explanation. . . . The assumption of inertia, that cultural and social continuity do not require explanation, obliterates the fact that both have to be recreated anew in each generation, often with great pain and suffering.[16]

---

[15]*SAUS* (1984), 302.

[16]Barrington Moore, *Social Origins of Dictatorship and Democracy: Lord and Peasant in the Making of the Modern World*, (Boston, 1966), 485–86.

Cultural persistence is not the same as stasis. Many things must *happen* if a culture is to be transmitted from one generation to the next. Whenever its continuance is challenged by events as large as a revolution, or as small as the birth of a child, some very complex cultural machinery instantly begins to operate.

This process of cultural persistence may be studied from many different perspectives. One obvious approach centers on the ways in which individual people learn their social roles. Some of the most important instruments of cultural persistence operate within schools, churches and families, where children learn to do what is expected of them. Other institutions continue the socializing process through every stage of life. Each of the four cultural regions of British America, as we have seen, kept its own customs of enculturation for many generations.

A second and very different perspective on persistence centers on the functional interdependence of a culture's various parts. Material and ethical structures, for example, tend to be mutually reinforcing. To change a culture in any fundamental way, one must transform many things at once—no easy task, as many a reformer has learned. Social institutions tend to perpetuate themselves, and have their own means of doing so. These institutional imperatives are powerful instruments of continuity in a cultural system.

Yet another perspective on cultural persistence focuses on the conduct of elites. There is a cultural equivalent of the iron law of oligarchy: small groups dominate every cultural system. They tend to do so by controlling institutions and processes, so that they become the "governors" of a culture in both a political and a mechanical sense.

This iron law of cultural elites is an historical constant, but the relation between elites and other cultural groups is highly variable. Every culture might be seen as a system of bargaining, in which elites maintain their hegemony by concessions to other groups. These bargaining processes worked differently in the four regions of British America. New England's town system, for example, gave each community a high degree of autonomy and also a common interest in supporting the system itself. Pennsylvania's system of reciprocal liberty became a basis for bargaining among different groups. In the back settlements, the idea of natural liberty functioned in the same way. These bargaining processes became exceptionally complex in the Chesapeake colonies;

historian Allan Kulikoff has brilliantly described the social trans-actions between gentry and yeomen, gentry and poor whites, and gentry and slaves.[17]

Finally, when all else fails, the ultimate instrument of cultural persistence is physical force, which every culture must sometimes use to maintain itself. Even the Quakers were compelled to use force against criminals and pirates in the Delaware Bay. Every other culture frequently resorted to violence against aliens and dissenters.

These various perspectives on cultural persistence—encultur-ation, institutional structures, elite solidarity, intergroup bargain-ing and physical force, are not alternative to one another. They are different ways of looking at a single cultural process of high complexity.

❧ Conclusion: The Cultural Determinants of a Voluntary Society

The persistence of regional cultures in America is more than merely a matter of antiquarian interest. Regional diversity has created a dynamic tension within a single republican system. It has also fostered at least four different ideas of liberty within a common cultural frame.

These four libertarian traditions were not forms of classical republicanism or European liberalism—even as those alien ideologies were often borrowed as rationales. American ideas of freedom developed from indigenous folkways which were deeply rooted in the inherited culture of the English-speaking world.

Considered in ethical terms, each of these four freedom ways began as a great and noble impulse, but all at first were limited in expression and defective in their operation. The Puritan idea of ordered freedom was no sooner brought to Massachusetts than it became an instrument of savage persecution. The cavalier conception of hegemonic freedom, when carried to Virginia, per-mitted and even required the growth of race slavery for its sup-port. The Quaker vision of reciprocal freedom was a sectarian impulse which could be sustained only by withdrawal from the

---

[17]Allan Kulikoff, *Tobacco and Slaves: The Development of Southern Cultures in the Chesapeake, 1680–1800* (Chapel Hill, 1986), 280–313, 408–20.

world. The backcountry belief in natural freedom sometimes dissolved into cultural anarchy.

But each of these four libertarian traditions proved capable of continuing growth. New England's Puritan faith in ordered freedom grew far beyond its original limits to become, in Perry Miller's words, "a constellation of ideas basic to any comprehension of the American mind." Virginia's cavalier conceit of hegemonic freedom transcended its association with inequalities of rank and race and gender to become an ethical idea that is relevant to all. Pennsylvania's Quaker inspiration of reciprocal freedom developed from a fragile sectarian vision into a libertarian creed remarkable for toughness of mind and tenacity of purpose. Border and backcountry notions of natural freedom evolved from a folk tradition into an elaborate ideology.

Each of these four freedom ways still preserves its separate existence in the United States. The most important fact about American liberty is that it has never been a single idea, but a set of different and even contrary traditions in creative tension with one another. This diversity of libertarian ideas has created a culture of freedom which is more open and expansive than any unitary tradition alone could possibly be. It has also become the most powerful determinant of a voluntary society in the United States. In time, this plurality of freedoms may prove to be that nation's most enduring legacy to the world.

ACKNOWLEDGMENTS

The University of Oxford keeps many curious folkways, one of which gave rise to this book. Every year the visiting Harmsworth Professor of American History is required to give an Inaugural Lecture. He is also instructed that this event should never occur at the beginning of his tenure. It must come at the middle or the end. Mine came toward the end—a valedictory-inaugural of sorts. Whatever the cause of this custom may be, its consequence was a year of preparation–time when I was free to do research in British archives. In that period, the lecture grew rapidly into the text of this book.

My year at Oxford also had a major impact on my work in another way. For more than a decade, I had been struggling with a problem of synthesis in the "new social history." Suddenly I was required to teach Oxford's excellent but very old-fashioned history syllabus. That experience revolutionized my thinking. It inspired this attempt to join the old history with the new.

The subject of this first volume had been stirring in my mind since 1975 when I gave a graduate seminar called "Determinants of a Voluntary Society" at the University of Washington in Seattle. I learned much from my students and colleagues there, and remember with pleasure the collegiality of Arthur Bestor, Vernon Carstensen, Arthur Ferrell, Douglas North, Otis Pease, David Pinkney, Max Savelle and Donald Treadgold, and also the stimulus of my students there, several of whom went on to graduate work in history—Edward Byers, Jan Lewis, and Terry Roper.

English research for this book began in East Anglian archives during the summers of 1976 and 1978, when I learned much from an all-too-brief association with Peter Laslett and members of the Cambridge Group, and especially from J. R. Pole, whose friendship and wise advice I have come to cherish through the years. Thanks are due to the Cambridge University Library, to the Cambridge History Faculty for office space, and to the Visiting Scholars Centre for many kindnesses to me and my family. We

899

specially remember the hospitality of Christopher and Judy Ricks and the people of Little Eversden, Cambridge, who made us feel so much at home.

Many distractions and difficulties caused this project to be laid aside from 1978 until 1985, when a call to Oxford allowed me to take up the English research again and turned my efforts in a new direction. Many friends and colleagues made that year one of the happiest periods of my life. Special thanks are due to Lord Blake, Provost of The Queens College, and to Lady Blake for acts of kindness to me and my wife that went far beyond the call of duty. This book is dedicated to them as a token of affection and respect.

I remember also the unstinting hospitality of the Fellows of Queens College and their families, all of whom without exception did something to make us feel welcome—especially Jonathan and Jill Cohen, Kenneth and Jane Morgan, Peter and Kate Miller, Peter and Sylvia Neumann, Alisdair and Julie Parker and John and Menna Prestwich. Special thanks are due to Paul Foote for introducing me to the beauty of his beloved Dorset countryside and providing a place to stay while doing research in Wessex, to Geoffrey Marshall for setting me straight on the North Midlands, and to John Blair for helping patiently with many tedious questions about medieval history.

Thanks also are due to my colleagues of the History Faculty, especially to J. R. Pole and Harry Pitt with whom I taught, and to my gifted Oxford students who taught their teacher. I am specially indebted to Keith Thomas and Gerald Aylmer, who found time to read this manuscript and were generous with their critical gifts at a time when both of them were very busy with other things. For many kindnesses, I remember John Rowett, Michael and Eleanor Williams, Peter Carey, Colin and Susan Matthew, Jose Harris, Alec Campbell, Byron and Wanda Shafer, Michael Brock, George Richardson, Ivon Asquith, Julian Roberts, David Vaisey, Henry and Evelyn Phelps-Brown, Don and Hattie Price, Roger and Moyra Bannister, Andrew Robertson, Charles Webster and especially Alan and Olivia Bell. Alan Bell and his efficient staff at Rhodes House Library supported the project in many ways, as did archivists at County Record Offices throughout England.

Thanks also to the Rothermere Foundation for putting a roof over our heads, and especially to Vyvyan and Alexandra Harmsworth for their kindness and friendship. I remember the hospitality of Diana Barraclough in Burford, Cora Lushington in

Sussex, John and Veronica Oldfield in Southampton, Peter Parish in London, Roger and Kit Thompson in Norwich, A. J. Warren in York, and David and Isabel Spence, Elizabeth Leyland, Edward and Sarah McCabe, Donald and Penny Richards in Old Headington.

At Oxford University Press, I have for twenty years cherished the friendship and wise advice of my editor Sheldon Meyer, who made the book better in many ways. So also did Leona Capeless who gave the project the benefit of her wisdom and experience. Stephanie Sakson-Ford did the copy editing to an exceptionally high standard. Rachel Toor kept the project moving with intelligence and grace; I don't know how it could have moved through the press without her. Joellyn Ausanka helped in many other ways.

Jennifer Brody contributed the original art work, with patience, sensitivity, good humor and the gift of her high talent. Once again, on this project as in others, it was a pleasure to work with her.

Andrew Mudryk designed the maps, and executed them to a very high standard. He gave the project the benefit of his skill and creative imagination, and I very much enjoyed working with him.

Much of the American research for this series was done with the help of students and research assistants at Brandeis University. Some of this work has been published separately in our Chronos monographs with the support of an endowment from the Harold Sherman Goldberg Fund. The Concord Group included Mark Harris, James Kimenker, Richard Weintraub, Susan Kurland and Joanne Levin, with much help from Robert Gross at Amherst College and Mrs. William H. Moss at the Concord Library. The Brookline Group consisted of Beth Linzner, Kenneth A. Dreyfuss, Alisa Belinkoff Katz, and Bethamy Dubitzky Weinberger. The Waltham Group involved Michael Clark, Wendy Gamber, Barry Lieber, Jill Mazur and Theodore Steinberg. In the Nantucket Group were Carol Shuchman, Mindy Berman, Jemma Lazerow and Edward Byers who carried forward the work in a dissertation which is now separately published. Sally Barrett and Audrey Neck did the family reconstitution project on Milford, Massachusetts. Lawrence Kilbourne completed three family reconstitution projects on Hampton, New Hampshire; New Paltz, New York, and the Pennsylvania Schwenckfelders. Susan Irwin, Donna Bouvier and Marc Orlofsky did much of the quantitative research on slave culture and black families, and Marc

Orlofsky also did the analysis of wealth distribution in Kentucky and Tennessee. Jonathan Schwartz compiled and checked statistics of transatlantic migration. Edward Richkind and Janice Bassil helped to compile religious statistics. David Gould compiled statistics of school enrollment. Helena Wall and Jeffrey Adler worked on age relations. Miriam Hibel did a project on gender relations. Marshall Schatz and Andrew Robertson worked on statistics of voting participation. Mark Saloman did the research on regional crime statistics. Mathew Shuchman helped with many problems of computer programming and Daniel Highkin worked with us on mathematical models that lie below the surface of this book. Robert Finkel, Scott Gladstone and Michael Reeves helped to check citations and quotations.

In its inception, this project was generously supported by Brandeis University. I am specially grateful to President Marver Bernstein and Dean of Faculty Jack Goldstein for their encouragement. In the history office, Ina Malaguti, Judy Brown, Betty Larsen and Diane Spellman have helped in many ways—most of all by their exceptional competence and unfailing good humor.

I wish that it were possible to thank by name the many American archivists, librarians, scholars, friends and colleagues whose published research and private advice made this project possible. I have a major debt to Daniel Scott Smith who read this manuscript, and offered many perceptive suggestions for its improvement. John Murrin also took time from his own work to read the work with great care, and gave me the benefit of his unrivalled critical skills, Bertram and Anne Wyatt-Brown also read parts of the manuscript and offered many helpful suggestions. I have learned much through the years in conversation with John Demos, Robert Gross, Maris Vinovskis, George Billias, Richard Bushman, Michael Zuckerman, Tamara Hareven, Ronald Formisano, Roger Lane, James McPherson, James Kloppenberg, Morton Keller, Christine Heyrman and Rupert Wilkinson. My parents, John and Norma Fischer, and my brother Miles Pennington Fischer were as always a source of wise advice and encouragement. Susanna, Anne and Fred were a source of unfailing good cheer. My wife Judith helped and supported in many ways.

                                                                    D.H.F.

ABBREVIATIONS

A	*Antiquary*
AAAG	*Annals of the Association of American Geographers*
AAS	American Antiquarian Society, Worcester, Mass.
AC	*Archaeologia Cantiana*
ACLS	*American Council of Learned Societies*
AHAR	*American Historical Association, Annual Report*
AHR	*American Historical Review*
AJLH	*American Journal of Legal History*
AJS	*American Journal of Sociology*
AL	*American Literature*
ALAR	*Alabama Review*
AM	*Atlantic Monthly*
AMST	*Ancient Monuments Society Transactions*
AQ	*American Quarterly*
AR	*Archaeological Review*
AS	*American Speech*
ASR	*American Sociological Review*
BERKRO	Berkshire Record Office, Reading
C	*Costume*
CAMBRO	Cambridgeshire Record Office, Cambridge
CAMBU	Cambridge University Library
CASP	*Cambridge Antiquarian Society Proceedings*
CH	*Church History*
CHESRO	Cheshire Record Office, Chester
CS	*Camden Society Publications*
CSMP	*Colonial Society of Massachusetts Proceedings*
CSP	*Calendar of State Papers*
CSSH	*Comparative Studies in Society and History*
CUMROC	Cumbria Record Office, Carlisle
CUMROK	Cumbria Record Office, Kendal
CWAAS	*Cambridge and Westmorland Antiquary and Archeological Society Transactions*
D	*Demography*
DERBRO	Derbyshire Record Office, Matlock
DEVRO	Devonshire Record Office, Exeter

DH	*Delaware History*
DN	*Dialect Notes*
DORSRO	Dorsetshire Record Office, Dorchester
DSNEF	*Dublin Seminar for New England Folklore*
EAL	*Early American Literature*
EANGU	University of East Anglia
EAST	*Transactions of the Essex Archeological Society*
ECHR	*Economic History Review*
EDD	*English Dialect Dictionary*
EHR	*English Historical Review*
EJ	*Essex Journal*
ELAST	*East Lothian Antiquarian Society Transactions*
ESSRO	Essex Record Office, Chelmsford
ESUSRO	East Sussex Record Office, Lewes
ETHSP	*East Tennessee Historical Society Publications*
F	*Forum*
FHSJ	*Friends Historical Society Journal*
FL	*Folklore*
FLL	Friends Library, London
G	*Gwerin*
GM	*Gentleman's Magazine*
GLOCRO	*Gloucestershire Record Office, Gloucester*
GR	*Geographical Review*
H	*History*
HAMPRO	Hampshire Record Office, Winchester
HARLSP	*Harleian Society Publications*
HAV	Quaker Collection, Haverford College Library
HJ	*Historical Journal*
HSLCT	*Historical Society of Lancashire and Cheshire Transactions*
HSP	Historical Society of Pennsylvania, Philadelphia
HSUS	*Historical Statistics of the United States*
HUNTRO	Huntingdonshire Record Office, Huntingdon
I	*Independent*
IBGT	*Institute of British Geographers Transactions*
JAF	*Journal of American Folklore*
JAH	*Journal of American History*
JAS	*Journal of American Studies*
JECH	*Journal of Ecclesiastical History*
JEH	*Journal of Economic History*
JEL	*Journal of English Linguistics*
JFH	*Journal of Family History*
JHG	*Journal of Historical Geography*
JIH	*Journal of Interdisciplinary History*
JMF	*Journal of Marriage and the Family*
JMH	*Journal of Modern History*

JSH	Journal of Southern History
JSOCH	Journal of Social History
JSPH	Journal of Sports History
KAO	Kent Archives Office, Maidstone
KSHSR	Kentucky State Historical Society Register
LANCRO	Lancashire Record Office, Preston
LC	Library of Congress, Washington
LINCRO	Lincoln Archives Office, Lincoln Castle, Lincoln
LNA	Lower Norfolk Antiquary
LNQ	Lincolnshire Notes and Queries
LRS	Lincolnshire Record Society Publications
MAHS	Massachusetts Historical Society, Boston
MAHSC	Massachusetts Historical Society Collections
MAHSP	Massachusetts Historical Society Proceedings
MDA	Archives of Maryland
MDHM	Maryland Historical Magazine
MDHS	Maryland Historical Society, Baltimore
MEHSQ	Maine Historical Society Proceedings
MH	Midland History
MLW	Mountain Life and Work
MQ	Mississippi Quarterly
MVHR	Mississippi Valley Historical Review
NA	Norfolk Archaeology
NAR	North American Review
NCHR	North Carolina Historical Review
NEHGR	New England Historic and Genealogical Register
NEQ	New England Quarterly
NH	Northern History
NHANTRO	Northamptonshire Record Office, Delapre Abbey, Northampton
NHANTRS	Northamptonshire Record Society Publications
NHHSC	New Hampshire Historical Society Collections
NJA	New Jersey Archives
NJH	New Jersey History
NOTTRO	Nottinghamshire Record Office, Nottingham
NYHS	New York Historical Society, New York City
NYPL	New York Public Library, New York City
OED	Oxford English Dictionary
OXBOD	Bodleian Library, Oxford
OXRO	Oxfordshire Record Office, Oxford
PA	Pennsylvania Archives
PF	Pennsylvania Folklife
PH	Pennsylvania History
PMA	Post Medieval Archeology
PMHB	Pennsylvania Magazine of History and Biography

PMLA	*Publications of the Modern Language Association*
PP	*Past and Present*
PRO	Public Record Office
PS	*Population Studies*
QH	*Quaker History*
RHST	*Royal Historical Society Transactions*
SAC	*Sussex Archaeological Collections*
SAHJ	*Society of Architectural Historians*
SANHSP	*Somerset Archeological and Natural History Society Proceedings*
SAUS	*Statistical Abstract of the United States*
SCHGM	*South Carolina Historical and Genealogical Magazine*
SDNQ	*Somerset and Dorset Notes and Queries*
SF	*Social Forces*
SFH	*Sussex Family History*
SFS	*Somerset Folklore Studies*
SH	*Southern History*
SHCUNC	Southern Historical Collection, University of North Carolina
SIAP	*Suffolk Institute of Archeology Publications*
SLHSJ	*Scottish Labor History Society Journal*
SOCH	*Social History*
SOMERO	Somerset Record Office, Taunton
SOMERSRS	*Somerset Record Society Publication*
SP	*Studies in Philology*
SSP	*Surtees Society Publication*
SUFROBS	Suffolk Record Office, Bury St. Edmunds
SUFROIP	Suffolk Record Office, Ipswich
SWAR	Friends Historical Library, Swarthmore College
THM	*Tennessee Historical Magazine*
VA	*Vernacular Architecture*
VCH	*Victoria County History*
VMHB	*Virginia Magazine of History and Biography*
WARRO	Warwickshire Record Office, Warwick
WILTRO	Wiltshire Record Office, Trowbridge
WMQ1	*William and Mary Quarterly, First Series*
WNQ	*Wiltshire Notes and Queries*
WVAH	*West Virginia History*
YAS	Yorkshire Archaeological Society, Leeds
YROL	Yorkshire Record Office, Leeds
YROW	Yorkshire Record Office, Wakefield

Note: Spelling and punctuation have been modernized throughout.

SOURCES FOR MAPS

Map 1 (p. 32): data in text.

Map 2 (p. 37): data in text.

Map 3 (p. 45): Malcolm Falkus and John Gillingham, *Historical Atlas of Britain* (New York, 1981); David Hill, *An Atlas of Anglo-Saxon England* (Oxford, 1984); H. C. Darby, *The Domesday Geographies of England* (Cambridge, 1969); H. L. Gray, *English Field Systems* (Cambridge, 1915); A.R.H. Baker and R. A. Butlin, eds., *Studies of Field Systems in the British Isles* (Cambridge, 1973).

Map 4 (p. 48): F. M. Stenton, *Anglo-Saxon England* (3rd ed., Oxford, 1971); Patrick Collinson, "The Puritan Classical Movement in the Reign of Elizabeth I" (thesis, Univ. of London, 1957); David Grayson Allen, *In English Ways* (Chapel Hill, 1981); Clive Holmes, *The Eastern Association in the English Civil War.*

Map 5 (p. 51): Lois Mathews, *The Expansion of New England* (rpt., New York, 1962); James Truslow Adams, *Atlas of American History* (New York, 1943); Lester J. Cappon, et al., *Atlas of Early American History: The Revolutionary Era* (Princeton, 1976).

Map 6 (p. 182): Charles M. Andrews, *The River Towns of Connecticut* (Baltimore, 1889); "A Trewe Platt of the Mannor and Towne of Chellmisforde," Essex Record Office, Chelmsford, England; Peter Benes, *New England Prospect; A Loan Exhibition of Maps at the Currier Gallery of Art* (Boston, 1981); Anthony N. B. Garvan, *Architecture and Town Planning in Colonial Connecticut* (New Haven, 1951).

Map 7 (p. 238): data in text.

Map 8 (p. 242): Malcolm Falkus and John Gillingham, *Historical Atlas of Britain* (New York, 1981); David Hill, *An Atlas of Anglo-Saxon England* (Oxford, 1984); Andrew Charlesworth, ed., *An Atlas of Rural Protest in Britain, 1548–1900* (London, 1983); Samuel R. Gardiner, *History of the Great Civil War, 1642–1649* (new ed., 4 vols. London, 1897), I, 254f; David Underdown, *Royalist Conspiracy in England 1649–1660* (New Haven, 1960).

Map 9 (p. 249): U.S. Coast and Geodetic Survey; Arthur P. Middleton, *Tobacco Coast; A Maritime History of Chesapeake Bay in the Colonial Era* (Newport News, 1953).

Map 10 (p. 391): British Ordnance Survey (sheet 162); military maps of Sebastian Baumann and Joachim du Perron, Comte de Revel, 1781, in Howard C. Rice, Jr., and Anne S. K. Brown, *The American Campaigns of Rochambeau's Army,* II, fig. 90; Sebastian Bauman, *Plan of the Investment of York and Gloucester* (Philadelphia, 1782); Kenneth Nebenzahl and Don Higginbotham, *Atlas of the American Revolution* (New York, 1975), 182–83.

Map 11 (p. 440): data in text.

Map 12 (p. 443): data in text.

Maps 13–14 (pp. 447–49): Malcolm Falkus and John Gillingham, *Historical Atlas of Britain* (New York, 1981); David Hill, *An Atlas of Anglo-Saxon England* (Oxford, 1984); William C. Braithwaite, *The Beginnings of Quakerism* (London, 1912); Hugh Barbour, *The Quakers in Puritan England* (New Haven, 1964).

Map 15 (p. 454): James Truslow Adams, *Atlas of American History* (New York, 1943); Lester J. Cappon, et al., *Atlas of Early American History: The Revolutionary Era* (Princeton, 1976); U.S. Coast and Geodetic Survey.

Map 16 (p. 579): Thomas Holme, *A Map of Ye Improved Part of Pensilvania . . .* (n.p., n.d.); Stephanie Grauman Wolf, *Urban Village; Population, Community and Social Structure in Germantown, Pennsylvania, 1683–1800* (Princeton, 1976); James T. Lemon, *The Best Poor Man's Country; A Geographical Study of Early Southeastern Pennsylvania* (Baltimore, 1972).

Maps 17–18 (pp. 607–19): Bernard Bailyn, *Voyagers to the West* (New York, 1986); Malcolm Falkus and John Gillingham, *Historical Atlas of Britain* (New York, 1981); Irish maps by Raymond Gillespie, Diarmid O'Muirithe and J. G. Simms.

Map 19 (p. 627): Sources for these maps include John W. Leopold, "The Levellers' Revolt in Galloway of 1724," in Andrew Charlesworth, ed., *An Atlas of Rural Protest in Britain* (London, 1983), 44–48; D.L.W. Tough, *The Last Years of a Frontier* (Oxford, 1928); T. I. Rae, *The Administration of the Scottish Frontier* (Edinburgh, 1966); George M. Fraser, *The Steel Bonnets* (New York, 1972); and various unpublished materials.

Map 20 (pp. 636–37): James Truslow Adams, *Atlas of American History* (New York, 1943); Lester J. Cappon, et al., *Atlas of Early American History: The Revolutionary Era* (Princeton, 1976).

Map 21 (p. 761): Robert Ramsay, *Carolina Cradle; Settlement of the Northwest Carolina Frontier, 1747–1762* (Chapel Hill, 1964).

Map 22 (p. 762): Banastre Tarleton, *History of the Campaigns of 1780 and 1781* (London, 1787).

Map 23 (p. 791): Malcolm Falkus and John Gillingham, *Historical Atlas of Britain* (New York, 1981); David Hill, *An Atlas of Anglo-Saxon England* (Oxford, 1984): H. C. Darby, *The Domesday Geographies of England* (Cambridge, 1969); H. L. Gray, *English Field Systems* (Cambridge, 1915); A.R.H. Baker and R. A. Butlin, eds., *Studies of Field Systems in the British Isles* (Cambridge, 1973); E. J. Dobson, *English Pronun-*

ciation, 1500–1700 (2 vols., Oxford, 1968); W. W. Skeat, *English Dialects from the Eighth Century to the Present Day* (Cambridge, 1911); Joan Thirsk, ed., *The Agrarian History of England and Wales* (Cambridge, 1984), vols. 4, 5.

Map 24 (p. 833): Hans Kurath, *A Word Geography of the Eastern United States* (Ann Arbor, 1949); Henry Glassie, *Pattern in the Material Folk Culture of the Eastern United States* (Philadelphia, 1968).

Maps 25–33 (pp. 846, 853, 858, 864, 869, 871, 876): U.S. Bureau of the Census, *Historical Statistics of the United States from Colonial Times to the Present* (New York, 1976); *Statistical Abstract of the United States;* New York *Times,* 10 Nov. 1988.

Map 34 (p. 891): *Statistical Abstract of the United States* (1988) table 119.

Map 35 (p. 893): Charles O. Paullin, *Atlas of the Historical Geography of the United States* (Washington, 1932), 127.

INDEX